Frommer's®

Japan

11th Edition

by Beth Reiber

with Andrew Bender

WILEY

John Wiley & Sons, Inc.

Published by:
JOHN WILEY & SONS, INC.
111 River St.
Hoboken, NJ 07030-5774

ISBN 978-1-118-25262-8 (pbk); 978-1-118-28335-6 (ebk); 978-1-118-28449-0 (ebk); 978-1-118-28715-6 (ebk)

Editor: Gene Shannon
Production Editor: Eric T. Schroeder
Cartographer: Liz Puhl
Photo Editor: Richard Fox
Production by Wiley Indianapolis Composition Services

Front Cover Photo: Red Footbridge leading to Matsumoto Castle in Nagano Prefecture, Tokyo
© M. Burgess / Classic Stock / Alamy Images
Back Cover Photo: Japanese macaque, snow monkey (Macaca fuscata), two animals sitting in warm spring. © Blickwinkel / Alamy Images

For information on our other products and services or to obtain technical support, please contact our Customer Care Department within the U.S. at 877/762-2974, outside the U.S. at 317/572-3993 or fax 317/572-4002.

Wiley also publishes its books in a variety of electronic formats. Some content that appears in print may not be available in electronic formats.

Manufactured in the United States of America

5 4 3 2 1

CONTENTS

9 SHIKOKU 440

10 KYUSHU 463

11 OKINAWA 524

12 NORTHEASTERN HONSHU: TOHOKU 540

LIST OF MAPS

To my parents, who, while I was growing up in Kansas, always encouraged me to look farther than my own backyard; to my sons, Matthias and Johannes, for providing a teenager's perspective on Japan; and to the Japanese people, who have taught me more about myself and life than I'd ever imagined.
—Beth Reiber

Dedication: To the people of Tohoku, whose spirit of ganbare (go for it!) is an inspiration.
—Andrew Bender

ACKNOWLEDGMENTS

I would like to thank some fine and very special people without whose generous assistance and advice this book could never be as comprehensive as it is. A special *arigato* goes to Nori Akashi, Satoshi Asano, Nozomi Tsuji, Yoko Tanaka, Zenbon Tei, and others at the Japan National Tourist Organization for their support and behind-the-scenes guidance. I would also like to thank the following for their regional expertise and the assistance they extended during my travels: Takao Chiba in Hiraizumi, Iwate Prefecture; Eri Yamada in Nagoya; Yoshikazu Kitaguchi in Ishikawa Prefecture; Atsuhi Murai in Takayama; Ichiro Nakamura in Osaka City; Fumiko Tanaka in Himeji; Atsushi Tabara and Mayuka Ito in Shimane Prefecture; Takashige Ishii and Ryoji Okue in Hiroshima Prefecture; Kosuke Nasagi, Kousaku Inoue, and Lisa Nakamura in Fukuoka Prefecture; Chieko Shiozuka, Yumi Tanaka, and Kenji Odawara in Nagasaki; Hisatoshi Sakamoto, Chihiro Ono, and Yohsuke Kurose in Kumamoto Prefecture; Shigeto Moto, Mikiko Morita, Moyuru Nagata, and Satsuki Watanabe in Kagoshima Prefecture; Takashi Naoyama in Oita Prefecture; and Takashi Kinjo and Aki Miyazato in Okinawa. A special thanks to the following, who were supportive in the aftermath of Japan's massive earthquake and tsunami in the belief that tourism would help Japan's road to recovery: Sue Brosseau, Don Brownstein, Norman and Helen Gee, Caryn Goldberg, Jack Graham, Denise Low, Norinaka J. Matsuya, Lizette Peters, Jürgen Schmidt, Roger Shimomura, Aimee Stewart, and Luella Vaccaro. Debbie Howard gets kudos for her moral support, not to mention her years as a partner in crime researching Tokyo's nightlife, while Junko Matsuda gets a huge thanks for her tireless fact-checking skills and valuable knowledge of Tokyo. Finally, I'd also like to thank Tak Nagaoka for encouraging me so many years ago to take on this mammoth project, which sent my life in a totally unexpected direction.

—Beth Reiber

First thanks go to Yohko Scott and her colleagues at the Japan National Tourism Organization in Los Angeles for their consistent assistance. Colleagues and new friends on the ground in Japan include Mayumi Togawa in Okayama, Akiko Okazaki of Tourism Shikoku in Takamatsu, Mie Kotooka in Kotohira, Ms. Nakaoka of Uchiko, Takuya Nishimatsu and Mai Sakai of Kyoto's Tourism Promotion Division, Eiju Nakamura of Matsushima Tourist Information and Aya Satoh of the Matsushima City Government, Naoko Osawa of the Kakunodate Film Commission, Kazushi Sato of the Tazawako Tourist Association and the entire staff of the Tazawako Tourist Information Center, Reiko Kondo of the Sapporo Hokkaido Tourist Information Center, Yoko Maeda of the Noboribetsu Tourist Information Center, Dameon Takada in Akanko, and the innumerable hoteliers and tourist information counters who put up with more than their share of niggling questions from me. And thanks to Marian Goldberg for always having the right connections.

—Andrew Bender

HOW TO CONTACT US

In researching this book, we discovered many wonderful places—hotels, restaurants, shops, and more. We're sure you'll find others. Please tell us about them, so we can share the information with your fellow travelers in upcoming editions. If you were disappointed with a recommendation, we'd love to know that, too. Please write to:

Frommer's Japan, 11th Edition
John Wiley & Sons, Inc. • 111 River St. • Hoboken, NJ 07030-5774
frommersfeedback@wiley.com

ADVISORY & DISCLAIMER

Travel information can change quickly and unexpectedly, and we strongly advise you to confirm important details locally before traveling, including information on visas, health and safety, traffic and transport, accommodations, shopping, and eating out. We also encourage you to stay alert while traveling and to remain aware of your surroundings. Avoid civil disturbances, and keep a close eye on cameras, purses, wallets, and other valuables.

While we have endeavored to ensure that the information contained within this guide is accurate and up-to-date at the time of publication, we make no representations or warranties with respect to the accuracy or completeness of the contents of this work and specifically disclaim all warranties, including without limitation warranties of fitness for a particular purpose. We accept no responsibility or liability for any inaccuracy or errors or omissions, or for any inconvenience, loss, damage, costs, or expenses of any nature whatsoever incurred or suffered by anyone as a result of any advice or information contained in this guide.

The inclusion of a company, organization, or website in this guide as a service provider and/or potential source of further information does not mean that we endorse them or the information they provide. Be aware that information provided through some websites may be unreliable and can change without notice. Neither the publisher nor author shall be liable for any damages arising herefrom.

ABOUT THE AUTHORS

After living four years in Germany, first as a university student and then as a freelance travel writer writing for many U.S. newspapers from the *Los Angeles Times* to the *Washington Post*, **Beth Reiber** moved to Tokyo, where she worked as editor of *Far East Traveler*. She is the author of several Frommer's guides, including *Frommer's Tokyo* and *Frommer's Hong Kong*, as well as travel apps *Hong Kong Explorations* and *Branson and Beyond Traveler*. In 2009 she was appointed a VISIT JAPAN AMBASSADOR by Japan's Ministry of Land, Infrastructure, Transport and Tourism for her many years of writing about Japan, the only recipient residing in the United States to receive the honorary award. When not on the road, she resides in an 1890 Victorian home in Lawrence, Kansas, where she tries to keep peace between her dog and cat and one step ahead of her teenage sons.

Andrew Bender first moved to Japan in 1985 and worked for Japanese companies in the finance, film, and consulting industries. Now based in Los Angeles, he's crossed the Pacific to Japan so many times he's lost count. He also writes the Seat 1A blog for Forbes.com and for dozens of other publications including the *Los Angeles Times* and the in-flight magazine of Singapore Airlines.

FROMMER'S STAR RATINGS, ICONS & ABBREVIATIONS

Every hotel, restaurant, and attraction listing in this guide has been ranked for quality, value, service, amenities, and special features using a **star-rating system.** In country, state, and regional guides, we also rate towns and regions to help you narrow down your choices and budget your time accordingly. Hotels and restaurants are rated on a scale of zero (recommended) to three stars (exceptional). Attractions, shopping, nightlife, towns, and regions are rated according to the following scale: zero stars (recommended), one star (highly recommended), two stars (very highly recommended), and three stars (must-see).

In addition to the star-rating system, we also use **seven feature icons** that point you to the great deals, in-the-know advice, and unique experiences that separate travelers from tourists. Throughout the book, look for:

special finds—those places only insiders know about

fun facts—details that make travelers more informed and their trips more fun

kids—best bets for kids and advice for the whole family

special moments—those experiences that memories are made of

overrated—places or experiences not worth your time or money

insider tips—great ways to save time and money

great values—where to get the best deals

The following abbreviations are used for credit cards:

AE	American Express	DISC	Discover	V	Visa
DC	Diners Club	MC	MasterCard		

TRAVEL RESOURCES AT FROMMERS.COM

Frommer's travel resources don't end with this guide. Frommer's website, **www.frommers. com**, has travel information on more than 4,000 destinations. We update features regularly, giving you access to the most current trip-planning information and the best airfare, lodging, and car-rental bargains. You can also listen to podcasts, connect with other Frommers.com members through our active-reader forums, share your travel photos, read blogs from guide-book editors and fellow travelers, and much more.

THE BEST OF JAPAN

The 2011 triple whammy of an earthquake, tsunami, and nuclear power plant meltdown will undoubtedly go down in history as one of this century's worst disasters, yet it also brought global attention to Japan's most admirable trait: the integrity, honesty and perseverance of the Japanese people themselves. That, coupled with the country's fascinating history, stunning mountain scenery, festivals, hot-spring spas, historic structures ranging from castles to temples, Japanese gardens, and trend-setting metropolises all combine to make Japan a destination like no other.

Sightseeing   With its sensory overload, Tokyo is the nation's trendsetter, whether it's avant-garde installations at the **Mori Art Museum** or knock-out views from **Sky Tree.** Kyoto is arguably Japan's most beautiful city, rife with historic structures like **Kiyomizu Temple** and **Katsura Imperial Villa.** Other top attractions include **Himeji Castle, Nara's Great Buddha,** and Kanazawa's **Kenrokuen Garden,** but not to be neglected are small villages, like **Mount Koya** with its many temples, the mountain resort of **Unzen Spa,** and **Uchiko** with its historic district.

Eating & Drinking   There's more to Japanese food than sushi, including tempura, yakitori, and shabu-shabu (see chapter 2 for more information), but part of what makes travel here so fascinating is the variety of national and regional dishes. Every prefecture, it seems, has its own style of noodles, its locally grown vegetables, its delicacies, and unique dishes, whether it's mountain vegetables in **Takayama** or hairy crabs in **Hokkaido.** Japan is also renowned for sake, with about 10,000 varieties available throughout the country.

Shopping   Japan is famous for crafts ranging from **lacquerware** to **ceramics** (with Kyoto and Kanazawa being top destinations), but other fun shopping experiences include browsing **department stores,** antique and flea **markets,** streets known for their electronics and anime stores (like **Akihabara** in Tokyo and **Den Den Town** in Osaka), and local shops selling **regional products**—like sake, toys, handbags and other items made from locally made cloth, sweets, dolls, and much more—virtually everywhere in Japan.

Arts & Culture   Japan is known for its highly ritualized **tea ceremony,** offered in teahouses at many gardens, and **ikebana** (Japanese flower arranging). The theatrics of **Kabuki,** should be at the top of anyone's list, but equally entertaining are **Bunraku** puppetry and **sumo**

wrestling matches. The nation's top museum for Japanese art and antiquities is the **Tokyo National Museum,** but top-notch contemporary art is visible throughout the country, including virtually the entire island of **Naoshima,** the I.M. Pei-designed **Miho Museum,** and Kanazawa's **21st Century Museum of Contemporary Art.**

THE most UNFORGETTABLE TRAVEL EXPERIENCES

- **Making a Pilgrimage to a Temple or Shrine:** From mountaintop shrines to neighborhood temples, Japan's religious structures rank among the nation's most popular attractions. They're often visited for specific reasons: Students flock to **Dazaifu Tenmangu Shrine** (p. 469) to pray for successful exams, while couples wishing for a happy marriage head to Kyoto's **Jishu Shrine,** devoted to the deity of love (p. 260). Shrines and temples are also sites for Japan's major festivals. See p. 24 for information on Buddhism and Shintoism and the regional chapters.

- **Taking a Communal Hot-Spring Bath:** No other people on earth bathe as enthusiastically, as frequently, and for such duration as the Japanese. Their many hot-spring baths—thought to cure all sorts of ailments as well as simply make you feel good—range from elegant, Zen-like affairs to rustic outdoor baths with views of the countryside. You'll find them all over Japan; see the "Bathing" section under "Minding Your P's & Q's" in chapter 2, and the regional chapters for more information.

- **Participating in a Festival:** With Shintoism and Buddhism as its major religions, and temples and shrines virtually everywhere, Japan has multiple festivals every week. Celebrations range from huge processions of wheeled floats to those featuring horseback archery; you may want to plan your trip around one (and book early for a hotel). See the "Japan Calendar of Events," in chapter 2, for a list of some of the most popular festivals.

- **Viewing the Cherry Blossoms:** Nothing symbolizes the approach of spring so vividly to Japanese as the appearance of the cherry blossoms—and nothing so amazes visitors as the way Japanese gather under the blossoms to celebrate the season with food, drink, and dance. See the "Japan Calendar of Events," in chapter 2, for cherry blossom details.

- **Riding the Shinkansen Bullet Train:** One of the world's fastest trains whips you across the countryside at up to 300km (187 miles) an hour as you relax, see Japan's rural countryside, and dine on boxed meals filled with local specialties. See "Getting Around" in chapter 14.

- **Staying in a Ryokan:** Japan's legendary service reigns supreme in a top-class *ryokan,* a traditional Japanese inn. You'll bathe in a Japanese tub or hot-spring bath, feast your eyes on lovely views past *shoji* screens, dine like a king in your *tatami* room, and sleep on a futon. See "Tips on Accommodations," in chapter 14, and the "Where to Stay" sections in the regional chapters for more on ryokan.

- **Attending a Kabuki Play:** Based on universal themes and designed to appeal to the masses, *kabuki* plays are extravaganzas of theatrical displays, costumes, and scenes—but mostly they're just plain fun. See "Japanese Arts in a Nutshell," in chapter 2, and the kabuki section of "Entertainment & Nightlife" in chapter 4.

- **Seeing Mount Fuji:** It may not seem like much of an accomplishment to see Japan's most famous and tallest mountain, visible from about 160km (100 miles) away. But, the truth is, it's hardly ever visible, except during winter months and rare occasions when the air is clear. Catching a glimpse of the giant peak is truly breathtaking, whether you see it from aboard the **Shinkansen,** a Tokyo skyscraper, or a nearby national park. If you want to climb it (possible only in July–Aug), be prepared for a group experience—400,000 people climb Mount Fuji every summer. See "Climbing Mount Fuji," in chapter 5.

THE best CITY & SMALL-TOWN EXPERIENCES

o **Feeling the Adrenalin Rush of Tokyo:** Tokyo is Japan's showcase for all that's high-tech, sophisticated, zany, and avant-garde, making this a must-see for just about everyone. Seeing main sights like the **Tokyo National Museum** and **Sensoji Temple** top the list, but wandering the metropolis' many neighborhoods adds a totally new dimension to a Tokyo experience. See chapter 4.

o **Spending a Few Days in Kyoto:** If you see only one city in Japan, Kyoto should be it. Japan's capital from 794 to 1868, Kyoto is one of Japan's finest ancient cities, boasting some of the country's best temples, imperial villas, Japanese-style inns, traditional restaurants, shops, and gardens. See chapter 7.

o **Wandering the Historic Streets of Takayama:** Nicknamed "Little Kyoto" of the **Hida Mountains,** this town invites exploration: you'll find streets lined with traditional wooden buildings and shops, a morning market, Japanese inns, and a wealth of museums. See chapter 6.

o **Pretending You're a Feudal Lord in Tsumago:** Back in the feudal days, this tiny village served as a stopover for feudal lords traveling between Kyoto and Edo (present-day Tokyo). To make your experience even richer, hike part of the old footpath between **Tsumago** and **Magome** and stay overnight in a *ryokan.* See chapter 6.

o **Exploring the Historic Quarters of Kurashiki:** With its willow-fringed canal and black-and-white old granaries, this former merchant town is a photographer's dream, though there are also museums (like the renowned **Ohara Museum** with its impressive collection of Western art) and plenty of shops to explore. See chapter 8.

o **Reliving History in Nagasaki:** This port town surely ranks as one of Japan's prettiest, with hills rising from the harbor and a plethora of sights tied to its past history of international trade. Best bet: restored Dejima, a small island that served as home to Japan's only foreigners during the country's 200-some years of isolation. See chapter 10.

o **Soaking in the Baths of Hell in Unzen:** This mountain-top hot-spring resort has served as a summer resort for international travelers for more than a century. With its sulfurous hot springs (the Hells) and *ryokan* spread along its one main street, it's still a great getaway for travelers needing some R&R. See chapter 10.

THE best FOOD & DRINK EXPERIENCES

o **Experiencing a Kaiseki Feast:** The ultimate in Japanese cuisine, *kaiseki* is a feast for the senses and spirit. Consisting of a variety of exquisitely prepared and arranged dishes, a kaiseki is a multicourse meal consisting of seasonal ingredients served on complementing tableware. There are hundreds of exceptional kaiseki restaurants in Japan, from old-world traditional to sleek modern. Traditional *ryokan* also serve kaiseki. See regional chapters as well as "Eating & Drinking in Japan," in chapter 2.

o **Spending an Evening in a Robatayaki:** Harkening back to the olden days when the Japanese cooked over an open fireplace, a *robatayaki* is a convivial place for a meal and drinks. One of the most famous is **Inakaya** in Tokyo, where diners sit at a counter; on the other side are two cooks, grills, and mountains of food. You'll love the drama of this place. See p. 138 as well as "Eating & Drinking in Japan," in chapter 2.

o **Dining on Western Food in Modern Settings:** Japan has no lack of great Western food, and some of the best places to dine are its first-class hotels. The **New York Grill,** on the 52nd floor of the Park Hyatt in Tokyo, epitomizes the best of the West with its sophisticated setting, and great views, food, and jazz. See p. 130.

o **Slurping Noodles in a Noodle Shop:** You're supposed to slurp when eating Japanese noodles, which are prepared in almost as many different ways as there are regions. Noodle shops range from stand-up counters to traditional restaurants; one of my favorites is **Raitei** in Kamakura. See p. 192 as well as "Eating & Drinking in Japan," in chapter 2, and the "Where to Eat" sections in regional chapters.

o **Rubbing Elbows in an Izakaya:** *Izakaya* are pubs in Japan—usually tiny affairs with just a counter, serving up skewered grilled chicken, fish, and other fare. They're good places to meet the natives and are inexpensive as well. You'll find them in every nightlife district in the country. See the regional chapters and also "Eating & Drinking in Japan," in chapter 2.

o **Feeling Adventuresome in the Hinterlands:** Virtually every region in Japan has its own local specialties, from oysters in Hiroshima, raw horse meat in Kumamoto, and *goya champuru* (a stir-fry of bittermelon, tofu, pork, and other ingredients) in Okinawa. You can even enjoy local specialties by ordering regional box lunches on the Shinkansen bullet train. See the regional chapters and also "Eating & Drinking in Japan," in chapter 2.

THE best WAYS TO SEE JAPAN LIKE A LOCAL

o **Buying Prepared Meals at a Department Store:** The basement floors of department stores are almost always devoted to foodstuffs, including takeout foods. Shopping for your meal is a fun experience: Hawkers yell their wares, wives buy food for the evening's dinner, samples are set out for you to nibble, and you can choose anything from tempura and sushi to boxed meals. See "Eating & Drinking in Japan," in chapter 2.

o **Using Local Transportation:** Sure, jumping in a taxi might be the quickest way to travel in a city, but you'll have more fun taking local subways, buses and trams (and save money, too). In fact, in some towns (like Nagasaki, Kumamoto, and Hakodate), streetcars are considered a star attraction. Some towns also have dedicated tourist buses—filled with Japanese tourists. See the regional chapters.

o **Renting a Bike:** Some towns just lend themselves to biking, like Kyoto, Takayama, Ise, Kanazawa, Himeji, Matsue, Hiroshima, Kakunodate, and Hiraizumi, making this slow form of transportation popular among locals and tourists alike. See the appropriate regional chapters.

o **Overnighting in a Hot-Spring Resort:** It's not unusual to see multi-generational families at Japan's many hot-spring resorts, where everyone from the youngest tyke to granny wander the halls in *yukata* (cotton robes), soak in the baths, and dine en-masse in noisy restaurants. See the regional chapters.

o **Joining the Crowds at a Local Festival:** Local festivals are big events for families, who come to peruse market stalls, dine on festival fare like octopus balls, and enjoy parades, flower shows, folk dancing, and other activities. While not as famous as Japan's major festivals, these local celebrations can be more accessible and equally fun. See "Japan Calendar of Events" in chapter 2 and the regional chapters for local tourist websites.

o **Spending a Sunday in a Local Park:** Parks are popular Sunday destinations for families with kids and young couples on dates, making for great people-watching and a restorative afternoon. Among my favorites: **Ueno Park** in Tokyo, **Yamashita Park** in Yokohama, and the extensive park surrounding **Osaka Castle.** See p. 95, 203, and 362.

o **Strolling Through Tokyo's Nightlife District:** A spin through one of Japan's famous nightlife districts, such as **Shinjuku** or **Roppongi** in Tokyo or **Dotombori** in Osaka, is a colorful way to rub elbows with the natives as you explore narrow streets with their whirls of neon, tiny hole-in-the-wall bars and restaurants, and all-night amusement spots. See "Entertainment & Nightlife," in chapter 4, and "Osaka After Dark," in chapter 8.

THE best FAMILY EXPERIENCES

o **Joining the Throngs at Sensoji Temple:** Tokyo's oldest temple is also its liveliest, with throngs of visitors and stalls selling both traditional and kitschy items, giving it a festival-like atmosphere every day of the year. There's enough excitement to keep everyone entertained, but top it off with a stop at nearby **Hanayashiki amusement park** for its old-fashioned rides. See p. 94 and 94.

o **Learning History at the Edo-Tokyo Museum:** Housed in a high-tech modern building, this ambitious museum chronicles the fascinating and somewhat tumultuous history of Tokyo (known as Edo during the Feudal Era) with models, replicas, artifacts, and dioramas. Not only can children climb into a palanquin and a rickshaw, but volunteers stand ready to give free guided tours in English. See p. 101.

o **Attending a Baseball Game:** After sumo, baseball is Japan's most popular spectator sport. Watching a game with a stadium full of avid Japanese fans and cheerleaders can shed new light on this favorite pastime. See p. 102 and "Take Me Out to the Ballgame" on p. 469.

o **Seeing Tokyo from the TMG:** On the 45th floor of the Tokyo Metropolitan Government Office (TMG), designed by well-known architect Tange Kenzo, this observatory offers a bird's-eye view of Shinjuku's cluster of skyscrapers, the never-ending metropolis, and, on fine winter days, Mount Fuji. Best of all, it's free. See p. 98.

o **Seeing Fish Eye-to-Eye in an Aquarium:** Because Japan is surrounded by sea, it's no surprise that it has more than its share of aquariums, many with innovative displays that put you eye-to-eye with the creatures of the deep. My favorites are the ones in Osaka and Okinawa. See p. 364 and 530.

o **Pretending You're a Ninja:** There are plenty of amusement parks in Japan, but for something uniquely Japanese, head to one that's themed around feudal Japan, where staff is dressed like ninja and courtesans, the setting harkens back to old Japan, and amusements like throwing ninja weapons at a target or navigating a ninja house keep little ones entertained. You'll find them in Futami and Noboribetsu. See p. 336 and 587.

- **Hanging Out in Harajuku:** If you have teenagers, nothing beats a day in teenybopper heaven with Tokyo's many clothing and accessory stores lining narrow streets packed with a never-ending flow of humanity. There are lots of restaurants geared to the younger generation, too, but for a bit of culture (and quietude) head to nearby **Meiji Shrine** enveloped in woods. See "Walking Tour 2: In the Heart of Trendy Tokyo, a Stroll Through Harajuku & Aoyama," in chapter 4.
- **Exploring a Japanese Castle:** The past comes alive when you tromp the many wooden stairs in a Japanese castle, gaze upon samurai helmets and gear, and pretend you're the feudal lord viewing his domain from the keep's top floor. Some are remakes (but still impressive, like towering Osaka Castle) and others are the original. My favorites: Himeji Castle, Matsue Castle, Matsuyama Castle, and Kumamoto Castle. See p. 394, 413, 454, and 494.

THE best TRADITIONAL JAPANESE-STYLE ACCOMMODATIONS

- **Hiiragiya Ryokan** (Kyoto): If ever there was an example of the quintessential *ryokan*, Hiiragiya is it. Located in the heart of old Kyoto, it's the ultimate in *tatami* luxury: a dignified enclave of polished wood and rooms with antique furnishings overlooking private gardens. Six generations of the same family have provided impeccable service and hospitality here since 1861. See p. 292.
- **Hakusuikan Ryokan** (Ibusuki): I'm usually partial to historic Japanese inns, but this sprawling complex right on the coast, with manicured lawns dotted by pine trees, offers an assortment of accommodations (the oldest building is 45 years old), along with one of the best hot-spring spas I've ever seen, modeled after a public bath of the Edo Era, as well as a museum filled with antiques. See p. 514.
- **Homeikan** (Tokyo): This is my top pick for an affordable, authentic Japanese inn in the capital. Rooms do not have private bathrooms, but pluses include a Japanese garden, nice public baths, and detailed *tatami* rooms adorned with traditional architectural features. Meals (optional) are served in your room. Another great plus: The owner speaks English. See p. 181.
- **Arai Ryokan** (Shuzenji): Fifteen historic structures, all registered as national cultural assets and situated around a river-fed pond, comprise this sprawling *ryokan*, in business since 1872. See p. 220.
- **Ryokan Fujioto** (Tsumago): This 100-year-old inn is nestled back from the main street of Tsumago, a delightful village on the Edo-era Nakasendo Highway. Meals feature local specialties, and the father-daughter team running it go out of their way to make guests feel at home. See p. 232.
- **Minshuku in Shirakawago's Ogimachi:** Nestled in a narrow valley of the Japan Alps, Ogimachi is a small village of paddies, flowers, irrigation canals, and 200-year-old thatched farmhouses, about two dozen of which offer simple tatami accommodations and meals featuring local cuisine. This is a great, inexpensive escape. See "Rural Shirakawa-go & Ogimachi," in chapter 6.
- **Temple Accommodations on Mount Koya:** If your vision of Japan includes temples, towering cypress trees, shaven-headed monks, and religious chanting at the crack of dawn, head for the religious sanctuary atop Mount Koya, where some 50 Buddhist temples offer tatami accommodations—some with garden views—and two vegetarian meals a day. See "The Temples of Mount Koya," in chapter 8.

- **Tsuru-no-yu Onsen** (Nyuto Onsen): This rustic inn, with a history stretching back to the Edo Period, complete with thatched-roof building and outdoor hot-spring baths, is as close as you can get to time travel. To really save money, opt for the self-cooking wing and prepare your own meals. See p. 560.

THE best HISTORIC EXPERIENCES

- **Paying Respects to the Shogun at Toshogu Shrine** (Nikko): Dedicated to Japan's most powerful shogun, Tokugawa Ieyasu, this World Heritage Site is the nation's most elaborate and opulent shrine, made with 2.4 million sheets of gold leaf. It's set in a forest of cedar in a national park. See p. 196.
- **Hiking the Old Nakasendo Highway:** Back in the days of the shogun, feudal lords were required to return to Edo (now Tokyo) every other year, traveling designated highways. Nakasendo was one of these highways, and an 8km (5-mile) stretch through a valley still exists between the old post towns of **Magome** and **Tsumago.** It's a beautiful walk, and the towns are historic relics. See p. 231.
- **Strolling Through a Japanese Garden:** Most of Japan's famous gardens are relics of the Edo Period, when the shogun, *daimyo* (feudal lords), imperial family, and even samurai and Buddhist priests developed private gardens for their own viewing pleasure. The garden at Katsura Imperial Villa in Kyoto is, in my view, Japan's most beautiful. A "strolling garden," its view changes with every step but is always complete, perfectly balanced, and in harmony. See p. 264 and 23 in chapter 2.
- **Attending a Traditional Tea Ceremony:** Developed in the 16th century as a means to achieve inner harmony with nature, the highly ritualized ceremony is carried out in teahouses throughout the country, including those set in Japan's many parks and gardens. See "The Tea Ceremony," in chapter 2, and the regional chapters.
- **Exploring Kyoto's Higashiyama-ku District:** Kyoto's eastern sector is a lovely combination of wooded hills, temples, shrines, museums, shops, and traditional restaurants, making it one of the best neighborhoods in Japan for a stroll. See "Walking Tour 1: A Stroll Through Higashiyama-ku," in chapter 7.
- **Exploring the Buddhist Pure Land in Hiraizumi:** Back in the 12th century, three generations of the Fujiwara clan devoted themselves to creating a Buddhist heaven on earth, filled with magnificent temples (like Chusonji's Golden Hall), sleeping quarters for monks, and the Pure Land Garden. Located in Tohoku, it was declared a World Heritage Site shortly after the Great East Japan Earthquake. See p. 549.
- **Walking to Kobo Daishi's Mausoleum on Mount Koya:** Ever since the 9th century, when Buddhist leader Kobo Daishi was laid to rest at Okunoin on Mount Koya, his faithful followers have followed him to their graves—and now tomb after tomb lines a 1.5km (1-mile) pathway to Daishi's mausoleum. Cypress trees, moss-covered stone lanterns, and thousands upon thousands of tombs make this the most impressive graveyard stroll in Japan, especially at night. See "Exploring Mount Koya," in chapter 8.

THE best OUTDOOR EXPERIENCES

- **Climbing Mount Fuji:** Okay, so climbing Japan's tallest—3,766m-high (12,355 ft.)—and most famous mountain is not the solitary, athletic pursuit you may have envisioned—but with 400,000 people climbing it annually, it's a great, culturally enriching group activity. Many opt to climb through the night with a flashlight and then cheer the sunrise from the top of the mountain. See "Climbing Mount Fuji," in chapter 5.

o **Cycling in Japan:** Hard to believe, but you can bike between Shikoku island and Hiroshima Prefecture via the 70km (43-mile) Shimanami Kaido route, which actually comprises six bridges and six islands in the Seto Inland Sea and follows a well-maintained, dedicated biking path. See "Cycling the Shimanami Kaido," in chapter 8, and "Exploring Sights of the Seto Inland Sea," in chapter 8. Another favorite: Cycling through the historic, rural Kibiji District in Okayama Prefecture on a path that takes you past paddies, ancient burial grounds, temples, and shrines. See p. 400.

o **Hiking:** With 70% of Japan covered with mountains, it should come as no surprise that there are many hiking trails lacing the country. Top hiking destinations include the Japan Alps, Tohoku, and Hokkaido, but there are also many temple pilgrimages (like on the island of Shikoku). See individual chapters.

o **Skiing in Honshu & Hokkaido:** Host of two winter Olympics (in Sapporo in 1972 and Nagano in 1998) and riddled with mountain chains, Japan is a great destination for skiing, the most popular winter sport in the country, and for snowboarding. The Japan Alps in Central Honshu and the mountains of Tohoku and Hokkaido are popular destinations. See chapters 6, 12, and 13.

o **Scuba Diving and Snorkeling in Okinawa:** Okinawa, an archipelago of 160 subtropical islands, is blessed with coral reefs, schools of manta rays, and operators offering excursions for all levels, not to mention some of the best dive spots in the world. Favorites include the Kerama Islands and Iriomote. See chapter 11.

THE best SHOPPING EXPERIENCES

o **Shopping in a Department Store:** Japanese department stores are microcosms of practically everything Japan produces, from the food halls in the basement to the departments selling clothing, accessories, office supplies, souvenirs, pottery, household goods, and cameras, to rooftop garden centers. What's more, service is great and purchases are beautifully wrapped. If you arrive when the store opens, staff will be lined up at the front door to bow as you enter. You'll be spoiled for life. See the "Shopping" sections throughout this book.

o **Finding Those Souvenirs:** Japanese are avid souvenir shoppers when they travel, so souvenirs are sold literally everywhere, even near shrines and temples. Nakamise Dori, a pedestrian lane leading to Tokyo's Sensoji Temple, is one of Japan's most colorful places to shop for paper umbrellas, toys, and other souvenirs. The two best places for one-stop memento shopping are the Oriental Bazaar (p. 148) in Tokyo and the Kyoto Handicraft Center (p. 280), both of which offer several floors of everything from fans to woodblock prints.

o **Appreciating Traditional Crafts:** Japan treasures its artisans so highly that it designates the best as National Living Treasures. Tokyo's **Japan Traditional Craft Center** (p. 148) offers a varied inventory of everything from knives and baskets to lacquerware, but there are many renowned shops in Kyoto and Kanazawa as well. Department stores also offer an excellent collection of traditional crafts. See "Shopping," in chapter 4, and the shopping sections for Kyoto in chapter 7 and Kanazawa on p. 350.

- **Hunting for Antiques & Curios:** Flea markets are great for browsing; you'll see everything from used kimono to Edo-era teapots for sale. Japan's largest and one of its oldest monthly markets is held the 21st of each month at Toji Temple in Kyoto. (A lesser flea market is held there the first Sun of each month.) Tokyo also has great weekend markets. See chapters 4 and 7.
- **Sizing Up the Latest Gizmos:** Looking for that perfect digital camera, MP3 player, calculator, or rice cooker? Then join everyone else in the country by going to one of the nation's two largest electronics and electrical-appliance districts. In Tokyo, it's Akihabara, where open-fronted shops beckon up to 50,000 weekday shoppers with whirring fans, blaring radios, and sales pitches. In Osaka, head to Den Den Town. Be sure to comparison-shop and bargain. See "Shopping," in chapters 4 and 8.
- **Searching for Local Specialties:** Many prefecture capitals have a government-owned exhibition hall where local products are displayed for sale. Often called a *kanko bussankan,* the hall may have everything from locally produced pottery to folk toys and foodstuffs. Cities with kanko bussankan include Kanazawa, Okayama, Matsuyama, and Kumamoto. See chapters 8, 9, and 10.
- **Buying That Special Porcelain & Pottery:** Porcelain and pottery are produced seemingly everywhere in Japan. Some of the more famous centers include Nagoya, home to Noritake, Japan's largest chinaware company; Kanazawa, known for its Kutani pottery with its distinctive colorful glaze; Bizen, with its unglazed pottery; Matsuyama, famous for its Tobe pottery (white porcelain with cobalt-blue designs); and Kagoshima, with Satsuma pottery available in white (used by the upper class in feudal Japan) and black (used by the common people). See chapters 8, 9, and 10.

THE best OFFBEAT TRAVEL EXPERIENCES

- **Visiting a Local Market:** Tsukiji Fish Market in Tokyo is Japan's largest (and most crowded), but there are local seafood and produce markets virtually everywhere. Those in Kyoto, Kanazawa, Takayama, Kagoshima, Hakodate, and Okinawa are among my favorites. See p. 282, 350, 235, 503, 570, and 532.
- **Watching the Big Guys Wrestle** (Tokyo, Osaka, Nagoya, Fukuoka): There's nothing quite like watching two monstrous sumo wrestlers square off, bluff, and grapple as they attempt to throw each other on the ground or out of the ring. Matches are great cultural events, but even if you can't attend one, you can watch them on TV during one of six annual 15-day tournaments. For more information, see "Spectator Sports," in chapter 4, and "Sumo," in chapter 2.
- **Getting a Shiatsu Massage:** Shiatsu, or pressure-point massage, is available in virtually all first-class accommodations in Japan and at most moderately priced ones as well. After a hard day of work or sightseeing, nothing beats a relaxing massage in the privacy of your room.
- **Watching Cormorant Fishing:** Every night in summer, wooden boats gaily decorated with paper lanterns will take you out on rivers outside Nagoya for an up-close look at cormorant fishing. The birds, maneuvered by fishermen in traditional garb, have tight collars around their necks to prevent them from swallowing their catch. Drinking and dining on board contribute to the festive air. See p. 326.
- **Joining the Otaku (Geeks) in Akihabara** (Tokyo): In addition to its electronics stores, Akihabara boasts Japan's largest concentration of shops devoted to *manga*

(Japanese comic books and graphic novels) and *anime* (Japanese animation), as well as "maid cafes," coffee shops with waitresses dressed as maids. See p. 146.

○ **Getting off the Beaten Path, Literally:** There are hiking paths throughout Japan, to mountain peaks, through forests leading to temples and shrines, and in national parks. Because most Japanese hikers tend to stick to famous trails, you can often have trails entirely to yourself. See individual chapters, including Hokkaido's national parks in chapter 13.

JAPAN IN DEPTH

Hardly a day goes by that you don't hear something about Japan, whether the subject is trade, travel, food, the arts, Japanese products, karaoke, anime, or, more recently, ongoing economic struggles and clean-up efforts as the country continues to deal with the aftermath of the 2011 Great East Japan Earthquake. Yet Japan remains something of an enigma to people in the Western world. What best describes this Asian nation? Is it the giant producer of cars and an entire array of sleek electronic goods that compete favorably with the best in the West? Or is it still the land of geisha and bonsai, the punctilious tea ceremony, and the delicate art of flower arrangement? Has it become, in its outlook and popular culture, a country more Western than Asian? Or has it retained its unique ancient traditions while forging a central place in the contemporary post-industrialized world?

In fact, Japan has long adopted the best of the West (and the East, for that matter) and then adapted it to its own needs. Its cities may look Westernized—often disappointingly so—but beyond first impressions, there's very little about this Asian nation that could lull you into thinking you're in the West. Japan also differs greatly from its Asian neighbors. Although it borrowed much from China in its early development, including Buddhism and its writing system, the island nation remained steadfastly isolated from the rest of the world throughout much of its history, usually deliberately so. Until World War II, it had never been successfully invaded; and for more than 200 years, while the West was stirring with the awakenings of democracy and industrialism, Japan completely closed its doors to the outside world and remained a tightly structured feudalistic society with almost no outside influence.

It's been only 150-some years since Japanese opened their doors, embracing Western products wholeheartedly, yet at the same time altering them and making them unquestionably their own. Thus, that modern high-rise may look Western, but it may contain a rustic-looking restaurant with open charcoal grills, corporate offices, a pachinko parlor, a high-tech bar with surreal city views, a McDonald's, an acupuncture clinic, a computer showroom, and a rooftop shrine. Your pizza may come with octopus, beer gardens are likely to be fitted with AstroTurf, and "parsley" refers to unmarried women older than 28 (because parsley is what's left on a plate). City police patrol on bicycles; garbage collectors attack their job with the vigor of a well-trained army; and white-gloved elevator operators, working in some of the world's swankiest department stores, bow and thank you as you exit.

Because of this unique synthesis of East and West into a culture that is distinctly Japanese, Japan is not easy for Westerners to comprehend. Discovering it is like peeling an onion—you uncover one layer only to discover more layers underneath. Thus, no matter how long you stay in Japan, you never stop learning something new about it—and to me that constant discovery is one of the most fascinating aspects of being here.

In any case, with a population of about 127 million, a history stretching back thousands of years, the world's longest-reigning monarchy, and unique forms of culture, art, food, etiquette, and religion, Japan merits more than this short chapter can deliver. I urge you to delve deeper with the recommendations in "Japan in Popular Culture: Books & Film," later in this chapter.

JAPAN TODAY

You can't talk about Japan today without mentioning its biggest earthquake in recorded history, known as the Great East Japan Earthquake, which struck off the Tohoku coast on March 11, 2011. While the consequences of the triple whammy—earthquake, tsunami, and meltdown of the Fukushima nuclear power plant—may not be entirely evident for years to come, it seems safe to say that for Japan, 3/11 will remain a defining moment in its history and its future.

The tangible losses, of course, are painfully clear: More than 19,000 dead or missing, entire towns and villages along the Tohoku coast obliterated, more than 1 million homes and buildings damaged or destroyed, and trillions of yen in damage.

Less clear is Japan's future relationship with nuclear power. The Fukushima nuclear reactors, owned by Tokyo Electric Power Co. (TEPCO), suffered the world's worst meltdown and radiation leakage since the 1986 disaster in Chernobyl, forcing the evacuation of more than 90,000 people from around the plant. It was later revealed that TEPCO and the Japanese government, fearing panic, had withheld computer forecasts about the spread of radiation, allowing thousands of people to stay in areas of high radiation for days. Two weeks after the disaster, the government also decided not to tell the public that if meltdowns spiraled out of control and radiation levels soared, as many as 35 million people in the Tokyo area would have to be evacuated. And this in a country that, having suffered the world's only atomic bombing, knows better than any other the long-lasting effects of radiation. (Discontent with how then prime minister Kan Naoto handled the aftermath of the March 2011 disaster led to his ouster in September of that year, with the new prime minister, Noda Yoshihiko, becoming the sixth person to hold the position in five years.)

Meanwhile, as the list of contaminated foods grew to include beef, produce, and even infant formula, many residents decided to take matters into their own hands, buying or renting Geiger counters and dosimeters to gauge radiation exposure. Anger over the cozy relationship between TEPCO and the government ministry that was supposed to regulate it has led to unprecedented mass protest in Tokyo, with as many as 60,000 people marching against nuclear power in September 2011.

Although the Fukushima power plant achieved a cold shutdown at the end of 2011, it still contains dangerously high radiation levels and was still suffering occasional leaks at the time of going to press; experts say it could take 40 years to decommission the plant. After the Great East Japan Earthquake, it was mandated that all nuclear reactors closing down for routine maintenance undergo tests to confirm they could withstand earthquakes and tsunamis with the force of Tohoku's disaster and then get the go-ahead from local governments before restarting. Although all nuclear power plants in Japan had been shut down by May 2012, two reactors at Ohi nuclear power plant, serving the Osaka area, were turned on in July despite nation-wide protests. Those in favor of nuclear power point out that Japan can not generate enough electricity from renewable resources alone, especially during Japan's hot, humid summers (before 3/11, nuclear power plants supplied 30% of Japan's energy). Compounding the problem is that Tokyo and all points to the northwest of Japan run on a different electric grid from the southeast part of the country, making the transfer of power between the two systems impossible without major upgrades. In other words, the direction of Japan's future energy needs remains in limbo.

The biggest challenges facing Japan, of course, remain in the Tohoku area. Like most TV viewers, I was devastated by broadcasts of the tsunami; I've traveled the Tohoku coast so often, it seemed like it was happening in my own backyard. When I traveled in Tohoku eight months after the disaster, debris had been cleared, but it was collected in huge piles; other prefectures have been reluctant to take it, especially from contaminated areas. In any case, the work still ahead is staggering: the removal of tons of debris, the decontamination of affected areas, and finding new housing for tens of thousands of people whose homes were destroyed or remain off-limits. The scale of decontamination alone is mind-boggling. According to a news report I saw on Japanese television, the cost of decontaminating one home costs about ¥170,000, and there are 110,000 contaminated houses in Fukushima Prefecture alone. Topsoil equal to the size of Connecticut has to be removed and replaced. Where villages once stood, there are now only wide, empty spaces. Although some towns hope to rebuild, many evacuees, especially families with children, have said they have no intention of ever returning.

Other challenges facing Japan include a large national debt, a government that seems powerless to instigate change, a high yen and an exchange rate that's devastating Japan's manufacturing base and making its products too expensive on the global market; not to mention a declining birthrate coupled with one of the most rapidly aging populations in the world. About 22% of Japan's population is 65 and older; by 2060, that number is expected to reach almost 40%, while Japan's children aged 14 and younger is expected to decline to 9.1%. Unless more women enter the workforce or immigration standards are relaxed, this will undoubtedly lead to a shortage of labor, severely straining the country's resources for tax revenues, pensions, and healthcare.

The one message I heard loud and clear from innkeepers, restaurant owners, and others while updating this book is that Japan needs visitors; after 3/11, the number of foreign visitors dropped about 25% in 2011 compared with a year earlier. With the exception of areas in Fuskushima Prefecture, radiation levels in Japan are considered normal. Japan's standards for measuring food and water safety for radioactive contamination are the same as in the United States and have not turned up any new scares since 2011. Hong Kong, Japan's largest importer of Japanese food, lifted import restrictions, including those from Fukushima Prefecture, in March 2012.

Indeed, with the exception of Matsushima, which received minor damage from the tsunami (p. 543), all other destinations covered in this guide are conducting business as usual. In fact, some areas, like southern Kyushu and ski areas in Hokkaido, have seen a boom in tourism, and virtually every prefecture is trying to figure out how to lure more international travelers. There are deals across the country that are only for foreigners, including regional rail passes and plane tickets. Now is a good time to visit Japan, not only to show support for the Japanese people, but to take advantage of lower prices.

In any case, the attributes that drew me to Japan in the first place and keep me coming back remain strongly in place: the country's unexpected physical beauty and its unique cuisine, customs, and culture. One of the things I love most about Japan is how safe I feel from crime. Indeed, after the Great East Japan Earthquake and tsunami, never once did it cross my mind that there might be looting or crime in its aftermath. I also like the ways Japan has changed over the years, how a younger generation of less inhibited Japanese has forever altered the social landscape. Whereas in the 1980s Japan was best known as an economic powerhouse, today it's known also for its cool pop culture, from *anime* and *manga* to fashion and food. It's still the land of the geisha, but it's also the land of Hello Kitty.

THE MAKING OF JAPAN

ANCIENT HISTORY (CA. 30,000 B.C.–A.D. 710)   According to mythology, Japan's history began when the sun goddess, Amaterasu, sent one of her descendants down to the island of Kyushu to unify the people of Japan. Unification, however, was not realized until a few generations later when Jimmu, the great-grandson of the goddess's emissary, succeeded in bringing all of the country under his rule. Because of his divine descent, Jimmu became emperor in 660 B.C. (the date is mythical), thus establishing the line from which all of Japan's emperors are said to derive. However mysterious the origin of this imperial dynasty, it is acknowledged as the longest reigning such family in the world.

Legend begins to give way to fact only in the 4th century A.D., when a family by the name of Yamato succeeded in expanding its kingdom throughout much of the country. At the core of the unification achieved by the Yamato family was the Shinto religion. Indigenous to Japan, **Shintoism** is marked by the worship of natural things—mountains, trees, stars, rivers, seas, fire, animals, even vegetables—as the embodiment of *kami* (gods) and of the spirits of ancestors. It is also marked by belief in the emperor's divinity. Along with Buddhism, Shintoism is still a driving belief in Japanese life.

Although the exact origin of Japanese people is unknown, we know Japan was once connected to the Asian mainland by a land bridge, and the territory of Japan was occupied as early as 30,000 B.C. From about 10,000 B.C. to 400 B.C., hunter-gatherers, called Jomon, thrived in small communities primarily in central Honshu; they're best known for their hand-formed pottery decorated with cord patterns. The Jomon Period was followed by the Yayoi Period, which was marked by metalworking, the pottery wheel, and the mastering of irrigated rice cultivation. The Yayoi Period lasted until about A.D. 300, after which the Yamato family unified the state for the first time and set up their court in what is now Nara Prefecture. Yamato (present-day Japan) began turning cultural feelers toward its great neighbor to the west, China.

In the 6th century, **Buddhism,** which originated in India, was brought to Japan via China and Korea, followed by the importation of Chinese cultural and scholarly knowledge—including art, architecture, and the use of Chinese written characters. In 604, the prince regent Shotoku, greatly influenced by the teachings of Buddhism and Confucianism and still a beloved figure today, drafted a document calling for political reforms and a constitutional government. By 607, he was sending Japanese scholars to China to study Buddhism, and he started building Buddhist temples. The most famous is **Horyuji Temple** near Nara, said to be the oldest existing wooden structure in the world. He also built **Shitennoji Temple** in what is now Osaka.

THE NARA PERIOD (710–84)   Before the 700s, the site of Japan's capital changed every time a new emperor came to the throne. In 710, however, a permanent capital was established at Nara. Although it remained the capital for only 74 years, seven successive emperors ruled from Nara. The period was graced with the expansion of Buddhism and flourishing temple construction throughout the country. Buddhism also inspired the arts, including Buddhist sculpture, metal casting, painting, and lacquerware. It was during this time that Emperor Shomu, the most devout Buddhist among the Nara emperors, ordered the casting of a huge bronze statue of Buddha to be erected in Nara. Known as the Daibutsu, it remains Nara's biggest attraction.

THE HEIAN PERIOD (794–1192) In 794, the capital was moved to Heiankyo (present-day Kyoto), and following the example of cities in China, Kyoto was laid out in a grid pattern with broad roads and canals. Heiankyo means "capital of peace and tranquility," and the Heian Period was a glorious time for aristocratic families, a time of luxury and prosperity during which court life reached new artistic heights. Moon viewing became popular. Chinese characters were blended with a new Japanese writing system, allowing for the first time the flowering of Japanese literature and poetry. The life of the times was captured in the works of two women: Sei Shonagon, who wrote a collection of impressions of her life at court known as the *Pillow Book;* and Murasaki Shikibu, who wrote the world's first major novel, *The Tale of Genji.*

Because the nobles were completely engrossed in their luxurious lifestyles, however, they failed to notice the growth of military clans in the provinces. The two most powerful warrior clans were the Taira (also called Heike) and the Minamoto (also called Genji), whose fierce civil wars tore the nation apart until a young warrior, Minamoto Yoritomo, established supremacy. (In Japan, a person's family name—here, Minamoto—comes first, followed by the given name; I have followed this order throughout this book.)

THE KAMAKURA PERIOD (1192–1333) Wishing to set up rule far away from Kyoto, Minamoto Yoritomo established his capital in a remote and easily defended fishing village called Kamakura, not far from today's Tokyo. In becoming the nation's first shogun, or military dictator, Minamoto Yoritomo laid the groundwork for 700 years of military governments—in which the power of the country passed from the aristocratic court into the hands of the warrior class—until the imperial court was restored in 1868.

The Kamakura Period is perhaps best known for the unrivaled ascendancy of the warrior caste, or **samurai.** Ruled by a rigid honor code, samurai were bound in loyalty to their feudal lord, and they became the only caste allowed to carry two swords. They were expected to give up their lives for their lord without hesitation, and if they failed in their duty, they could regain their honor only by committing ritualistic suicide, or *seppuku.* Spurning the soft life led by court nobles, samurai embraced a spartan lifestyle. When **Zen Buddhism,** with its tenets of mental and physical discipline, was introduced into Japan from China in the 1190s, it appealed greatly to the samurai. Weapons and armor achieved new heights in artistry, while *Bushido,* the way of the warrior, contributed to the spirit of national unity.

In 1274, Mongolian forces under Kublai Khan made an unsuccessful attempt to invade Japan. They returned in 1281 with a larger fleet, but a typhoon destroyed it. Regarding the cyclone as a gift from the gods, Japanese called it *kamikaze,* meaning "divine wind," which took on a different significance at the end of World War II when Japanese pilots flew suicide missions in an attempt to turn the tide of war.

THE MUROMACHI & AZUCHI-MOMOYAMA PERIODS (1336–1603) After the fall of the Kamakura shogunate, a new feudal government was set up at Muromachi in Kyoto. The next 200 years, however, were marred by bloody civil wars as *daimyo* (feudal lords) staked out their fiefdoms. Similar to the barons of Europe, the daimyo owned tracts of land, had complete rule over the people who lived on them, and had an army of retainers, the samurai, who fought his enemies. This period of civil wars is called Sengoku-Jidai, or **Age of the Warring States.**

Yet these centuries of strife also saw a blossoming of art and culture. Kyoto witnessed the construction of the extravagant Golden and Silver pavilions as well as the artistic arrangement of Ryoanji Temple's famous rock garden. Noh drama, the tea ceremony, flower arranging, and landscape gardening became the passions of the upper class. At the end of the 16th century, a number of castles were built on mountaintops to demonstrate the strength of the daimyo, guard their fiefdoms, and defend themselves against the firearms introduced by the Portuguese.

In the second half of the 16th century, a brilliant military strategist by the name of Oda Nobunaga almost succeeded in ending the civil wars. Upon Oda's assassination by one of his own retainers, one of his best generals, Toyotomi Hideyoshi, took up the campaign, built magnificent Osaka Castle, and crushed rebellion to unify Japan. Oda and Toyotomi's successive rules are known as the **Azuchi-Momoyama Period,** after the names of their castles.

THE EDO PERIOD (1603–1867) Upon Toyotomi's death (1598), power was seized by Tokugawa Ieyasu, a statesman so shrewd and skillful in eliminating enemies that his heirs would continue to rule Japan for the next 250 years. After defeating his greatest rival in the famous battle of Sekigahara, Tokugawa set up a shogunate government in 1603 in Edo (present-day Tokyo), leaving the emperor intact but virtually powerless in Kyoto. In 1615, the Tokugawa government assured its supremacy by getting rid of Toyotomi's descendants in a fierce battle at Osaka Castle that destroyed the castle and annihilated the Toyotomi clan.

Meanwhile, European influence in Japan was spreading. The first contact with the Western world had occurred in 1543, when Portuguese merchants (with firearms) arrived, followed by Christian missionaries. St. Francis Xavier landed in Kyushu in 1549, remaining for 2 years and converting thousands of Japanese; by 1580, there were perhaps as many as 150,000 Japanese Christians. Although Japan's rulers at first welcomed foreigners and trade (three Kyushu daimyo even went so far as to send emissaries to Rome, where they were received by the pope), they gradually became alarmed by the Christian missionary influence. Hearing of the Catholic Church's power in Rome and fearing the expansionist policies of European nations, Toyotomi banned Christianity in the late 1500s. In 1597, 26 Japanese and European Christians were crucified in Nagasaki.

The Tokugawa shogunate intensified the campaign against Christians in 1639 when it closed all ports to foreign trade. Adopting a policy of **total isolation,** the shogunate forbade foreigners from landing in Japan and Japanese from leaving; even Japanese who had been living abroad in overseas trading posts were never allowed to return. The only exception was in Nagasaki, home to a colony of tightly controlled Chinese merchants and a handful of Dutch confined to a tiny island trading post.

Thus began an amazing 215-year period in Japanese history during which Japan was closed to the rest of the world. It was a time of political stability at the expense of personal freedom, as all aspects of life were strictly controlled by the Tokugawa government. Japanese society was divided into four distinct **classes:** samurai, farmers, craftspeople, and merchants. Class determined everything in daily life, from where a person could live to what he was allowed to wear or eat. Samurai led the most exalted social position, and it was probably during the Tokugawa Period that the samurai class reached the zenith of its glory. At the bottom of the social ladder were the merchants, but as they prospered under the peaceful regime, new forms of entertainment arose to occupy their time. Kabuki drama and woodblock prints became the rage, while stoneware and porcelain, silk brocade for kimono, and lacquerware improved in quality. In fact, it was probably the shogunate's rigid policies that actually fostered the arts. Because anything new was considered dangerous and quickly suppressed, Japanese were forced to retreat inward, focusing their energies in the arts and perfecting handicrafts down to the minutest detail whether it was swords, kimono, or lacquered boxes. Only Japan's many festivals and pilgrimages to designated religious sites offered relief from harsh and restrictive social mores.

To ensure that no daimyo in the distant provinces would become too powerful and a threat to the shogun's power, the Tokugawa government ordered each daimyo to leave his family in Edo as permanent residents (effectively as hostages) and required the lord to spend a prescribed number of months in Edo every year or two. Inns and townships sprang up along Japan's major highways to accommodate the elaborate processions of palanquins, samurai, and footmen traveling back and forth between Edo and the provinces. In expending so much time and money traveling back and forth and maintaining elaborate residences both in the provinces and in Edo, the daimyo had no resources left with which to wage a rebellion.

Yet even though the Tokugawa government took such extreme measures to ensure its supremacy, by the mid–19th century it was clear that the feudal system was outdated and economic power had shifted into the hands of the merchants. Many samurai families were impoverished, and discontent with the shogunate became widespread.

In 1853, American Commodore Matthew C. Perry sailed to Japan, seeking to gain trading rights. He left unsuccessful, but returning a year later he forced the Shogun to sign an agreement despite the disapproval of the emperor, thus ending Japan's 2 centuries of isolation. In 1867, powerful families toppled the Tokugawa regime and restored the emperor as ruler, thus bringing the Feudal Era to a close.

MEIJI PERIOD THROUGH WORLD WAR II (1868–1945) In 1868, Emperor Meiji moved his imperial government from Kyoto to Edo, renamed it Tokyo (Eastern Capital), and designated it the official national capital. During the next few decades, known as the **Meiji Restoration,** Japan rapidly progressed from a feudal agricultural society of samurai and peasants to an industrial nation. The samurai were stripped of their power and no longer allowed to carry swords, thus ending a privileged way of life begun almost 700 years earlier in Kamakura. A prime minister and a cabinet were appointed, a constitution was drafted, and a parliament (called the Diet) was elected. With the enthusiastic support of Emperor Meiji, the latest in Western technological know-how was imported, including railway and postal systems, along with specialists and advisers: Between 1881 and 1898, about 10,000 Westerners were retained by the Japanese government to help modernize the country.

Meanwhile, Japan made incursions into neighboring lands. In 1894 to 1895, it fought and won a war against China; in 1904 to 1905, it attacked and defeated Russia; and in 1910, it annexed Korea. After militarists gained control of the government in the 1930s, these expansionist policies continued; Manchuria was annexed, and Japan went to war with China again in 1937. On the other side of the world, as **World War II** flared in Europe, Japan formed a military alliance (Axis) with Germany and Italy and attacked French Indochina.

After several years of tense diplomatic confrontations between Japan and America, Japanese extremists decided to attack Pearl Harbor in the hope that by striking first they could prevent U.S. mobilization. On December 7, 1941, Japan bombed Pearl Harbor, entering World War II against the United States. Although Japan went on to conquer Hong Kong, Singapore, Burma, Malaysia, the Philippines, the Dutch East Indies, and Guam, the tide eventually turned, and American bombers reduced every major Japanese city to rubble with the exception of historic Kyoto. On August 6, 1945, the United States dropped the world's first atomic bomb over Hiroshima, followed on August 9 by a second over Nagasaki. Japan submitted to unconditional surrender on August 14, with Emperor Hirohito's radio broadcast telling his people the time had come for "enduring the unendurable and suffering what is insufferable." American and other **Allied occupation** forces arrived and remained until 1952. For the first time in history, Japan had suffered defeat by a foreign power; the country had never before been invaded or occupied by a foreign nation.

POSTWAR JAPAN (1946–1989) The experience of World War II had a profound effect on the Japanese, yet they emerged from their defeat and began to rebuild. In 1946, under the guidance of the Allied military authority headed by U.S. Gen. Douglas MacArthur, they adopted a democratic constitution renouncing war and the use of force to settle international disputes and divesting the emperor of divinity. A parliamentary system of government was set up, and 1947 witnessed the first general elections for the National Diet, the government's legislative body. After its founding in 1955, the **Liberal Democratic Party (LDP)** remained the undisputed majority party for decades, giving Japan the political stability it needed to grow economically and compete in world markets.

To the younger generation, the occupation was less a painful burden to be suffered than an opportunity to remake their country, with American encouragement, into a modern, peace-loving, and democratic state. A relationship developed between Japanese and their American occupiers. In the early 1950s, as the Cold War between the United States and the Communist world erupted in hostilities in Korea, that relationship grew into a firm alliance, strengthened by a security treaty. In 1952, the occupation ended, and Japan joined the United Nations as an independent country.

Avoiding involvement in foreign conflicts as outlined by its constitution, Japanese concentrated on economic recovery. Through a series of policies favoring domestic industries and shielding Japan from foreign competition, they achieved **rapid economic growth.** In 1964, Tokyo hosted the Summer Olympic Games, showing the world that the nation had transformed itself into a formidable industrialized power. Incomes doubled during the 1960s, and a 1967 government study found that 90% of Japanese considered themselves middle class. By the 1980s, Japan was by far the richest industrialized nation in Asia and the envy of its neighbors, who strove to emulate Japan's success. Sony was a household word around the globe; books flooded the international market touting the economic secrets of Japan, Inc. After all, Japan seemed to have it all: a good economy, political stability, safe streets, and great schools. As the yen soared, Japanese traveled abroad as never before, and Japanese companies gained international attention as they gobbled up real estate in foreign lands and purchased works of art at unheard-of prices.

Meanwhile, a snowballing trade surplus had created friction between Japan and the United States, its chief trading partner. In the 1980s, as Japanese auto sales in the United States soared and foreign sales in Japan continued to be restricted, disagreements between Tokyo and Washington heated up. In 1989, Emperor Hirohito died of cancer at age 87, bringing the 63-year Showa Era to an end and ushering in the **Heisei Period** under Akihito, the 125th emperor, who proclaimed the new "Era of Peace" (Heisei).

AFTER THE BUBBLE BURST (1990–PRESENT DAY) In the early 1990s, shadows of financial doubt began to spread over the Land of the Rising Sun, with alarming reports of bad bank loans, inflated stock prices, and overextended corporate investment abroad. In 1992, **recession** hit Japan, bursting the economic bubble and plunging the country into its worst recession since World War II. The Nikkei (the Japanese version of the American Dow) fell a gut-churning 63% from its 1989 peak, and, over the next decade, bankruptcies reached an all-time high and unemployment climbed to its highest level since World War II. Public confidence was further eroded in 1995, first by a major earthquake in Kobe that killed more than 6,000 people and proved that Japan's cities were not as safe as the government had maintained, and then by an attack by an obscure religious sect that released the deadly nerve gas sarin on Tokyo's subway system during rush hour, killing 12 people and sickening thousands.

On the international front, Japan's most immediate worry continued to be its neighbor, North Korea, which lobbed its first missile over Japan in 1998, declared in 2002 that it had never halted its nuclear-weapons program despite a 1994 nuclear accord, and in 2008 launched its first satellite rocket over Japan. In 2002, North Korea admitted that it had abducted 13 young Japanese in the '70s and '80s to teach its spies the Japanese language and customs. Five of the abductees were subsequently repatriated back to Japan; North Korea maintains the others died of natural causes.

In 1999, Japan, which did not have a legally recognized national flag nor an anthem, adopted a World War II hymn, *Kimigayo,* as its national anthem and declared the traditional Japanese sun flag, a red disk in a field of white, its official flag. But any overt displays of Japanese nationalism have always spurred criticism from Asian neighbors, who maintain that despite an official apology in 1995 for wartime aggression, Japan has never truly shown remorse for invading and occupying its neighbors. Relations became further strained in 2005, when Japan's Education Ministry approved revised history textbooks that glossed over Japan's war crimes, sparking outrage in China and South Korea that erupted into anti-Japanese street riots. In 2007, an international furor arose when then-prime minister Abe Shinzo claimed that no evidence existed of women being forced to work in Asian brothels established by the Japanese military during World War II.

Although Japan, whose foremost trading partner had shifted from the United States to China, seemed to be on the economic mend by the mid-2000s, the 2008 global financial meltdown (referred to in Japan as the "Lehman Shock"), hijacked its recovery by causing a downward spiral in foreign trade as demand for Japanese cars, electronics, and other exports dropped dramatically around the world. Major companies were forced to curtail production and close plants, causing thousands of workers to lose their jobs. Even though widespread dissatisfaction with the status quo brought a landslide victory for the opposition Democratic Party of Japan in 2009 and defeat for the business-friendly Liberal Democratic party, which had ruled for more than a half-century, the new government failed to restore vitality to a country struggling with almost 20 years of deflation, political and corporate scandals, an aging population, a rising yen, and the world's largest debt. For Japan's young generation, economic stagnation was all they'd known. Instead of being envied as an Asian superpower, Japan had become an example of an economy other nations wished to avoid.

But everything that had come before paled to what happened on March 11, 2011, when Japan's strongest quake in recorded history struck off the Tohoku coast with a magnitude of 9.0, unleashing a massive tsunami up to three stories high that raced up to 10km (6 miles) inland, washing away entire villages and their inhabitants, causing severe damage to the Fukushima nuclear power plant, and leaving more than 4 million homes without electricity. News helicopters, cell phones, and surveillance cameras captured horrifying footage of the tsunami carrying boats, cars, houses and debris, making the catastrophe one of the most filmed natural disasters ever. Survivors, many of them elderly, made their way to schools, hospitals, and evacuation centers that had no electricity, no running water, no heat, and no help in sight.

In the days that followed, a dazed population mourned the loss of life and grew ever more fearful over reports of radiation leakage from the damaged plant, despite heroic onsite efforts. Then, due to increased concern over radiation, lack of transparency from both the Tokyo Electric Power Co. (owners of the Fukushima power plant) and the Japanese government, and more than 300 unnerving aftershocks in the days after the quake, several embassies, including those of the United States and Britain, advised its citizens to leave Tokyo and even Japan, causing a huge exodus of foreigners from the capital. All this was accompanied by rolling blackouts in the Tokyo area, a run on food staples, and a growing sense of gloom and doom. Foreign tourists in Japan all but vanished, with the Japan National Tourism Organization reporting a 62.5% plummet in April visits compared to a year earlier.

To deal with the 2011 energy shortage caused by the defunct Fukushima power plant, as well as other plants that were subsequently shut down, the government ordered businesses and asked residents in Tokyo to reduce energy usage by 15%, especially during the hot, humid summer. Lights went dim in train stations and stores, some escalators and elevators were turned off, lighted billboards went blank, rail service was curtailed in Tokyo and surrounding areas, thermostats were cranked up, and many Tokyo businessmen embraced the Super Cool Biz campaign that eschewed the traditional suit in favor of more casual (and cooler) business attire, with some even sporting polo and Hawaiian shirts. Seven prefectures in western Japan also launched energy-saving campaigns, such as implementing earlier work schedules for government employees or switching off elevators.

Meanwhile, as the count of the dead and missing climbed to more than 19,000, the unfolding saga of the Fukushima nuclear power plant made clear that the catastrophe was far from over, with leakage from the plant adding to a growing list of contaminated food, including spinach, tea leaves, beef, rice, mushrooms, rice, milk, fish, and even infant formula, mostly from affected areas in Tohoku. Although the Fukushima power plant achieved a cold shutdown in December 2011, experts say it could take 40 years to clean up and fully decommission the facility.

Just as 9/11 remains seared in American minds, 3/11 is the day that for most Japanese changed their nation forever.

JAPANESE ARTS IN A NUTSHELL

Traditional Theater

KABUKI   Japan's best-known traditional theater art, *kabuki* is also one of the country's most popular forms of entertainment. Visit a performance and it's easy to see why— kabuki is fun! The plays are dramatic, the costumes are gorgeous, the stage settings are often fantastic, and the themes are universal—love, revenge, and the conflict between duty and personal feelings. Probably one of the reasons kabuki is so popular even today is that it developed centuries ago as a form of entertainment for the common people in feudal Japan, particularly the merchants. And one of kabuki's interesting aspects is that all roles—even those depicting women—are played by men.

Kabuki has changed little in the past 100-some years. Altogether there are more than 300 kabuki plays, all written before the 20th century. Kabuki stages almost always revolve and have an aisle that extends from the stage to the back of the spectator theater. For a Westerner, one of the more arresting things about a kabuki performance is the audience itself. Because this has always been entertainment for the masses, the audience can get quite lively with yells, guffaws, shouts of approval, and laughter. In fact, old woodcuts of cross-eyed men apparently stemmed from kabuki— when things got a little too rowdy, actors would stamp their feet and strike a cross-eyed pose in an attempt to gain the audience's attention.

Of course, you likely won't be able to understand what's being said. Indeed, because much of kabuki drama dates from the 18th century, even many Japanese sometimes have difficulty understanding the language. But it doesn't matter, as plots are easy to follow, though some theaters have English-language programs and earphones that describe the plots in minute detail. The best place to enjoy kabuki is Tokyo, where performances are held throughout much of the year.

NOH Whereas *kabuki* developed as a form of entertainment for the masses, Noh was a much more traditional and aristocratic form of theater. Most of Japan's shogun were patrons of Noh; during the Edo Period, it became the exclusive entertainment of the samurai class. In contrast to kabuki's extroverted liveliness, Noh is very calculated, slow, and restrained. The oldest form of theater in Japan, it has changed very little in the past 600 years, making it the oldest theater art in the world. The language is so archaic that Japanese cannot understand it at all, which explains in part why Noh does not have the popularity that kabuki does.

As in kabuki, all Noh performers are men, with the principal characters consisting mostly of ghosts or spirits, who illuminate foibles of human nature or tragic-heroic events. Performers often wear masks. Spoken parts are chanted by a chorus of about eight; music is provided by a Noh orchestra that consists of several drums and a flute.

Because the action is slow, watching an entire evening can be quite tedious unless you are particularly interested in Noh dance and music. In addition, most Noh plays do not have English translations. You may want to drop in for just a short while. In between Noh plays, short comic reliefs, called *kyogen,* usually make fun of life in the 1600s, depicting the lives of lazy husbands, conniving servants, and other characters with universal appeal.

BUNRAKU *Bunraku* is traditional Japanese puppet theater. But contrary to what you might expect, bunraku is for adults, and themes center on love and revenge, sacrifice and suicide. Many dramas now adapted for *kabuki* were first written for the bunraku stage.

Popular in Japan since the 17th century—at times even more popular than kabuki— bunraku is fascinating to watch because the puppeteers are right onstage with their puppets. Dressed in black, they're wonderfully skilled in making the puppets seem like living beings. Usually, there are three puppeteers for each puppet, which is about three-fourths human size: One puppeteer is responsible for movement of the puppet's head,the expression on its face, and for the movement of the right arm and hand; another puppeteer operates the puppet's left arm and hand; while the third moves the legs. Although at first the puppeteers are somewhat distracting, after a while you forget they're

SUMO

The Japanese form of wrestling known as **sumo** was first mentioned in written records in the 6th century but was probably popular long before that. Today it's still popular, with the best wrestlers revered as national heroes, much as baseball or basketball players are in North America. Often taller than 1.8m (6 ft.) and weighing well over 136 kilograms (300 lb.), sumo wrestlers follow a rigorous training period, which usually begins when they're in their teens and includes eating special foods to gain weight. Unmarried wrestlers even live together at their training schools, called sumo stables.

A sumo match takes place on a sandy-floored ring less than 4.5m (15 ft.) in diameter. Wrestlers dress much as they did during the Edo Period—their hair in a samurai-style topknot, an ornamental belt/loincloth around their huge girths. Before each bout, the two contestants scatter salt in the ring to purify it from the last bout's loss; they also squat and then raise each leg, stamping it into the ground to crush, symbolically, any evil spirits. They then squat down and face each other, glaring to intimidate their opponent. Once they rush each other, each wrestler's object is to either eject his opponent from the ring or cause him to touch the ground with

any part of his body other than his feet. This is accomplished by shoving, slapping, tripping, throwing, and even carrying the opponent, but punching with a closed fist and kicking are not allowed. Altogether, there are 48 holds and throws, and sumo fans know all of them.

Most bouts are very short, lasting only 30 seconds or so. The highest-ranking players are called *yokozuna*, or grand champions; in 1993, a Hawaiian named Akebono was promoted to the highest rank, the first non-Japanese ever to be so honored. Nowadays foreign-born sumo wrestlers are common, though their numbers are restricted by the Japan Sumo Association.

There are six 15-day sumo tournaments in Japan every year: Three are held in Tokyo (Jan, May, and Sept); the others are held in Osaka (Mar), Nagoya (July), and Fukuoka (Nov). Each wrestler in the tournament faces a new opponent every day; the winner of the tournament is the wrestler who maintains the best overall record.

If you'd like to attend a sumo match while you're in Tokyo, see the "Spectator Sports" section of chapter 4. Tournament matches are also widely covered on television.

there as the puppets assume personalities of their own. The narrator, who tells the story and speaks the various parts, is an important figure in the drama. The narrator is accompanied by a traditional three-stringed Japanese instrument called a *shamisen*. By all means, try to see bunraku. The most famous presentations are at the Osaka Bunraku Theater, but there are performances in Tokyo and other major cities, too.

The Tea Ceremony

Tea was brought to Japan from China more than 1,000 years ago. It first became popular among Buddhist priests as a means of staying awake during long hours of meditation; gradually, its use filtered down among the upper classes, and in the 16th century, the tea ceremony was perfected by a merchant named Sen-no-Rikyu. Using the principles of Zen and the spiritual discipline of the samurai, the tea ceremony became a highly stylized ritual, with detailed rules on how tea should be prepared, served, and drunk. The simplicity of movement and tranquility of setting are meant to free the mind from the banality of everyday life and to allow the spirit to enjoy peace. In a way, it is a form of spiritual therapy.

The tea ceremony, *cha-no-yu*, is still practiced in Japan today and is regarded as a form of disciplinary training for mental composure and for etiquette and manners. In Kyoto, I once met a fellow guest in an inexpensive Japanese inn who asked whether she could serve me Japanese tea and a sweet after breakfast. She apologized for her ineptitude, saying she was only a mere apprentice of tea. When I asked how long she'd been studying cha-no-yu, she replied 7 years. That may seem like a long time, but the study of the tea ceremony includes related subjects, including the craftsmanship of tea vessels and implements, the design and construction of the teahouse, the landscaping of gardens, and literature related to the tea ceremony.

Several of Japan's more famous landscape gardens have teahouses on their grounds where you can sit on *tatami*, drink the frothy green tea (called *maccha*), eat sweets (meant to counteract the bitter taste of the tea), and contemplate the view. Traditionally, teahouses are quite small, with space for five or fewer people, and with two entrances: one for the host and the other for guests, so small that they must crawl through it to enter. In the center of the room is a small brazier for the teapot along with utensils needed for the making of tea—tea bowl, tea caddy, bamboo whisk, and bamboo spoon. Tea etiquette requires that guests compliment the host on the excellent flavor of the tea and on the beauty of the tea implements, which of course change with the seasons and are often valuable art objects.

Although several first-class hotels in Tokyo hold tea ceremonies in special tea-ceremony rooms (see chapter 4 for more information), nothing beats the atmosphere of a landscaped Japanese garden, many of which serve tea.

Floral & Landscape Arts

IKEBANA   Whereas a Westerner is likely to put a bunch of flowers into a vase and be done with it, the Japanese consider the arrangement of flowers an art in itself. Most young girls have at least some training in flower arranging, known as *ikebana*. First popularized among aristocrats during the Heian Period (A.D. 794–1192) and spreading to the common people in the 14th to 16th centuries, traditional ikebana, in its simplest form, is supposed to represent heaven, man, and earth; it's considered a truly Japanese art without outside influences. As important as the arrangement itself is the vase chosen to display it. Department store galleries sometimes have ikebana exhibitions, as do shrines; otherwise, check with the local tourist office.

GARDENS   Nothing is left to chance in a Japanese landscape garden: The shapes of hills and trees, the placement of rocks and waterfalls—everything is skillfully arranged in a faithful reproduction of nature. To Westerners, it may seem a bit strange to arrange nature to look like nature; but to Japanese, even nature can be improved upon to make it more pleasing through the best possible use of limited space. Japanese are masters at this, as a visit to any of their famous gardens will testify.

In fact, Japanese have been sculpting gardens for more than 1,000 years. At first, gardens were designed for walking and boating, with ponds, artificial islands, and pavilions. As with almost everything else in Japanese life, however, Zen Buddhism exerted an influence, making gardens simpler and attempting to create the illusion of boundless space within a small area. To the Buddhist, a garden was not for merriment but for contemplation—an uncluttered and simple landscape on which to rest the eyes. Japanese gardens often use the principle of "borrowed landscape"—that is, the incorporation of surrounding mountains and landscape into the overall design and impact of the garden.

THE MAGICAL WORLD OF vending MACHINES

One of the things that usually surprises visitors to Japan is the number of vending machines in the country, estimated to be more than 5.5 million—one for every 20 people. They're virtually everywhere—in train stations, in front of shops, on the back streets of residential neighborhoods. Most will take bills and give back change. Many have almost nonsensical English-language promotional lines on them, such as ENJOY REFRESHING TIME. Some will even talk to you.

And what can you buy in these vending machines? First, there are the obvious items—drinks and snacks, including hot or cold coffee in a can or a cup. But if you're on your way to someone's house, you might be able to pick up a bouquet of flowers from a machine. Your camera is out of batteries? You may be able to find those, too, along with eggs for breakfast. Vending machines outside post offices sell stamps and postcards,

while those in business hotels sell razors, cup noodles, beer, and even underwear.

In the not-too-distant past, things were also sold from sidewalk vending machines that would have met with instant protest in other countries around the world. Cigarettes and beer were available on almost every corner, where even children could buy them if they wanted to; nowadays, however, shoppers must first insert a computer-readable card certifying they're at least 20 years old. I remember a vending machine in my Tokyo neighborhood: By day, it was blank, with no sign as to what was inside; at night, however, the thing would light up, and on display were pornographic comics. Nowadays, pornographic vending machines are very rare, not for moral reasons, but because of the Internet.

Still, if it's available in Japan, it's probably in a vending machine somewhere.

Basically, there are three styles of Japanese gardens. One style, called **tsukiyama,** uses ponds, hills, and streams to depict nature in miniature. Another style, known as the **karesansui,** uses stones and raked sand in place of water and is often seen at Zen Buddhist temples; it was developed during the Muromachi Period as a representation of Zen spiritualism. The third style, called **chaniwa,** emerged with the tea ceremony; built around a teahouse with an eye toward simplicity and tranquility, such a garden will often feature stone lanterns, a stone basin filled with water, or water flowing through a bamboo pipe.

Famous gardens in Japan include Kenrokuen Park in Kanazawa, Korakuen Park in Okayama, Ritsurin Park in Takamatsu, and the grounds of the Adachi Museum. Kyoto alone has about 50 gardens, including the famous Zen rock gardens at Daitokuji and Ryoanji temples, the gardens at both the Golden and Silver pavilions, and those at Heian Shrine, Nijo Castle, and the Katsura Imperial Villa.

SHRINES & TEMPLES: RELIGION IN JAPAN

The main religions in Japan are Shintoism and Buddhism, and many Japanese consider themselves believers in both. Most Japanese, for example, will marry in a Shinto ceremony, but when they die, they'll have a Buddhist funeral.

A native religion of Japan, **Shintoism** is the worship of ancestors and national heroes, as well as of all natural things, both animate and inanimate. These natural things are thought to embody gods and can be anyone or anything—mountains, trees, the moon, stars, rivers, seas, fires, rocks, and animals. Shintoism also embraces much of Confucianism, which entered Japan in the 5th century and stressed the importance of family and loyalty. There are no scriptures in Shintoism, nor any ordained code of morals or ethics.

The place of worship in Shintoism is called a *jinja,* or shrine. The most obvious sign of a shrine is its *torii,* an entrance gate, usually of wood, consisting of two tall poles topped with either one or two crossbeams. Another feature common to shrines is a water trough with communal cups, where the Japanese will wash their hands and sometimes rinse out their mouths. Purification and cleanliness are important in Shintoism because they show respect to the gods. At the shrine, worshipers will throw a few coins into a money box, clap their hands twice to get the gods' attention, and then bow their heads and pray for whatever they wish—good health, protection, the safe delivery of a child, or a prosperous year.

Founded in India in the 6th to 5th centuries B.C., **Buddhism** came to Japan in the 6th century A.D. via China and Korea, bringing with it the concept of eternal life. By the end of the 6th century, Buddhism had gained such popularity that the prince regent Shotoku, one of Japan's most remarkable historical figures, declared Buddhism the state religion and based many of his governmental policies on its tenets. Another important Buddhist leader to emerge was a priest called Kukai, known posthumously as Kobo Daishi. After studying Buddhism in China in the early 800s, he returned and built temples throughout Japan, including the famous 88 temples on Shikoku island and those on Mount Koya, which continue to attract millions of pilgrims today.

Of the various Buddhist sects in Japan today, Zen Buddhism is probably the most well known in the West. Considered the most Japanese form of Buddhism, Zen is the practice of meditation and a strictly disciplined lifestyle to rid yourself of desire so that you can achieve enlightenment. There are no rites in Zen Buddhism, no dogmas, no theological conceptions of divinity. You do not analyze rationally, but rather know things intuitively. The strict and simple lifestyle of Zen appealed greatly to Japan's samurai warrior class, and many of Japan's arts, including the tea ceremony, arose from the practice of Zen.

Whereas Shintoists have shrines, Buddhists have temples, called *otera.* Instead of torii, temples will often have an entrance gate with a raised doorsill and heavy doors. Temples may also have a cemetery on their grounds (which Shinto shrines never have) as well as a pagoda.

MINDING YOUR P'S & Q'S

As an island nation with few natural resources, Japan's 127 million people are its greatest asset. Hardworking, honest, and proud about performing every task well no matter how insignificant it may seem, Japanese are well known for their politeness and helpfulness to strangers. Indeed, hardly anyone returns from a trip to Japan without stories of extraordinary kindnesses extended by Japanese.

With almost 99% of its population consisting of ethnic Japanese, Japan is one of the most homogeneous nations in the world. That—coupled with Japan's actual physical isolation as an island nation—has more than anything else led to a feeling among Japanese that they belong to a single huge tribe different from any other people on earth, and that all people can basically be divided into two categories: Japanese and non-Japanese. You'll often hear a Japanese preface a statement or opinion with the words "We Japanese," implying that all Japanese think alike.

While in the West the attainment of "happiness" is the elusive goal for a full and rewarding life, in Japan, it's satisfactory performance of **duty.** From the time they are born, Japanese are instilled with a sense of duty that extends toward parents, spouses, bosses, co-workers, neighbors, and society as a whole. In a nation as crowded as Japan, consideration of others is essential, and consideration of the group always wins out over the desire of the individual. In fact, I have had Japanese tell me they consider individuality synonymous with selfishness and a complete disregard for the feelings of others.

Meeting the Japanese People

On a personal level, Japanese are among the most likable people in the world. They are kind, thoughtful, and adept in perceiving another person's needs, traits that gained worldwide admiration in the days following the 2011 disaster. Japanese also have an unerring eye for beauty, whether it be food, architecture, or landscaped gardens; it's impossible to visit Japan and not have some of the Japanese appreciation of beauty rub off.

If you're invited to Japan by an organization or business, you'll receive the royal treatment and will most likely be wined and dined so wonderfully and thoroughly that you'll never want to leave. If you go to Japan on your own as an ordinary tourist, however, chances are that your experiences will be much different. Except for those who have lived or traveled abroad, few Japanese have had much contact with foreigners, especially in rural areas. And although most Japanese have studied English, not

 THE home-visit **SYSTEM**

Recognizing the difficulty foreigners can face in meeting Japanese people, some cities offer a **Home Visit,** allowing overseas visitors the chance to visit an English-speaking Japanese family in their home for a few hours. Not only does such an encounter bring you in direct contact with Japanese, it also offers a glimpse into their lifestyle. You can even request that a family member share your occupation, though such requests are, of course, sometimes impossible to fulfill. The program doesn't cost anything, but you must make arrangements in advance, which differs from city to city and can range from 1 day in advance to 2 weeks in advance by calling or applying in person at the local administrative authority or private organization (which is sometimes the local tourist office) that handles the city's home-visit program. After contacting a

local family, the office will inform you of the family and the time to visit. Most visits take place for a few hours in the evening (dinner is not served). You should bring a small gift such as flowers, fruit, or a small souvenir from your hometown. Here are a few contact numbers for cities participating in the Home-Visit System: **Narita** (℡ 0476/24-3232 or 24-3198; you can also apply in person at the Tourist Information Center in Terminal 2 at Narita airport), **Nagoya** (℡ 052/581-5689), **Kyoto** (℡ 075/752-3511), **Osaka** (℡ 06/6345-2189), **Kobe** (℡ 078/303-1010), **Kurashiki** (℡ 086/475-0543), **Hiroshima** (℡ 082/242-8879), **Fukuoka** (℡ 092/733-2220), and **Kumamoto** (℡ 096/359-2121). Note that application offices may be closed on weekends and holidays. For more information, contact local tourist information offices.

as many have had the opportunity to use the language and cannot (or are too shy to) communicate in it. So don't be surprised if you find the empty seat beside you on the subway the last one to be occupied—most Japanese are deathly afraid you'll ask them a question they won't understand.

In many respects, therefore, it's much harder to meet the locals in Japan than in many other countries. Japanese are simply much shyer than North Americans. Although they will sometimes approach you to ask whether they might practice English with you, for the most part you're left pretty much on your own unless you make the first move.

Probably the easiest way to meet Japanese is to go where they play—namely, the country's countless **bars,** including those that serve *yakitori* (skewered chicken). Usually small affairs, each with perhaps just a counter and some tables, they're often filled with both younger and older Japanese, many of whom are regulars. As the evening wears on, you'll encounter Japanese who do want to speak to you if they understand English, and other slightly inebriated Japanese who will speak to you even if they don't. If you're open to them, such chance encounters may prove to be the highlight of your trip or, at the very least, an evening of just plain fun.

Another good way to meet Japanese people is to stay in a *minshuku,* an inexpensive lodging in a private home (see "Tips on Accommodations" in chapter 14). Also, national newspapers and local English-language newsletters list **international club activities;** you may be able to hook up with, say, a hiking or skiing group composed of both Japanese and international members.

Finally, you can meet locals and learn about destinations at the same time through **Goodwill Guides,** a national organization of volunteers (mostly retirees, housewives, and students) who donate their time to guide you around their city free of charge (you pay their travel expenses, admission fees to sights, and meals). There are Goodwill Guides in cities throughout Japan, including Fukuoka, Kumamoto, Beppu, Kagoshima, Takamatsu, Matsuyama, Hiroshima, Himeji, Kurashiki, Matsue, Kobe, Osaka, Kyoto, Nara, Kanazawa, Matsumoto, Nagoya, Tokyo, Yokohama, Kamakura, Hakone, Nikko, and Matsushima. Reservations for a guide must be made in advance—usually a week or more. For information, including contact information, ask for the pamphlet "Goodwill Guide Groups of Japan Welcome You," at Tourist Information Centers in Tokyo or Narita and Kansai international airports; or go to JNTO's website at www.jnto.go.jp, and click "Essential Info" (under "Arrange Your Journey"), "Tourist Information Centers," and then "List of Volunteer Guide."

Etiquette

Much of Japan's system of etiquette and manners stems from its feudal days, when the social hierarchy dictated how a person spoke, sat, bowed, ate, walked, and lived. Failure to comply with the rules would bring severe punishment, even death. Many Japanese have literally lost their heads for committing social blunders.

Of course, nowadays it's quite different, although Japanese still attach much importance to proper behavior. As a foreigner, however, you can get away with a lot. After all, you're just a "barbarian" and, as such, can be forgiven for not knowing the rules. There are two cardinal sins, however, you should never commit: One is you should **never wear your shoes into a Japanese home, traditional inn, temple, or any room with *tatami*;** the other is that you should **never wash with soap inside a communal Japanese bathtub.** Except for these two horrors, you will probably be forgiven any other social blunders (such as standing with your arms folded or your hands in your pockets).

As a sensitive traveler, however, you should try to familiarize yourself with the basics of Japanese social etiquette. Japanese are very appreciative of foreigners who take the time to learn about their country and are quite patient in helping you. Remember, if you do commit a faux pas, apologize profusely and smile.

Most forms of behavior and etiquette in Japan developed to allow relationships to be as frictionless as possible—a pretty good idea in a country as crowded as Japan. Japanese don't like confrontations, and fights are extremely rare. Japanese are very good at covering almost all unpleasantness with a smile. Foreigners find the smile hard to read; a smiling Japanese face can mean happiness, sadness, embarrassment, or even anger. My first lesson in such physiognomic inscrutability happened on a subway in Tokyo, where I saw a middle-aged Japanese woman who was about to board the subway brutally knocked out of the way by a Japanese man rushing off the train. She almost lost her balance, but she gave a little laugh, smiled, and got on the train. A few minutes later, as the train was speeding through a tunnel, I stole a look at her and was able to read her true feelings on her face. Lost in her thoughts, she knitted her brow in consternation and looked most upset and unhappy. The smile had been a put-on.

Another aspect of Japanese behavior that sometimes causes difficulty for foreigners, especially in business negotiations, is **the reluctance of Japanese to say no when they mean no.** Many consider such directness poor manners. As a result, they're much more apt to say your request is very difficult, or they'll simply beat around the bush without giving a definite answer. At this point, you're expected to let the subject drop. Showing impatience, anger, or aggressiveness rarely gets you anywhere; apologizing sometimes does. And if someone does give in to your request, you can't thank him enough.

If you're invited to a Japanese home, you should know that it's both a rarity and an honor. Most Japanese consider their homes too small and humble for entertaining guests, which is why there are so many restaurants, coffee shops, and bars. **If you're invited to a home, don't show up empty-handed.** Bring a small gift such as candy, fruit, flowers, or perhaps a souvenir from your hometown. Alcohol is also appreciated. And if someone does extend you a favor, be sure to thank him again the next time you see him—even if it's a year later.

BOWING The main form of greeting in Japan is the bow rather than the handshake. Although at first glance it may seem simple enough, the bow—together with its implications—is actually quite complicated. The depth of the bow and the number of seconds devoted to performing it, as well as the total number of bows, depend on who you are, to whom you're bowing, and how he's bowing back. In addition to bowing in greeting, Japanese also bow upon departing and to express gratitude. The proper form for a bow is to bend from the waist with a straight back and to keep your arms at your sides if you're a man or clasped in front of you if you're a woman, but if you're a foreigner, a simple nod of the head is enough. Knowing foreigners shake hands, a Japanese may extend his hand, although he probably won't be able to stop himself from giving a little bow as well. (I've even seen Japanese bow when talking on the telephone.) Although I've occasionally witnessed Japanese businessmen shaking hands among themselves, the practice is still quite rare. Kimono-clad hostesses of a high-end traditional Japanese inn will often kneel on *tatami* and bow to the ground as they send you off on your journey.

VISITING CARD   You're a nonentity in Japan if you don't have a visiting card, called a **meishi.** Everyone—from housewives to bank presidents—carries meishi to give out during introductions. If you're trying to conduct business in Japan, you'll be regarded suspiciously—even as a phony—if you don't have business cards. Meishi are very useful business tools for Japanese. Likewise, a meishi can be used as an introduction to a third party—a Japanese may give you his meishi, scribble something on it, and tell you to present it to his cousin who owns a restaurant in Fukuoka. *Voilà*—the cousin will treat you like a royal guest.

As a tourist, you don't have to have business cards, but it certainly doesn't hurt, and Japanese people will be greatly impressed by your preparedness. The card should have your address and occupation on it; you might even consider having your meishi made in Japan, with *katakana* (Japanese syllabic script) written on the reverse side.

Needless to say, there's a proper way to present a meishi. Turn it so that the other person can read it (that is, upside-down to you) and present it with both hands and a slight bow. If you are of equal status, you exchange meishi simultaneously; otherwise, the lower person on the totem pole presents the meishi first and delivers it underneath the card being received, to show deference. Afterward, don't simply put the meishi away. Rather, it's customary for both of you to study the meishi for a moment and, if possible, to comment on it (such as, "You're from Kyoto? My brother lived in Kyoto!" or "Sony! What a famous company!"). If you're at a business meeting, you should place the card in front of you on the table.

SHOES   Nothing is so distasteful to Japanese as the soles of shoes. Therefore, you should take off your shoes before entering a home, a Japanese-style inn, a temple, and even some museums and restaurants. Usually, there will be plastic slippers at the entryway for you to slip on, but whenever you encounter *tatami,* you should take off even these slippers—only bare feet or socks are allowed to tread upon tatami.

Restrooms present another set of slippers. If you're in a home or a Japanese inn, you'll notice another pair of slippers—again plastic or rubber—sitting right inside the restroom door. Step out of the hallway plastic shoes and into the bathroom slippers, and wear these entire time you're in the restroom. When you're finished, change back into the hallway slippers. If you forget this last changeover, you'll regret it— nothing is as embarrassing as walking into a room wearing toilet slippers and not realizing what you've done until you see the mixed looks of horror and mirth on the faces of Japanese people.

BATHING   On my very first trip to Japan, I was certain I would never enter a Japanese bath. I was under the misconception that men and women bathed together, and I couldn't imagine getting into a tub with a group of smiling and bowing Japanese men. I needn't have worried—in almost all circumstances, bathing is gender segregated. There are some exceptions, primarily at outdoor hot-spring spas in the countryside, but the women who go to these are usually grandmothers who couldn't care less. Young Japanese women wouldn't dream of jumping into a tub with a group of male strangers.

Japanese baths are delightful—I'm addicted to them. You'll find them at Japanese-style inns, at *onsen* (hot-spring spas), and at *sento* (neighborhood baths). Sometimes they're elaborate affairs with indoor and outdoor tubs, and sometimes they're nothing more than a tiny tub. Public baths have long been regarded as social centers for Japanese—friends and co-workers will visit hot-spring resorts together; neighbors exchange gossip at the neighborhood bath. Sadly, neighborhood baths have been in great decline over the past decades, as most Japanese now have private baths in their homes. Hot-spring spas, however, remain hugely popular.

In any case, whether large or small, the procedure at all Japanese baths is the same. After completely disrobing in the changing room and putting your clothes in either a locker or a basket, hold a washcloth (provided free or available for sale at the bathhouse) in front of you so that it covers your vital parts and walk into the bathing area. There you'll find plastic basins and stools (sometimes they're still made of wood), and faucets along the wall. Sit on the stool in front of a faucet and repeatedly fill your basin with water (or use the hand-held faucet if available), splashing water all over you. If there's no hot water from the faucet, it's acceptable to dip your basin into the hot bath, but your washcloth should never touch the tub water. Rinsing yourself thoroughly is not only proper onsen manners; it also acclimatizes your body to the bath's hot temperature so you don't suffer a heart attack. While some Japanese just throw a bit of water over themselves, others soap down completely—and I mean completely—and then rinse away all traces of soap before getting into the tub. At any rate, only when you feel squeaky-clean should you enter the tub.

As in a Jacuzzi, everyone uses the same bath water. For that reason, you should never wash yourself in the tub, never put your washcloth into the bath (place it on your head or lay it beside the bath), and never pull the plug when you're done. After your bath is when you scrub your body and wash your hair. I have never seen a group of people wash themselves so thoroughly as the Japanese, from their ears to their toes. All sento provide shampoo and body soap, along with interesting products provided free by companies hoping to rope in new customers, but in small public baths you might have to provide your own.

Your first attempt at a Japanese bath may be painful—simply too scalding for comfort. It helps if you ease in gently and then sit perfectly still. You'll notice all tension and muscle stiffness ebbing away, a decidedly relaxing way to end the day. The Japanese are so fond of baths that many take them nightly, especially in winter when a hot bath keeps them toasty warm for hours. At an onsen, where hot-spring waters are considered curative, Japanese will bathe both at night and again in the morning, often making several trips between the faucet and the tubs and being careful not to rinse off the curative waters when they're done. With time, you'll probably become addicted, too. **Note:** Because tattoos in Japan have long been associated with *yakuza* (Japanese mafia), most public baths do not admit people with tattoos. However, if your tattoo is discreet and you're at, say, a small Japanese inn, you probably won't have any problems.

DEALING WITH THE LANGUAGE BARRIER

Without a doubt, the hardest part of traveling in Japan is the language barrier. Suddenly you find yourself transported to a crowded land of 127 million people where you can neither speak nor read the language. To make matters worse, many Japanese cannot speak English. And outside big cities and major tourist sites, menus, signs at train stations, and shop names are often in Japanese only.

However, millions of foreign visitors before you who didn't speak a word of Japanese have traveled throughout Japan on their own with great success. Much of the anxiety travelers experience elsewhere is eliminated in Japan because the country is safe and the people are kind and helpful to foreigners. In addition, the country has done a mammoth job during the past couple of decades updating street signs, subway directions, and addresses in Roman letters, especially in Tokyo, Osaka, Kyoto, and other destinations popular with tourists. There are local **tourist information offices,** called *kanko annaijo,* in almost all cities and towns, usually at train stations. While not all staff speak English, they can provide maps, point out directions, and help with hotel reservations.

In addition, the **Japan National Tourist Organization (JNTO)** does a super job publishing helpful brochures, leaflets, and maps, including a nifty booklet called *The Tourist's Language Handbook.* It contains sentences in English and their Japanese equivalents for almost every activity, from asking directions, to shopping, to ordering in a restaurant, to staying in a Japanese inn. Pick up a copy at a Tourist Information Center in Tokyo or at Narita or Kansai airports. Otherwise, a glossary of common phrases and words appears in chapter 15 of this book. For more in-depth coverage, there are many language books geared toward travelers, including *Japanese for Travelers* by Scott Rutherford (Tuttle, 2009), with useful phrases and travel tips. It also doesn't hurt to be armed with a small pocket dictionary.

If you need to ask directions of strangers in Japan, your best bet is to **ask younger people.** They have all studied English in school and are most likely to be able to help you. Japanese businessmen also often know some English. And as strange as it sounds, if you're having problems communicating with someone, **write it down** so he or she can read it. The emphasis in schools is on written rather than oral English (many English teachers can't speak English well themselves), so Japanese who can't understand a word you say may know all the subtleties of syntax and English grammar. If you still have problems communicating, you can always call the **Tourist Information Center** (© 03/3201-3331) to help with translation.

If you're heading out for a particular restaurant, shop, or sight, have your destination written down in Japanese by someone at your hotel. If you get lost along the way, look for one of the police boxes, called *koban,* found in virtually every neighborhood. They have maps of particular districts and can pinpoint exactly where you want to go if you have the address with you.

THE WRITTEN LANGUAGE No one knows the exact origins of the Japanese language, but we do know it existed only in spoken form until the 6th century. That's when the Japanese borrowed the Chinese pictorial characters, called *kanji,* and used them to develop their own form of written language. Later, two phonetic alphabet systems, *hiragana* and *katakana,* were added to kanji to form the existing Japanese writing system. Thus, Chinese and Japanese use some of the same pictographs, but otherwise there's no similarity between the languages; while they may be able to recognize parts of each other's written language, the Chinese and Japanese cannot communicate verbally.

The Japanese written language—a combination of kanji, hiragana, and katakana—is probably one of the most difficult in the modern world. As for the spoken language, there are many levels of speech and forms of expression relating to a person's social status and sex. Even nonverbal communication is a vital part of understanding Japanese, because what isn't said is often more important than what is. It's little wonder that St. Francis Xavier, a Jesuit missionary who came to Japan in the 16th century, wrote that Japanese was an invention of the devil designed to thwart the spread of Christianity. And yet, astoundingly, adult literacy in Japan is estimated to be 99%.

A note on establishment names: Many hotels and restaurants in Japan now have signs in *romaji* (Roman, or English-language, characters) in addition to their

Japanese-character signs. For those that don't, the Japanese-character names are provided for each establishment in this book that have signs in Japanese only.

OTHER HELPFUL TIPS It's worth noting that Japanese nouns do not have plural forms; thus, for example, *ryokan,* a Japanese-style inn, can be both singular and plural, as can kimono. Plural sense is indicated by context.

In addition, the Japanese custom is to list the family name first followed by the given name. That is the format I have followed in this book (with the exception of a few celebrities known outside of Japan), but note that many things printed in English—business cards, city brochures, and so on—increasingly follow the Western custom of listing the family name last.

And finally, you may find yourself confused because of suffixes attached to Japanese place names. For example, *dori* can mean street, avenue, or road; and sometimes it's attached to a street name with a hyphen, while at other times it stands alone. Thus, you may see Chuo-dori, Chuo Dori, or even Chuo-dori Avenue on English-language maps and street signs, but they're all one and the same street. Likewise, *dera* means "temple" and is often included at the end of the name, as in Kiyomizudera, which may be translated into English as Kiyomizu Temple; *jo* means "castle" and may appear at the end of a castle's name, as in Nijojo, or it may be left off and appear as Nijo Castle.

WRITTEN ENGLISH IN JAPAN English-language words are quite fashionable in Japanese advertising, with the result that you'll often see them on shop signs, posters, shopping bags, and T-shirts. However, the words are often wonderfully misspelled or are used in such unusual contexts that you can only guess at the original intent. What, for example, can possibly be the meaning behind TODAY BIRDS, TOMORROW MEN, which appeared below a picture of birds on a shopping bag? I have treasured ashtrays that read THE YOUNG BOY GRASPED HER HEART FIRMLY and LET'S TRIP IN HOKKAIDO. In Okayama, I saw a shop whose name was a stern admonition to customers to GROW UP, while in Gifu you can only surmise at the pleasures to be had at HOTEL JOYBOX. A staff member of the Hokkaido Tourist Association whose business card identified him working for the PROPAGANDA SECTION was probably more truthful than most. And imagine my consternation upon stepping onto a bathroom scale that called itself the BEAUTY-CHECKER. But the best sign I've seen was at Narita Airport years ago, where each check-in counter displayed a notice advising passengers they would have to pay a service-facility charge at THE TIME OF CHECK-IN FOR YOUR FRIGHT. I explained the cause of my amusement to the person behind the counter, and when I came back 2 weeks later, I was almost disappointed to find that all signs had been corrected. That's Japanese efficiency.

JAPAN IN POPULAR CULTURE: BOOKS & FILM

Although **Kodansha International,** which published more books on Japan in English than any other publisher, ceased operations in 2011, its considerable backlist of titles is still available at www.kodanshausa.com and www.amazon.com. **Tuttle Publishing Company** (www.tuttlepublishing.com), established in 1948 in both Vermont, USA, and Tokyo, is a leading publisher of books on Asia, including many titles about Japan.

HISTORY The definitive work of Japan's history through the ages is *Japan: The Story of a Nation* (Alfred A. Knopf, 1991) by Edwin O. Reischauer, a former U.S. ambassador to Japan. *A Modern History of Japan* (Oxford University Press, 2002), by Andrew

Gordon, covers the past 200-some years beginning with the Tokugawa shogunate. Ivan Morris's *The World of the Shining Prince: Court Life in Ancient Japan* (Kodansha Globe, 1994) highlights the golden age of the imperial court through diaries and literature of the Heian Period (794–1192), while *Everyday Life in Traditional Japan* (Tuttle, 2000) details the daily lives of samurai, farmers, craftsmen, merchants, courtiers, and outcasts during the Edo Period. Japan's 2011 earthquake and tsunami are captured in first-person accounts, essays, photographs and artwork in contributions sent from around the world in *2:46: Aftershocks: Stories from the Japan Earthquake* (Enhanced Editions, 2011), with proceeds going to the Japanese Red Cross.

For personal accounts of Japan in ages past, there's no better anthology than Donald Keene's *Travelers of a Hundred Ages: The Japanese as Revealed Through 1,000 Years of Diaries* (Holt, 1989). Written by Japanese from all walks of life, the journals provide fascinating insight into the hidden worlds of imperial courts, Buddhist monasteries, isolated country inns, and more. Lafcadio Hearn, a prolific writer about things Japanese, describes life in Japan around the turn of the 20th century in *Writings from Japan* (Penguin, 1985), while Isabella Bird, an Englishwoman who traveled in Japan in the 1870s, writes a vivid account of rural Japanese life in *Unbeaten Tracks in Japan* (Cornell University Library, 2009). *Autobiography of a Geisha* (Columbia University Press, 2003), first published in 1957, is Masuda Sayo's account of being sold to a geisha house as a child, working at a hot-spring spa, and living under harsh conditions during and after World War II.

SOCIETY   Reischauer's *The Japanese Today: Change and Continuity* (Belknap Press, 1995) offers a unique perspective on the historical events that have shaped and influenced Japanese behavior and the role of the individual in Japanese society. A classic description of Japanese and their culture is found in Ruth Benedict's brilliant *The Chrysanthemum and the Sword: Patterns of Japanese Culture* (Mariner Books, 2006), first published in the 1940s but reprinted many times since. *The Japanese Mind: Understanding Contemporary Japanese Culture* (Tuttle Publishing, 2002) was written by Japanese university students and covers everything from the meaning of silence in communication to group mentality. Debunking theories that have long shaped the outside world's views of Japan (many of which are espoused by the books above) is *Japan: A Reinterpretation* (Pantheon, 1997) by former *International Herald Tribune* Tokyo bureau chief Patrick Smith, who gives a spirited reinterpretation of Japan's economic miracle and demise; and Alex Kerr's *Dogs and Demons: Tales From the Dark Side of Modern Japan* (Hill and Wang, 2001), who writes a scathing, controversial indictment of a country he loves but says was ruined by corrupt bureaucracy. Jake Adelstein, a former Tokyo crime reporter, writes a gripping account of his run-in with Japanese mafia and the threat on his life in *Tokyo Vice: An American Reporter on the Police Beat in Japan* (Pantheon, 2009).

CULTURE & THE ARTS   For a cultural overview in one book, see *Introduction to Japanese Culture*, edited by Daniel Sosnoski (Tuttle, 1996), which covers major festivals, the tea ceremony, flower arranging, kabuki, sumo, Japanese board games, Buddhism, kanji, and much more. Elizabeth Kiritani's *Vanishing Japan: Traditions, Crafts & Culture* (Tuttle, 1995) covers a wide spectrum of traditional Japanese crafts and professions that were once a part of daily life, from potato vendors, shoe shiners, and *tatami* makers to Japanese umbrellas and handmade paper, many of which are fast disappearing in today's Japan.

The Japan Travel Bureau puts out nifty pocket-size illustrated booklets on things Japanese, including *A Look into Japan, Living Japanese Style, Eating in Japan, Festivals of Japan,* and *Japanese Family & Culture,* which covers everything from marriage in Japan to problems with mothers-in-law and explanations of why Dad gets home so late. My favorite is *Salaryman in Japan* (JTB, 1987), which describes the private and working lives of Japan's army of white-collar workers who receive set salaries.

And while some might argue it's not art, there's no denying the power *manga* (Japanese comics) has over Japanese readers and the graphic novel industry worldwide. Although dated, *Manga! Manga! The World of Japanese Comics* (Kodansha, 1986), written by Frederik L. Schodt with an introduction by Tezuka Osamu, is the bible of Japan's graphic storytelling, with excerpts from famous works. Other primers in *manga* history and its various genre are Schodt's follow-up *Dreamland Japan: Writings on Modern Manga* (Stone Bridge Press, 1996), and Paul Gravett's *Manga: 60 Years of Japanese Comics* (Collins Design, 2004).

FICTION Whenever I travel in Japan, I especially enjoy reading fictional accounts of the country; they help put me in tune with my surroundings and increase my awareness and perception. The world's first major novel was written by a Japanese woman, Murasaki Shikibu, whose classic, *The Tale of Genji* (Knopf, 1978), dating from the 11th century, describes the aristocratic life of Prince Genji.

Tokyo bookstores have entire sections dedicated to English-language translations of Japan's best-known modern and contemporary authors, including Mishima Yukio, Soseki Natsume, Abe Kobo, Tanizaki Junichiro, and Nobel Prize winners Kawabata Yasunari and Oe Kenzaburo. An overview of Japanese classical literature from the earliest times to the mid–19th century is provided in *Anthology of Japanese Literature* (Grove Press, 1988), edited by Donald Keene. Likewise, *The Showa Anthology: Modern Japanese Short Stories* (Kodansha, 1992), edited by Van C. Gessel and Tomone Matsumoto, covers works by Abe Kobe, Mishima Yukio, Kawabata Yasunari, Oe Kenzaburo, and others written between 1929 and 1984, while *Modern Japanese Stories: An Anthology* (Tuttle, 1962), edited by Ivan Morris, introduces short stories by some of Japan's top modern writers, including Mori Ogai, Tanizaki Junichiro, Kawabata Yasunari, and Mishima Yukio.

For novels, you might read Mishima's *The Sea of Fertility* (Knopf), a collection of four separate works, the last of which, *The Decay of the Angel,* was delivered to his publisher on the day of his suicide; or *The Sound of Waves* (Knopf, 1956), about young love in a Japanese fishing village. Other famous works by Japanese authors include Soseki Natsume's first novel, *I am a Cat* (Tuttle, 1972), which describes the foibles of upper-middle-class Japanese during the Meiji Era through the eyes of a cat; and his later novel, *Kokoro* (Regnery Gateway Co., 1985), as well as Kawabata Yasunari's *Snow Country* (Knopf, 1956), translated by Edward G. Seidensticker. Although not well known in the West, Enchi Fumiko wrote an absorbing novel about women in an upper-class, late-19th-century family in *The Waiting Years* (Kodansha, 2002), first published in 1957. Tanizaki Junichiro's *Makioka Sisters* (Vintage, 1995) is an epic tale of four Japanese sisters during the turbulent 1940s and '50s.

Oe Kenzaburo gained international recognition when he became the second Japanese to win the Nobel Prize for literature in 1994. One of his best-known novels is *Nip the Buds, Shoot the Kids* (Grove Press, 1996), a disturbing tale of a group of reform-school boys in the waning days of World War II. *A Personal Matter* (Grove Press, 1968) is about a man in search of himself after the birth of a handicapped son. *Hiroshima Notes* (Grove/Atlantic, 1996), featuring personal accounts of atomic bomb survivors, is a moving commentary on the meaning of the Hiroshima bombing, while *The Changeling* (Grove Press, 2011) merges fact with fiction in this story about the narrator's releationship with his filmmaker brother-in-law who leaps to his death (Oe's famous brother-in-law Juzo Itami also jumped to his death).

Favorite writers of Japan's baby-boom generation include Murakami Ryu, who burst onto the literary scene with *Almost Transparent Blue* (Kodansha, 1977), and later captured the undercurrent of decadent urban life in his best-selling *Coin Locker Babies* (Kodansha, 1995). He wrote a shocking exposé of Tokyo's sex industry, *In the Miso Soup* (Kodansha, 2003), though its murder descriptions might be too graphic for some. Ditto for *Popular Hits of the Showa Era* (W.W. Norton, 2011), a story of murder and revenge that erupts between a group of six teenage boys and six middle-aged divorced women. Murakami Haruki's writings include *Dance Dance Dance* (Kodansha, 1994); *Hard-Boiled Wonderland and the End of the World* (Vintage, 1993); *The Wind-Up Bird Chronicle* (Knopf, 1997); *South of the Border, West of the Sun* (Knopf, 1999); and *Norwegian Wood* (Vintage, 2000), a coming-of-age story set during the 1969 student movement in Japan. His *1Q84* (Knopf, 2011) is a fantasy novel set in 1984 Tokyo about a woman and man whose lives grow increasingly intertwined.

For works of fiction about Japan by Western writers, most Westerners are familiar with James Clavell's *Shogun* (Dell, 1975), a fictional account based on the lives of Englishman William Adams and military leader Tokugawa Ieyasu around 1600, but more recent is David Mitchell's *The Thousand Autumns of Jacob de Zoet* (Random House, 2010), set at the turn of the 18th century when the Dutch were confined to Dejima island in Nagasaki. The best-selling *Memoirs of a Geisha* (Knopf, 1997), by Arthur Golden and also a movie, is the fictional autobiography of a fisherman's daughter sold to a geisha house, later becoming one of Kyoto's most celebrated geisha of the 1930s.

For fictional yet personal contemporary accounts of what it's like for Westerners living in Japan, entertaining novels include *Ransom* (Vintage, 1985) by Jay McInerney and *Pictures from the Water Trade* (Harper & Row, 1986) by John D. Morley. Pico Iyer taps into the mysterious juxtaposition of the old Japan vs. the new in *The Lady and the Monk: Four Seasons in Kyoto* (Knopf, 1991). *Audrey Hepburn's Neck* (Simon & Schuster, 1996) is Alan Brown's poignant portrait of Japan's mishmash of Western and Japanese culture, as seen through the eyes of a confused young Japanese comic illustrator. Mystery fans should read Sujata Massey's 10 novels following the adventures of Japanese-American Rei Shimura; her *Girl in a Box* (HarperCollins, 2006), follows Rei's cross-cultural escapades as she works undercover in a Japanese department store. Anyone who has taught English in Japan will identify with Melana Watrous' main character in *If You Follow Me* (Harper Perennial, 2010), who spends a year in a rural town and learns as much about herself as her adopted country.

Films

For an overview of Japanese movies, an excellent reference is Donald Richie's *A Hundred Years of Japanese Film* (Kodansha, 2005). The classic samurai film is probably Kurosawa Akira's *The Seven Samurai* (1954), remade into the western *The Magnificent Seven*. Other films by what some consider to be Japan's greatest filmmaker include *Rashomon* (1951), about a murder and a rape and that raises as many questions as it answers about human nature; *Kagemusha* (1980), about warlords battling for control at the end of feudal Japan; *Ran* (1985), an epic drama set in 16th-century Japan and based on Shakespeare's *King Lear;* and *Dreams* (1990), which explores the meaning of life through eight vignettes that unfold in dreamlike settings. For a look at Japan's mountain people in the 1880s, nothing can beat Kinoshita Keisuke's *Ballad of Narayama* (1958), with its unsentimental portrait of an elderly woman who goes off into the snowy countryside to die, as was the custom of her people.

Director Oshima Nagisa created a stir in the film world with *In the Realm of the Senses* (1976), a story of obsessive love so graphic and erotic it remains censored in Japan. Juzo Itami, a famous Japanese director who purportedly leapt to his death in Tokyo in 1997 (the circumstances are mysterious), is remembered for his humorous satires on Japanese life, including *Tampopo* (1985), about sex and food and a Japanese woman who achieves success with a noodle shop; *The Funeral* (1984), which takes a comic look at death in Japan, including the surviving family's helplessness when it comes to arranging the complex rituals of the Buddhist ceremony; and *A Taxing Woman* (1987), about a female tax auditor.

Love and Pop (1998), by director Anno Hideaki, best known for *anime* films, is a low-budget film based on a novel by Murakami Ryu about "compensated dating," in which teenage girls are paid to go out with older businessmen. Another film dealing with this phenomenon rarely covered in the Western press is Harada Masato's *Bounce Ko Gals* (1998), which presents a shocking but heartfelt story of sexual exploitation and loss of innocence.

A commentary on Japan's economic woes on a personal level is *Tokyo Sonata* (2008), directed by Kurosawa Kiyoshi, about a father who loses his job but is too ashamed to tell his family and thus pretends he's going to work every day. *Departures* (2008) is Takita Yojiro's moving Academy Award–winning film (for best foreign film) about a musician who takes a job preparing corpses; the dignity with which he handles the dead and tenderness he imparts to the grieved ones make it clear that this is his true calling.

Probably the most internationally well-known film shot in Tokyo in recent years is Sophia Coppola's *Lost in Translation* (2003), in which two lost characters take solace in each other's company as they drift through an incomprehensible—and at times hilarious—Tokyo, while *The Harimaya Bridge* (2009), by Aaron Woolfolk, is a moving story about a man whose hatred for Japanese (his father died in a Japanese POW camp) slowly dissolves when he travels to Kochi to pick up his dead son's belongings. *The Cove* (2009), which won a 2010 Academy Award for best documentary film, is a shocking documentary about the slaughter of Japanese dolphins by fishermen in a small coastal village.

Those who want to know more about *anime* (Japanese animation) should take a look at *Anime from Akira to Howl's Moving Castle* by Susan J. Napier (Palgrave Macmillan, 2005), and Gilles Poitras' *Anime Essentials: Everything a Fan Needs to Know* (Stone Bridge Press, 2000). One of Japan's most famous animated films is Miyazaki Hayao's *Spirited Away* (2001), about a young girl who must call upon her inner strength to save herself and her family.

EATING & DRINKING IN JAPAN

Japanese Cuisine

Altogether, there are more than a dozen different and distinct types of Japanese cuisine, plus countless regional specialties. A good deal of what you eat may be completely new to you as well as completely unidentifiable. Sometimes Japanese themselves don't even know what they're eating, so varied and so wide is the range of available edibles. The rule is simply to enjoy, and enjoyment begins even before you raise your chopsticks to your mouth.

Keep in mind that first-class restaurants will also add a 10% to 15% service charge, as do most hotel restaurants.

Whenever I leave Japan, it's the food I miss the most. Sure, there are sushi bars and other Japanese specialty restaurants in many major cities around the world, but they don't offer nearly the variety available in Japan (and often they aren't nearly as good). For just as America has more to offer than hamburgers and steaks and England more than fish and chips, Japan has more than just sushi and *teppanyaki*. For both the gourmet and the uninitiated, Japan is a treasure-trove of culinary surprises and a foodie's delight.

To the Japanese, **presentation** of food is as important as the food itself, and dishes are designed to appeal not only to the palate but to the eye. In contrast to the American way of piling as much food as possible onto a single plate, Japanese use lots of small plates, each arranged artfully with bite-size morsels of food. After you've seen what can be done with maple leaves, flowers, bits of bamboo, and even pebbles to enhance the appearance of food, your relationship with what you eat may change forever. If there's such a thing as designer cuisine, Japan is its home.

Below are explanations of some of the most common types of Japanese cuisine. Generally, only one type of cuisine is served in a given restaurant—for example, only raw seafood is served in a sushi bar, whereas tempura is featured at a tempura counter. There are exceptions to this, especially in regards to raw fish, which is served as an appetizer in many restaurants, and set meals, which contain a variety of dishes. In addition, Japanese restaurants in hotels may offer a great variety, and some Japanese drinking establishments (called *izakaya* or *nomiya*) offer a wide range of foods from soups to sushi to skewered pieces of chicken known as *yakitori*.

FUGU　Known as blowfish, puffer fish, or globefish in English, *fugu* is one of the most exotic and adventurous foods in Japan: If it's not prepared properly, it means almost certain death for the consumer. Every year a few dozen people are hospitalized from fugu poisoning and a handful die, usually fishermen who tried preparing it at home. The fugu's ovaries and intestines are deadly and must be entirely removed without puncturing them. So why eat fugu if it can kill you? Well, for one thing, it's delicious; for another, fugu chefs are skilled in preparing fugu dishes. Ways to order it include *fugu-sashi* (raw), when it's sliced paper thin and dipped into soy sauce with bitter orange and chives; in *fugu-chiri* (stew) cooked with vegetables at your table; and as *fugu-zosui* (rice porridge). The season for fresh fugu is October or November through March, but some restaurants serve it throughout the year.

KAISEKI　The king of Japanese cuisine, *kaiseki* is the epitome of delicately and exquisitely arranged food, the ultimate in Japanese aesthetic appeal. It's also among the most expensive meals you can eat and can cost ¥25,000 or more per person; some restaurants, however, do offer more affordable mini-kaiseki courses. In addition, the better Japanese inns serve kaiseki, a reason for their high cost. Kaiseki, which is not a specific dish but rather a complete meal, is expensive because much time and skill are involved in preparing each of the many dishes, with the ingredients cooked to preserve natural flavors. Even the plates are chosen with great care to enhance the color, texture, and shape of each piece of food.

Kaiseki cuisine is based on the four seasons, with the selection of ingredients and their presentation dependent on the time of the year. In fact, so strongly does a kaiseki preparation convey the mood of a particular season, the kaiseki gourmet could tell what season it is just by looking at a meal.

A kaiseki meal is usually a lengthy affair with various dishes appearing in set order. First come the appetizer, clear broth, and one uncooked dish. These are followed by boiled, broiled, fried, steamed, heated, and vinegary dishes and finally by another soup, rice, pickled vegetables, and fruit. Although meals vary greatly depending upon the region and what's fresh, common dishes include some type of sashimi, tempura, cooked seasonal fish, and bite-size pieces of various vegetables. Because kaiseki is always a set meal, there's no problem in ordering. Let your budget be your guide.

KUSHIAGE Kushiage foods are breaded and deep-fried on skewers and include chicken, beef, seafood, and lots of seasonal vegetables (snow peas, green pepper, gingko nuts, lotus root, and the like). They're served with a slice of lemon and usually a specialty sauce. The result is delicious, and I highly recommend trying it. You'll find it at shops called *kushiage-ya* (*ya* means "shop"), which are often open only at night. Ordering the set meal is easiest, and what you get is often determined by both the chef and the season.

OKONOMIYAKI *Okonomiyaki,* which originated in Osaka after World War II and literally means "as you like it," is often referred to as Japanese pizza. To me, it's more like a pancake to which meat or fish, shredded cabbage, and vegetables are added, topped with Worcestershire sauce. Because it's a popular offering of street vendors, restaurants specializing in this type of cuisine are very reasonably priced. At some places the cook makes it for you, but at other places it's do-it-yourself, which can be quite fun if you're with a group. *Yakisoba* (fried Chinese noodles with cabbage) is also usually offered at okonomiyaki restaurants.

RICE As in other Asian countries, rice has been a Japanese staple for about 2,000 years. In fact, rice is so important to the Japanese diet that *gohan* means both "rice" and "meal." There are no problems here—everyone is familiar with rice. The difference, however, is that in Japan it's quite sticky, making it easier to pick up with chopsticks. It's also just plain white rice—no salt, no butter, no soy sauce (it's thought to be rather uncouth to dump a lot of sauces in your rice)—though trendy restaurants may sprinkle rice bowls with black sesame seeds, plum powder, or other seasoning. In the old days, not everyone could afford the expensive white kind, which was grown primarily to pay taxes or rent to the feudal lord; peasants had to be satisfied with a mixture of brown rice, millet, and greens. Today, some Japanese still eat rice three times a day, although they're now just as apt to have bread and coffee for breakfast. Restaurants specializing in organic foods often offer *genmai* (unpolished brown rice).

ROBATAYAKI *Robatayaki* refers to restaurants in which seafood and vegetables are cooked over an open charcoal grill. In the olden days, an *robata* (open fireplace) in the middle of an old Japanese house was the center of activity for cooking, eating, socializing, and simply keeping warm. Therefore, today's robatayaki restaurants are like nostalgia trips back into Japan's past and are often decorated in rustic farmhouse style with the staff dressed in traditional clothing. Robatayaki restaurants—mostly open only in the evening—are popular among office workers for both eating and drinking.

There's no special menu in a robatayaki restaurant—rather, it includes just about everything eaten in Japan. The difference is that most of the food will be grilled. Favorites of mine include *ginnan* (gingko nuts), asparagus wrapped in bacon, *piman* (a type of green pepper), mushrooms (various kinds), *jagabataa* (potatoes), and just about any kind of fish. You can usually get skewers of beef or chicken as well as *nikujaga* (a stew of meat and potatoes)—delicious during cold winter months. Because ordering is often a la carte, you'll just have to look and point.

SASHIMI & SUSHI It's estimated that the average Japanese eats 38 kilograms (84 lb.) of seafood a year—that's six times the average American consumption. Although this seafood may be served in any number of ways from grilled to boiled, a great deal of it is eaten raw.

Sashimi is simply raw seafood, usually served as an appetizer and eaten alone (that is, without rice). If you've never eaten it, a good choice to start out with is *maguro,* or lean tuna, which doesn't taste fishy at all and is so delicate in texture that it almost melts in your mouth. The way to eat sashimi is to first put *wasabi* (pungent green horseradish) into a small dish of soy sauce and then dip the raw fish in the sauce using your chopsticks (some purists maintain that wasabi and soy sauce shouldn't be mixed, but that's what my Japanese friends do).

Sushi, which is raw fish with vinegared rice, comes in many varieties. The best known is *nigiri-zushi:* raw fish, seafood, or vegetables placed on top of vinegared rice with just a touch of wasabi. It's also dipped in soy sauce. Use chopsticks or your fingers to eat sushi; remember you're supposed to eat each piece in one bite—quite a mouthful, but about the only way to keep it from falling apart. Another trick is to turn it upside down when you dip it in the sauce, to keep the rice from crumbling.

Also popular is *maki-zushi,* which consists of seafood, vegetables, or pickles rolled with rice inside a sheet of *nori* seaweed. *Inari-zushi* is vinegared rice and chopped vegetables inside a pouch of fried tofu bean curd.

Typical sushi includes *maguro* (tuna), *hirame* (flounder), *tai* (sea bream), *ika* (squid), *tako* (octopus), *ebi* (shrimp), *anago* (sea eel), and *tamago* (omelet). Ordering is easy because you usually sit at a counter where you can see all the food in a refrigerated glass case in front of you. You also get to see the sushi chefs at work. The typical meal begins with sashimi and is followed by sushi, but if you don't want to order separately, there are always various *seto* (set meals or courses). Pickled ginger is part of any sushi meal.

By the way, the least expensive sushi is *chirashi,* which is a selection of fish, seafood, and usually tamago on a large shallow bowl of rice. Because you get more rice, those of you with bigger appetites may want to order chirashi. Another way to enjoy sushi without spending a fortune is at a *kaiten* sushi shop, in which plates of sushi circulate on a conveyor belt on the counter—customers reach for the dishes they want and pay for the number of dishes they take.

SHABU-SHABU & SUKIYAKI Until the Meji Restoration beginning in 1868, which brought foreigners to Japan, Japanese could think of nothing as disgusting as eating the flesh of animals (fish was okay). Meat was considered unclean by Buddhists, and consuming it was banned by the emperor way back in the 7th century. Imagine the horror of Japanese when they discovered that Western "barbarians" ate bloody meat! It wasn't until Emperor Meiji himself announced his intention to eat meat that Japanese accepted the idea. Today, Japanese have become skilled in preparing a number of beef dishes.

Sukiyaki is among Japan's best-known beef dishes and is one many Westerners seem to prefer. Whenever I'm invited to a Japanese home, this is the meal most often served. Like fondue, it's cooked at the table.

Sukiyaki is thinly sliced beef cooked in a broth of soy sauce, stock, and sake along with scallions, spinach, mushrooms, tofu, bamboo shoots, and other vegetables. All diners serve themselves from the simmering pot and then dip their morsels into their own bowl of raw egg. You can skip the raw egg if you want (most Westerners do), but it adds to the taste and also cools the food down enough so that it doesn't burn.

Shabu-shabu is also prepared at your table and consists of thinly sliced beef cooked in a broth with vegetables in a kind of Japanese fondue. (It's named for the swishing sound the beef supposedly makes when cooking.) The main difference between the two dishes is the broth: Whereas in sukiyaki it consists of stock flavored with soy sauce and sake and is slightly sweet, in shabu-shabu it's relatively clear and has little taste of its own. The pots used are also different.

Using their chopsticks, *shabu* diners submerge pieces of meat in the watery broth until they're cooked. This usually takes only a few seconds. Vegetables are left in longer to swim around until fished out. For dipping, there's either sesame sauce with diced green onions or a more bitter fish stock sauce. Restaurants serving sukiyaki usually serve shabu-shabu as well, and they're usually happy to show you the right way to prepare and eat it.

SHOJIN RYORI   **Shojin Ryori** is the ultimate vegetarian meal, created centuries ago to serve the needs of Zen Buddhist priests and pilgrims. Dishes may include *yudofu* (simmered tofu) and an array of local vegetables. Kyoto is the best place to experience this type of cuisine.

SOBA & UDON NOODLES   Japanese love eating noodles, but I suspect at least part of the fascination stems from the way they eat them—they slurp, sucking in the noodles with gravity-defying speed. What's more, slurping noodles is considered proper etiquette. Fearing it would stick with me forever, however, slurping is a technique I've never quite mastered.

There are many different kinds of noodles, and it seems like almost every region of Japan has its own special style or kind—some are eaten plain, some in combination with other foods such as shrimp tempura, some served hot, some served cold. **Soba,** made from unbleached buckwheat flour and enjoyed for its nutty flavor and high nutritional value, is eaten hot *(kake-soba)* or cold *(zaru-soba)*. **Udon** is a thick white wheat noodle originally from Osaka; it's usually served hot. **Somen** is a fine white noodle eaten cold in the summer and dunked in a cold sauce. Establishments serving noodles range from stand-up eateries to more refined noodle restaurants with *tatami* seating. Regardless of where you eat them, noodles are among the least expensive dishes in Japan.

TEMPURA   Today a well-known Japanese food, tempura was actually introduced by the Portuguese in the 16th century. Tempura is fish and vegetables coated in a batter of egg, water, and wheat flour and then deep-fried; it's served piping hot. To eat it, dip it in a sauce of soy, fish stock, *daikon* (radish), and grated ginger; in some restaurants, only some salt, powdered green tea, or a lemon wedge is provided as an accompaniment. Various tempura specialties may include *nasu* (eggplant), *shiitake* (mushroom), *satsumaimo* (sweet potato), *shishito* (small green pepper), *renkon* (sliced lotus root), *ebi* (shrimp), *ika* (squid), *shisho* (lemon-mint leaf), and many kinds of fish. Again, the easiest thing to do is to order the *teishoku* (set meal).

TEPPANYAKI   A *teppanyaki* restaurant is a Japanese steakhouse. As in the famous Benihana restaurants in many U.S. cities, the chef slices, dices, and cooks your meal of tenderloin or sirloin steak and vegetables on a smooth, hot grill right in front of you—though with much less fanfare than his U.S. counterpart. Because beef is relatively new in Japanese cooking, some people categorize teppanyaki restaurants as "Western." However, I consider this style of cooking and presentation special enough to be referred to as Japanese. Teppanyaki restaurants also tend to be expensive, simply because of the price of beef in Japan, with Kobe beef the most prized.

TOFU Originally from China, tofu, or bean curd, is made from soy milk. It has little flavor of its own and is served cold in summer and *yudofu* (boiled) in winter. A byproduct of tofu is *yuba,* thin sheets rich in protein.

TONKATSU *Tonkatsu* is the Japanese word for "pork cutlet," made by dredging pork in wheat flour, moistening it with egg and water, dipping it in bread crumbs, and deep-frying it in vegetable oil. Because tonkatsu restaurants are generally inexpensive, they're popular with office workers and families. It's easiest to order the *teishoku,* which usually features either the *hirekatsu* (pork filet) or the *rosukatsu* (pork loin). In any case, tonkatsu is served on a bed of shredded cabbage, and one or two different sauces will be at your table, a Worcestershire sauce and perhaps a specialty sauce. If you order the teishoku, it will come with rice, miso soup, and pickled vegetables. Pork cutlet served on a bowl of rice is *katsudon.*

UNAGI I'll bet that if you eat *unagi* without knowing what it is, you'll find it very tasty—and you'll probably be very surprised to find out you've just eaten eel. Popular as a health food because of its rich protein and high vitamin A content, eel is supposed to help you fight fatigue during hot summer months but is eaten year-round. *Kabayaki* (broiled eel) is prepared by grilling filet strips over a charcoal fire; the eel is repeatedly dipped in a sweetened barbecue soy sauce while cooking. A favorite way to eat broiled eel is on top of rice, in which case it's called *unaju* or *unagi donburi.* Do yourself a favor and try it.

YAKITORI *Yakitori* is chunks of chicken or chicken parts basted in a sweet soy sauce and grilled over a charcoal fire on thin skewers. Places that specialize in yakitori (*yakitori-ya,* often identifiable by a red paper lantern outside the front door) are technically not restaurants but drinking establishments; they usually don't open until 5 or 6pm. Most yakitori-ya are popular with workers as inexpensive places to drink, eat, and be merry.

The cheapest way to dine on yakitori is to order a set course, which will often include various parts of the chicken including the skin, heart, and liver. If this isn't entirely to your taste, you may wish to order a la carte, which is more expensive but gets you exactly what you want. In addition to chicken, other skewered, charcoaled delicacies are usually offered (called *kushi-yaki*). If you're ordering by the stick, you might want to try *sasami* (chicken breast), *tsukune* (chicken meatballs), *piman* (green peppers), *negima* (chicken and leeks), *shiitake* (mushrooms), or *ginnan* (gingko nuts).

OTHER CUISINES During your travels you might also run into these types of Japanese cuisine: **Kamameshi** is a rice casserole served in individual-size cast-iron pots with different toppings that might include seafood, meat, or vegetables. **Donburi** is also a rice dish, topped with tempura, eggs, and meat such as chicken or pork. **Nabe,** a stew cooked in an earthenware pot at your table, consists of chicken, sliced beef, pork, or seafood; noodles; and vegetables. **Oden** is a broth with fish cakes, tofu, eggs, and vegetables, served with hot mustard. If a restaurant advertises that it specializes in **Kyodo-Ryori,** it serves local specialties for which the region is famous and is often very rustic in decor. A more recent trend is **crossover fusion cuisine**—creative dishes inspired by ingredients from both sides of the Pacific. Upmarket *izakaya* may also serve nouvelle dishes.

Although technically considered Chinese fast-food restaurants, **ramen shops** are a big part of dining in Japan. Serving what I consider to be generic Chinese noodles, soups, and other dishes, ramen shops can be found everywhere; they're easily recognizable by red signs and often pictures of various dishes displayed right by the front door. Many are stand-up affairs—just a high counter to rest your bowl on. In addition to *ramen* (noodle and vegetable soup), you can also get such things as *yakisoba* (fried noodles) or—my favorite—*gyoza* (fried pork dumplings). What these places lack in atmosphere is made up for in price: Dishes average less than ¥700, making them some of the cheapest places in Japan for a meal.

Drinks

All Japanese restaurants serve complimentary **green tea** with meals. If that's too weak, you might want to try **sake** (also known as *nihonshu*), an alcoholic beverage made from rice and served either hot or cold. It goes well with most forms of Japanese cuisine. Produced since about the 3rd century, sake varies by region, production method, alcoholic content, color, aroma, and taste. There are more than 1,800 sake brewers in Japan producing about 10,000 varieties. Miyabi is a prized classic sake; other brands are Gekkeikan, Koshinokanbai, Hakutsuru (meaning White Crane), and Ozeki. A good place to try a good variety of sake is at a Japanese-style pub, an *izakaya*.

Japanese **beer** is also very popular. The biggest sellers are Kirin, Sapporo, Asahi, and Suntory, with each brand offering a bewildering variety of brews. They enjoyed exclusive brewing rights until deregulation in the 1990s opened the gates to competition; now microbreweries are found everywhere in Japan. Businessmen are fond of **whiskey,** which they usually drink with ice and water. Popular in recent years is *shochu,* a clear, distilled spirit usually made from rice but sometimes from wheat, sweet potatoes, barley, or sugar cane. It used to be considered a drink of the lower classes, but sales have increased so much that it's threatening the sake and whiskey businesses. A clear liquid comparable, perhaps, to vodka, it can be consumed straight but is often combined with soda water in a drink called *chuhai*. My personal favorite is *ume-shu,* a plum-flavored shochu. But watch out—the stuff can be deadly. **Wine,** usually available only at restaurants serving Western food, has gained in popularity in recent years, with both domestic and imported brands available. Although **cocktails** are available in dance clubs, hotel lounges, and fancier bars at rather inflated prices, most Japanese stick with beer, wine, sake, shochu, or whiskey.

Tips on Dining in Japan
RESTAURANT ESSENTIALS

ORDERING The biggest problem facing the hungry foreigner in Japan is ordering a meal in a restaurant without an English-language menu. This book alleviates the problem to some extent by recommending sample dishes and giving prices for restaurants throughout Japan; we've also noted which restaurants offer English-language menus.

One aid to simplified ordering is the use of plastic food models in glass display cases either outside or just inside the front door of many restaurants, especially those in tourist areas and department stores. Sushi, tempura, daily specials, spaghetti—they're all there in mouthwatering plastic replicas along with corresponding prices. Simply decide what you want and point it out to staff.

Unfortunately, not all restaurants in Japan have plastic display cases, especially the more exclusive or traditional ones. In fact, you'd be missing a lot of Japan's best cuisine if you restrict yourself to eating only at places with displays. If there's no display from which to choose, the best thing to do is see whether the Japanese-language menu has photos or to look at what people around you are eating and order what looks best. Or, order the *teishoku,* or daily special meal (also called "set course" or simply "course," especially in restaurants serving Western food); these fixed-price meals consist of a main dish and several side dishes, including soup, rice, and Japanese pickles. Although most restaurants have set courses for dinner as well, lunch is the usual time for the teishoku, generally from 11 or 11:30am to 1:30 or 2pm.

In any case, once you've decided what you want to eat, flag down a waiter or waitress; they will not hover around your table waiting for you to order but come only when summoned. In most restaurants there are no assigned servers to certain tables; rather, servers are multitaskers, so don't be shy about stopping any who pass by.

HOURS In larger cities, most restaurants are open from about 11am to 10 or 11pm. Of course, some establishments close earlier at 9pm, while others stay open past midnight; the majority close for a few hours in the afternoon (2–5pm). In big cities like Tokyo or Osaka, try to avoid the lunchtime rush from noon to 1pm. In rural areas and small towns, restaurants tend to close early, often by 7:30 or 8pm. Traditional Japanese restaurants hang a *noren* (split curtain) over the front door to signify they're open.

Another thing to keep in mind is that the closing time posted for most restaurants is exactly that—everyone is expected to pay his or her bill and leave. A general rule of thumb is that the last order is taken at least a half-hour before closing time, sometimes an hour or more for *kaiseki* restaurants (staff will usually alert you they're taking last orders). To be on the safe side, try to arrive at least an hour before closing time so you have time to relax and enjoy your meal.

EXTRA CHARGES & TAXES Although there's talk about raising Japan's consumption tax, at the time of going to press the current tax imposed on goods and services, including restaurant meals, is 5% (generally already included in menu prices. In finer restaurants and nightlife establishments, a 10% to 15% service charge may also be levied (there is no tipping in Japan). You should also be aware of the **"table charge"** imposed on customers by some bars (especially *nomiya*), many cocktail lounges, and, only rarely, restaurants. Included in the table charge is usually a small appetizer—maybe nuts, chips, or a vegetable; for this reason, some locales call it an *otsumami*, or snack charge. At any rate, the charge is usually between ¥300 and ¥500 per person. Some establishments levy a table charge only after a certain time in the evening; others may add it only if you don't order food from the menu.

ETIQUETTE

UPON ARRIVAL As soon as you're seated in a Japanese restaurant (that is, a restaurant serving Japanese food), you'll be given a wet towel, which will be steaming hot in winter or pleasantly cool in summer. Called an *oshibori,* it's for wiping your hands. In all but the fancy restaurants, men can get away with wiping their faces as well, but women are not supposed to (I ignore this if it's hot and humid outside). Sadly, some cheaper Japanese restaurants now resort to a paper towel wrapped in plastic, which isn't nearly the same. Oshibori are generally not provided in Western restaurants.

CHOPSTICKS The next thing you'll probably be confronted with is chopsticks (though knives and forks are used in restaurants serving Western food). The proper way to use a pair is to place the first chopstick between the base of the thumb and the top of the ring finger (this chopstick remains stationary) and the second one between the top of the thumb and the middle and index fingers. (This second chopstick is the one you move to pick up food.)

The best way to learn to use chopsticks is to have a Japanese person show you how. It's not difficult, but if you find it impossible, some restaurants might have a fork as well. How proficiently foreigners handle chopsticks is a matter of great curiosity for Japanese, and they're surprised if you know how to use them; even if you were to live in Japan for 20 years, you would never stop receiving compliments on how talented you are with chopsticks.

CHOPSTICK ETIQUETTE If you're taking something from a communal bowl or tray, you're supposed to turn your chopsticks upside down and use the part that hasn't been in your mouth; after transferring the food to your plate, you turn the chopsticks back to their proper position. The exception is *shabu-shabu* and sukiyaki.

Never point at someone with your chopsticks, and never stick them down vertically into your bowl of rice and leave them there, and never pass anything from your chopsticks to another person's chopsticks—both actions have origins relating to funerary rites but are now mostly considered bad manners.

EATING SOUP & NOODLES You don't use a spoon with Japanese soup. Rather, you'll pick up the bowl and drink from it, using your chopsticks to fish out larger pieces of food. You should also pick up a bowl of rice to eat it. It's considered good taste to slurp with gusto, especially if you're eating hot noodles. Noodle shops in Japan are always well orchestrated with slurps and smacks.

DRINKING Women should hold their glass or cup with both hands, but men do not. If you're drinking in Japan, the main thing to remember is that you never pour your own glass. Bottles of beer are so large that people often share one. The rule is that in turn, one person pours for everyone else in the group, so be sure to hold up your glass when someone is pouring for you. As the night progresses Japanese get sloppy about this rule. It took me awhile to figure this out, but if no one notices your empty glass, the best thing to do is to pour everyone else a drink so that someone will pour yours. If someone wants to pour you a drink and your glass is full, the proper thing to do is to take a few gulps so that he or she can fill your glass. Because each person is continually filling everyone else's glass, you never know exactly how much you've had to drink, which (depending on how you look at it) is either very good or very bad. If you really don't want more to drink, leave your glass full and refuse refills.

PAYING THE BILL If you go out with a group of friends (not as a visiting guest of honor and not with business associates), it's customary to split the dinner bill equally, even if you all ordered different things. Even foreigners living in Japan adopt the practice of splitting the bill; it certainly makes figuring everyone's share easier, especially since **there's no tipping in Japan.** But it can be hard on frugal diners on a budget. If you're with friends who do wish to pay for only what they ate, tell the cashier you want to pay *"betsu, betsu."*

OTHER TIPS It's considered bad manners to walk down the street eating or drinking (except at a festival). You'll notice that if a Japanese buys a drink from a vending machine, he'll stand there, gulp it down, and throw away the container before going on. To the chagrin of their elders, young Japanese sometimes ignore this rule.

HOW TO EAT WITHOUT SPENDING A FORTUNE

During your first few days in Japan—particularly if you're in Tokyo—money will seem to flow from your pockets like water. In fact, money has a tendency to disappear so quickly that many people become convinced they must have lost some of it somehow. At this point, almost everyone panics (I've seen it happen again and again), but with time they slowly realize that because prices are markedly different here (steeper), a bit of readjustment in thinking and habits is necessary. Coffee, for example, is something of a luxury, and some Japanese are astonished at the thought of drinking four cups a day. Here are some tips for getting the most for your yen.

BREAKFAST Buffet breakfasts are popular at Japanese hotels and can be an inexpensive way to eat your fill. Otherwise, coffee shops offer what's called "morning service" until 10 or 11am; it generally consists of a cup of coffee, a small salad, a boiled egg, and the thickest slice of toast you've ever seen for about ¥650. That's a real bargain when you consider that just one cup of coffee can cost ¥250 to ¥500. (Except at most hotel breakfast buffets, there's no such thing as the bottomless cup in Japan.) There are many coffee-shop chains in Japan, including Doutour, Pronto, and the ever-expanding Starbucks (854 in Japan at last count).

SET LUNCHES **Eat your biggest meal at lunch.** Many restaurants serving Japanese food offer a daily set lunch, or *teishoku,* at a fraction of what their set dinners might be. Usually ranging in price from ¥800 to ¥2,000, they're generally available from about 11am to around 2pm. A Japanese teishoku will include the main course (such as tempura, grilled fish, or the specialty of the house), soup, pickled vegetables, rice, and tea, while the set menu in a Western-style restaurant (often called set lunch) usually consists of a main dish, salad, bread, and coffee.

CHEAP EATS Inexpensive restaurants can be found in department stores (often one whole floor will be devoted to various kinds of restaurants, most with plastic-food displays), underground shopping arcades, nightlife districts, and in and around train and subway stations. Some of the cheapest establishments for a night out on the town are **yakitori-ya, izakaya** (Japanese pubs), **noodle** and **ramen shops, coffee shops** (which often offer inexpensive pastries and sandwiches), and **conveyor-belt sushi restaurants** where you reach out and take the plates that interest you. Restaurants serving **gyudon** (beef bowl) are also cheap, with Yoshinoya the largest chain. Japan also has American **fast-food chains,** such as McDonald's (where Big Macs cost about ¥320) and KFC, as well as Japanese chains—Freshness Burger, MOS Burger, and First Kitchen, among them—that sell hamburgers.

Ethnic restaurants, particularly those serving Indian, Korean, Chinese, Italian, and other cuisines, are plentiful and usually inexpensive. **Hotel restaurants** can also be good bargains for inexpensive set lunches or buffets (called *viking* in Japanese; buffets always give price breaks for children), while inexpensive drinking places are good bets for dinner.

Street-side stalls, called **yatai,** are also good sources of inexpensive meals. These restaurants-on-wheels sell a variety of foods, including *oden* (fish cakes), *yakitori* (skewered barbecued chicken), and *yakisoba* (fried noodles), as well as sake and beer. They appear mostly at night, lighted by a single lantern or a string of lights, and most have a counter with stools as well, protected in winter by a wall of tarp. These can be great, cozy places for rubbing elbows with the locals. Fukuoka, in Kyushu, is famous for its yatai, but you may find them also near other cities' nightlife districts. Sadly, traditional pushcarts are being replaced by motorized vans, which are not nearly as romantic and do not offer seating.

PREPARED FOODS You can save even more money by avoiding restaurants altogether. There are all kinds of prepared foods you can buy; some are even complete meals, perfect for picnics in a park or right in your hotel room.

Perhaps the best known is the **obento,** or box lunch, commonly sold on express trains, on train-station platforms, in food sections of department stores, and at counter windows of tiny shops throughout Japan. In fact, the obento served by vendors on trains and at train stations are an inexpensive way to sample regional cuisine since they often include food typical of the region you're passing through. Costing between

¥800 and ¥1,500, the basic obento contains a piece of meat (generally fish or chicken), various side dishes, rice, and pickled vegetables. Sushi boxed lunches are also readily available.

My favorite place to shop for prepared foods is **department stores.** Located in basements, these enormous food and produce sections harken back to Japanese markets of yore, with vendors yelling out their wares and crowds of housewives deciding on the evening's dinner. Different counters specialize in different items—tempura, *yakitori,* eel, Japanese pickles, cooked fish, sushi (sometimes made by robots!), salads, vegetables, and desserts. Almost the entire spectrum of Japanese cuisine is available, as are numerous samples. There are also counters selling obento box meals. In any case, you can eat for less than ¥1,200, and there's nothing like milling with Japanese housewives to make you feel like one of the locals. Though not as colorful, **24-hour convenience stores** and grocery stores also sell packaged foods like sandwiches and obento.

WHEN TO GO

Because Japan stretches in an arc from northeast to southwest at about the same latitudes as Maine and Florida, you can travel in the country virtually any time of year. Winters in southern Kyushu and Okinawa are mild, while summers in northern Hokkaido are cool. There are, however, peak seasons to avoid, including April 29 to May 5, mid-July through August, and New Year's.

CLIMATE   Most of Japan's islands lie in a temperate seasonal wind zone similar to that of the East Coast of the United States, which means there are four distinct seasons. Japanese are very proud of their seasons and place much more emphasis on them than people do in the West. Kimono, dishes and bowls used for *kaiseki,* and even *noh* plays change with the season. Certain foods are eaten during certain times of the year, such as eel in summer and *fugu* (blowfish) in winter. Almost all haiku have seasonal references. The cherry blossom signals the beginning of spring, and most festivals are tied to seasonal rites. Even urban dwellers note the seasons; almost as though on cue, businessmen will change virtually overnight from their winter to summer attire.

Summer, which begins in June, is heralded by the rainy season, which lasts from about mid-June to mid-July (there's no rainy season in Hokkaido). Although it doesn't rain every day, it does rain a lot, sometimes quite heavily, making umbrellas imperative. After the rain stops, it turns unbearably hot and uncomfortably humid throughout the country, with the exception of Hokkaido, mountaintop resorts such as Hakone, and the Japan Alps. You'll be more comfortable in light cottons, though you should bring a light jacket for unexpected cool evenings or air-conditioned rooms. You should also pack sunscreen and a hat (Japanese women are also fond of parasols).

The period from the end of August to September is **typhoon season,** although the majority of storms stay out at sea and generally vent their fury on land only in thunderstorms.

Autumn, lasting through November, is one of the best times to visit Japan. The days are pleasant and slightly cool, and the changing red and scarlet of leaves contrast brilliantly with the deep blue skies. There are many chrysanthemum shows in Japan at this time, popular maple-viewing spots, and many autumn festivals. Bring a warm jacket.

Winter, lasting from December to March, is marked by snow in much of Japan, especially in the mountain ranges where the skiing is superb. Many tourists also flock to hot-spring resorts during this time. The climate is generally dry, and on the Pacific coast the skies are often blue. Tokyo doesn't get much snow, though it can be crisp, cold, and wet. Northern Japan's weather, in Tohoku and Hokkaido, can be quite severe, while southern Japan, especially Kyushu and Okinawa, enjoys generally mild, warm weather. Wherever you are, you'd be wise to bring warm clothing throughout the winter months.

Spring arrives with a magnificent fanfare of plum and cherry blossoms in March and April, an exquisite time when all of Japan is ablaze in whites and pinks. The **cherry-blossom season** starts in southern Kyushu around mid-March and reaches Hokkaido by early May. The blossoms themselves last only a few days, symbolizing to Japanese the fragile nature of beauty and of life itself. Other flowers also bloom through May or June, including azaleas and irises. During spring, numerous festivals throughout Japan celebrate the rebirth of nature.

Tokyo's Average Daytime Temperatures & Rainfall

	JAN	FEB	MAR	APR	MAY	JUNE	JULY	AUG	SEPT	OCT	NOV	DEC
TEMP. (°F)	42	45	50	61	69	71	78	81	76	68	57	48
TEMP. (°C)	5	7	10	16	21	22	26	27	24	20	14	9
DAYS OF RAIN	4.3	6.1	8.9	10	9.6	12.1	10	8.2	10.9	8.9	6.4	3.8

BUSY SEASONS   Japanese have a passion for travel, and they generally travel at the same time, resulting in jampacked trains and hotels. The worst times to travel are around **New Year's,** from the end of December to January 4; **Golden Week,** from April 29 to May 5; and during the **Obon Festival,** about a week in mid-August. Avoid traveling on these dates at all costs, since all long-distance trains, domestic airlines, and most accommodations are booked solid and prices are higher. The weekends before and after these holidays are also likely to be crowded or booked. Exceptions are major cities like Tokyo or Osaka—since the major exodus is back to hometowns or the countryside, metropolises can be downright blissful during major holidays such as Golden Week, especially since most restaurants and municipal and national museums do not close.

Another busy time is during the **school summer vacation,** from around July 19 or 20 through August. It's best to reserve train seats and book accommodations during this time in advance. In addition, you can expect destinations to be packed during major festivals, so if one of these is high on your list, make plans well in advance.

HOLIDAYS   National holidays are January 1 (New Year's Day), second Monday in January (Coming-of-Age Day), February 11 (National Foundation Day), March 20 (Vernal Equinox Day), April 29 (Showa Day, after the late Emperor Showa), May 3 (Constitution Memorial Day), May 4 (Greenery Day), May 5 (Children's Day), third Monday in July (Maritime Day), third Monday in September (Respect-for-the-Aged Day), September 23 (Autumn Equinox Day), second Monday in October (Health Sports Day), November 3 (Culture Day; many municipal museums are free), November 23 (Labor Thanksgiving Day), and December 23 (Emperor's Birthday).

When a national holiday falls on a Sunday, the following Monday becomes a holiday. Although government offices and some businesses are closed on public holidays, most stores and restaurants remain open. The exception is during the New Year's celebration, January 1 through January 3 or 4, when virtually all restaurants, public and private offices, stores, and even ATMs close; during that time, you'll have to dine in hotels.

All museums close for New Year's for 1 to 4 days, but most major museums remain open for the other holidays. If a public holiday falls on a Monday (when most museums are closed), many museums will remain open but will close instead the following day, Tuesday. Note, however, that privately owned museums, such as art museums or special-interest museums, generally close on public holidays. To avoid disappointment, be sure to phone ahead if you plan to visit a museum on a holiday or the day following it.

FESTIVALS With Shintoism and Buddhism the major religions in Japan, it seems as though there's a *matsuri* (festival) going on somewhere in the country almost every day, especially in summer. Every major shrine and temple has at least one annual festival. Such festivals are always free, though admission may be charged for special exhibitions such as flower shows. There are also a number of national holidays observed throughout the country with events and festivals, as well as annual seasonal events like cormorant fishing and cherry-blossom viewing.

The larger, better-known festivals are exciting to attend but do take some advance planning since hotel rooms may be booked 6 months in advance. If you haven't made prior arrangements, you may want to let the following schedule be your guide in avoiding certain cities on certain days. ***A note on festival dates:*** If you plan your trip around a certain festival, be sure to double-check the exact dates since they can change. Check the JNTO website and the tourist website of the city hosting the festival. In addition, for an exhaustive list of events beyond those listed here, check http://events.frommers.com, where you'll find a searchable, up-the-minute roster of what's happening in cities all over the world.

Japan Calendar of Events

For an exhaustive list of events beyond those listed here, check http://events.frommers.com, where you'll find a searchable, up-to-the-minute roster of what's happening in cities all over the world.

JANUARY

New Year's Day is the most important national holiday in Japan. Because this is a time when Japanese are with their families and because virtually all businesses, restaurants, museums, and shops close down, it's not a particularly rewarding time of the year for foreign visitors. Best bets are shrines and temples, where Japanese come in their best kimono or dress to pray for good health and happiness in the coming year. January 1.

Tamaseseri (Ball-Catching Festival), Hakozaki Shrine, Fukuoka. The main attraction at this 500-year-old tradition is a struggle between two teams of men, representing farmers and fishermen and dressed only in loincloths, who try to capture a sacred wooden ball. The winning team is supposed to have good luck the entire year. January 3.

Dezomeshiki (New Year's Parade of Firemen), Tokyo Big Sight, Odaiba, Tokyo. Agile firemen dressed in Edo-Era costumes prove their worth with acrobatic stunts atop tall bamboo ladders in this parade, with fire

trucks, helicopters, and emergency drills adding to the excitement. January 6.

Usokae (Bullfinch Exchange Festival), Dazaifu Tenmangu Shrine, Fukuoka Prefecture. The object here is to pass wooden bullfinches from person to person, hopefully ending up with the golden bullfinch, thought to bring good luck. A giant fire is lit in the evening to drive away evil spirits. January 7.

Coming-of-Age Day, a national holiday. This day honors young people who have reached the age of 20, when they can vote, drink alcohol, and assume other responsibilities. On this day, they visit shrines throughout the country to pray for their future, with many women dressed in kimono. In Tokyo, the most popular shrine is Meiji Shrine near Harajuku Station. Second Monday in January.

Toka Ebisu Festival, Imamiya Ebisu Shrine, Osaka. Ebisu is considered the patron saint of business and good fortune, so this is the time when businesspeople pray for a successful year. The highlight of the festival is a parade of women dressed in colorful kimono and carried through the streets in palanquins (covered litters). Stalls sell good-luck charms. January 9 to January 11.

Toh-shiya, Kyoto. This traditional Japanese archery contest is held in the back corridor of Japan's longest wooden structure, Sanjusangendo Hall. Sunday closest to January 15.

Yamayaki (Grass Fire Ceremony), Nara. As evening approaches, Wakakusayama Hill is set ablaze and fireworks are displayed. The celebration marks a time more than 1,000 years ago when a dispute over the boundary of two major temples in Nara was settled peacefully. Fourth Sunday in January.

Ice Falls Festival, Sounkyo Onsen. Ice sculptures, ice slides, frozen waterfalls lit in various colors, and evening fireworks are the highlights of this small-town festival. Mid-January to Mid-March.

FEBRUARY

Oyster Festival, Matsushima. Matsushima is famous for its oysters, and this is the time they're considered to be at their best. Oysters are given out free at booths set up at the seaside park along the bay. First Sunday in February.

Setsubun (Bean-Throwing Festival), at leading temples throughout Japan. According to the lunar calendar, this is the last day of winter; people throng to temples to participate in the traditional ceremony of throwing beans to drive away imaginary devils, yelling, "Evil go out, good luck come in." If they then eat the same number of soybeans as their age, they'll have good luck. February 3 or 4.

Setsubun Mantoro (Lantern Festival), Kasuga Shrine, Nara. A beautiful sight in which more than 3,000 stone and bronze lanterns are lit from 6:30 to 9pm. February 3 and August 14 and 15.

Nagasaki Lantern Festival, Nagasaki. Begun by Chinese residents to celebrate the Chinese New Year, this festival now features 15,000 lanterns in around Chinatown, a parade honoring the Qing Dynasty, dragon and lion dances, Chinese acrobatics, and Chinese music. Chinese New Year (date varies according to the lunar calendar).

Sapporo Snow Festival, Odori Park, and Susukino, in Sapporo. This famous 7-day Sapporo festival features huge, elaborate statues and figurines carved in snow and ice. Competitors come from around the world. Second week in February.

Saidaiji Eyo, Saidaiji Kannon-in Temple, Okayama Prefecture. Thousands of loincloth-clad men grapple for sacred wooden sticks tossed by priests. Third Saturday of February at midnight.

MARCH

Omizutori (Water-Drawing Festival), Todaiji Temple, Nara. This festival includes a solemn evening rite in which young ascetics brandish large burning torches and draw circles of fire. The biggest ceremony takes place on the night of March 12; on the next day, the ceremony of drawing water is held to the accompaniment of ancient Japanese music. March 1 to March 14.

Hinamatsuri (Doll Festival), observed throughout Japan. It's held in honor of young girls to wish them a future of happiness. In homes where there are girls, dolls dressed in ancient costumes representing the emperor, empress, and dignitaries are set up on a tier of shelves along with miniature household articles. Many hotels also display dolls in their lobbies. March 3.

Tokyo International Anime Fair, Tokyo Big Sight, Odaiba (www.tokyoanime.jp). One of the world's largest Japanese animation events draws more than 100 production companies, TV and film agencies, toy and game software companies, publishers, and other *anime*-related companies. Usually last weekend in March.

APRIL

Kanamara Matsuri, Kanayama Shrine, Kawasaki (just outside Tokyo). This festival extols the joys of sex and fertility (and more recently, raises awareness about AIDS), featuring a parade of giant phalluses, some carried by transvestites. You'll definitely get some unusual photographs here. First Sunday in April.

Buddha's Birthday (also called Hana Matsuri, or Floral Festival), observed nationwide. Ceremonies are held at all Buddhist temples. April 8.

Kamakura Matsuri, Tsurugaoka Hachimangu Shrine, Kamakura. This festival honors heroes from the past, including Minamoto Yoritomo, who made Kamakura his shogunate capital back in 1192. Highlights include horseback archery (truly spectacular to watch, though fewer and fewer men have the skill), a parade of portable shrines, and sacred dances. Second to third Sunday of April.

Takayama Spring Festival, Takayama. Supposedly dating from the 15th century, this festival is one of Japan's grandest with a dozen huge, gorgeous floats that are wheeled through the village streets. April 14 and 15.

Gumonji-do (Firewalking Ceremonies), Miyajima. Walking on live coals is meant to show devotion and to pray for purification and protection from illness and disaster. Daishoin Temple. April 15 and November 15.

Yayoi Matsuri, Futarasan Shrine, Nikko. Yayoi Matsuri features a parade of floats embellished with artificial cherry blossoms and paper lanterns. April 16 and 17.

Golden Week is a major holiday period throughout Japan, when many Japanese offices and businesses close down and families go on vacation. It's a crowded time to travel; reservations are a must. April 29 to May 5.

MAY

Hakata Dontaku Port Festival, Fukuoka. Citizens, dressed as deities, parade through the streets clapping wooden rice paddles— you're welcome to join in. May 3 and 4.

Children's Day is a national holiday honoring all children, especially boys. The most common sight throughout Japan is colorful streamers of carp—which symbolize perseverance and strength—flying from poles. May 5.

Takigi Noh Performances, Kofukuji Temple, Nara. These *noh* plays are presented outdoors after dark under the blaze of torches. May 11 and 12.

Kanda Festival, Kanda Myojin Shrine, Tokyo. This festival, which commemorates Tokugawa Ieyasu's famous victory at Sekigahara in 1600, began during the Feudal Period as the only time townspeople could enter the shogun's castle and parade before him. Today this major Tokyo festival features a parade of dozens of portable shrines carried through the district, plus geisha dances and a tea ceremony. Held in odd-numbered years (with a smaller festival held in even years) on the Saturday and Sunday closest to May 15.

Aoi Matsuri (Hollyhock Festival), Shimogamo and Kamigamo Shrines, Kyoto. This is one of Kyoto's biggest events, a colorful parade with 500 participants wearing ancient costumes to commemorate the days when the imperial procession visited the city's shrines. May 15.

Kobe Matsuri, Kobe. This relatively new festival celebrates Kobe's international past with fireworks at Kobe Port, street markets, and a parade on Flower Road with participants wearing native costumes. Mid-May.

Shunki Reitaisai (Grand Spring Festival), Nikko. Commemorating the day in 1617 when Tokugawa Ieyasu's remains were brought to his mausoleum in Nikko, this festival re-creates that drama with more than 1,000 armor-clad people escorting three palanquins through the streets. May 17 and 18.

Sanja Matsuri, Asakusa Shrine, Tokyo. Tokyo's most celebrated festival features about 100 portable shrines carried through the district on the shoulders of men and women in traditional garb. Third Sunday and preceding Friday and Saturday of May.

Mifune Matsuri, Arashiyama, on the Oigawa River outside Kyoto, is when the days of the Heian Period (during which the imperial family used to take pleasure rides on the river) are reenacted by some 20 boats and people in costume. Third Sunday in May.

JUNE

Takigi Noh Performances, Kyoto. Evening performances of *noh* are presented on an open-air stage at the Heian Shrine. June 1 and 2.

Hyakumangoku Matsuri (One Million Goku Festival), Kanazawa. Celebrating Kanazawa's production of one million *goku* of rice (1 goku is about 150kg/330 lb.), this extravaganza features folk songs and traditional dancing in the streets, illuminated paper lanterns floating downriver, public tea ceremonies, geisha performances, and— the highlight—a parade that winds through the city in reenactment of Lord Maeda Toshiie's triumphant arrival in Kanazawa on June 14, 1583, with lion dances, ladder-top acrobatics by firemen, and a torch-lit outdoor *noh* performance. June 8 to June 14.

Sanno Festival, Hie Shrine, Tokyo. This Edo Period festival, one of Tokyo's largest, features the usual portable shrines, transported through the busy streets of the Akasaka District. June 10 to June 16.

Otaue Rice-Planting Festival, Sumiyoshi Taisha Shrine, Osaka. In hopes of a successful harvest, young girls in traditional farmers' costumes transplant rice seedlings in the shrine's rice paddy to the sound of traditional music and songs. June 14.

Ukai (Cormorant Fishing), Nagara River near Gifu and Kiso River in Inuyama (near Nagoya). Visitors board small wooden boats after dark to watch cormorants dive into the water to catch *ayu,* a kind of trout. Generally mid-May to October.

JULY

Tanabata Matsuri (Star Festival), celebrated throughout Japan. According to myth, the two stars Vega and Altair, representing a weaver and a shepherd, are allowed to meet once a year on this day. If the skies are cloudy, however, the celestial pair cannot meet and must wait another year. Celebrations differ from town to town, but in addition to parades and food/souvenir stalls, look for bamboo branches with colorful strips of paper bearing children's wishes. July 7.

Hozuki Ichi (Ground-Cherry Pod Fair), Tokyo. This colorful affair at Sensoji Temple in Asakusa features hundreds of stalls selling ground-cherry pods and colorful wind bells. July 9 and 10.

Yamakasa, Fukuoka. Just before the crack of dawn, seven teams dressed in loincloths and *happi* coats (short, colorful, kimono-like jackets) race through town, bearing 1-ton floats on their shoulders. In addition, elaborately decorated, 9m-tall (30-ft.) floats designed by Hakata doll masters are on display throughout town. July 15.

Gion Matsuri, Kyoto. One of the most famous festivals in Japan, this dates back to the 9th century, when the head priest at Yasaka Shrine organized a procession to ask the gods' assistance in a plague raging in the city. Although celebrations continue throughout the month, the highlight is on the 17th, when more than 30 spectacular wheeled floats wind their way through the city streets to the accompaniment of music and dances. Many visitors plan their trip to Japan around this event. July 16 and 17.

Obon Festival, nationwide. This festival commemorates the dead who, according to Buddhist belief, revisit the world during this period. Many Japanese return to their hometowns for religious rites, especially if a family member has died recently. As one Japanese whose grandmother had died a few months before told me, "I have to go back to my hometown—it's my grandmother's first Obon." Mid-July or mid-August, depending on the region.

Tenjin Matsuri, Temmangu Shrine, Osaka. One of Japan's biggest festivals, this dates from the 10th century when the people of Osaka visited Temmangu Shrine to pray for protection against diseases prevalent during the long, hot summer. They would take pieces of paper cut in the form of human beings and, while the Shinto priest said prayers, would rub the paper over themselves in ritual cleansing. Afterward, the pieces of paper were taken by boat to the mouth of the river and disposed of. Today, events are reenacted with a procession of more than 100 sacred boats making their way downriver, followed by a fireworks display. There's also a parade of some 3,000 people in traditional costume. July 24 and 25.

Kangensai Music Festival, Itsukushima Shrine, Miyajima. There are classical court music and *Bugaku* dancing, and three barges carry portable shrines, priests, and musicians across the bay along with a flotilla of other boats. Because this festival takes place according to the lunar calendar, the actual date changes each year. Late July or early August.

Hanabi Taikai (Fireworks Display), Tokyo. This is Tokyo's largest summer celebration, and everyone sits on blankets along the banks of the Sumida River near Asakusa to see the show. It's great fun! Last Saturday of July.

Fuji Rock Festival, Naeba Ski Resort, Niigata. Japan's biggest outdoor rock festival, with an impressive lineup of international acts in a beautiful mountain setting. Last weekend in July.

AUGUST

Oshiro Matsuri, Himeji. This celebration is famous for its *noh* dramas lit by bonfire and performed on a special stage on the Himeji Castle grounds, as well as a procession from the castle to the city center with participants dressed as feudal lords and ladies in traditional costume. First Friday and Saturday of August.

Peace Ceremony, Peace Memorial Park, Hiroshima. This ceremony is held annually at 8:15am in memory of those who died in the atomic bomb blast of August 6, 1945. In the evening, thousands of lit lanterns are set adrift on the Ota River in a plea for world peace. A similar ceremony is held on August 9 in Nagasaki. August 6.

Tanabata Matsuri, Sendai. Sendai holds its Star Festival 1 month later than the rest of Japan. It's the country's largest, and the entire town is decorated with colored paper streamers. August 6 to August 8.

Matsuyama Festival, Matsuyama. Jubilant festivities include dances, fireworks, a parade, and a night fair. August 11 to August 13.

Sanuki Takamatsu Festival, Takamatsu. About 4,000 people participate in a dance procession that threads its way along Chuo Dori Avenue; anyone can join in. Food stalls are set up in Chuo Park, and there's also a fireworks display. August 12 to August 14.

Toronagashi and Fireworks Display, Matsushima. A fireworks display is followed by the setting adrift on the bay of about 5,000 small boats with lanterns, which are meant to console the souls of the dead; another 3,000 lanterns are lit on islets in the bay. Evening of August 15.

Yamaga Toro Matsuri (Lantern Festival), Kumamoto. Women dressed in *yukata* dance through town with illuminated paper lanterns on their heads, and there's also a fireworks display. August 15 and 16.

Daimonji Bonfire, Mount Nyoigadake, Kyoto. A huge bonfire in the shape of the Chinese character *dai*, which means "large," and other motifs are lit near mountain peaks; it's the highlight of the Obon Festival (see July, above). August 16.

Eisa Festival, Okinawa Island. Dance teams compete in lively folk performances to the accompaniment of drums, three-stringed *sanshin*, and other instruments. Late August.

SEPTEMBER

Yabusame, Tsurugaoka Hachimangu Shrine, Kamakura. Archery performed on horseback recalls the days of the samurai, along with classical Japanese dance and a parade of portable shrines. September 16.

OCTOBER

Okunchi Festival, Suwa Shrine, Nagasaki. This 370-year-old festival, one of Kyushu's best, illustrates the influence of Nagasaki's Chinese population through the centuries. Highlights include a parade of floats and dragon dances. October 7 to October 9.

Marimo Matsuri, Lake Akan, Hokkaido. This festival is put on by the native Ainu population to celebrate *marimo* (a spherical weed found in Lake Akan) and includes a pine torch parade and fireworks. Early October.

Takayama Matsuri (Autumn Festival), Takayama. As in the festival held here in April, huge floats are paraded through the streets. October 9 and 10.

Nagoya Festival, Nagoya. Nagoya's biggest event commemorates three of its heroes—Tokugawa Ieyasu, Toyotomi Hideyoshi, and Oda Nobunaga—in a parade that goes from City Hall to Sakae and includes nine floats with mechanical puppets, marching bands, and a traditional orchestra. Second weekend in October.

Naha Tug of War, Naha, Okinawa. Anyone can join in this tug of war with the world's largest rope (186m/619 ft.), once held to welcome Chinese ambassadors. Second Sunday in October.

Nada no Kenka Matsuri (Nada Fighting Festival), Matsubara Hachiman Shrine, Himeji. Men shouldering portable shrines jostle each other as they attempt to show their skill in balancing their heavy burdens. October 14 and 15.

Doburoku Matsuri, Ogimachi, Shirakawago. This village festival honors unrefined sake, said to represent the spirit of God, with a parade, an evening lion dance, and plenty of eating and drinking. October 14 to October 19.

Nikko Toshogu Shrine Festival, Nikko. A parade of warriors in early-17th-century dress are accompanied by spear-carriers, gun-carriers, flag-bearers, Shinto priests, pages, court musicians, and dancers as they escort a sacred portable shrine. October 17.

Jidai Matsuri (Festival of the Ages), Kyoto. Another of Kyoto's grand festivals, this one began in 1894 to commemorate the founding of the city in 794. It features a procession of more than 2,000 people dressed in ancient costumes representing different epochs of Kyoto's 1,200-year history, who march from the Imperial Palace to Heian Shrine. October 22.

NOVEMBER

Ohara Matsuri, Kagoshima. About 20,000 people parade through the town in cotton *yukata* and other traditional garb, dancing to the tune of local folk songs. A sort of Japanese Mardi Gras, this event attracts around 200,000 spectators each year. November 2 and 3.

Daimyo Gyoretsu (Feudal Lord Procession), Yumoto Onsen, Hakone. The old Tokaido Highway that used to link Kyoto and Tokyo comes alive again with a faithful reproduction of a feudal lord's procession in the olden days. November 3.

Shichi-go-san (Children's Shrine-Visiting Day), held throughout Japan. Shichi-go-san literally means "seven-five-three" and refers to children of these ages who are dressed in their kimono best and taken to shrines by their elders to express thanks and pray for their future. November 15.

Tori-no-Ichi (Rake Fair), Otori Shrine, Tokyo. This fair in Asakusa (and other Otori shrines throughout Japan) features stalls selling rakes lavishly decorated with paper and cloth, which are thought to bring good luck and fortune. Based on the lunar calendar, the date changes each year. Mid-November.

DECEMBER

Gishi-sai, Sengakuji Station, Tokyo. This memorial service honors 47 *ronin* (masterless samurai) who avenged their master's death by killing his rival and parading his head; for their act, all were ordered to commit suicide. Forty-seven men dressed as the ronin travel to Sengakuji Temple (the site of their and their master's burial) with the enemy's head to place on their master's grave. December 14.

Kasuga Wakamiya On-Matsuri, Kasuga Shrine, Nara. This festival features court music with traditional dance and a parade of people dressed as courtiers, retainers, and wrestlers of long ago. December 15 to December 18.

Hagoita-Ichi (Battledore Fair), Sensoji Temple, Tokyo. Popular since Japan's feudal days, this Asakusa festival features decorated paddles of all types and sizes. Most have designs of kabuki actors—images made by pasting together padded silk and brocade—and make great souvenirs and gifts. December 17 to December 19.

New Year's Eve. At midnight, many temples ring huge bells 108 times to signal the end of the old year and the beginning of the new. Families visit temples and shrines throughout Japan to pray for the coming year. December 31.

RESPONSIBLE TRAVEL

Japan is not the same since the 2011 Great East Japan Earthquake. Following the shutdown of the Fukushima nuclear power plants about 220 km (137 miles) north of Tokyo, Tokyo and other cities embraced energy-saving measures, some mandated by the government, others voluntarily for the greater good. To be sure, there was waste that should have been curbed long ago (I've always wondered how open-fronted shops can afford to air-condition the outside world), but I was heartened to see energy-saving measures adopted in Tokyo in the summer months following the disaster, including dimmed lights in subway stations, thermostats turned high in summer, businessmen eschewing suits for more casual, lighter attire, and products introduced to conserve energy, including—my favorite—exterior walls covered with plants; in all, Tokyo residents reduced energy usage by 16% the summer of 2011. Although it's hard to predict whether conservation measures will continue to grow, growing opposition to nuclear energy seems to forecast alternative energy sources for Japan's future.

Perhaps Fukuoka, on the island of Kyushu, will serve as a model green city. Over the years it has introduced a variety of programs to reduce its carbon footprint, including a "Morning Glory Curtain Project" to cover building walls with greenery (the city's ACROS Fukuoka Building is well-known for its terraced façade covered with plants and shrubs), a seawater desalination center, and its own "Fukuoka Method" of waste landfill that reduces greenhouse gases by 50%. Fukuoka also hopes to become the first city in the world powered by hydrogen.

In any case, it will be a while—if not years—before the country's energy output is fully up to speed. What that means for Japan's hot and humid summers and cold winters is anybody's guess.

In other respects, Japan may be crowded and land may be scarce, but it has always been clean and cared for. Littering is rare in Japan, and Japanese are taught practically at birth about separating trash for recycling.

You can do your part by depositing all your trash—newspapers, plastic water bottles, cans—into the appropriate recycle bins found in parks, subway stations, and other public places. Other actions you can take include refusing extra packaging at department stores (which may otherwise wrap your purchase and then place it in a shopping bag), carrying your own chopsticks (in cheap restaurants they are likely to be disposable), reusing your towels and sheets in hotels, turning off unused lights, and opting for public transportation over taxis.

Luckily, public transportation in Japan is efficient, whether it's from city to city or getting around a particular city. Most people I know in Tokyo don't own a car, but Japan is no newcomer to the idea of hybrids, either, with Toyota introducing the Prius many years back, followed by Honda's Insight and 125-cc scooters that are 25% more efficient than conventional ones. There are even electric-powered taxis; you'll find an e-cab stand west of Tokyo Station, in front of the Shin Marunouchi Building.

The report card on Japan's relationship with its natural surroundings, however, is mixed. I was aghast the first-time I traveled in Japan and saw roadside hills and river banks plastered with unsightly cement in an effort to curb erosion and avalanches, and Japan has long drawn worldwide criticism for its annual whale hunting and for its annual slaughter of dolphins in a coastal fishing village.

As for grass-roots organizations that support sustainability in Japan, **Ecotourism Japan** (www.ecoutourism-center.jp) is a non-profit organization that works with tour operators, researchers and other professionals with the goal of preserving Japan's natural environment and revitalizing local communities through ecotourism. See, also, www.greenz.jp, which is in Japanese but has some English references.

In addition to the information above, see www.frommers.com/planning for more tips on responsible travel.

TOURS

Academic Trips & Language Classes

If your primary interest lies with *ikebana* (Japanese flower arranging), the tea ceremony, or other cultural pursuits, Tokyo and Kyoto are your best bets for finding instruction in English. For short introductions, **Sunrise Tours** (www.jtb-sunrisetours.jp) offers the chance to experience the tea ceremony on 2- or 3-hour tours in Tokyo, along with other cultural pursuits such as making sushi. In Tokyo, there are several **ikebana schools** offering one-time or on-going instruction in English (see p. 104 for more information). In Kyoto, the **Women's Association of Kyoto** (www.wakjapan.com) offers short, one-time classes on the tea ceremony, flower arranging, origami, Japanese calligraphy, Japanese cooking, and other cultural activities. The tourist offices in both Tokyo and Kyoto have information on temples that provide *zazen* (sitting meditation) in English.

You won't become fluent in Japanese in a week or two, but for longer stays there are language schools in major cities across Japan that cater to both the beginner and the intermediate. Long-established ones, with courses that last one week to a year or more, include **Akamonkai Japanese Language School** (www.akamonkai.ac.jp; ✆ 03/3806-6102); **Arc Academy** (http://en.arc-academy.net; (✆ 03/3409-0391); **Intercultural Institute of Japan** (www.incul.com; ✆ 03/5816-4861); **Kai Japanese Language School** (www.kaij.jp/e; ✆ 03//3206-1356); **Tokyo Central Japanese Language School** (www.tcj-nihongo.com; ✆ 03/5411-3331); and **We Japanese Language School** (www.we-japan.com; ✆ 03/5489-6480). Check the classified sections of city magazines such as *Metropolis* for lists of language schools.

Outside Tokyo and Kyoto, local international centers in larger cities, founded to promote multi-cultural harmony and to assist foreigners living in their communities, are good resources for cultural activities and events. The **Nagoya International Center** (www.nic-nagoya.or.jp), for example, provides a list of schools and clubs offering Japanese instruction throughout Nagoya, from conversation for beginners to writing kanji, at reasonable prices. In Kanazawa, the **Ishikawa International Lounge** (www.ifie.or.jp) schedules cultural events and classes that might cover origami, calligraphy, the tea ceremony, Japanese flower arranging, Japanese folk dancing, Japanese cooking, and Japanese language; classes themselves are free, but materials for the class cost extra. Other cities with similar institutions, all offering Japanese language classes and sometimes cultural classes as well, include the **International House, Osaka** (www.ih-osaka.or.jp), Kobe's **Hyogo International Association** (www.hyogo-ip.or.jp/en), the **Okayama Prefectural International Exchange Foundation** (www.opief.or.jp), and the **Hiroshima International Center** (http:/hiroshima-ic.or.jp). See individual cities in this guide for more information.

Alternatively, you can start learning Japanese even before your trip at the **Japan Online School** (http://j-os.com), which uses Skype to connect students to teachers. There are also many online sites offering free Japanese lessons, including www.japanese-online.com and www.easyjapanese.org.

Adventure & Wellness Trips

If you're into hiking, **Walk Japan** (www.walkjapan.com) has been offering guided walks since 1992, with the first one covering Nakasendo Highway (p. 230). Other hikes take place in Hokkaido, Kyushu, and in the Hakone area near Mt. Fuji. For those who prefer to bike, **Bike Tours Japan** (www.biketoursjapan.com) offers guided and self-guided tours in Hokkaido, which offers plenty of space and a cooler summer climate than the rest of Japan. **Jouney into Japan** (www.journeyintojapan.com.au) was founded by an Aussie who first came to Japan in 1981 and now offers walking, hiking, and skiing tours of Japan.

Cooking & Sake Classes

Many people become so enamored of Japanese cuisine that they want to try making some dishes at home. In Tokyo, the **Tsukiji Soba Academy** (http://soba.specialist.co.jp) offers instruction on how to make buckwheat noodles from scratch, but for a more personalized cooking experience, including trips to markets, tasting sessions to familiarize participants with traditional foods, and hands-on cooking classes, Elizabeth Andoh offers **A Taste of Culture;** check her website, http://tasteofculture.com, for more information.

If you want to know more about sake, take the 5-day **Sake Brewery Tour** offered by sake expert John Gauntner (www.sake-world. com.), who also leads seminars and other events centering on sake.

Guided Tours

Lots of tour companies offer group trips to Japan. **Esprit Travel & Tours** (www.esprittravel.com) specializes in small-group and custom tours to Japan. Although programs can change, it currently offers an art tour that covers art in Kyoto, Tokyo, and Naoshima's Benesse Art Site, as well as a ceramics tour that includes visits to galleries, the Bizen pottery village, and studios. **Artisans of Leisure** (www.artisansofleisure.com) provides luxury tours with private guides that are tailored to your interests. UK-based **InsideJapan Tours** (www.insidejapantours.com) offers small escorted tours to both known destinations and places off the beaten track. For more ideas on escorted tours departing from North America, go to www.japantravelinfo.com; for tours departing from England, go to www.seejapan.co.uk. For more information on escorted tours, including questions to ask before booking your trip, see www.frommers.com/planning.

Volunteer & Working Trips

Japan was never a big destination for people wishing to volunteer—until, of course, the Great East Japan Earthquake. **Foreign Volunteers Japan** (www.foreignvolunteersjapan.org) was created after the disaster for foreign volunteers wishing to take an active role in Tohoku relief efforts and has links to other volunteer opportunities such as https://japanvolunteers.wordpress.com. **Peace Boat** (www.peaceboat.org) is a non-profit dedicated to responsible travel, human rights, and social awareness, with programs in Japan and abroad; at the time of going to press, it offered volunteer opportunities in Tokyo lasting a day or longer, as well as one-week trips to the Tohoku area. Organizations stress that it's essential to be part of a group for relief efforts in Tohoku, and being able to speak Japanese is often mandatory.

Travelers with an interest in helping a family-run business, such as organic farming or an inn, in exchange for room and board can contact **Wwoof Japan** (www.wwoof japan.com), with most stays lasting two weeks or more.

Otherwise, in Tokyo, **Second Harvest** (www.2hj.org), Japan's first food bank, collects food that would otherwise go to waste from food manufacturers, farmers, restaurants, and other sources and distributes it to soup kitchens, the homeless, emergency shelters and other places. Anyone 12 and older can help the organization's main volunteering event at Ueno Park, where Saturday lunch is served to the homeless.

SUGGESTED JAPAN ITINERARIES

3

Japan, with its rich culture, stunning mountain and coastal scenery, and varied climates, has much to offer the curious visitor, not only in and around the major cities but in many outlying regions as well. If you want to see everything, you should plan on spending about a year in Japan. More likely, your time will be limited to a week or two, so you'll have to be selective. This section will help you decide on an itinerary and whether you're better off buying one of several options for rail passes or flying (outlined in chapter 14).

If you're in Japan for several weeks, you can fashion a personalized tour by combining several of these suggested itineraries, adding, perhaps, a town or two from the chapters that follow. But regardless of what itinerary you plan, *Kyoto is a must for first-time visitors.* It served as the nation's capital for more than 1,000 years and has more temples, shrines, and historic sights than any other Japanese city.

THE REGIONS IN BRIEF

Separated from mainland China and Korea by the Sea of Japan, the nation of Japan stretches in an arc about 2,900km (1,800 miles) long from northeast to southwest, yet it is only 403km (250 miles) wide at its broadest point. Japan consists primarily of four main islands—**Honshu, Hokkaido, Shikoku,** and **Kyushu.** Surrounding these large islands are more than 6,000 smaller, mostly uninhabited islands and islets. Far to the southwest are the **Okinawan islands,** perhaps best known for the fierce fighting that took place there during World War II and for their continued (and controversial) use as an American military base. If you were to superimpose Japan's four main islands onto a map of the United States, they would stretch all the way from Boston to Atlanta, which should give you an idea of the diversity of Japan's climate, flora, and scenery—Hokkaido in the north is subarctic, while Kyushu is subtropical. Honshu, Japan's most populous island and home to Tokyo, Kyoto, and Osaka, is connected to the other three islands by tunnel or bridge, which means you can travel to all four islands by train.

As much as 70% of Japan consists of **mountains.** They are found on all four main islands and most are volcanic in origin. Altogether, there are some 265 **volcanoes,** more than 30 of them still active. Mount Fuji (on

Honshu), dormant since 1707, is Japan's highest and most famous volcano, while Mount Aso (on Kyushu) boasts the largest caldera in the world. Because of these volcanic origins, earthquakes have plagued Japan throughout history. In the 20th century, the two most destructive earthquakes were the 1923 Great Kanto Earthquake, which killed more than 100,000 people in the Tokyo area, and the 1995 Great Hanshin Earthquake, which claimed more than 6,000 lives in Kobe. They were followed in 2011 by Japan's largest earthquake in recorded history, the Great East Japan Earthquake, which struck off the northeast Honshu coast and triggered a massive tsunami that contributed to the loss of more than 19,000 lives.

Japan is divided into 47 regional divisions, or **prefectures.** Each prefecture has its own capital and is comparable to the U.S. state or the British county, though prefectures vary greatly in size (greater Tokyo is one prefecture; all of Hokkaido is another). Japan's total landmass is slightly smaller than California in area, yet Japan has almost 41% the population of the United States. And because three-fourths of Japan is mountainous and therefore uninhabitable, its people are concentrated primarily in only 10% of the country's landmass, with the rest of the area devoted to agriculture. In other words, imagine 41% of the U.S. population living in California—primarily in San Diego County—and you get an idea of how crowded Japan is. For this island nation—isolated physically from the rest of the world, struck repeatedly through the centuries by earthquakes, fires, and typhoons, and possessed of only limited space for harmonious living—geography and topography have played major roles both in determining its development and in shaping its culture, customs, and arts.

Honshu

Of the four main islands, Honshu is the largest and most populated. Because it's also the most important historically and culturally, it's where most visitors spend the bulk of their time.

KANTO DISTRICT

Located in east-central Honshu and comprising metropolitan **Tokyo** and six prefectures, this district is characterized by the Kanto Plain, the largest flatland in Japan. Although development of the district didn't begin in earnest until the establishment of the shogunate government in Edo (present-day Tokyo) in 1603, Tokyo and surrounding giants such as **Yokohama** make this the most densely populated region in Japan.

KANSAI DISTRICT

Also called the Kinki District and encompassing seven prefectures, this is Japan's most historic region. **Nara** and **Kyoto**—two of Japan's ancient capitals—are here, as are two of Japan's most important port cities, **Kobe** and **Osaka.** Since the 1994 opening of Kansai International Airport outside Osaka, many foreign visitors opt to bypass Tokyo altogether in favor of Kansai's many historic spots, including **Mount Koya** with its many temples, **Himeji** with what I consider to be Japan's most beautiful castle, **Ise-Shima National Park** with Japan's most revered Shinto shrine, Nara with its Great Buddha and temples, and, of course, Kyoto, the former capital for more than 1,000 years with so many temples, imperial villas, and gardens that it ranks as Japan's foremost tourist destination.

CHUBU DISTRICT

The Chubu District lies between Tokyo and Kyoto and straddles central Honshu from the Pacific Ocean to the Japan Sea, encompassing nine prefectures. **Nagoya,** Japan's fourth-largest city and home to an international airport nicknamed Centrair, is Chubu's most important city and a gateway to its other destinations. The district features mountain ranges (including the **Japan Alps,** see below), volcanoes (including **Mount Fuji**), large rivers, and coastal regions on both sides of the island. It's popular for skiing and hiking, for quaint mountain villages such as **Takayama** and **Shirakawa-go,** and for tourist attractions that include the open-air Museum Meiji Mura (near Nagoya), the castle in **Matsumoto,** and Kenrokuen Garden in **Kanazawa,** considered one of Japan's finest.

THE JAPAN ALPS

Spreading over central Honshu in the Chubu District, the Japan Alps are among Japan's most famous mountain ranges, especially since hosting the 1998 XVIII Winter Olympics in **Nagano. Chubu-Sangaku National Park** (also called the Japan Alps National Park) contains some of the nation's most beautiful mountain scenery and the country's best skiing, while destinations like **Takayama** and **Shirakawa-go** boast quaint historic districts and thatched-roof farmhouses.

ISE-SHIMA

Shima Peninsula, in Mie Prefecture, juts into the Seto Inland Sea and is famous for **Ise-Shima National Park,** noted for its coastal scenery and Ise Jingu Shrines. **Toba,** birthplace of the cultured pearl, is popular for its Mikimoto Pearl Island and the Toba Aquarium. Shima Peninsula also boasts two theme parks, one fashioned after Japan's Warring States Era and the other an amusement park with a Spanish theme.

CHUGOKU DISTRICT

Honshu's southwestern district has five prefectures and is divided by the Chugoku Mountain Range. Industrial giants such as **Hiroshima** and **Okayama** lead as the major cities, drawing tourists with reconstructed castles, Korakuen Garden, and the sobering Peace Memorial Park in Hiroshima, dedicated to victims of the world's first atomic bomb. **Kurashiki** is a must for its photogenic, historic warehouse district, while **Miyajima,** part of the Seto-Naikai (Inland Sea) National Park, is considered one of Japan's most beautiful islands.

TOHOKU DISTRICT

Northeastern Honshu, with **Sendai** as its regional center, encompasses six prefectures. Known as the Tohoku District, it isn't nearly as developed as the central and southern districts of Honshu, due in large part to its rugged, mountainous terrain and harsh climate. **Matsushima,** about halfway up the coast between Tokyo and the northern tip of Honshu, is the district's major tourist destination; with its pine-clad islets dotting the bay, it's considered one of Japan's most scenic spots. **Kakunodate,** located inland, is a former castle town offering preserved samurai houses and, during cherry-blossom season, a stunning show of pink flowers to travelers willing to take a road less traveled. **Hiraizumi** boasts the Golden Hall, Pure Land Garden, and other 12th-century relics that were declared a World Heritage Site in 2011, while **Towada-Hachimantai National Park,** which extends over three prefectures, boasts scenic lakes, rustic hot-spring spas, hiking, and skiing. Of these destinations, only Matsushima was hit by the tsunami but was spared large-scale damage due to its islets and is now largely recovered.

Hokkaido

Japan's second-largest island, Hokkaido lies to the north of Honshu and is regarded as the country's last frontier with its wide-open pastures, evergreen forests, mountains, gorges, crystal-clear lakes, and wildlife, much of it preserved in national parks. Originally occupied by the indigenous Ainu, it was colonized by Japanese settlers mostly after the Meiji Restoration in 1868. Today it's home to 5.5 million people, 1.9 million of whom live in **Sapporo.** With a landmass that accounts for 22% of Japan's total area, Hokkaido has the nation's lowest population density: about 4.3% of the total population. That, together with the island's cold, severe winters but mild summers, and its unspoiled natural beauty make this island a nature lover's paradise.

Shikoku

Shikoku, the smallest of the four main islands, is off the beaten path for many foreign visitors. It's famous for its 88 Buddhist temples founded by one of Japan's most interesting historical figures, the Buddhist priest Kukai, known posthumously as Kobo Daishi. Other major attractions are Ritsurin Park in **Takamatsu,** Matsuyama Castle in **Matsuyama,** and **Dogo Spa,** one of Japan's oldest hot-spring spas. For active travelers, the **Shimanami Kaido route** offers 70 scenic kilometers (43 miles) of dedicated biking trails that connect Shikoku with Hiroshima Prefecture via six islands and a series of bridges in the Seto Inland Sea.

Kyushu

The southernmost of the four main islands, Kyushu boasts a mild subtropical climate, active volcanoes, and hot-spring spas. Because it's the closest major island to Korea and China, Kyushu served as a gateway to the continental mainland throughout much of Japan's history, later becoming the springboard for both traders and Christian missionaries from the West. **Fukuoka,** Kyushu's largest city, serves as a rail gateway from Honshu, dispersing travelers to hot springs in **Beppu, Unzen,** and **Ibusuki** and to such major attractions as Kumamoto Castle in **Kumamoto** and Sengan-en Garden in **Kagoshima. Nagasaki,** victim of the world's second atomic bomb, is one of Japan's most cosmopolitan and most attractive cities.

Okinawa

Okinawa is comprised of 160 islands stretching 400km (248 miles) north to south and 1,000km (620 miles) east to west. Part of the Ryukyu Island chain, Okinawa developed its own languages, culture, cuisine, and architecture under the Ryukyu Kingdom, which traded extensively with both Japan and China before being annexed to Japan after the 1868 Meiji Restoration. **Okinawa Island,** the largest Ryukyu island and almost 1,000 miles away from Tokyo, is home to **Naha** (Okinawa Prefecture's capital), U.S. military bases, war memorials, and natural attractions, including white sandy beaches and coral reefs popular with divers and snorkelers. Other destinations include the laid-back, mostly rural **Kume Island** and **Iriomote Island,** 80% of it protected in state and national parks and boasting dense forests, mangroves, and pristine beaches.

JAPAN HIGHLIGHTS

This trip, designed for first-timers, takes you to Japan's highlights, from fast-paced Tokyo to the quiet temples of Kyoto, along with a couple of other worthwhile destinations. Plan on about a week, but if time permits, add one of the small-town destinations recommended in "Small Towns and Villages."

Days 1 & 2: Tokyo ★★★

No one should miss this adrenaline-rush of a metropolis; you'll need at least two days to do it justice. Hit the highlights like the **Tsukiji Fish Market,** the 45th-floor **observatory** in Shinjuku for its eye-popping views, and the **Tokyo National Museum** with the world's largest collection of Japanese art. Be sure to allow time wandering its diverse neighborhoods, including **Asakusa** with its famous temple and old downtown atmosphere, electrifying **Akihabara** with stores selling everything from cameras to anime figurines, and **Harajuku** with its vibrant teeny-bopper scene and Oriental Bazaar souvenir shop. Top it off with a stroll through **Kabuki-cho,** Japan's most notorious and crazy nightlife district.

Day 3: Hakone ★★★

Take an early train to Hakone Yumoto, gateway to the wonderful **Fuji-Hakone-Izu National Park.** Here you can see some of Japan's most scenic countryside via a circuitous route that includes a three-car mountain train, a cable car, ropeway, and a boat, while seeing such sights as the wonderful **Hakone Open-Air Museum** and, if you're lucky, the elusive **Mount Fuji.** Be sure to schedule some time for a dip in a hot-spring bath, and spend the night in the historic **Fujiya Hotel** or a Japanese inn.

Days 4, 5 & 6: Kyoto ★★★

Capital for more than 1,000 years, Kyoto is Japan's number-one must see. Top historic sites include **Nijo Castle,** former home of the shogun; **Ryoanji Temple** with its famous Zen rock garden; and the **Golden Pavilion.** Take a self-guided walk through eastern Kyoto, seeing **Sanjusangendo Hall** with its 1,001 wooden statues, **Kiyomizu Temple,** and **Heian Shrine,** followed by shopping at the **Kyoto Handicraft Center.** Be sure to sample Kyoto's legendary Buddhist vegetarian cuisine, stroll through its famous geisha quarters, and spend at least one night in a Japanese-style inn.

Day 7: Hiroshima ★★

The top destination in Hiroshima is **Peace Memorial Park** with its sobering memorials and museum that detail events surrounding the explosion of the atomic bomb. If you have another day, be sure to include a trip to the nearby island of **Miyajima,** home of a famous shrine and considered one of Japan's most scenic places.

SMALL TOWNS & VILLAGES

If you've seen Japan's big cities and want to escape to a slower pace of life, let the suggestions below be your guide. Because some of them are easily accessible from cities recommended in the itineraries above and below, they can be combined to create your own memorable trip in Japan.

Day 1: Nikko ★★★

About 2 hours north of Tokyo, **Nikko** is famous for its sumptuous mausoleum of Tokugawa Ieyasu, Japan's most famous shogun, set in a forest of majestic cedars. Throw in other worthwhile sites like a temple, shrine, garden, and

imperial villa, and there's more than enough to occupy a full day. Spend the night in the old Nikko Kanaya Hotel or in a Japanese inn with hot-spring baths.

Days 2 & 3: Takayama & the Japan Alps ★★★

The **Miyagawa Morning Market** is a great way to start the day, followed by explorations through the picturesque, narrow streets of this old castle town. Highlights include **Hida Folk Village** with its rural architecture, old **merchant homes,** and the **Hirata Folk Art Museum** filled with items used in times past. Also not to be missed is the **Historical Government House,** the only regional administrative building from the shogun era still in existence. Takayama is also the perfect place to experience *tatami* living, with accommodations available at various price ranges.

Day 4: Shirakawa-go ★

It's a 1-hour bus ride onward to Shirakawa-go, where you'll find the village of **Ogimachi,** a UNESCO World Cultural and Natural Heritage Site with thatch-roofed houses. Several farmhouses are open to the public as museums, but your reason for coming here is to actually spend the night in one so you can explore this unique place after day-trippers have gone.

Days 5 & 6: Nakasendo Highway ★★

The small village of Magome is the start of the old **Nakasendo Highway,** once traversed by feudal lords and samurai. After a 3-hour hike through woods along a rushing river, you'll find yourself in the quaint village of **Tsumago,** where you'll sleep in a traditional inn. My then-14-year-old son declared this hike the highlight of his Japan trip. I absolutely love this whole experience.

Day 7: Mount Koya ★★★

Accessible from Osaka via train and cable car, **Mount Koya** is Japan's most sacred religious site, achingly beautiful with more than 115 Buddhist temples spread through the forests. Be sure to take both a day and a nighttime stroll past towering cypress trees and countless tombs and memorial tablets to **Okunoin,** the burial ground of Kobo Daishi, one of Japan's most revered Buddhist priests. Spend the night in a temple, dining on vegetarian food.

Days 8 & 9: Nara ★★

Nara is even older than Kyoto and served as the nation's capital for 74 years. Most of its impressive sights are within expansive **Nara Park,** where deer (considered divine messengers) roam free; foremost here is the **Great Buddha,** housed inside the largest wooden structure in the world. Staying overnight allows time also to see magnificent **Horyuji Temple** (Japan's first UNESCO site), and, from mid-July through September, the nightly illumination of many historic buildings.

Day 10: Miyajima ★★★

Most visitors see **Miyajima** on a day trip from Hiroshima, but you'll get more out of this gem of an island by spending the night, seeing its famous Itsukushima Shrine lit at night, and taking the cable car up to Mount Misen, where you'll be rewarded with great views of the Inland Sea and hiking paths to religious sites. If it's summer, you might also want to hit Miyajima's beaches.

NORTHERN JAPAN IN 2 WEEKS

Tohoku and Hokkaido are usually ignored by travelers. Though it's true that the country's most significant historic treasures lie in the southern regions, Northern Japan, where the emphasis is on natural wonders and hot-spring spas, offers a more relaxed vacation for those who have already seen the country's must-sees. With the exception of Sapporo, most destinations on this itinerary are villages that can be seen on an overnight stopover, but for real relaxation you'll probably want to pick at least one place to linger longer.

Day 1: Matsushima ★

Take the Shinkansen to Sendai (about 2 hr. from Tokyo) and then board a sight-seeing boat for a 50-minute trip to **Matsushima,** famous for its scenic coastline of pine-studded islets. Visit the venerable **Zuiganji Temple,** northern Japan's most famous Zen temple; **Entsuin Temple,** with its nice gardens and restaurant serving Buddhist vegetarian cuisine; and a museum detailing the life of Tohoku's most famous feudal lord.

Day 2: Hiraizumi ★

Fame has come only recently to this small village, when a collection of its sights dating from the 12th century were declared a World Heritage Site shortly after the 2011 Great East Japan Earthquake. Outstanding are the Golden Hall and Pure Land Garden, but to me it's the concept of a Buddhist utopia on earth that gives inspiration. Hiraizumi itself, while popular among Japanese day-trippers, is unassuming and remarkably free of sprawling hotels and souvenir shops.

Day 3: Kakunodate ★

Kakunodate is a small and relatively unspoiled castle town famous for its samurai district and cherry trees. Be sure to see the **Aoyagi Samurai Manor,** a compound of traditional buildings packed with Edo Period memorabilia. Spend the night here or head onward to Nyuto Onsen.

Day 4: Nyuto Onsen ★★

Just one stop away from Kakunodate on the Shinkansen is Tazawako Station, where you then board a local bus for **Nyuto Onsen,** a secluded valley of hot springs and rustic inns. This is a wonderful base from which to explore the many wonders of Towada-Hachimantai National Park, including skiing in winter and hiking, biking, and swimming in summer. For the ultimate *ryokan* experience, spend the night in **Tsuru-no-yu Onsen,** a rustic and remote Japanese inn with both indoor and outdoor baths.

Days 5 & 6: Lake Towada ★★

There's a sightseeing bus that departs Tazawako Station every morning from late April to October, arriving at Lake Towada 7 hours later. Popular activities here include taking a **boat cruise** of the lake and visiting **Towada Jinja Shrine,** but the absolute winner of a stay here is a hike along the **Oirase Stream,** a coursing river shaded by trees and marked by huge boulders. I find this walk magical, especially early in the morning before others hikers arrive.

Day 7: Hakodate ★

Wander the **waterfront warehouse district** and historic **Motomachi,** a picturesque neighborhood of steep slopes and turn-of-the-20th-century clapboard homes and other buildings, all relics of Hakodate's days as one of Japan's first international ports following 2 centuries of isolation. In the evening, take a cable car to the top of **Mount Hakodate,** renowned for its night view of Hakodate. The next day, visit Hakodate's **morning market,** famous for its hairy crabs and other sea creatures.

Day 8: Noboribetsu Spa

In **Noboribetsu Onsen,** famous for its curative hot springs, hike through **Hell Valley** for a view of the bubbling hot water that has made Noboribetsu famous, and then experience its magic at the Dai-ichi Takimotokan hot-spring baths.

Days 9 & 10: Sapporo

En route to Sapporo, stop off at the **Poroto Kotan and Ainu Museum** in Shiraoi with its impressive collection of indigenous Ainu artifacts. Capital of Hokkaido Prefecture and the island's largest city, Sapporo is an easygoing city that's a snap to navigate. Top on a list of must-sees is **Nopporo Forest Park,** where you can visit the **Historical Museum of Hokkaido** and see vintage homes and buildings at the **Historical Village of Hokkaido.** Be sure, too, to dine at the **Sapporo Bier Garten** on the grounds of the old Sapporo brewery. If it's winter, hit the ski slopes on the city's perimeter or travel farther afield to Niseko.

Days 11 & 12: Sounkyo Onsen ★

If hiking's your thing, you're going to want to make this mountain village a priority. Located in Daisetsuzan National Park, it offers easy access to trails that take from 1 to 8 hours to hike (and even overnight trips to neighboring towns). In winter, it also offers skiing and the Ice Falls Festival. Best of all, you can soak your weary bones in hot-springs baths after a strenuous day.

Days 13 & 14: Akanko Onsen

This lakeside hot-spring resort is a natural playground for outdoor enthusiasts, offering fishing, canoeing, hiking, and winter activities from ice fishing to skiing. You can also take a boat cruise of **Lake Akan,** famous for its *marimo,* a spongelike ball of duckweed, and tour the marimo museum. A must-see is the **Ainu Kotan Village** with its shops and traditional Ainu dancing, while the nearby

Northern Japan in 2 Weeks

① Osaka
② Kanazawa
③ Kyoto
④ Himeji
⑤ Okayama
⑥ Matsue

Akan International Crane Center explains all you'd ever want to know about the red-crested crane. From Akanko Onsen you can take a bus to Kushiro Airport for the flight back to Tokyo.

HONSHU'S BEST GARDENS & CASTLES

Once upon a time, Japan was divided into a patchwork of feudal kingdoms, each ruled by a *daimyo* (feudal lord) who had complete control over his samurai retainers and the farmers who worked his land. To protect their fiefdoms, the daimyo built castles of various proportions; many of them also had well-maintained gardens in which they could escape from their worries and enjoy such aesthetic pursuits as the tea ceremony. Many such castles and gardens still exist, either as originals or as reconstructions (many castles were destroyed by the imperial government during or after the fall of the shogun and during World War II). A few gardens are much newer but are so spectacular they are not to be missed. Use Osaka as your international gateway.

Day 1: Osaka

Although **Osaka Castle** was destroyed in 1868 during fierce fighting that took place between shogun loyalists and imperial troops, this remake has a wow factor due to its massive size, surrounding park filled with cherry trees, and high-tech museum that captures the life and times of Toyotomi Hideyoshi, the brilliant general who built Osaka Castle in 1580 and unified Japan under his command.

Day 2: Kanazawa ★★

Kenrokuen Garden is considered one of Japan's best landscape gardens and is one of my favorites. Because of its lofty position, there are no skyscrapers to detract from its gorgeous setting of ponds, streams, and strategically placed trees and rocks. It once served as the outer garden of **Kanazawa Castle,** of which only the original Ishikawa Gate remains, along with reconstructed fortifications built using traditional methods. While in Kanazawa you'll also want to visit other sights related to Japan's feudal era, including its well-preserved former geisha and samurai districts and Myoryuji Temple (known as the Ninja Temple).

Days 3 & 4: Kyoto ★★★

One of the few castles built by the mighty Tokugawa shogunate as a residence rather than for defense, **Nijo Castle** is where the shogun stayed whenever he was in Kyoto. Considered the quintessence of Momoyama architecture, it's famous for its nightingale (creaking) floorboards that warned of enemy intruders; its adjoining garden was designed by one of Japan's most renowned gardeners, Kobori Enshu. Also designed by Kobori is the garden at **Katsura Imperial Villa,** largely considered Japan's most beautiful. A "strolling garden," its view changes with every step but is always perfectly balanced and in harmony. Also in Kyoto is Japan's most famous Zen rock garden, at **Ryoanji Temple.**

Day 5: Himeji ★

If you see only one castle in town, **Himeji Castle** is the one. Said to resemble a white heron poised in flight over the plains, it is quite simply Japan's most beautiful castle, with extensive gates, moats, turrets, and maze of passageways that have survived virtually intact since feudal times. Note that the main keep is under renovation until March 2014, but a special exhibition area allows visitors to watch the painstaking process of renovation using traditional methods. Nearby is **Koko-en,** laid out in 1992 but worth a visit for its nine different gardens typical of those during the Edo Period.

Day 6: Okayama

Along with Kenrokuen (above), Okayama's **Korakuen** is rated as one of Japan's most beautiful gardens, but I personally don't think it's quite as captivating. Still, completed in 1700 and incorporating the surrounding hills and **Okayama Castle** (a remake) into its design, it's worth a stopover, especially since it serves as the gateway to Matsue.

Day 7 & 8: Matsue ★

Off the beaten path of most travelers, Matsue is dominated by **Matsue Castle,** surrounded by a moat and containing many interesting defensive details (such as drop chutes for rocks and stairs that could be raised). It's surrounded by many

Honshu's Best Gardens & Castles

WEEK 1
1. Matsushima
2. Hiraizumi
3. Kakunodate
4. Nyuto Onsen
5. Lake Towada
6. Hakodate Port Town
7. Noboribetsu Spa

WEEK 2
8. Sapporo
9. Sounkyo Onsen
10. Akanko Onsen

historic sights related to life in a former castle town, but gardeners will want to hightail it to the **Adachi Museum.** Although modern art is the focus indoors, the perfectly landscaped garden—one of Japan's best—comes into view through framed windows, making it part of the art in a very surreal way.

4

TOKYO

To the uninitiated, Tokyo may seem like a whirlwind of traffic and people, so confusing that visitors might think they have somehow landed on another planet. Little wonder first-time visitors are almost invariably disappointed. They come expecting an exotic Asian city, but instead they find a city Westernized and modernized to the point of ugliness, much of it a drab concrete jungle of unimaginative buildings clustered so close together that there's hardly room in which to breathe.

Simply stated, Tokyo is a crush of humanity. Its subways are often packed, its sidewalks are crowded, its streets are congested, and its air is filled with noise, pollution, and what can only be called mystery smells. Almost 13 million people reside in Greater Tokyo's 2,188 sq. km (844 sq. miles), many of them in bedroom towns from which they have to commute to work for an average of 2 to 3 hours every day. No matter where you go in Tokyo, you're never alone. After you've been here for a while, Paris, London, and even New York will seem deserted.

Crowds and urban ugliness, however, are what you'll see only if you don't bother to look beneath the surface. For Tokyo is alluring in its own way; and if you open yourself to it, you'll find a city unlike any other in the world, humming with energy and vitality.

A LOOK AT THE PAST   Though today the nation's capital, Tokyo is a relative newcomer to the pages of Japanese history. For centuries it was nothing more than a rather unimportant village called Edo, which means simply "mouth of the estuary." In 1603, Edo was catapulted into the limelight when the new shogun, Tokugawa Ieyasu, made the sleepy village the seat of his government. He expanded Edo Castle, making it the largest and most impressive castle in the land, and surrounded it with an ingenious system of moats that radiated from the castle in a great swirl, giving him easy access to the sea and an upper hand in thwarting enemy attack.

The town developed quickly, due largely to the shogun's decree requiring all *daimyo* (feudal lords) to permanently leave their families in Edo, a shrewd move to thwart insurrection in the provinces. There were as many as 270 daimyo in Japan in the 17th century, all of whom maintained several mansions in Edo, complete with elaborate compounds and expansive gardens. The daimyo's trusted samurai soon accounted for more than half of Edo's population, and the merchant class expanded as well. By 1787 the population had grown to 1.3 million, making Edo—even then—one of the largest cities in the world.

When the Tokugawas were overthrown in 1868, the Japanese emperor was restored to power and moved the capital from Kyoto to Edo, now renamed Tokyo (Eastern Capital). Japan's Feudal Era—and its isolation from the rest of the world—was over. As the capital city, Tokyo was the hardest hit in this new era of modernization, with fashion, architecture, food, and even people imported from the West. West was best, and things Japanese were forgotten or ignored.

It didn't help that Tokyo was almost totally destroyed twice in the first half of the 20th century: In 1923, a massive earthquake measuring 7.9 on the Richter scale destroyed more than a third of the city and claimed more than 140,000 lives in Tokyo and Yokohama; disaster struck again in 1945, toward the end of World War II when Allied incendiary bombs laid more than half the city to waste and killed another 100,000 people.

TOKYO TODAY   Perhaps that's why most visitors are disappointed with Tokyo: It has almost nothing of historical importance to match Kyoto or Kamakura. So put your notions of quaint Japan out of your mind and plunge headfirst into the 21st century, because that's what Tokyo is all about. In fact, in the past few years, skyscrapers and new developments have been mushrooming faster than you can say shiitake, some of them the most ambitious land projects Japan has ever seen.

As the financial nerve center of Japan, Tokyo has long set the pace for what happens in the rest of Asia. The city is the reigning capital of Asian pop art and kitsch, fads, fashions, and trends.

But even though the city has a fast-paced, somewhat zany side, it also has a quieter and often overlooked side that makes the city both lovable and livable. Although formidable at first glance, Tokyo is nothing more than a series of small towns and neighborhoods clustered together, each with its own atmosphere, narrow, winding streets, mom-and-pop shops, fruit stands, and stores. Look for the details, and you'll notice carefully pruned bonsai adorning the sidewalks; traditional wooden houses tucked between massive apartment complexes; everywhere, neatness and order. Peer inside those concrete high-rises, and you're apt to find Japanese restaurants that are perfect replicas of wood-beamed farmhouses side by side with cocktail bars that epitomize high-tech avant-garde.

I love Tokyo. Despite its daily frustrations, Tokyo is exhilarating, often exciting, and unceasingly interesting. Best of all, it's one of the world's safest metropolises, with the lowest theft rate of any large city on the planet. As for the 2011 Great East Japan Earthquake, although the six-minute quake was the most terrifying most Tokyoites had ever experienced, there was virtually no damage to the city itself. After a short period of rolling blackouts, followed by energy conservation measures through the long, hot summer that included limited commuter train service, cranked up thermostats, and dimmed public lighting, Tokyo seems back to business as usual. Of course, the biggest energy hump for Tokyo will remain its summers; whether austerity measures will be a part of the city's future is anyone's guess.

THE BEST TOKYO EXPERIENCES

○ **Catching the Action at Tsukiji Fish Market.** Get up your first morning in Japan (you'll probably be wide awake with jet lag anyway) and head straight for the country's largest fish market, where you can eat the freshest sushi breakfast you'll ever have and then browse through stalls of seafood. See p. 93.

○ **Sitting Pretty Above Tokyo.** On the 45th floor of the Tokyo Metropolitan Government Office in Shinjuku, an observatory offers a bird's-eye view of the never-ending metropolis, and, on fine winter days, Mount Fuji. Best of all, it's free. Other perches include Tokyo Tower, The Mori Art Museum, and Sky Tree, but you have to pay for those. See p. 98, 100, 99, and 106.

o **Strolling Through Asakusa.** No place better conveys the atmosphere of old Tokyo than Asakusa. Sensoji Temple is the city's oldest and most popular temple, and Nakamise Dori, the pedestrian lane leading to the temple, is lined with shops selling souvenirs and traditional Japanese goods. See the walking tour on p. 108.

o **Ogling Treasures at the Tokyo National Museum.** Even professed museumphobes should make a point of visiting the largest museum of Japanese art in the world, where you can see everything from samurai armor and lacquerware to kimono and woodblock prints. If you visit only one museum in Tokyo, this should be it. See p. 96.

o **Hanging Out in Harajuku on Sunday.** Start with brunch, and after watching the kids in costume near the station dancing and posing for pictures, stroll Omotesando Dori, shop the area's boutiques, visit a museum and Meiji Shrine, or just sit back and take it all in from a sidewalk café. See the walking tour on p. 112.

o **Browsing the Electronics & Anime Shops of Akihabara.** Even if you don't buy anything, it's great fun—and very educational—to see the latest in electronic gadgetry in Japan's largest electronics district. In recent years, shops specializing in *manga* (Japanese comic books and graphic novels) and *anime* (Japanese animation) have also opened, along with so-called "maid cafes." See p. 151 and 146.

ESSENTIALS

Arriving
BY PLANE

Tokyo is served by two international airports. Narita International Airport, located in Narita about 66km (41 miles) east of Tokyo, is by far the largest and serves the most flights. More convenient (and closer) is Haneda Airport, which operates as Tokyo's domestic airport but also started receiving international flights in 2010.

FACILITIES AT NARITA AIRPORT   Narita International Airport (NRT; www. narita-airport.jp; 🕐 0476/34-8000) consists of two terminals (1 and 2). Arrival lobbies in both terminals have ATMs and counters for money exchange (both offer about the same rates), open daily 6:30am to 11pm (change enough money here to last several days, as the exchange rate is the same as in town, the process is speedy, and facilities in town are somewhat limited). Both are connected to all ground transportation into Tokyo.

A **Tourist Information Center (TIC),** managed by the Japan National Tourist Organization, is located in the arrival lobbies of both Terminal 1 (www.jnto.go.jp; 🕐 0476/30-3383) and Terminal 2 (🕐 0476/34-5877). The TIC offers free maps and pamphlets and can direct you to your hotel or inn. Both are open daily 8am to 8pm; if you don't yet have a hotel room and want one at a modest price, you can make reservations here free of charge until 7:30pm.

If you've purchased a Japan Rail Pass, you can turn in your voucher at one of the **Japan Railways (JR) View Plazas** (Travel Service Centers), located in both terminals and open daily 6:30am to 9:45pm. Other facilities at both terminals include post offices, medical clinics, shower rooms, day rooms for napping, children's playrooms, luggage storage and lockers, cellular phone rentals, and coin-operated computers with Internet capabilities (¥100 for 10 min.). Wi-Fi access is free.

GETTING TO TOKYO FROM NARITA AIRPORT   Jumping into a **taxi** is the easiest way to get to Tokyo, but it's also prohibitively expensive—and may not even be the quickest if you happen to hit rush hour. Expect to spend around ¥19,000 to ¥21,000 for a 1½- to 2-hour taxi ride to central Tokyo. If you plan ahead, however, **Anzen Taxi** (www.anzentaxi.co.jp; ✆ **05/5532-9807**) provides fixed-fare service between Narita and Tokyo for ¥16,000 to ¥17,000 (highway toll charges and rides from 10pm to 5am cost more). Only online reservations are accepted and must be made at least 72 hours in advance.

BY BUS   The most popular and stress-free way to get from Narita to Tokyo is via the **Airport Limousine Bus** (www.limousinebus.co.jp; ✆ **03/3665-7220**), which picks up passengers and their luggage from just outside the arrival lobbies of Terminals 1 and 2 and delivers them to downtown hotels. This is the best mode of transportation if you have heavy baggage or are staying at one of the 40 or so major hotels served by the bus. Buses depart for the various hotels generally once an hour, and it can take almost 2 hours to reach a hotel in Shinjuku. Buses also travel to both Tokyo and Shinjuku stations, Haneda Airport, and the **Tokyo City Air Terminal (TCAT)** in downtown Tokyo, with more frequent departures (up to four times an hour in peak times); all are served by public transportation. TCAT is connected to the subway Hanzomon Line via moving walkways and escalators; Shinjuku and Tokyo stations are hubs for subway lines and commuter trains, but if it's your first trip to Japan, you might want to avoid these big, crowded stations. Even if your hotel is not served by limousine bus, you can still take it to the hotel or station nearest your destination.

Check with the staff at the Airport Limousine Bus counter in the arrival lobbies to inquire which bus stops nearest your hotel and its departure time. The fare to most destinations is ¥3,000. Children 6 to 12 are charged half fare; those 5 and under ride free.

 Saving on Transportation

If you're going to be traveling around Tokyo by public transportation (and who doesn't?), you can save money by purchasing a combination N'EX and Suica card for ¥3,500, which includes the Narita Express into Tokyo plus ¥2,000 worth of travel in Tokyo. A combination card that includes roundtrip N'EX travel from and to the airport costs ¥5,500. The discount tickets, available only at Narita Airport to foreign visitors, can be purchased at JR East Travel Service Centers in the basement of both terminals. Likewise, there's an Airport Limousine & Metro Pass combination ticket that includes one Airport Limousine trip to or from the airport plus 1 day of unlimited rides on Metro subways (it doesn't have to be the same day of arrival) for ¥3,100. This ticket is available at Airport Limousine counters at the airport, TCAT, Shinjuku Station West Exit, and Tokyo Metro Pass offices around town. A round-trip from and to the airport plus 2 days traveling on Metro subways costs ¥6,000; this one is available only at Narita Airport. There are also 1- and 2-day Metro passes available only in the arrival lobbies of both terminals at Narita for ¥600 and ¥980, respectively (these do not include transportation from the airport). The Keisei Skyliner offers its own combination train/metro ticket, charging ¥2,600 for the train from the airport to Ueno plus 1 day of unlimited Metro subway rides; roundtrip tickets and 2-day Metro passes are also available. For more information on the Suica and Metro cards, see "Getting Around," later.

4

TOKYO | Essentials

BY TRAIN   The quickest way to reach Tokyo is by train, with several options available. Trains depart directly from the airport's two underground stations, called Narita Airport Station (which is in Terminal 1) and Airport Terminal 2 Station. The JR **Narita Express (N'EX;** www.jreast.co.jp; ✆ **03/3423-0111)** is the fastest way to reach Tokyo Station, Shinagawa, Shibuya, Shinjuku, or Ikebukuro, with departures approximately twice an hour. The 53-minute trip to Tokyo Station costs ¥2,940 one-way. At Tokyo Station, the train splits, with the front cars going to Shibuya, Shinjuku, and, less frequently, to Ikebukuro, and rear cars going to Shinagawa (cost to these stations: ¥3,110). Note, however, that if you have a validated JR Rail Pass, you can ride the N'EX free (as mentioned above, you must first validate your rail pass at the JR Travel Service Center, located in both terminals). *Note:* Although passengers can buy their N'EX tickets only upon arrival at Narita Airport, I suggest you purchase your return ticket to Narita Airport at least a week or more before your departure, which you can easily do at major JR stations in Tokyo, at a travel agency or online; time your arrival to the airport at least 2 hours before your plane's departure.

If the N'EX is sold out and you're still determined to use your rail pass, you can take the slower **JR Airport Liner,** which will get you to Tokyo Station in 80 minutes. Without a rail pass, this rapid train will cost you ¥1,280.

Another train option, especially if your destination is Ueno, is the privately owned **Keisei Skyliner** (www.keisei.co.jp; ✆ **03/3831-0131),** which departs directly from both Narita Airport Station (Terminal 1) and Airport Terminal 2 and travels to Ueno Station in Tokyo in as little as 36 minutes. You'll find Keisei Skyliner counters in the arrival lobbies of both terminals. Trains depart Narita approximately every 20 to 40 minutes between 8:17am and 10:18pm (6:30am to 5:45pm from Ueno to Narita). The fare between Narita Airport and Ueno Station is ¥2,400 one-way. Cheaper, but with more stops, is Keisei's **Cityliner,** which travels between Ueno and Narita Airport in about 75 minutes and costs ¥1,920 one-way. Finally, travelers on a budget can take one of Keisei's slower limited express trains to Ueno Station; fares start at ¥1,000 for the 80-minute trip.

FACILITIES AT HANEDA AIRPORT   Haneda Airport (HND; www.tokyo-airport-bldg.co.jp; ✆ **03/5757-8111)** is officially named Tokyo International Airport, but everyone calls it Haneda. It has served as Tokyo's city airport for domestic flights for decades; if you're connecting to a domestic flight from Narita, you may need to transfer to Haneda Airport. The **Airport Limousine Bus** makes runs between Narita and Haneda for ¥3,000 for the 75-minute trip.

In 2010 Haneda Airport added a new international terminal. Check airline websites to see whether plane tickets are competitive with Narita, taking into account you'll save time and transportation costs by landing in Haneda. It offers the usual passenger facilities, including a **Tokyo Tourist Information Center** on the second floor of the International Terminal (✆ **03/6428-0653;** daily 9am–11pm), currency exchange, free Wi-Fi, and cell phone rental. But the overriding benefit to Haneda is its central location just 16 minutes via monorail to the useful Yamanote Line.

GETTING FROM HANEDA AIRPORT INTO CENTRAL TOKYO   Like Narita, Haneda Airport is served by the **Airport Limousine Bus,** with service to Shinjuku Station, Tokyo Station, the Tokyo City Air Terminal (TCAT) in downtown Tokyo, and selected hotels in Ginza, Hibiya, Shinjuku, Ikebukuro, Shibuya, and Akasaka. Fares run ¥900 to ¥1,200. Locals, however, are more likely to take the **monorail** from Haneda Airport 16 minutes to Hamamatsucho Station (fare: ¥470), or the **Keikyu**

Line 19 minutes to Shinagawa (fare: ¥400). Both Hamamatsucho and Shinagawa connect to the very useful Yamanote Line, which travels to major stations, including Tokyo and Shinjuku stations.

BY LAND OR SEA

BY TRAIN   If you're traveling to Tokyo from elsewhere in Japan, you'll most likely arrive via Shinkansen bullet train at Tokyo, Ueno, or Shinagawa stations (avoid Tokyo Station if you can; it's very big and confusing). All are well served by trains (including the useful JR Yamanote Line), subways, and taxis.

BY BUS   Long-distance bus service from Hiroshima, Nagoya, Osaka, Kyoto, and other major cities delivers passengers mostly to Tokyo and Shinjuku stations, both of which are connected to the rest of the city via subway and commuter train, including the JR Yamanote Line, which loops around the city. For more information on long-distance bus service, check websites www.bus.or.jp, www.jrbuskanto.co.jp, and http://travel.willer.co.jp/endex.php.

BY FERRY   There are no international ferry services to Tokyo, but domestic long-distance ferries arrive at Ariake Ferry Terminal, located on an artificial island adjacent to Odaiba in Tokyo Bay; the nearest station is Kokusai-Tenjijo-Seimon. Cruise lines usually dock at Harumi Terminal.

Visitor Information

In addition to tourist offices located at both airports (see above), the **Tourist Information Center (TIC)** is in the heart of Tokyo in the Shin-Tokyo Building, 3–3–1 Marunouchi (www.jnto.go.jp; ✆ **03/3201-3331;** station: Yurakucho), within walking distance of the Ginza. The TIC staff is courteous and efficient; I cannot recommend them highly enough. In addition to city maps and sightseeing materials, the office has more information on the rest of Japan than any other tourist office, including pamphlets and brochures on major cities and attractions such as Nikko and Kamakura. Hours are daily 9am to 5pm.

Near Tokyo Station, there's the **TIC TOKYO,** facing the Nihombashi exit of Tokyo Station's north end at 1–8–1 Marunouchi (www.tictokyo.jp; ✆ **03/5220-7055**). Open daily 10am to 7pm, it dispenses information on traveling in Tokyo and Japan.

Another great source of information is the **Tokyo Tourist Information Center,** operated by the Tokyo Metropolitan Government and located on the first floor of the Tokyo Metropolitan Government (TMG) Building no. 1, 2–8–1 Nishi-Shinjuku (www.tourism.metro.tokyo.jp; ✆ **03/5321-3077;** station: Tochomae or Shinjuku). You'll probably want to come here anyway for the great views from TMG's free observation floor. The center dispenses pamphlets, its own city map (which is a great complement to the one issued by JNTO), and handy one-page detailed maps of various city districts, from Ueno to Roppongi. It's open daily 9:30am to 6:30pm. Other city-run information counters are located at Keisei Ueno Station (✆ **03/3836-3471**), open daily 9:30am to 6:30pm, and at Haneda Airport's International Terminal (✆ **03/6428-0653**), open daily 9am to 11pm.

Tourist Publications: Be sure to pick up *Event Calendar* at the TIC, a monthly leaflet listing festivals, antiques and crafts fairs, and other events throughout the metropolitan area. Of the many free giveaways available at the TICs, restaurants, bars, bookstores, hotels, and other establishments visitors and expats are likely to frequent, the best is the weekly ***Metropolis*** (http://metropolis.co.jp), with features on Tokyo, club listings, and restaurant and movie reviews. Look also for the free *Japan-i.jp* (www.japan-i.jp) and *att.Japan* (www.att-japan.net). Weekly entertainment sections on theater, films, and special events are published in the English-language newspapers, appearing on Friday in the *Japan Times* and on Thursday in the *Daily Yomiuri.*

City Layout

Your most frustrating moments in Tokyo will probably occur when you find that you're totally lost. Maybe it will be in a subway or train station, when all you see are signs in Japanese, or on a street somewhere as you search for a museum, restaurant, or bar. At any rate, accept it here and now: You *will* get lost if you are at all adventurous and strike out on your own. It's inevitable. But take comfort in the fact that Japanese get lost, too—even taxi drivers! And don't forget that most of the hotel and restaurant listings in this book have the number of minutes (in parentheses) it takes to walk there from the nearest station; if you take note, you'll at least know the radius from the station to your destination. It's wise, too, to always allow extra time to find your way around.

Tokyo, situated at one end of Tokyo Bay and spreading across the Kanto Plain, still retains some of its Edo Period features. If you look at a map, you'll find a large green oasis in the middle of the city, site of the Imperial Palace and its grounds. Surrounding it is the castle moat; a bit farther out are remnants of another circular moat built by the Tokugawa shogun. The JR Yamanote Line forms another loop around the inner city; most of Tokyo's major hotels, nightlife districts, and attractions are near or inside this oblong loop.

For administrative purposes, Tokyo is broken down into **23 wards,** known as *ku.* Its business districts of Marunouchi and Hibiya, for example, are in Chiyoda-ku, while Ginza is part of Chuo-ku (Central Ward). These two ku are the historic hearts of Tokyo, for it was here that the city had its humble beginnings. Greater Tokyo is also a prefecture (similar to a state or province), with a population of almost 13 million, and includes 26 cities, five towns, and eight villages in addition to its 23 wards, as well as Pacific islands. For most purposes, however, references to Tokyo in this guide pertain mostly to central Tokyo's 23 wards, home to 8.8 million residents.

MAIN STREETS & ARTERIES   One difficulty in finding your way around Tokyo is that hardly any streets are named. Think about what that means: almost 9 million people living in a huge metropolis of nameless streets. Granted, major thoroughfares and some well-known streets in areas such as Ginza and Shinjuku received names after World War II at the insistence of American occupation forces, and more have been labeled or given nicknames that only the locals know, but for the most part, Tokyo's address system is based on a complicated number scheme that must make the postal worker's job here a nightmare. To make matters worse, most streets in Tokyo zigzag—an arrangement apparently left over from olden days, to confuse potential attacking enemies. Now they confuse Tokyoites and visitors alike.

Among Tokyo's most important named streets are **Meiji Dori,** which follows the loop of the Yamanote Line and runs from Minato-ku in the south through Ebisu, Shibuya, Harajuku, Shinjuku, and Ikebukuro in the north; **Yasukuni Dori** and **Shinjuku Dori,** which cut across the heart of the city from Shinjuku to Chiyoda-ku; and **Sotobori Dori, Chuo Dori, Harumi Dori,** and **Showa Dori,** which pass through Ginza. Other major thoroughfares are named after the districts they're in, such as **Roppongi Dori** in Roppongi and **Aoyama Dori** in Aoyama (*dori* means avenue or street, as does *michi*).

Intersections in Tokyo are called a crossing; it seems every district has a famous crossing. **Ginza 4-chome Crossing** is the intersection of Chuo Dori and Harumi Dori. **Roppongi Crossing** is the intersection of Roppongi Dori and Gaien-Higashi Dori.

ADDRESSES   Because streets did not have names when Japan's postal system was established, the country has a unique address system. A typical Tokyo address might read 8–4–21 Ginza, Chuo-ku, which is the address of the Ginza Nikko Hotel. Chuo-ku is the name of the ward. Wards are further divided into named districts, in this case Ginza. Ginza itself is broken down into *chome* (numbered subsections), the first number in the series, here 8–chome. The second number (4 in the example) refers to a smaller area within the *chome*—usually an entire block, sometimes larger. Thus, houses on one side of the street will usually have a different middle number from houses on the other side. The last number, in this case 21, refers to the actual building. Although it seems reasonable to assume that next to a no. 21 building will be a no. 22, that's not always the case; buildings were assigned numbers as they were constructed, not according to location.

Addresses are usually, but not always, posted on buildings beside doors, on telephone poles, and at major intersection traffic lights, but sometimes they are written in kanji only. One frustrating trend is that new, modern buildings omit posting any address whatsoever on their facades, perhaps in the belief that no one understands the address system anyway.

FINDING YOUR WAY AROUND   If you're traveling by subway or JR train, the first thing you should do upon exiting your compartment is to look for **yellow signs** posted on every platform that tell you which exit to take for particular buildings, attractions, and *chome*. At Roppongi Station, for example, you'll find yellow signboards that tell you the exit to take for Roppongi Hills, which will at least get you pointed in the right direction once you emerge from the station. Stations also have maps of the areas either inside the station or at the exit; these are your best plan of attack when trying to find a particular address.

As you walk around Tokyo, you will also notice **map boards** posted beside sidewalks (look for a white circle with an "i" in the middle) giving a breakdown of the postal number system for that particular neighborhood. The first time I tried to use one, I stopped one Japanese, then another, and asked them to locate a specific address on the map. They both studied the map and pointed out the direction. Both turned out to be wrong. Not very encouraging, but if you learn how to read these maps, they're invaluable. Nowadays, many of them include landmarks translated in English.

Another invaluable source of information is the numerous **police boxes,** called *koban,* located in major neighborhoods and beside major train and subway stations throughout the city. Police officers have area maps and are very helpful (helping lost souls seems to occupy much of their time). You should also never hesitate to ask a Japanese the way, but be sure to ask more than one. You'll be amazed at the conflicting directions you'll receive. Apparently, Japanese would rather hazard a guess than impolitely shrug their shoulders and leave you standing there. The best thing to do is ask directions of several Japanese and then follow the majority opinion. You can also duck into a shop and ask someone where a nearby address is, although in my experience employees do not even know the address of their own store. However, they may have a map of the area.

MAPS   Before setting out on your own, arm yourself with a few maps. Maps are so much a part of life in Tokyo that they're often included in shop or restaurant advertisements or brochures, on business cards, and even in private party invitations. Even though I've spent years in Tokyo, I rarely venture forth without a map. You can pick up free maps at Tokyo's tourist information centers (see p. 75 for locations), many with a subway map. Tokyo Tourist Information Centers, run by the Tokyo Metropolitan Government, also have detailed leaflets of Tokyo's many districts, including Shinjuku, Roppongi, Ueno, and other areas you'll probably visit. Armed with these maps, you should be able to locate at least the general vicinity of every place mentioned in this book. Hotels sometimes distribute their own maps. In short, never pass up a free map.

For more detailed maps, head for Tower Books, Kinokuniya, or one of the other bookstores with an English-language section, where you'll find several variations of city maps. My favorite is Shobunsha's Bilingual Map of Tokyo, listing chome and chome subsections for major areas; the compact folded map can be carried in a purse or backpack. If you plan to write a guidebook, consider Shobunsha's Tokyo Metropolitan Atlas, or Kodansha International's Tokyo City Atlas—A Bilingual Guide, both of which cover all 23 of Tokyo's wards with specific postal maps, provide both Japanese and English-language place names, rail and subway maps, and an index to important buildings, museums, and other places of interest. For online maps, www.tokyomap. com has maps of a handful of neighborhoods, including Ginza, Harajuku, and Shibuya, while Google Maps gives detailed satellite maps of the city at www. 24timezones.com/onlinemap/japan_tokyo.php.

Tokyo's Neighborhoods in Brief

Taken as a whole, Tokyo seems formidable and unconquerable. It's best, therefore, to think of it as nothing more than a series of villages scrunched together, much like the pieces of a jigsaw puzzle. Holding the pieces together, so to speak, is the **Yamanote Line,** a commuter train loop around central Tokyo that passes through such important stations as Yurakucho, Tokyo, Ueno, Ikebukuro, Shinjuku, Harajuku, Shibuya, and Shinagawa.

MARUNOUCHI Bounded by the Imperial Palace to the west and Tokyo Station to the east, Marunouchi is one of Tokyo's oldest business districts but has undergone a massive revival since the turn of this century. It's home to office buildings, swanky hotels, and wide avenues like the fashionable, tree-lined **Marunouchi Naka Dori,** home to international designer boutiques from Armani and Burberry to Tiffany.

HIBIYA This is not only the business heart of Tokyo, but its spiritual heart as well. This is where the Tokugawa shogun built his magnificent castle and was thus the center of old Edo. Today, Hibiya, in Chiyoda-ku, is no less important as the home of the **Imperial Palace,** built on the ruins of Edo Castle and the residence of Japan's 125th emperor. Bordering the palace is the wonderful East Garden and Hibiya Park, both open free to the public.

GINZA Ginza is the swankiest and most expensive **shopping area** in all Japan. When the country opened to foreign trade in the 1860s, following 2 centuries of self-imposed seclusion, it was here that Western imports and adopted Western architecture were first displayed. Today, Ginza is where you'll find a multitude of department stores, international name-brand boutiques, exclusive restaurants, hotels, art galleries, and drinking establishments.

TSUKIJI Located only two subway stops from Ginza, Tsukiji was born from reclaimed land during the Tokugawa shogunate; its name, in fact, means "reclaimed land." Today it's famous for the **Tsukiji Fish Market,** one of the largest wholesale fish markets in the world. Nearby is Hama Rikyu Garden, one of Tokyo's most famous gardens.

AKIHABARA Two stops north of Tokyo Station on the Yamanote Line, Akihabara has long been Japan's foremost shopping destination for electronic and electrical appliances, with hundreds of shops offering a look at the latest in gadgets and gizmos, including

Yodobashi Camera, Japan's largest appliance store. In recent years, Akihabara has also become a mecca for *otaku* (geek) culture, home of *anime* and *manga* stores. This is a fascinating area for a stroll, even if you don't buy anything. About a 12-minute walk to the west is **Kanda,** with many stores specializing in new and used books.

ASAKUSA   In the northeastern part of central Tokyo, Asakusa and areas to its north served as the pleasure quarters for old Edo. Today it's known throughout Japan as the site of the famous **Sensoji Temple,** one of Tokyo's top and oldest attractions. It also has a wealth of tiny shops selling traditional Japanese crafts. When Tokyoites talk about old *shitamachi* (downtown), they are referring to the traditional homes and tiny narrow streets of the Asakusa and Ueno areas.

UENO   Located just west of Asakusa, on the northern edge of the JR Yamanote Line loop, Ueno is also part of the city's old downtown. Ueno boasts **Ueno Park,** a huge green space comprising a zoo and several acclaimed museums, including the **Tokyo National Museum,** which houses the largest collection of Japanese art and antiquities in the world. Ueno Station serves as a stop for major train lines heading north and eastward, including some lines of the Shinkansen bullet train. Under the train tracks of the JR Yamanote Line loop is the spirited **Ameya Yokocho,** a thriving market for food, clothing, and accessories.

SHINJUKU   Originating as a post town in 1698 to serve the needs of feudal lords and their retainers traveling between Edo and the provinces, Shinjuku was hardly touched by the 1923 Great Kanto Earthquake, making it an attractive alternative for businesses wishing to relocate following the destruction. In 1971, Japan's first skyscraper was erected with the opening of the Keio Plaza Hotel in western Shinjuku, setting a dramatic precedent for things to come. Today more than a dozen skyscrapers, including several hotels, dot the Shinjuku skyline, and with the opening of the **Tokyo Metropolitan Government Office (TMG)** in 1991 (with a tourist office and a great free observation floor), Shinjuku's transformation into the capital's upstart business district was complete. Separating eastern and western Shinjuku is **Shinjuku Station,** the nation's busiest commuter station, located on the western end of the Yamanote Line loop. Surrounding the station is a bustling shopping district, particularly the huge **Takashimaya Shinjuku** complex and the many discount electronics stores. Shinjuku is also known for its nightlife, especially in **Kabuki-cho,** one of Japan's most famous—and naughtiest—amusement centers; and in **Shinjuku 2–chome,** Tokyo's premier gay nightlife district. An oasis in the middle of Shinjuku madness is **Shinjuku Gyoen Park,** a beautiful garden for strolling and with a tranquil Japanese garden at its center.

IKEBUKURO   Located north of Shinjuku on the Yamanote Line loop, Ikebukuro is the working person's Tokyo, less refined and a bit rougher around the edges. Ikebukuro is where you'll find **Seibu** and **Tobu,** two of the country's largest department stores, as well as the **Japan Traditional Craft Center** with its beautifully crafted traditional items. The **Sunshine City Building,** one of Tokyo's tallest skyscrapers, is home to a huge indoor shopping center.

HARAJUKU   The mecca of Tokyo's younger generation, Harajuku swarms throughout the week with teenagers in search of fashion and fun. **Takeshita Dori** is a narrow pedestrian lane packed elbow to elbow with young people looking for the latest in inexpensive clothing; at its center is Harajuku Daiso, a ¥100 discount shop. Harajuku is also home to one of Japan's major attractions, the **Meiji Jingu Shrine,** built in 1920 to deify Emperor and Empress Meiji; and to the small but delightful **Ukiyo-e Ota Memorial Museum of Art,** with its woodblock prints. Another draw is the **Oriental Bazaar,** Tokyo's best shop for products and souvenirs of Japan. Linking Harajuku with Aoyama (below) is **Omotesando Dori,** a fashionable tree-lined avenue flanked by trendy shops, restaurants, and sidewalk cafes, making it a premier promenade for people-watching. The upscale **Omotesando Hills** shopping center on Omotesando Dori stretches from Harajuku to Aoyama.

AOYAMA While Harajuku is for Tokyo's teeny-boppers, nearby chic Aoyama is its playground for trendsetting yuppies, boasting sophisticated restaurants, pricey boutiques, and more cutting-edge designer-fashion outlets than anywhere else in the city. It's located on the eastern end of **Omotesando Dori** (and an easy walk from Harajuku), centered on Aoyama Dori.

SHIBUYA Located on the southwestern edge of the Yamanote Line loop, Shibuya serves as a vibrant nightlife and shopping area for the young. More subdued than Shinjuku, more down-to-earth than Harajuku, and less cosmopolitan than Roppongi, it's home to more than a dozen department stores specializing in everything from designer clothing to housewares and CDs. Shibuya's backwater status may change, however, with the 2012 opening of **Hikarie,** a 34-story complex across from the station designed to attract an older commuter crowd with shopping (including a new Tokyu department store), restaurants, a 2,000-seat theater showcasing Broadway musicals, and a gallery for artists and artisans from around Japan. Don't miss the light change at Shibuya Crossing, reportedly Japan's busiest intersection, with its hordes of pedestrians, neon, and five video billboards that have earned it the nickname "Times Square of Tokyo" (and a spot in the movie *Lost in Translation*).

EBISU One station south of Shibuya on the JR Yamanote Line, Ebisu was a minor player in Tokyo's shopping and nightlife league until the 1995 debut of **Yebisu Garden Place,** a smart-looking complex of apartments, concert halls, two museums, restaurants, a department store, and a first-class hotel, all connected to Ebisu Station via moving walkway. The vicinity east of Ebisu Station, once a sleepy residential and low-key shopping district, is now a small but thriving nightlife mecca popular with ex-pats who find Roppongi too crass or commercial.

ROPPONGI Tokyo's best-known nightlife district for young Japanese and foreigners, Roppongi has more bars and nightclubs than any other district outside Shinjuku, as well as a multitude of restaurants serving international cuisines. It's anchored by two sprawling developments: the eye-popping, 11-hectare (28-acre) **Roppongi Hills,** Tokyo's largest urban development housing 230 shops and restaurants, a first-class hotel, a garden, apartments, offices, a cinema complex, and Tokyo's highest art museum, on the 53rd floor of Mori Tower; and the 10-hectare (25-acre) **Tokyo Midtown,** which boasts Tokyo's tallest building, a luxury hotel, medical center, 130 restaurants and fashion boutiques, apartments, offices, a garden, and the Suntory Museum of Art.

AKASAKA Bordering Japan's seat of government and home to several large hotels and a small nightlife district, Akasaka caters mostly to businessmen and bureaucrats, making it of little interest to tourists. It does, however, boast some good restaurants; in recent years, so many Koreans have opened restaurants and other establishments here that it has been dubbed "Little Korea."

SHINAGAWA Once an important post station on the old Tokaido Highway, Shinagawa remains an important crossroads due to **Shinagawa Station,** a stop on the Shinkansen bullet train route and on the southern end of the Yamanote Line loop. Home to several major hotels, it has also witnessed a major blossoming of office construction in recent years, making it a serious rival to Shinjuku's business district.

ODAIBA This is Tokyo's newest district, constructed from reclaimed land in Tokyo Bay. Connected to the mainland by the **Rainbow Bridge** (famous for its chameleon colors after nightfall), the Yurikamome Line monorail, the Rinkai Line, and a vehicular harbor tunnel, Odaiba is home to hotels, Japan's largest convention space, several shopping complexes (including VenusFort with its outlet shops), and museums, a monolithic Ferris wheel, and **Megaweb,** a huge multimedia car amusement and exhibition center sponsored by Toyota. For young Japanese, it's one of Tokyo's hottest date spots.

GETTING AROUND

The first rule of getting around Tokyo: It will always take longer than you think. For short-term visitors, calculating travel times in Tokyo is a tricky business. Taking a taxi is expensive and involves the probability of getting stuck interminably in traffic, with the meter ticking away. Taking the subway is usually more efficient, even though it's more complicated and harder on your feet: Choosing which route to take isn't always clear, and transfers between lines are sometimes quite a hike in themselves. If I'm going from one end of Tokyo to the other by subway, I usually allow anywhere from 30 to 60 minutes, depending on the number of transfers and the walking distance to my final destination. If you don't have to change trains, you can travel from one end of central Tokyo to the other (say, from Shibuya to Ueno) in about 30 minutes or less. In any case, travel times to destinations within each line are posted on platform pillars, along with diagrams showing which train compartments are best for making quick transfers between lines.

Your best bet for getting around Tokyo is to take the subway or a Japan Railways (JR) commuter train such as the Yamanote Line to the station nearest your destination. From there you can either walk, using a map and asking directions along the way, or take a taxi.

By Public Transportation

Each mode of transportation in Tokyo—subway (with two different companies), JR train (such as the Yamanote Line), and bus—has its own fare system and therefore requires a new ticket each time you transfer from one mode of transport to another. If you're going to be in Tokyo for a few days, it's much more convenient to purchase a **Suica,** a contactless card issued by JR East that automatically deducts fares and can be used on virtually all modes of transportation, including JR trains (excluding the Shinkansen), private railways (such as the Rinkai Line to Odaiba or Minato Mirai Line to Yokohama), subways, and buses in the greater Tokyo area (including trips to Kamakura). It can even be used for purchases at designated vending machines, convenience stores, and fast-food outlets that display the Suica sign. First-time buyers must purchase the Suica from vending machines for ¥2,000, which includes a ¥500 deposit. The Suica is rechargeable, at amounts ranging from ¥1,000 to ¥10,000. Note, however, that when you return your Suica to get your deposit back, you must be sure that the card is depleted, or you'll be charged a ¥210 handling fee for any remaining stored balance on the card. A similar card to the Suica is the **Pasmo** (also available from vending machines), which can also be used on various modes of transportation throughout Tokyo. Although there are other options available, including 1-day cards and metro-only cards, the Suica and the Pasmo are by far my favorites.

If you think you're going to be traveling a lot by public transportation on any given day, consider purchasing a **Tokyo Free Kippu** (Tokyo Round Tour Ticket), which, despite its name, costs ¥1,580, but does allow unlimited travel for 1 day on all subways, JR trains, and Toei buses within Tokyo's 23 wards. It's available at all JR stations with a *midori-no-madoguchi* (reservation ticket office) or View Plaza (Travel Service Center), and most Metro subway stations.

Avoid taking the subway or JR train during the weekday morning **rush hour,** from 8 to 9am—the stories you've heard about commuters packed into trains like sardines are all true. There are even "platform pushers," men who push people into compartments so that the doors can close. If you want to witness Tokyo at its craziest, go to

Shinjuku Station at 8:30am—but go by taxi unless you want to experience the crowding firsthand. Most lines provide women-only compartments weekdays until 9:30am.

Finally, please note that all cellphones should be switched to silent mode (called "manner mode" in Japanese) on public conveyances.

BY SUBWAY

To get around Tokyo on your own, it's imperative to learn how to ride its subways. Fortunately, the Tokyo Metro system (which uses a symbol "M" vaguely reminiscent of McDonald's famous arches) is efficient, modern, clean, and easy to use; in fact, I think it's one of the most user-friendly systems on the planet. All station names are written in English. Many cars also display the next station in English on digital signs above their doors and announce stops in English.

Altogether, there are 13 underground subway lines crisscrossing the city, operated by two companies: Tokyo Metro (the bigger of the two) and Toei (which operates four lines). Each line is color-coded. The Ginza Line, for example, is orange, which means that all its trains and signs are orange. If you're transferring to the Ginza Line from another line, follow the orange signs and circles to the Ginza Line platform. Each line is also assigned a letter (usually its initial), so that Ginza has the letter "G" and Hibiya the letter "H." Additionally, each station along each line is assigned a number in chronological order beginning with the first station (Asakusa Station, for example, is G19, the 19th stop from Shibuya on the Ginza Line), so you always know how many stops to your destination. Before boarding, however, make sure the train is going in the right direction—signs at each station show both the previous and the next stop, so you can double-check you're heading in the right direction. Tokyo's newest line, Toei's Oedo Line, makes a zigzag loop around the city and is useful for traveling between Roppongi and Shinjuku; be aware, however, that it's buried deep underground and that platforms take a while to reach, despite escalators.

Whereas it used to be a matter of skill to know exactly which train compartment to board if making transfers down the line, diagrams at each station (usually on a pillar at the entrance to each platform) show which end of the train and compartment is most useful for connections. There are also signs that show exactly how many minutes it takes to reach every destination on that line.

Remember, once you reach your destination, look for the yellow signs on station platforms designating which exit to take for major buildings, museums, and addresses. If you're confused about which exit to take, ask someone at the window near the ticket gate. Taking the right exit can make a world of difference, especially in Shinjuku, where there are some 60 station exits.

TICKETS Vending machines at all subway stations sell tickets; fares begin at ¥160 for the shortest distance and increase according to how far you're traveling. Children 6 to 11 pay half fare; children 5 and under ride free. Vending machines give change, even for a ¥10,000 note. **To purchase your ticket,** insert money into the vending machine until the fare buttons light up, and then push the amount for the ticket you want. Your ticket and change will drop onto a little platform at the bottom of the machine.

Before purchasing your ticket, you first have to figure out your **fare.** Fares are posted on a large subway map above the vending machines, but they're generally in Japanese only; major stations also post a smaller map listing fares in English, but you may have to search for it. An alternative is to look at the subway map contained in the "Tokyo Handy Map" issued by the Tokyo Metropolitan Government—it lists most stations in both Japanese and English. When you know what the Japanese characters look like, you may be able to locate your station and the corresponding fare. If you still don't know the fare, just buy a basic-fare ticket for ¥160. When you exit at your destination, look for the **fare adjustment machine;** insert your ticket to find out how much more you owe, or look for a subway employee at the ticket window to tell you how much extra you owe. In any case, be sure to hang onto your ticket, as you must give it up at the end of your journey. Since buying individual tickets is a hassle (and vending machines are unfortunately not as user-friendly as the subway system is), I suggest buying either a Suica or Pasmo card (see above).

HOURS Most subways run from about 5am to midnight, although the times of the first and last trains depend on the line, the station, and whether it's a weekday or a weekend. Schedules are posted in the stations, and throughout most of the day, trains run every 3 to 5 minutes.

For more information on tickets, passes, and lines for the subway, as well as a detailed subway map and brochure, stop by **Metro Information desks** located at Ginza, Shinjuku, Omotesando, and other major stations in Tokyo. Or check the website **www.tokyometro.jp**. Staff at the Metro's Customer Relations Center (© 03/3941-2004) speak Japanese only. Information on **Toei Subway** is available at © 03/3812-2011 or by checking its website at **www.kotsu.metro.tokyo.jp**.

BY JR TRAIN

In addition to subway lines, commuter trains operated by the **East Japan Railways Company (JR)** run aboveground throughout greater Tokyo. These are also color-coded, with fares beginning at ¥130. Buy your ticket from vending machines just as you would for the subway, but more convenient is the Suica. Otherwise, if you think you'll be traveling a lot by JR lines on any given day, consider purchasing a **1-Day Tokunai Pass,** which allows unlimited travel within Tokyo's 23 wards for ¥730. If you have a validated Japan Rail Pass, you can travel on JR trains for free.

The **Yamanote Line** (green-colored coaches) is the best-known and most convenient JR line. It makes an oblong loop around the city, stopping at 29 stations along the way, all of them announced in English and with digital signboards in each compartment. In fact, you may want to take the Yamanote Line and stay on it for a roundup view of Tokyo; the entire trip takes about an hour, passing such stations as Shinjuku, Tokyo, Akihabara, Ueno, Harajuku, and Shibuya on the way.

Another convenient JR line is the orange-colored **Chuo Line;** it cuts across Tokyo between Shinjuku and Tokyo stations, with both express (which doesn't make as many stops) and local trains available. The yellow-colored **Sobu Line** runs between Shinjuku and Akihabara and beyond to Chiba. Other JR lines serve outlying districts for the metropolis's commuting public, including Yokohama and Kamakura. Because the Yamanote, Chuo, and Sobu lines are rarely identified by their specific names at major stations, look for signs that say JR LINES.

For more information on JR lines and tickets, stop by one of JR's **Information Centers** at Tokyo Station, Ueno, Shinjuku, Shibuya, or Shinagawa or call the English-language **JR East Infoline** at © 050/2016-1603 daily from 10am to 6pm. You can also check its website at **www.jreast.co.jp/e**.

In addition to JR, there are private train companies that provide service from Tokyo to outlying areas. **Tobu Railway** (www.tobu.co.jp; (© **03/3841-2871**), for example, operates trains to Nikko, while **Odakyu Electric Railway** (www.odakyu.jp; © **03/5321-7887**) covers the Hakone area. Both offer discount travel passes. For more information, see individual destinations in chapter 5.

4

TOKYO | Getting Around

You can transfer between most subway lines without buying another ticket, and you can transfer between JR train lines on one ticket. However, your ticket or prepaid card does not allow a transfer between Tokyo's two subway companies (Metro and Toei), JR train lines, and private train lines connecting Tokyo with outlying destinations such as Nikko. You usually don't have to worry about this, though, because if you exit through a wicket and have to give up your ticket, you'll know you have to buy another one.

The general rule is that if your final destination and fare are posted above the ticket vending machines, you can travel all the way to your destination with only one ticket. But don't worry about this too much; the ticket collector will set you straight if you've miscalculated. Note, however, that if you pay too much for your ticket, the portion of the fare that's left unused is not refundable—so, again, the easiest thing to do if in doubt is to buy the cheapest fare. Even better, buy a Suica.

BY BUS

Buses are not as easy to use as trains or subways unless you know their route, because only the end destination is written on the bus and routes listed at bus stops are usually not in English. In addition, many bus drivers don't speak English. Buses are sometimes convenient for short distances, however (such as traveling between Roppongi and Aoyama). If you're feeling adventurous, board the bus at the front and drop the exact fare (usually ¥200) into the box. If you don't have the exact amount, fare boxes accept coins or bills; your change minus the fare will come out below. Suica and Pasmo cards are also accepted. A signboard at the front of the bus displays the next stop, usually in English. When you wish to get off, press one of the purple buttons on the railing near the door or the seats. You can pick up an excellent Toei bus map showing all major routes at one of the Tokyo Tourist Information Centers operated by the Tokyo Metropolitan Government (see "Visitor Information," earlier). Or check the Toei website at **www.kotsu.metro.tokyo.jp**.

An exception to the city buses above is Toei's **Tokyo Shitamachi Bus,** a user-friendly sightseeing bus that follows a fixed route to seven major sightseeing spots. Departing from the Marunouchi north exit of Tokyo Station, buses stop at Nihombashi's Mitsukoshi Department Store, Akihabara with its many *anime* and electronics stores, Ueno Park, Kappabashi-dougugai Dori with its many kitchen stores, and Asakusa before terminating at Ryogoku Station with the Edo-Tokyo Museum. Buses travel in both directions at 30-minute intervals daily between 9am and 6:30pm. The fare is ¥200 each time you board (you can use a Suica card); or purchase a 1-day Toei bus pass for ¥500. For information about the Tokyo Shitamachi Bus, including a schedule and map, stop by the Tokyo Tourist Information Center in Shinjuku or Ueno.

By Taxi

Taxis are shamefully expensive in Tokyo. **Fares** start at ¥710 for the first 2km (1¼ miles) and increase ¥90 for each additional 288m (950 ft.) or 90 seconds of waiting time. There are also smaller, more compact taxis for a maximum of four persons that charge slightly less, but they are fewer in number. Fares are posted on the back of the front passenger seat. If you're like me, you probably won't shop around—you'll gratefully jump into the first taxi that stops. Note that from 10pm to 5am, an extra 20% is added to your fare.

Perhaps as an admission of how expensive taxis are, fares can also be paid by all major credit cards, though some companies require a minimum fare of ¥5,000.

With the exception of some major thoroughfares in the downtown area, you can hail a taxi from any street or go to a taxi stand or a major hotel. A red light above the dashboard shows if a taxi is free to pick up a passenger; a yellow light indicates that the taxi is occupied. *Note:* Be sure to stand clear of the back left door—it swings open automatically. Likewise, it shuts automatically once you're in. Taxi drivers are quite perturbed if you try to maneuver the door yourself. The law requires that back-seat passengers wear seat belts.

Unless you're going to a well-known landmark or hotel, it's best to have your destination written out in Japanese, since most taxi drivers don't speak English. But even that may not help. Tokyo is so complicated that taxi drivers may not know a certain area, although many now have navigation systems or will call their central office to inquire about a specific address.

There are so many taxis cruising Tokyo that you can hail one easily on most thoroughfares—except when you need it most: when it's raining, or just after 1am on weekends, after all subways and trains have stopped. To call a major taxi company for a pickup, try **Nihon Kotsu** (www.nihon-kotsu.co.jp; ✆ 03/5755-2336) for an English-speaking operator or **Kokusai** (✆ 03/3505-6001; Japanese only). Note, however, that you'll be required to pay extra (usually not more than ¥400 for an immediate pickup). I have rarely telephoned for a taxi—as in the movies, one usually cruises by just when I raise my hand.

[FastFACTS] TOKYO

If you can't find answers to your questions here, check "Fast Facts: Japan," in chapter 14. If you still can't find an answer, call one of the tourist information offices listed earlier under "Visitor Information." Another good source is the **Foreign Residents' Advisory Center** (✆ 03/5320-7744), which can answer questions on a wide range of topics concerning daily life in Japan, including legal matters, taxes, traffic accidents, emergency numbers and even Japanese customs; it's open Monday to Friday from 9:30am to noon and 1 to 5pm. Finally, if you're staying in a first-class hotel, another valuable resource is the concierge or guest-relations desk, where the staff can tell you how to reach your destination, answer general questions, and even make restaurant reservations.

ATMs/Banks **Narita Airport** and **Haneda Airport** have exchange counters for all incoming international flights that offer better exchange rates than what you'd get abroad, as well as ATMs. Change enough money to last several days, since the exchange rate is the same as in town. Otherwise, all banks displaying an AUTHORIZED FOREIGN EXCHANGE sign can exchange currency and traveler's checks, with exchange rates usually displayed at the appropriate foreign-exchange counter. More convenient—and quicker—are **Travelex** foreign-exchange kiosks, with more than a dozen locations across town, including Tokyo Station (✆ 03/5220-5021), open daily from 9am to 8pm; 3rd floor of Tokyo Midtown Tower, 9–7–1 Akasaka (✆ 03/3408-2280; station: Roppongi), open Monday to Friday from 11am to 3pm and 4 to 7pm and Saturday from 10am to 5pm; and Keisei Ueno Station (✆ 03/5708-0832), open daily 6:15am to 7pm. Other locations are in Shinjuku, Shibuya, Shimbashi, Akihabara, Ikebukuro, and Odaiba. See www.travelex.com for more information. **WORLD CURR€NC¥$HOP**

is a Japanese money exchange company offering similar services, with counters in the Ginza Core Building, 5–8–20 Ginza (© **03/6254-6851;** station: Ginza), open daily from 11am to 8pm; in Roppongi Hills, 6–19–1 Roppongi (© **03/5413-9722;** station: Roppongi), open Monday to Friday from 11am to 7pm and Saturday, Sunday and holidays from noon to 5pm; and in Shinjuku, Shibuya, Ikebukuro, Ueno, Marunouchi and other locations. Call © **03/5275-7610** for more information. For ATMs that accept foreign credit cards, head to any post office or 7-Eleven. For more information on changing money, see "Money & Costs," in chapter 14.

Dentists The **Tokyo Clinic Dental Office,** 3–4–30 Shiba-koen, Minato-ku (© **03/3431-4225;** Mon–Thurs 9am–6pm and Sat 9am–5pm), is near Kamiyacho, Onarimon, or Shiba-koen stations and across from Tokyo Tower. Just a 3-minute walk away is the **United Dental Office,** 2–3–8 Azabudai, Minato-ku (http://uniteddentaloffice. com; © **03/5570-4334;** Mon–Tues and Thurs–Sat 9am–1pm and 2–6pm). Tokyo Midtown Medical Center (see "Doctors & Hospitals," below) also has a **Dental Clinic;** call © **03/5413-7912** for an appointment. The **Tokyo Adventist Dental Clinic,** 1–11–1 Jingumae (www. adventistdental.jp; © **03/3402-1501;** station:

Harajuku or Meiji-Jingumae, is open Monday, Wednesday and Friday from 9am to 4:30pm.

Doctors & Hospitals
Many first-class hotels offer medical facilities or an in-house doctor. Otherwise, your embassy, the **Tokyo Metropolitan Medical Institution Information** (www.himawari.metro.tokyo. jp/qq/qq13enmnlt.asp; © **03/5285-8181;** daily 9am–8pm) can refer you to medical professionals who speak English. The latter has staff who can also explain the health insurance system in Japan; its emergency translation services at © **03/5285-8185** is staffed with translators who can act as go-betweens during treatment if problems arise, available Monday to Friday from 5 to 8pm and weekends and holidays from 9am to 8pm.

The following clinics have some English-speaking staff and are popular with foreigners living in Tokyo: **Tokyo Midtown Medical Center,** an affiliate of Johns Hopkins and located on the sixth floor of Midtown Tower, 9–7–1 Akasaka, Minato-ku, near Roppongi Station (www.tokyomidtown-mc.jp; © **03/5413-0080;** Mon–Fri 10:20am–1pm and 2:50–7pm; Sat 9am–noon; accepts walk-ins, appointments, and emergencies); **The International Clinic,** 1–5–9 Azabudai, Minato-ku, within walking distance of Roppongi or Azabu-Juban stations (© **03/3582-2646;** Mon–Fri 9am–noon and

2–5pm, Sat 9am–noon; walk-ins only); and **Tokyo Medical & Surgical Clinic** (www.tmsc.jp; © **03/3436-3028;** Mon–Fri 8:30am–5:30pm, Sat 8:30am–noon; appointments only).

Large hospitals in Japan are open only a limited number of hours (designated hospitals remain open for emergencies, however, and an ambulance will automatically take you there). Otherwise, you can make appointments at these hospital clinics to see a doctor: **The International Catholic Hospital (Seibo Byoin),** 2–5–1 Naka-Ochiai, Shinjuku-ku, near Mejiro Station on the Yamanote Line (http:// catholic-toshima.web9. jp/english/seibohospital. html; © **03/3951-1111;** clinic hours Mon–Sat 8–11am; closed third Sat each month; walk-ins accepted); **St. Luke's International Hospital (Seiroka Byoin),** 9–1 Akashi-cho, Chuo-ku, near Tsukiji Station on the Hibiya Line (www. luke.or.jp; © **03/3541-5151;** Mon–Fri 8:30–11am; appointment necessary for some treatments); and **Japan Red Cross Medical Center (Nihon Sekijujisha Iryo Center),** 4–1–22 Hiroo, Shibuya-ku (www.med.jrc. or.jp; © **03/3400-1311;** Mon–Fri 8:30–11am; walk-ins only), whose closest subway stations are Roppongi, Hiroo, and Shibuya—from there, you should take a taxi.

Embassies & Consulates Visa or passport sections of most embassies are open only at certain times during the day, so it's best to call in advance.

Australian Embassy: 2–1–14 Mita, Minato-ku, near Azabu-Juban Station, exit 2 (www.australia.or.jp; ℂ **03/5232-4111;** consular section Mon–Fri 9am–12:30pm and 1:30–5pm).

British Embassy: 1 Ichiban-cho, Chiyoda-ku, near Hanzomon Station (http://ukin japan.fco.gov.uk/en; ℂ **03/5211-1100;** Mon–Fri 9am–4:30pm).

Canadian Embassy: 7–3–38 Akasaka, Minato-ku, near Aoyama-Itchome Station (www.canadainternational. gc.ca/missions/japan-japon/; (ℂ **03/5412-6200;** Mon–Fri 9am–5:30pm).

Embassy of Ireland: Ireland House, 2–10–7 Kojimachi, Chiyoda-ku, near Hanzomon Station, exit 3 (www.irish embassy.jp; ℂ **03/3263-0695;** Mon–Fri 10am–12:30pm and 2–4pm).

New Zealand Embassy: 20–40 Kamiyama-cho, Shibuya-ku, a 15-minute walk from Shibuya Station (www.nzembassy.com/japan; ℂ **03/3467-2271;** Mon–Fri 9am–5:30pm).

U.S. Embassy: 1–10–5 Akasaka, Minato-ku, near Toranomon subway station (http://japan.usembassy. gov; ℂ **03/3224-5000;** Mon–Fri 8:30am–5:30pm).

Emergencies The national emergency numbers are ℂ **110** for **police** and ℂ **119** for **ambulance** and **fire** (ambulances are free in Japan unless you request a specific hospital). You do not need to insert any money into public telephones to call these numbers. However, if you use a green public telephone, it's necessary to push a red button before dialing. If you call from a gray public telephone or one that accepts only prepaid cards, you won't see a red button; in that case simply lift the receiver and dial. The Metropolitan Police Department also maintains a telephone counseling service for foreigners at ℂ **03/3501-0110,** Monday through Friday from 8:30am to 5:15pm.

Internet Access A good place to set up a temporary office is at the sophisticated **Gran Cyber Café Bagus,** on the 12th floor of the Roi Building, 5–5–1 Roppongi (ℂ **03/5786-2280;** station: Roppongi). Open 24 hours, it offers individual cubicles with prices that depend on the chair you select: ¥500 for the first hour for a straight-back chair, ¥530 for a recliner, and ¥600 for a massage chair. Unsurprisingly, given Tokyo's high taxi prices, it also offers a "night pack" in a reclining chair, available for a maximum of 6 hours between 11pm to 8am for ¥1,500, as well as—brace yourself—booths for couples. You have to wonder how many people actually work. Ladies take note: There's a section just for you. Another 24-hour Gran Cyber Café Bagus is located in Shibuya, on the seventh floor of Forever 21 at 24–1 Udagawacho (ℂ **03/5456-8922**). For free access, try **Marunouchi Café,** located on the tree-lined Marunouchi Naka Dori avenue in the Shin Tokyo Building, 3–3–1 Marunouchi (ℂ **03/3212-5025;** stations: Marunouchi or Tokyo), with four chest-high computers (you have to stand) available Monday to Friday 8am to 9pm and Saturday and Sunday 11am to 8pm (you'll need to show a photo ID, such as a passport). Or try the **Apple Store,** 3–5–12 Ginza (ℂ **03/5159-8200;** station: Ginza), with demonstration Macs and iPads connected to the Internet you can try out for free daily from 10am to 9pm (the store also has free Wi-Fi).

Mail & Postage Although all post offices are open Monday through Friday from 9am to 5pm, major post offices in each ward remain open to 7pm. The **Shibuya Central Post Office,** 1–12–13 Shibuya (ℂ **03/5469-9908;** station: Shibuya), has longer business hours than most: Monday through Friday 9am to 9pm; and Saturday, Sunday, and holidays 9am to 7pm. An after-hours counter remains open throughout the night for mail and packages, making it the only 24-hour post office in town. *Note:* The **Central Post Office,** built in 1931 southwest of Tokyo Station at 2–7–2 Marunouchi, Chiyoda-ku (ℂ **03/3284-9527**), is closed for major renovation until late 2012. Upon completion, it's expected to be open the same hours as the Shibuya facility, including an after-hours counter open throughout the night for mail and packages. For information on domestic and international postage rates, see chapter 14.

Newspapers & Magazines In addition to two English-language newspapers published daily in Japan—the *Japan Times* (www.japantimes.co.jp) and the *Daily Yomiuri* (www. yomiuri.co.jp/dy), *Metropolis* (http://metropolis.co.jp) is a free weekly with features on Tokyo, club listings, and restaurant and movie reviews.

Pharmacies There are no 24-hour drugstores (*kusuri-ya*) in Tokyo, but ubiquitous 24-hour convenience stores such as 7-Eleven, Lawson, and Family Mart carry things like aspirin. If you're looking for specific pharmaceuticals, a good bet is the **American Pharmacy,** in the basement of the Marunouchi Building, 2–4–1 Marunouchi, Chiyoda-ku (✆ **03/5220-7716;** station: Tokyo; Mon–Sat 10:30am–9pm and Sun and holidays 10am–8pm), which has many of the same over-the-counter drugs you can find at home (many of them imported from the United States) and can fill American prescriptions—but note that you *must first visit a doctor in Japan* before foreign prescriptions can be filled, so it's best to bring an ample supply of any prescription medication with you.

Police The national emergency telephone number is ✆ **110.** For nonemergency criminal matters or concerns, the **Metropolitan Police Department** maintains an English-language telephone counseling service for foreigners at ✆ **03/3501-0110** Monday through Friday from 8:30am to 5:15pm.

Safety Tokyo is one of the safest cities in the world. However, crime is on the increase, and there are precautions you should always take when traveling: Stay alert and be aware of your immediate surroundings. Be especially careful with cameras, purses, and wallets, particularly in crowded subways, department stores, or tourist attractions (such as the retail district around Tsukiji Fish Market), especially because pickpocketing has been on the rise. Some Japanese also caution women against walking through parks alone at night.

EXPLORING TOKYO

Tokyo hasn't fared very well over the centuries. Fires and earthquakes have taken their toll, old buildings have been torn down in the zeal of modernization, and World War II left most of the city in ruins. Save your historical sightseeing, therefore, for places such as Kyoto, Nikko, and Kamakura, and consider Tokyo your introduction to the newest of the new in Japan, the showcase of the nation's accomplishments in the arts, technology, fashion, pop art, and design. It's also the best place in the world to take in Japan's performing arts, such as *kabuki,* and offers such diverse activities as the tea ceremony, flower arranging, and sumo. Tokyo also has more museums than any other city in Japan, as well as a wide range of other attractions, including parks, temples, and shrines. In Tokyo you can explore mammoth department stores, sample unlimited cuisines, walk around unique neighborhoods, revel in kitsch, and take advantage of glittering nightlife. There's so much to do in Tokyo that I can't imagine ever being bored—even for a minute.

There are two things to remember when planning your sightseeing itinerary: The city is huge, and it takes time to get from one end to the other. Plan your days so you cover Tokyo neighborhood by neighborhood, coordinating sightseeing with dinner and evening plans. Keep in mind that most museums in Tokyo are closed 1 day of the week (usually Monday) and for New Year's (generally the last day or two in December and the first 1 to 3 days of January). If Monday happens to be a national holiday, most national and municipal museums will remain open but will close Tuesday instead.

Some of the privately owned museums, however, are closed on national holidays, as well as for exhibition changes. Call beforehand or check websites to avoid disappointment. Remember, too, that you must enter museums at least 30 minutes before closing time. For a listing of current exhibitions, including those being held at major department stores, consult *Metropolis,* an English-language weekly available in hotels, restaurants, and bars around town as well as online at www.metropolis.co.jp.

Central Tokyo: Ginza & the Vicinity of the Imperial Palace

East Garden (Higashi Gyoen) ★★ PARK/GARDEN   The 21 hectares (52 acres) of the formal Higashi Gyoen—once the main grounds of Edo Castle and located next to the Imperial Palace—are a wonderful respite in the middle of the city. Yet surprisingly, this garden is hardly ever crowded (except when cherry trees, azaleas, and other blossoms are in full bloom or at lunchtime when *obento*-eating office workers fill the benches). **Ninomaru ★★★**, my favorite part, is laid out in Japanese style with a pond, steppingstones, and winding paths; it's particularly beautiful when the wisteria, azaleas, irises, and other flowers are at their peak. Near Ninomaru is the **Sannomaru Shozokan,** with free, changing exhibitions of art treasures belonging to the imperial family.

On the highest spot of East Garden is the **Honmaru** (inner citadel), where Tokugawa's main castle once stood. Built in the first half of the 1600s, the castle was massive, surrounded by a series of whirling moats and guarded by 23 watchtowers and 99 gates around its 15km (10-mile) perimeter. At its center was Japan's tallest building at the time, the five-story castle keep, soaring 50m (168 ft.) above its foundations and offering an expansive view over Edo. This is where Tokugawa Ieyasu would have taken refuge, had his empire ever been seriously threatened. Although most of the castle was a glimmering white, the keep was black with a gold roof, which must have been quite a sight in old Edo as it towered above the rest of the city. All that remains today of the shogun's castle are a few towers, gates, stone walls, moats, and the stone foundations of the keep.

Free guided tours of the garden, run by volunteers, are given Saturday from 1 to 3pm. No appointments are necessary; just show up at the meeting point outside Tokyo Station's Marunouchi Central Exit and look for the sign *Tokyo Free Walking Tour.* For more information, see the website http://tfwt.web.officelive.com/default.aspx.

1–1 Chiyoda, Chiyoda-ku. (✆ **03/3213-1111.** Free admission. Tues–Thurs and Sat–Sun 9am–5pm (to 4:30pm Mar to mid-Apr and Sept–Oct; to 4pm Nov–Feb). You must enter 30 min. before closing. Closed Dec 23 and Dec 28–Jan 3; open other national holidays. Station: Otemachi, Takebashi, or Nijubashi-mae.

The Imperial Palace (Kyokyo) ★ ICON   The Imperial Palace, home of the imperial family, is the heart and soul of Tokyo. Built on the very spot where Edo Castle used to stand during the days of the Tokugawa shogunate, it became the imperial home upon its completion in 1888 and is now the residence of Emperor Akihito, 125th emperor of Japan. Destroyed during air raids in 1945, the palace was rebuilt in 1968 using the principles of traditional Japanese architecture. But don't expect to get a good look at it; most of the palace grounds' 114 hectares (282 acres) are off-limits to the public, with the exception of 2 days a year when the royal family makes an appearance before the throngs: January 2 and December 23 (the emperor's birthday). Or, you can visit Imperial Palace grounds on free **guided tours** Monday through

Tokyo Attractions

Amuse Museum **11**
East Garden **17**
Edo-Tokyo Museum **13**
Fukugawa Edo Museum **14**
Hama Rikyu Garden **29**
Hanayashiki **9**
Imperial Palace **18**
Kiyomizu Kannon-do
  Temple **6**
Kokugikan
  (Sumo Stadium) **12**
Meiji Jingu Shrine **21**
Mori Art Museum **28**
Museum of Contemporary
  Art, Tokyo (MOT) **14**
The National Art Center,
  Tokyo **24**
National Children's
  Castle **23**
National Museum of
  Modern Art **16**
National Museum of
  Nature and Science **3**
National Museum of
  Western Art **7**
Oedo-Onsen Monogatari **31**
Rikugien Garden **1**
Sensoji Temple **10**
Shinjuku Gyoen **20**
Suntory Museum of Art **25**
TMG Observation
  Platform **19**
Tokyo National Museum **2**

Key continues below

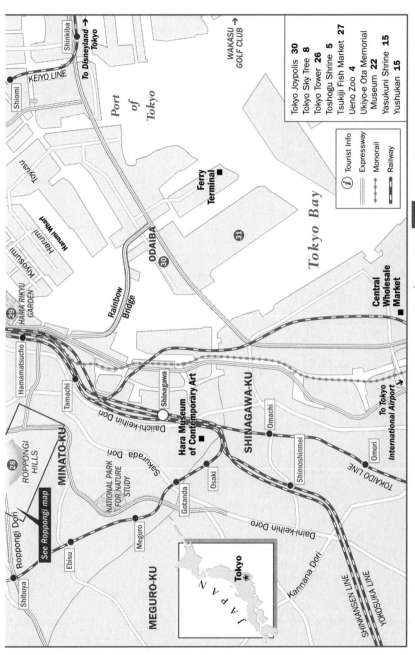

Tokyo Joypolis **30**
Tokyo Sky Tree **8**
Tokyo Tower **26**
Toshogu Shrine **5**
Tsukiji Fish Market **27**
Ueno Zoo **4**
Ukiyo-e Ota Memorial
Museum **22**
Yasukuni Shrine **15**
Yushukan **15**

ⓘ Tourist Info
Expressway
Monorail
Railway

Friday at 10am and 1:30pm (1:30pm tour not available July 21–Aug 31), but you must make a reservation (reservations are accepted up to 1 month in advance). Easiest is to book online, which you must do at least 4 days in advance at **http://sankan.kunaicho. go.jp.** Alternatively, you can make a reservation up to 1 day in advance by calling ✆ **03/3213-1111** and then stopping by the Imperial Household Agency (located at the Sakashita-mon Gate, on the east side of the palace grounds) to show your passport number and provide nationality, name, age, gender, and home address. Tours, conducted in Japanese but with English-language audio guides, last about 75 minutes and lead past official buildings, the inner moat, historic fortifications, and Nijubashi Bridge. I recommend this tour only if you have seen Tokyo's other top attractions (and it doesn't come close to the more impressive imperial palace tours in Kyoto).

Otherwise, you'll have to console yourself with a camera shot of the palace from the southeast side of **Nijubashi Bridge,** where the moat and the palace turrets show above the trees. Most Japanese tourists make brief stops here to pay their respects. The wide moat, lined with cherry trees, is especially beautiful in the spring. You might even want to spend an hour strolling or jogging the 5km (3 miles) around the palace and moat. But the most important thing to do in the palace's vicinity is visit its **East Garden (Higashi Gyoen),** where you'll find what's left of the central keep of old Edo Castle, the stone foundation (see above).

Hibiya Dori Ave. Station: Nijubashi-mae (1 min.) or Hibiya (5 min.).

National Museum of Modern Art (Tokyo Kokuritsu Kindai Bijutsukan) ★★

ART MUSEUM   This museum houses the largest collection of modern Japanese art under one roof, including both Japanese- and Western-style paintings, prints, watercolors, drawings, and sculpture, all dating from the Meiji Period through the 20th century. Names to look for include Munakata Shiko, Kuroda Seiki, and Yokoyama Taikan. A few works by Western artists, such as Picasso, Klee, and Kandinsky, are also on display as examples of Western artistic styles of the same period. Expect to spend about 1 hour here.

3 Kitanomaru Koen Park, Chiyoda-ku. www.momat.go.jp. ✆ **03/3214-2561.** Admission ¥420 adults, ¥130 college students, free for children; special exhibits cost more. Tues–Sun 10am–5pm (Fri to 8pm). Station: Takebashi (exit 1b, 3 min.).

Yushukan ★ MUSEUM   Located on the grounds of **Yasukuni Shrine,** built in 1869 to commemorate some 2.5 million Japanese war dead, this war memorial museum chronicles the rise and fall of the samurai, Sino-Japanese War, Russo-Japanese War, and World Wars I and II, though English-language explanations are rather vague and Japan's military aggression in Asia is glossed over. Still, a fascinating 90 minutes can be spent here gazing at samurai armor, uniforms, tanks, guns, and artillery, as well as such thought-provoking displays as a human torpedo (a tiny submarine guided by one occupant and loaded with explosives) and a suicide attack plane. But the most chilling displays are the seemingly endless photographs of war dead, some of them young teenagers. In stark contrast to the somberness of the museum, temporary exhibits of beautiful *ikebana* (Japanese flower arrangements) and bonsai are often held on shrine grounds in rows of glass cases. The shrine is also famous for its cherry blossoms and for its Sunday flea market held from 6am to 3pm. Yasukuni Shrine is most well known, however, for the controversy that erupts every August 15 when World War II memorials are held and top government officials stop by, causing outrage among Japan's Asian neighbors.

Yasukuni Shrine, 3–1–1 Kudan-kita, Chiyoda-ku. www.yasukuni.or.jp. ✆ **03/3261-8326.** Free admission to shrine; Yushukan ¥800 adults, ¥500 students, ¥300 junior-high and high-school

Tsukiji & Shiodome

Hama Rikyu Garden ♨ PARK/GARDEN   Considered by some to be the best garden in Tokyo (but marred, in my opinion, by skyscrapers in Shiodome that detract from its charm; there ought to be a law), this urban oasis has origins stretching back 300 years, when it served as a retreat for a former feudal lord and as duck-hunting and falconry grounds for the Tokugawa shoguns. In 1871, possession of the garden passed to the imperial family, which used it to entertain such visiting dignitaries as Gen. Ulysses S. Grant. Come here to see how the upper classes enjoyed themselves during the Edo Period; to gain a better understanding, pick up the park's free audio guide. The garden contains an inner tidal pool, spanned by three bridges draped with wisteria (views from the south end of the garden are the most picturesque). There are also other ponds; a refuge for ducks, herons, and migratory birds; a promenade along the bay lined with pine trees; a 300-year-old pine; moon-viewing pavilions; and teahouses (powdered green tea and a sweet will cost you ¥500). Plan on at least an hour's stroll to see everything, but the best reason for coming here is to board a ferry from the garden's pier bound for Asakusa, with departures every hour (or more often) between 10:35am and 4:15pm; the fare is ¥720 one-way.

1–1 Hamarikyuteien, Chuo-ku. www.tokyo-park.or.jp. ✆ **03/3541-0200.** Admission ¥300 adults, ¥150 seniors, free for children 12 and under. Daily 9am–5pm. Station: Shiodome (exit 5, 5 min.) or Tsukiji-shjjo (7 min.).

Tsukiji Fish Market ★★★ MARKET   This huge wholesale fish market—the largest in Japan and one of the largest in the world—is a must for anyone who has never seen such a market in action. The action here starts early: Throughout the night, boats begin arriving from the seas around Japan, from Africa, and even from America, with enough fish to satisfy the demands of a nation where seafood reigns supreme. To give you some idea of its enormity, this market handles almost all the seafood—about 450 kinds of seafood amounting to more than 2,000 tons daily—consumed in and around Tokyo. The king is tuna, huge and frozen, unloaded from the docks at around 3am, laid out on the ground, and numbered. Wholesalers walk up and down the rows, jotting down the numbers of the best-looking tuna, and by 5:30am, the tuna auctions are well underway. The entire auction of sea products takes place from about 4:40 to 6:30am, with auctions of vegetables at a corner of the market starting at 6:30am. The wholesalers then transfer what they've bought to their own stalls in the market, subsequently selling fish and produce to their regular customers, usually retail stores and restaurants.

Although I used to be able to arrive before dawn and visit the entire market freely, an increasing number of tourists over the years has prompted authorities to close tuna auctions to visitors, except for a small viewing area open 5–6:15am to the first 120 visitors on a first-come first-serve basis (apply at the Fish Information Center, located on Harumi Dori near the Kochidoki-bashi Bridge, before 5am and expect to wait in line). Otherwise, I think it's just as fun to arrive after 9am to visit the wholesale market area, held in a cavernous, hangarlike building, which means you can visit it even on a dismal rainy morning. There's a lot going on—men in black rubber boots rushing wheelbarrows and forklifts through the aisles, hawkers shouting, knives chopping and slicing. Wander the aisles and you'll see things you never dreamed were edible. This is a good place to bring your camera, but note that no flash photography of auctions or the

4

TOKYO | Exploring Tokyo

market is allowed. Also, the floors are wet, so leave your fancy shoes at the hotel. Finally, be mindful of the many forklifts and carts, and please don't touch the fish.

Tsukiji is also a good place to come if you want sushi for breakfast. Alongside the covered market are rows of barracklike buildings divided into sushi restaurants and shops related to the fish trade. In addition, in between the market and Tsukiji Station is the Outer Market (*Jogai*), a delightful district of tiny retail shops and stalls where you can buy the freshest seafood in town, plus dried fish and fish products, seaweed, vegetables, knives, and other cooking utensils. **Warning:** While walking through the Outer Market, my Japanese friend and I were warned several times by local shop-keepers to watch our purses, advice we didn't take lightly. Apparently, pickpockets have been at work here on unsuspecting tourists.

5–2–1 Tsukiji, Chuo-ku. www.tsukiji-market.or.jp. ✆ **03/3542-1111.** Free admission. Mon–Sat 9–11am. Closed some Wed, holidays, several days around New Year's, and 3 days in mid-Aug. Station: Tsukijishijo (exit A2, 2 min.) or Tsukiji (Honganji Temple exit, 10 min.).

Asakusa

Amuse Museum ★★ 🏛MUSEUM   This great museum's sole purpose is to high-light items and traditions from Japan's past that might otherwise slip from public view. Most fascinating to me is the display of *boro*, which is clothing originating in Japan's snowy north, mended through the years with additional stitching and various pieces of fabric, and passed down from generation to generation. These patchwork garments would have probably disappeared altogether had it not been for Tanaka Chuzaburo, a private collector who scoured the countryside searching for boro, kimono, folk art, and antiques. In fact, Tanaka's collection of authentic clothing is so rare, Kurosawa Akira used some of it in his movie *Dreams;* a room in the museum shows scenes from the movie and artifacts. Other rooms display antique clocks, iron kettles, Jomon pottery, and other household goods and crafts, while the Kimono Gallery pays tribute to women of lore who were involved in every single step in producing their own clothing, from planting seeds, weaving their cloth, and sewing together their garments. On the first floor is the Ukiyo-e Theather, where a 28-minute educational film highlights individual woodblock prints and points out details that tell us about life during the Edo Period, from clothing worn by fishermen to hairstyles of the time. On the roof is a viewing deck providing a unique perspective of Sensoji Temple's grounds, while on the sixth floor is Bar Six, open from 6pm and also providing views of Asakusa.

2–34–3 Asakusa, Taito-ku. www.amusemuseum.com. ✆03/5806-1181. Admission ¥1,000 adults, ¥800 university and high-school students, ¥500 children. Tues–Sun 10am–6pm. Station: Asakusa (5 min.). Tokyo Shitamachi Bus: Asakusa Kaminarimon. Just east of Sensoji Temple, past Nitemmon Gate.

Hanayashiki ☺AMUSEMENT PARK   Opened in 1853 while the shogun still reigned, this small and rather corny amusement park is Japan's oldest. It offers a small roller coaster, a kiddie Ferris wheel, a carousel, a haunted house, a 3-D theater, samu-rai and ninja shows, and other diversions that appeal to younger children. Note, however, that after paying admission, you must still buy tickets for each ride; tickets are ¥100 each, and most rides require three to four tickets.

2–28–1 Asakusa (northwest of Sensoji Temple), Taito-ku. www.hanayashiki.net. ✆03/3842-8780. Admission ¥900 adults, ¥400 children 5–12 and seniors, free for children 4 and under. Daily 10am–6pm (to 5pm in winter). Station: Asakusa (5 min.). Tokyo Shitamachi Bus: Asakusa Kaminarimon.

Sensoji Temple ★★★TEMPLE   Also popularly known as Asakusa Kannon, this is Tokyo's oldest and most popular temple, with a history dating back to A.D. 628. That was when, according to popular lore, two brothers fishing in the nearby Sumida River netted the catch of their lives: a tiny golden statue of Kannon, the Buddhist goddess of mercy and happiness who is empowered with the ability to release humans from all suffering. Sensoji Temple was erected in her honor, and although the statue is housed here, it's never shown to the public. Still, through the centuries, worshipers have flocked here seeking favors of Kannon; and when Sensoji Temple burned down during a 1945 bombing raid, the present structure was rebuilt with donations from the Japanese people.

Colorful **Nakamise Dori,** a pedestrian lane leading to the shrine, is lined with more than 80 stalls selling souvenirs and traditional Japanese goods. In fact, the whole Asakusa area is one of my favorite neighborhoods, and you can easily spend half a day here; see the walking tour on p. 108 for more on this fascinating part of old Tokyo.

2–3–1 Asakusa, Taito-ku. ✆ **03/3842-0181.** Free admission. Daily 6:30am–5pm. Station: Asakusa (2 min.). Tokyo Shitamachi Bus: Asakusa Kaminarimon.

Ueno

National Museum of Nature and Science (Kokuritsu Kagaku Hakubutsukan) ★ ☺ MUSEUM   Japan's largest science museum covers everything from

ueno park: **TOKYO'S BEST FAMILY OUTING**

Ueno Park—on the northeast edge of the Yamanote Line—is one of the largest parks in Tokyo and one of the most popular places in the city for Japanese families on a day's outing. It's a cultural mecca with a number of attractions, including the prestigious Tokyo National Museum; the National Museum of Western Art; the delightful Shitamachi Museum with its displays of old Tokyo; Ueno Zoo; and Shinobazu Pond, a bird sanctuary. For a map of the Ueno area, see p. 183.

A landmark in the park is the small Toshogu Shrine. Erected in 1651, it's dedicated to Tokugawa Ieyasu, founder of the Tokugawa shogunate. Stop here to pay respects to the man who made Edo (present-day Tokyo) the seat of his government and thus elevated the small village to the most important city in the country. The pathway to the shrine is lined with massive stone lanterns, as well as 50 copper lanterns donated by *daimyo* (feudal lords) from all over Japan; unfortunately, the shrine itself is closed for renovations until 2014. Also in the park is Kiyomizu Kannon-do Temple, completed in 1631 as a copy of the famous Kiyomizu Temple in

Kyoto (but on a much less grand scale). It enshrines Kosodate Kannon, protector of childbearing and child-raising. Women hoping to become pregnant come here to ask for the goddess's blessing; those whose wishes have been fulfilled return to pray for their children's good health and protection. Many leave behind dolls as symbols of their children. Once a year, a requiem service is held for all the dolls at the temple, after which they are cremated.

The busiest time of the year at Ueno Park is April, during the cherry-blossom season, when people come en masse to celebrate the birth of the new season. It's not the spiritual communion with nature that you might think, however. On weekends and in the evenings during cherry-blossom time (which only lasts for a few days), havoc prevails as entire companies converge on the park to sit under the cherry trees on plastic or cardboard and to drink sake and beer, seemingly oblivious to the fragile pink blossoms shimmering above. Incidentally, Ueno Park is also a popular refuge for Tokyo's homeless.

the evolution of life to Japanese inventions and technology, in expansive, imaginative displays, with plenty of exhibits geared toward children. A highlight is an entire arena of 100-some taxidermic animals from around the world, including a polar bear, camel, gorilla, tiger, and other creatures (some are animals that died at Ueno Zoo). Other highlights include a dinosaur display; a hands-on discovery room for children exploring sound, light, magnetism, and other scientific phenomena; re-created wood and marine habitats; a Japanese mummy from the Edo Period curled up in a burial jar; Hachiko (stuffed, on the second floor of the main building—there's a famous statue of this dog at Shibuya Station); and an extensive exhibition that allows visitors to stroll through some 4 billion years of evolutionary history. You'll want to spend about 2 hours here, more if you have children in tow or if you opt for the audio guide (¥200 extra), recommended since English-language explanations are limited.

Ueno Park, Taito-ku. www.kahaku.go.jp. 📞 **03/5777-8600.** Admission ¥600 adults, free for children. Tues–Sun 9am–5pm (Fri to 8pm). Station: Ueno (5 min.). Tokyo Shitamachi Bus: Ueno Koen Yamashita/Ueno Station.

The National Museum of Western Art (Kokuritsu Seiyo Bijutsukan) ★

ART MUSEUM   Japan's only national museum dedicated to Western art is housed in a main building designed by Le Corbusier and in two more recent additions. It presents a chronological study of sculpture and art from the end of the Middle Ages through the 20th century, beginning with works by Old Masters, including Lucas Cranach the Elder, Rubens, El Greco, Murillo, and Tiepolo. French painters and Impressionists of the 19th and 20th centuries are well represented, including Delacroix, Monet (with a whole room devoted to his work), Manet, Renoir, Pissarro, Sisley, Courbet, Cézanne, and Gauguin. The museum's 20th-century collection includes works by Picasso, Ernst, Miró, Dubuffet, and Pollock. The museum is also famous for its 50-odd sculptures by Rodin, one of the largest collections in the world, encompassing most of his major works including *The Kiss, The Thinker, Balzac,* and *The Gates of Hell.* Plan on spending at least an hour here, though frequent—and ambitious—special exhibitions may entice you to linger longer.

Ueno Park, Taito-ku. www.nmwa.go.jp. 📞 **03/3828-5131.** Admission ¥420 adults, ¥130 college students, free for children 17 and under and seniors; special exhibits require separate admission fee. Free admission to permanent collection 2nd and 4th Sat of the month. Tues–Sun: 9:30am–5:30pm in summer, 9:30am–5pm in winter (to 8pm Fri year-round). Station: Ueno (4 min.). Tokyo Shitamachi Bus: Ueno Koen Yamashita/Ueno Station.

Tokyo National Museum (Tokyo Kokuritsu Hakubutsukan) ★★★

MUSEUM   The National Museum is not only the largest and oldest museum in Japan, it boasts the largest collection of Japanese art in the world. This is where you go to see antiques from Japan's past—old kimono, samurai armor, priceless swords, lacquerware, metalwork, pottery, scrolls, screens, *ukiyo-e* (woodblock prints), calligraphy, ceramics, archaeological finds, and more. Items are shown on a rotating basis with about 3,000 on display at any one time—so no matter how many times you visit the museum, you'll always see something new. There are also frequent special exhibitions. Schedule at least 2 hours to do the museum justice.

The museum comprises five buildings. The **Japanese Gallery (Honkan),** straight ahead as you enter the main gate, is the most important one, devoted to Japanese art. Here you'll view Japanese ceramics; Buddhist sculptures dating from about A.D. 538 to 1192; samurai armor, helmets, and decorative sword mountings; swords, which throughout Japanese history were considered to embody spirits all their own;

textiles and kimono; lacquerware; ceramics; and paintings, calligraphy, ukiyo-e, and scrolls. Be sure to check out the museum shop in the basement; it sells reproductions from the museum's collections as well as traditional crafts by contemporary artists.

The **Heiseikan Gallery** is where you'll find archaeological relics of ancient Japan, including pottery and Haniwa clay burial figurines of the Jomon Period (10,000 B.C.–1000 B.C.) and ornamental, keyhole-shaped tombs from the Yayoi Period (400 B.C.–A.D. 200). The **Gallery of Horyuji Treasures (Horyuji Homotsukan)** displays priceless Buddhist treasures from the Horyuji Temple in Nara, founded by Prince Shotoku in A.D. 607. Although the building's stark modernity (designed by Taniguchi Yoshio, who also designed the expansion of the New York Museum of Modern Art) seems odd for an exhibition of antiquities, the gallery's low lighting and simple architecture lend dramatic effect to the museum's priceless collection of bronze Buddhist statues, ceremonial *gigaku* masks used in ritual dances, lacquerware, and paintings. *Note:* The **Asian Gallery (Toyokan),** housing art and archaeological artifacts from everywhere in Asia outside Japan, is closed for renovation until 2013. Until its reopening, a limited selection from the collection is on display in the **Hyokeikan,** built on the museum grounds in 1909 to commemorate the marriage of Emperor Taisho.

Ueno Park, Taito-ku. www.tnm.jp. ⏰ **03/3822-1111.** Admission ¥600 adults, ¥400 college students, free for seniors and children. Special exhibits cost more. Tues–Sun 9:30am–5pm (enter by 4:30pm); Apr–Dec open to 8pm Fri during special exhibitions; Apr–Sept open to 6pm weekends and holidays). Closed Dec 28–Jan 1. Station: Ueno (10 min.). Tokyo Shitamachi Bus: Ueno Koen Yamashita/Ueno Station.

Ueno Zoo ☺ ZOO   Founded in 1882, Japan's oldest zoo is small by today's standards but remains one of the most well-known zoos in Japan. Its most celebrated residents are Li-Li and Shin-Shin, two pandas on loan from a wildlife sanctuary in China's Sichuan province. A vivarium houses amphibians, fish, and reptiles, including snakes and crocodiles. Also of note is the five-storied pagoda dating from the Edo era, along with a teahouse built 350 years ago to receive the shogun when visiting nearby Toshogu Shrine. Shinobazu Pond, on the west end of the zoo, serves as a sanctuary for wild cormorants and other birds. Personally, I can't help but feel sorry for some of the animals in their small spaces, but children will enjoy the Japanese macaques, polar and Hokkaido brown bears, California sea lions, penguins, gorillas, giraffes, zebras, elephants, hippos, deer, and tigers. Expect to spend a minimum of 2 hours here.

Ueno Park, Taito-ku. www.tokyo-zoo.net/english. ⏰ **03/3828-5171.** Admission ¥600 adults, ¥300 seniors, ¥200 children 13–15, free for children 12 and under. Tues–Sun 9:30am–5pm (enter by 4pm). Closed some holidays. Station: Ueno (4 min.). Tokyo Shitamachi Bus: Ueno Koen Yamashita.

Shinjuku

Shinjuku Gyoen ★★ ☺ PARK/GARDEN   Formerly the private estate of a feudal lord and then of the imperial family, this is considered one of the most important parks of the Meiji Era. It's wonderful for strolling because of the variety of its planted gardens; styles range from French and English to Japanese traditional. The park's 58 hectares (143 acres) make it one of the city's largest, and each bend in the pathway brings something completely different: Ponds and sculpted bushes give way to a promenade lined with sycamores that opens onto a rose garden. This place amazes me every time I come here. Cherry blossoms, azaleas, chrysanthemums, and other flowers provide splashes of color from spring through autumn. The Japanese garden, buried in the center, is exquisite; if you have time only for a quick look at traditional landscaping, you won't be disappointed here. There are also wide grassy expanses, popular for picnics and playing, and a greenhouse filled with tropical plants. You could easily spend a half-day of leisure here, but for a quick fix of rejuvenation, 1 hour will do.

11 Naitocho, Shinjuku-ku. www.env.go.jp/garden/shinjukugyoen/english/index.html. © **03/3350-0151.** Admission ¥200 adults, ¥50 children. Tues–Sun 9am–4:30pm. Station: Shinjuku Gyoen-mae (2 min.) or Sendagaya (5 min.).

Tokyo Metropolitan Government Office (TMG) ★★★ ☺ OBSERVATION DECK   Tokyo's city hall—designed by one of Japan's best-known architects, Kenzo Tange—comprises three buildings—TMG no. 1, TMG no. 2, and the Metropolitan Assembly Building—and together they contain everything from Tokyo's Disaster Prevention Center to the governor's office. Most important for visitors is TMG no. 1, the tall building to the north that offers the best free view of Tokyo. This 48-story, 240m (787-ft.) structure, the tallest building in Shinjuku, boasts two observatories located on the 45th floors of both its north and south towers. Both observatories offer the same spectacular views—on clear winter days you can even see Mount Fuji—as well as a small souvenir shop and coffee shop (the North Tower also has a Hakuhinkan Toy Park, with fun souvenirs, but a large restaurant annoyingly takes up the entire east side of the observatory). In expensive Tokyo, this is one of the city's best bargains, and kids love it. On the first floor is a Tokyo Tourist Information Center, open daily 10am to 6:30pm.

2–8–1 Nishi-Shinjuku. © **03/5321-1111.** Free admission. Daily 9:30am–10:30pm. Closed Dec 29–Jan 3. Station: Tochomae (1 min.), Shinjuku (10 min.), or Nishi-Shinjuku (5 min.).

Harajuku & Aoyama

Meiji Jingu Shrine ★★ SHRINE   This is Tokyo's most venerable Shinto shrine, opened in 1920 in honor of Emperor and Empress Meiji, who were instrumental in opening Japan to the outside world more than 120 years ago. Japan's two largest *torii* (the traditional entry gate of a shrine), built of cypress more than 1,700 years old, give dramatic entrance to the grounds, once the estate of a *daimyo*. The shaded pathway is lined with trees, shrubs, and dense woods. In late May/June, the **Iris Garden** is in spectacular bloom (admission fee charged). About a 10-minute walk from the first torii, the shrine is a fine example of dignified and refined Shinto architecture. It's made of plain Japanese cypress and topped with green-copper roofs. Meiji Jingu Shrine is the place to be on New Year's Eve, when more than two million people crowd onto the grounds to usher in the new year.

Meiji Shrine Inner Garden, 1–1 Kamizono-cho, Yoyogi, Shibuya-ku. www.meijijingu.or.jp. © **03/3379-5511.** Free admission. Daily sunrise to sunset (about 6:40am–4pm in December, 5am–6:30pm in June). Station: Harajuku or Meiji-Jingumae (1 min.).

National Children's Castle (Kodomo-no-Shiro) ★ ☺ MUSEUM   Conceived by the Ministry of Health and Welfare to commemorate the International Year of the Child in 1979, the Children's Castle holds various activity rooms for children of all ages (though most are geared to elementary-age kids and younger). The third floor, designed for spontaneous and unstructured play, features a large climbing gym, building blocks, a playhouse, dolls, books, and a preteen corner with billiards, Foosball, and other age-appropriate games; there's also an art room staffed with instructors to help children with projects suitable for their ages. On the fourth floor is a music room with instruments the kids are invited to play, as well as a video room with private cubicles where visitors can make selections from a library of English-language and Japanese DVDs, including Disney films. On the roof is an outdoor playground complete with a wading pool (open summer only; ¥200 extra admission) and tricycles. Various programs are offered throughout the week, including puppet shows, fairy tales, live music performances, and origami presentations.

5–53–1 Jingumae, Shibuya-ku. www.kodomono-shiro.com/english/index.shtml. ☏ **03/3797-5666.** Admission ¥500 adults, ¥400 children 3–17, free for children 2 and under. Tues–Fri 12:30–5:30pm; Sat–Sun and holidays (including school holidays) 10am–5:30pm. Station: Omotesando (exit B2, 8 min.) or Shibuya (10 min.). On Aoyama Dori btw. Omotesando and Shibuya stations.

Ukiyo-e Ota Memorial Museum of Art (Ota Kinen Bijutsukan) ★ 🎒 ART MUSEUM

This great museum features the private ukiyo-e (woodblock print) collection of the late Ota Seizo, who, early in life, recognized the importance of ukiyo-e as an art form and dedicated himself to its preservation. Although the collection contains 12,000 prints, only 80 to 100 are displayed at any given time, in thematic exhibitions that change monthly and include English-language descriptions. The museum itself is small but delightful. You can tour it in about 30 minutes, and be sure to take a peek in the basement shop with its *furoshiki* (traditional wrapping cloth), handkerchiefs, and other items.

1–10–10 Jingumae, Shibuya-ku. www.ukiyoe-ota-muse.jp. ☏ **03/3403-0880.** Admission ¥700–¥1,000 adults, ¥500–¥700 high-school and college students, free–¥200 children; price depends on the exhibit. Tues–Sun 10:30am–5:30pm (enter by 5pm). Closed from the 27th to end of each month. Station: Harajuku (2 min.) or Meiji-Jingumae (exit 5, 1 min.). Near the Omotesando Dori and Meiji Dori intersection, behind La Forêt.

Roppongi

Mori Art Museum (Mori Bijutsukan) ★★ ART MUSEUM/OBSERVATION DECK

This is Tokyo's highest museum, on the 53rd floor of the Roppongi Hills Mori Tower. It features state-of-the-art galleries with 6m-tall (20-ft.) ceilings, controlled natural lighting, a free audio guide, and great views of Tokyo. Innovative exhibitions of emerging and established artists from around the world are shown four times a year, with past shows centering on contemporary Asian, African, and Japanese art. Although the installations alone, ranging from paintings and fashion to architecture and design, are worth a visit, an extra incentive is the attached Tokyo City View observatory, usually included in the museum admission and providing eye-popping views over Tokyo (the rooftop Sky Deck costs ¥300 extra). Plan on at least 90 minutes up here.

Roppongi Hills Mori Tower, 6–10–1 Roppongi, Minato-ku. www.mori.art.museum/eng/index.html. ☏ **03/5777-8600.** Admission varies according to the exhibit but averages ¥1,500 adults, ¥1,000 high-school and college students, and ¥500 children. Wed–Mon 10am–10pm; Tues 10am–5pm. Station: Roppongi (Roppongi Hills exit, 1 min.) or Azabu Juban (5 min.).

The National Art Center, Tokyo ★ ART MUSEUM

This national museum doesn't have a collection of its own. Rather, its purpose is to exhibit works organized by Japanese artists' associations, its own curators, and joint efforts by mass media companies and other art institutions. The range of changing exhibitions, therefore, can be staggering, with past exhibitions showing masterworks from the Rijksmuseum Amsterdam; fashion and architecture organized by the Museum of Contemporary Art, Los Angeles; works by Monet and Lalique; and a retrospective on Japanese government-sponsored art exhibitions held during the past 100 years. Even the building itself—with an undulating, seductive facade of glass—attracts crowds with its Paul Bocuse restaurant, museum shop, and changing exhibitions by national artists' associations. This museum, the nearby Mori Art Museum, and Suntory Museum of Art, all within walking distance of one another, have been dubbed Art Triangle Roppongi.

7–22–2 Roppongi, Minato-ku. www.nact.jp. ℂ **03/5777-8600.** Admission ¥500–¥1,500 for most exhibitions. Wed–Mon 10am–6pm (Fri to 8pm). Station: Nogizakai (exit 6, 1 min.) or Roppongi (exit 4A or 7, 5 min.)

Suntory Museum of Art (Suntory Bijutsukan) ★ ART MUSEUM   This private museum boasts a collection of 3,000 Japanese antique arts and crafts, including lacquerware, ceramics, paintings, glassware, Noh costumes, kimono, scrolls, teaware, and other items, which it displays in themed exhibitions, along with visiting collections. Although modern in design, the museum incorporates such traditional Japanese materials as wood and paper in darkened rooms to create a soothing, inviting atmosphere. That's in keeping with its basic philosophy and mission: to make us see ancient art in a renewed way, to bridge the differences of time, place and culture.

Tokyo Midtown, 9–7–4 Akasaka, Minato-ku. www.suntory.com/culture-sports/sma. ℂ **03/3479-8600.** Admission varies, averaging ¥1,300 adults, ¥1,000 high-school and college students, free for children. Sun–Mon and Wed–Thurs 10am–6pm; Fri–Sat 10am–8pm. Station: Roppongi (2 min.) or Nogizaka (exit 3, 3 min.).

Tokyo Tower ★ ♨ ☺ OBSERVATION DECK   Japan's most famous observation tower was built in 1958 and was modeled after the slightly smaller Eiffel Tower in Paris. Lit up at night, this 330m (1,083-ft.) tower, a relay station for TV and radio stations, is a familiar and beloved landmark in the city's landscape; but with the construction of skyscrapers over the past few decades (including the TMG, above, with its free observatory, and Sky Tree, p. 106), it has lost some of its appeal as an observation platform and seems more like a relic from the 1950s. With its tacky souvenir shops and assorted small-time attractions, this place is about as kitsch as kitsch can be.

The tower has two observatories: the main one at 149m (489 ft.) and the top observatory at 248m (814 ft.). The best time of year for viewing is said to be during Golden Week at the beginning of May. With many Tokyoites gone from the city and most factories and businesses closed down, the air at this time is thought to be the cleanest and clearest. There are several offbeat tourist attractions in the tower's base building, including a wax museum (where you can see the Beatles, a wax rendition of Leonardo's *Last Supper*, Hollywood stars, and a medieval torture chamber), a small aquarium, and a Guinness World Records Museum, all with separate admission fees and appealing mainly to children.

4–2 Shiba Koen, Minato-ku. www.tokyotower.co.jp. ℂ **03/3433-5111.** Admission to both observatories ¥1,420 adults, ¥860 children. Daily 9am–10pm. Station: Onarimon or Kamiyacho (6 min.).

Odaiba

Ooedo-Onsen Monogatari ★★ SPA   For a unique bathing experience, nothing beats a 3- or 4-hour respite at this re-created Edo-Era bathhouse village, which tapped mineral-rich hot-spring waters 1,380m (4,528 ft.) below ground to supply its various baths. After changing into a *yukata* (cotton kimono) and depositing your belongings in a locker (your key is bar-coded, so there's no need to carry any money), you'll stroll past souvenir shops and restaurants on your way to massage rooms, sand baths (extra fee charged), and *onsen* (hot-spring baths) complete with outdoor baths, Jacuzzi, steam baths, foot baths, and saunas. Because it can be quite crowded on weekends, try to come on a weekday. Also, signs in English are virtually nonexistent, so observe gender before entering bathing areas (a hint: women's baths usually have pink or red curtains, men's blue). Finally, because tattoos are associated with the Japanese mafia, people with tattoos are prohibited here, as they are in most public baths in Japan.

2–57 Aomi, Odaiba. www.ooedoonsen.jp/higaeri/english/index.html. © **03/5500-1126.** Admission ¥2,900 adults, ¥1,600 children 4–11; reduced prices after 6pm. Daily 11am–9am the next day. Station: Telecom Center Station (2 min.).

Tokyo Joypolis ☺ GAMES ARCADE Bored teenagers in tow, grumbling at yet another temple or shrine? Bring them to life at Tokyo's most sophisticated virtual amusement arcade, outfitted with the latest in video games and high-tech virtual-reality attractions, courtesy of Sega. Video games include bobsledding, snowboarding, river rafting and car races, in which participants maneuver curves utilizing virtual-reality equipment, as well as numerous aeronautical battle games. There's also a 3-D sightseeing tour with seats that move with the action on the screen, several virtual reality rides (sky diving, anyone?), a virtual aquarium, and much, much more. Most harmless are the Print Club machines, which will print your face on stickers with the background (Mt. Fuji, perhaps?) of your choice. If you think your kids will want to try everything, buy them a passport for ¥3,500 for those 15 and older or ¥3,100 for those under 15 (after 5pm, a passport costs ¥2,500 and ¥2,100, respectively). Children younger than 7 and seniors over 60 get in free but are charged for attractions; note, too, that some activities have height restrictions.

Tokyo Decks, 3rd floor, Odaiba. http://tokyo-joypolis.com. © **03/5500-1801.** Admission ¥500 adults, ¥300 children; individual attractions an additional ¥500–¥600 each. Daily 10am–11pm. Station: Odaiba Kaihin Koen (2 min.).

Outlying Areas

Edo-Tokyo Museum (Edo-Tokyo Hakubutsukan) ★★★ ☺ MUSEUM The building housing this impressive museum is said to resemble a rice granary when viewed from afar, but to me it looks like a modern *torii,* the entrance gate to a shrine. This is the metropolitan government's ambitious attempt to present the history, art, disasters, science, culture, and architecture of Tokyo from its humble beginnings in 1590—when the first shogun, Tokugawa Ieyasu, made Edo (old Tokyo) the seat of his domain—to 1964, when Tokyo hosted the Olympics. All in all, the museum's great visual displays create a vivid portrayal of Tokyo through the centuries. I wouldn't miss it. Plan on spending 2 hours here.

After purchasing your ticket and going to the sixth floor, you'll enter the museum by walking over a replica of Nihombashi Bridge, the starting point for all roads leading out of old Edo. Exhibits covering the Edo Period portray the lives of the shoguns, merchants, craftsmen, and townspeople. Explanations are mostly in Japanese, but there's plenty to look at, including a replica of an old kabuki theater, models of Edo Castle and a *daimyo's* (feudal lord's) mansion, portable floats used during festivals, maps and photographs of old Edo, and—perhaps most interesting—a row-house tenement where Edo commoners lived in cramped quarters measuring only 10 sq. m (108 sq. ft.). Other displays cover the Meiji Restoration, the Great Kanto Earthquake of 1923, and the bombing raids of World War II (Japan's own role as aggressor is disappointingly glossed over), with plenty of old-style conveyances—from a palanquin to a rickshaw—for kids to climb in and have parents take their picture.

If you wish, take advantage of a free museum tour offered by volunteers (in English) daily 10am to 3pm (last tour). Most tours last 1 to 2 hours, depending on the level of visitor interest, and are insightful for their explanations of the Japanese-only displays. However, tours are necessarily rushed and focus on particular displays; you may wish to tour the museum afterward on your own.

spectator **SPORTS**

For information on current sporting events, ranging from kickboxing and pro wrestling to soccer, table tennis, martial arts, and golf classics, contact the Tourist Information Center or pick up a copy of the free weekly Metropolis magazine (www.metropolis.co.jp). Tickets for many events can be purchased at convenience stores like Lawson, Family Mart, and 7-Eleven.

Baseball Japanese are so crazy about baseball, you'd think they invented the game. Actually, it was introduced to Japan by the United States way back in 1873. Today, it's as popular among Japanese as it is among Americans. Even the annual high-school playoffs keep everyone glued to the TV set. As with other imports, the Japanese have added their modifications, including cheerleaders. Several American players have proven very popular with local fans; but according to the rules, no more than four foreigners may play on any one team. More recently, there's been a reverse exodus of top Japanese players defecting to American teams.

There are two professional leagues, the Central and the Pacific, which play from April to October and meet in the Japan Series. In Tokyo, the home teams are the **Yomiuri Giants,** who play at Tokyo Dome (✆ **03/5800-9999;** station: Korakuen or Suidobashi), and the **Yakult Swallows,** who play at Jingu Stadium (✆ **03/3404-8999;** station: Gaienmae). Other teams playing in the vicinity of Tokyo are the **Chiba Lotte Marines,** who play at Chiba Marine Stadium in Chiba (✆ **043/296-8900**), and the **Yokohama BayStars,** who play in downtown Yokohama Stadium (✆ **045/661-1251**). Good English-language websites that follow Japanese baseball are http://japanesebaseball.com and www.japanball.com.

Except for the Giants, who often sell out, you can usually get tickets at the ball park before the game. Otherwise, advance tickets go on sale Friday, 2 weeks prior to the game, and can be purchased at one of many **Ticket Pia** locations around town (such as the Sony building in Ginza or the Isetan department store annex in Shinjuku; ask your hotel for the one nearest you). But probably the easiest method for obtaining tickets is through the website www.japanballtickets.com; tickets must be ordered at least four days in advance and can even be delivered to your hotel. Prices for Tokyo Dome, all for reserved seating, range from ¥1,700 in the outfield to ¥5,900 for seats behind home plate. The Giants are so popular, however, that tickets are sometimes hard to come by. Tickets for Jingu Stadium range from ¥1,500 for an unreserved seat in the outfield to ¥4,500 for seats behind home plate.

Sumo Sumo matches are held in Tokyo at the **Kokugikan,** 1–3–28 Yokoami, Sumida-ku (www.sumo.or.jp; ✆ **03/3622-1100;** station: Ryogoku, then a 1-min. walk; Tokyo Shitamachi Bus: Ryogoku Station). Matches are held in January, May, and September for 15 consecutive days, beginning at around 9:30am and lasting until 6pm; the top wrestlers compete after 3:30pm. The best seats are ringside box seats, but they're snapped up by companies or the friends and families of sumo wrestlers. Usually available are balcony arena seats, which can be purchased at Ticket Pia locations around town or through the website www.japanballtickets.com. You can also purchase tickets directly at the Kokugikan ticket office beginning at 9am every morning of the tournament. Prices range from about ¥2,100 for an unreserved seat (sold only on the day of the event at the stadium, with about 400 seats available) to ¥8,200 for a good reserved seat.

If you can't make it to a match, watching on TV is almost as good. Tournaments in Tokyo, as well as those that take place annually in Osaka, Nagoya, and Fukuoka, are broadcast on the NHK channel from 4 to 6pm daily while tournaments are taking place. For more information on sumo, see p. 22.

1–4–1 Yokoami, Sumida-ku. www.edo-tokyo-museum.or.jp. © **03/3626-9974.** Admission ¥600 adults, ¥480 college students, ¥300 seniors and junior-high/high-school students, free for younger children. Tues–Sun 9:30am–5:30pm. Station: Ryogoku on the JR Sobu Line (west exit, 3 min.) and Oedo Line (exit A4, 1 min.). Tokyo Shitamachi Bus: Ryogoku Station.

Fukagawa Edo Museum (Fukagawa Edo Shiryokan) ★☺MUSEUM   This is the Tokyo of your dreams, the way it appears in all those samurai flicks on Japanese TV: a reproduction of a 19th-century neighborhood in Fukagawa, a prosperous community on the east bank of the Sumida River during the Edo Period. This delightful museum is located off Kiyosumi Dori on a pleasant tree-lined, shop-filled street called Fukagawa Shiryokan Dori. The museum's hangarlike interior contains 11 full-scale replicas of traditional houses, vegetable and rice shops, a fish store, two inns, a fire watchtower, and tenement homes, all arranged to resemble an actual neighborhood. There are lots of small touches and flourishes to make the community seem real and believable—a cat sleeping on a roof, a snail crawling up a fence, a dog relieving itself on a pole, birdsong, and a vendor shouting his wares. The village even changes with the seasons (with trees sprouting cherry blossoms in spring and threatened by thunderstorms in summer) and, every 45 minutes or so, undergoes a day's cycle from morning (roosters crow, lights brighten) to night (the sun sets, the retractable roof closes to make everything dark). Of Tokyo's museums, this one is probably the best for children; plan on spending about an hour here. Don't confuse this museum with the much larger Edo-Tokyo Museum, which traces the history of Tokyo. *Note:* After the Great East Japan Earthquake, the museum suspended its lighting show mimicking the course of a day until further notice in order to conserve energy.

1–3–28 Shirakawa, Koto-ku. ©**03/3630-8625.** Admission ¥300 adults, ¥50 children. Daily 9:30am–5pm. Station: Kiyosumi-Shirakawa (3 min.).

MOT or Museum of Contemporary Art, Tokyo (Tokyo-to Gendai Bijut-sukan) ★ART MUSEUM   The MOT is inconveniently located but well worth the trek if you're a fan of the avant-garde (you'll pass the Fukagawa Edo Museum, described above, on the way, so you may wish to visit both). This modern structure of glass and steel, with a long corridor entrance that reminds me of railroad trestles, houses both permanent and temporary exhibits of Japanese and international postwar art in rooms whose sizes lend themselves to large installations. Although temporary exhibits, which occupy most of the museum space, have ranged from Southeast Asian art to a retrospective of Jasper Johns, the smaller permanent collection presents a chronological study of 40 years of contemporary art, beginning with anti-artistic trends and pop art in the 1960s and continuing with minimalism and cutting-edge contemporary works, with about 100 works displayed on a rotating basis. Included may be works by Andy Warhol, Gerhard Richter, Roy Lichtenstein, David Hockney, Frank Stella, Sandro Chia, Mark Rothko, Julian Schnabel, and Ishida Takashi. Depending on the number of exhibits you visit, you'll spend anywhere from 1 to 2 hours here, unless you decide to stay longer to take advantage of the museum's pleasant café or restaurant.

4–1–1 Miyoshi, Koto-ku. www.mot-art-museum.jp. © **03/5245-4111.** Admission to permanent collection ¥500 adults, ¥400 college students, ¥250 high-school students and seniors, free for children; special exhibits cost more. Tues–Sun 10am–6pm. Station: Kiyosumi-Shirakawa (exit A3, 15 min.). On Fukagawa Shiroyokan-dori, just off Mitsume Dori.

Rikugien Garden ★★ ▮PARK/GARDEN   Though not as centrally located nor as easy to reach as Tokyo's other famous gardens, this one is a must for fans of

IMMERSING YOURSELF IN JAPANESE culture

Just walking down the street could be considered a cultural experience in Japan, but there are more concrete ways to learn more about this country's cultural life: The best is by participating in some of its time-honored rituals and traditions. For some background information on Japanese flower arranging, the tea ceremony, and other activities recommended below, see "Japanese Arts in a Nutshell," in chapter 2.

In addition to the recommendations below, JTB's **Sunrise Tours** (www.jtb-sunrisetours.jp; ✆ **03/5796-5454**) offers several cultural activities, like trying your hand at making sushi, participating in a tea ceremony, and trying on samurai and ninja outfits. Prices range from ¥6,000 for the Tea Ceremony Experience to ¥13,900 for the Ninja and Samurai Tour. Similarly, the **Institute for Japanese Cultural Exchange and Experience** (www.ijcee.com/e.html; ✆ **080/3313-1107**) provides a variety of cultural immersion experiences, including a visit to a sumo stable to watch wrestlers train or to Tsukiji Market's tuna auction followed by a lesson in making sushi; participating in the tea ceremony; learning calligraphy or how to play the *shamisen* (a three-stringed Japanese instrument); how to wear a kimono; and attending a ninja training workshop. Prices for one person range from ¥8,000 for the lessons in tea ceremony, shamisen, or how to wear a kimono to ¥18,000 for the ninja workshop; prices are lower if there is more than one participant.

Ikebana Instruction in *ikebana,* or Japanese flower arranging, is available at several schools in Tokyo, a few of which offer classes in English on a regular basis. (Note that you should call beforehand to enroll.) **Sogetsu Ikebana School,** 7–2–21 Akasaka (www.sogetsu.or.jp; ✆ **03/3408-1209** or 3408-1551; station: Aoyama-Itchome, a 5-min. walk from exit 4), offers instruction in English on Monday from 10am to noon (closed in Aug). The cost of one lesson for first-time participants is ¥3,800, including flowers. The **Ohara Ikebana School,** 5–7–17 Minami Aoyama (www.ohararyu.or.jp; ✆ **03/5774-5097;** station: Omotesando, 3-min. walk from exit B1), offers 2-hour instruction in English at 10am on Wednesday and a 3-hour class at 11am on Thursday for ¥4,000 (no classes from mid-July–Sept); if you wish to observe the class but not participate, you can do so for ¥800.

If you wish to see ikebana, ask at the **Tourist Information Office** whether there are any special exhibitions. Department stores sometimes have special ikebana exhibitions in their galleries. Another place to look is **Yasukuni Shrine,** located on Yasukuni Dori northwest of the Imperial Palace (station: Ichigaya or Kudanshita). Dedicated to Japanese war dead, the shrine is also famous for ongoing ikebana exhibitions.

Tea Ceremony **Waraku-an** is a Japanese-style tea room located at the headquarters of KSA International Inc., behind the Canadian Embassy at 7–4–25 Akasaka, Minato-ku (www.ksa.co.jp/e/cul.html; ✆ **03/3505-8622;** station: Aoyama-Itchome, 8 min.), where you can either have a 90-minute lesson in the Japanese tea ceremony for ¥3,000 or simply observe the tea ceremony for ¥2,000; both options include tea and a sweet. Reservations are required, and ceremonies can be held Monday to Friday from 10am to 8pm. Although not as atmospheric, you can experience the tea ceremony and even try your hand at making tea in a corner of **Kyoto-Kan,** a shop selling products from Kyoto located across from the Yaesu Central Exit of Tokyo Station, on the corner of Yaesu Dori and Sotobori Dori, 2–1–1 Yaesu, Chuo-ku (✆ **03/5204-2260**). Available from 12:30 to 4:30pm

Saturday to Tuesday, it costs only ¥500, and reservations are required only for groups of more than five people.

In addition, several first-class hotels hold tea-ceremony demonstrations in special tea-ceremony rooms. Reservations are usually required, and because ceremonies are often booked by groups, you'll want to call in advance to see whether you can participate. These include **Seisei-an** in Hotel New Otani (see p. 171), which holds 20-minute demonstrations Thursday through Saturday from 11am to 4pm; **Chosho-an** in Hotel Okura (see p. 171), with 40-minute demonstrations given anytime between 11am and noon and between 1 and 4pm Monday, Tuesday, and Thursday through Saturday except holidays; and **Toko-an** in the Imperial Hotel (see p. 170), which gives demonstrations from 10am to 4pm Monday through Saturday except holidays. Fees range from ¥1,050 to ¥1,500, including tea and sweets.

Acupuncture & Shiatsu

Although most Westerners have heard of acupuncture, they may not be familiar with *shiatsu* (Japanese pressure-point massage). Most first-class hotels in Japan offer shiatsu in the privacy of your room. There are acupuncture clinics everywhere in Tokyo, and the staff of your hotel may be able to tell you of one nearby. As it's not likely the clinic's staff will speak English, it might be a good idea to have the hotel guest relations officer not only make the reservation but specify the treatment you want. Otherwise, English is spoken at **Yamate Acupuncture Clinic,** second floor of the ULS Nakameguro Building, 1–3–3 Higashiyama, Meguro-ku (www.yamate-st.com; ℂ 03-3792-8989; station: Nakameguro, 6 min.), open Monday to Friday 9am to 8pm and Saturday 9am to 2pm. Specializing in athletic injuries, it charges ¥3,000 for a specific treatment or ¥5,000 for the

whole body, plus a ¥1,000 initial fee. English is also spoken at **ACURA Acupuncture Clinic,** eighth floor of the Daini Eirai Building, 1–3–8 Shibuya, Shibuya-ku (ℂ 03/5469-0810; station: Shibuya or Omotesando, 8 min. from both), open Monday to Friday from 10am to 1:30pm and 2:30 to 8:30pm, and Saturday 10am to 1:30pm and 2:30 to 7pm. It charges ¥3,000 for an initial consultation and ¥7,000 for acupuncture. The **Edward Obaidey Acupuncture Clinic,** 2–17–12 Sangenjaya, Setagaya-ku (www.edward shinkyu.com; ℂ 03/3418-8989; station: Sangenjaya, 3 min.), has an international staff and is open Monday 2:30 to 5:30pm, Tuesday to Friday 10am to 5:30pm, and Saturday from 9am to 5:30pm. It charges ¥3,000 for the first consultation and ¥7,000 for treatment.

Zazen A few temples in the Tokyo vicinity occasionally offer sitting meditation with instruction in English. You should call in advance to make a reservation and arrive 30 minutes early for instructions. The **Toshoji International Zen Center,** 4–5–18 Yutaka-machi, Shinagawa-ku (ℂ 03/3781-4235; station: Togoshikoen, 5 min.), offers free zazen at 5am every morning (except Sun and holidays), as well as Zen training meetings Saturday from 6 to 8pm, including zazen, a lecture, and tea. Accommodations are also available to those who wish to stay for longer periods to practice Zen. **Sounin Temple,** 4–1–12 Higashi-Ueno, Taito-ku (ℂ 03/3844-3711; station: Ueno, 5 min.), holds free zazen the second Sunday and Monday (and preceding Sat) from 7 to 8:30pm (first-time visitors are requested to arrive at 6:30pm), followed by a talk and tea. **Daido Gakusha** (Zen Center), 4–26–5 Ikenohata, Taito-ku (ℂ 03/3824-0030; www.daidozen.net; station: Nezu, 5 min.), offers zazen every Sunday from 9am to noon and Wednesday from 6:30 to 8:30pm for ¥300.

traditional Japanese gardens and is probably my favorite. It was created in 1702 by a trusted confidante of the shogun, who began as a page and rose to the highest rank as a feudal lord. During the Meiji Era, the founder of Mitsubishi took it over for his second residence and later donated it to the city. What I like most about the garden is that it's dominated by a pond in its center, complete with islands and islets, viewing hills, and strolling paths around its perimeter, providing enchanting views. The garden is especially famous for its changing maple leaves in autumn. Since it takes some effort to reach, you'll probably want to enjoy at least an hour here.

6–16–3 Hon-Komagome, Bunkyo-ku. www.tokyo-park.or.jp. ✆ **03/3941-2222.** Admission ¥300 adults, ¥150 seniors, free for children 12 and under. Daily 9am–5pm. Station: Komagome (8 min.) or Sengoku (10 min.).

Tokyo Disneyland & Tokyo DisneySea ★★★ ☺ THEME PARK Virtually a carbon copy of Disneyland in California, this one also boasts the Jungle Cruise, Pirates of the Caribbean, the Haunted Mansion, and Space Mountain. Other hot attractions include Toontown, a wacky theme park where Mickey and other Disney characters work and play; MicroAdventure, which features 3-D glasses and special effects; and Star Tours, a thrill adventure created by Disney and George Lucas.

Adjacent to Disneyland is **DisneySea,** a theme park based on ocean legends and myths. It offers seven distinct "ports of call," including the futuristic Port Discovery marina with its StormRider that flies straight into the eye of a storm; the Lost River Delta with its Indiana Jones Adventure; Mermaid Lagoon based on the film *The Little Mermaid*; the Arabian Coast, with its Sinbad's Seven Voyages boat ride; and the American Waterfront with its Tower of Terror. Because DisneySea is unique to Tokyo, I personally think this is the one to see; its installations are a class act.

1–1 Maihama, Urayasu-shi, Chiba. www.tokyodisneyresort.co.jp. ✆ **047/310-0733.** 1-day passport to either Disneyland or DisneySea, including entrance to and use of all attractions, ¥6,200 adults, ¥5,500 seniors, ¥5,300 children 12–17, ¥4,100 children 4–11, free for children 3 and under. Daily 8 or 9am to 10pm, with slightly shorter hours in winter. Station: Maihama, on the JR Keiyo Line from Tokyo Station (1 min.).

Tokyo Sky Tree OBSERVATION DECK I used to think Tokyo Tower was expensive (p. 100), but then the world's tallest free-standing telecommunications tower (documented by Guinness World Records) took over as Japan's tallest structure, with sky-high admission fees to boot. Opened May 2012 to handle digital broadcasting (Japan switched from analog to digital broadcasting in July 2011) and cellphone transmission, the 634-m (2,080-ft) tower contains two observatories, one at 350m (1,150 ft.) high and another at 450 m (1,476 ft.), as well as shops and restaurants. Visible from many areas of Tokyo, it makes Tokyo Tower seem downright diminutive.

1–32–3 Mukojima, Sumida-ku. www.tokyo-skytree.jp. ✆ **03/6658-8012.** Admission ¥2,000 to lower observatory, ¥3,000 to top observatory. Daily 8am–10pm. Station: Tokyo Sky Tree or Oshiage (2 min.).

Organized Tours

With the help of this book and a good map, you should be able to visit Tokyo's major attractions easily on your own. Should you be pressed for time, however, you might consider taking a group tour of Tokyo and its environs offered by the **Japan Travel Bureau (JTB;** www.jtb-sunrisetours.jp; ✆ **03/5796-5454**). Day tours may include Tokyo Tower, the Imperial Palace and Ginza districts, Asakusa Sensoji Temple, Meiji Jingu Shrine, and a harbor or river cruise. There are also specialized tours that take in local festivals, Kabuki, Tsukiji Fish Market, neighborhoods like Harajuku or Akihabara, sumo wrestling, or Tokyo's nightlife, as well as cultural-themed tours that allow participants to experience such activities as the tea ceremony, making sushi, or dressing up in a kimono. Be warned, however, that tours are very tourist-oriented, do not allow much time for exploration, and are more expensive than touring Tokyo on your own. Prices range from about ¥4,500 for a half-day tour to ¥12,000 or more for a full-day tour including lunch (children pay half fare). You can easily book tours through most hotels and travel agencies like JTB. Although its offerings are not nearly as extensive, **Japan Gray Line** (www.jgl.co.jp/inbound/index.htm; (✆ **03/3595-5939**) also offers a morning, afternoon and full-day tour.

Although they cover less ground, 10 tours offered by the **Tokyo Metropolitan Government** concentrate on specific areas or themes, such as Japanese gardens, Asakusa, or Harajuku. What I like most about these tours is that they are more personable than those above, with a maximum tour group size of only 5 persons. Lasting 2 to 3½ hours, they are conducted mostly on foot or utilize public transportation and vary in price from free (a walking tour of Shinjuku and the food floor of Isetan department store) to ¥3,540 (a tour taking in the Ginza, Tsukiji Outer Market, Hama Rikyu Garden, and Odaiba), plus admission costs of the volunteer guides. Prices may be cheaper for some tours if there's more than one participant. Tours depart from the Tokyo Tourist Information Center in the TMG Building No. 1 in Shinjuku (the same building as the free observatory; see p. 75) at 1pm Monday to Friday (excluding public holidays; some tours depart also at 10am). Preregistration 3 days in advance of the tour is required, and a minimum of one participant must be at least 20 years old. For more information, go to www.tourism.metro.tokyo.jp/english/tourists/guideservice/guideservice/index.html or contact the tourist office (see p. 75 earlier in this chapter).

Volunteer guides are also on hand at the Ueno Green Salon in Ueno Park every Wednesday, Friday, and Sunday for free 90-minute walking tours departing at 10:30am and 1:30pm; and at the Asakusa Information Center every Saturday and Sunday for 1-hour tours departing at 11am and 2pm (for location of the latter, see the walking tour of Asakusa beginning on p. 108). No registration is required. For more information, call ✆ **03/3842-5566.**

Free guided tours are also offered through www.tokyofreeguide.com, staffed by volunteers ranging from students and housewives to retirees and businesspeople. You're expected to pay for the guide's entrance to museums, meals, and transportation fees if applicable, but you get to choose what you'd like to see; because many of these volunteers work, weekends are the best days to book a tour.

One tour I especially like is a **boat trip on the Sumida River ★★** between Hama Rikyu Garden and Asakusa. Commentary on the 45-minute trip is in both Japanese and English (be sure to pick up the English-language leaflet, too). You'll get descriptions of the 12 bridges you pass along the way and views of Tokyo you'd otherwise miss. Boats depart Hama Rikyu Garden hourly or more frequently between 10:35am and 4:15pm, with the fare to Asakusa costing ¥720 one-way. There are also other cruise routes, including those between Hinode Pier (closest station: Hinode, about a 1-min. walk) and Asakusa (fare: ¥760), Asakusa and Odaiba (fare: ¥1,520), and Hinode Pier and Odaiba (fare: ¥460). For more information, contact the **Tokyo Cruise Ship Co.** (✆ **0120-977311;** www.suijobus.co.jp).

Finally, for personalized, one-on-one tours of Tokyo, contact **Jun's Tokyo Discovery Tours,** managed by Tokyoite Junko Matsuda, which offers tailored sightseeing trips to Tsukiji, Asakusa, Harajuku, Aoyama, Shibuya, Shinjuku, and Kamakura, as well as shopping trips and special trips designed to fit your interests. Tours utilize public transportation and are especially useful if you wish to communicate with shopkeepers and the locals, want to learn more about what you're seeing, or are timid about finding your way on public transportation (if you wish, you'll be met at your hotel). The cost is ¥25,000 for 1 day (7 hr.) for up to four adults or a family. Reserve tours at least 3 days in advance (1 week preferred) by e-mail (me2@gb3.so-net.ne.jp) or fax (✆ 03/3429-8664), stating the desired tour date and what you'd like to see; messages can also be left at ✆ 090/7734-0079 (if you're calling from abroad, drop the initial 0).

WALKING TOUR 1: SEARCHING FOR OLD EDO, A WALKING TOUR OF ASAKUSA

START:	**Asakusa Station (exit 1 or 3).**
FINISH:	**Kappabashi Dori (Station: Tawaramachi).**
TIME:	**Allow approximately 3 hours.**
BEST TIMES:	**Tuesday through Friday, when the crowds aren't as big, or Saturday, when you can join a free tour.**
WORST TIMES:	**Monday, when Amuse Museum is closed, and Sunday, when the shops on Kappabashi Dori are closed.**

If anything remains of old Tokyo, Asakusa is it. This is where you'll find narrow streets lined with small residential homes, Tokyo's oldest and most popular temple, and quaint shops selling boxwood combs, fans, kitchen knives, sweet pastries, and other products of yore. With its temple market, rickshaw drivers vying for the tourist trade, old-fashioned amusement park, traditional shops, and restaurants, Asakusa preserves the charm of old downtown Edo better than anyplace else in Tokyo. For many older Japanese, a visit to Asakusa is like stepping back to the days of their childhood; for tourists, it provides a glimpse of the way things were.

Pleasure-seekers have been flocking to Asakusa for centuries. Originating as a temple town back in the 7th century, it grew in popularity during the Tokugawa regime as merchants became wealthy and entirely new forms of popular entertainment arose to cater to them. Theaters for *kabuki* and *bunraku* flourished in Asakusa, as did restaurants and shops. By 1840, Asakusa had become Edo's main entertainment district. In stark contrast to the solemnity surrounding places of worship in the West, Asakusa's temple market had a carnival atmosphere reminiscent of medieval Europe, complete with street performers and exotic animals. It retains some of that festive atmosphere even today.

Take the subway to Asakusa Station and start your tour at the corner of Kaminarimon Dori and Asakusa Dori, where you'll find the:

1 Asakusa Information Center
Located at 2–18–9 Kaminarimon (✆ 03/6280-6710), the center is open daily from 9:30am to 8pm but is staffed by English-speaking volunteers only from 10am to 5pm. Stop here to pick up a map of the area, use the restroom, and ask for directions to restaurants and sights. On Saturdays and Sundays, volunteers

Walking Tour 1: Asakusa

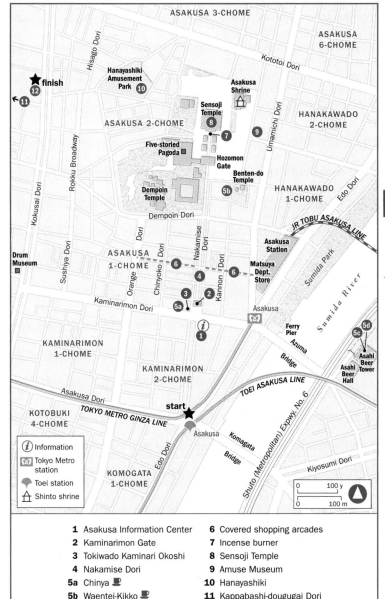

1 Asakusa Information Center
2 Kaminarimon Gate
3 Tokiwado Kaminari Okoshi
4 Nakamise Dori
5a Chinya ☕
5b Waentei-Kikko ☕
5c La Ranarita Azumabashi ☕
5d Sky Room ☕

6 Covered shopping arcades
7 Incense burner
8 Sensoji Temple
9 Amuse Museum
10 Hanayashiki
11 Kappabashi-dougugai Dori
12 Asakusa View Hotel ☕

giving free 1-hour guided tours of Asakusa depart here at 11am and 2pm (arrive 10 min. earlier).

Then it's time to head across the street to the:

2 Kaminarimon Gate

The gate is unmistakable with its bright red colors and 100-kilogram (220-lb.) lantern hanging in the middle. The statues inside the gate are the god of wind to the right and the god of thunder to the left, ready to protect the deity enshrined in the temple. The god of thunder is particularly fearsome: He supposedly has an insatiable appetite for navels.

To the left of the gate, on the corner, is:

3 Tokiwado Kaminari Okoshi

This open-fronted confectionery has been selling *okoshi* (rice-based sweets) for 250 years and is popular with visiting Japanese buying gifts for the folks back home. It's open daily from 9am to 9pm.

Once past Kaminarimon Gate, you'll find yourself immediately on a pedestrian lane called:

4 Nakamise Dori

The lane leads straight to the Sensoji Temple. *Nakamise* means "inside shops," and historical records show that vendors have sold wares here since the late 17th century. Today Nakamise Dori is lined on both sides with tiny stall after tiny stall, many owned by the same family for generations. If you're expecting austere religious artifacts, however, you're in for a surprise: sweets, shoes, barking toy dogs, *sembei* (Japanese crackers), bags, umbrellas, Japanese dolls, T-shirts, fans, masks, and traditional Japanese accessories are all sold. How about a brightly colored straight hairpin—and a black hairpiece to go with it? Or a temporary tattoo in the shape of a dragon? This is a great place to shop for souvenirs, gifts, and items you have no earthly need for—a little bit of unabashed consumerism on the way to spiritual purification.

5 Kaminarimon Gate restaurants 🍵

If you're hungry for lunch, there are many possibilities in the neighborhood. Chinya (p. 126), 1–3–4 Asakusa, just west of Kaminarimon Gate on Kaminarimon Dori, has been serving sukiyaki and shabu-shabu since 1880. Northeast of Kaminarimon Gate is Waentei-Kikko (p. 127), 2–2–13 Asakusa, offering obento lunch boxes and shamisen performances. For Western food, head to the other side of the Sumida River, where on the 22nd floor of the Asahi Beer Tower is La Ranarita Azumabashi (p. 126), 1–23–1 Azumabashi, a moderately priced Italian restaurant with great views of Asakusa; and the utilitarian Sky Room (p. 164) with inexpensive beer, wine, and snacks.

Before reaching the end of Nakamise Dori, there are a couple of interesting side streets worth exploring. Just 2 blocks north of Kaminarimon Gate are two:

6 Covered Shopping Arcades

Stretching to both the right and left of Nakamise Dori, these pedestrian-only covered lanes are typical of what you'll see everywhere in Japan—regular streets that became instant shopping centers by covering them with roofs and banning vehicular traffic. This is where locals come to shop, with stores selling clothing, household goods, souvenirs, and more.

Farther along Nakamise Dori is the second gate, which opens onto a square filled with pigeons and a large:

7 Incense Burner

This is where worshipers "wash" themselves to ward off or help cure illness. If, for example, you have a sore throat, be sure to rub some of the smoke over your throat for good measure.

The building dominating the square is:

8 Sensoji Temple

Sensoji is Tokyo's oldest temple. Founded in the 7th century and therefore already well established long before Tokugawa settled in Edo, Sensoji Temple is dedicated to Kannon, the Buddhist goddess of mercy, and is therefore popularly called the Asakusa Kannon Temple. According to legend, the temple was founded after two fishermen pulled a golden statue of Kannon from the sea. The sacred statue is still housed in the temple, carefully preserved inside three boxes; even though it's never on display, an estimated 20 million people flock to the temple annually to pay their respects.

Within the temple is a counter where you can buy your fortune by putting a 100-yen coin into a wooden box and shaking it until a long bamboo stick emerges from a small hole. The stick will have a Japanese number on it, which corresponds to one of the numbers on a set of drawers. Take the fortune, written in both English and Japanese, from the drawer that has your number. But don't expect the translation to clear things up; my fortune contained such cryptic messages as "Getting a beautiful lady at your home, you want to try all people know about this" and "Stop to start a trip." If you find that your fortune raises more questions than it answers or you simply don't like what it has to say, you can conveniently negate it by tying it to one of the wires provided for this purpose just outside the main hall.

To the right (east) of the temple is the rather small Nitemmon Gate, built in 1618 and the only structure on temple grounds remaining from the Edo Period. Just past Nitemmon Gate, to the left, is the:

9 Amuse Museum

The name of this gem doesn't do it justice, because rather than being amused, you'll be amazed by the simple elegance of what you see. It houses an astounding collection of *boro*, clothing from the Edo Period that was passed down from generation to generation, lovingly mended, restitched and patched. Not only is it rare that such garments from Japan's lower class still exist, but here they are strikingly displayed like treasures. Kimono and antiques round out the collection; there's also a small theater that displays digital images of woodblock prints, complete with commentary about what the prints tell us about life during the Edo Period. A bonus: the museum's rooftop terrace, with views overlooking the grounds in front of Sensoji Temple.

West of Sensoji Temple is a gardenlike area of lesser shrines and memorials, flowering bushes, and a stream filled with carp. The most picturesque photos of Sensoji Temple can be taken from here. Farther west still is:

10 Hanayashiki

This is a small and corny amusement park that first opened in 1853 and still draws in the little ones. (See p. 94 for more details.)

Most of the area west of Sensoji Temple (the area to the left if you stand facing the front of the temple) is a small but interesting part of Asakusa popular among Tokyo's older working class. This is where several of Asakusa's old-fashioned pleasure houses remain, including bars, restaurants, strip shows, traditional Japanese vaudeville, and so-called "love hotels," which rent rooms by the hour.

If you keep walking west, past the Asakusa View Hotel, within 10 minutes you'll reach:

11 Kappabashi-dougugai Dori

This district, generally referred to as Kappabashi Dori, is Tokyo's wholesale district for restaurant items. Shop after shop sells pottery, chairs, tableware, cookware, lacquerware, rice cookers, *noren* (short curtains hung outside shops and restaurants to signify they are open), and everything else needed to run a restaurant. And yes, you can even buy those models of plastic food you've been drooling over in restaurant displays. Ice cream, pizza, sushi, mugs foaming with beer—they're all here, looking like the real thing. (Stores close about 5pm and are closed Sun.)

12 Asakusa View Hotel 🍺

The Asakusa View Hotel, on Kokusai Dori Avenue between Sensoji Temple and Kappabashi Dori, has several restaurants and bars. In the basement is the clubby Ice House, the hotel's main bar.

WALKING TOUR 2: IN THE HEART OF TRENDY TOKYO, A STROLL THROUGH HARAJUKU & AOYAMA

START:	**Meiji Jingu Shrine (Station: Harajuku).**
FINISH:	**Aoyama (Station: Omotesando).**
TIME:	**Allow approximately 3 hours (shopping hounds might require longer).**
BEST TIME:	**Every Sunday when teenagers dressed in *cosplay* (costume play) and other costumes hang out near Meiji Jingu Shrine.**
WORST TIMES:	**Monday, from the 27th to the end of every month (when the Ota Memorial Museum of Art is closed), and Thursday (when the Oriental Bazaar is closed).**

Harajuku is one of my favorite neighborhoods in Tokyo, though I'm too old to really fit in. In fact, anyone over 25 is apt to feel ancient here, as this is Tokyo's most popular hangout for Japanese high-school and college students. The young come here to see and be seen; you're sure to spot Japanese punks, girls decked out in the fashions of the moment, and young couples out on dates. I like Harajuku for its vibrancy, its sidewalk cafes, its street hawkers, and its trendy clothing boutiques. It's also the home of Tokyo's most important Shinto shrine, as well as a delightful woodblock-print museum and an excellent souvenir shop of traditional Japanese items. If you have teenagers in tow, you'll definitely want to make Harajuku a top priority.

Nearby is **Aoyama**, a yuppified version of Harajuku, where the upwardly mobile dine and shop for designer clothing. Connecting Harajuku and Aoyama is **Omotesando Dori**, a wide, tree-lined, European-style shopping boulevard that forms the heart of this area; its many sidewalk cafes make it a popular promenade for people-watching.

Walking Tour 2: Harajuku & Aoyama

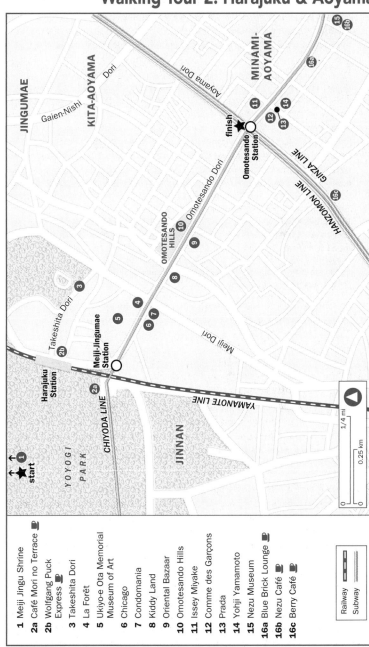

1 Meiji Jingu Shrine
2a Café Mori no Terrace 🍴
2b Wolfgang Puck Express 🍴
3 Takeshita Dori
4 La Forêt
5 Ukiyo-e Ota Memorial Museum of Art
6 Chicago
7 Condomania
8 Kiddy Land
9 Oriental Bazaar
10 Omotesando Hills
11 Issey Miyake
12 Comme des Garçons
13 Prada
14 Yohji Yamamoto
15 Nezu Museum
16a Blue Brick Lounge 🍴
16b Nezu Café 🍴
16c Berry Café 🍴

Railway
Subway

From Harajuku Station, take the south exit (the one closer to Shibuya) and turn right over the bridge, where you will immediately see the huge cypress *torii* marking the entrance to:

1 Meiji Jingu Shrine

Dedicated to Emperor and Empress Meiji, Meiji Jingu Shrine (p. 98) opened in 1920 and remains the most venerable shrine in Tokyo. The shrine is surrounded by a dense forest of 245 different species totaling 170,000 trees, donated by people from all over Japan and planted by 110,000 volunteers. If it's June, stop off at the Iris Garden, located halfway on the 10-minute tree-shaded path to the shrine.

2 Café Mori no Terrace & Wolfgang Puck Express 🍵

If the hike to Meiji Shrine has made you thirsty, stop off at the rustic Café Mori no Terrace outdoor pavilion just inside the entryway to the shrine grounds. Open daily 9am to sunset, it offers coffee, beer, pastries, and ice cream. For something more substantial, wait until you get to Takeshita Dori (described below), where you'll find a Wolfgang Puck Express, 1–17–1 Jingumae, good for burgers and pizza (p. 137).

After visiting the shrine, retrace your steps to Harajuku Station. If it's Sunday, you'll see groups of teenagers—many bizarrely dressed—gathered on the bridge over the train tracks. They're all that's left of the masses of teens that used to congregate on nearby Yoyogi Dori back when it was closed to vehicular traffic on Sundays. Sadly, authorities decided to open Yoyogi and Omotesando Dori streets to traffic, thereby putting an end to Tokyo's most happening Sunday scene.

At Harajuku Station, continue walking north beside the station to its north exit. Across the street from Harajuku Station's north exit is:

3 Takeshita Dori

This pedestrian-only street is lined nonstop with stores that cater to teenagers. It's packed—especially on Sunday afternoons—with young people hunting for bargains on inexpensive clothing, shoes, music, sunglasses, jewelry, watches, cosmetics, and more. One shop worth pointing out is **Harajuku Daiso** (© **5775-9641;** daily 10am–9pm) on the left, one of many bargain variety stores to hit Japan after the recession; there are now more than 2,500 Daiso in the country. It offers four floors of kitchenware, tableware, cosmetics, office supplies, and more, most priced at ¥100.

After inching your way through the flow of humanity along this narrow lane, you'll eventually find yourself on a busy thoroughfare, Meiji Dori, where you should turn right. Farther along, on your right just before the big intersection is:

4 La Forêt

This building, housing trendy shoe and clothing boutiques, is the ultimate in Tokyo teen cool. The less expensive boutiques tend to be on the lower floors, more exclusive boutiques higher up. (See "Shopping," later in this chapter, for details on many of the shops and department stores listed in this walking tour.)

Behind La Forêt is one of my favorite museums, the:

5 Ukiyo-e Ota Memorial Museum of Art

Located at 1–10–10 Jingumae, this museum features the private *ukiyo-e* (woodblock prints) collection of the late Ota Seizo. Exhibitions of the museum's 12,000 prints change monthly and are always worth checking out (p. 99).

Across Omotesando Dori is:

6 Chicago

This store specializes in used American clothing but also stocks hundreds of used and new kimono and *yukata* in the far back corner of its basement.

Near La Forêt is Harajuku's major intersection, Meiji Dori and Omotesando Dori. Here, at the intersection at 6–30–1 Jingumae, is one of Harajuku's more unusual shops:

7 Condomania

Condoms are for sale here in a wide range of sizes, colors, and styles, from glow-in-the-dark to scented, as well as gag gifts and novelties. It's open daily 10:30am to 10:30pm.

Heading east on Omotesando Dori (away from Harajuku Station), you'll soon see, to your right:

8 Kiddy Land

Located at 6–1–9 Jingumae, this store sells gag gifts and a great deal more than just toys, including enough to amuse less discerning adults. You could spend an hour browsing here, but the store is so crowded with teenagers that you may end up rushing for the door.

Continue east on Omotesando Dori (where sidewalk vendors selling jewelry and ethnic accessories set up shop on weekends); to your right will soon be Harajuku's most famous store:

9 Oriental Bazaar

Located at 5–9–13 Jingumae, this is Tokyo's best one-stop shopping spot for Japanese souvenirs. Several floors offer antiques, old and new kimono, Japanese paper products, fans, jewelry, woodblock prints, screens, chinaware, and much more at reasonable prices. I always stock up on gifts here for the folks back home.

On the other side of Omotesando Dori is:

10 Omotesando Hills

This posh commercial and residential shopping center, designed by Tadao Ando, houses upscale clothing and accessory shops, as well as restaurants. Unique is **Hasegawa Sake Shop** (はせがわ; © **03/5785-0833**), with selected offerings from sake breweries across Japan. You can sample sake at its stand-up bar for ¥400 and up a cup.

Back on Omotesando Dori and continuing east, you'll pass shops dedicated to the wares of Gucci, Fendi, Armani, Louis Vuitton, and Tod's. At the end of Omotesando Dori, where it connects with Aoyama Dori, is Omotesando Station. You can board the subway here or, for more shopping, cross Aoyama Dori and continue heading east, where you'll pass a number of designer shops. First, on the left at 3–18–11 Minami-Aoyama, is:

11 Issey Miyake

The clothes here are known for their richness in texture and fabrics.

To the right, at 5–2–1 Minami-Aoyama, is:

12 Comme des Garçons

Rei Kawakubo's designs for both men and women are showcased here.

Farther down the street, on the right at 5–2–6 Minami-Aoyama, is:

13 Prada

By far the most interesting design on the block, the building looks like a giant bug eye (to me, at least), with its dome structure comprising hundreds of glass bubbles.

Just past Prada, on the right at 5–3–6 Minami-Aoyama, is:

14 Yohji Yamamoto

As with all Yamamoto shops, this store has an interesting avant-garde interior.

Continue walking east, past the elementary school and From 1st shopping complex, where at the next larger intersection is the:

15 Nezu Museum

This private museum at 6–5–1 Minami Aoyama (www.nezu-muse.or.jp; ✆ 03/3400-2536) shows changing exhibits of Japanese and East Asian art, from lacquerware and ceramics to textiles, paintings and ceremonial tea instruments. Most wondrous of all, it boasts a peaceful garden, complete with a pond; the surrounding megalopolis hardly seems present. It's open Tuesday to Sunday from 10am to 5pm; admission ranges from ¥1,000 to ¥1,200, depending on the exhibit.

Return to Aoyama Dori, where you'll find the Omotesando subway station.

16 Museum-area Restaurants

Between Comme des Garçons and Yohji Yamamoto is Blue Brick Lounge, easy to find at 5–3–3 Minami-Aoyama (✆ 03/5485-3330) with its bright blue exterior and terrace. It serves lunch from 11:30am to 2pm and operates as a bar from 6 to 10pm. Its adjoining shop is famous for pastries and desserts. I also like Nezu Café, a glass-enclosed café on the grounds of Nezu Museum (see no. 14, above), which you can visit by paying museum admission. For more sinful pleasures, head to Berry Café, 5–10–19 Minami-Aoyama (✆ 03/5774-7130), on the left side of Aoyama Dori in the direction of Shibuya. Its berry-topped cakes have to be seen to be believed; even its plastic-food displays look good enough to eat.

WHERE TO EAT

From stand-up noodle shops and pizzerias to exclusive *kaiseki* restaurants and sushi bars, there are at least 80,000 restaurants in Tokyo—which gives you some idea of how fond Japanese are of eating out. In a city where apartments are so small and cramped that entertaining at home is almost unheard of, restaurants serve as places for socializing, meeting friends, and wooing business associates—as well as great excuses for drinking a lot of beer, sake, and whiskey.

HOW TO DINE IN TOKYO WITHOUT SPENDING A FORTUNE I know people in Tokyo who claim they haven't cooked in years—and they're not millionaires. They simply take advantage of one of the best deals in Tokyo—the fixed-price lunch, usually available from 11am to 2pm. Called a *teishoku* in a Japanese restaurant, a fixed-price meal is likely to include soup, a main dish such as tempura or whatever the restaurant specializes in, pickled vegetables, rice, and tea. In restaurants serving Western food, the fixed-price lunch is variously referred to as a set lunch, *seto coursu,* or simply *coursu,* and usually includes an appetizer, a main course with one or two side dishes, coffee or tea, and sometimes dessert. Even restaurants listed under **Very**

Mapping Out Tokyo's Restaurants

You can locate the restaurants reviewed below using the following neighborhood maps:

- To locate restaurants in **Shinjuku,** p. 130.
- To locate restaurants in **Asakusa,** p. 126.

- To locate restaurants in **Ueno,** p. 128.
- To locate restaurants in **Hibiya** and **Ginza,** p. 120.
- To locate restaurants in **Harajuku,** p. 133.
- To locate restaurants in **Roppongi,** p. 138.

Expensive—where you'd otherwise spend at least ¥13,000 or more per person for dinner, excluding drinks—and **Expensive**—where you can expect to pay ¥9,000 to ¥13,000 for dinner—usually offer set-lunch menus, allowing you to dine in style at very reasonable prices. To keep your costs down, therefore, try having your biggest meal at lunch, avoiding, if possible, the noon-to-1pm weekday crush when Tokyo's army of office workers flood area restaurants. Because Japanese tend to order fixed-price meals rather than a la carte, set dinners are also usually available (though they're not as cheap as set lunches). All-you-can-eat buffets (called *viking* in Japanese, probably because Japan's first buffet was in a restaurant called Viking in Tokyo's Imperial Hotel), offered by many hotel restaurants, are also bargains for hearty appetites.

So many of Tokyo's good restaurants fall into the **Moderate** category that it's tempting to simply eat your way through the city—and the range of cuisines is so great you could eat something different at each meal. Dinner in this category will average ¥4,000 to ¥9,000, lunch likely half as much.

Many of Tokyo's most colorful, noisy, and popular restaurants fall into the **Inexpensive** category, where meals usually go for less than ¥4,000; indeed, many offer meals for less than ¥2,000 and lunches for ¥1,000 or less. The city's huge working population heads to these places to catch a quick lunch or to socialize with friends after hours. There are also many excellent yet inexpensive French bistros, Italian trattorie, and ethnic restaurants, particularly those serving Indian, Chinese, and other Asian cuisines. Hotel restaurants are good bargains for inexpensive set lunches and buffets. Finally, see "Entertainment & Nightlife" later in this chapter for suggestions on inexpensive drinking places that serve food. And because I can cover only a limited number of cheap restaurants in each neighborhood, I also suggest you ask your concierge or hotel manager for recommendations; there's probably a great little place just around the corner.

OTHER DINING NOTES The restaurants listed below are organized first by neighborhood and then by price category. For information on Japanese food, see "Tips on Dining in Japan," in chapter 2.

Note that the 5% consumption tax is included in menu prices. However, many first-class restaurants, as well as hotel restaurants, will add a 10% to 15% service charge to the bill. Unless otherwise stated, the prices given below include the tax but not the service charge.

Finally, keep in mind that the **last order** is taken at least 30 minutes before the restaurant's actual closing time, sometimes even an hour before closing at the more exclusive restaurants.

Ginza & Hibiya

HOTELS ■
Hotel Com's Ginza **4**
Hotel Gracery **11**
Imperial Hotel **1**
Mitsui Garden Hotel
   Premier **6**
Park Hotel Tokyo **5**
The Peninsula Tokyo **15**
remm Hibiya **13**

RESTAURANTS ◆
Andy's Shin Hinomoto **18**
Donto **16**
Ginza Daimasu **25**
Gonpachi **35**
The Imperial Viking Sal **1**
Inakaya **8**
Kamon **1**
Kihachi **24**
La Boheme **20, 35**
Manpuku **17**
Meal Muji **21**
Monsoon **35**
Ohmatsuya **27**
Ohmatsuya Kura **23**
Rangetsu **33**
Shabusen **28**
Ten-ichi **2, 22**
Tsukiji Sushi Sen **30**
Yakitori stands **14**
Zest Cantina **35**

NIGHTLIFE ◆
300 Bar **3, 29**
Cotton Club **19**
Ginza Sapporo Lion **10**
Kabuki-za **32**
Kento's **9**
Lupin **26**
Nelson's Bar Gabbiano **34**
Old Imperial **1**
Shinbashi Enbujo
   Theater **31**
Show Dining Konparuza **7**
Takarazuka Gekijo **12**

4

Railway
Subway
Tourist Info ⓘ

HIBIYA PARK
HIBIYA LINE

Imperial
Tower

KEIHIN-TOHOKU LINE

New Ginza
Bldg.

Sotobori Dori

Soni Dori

Namiki Dori

Metropolitan (Shuto) Expressway

Nishi-Go-Bangai (West 5th St.)

Azuma Dori

0   1/10 mi
0   100 m

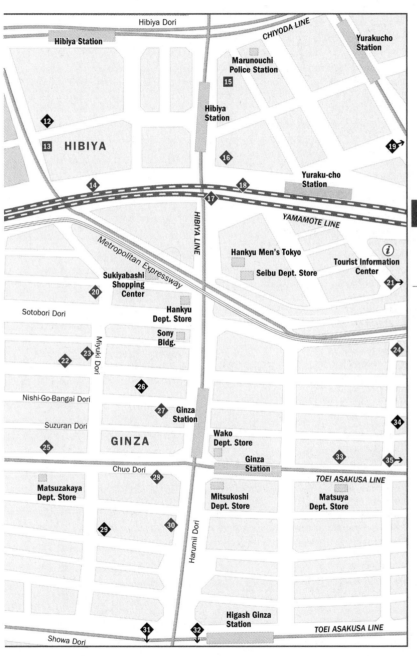

Ginza & Hibiya
VERY EXPENSIVE

In addition to the recommendations here, there's also a branch of **Inakaya**, 8–7–4 Ginza (📞 **03/3569-1708**), a *robatayaki* restaurant serving grilled foods (see p. 138 for a review).

Kamon ★★★ TEPPANYAKI   Kamon, which means "Gate of Celebration," has an interior that could be a statement on Tokyo itself—traditionally Japanese yet ever so high-tech. Located on the 17th floor of the Imperial Hotel, the restaurant offers seating at one of several large counters (some with views over Hibiya) centered around grills where expert chefs prepare excellent teppanyaki before your eyes according to your wishes. Japanese sirloin steaks or filets, cooked to succulent perfection, are available, as well as seafood ranging from fresh prawns and scallops to crabmeat and fish, and seasonal vegetables, served with traditional Japanese accompaniments. The service is, of course, imperial.

Imperial Hotel, 17th floor, 1–1–1 Uchisaiwai-cho. www.imperialhotel.co.jp. 📞 **03/3539-8116.** Reservations recommended for dinner. Set dinners ¥12,500–¥24,000; set lunches ¥4,200–¥7,875. AE, DC, MC, V. Daily 11:30am–2:30pm and 5:30–9:30pm. Station: Hibiya (1 min.).

EXPENSIVE

Ten-ichi ★★ TEMPURA   In this restaurant, located on Namiki Dori in the heart of Ginza's nightlife, you can sit at a counter and watch the chef prepare your meal. This is the main outlet of an 80-year-old restaurant chain that helped the tempura style of cooking gain worldwide recognition by serving important foreign customers. Today Ten-ichi still has one of the best reputations in town for serving the most delicately fried foods, along with its special sauce (or, if you prefer, you can dip the morsels in lemon juice with a pinch of salt).

Other Ten-ichi restaurants in Tokyo are in the Imperial Hotel's Tower basement (📞 **03/3503-1001;** station: Hibiya); Akasaka Tokyu Plaza (📞 **03/3581-2166;** station: Akasaka-mitsuke); and Isetan department store, 3–14–1 Shinjuku (📞 **03/5379-3039;** station: Shinjuku Sanchome).

6–6–5 Ginza. www.tenichi.co.jp. 📞 **03/3571-1949.** Reservations recommended for lunch, required for dinner. Set dinners ¥10,500–¥18,900; set lunches ¥8,400–¥12,600. AE, DC, MC, V. Daily 11:30am–9:30pm. Station: Ginza (3 min.). On Namiki Dori.

MODERATE

Donto (どんと) ★★ 🍴 VARIED JAPANESE   Located in Hibiya on Harumi Dori in the basement of an unlikely looking office building, this is a great place for lunch. Popular with the local working crowd (and therefore best avoided noon–1pm), it's pleasantly decorated in a rustic style with *shoji* screens, wooden floors, and an open kitchen. Take off your shoes at the entryway and put them into one of the wooden lockers. Choose what you want from the plastic display case by the front door, which shows various *teishoku* and set meals. Everything from noodles, sashimi, tempura, and *obento* to *kaiseki* is available. Unfortunately, the best deals are daily specials written in Japanese only; ask about them or look around at what others are eating.

There are other Donto restaurants at 2–6–1 Shimbashi (📞 **03/3501-0123;** station: Shimbashi) and on the 49th floor of the Sumitomo Building in Shinjuku (📞 **03/3344-6269;** station: Tochomae).

Yurakucho Denki Building basement. 1–7–1 Yurakucho. 📞 **03/3201-3021.** Set dinners ¥3,500–¥5,000; set lunches ¥700–¥1,000. AE, DC, MC, V. Mon–Sat 11am–2pm and 5–11pm. Closed holidays. Station: Hibiya (1 min.). On Harumi Dori.

A Note on Establishments with Japanese Signs

Many establishments and attractions in Japan do not have signs in Roman (English-language) letters. Those that don't are provided with the Japanese equivalent to help you locate them.

Ginza Daimasu (銀座大増) KAISEKI/OBENTO   This 90-year-old restaurant has a simple, modern decor with Japanese touches. Experienced, kimono-clad waitresses serve artfully arranged set meals from the English-language menu. The *Fukiyose-zen obento*—many delicate dishes served in three courses—includes beautiful tempura delicacies for ¥3,675. A plastic-food display in the front window will help you recognize the restaurant. Set lunches are served until 4pm.

6–9–6 Ginza. 🕐 **03/3571-3584.** Reservations required for kaiseki meals costing more than ¥9,450. Kaiseki ¥5,250–¥12,600; obento ¥2,415–¥3,675; set lunches ¥2,100–¥2,940. AE, DC, MC, V. Daily 11:30am–8:30pm (last order). Station: Ginza (2 min.). On Chuo Dori, across from Matsuzakaya department store.

The Imperial Viking Sal ★ INTERNATIONAL   No, this has nothing to do with Scandinavian invaders; rather, *viking* is the Japanese word for "all-you-can-eat buffet." Although lots of Tokyo hotels now offer such spreads, this 17th-floor restaurant was the first and has been serving buffets since 1953 (as you might imagine, it's offerings have changed a great deal since then). It boasts more than 40 mostly European and some international dishes, which vary according to seasonal food promotions spotlighting a country's cuisine, from Indonesian to Swiss. Views are of the Ginza and Hibiya Park, and there's live jazz in the evenings. This restaurant has enjoyed great popularity for decades, making reservations a must.

Imperial Hotel, 17th floor, 1–1–1 Uchisaiwai-cho. www.imperialhotel.co.jp. 🕐 **03/3504-1111.** Reservations strongly recommended. Buffet dinner Mon–Fri ¥7,900, Sat–Sun and holidays ¥8,400; buffet lunch Mon–Fri ¥5,300, Sat–Sun and holidays ¥5,800. AE, DC, MC, V. Daily 11:30am–2:30pm; Mon–Fri 5:30–9:30pm; Sat–Sun and holidays 5–9:30pm. Station: Hibiya (1 min.).

Kihachi ★★ FUSION   With a cool, crisp interior accented with Art Nouveau trimmings, this second-floor restaurant offers an interesting French-influenced menu that combines flavors of the West with Japanese and Asian ingredients, creations of its French-trained chef. Past choices on the English-language menu have included such starters as pan-fried foie gras or half-baked egg wrapped in smoked salmon and topped with carrot and crab; mains have included grilled sea bream with cumin and roasted vegetables or Japanese-flavored duck breast. The hardest part of dining here? Limiting yourself to one meal—you just might have to come back. To spare your wallet, consider dining in the first-floor cafe, which offers set lunches beginning at ¥2,000 and dinner entrees ranging from a fish of the day to grilled duck with *yuza* pepper and lemon.

2–2–6 Ginza. 🕐 **03/3567-6281.** Main dishes ¥2,650–¥3,150; set dinners ¥5,250–¥10,500; set lunches ¥2,625–¥3,675. AE, DC, MC, V. Daily 11:30am–2:30pm and 6–9:30pm (last order; 8pm Sun and holidays). Station: Yurakucho (5 min.). Near Printemps department store.

Ohmatsuya (大松屋) **★★ 🍴** JAPANESE GRILL   Enter this restaurant of a nondescript building and you're instantly back in time: After you're greeted by waitresses clad in traditional country clothing, you'll find yourself enveloped in an old farmhouse atmosphere. (Part of the decor is from a 17th-c. samurai house in northern

Japan.) Even the style of cooking is traditional, as customers grill their own food over a hibachi. Sake, served in a length of bamboo, is drunk from bamboo cups. Dinner menus (in English) include such delicacies as grilled fish, skewered meat, and vegetables. This is a true find—and easy to find at that—just off Harumi Dori on West 5th Street. If this place is full, there's a nearby sister restaurant, **Ohmatsuya Kura,** 6–6–19 Ginza (© 03/3574-4200), with the same atmosphere and two set meals starting at ¥5,250; it's open Monday to Friday from 5 to 10pm.

5–6–13 Ginza, 7th floor. © **03/3571-7053.** Reservations required. Set dinners ¥5,040–¥9,450, plus a ¥500 table charge. AE, DC, MC, V. Mon–Sat 5–10pm (last order). Closed holidays. Station: Ginza (3 min.). On W. 5th St.

Rangetsu (らん月) SUKIYAKI/SHABU-SHABU/KAISEKI/OBENTO   This well-known Ginza restaurant has been dishing out sukiyaki, shabu-shabu, obento (traditional box meals), and steaks since 1947. It uses A5-grade Japanese wagyu beef for its sukiyaki and shabu-shabu, which you cook yourself at your table. There are also crab dishes (including a crab shabu-shabu set meal for ¥8,000), kaiseki, and much more. Especially good deals are the obento box meals (available day and night and offering a variety of small dishes) and the set lunches served until 2:30pm. In the basement is a sake bar with more than 80 different kinds of sake from all over Japan, which you can also order with your meal.

3–5–8 Ginza. © **03/3567-1021.** Reservations recommended. Beef sukiyaki or shabu-shabu set meals from ¥8,000 for dinner, ¥2,500 for lunch; obento meals and mini-kaiseki ¥2,400–¥5,800. AE, DC, MC, V. Daily 11:30am–10pm. Station: Ginza (3 min.). On Chuo Dori, across from the Matsuya department store.

INEXPENSIVE

In addition to the restaurants here, check out **Meal Muji,** 3–8–3 Marunouchi (© 03/5208-8241), a cafeteria on the second floor of the popular minimalist Muji clothing and housewares store, where you can load up on mostly salads and veggies daily from 10am to 8pm. There are also a number of restaurants on the eighth floor of **Matsuya Ginza department store** serving everything from French and Chinese food to sushi, tempura, noodles, and more.

For atmospheric dining, head to an arch underneath the elevated Yamanote railway tracks located about halfway between Harumi Dori and the Imperial Hotel Tower; it has a handful of tiny *yakitori* **stands,** each with a few tables and chairs. They cater to a rather boisterous working-class clientele, mainly men. The atmosphere, unsophisticated and dingy, harks back to prewar Japan, somewhat of an anomaly in the otherwise chic Ginza. Stalls are open from about 5pm to midnight Monday through Saturday.

Andy's Shin Hinomoto ✦ VARIED JAPANESE   Occupying its own arch underneath the Yamanote tracks, this Japanese-style pub is owned by Andy, a Brit, who buys all his seafood and vegetables fresh daily at Tsukiji Market. The upstairs is the place to be, with its arched ceiling and mixed foreign and Japanese crowd. If you don't have reservations, you'll be shunted into the less ambient downstairs, where you'll feel like a refugee in a fallout shelter as you sit elbow-to-elbow with local office workers at long tables under fluorescent lighting. Sashimi, grilled fish, tempura, sautéed vegetables, deep-fried chicken, tofu, salad, and much more are offered on the English-language menu.

2–4–4 Yurakucho. © **03/3214-8021.** Reservations strongly recommended. Main dishes ¥500–¥1,600. No credit cards. Mon–Sat 5pm–midnight. Station: Yurakucho or Ginza (1 min.). Underneath the Yamanote elevated tracks, across from the Yurakucho Denki Building.

family-FRIENDLY RESTAURANTS

Hard Rock Cafe (p. 142)   This internationally known establishment should pacify grumbling teenagers. They can munch on hamburgers, gaze at famous guitars and other rock-'n'-roll memorabilia and, most important, buy that Hard Rock Cafe T-shirt.

Kua' Aina (p. 136)   When your kids start asking for "real food," take them here for some of the best burgers in town, as well as unusual creations.

Sometaro (p. 128)   This traditional restaurant specializes in Japanese-style pancakes filled with meat and vegetables and fried noodles that you cook yourself at your table, which might delight more adventuresome little eaters, especially because they get to pick their own ingredients.

Tokyo Catering (p. 132)   This inexpensive cafeteria won't break the bank, and with everything from sushi to noodles, offers enough to satisfy most diners. Your kids will be impressed, too, with the views from its location on the 32nd floor, but to really wow the little ones, take them also to the free observatory on the 45th floor.

4

TOKYO | Where to Eat

La Boheme ITALIAN   The food is passable, but what sets La Boheme apart is that it's open every day until 5am, making it a good bet for a late-night meal. The pasta ranges from spaghetti with eggplant and tomato sauce to spaghetti Bolognese, along with Japanese-style versions like steamed breast of chicken with Japanese leek, spinach, and sesame oil. This restaurant is actually one of four restaurants ensconced under a freeway in a nifty dining complex called **G-Zone.** Southeast Asian fare is offered in **Monsoon** (www.monsoon-café.jp; ✆ **03/5524-3631**); burritos, shrimp enchiladas, tacos, and other Tex-Mex food is served at **Zest Cantina** (www.zest-cantina.jp; ✆ **03/5524-3621**); and Japanese food in **Gonpachi** (p. 141). English-language menus, inexpensive food, friendly and polished staff, and late opening hours make these restaurants winners whether you're a Tokyo novice or a pro. Check websites for other locations at many popular spots around Tokyo.

1–2–3 Ginza. www.boheme.jp. ✆ **03/5524-3616.** Pizza and pasta ¥650–¥1,480; set lunches ¥900–¥1,100. AE, DC, MC, V. Daily 11:30am–5am. Station: Kyobashi (exit 3, 2 min.) or Ginza-Itchome (exit 7, 1 min.). On Chuo Dori, at the northern edge of Ginza.

Manpuku 🏮YAKITORI   This yakitori restaurant differs from the others under the Yamanote tracks in that it offers tables along a covered passageway where you can watch office workers bustling by. Decorated with old posters inside and out, it has a slight post–World War II retro feel; its sign even boasts RETRO DINING. Manpuku offers an English-language menu of yakitori, garlic shrimp, soba noodles, sashimi, tempura, and other pub grub. The food isn't the greatest, but prices are cheap and it's often packed. Note that in the evenings there's a ¥300 snack charge per person.

2–4–1 Yurakucho. ✆03/3211-6001. Main dishes ¥580–¥1,280; set lunches ¥680–¥1,449. No credit cards. 24 hr., except 1st and 3rd Sun when it's closed 1am–6am. Station: Yurakucho or Hibiya (1 min.). On Harumi Dori, underneath the elevated Yamanote tracks btw. Hankyu department store and Yurakucho Denki buildings.

Shabusen (しゃぶせん) ★ 🍴 SHABU-SHABU   With an improbable location in the basement of a fashion department store just a stone's throw from Ginza 4–chome Crossing (the Harumi Dori–Chuo Dori intersection), this is a fun restaurant where you can cook your own sukiyaki or shabu-shabu in a boiling pot as you sit at a round counter or at your private table. It's also one of the few restaurants that caters to individual diners (shabu-shabu is usually shared by a group). Orders are shouted back and forth among the staff, service is rapid, and the place is lively. There's an English-language menu, complete with cooking instructions, so it's user-friendly. The special shabu-shabu dinner for ¥3,400, with tomato ("super dressing") salad, beef, vegetables, noodles or rice porridge, and dessert, is enough for most appetites.

Core Building 2nd basement, 5–8–20 Ginza. ℂ **03/3572-3806.** Set dinners ¥2,200–¥4,300; set lunches ¥1,200–¥3,150. AE, DC, MC, V. Daily 11am–9pm (last order). Station: Ginza (1 min.). On Chuo Dori, next to the Nissan Gallery.

Tsukiji Sushi Sen (築地すし鮮) SUSHI   Too brightly lit and possessing as much charm as an interrogation room, this second-floor Ginza branch nevertheless offers fresh sushi at bargain prices, served at a counter or at tables overlooking busy Harumi Dori. Other dishes are also available on the English-language menu, including salads, tofu, grilled seafood, tempura, and sushi rolls. If you find yourself hungry in Ginza in the dead of night, this all-nighter is a good choice.

5–9–1 Ginza. ℂ **03/5537-2878.** Sushi a la carte ¥52–¥514; set lunches ¥892–¥945; set dinners ¥1,260–¥3,150. AE, MC, V. 24 hr. Station: Higashi Ginza or Ginza (2 min.). On the south side of Harumi Dori, btw. Chuo Dori and Showa Dori.

Near Tokyo Station
MODERATE
Aux Amis Tokyo ★ FRENCH   This small, tony restaurant specializing in creative French cuisine is one of several on the top two floors of the Marunouchi Building (called *Maru Biru* by locals), located on the Marunouchi (west) side of Tokyo Station. Sweeping views make it a popular dining spot (reserve one of the few coveted window seats), as do an extensive wine list and a changing French/Japanese menu that might include such entrees as roast lamb with shiitake mushrooms or pork filet in a red-wine sauce. It's also a great spot for lunch, but note that the rather bare dining room fails to absorb the constant chatter of this popular venue. Other restaurants on the two floors serve shabu-shabu, sushi, tempura, and kaiseki, as well as Italian, Thai, French, and Chinese cuisines. There are many more inexpensive eateries in the basement.

Marunouchi Building, 35th floor, 2–4–1 Marunouchi. ℂ **03/5220-4011.** Main dishes ¥2,940–¥5,145; set dinners ¥6,300–¥12,600; set lunches ¥2,940–¥7,140, plus a weekday lunch for ¥1,890. AE, DC, MC, V. Daily 11am–2:30pm and 5:30–11pm (last order). Station: Tokyo (Marunouchi exit, 2 min.).

INEXPENSIVE
There's a **Kua' Aina** (p. 136) outlet selling burgers in the Marunouchi Building on the fifth floor, across from Tokyo Station at 2–4–1 Marunouchi (ℂ **03/5220-2400**).

A16 ★ ITALIAN   This San Francisco transplant serves south Italian fare via California, mostly pizza and pasta. What I like most about this open-fronted restaurant is that it offers terrace seating on leafy Brick Square, a rarity in this neck of the woods and making you feel like you've landed in a European village rather than downtown Tokyo. Pasta, available in half and regular sizes, includes the like of squid ink tonnarelli with shrimp, zucchini, garlic, mint, anchovies, and chiles. Pizzas, baked in a brick oven, are seriously large, meaning two can share if they order a salad or appetizer as well. There are also a few main dishes, like roasted chicken and braised pork meatballs with tomato, grana padano and basil. From 2:30 to 5pm it's open as a café, making it a good place also to chill in the afternoon.

Marunouchi Park Building, Brick Square, 2–6–1 Marunouchi. www.giraud.co.jp/a16/index/html. *℃* **03/3212-5215.** Pizza and pasta ¥1,200–¥2,700; main dishes ¥1,200–¥2,700; set lunches ¥2,100–¥2,600. AE, DC, MC, V. Mon–Sat 11am–11pm; Sun 11am–10pm. Station: Tokyo (Marunouchi exit, 5 min.) or Nijubashimae (5 min).

Dhaba India ★ 🍴 SOUTH INDIAN   A brisk lunchtime business, which brings in both Japanese and expats (including those from India and surrounding countries) is testimony to this restaurant's popularity and good food. Although the wait staff is Japanese, those in the open kitchen hail from southern India, turning out spicy dishes and weekday set lunches that don't scrimp on ingredients (unlike some Indian restaurants in Tokyo that offer lunch curries that more resemble soup). The a-la-carte menu, available evenings and all day on weekends, offers tandoori and about 20 different curries, from Kerala fish curry and dry mutton curry to *moong dal* and green banana curry.

2–7–9 Yaesu. *℃* **03/3272-7160.** Main dishes ¥950–¥1,470; set dinners ¥2,000–¥2,800; set lunches ¥800–¥1,200. AE, DC, MC, V (no credit cards during weekday lunch). Mon–Fri 11:15am–3pm and 5–11pm; Sat–Sun noon–3pm and 5–10pm. Station: Tokyo (Yaesu exit, 2 min.) or Kyobashi (2 min.). One block east of Tokyo Station. From Pacific Century Place (south of Tokyo Station), cross Sotobori Dori and continue east on Kajibashi Dori, taking the first left.

Tsukiji

Because Tsukiji is home to the nation's largest wholesale fish market, it's not surprising that this area abounds in sushi and seafood restaurants. In addition to the recommendations here, don't neglect the many stalls in and around the market where you can eat everything from noodles to fresh sashimi.

MODERATE

Tentake (天竹) FUGU   People who really know their fugu, or blowfish, will tell you that the proper time to eat it is October through March, when it's fresh. You can eat fugu year-round, however, and a good place to try this Japanese delicacy is Tentake, popular with the Tsukiji working crowd. An English-language menu lists dishes such as tempura fugu and blowfish sashimi, along with complete fugu dinners with all the trimmings. Otherwise, if you want suggestions, try the fugu-chiri for ¥2,800, a do-it-yourself blowfish-and-vegetable stew in which you cook raw blowfish, cabbage, dandelion leaves, and tofu in a pot of boiling water in front of you—this was more than I could eat, but you can make a complete meal of it by ordering the Tsukiji course for ¥6,500, which adds tempura, salad, and other dishes. Wash it all down with fugu sake. There are options for those who don't like fugu, such as the crab set menu for ¥4,090. And yes, that's fugu swimming in the fish tank. (Before you eat here, be sure you read about fugu, in "Japanese Cuisine," in chapter 2.)

6–16–6 Tsukiji. *℃* **03/3541-3881.** Fugu dishes ¥520–¥2,050; fugu set dinners ¥4,800–¥13,500; set lunches ¥630–¥1,570. AE, DC, MC, V. Daily 11:30am–9:30pm (last order). Station: Tsukiji (7 min.). From the Harumi Dori/Shinohashi intersection, walk on Harumi Dori in the opposite direction of Ginza; the restaurant is on the left in a modern building just before the Kachidoki-bashi Bridge, with a picture of a giant blowfish above the door.

INEXPENSIVE

There's a **Tsukiji Sushi Sen,** 12–23–6 Tsukiji (*℃* **03/3549-1136**), open 24 hours with an English menu, that offers set meals starting at ¥1,365 and other dishes like tempura and grilled fish. From the Harumi/Shinohashi Dori intersection, walk toward Tsukiji Market on Shinohashi Dori and turn left at the carpark onto Namiyoke Dori (p. 124).

Edogin (江戸銀) SUSHI   There are two Edogin sushi restaurants in Tsukiji, within walking distance of one another. Because they're close to the famous fish market, you can be sure that the fish will be fresh. There's nothing aesthetic about the main Edogin, first established about 80 years ago—the lights are bright, it's packed with the locals, and it's noisy and busy. It's particularly crowded during lunch and dinnertime because the food is dependably good and plentiful. The menu is in Japanese only, but an illustrated menu outside displays some of the set meals, with most prices ¥3,700 or less. There are also sushi platters for ¥1,600 to ¥4,200. As an alternative, look at what the people around you are eating or, if it's lunchtime, order the teishoku (served until 2pm Mon–Fri and all day Sat). The nigiri-zushi teishoku for ¥1,050 offers a variety of sushi, along with soup and pickled vegetables; if you're really hungry, a more plentiful nigiri-zushi teishoku is available for ¥1,470.

4–5–1 Tsukiji. ☏ **03/3543-4401.** Set meals ¥1,650–¥5,500; lunch teishoku ¥1,050–¥1,470. AE, DC, MC, V. Mon–Sat 11:30am–9:30pm; Sun and holidays 11:30am–8pm. Station: Tsukiji or Tsukijijo (3 min.). Located near the Harumi and Shinohashi Dori intersection behind Tsukiji Bon Marche; anyone in the neighborhood can point you in the right direction.

Sushi Dai (寿司大) ★ SUSHI   Located right in the Tsukiji Fish Market, this sushi bar boasts some of the freshest fish in town. The easiest thing to do is order the *seto*, a set sushi course that usually comes with tuna, eel, shrimp, and other morsels, plus six rolls of tuna and rice in seaweed (*onigiri*). You won't get plates here—food is served directly on the raised counter in front of you. Unfortunately, although I used to be able to sail right in, this tiny restaurant with only a dozen or so seats has since been "discovered" and waits can be up to an hour. There are dozens of other tiny sushi restaurants surrounding it, any of which also serve sushi right from the market.

Tsukiji Fish Market. ☏ **03/3547-6797.** Sushi a la carte ¥315–¥1,000; sushi seto ¥2,500–¥3,900. No credit cards. Mon–Sat 5am–2pm. Closed Wed if the market is closed, and on holidays. Station: Tsukijijo (2 min.) or Tsukiji (10 min.). Located in a row of barracks housing other restaurants and shops beside the covered market, in Building no. 6 in the 3rd alley (just past the mailbox); it's the 3rd shop on the right.

Asakusa

MODERATE

Chinya (ちんや) ★ 🍴 SHABU-SHABU/SUKIYAKI   Established in 1880, Chinya is an old sukiyaki restaurant with a new home in a seven-story building to the left of Kaminarimon Gate, adjacent to its own butcher shop. The entrance to this place is open-fronted; all you'll see is a man waiting to take your shoes and a hostess in a kimono ready to lead you to one of the tatami-floored dining areas above. Chinya offers very good shabu-shabu and sukiyaki set lunches for ¥4,300, available until 3:30pm and including an appetizer, miso soup, rice or noodles, and side dishes. Otherwise, dinner set meals of shabu-shabu or sukiyaki, including sashimi, rice, and soup, begin at ¥5,500 (reservations required). The English-language menu and an English pamphlet include instructions, making this a good bet for the sukiyaki/shabu-shabu novice.

1–3–4 Asakusa. www.chinya.co.jp. ☏ **03/3841-0010.** Reservations required for set dinners. Sukiyaki or shabu-shabu set dinners ¥5,500–¥12,000; set lunch ¥4,300. AE, DC, MC, V. Mon–Sat noon–9pm; Sun and holidays 11:30am–9pm (last order 7pm). Station: Asakusa (1 min.). On Kaminarimon Dori; located to the left of the Kaminarimon Gate, if you stand facing Asakusa Kannon Temple (look for the SUKIYAKI sign).

La Ranarita Azumabashi ★ ITALIAN   The Asahi Beer Tower may not mean anything to you, but if I mention the building with the golden hops poised on top, you'll certainly know it when you see it (the building was designed by Philippe Starck). The Asahi Beer Tower is the high-rise next to the golden hops, looking like . . .a foaming beer mug? On the top floor (in the foam), this Italian restaurant has soaring walls and great views of Asakusa. It's a perfect perch from which to watch barges on the river or the sun set over Asakusa as you dine on everything from pasta and grilled lamb with rosemary to fresh fish of the day prepared baked, grilled, or meunière. The set lunches include an antipasto, salad, a main dish, and coffee; on weekdays there's also a pizza or pasta set for ¥1,000. If you want a ringside seat, make a reservation at least 3 days in advance, avoid weekends and holidays, or arrive just when they open.

Asahi Beer Tower (on the opposite side of the Sumida River from Sensoji Temple), 22nd floor, 1–23–1 Azumabashi. 🕿 **03/5608-5277.** Reservations recommended on weekends. Pizza and pasta ¥1,400–¥2,000; main dishes ¥2,200–¥5,500; set lunches ¥2,000–¥4,800 (from ¥1,000 on week-days). AE, DC, MC, V. Mon–Sat 11:30am–2pm and 5–9pm; Sun and holidays 11:30am–3pm and 5–9pm (last order). Station: Asakusa (4 min.).

Mugitoro (むぎとろ) YAM/KAISEKI Founded about 65 years ago but now housed in a new building, this restaurant specializes in *tororo-imo* (yam) kaiseki and has a wide following among middle-age Japanese women. Popular as a health food, the yams used here are imported from the mountains of Akita Prefecture and are featured in almost all the dishes. If you're on a budget or want a quick meal, come for the weekday lunch buffet offered until 1pm on the ground floor; it includes a main dish such as fish or beef, yam in some form, vegetable, soup, and rice—just deposit ¥1,000 into the pot on the table and help yourself.

2–2–4 Kaminarimon. 🕿 **03/3842-1066.** Reservations recommended. Set dinners ¥4,200–¥10,500; set lunches ¥2,625–¥3,675 (also for ¥1,000 weekdays). AE, DC, MC, V. Mon–Fri 11:30am–9pm; Sat–Sun and holidays 11am–9pm (last order). Station: Asakusa (2 min.). From Sensoji Temple, walk south (with your back to Kaminarimon Gate) until you reach the 1st big intersection with the stop-light. Komagata-bashi Bridge will be to your left; Mugitoro is beside the bridge on Edo Dori, next to a tiny temple.

Waentei-Kikko (和えん亭 吉幸) ★★★ KAISEKI/OBENTO Just southeast of Sensoji Temple, Waentei-Kikko is actually a tiny, traditional house tucked behind a tiny garden. Inside, it's like a farmhouse in the countryside with its flagstone entry, wooden rafters, and tatami seating. A warm and friendly husband-and-wife team manage it, but what makes this establishment especially compelling are the shamisen performances by the husband, Fukui Kodai, playing with the fervor of a rock star, or by other staff members, as well as performances of other traditional Japanese music (performances are at 12:15, 1:30, 3, 6:30, and 8pm). Of course, the food shines, too, with obento lunchboxes and kaiseki dinners that change with the seasons. Fugu kaiseki dinners, beginning at ¥9,975, are also available with advance reservations. This place is a true find.

2–2–13 Asakusa. www.waentei-kikko.com. 🕿 **03/5828-8833.** Reservations recommended. Obento lunches ¥2,500 and ¥3,500; kaiseki dinners ¥6,825–¥14,175. AE, DC, MC, V. Thurs–Tues 11:30am–1:30pm and 5–8:30pm (last order). Station: Asakusa (5 min.). Walk on Nakamise Dori toward Sensoji Temple, turning right after the last shop; go past the 2 stone Buddhas, and then turn right again at the tiny Benten-do Temple with the large bell. The restaurant is on the right side of the street across from the playground.

INEXPENSIVE

Kamiya Bar VARIED JAPANESE/WESTERN This inexpensive restaurant, established in 1880 as the first Western bar in Japan, serves both Japanese and Western fare on its three floors. The first floor is the bar, popular with older, tobacco-smoking Japanese men and famous for its Denki Bran (a concoction of brandy, gin, wine, vermouth, Curacao, and herbs). The second floor offers Western food of a sort (that is, the Japanese version of Western food), including fried chicken, smoked salmon, spaghetti, fried shrimp, and hamburger steak. The third floor serves Japanese food ranging from udon noodles and yakitori to tempura and sashimi. I personally prefer the third floor for both its food and its atmosphere. Although the menus are in Japanese only, extensive plastic-food display cases show set meals of Japanese food costing ¥1,500 to ¥3,500. This is a very casual restaurant, very much a place for older locals, and it can be quite noisy and crowded.

1–1–1 Asakusa. ✆ **03/3841-5400.** Main dishes ¥700–¥1,500. AE, DC, MC, V (2nd/3rd floors only). Wed–Mon 11:30am–9:30pm (last order). Station: Asakusa (1 min.). Located on Kaminarimon Dori in a plain, brown-tiled building btw. Kaminarimon Gate and the Sumida River.

Sansado (三定) TEMPURA Located right beside Kaminarimon Gate, next to the Kurodaya paper shop, this simple tempura restaurant specializes in Edo-style tempura, fried in a light oil. On the first floor, seating is either at tables or on tatami, while the upstairs is more traditional with tatami seating; one room overlooks the temple gate. Sansado is run by an army of very able grandmotherly types, and because the menu is in Japanese only, they're more than happy to go outside with you to help you make a selection from the plastic-food display case.

1–2–2 Asakusa. ✆ **03/3841-3400.** Set meals ¥1,385–¥4,100. AE, DC, MC, V. Daily 11:30am–9:30pm (last order). Station: Asakusa (1 min.). East of Kaminarimon Gate, with entrances beside Kurodaya paper shop and on Kaminarimon Dori.

Sometaro (染太郎) ★ ☺ OKONOMIYAKI This very atmospheric neighborhood restaurant specializes in okonomiyaki, a working-class meal that is basically a Japanese pancake filled with beef, pork, and vegetables, and prepared by the diners themselves as they sit on tatami at low tables inset with griddles. Realizing that some foreigners may be intimidated by having to cook an unfamiliar meal, this restaurant makes the process easier with an English-language menu complete with instructions. The busy but friendly staff can help you get started. In addition to okonomiyaki, *yakisoba* (fried noodles) with meat or vegetables and other do-it-yourself dishes are available. This is a fun, convivial way to enjoy a meal, especially for kids who might like to try their own hand in cooking their meal (and selecting their own ingredients). Before entering the restaurant, be sure to deposit your shoes in the proffered plastic sacks by the door.

2–2–2 Nishi-Asakusa. ✆ **03/3844-9502.** Main dishes ¥600–¥1,080. No credit cards. Daily noon–10pm (last order). Station: Tawaramachi (2 min.) or Asakusa (5 min.). Just off Kokusai Dori, on the side street that runs btw. the Drum Museum and the police station, in the 2nd block on the right.

Ueno
EXPENSIVE
Grill Fukushima ★ CLASSIC FRENCH Parent company Seiyoken opened one of Japan's first restaurants serving Western food in 1876. Its restaurant here, ensconced in a nondescript building dating from the 1950s, is nonetheless the classiest place to eat in Ueno Park, serving pricey but quite good French cuisine, with a relaxing view of greenery outside its large windows and classical music playing softly in the background. The a la carte menu, in French and Japanese, includes seafood such as lobster in an orange sauce and meat dishes ranging from filet mignon in red-wine sauce to roast lamb, but most people order one of the many fixed-price meals.

There's a varied selection of French wines as well as wines from Germany, California, and Australia. The Grill is located to the right as you enter the building and is not to be confused with the much cheaper utilitarian restaurant to the left.

In Ueno Park. 📞 **03/3821-2181.** Main dishes ¥4,200–¥7,875; set dinners ¥8,400–¥16,800; set lunches ¥4,800–¥10,500. AE, DC, MC, V. Daily 11am–8pm (last order). Station: JR Ueno (6 min.). Btw. Kiyomizu Temple and Toshogu Shrine.

MODERATE

Innsyoutei (韻松亭) ★ KAISEKI/OBENTO   This traditional Japanese restaurant in Ueno Park has been a Tokyo landmark since 1875. Downstairs is a simple tearoom, but for a meal you'll be ushered upstairs to a dining room with tables overlooking trees or a private tatami room. For lunch, it offers a variety of set meals (including a vegetarian meal), obento, and kaiseki meals from an English-language menu, while dinner features kaiseki and chicken sukiyaki. If you've never had kaiseki, this is a good choice, but it's also a convenient lunch spot after visiting Ueno Park's many museums.

In Ueno Park. 📞 **03/3821-8126.** Reservations recommended. Set dinners ¥5,300–¥10,500; set lunches ¥1,680–¥6,300. No credit cards. Daily 11am–4pm and 5–11pm (to 10pm Sun). Station: JR Ueno (6 min.). Btw. Grill Fukushima (see above) and the row of orange torii leading downhill.

Tokori KOREAN BARBECUE   One of three restaurants in a modern concrete building called Bamboo Garden (the other two restaurants serve Chinese and Japanese food), this friendly establishment offers Korean-style barbecued meats, which you grill yourself at your table, as well as salads, kimchi (spicy Korean cabbage), Korean-style pancakes, rice porridge, noodles, and soups from an English-language menu with photographs. Set lunches feature one-pot meals or grilled beef, along with side dishes of soup, salad, and *kimchi*.

1–52 Ueno Park. 📞 **03/5807-2255.** Main dishes ¥840–¥1,880; set lunches ¥1,000–¥2,200. AE, DC, MC, V. Daily 11am–11:30pm. Station: JR Ueno (2 min.). On a steep hillside across the street from JR Ueno Station's west side, in Ueno Park next to the Ueno Royal Museum.

Unagi Kappo Izu'ei Honten (鰻割烹伊豆栄本店) EEL   Put aside all your prejudices about eels and head for this modern yet traditionally decorated multistoried restaurant with a 265-year history dating back to the Edo Period (there's a model of the old restaurant in the entryway), and with views of Shinobazu Pond. Because eels are grilled over charcoal, the Japanese place a lot of stock in the quality of the charcoal used, and this place boasts its own furnace in the mountains of Wakayama Prefecture, which is said to produce the best charcoal in Japan. The English menu, complete with photos, shows 15 set meals that include eel, as well as individual eel dishes like *unagi donburi* (rice topped with strips of eel) and tempura and sashimi set meals.

2–12–22 Ueno. 📞 **03/3831-0954.** Reservations recommended. Set meals ¥1,575–¥3,675. AE, DC, MC, V. Daily 11am–9:30pm (last order). Station: JR Ueno (3 min.). On Shinobazu Dori, across the street from Shinobazu Pond and the Shitamachi Museum, next to KFC.

INEXPENSIVE

The **Hard Rock Cafe Ueno** (see p. 142 for a review), 7–1–1 Ueno (📞 **03/5826-5821**), is located in JR Ueno Station, while **Kohmen** (p. 142), 4–8–8 Ueno (📞 **03/5807-4535**), offers tasty ramen and *gyoza*.

Mantra INDIAN   Decorated in pink, with etched mirrors and lots of brass, this tiny, spotless restaurant offers curries, tandoori, and Halal food at inexpensive prices. A good way for lone diners to try a variety of dishes is the all-you-can-eat lunch buffet served from 11am to 4pm, or one of the meat or vegetarian set meals *(thali)*. Another good choice for budget travelers: a set dinner for ¥1,950 that's all you can eat within 120 minutes; add ¥1,050 for all you can drink.

Nagafuji Building Annex, 3rd floor, 4–9–6 Ueno. © **03/3835-0818.** Main dishes ¥890–¥1,680; set meals ¥1,680–¥2,650; set lunches ¥1,360–¥1,680; lunch buffet ¥980 Mon–Fri, ¥1,200 Sat–Sun and holidays. AE, DC, MC, V. Daily 11am–10pm (last order). Station: JR Ueno (2 min.). From the south end of Ueno Park, look for the modern Nagafuji Building on Chuo Dori; the annex is in the back, facing the north end of Ameyokocho shopping street.

Shinjuku

In addition to the suggestions below, be sure to check out the restaurant floors of several buildings in Shinjuku, where you can find restaurants in all price categories serving a variety of Japanese and international cuisine, some with very good views. These include the 29th and 30th floors of the **N. S. Building** where, in addition to Hakkaku (described below), there are restaurants serving tempura, tonkatsu, teppanyaki, and Italian fare; the top four floors of the **Sumitomo Building** where, in addition to Donto (p. 120), you'll find more than 20 outlets offering everything from tempura to Chinese cuisine; and the 12th, 13th, and 14th floors of **Takashimaya Shinjuku** where restaurants serve sushi, eel, *tonkatsu,* noodles, tempura, hamburgers, and more.

VERY EXPENSIVE

New York Grill ★★★ AMERICAN   On the 52nd floor of one of Tokyo's most exclusive hotels, the New York Grill has remained one of *the* places to dine ever since its 1994 opening; some swear it's the most sophisticated restaurant in all of Japan. Surrounded on four sides by glass, it features stunning views (especially at night), live jazz in the evenings from an adjacent bar, and a 1,600-bottle wine cellar (with an emphasis on California wines). The restaurant backs up its dramatic setting with generous portions of steaks, seafood, and other fare, ranging from tuna steak to Australian tenderloin, all prepared in an open kitchen with counter seating for close-up views of the action. Both the set lunch and the weekend and holiday brunches are among the city's best and most sumptuous—and are great options for those who don't want to pawn their belongings to eat dinner here. I wouldn't miss it.

Park Hyatt Tokyo, 3–7–1–2 Nishi-Shinjuku. www.tokyo.park.hyatt.com. © **03/5323-3458.** Reservations required. Main dishes ¥4,400–¥13,000; set lunches ¥5,200; set dinners ¥11,000–¥21,000; Sat–Sun and holiday brunch ¥6,600. AE, DC, MC, V. Daily 11:30am–2:30pm and 5:30–10:30pm. Station: Shinjuku (west exit, 13-min. walk or 5-min. free shuttle ride), Hatsudai on the Keio Line (7 min.), or Tochomae on the Oedo Line (8 min.).

EXPENSIVE

In addition to the listing here, there's a branch of the famous tempura restaurant **Ten-ichi** (p. 120) on the seventh floor of Isetan department store, 3–14–1 Shinjuku (© **03/5379-3039**).

Kakiden (柿伝) ★★ KAISEKI   Although it's located on the eighth floor of a rather uninspiring building, Kakiden has a relaxing teahouse atmosphere, with low chairs, shoji screens, bamboo trees, and soothing traditional Japanese music playing softly in the background. Sibling restaurant to one in Kyoto founded more than 270 years ago as a catering service for practitioners of the tea ceremony, this kaiseki restaurant serves set meals that change with the seasons, according to what's fresh and available. An English-language menu lists the set meals, but it's probably best to simply pick a meal to fit your budget. The set lunch is available until 3pm. Set dinners include box kaiseki starting at ¥5,250, mini-kaiseki for ¥8,400, and kaiseki courses starting at ¥8,400. Some of the more common dishes here include fish, seasonal vegetables, sashimi, shrimp, and mushrooms, but don't worry if you can't identify everything—I've found that even the Japanese don't always know what they're eating.

Yasuo Building 8F, 3–37–11 Shinjuku, 8th floor. www.kakiden.com. **03/3352-5121.** Reservations recommended for lunch. Set dinners ¥5,250–¥21,000; set lunches ¥4,200–¥6,300. AE, DC, MC, V. Daily 11am–9pm (last order). Station: Shinjuku (east exit, 1 min.). Next to Shinjuku Station's east side.

MODERATE

In addition to the suggestions here, **Kushinobo** (p. 140) is a kushikatsu restaurant at 1–10–5 Kabuki-cho (**03/3232-9744).**

Ban-Thai (バンタイ) THAI   One of Tokyo's longest-running Thai restaurants and credited with introducing authentic Thai food to the Japanese, Ban-Thai prepares excellent Thai fare, with 90 mouthwatering items on the menu. My favorites are the cold and spicy meat salad, the chicken soup with coconut and lemongrass, the deep-fried flatfish with sweet and spicy topping, and the pad Thai. Note that set dinners are available only for parties of two or more; also, portions are not large, so if you order several portions and add beer, your tab can really climb. Finally, the service is indifferent. Yet this place is packed every time I come here.

1–23–14 Kabuki-cho, 3rd floor. **03/3207-0068.** Reservations recommended. Main dishes ¥1,200–¥1,800; set dinners ¥3,000–¥6,000; set lunches ¥683–¥1,365 (Mon–Fri only). AE, DC, MC, V. Mon–Fri 11:30am–3pm and 5–11:30pm; Sat–Sun and holidays 11:30am–11:45pm. Station: Shinjuku (east exit, 7 min.). In East Shinjuku, in the seediest part of Kabuki-cho (don't worry, the interior is nicer than the exterior). From Yasukuni Dori, take the pedestrian street beside 7-Eleven with a red neon archway and walk north toward Koma Stadium (a Kabuki-cho landmark); it's on the left side, above St. James Bar.

daidaiya ★★ 🎎 VARIED JAPANESE/NOUVELLE JAPANESE   daidaiya's dark, theatrical entrance is the first clue that this is not your ordinary Japanese restaurant. Its dining room, a juxtaposition of contemporary and traditional decor, is rather like the cuisine—a curious mix of traditional Japanese food and original nouvelle creations, all mouthwateringly good. An English-language seasonal menu lists such intriguing starters as grilled bamboo shoots with a miso-mayonnaise sauce and sesame tofu béchamel sauce mixed with lotus root and soy bean curds. In addition to fresh fish of the day, you'll find the likes of grilled salmon marinated with saikyou miso and grilled Kirishima pork. Set lunches, available only weekends and holidays, lets you add a buffet of healthy desserts for ¥300. I love this place.

Nowa Building 3F, 3–37–12 Shinjuku. **03/5362-7173.** Reservations recommended for dinner. Main dishes ¥1,050–¥3,500; set dinners ¥4,500–¥8,000; set lunches ¥980–¥3,500 (Sat–Sun and holidays only). AE, DC, MC, V. Sat–Sun and holidays 11:30am–2pm; Mon–Thurs and Sat 5–11pm; Fri and holidays 5pm–midnight (last order). Station: Shinjuku (central east exit, 1 min.). Next to the JR station.

Hayashi (はやし) ★★ 🎎 ROBATAYAKI   This restaurant has been specializing in Japanese set meals cooked over your own hibachi grill for 35 years. It's small and cozy, with only five grills and a woman in a kimono overseeing the cooking operations, taking over if customers seem the least bit hesitant. The rustic interior was imported intact from the mountain region of Takayama. Four set meals are offered (vegetarian meals are available on request). My ¥5,250 meal came with sashimi, yakitori, tofu steak, scallops cooked in their shells, shrimp, and vegetables, all grilled one after the other. Watch your alcohol intake—drinks can really add to your bill.

Jojoen Daini Shinjuku Building, 2–22–5 Kabuki-cho. **03/3209-5672.** Reservations recommended. Set dinners ¥4,200–¥7,350. AE, DC, MC, V. Mon–Sat 5–11:30pm. Closed holidays. Station: Shinjuku (east exit, 10 min.). On the northern edge of Kabuki-cho; you'll know you're getting close when you see Godzilla hanging from a building; the restaurant is just a bit farther to the north, on a corner.

Tsunahachi (つな八) ★ TEMPURA Inside a small, old-fashioned brown building in the heart of fashionable East Shinjuku is the main branch of a restaurant that has been serving tempura since 1923. Now there are several dozen outlets in Japan, including one on the 13th floor of Takashimaya Shinjuku (✆ **03/5361-1860**). The Shinjuku location is the largest outlet, with an open kitchen and counter plus table seating. Though it has an English menu, the easiest option is to order one of three set meals, the least expensive of which includes six pieces of tempura, including deep-fried shrimp, conger eel, seasonal fish, shrimp balls, and vegetables, along with miso soup, Japanese pickles, and rice.

3–31–8 Shinjuku. www.tsunahachi.co.jp. ✆ **03/3352-1012.** Reservations recommended. Tempura a la carte ¥470–¥1,200; tempura set meals ¥1,995–¥3,990; set lunches from ¥1,260. AE, DC, V. Daily 11am–10pm. Station: Shinjuku Sanchome (2 min.) or Shinjuku (east exit, 5 min.). Off Shinjuku Dori on the side street that runs along the east side of Mitsukoshi department store.

INEXPENSIVE

Donto, on the 49th floor of the Sumitomo Building (✆ **03/3344-6269**), offers a Japanese lunch buffet and set meals for dinner (p. 120), while **Kohmen,** 1–17–5 Shinjuku (✆ **03/5292-6922**), serves tasty and cheap ramen (p. 142).

Hakkaku (八角) ★ 🍴 VARIED JAPANESE/ROBATAYAKI This lively, crowded establishment has a lot going for it: a corner location in a skyscraper with expansive views over Yoyogi Park, inexpensive dishes and meals on an English-language menu, and Kirin beer on tap. Its decor and food resemble those of an *izakaya* (Japanese-style bar). During lunch, only set meals are available; choose from the likes of grilled fish, fried chicken, tempura, or from the display case. Dinner offers a wider range of possibilities, including sashimi, grilled fish, fried noodles, and salads. Yakitori, beginning at ¥399 per two skewers, includes asparagus wrapped in bacon and *tsukune* (chicken meatballs), two of my favorites. There's also a robatayaki counter, where you can point at various dishes, watch them be prepared on the open grill, and then receive them from a wooden paddle passed in your direction.

N. S. Building, 29th floor (be sure to take the dedicated SKY RESTAURANT elevator), 2–4–1 Nishi-Shinjuku. ✆ **03/3345-1848.** Main dishes ¥700–¥1,869; set lunches ¥780–¥900. AE, DC, MC, V. Mon–Fri 11am–2:30pm; Sat–Sun and holidays 11am–2pm; Mon–Sat 5–10pm; Sun and holidays 5–9pm (last order). Station: Tochomae (3 min.) or Shinjuku (west exit, 8 min.).

Tokyo Catering 🍴 VARIED JAPANESE This is probably the cheapest place in town for a meal with a view. Located on the 32nd floor in the north tower of the Tokyo Metropolitan Government Office (TMG), which offers a free observation room on its 45th floor, this cafeteria is for public employees but is open to everyone. Choose your meal—which can include pork cutlet, fried fish, sushi, tempura, curry rice, or noodles—from the cart laden with displays of daily set meals or the display case, where every item is identified by a number. You then purchase your selections from a vending machine and take your tickets to the cafeteria window. My last set meal consisted of fish tempura, rice, soup and salad. The cafeteria lacks charm, but if you can get a table by the window, you'll have a good view of Tokyo. On the same floor is also a cafe, open Monday to Friday from 10am to 5pm for drinks and dessert.

TMG, 32nd floor of North Tower (take the office elevator, not the elevator to the observatory), 2–8–1 Nishi-Shinjukuku. ✆ **03/5320-7510.** Set meals ¥580–¥660. No credit cards. Mon–Fri 11:30am–2pm. Closed holidays. Station: Tochomae (1 min.), Shinjuku (10 min.), or Nishi-Shinjuku (5 min.).

Harajuku & Aoyama

EXPENSIVE

Casita ★★★ 💼 FUSION   One of the reasons I'm a great fan of Casita is that I feel truly pampered here. Who wouldn't, with a staff that proffers flashlights to the aged among us who have difficulty reading menus in dim lighting, stands ready to carry out every whim, and, on chilly nights, tucks us under electric blankets so that we can enjoy after-dinner drinks on the deck before we head over to the massage chairs? Casita aims to please, carving its own niche in Tokyo's fiercely competitive market by creating a tropical, resortlike atmosphere, bolstered by great service and a year-round outdoor deck that's heated in winter and covered when it rains. Of course, none of that matters if the food falls short, but Casita turns out seasonal dishes that border on awesome, whether it's the Caesar salad with serious shavings of Parmesan or the grilled Japanese beef sirloin with seasonal vegetables in a wasabi-flavored red wine sauce. Who wouldn't be a fan?

La Porte Aoyama, 5th floor, 5–51–8 Jingumae. www.casita.jp. ℂ **03/5485-7353.** Reservations required. Main dishes ¥3,200–¥5,800; set dinners ¥8,400–¥13,600. AE, DC, MC, V. Daily 5–11pm (last order). Station: Omotesando (3 min.). Head toward Shibuya on Aoyama Dori; it will be on your right, buried in an unlikely looking building past Kinokuniya and the stoplight.

Shiro (しろう) ★★ 💼 KAISEKI   You know you're in for a treat when you spot this traditional two-story Japanese house tucked away on a side street. Decorated with Japanese antiques and offering counter and table seating, it serves elaborate seasonal kaiseki, along with seasonal dinner courses like shabu-shabu in spring and summer and *fugu* (blowfish) courses in winter. Surprisingly, you don't have to empty your bank account to dine here for lunch, when an English-language menu with photos shows set lunches featuring tempura, sashimi and more.

3–5–1 Jingumae. ℂ **03/5414-2311.** Reservations recommended. Set dinners ¥10,000–¥25,000; set lunches ¥1,800–¥2,800. AE, DC, MC, V. Mon–Sat 11am–3pm and 6–11pm. Station: Omotesando (exit A2, 5 min.). Head toward Harajuku on Omotesando Dori and take the first right (there's an archway with FITNESS CLUB GOLD'S GYM above the street); take the 1st left, and then an immediate right. After about 3 blocks you'll see it on the left.

Two Rooms Grill/Bar ★★ CONTINENTAL   There's been lots of buzz about this striking restaurant/bar combo with its dramatic, open setting; contemporary design featuring glass, steel and wood (the restaurant prides itself in using 50,000-year-old swamp kauri timber from New Zealand); and a who's who roster of well-moneyed regulars. Wagyu beef is the obvious king of the menu, but there are also other temptations, like rare blue fin tuna with burnt okra and white celery in a blue honey miso, or duck breast and confit with artichokes and truffle Dijon. Still, what really sets this venue apart in my mind is its bar, reached via an open-air walkway over an infinity pool and with an outdoor terrace affording outstanding views of Tokyo's skyline, making this, quite possibly, the best place in town on a fine summer's night.

AO Building, 5th floor, 3–11–7 Kita-Aoyama. www.tworooms.jp. ℂ **03/3498-0002.** Reservations required. Main dishes ¥3,300–¥7,600; set dinners ¥7,500–¥9,500; set lunches ¥1,850–¥2,950. AE, DC, MC, V. Daily 11:30am–2:30pm; Mon–Sat 6–10pm; Sun 6–9pm (last order). Station: Omotesando (exit B2, 1 min.). It's on the right side of Aoyama Dori in the direction of Shibuya, in the striking, trapezoidal AO Building.

MODERATE

Maru (圓) ★ 💼 VARIED/NOUVELLE JAPANESE   Tucked away on a side street, this small gem offers an English menu of intriguing seasonal choices, from traditional dishes like noodles topped with nameko mushrooms to those with added ingredients that give them a contemporary twist. You might want to start, for example, with simmered vegetables in a Japanese version of Ratatouille, or wild duck cooked in soy sauce and sake. Although the menu changes often, main choices may include the likes of free-range chicken with salt and yuzu pepper, beef preserved in Kyoto miso, or simmered pork belly and eggplant topped with sweet white miso. Don't miss the *donabe*, the restaurant's signature rice simmered in a clay pot and served with a choice of toppings. There's also a good selection of wines, sake, and shochu (there's even *awamori*, an Okinawan shochu made of Thai rice). The young staff is friendly, and you'll dine either at the long counter overlooking the open kitchen or at one of the couple wooden tables (the restaurant is smoke-free).

5–50–8 Jingumae. www.maru-mayfont.jp. ☎ **03/6418-5572.** Reservations recommended. Main dishes ¥1,000–¥2,500. AE, DC, MC, V. Mon–Sat 6pm–1am; Sun and holidays 6pm–midnight. Station: Omotesando (3 min.). Walk toward Shibuya on Aoyama Dori and turn right at Muji; it's on the right, in a basement.

Yasaiya Mei (やさい家めい) ★ VARIED JAPANESE/VEGETARIAN   If you like veggies, this restaurant specializing in fresh, seasonal vegetables is a must. For starters you might choose the green papaya kimchi or the Mei Special bagna cauda, which comes with a variety of veggies—such as eggplant, radish and asparagus—plus a dipping sauce. Not to be missed is the wild plant tempura, which changes with the seasons; spring might feature young bamboo shoots, while autumn may include eggplant and water chestnuts. Although the emphasis here is clearly on things that grow in the ground, a few meat dishes are also available, such as grilled pork with mashed potatoes. Set lunches feature a vegetable curry or fish, along with an obento served in a charming box with drawers. Seating is either at the U-shaped open kitchen or a table (try to snag one beside the large windows overlooking the trees of Omotesando Dori). There's a branch in Roppongi Hills, on the fifth floor of Mori Tower, in an area called West Walk (☎ **03/5775-2960;** station: Roppongi).

Omotesando Hills, 3rd floor, 4–12–10 Jingumae. ☎ **03/5785-0606.** Reservations required. Main dishes ¥1,000–¥1,800; set dinners ¥3,500–¥5,800; set lunches ¥1,380–¥1,980. AE, DC, MC, V. Mon–Sat 11am–11pm; Sun 11am–10pm (last order). Station: Meiji-Jingumae or Omotesando (4 min). On Omotesando Dori.

INEXPENSIVE

In addition to the choices below, consider **La Boheme** (p. 123) serving pizza and pasta, with locations at 7–11–4 Minami Aoyama (☎ 03/3499-3377), 6–2–2 Minami Aoyama (☎ 03/6418-4242), 3–6–25 Kita-Aoyama (☎ 03/5766-1666), and on Omotesando Dori at 5–8–5 Jingumae (☎ 03/5467-5666). **Kohmen** (p. 142), 6–2–8 Jingumae (☎ 03/5468-6344), serves tasty ramen and *gyoza*.

Fonda de la Madrugada MEXICAN   Serving what is probably Tokyo's most authentic Mexican food, this dark basement restaurant has a cavernous main dining room, several small and cozy offshoots, and a strolling mariachi band, making it seem like you're dining in a Mexican villa. Shrimp marinated in tequila, chicken mole, and soft-tortilla tacos served with chicken, fish, beef, or pork are just some of the items on the trilingual (Japanese/Spanish/English-language) menu, along with the requisite Mexican beers, tequila shots and shooters, margaritas, rum and vodka cocktails, and wine from Mexico, Chile, and Argentina.

2–33–12 Jingumae. ☎ **03/5410-6288.** Reservations required. Main dishes ¥1,050–¥3,045. AE, DC, MC, V. Sun–Thurs 5:30pm–2am; Fri–Sat 5:30pm–5am. Station: Meiji-Jingumae (10 min.). From the

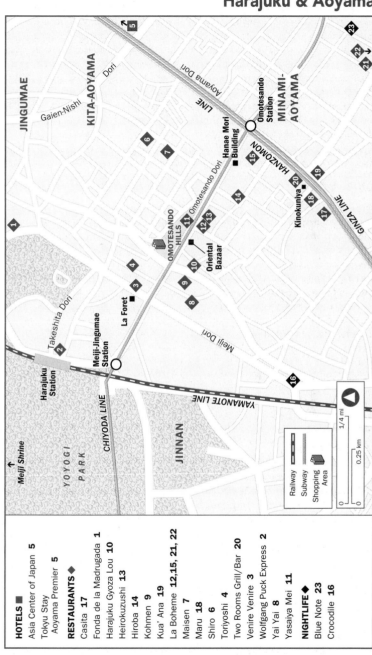

4

Meiji Dori/Omotesando intersection, walk north on Meiji Dori (toward Shinjuku); it will be on your right after the pedestrian overpass.

Harajuku Gyoza Lou (原宿餃子樓) ★ GYOZA   If you like *gyoza* (pork dumplings), you owe yourself a meal here. Unlike most greasy spoons that specialize in fast-food Chinese (and tend to be on the dingy side), this restaurant in the heart of Harajuku is hip yet unpretentious and draws a young crowd with its straightforward menu posted on the wall (an English-language menu is also available). Only four types of gyoza are offered: steamed *(sui-gyoza)* or fried *(yaki-gyoza),* and with or without garlic *(ninniku).* A few side dishes, such as cucumber, boiled cabbage with vinegar, sprouts with a spicy meat sauce, and rice, are available, as are beer and sake. A U-shaped counter encloses the open kitchen, which diners can watch as they chow down on the very good gyoza.

6–2–4 Jingumae. ℂ **03/3406-4743.** Gyoza ¥290 for a plate of 6. No credit cards. Mon–Sat 11:30am–4:30am; Sun and holidays 11:30am–10:30pm (last order). Station: Meiji-Jingumae (3 min.) or Harajuku (5 min.). From the Meiji/Omotesando Dori intersection, walk on Omotesando Dori toward Aoyama and take the 3rd right just before Kiddy Land; it's at the end of this alley, on the right.

Heirokuzushi (平禄寿司) SUSHI   Bright (a bit too bright), clean, and modern, this is one of those fast-food sushi bars where plates of food are conducted along a conveyor belt on the counter. Customers help themselves to whatever strikes their fancy. To figure your bill, the cashier counts the number of plates you took from the conveyor belt: Green plates cost ¥130, for example, blue ones ¥160, and so on. You can also order takeout; you might want to eat in nearby Yoyogi Park.

5–8–5 Jingumae. ℂ **03/3498-3968.** Plates of sushi ¥130–¥480. No credit cards. Daily 11am–9pm. Station: Meiji-Jingumae (2 min.) or Omotesando (5 min.). On Omotesando Dori close to Oriental Bazaar.

Hiroba VARIED JAPANESE/VEGETARIAN   Located in the basement of the Crayon House, which specializes in Japanese children's books, this natural-food restaurant offers buffet lunches and dinners of organic veggies, fish, brown rice, and other health foods. The dining hall, next to an organic food store, is very simple (its atmosphere reminds me of a potluck supper in a church basement), and because of the upstairs bookstore, there are likely to be families here.

Crayon House, 3–8–15 Kita-Aoyama. ℂ **03/3406-6409.** Dinner buffet ¥2,000; lunch buffet ¥1,260. No credit cards. Daily 11am–2pm and 5:30–10pm. Station: Omotesando (2 min.). From the Omotesando/Aoyama Dori intersection, walk on Omotesando Dori toward Harajuku and take the first left.

Kua' Aina ☺ AMERICAN   How far will you go for a burger? Quite simply, one of the most popular burger chains in town makes this Hawaiian import a smashing success. In fact, if you come at mealtime, you'll probably have to wait for a table in one of the tiny upstairs dining rooms. Burgers come as third- and (whopping) half-pounders. There are also sandwiches ranging from BLTs with avocado to roast beef to tuna. A good carnivore fix.

Branches can be found at 1–10–4 Shibuya (ℂ **03/3409-3200;** station: Shibuya); in the Marunouchi Building across from Tokyo Station at 2–4–1 Marunouchi (ℂ **03/5220-2400;** station: Tokyo); and in Aqua City on Odaiba (ℂ **03/3599-2800;** station: Daiba).

5–10–21 Minami Aoyama. ℂ **03/3407-8001.** Burgers and sandwiches ¥750–¥1,330. No credit cards. Daily 11am–10pm. Station: Omotesando (2 min.). On Aoyama Dori (heading toward Shibuya), at its busy intersection with Kotto Dori.

Maisen (まい泉) ★ 🍴 TONKATSU   Extremely popular with the locals, this restaurant has been dishing out *tonkatsu* (deep-fried breaded pork cutlet) for more than

25 years and is especially known for its black pork, originally from China and prized for its sweet, intense flavor. But what makes this restaurant a real standout is that it occupies a former pre–World War II public bathhouse; its main dining hall, once the changing room, sports a high ceiling and original architectural details. There's an English-language menu, but lunch specials (available until 4pm) are listed in Japanese only, though there are photos. It's easiest to order a set meal.

4–8–5 Jingumae. ℂ **03/3470-0071.** Set meals ¥1,420–¥2,995; set lunches ¥840–¥1,420. AE, DC, MC, V. Daily 11am–10pm (last order). Station: Omotesando A2 exit, (4 min.). Heading toward Harajuku on Omotesando Dori, take the first right (there's an archway here with FITNESS CLUB GOLD'S GYM written on it), then the 1st left and an immediate right. It will be in the next block on the left.

Toriyoshi (鳥良) VARIED JAPANESE/INTERNATIONAL This hip, upscale bar is a popular dining spot as well, especially for its chicken specialties such as fried chicken wings and half a fried chicken. The huge English-language menu, complete with photos, lists a variety of Japanese and Asian pub fare as well, including salads, yakitori, tofu (I love the black sesame tofu, called *kuroi gomadofu*), kimchi, and more. A good place for a convivial evening.

4–28–21 Jingumae. www.samukawa.co.jp/toriyoshi/en/. ℂ **03/3470-3901.** Main dishes ¥480–¥700. AE, DC, MC, V. Mon–Fri 5–11pm; Sat–Sun 4–11pm (last order). Station: Meiji-Jingumae (3 min.). From the Meiji Dori/Omotesando intersection, walk on Omotesando Dori toward Aoyama and take the 1st left (there's a Wendy's here); Toriyoshi is down this street, on the right side, beside a willow tree.

Venire Venire ITALIAN You'll have to see for yourself how inexpensive doesn't necessarily mean drab. This tall-ceilinged trattoria is light and airy, with a large outdoor terrace (open from Golden Week to October) affording sweeping views over the surrounding rooftops. It offers mostly pizzas and pastas, such as fettuccini with scampi or pizza topped with prosciutto ham and mozzarella cheese, as well as a handful of main dishes like grilled chicken or pork with rosemary. Lunch gives a choice of pizza, pasta, or a main dish such as fish, along with a trip through the appetizer and salad bar. There's a large selection of Italian wines.

Y.M. Square, 5th floor; 4–31–10 Jingumae. ℂ **03/5775-5333.** Pizza and pasta ¥1,300–¥2,200; main dishes ¥1,400–¥3,000; set lunch ¥1,680. AE, DC, MC, V. Mon–Fri 11:30am–3pm and 5–11pm; Sat–Sun and holidays 11:30am–3:30pm and 5–10:30pm. Station: Harajuku (1 min.). On Meiji Dori, just north of Gap and across from La Foret.

Wolfgang Puck Express AMERICAN This is the most casual and least expensive of Puck's invasion of eateries in Japan. It concentrates on burgers, pizza, pasta, roast chicken, salads, and other fast foods. What I like about this location is that it's easy to find, right at the top of Takeshita Dori (Harajuku's most popular shopping street) across from the station, and it's more stylish than other fast-food competitors that shall remain nameless. Fast service, pop music, and beer—what more could you ask for?

1–17–1 Jingumae. ℂ **03/5786-4690.** Main dishes ¥980–¥1,480; set lunches ¥880–¥1,480. AE, DC, MC, V. Daily 11am–11pm. Station: Harajuku (1 min.). Across the street from Harajuku Station's north exit, at the top of Takeshita Dori.

Yai Yai (やいやい) OKONOMIYAKI Instead of having to cook your own okonomiyaki, all you have to do here is order, whereupon the young staff sets to work cooking your meal on a griddle in front of you. You choose your toppings—such as pork and leek, seafood mix, and kimchi—which are then added to the pancakelike base, cabbage, and egg. Fried noodles and negi-yaki (flat dough with leeks, also cooked with a choice of toppings) are also available.

6–8–7 Jingumae. ☏ **03/3406-8181.** Okonomiyaki or fried noodles ¥924–¥1,564. AE, DC, MC, V. Mon–Fri 5pm–3am; Sat–Sun and holidays noon–11pm. Station: Meiji-Jingumae (3 min.) or Harajuku (7 min.). From the Meiji Dori/Omotesando intersection, walk on Omotesando Dori toward Aoyama and take the 2nd right; it will be on the left.

Roppongi

Because Roppongi is such a popular nighttime hangout for young Tokyoites and foreigners, it boasts a large number of both Japanese and Western restaurants. To find the location of any of the Roppongi addresses below, stop by the tiny police station on Roppongi Crossing (Roppongi's main intersection of Roppongi Dori and Gaien-Higashi Dori), where you'll find a map of the area. If you still don't know where to go, ask one of the policemen. Opposite the police station, on the other side of the overhead expressway, is the number-one meeting spot in Roppongi, in front of Almond coffee shop with its pink sign and façade. If you are asked to meet someone in Roppongi, this will likely be the spot.

About a 10-minute walk west of Roppongi (via Roppongi Dori in the direction of Shibuya) is **Nishi Azabu** with more restaurants and bars. Between Roppongi Crossing and Nishi Azabu is **Roppongi Hills,** a sprawling urban development with many choices in dining. **Tokyo Midtown,** Tokyo's newest urban development, also offers dining.

VERY EXPENSIVE

Inakaya (田舎屋) ★★ ROBATAYAKI   Whenever I host first-time foreign visitors in Tokyo, I take them to this festive restaurant, and they've never been disappointed. Although tourist-oriented and overpriced, it's still great fun; the drama of the place alone is worth it. Customers sit at a long, U-shaped counter, on the other side of which are mountains of fresh vegetables, beef, and seafood. And in the middle of all that food, seated in front of a grill, are male chefs—ready to cook whatever you point to in the style of robatayaki. Orders are yelled out by your waiter and are repeated in unison by all the other waiters, resulting in ongoing, excited yelling. Sounds strange, I know, but actually it's a lot of fun. Food offerings may include yellowtail, red snapper, sole, scallops, king crab legs, giant shrimp, steak, meatballs, gingko nuts, potatoes, eggplant, and asparagus, all piled high in wicker baskets and ready for the grill. Although prices for individual dishes may not seem high, they quickly add up. Most meals here average around ¥15,000, including a ¥800 per person table charge.

Other branches are at 5–3–4 Roppongi (☏ **03/3408-5040;** station: Roppongi) and at 8–7–4 Ginza (☏ **03/3569-1708;** station: Ginza), both open daily 5 to 11pm, but only the one detailed here has an English-language menu.

4–10–11 Roppongi. www.roppongiinakaya.jp. ☏ **03/5775-1012.** Grilled vegetables ¥650–¥900; grilled seafood and meats ¥1,050–¥5,100. AE, DC, MC, V. Daily 5–10:30pm (last order). Station: Roppongi (2 min.). Off Gaien-Higashi Dori on a side street opposite Ibis Hotel; from Roppongi Crossing, walk on Gaien-Higashi Dori in the direction of Midtown and take the 2nd right.

EXPENSIVE

Fukuzushi (福鮨) ★★ SUSHI   This is one of Tokyo's classiest sushi bars, attracting a cosmopolitan crowd. Although it has a traditional entrance through a small courtyard with lighted lanterns and the sound of trickling water, the interior is slick and modern with bold colors of black and red. Some people swear it has the best sushi in Tokyo, although with 7,000 sushi bars in the city, I'd be hard-pressed to say which one is tops. Certainly, you can't go wrong here. Three different set lunches are available, featuring sushi, *chirashi-zushi* (assorted sashimi with rice), or eel as the

Roppongi

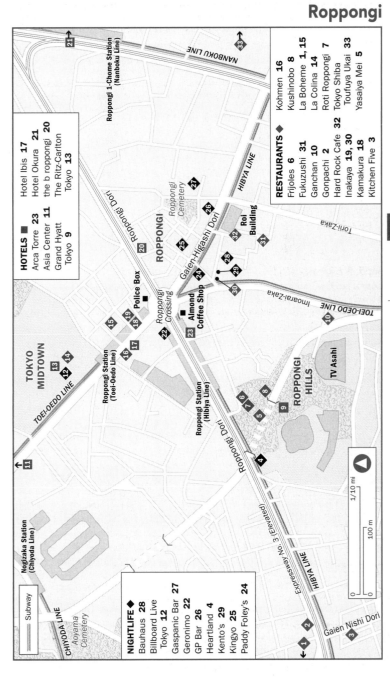

HOTELS ■
Arca Torre **23**
Asia Center **11**
Grand Hyatt Tokyo **9**
Hotel Ibis **17**
Hotel Okura **21**
the b roppongi **20**
The Ritz-Carlton Tokyo **13**

RESTAURANTS ◆
Frijoles **6**
Fukuzushi **31**
Ganchan **10**
Gonpachi **2**
Hard Rock Cafe **32**
Inakaya **19, 30**
Kamakura **18**
Kitchen Five **3**
Kohmen **16**
Kushinobo **8**
La Boheme **1, 15**
La Colina **14**
Roti Roppongi **7**
Tokyo Shiba Toufuya Ukai **33**
Yasaiya Mei **5**

NIGHTLIFE ◆
Bauhaus **28**
Billboard Live Tokyo **12**
Gaspanic Bar **27**
Geronimo **22**
GP Bar **26**
Heartland **4**
Kento's **29**
Kingyo **25**
Paddy Foley's **24**

main course. Dinners are more extensive, with the ¥8,400 set course consisting of salad, sashimi, steamed egg custard, grilled fish, sushi, miso soup, dessert, and coffee (set dinners require orders by a minimum of two people).

5–7–8 Roppongi. www.roppongifukuzushi.com. ☏ **03/3402-4116.** Reservations recommended, especially for dinner. Set dinners ¥6,300–¥8,400; set lunches ¥2,625–¥4,725. AE, DC, MC, V. Mon–Sat 11:30am–1:30pm and 5:30–10pm (last order); holidays 5:30–9pm. Closed 1 week in mid-Aug. Station: Roppongi (4 min.). From Roppongi Crossing, walk toward Tokyo Tower on Gaien-Higashi Dori, turning right at McDonald's, left in front of Hard Rock Cafe, and then right.

Tokyo Shiba Toufuya Ukai ★★★ 🏠 TOFU   It's hard to imagine you're in Tokyo when you enter the lush grounds of this exquisite restaurant. Indeed, though it's located at the foot of Tokyo Tower (about a 15-min. walk from Roppongi), it's a world apart from the bustling city, with a landscaped garden complete with ponds (and three fulltime gardeners) and traditional Japanese structures that include a main building constructed with heavy beams and foot-thick lacquered pillars imported from a 200-year-old Takayama farmhouse. Yet despite its aristocratic atmosphere, this restaurant specializes in classic tofu cuisine, with set meals that change with the seasons and are described on an English-language menu. The least expensive set lunch, for example, may start with an egg custard, deep-fried tofu with sweet miso sauce, and assorted sashimi, followed by deep-fried simmered tofu, tofu seasoned in soy milk, rice, and sweet red-bean soup with rice cake.

4–4–13 Shibakoen. www.ukai.co.jp. ☏ **03/3436-1028.** Reservations required. Set dinners ¥8,400–¥12,600; set lunches ¥5,500–¥6,500. Prices exclude tax. AE, DC, MC, V. Daily 11am–10pm (last order 8pm). Station: Akabanebashi (5 min.). Behind Tokyo Tower's main entrance, to the left.

MODERATE

Yasaiya Mei (p. 134) specializes in fresh vegetables and is located in Roppongi Hills on the fifth floor of Mori Tower in an area called West Walk (☏ **03/5775-2960**).

Kushinobo KUSHIKATSU   First opened in Osaka in 1950, this small and cozy restaurant specializing in *kushikatsu* (deep-fried skewers of food) is ensconced in Roppongi Hills. Every day it prepares more than 30 different kinds of meat, seafood, and vegetable kushikatsu, drawn from more than 100 in-house recipes. If you order the Omakase set meal ("chef's choice," available all day), you'll be served a progression of skewers one at a time until you say stop (if you like one especially well, you can ask for it again), along with the restaurant's own special tartar sauce, miso sauce, sweet-and-sour sauce, and other sauces for dipping. Most people average about 16 skewers, which cost about ¥4,500, including a side dish and dessert. By the way, this is the first restaurant I've seen that charges a 10% "night charge," levied to those entering after 10pm or departing after 11pm. Still, I really like kushikatsu and wish there were more restaurants serving it in Tokyo. There's also a Kushinobo in Shinjuku, at 1–10–5 Kabuki-cho (☏ **03/3232-9744**; station: Shinjuku).

Roppongi Hills, 5th floor of West Walk, 6–10–1 Roppongi. www.kushinobo.jp. ☏ **03/5771-0094.** Set dinners ¥2,940–¥4,620; set lunches ¥1,575–¥3,150. AE, DC, MC, V. Daily 11am–10:30pm (last order). Closed holidays. Station: Roppongi (Roppongi Hills exit, 2 min.) or Azabu Juban (5 min.).

La Colina MEXICAN   A marked contrast to its sister restaurant Fonda de la Madrugada in Harajuku (p. 134), this stylish restaurant with its modern decor, strolling musicians, and wonderful outdoor terrace offers a limited menu of traditional and creative dishes, including tacos, sautéed shrimp with garlic, guaillo chili and roasted tomatoes, and grilled chicken with mole. If it's a weekend or holiday, when Tokyo Midtown buzzes with shoppers and sightseers, you might be able to secure a seat here without a reservation simply because Mexican food remains unknown to many Japanese.

Tokyo Midtown, Garden Terrace (shop D-0118), 1st floor, 9–7–4 Akasaka. ℂ **03/5413-0092.** Reservations strongly recommended. Main dishes ¥1,600–¥2,600; set lunches ¥1,200–¥1,800. AE, DC, MC, V. Daily 11am–3pm and 5–11pm. Station: Roppongi (Oedo exit, 2 min.). From Roppongi Crossing, walk on Gaien-Higashi Dori to Midtown, and then head to Garden Terrace.

INEXPENSIVE

In addition to the recommendations below, **La Boheme** (p. 123), 2–25–18 Nishi Azabu (ℂ **03/3407-1363**) and 4–11–13 Roppongi (ℂ **03/3478-0222**), serves pizza and pasta.

Frijoles ★ MEXICAN   Next to Roti (below), this casual eatery serves only a few dishes—burritos, tacos, and salads—but it does it extremely well, making this a very popular choice for lunch and takeout. Head to the counter and choose your medium (taco, burrito or salad), your meat (chicken, steak, or seasoned pork; vegetarian also available), toppings (black beans, pinto beans, cheese, etc.), and salsa (from mild to fiery hot), and then head to the small dining counter or one of the outdoor tables. Most of the food is prepared on-site, and it shows.

6–6–9 Roppongi. www.frijoles.jp. ℂ **03/6447-1433.** Main dishes ¥850–¥1,000. AE, DC, MC, V. Daily 11am–10pm. Closed 2nd Sun of every month. Station: Roppongi (A1 exit, 1 min.). On a side street that parallels Roppongi Dori, a stone's throw from Roppongi Hills.

Ganchan (がんちゃん) ★ ▮YAKITORI   This is one of my favorite yakitori-ya. Small and intimate, with seating along a single counter with room for only a dozen or so people, it has a young and fun-loving staff. Though there's an English-language menu, it's easiest to order the yakitori seto, a delicious set course that comes with salad and soup and eight skewers of such items as chicken, beef, meatballs, green peppers, and asparagus rolled with bacon. There's a table charge of ¥600 per person, but it includes an appetizer.

6–8–23 Roppongi. ℂ **03/3478-0092.** Yakitori skewers ¥315–¥735; yakitori set course ¥2,625. AE, MC, V. Daily 5pm–1:30am. Station: Roppongi (7 min.). From Roppongi Crossing, take the small street going downhill to the left of the Almond coffee shop; Ganchan is at the bottom of the hill on the right.

Gonpachi ★★ VARIED JAPANESE/YAKITORI   Housed in a re-created *kura* (traditional Japanese warehouse) with a high ceiling, three-tiered seating, and a central, open kitchen, this is one of Tokyo's most imaginative inexpensive Japanese restaurants (it's said to have served as the inspiration for the animated restaurant scene in the movie *Kill Bill*). It offers a wide variety of dishes, including yakitori (such as duck breast with wasabi), fish (such as miso-glazed black cod), sushi (on the third floor), noodles, and more. From the outside, you'd expect this place to be much more exclusive than it is—and you probably will be excluded if you fail to make reservations for dinner.

There are branches of Gonpachi at the G-Zone, 1–2–3 Ginza (ℂ **03/5524-3641;** station: Kyobashi or Ginza-Itchome); in Shibuya on the 14th floor of E-Space Tower, 3–6 Maruyama-cho (ℂ **03/5784-2011;** station: Shibuya); and at Mediage on Odaiba (ℂ **03/3599-4807;** station: Daiba), all open from 11:30am to 3:30am or later. However, they don't match the Nishi Azabu location's atmosphere.

1–13–11 Nishi Azabu. www.gonpachi.jp. ℂ **03/5771-0170.** Reservations recommended for dinner. Yakitori ¥300–¥1,500; main dishes ¥1,200–¥3,200; set dinners ¥4,500–¥6,000; set lunches ¥1,000–¥3,000. AE, DC, MC, V. Daily 11:30am–3:30am. Station: Roppongi (12 min.). From Roppongi Crossing, walk toward Shibuya on Roppongi Dori. It will be on your right, at the corner of Gaien-Nishi Dori.

Hard Rock Cafe ☺ AMERICAN   Founded by two American expatriates in London in 1971, Hard Rock Cafe has more than half a dozen locations in Japan; this was the first. If you have disgruntled teenagers in tow, bring them to this world-famous hamburger joint dedicated to rock 'n' roll to ogle the memorabilia on the walls, chow down on burgers, and check out the T-shirts for sale. In addition to hamburgers, the menu includes salads, sandwiches, steaks, barbecued ribs, barbecued chicken, fish of the day, fajitas, and a few Asian dishes. Be prepared: The music is loud.

A branch is located in JR Ueno Station at 7–1–1 Ueno (☏ **03/5826-5821;** station: Ueno).

5–4–20 Roppongi. www.hardrockjapan.com. ☏ **03/3408-7018.** Main dishes ¥1,480–¥3,780; set lunch ¥1,000. AE, DC, MC, V. Sun–Thurs 11:30am–2am; Fri–Sat 11:30am–4am. Station: Roppongi (3 min.). From Roppongi Crossing, walk on Gaien-Higashi Dori toward Tokyo Tower and take a right at McDonald's.

Kamakura ★ 🍢 YAKITORI   Much more refined than most yakitori-ya, this basement establishment is decorated with paper lanterns and sprigs of fake but cheerful spring blossoms, with traditional koto music playing softly in the background. The English-language menu lists skewers with chicken, shrimp, meatballs, gingko, squid, eggplant, mushrooms, and more, but I usually go with one of the set meals.

4–10–11 Roppongi. ☏ **03/3405-4377.** Yakitori skewers ¥240–¥550; set dinners ¥2,300–¥4,300. AE, DC, MC, V. Mon–Sat 5:30–11:30pm. Station: Roppongi (2 min.). From Roppongi Crossing, walk on the right side of Gaien-Higashi Dori in the direction of Tokyo Midtown and take the 2nd right.

Kitchen Five ★ 🍴 INTERNATIONAL   If it's true that love is the best spice for cooking, then perhaps that's why Yuko Kobayashi's 25-year-old, 18-seat restaurant is so popular. She goes to market every morning to fetch ingredients for a dozen main dishes, which may include stuffed eggplant, lasagna, moussaka, and other casseroles and curries that are spread on a counter along with their prices. Every year Kobayashi goes off to search for recipes in Sicily, South America, northern Africa, and other countries that feature garlic, tomatoes, and olive oil in their cuisine. The love for what she does shines in her eyes as she cooks, serves, and walks you through the menu of daily dishes displayed. ***Warning:*** The food is so delicious, it's tempting to over-order. Highly recommended.

4–2–15 Nishi Azabu. ☏ **03/3409-8835.** Dishes ¥1,300–¥1,900. No credit cards. Tues–Sat 6–9:30pm (last order). Closed holidays, Jan, Golden Week, and late July to early Sept. Station: Hiroo (10 min.) or Roppongi (13 min.). Opposite Gaien-Nishi Dori from the gas station, down a side street.

Kohmen (光麺) 🍜 RAMEN   Famished in the wee hours of the morning but spent most of your cash carousing? Head to this quirky ramen restaurant, where black-clad staff move around the dark interior like ninjas, fish swim in a birdcage, and personal-sized TVs at counters and tables broadcast Kohmen commercials, concerts, and movie previews. An English-language menu gives a good choice of various ramen noodles, from thick or thin to crispy, along with various broths and extra toppings ranging from grilled pork to fried leek. I'm crazy about the *kogashi-tantanmen*, a creamy sesame soup with noodles, hot chili and chargrilled marinated pork. There are branches across the city, including those at 6–2–8 Jingumae in Harajuku (☏ **03/5468-6344;** station: Harajuku); 1–9–5 Ebisu (☏ **03/5475-0185;** station: Ebisu); 4–8–8 Ueno (☏ **03/5807-4535;** station: Ueno); and 1–17–5 Kabuki-cho (☏ **03/5292-6922;** station: Shinjuku).

7–14–3 Roppongi. ☏ **03/6406-4565.** Ramen ¥730–¥1,080. No credit cards. Daily 11am–6am. Station: Roppongi (1 min.). From Roppongi Crossing, head away from Tokyo Tower on Gaien-Higashi Dori; it will be on the left, just past the Ibis Hotel.

Roti Roppongi ★ AMERICAN   A casual brasserie with both indoor (nonsmoking) and outdoor seating, Roti counts many expats among its loyal customers, due in part to its quiet, tucked-away location just a minute's walk from Roppongi Hills and also to its bilingual staff and modern American fare, which includes free-range rotisserie chicken, grilled steaks, a variety of burgers, serious Caesar salads, and many other delectable dishes too numerous to mention. More than 90 bottles of New World, Australian, and New Zealand wines, as well as American ales and Belgian microbrews, round out the menu.

6–6–9 Roppongi. www.roti.jp. (✆ **03/5785-3671.** Main dishes ¥1,600–¥2,800; set lunches (Mon–Fri only) ¥1,000–¥2,200. AE, DC, MC, V. Daily 11:30am–5pm and 6–11pm. Station: Roppongi (A1 exit, 1 min.). On a side street that parallels Roppongi Dori, a stone's throw from Roppongi Hills.

Shibuya

Good Honest Grub ★ 🎁AMERICAN/VEGETARIAN   The owner is Canadian and the food is a compilation of homegrown favorites expatriates—including the health conscious—are likely to crave: eggs Benedict, omelets, and French toast for the weekend brunch (with bottomless coffee refills), and sandwiches, wraps, and daily specials for lunch. Produce, from the restaurant's own organic garden at the foot of Mt. Fuji, is used in recipes and fresh juices. Located in a cute Lilliputian house, with seating on a small terrace and upstairs in a sunny, cozy room with hanging plants, it would be right at home at any North American college campus.

2–20–8 Higashi. (✆ **03/3797-9877.** Main dishes ¥700–¥1,700. No credit cards. Mon–Fri 11:30am–3pm; Sat–Sun and holidays 10:30am–4:30pm. Station: Shibuya or Ebisu (10 min.). Just off Meiji Dori midway btw. Ebisu and Shibuya stations, on a side street beside the Lawson 100 store.

Legato ★★ 🎁 ITALIAN/FUSION   Walk past the tear-shaped bar with its view over Shibuya (or stop for an aperitif), and then head downstairs to the theatrical setting of this elegant yet low-key restaurant. Dim lighting, an open kitchen, knowledgeable service, and reasonable prices make this a great choice for a splurge without spending a fortune. The menu blends ingredients from Italy and Asia, with starters that range from grilled tuna and avocado crispy tacos with salsa to caramelized foie gras with fig balsamic sauce. Main dishes offer pasta, fish, and meat choices, such as roasted cod with miso glazed grated radish sauce, and roasted New Zealand lamb with mustard sauce. Set lunches give a choice of main dish plus a buffet table of appetizers and desserts.

E-Space Tower, 15th floor, 3–6 Maruyama-cho. www.legato-tokyo.jp. (✆ **03/5784-2121.** Main dishes ¥1,600–¥4,200; set dinner ¥4,980; set lunches ¥1,200–¥2,200. AE, DC, MC, V. Mon–Fri 11:30am–2pm; daily 5:30–10:30pm (last order). Station: Shibuya (Hachiko, 8 min.). From the station, walk straight up Dogenzaka; it will be on the right, just past the koban police box.

Akasaka

Ninja ★ VARIED JAPANESE   At this themed restaurant, diners enter the secret world of the ninja as soon as they step inside the darkened entrance, where costumed waiters appear out of nowhere to lead the hungry through a labyrinth of twisting passageways to private dining nooks. A scroll unrolls to reveal an English-language menu listing various set dinner menus that may include shabu-shabu, as well as a la carte items such as salmon grilled with saikyo miso in rice porridge sauce, and roast lamb with Korean flavoring. On most nights a roaming ninja will come to your table to entertain with magic acts (tipping is at your own discretion). A fun place for a meal, but book early to reserve a seat.

Akasaka Tokyu Plaza, 1st floor, 2–14–3 Nagata-cho. (C) **03/5157-3936.** Reservations required. Main dishes ¥1,500–¥6,800; set dinners ¥5,000–¥20,000. AE, DC, MC, V. Mon–Sat 5pm–2am; Sun and holidays 5–11pm. Station: Akasaka-mitsuke (1 min.). In the candy cane–striped building, below the Akasaka Excel Tokyu Hotel.

Soba Giro NOODLES   This simple restaurant, with indoor tables partitioned by bamboo and outdoor seating, does a brisk lunchtime business but has also found a niche as an after-hours *izakaya* (Japanese pub), when it dims the lights, plays soft background jazz, and offers a large drink menu. The focus, however, is always on the food, with contemporary interpretations of soba, like soba in a basket with pork and vegetables and a curry dipping sauce, as well as more traditional dishes like soba with shrimp tempura. The evening menu adds yakitori, tempura (the avocado tempura, unfortunately, falls short), salads, and other popular bar food.

Prudential Plaza, 2–13–10 Nagata-cho. www.ystable.co.jp/restaurant/sobagiro/index.html. (C) **03/3500-5720.** Main dishes ¥700–¥1,480. AE, DC, MC, V. Mon–Fri 11am–2:30pm and 5–10pm; Sat–Sun 11am–10pm. Station: Akasaka-mitsuke (2 min.). On the east side of Sotobori Dori, to the back of a small square btw. 2 glass office buildings that contain Citibank and Prudential Financial.

Akihabara

Gundam Cafe ♨ VARIED JAPANESE   The gimmick at this tribute to the anime series with its robot characters is that dishes are decorated and named after specific characters, like the *Gunpla-yaki* (sweet-bean pastry in the shape of Gundam). The menu, however, is extremely limited (just a few pasta and rice dishes) and the food is ho-hum. I suggest coming instead just for dessert or a drink (alcoholic drinks are served from 5pm) so you can ogle the life-size Gundam character, admire the die-hard fans braving their meals, and, of course, purchase a souvenir.

1–1 Kanda-Hanaoka-cho. http://g-cafe. (C) **03/3251-0078.** Main dishes ¥590–¥890. AE, DC, MC, V. Mon–Fri 11am–11pm; Sat 8:30am–11pm; Sun and holidays 8:30am–9:30pm. Station: Akihabara (1 min.). Underneath the JR train tracks, across from UDX.

SHOPPING

It won't take you long to become convinced that shopping is the number-one pastime in Tokyo. Women, men, couples, and even entire families go on buying expeditions in their free time, making Sunday the most crowded shopping day of the week—though with today's economic climate, many of them may just be window-shopping. But even those on a budget can shop; 100-Yen discount stores are virtually everywhere.

The Shopping Scene

BEST BUYS   Tokyo is the country's showcase for everything from the latest in camera, computer, or music equipment to original woodblock prints, anime products, and designer fashions. Traditional Japanese crafts and souvenirs that make good buys include toys (both traditional and the latest in technical wizardry), kites, Japanese dolls, carp banners, swords, lacquerware, bamboo baskets, *ikebana* (flower arranging) accessories, ceramics, pottery, iron teakettles, chopsticks, fans, masks, knives, scissors, sake, incense, and silk and cotton kimono. And you don't have to spend a fortune: You can pick up handmade Japanese paper *(washi)* products, such as umbrellas, lanterns, boxes, stationery, and other souvenirs, for a fraction of what they would cost in import shops in the United States. In Harajuku, stores sell the latest fashion craze at cheap prices, and I can't even count the number of pairs of fun, casual shoes I've bought for a song. Reproductions of famous woodblock prints make great inexpensive gifts, and many items—from pearls to electronic video and audio equipment—can be bought tax-free (see "Taxes," below).

Japan is famous for its electronics, but if you're buying new you can probably find these products just as cheaply, or even more cheaply, in the United States. If you think you want to shop for electronic products while you're in Tokyo, it pays to do some comparison shopping before you leave home so that you can spot a deal when you see one. On the other hand, one of the joys of shopping for electronics in Japan is discovering new, advanced models; you might decide you want that new Sony HD digital camcorder simply because it's the coolest thing you've ever seen, no matter what the price.

GREAT SHOPPING AREAS   Another enjoyable aspect of shopping in Tokyo is that specific areas are often devoted to certain goods, sold wholesale but also available to the individual shopper. **Kappabashi-dougugai Dori** (station: Tawaramachi), for example, is where you'll find shops specializing in kitchenware, while **Kanda** (station: Jimbocho) is known for its bookstores. **Akihabara** (station: Akihabara) is packed with stores selling the latest in electronics, as well as *anime*-related items. **Ginza** (station: Ginza) is the chic address for high-end international designer brands and art galleries. **Aoyama** (station: Omotesando) boasts the city's largest concentration of Japanese designer-clothing stores and an ever-increasing number of international names, while nearby **Harajuku** (stations: Harajuku, Meiji-Jingu-mae, or Omotesando) and **Shibuya** (station: Shibuya) are the places to go for youthful, fun, and inexpensive fashions. Department stores, good for one-stop shopping, are spread throughout the city.

SALES   Department stores have sales throughout the year, with bargains on everything from electronic goods and men's suits to golf clubs, toys, kitchenware, food, and lingerie; there are even sales for used wedding kimono. Sales are generally held on one of the top floors of the department store in what's usually labeled the "Exhibition Hall" or "Promotion Hall" in the store's English-language brochure. Stop by the store's information desk, usually located near the main entrance, for the brochure as well as fliers listing current sales promotions.

TAXES   A 5% consumption tax (which is being considered for an increase due to the economic repercussions of the 2011 earthquake) is included in the price of marked goods, but all major department stores and tourist shops will refund the tax to foreign visitors if total purchases in that store amount to more than ¥10,001 in one day, excluding tax (including tax, purchases must exceed ¥10,501). Exemptions include food, beverages, tobacco, pharmaceuticals, cosmetics, and batteries. When you've finished shopping, take the purchased goods and receipts to the tax refund counter in the store. There are forms to fill out (you'll need your passport). Upon completion, a record of your purchase is placed on the visa page of your passport, and you are given the tax refund on the spot. When you leave Japan, make sure you have your purchases with you (pack them in your carry-on); you may be asked by Customs to show them, though I've never been asked.

SHIPPING IT HOME   Most first-class hotels provide a packing and shipping service. In addition, most large department stores, tourist shops like Oriental Bazaar, and antiques shops, will ship your purchases overseas, including antique furniture.

If you wish to ship packages yourself, the easiest method is to go to a post office and purchase an easy-to-assemble cardboard box, available in several sizes (along with the necessary tape). Keep in mind that packages mailed abroad cannot weigh more than 20 kilograms (about 44 lb.), and that only the larger international post offices accept packages to be mailed overseas (ask your hotel concierge for the closest one). Remember, too, that mailing packages from Japan is expensive (for details, see "Fast Facts" earlier in this chapter and in chapter 14).

Shopping from A to Z
ANIME & MANGA
Although **Akihabara** has long boasted Japan's largest concentration of electronics shops, in the past decade it has also gained a reputation as *the* place to shop for manga (Japanese comic books and graphic novels) and items related to anime (Japanese animation) and cosplay (costume play). One of the best anime/manga chain stores in Japan is **Mandarake,** which first opened in 1987 as a second-hand shop for manga. It's shop in Akihabara, about 4 minutes from JR Akihabara Station at 3–11–2 Soto-Kanda (www.mandarake.co.jp; (✆ **03/3252-7007**), offers eight floors of both new and second-hand goods, including pop and vintage figurines, video games, manga, and posters (some products are definitely X-rated). There's also a branch in Shibuya, deep underground beneath Shibuya BEAM on Inokashira Dori, 31–2 Udagawacho (✆ **03/3477-0777;** station: Shibuya). Serious shoppers, however, will want to make a pilgrimage to **Nakano Broadway Mall** at 5–52–15 Nakano (✆ **03/3388-7004**), a 5-minute walk from the north exit of Nakano Station and known throughout the country as *otaku* (geek) heaven for its slew of shops dedicated to both new and retro pop goods from Japan and overseas, including software, games, manga, figures, and anima and cosplay fare. Mandarake (✆ **03/3228-0007**) is the biggest player here, with more than a dozen departments spread throughout the mall, each specializing in particular products, from manga and cosplay clothing to anime song CDs and figurines. All Mandarake stores are open daily from noon to 8pm.

Back in Akihabara, **Akihabara Gamers,** in front of Akihabara Station at 1–14–7 Soto-Kanda (http://akiba.kaku.com/en/shopinfo/en_gameres.php; ✆ **03/5298-8720**), sells anime-related goods, including figurines, game software, cards, books, and DVDs from 10am to 9pm daily. It's also worth popping into **Don Quijote** (ドン・キホーテ) on Chuo Dori at 4–3–3 Soto-Kanda (www.donki.com; (✆ **03/5298-5411**), open daily from 10am to an astonishing 5am. It has to be seen to appreciate its jumble of everyday goods too numerous to mention, including maid costumes and even a maid cafe (I don't even want to get into why these are so popular) on the fifth floor.

ANTIQUES & CURIOS
In recent years, it has become a buyer-beware market in Japan, with fake antiques produced in China infiltrating the Japanese market. You shouldn't have any problems with the reputable dealers listed here, but if you're buying an expensive piece, be sure to ask whether there are any papers of authenticity.

In addition to the listings here, other places to look for antiques include **Oriental Bazaar** (p. 148) and Tokyo's outdoor **flea markets** (see later in this section).

Antique Mall Ginza   Japanese, European, and some American antiques, collectibles, and odds and ends crowd three floors of Tokyo's largest antiques mall, where you could spend hours browsing among furniture, jewelry, watches, porcelain, pottery, dolls, *netsuke,* scrolls, glassware, kimono, folk art, and much more. Open Thursday to Tuesday 11am to 7pm. 1–13–1 Ginza, Chuo-ku. www.antiques-jp.com. ✆ **03/3535-2115.** Station: Ginza-Itchome or Kyobashi (3 min.). Btw. Chuo Dori and Showa Dori.

Kinokuniya 🎁   This tiny store, tucked away on the third floor of a nondescript office building near Tokyo Station, contains an amazing collection of samurai armor and accessories that make it seem more like a museum. There are complete sets, from the helmet and mask to the breastplate and leggings, as well as individual masks, helmets, leg and arm coverings, swords, accessories, and even horse saddles and stirrups. In business for about 40 years, it usually has 40 to 50 samurai sets on hand, which sell from about ¥350,000 to 1 million yen, though individual items are cheaper. Open Monday to Saturday 10am to 5:30pm. 1–6–15 Yaesu, Chuo-ku www.kinokuniya.tv/en. © **03/5202-8688.** Station: Tokyo (North Yaesu exit, 3 min.). On the other side of Sotobori Dori, on a side street called Yaesu Kitaguchi Dori.

Kurofune Antiques 🏠 Located in a large house in Roppongi, Kurofune is owned by American John Adair, who for more than 25 years has specialized in Japanese antique furniture in its original condition. The largest collection here is of mid- to top-quality pieces, but browsing is a delight even if you can't afford to buy; stock in addition to furniture includes hibachi, fabrics, prints, maps, lanterns, screens, folk art, and the country's largest collection of Japanese baskets. Open Monday to Saturday 10am to 6pm. Closed early April through Golden Week. 47–7–4 Roppongi, Minato-ku. www.kurofuneantiques.com. © **03/3479-1552.** Station: Roppongi (5 min.). From Roppongi Crossing, walk away from Tokyo Tower on Gaien-Higashi Dori, take the diagonal street (Ryudocho-Bijitsukan-dori) to the left (across from Tokyo Midtown), and then take a right at 7-Eleven.

ARCADES & SHOPPING MALLS

UNDERGROUND ARCADES Underground shopping arcades are found around several of Tokyo's train and subway stations; the biggest are at **Tokyo Station** (the Yaesu side) and **Shinjuku Station** (the east side). They often have great sales and bargains on clothing, accessories, and electronics. My only complaint is that once you're in them, it sometimes seems as if you'll never find your way out again.

SHOPPING MALLS **Sunshine City** (station: Higashi Ikebukuro or Ikebukuro) is one of Tokyo's oldest shopping malls, with more than 200 shops and restaurants spread through several adjoining buildings. Its popularity, however, is now challenged by newer and grander shopping centers, including chic **Omotesando Hills** (station: Harajuku, Omotesando, or Meiji-Jingumae) with a varied mix of upscale boutiques and restaurants; **Roppongi Hills** (station: Roppongi), an urban renewal project with approximately 130 shops spread throughout several buildings and along tree-lined streets; and **Tokyo Midtown** (station: Roppongi) with its mix of tony shops, restaurants, and offices. In the harbor, on man-made island Odaiba (station: Odaiba Kaihin Koen), is **Palette Town,** an amusement/shopping center that contains the sophisticated, upscale Italian-themed **Venus Fort,** an indoor mall that evokes scenes from Italy with its store-fronted lanes, painted sky, fountains, plazas, and Italian name-brand boutiques. On the first floor are shops for kids, pets, and households; the second floor is devoted to women's clothing and accessories; and the third floor serves as Tokyo's first outlet mall. Nearby **Tokyo Decks** targets Japanese youths with its international goods, including imports from the United States, Europe, China, and Hong Kong; I especially like its Daiba 1-chome Syoutengai section (on the fourth floor of Tokyo Deck's "Seaside Mall" section), a remake of mid-1900s Japan, with crafts, food, and an old-fashioned games arcade.

CRAFTS & TRADITIONAL JAPANESE PRODUCTS

If you want to shop for traditional Japanese folk crafts in a festival-like atmosphere, nothing beats **Nakamise Dori** (station: Asakusa), a pedestrian lane leading to Sensoji Temple in Asakusa. It's lined with stall after stall selling souvenirs galore, from wooden *geta* shoes and hairpins worn by geisha to T-shirts, fans, umbrellas, toy swords, and dolls. Most are open daily from 10am to 6pm; some may close 1 day a week. The side streets surrounding Nakamise Dori, including Demboin Dori and a covered pedestrian lane stretching from both sides of Nakamise Dori, are also good bets.

Another good place to search for traditional crafts are **department stores,** which usually have sections devoted to ceramics, pottery, bambooware, flower-arranging accessories, and kimono, and **flea markets.**

Japan Sword   Coming here is like visiting a museum. Established more than 100 years ago, this is the best-known sword shop in Tokyo, with a knowledgeable staff and an outstanding collection of fine swords, daggers, sword guards, fittings, and other sword accessories, as well as antique samurai armor. The place also sells copies and souvenir items of traditional swords at prices much lower than those of the very expensive historic swords. Note that antique and modern swords require permission to export, which takes about 2 weeks (the company can ship purchases to you), but you can take replicas with you—just be sure to pack them in checked bags. Open Monday to Friday 9:30am to 6pm, Saturday 9:30am to 5pm. Closed holidays. 3–8–1 Toranomon, Minato-ku. www.japansword.co.jp. ⓒ **03/3434-4321.** Station: Toranomon (exit 2, 5 min.) or Kamiyacho (exit 3, 5 min.).

Japan Traditional Craft Center (Zenkoku Dentoteki Kogeihin Senta) 🎁 Established to promote the country's artisans, this two-story center is a great introduction to both traditional and contemporary Japanese design, with explanations in English. It sells various top-quality crafts from all over Japan on a rotating basis, so there are always new items on hand. Crafts for sale may include lacquerware, ceramics, textiles, paper products, bamboo items, calligraphy brushes, fans, metalwork, knives, furniture, and sometimes even stone lanterns or Buddhist family altars. Prices are high, but rightfully so. Unfortunately, its location in out-of-the-way Ikebukuro makes a trip here feasible only if you have the time; otherwise, you're probably better off shopping in the crafts section of a department store. Open daily 11am to 7pm. 1st floor of Metropolitan Plaza Building, 1–11–1 Nishi-Ikebukuro. www.kougeihin.jp. ⓒ **03/5954-6066.** Station: Ikebukuro (1 min.).

Oriental Bazaar   If you have time for only one souvenir shop in Tokyo, this should be it. This is the city's best-known and largest souvenir/crafts store, selling products at reasonable prices and offering three floors of souvenir and gift items, including cotton *yukata,* kimono (new and used), woodblock prints, paper products, fans, chopsticks, Imari chinaware, sake sets, Japanese dolls, pearls, books on Japan, and antique furniture. This store will also ship things home for you. Open Monday to Wednesday and Friday 10am to 6pm; Saturday and Sunday 10am to 7pm. 5–9–13 Jingumae, Shibuya-ku. ⓒ **03/3400-3933.** Station: Meiji-Jingumae (3 min.), Harajuku (4 min.), or Omotesando (5 min.). On Omotesando Dori in Harajuku; look for an Asian-looking facade of orange and green.

Sakai Kokodo Gallery   This gallery claims to be the oldest woodblock print shop in Japan. It was first opened back in 1870 in the Kanda area of Tokyo by the present owner's great-grandfather; altogether four generations of the Sakai family have tended the store. It's a great place for original prints, as well as reproductions of great masters like Hiroshige. (If you're really a woodblock print fan, you'll want to visit the Sakai family's excellent **Japan Ukiyo-e Museum,** in the small town of Matsumoto in the Japan Alps.) Open daily 11am to 6pm. 1–2–14 Yurakucho, Chiyoda-ku (across from the Imperial Hotel's Tower). www.ukiyo-e.co.jp/index-e.html. ⓒ **03/3591-4678.** Station: Hibiya (1 min.).

DEPARTMENT STORES

Japanese department stores are institutions in themselves. Usually enormous, well designed, and chock-full of merchandise, they have about everything you can imagine, including museums and art galleries, travel agencies, restaurants, grocery markets, and, on the rooftop, playgrounds, greenhouses or even shrines. You could easily spend an entire day in a department store—eating, attending cultural exhibitions, planning your next vacation, exchanging money, and, well, shopping.

One of the most wonderful aspects of the Japanese department store is the **courteous service.** If you arrive at a store as its doors open at 10 or 10:30am, you'll witness a daily rite: Lined up at the entrance are staff who bow in welcome. Some Japanese shoppers arrive just before opening time so as not to miss this favorite ritual. Sales clerks are everywhere, ready to help you. In some stores, you don't even have to go to the cash register once you've made your choice; just hand over the product, along with your money, to the sales clerk, who will return with your change, your purchase neatly wrapped, and an *"Arigato gozaimashita"* ("Thank you very much"). Many department stores will also ship your purchases home for you, send them to your hotel, or hold them until you're ready to leave the store. A day spent in a Japanese department store could spoil you for the rest of your life.

Most department stores include **boutiques** by famous Japanese and international fashion designers, like Issey Miyake, Rei Kawakubo (creator of Comme des Garçons), Tsumori Chisato, Yohji Yamamoto, Takeo Kikuchi, Vivienne Westwood, Armani, and Paul Smith, as well as a department devoted to the kimono. Near the **kimono department** may also be the section devoted to **traditional crafts,** including *ikebana* vases, pottery, and lacquerware. Many famous **restaurants** maintain branches in department stores, but not to be missed is the basement (nicknamed a *depachika,* which is a combination *depa*—from department store—and *chika,* meaning basement), where you'll find one or two levels devoted to **foodstuffs:** fresh fish, produce, green tea, sake, prepared snacks and dinners, and delectable pastries. There are often free samples of food; if you're hungry, walking through the food department could do nicely for a snack.

To find out what's where, stop by the store's information booth located on the ground floor near the front entrance and ask for the floor-by-floor English-language pamphlet. Be sure, too, to ask about **sales** on the promotional floor—you never know what bargains you may chance upon.

Hours are generally daily from 10 or 10:30am to 8pm. Department stores used to close 1 day a week, but now they rarely close, or close irregularly on the same day of the week (say, on Tues) but in no apparent pattern. One month they may be closed the second and third Tuesday of the month, but the next month only the first or not at all. In any case, you can always find department stores that are open, even on Sundays and holidays (major shopping days in Japan).

Isetan   With a history stretching 120 years, Isetan is a favorite among foreigners living in Tokyo. Part of the Isetan-Mitsukoshi conglomerate, it has a good line of conservative work clothes, as well as contemporary and fashionable styles, including designer goods by Issey Miyake, Yohji Yamamoto, Hanae Mori, Comme des Garçons, Marc Jacobs, Junya Watanabe, and Salvatore Ferragamo, as well as large dress sizes (on the second floor). It has a great kimono section along with all the traditional accessories (*obi,* shoes, purses), but following a recent trend wooing male shoppers, a 9-floor annex behind the main building caters entirely to men (there's even a golf school on its roof). Its basement food hall is legendary, with its dessert and massive chocolate sections an especially illuminating commentary on Japan's obsession with food. Open daily 10am to 8pm.

3–14–1 Shinjuku, Shinjuku-ku. ✆ **03/3352-1111.** Station: Shinjuku Sanchome (1 min.) or Shinjuku (east exit, 6 min.). On Shinjuku Dori, east of Shinjuku Station.

Matsuya Ginza   This is one of my favorite department stores in Tokyo; if I were buying a wedding gift, Matsuya is one of the first places I'd look. It has a good selection of Japanese folk crafts items, kitchenware, kimono, and beautifully designed contemporary household goods, in addition to the usual designer clothes and accessories ("queen" sizes are on the sixth floor). I always make a point of stopping by the seventh floor's Design Collection, which displays items from around the world selected by the Japan Design Committee as examples of fine design, from the Alessi teapot to Braun razors. Two basement floors are devoted to food. Open daily 10am to 8pm. There's a branch in Asakusa at 1–41–1 Hanakawado (✆ **03/3842-1111;** daily 10am–7:30pm). 3–6–1 Ginza, Chuo-ku. ✆ **03/3567-1211.** Station: Ginza (2 min.). On Chuo Dori, just a long block north of Ginza 4–chome Crossing.

Mitsukoshi   This Nihombashi department store is one of Japan's oldest and grandest, founded in 1673 by the Mitsui family as a kimono store. In 1683, it became the first store in the world to deal only in cash sales; it was also one of the first stores in Japan to display goods on shelves rather than have merchants fetch bolts of cloth for each customer, as was the custom of the time. Today, housed in a building dating from 1935, it remains one of Tokyo's loveliest department stores, with a beautiful and stately Renaissance-style facade and an entrance guarded by two bronze lions, replicas of the lions in Trafalgar Square. The store carries many name-brand boutiques, from Chanel to Christian Dior. Its kimono, by the way, are still hot items. Open daily 10am to 7pm (basement food floors and the first 3 floors open to 8pm). A branch, located at Ginza 4–chome Crossing (✆ **03/3562-1111;** open daily 10am–8pm), is popular with young shoppers. 1–4–1 Nihombashi Muromachi, Chuo-ku. ✆ **03/3241-3311.** Station: Mitsukoshimae (1 min.).

Seibu   Once the nation's largest department store—and still one of the biggest—Seibu offers clothing, furniture, art galleries, jewelry, household goods, kitchenware, and a million other things. Loft, Seibu's department for household goods and interior design marketed to the younger set, occupies the top three floors of the main building. Many of the best Japanese and Western designers have boutiques here; it also carries large, tall, and petite sizes on the fourth floor. Two basement floors are devoted to foodstuffs—you can buy everything from taco shells to octopus to seaweed there. Dishes are set out so you can nibble the food as you move along, and hawkers yelling out their wares give the place a marketlike atmosphere.

There's also a Seibu in **Shibuya** at 21–1 Udagawacho (✆ **03/3462-0111;** open Sun–Wed 10am–8pm, Thurs–Sat 10am–9pm; station: Shibuya, Hachiko exit). It consists of two buildings connected by pedestrian skywalks, with lots of designer boutiques like Issey Miyake, Comme des Garçons, Helmut Lang, Vivienne Westwood, and Vivienne Tam. Nearby are Loft, with household goods, and Movida, a fashion department store with fun young fashions for waifs.

Open Monday to Saturday 10am to 9pm, Sunday 10am to 8pm. 1–28–1 Minami Ikebukuro, Toshima-ku. ✆ **03/3981-0111.** Station: Ikebukuro (underneath the store).

Takashimaya   This department store has always provided stiff competition for Mitsukoshi, with a history just as long. It was founded as a kimono shop in Kyoto during the Edo Period and opened in Tokyo in 1933. Today it's one of the city's most attractive department stores, with a Renaissance-style building and gloved elevator operators whisking customers to eight floors of shopping and dining. Naturally, it features boutiques by such famous designers as Chanel, Louis Vuitton, Gucci, Issey Miyake, and more. Its sale of used kimono draws huge crowds (look for advertisements in the *Japan Times*). A branch, **Takashimaya Shinjuku**, 5–24–2 Sendaygaya, Shinjuku (*C* **03/53610111;** open daily 10am–8pm; station: Shinjuku), boasts 14 floors of clothing and restaurants (lower floors target affluent seniors, while upper floors appeal to younger shoppers and families; petite and "queen-size" clothing are on the sixth floor). There's also Tokyu Hands with everything imaginable for the home hobbyist, and Kinokuniya bookstore with English-language books on the sixth floor. Open daily 10am to 8pm. 2–4–1 Nihombashi (on Chuo Dori Ave.), Chuo-ku. www.takashimaya. co.jp/tokyo/store_information/index.html. *C* **03/3211-4111.** Station: Nihombashi (1 min.).

Tokyu Honten (Main Store)   With its conservative styles in clothing and housewares and elegant layout, the Tokyu chain's flagship store appeals mainly to a 40s-and-older age group. You'll find women's fashions (including departments for larger sizes), men's fashions, children's clothing and toys, arts and crafts, and restaurants. It adjoins the ultramodern Bunkamura complex, a cultural center with cinemas, theater and concert halls, a museum, a bookstore, and cafes. Open daily 11am to 7pm (the basement food floor open to 8pm). 2–24–1 Dogenzaka. *C* **03/3477-3111.** Station: Shibuya (Hachiko exit, 7 min.).

Wako   This is one of Ginza's smallest department stores but also one of its classiest, housed in one of the few area buildings that survived World War II. It was erected in 1932 by the Hattori family, founders of the Seiko watch company, and is famous for its distinctive clock tower, graceful curved facade, and innovative window displays. The store's ground floor carries a wide selection of Seiko watches and handbags, while the upper floors carry imported and domestic fashions and luxury items with prices to match. It caters to older, well-to-do customers; you won't find hordes of young Japanese girls shopping here. Open Monday to Saturday 10:30am to 6pm; closed holidays. 4–5–11 Ginza (at Ginza 4–chome Crossing), Chuo-ku. www.wako.co.jp. *C* **03/3562-2111.** Station: Ginza (1 min.).

ELECTRONICS

The largest concentration of electronics and electrical-appliance shops in Japan is in an area of Tokyo called **Akihabara,** also known simply as Akiba and centered around Chuo Dori (station: Akihabara). Although you can find good deals on video and audio equipment elsewhere (especially just west of Shinjuku Station, where Yodobashi dominates with several stores devoted to electronics), Akihabara is a must-see simply for its sheer volume. With hundreds of multilevel stores, shops, and stalls, Akihabara accounts for one-tenth of the nation's electronics and electrical-appliance sales. An estimated 50,000 shoppers come here on a weekday, 100,000 per day on a weekend. Even if you don't buy anything, it's great fun walking around. Most stores and stalls are open-fronted, and many are painted neon green and pink. Salespeople yell out their wares, trying to get customers to look at cellular phones, computers, digital cameras, MP3 players, TVs, calculators, watches, and rice cookers. This is the best place to see the latest models of everything electronic; it's an educational experience in itself.

If you do intend to buy, make sure you know what the item would cost back home. Or, you may be able to pick up something that's unavailable back home. Be sure to bargain and don't buy at the first place you hit. One woman I know who was looking for a portable music device bought it at the third shop she went to for ¥4,000 less than what was quoted to her at the first shop. Make sure, too, that whatever you purchase is made for export—that is, with instructions in English, an international warranty, and the proper electrical connectors. All the larger stores have duty-free floors where products are made for export, and most shops are open daily from about 10am to 8pm or later.

The largest store here is **Yodobashi Akiba,** just east of JR Akihabara Station at 1–1 Hanaoka-cho (✆ **03/5209-1010;** open daily 9:30am–10pm), which offers a staggering number of electronic-related goods such as cameras, computers, TVs, and rice cookers, but it also offers a slew of other leisure-related items like games and bicycles (some people fear this monolith will put independent Akiba shop owners out of business). Other reputable stores, with English-speaking staff and models for export, include **Laox,** 15–3 Soto-Kanda (✆ **03/3255-5301**), and **AKKY International,** 1–12–5 Soto-Kanda (✆ **03/5207-5027**), both on Chuo Dori (the latter store also with Japanese souvenirs in its basement). If you're serious about buying, check these stores first.

Cameras

You can purchase cameras at many duty-free shops, including those in Akihabara, but if you're serious about photographic equipment, make a trip to a shop dealing specifically in cameras, including Akihabara's **Yodobashi Akiba,** above. If a new camera is too formidable an expense, consider buying a used camera. New models come out so frequently that older models can be snapped up for next to nothing (though the current exchange rate makes even used cameras no longer the bargain they once were).

Bic Camera This huge, eight-floor store near Ginza offers not only single-lens reflex and digital cameras, but also computers, DVD and MP3 players, camcorders, watches, toys, and much more. Note, however, that it caters primarily to Japanese; English-speaking sales clerks are scarce, and export models are limited (duty-free overseas models are in the second basement). Ask for the English-language brochure, and if you're buying sensitive equipment, make sure it will work outside Japan and comes with English-language instructions. Open daily 10am to 10pm. There's a branch in Shibuya at 1–24–12 Shibuya (✆ **03/5466-1111;** open daily 10am–10pm; station: Shibuya, 2 min.). 1–11–1 Yurakucho, Chiyoda-ku. www.biccamera.co.jp/shoplist/yurakucho_english.html. ✆ **03/5221-1112.** Station: Yurakucho (1 min.).

Lemon (レモン) Its name doesn't inspire confidence, but this company specializes in used and new cameras and lenses from around the world, including digital cameras and large-format models. Leica, Hasselblad, Rolleiflex, Canon, Pentax, and Nikon are just some of the brands available, along with watches and eyeglasses. A camera buff's paradise. There's a branch in Shinjuku, a 3-minute walk west of Shinjuku Station not far from Yodobashi Camera (below), at 1–15–4 Nishi-Shinjuku (✆ **03/5909-2333;** daily 10:30am–10pm). Open Monday to Saturday 11am to 8pm, Sunday 11am to 5pm. 4–2–2 Ginza, Chuo-ku. www.lemonsha.com/english. ✆ **03/3567-3131.** Station: Ginza (1 min.). In a green glazed-brick building also housing the Ginza Methodist Church, on the 8th floor.

Yodobashi Camera Shinjuku is the photographic equipment center for Tokyo, and this store, 1 block west of the station, is the biggest in the area. It ranks as one of the largest discount camera shops in the world (though the new Yodobashi in Akihabara, above, now surpasses it), with around 30,000 items in stock, and it reputedly sells approximately 500 to 600 cameras daily. Prices are marked, but you can bargain here. It also sells watches, calculators, computers, and other electronic equipment, though if you're interested specifically in watches, clocks, audio/video equipment, games, and other wares, nearby branches specialize in all of these (ask the main shop for a map of shops in the area). Open daily 9:30am to 10pm. 1–11–1 Nishi-Shinjuku, Shinjuku-ku. ✆ **03/3346-1010.** Station: Shinjuku (west exit, 3 min.).

FASHION

The **department stores** and **shopping malls** listed earlier are all good places to check out the latest trends. For international designers, chic boutiques abound in the **Ginza** and neighboring **Marunouchi.** Otherwise, **Harajuku** and **Shibuya** are the places to go for hundreds of small shops selling inexpensive designer knockoffs, as well as fashion department stores—multistoried buildings filled with concessions of various designers and labels.

For inexpensive, basic clothing (think Japanese version of Gap), look for one of the 40-some **Uniqlo** shops in Tokyo selling T-shirts, jeans, socks, shirts, and other clothing for the whole family. Its 12-story flagship store is just off Chuo Dori at 6–9–5 Ginza (✆ **03/6252-5161**; station: Ginza). Another popular chain, selling minimalist yet hip cotton clothing in basic colors, is **Muji,** with its flagship located at 3–8–3 Marunouchi (✆ **03/5208-8241**; station: Yurakucho).

La Forêt This is not only the largest store in Harajuku but also one of the most fashionable, appealing mostly to teenage and 20-something shoppers. Young and upcoming Japanese designers are here as well as established names, in boutiques spread on several floors. In addition to men's and women's fashions there are also shops selling jewelry, shoes, handbags, and other accessories. There's so much to see—from pink frilly dresses to Goth—you can easily kill a few hours here. Open daily 11am to 8pm. 1–11–6 Jingumae, Shibuya-ku. www.laforet.ne.jp. ✆ **03/3475-0411.** Station: Meiji-Jingumae (1 min.) or Harajuku (3 min.). On Meiji Dori, just off Harajuku's main intersection of Omotesando Dori and Meiji Dori.

Parco A division of Seibu, Parco is actually two buildings clustered together and called Parco Part 1 and Part 3 (Part 2 closed). Parco Part 1 is the place to go for designer boutiques for men and women, with clothes and accessories by Japanese designers such as Junya Watanabe and Tsumori Chisato, and such foreign designers as Anna Sui and Vivienne Westwood. Part 3 is devoted to casual, young fashions. Parco has two sales a year that you shouldn't miss if you're in town—one in January and one in July. Open daily 10am to 9pm. 15–1 Udagawacho, Shibuya-ku. ✆ **03/3464-5111.** Station: Shibuya (Hachiko exit, 4 min.)

Designer Boutiques

Ginza is home to international designer names, including Prada, Bally, Cartier, Chanel, Christian Dior, and Louis Vuitton. Nearby, on Marunouchi Naka Dori, there are outlets for Hermes, TOD's, Tiffany & Co., Armani, and Issey Miyake, among others.

For top Japanese designers, the blocks between Omotesando Crossing and the Nezu Museum in **Aoyama** (station: Omotesando, 2 min.) are the Rodeo Drive of Japan. Even if you can't buy here (steep prices for most pocketbooks), a stroll is de rigueur for clothes hounds and those interested in design. Most shops are open daily from 11am to 8pm. **Issey Miyake** (www.isseymiyake.com; (✆ **03/3423-1408**), on the left side as you walk from Aoyama Dori, offers two floors of cool, spacious displays of Miyake's interestingly structured designs for men and women. His very popular Pleats Please line is next door (✆ **03/5772-7750**); a shop offering all Issey Miyake brands in one location is ELTTOB TEP ISSEY MIYAKE, 4–4–5 Ginza (✆ **03/3566-5225**). Across the street is **Comme des Garçons** (www.comme-des-garcons.com; (✆ **03/3406-3951**), Rei Kawakubo's showcase for her daring—and constantly evolving—men's and women's designs. The goddess of Japanese fashion and one of the few females in the business when she started, Kawakubo has remained on the cutting edge of design for more than 3 decades. One of Japan's newer designers, **Tsumori**

Chisato, has a shop on the left side of the street (www.tsumorichisato.com; ℭ 03/3423-5170). Also worth seeking out is **Yohji Yamamoto** on the right (www.yohjiyamamoto.co.jp; ℭ 03/3409-6006), where Yamamoto's unique, classically wearable clothes are sparingly hung, flaunting the avant-garde interior space.

Of the many non-Japanese designers to have invaded this trendy neighborhood in recent years, none stands out as much as **Prada** (ℭ 03/6418-0400), a bubble of convex/concave windows on the right side of the street. On a back street behind Prada are up-and-coming design houses, including **A Bathing Ape** (ℭ 03/3407-2145), where DJ/fashion designer Nigo sells limited editions of his hip street wear, including T-shirts and shoes, at prices most kids can't afford. Down the street, **Y-3** (ℭ 03/5464-1930), a collaboration between Yohji Yamamoto and Adidas, is a must for those who wish to look fashionable while working out. Nearby, at **10 Corso Como Comme des Garcons** (ℭ 03/5774-7800), special editions of clothing and accessories for both men and women, designed by Rei Kawakubo, Junya Watanabe, Diesel, and others, are sold.

FLEA MARKETS

Flea markets are good places to shop for antiques as well as for delightful junk. You can pick up secondhand kimono at very reasonable prices, as well as kitchenware, vases, cast-iron teapots, small chests, woodblock prints, dolls, household items, and odds and ends. (Don't expect to find any good buys in furniture.) The markets usually begin as early as dawn or 6am and last until 3 or 4pm or so, but go early if you want to pick up bargains. Bargaining is expected. Note that since most markets are outdoors, they tend to be canceled if it rains.

Nogi Shrine, a 1-minute walk from Nogizaka Station at 8–11–27 Akasaka (ℭ 03/3478-3001), has an antiques flea market from dawn to about 3pm the second Sunday of each month except November. It has a lovely setting; the shrine commemorates General Nogi and his wife, both of whom committed suicide on September 13, 1912, to follow the Meiji emperor into the afterlife. Their simple home and stable are on shrine grounds.

Hanazono Shrine, 5–17–3 Shinjuku (ℭ 03/3200-3093), near the Yasukuni Dori/Meiji Dori intersection east of Shinjuku Station (Shinjuku Sanchome Station, 5 min.), has a flea market every Sunday from dawn to about 2pm (except in May and Nov, due to festivals).

Yasukuni Shrine, a 3-minute walk from Kudanshita Station at 3–1–1 Kudanshita (ℭ 03/3261-8326), holds a flea market every Sunday from 6am to about 3pm on the long walkway to this very famous shrine (see p. 92 for information on the shrine and its military museum).

The **Oedo Antique Fair,** held at 3–5–1 Marunouchi (ℭ 03/5805-1093), in the courtyard of the Tokyo International Forum beside Yurakucho Station, claims to be the largest outdoor antiques market in Japan (it has also taken away vendors from Tokyo's other flea markets). Held the first and third Sunday of the month from 9am to 5pm, it features Western antiques (at highly inflated prices), as well as Japanese glassware, furniture, ceramics, furniture, kimono, woodblock prints, and odds and ends. If you hit only one flea market, this should be it.

Finally, the closest thing Tokyo has to a permanent flea market is **Ameya Yokocho** (also referred to as Ameyoko, Ameyokocho or Ameyacho), a narrow street near Ueno Park that runs along and underneath the elevated tracks of the JR Yamanote Line between Ueno and Okachimachi stations. Stalls here sell discounted items ranging from vegetables and cosmetics to handbags, tennis shoes, watches, and casual clothes. The scene retains something of the *shitamachi* spirit of old Tokyo. Although housewives have been coming here for years, young Japanese recently discovered the market as a good bargain spot for young fashions, accessories like shoes and baseball caps, luggage, perfume, and cosmetics. Some shops close on Wednesdays, but hours are usually daily from 10am to 7pm; early evening is the most crowded time. Don't even think of coming here on a holiday—it's a standstill pedestrian traffic jam.

KIMONO

Chicago, on Omotesando Dori in Harajuku (📞 **03/3409-5017;** station: Meiji-Jingumae or Harajuku), is a good place for used kimono. It stocks hundreds of affordable used kimono, cotton *yukata* (casual kimono), and *obi* (sashes) back in the far left corner of the basement shop, past the used American clothes. It's open daily from 11am to 8pm. The nearby **Oriental Bazaar** (p. 148) also has a decent selection of new and used kimono at affordable prices, including elaborate wedding kimono. On weekends and holidays, there's a **secondhand kimono stand** on the corner of Meiji Dori and Omotesando Dori in Harajuku from 11am to 5pm, with very good prices.

In addition, department stores sell new kimono, notably **Takashimaya** and **Mitsukoshi** in Nihombashi and **Isetan** in Shinjuku. They also hold sales for rental wedding kimono. **Flea markets** are also good for used kimono and yukata.

Established in 1913, **Hayashi Kimono** (📞 **03/3501-4012**), in the International Arcade (near the Imperial Hotel under the elevated JR Yamamote train tracks; station: Hibiya), sells all manner of kimono, including antique kimono, yukata, and *tanzen* (the heavy winter overcoat that goes over the yukata), as well as used and antique kimono. If you're buying a gift for someone back home, this is a good place to start. Open daily from 10am to 7pm (to 6pm on Sun).

KITCHENWARE & TABLEWARE

In addition to the department stores listed earlier, the best place to shop for items related to cooking and serving is **Kappabashi-dougugai Dori** (station: Tawaramachi), popularly known as Kappabashi; this is Japan's largest wholesale area for cookware. There are approximately 150 specialty stores here selling cookware, including sukiyaki pots, woks, lunch boxes, pots and pans, aprons, knives, china, lacquerware, rice cookers, plastic food (the kind you see in restaurant display cases), *noren* (Japanese curtains), and disposable wooden chopsticks in bulk. Although stores are wholesalers selling mainly to restaurants, you're welcome to browse and purchase as well. Stores are closed on Sunday but are otherwise open from about 10am to 5pm.

PEARLS

Mikimoto, on Chuo Dori not far from Ginza 4-chome Crossing, past Wako department store (📞 **03/3535-54611;** station: Ginza), is Japan's most famous pearl shop. It was founded by Mikimoto Koichi, the first to produce a really good cultured pearl, in 1905. Open Thursday to Tuesday 11am to 7pm. Also, there's a Mikimoto branch (📞 **03/3591-5001**) in the **Imperial Hotel Arcade,** under the Imperial Hotel (station: Hibiya), where you'll also find **Asahi Shoten** (📞 **03/3503-2528**), with a good selection in the moderate price range; and **Uyeda Jeweller** (📞 **03/3503-2587**), with a wide selection of pearls in many price ranges.

ENTERTAINMENT & NIGHTLIFE

By day, Tokyo's sprawl makes it arguably one of the least attractive cities in the world. Come dusk, however, Tokyo comes into its own. The drabness fades, the city blossoms into a profusion of giant neon lights and paper lanterns, and its streets fill with millions of overworked Japanese out to have a good time. If you ask me, Tokyo at night is one of the craziest cities in the world, a city that never gives up and never sleeps. Entertainment districts are as crowded at 3am as they are at 10pm, with many establishments open until the first subways start running after 5am. Whether it's jazz, reggae, gay bars, sex shows, dance clubs, mania, or madness that you're searching for, Tokyo has them all.

GETTING TO KNOW THE SCENE Tokyo has several nightlife districts spread throughout the city, each with its own atmosphere, price range, and clientele. Most famous are probably **Ginza, Kabuki-cho** in Shinjuku, and **Roppongi.** Before visiting any of the locales suggested below, be sure to just walk around one of these neighborhoods and absorb the atmosphere. The streets will be crowded, the neon lights will be overwhelming, and you never know what you might discover on your own.

Although there are many bars, dance clubs, and nightclubs packed with young Japanese of both sexes, nightlife in Japan for the older generations is still pretty much a man's domain, just as it has been for centuries. At the high end of this domain are the **geisha bars,** concentrated primarily in Kyoto. All Japanese cities, however, have so-called **hostess bars;** in Tokyo these are concentrated in Ginza, Roppongi, Shinjuku, and Akasaka. A woman will sit at your table, talk to you, pour your drinks, listen to your problems, and boost your ego. You buy her drinks as well, which is one reason the tab can be so high. Hostess bars in various forms have been a part of Japanese society for centuries. Most foreign visitors find the cost of visiting a hostess bar not worth the price, as hostesses usually speak Japanese only, but such places provide Japanese males with sympathetic ears and the chance to escape the world of both work and family. Men usually have their favorite hostess bar, often a small place with just enough room for regular customers. In the more exclusive hostess bars, only those customers with an introduction are allowed entrance.

The most popular nightlife spots are **drinking establishments,** where the vast majority of Japan's office workers, college students, and expatriates go for an evening out. These places include Western-style bars as well as Japanese-style watering holes, called *nomi-ya* (literally "drinking place) or *izakaya,* a Japanese-style pub also serving food. *Yakitori-ya,* restaurant-bars that serve yakitori and other snacks, are included in this group. Dancing and live-music venues are also hugely popular with young Tokyoites. At the low end of the spectrum are Tokyo's topless bars, strip shows, massage parlors, and porn shops, with the largest concentration of such places in Shinjuku's **Kabuki-cho District.**

In addition to the establishments listed below, be sure to check the restaurants listed in the inexpensive category under "Where to Eat" earlier in this chapter for a relatively cheap night out on the town. Many places serve as both eateries and watering holes, especially yakitori-ya.

EXTRA CHARGES & TAXES One more thing you should be aware of is the **"table charge"** imposed on customers by some bars (especially *nomiya*) and many cocktail lounges. Included in the table charge is usually a small appetizer—maybe nuts, chips, or a vegetable; for this reason, some locales call it an *otsumami,* or snack charge. At any rate, the charge is usually between ¥300 and ¥500 per person. Some establishments levy a table charge only after a certain time in the evening; others may add it only if you don't order food from the menu. If you're not sure and it matters to you, be sure to ask before you order anything. Remember, too, that there's a 5% consumption tax, though most menus already include it in their price. Some higher-end establishments, especially nightclubs, hostess bars, and dance clubs, will add a service charge ranging anywhere from 10% to 20%.

FINDING OUT WHAT'S ON   Keep an eye out for *Metropolis* (www.metropolis.co.jp), a free weekly that carries a nightlife section covering concerts, theaters, and events and is available at bars, restaurants, and other venues around town. The *Japan Times* and *Daily Yomiuri* also have entertainment sections. For an online rundown of what's happening at Tokyo's hundreds of venues, live houses and clubs every week, check out www.tokyogigguide.com.

GETTING TICKETS   If you're staying in a higher-end hotel, the concierge or guest-relations manager can usually get tickets for you. Otherwise, you can head to the theater or hall itself. An easier way is to go through one of many ticket services available such as **Ticket PIA,** which has outlets on the first floor of the Sony Building in Ginza, the Isetan department store annex in Shinjuku, and many other locations in Tokyo; ask your hotel concierge for the one nearest you. Lawson convenient stores also sell tickets to many events from kiosks, but instructions are in Japanese only.

The Major Entertainment Districts

GINZA   A chic and expensive shopping area by day, Ginza transforms itself into a dazzling entertainment district of restaurants, bars, and first-grade hostess bars at night. It's the most sophisticated of Tokyo's nightlife districts and is also one of the most expensive. However, because Ginza does have some fabulous restaurants and several hotels, I've included some reasonably priced recommendations for a drink in the area if you happen to find yourself here after dinner. The cheapest way to absorb the atmosphere in Ginza is simply to wander about, particularly around **Namiki Dori** and its side streets.

SHINJUKU   Northeast of Shinjuku Station is an area called **Kabuki-cho,** which undoubtedly has the craziest nightlife in all of Tokyo, with block after block of strip joints, massage parlors, pornography shops, peep shows, love hotels, bars, restaurants, and, as the night wears on, lots of drunk revelers. A world of its own, it's sleazy, chaotic, crowded, vibrant, and fairly safe. Despite its name, Shinjuku's primary night hot spot has nothing to do with kabuki, though at one time, there was a plan to bring some culture to the area by introducing a kabuki theater. The plan never materialized but the name stuck. Although Kabuki-cho used to be the domain of businessmen out on the town, nowadays young Japanese, including college-age men and women, have claimed parts of it as their own; the result is a growing number of inexpensive drinking and live-music venues well worth a visit.

To the east of Kabuki-cho, just west of Hanazono Shrine, is a smaller district called **Goruden Gai,** which is "Golden Guy" mispronounced. It's a warren of tiny alleyways leading past even tinier bars, each consisting of just a counter and a few chairs. Many of these closet-size bars are closed to outsiders, catering to regular customers, though others welcome strangers as well. Although many thought Goruden Gai would succumb to land-hungry developers in the 1980s, the economic recession brought a stay of execution and now Goruden Gai has experienced a revival, with more than 100 tiny drinking dens lining the tiny streets. Still, it occupies such expensive land that I still fear for the life of this tiny enclave, one of Tokyo's most fascinating.

Even farther east is **Shinjuku Ni-chome** (pronounced "*nee*-chomay"), officially recognized as the gay-bar district of Shinjuku. Its lively street scene of mostly gays and some straights of all ages (but mostly young) make this one of the most vibrant nightlife districts. It's here that I was once taken to a host bar featuring young men in crotchless pants. The clientele included both gay men and groups of young, giggling office girls. That place has since closed down, but Shinjuku is riddled with other spots bordering on the absurd.

The best thing to do in Shinjuku is to simply walk about. In the glow of neon light, you'll pass everything from smoke-filled restaurants to hawkers trying to get you to step inside so they can part you from your money. If you're looking for strip joints, topless or bottomless coffee shops, peep shows, or porn, I leave you to your own devices, but you certainly won't have any problems finding them. In Kabuki-cho alone there are an estimated 200 sex businesses in operation, including bathhouses where women are available for sex at a high price. Although prostitution is illegal in Japan, everyone seems to ignore what goes on behind closed doors. Just be sure you know what you're getting into; your bill may end up much higher than you bargained for.

A word of **warning** for women traveling alone: Forgo the experience of strolling around Kabuki-cho. The streets are crowded and therefore relatively safe, but you may not feel comfortable with so many inebriated men stumbling around. If there are two of you, however, go for it. I took my mother to Kabuki-cho for a spin around the neon, and we escaped relatively unscathed. You're also fine walking alone to any of my recommended restaurants.

ROPPONGI   To Tokyo's younger crowd, Roppongi is the city's most fashionable place to hang out. It's also a favorite with the foreign community, including models, business types, English-language teachers, and tourists staying in Roppongi's posh hotels. Roppongi has more than its fair share of live-music houses, restaurants, dance clubs, expatriate bars, and pubs. **Roppongi Hills** is a massive urban development with many restaurants and some bars of its own, while the newest kid on the block, **Tokyo Midtown,** has brought gentrification—and an influx of affluent customers—to Roppongi's nightlife. Some Tokyoites complain that Roppongi is too crowded, too crass, and too commercialized (and has too many foreigners). However, for the casual visitor, Roppongi offers an excellent opportunity to see what's new and hot in the capital city and is easy to navigate because nightlife activity is so concentrated. There is one huge **caveat,** however: Roppongi's concentration of foreigners has also attracted the unscrupulous, with reports of spiked drinks causing patrons to pass out, only to awaken hours later to find their credit cards missing or fraudulently charged for huge amounts. In other words, never leave your drinks unattended, and you're best off following the buddy system.

Mapping Out Tokyo's Nightlife

Once you've chosen a nightlife spot that appeals to you, you can locate it using the following neighborhood maps:

- To locate bars and clubs in **Shinjuku,** p. 172.
- To locate bars and clubs in **Asakusa,** p. 177.
- To locate bars and clubs in **Ginza and Hibiya,** p. 118.
- To locate bars and clubs in **Harajuku,** p. 135.
- To locate bars and clubs in **Roppongi,** p. 139.

The center of Roppongi is **Roppongi Crossing** (the intersection of Roppongi Dori and Gaien-Higashi Dori), at the corner of which sits the Almond Coffee Shop with its pink flags and decor. The shop has mediocre coffee and desserts at inflated prices, but the sidewalk in front is the number-one meeting spot in Roppongi.

If you need directions, there's a conveniently located *koban* (police box) catty-corner from the Almond Coffee Shop and next to a bank. It has a big map of the Roppongi area showing the address system, and someone is always there to help.

The Performing Arts

For descriptions of Japanese traditional performance arts such as *kabuki* and *noh,* see "Japanese Arts in a Nutshell," in chapter 2. In addition to the performance art listings below, Tokyo also has occasional shows of more avant-garde or lesser-known performance art productions, including highly stylized Butoh dance performances from such companies as Sankai Juku and percussion demonstrations by Kodo drummers and other Japanese drum groups. See publications listed above for complete listings.

KABUKI   One of Japan's most prestigious theaters for Kabuki is **Kabuki-za,** 4–12–15 Ginza, which unfortunately closed for demolition in April 2010, with an expected resurrection in a new building in April 2013. Although I lament the destruction of the handsome older structure, which boasted a Momoyama-style facade influenced by 16th-century castle architecture, the new theater will undoubtedly incorporate the usual Kabuki stage fittings, including a platform that can be raised above and lowered below the stage for dramatic appearances and disappearances of actors, a revolving stage, and a runway stage extending into the audience. For more information on its exact reopening date and subsequent performance schedule, check the website www.kabuki-bito.jp/eng.

In any case, until the Kabuki-za's reopening, kabuki is performed at the nearby **Shinbashi Enbujo Theater,** 6–18–2 Ginza (www.kabuki-bito.jp/eng; © **03/3541-2600,** or 03/6745-0333 for advance reservations; station: Higashi-Ginza), as well as other venues in town. There are about eight or nine Kabuki productions a year; each production begins between the first and third of each month and runs about 25 days. Usually, two different programs are shown; matinees run from about 11 or 11:30am to 4pm, and evening performances run from about 4:30 or 5pm to about 9pm. It's considered perfectly okay to come for only part of a performance. Your appreciation for Kabuki will be greatly enhanced if you spring for an **English-language earphone,** which rents for ¥650, plus a ¥1,000 refundable deposit. Not only does it give a translation of the play's dialogue, but it also provides a running commentary on the story, music, actors, stage properties, and other aspects of Kabuki.

Tickets generally range from ¥2,500 to ¥15,000, depending on the program and seat location. Tickets can be purchased at the theater box office from 10am to 6pm. You may also make advance reservations by phone (same-day bookings are not accepted) and online.

Another venue for Kabuki is the **National Theatre of Japan (Kokuritsu Gekijo),** 4–1 Hayabusacho, Chiyoda-ku (www.ntj.jac.go.jp; © **03/3230-3000;** station: Hanzomon, 6 min.). Kabuki is scheduled throughout the year except during February, May, August, and September, when Bunraku (see below) is staged. Matinees usually begin at 11:30am or noon, and afternoon performances at 4:30pm. Most tickets range from about ¥1,500 to ¥8,500, with earphones available for ¥700 plus a ¥1,000 deposit. Tickets can be purchased at the box office (daily 10am to 6pm), by phone, or online.

NOH   *Noh* is performed at a number of locations in Tokyo, but most famous is the **National Noh Theater (Kokuritsu Nohgakudo),** 4–18–1 Sendagaya, Shibuya-ku (www.ntj.jac.go.jp; ℂ **03/3423-1331** or 3230-3000 for reservations; station: Sendagaya, 5 min.). Opened in 1983, it's dedicated to presenting classical noh and *kyogen,* with about three to five performances monthly. Tickets range from about ¥2,600 to ¥4,800 but are often sold out in advance. However, about 30 tickets are held back to be sold on the day of the performance. In addition, privately sponsored noh performances are also held here, for which the admission varies. Check the *Japan Times* or *Daily Yomiuri* for performance dates and times, or go to www.theatrenohgaku.org for information on noh performances being staged throughout Japan.

BUNRAKU   Although the main *bunraku* theater in Japan is in Osaka, the **National Theatre of Japan** (see above for information) stages about four bunraku plays a year (in Feb, May, Aug, and Sept). There are usually two to three performances daily, beginning at 11am, with tickets costing ¥1,500 to ¥6,500. Earphones with English-language explanations are available for ¥550, plus a ¥1,000 deposit.

TAKARAZUKA KAGEKIDAN   This world-famous, all-female troupe stages elaborate musical revues with dancing, singing, and gorgeous costumes. Performances range from Japanese versions of Broadway hits to original Japanese works based on local legends. The first Takarazuka troupe, formed in 1912 at a resort near Osaka, gained instant notoriety because all its performers were women, in contrast to the all-male kabuki. When I went to see this troupe perform, I was surprised to find that the audience also consisted almost exclusively of women; indeed, the troupe has an almost cultlike following.

Performances, with story synopses available in English, are generally held in March, April, July, August, November, December, and sometimes in June, at **Tokyo Takarazuka Gekijo,** 1–1–3 Yurakucho, Chiyoda-ku (www.kageki.hankyu.co.jp/english; ℂ **03/5251-2001;** station: Hibiya, 1 min.). Tickets, available at the box office or through **Ticket Pia,** usually range about ¥3,500 to ¥11,000.

SHOW NIGHTCLUBS ★   For unique, casual entertainment, nothing beats an evening at an entertainment nightclub, featuring fast-paced dancing in intimate venues. Although the emcee may speak Japanese only, no translation is necessary for the stage productions, which center on easy-to-understand themes or include humorous antics. One of the oldest show nightclubs is **Kingyo,** 3–14–17 Roppongi, Minato-ku (www.kingyo.co.jp; ℂ **03/3478-3000;** station: Roppongi, 4 min.), which stages one of the most high-energy, visually charged acts I've seen—nonstop action of ascending and receding stages and stairs, fast-paced choreography, elaborate costumes, and loud music. In addition to female dancers, there are also male dancers assuming female parts, just like in Kabuki (and I swear, it's difficult to tell the difference). Some of the acts center on traditional Japanese themes with traditional dress and kimono (a perennial favorite is a well-known song from Okinawa), but there are also satires and social commentaries. It's great fun, and you'll admire the cast not only for their talent but for their quick costume changes. It's located in the Roppongi nightlife district near the Roppongi Cemetery. (From Roppongi Crossing, walk toward Tokyo Tower on Gaien-Higashi Dori and take the second left; it's on the right.) The cover is ¥3,500 for shows Tuesday through Saturday at either 7:30 (doors open at 6pm) or 10pm (doors open at 9pm). Reservations are recommended. You are also required to purchase one drink and one food item. Or you can opt for admission packages that include a set meal and drinks beginning at ¥4,800. Prices do not include tax and service charge.

I also like **Show Dining Konparuza,** 8–7–5 Ginza, Chuo-ku (📞 **03/6215-8593;** station: Ginza or Shimbashi), also with moving stages and with lively choreography by Makato-san, who also performs. Productions change twice a year, but there's always a traditional number with dancers dressed in kimono, along with performances that act out popular songs or movies. Doors open daily at 6pm, with the first show at 7:30pm and the second show at 9pm. Cover charge is ¥3,000, plus a minimum of one drink and one food purchase. Alternatively, there's an all-you-can-drink set that includes three dishes and the cover charge for ¥5,800.

Live Music Clubs

The live music scene exploded in the 1990s and is now located throughout the metropolis. In addition to the dedicated venues below, which represent only the tip of the iceberg, be sure to check out http://metropolis.co.jp and www.tokyogigguide.com for more suggestions.

Bauhaus Since 1981, this small club has had the same great house band that plays mostly 1970s and 1980s British and American hard rock, including the music of Led Zeppelin, Queen, Jimi Hendrix, the Who, Aerosmith, the Eagles, Van Halen, Santana, Red Hot Chili Peppers, and others, with music beginning around 8pm. The band puts on quite a show—a bit raunchy at times but very polished. Open Monday to Saturday 7pm to 1am. Closed holidays. Reine Roppongi, 2nd floor, 5–3–4 Roppongi, Minato-ku. www.bauhaus.jp. 📞 **03/3403-0092.** Cover ¥2,835. Station: Roppongi (3 min.). From Roppongi Crossing, walk toward Tokyo Tower on Gaien-Higashi Dori and turn right at McDonald's. It's to the right of the parking lot.

Billboard Live Tokyo Unsurprisingly, this 300-seat, split-level venue is Tokyo's number-one place to hear top-class musicians from Japan and around the world, with past performances by Melissa Manchester, Pyramid, Air Supply, Cheryl Lynn, and many more on a stage against a backdrop of the city skyline. The best seats cost more (from ¥3,000 for two people on top of the ticket price), while the cheapest way to enjoy a show is standing on the top level, where you're even entitled to one free drink. There are two sets most nights of the week, with the first stage at 7pm weekdays, 6pm Saturdays, and 4:30pm Sundays and holidays (tickets are for one show). Doors open about an hour or so before each show. Tokyo Midtown, 4th floor of Garden Terrace, 9–7–4 Roppongi, Minato-ku. 📞 **03/3405-1133.** Cover ¥5,000–¥12,600 for most acts; big names cost more. Station: Roppongi (Oedo exit, 2 min.).

Blue Note This expensive, elegant jazz venue is cousin to the famous Blue Note in New York. The musicians are top-notch; Natalie Cole, Sarah Vaughan, Tony Bennett, Chick Corea, David Sanborn, Roberta Flack, the Milt Jackson Quartet, and Tower of Power have all performed here. However, the 300-seat establishment follows the frustrating Japanese practice of selling tickets good for only one set, and you'll pay extra for the best seats. There are usually two sets nightly, generally at 7 and 9:30pm Monday to Saturday and 6:30 and 9pm Sunday and holidays. 6–3–16 Minami Aoyama, Minato-ku. www.bluenote.co.jp. 📞 **03/5485-0088.** Cover ¥6,300–¥8,400 for most performances, more for top names. Station: Omotesando (8 min.). Off Kotto Dori, on the same street as the Nezu Museum.

Cotton Club This cool venue is the best proof yet that Marunouchi, which already boasts new skyscrapers, hotels, and designer shops, is on its way to becoming an urban destination. Taking its name from Harlem's legendary establishment and attracting well-heeled business types, this sophisticated supper club, ensconced on the second floor of an office building, offers a wide range of musical entertainment, from traditional and fusion jazz to salsa and modern Hawaiian music, performed by trios, quartets, bands, solo guitarists, and vocalists. Past performers include Rickie Lee Jones, Rita Coolidge, and the Duke Ellington Orchestra. There are usually two seatings, at 7 and 9:30pm (5 and 8pm Sun and holidays), with prices dependent on the performances and seating. 2–7–3 Marunouchi, Chiyoda-ku. www.cottonclubjapan.co.jp. ✆ **03/3215-1555.** Cover ¥5,500–¥9,000 for most performances. Station: Tokyo (Marunouchi south exit, 2 min.). Behind (south of) the Central Post Office.

Crocodile   Popular with a young Japanese crowd, the eclectic Crocodile describes itself as a casual rock-'n'-roll club, with live bands ranging from rock and blues to fusion jazz, reggae, soul, experimental, salsa, and even country and Hawaiian. It's a good place to check out new Japanese bands; on the first Saturday and fourth Sunday of the month, the Tokyo Comedy Store (www.tokyocomedy.com) provides more than 2 hours of live stand-up and improv comedy in English. The club has a good, laid-back atmosphere; although it's a not a dance club per se, no one will mind if you just can't help yourself. Open daily 6pm to 2am; performances start around 8pm. 6–18–8 Jingumae, Shibuya-ku. www.crocodile-live.jp. ✆ **03/3499-5205.** Cover ¥2,000–¥4,000, occasionally more for big acts. Station: Meiji-Jingumae or Shibuya (10 min.). On Meiji Dori halfway btw. Harajuku and Shibuya.

Kento's   Kento's was one of the first places to open when the wave of 1950s nostalgia hit Japan in the 1980s; it has even been credited with creating the craze. This is the place to come if you feel like bopping the night away to tunes of the 1950s and 1960s played by live bands. Although there's hardly room to dance, that doesn't stop the largely over-30 Japanese audience from twisting in the aisles as the night wears on. Hours are Monday to Saturday from 6pm to 2am, Sunday and holidays from 6pm to 11:30pm. (Also at 8–2–1 Ginza, on the 9th floor, ✆ **03/3572-9161;** and in east Shinjuku at 3–18–4 Shinjuku, on the 6th floor, www.kentos-tokyo.jp. ✆ **03/3355-6477.**) Daini Reine Building, 5–3–1 Roppongi. ✆ **03/3401-5755.** Cover ¥2,100, plus 10% service charge and 1-drink minimum. Station: Roppongi (4 min.). Take the side street going downhill on the left side of Almond Coffee Shop, and then take the 1st left; the club is on the right.

Liquidroom   This is the most happening place in Ebisu (if not all of Tokyo) for live events, with concerts, well-known DJs, and stage events most nights of the week. Lots of groups kick off their world tours here, in a huge, cavernous room where the energy is so pervasive that the floor vibrates. On the second floor is Time Out Café & Diner (www.timeoutcafe.jp; (✆ **03/5774-0440**), with decent food and free Wi-Fi, open Monday to Friday noon to 11:30pm, Saturday 1 to 11:30pm, and Sunday 3 to 10pm. Liquidroom usually opens around 6pm, with live events from about 7 to 10pm or later. 3–16–6 Higashi, Shibuya-ku. www.liquidroom.net. ✆ **03/5464-0800.** Cover ¥3,000–¥6,000, depending on the event. Station: Ebisu (3 min.). Take the west exit, cross Komazawa Dori and turn right, and then turn left at Meiji Dori; it will be almost immediately on your left.

New York Bar   This is one of Tokyo's most sophisticated venues, boasting Manhattan-style jazz and breathtaking views of glittering west Shinjuku. Unfortunately, it's also one of the city's smallest. Consider coming for dinner in the adjacent **New York Grill** (p. 130); it costs a small fortune, but you'll save the cost of the cover. Hours are daily from 5pm, with live music 8pm to midnight (from 7pm on Sun). Park Hyatt Hotel, 52nd floor, 3–7–1–2 Nishi-Shinjuku, Shinjuku-ku. http://tokyo.park.hyatt.com. ✆ **03/5322-1234.** Cover ¥2,200. Station: Shinjuku (13 min.), Hatsudai on the Keio Line (7 min.), or Tochomae (8 min.).

The Ruby Room   I've seen living rooms larger than this second-floor venue, home to local acts, open-mic Tuesdays, house and techno DJs, and other events. The crowd depends on the music, but because there's no room to move, people dance where they are. The band is close, close, close—any closer and you'd be in the drummer's lap. Open Monday, Tuesday, Thursday, Friday and Saturday from 7pm or later, depending on the event (some concerts get underway at midnight), until 5am. 2–25–17 Dogenzaka, Shibuya-ku. www.rubyroomtokyo.com. ✆ **03/3780-3022.** Cover ¥1,500–¥2,000 Fri–Sat only, including 1 drink; Tues open mike ¥1,000, including 2 drinks. Station: Shibuya (Hachiko exit, 4 min.). Walk on Dogenzaka to the Prime Building and Royal Host and take the 1st right; keep to the left at the Y intersection.

Shinjuku Pit Inn   This is one of Tokyo's most famous and longest-running jazz, fusion, and blues clubs, featuring both Japanese and foreign musicians. There are two programs daily—from 2:30 to 5pm and from 7:30 or 8pm—making it a great place to stop for a bit of music in the middle of the day. 2–12–4 Shinjuku, Shinjuku-ku. www.pit-inn. com. ✆ **03/3354-2024.** Cover, including 1 drink, ¥1,300 for the 2:30pm show (¥2,500 Sat–Sun and holidays), ¥3,000 for the evening shows. Station: Shinjuku Sanchome (3 min.). Northeast of the Shinjuku Dori/Meiji Dori intersection.

What the Dickens!   One of Tokyo's most popular expat bars, What the Dickens! packs 'em in with live bands nightly from 8:30 to 11:30pm (everything from rock and pop to reggae, jazz, blues, Dixieland, and folk), no cover, British beer on tap, and hearty servings of pub grub. Come early for happy hour, available every day except Sunday and holidays from 5 to 7pm. Hours are Tuesday to Thursday 5pm to 1am, Friday and Saturday 5pm to 2am, and Sunday 3pm to midnight. 1–13–3 Ebisu Nishi, Shibuya-ku. 4th floor of the Roob Building. www.whatthedickens.jp. ✆ **03/3780-2099.** Station: Ebisu (west exit, 3 min.). On the other side of Komazawa Dori street, take the small street beside St. Marc Café; it's at the end of the 2nd block on the left, on the corner.

Bars & Clubs
GINZA

Ginza Sapporo Lion   Yebisu and Sapporo beer are the draw at this large beer hall, a Ginza institution since 1934 and popular with older Japanese for its mock Gothic ceiling, wall murals, colored mosaic tiles, and German decor. A large display of plastic foods and an English-language menu offer snacks ranging from yakitori to sausage and spaghetti. Hours are Monday to Saturday from 11:30am to 11pm, Sunday and holidays from 11:30am to 10:30pm. 7–9–20 Ginza. ✆ **03/3571-2590.** Station: Ginza (3 min.). On Chuo Dori not far from the Matsuzakaya department store.

Lupin (ルパン) 👔   You couldn't find a more subdued place than this tiny basement bar. First opened in 1928, it has an interesting history, including the fact that it was forced to temporarily change its name during World War II (foreign names were banned) and then had to procure and sell liquor secretly after the war. In any case, with its long wooden bar and booths, it seems little changed over the decades; even the staff looks like they've been here since it opened. Because no music is ever played here, it's a great place for conversation. Very civilized. There's a table charge of ¥800 per person, which includes a snack. The local Heartland beer is on tap. Hours are Tuesday to Saturday from 5 to 11:30pm. 5–5–11 Ginza. ✆ **03/3571-0750.** Station: Ginza (2 min.). In a tiny alley btw. Namiki and Ginza W. 5th St. (look for a nearby torigin sign).

Nelson's Bar Gabbiano ⚓   You could spend a fortune in the Ginza, or you could come here and pay only ¥500 for a glass of beer, wine or mixed drink. Decorated like an old sailor's bar with its rustic decor, hurricane lamp, wooden parrot, and other memorabilia, the two-level bar is small and usually crowded, a favorite haunt of Japanese and expats alike. It's open Monday to Thursday from 5pm to 1am, Friday from 5pm to 5am, and Saturday and Sunday from 4pm to midnight. 2–5–16 Ginza. ✆ **03/3564-8600.** Station: Ginza (4 min.). From Ginza Crossing, walk north on Chuo Dori past Apple, turn left at Chanel, take the first right, and then turn left at Sapporo Lion Bar; it will be on the right of this small alleyway, up on the second floor.

Old Imperial   This is the Imperial Hotel's tribute to its original architect, Frank Lloyd Wright, and is the only place in the hotel that contains Wright originals—the Art Deco terra-cotta wall behind the bar, the mural, and the small desk at the entrance. Its clubby atmosphere, low lighting, and comfortable chairs and tables (copies of Wright originals) make it perfect for a lunchtime sandwich or a quiet drink. Try the Mount Fuji, the bar's own 1924 creation: dry gin, lemon juice, pineapple juice, egg white, and maraschino cherry. Hours are daily 11:30am to midnight. Imperial Hotel, 1–1–1 Uchisaiwai-cho. www.imperialhotel.co.jp. ✆ **03/3539-8088.** Station: Hibiya (1 min.).

300 Bar   You don't want to come here when you're drop-dead tired, because there are no seats in this standing bar. Rather, with all drinks and appetizers priced at ¥315 (including tax), this is a good place for a quick drink or a place to meet up with friends in the Ginza. It's self-service and, upon entry you're required to purchase two tickets totaling ¥630, which can be redeemed for two drinks or food items from the 100-plus menu listing everything from cocktails to such snacks as tofu gratin and fried rice balls. There are two locations in the Ginza, the one below and at 8–3–12 Ginza (✆ **03/3571-8300**). Both are open Monday to Saturday 5pm to 2am, Sunday and holidays 5 to 11pm. 5–9–11 Ginza. www.300bar.com. ✆ **03/3572-6300.** Station: Ginza (2 min.). On a side street southeast of the Ginza 4–chome Crossing.

ASAKUSA

Bar Six 🎁   Looking for a place to chill after a day of sightseeing in Asakusa? Better yet, a place with a view? Bar Six, located on the sixth floor of Amuse Museum (p. 94), is conveniently located next to Sensoji Temple and even boasts a terrace overlooking temple grounds. Belgian beers, whiskey, and other drinks are available; note that there's a ¥800 per-person seat charge. Open daily 6pm to 2am. Amuse Museum, 6th floor, 2–34–3 Asakusa. ✆ **03/5806-5106.** Station: Asakusa (5 min.). Just east of Sensoji Temple, past Nitemmon Gate.

Daimasu   This sake bar offers more than 100 different kinds of sake and shochu by the glass, allowing you to try a variety of different kinds, including seasonal and regional varieties. Or, sample three different kinds of sake for ¥1,000. Alternatively, purchase alcohol at the shop's adjoining liquor store and drink it at the sake bar; corkage fee is ¥200 for beer and ¥500 for wine or sake. Open daily noon to 11:30pm. 1–2–8 Asakusa. ✆ **03/5806-3811.** Station: Asakusa (3 min.).Just off Nakamise Dori, to the right if walking from Kaminarimon Gate toward Sensoji Temple.

Sky Room 🍸   This is a great—albeit simple—place for an inexpensive drink after an active day in Asakusa. The Asahi Beer Tower, which sits next to the distinctive building with the golden hops perched on top, belongs to the Asahi Beer company; it's thought to represent a mug of foaming beer. The plain, cafeteria-style bar, perched at the top of the building in the foam next to **La Ranarita Azumabashi** (p. 126), offers great views of the Sumida River with its barge traffic, Asakusa, and Sky Tree, as well as different kinds of Asahi beer, wine, coffee, tea, and sodas, all priced at ¥600 or less, and a very limited snack menu. With seating for only 26 at a window-side counter, it can be crowded on weekends. Open daily 10am to 9:30pm. Asahi Beer Tower, 22nd floor, 1–23–1 Azumabashi. ✆ **03/5608-5277.** Station: Asakusa (exit 5, 4 min.). On the opposite side of the Sumida River from Sensoji Temple.

SHINJUKU

Albatross 🍴 This tiny bar is one of the 100 or so miniature establishments nestled in Goruden Gai. Painted a blood red and eclectically decorated with chandeliers, a deer head, and other memorabilia, it attracts a mostly young crowd—though there's room for only a handful of patrons squeezed along the counter, with additional two tiers of seating up the narrow flight of stairs. There's a ¥300 snack charge per person. Open daily 8pm to 5am. 1-1-7 Kabuki-cho. ℂ **03/3203-3699.** Station: Shinjuku Sanchome (7 min.). In Goruden Gai, on 5th St. (Gobangai).

Dubliners' Irish Pub Attracting expats and locals alike—mostly in their 30s and 40s—is this chain Irish bar, especially for its weekday happy hour from 3 to 7pm. A menu lists such perennial favorites as fish and chips and minced lamb shepherd's pie. Open Monday to Thursday 3 to 11:30pm, Friday 3pm to 1am, Saturday noon to 1am, Sunday noon to 11pm. 3-28-9 Shinjuku. ℂ **03/3352-6606.** Station: Shinjuku (east exit, 3 min.). In east Shinjuku, behind Mitsukoshi department store to the southwest, above Sapporo Lion.

Tokyo Loose Young Tokyoites who work in Shinjuku come here after hours to hang out and to dance to trance, hip-hop, techno, soul, R&B, and house music spun by local DJs. Things don't get hopping until after midnight, and even when the sun comes up it's night at this small basement club that attracts a good mix of Japanese and foreigners, most in their twenties. Happy hour is until 11pm Monday to Thursday, when drinks cost ¥500. Open daily at 8pm, closing when the crowd thins out (about 10am on weekends). 2-37-3 Kabuki-cho. www.tokyoloose.com. ℂ **03/3207-5677.** Cover (Fri–Sat only) ¥1,000, including 1 drink for men, 2 drinks for women. Station: Shinjuku (east exit, 10 min.). North of Koma Stadium, on Hanamichi Dori.

ROPPONGI

Gaspanic Bar This has long been *the* bar for foreign and Japanese 20-somethings (it claims that its four properties, three listed here and one in Shibuya, receive150,000 people a month). The music is loud, and after midnight the place gets so crowded that you may see female patrons dancing on the countertops. Thursdays are especially packed—all drinks are only ¥300. Drinks are also just ¥300 daily during happy hour to 10pm. In the basement is **Club 99,** open Thursday to Saturday from 9pm to 9am for dancing. Nearby, **GP Bar,** on Gaien-Higashi Dori, across from the Roi Building at 3-10-5 Roppongi (ℂ **03/3402-7054**), is open daily 6pm to 5am for dancing. All offer the same Thursday and happy-hour drink specials. Large bouncers at all the doors serve as clues that these places can get rough. Hours for Gaspanic Bar are daily 6pm to 5am. 3-15-24 Roppongi. www.gaspanic.co.jp. ℂ **03/3405-0633.** Station: Roppongi (4 min.). From Roppongi Crossing, walk toward Tokyo Tower on Gaien-Higashi Dori, and turn left at Family Mart.

Geronimo Shot Bar People seem to either love or hate this place. It's tiny, dominated by a bar in the middle that's surrounded by people who come to drink, dance, and socialize, making it a good place to meet people. If the gong sounds, it means someone has bought a shot for everyone there, and this happens more than you might think. Happy hour is until 9pm. Open Monday to Friday 6pm to 5am, Saturday and Sunday 7pm to 5am. 7-14-10 Roppongi. www.geronimoshotbar.com. ℂ **03/3478-7449.** Station: Roppongi (1 min.). On Roppongi Crossing, across from Almond Coffee Shop.

Heartland This is the New Age reincarnation of a former popular dive, occupying a corner of Roppongi Hills and attracting crowds of mostly expats, from bankers and investors to artistic types. Artwork not only fills the walls but also is projected onto a curved wall behind the bar that acts as a screen. Seating is limited, forcing people to mill around as though it were a private cocktail reception every night of the week, and a DJ on weekends keeps things hopping. What to order? Try the bar's namesake Heartland microbrew (produced by Kirin). Hours are daily 5pm to 4am. 6–10–1 Roppongi. ℂ **03/5772-7600.** Station: Roppongi (3 min.). From Roppongi Crossing, walk on Roppongi Dori to the end of Roppongi Hills; it will be on the left.

Paddy Foley's   Easy to find, Tokyo's first Irish pub is still popular with both Japanese and foreigners. Happy hour is until 8pm Monday to Thursday, 7pm Friday, and 6pm Saturday and Sunday; several screens show live sports events (mainly soccer and rugby); and there's occasional live music (usually on the second and last Friday of every month) and even live dancers (from Irish to belly dancing). It's open Monday to Thursday 6pm to 2am, Friday 5pm to 4am, Saturday 1pm to 4am, and Sunday 3pm to 2am. Roi Building basement, 5–5–1 Roppongi. www.paddyfoleystokyo.com. ℂ **03/3497-9900.** Station: Roppongi (3 min.). On Gaien-Higashi Dori, on the right as you walk from Roppongi Crossing toward Tokyo Tower.

Gay & Lesbian Bars

Shinjuku Ni-chome (pronounced "*nee*-chomay"), southeast of the Yasukuni-Gyoen Dori intersection (station: Shinjuku Sanchome), is Tokyo's gay and lesbian quarter, with a lively street scene and countless establishments catering to a variety of age groups and preferences. The following are good starting points, but you'll find a lot more in the immediate area by exploring on your own. Attracting both gays and straights, **Advocates,** 2–18–1 Shinjuku (ℂ **03/3358-3988**), is a crowded, small bar open to the street with a few sidewalk tables, making this a good vantage point from which to watch the street action. It's also a good place to network and find out about neighboring bars. **Kinsmen,** on the second floor at 2–18–5 Shinjuku (ℂ **03/3354-4949**), has been welcoming customers of all persuasions for as long as I can remember. It's a pleasant oasis, small and civilized. It's closed on Monday. The casual, laid-back, women-only **Kinswomyn,** 2–15–10 Shinjuku (ℂ **03/3354-8720**), attracts a regular clientele of mainly Japanese lesbians and has a friendly, welcoming atmosphere. It's closed on Tuesday. **Arty Farty,** 2–11–7 Shinjuku (ℂ **03/5362-9720**), one of Ni-chome's larger gay bars, is also one of the best places to dance, due to a good sound system and music that ranges from house to hip-hop. Although it used to be strictly males only, it recently moved to a new location (across from the legendary Pit Inn jazz house; p. 163) and threw open its doors to all. A fun climax to a pub-crawl in Shinjuku.

WHERE TO STAY

Tokyo has no old, grand hotels in the tradition of Hong Kong's Peninsula or Bangkok's Oriental; it has hardly any old hotels, period. But what the city's hotels may lack in quaintness or old grandeur is more than made up for by excellent service—for which Japanese are legendary—as well as cleanliness and efficiency. Be prepared, however, for small rooms. Space is at a premium in Tokyo, so with the exception of some of Tokyo's most expensive hotels, rooms seem to come in only three sizes: small, minuscule, and barely adequate.

Unfortunately, Tokyo also doesn't have many first-class *ryokan,* or Japanese-style inns. I suggest, therefore, that you wait for your travels around the country to experience a first-rate ryokan. Otherwise, there are moderate and inexpensive Japanese-style inns in Tokyo. In fact, if you're traveling on a tight budget, a simple Japanese-style

Mapping out Tokyo's Hotels

Once you've chosen a hotel or inn that appeals to you, you can locate it using the following neighborhood maps:

- To locate accommodations in **Shinjuku,** p. 172.
- To locate accommodations in **Asakusa,** p. 177.

- To locate accommodations in **Ueno,** p. 183.
- To locate accommodations in **Hibiya** and **Ginza,** p. 118.
- To locate accommodations in **Harajuku,** p. 135.
- To locate accommodations in **Roppongi,** p. 139.

inn is often the cheapest way to go, though don't expect much in the way of service or amenities. In addition, most of the upper-bracket hotels offer at least a few Japanese-style rooms, with *tatami* mats, a Japanese bathtub (deeper and narrower than the Western version), and a futon. Although these rooms tend to be expensive, they're usually large enough for four people.

For more on available types of accommodations, see "Tips on Accommodations" in chapter 14.

PRICE CATEGORIES   The recommended hotels that follow are arranged first according to price, then by location. After all, because attractions are spread throughout the city, and Tokyo's public transportation service is fast and efficient (I've provided nearest subway or train stations for each listing)—and as this is one of the most expensive hotel cities in the world—the overriding factor in selecting accommodations will likely be cost. I've divided Tokyo's hotels into price categories based upon two people per night, including tax: **Very Expensive** hotels charge ¥50,000 and above, **Expensive** hotels charge ¥32,000 to ¥50,000, **Moderate** hotels offer rooms for ¥16,000 to ¥32,000, and **Inexpensive** accommodations offer rooms for less than ¥16,000. Keep in mind that these are rack rates; you're likely to find cheaper rates posted on hotel websites.

Unless otherwise indicated, units have private bathrooms. Note, too, that in Japan, a **twin room** refers to a room with two twin beds, while a **double room** refers to a room with one double bed. For convenience's sake, however, the "double" rates for hotels listed below refer to two people in one room and include both twin and double beds. Most hotels charge more for a twin room, but sometimes the opposite is the case. When making your reservation, therefore, inquire about the differences in rates and what they entail.

TAXES & SERVICE CHARGES   All hotel rates below include a 5% government **tax.** An additional local hotel tax will be added to bills that cost more than ¥10,000 per person per night. ¥100 is levied per person per night for rates between ¥10,000 and ¥14,999; rates of ¥15,000 and up are taxed at ¥200. Furthermore, upper-class hotels and most medium-range hotels add a **service charge** of 10% to 15% (cheaper establishments do not add a service charge, because no service is provided). Unless otherwise stated, prices for accommodations include all taxes and service charge.

RESERVATIONS   Although Tokyo doesn't suffer from a lack of hotel rooms during peak holidays (when most Japanese head for the hills and beaches), rooms may be in short supply at other times because of conventions and other events. If possible, avoid coming to Tokyo in mid-February unless you book well in advance; that's when university entrance exams bring aspiring high-school students and their parents flocking to the capital for a shot at one of the most prestigious universities in the country. And in summer, when most foreign tourists visit Japan, the cheaper accommodations are likely to fill up first. It's always best, therefore, to make your hotel reservations in advance, especially if you're arriving in Japan after a long transoceanic flight and don't want the hassle of searching for a hotel room. See "Tips on Accommodations" in chapter 14 for information on securing rooms.

Very Expensive

NEAR GINZA

The Peninsula Tokyo ★★★   Travelers who love the ornate lobby of Hong Kong's The Peninsula may experience culture shock here. While the lobby layouts are the same—dominated by a restaurant popular for people-watching—here the decor is Zen-like, and the emphasis is on the rooms. Rooms begin at 51 sq. m. (544 sq. ft.), with the most expensive facing the Imperial Palace and Hibiya Park, and amenities include bedside controls that light up with the slightest touch, gorgeous bathrooms with mood lighting (and tubs big enough for two), and dryers just for nails. Add a fantastic location between the Imperial Palace and Ginza, gratis transportation via Rolls-Royce within a 2km (1¼-mile) radius, free iPod tours of the surrounding area, and the Peninsula Academy offering classes for cooking and flower arranging, and it's clear this hotel is in a class all its own.

1–8–1 Yurakucho, Chiyoda-ku, Tokyo 100-0006. www.peninsula.com. ✆ **866/382 8388** in the U.S., or 03/6270-2888. Fax 03/6270-2000. 314 units. ¥60,000–¥80,000 single or double; from ¥120,000 suite. Rates exclude taxes and service charge. AE, DC, MC, V. Station: Yurakucho (3 min.); Hibiya (1 min.). **Amenities:** 5 restaurants; bar; babysitting; free use of bikes; concierge; health club and spa; 20m indoor pool w/outdoor terrace; room service. *In room:* A/C, TV/DVD and DVD library, CD player, fax/printer, hair dryer, minibar, Wi-Fi.

NEAR TOKYO STATION

Shangri-La Hotel, Tokyo ★★★   This was the third Hong Kong-based property to debut in Tokyo in almost as many years (following The Peninsula and Mandarin Oriental), and like its predecessors, it spares no expense in luxury and services. Located adjacent to Tokyo Station on the top 11 floors of a 37-floor office and retail building, it wows with the Shangri-La's trademark dedication to art, with 2,000 pieces adorning the hotel along with 50 chandeliers. Rooms, the smallest of which are 50 sq. m (538 sq. ft.), are opulently decorated, with low windows and chaise lounges taking advantage of the view (I was told Japanese prefer views toward Tokyo Bay, while foreigners seem partial to views of Tokyo Station and the Imperial Palace park.). If you wish, there's a free escort from and to any train platform at Tokyo Station.

1–8–3 Marunouchi, Chiyoda-ku, Tokyo 100-8283. www.shangri-la.com. ✆ **866/565-5050** in the U.S. and Canada, or 03/6739-7888. Fax 03/6739-7889. 200 units. ¥70,000–¥82,000 single or double; from ¥100,000 Horizon Club; from ¥250,000 suite. Rates exclude taxes and service charge. Off-season discounts available. AE, DC, MC, V. Station: Tokyo Station (1 min.). **Amenities:** 2 restaurants; lounge; babysitting; concierge; health club w/indoor pool overlooking Imperial Palace garden and Jacuzzi; room service; spa. *In room:* A/C, TV/DVD, hair dryer, minibar, Wi-Fi.

SHINJUKU

Park Hyatt Tokyo ★★★   Located on the 39th to 52nd floors of Kenzo Tange's granite-and-glass Shinjuku Park Tower, the Park Hyatt is among the most gorgeous hotels in Japan, a perfect reflection of high-tech Tokyo. If you can afford it, stay here.

Though it doesn't attract as much off-the-street foot traffic as Shinjuku's other hotels, the Park Hyatt's debut in *Lost in Translation* assures a steady stream of curious fans to its lounges and restaurants. Be sure to book early, therefore, for the 52nd-floor New York Grill, one of Tokyo's best restaurants. All rooms average at least 45 sq. m (484 sq. ft.) and have original artwork, stunning views (including Mount Fuji on clear days), bathrooms to die for with deep tubs and separate showers, walk-in closets, and even Japanese/English-language dictionaries. Although no longer the only high-in-the-sky luxury hotel, this property remains high on my short list of great places to stay.

3–7–1–2 Nishi-Shinjuku, Shinjuku-ku, Tokyo 163-1055. www.tokyo.park.hyatt.com. © **800/233-1234** in the U.S. and Canada, or 03/5322-1234. Fax 03/5322-1288. 177 units. ¥70,455–¥90,000 single or double; from ¥170,940 suite. Rates exclude hotel tax. AE, DC, MC, V. Station: Shinjuku (a 13-min. walk or 5-min. free shuttle ride); Hatsudai, on the Keio Line (7 min.); or Tochomae (8 min.). **Amenities:** 3 restaurants, including New York Grill (p. 130); 3 bars; lounge; babysitting; concierge; health club and spa; dramatic 20m indoor pool w/great views; room service; free shuttle service to Shinjuku Station up to 3 times an hr. *In room:* A/C, TV/DVD, CD player and CD library, hair dryer, minibar, Wi-Fi.

ROPPONGI

Grand Hyatt Tokyo ★★★   Depending on surrounding Roppongi Hills with its 200-some shops and restaurants to act as a major draw, this stylish hotel gets kudos for its wide range of recreational and dining facilities, as well as its technically advanced rooms that older hotels can only dream about. In contrast to sister Park Hyatt's subdued, sophisticated atmosphere that attracts bigwigs hoping to escape the limelight, the Grand Hyatt strives for a livelier clientele who relish being in the center of it all. Those seeking pampering can opt for the Grand Club floor. Rooms, starting at 42 sq. m (452 sq. ft.), feature large mahogany desks, blackout blinds activated by a button, and bedside focused reading lights. One-quarter of each unit's space is taken up by a huge bathroom equipped with separate shower and tub areas and a small TV that swivels from the tub to the sink.

Roppongi Hills, 6–10–3 Roppongi, Minato-ku, Tokyo 106-0032. www.tokyo.grand.hyatt.com. © **800/233-1234** in the U.S. and Canada, or 03/4333-1234. Fax 03/4333-8123. 389 units. ¥50,820–¥58,905 single; ¥56,595–¥64,680 double; from ¥68,145 Grand Club double; from ¥103,950 suite. Rates exclude hotel tax. Children 12 and under stay free in parent's room. AE, DC, MC, V. Station: Roppongi (exit 1, 3 min.) or Azabu-Juban (exit A3, 5 min.). **Amenities:** 7 restaurants; 3 bars; babysitting; concierge (plus technology concierge to address your computer woes); executive-level rooms; health club w/20m red granite indoor pool and spa (fee: ¥4,200); room service. *In room:* A/C, TV/DVD and DVD library, hair dryer, minibar, Wi-Fi.

The Ritz-Carlton, Tokyo ★★★   Of the several luxury hotels to come online the past few years, the Ritz-Carlton literally tops them all: It occupies the lofty upper reaches of Tokyo's tallest building, making it the highest hotel in a city that prides itself on skyscraper hotels. The crowning glory of Roppongi's Midtown urban renewal project, it boasts Tokyo's largest rooms (starting at 52 sq. m/560 sq. ft.) and its most expensive suite (¥2,100,000 in case you're considering it). Rooms, from the 47th to 53rd floors, provide eye-popping views of Tokyo and come with everything you'd expect from a top-rated hotel, including—great for couples—two large closets and humongous bathrooms which account for a third of the room's space.

Tokyo Midtown, 9–7–1 Akasaka, Minato-ku, Tokyo 107-6245. www.ritzcarlton.com. © **800/241-3333** in the U.S. and Canada, or 03/3423-8000. Fax 03/3423-8001. 248 units. ¥73,500–¥76,650 single; ¥78,750–¥81,900 double; Club floors from ¥89,250 single, ¥99,750 double; from ¥126,000 suite. Rates exclude service charge and hotel tax. AE, DC, MC, V. Station: Roppongi or Nogizaka (3 min.). **Amenities:** 3 restaurants; bar; lounge; babysitting; concierge; executive-level rooms; health club

family-FRIENDLY HOTELS

Four Seasons Hotel Tokyo at Chinzan-So (p. 174)   If money is no object, little princes and princesses receive the royal treatment here, including a welcome amenity, child-size robes, children's menus, complimentary toiletries, and bedtime cookies and milk.

Hotel New Otani (p. 171)   This huge hotel has an outdoor swimming pool (which you can use free of charge by becoming a Hotel Club member), but best for parents is the babysitting room for children ages 1 month to 5 years. For a small fortune, you can even leave the darlings overnight.

Imperial Hotel (p. 170)   This famous hotel makes it easier to bring the family along, with its day-care center for children ages 2 weeks to 6 years, its babysitting service, and an indoor pool, which you can use free of charge by becoming a member of the Imperial Club.

Ryokan Kamogawa (p. 181)   Located in colorful Asakusa with its famous Sensoji Temple and small Hanayashiki amusement park, this Japanese inn offers *tatami* rooms large enough for up to six persons, plus a private family bath.

Shinagawa Prince (p. 179)   Japan's largest hotel boasts a children's day-care center, cinema complex, amusement arcade, indoor and outdoor pools, aquarium, bowling alley, sports center, and much more.

w/20m indoor lap pool and spa (free entrance to health club; spa entrance fee: ¥5,250); room service. *In room:* A/C, TV/DVD, CD player, hair dryer, minibar, Wi-Fi.

Expensive

GINZA & HIBIYA

Imperial Hotel ★★★ ☺   Located across from Hibiya Park, this is one of Tokyo's best-known hotels. Its history dates from 1890, when it opened at the request of the imperial family to house foreigners visiting Japan; it was rebuilt in 1922 by Frank Lloyd Wright, but the present hotel dates from 1970. Wright's legacy lives on in the hotel's Art Deco Old Imperial bar and Wright-inspired designs and furniture in public spaces. (Part of Wright's original structure survives as Meiji Mura, an architectural museum outside Nagoya.) Rooms are large for Tokyo, with all the first-class amenities you'd expect from one of Tokyo's top hotels. For the best views, ask for a room facing Hibiya Park. *Tip:* Become a member of the Imperial Club International (membership is free), and you can use the small pool and gym free of charge as well as qualify for other discounts.

1–1–1 Uchisaiwaicho, Chiyoda-ku, Tokyo 100-8558. www.imperialhotel.co.jp/e/tokyo. © **800/223-6800** in the U.S. and Canada, or 03/3504-1111. Fax 03/3581-9146. 1,019 units. ¥39,900—¥63,000 single; ¥45,150–¥68,250 double; from ¥73,500 suite. Imperial Floor ¥45,150–¥68,250 single; ¥50,400–¥73,500 double. Rates exclude service charge and hotel tax. AE, DC, MC, V. Station: Hibiya (1 min.). **Amenities:** 13 restaurants, including Kamon, Ten-ichi, and the Imperial Viking Sal (p. 120, 120 and 121); 2 bars, including the Old Imperial Bar (p. 164); lounge; babysitting; children's day-care center for ages 2 weeks to 6 years (fee: ¥5,250 for 2 hr.); concierge; executive-level rooms; exercise room (fee: ¥1,050; free for Imperial Club International members); 20th-floor indoor pool (fee: ¥1,050; free for Imperial Club International members); room service; sauna; in-house doctor; tea-ceremony room; post office. *In room:* A/C, TV, hair dryer, Internet, minibar.

SHINJUKU

Hyatt Regency Tokyo ★   Located on Shinjuku's west side next to Shinjuku Chuo (Central) Park (popular with joggers), this is the least expensive and oldest of the

Hyatt's three Tokyo properties, with three of the most massive chandeliers you're likely to see anywhere a trademark of its seven-story atrium lobby. Many foreigners (mostly American) have passed through the hotel's doors, ably assisted by the excellent staff, which meets the Hyatt's usual high standards. However, because this hotel is popular with both business and leisure groups, those seeking a quieter, more personalized experience will want to book elsewhere. Rates are based on size; even the cheapest units are adequate, but they do face another building and don't receive much sunshine. If you can afford it, spring for a more expensive room on a high floor with bay windows overlooking the park (in winter, you might also have a view of Mt. Fuji).

2–7–2 Nishi-Shinjuku, Shinjuku-ku, Tokyo 160-0023. http://tokyo.regency.hyatt.com. ℂ **800/233-1234** in the U.S. and Canada, or 03/3348-1234. Fax 03/3344-5575. 744 units. ¥35,700 single; ¥38,850–¥43,050 double. Regency Club from ¥45,150 single; ¥48,300 double. Rates exclude service charge and hotel tax. AE, DC, MC, V. Station: Tochomae (1 min.), Nishi-Shinjuku (3 min.), or Shinjuku (a 10-min. walk, or a free 3-min. shuttle ride). **Amenities:** 6 restaurants; bar; concierge; executive-level rooms; health club w/indoor pool (fee: ¥2,000) and spa; room service; free shuttle service to Shinjuku Station every 20 min; Wi-Fi (free, in lobby). *In room:* A/C, TV, hair dryer, Internet, minibar.

AKASAKA

Hotel New Otani ★★ ☺   This hotel's most splendid feature is a 400-year-old Japanese garden that once belonged to a feudal lord, with 4 hectares (10 acres) of ponds, waterfalls, bridges, bamboo groves, and manicured bushes. Note, however, that the New Otani is so big, two information desks are needed to assist lost souls searching for a particular restaurant or one of the shops in the meandering arcade. Rooms range from those in the main building (built for the 1964 Olympics) with full-length windows to take advantage of city and garden views to tower rooms that offer the best views—of the garden, the skyscrapers of Shinjuku, and, on clear days, Mount Fuji. Since rates are the same no matter which way you face, be sure to request a room overlooking the garden. Parents appreciate the 24-hour Baby Room and the fact that the outdoor pool is free for those who become Club International members (membership is free).

4–1 Kioi-cho, Chiyoda-ku, Tokyo 102-8578. www.newotani.co.jp. ℂ **800/421-8795** in the U.S. and Canada, or 03/3265-1111. Fax 03/3221-2619. 1,533 units. ¥32,500–¥39,900 single; ¥37,800–¥45,100 double; from ¥50,400 Executive House Zen; from ¥89,250 suite. Rates exclude service charge and hotel tax. AE, DC, MC, V. Station: Akasaka-mitsuke or Nagatacho (3 min.). **Amenities:** 31 restaurants and cafes; 7 bars and lounges; children's day-care center for ages 2 months to 5 years old (fee: ¥6,300 for 2 hr.); concierge; executive-level rooms; small exercise room; health club w/indoor pool and spa (fee: ¥5,250); outdoor pool (fee: ¥2,000; free for Club International members); room service; lighted outdoor tennis courts; medical and dental clinics; art museum (free for hotel guests); post office; tea-ceremony room. *In room:* A/C, TV, hair dryer, Internet (fee: ¥1,260 for 24 hr.), minibar.

Hotel Okura ★★★   Located across from the U.S. Embassy and long considered one of Tokyo's most venerable hotels, the Okura is a favorite home-away-from-home of visiting U.S. dignitaries, and the service is gracious and impeccable. Rich decor elegantly combines Japanese traditions with an old-fashioned Western spaciousness. The atmosphere is low-key, with none of the flashiness inherent in some newer hotels. All rooms are comfortable, with opaque windows designed to resemble *shoji* and gold colors offset by fuchsia or other bright-colored armchairs and pillows. My favorite rooms are in the main building facing the garden; some on the fifth floor here have balconies overlooking the garden and pool. Other rooms have views of a rooftop garden or Tokyo Tower, while "Grand Comfort rooms" on the 9th and 10th floors offer free entrance to the spa. *Tip:* Become a member of Okura Club International (membership is free) and you can use the health club and pools for free.

Shinjuku

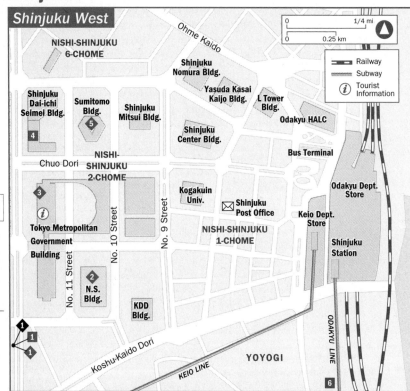

Shinjuku West

NISHI-SHINJUKU 6-CHOME

Ohme Kaido

Shinjuku Nomura Bldg.

Yasuda Kasai Kaijo Bldg.

L Tower Bldg.

Odakyu HALC

Shinjuku Dai-ichi Seimei Bldg.

Sumitomo Bldg.

Shinjuku Mitsui Bldg.

Shinjuku Center Bldg.

Bus Terminal

Chuo Dori

NISHI-SHINJUKU 2-CHOME

Kogakuin Univ.

Shinjuku Post Office

Odakyu Dept. Store

Keio Dept. Store

Tokyo Metropolitan Government Building

No. 10 Street

No. 9 Street

NISHI-SHINJUKU 1-CHOME

Shinjuku Station

No. 11 Street

N.S. Bldg.

KDD Bldg.

Koshu-Kaido Dori

YOYOGI

ODAKYU LINE

KEIO LINE

Railway · Subway · (i) Tourist Information

0 — 1/4 mi
0 — 0.25 km

4

TOKYO | **Where to Stay**

2–10–4 Toranomon, Minato-ku, Tokyo 105-0001. www.okura.com/tokyo. © **03/3582-0111.** Fax 03/3582-3707. 833 units. ¥36,750–¥44,100 single; ¥42,000–¥49,350 double; from ¥94,500 suite. Grand Comfort rooms ¥52,500 single; ¥66,150 double. Rates exclude service charge and hotel tax. AE, DC, MC, V. Station: Toranomon or Kamiyacho (5 min.). **Amenities:** 9 restaurants; 3 bars; children's day-care center (fee: ¥6,300 for 2 hr.); concierge; health club w/indoor 20m pool (fee: ¥5,775) and spa; nicely landscaped outdoor pool (fee: ¥2,100); room service; free shuttle service to the nearest subways (Sat–Sun only); tea-ceremony room; in-house dentist; private museum showcasing Japanese art (free for hotel guests); pharmacy; packing and shipping service; post office. *In room:* A/C, TV, hair dryer, Internet (fee: ¥1,500 for 1 day), minibar.

NEAR SHINAGAWA

Sheraton Miyako Hotel Tokyo ★★ ✦   This hotel is one of my favorites in Tokyo, for its calm peacefulness as well as its small-luxury-hotel service. Because it's a bit off the beaten path, it has a quieter, more relaxed atmosphere than those found at more centrally located hotels, evident the moment you step into its lobby lounge with its gas-flame fireplace (winter only) on one end and the lush greenery of a garden on its other. It offers average-size rooms, with good bedside reading lamps and beds so comfortable you'd sneak them into your luggage if you could. The best rooms are on higher floors with huge floor-to-ceiling windows overlooking the hotel's own lush

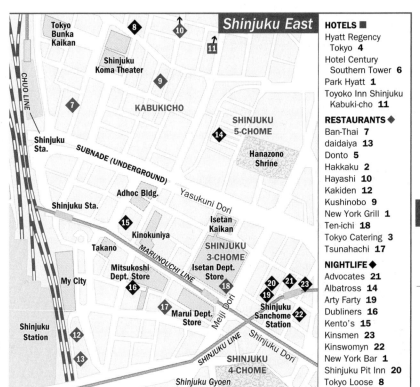

Shinjuku East

HOTELS ■
Hyatt Regency Tokyo **4**
Hotel Century Southern Tower **6**
Park Hyatt **1**
Toyoko Inn Shinjuku Kabuki-cho **11**

RESTAURANTS ◆
Ban-Thai **7**
daidaiya **13**
Donto **5**
Hakkaku **2**
Hayashi **10**
Kakiden **12**
Kushinobo **9**
New York Grill **1**
Ten-ichi **18**
Tokyo Catering **3**
Tsunahachi **17**

NIGHTLIFE ◆
Advocates **21**
Albatross **14**
Arty Farty **19**
Dubliners **16**
Kento's **15**
Kinsmen **23**
Kinswomyn **22**
New York Bar **1**
Shinjuku Pit Inn **20**
Tokyo Loose **8**

Map labels: Tokyo Bunka Kaikan, Shinjuku Koma Theater, CHUO LINE, KABUKICHO, Shinjuku Sta., SUBNADE (UNDERGROUND), SHINJUKU 5-CHOME, Hanazono Shrine, Adhoc Bldg., Yasukuni Dori, Shinjuku Sta., Isetan Kaikan, Kinokuniya, SHINJUKU 3-CHOME, Takano, MARUNOUCHI LINE, Mitsukoshi Dept. Store, Isetan Dept. Store, My City, Marui Dept. Store, Meiji Dori, Shinjuku Sanchome Station, Shinjuku Station, SHINJUKU LINE, Shinjuku Dori, SHINJUKU 4-CHOME, Shinjuku Gyoen

4

TOKYO | Where to Stay

garden, a famed garden next door, or Tokyo Tower (Luxury Rooms even have balconies). This is a fine choice of hotel, despite its out-of-the-way location (mitigated by frequent complimentary shuttle service to Meguro Station).

1–1–50 Shirokanedai, Minato-ku, Tokyo 108-8640. www.miyakohotels.ne.jp/tokyo. **℡ 800/325-3535** in the U.S. and Canada, or 03/3447-3111. Fax 03/3447-3133. 495 units. ¥28,350–¥44,100 single; ¥31,500–¥47,250 double; from ¥74,550 suite. Rates exclude service charge and hotel tax. AE, DC, MC, V. Station: Shirokanedai (4 min.), Shirokane-Takanawa (5 min.), or free shuttle from Meguro Station (outside the Central Gate to the right). **Amenities:** 3 restaurants; bar; lounge; concierge; health club w/25m indoor heated pool and spa (fee: ¥1,600); room service; free shuttle service to Meguro Station every 15 min. and Shinagawa Station (mornings only); dental/medical clinics. *In room:* A/C, TV, hair dryer, Internet, minibar.

ODAIBA

Hotel Nikko Tokyo ★ This is the most un-Tokyo-like hotel in the city. Located on Odaiba in Tokyo Bay with its convention center, shopping malls, and sightseeing attractions, this grand lodging is surrounded by parks and sea. Billing itself as an "urban resort," it's especially popular with young well-to-do Japanese in search of an exotic weekend getaway. A curved facade assures waterfront views from most rooms, which have the added benefit of private balconies. The most expensive rooms offer commanding views of Tokyo Bay, Rainbow Bridge, and the city skyline (impressive at night); the least expensive rooms face another hotel or the Maritime Museum and Haneda Airport across the bay. This is a great choice if you want to get away from the bustle of Tokyo, but the location can be a disadvantage; it's served only by the expensive monorail Yurikamome Line, the JR Saikyo Line to Shibuya, and the inconvenient Rinkai Line, all of which can be quite crowded on weekends.

1–9–1 Daiba, Minato-ku, Tokyo 135-8625. www.hnt.co.jp. © **800/645-5687** in the U.S. and Canada, or 03/5500-5500. Fax 03/5500-2525. 452 units. ¥36,000–¥62,000 single; ¥42,000–¥68,000 double; from ¥150,000 suite. Rates exclude hotel tax. AE, DC, MC, V. Station: Daiba (1 min.) or Tokyo Teleport Station (10 min., or free shuttle bus to hotel). **Amenities:** 6 restaurants; bar; lounge; babysitting; concierge; room service; spa w/indoor pool linked to outdoor heated tub, Jacuzzi, and sun terrace overlooking Rainbow Bridge (fee: ¥3,150 the 1st day; thereafter ¥1,050); free shuttle service from Tokyo Teleport Station every 30 min. *In room:* A/C, TV, hair dryer, Internet (fee: ¥2,100 per stay), minibar.

OTHER NEIGHBORHOODS

Four Seasons Hotel Tokyo at Chinzan-So ★★★ 🎒 ☺
Although inconveniently located in northwest Tokyo (about a 15-min. taxi ride from Ikebukuro), the Four Seasons Tokyo is a superb hotel set in the luscious 6.8-hectare (17-acre), 100-year-old Chinzan-So Garden, making it extremely inviting after a bustling day in Tokyo. It also has what may be Tokyo's best spa, including a gorgeous glass-enclosed indoor pool surrounded by greenery with a glass ceiling that opens in summer and a Japanese hot-springs bath (the water is shipped in from Izu Peninsula). Its luxurious interiors make this one of the most beautiful European-style hotels in Japan, and because the hotel embraces the park, most rooms have peaceful garden views from their V-shaped bay windows (those that don't are cheaper, but the garden views are worth the splurge). Don't miss a stroll through the garden, which contains several charming, traditional Japanese restaurants; a pagoda; and stone monuments.

2–10–8 Sekiguchi, Bunkyo-ku, Tokyo 112-8667. www.fourseasons.com/tokyo. © **800/819-5053** in the U.S. and Canada, or 03/3943-2222. Fax 03/3943-2300. 259 units. ¥45,150–¥65,100 single or double; from ¥72,450 suite. Rates exclude service charge and hotel tax. AE, DC, MC, V. Station: Edogawabashi (exit 1a, a 10-min. walk along a cherry-tree-lined canal or a 2-min. ride). **Amenities:** 3 restaurants (plus 3 tenant restaurants in the garden); 2 lounges; babysitting; concierge; executive-level rooms; health club w/indoor pool and spa (fee: ¥5,250); room service. *In room:* A/C, TV/DVD and DVD library, CD player, hair dryer, Internet, minibar, MP3 docking station.

Moderate

GINZA & HIBIYA

Hotel Com's Ginza Because of its great location, convenient to the Ginza, Shimbashi, and Hibiya shopping and business centers, this attractive hotel caters mostly to business travelers, but tourists like it, too. The lobby, on the second floor, has a friendly staff and an exceptionally long front desk, which hopefully translates into quicker service. Rooms, from the 3rd to 11th floors, are tiny but pleasant. Note that the cheapest rooms don't have desks, closets or space to unpack, a good example of what ¥25,000 buys for two people in Tokyo (though you can probably snag a deal on the hotel's website). If you can, spring for one of the five so-called Urban Rooms sporting comfortable leather chairs, good-size desks, espresso machines, a TV with headphones, and duvet-covered beds (but still no closets). In any case, I suggest asking for a room away from the highway overpass beside the hotel.

8–6–15 Ginza, Chuo-ku, Tokyo 104-0061. www.granvista.co.jp. © **03/3572-4131.** Fax 03/3572-4254. 267 units. ¥14,500–¥21,500 single; ¥25,000–¥34,800 double. AE, DC, MC, V. Station: Shimbashi (3 min.). **Amenities:** 3 restaurants; bar; lounge; lobby computer w/free Internet. *In room:* A/C, TV, hair dryer, Internet.

For the sake of convenience, the price for two people in a room is listed as a "double" in this book. Japanese hotels, however, usually differentiate between rooms with a double bed or two twin beds, often with different prices. Most hotels charge more for a twin room, but sometimes the opposite is true; if you're looking for a bargain, therefore, be sure to inquire about prices for both. Note, too, that hotels usually have more twin rooms than doubles, for the simple reason that Japanese couples, used to their own futon, traditionally prefer twin beds.

Hotel Gracery ★★ 🌶 You can't beat the rates and prime Ginza location of this budget hotel, just off Chuo Dori behind Ginza Sapporo Lion. Part of a business hotel chain targeting downtown metropolises, it offers tiny rooms smartly decorated in beige and red, with duvet-covered beds, unit bathrooms, and clothes racks filling in for closets. Female travelers may opt for the Lady's Floor, which features wooden floors in most rooms (in the belief that walking barefoot makes one feel more relaxed) and amenities geared toward women, while those looking for an upgrade can try the Executive Floor, with massage chairs and TVs that double as computers.

7–10–1 Ginza, Chuo-ku, Tokyo 104-0061. www.gracery-ginza.com. ℂ **03/6686-1000.** Fax 03/6858-1020. 270 units. ¥15,600–¥22,200 single; ¥22,200–¥24,200 double. AE, DC, MC, V. Station: Ginza (3 min.) or Shimbashi (7 min.). **Amenities:** Restaurant; Wi-Fi (free, in lobby). *In room:* A/C, TV, fridge, hair dryer, Internet.

Mitsui Garden Hotel Ginza Premier ★★★ 📖 This chic hotel is a notch above older Ginza properties and a good choice for business travelers looking for stylish rooms with good views. Located at the edge of Ginza close to Shimbashi, it occupies the upper floors of an office building (reception is on the 16th floor), with guest rooms providing panoramic views of Tokyo Bay, Tokyo Tower (the most requested) or the Ginza with its glittering night scenes. Room desks and love seats are both placed strategically at windows to take advantage of the hotel's best feature. Even bathrooms take advantage of the views, with those in single rooms boasting windows that look out past the bedroom toward the views beyond (thankfully, the glass can be switched from transparent to opaque with the flip of a switch), while those in the more expensive double and twin rooms have windows that let you gaze upon Tokyo right from the tub (called the View Bath Twin or Double).

8–13–1 Ginza, Chuo-ku, Tokyo 104-0061. www.gardenhotels.co.jp/eng/ginzapremier. ℂ **03/3543-1131.** Fax 03/3543-5531. 361 units. ¥18,900–¥21,000 single; ¥25,200–¥34,650 double. Rates exclude hotel tax. AE, DC, MC, V. Station: Shimbasi (5 min.) or Ginza (7 min). **Amenities:** Restaurant; bar. *In room:* A/C, TV, fridge, hair dryer, Internet.

Park Hotel Tokyo ★★ 📖 Occupying the top 10 floors of a building it shares with international media organizations, this hotel is well located within walking distance of the Ginza, Tsukiji Fish Market, and Hama Rikyu Garden. Its lobby, on the 25th floor and decorated with large trees and dark woods in a theme of "nature and health," is bathed in the natural sunlight afforded by its 10-story atrium topped with an opaque ceiling. The front desk is one of the most dramatic I've seen, backed by nothing but great views of Tokyo Tower and the city. Rooms, simply decorated with original art, also provide views, the best of which can be found on the 30th floor and above facing Hama Rikyu Garden and Tokyo Bay or facing Tokyo Tower (and Mt. Fuji on clear winter days).

Shiodome Media Tower, 1–7–1 Higashi Shimbashi, Minato-ku, Tokyo 105-7227. www.parkhotel tokyo.com. ✆ **03/6252-1111.** Fax 03/6252-1001. 273 units. ¥21,000 single; ¥26,250–¥37,800 double. Rates exclude service charge and hotel tax. AE, DC, MC, V. Station: Shiodome (1 min.) or Shimbashi (8 min.). **Amenities:** 2 restaurants; bar; lounge; room service; Wi-Fi (free, in lobby). *In room:* A/C, TV, hair dryer, Internet, minibar.

remm Hibiya 🗡 This low-key business hotel slips under the radar of most passersby, despite its prime location across from the Imperial Hotel and just steps away from the Ginza. Its second-floor reception shares space with a branch of Muji Café & Meal, known for its inexpensive salads and healthy dishes and open from 6:30am for breakfast. Rooms are equipped with massage chairs and are expectedly small, but some single and double rooms provide glimpses of Hibiya Park or the Imperial Palace between buildings (note that twin rooms do not have windows) and bathrooms (equipped with showers only) have glass walls that give the illusion of space. Incidentally, the fact that the hotel advertises that it carries the Takarazuka Sky Stage cable channel free of charge is a clue that it caters to women attending this very popular theater just down the street (see p. 160).

1–2–1 Yurakucho, Chiyoda-ku, Tokyo 100-0006. www.hankyu-hotel.com/english/sitemap.html. ✆ **03/3507-0606.** Fax 03/3507-0607. 225 units. ¥15,950–¥17,000 single; ¥18,900–¥25,400 double. AE, DC, MC, V. Station: Hibiya (2 min.) **Amenities:** 1 restaurant. *In room:* A/C, TV, hair dryer, Internet.

NEAR TOKYO STATION

Marunouchi Hotel ★ This low-key accommodation is well situated in the heart of Tokyo's business district; its location, just north of Tokyo Station's Marunouchi exit, makes it also convenient to both train and plane travel. Occupying the top 11 floors of a glass high-rise, it exudes an almost Zen-like solemnity, with bare wooden floors and shoji-like walls in a lobby that overlooks a rooftop garden that seems almost surreal. Rooms range from standards and so-called Comfort Rooms (on higher floors and decorated with plants) to roomy deluxe twins with "Japanese corners," a tatami area with a low table (and a "leg well" under the table for those errant limbs), but for the best view ask for a room facing Tokyo Station, where triple-pane glass allows you to watch bullet trains silently glide by. Though classy (and pricey), the Marunouchi is lacking in facilities and services, placing it more squarely in the business-hotel category.

Marunouchi Oazo Building, 1–6–3 Marunouchi, Chiyoda-ku, Tokyo 100-0005. www.marunouchi-hotel.co.jp. ✆ **03/3217-1111.** Fax 03/3217-1115. 205 units. ¥23,300–¥29,075 single; ¥31,385–¥52,375 double; ¥115,900 suite. AE, DC, MC, V. Station: Tokyo (1 min. via underground passageway) or Otemachi (2 min.). **Amenities:** 3 restaurants; bar; concierge; room service; Wi-Fi (free in lobby). *In room:* A/C, TV, fridge, Internet.

ASAKUSA

Sadachiyo Sukeroku-no-yado ★★ 🎒 Located in the heart of Asakusa's traditional neighborhood, this 67-year-old ryokan entices with its whitewashed walls, stone and paper lanterns, bamboo screens, traditionally clad staff, and rickshaw beside its front door. Inside, antiques line hallways that lead to tatami guest rooms (rooms sleeping up to six persons are available). Even the public areas and cypress-and-granite public baths are Japanese-style, and Japanese dinners typical of old Tokyo are available, beginning at ¥7,000 (make dinner reservations when you reserve your room), making this inn a great choice for those wishing to experience a bit of old Edo in the modern metropolis.

Asakusa

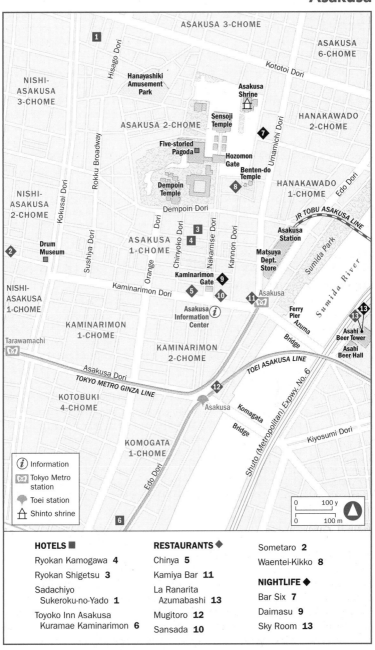

Information

Tokyo Metro station

Toei station

Shinto shrine

HOTELS ■	RESTAURANTS ◆	Sometaro **2**
Ryokan Kamogawa **4**	Chinya **5**	Waentei-Kikko **8**
Ryokan Shigetsu **3**	Kamiya Bar **11**	
Sadachiyo Sukeroku-no-Yado **1**	La Ranarita Azumabashi **13**	**NIGHTLIFE ◆**
Toyoko Inn Asakusa Kuramae Kaminarimon **6**	Mugitoro **12**	Bar Six **7**
	Sansada **10**	Daimasu **9**
		Sky Room **13**

2–20–1 Asakusa, Taito-ku, Tokyo 111-0032. www.sadachiyo.co.jp. © **03/3842-6431.** Fax 03/3842-6433. 20 units. ¥14,000 single; ¥19,000 double. ¥1,000 extra Fri, Sat, and night before holidays. AE, MC, V. Station: Tawaramachi (8 min.) or Asakusa (15 min.) or Tsukuba Express Asakusa (3 min.). **Amenities:** Restaurant; Wi-Fi (free, in the lounge). *In room:* A/C, TV, fridge.

SHINJUKU

Hotel Century Southern Tower ★★★ 🏨
This chic, modern hotel is located just southwest of Shinjuku Station and just a footbridge away from the huge Takashimaya Shinjuku shopping complex. Because it occupies the top floors of a sleek white building, it seems far removed from the hustle and bustle of Shinjuku below. Its 20th-floor lobby is simple and uncluttered and boasts almost surreal views of Tokyo stretching in the distance. Ask for a room on a higher floor. Rooms facing east or south are considered best (and are therefore pricier), especially at night when neon is in full regalia. Rooms facing west have views of Shinjuku's skyscrapers and, on clear days (mostly in winter), of Mount Fuji. A playful touch: Maps in each room outline the important buildings visible from your room. Newly installed TVs double as in-room computers.

2–2–1 Yoyogi, Shibuya-ku, Tokyo 151-8583. www.southerntower.co.jp. © **03/5354-0111.** Fax 03/5354-0100. 375 units. ¥18,480–¥20,790 single; ¥27,720–¥34,650 double. Rates exclude hotel tax. AE, DC, MC, V. Station: Shinjuku (south exit, 3 min.). **Amenities:** 3 restaurants; lounge; executive-level rooms; exercise room. *In room:* A/C, TV w/computer capability, fridge, hair dryer, Wi-Fi.

AOYAMA

Tokyu Stay Aoyama Premier ★★ 🏨
Finally, a Tokyo hotel chain that provides discounts for guests staying longer than a week, plus in-room extras road-weary travelers can appreciate. All Tokyu Stay hotels offer rooms with kitchenettes (complete with cooking and dining utensils) in all but the cheapest singles (which come instead with microwaves but no hot plates), as well as combination washer/dryers and plenty of storage space, but this Aoyama property is the cream of the crop, with a central location convenient to both Aoyama and Roppongi and high floors affording expansive city views. Of course, these advantages also come with a price. To save money, couples can opt to stay in one of the more expensive single rooms by paying ¥3,150 extra a night. Otherwise, cheaper alternatives include **Tokyu Stay Shibuya Shin-Minamiguchi,** 3–26–21 Shibuya (© **03/5466-0109;** station: Shibuya), **Tokyu Stay Nihombashi,** 4–7–9 Nihombashi-Honcho (© **03/3231-0109;** station: Shin-Nihombashi or Kodemmacho), and **Tokyu Stay Higashi-Ginza,** with a colorful location near the Tsukiji Fish Market at 4–11–5 Tsukiji (© **03/5551-0109;** station: Tsukiji or Tsukijijo). Check the website for more than a dozen other Tokyo locations.

2–27–18 Minami-Aoyama, Minato-ku, Tokyo 107-0062. www.tokyustay.co.jp. © **03/3497-0109.** Fax 03/3497-1091. 170 units. ¥14,000–¥16,500 single; ¥24,500–¥26,500 double. Rates exclude hotel tax. Rates include breakfast. Discounts for stays longer than 6 nights. AE, DC, MC, V. Station: Gaienmae (exit 1a, 2 min.). **Amenities:** Restaurant; lobby computer w/free Internet; Wi-Fi (free, in lobby). *In room:* A/C, TV/DVD, hair dryer, Internet, kitchenette (most rooms), trouser press.

ROPPONGI

the b roppongi ★★ 🏨
This boutique business hotel, within walking distance of both Roppongi and Akasaka, has more style than most business-oriented hotels, making it attractive to business and leisure travelers alike. Although it doesn't offer much in the way of facilities, rooms are functional and pleasant, with comfortable beds, good bedside reading lamps, and shades that can be drawn for added darkness. If you're claustrophobic, spring for a deluxe room (the most expensive of which has a kitchenette), as standard and superior choices are quite small. Free coffee in the lobby is a plus, not to mention that it's only a short walk from Roppongi's nighttime

madness. Other locations of this chain are **the b akasaka,** 7–6–13 Akasaka (*📞* **03/3586-0811;** station: Akasaka), and **the b ikebukuro,** 1–39–4 Higashi-Ike-bukuro (*📞* **03/3980-1911;** station Ikebukuro).

3–9–8 Roppongi, Minato-ku, Tokyo 106-0032. www.ishinhotels.com. *📞* **03/5412-0451.** Fax 03/5412-9353. 76 units. ¥18,000–¥23,000 single; ¥22,000–¥43,000 double. Rates exclude hotel tax. AC, MC, V. Station: Roppongi (1 min.). **Amenities:** Restaurant; lobby computer w/free Internet; Wi-Fi (free, in lobby). *In room:* A/C, TV, fridge, hair dryer, Internet.

SHIBUYA

Shibuya Excel Hotel Tokyu ★ Across from bustling Shibuya Station and con-nected by a footbridge and underground passage, this busy, modern hotel has an excel-lent location above Mark City shopping mall (reception is on the fifth floor). The hotel tries hard to appeal to everyone with a variety of room types, including two women-only floors accessed by a special key and with special in-room amenities such as face cream and jewelry boxes; rooms for visitors with disabilities; and rooms that sleep up to four persons. More than half its rooms are for nonsmokers. Ask for an upper-floor room fac-ing Shinjuku (rooms run from the 7th to 24th floors); the night view is great.

1–12–2 Dogenzaka, Shibuya-ku, Tokyo 150-0043. www.tokyuhotelsjapan.com. *📞* **800/428-6598** in the U.S., or 03/5457-0109. Fax 03/5457-0309. 408 units. ¥22,500–¥25,000 single; ¥29,000–¥45,000 double. Rates exclude hotel tax. AE, DC, MC, V. Station: Shibuya (1 min. by footbridge). **Ameni-ties:** 3 restaurants, plus many more in Mark City mall; room service. *In room:* A/C, TV, hair dryer, Internet, minibar.

SHINAGAWA

Shinagawa Prince Hotel ☺ With four gleaming white buildings added at vari-ous stages (each with its own check-in), the Shinagawa Prince Hotel is a virtual city within a city, with an 11-screen cinema complex, a small aquarium with dolphin shows, a sports center with nine indoor tennis courts, an 80-lane bowling center, an indoor golf practice center, indoor and outdoor pools, and a fitness center. Rooms and prices vary widely depending on which building you select. Assuming you can find it, be sure to have a drink or meal at the 39th-floor Top of Shinagawa; its views of Tokyo Bay and the city are among the best in town. With its many diversions, this hotel is like a resort getaway, but is too big and busy for my taste.

4–10–30 Takanawa, Minato-ku, Tokyo 108-8611. www.princehotels.com/en/shinagawa. *📞* **800/542-8686** in the U.S. or Canada, or 03/3440-1111. Fax 03/3441-7092. 3,679 units. ¥9,300–¥20,500 single; ¥16,300–¥36,000 double. Rates exclude hotel tax. AE, DC, MC, V. Station: Shinagawa (2 min.). **Amenities:** 10 restaurants; bar; lounge; sports center (various fees charged: ¥1,050 for indoor pool, ¥1,500 for outdoor pool); children's day-care center (fee: ¥1,800 for 1 hr. 10am–6pm; ¥2,300 after 6pm); cinema complex; aquarium (¥1,800 for adults, ¥600– ¥1,000 for children). *In room:* A/C, TV, fridge, hair dryer, Internet (some rooms; fee: ¥1,050 for 24 hr.).

OTHER NEIGHBORHOODS

The Hilltop Hotel (Yama-no-Ue Hotel) ★★ 🛍 This is a delightfully old-fashioned, unpretentious (some might say dowdy) hotel with character. Built in 1937 and boasting an Art Deco facade, it was once the favorite haunt of writers, including novelist Mishima Yukio. Avoid the cheaper, boring rooms in the 1954 annex unless you spring for the higher-priced Art Septo rooms with their flower boxes outside the windows, black leather furnishings, TV with CD player, and fancier bathrooms. Oth-erwise, rooms in the main building have such endearing, homey touches as fringed lampshades, doilies, cherrywood furniture (and mahogany desks), velvet curtains, vanity tables, and old-fashioned heaters with intricate grillwork. Some twins even combine a tatami area and shoji with beds; the most expensive twin overlooks its own

narita STOPOVER

An early departure out of Narita Airport? A late-night arrival? It might make sense to spend the night near the airport (plus, rates have fallen dramatically since the 2011 earthquake). Topping the list is the **Hilton Narita,** 456 Kosuge, Narita, Chiba 286-0127 (www.hilton.com; ℂ **800/445-8667** in the U.S. and Canada, or 0476/33-1121), a 10-minute free shuttle ride from the airport and downtown Narita rail stations. With a glass-enclosed garden and waterfall centered in its lobby, it's the only airport hotel that imparts an Asian flair. Facilities include three restaurants, a health club with gym and outdoor pool, and 548 good-size rooms with all the amenities you'd expect. Rates average ¥13,000 to ¥20,000 for a single or double.

The 484-room **Narita Tobu Hotel Airport,** 320–1 Tokko, Narita, Chiba 286-0106 (www.naritatobuhotel.com;

ℂ **0476/32-1234**), a 5-minute free shuttle ride from the airport, offers singles starting at ¥8,400 and doubles at ¥13,000. Facilities include a coffee shop, Chinese restaurant, and health club with indoor pool and gym. A good budget choice is the 142-room downtown **Comfort Hotel Narita,** near the Keisei and JR Narita stations at 968 Hanazaki-cho (www.choicehotels.com; ℂ **0476/24-6311**). Singles here begin at ¥5,800 and twins at ¥11,000, including Continental breakfast.

If you have 3 hours to spare, consider an excursion to downtown **Narita** (10 min. by train from the airport; most airport hotels also offer shuttle buses), a quaint village with a winding, shop-lined street leading to Narita-san Temple, an impressive complex consisting of a main hall, several pagodas, and a nice park.

Japanese garden. Don't be surprised if the reception desk remembers you by name. Although the Hilltop is not as up-to-date as other hotels, nearby Meiji University brings lots of young people and liveliness to the area.

1–1 Surugadai, Kanda, Chiyoda-ku, Tokyo 101-0062. www.yamanoue-hotel.co.jp. ℂ **03/3293-2311.** Fax 03/3233-4567. 74 units. ¥12,600–¥21,000 single; ¥23,100–¥33,600 double. Rates exclude service charge and hotel tax. AE, DC, MC, V. Station: Ochanomizu or Shin-Ochanomizu (8 min.) or Jimbocho (5 min.). **Amenities:** 7 restaurants; 3 bars; room service. *In room:* A/C, TV, hair dryer, Internet, minibar.

Inexpensive

ASAKUSA

Ryokan Asakusa Shigetsu ★ Whenever a foreigner living in Tokyo, soon to host first-time visitors to Japan, asks me to recommend a moderately priced Japanese-style inn in Tokyo, this is the one I often suggest due to its great location in Asakusa, an area that gives you a feel for the older Japan. It represents the best of modern yet traditional Japanese design—simple yet elegant, with shoji, unadorned wood, and artwork throughout. Two public Japanese baths have views of the nearby five-story pagoda. There are six Western-style single rooms, but I prefer the 15 slightly more expensive Japanese-style tatami rooms, which include Japanese-style mirrors and comfortable chairs for those who don't like relaxing on the floor. This ryokan costs no more than a regular business hotel but has much more class. What a pity that the front-desk staff can be brusque.

1–31–11 Asakusa, Taito-ku, Tokyo 111-0032. www.shigetsu.com. ℂ **03/3843-2345.** Fax 03/3843-2348. 22 units. ¥6,700–¥9,450 single; ¥14,700–¥15,750 double. Japanese or Western breakfast

¥1,300 extra. AE, DC, MC, V. Station: Asakusa (4 min.). **Amenities:** Restaurant; lobby computer w/ free Internet. *In room:* A/C, TV, hair dryer, Internet, minibar.

Ryokan Kamogawa ★ ☺ If Ryokan Asakusa Shigetsu (see above) is full, this is a very good alternative. Established in 1948 by the present owner's parents and located just off Nakamise Dori, it's small and personable, with a coffee shop and tatami rooms with shoji screens. Four room sizes are available, with and without private bathrooms. The largest sleep four to six persons, making them a good choice for families, as is the family bath you can use privately (reserve in advance). Note that the inn is usually fully booked in April and December, so if you hope to stay here then, book far ahead. Note, too, that it locks its front door at 11:30pm; if you wish to stay out later be sure to ask for the back-door key.

1–30–10 Asakusa, Tokyo 111-0032. www.f-kamogawa.jp. © **03/3843-2681.** Fax 03/3843-2683. 12 units (8 with bathroom). ¥6,400 single without bathroom; ¥6,800–¥8,200 single with bathroom; ¥12,600–¥13,000 double without bathroom, ¥12,800–¥14,600 double with bathroom; ¥19,200 triple without bathroom, ¥21,300 triple with bathroom. Rates include coffee and toast. Japanese breakfast ¥1,000 extra. Japanese dinner ¥4,000 extra (reservations required). AE, DC, MC, V. Station: Asakusa (3 min.). **Amenities:** Coffee shop w/computer and free Internet; Wi-Fi (free, in lobby). *In room:* A/C, TV, fridge, hair dryer (in rooms w/bathroom), Internet.

UENO

Annex Katsutaro ★★ 🛏 This thoroughly modern concrete ryokan is a standout for its simple yet chic designs, spotless Japanese-style rooms and location—right in the heart of Yanaka with its old-fashioned neighborhood and about a 20-minute walk northwest of Ueno Park (the Keisei Skyliner from Narita Airport stops at nearby Nippori Station). The English-speaking proprietress, Arakawa-san, distributes a free map of the area showing the best way to get around and offers free coffee in the lobby. If the ryokan is full, don't let management talk you into taking a room in its much older main Ryokan Katsutaro; it's not nearly as nice as the annex.

3–8–4 Yanaka, Taito-ku, Tokyo 110-0001. www.katsutaro.com. © **03/3828-2500.** Fax 03/3821-5400. 17 units. ¥6,300 single; ¥10,500–¥12,600 double; ¥14,700–¥16,800 triple. Continental breakfast ¥840 extra. MC, V. Station: Sendagi (2 min.) or Nippori (7 min.). **Amenities:** Lobby computers w/ free Internet. *In room:* A/C, TV, fridge, hair dryer, Internet.

Homeikan ★★★ 🛏 Although a bit of a hike from Ueno Park (about 30 min.) this lovely place is my number-one choice if you want to experience an authentic, traditional ryokan in a traditional neighborhood. It consists of three separate buildings acquired over the last century by the present owner's grandfather, including the Homeikan, the main building (Honkan), purchased 100 years ago and listed as a "Tangible Cultural Property." Most foreigners choose to stay across the street in the Daimachi Bekkan, built after World War II to serve as the family home. A beautiful, 31-room property, it boasts a private Japanese garden with a pond, public baths (including one open 24 hr.), and wood-inlaid and pebbled hallways leading to nicely detailed tatami rooms adorned with such features as gnarled wood trim and sitting alcoves, as well as simpler tatami rooms for budget travelers. If you opt for meals, they will be served in your room in true ryokan fashion. Owner Koike-san, who speaks excellent English, points out that travelers who need the latest in creature comforts (including private bathrooms) should go elsewhere; those seeking a traditional ryokan experience, however, will not be disappointed.

5–10–5 Hongo, Bunkyo-ku, Tokyo 113-0033. www.homeikan.com. © **03/3811-1187.** Fax 03/3811-1764. 89 units (none with private bathroom). ¥7,350 single; ¥12,600 double; ¥15,750 triple. ¥525 more per person in peak season; ¥525 less per person in off season. Western- or Japanese-style

4

TOKYO Where to Stay

breakfast ¥1,050; Japanese dinner ¥3,150 (not available 1st night of stay). AE, DC, MC, V. Station: Hongo Sanchome (8 min.) or Kasuga (5 min.). *In room:* A/C, TV, minibar.

Hotel Coco Grand ★★ 🗡 Located across from the south end of Shinobazu Pond, this chic, boutique-like hotel has a good location near Ueno Park's many attractions. Decorated with bright, up-beat colors and furnishings, it offers mostly singles, some of which have views of the pond and all with foot massager and massage cushion. There are also doubles and twins, including Zen Twins featuring raised beds on tatami and shoji-like window coverings, but for a real splurge go with the Villa Suite Twin (¥39,000 for two persons), which comes with its own private outdoor terrace complete with Jacuzzi, sofa and TV, as well as a steam room and bathrooms with two sinks and a deep tub big enough for two. By the way, at last check the hotel website is in Japanese only, but there are photos of its rooms.

2–12–14 Ueno, Taito-ku, Tokyo 110-0005. www.cocogrand.co.jp/uenoshinobazu. © **03/5812-1155.** Fax 03/5812-1156. 58 units. ¥8,800–¥11,800 single; ¥15,800–¥24,800 double. Rates exclude hotel tax. Rates include breakfast. AE, DC, MC, V. Station: Ueno (4 min.). **Amenities:** Cake shop. *In room:* A/C, TV, fridge, hair dryer, Internet.

Ryokan Sawanoya ★ Although this family-run, smoke-free ryokan, open since 1949, looks unexciting, it's delightfully located in a wonderful residential area of old Tokyo, northwest of Ueno Park and within walking distance of the park's attractions and Nezu Shrine. Upon your arrival, English-speaking Sawa-san or his son give a short tour of the establishment before taking you to your tatami room; throughout the ryokan are written explanations to help the novice. You'll be given a map outlining places of interest in the vicinity; in the lobby is a huge map of Japan along with pamphlets from all over the country. Several times a month, guests are treated to a traditional Japanese lion dance, free of charge. The nice public baths (which you can lock for privacy) have a view of a small garden, and there's free coffee in the lobby. This is a great place to stay thanks to Sawa-san's enthusiastic devotion to his neighborhood (he's even written a book about his years as an innkeeper). Highly recommended.

2–3–11 Yanaka, Taito-ku, Tokyo 110-0001. www.sawanoya.com. © **03/3822-2251.** Fax 03/3822-2252. 12 units (2 with bathroom). ¥5,040 single without bathroom; ¥9,450 double without bathroom, ¥10,080 double with bathroom, ¥12,915 triple without bathroom, ¥14,490 triple with bathroom. AE, MC, V. Closed Dec 29–Jan 3. Station: Nezu (exit 1, 7 min.). **Amenities:** 2 rental bikes (¥200 for 1 day); lobby computer w/free Internet; and trouser press (on 3rd floor); Wi-Fi (free, in lobby). *In room:* A/C, hair dryer, Internet.

SHINJUKU

Tokyo Central Youth Hostel (formerly Tokyo International Hostel) 🗡 This spotless hostel is definitely the best place to stay in its price range—situated on the 18th and 19th floors of a high-rise, it offers fantastic Tokyo views. Even the public baths boast good views (especially at night). All beds are dormitory style, with two, four, or more bunk beds to a room. Rooms are very pleasant, with big windows, and each bed has its own curtain for privacy. If there are vacancies, you can stay longer than the normal 6-day maximum. In summer, it's a good idea to reserve about 2 months in advance (reservations can be made up to 3 months in advance). The hostel is closed from 10am to 3pm and locked at 11pm (lights out also at 11pm).

1–1 Kagura-kashi, Shinjuku-ku, Tokyo 162-0823. www.jyh.gr.jp/tcyh. © **03/3235-1107.** Fax 03/3267-4000. www.tokyo-yh.jp. 158 beds. ¥3,960 adult, ¥2,800 child. Breakfast ¥500; dinner ¥1,050. No youth-hostel card required; no age limit. AE, MC, V. Closed Dec 29–Jan 3. Station: Iidabashi (take the west exit from the JR station or the B2b subway exit, 2 min.). Reception is on the 18th floor of the Central Plaza Building. **Amenities:** Communal kitchen. *In room:* A/C, no phone.

Ueno

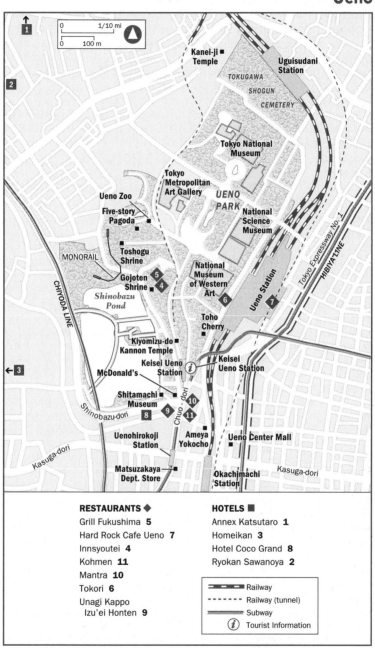

RESTAURANTS ◆

Grill Fukushima **5**
Hard Rock Cafe Ueno **7**
Innsyoutei **4**
Kohmen **11**
Mantra **10**
Tokori **6**
Unagi Kappo
Izu'ei Honten **9**

HOTELS ■

Annex Katsutaro **1**
Homeikan **3**
Hotel Coco Grand **8**
Ryokan Sawanoya **2**

━◼━◼━ Railway
------- Railway (tunnel)
▨▨▨▨ Subway
ⓘ Tourist Information

4

TOKYO | Where to Stay

ROPPONGI & AKASAKA

Arca Torre ☙ This smart-looking, 10-story business hotel has a great location on Roppongi Dori between Roppongi Crossing and Roppongi Hills, making it popular with business types and tourists on a budget. Its (mostly single) rooms are small but cheerful, with flatscreen TVs and complimentary bottled water in the otherwise empty fridge. Rooms facing the back are quiet but face another building with glazed windows and are rather dark. If you opt for a room facing the front, spring for more expensive rooms on higher floors above the freeway; otherwise, from the cheaper rooms on lower floors your view will be of cars and, at certain times of the day, traffic jams.

6–1–23 Roppongi, Minato-ku, Tokyo 106-0032. www.arktower.co.jp/arcatorre. ℂ **03/3404-5111.** Fax 03/3404-5115. 77 units. ¥11,550–¥13,650 single; ¥14,700–¥22,050 double. AE, DC, MC, V. Station: Roppongi (1 min.). **Amenities:** Restaurant. *In room:* A/C, TV, fridge, hair dryer, Internet.

Asia Center of Japan (Asia Kaikan) ★ ☙ Great rates make this a top choice if you're looking for inexpensive Western-style accommodations in the center of town (reserve months in advance). Everyone from businessmen to students to travelers to foreigners teaching English stays here. Established in 1957 and resembling a college dormitory, the Asia Center is popular with area office workers for its inexpensive cafeteria with outdoor seating. Accommodations are basic, with few frills, and in the singles you can almost reach out and touch all four walls. The cheapest doubles are actually single rooms with small, semi-double-size beds (not quite full size but larger than single/twin size). Avoid rooms on the ground floor—windows can open, and in Japan there are no screens. Tucked on a side street off Gaien-Higashi Dori not far from Aoyama Dori, the center is a 15-minute walk to the nightlife of Roppongi or Akasaka, one station away by subway.

8–10–32 Akasaka, Minato-ku, Tokyo 107-0052. www.asiacenter.or.jp. ℂ **03/3402-6111.** Fax 03/3402-0738. 173 units. ¥8,610–¥10,290 single; ¥12,390–¥18,690 double. AE, MC, V. Station: Aoyama-Itchome (exit 4, 5 min.) or Nogizaka (exit 3, 5 min.). **Amenities:** Restaurant; Wi-Fi (free, in lobby). *In room:* A/C, TV, fridge, hair dryer, Internet.

SHINAGAWA

Toyoko Inn Shinagawa-Eki Takanawaguchi ★ ☙ I like this hotel chain for its clean functional rooms, complimentary breakfast of coffee and pastries served in the lobby, free in-room Internet connections, free Wi-Fi access in the lobby (and for those who don't have their own laptops, free use of computers in the lobby), and coin laundry. Rooms are all very small singles and doubles. Other convenient Tokyo locations of this popular chain offering similar rooms at similar costs and the same freebies include **Toyoko Inn Shinjuku Kabuki-cho,** 2–20–15 Kabuki-cho (ℂ **03/5155-1045;** station: Shinjuku); **Toyoko Inn Ikebukuro Kita-guchi No. 1,** 2–50–5 Ikebukuro (ℂ **03/5960-1045;** station: Ikebukuro); and **Toyoko Inn Asakusa Kuramae Kaminarimon,** 1–3–13 Komagata (ℂ **03/3841-1045;** station: Kuramae or Asakusa). Check the website for other Toyoko Inns in Nihombashi, Akihabara, and other locations.

4–23–2 Takanawa, Minato-ku, Tokyo 108-0074. www.toyoko-inn.com. ℂ **03/3280-1045.** Fax 03/3280-1046. 180 units. ¥7,480 single; ¥8,690–¥9,740 double. Rates include continental breakfast. AE, DC, MC, V. Station: Shinagawa (3 min.). From JR station's Takanawa (west) exit, cross the street and turn left. **Amenities:** Lobby computers w/free Internet. *In room:* A/C, TV, fridge, hair dryer, Internet.

IKEBUKURO

Kimi Ryokan ★★ ☖ This has long been a Tokyo favorite for inexpensive Japanese-style lodging. Spotlessly clean and with traditional touches like sliding screens, a cypress public bath, flower arrangements in public spaces (created by the owner himself), and Japanese music playing softly in the hallways, it caters almost exclusively to foreigners (mostly 20-somethings), which means it was especially hard hit after the 2011 disaster (before that, there was sometimes a waiting list). A bulletin board and newsletter list rental apartments and job opportunities (primarily teaching English); a lounge with cable TV is a favorite hangout and a good place to network with other travelers; and a rooftop terrace is a good place to relax. Rooms are Japanese style, with the single and the cheapest double the size of four and one-half tatami mats, and the larger double the size of six tatami mats (a single tatami measures 1m×1.8m/3¼ ft.×6 ft.). Note that there's a 2am curfew.

2–36–8 Ikebukuro, Toshima-ku, Tokyo 171-0014. www.kimi-ryokan.jp. © **03/3971-3766.** Fax 03/3987-1326. 38 units (none with private bathroom). ¥4,000 single; ¥5,800–¥6,700 double; ¥8,900 triple. No credit cards. Station: Ikebukuro (west exit; 7 min.). The police station (take the west exit from Ikebukuro Station and turn right) has maps that will guide you to Kimi; there's also an area map outside the station. *In room:* A/C, Wi-Fi.

SIDE TRIPS FROM TOKYO

I f your stay in Tokyo is long enough, you should consider taking an excursion or two. Kamakura and Nikko rank as two of the most important historical sites in Japan. Yokohama, with its thriving port, waterfront development, and several museums and attractions, also makes an interesting day trip. **Fuji-Hakone-Izu National Park** serves as a huge recreational playground for the residents of Tokyo. For overnight stays, I heartily recommend **Hakone** or **Izu Peninsula,** both with *ryokan* (Japanese-style inns) where you'll be able to experience the atmosphere of old Japan. Active travelers may want to hike to the top of **Mount Fuji** in summer.

5

Before departing Tokyo, stop by the **Tourist Information Center (TIC)** for pamphlets on Kamakura, Nikko, Hakone, and the Mount Fuji area, some of which give train schedules and other useful information; see "Visitor Information," in chapter 14, for the TIC location.

THE BEST TOKYO SIDE TRIP EXPERIENCES

- **Coming Face to Face with the Great Buddha in Kamakura.** There are larger bronze Buddhas in Japan, but this one with its serene expression and backdrop of wooded hills is the most memorable (and my favorite). See p. 188.
- **Exploring Nikko.** With thousands of majestic cedars standing sentinel, the Nikko Sannai World Heritage Site contains opulent **Toshogu Shrine** and the mausoleum of Japan's most famous shogun, as well as the mausoleum of the shogun's grandson, a temple, shrine, and garden. Nearby are an imperial villa and Nikko's small downtown with craft stores and restaurants. See p. 192.
- **Learning About Japanese Emigration in Yokohama.** Anyone of Japanese descent should make a point of visiting the **Japanese Overseas Migration Museum,** where they'll learn about life and hardships for early emigrants to the Americas. Many such emigrants were passengers on the *Hikawa Maru,* now moored at Yamashita Park as a floating museum. See p. 203 and 204.
- **Traveling in Hakone.** With its mountain railway, cable car, ropeway, and sightseeing boat, this circuitous route through scenic Hakone is my favorite overnight trip outside Tokyo. The best place to stay? The historic **Fujiya Hotel,** hands down my favorite hotel in Japan. See p. 215.

- **Recuperating in Shuzenji.** This small mountain village is a perfect weekend getaway for those seeking respite from big-city life. Stay in a Japanese inn, dine on local cuisine, and soak cares away in hot-spring baths. See p. 218.

KAMAKURA, ANCIENT CAPITAL ★★★

51km (32 miles) S of Tokyo

If you take only one day trip outside Tokyo, it should be to Kamakura, especially if you're unable to include the ancient capitals of Kyoto and Nara in your travels. (If you are going to Kyoto and Nara, I would probably choose Nikko, below.) Kamakura is a delightful hamlet with no fewer than 65 Buddhist temples and 19 Shinto shrines spread throughout the town and surrounding wooded hills. Most of these were built centuries ago, when a warrior named Minamoto Yoritomo seized political power and established his shogunate government in Kamakura back in 1192. Wanting to set up his seat of government as far away as possible from what he considered to be the corrupt imperial court in Kyoto, Yoritomo selected Kamakura because it was easy to defend. The village is enclosed on three sides by wooded hills and on the fourth by the sea—a setting that lends a dramatic background to its many temples and shrines.

Although Kamakura remained the military and political center of the nation for a century and a half, the Minamoto clan was in power for only a short time. After Yoritomo's death, both of his sons were assassinated, one after the other, after taking up military rule. Power then passed to the family of Yoritomo's widow, the Hojo family, which ruled until 1333, when the emperor in Kyoto sent troops to crush the shogunate government. Unable to stop the invaders, 800 soldiers retired to the Hojo family temple at Toshoji, where they disemboweled themselves in ritualistic suicide known as *seppuku*.

Today Kamakura is a thriving seaside resort (pop. 173,500), with old wooden homes, temples, shrines, and wooded hills—a pleasant 1-day trip from Tokyo. (There's also a beach in Kamakura called Yuigahama Beach, but I find it unappealing; it's often strewn with litter and unbelievably crowded in summer. Skip it.)

Essentials

GETTING THERE　Take the **JR Yokosuka Line** bound for Zushi, Kurihama, or Yokosuka; it departs every 10 to 15 minutes from Yokohama, Shinagawa, Shimbashi, and Tokyo JR stations. The trip takes almost 1 hour from Tokyo Station and costs ¥890 to Kamakura Station. From Shinjuku, take the JR Shonan-Shinjuku Line 1 hour to Kamakura for the same price. Suica cards and Japan Rail Passes can be used for both lines.

VISITOR INFORMATION　In Kamakura, there's a **tourist information window** (✆ 0467/22-3350; www.city.kamakura.kanagawa.jp) inside Kamakura Station near the east (main) exit. You can pick up a map here and get directions to the village's most important sights and restaurants. It's open daily 9am to 5:30pm April to September, and 9am to 5pm October to March.

ORIENTATION & GETTING AROUND　Kamakura's major sights are clustered in two areas: **Kamakura Station,** the town's downtown with the tourist office, souvenir shops spread along Komachi Dori and Wakamiya Oji, restaurants, and Tsurugaoka Hachimangu Shrine; and **Hase,** with the Great Buddha and Hase Kannon

Temple. You can travel between Kamakura Station and Hase Station via the **Enoden Line,** a wonderful small train, or you can walk the distance in about 20 minutes. Destinations are also easily reached by buses departing from Kamakura Station.

Exploring Kamakura

AROUND KAMAKURA STATION About a 12-minute walk from Kamakura Station, **Tsurugaoka Hachimangu Shrine ★★★** (© **0467/22-0315**) is the spiritual heart of Kamakura and one of its most popular attractions. It was built by Yoritomo and dedicated to Hachiman, the Shinto god of war who served as the clan deity of the Minamoto family. The pathway to the shrine is along Wakamiya Oji, a cherry tree–lined pedestrian lane that was constructed by Yoritomo in the 1190s so that his oldest son's first visit to the family shrine could be accomplished in style with an elaborate procession. The lane stretches from the shrine all the way to Yuiga-hama Beach, with three massive *torii* gates set at intervals along the route to signal the approach to the shrine. On both sides of the pathway are souvenir and antiques shops selling lacquerware, pottery, and folk art (I suggest returning to Kamakura Station via Komachi Dori, a pedestrian shopping lane that parallels Wakamiya Oji to the west).

At the top of the stairs, which afford a panoramic view toward the sea, is the ver-milion-colored shrine with its small shrine museum (admission here is ¥100). You can also get your fortune in English for ¥100 by shaking out a bamboo stick with a number on it and giving it to the attendant. You can also buy a charm to assure good luck in health, driving a car, business, or other ventures. Shrine grounds are always open, free to the public.

AROUND HASE STATION To get to these attractions, you can go by bus, which departs from in front of Kamakura Station (take any bus from platform no. 1 or 6 to the Daibutsuen-mae stop). Or, for a more romantic adventure, you can go by the **JR Enoden Line,** a tiny train that putt-putts its way seemingly through backyards on its way from Kamakura Station to Hase and beyond. Since it's mostly only one track, trains have to take turns going in either direction. I suggest that you take the bus from Kamakura Station directly to the Great Buddha, walk to Hase Shrine, and then take the Enoden train back to Kamakura Station.

Probably Kamakura's most famous attraction is the **Great Buddha ★★★** (www. kotoku-in.jp; © **0467/22-0703**), called the Daibutsu in Japanese and located at **Kotokuin Temple.** Eleven meters (36 ft.) high and weighing 93 tons, it's the third-largest bronze image in Japan. The second-largest Buddha is in Nara and the largest (erected in the 1990s) is near Ushiku Station outside Tokyo, but in my opinion the Kamakura Daibutsu is much more impressive. For one thing, the Kamakura Buddha sits outside against a dramatic backdrop of wooded hills. Cast in 1252, the Kamakura Buddha was indeed once housed in a temple like the Nara Buddha, but a huge tidal wave destroyed the wooden structure—and the statue has sat under sun, snow, and stars ever since. I also prefer the face of the Kamakura Buddha; I find it more inspir-ing and divine, as though with its half-closed eyes and calm, serene face it's above the worries of the world. It seems to represent the plane above human suffering, the point at which birth and death, joy and sadness merge and become one. Open daily from 7am to 6pm (to 5:30pm Oct–Mar). Admission is ¥200 for adults and ¥150 for children. If you want, you can pay an extra ¥20 to go inside the statue—it's hollow—but there's usually a line and I find it claustrophobic.

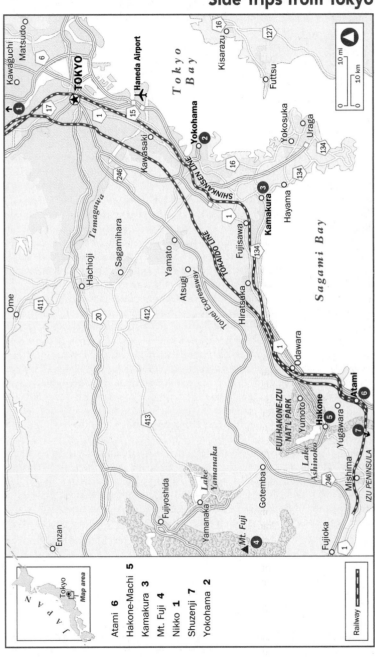

5

Atami **6**
Hakone-Machi **5**
Kamakura **3**
Mt. Fuji **4**
Nikko **1**
Shuzenji **7**
Yokohama **2**

Railway

About a 10-minute walk from the Daibutsu is **Hase Kannon Temple (Hasedera)** ★★★ (www.hasedera.jp; ✆ **0467/22-6300**), located on a hill with sweeping views of the sea. This is the home of an 11-headed gilt statue of Kannon, the goddess of mercy, housed in the Kannon-do (Kannon Hall). More than 9m (30 ft.) high and the tallest wooden image in Japan, it was made in the 8th century from a single piece of camphor wood. The legend surrounding this Kannon is quite remarkable. Supposedly, two wooden images were made from the wood of a huge camphor tree. One of the images was kept in Hase, not far from Nara, while the second was given a short ceremony and then tossed into the sea to find a home of its own. The image drifted about 483km (300 miles) eastward and washed up on shore but was thrown back in again when all who touched it became ill or incurred bad luck. Finally, the image reached Kamakura, where it gave the people no trouble. This was interpreted as a sign that the image was content with its surroundings, and Hase Kannon Temple was erected at its present site. Note how each face has a different expression, representing the Kannon's compassion for various kinds of human suffering. Also in the Kannon-do is a museum with religious treasures from the Kamakura, Heian, Muromachi, and Edo periods.

Another golden statue housed here is of **Amida,** a Buddha who promised rebirth in the Pure Land to the West to all who chanted his name. It was created by order of Yoritomo Minamoto upon his 42nd birthday, considered an unlucky year for men. You'll find it housed in the Amida-do (Amida Hall) beside the Kannon-do to the right. Also of interest is the **Kyozo,** with rotating book racks containing sutras (if you give the book racks a spin, it's considered just as auspicious as reading the sutras; but alas, you can do so only on the 18th of each month). **Benten-kutsu Cave** contains many stone images, including one of Benzaiten (seated, with a lute and a money box in front). A sea goddess and patroness of music, art, and good fortune, she is the only female of Japan's Seven Lucky Gods. **Prospect Road** is a 10-minute hiking path featuring flowers in bloom and panoramic views.

As you climb the steps to the Kannon-do, you'll encounter statues of a different sort. All around you will be likenesses of **Jizo,** the guardian deity of children. Although parents originally came to Hase Temple to set up statues to represent their children in hopes the deity would protect and watch over them, through the years the purpose of the Jizo statues changed. Now they represent miscarried, stillborn, or aborted infants. The hundreds or so you see here will remain only a year before being burned or buried to make way for others. Some of the statues are fitted with hand-knitted caps, bibs, and sweaters; the effect is quite chilling.

Hase Temple is open daily 8am to 5pm (to 4:30pm Oct–Feb); admission is ¥300 for adults, ¥100 for children.

Where to Eat

Milano a Riccione ITALIAN   This is the Japanese branch of a Milan restaurant known for its handmade pasta, seafood, and good selection of wines. Although located in a basement, it opens onto a subterranean courtyard, making it brighter and more cheerful than you might expect. There's an English-language seasonal menu,

Kamakura

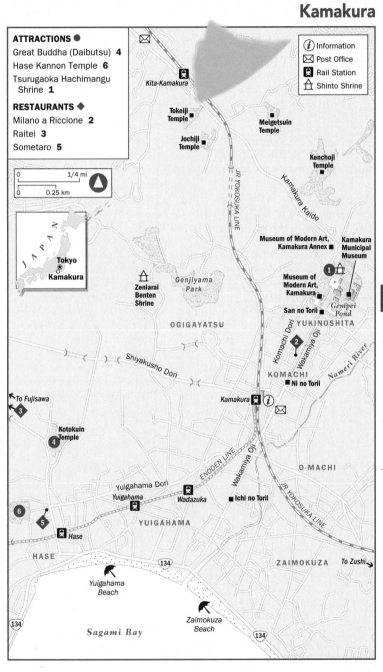

ATTRACTIONS ●
Great Buddha (Daibutsu) **4**
Hase Kannon Temple **6**
Tsurugaoka Hachimangu
  Shrine **1**

RESTAURANTS ◆
Milano a Riccione **2**
Raitei **3**
Sometaro **5**

0 ——— 1/4 mi
0 ——— 0.25 km

ⓘ Information
☒ Post Office
🚉 Rail Station
⛩ Shinto Shrine

JAPAN

Tokyo
Kamakura

☒
Kita-Kamakura

Tokeiji
Temple

Meigetsuin
Temple

Jochiji
Temple

Kenchoji
Temple

JR YOKOSUKA LINE

Kamakura Kaido

Museum of Modern Art,
Kamakura Annex ■

Kamakura
Municipal
Museum

Zeniarai
Benten
Shrine

Genjiyama
Park

Museum of
Modern Art,
Kamakura ■

❶ ⛩

San no Torii ■

Genpei
Pond

OGIGAYATSU

YUKINOSHITA

Shiyakusho Dori

❷

KOMACHI

Nameri River

Komachi Dori

Wakamiya Oji

← To Fujisawa

❸

■ Ni no Torii

Kotokuin
Temple

❹

Kamakura 🚉 ⓘ

☒

ENODEN LINE

Wakamiya Oji

O-MACHI

JR YOKOSUKA LINE

Yuigahama Dori

Yuigahama 🚉

Wadazuka

■ Ichi no Torii

❻

❺

YUIGAHAMA

🚉 Hase

HASE

ZAIMOKUZA

To Zushi →

134

Yuigahama
Beach

Zaimokuza
Beach

134

Sagami Bay

134

5

SIDE TRIPS FROM TOKYO | Kamakura, Ancient Capital

but the best bargain is the daily set lunch for ¥2,300, which includes an appetizer; soup; a choice of pasta or pizza; a choice of main dish like grilled fish or chicken; and coffee, espresso, or tea. There's also a salad and pasta lunch set for ¥1,200; this is the quickest meal you can order, but if you're in a hurry, you should dine elsewhere, as care and time are devoted to the preparation of such meals as sautéed Nagoya cochin chicken with gorgonzola or simmered whole fish. At dinner time, a table charge of ¥315 is levied per person and set meals are available only for two or more diners.

2–12–30 Komachi, Kamakura. ✆ **0467/24-5491.** Reservations required for lunch. Pizza and pasta ¥1,000–¥1,785; main dishes ¥1,500–¥2,800; set dinners ¥4,200–¥4,935; set lunches ¥1,200–¥2,730. AE, DC, MC, V. Thurs–Tues 11am–2:30pm; Mon–Tues and Thurs–Fri 5–8pm; Sat–Sun 5–9pm (last order). Station: Kamakura (6 min.). On the left side of Wakamiya Oji when walking from Kamakura Station to Tsurugaoka Hachimangu Shrine.

Raitei (擂亭) ★★★ 🍴 NOODLES/OBENTO   Though it's a bit inconveniently located, this is the absolute winner for a meal in Kamakura. Visiting Raitei is as much fun as visiting the city's temples and shrines. The restaurant is situated in the hills on the edge of Kamakura, surrounded by verdant countryside, and the wonder is that it serves inexpensive *soba* (Japanese noodles) and *obento* lunch boxes, as well as priestly *kaiseki* feasts. Take the stone steps on the right to the back entry, where you'll be given an English-language menu with such offerings as noodles with chicken, various obento, and kaiseki. The pottery used here comes from the restaurant's own kiln, and you'll sit on roughly hewn wood stools or on *tatami*. If you make a reservation in advance for kaiseki, you'll dine upstairs in your own private room in a refined traditional setting with great views. The house, once owned by a wealthy landowner, was moved to this site in 1929. Be sure to take the 20-minute looping path through the garden, past a bamboo grove, Buddhist stone images, and a miniature shrine.

Takasago. ✆ **0467/32-5656.** Reservations required for kaiseki. Noodles ¥900–¥1,522; obento ¥3,675; soba set meals ¥2,625; kaiseki from ¥6,300. Entry fee ¥500, which counts toward the price of your meal. AE, DC. Daily 11am–sundown (about 7pm in summer). Closed last week of July. Bus: 4 from platform no. 6 at Kamakura Station or Daibutsuen-mae to Takasago stop (or a 15-min. taxi ride).

Sometaro (染太郎) 🍴 OKONOMIYAKI   Located near the approach to Hase Temple, this small, second-floor restaurant offers do-it-yourself *okonomiyaki* (a kind of Japanese pancake; cooking instructions are available in English) stuffed with cabbage, bean sprouts, and a choice of a main ingredient like beef, pork, or shrimp. It also serves *yakisoba* (fried noodles) and *teppanyaki* (grilled steak, seafood, or vegetables), all from an English-language menu. The lone waitress is a bit gruff, but if you can ignore that, you'll enjoy the conviviality of dining here.

3–12–11 Hase. ✆ **0467/22-8694.** Reservations recommended for lunch. Main dishes ¥900. No credit cards. Thurs–Tues 11:30am–9pm (last order). Station: Hase (2 min.). On the slope leading to the entrance of Hase Temple, at the beginning on the left side.

SHOGUN COUNTRY: NIKKO ★★★

150km (93 miles) N of Tokyo

After the publication of James Clavell's novel *Shogun,* many people became familiar with Tokugawa Ieyasu, the powerful real-life shogun of the 1600s on whom Clavell's fictional shogun was based. Quashing all rebellions and unifying Japan under his leadership, Tokugawa established such a military stronghold that his heirs continued to rule Japan for the next 250 years without serious challenge.

Nikko

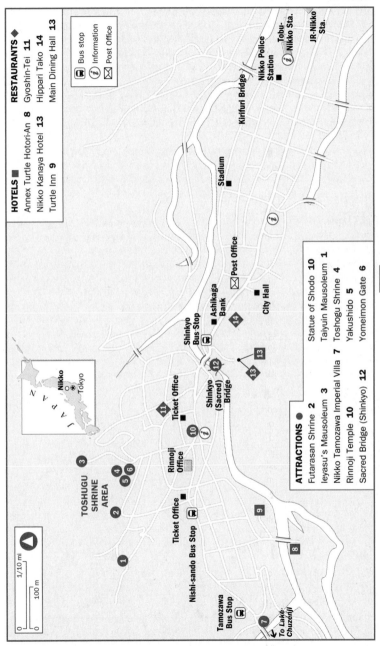

HOTELS ■
Annex Turtle Hotori-An **8**
Nikko Kanaya Hotel **13**
Turtle Inn **9**

RESTAURANTS ◆
Gyoshin-Tei **11**
Hippari Tako **14**
Main Dining Hall **13**

🚌 Bus stop
ⓘ Information
⊠ Post Office

ATTRACTIONS ●
Futarasan Shrine **2**
Ieyasu's Mausoleum **3**
Nikko Tamozawa Imperial Villa **7**
Rinnoji Temple **10**
Sacred Bridge (Shinkyo) **12**
Statue of Shodo **10**
Taiyuin Mausoleum **1**
Toshogu Shrine **4**
Yakushido **5**
Yomeimon Gate **6**

TOSHUGU
SHRINE
AREA

1/10 mi
100 m

JAPAN
Nikko
Tokyo

Tamozawa
Bus Stop

To Lake
Chuzenji

Nishi-sando Bus Stop

Ticket Office

Rinnoji
Office

Shinkyo
(Sacred)
Bridge

Shinkyo
Bus Stop

Ashikaga
Bank

Post Office

City Hall

Stadium

Kirifuri Bridge

Nikko Police
Station

Tobu-
Nikko Sta.

JR-Nikko
Sta.

If you'd like to join the millions of Japanese who through the centuries have paid homage to this great man, head north of Tokyo to Nikko, where **Toshogu Shrine ★★★** was constructed in his honor in the 17th century and where Tokugawa's remains were entombed in a mausoleum. Nikko means "sunlight"—an apt description of the way the sun's rays play upon this sumptuous shrine of wood and gold leaf. In fact, nothing else in Japan matches Toshogu Shrine for its opulence. Nearby is another mausoleum containing Tokugawa's grandson, as well as a temple, a shrine, and a garden. Surrounding the sacred grounds, known collectively as Nikko Sannai and designated a World Heritage Site by UNESCO in 1999, are thousands of majestic cedar trees in the 80,000-hectare (200,000-acre) **Nikko National Park ★★**. Another worthwhile sight is the **Nikko Tamozawa Imperial Villa ★★**, built in 1899.

I've included a few recommendations for an overnight stay. Otherwise, you can see Nikko in a very full day. Plan on 4 to 5 hours for round-trip transportation, 2½ hours to see Toshogu Shrine and vicinity, and 1 hour to see the imperial villa.

Essentials

GETTING THERE   The easiest, fastest, and most luxurious way to get to Nikko is on the privately owned Tobu Line's Limited Express **Spacia,** which departs every hour or more frequently from Tobu's Asakusa Station. The cost is ¥2,620 one-way for the 1-hour-and-50-minute trip on weekdays and ¥2,720 on weekends and holidays. All seats are reserved, which means you are guaranteed a seat; if you're traveling on a holiday or a summer weekend, you may wish to purchase and reserve your ticket in advance. Another plus is that there's usually an English-speaking hostess on board who passes out pamphlets on the area and can answer sightseeing questions about Nikko.

Otherwise, you can reach Nikko on Tobu's slower **rapid train** from Asakusa, which costs ¥1,320 one-way and takes 2 hours and 10 minutes, with trains departing every hour or more frequently. There are no reserved seats, which means you might have to stand if trains are crowded. Make sure to board cars no. 5 and 6 at the back of the train, as train cars are separated at Shimo-Imaichi Station.

To save yourself the trouble of buying individual tickets (money-wise, it's a bargain only if you wish to take the Spacia and use Nikko's buses), consider purchasing Tobu's World Heritage Pass, which provides round-trip train travel between Asakusa and Nikko via rapid train, unlimited bus travel in Nikko, and admission to Toshogu Shrine (excluding Ieyasu's mausoleum), Rinnoji Temple, and Futarasan Shrine. Cost of the pass, valid for 2 days and available only to foreign visitors, is ¥3,600 for adults, ¥3,200 for senior high students, ¥3,000 for junior high students, and ¥1,700 for children (you can upgrade to the Limited Express Spacia by paying an extra ¥1,040 weekdays and ¥1,120 Saturday and Sundays, one way). You can purchase the pass online at www.tobu.co.jp/foreign if you buy it at least four days before your trip, or at the Tobu Sightseeing Service Center at Asakusa Station (✆ **03/3841-2871**), open daily 7:45am to 5pm.

If you have a Japan Rail Pass, take the Tohoku Shinkansen bullet train from Tokyo Station to Utsunomiya (there are departures every 20–40 min. and the trip takes about 55 min.), where you change for the JR train to Nikko (45 min., with departures every hour or less).

VISITOR INFORMATION   Before leaving Tokyo, pick up the leaflet "Nikko" from the Tourist Information Center (TIC). It gives the train schedule for both the Tobu

Line departing from Asakusa Station, and JR trains from Shinjuku. The TIC also has color brochures with maps of the Nikko area.

Nikko's Tobu and JR stations are located almost side by side in the village's downtown area. **Nikko Tobu Station tourist information counter** (✆ **0288/53-4511;** www.nikko-jp.org; daily 8:30am–5pm), located inside Tobu Station, has staff who can give you a map, answer basic questions, and point you in the right direction. If you arrive before noon, you can also leave your luggage here for delivery by 3pm to a limited list of area hotels and ryokan for ¥500 per bag (Turtle Inn Nikko and Annex Turtle Hotori-an are on the list, but Nikko Kanaya Hotel, which is on the way to Toshogu Shrine, is not). Next to the tourist office is a hotel reservation counter, open daily from 9am to 5pm, which can make reservations at some 50 member hotels and ryokan for ¥100 per person.

Another tourist office, the **Nikko Information Center** (✆ **0288/54-2496**), is located on the left side of the main road leading from the train station to Toshogu Shrine. It has English-speaking staff and lots of information in English, including information on public hot springs and hiking trails. Open daily from 9am to 5pm.

GETTING AROUND Toshogu Shrine and its mausoleum are on the edge of town, but you can walk from either the JR or Tobu train stations to the shrine in about half an hour, passing souvenir shops and restaurants along the way. Head straight out the main exit, pass the bus stands, and then turn right. English-language signs point the way throughout town. Keep walking on this main road (you'll pass the Nikko Information Center about halfway down on the left side) until you come to a T-intersection with a vermilion-colored bridge spanning a river to the left (about a 15-min. walk from the train stations). The stone steps opposite lead up the hill into the woods and to Toshogu Shrine in 15 minutes. You can also travel from Tobu Station by bus from bus stop 1-A, getting off at either the Shinkyo (a 7-min. ride; fare: ¥190) or Omotesando (a 9-min. ride; fare: ¥280). I almost always walk.

Exploring Nikko

ON THE WAY TO THE SHRINE The first indication that you're nearing the shrine is the vermilion-painted **Sacred Bridge (Shinkyo)** arching over the rushing Daiyagawa River. It was built in 1636 for visiting shogun and their emissaries. Across the road from the Sacred Bridge, steps lead uphill into a forest of cedar where, after a 5-minute walk, you'll see a statue of **Shodo,** a priest who founded Nikko 1,200 years ago when mountains were revered as gods. In the centuries that followed, Nikko became one of Japan's greatest mountain Buddhist retreats, with 500 subtemples spread through the area. Behind Shodo is the first major temple, Rinnoji Temple, where you can buy a **combination ticket** for ¥1,000 for adults, ¥600 for high-school students, and ¥400 for children; it allows entry to Rinnoji Temple (but not Shoyo-en Garden), Toshogu Shrine, neighboring Futarasan Shrine, and the other Tokugawa mausoleum, Taiyuin. Once at Toshogu Shrine, you'll have to pay an extra ¥520 to see Ieyasu's tomb. Otherwise, if time is limited, you can buy a ticket only for Toshogu Shrine for ¥1,300 for adults and ¥450 children, including Ieyasu's tomb. It doesn't really matter where you buy your combination ticket, since you can always pay the extra fee to see sights not covered.

Toshogu Shrine and the other sights in Nikko Sannai are open daily from 8am to 5pm April through October (to 4pm the rest of the year); you must enter at least 30 minutes before closing time.

RINNOJI TEMPLE   Rinnoji Temple (✆ **0288/54-0531**) was founded by the priest Shodo in the 8th century, long before the Toshogu clan came onto the scene. Here you can visit **Sanbutsudo Hall,** a large building that enshrines three 8.4m-high (28-ft.) gold-plated wooden images of Buddha, considered the "gods of Nikko"; today people pray here for world peace (***Note:*** Sanbutsudo Temple is undergoing restoration until 2021, but you can still go inside). Perhaps the best thing to see at Rinnoji Temple is **Shoyo-en Garden** (opposite Sanbutsudo Hall), which costs ¥300 extra. Completed in 1815 and typical of Japanese landscaped gardens of the Edo Period, this small strolling garden provides a different vista with each turn of the path, making it seem much larger than it is. Your ticket to the garden also gains entrance to a small treasure house, where relics are displayed on a rotating basis.

TOSHOGU SHRINE ★★★   The most important and famous structure in Nikko is Toshogu Shrine (✆ **0288/54-0560**). When Ieyasu died in 1616 at the age of 75, his wish was to be enshrined in Nikko so that he could serve as a guardian from evil demons, who were thought to come from the north, and thereby ensure the safety and long reign of the Tokugawa regime. Although Ieyasu requested a small shrine, Tokugawa's grandson (and third Tokugawa shogun), Tokugawa Iemitsu, erected this grand complex as an act of devotion. It seems that no expense was too great in creating the monument. It took some 4.5 million artisans, craftspeople and other workers 1½ years to erect a group of buildings more elaborate and gorgeous than any other Japanese temple or shrine. Rich in colors and carvings, Toshogu Shrine is gilded with 2.4 million sheets of gold leaf (they could cover an area of almost 2.4 hectares/6 acres). The mausoleum was completed in 1636, almost 20 years after Ieyasu's death, and was most certainly meant to impress anyone who saw it as a demonstration of the Tokugawa shogunate's wealth and power. The shrine is set in a grove of magnificent ancient **Japanese cedars** planted over a 20-year period during the 1600s by a feudal lord named Matsudaira Masatsuna. Some 13,000 of the original trees still stand, adding a sense of dignity to the mausoleum and shrine.

You enter Toshogu Shrine via a flight of stairs that passes under a huge stone *torii* gateway, one of the largest in Japan. On your left is a five-story, 35m-high (115-ft.) **pagoda.** Although normally pagodas are found only at temples, this pagoda is just one example of how Buddhism and Shintoism are combined at Toshogu Shrine. After climbing a second flight of stairs, turn left and you'll see the **Sacred Stable,** which houses a sacred white horse. Horses have long been dedicated to Shinto gods and are kept at shrines. Shrines also kept monkeys as well, since they were thought to protect horses from disease; look for the three monkeys carved above the stable door, fixed in the poses of "see no evil, hear no evil, speak no evil"—they're considered guardians of the sacred horse. Across from the stable is **Kami-Jinko,** famous for its carving by Kano Tanyu, who painted the images of the two elephants (under the eaves) after reading about them but without seeing what they actually looked like.

The central showpiece of Nikko is **Yomeimon Gate,** popularly known as the Twilight Gate, implying that it could take you all day (until twilight) to see everything carved on it. Painted in red, blue, and green, and gilded and lacquered, this gate is carved with more than 500 flowers, dragons, birds, and other animals. It's almost too much to take in at once and is very un-Japanese in its opulence, having more in common with Chinese architecture than with the usual austerity of most Japanese shrines.

You can visit the shrine's main sanctuary, **Haiden,** comprising three halls: One was reserved for the Imperial family, one for the shogun, and one (the central hall) for conducting ceremonies. You can buy good-luck charms here that will guard against such misfortunes as traffic accidents, or that will ensure good health, success in business, easy childbirth, or other achievements in daily life. To the right of the main hall is the entrance to **Tokugawa Ieyasu's mausoleum.** If it's not already included in your combination ticket, admission is ¥520 extra. After the ticket counter, look for the carving of a sleeping cat above the door, dating from the Edo Period and famous today as a symbol of Nikko (you'll find many reproductions in area souvenir shops). Beyond that are 200 stone steps leading past cedars to Tokugawa's tomb. After the riotous colors of the shrine, the tomb seems surprisingly simple.

On the way out you'll pass **Yakushido,** famous for its dragon painting on the ceiling. A monk gives a brief explanation (in Japanese) and demonstrates how two sticks struck together produce an echo that supposedly resonates like a bell. Twelve statues here represent the Chinese zodiac calendar.

FUTARASAN SHRINE   Directly to the west of Toshogu Shrine is Futarasan Shrine (© 0288/54-0535), the oldest building in the district (ca. 1617), which has a pleasant garden and is dedicated to the gods of mountains surrounding Nikko. You'll find miniature shrines dedicated to the god of fortune, god of happiness, god of trees, god of water, and god of good marriages. On the shrine's grounds is the so-called **ghost lantern,** enclosed in a small vermilion-colored wooden structure. According to legend, it used to come alive at night and sweep around Nikko in the form of a ghost. It apparently scared one guard so much that he struck it with his sword 70 times; the marks are still visible on the lamp's rim. Entrance to the miniature shrines and ghost lantern is ¥200 extra.

TAIYUIN MAUSOLEUM ★   Past Futarasan Shrine is **Taiyuin Mausoleum** (© 0288/53-1567), the final resting place of Iemitsu, the third Tokugawa shogun (look for his statue). Completed in 1653, it's not nearly as large as Toshogu Shrine, but it's ornate and serenely elegant nevertheless. To show respect for the first shogun, Taiyuin's buildings face Toshogu Shrine. Tourists usually bypass this shrine, making it a pleasant last stop on your tour of Nikko Sannai.

NIKKO TAMOZAWA IMPERIAL VILLA (TAMOZAWA GOYOUTEI KINEN KOEN) ★★   If you haven't seen the Imperial villas of Kyoto (which require advance planning), this villa, at 8–27 Honcho (© 0288/53-6767), is a great alternative. It's not as old, having been built in 1899 for Prince Yoshihito (who later became the Taisho emperor), and was recently painstakingly restored so that it looks brand-new. It has the distinction of being the largest wooden Imperial villa of its era, with 106 rooms, 37 of which are open to the public. In addition, the central core of the villa is actually much older, constructed in 1632 by a feudal lord and brought to Nikko from Edo (present-day Tokyo). Altogether, three emperors and three princes used the villa between 1899 and 1947. A self-guided tour of the villa provides insight into traditional Japanese architectural methods—from its 11 layers of paper-plastered walls to its nail-less wood framing—as well as the lifestyle of Japan's aristocracy. Be sure to wander the small outdoor garden. Admission is ¥500 for adults, half-price for children. Open Wednesday to Monday 9am to 4:30pm. It's about a 20-minute walk from Toshogu Shrine, or take the bus to Tamozawa stop.

Where to Eat

In addition to rainbow trout, Nikko is also famous for *yuba,* a high-protein byproduct formed by boiling soymilk, which causes a thin film to rise to the liquid's surface. Thought to have originated in Kyoto, it was popular among monks training at Rinnoji

Temple for its nutrition, meat-like protein, and light weight for carrying on mountain retreats. Only priests and members of the Imperial family were allowed to consume it until the Meiji Period. Now you can enjoy it, too, at many restaurants in Nikko. Another popular dish is *Mizu-yokan*, a traditional sweet made from the Azuki bean.

Gyoshin-Tei ★★ VEGETARIAN/KAISEKI   This lovely Japanese restaurant, with a simple tatami room and a view of pines, moss, and bonsai, serves two kinds of set meals—kaiseki and Buddhist vegetarian cuisine (Shojin Ryori)—both of which change monthly and include the local specialty, *yuba* (see above). It's one of several restaurants in a parklike setting under the same management and with the same open hours. Meiji-no-Yakata (closed Wed), occupying a stone house built 110 years ago as the private retreat of an American businessman, serves Western food such as grilled rainbow trout, veal cutlet, and steak, with set meals ranging from ¥3,990 to ¥8,400. The drawback: This place is harder to find than my other recommendations, but it's only a 4-minute walk northeast of Rinnoji Temple, on the other side of a parking lot.

2339–1 Sannai, Nikko City. ✆ **0288/53-3751.** Reservations recommended. Vegetarian/kaiseki meals ¥3,990–¥5,775. AE, DC, MC, V. Fri–Wed 11am–7pm (from 11:30am in winter). A 25-min. walk from Nikko Tobu Station; or bus from Nikko Station to Shinkyo (then a 7-min. walk).

Hippari Tako (ひっぱり凧) NOODLES   This tiny, three-table establishment is under the caring supervision of motherly Miki-san, who serves a limited selection of noodle dishes, including ramen and stir-fried noodles with vegetables, as well as *onigiri* (rice balls), vegetarian tempura, and *yakitori* (skewered barbecued chicken). There's an English-language menu, and the walls, covered with business cards and messages left by appreciative guests from around the world, are testimony to both the tasty meals and Miki-san's warm hospitality. A computer allows guests access to the Internet for 30 minutes for free.

1011 Kami-Hatsuishi, Nikko City. ✆**0288/53-2933.** Main dishes ¥650–¥850. No credit cards. Daily 11am–7pm (last order). A 15-min. walk from Nikko Tobu Station. On the left side of the main street leading from the station to Toshogu Shrine, 1 min. before the Nikko Kanaya Hotel and the Sacred Bridge.

Main Dining Hall at Nikko Kanaya Hotel ★★ CONTINENTAL   Even if you don't spend the night here, the Kanaya Hotel's quaint dining hall with its colorful wood-carved pillars is a great place for lunch. Because it's beside the Sacred Bridge, only a 15-minute walk from Toshogu Shrine, you can easily combine it with your sightseeing tour. I suggest Nikko's specialty: locally caught rainbow trout available three different ways. I always order mine cooked Kanaya style—covered with soy sauce, sugar, and sake; grilled; and served whole. The best bargain is the set lunch for ¥3,500, available until 3pm, which comes with soup, salad, a main dish such as trout, bread or rice, and dessert. Steak, beef stroganoff, lobster, salmon, chicken, and other Western fare are also listed on the English-language menu.

Nikko Kanaya Hotel, 1300 Kami-Hatsuishi, Nikko City. ✆ **0288/54-0001.** Reservations recommended during peak season. Main dishes ¥2,887–¥9,240; set lunches ¥3,500–¥10,500; set dinners ¥9,800. AE, DC, MC, V. Daily 11:30am–2:30pm and 6–8pm (last order). A 20-min. walk from Nikko Tobu Station.

Where to Stay

If it's peak season (Golden Week, Aug, or Oct.) or a weekend, it's best to reserve a room in advance, which you can do by calling a lodging either directly or through a travel agency in Tokyo. Off-peak, you can make a reservation for ¥100 per person upon arrival at Nikko Tobu Station, at the **accommodations-reservation window** (☎ **0288/54-0864;** daily 9am–5pm), which is familiar with hotels and ryokan throughout the area.

Annex Turtle Hotori-An ★★ ☺   Owned by the super-friendly family that runs Turtle Inn (see below), this is one of my favorite places to stay in Nikko. One dip in the hot-spring bath overlooking the Daiyagawa River (which you can lock for privacy) will tell you why; at night, you're lulled to sleep by the sound of the rushing waters. A simple but spotless modern structure (all nonsmoking), it's located in a nice rural setting on a quiet street with a few other houses; an adjoining park and playground provide plenty of space for kids to play. All its rooms except one are Japanese style. A plentiful Western-style breakfast costs ¥1,050 in the pleasant living area/dining room. For dinner, you can go to the nearby Turtle Inn (not available Sun, Tues, or Thurs; reservations should be made the day before), or buy a pizza from the freezer and microwave it yourself. There's also a communal refrigerator where you can store food.

8–28 Takumi-cho, Nikko City, Tochigi 321-1433. www.turtle-nikko.com. ☎ **0288/53-3663.** Fax 0288/53-3883. 11 units. ¥6,650 single; ¥12,700 double. Special rates for children. AE, MC, V. Bus: From Nikko Station to the Sogo Kaikan-mae stop, a 7-min. ride; then a 9-min. walk. **Amenities:** Hot-spring baths; Wi-Fi (free, in lobby); computer w/free Internet access at Turtle Inn. *In room:* A/C, TV.

Nikko Kanaya Hotel ★★ ⛪   Founded in 1873, this distinguished-looking place on a hill above the Sacred Bridge is the most famous hotel in Nikko, combining the rustic heartiness of a European country lodge with elements of old Japan. The present complex, built in spurts over the past 140 years, has a rambling, delightfully old-fashioned atmosphere that fuses Western architecture with Japanese craftsmanship. Through the decades it has played host to a number of VIPs, from Charles Lindbergh to Indira Gandhi to Shirley MacLaine; Frank Lloyd Wright left a sketch for the bar fireplace, which was later built to his design. Even if you don't stay here, you might want to drop by for lunch (see review above). Pathways lead to the Daiyagawa River and several short hiking trails. All rooms are Western-style twins, with the differences in price based on room size, view (river view is best), and facilities. Some 10 rooms have been updated, but I prefer the older, simpler rooms because they have more character; some have antiques and claw-foot tubs. The best (and priciest) room is the annex corner room in the 77-year-old wing where the emperor once stayed.

1300 Kami-Hatsuishi, Nikko City, Tochigi 321-1401. www.kanayahotel.co.jp. ☎ **0288/54-0001.** Fax 0288/53-2487. 70 units. ¥15,015–¥46,200 single; ¥17,325–¥51,975 double. ¥3,465–¥4,620 extra on Fri, Sat, and eve before national holidays; ¥5,775–¥6,930 extra in peak season. AE, DC, MC, V. Bus: From Nikko Tobu Station to the Shinkyo stop, a 5-min. ride. On foot: 17 min. from Nikko Tobu Station. **Amenities:** 3 restaurants, including the Main Dining Hall (p. 198); bar; small outdoor heated pool (mid-July to Aug only); outdoor skating rink (Dec–Feb, free for guests, including shoes); shuttle bus from Tobu Nikko Station 2–4 times a day. *In room:* A/C, TV, minibar.

Turtle Inn ★   This excellent, nonsmoking pension, a Japanese Inn Group member, is located within walking distance of Toshogu Shrine in a newer two-story house on a quiet side street beside the Daiyagawa River. The friendly owner, Mr. Fukuda, speaks English and is very helpful in planning a sightseeing itinerary. Rooms are bright and cheerful in both Japanese and Western styles; the five tatami rooms are without a private bathroom. Excellent Japanese dinners (served on local Mashiko pottery) are available for ¥2,100, as are Western breakfasts for ¥1,050. Be sure to order dinner the day before, and note that it's not available on Sunday, Tuesday, or Thursday.

2–16 Takumi-cho, Nikko City, Tochigi 321-1433. www.turtle-nikko.com. ☏ **0288/53-3168.** Fax 0288/53-3883. 10 units (3 with bathroom). ¥4,950 single without bathroom, ¥5,750 single with bathroom; ¥9,300 double without bathroom, ¥10,900 double with bathroom. Special rates for children. AE, MC, V. Bus: From Nikko Station to the Sogo Kaikan-mae stop, a 7-min. ride; then a 5-min. walk. **Amenities:** Hot-spring baths; Wi-Fi (free, in lobby); computer w/free Internet access. *In room:* A/C, TV, no phone.

YOKOHAMA, CITY OF THE 21ST CENTURY

29km (18 miles) S of Tokyo

Few attractions in Yokohama warrant a visit if your time is limited. If you find yourself in Tokyo for an extended period, however, Yokohama is a pleasant destination for an easy day trip. Be sure to make time for wonderful Sankeien Garden; although only a century old, it ranks on my long list as one of the top gardens in Japan.

A rather new city in Japan's history books, Yokohama was nothing more than a tiny fishing village when Commodore Perry arrived in the mid-1800s and demanded that Japan open its doors to the world. The village was selected by the shogun as one of several ports to be opened for international trade, transforming it from a backwater to Japan's most important gateway. Yokohama subsequently grew by leaps and bounds and was a pioneer when it came to Western goods and services, boasting Japan's first bakery (1860), photo studio (1862), beer brewery (1869), cinema (1870), daily newspaper (1870), public restroom (1871), and ice cream (1879).

Now Japan's second-largest city with a population of 3.6 million, Yokohama remains the nation's largest international port and supports a large international community, with many foreigners residing in the section called the Bluff. Yokohama has an especially large Chinese population and Japan's largest Chinatown, whose restaurants serve as a mecca for hungry Tokyoites. Befitting a city known for its firsts, Yokohama constructed Japan's first and largest urban development project more than a decade ago—**Minato Mirai 21,** with a conference center, museums, hotels, shopping centers, and restaurants. Hard to imagine that a mere 150-some years ago, Yokohama was a village of 100 houses.

Essentials

GETTING THERE   Because many Yokohama residents work in Tokyo, it's as easy to get to Yokohama as it is to get around Tokyo. Although Yokohama Station is the city's main train station, I suggest taking a train from Tokyo that will take you farther to Sakuragicho, Minato Mirai, or Motomachi Chukagai station, since most attractions are clustered here. (However, if you're headed first to Sankeien Garden, you can disembark at Yokohama Station and transfer to bus no. 8 at the east exit, though you can also catch the same bus elsewhere in town.) Best is the **Minato Mirai Line** (of the Tokyu-Toyoko private company), which departs from Shibuya and reaches Minato Mirai in about 30 minutes on the limited express. A one-way fare costs ¥440; an all-day Minato Mirai Line pass, including transportation from Shibuya and back, is worth the cost of ¥840. Alternatively, the **JR Keihin-Tohoku Line** travels through Ueno, Tokyo, Yurakucho, Shimbashi, and Shinagawa stations before continuing on to Sakuragicho, with the journey from Tokyo Station taking approximately 40 minutes and costing ¥540 one-way (free with a Japan Rail Pass).

Yokohama

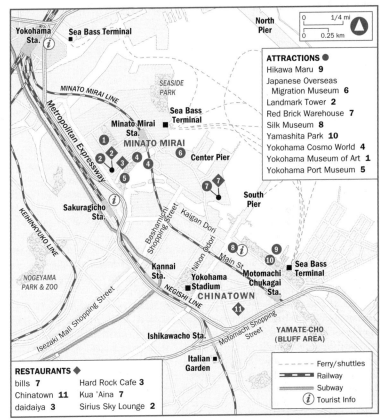

ATTRACTIONS ●
Hikawa Maru **9**
Japanese Overseas
  Migration Museum **6**
Landmark Tower **2**
Red Brick Warehouse **7**
Silk Museum **8**
Yamashita Park **10**
Yokohama Cosmo World **4**
Yokohama Museum of Art **1**
Yokohama Port Museum **5**

- - - - - Ferry/shuttles
▬▬▬ Railway
▬▬▬ Subway
ⓘ Tourist Info

RESTAURANTS ◆
bills **7**   Hard Rock Cafe **3**
Chinatown **11**   Kua 'Aina **7**
daidaiya **3**   Sirius Sky Lounge **2**

VISITOR INFORMATION   There are several Tourist Information Centers in Yoko-hama, but probably the most convenient and easiest to find is **Sakuragicho Station Tourist Information Center** (✆ **045/211-0111;** daily 9am–7pm), located in a kiosk outside JR Sakuragicho Station in the direction of Minato Mirai and its Land-mark Tower. The main office, the **Yokohama Convention & Visitors Bureau,** is located in the Sangyo Boeki Center (nicknamed Sambo Center), 2 Yamashita-cho, Naka-ku (www.welcome.city.yokohama.jp/eng/tourism; ✆ **045/641-4759;** Mon–Fri 9am–5pm), close to the Silk Center and Yamashita Park. Both have excellent city maps and brochures.

Next door to the Convention & Visitors Bureau, in the Silk Center, is the **Kanagawa Prefectural Tourist Office** (www.kanagawa-kankou.or.jp; ✆ **045/681-0007;** Tues–Sun 10am–6pm), with information on Hakone and Kamakura, both in Kanagawa Prefecture.

GETTING AROUND   If you start your day in Yokohama at either Sakuragicho or Minato Mirai Station, you can visit the museums and attractions there and then walk onward to Yamashita Park via a waterfront promenade in about 30 minutes (though you might want to stop at a museum on Japanese emigration and the Red Brick Warehouse shopping mall on the way). Alternatively, there's a red retro-looking tourist bus called the **Akai Kutsu,** which makes the rounds of central Yokohama, including Sakuragicho Station, Minato Mirai, Red Brick Warehouse, Yamashita Park, and Chinatown throughout the year, with departures every 20 to 30 minutes and costing ¥100 per ride (pick up a map and timetable at the Sakuragicho Station tourist office). To reach Sankeien Garden, take bus no. 8, which departs from Yokohama Station's east exit and passes Minato Mirai, Chinatown, and Yamashita Park on its way to the garden. If you end the day with a meal at Chinatown, you can catch the Minato Mirai Line back to Shibuya at nearby Motomachi Chukagai Station.

What to See & Do

MINATO MIRAI   There's no mistaking **Minato Mirai 21** (www.minatomirai21.com) when you see it—it looks like a vision of the future with its dramatic monolithic buildings. It boasts a huge state-of-the-art convention facility, three first-class hotels, Japan's tallest building, office buildings, two great museums, and an amusement park. It's all a bit too sterile for my taste, but its museums make a visit here worthwhile.

If you arrive at Sakuragicho Station, take the moving walkway that connects the station to the Landmark Tower in Minato Mirai in 5 minutes. Otherwise, the Minato Mirai Line will deposit you directly in the middle of the massive urban development.

There are several shopping malls in Minato Mirai, including Queen's Square, Yokohama World Porter's, Landmark Plaza, Jack Mall, and the restored Red Brick Warehouse, but the area's most conspicuous building is **Landmark Tower,** Japan's tallest building and also with Japan's highest observatory in a building (as opposed to a communications tower). The fastest elevator in the world will whisk you up 270m (886 ft.) in about 40 seconds to the 69th floor, where there's an observation room called **Sky Garden** (www.yokohama-landmark.jp/skygarden; ✆ **045/222-5030;** daily 10am–9pm, to 10pm Sat). From here you can see the harbor with its container port and Yokohama Bay Bridge, as well as almost the entire city and even, on clear days in winter, Mount Fuji. However, its admission fees—¥1,000 for adults, ¥800 for seniors and high-school students, ¥500 for elementary and junior-high students, and ¥200 for children—make it too expensive in my book. Better is Landmark Tower's 70th-floor **Sirius Sky Lounge;** although there's a cover charge, its atmosphere is more relaxing (see below).

Maritime buffs should spend an hour checking out the **Yokohama Port Museum (Yokohama Minato Hakubutsukan),** 2–1–1 Minato Mirai (www.nippon-maru.or.jp; ✆ **045/221-0280**), which concentrates on Yokohama's history as a port, beginning with the 1853 arrival of Perry's "Black Ships" and the establishment of Yokohama Port in 1859, followed by displays related to Japan's subsequent oceanic trading routes to Europe and America, which also spurred Japanese emigration to other countries. Other displays chart Yokohama's rise in the 1950s and '60s into a major ship-building yard and its role in the rise of container and cruise ships, with lots of models of everything from passenger ships to oil tankers and—I love this one!—a full-scale simulator that lets you bring a ship into Yokohama's port in all kinds of weather conditions. Sailing fans enjoy touring the 96m (315-ft.), four-masted

Nippon-Maru moored out front, built in 1930 as a sail-training ship for students of the merchant marines and complete with bridge, engine room, sleeping quarters, mess hall, and more. Admission is ¥600 for adults and ¥300 for children. The museum is open Tuesday to Sunday 10am to 5pm.

The most important thing to see in Minato Mirai is the **Yokohama Museum of Art ★**, 3–4–1 Minato Mirai (www.yaf.or.jp/yma/english; ℂ **045/221-0300**), which emphasizes 20th-century art by Western and Japanese artists in its ambitious goal to collect and display works reflecting the mutual influence of Europe and Japan on modern art since the opening of Yokohama's port in 1859. The light and airy building, designed by Kenzo Tange and Urtec, Inc., features exhibits from its permanent collection—which includes works by Cézanne, Picasso, Matisse, Leger, Max Ernst, Dalí, and Japanese artists, as well as photography—that change three times a year (you can tour its four rooms in about 30 min.), as well as special exhibitions on loan from other museums. Open Friday through Wednesday from 10am to 6pm. Admission is ¥500 for adults, ¥300 for high-school and college students, and ¥100 for children. Special exhibitions cost more.

It would be hard to miss **Yokohama Cosmo World** (℃ **045/641-6591**), an amusement park spread along both sides of a canal: It boasts one of the largest Ferris wheels in the world. Other diversions include a roller coaster that looks like it dives right into a pond (but vanishes instead into a tunnel), a haunted house, a simulation theater with seats that move with the action, kiddie rides, a games arcade, and much more. Admission is free but rides cost ¥300 to ¥700 apiece. The park opens at 11am, closing at 8pm in winter, 9pm in summer, and 10pm most weekends and holidays; closed most Thursdays (except in summer).

Just a few minutes' walk east of Cosmo World (in the direction of Yamashita Park) is the **Japanese Overseas Migration Museum (Kaigai Iju Shiryokan)**, 2–3–1 Shinko, Naka-ku (℃ **045/663-3257**), a must if you're of Japanese descent. Beginning in 1866 when Japanese were first able to apply for a passport and travel abroad, Japanese started emigrating to the Americas as working students (*shosei*) and laborers, many finding employment in the fishing and food processing industries, at Brazilian coffee plantations, and as field workers and gardeners before eventually branching out as doctors, teachers, lawyers, store proprietors, and other professionals, often serving the Japanese community. As many as 29,000 Japanese emigrated to Hawaii between 1885 and 1894; from 1908 to 1941 about 188,000 Japanese emigrated to Brazil. Displays include photographs, videos, newspaper articles, and personal artifacts, such as the sewing kit, *tabi* (traditional socks with a separation for the big toe), umbrella, and other items brought to Brazil by the Kawase family in 1931. The museum also covers the discrimination many immigrants experienced in the US, from the 1924 National Origins Act that effectively put a stop to Japanese immigration to the World War II internment camps which contained 120,000 *issei* and *nisei* (first- and second-generation immigrant Japanese). Admission is free, and it's open Tuesday to Sunday from 10am to 6pm.

Nearby is the **Red Brick Warehouse (Aka Renga)**, 1–1–2 Shinko (℃ **045/227-2002**). This restored waterfront warehouse is home to dozens of shops selling crafts, furniture, housewares, clothing, and jewelry, as well as restaurants, with most shops open daily 11am to 8pm.

IN & AROUND YAMASHITA PARK   From Aka Renga it's a 10-minute walk to Yamashita Park via the elevated Yamashita Rinko-sen waterfront promenade. Laid out after the huge 1923 earthquake that destroyed much of Tokyo and Yokohama, Yamashita Park was Japan's first seaside park. A popular destination for families, it provides great views of the city's mighty harbor and Bay Bridge. The most impressive landmark here is the **Hikawa Maru** (www.nyk.com/rekishi/e/exhibitions/hikawa. htm; ☎ **045/641-4362**), a passenger/cargo ship built in Yokohama Port in 1930 for the Yokohama–Seattle route. It was retired in 1960 after crossing the Pacific 254 times and carrying about 25,000 passengers. After paying the ¥200 admission fee (¥100 for seniors and children), you can learn about the ship's history and see the first- and third-class cabins, crew's quarters, first-class dining room with its Art Deco decor, outdoor deck, galley, engine room, and captain's office. It's open Tuesday to Sunday from 10am to 5pm.

Across the gingko-lined street from Yamashita Park is the Silk Center, where you'll find both the prefectural tourist office and the excellent **Silk Museum ★★**, 1 Yamashita-cho, Naka-ku (www.silkmuseum.or.jp; ☎ **045/641-0841;** station: Nihon Odori). For many years after Japan opened its doors, silk was its major export, and most of it was shipped to the rest of the world from Yokohama, the nation's largest raw-silk market. In tribute to the role silk has played in Yokohama's history, this museum has displays showing the metamorphosis of the silkworm and the process by which silk is obtained from cocoons, all well documented in English; from April to October you can even observe live cocoons and silkworms at work (compared to the beauty they produce, silkworms are amazingly ugly). The museum also displays various kinds of silk fabrics, as well as gorgeous kimono and reproduction Japanese costumes from the Nara, Heian, and Edo periods. Don't miss this museum, which takes about 30 minutes to see; surprisingly, it's never crowded. Open Tuesday through Sunday from 9am to 4:30pm; admission is ¥500 for adults, ¥300 for seniors, ¥200 for students, and ¥100 for children.

Not far from Yamashita Park is **Chukagai,** Japan's largest Chinatown with hundreds of souvenir shops and restaurants; see "Where to Dine," below.

SANKEIEN GARDEN ★★★ In my opinion, **Sankeien Garden** (www. sankeien.or.jp; (☎ **045/621-0634**) is the best reason to visit Yokohama. Although not old itself, this lovely park contains more than a dozen historic buildings that were brought here from other parts of Japan, including Kyoto and Nara, all situated around streams and ponds and surrounded by Japanese-style landscape gardens. The park, divided into an Inner Garden and Outer Garden, was laid out in 1906 by Tomitaro Hara, a local millionaire who made his fortune exporting silk. As you wander along the gently winding pathways, you'll see a villa built in 1649 by the Tokugawa shogunate clan, tea arbors, a 500-year-old three-story pagoda, and a farmhouse built in 1750 without the use of nails. The gardens are well known for their blossoms of plums, cherries, wisteria, azaleas, irises, and waterlilies, but no matter what the season, the views here are beautiful.

Plan on at least 2 hours to see both gardens. Sankeien is open daily from 9am to 5pm (you must enter the Inner Garden by 4pm, the Outer Garden by 4:30pm). Admission is ¥500 for adults, ¥300 for seniors, and ¥200 for children. The easiest way to reach Sankeien Garden is by bus no. 8, which departs from platform no. 2 at Yokohama Station's east exit (near Sogo department store) and winds its way past Sakuragicho Station, past Chinatown (via Hon-cho Dori), and through Kannai before it reaches the Honmoku-Sankeien-mae bus stop 30 minutes later (the bus stop is announced in English).

Where to Eat

CHINATOWN (CHUKAGAI)   Located in Yamashita-cho, a couple blocks inland from Yamashita Park and next to Motomachi Chukagai Station of the Minato Mirai Line, Chinatown has more than 500 restaurants and shops lining two main streets and dozens of offshoots. Tokyoites have long been coming to Yokohama just to dine; many restaurants have been owned by the same families for generations. Most serve Cantonese food and have plastic-food displays, English-language menus, or pictures of their dishes, so your best bet is to wander around and let your budget be your guide. Restaurants are open from about 11 or 11:30am to 9:30pm or later.

MINATO MIRAI   For sophisticated surroundings or just a romantic evening cocktail, take the elevator up to the 70th floor of Landmark Tower, where you'll find the Yokohama Royal Park Hotel's **Sirius Sky Lounge ★** (✆ **045/221-1111**), with stunning seaside views. It serves a buffet lunch for ¥4,042 daily from 11:30am to 2:30pm, which often centers on a changing, ethnic cuisine but also offers items such as salmon, lamb, and pizza. After lunch, it's teatime until 5pm. From 5pm to 1am daily, Sirius is a cocktail lounge (no one under 20 years old allowed) and levies a cover charge: ¥1,050 per person from 5 to 7pm and again from 11pm to 1am; ¥2,100 for live music from 7 to 11pm. It offers a small, a la carte dinner menu, as well as set dinners starting at ¥7,350.

Nearby, a good place for a drink or a hamburger is the local branch of the **Hard Rock Cafe,** located on the first floor of Queen's Square Yokohama Tower A (✆ **045/682-5626;** open daily 11am–11pm). Nearby, on the fourth and fifth floors of the Queen's Square Yokohama, is a branch of **daidaiya** (✆ **045/228-5035;** open daily 11am–3pm and 5–10:30pm). See p. 142 and 131 for reviews of these restaurants.

The 1911 renovated Red Brick Warehouse (see above) also has fast-food outlets, including a **Kua'Aina** burger shop (✆ **045/227-5300;** p. 136). For something more substantial, head to **bills** (✆ **045/650-1266;** daily 9am–10pm [last order]), featuring cuisine by Australian Bill Granger. With a crisp interior and outdoor seating, it serves breakfast (from scrambled organic eggs to blueberry pancakes), lunch (mainly salads, sandwiches, and pasta), and dinner entrees ranging from Parmesan chicken schnitzel with garlic mashed potatoes to grilled swordfish, most priced from ¥2,000 to ¥3,000.

MOUNT FUJI ★★

100km (62 miles) SW of Tokyo

Mount Fuji, affectionately called "Fuji-san," has been revered since ancient times. Throughout the centuries Japanese poets have written about it, painters have painted it, pilgrims have flocked to it, and more than a few people have died on it. Without a doubt, this mountain has been photographed more than anything else in Japan.

Mount Fuji is stunningly impressive. At 3,766m (12,355 ft.), it's the tallest mountain in Japan, towering far above anything else around it—a cone of almost perfectly symmetrical proportions. It is majestic, grand, and awe-inspiring. To the Japanese it symbolizes the very spirit of their country. Though it's visible on clear days (mostly in winter) from as far away as 160km (100 miles), Fuji-san, unfortunately, is almost always cloaked in clouds. If you catch a glimpse of this mighty mountain, consider yourself extremely lucky. One of the best spots for views of Mount Fuji is **Hakone** (see below).

Essentials

There are four ascents to the summit of Mount Fuji (and four descents), each divided into 10 stations of unequal length, with most climbs starting at the Go-go-me, or the Fifth Station level. From Tokyo, the **Kawaguchiko-Yoshidaguchi Trail** is the most popular and most easily accessible, as well as the least steep. The "official" climbing season is very short, only from July 1 to August 31. Climbers are discouraged from climbing outside the season, due to low temperatures, super-strong winds, and no emergency services. To beat the crowds—and I do mean crowds—try to schedule your climb on a weekday during the first 2 weeks of July, before the start of Japan's school vacation (around July 20). Otherwise, if you choose to climb during the busiest weeks of the season (the first two weeks of August), you'll be climbing with an estimated 8,000 hikers daily on the Kawaguchiko-Yoshidaguchi Route, including many foreigners.

GETTING THERE The easiest way to reach the Kawaguchiko Fifth Station is by **bus** from Shinjuku Station. There are two bus companies that operate the route, the **Keio Highway Bus** (www.highwaybus.com; (© 03/5376-2222) and the **Fujikyu Bus** (http://transportation.fujikyu.co.jp; (© 0555/72-5111). In July and August, there are six buses daily that travel directly from Shinjuku Station to Kawaguchiko Trail's 5th Station, costing ¥2,600 one-way and taking almost 2½ hours. Otherwise, in the off season (spring and autumn), there is limited bus service to the Fifth Station only on weekends. More frequent are buses that travel from Shinjuku to Kawaguchiko Station in 1 hour and 45 minutes and cost ¥1,700 one-way; from Kawaguchiko Station there are buses onward to the Fifth Station, with this trip taking approximately 45 minutes and costing another ¥1,500 one-way or ¥2,000 round-trip. Fujikyu also operates buses that depart from Tokyo Station's Yaesu south exit for Kawaguchiko Station for ¥1,700, but the trip takes an hour longer than from Shinjuku (obviously, life is easier if you can catch a bus directly to Mt. Fuji's Fifth station). Reservations for seats can be made from one month to 30 minutes before departure time, by telephone, online, or directly at the bus station (in peak season you'll want to make a reservation as early as possible).

VISITOR INFORMATION More information and train and bus schedules can be obtained from the **Tourist Information Center,** including a leaflet called "Mount Fuji and Fuji Five Lakes." See "Visitor Information," in chapter 4. Another good source is Fujiyoshida City's official website, www.city.fujiyoshida.yamanashi.jp, which carries information on the Kawaguchiko-Yoshidaguchi Trail, bus schedules from Tokyo, mountain huts, and other information. Finally, there's a tourist information office at Kawaguchiko Station (© 0555/72-6700), open daily 9am to 5pm during climbing season.

Climbing Mount Fuji

Mount Fuji is part of a larger national park called **Fuji-Hakone-Izu National Park.** Of the handful of trails leading to the top, most popular for Tokyoites is the **Kawaguchiko-Yoshidaguchi Trail,** which is divided into 10 different stages; the Fifth Station, located about 2,475m (8,120 ft.) up and served by bus, is the usual starting point. Although it's only 6km (about 3½ miles) from the Fifth Station to the summit, the trail climbs almost 1,500m (4,900 ft) and is very steep. It generally takes about 6 hours to reach the summit and 3 hours for the descent.

PREPARING FOR YOUR CLIMB Because of snow and inclement weather from fall through late spring, the best time to make an ascent is during the "official" climbing season from July through August. Keep in mind that this is not a solitary pursuit. Rather, more than 400,000 people climb Fuji-san every year, mostly in July and August and mostly on weekends—so if you plan on climbing Mount Fuji on a Saturday or a Sunday in summer, go to the end of the line, please.

You don't need climbing experience to ascend Mount Fuji (you'll see everyone from grandmothers to children making the pilgrimage), but you do need stamina and a good pair of hiking shoes. The climb is possible in tennis shoes, but if the rocks are wet, they can get awfully slippery. You should also bring a light plastic raincoat (which you can buy at souvenir shops at the Fifth Station), since it often rains on the mountain, a sun hat, sunglasses, sunscreen, water, snacks, a sweater for the evening, gloves, socks, tissues (for pay toilets, which may not have toilet paper), and a flashlight (or headlamp) if you plan on hiking at night. Keep in mind, too, that it gets very chilly on Mount Fuji at night. Even in August, the average temperature on the summit is 41°F (5°C). Finally, there are places to eat and rest on the way to the top, but prices are high, so bring as many snacks and liquids as you can. To avoid altitude sickness, walk at a slow pace, being sure to take frequent water breaks.

Don't be disappointed when your bus deposits you at **Kawaguchiko Fifth Station,** where you'll be bombarded with souvenir shops, restaurants, and busloads of tourists; most of these tourists aren't climbing to the top. As soon as you get past them and the blaring loudspeakers, you'll find yourself on a steep rocky path, surrounded only by scrub brush and the hikers on the path below and above you. After a couple of hours, you'll probably find yourself above the roiling clouds, which stretch in all directions. It will be as if you are on an island, barren and rocky, in the middle of an ocean.

STRATEGIES FOR CLIMBING TO THE TOP The usual procedure for climbing Mount Fuji is to take a morning bus, start climbing in early afternoon, spend the night near the summit, get up early in the morning to climb the rest of the way to the top, and then watch the sun rise (about 4:30am) from atop Mount Fuji. (You can, of course, also wake up in time to see the sun rise from your hut and then continue climbing.) At the summit is a 1-hour hiking trail that circles the crater. Hikers then begin the descent, reaching the Fifth Station before noon.

There are about 16 **mountain huts** along the Kawaguchiko Trail above the Fifth Station, but they're very primitive, providing only a futon and toilet facilities. Some have the capacity to house 500 hikers. The cost averages ¥5,500 per person without meals, ¥7,500 with two meals. Some huts charge ¥1,000 extra for Friday or Saturday night. When I stayed in one of these huts, dinner consisted of dried fish, rice, miso soup, and pickled vegetables; breakfast was exactly the same (many huts supply to-go breakfasts to be eaten on the trail). Still, unless you want to carry your own food, I'd opt for the meals. Note that most huts are open only in July and August; book as early as you can to ensure a place. I recommend **Seikanso** at the Sixth Station (www.seikanso.jp; © 0555/24-6090), with flush toilets and open from July to mid-October; **Toyokan Hut** at the Seventh Station (www.fuji-toyokan.jp; © **0555/22-1040**), or **Taishikan Hut** at the Eighth Station ((© **0555/22-1947**).

Mount Fuji or Bust

The first documented case of someone scaling Mount Fuji is from the early 8th century. During the Edo Period, pilgrimages to the top were considered a purifying ritual, with strict rules governing dress and route. Women, thought to defile sacred places, were prohibited from climbing mountains until 1871.

In the past few decades, there's been a trend in which climbers arrive at the Fifth Station late in the evening and then climb to the top during the night with the aid of flashlights. After watching the sunrise, they then make their descent. That way, they don't have to spend the night in one of the huts. My days of walking up a mountain through the night, however, are far behind me, but this is certainly an option if your time is limited.

Climbing Mount Fuji is definitely a unique experience, but there's a saying in Japan: "Everyone should climb Mount Fuji once; only a fool would climb it twice."

HAKONE ★★★

97km (60 miles) SW of Tokyo

Part of **Fuji-Hakone-Izu National Park,** Hakone is one of the closest and most popular weekend destinations for residents of Tokyo. Beautiful Hakone has about everything a vacationer could wish for—hot-spring resorts, mountains, lakes, breathtaking views of Mount Fuji when the weather is clear (visible mostly in winter), and interesting historical sites. You can tour Hakone as a day trip if you leave early in the morning and limit your sightseeing to a few key attractions, but adding an overnight stay—complete with a soak in a hot-spring tub—is much more rewarding. If you can, travel on a weekday, when modes of transportation are less crowded and some hotels offer cheaper weekday rates.

Essentials

GETTING THERE & GETTING AROUND   Getting to and around Hakone is half the fun! An easy loop tour you can follow through Hakone includes various forms of unique transportation: Starting out by train from Tokyo, you switch to a three-car mountain railway that zigzags up the mountain, then change to a cable car, and then to a smaller ropeway, and end your trip with a boat ride across Lake Ashi, stopping to see major attractions along the way. From Lake Ashi (that is, from the villages of Togendai, Hakone-machi, or Moto-Hakone), you can then take a bus to Odawara Station (an hour's ride), where you board the train back to Tokyo. These same buses also pass by all the recommendations listed below, which is useful if you wish to complete most of your sightseeing the first day before going to your hotel for the evening. A bus also runs directly between Togendai and Shinjuku in about 2 hours.

Odakyu operates the most convenient network of trains, buses, trams, cable cars, and boats to and around Hakone. The most economical and by far easiest way to see Hakone is with Odakyu's **Hakone Free Pass,** which, despite its name, isn't free but does give you a round-trip ticket on the express train from Shinjuku Station to Odawara or Hakone Yumoto and includes all modes of transportation in Hakone listed above and described below. The pass lets you avoid the hassle of buying

Hakone

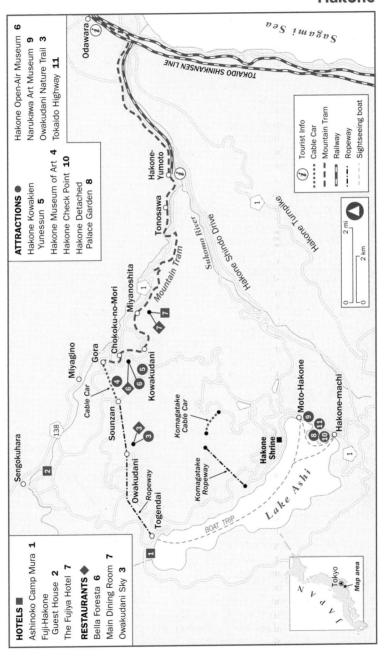

ATTRACTIONS ●
Hakone Kowakien
  Yunessun **5**
Hakone Museum of Art **4**
Hakone Check Point **10**
Hakone Detached
  Palace Garden **8**
Hakone Open-Air Museum **6**
Narukawa Art Museum **9**
Owakudani Nature Trail **3**
Tokaido Highway **11**

HOTELS ■
Ashinoko Camp Mura **1**
Fuji-Hakone
  Guest House **2**
The Fujiya Hotel **7**

RESTAURANTS ◆
Bella Foresta **6**
Main Dining Room **7**
Owakudani Sky **3**

Tourist Info
Cable Car
Mountain Tram
Railway
Ropeway
Sightseeing boat

2 mi
2 km

Sagami Sea

TOKAIDO SHINKANSEN LINE

Odawara
Hakone-Yumoto
Tonosawa
Miyanoshita
Chokoku-no-Mori
Gora
Miyagino
Sengokuhara
138
Sounzan
Owakudani
Togendai
Kowakudani
Cable Car
Mountain Tram
Sukomo River
Hakone Shinpo Drive
Hakone Turnpike
Komagatake Cable Car
Komagatake Ropeway
Hakone Shrine
Moto-Hakone
Hakone-machi
Lake Ashi
BOAT TRIP
Ropeway

JAPAN
Tokyo
Map area
N

5

SIDE TRIPS FROM TOKYO | Hakone

209

individual tickets and gives nominal discounts on most Hakone attractions. A 2-day pass costs ¥5,000 and a 3-day pass is ¥5,500. Children pay ¥1,500 and ¥1,750 respectively.

The trip from Shinjuku to Odawara via Odakyu Express takes 90 minutes, with departures two to four times an hour. In Odawara, you then transfer to another train for a 15-minute trip to Hakone Yumoto; trains depart four times an hour. If time is of the essence or if you want to ensure a seat during peak season, reserve a seat on the faster and more luxurious **Odakyu Romance Car,** which travels from Shinjuku all the way to Hakone Yumoto in 1½ hours and costs an extra ¥870 one-way with a Hakone Pass.

If you have a **Japan Rail Pass,** you should take the Shinkansen bullet train first to Odawara (not all bullet trains stop here, so make sure yours does). From there, you can buy a 2-day Hakone Free Pass for ¥3,900 or a 3-day Pass for ¥4,400. Children pay ¥1,000 and ¥1,250 respectively.

All passes described above can be purchased at any station of the Odakyu Railway, including Shinjuku and Odawara. In Tokyo, the best place to purchase Hakone Free Pass tickets is at the **Odakyu Sightseeing Service Center,** located on the ground floor near the west exit of Odakyu Shinjuku Station (www.odakyu.jp/english; (✆ **03/5321-7887;** daily 8am–6pm), where you can obtain sightseeing information in English in addition to purchasing tickets.

VISITOR INFORMATION   Before leaving Tokyo, pick up the "Hakone and Kamakura" leaflet available from the Tourist Information Center; it provides transportation information for throughout the Hakone area. A color brochure called "Hakone National Park" includes sightseeing information and contains a map of the Hakone area. See "Visitor Information" in chapter 4 for TIC locations. The Odakyu Sightseeing Service Center, above, also has a wealth of information, including the useful *Timetable of Traffic in Hakone,* a booklet that lists the schedules for all forms of transportation in Hakone.

In Hakone Yumoto, the **Yumoto Tourist Office** (✆ **0460/85-8911;** daily 9am–5:45pm) is across the street from Hakone Yumoto Station. Information on Hakone is also available at www.hakone.or.jp/english.

LUGGAGE   If you plan to return to Tokyo, I suggest you leave your luggage in storage at your Tokyo hotel or at Shinjuku Station and travel to Hakone with only an overnight bag. If you're traveling onward to, say, Kyoto, you can leave your bags at a check-in counter at Hakone Yumoto Station, open daily 8am to 10pm (a large bag costs ¥500 a day). Or, if you deliver your bags to the **Hakone Carry Service** (✆ **0460/86-4140**) at Hakone Yumoto Station between 8:30am and noon, it will transport your bags to your Hakone accommodations by 3pm. The next day, it can also pick up your bags at your hotel at 10am and deliver them to Yumoto Station by 1pm, where they will keep them until 7pm. The service costs ¥700 to ¥1,000 per bag, depending on the size and weight, and is available daily year-round.

Exploring Hakone

If you plan on spending only a day in Hakone, you should leave Tokyo very early in the morning and plan on visiting only a few key attractions—I recommend the **Hakone Open-Air Museum, Owakudani Nature Trail,** and, if time permits, **Hakone Check Point** and/or **Narukawa Art Museum.** Keep in mind that most forms of transportation (like the ropeway), as well as museums, close at 5pm.

If you're spending the night—and I strongly urge that you do—you can arrange your itinerary in a more leisurely fashion and devote more time to Hakone's attractions. You may wish to travel only as far as your hotel the first day, stopping at sights along the way and in the vicinity. The next day you could continue with the rest of the circuit through Hakone. Or, you can opt to complete most of your sightseeing the first day, and then backtrack to your accommodations or reach it by bus from Togendai, Hakone-machi, or Moto-Hakone. Finally, if it's a clear day and there's a chance Mt. Fuji is visible, you might want to do this tour in reverse from what's given below to make sure you get to Hakone-machi in the morning, as clouds sometimes cloak the mountain by afternoon.

SCENIC RAILWAY TO GORA   Regardless of whether you travel via the Odakyu Romance Car or the ordinary Odakyu express, you'll end up at Hakone Yumoto Station. Here you'll transfer to the **Hakone Tozan Railway,** in operation since 1919. This delightful, mountain-climbing, three-car electric train winds its way through forests and over streams and ravines as it travels upward to Gora, making several switchbacks along the way. The entire trip from Hakone Yumoto Station to Gora takes only 40 minutes, but the ride through the mountains is beautiful and this is my favorite part of the whole journey. The railway, which runs every 10 to 15 minutes, makes about a half-dozen stops before reaching Gora, including **Tonosawa** and **Miyanoshita,** two hot-spring spa resorts with a number of old *ryokan* and hotels. Some of the ryokan date back several centuries, to the days when they were on the main thoroughfare to Edo, called the old Tokaido Highway. Miyanoshita is the best place for lunch. See "Where to Stay & Eat," below.

For relaxing hot-springs bathing en route, visit the thoroughly modern, sophisticated public bath called **Hakone Kowakien Yunessun ★★** (www.yunessun.com/english; ✆ **0460/82-4126**). To reach it, disembark from the Hakone Tozan Railway at Kowakudani, and then take a 15-minute taxi or bus ride (bus stop: Kowaki-en). This self-described "Hot Springs Amusement Park & Spa Resort" offers a variety of both indoor and outdoor family baths, which means you wear your bathing suit. In addition to indoor Turkish, Roman, and salt baths, there's also a children's play area with slides and a large outdoor area with a variety of small baths, including those mixed with healthy minerals and—I am not making this up—coffee, green tea, sake, and wine. For those who desire more traditional bathing, there's the Mori No Yu, with both indoor and outdoor baths separated for men and women (you don't wear your suit here). Most people who come stay 2 to 3 hours. As with most public bathhouses, people with tattoos are not allowed. Admission to Yunessun is ¥1,800 Monday to Friday, and ¥2,600 Friday, Saturday and Sunday. Admission to Mori No Yu is ¥1,000 weekdays, ¥1,400 on weekends and holidays. Admission to both is ¥2,600 Monday to Friday and ¥3,600 weekends and holidays. Children pay half fare of the adult weekend price, regardless of which day they visit. If you have a Hakone Free Pass, you'll receive a slight discount. Upon admission, you'll be given a towel, robe, and wristband to pay for drinks and extras (rental suits are available), so you can leave all valuables in your assigned locker. Yunessun is open daily 9am to 7pm March to October, 9am to 6pm in November to February; Mori No Yu is open daily 11am to 8pm year-round.

The most important stop on the Hakone Tozan Railway is the next-to-the-last stop, Chokoku-no-Mori, where you'll find the famous **Hakone Open-Air Museum (Chokoku-no-Mori Bijutsukan) ★★★** (www.hakone-oam.or.jp; ✆ **0460/82-1161**), a minute's walk from the station. With the possible exception of views of

Mount Fuji, this museum is, in my opinion, Hakone's number-one attraction. Using nature as a dramatic backdrop, it showcases sculpture primarily of the 20th century in a spectacular setting of glens, formal gardens, ponds, and meadows. There are 400 sculptures on display, both outdoors and in several buildings, with works by Carl Milles, Manzu Giacomo, Jean Dubuffet, Willem de Kooning, Barbara Hepworth, and Joan Miró, as well as more than 25 pieces by Henry Moore, shown on a rotating basis. Several installations geared toward children allow them to climb and play. The Picasso Pavilion contains works by Picasso from pastels to ceramics (it's one of the world's largest collections) and photographs of the artist's last 17 years of life taken by David Douglas Duncan. I could spend all day here; barring that, count on staying at least 2 hours. Be sure to stop off at the "foot *onsen*," where you can immerse your tired feet in soothing, hot-spring water. The museum is open daily 9am to 5pm; admission is ¥1,600 adults, ¥1,100 university and high-school students and seniors, and ¥800 children (children are free on Saturday). Your Hakone Free Pass gives you a ¥200 discount.

BY CABLE CAR TO SOUNZAN Hakone Tozan Cablecars leave Gora every 20 minutes or so and arrive 9 minutes later at the end station of Sounzan, making several stops along the way as they travel steeply uphill. One of the stops is Koen-Kami, from which it's only a minute's walk to the **Hakone Museum of Art** (www.moaart.or.jp/english/hakone/index.html; ✆ **0460/82-2623**). This five-room museum displays Japanese pottery and ceramics from the Jomon Period (around 4000–2000 B.C.) to the Edo Period, including terra-cotta *haniwa* burial figures, huge 16th-century Bizen jars, and Imari ware. What makes this place particularly rewarding are the bamboo grove and small but lovely moss garden, shaded by Japanese maples, with a teahouse where you can sample Japanese tea for ¥630. Open Friday through Wednesday from 9:30am to 4:30pm (to 4pm Dec–Mar); admission is ¥900 for adults, ¥700 for seniors, ¥400 for university and high-school students, and free for children. The Hakone Free Pass gives you a ¥200 discount. Plan on spending about a half-hour here, more if you opt for tea.

BY ROPEWAY TO TOGENDAI From Sounzan, you board the Hakone Ropeway with gondolas for a 30-minute haul over a mountain to Togendai on the other side, which lies beside Lake Ashi, known as Lake Ashinoko in Japanese. Note that the ropeway stops running at around 5:15pm in summer and 4pm in winter.

Before reaching Togendai, however, get off at the first stop, Owakudani, the ropeway's highest point, to hike the 30-minute **Owakudani Nature Trail ★**. Owakudani means "Great Boiling Valley," and you'll soon understand how it got its name when you see (and smell) the sulfurous steam escaping from fissures in the rock, testimony to the volcanic activity still present here. Most Japanese commemorate their trip by buying boiled eggs cooked here in the boiling waters, available at the small hut midway along the trail.

ACROSS LAKE ASHI BY BOAT From Togendai you can take a pleasure boat across Lake Ashi, also referred to as "Lake Hakone" in some English-language brochures. Believe it or not, a couple of the boats plying the waters are replicas of a man-of-war pirate ship. It takes about half an hour to cross the lake to Hakone-machi (also called simply Hakone; *machi* means city) and Moto-Hakone, two resort towns right next to each other on the southern edge of the lake. This end of the lake affords the best view of Mount Fuji, one often depicted in tourist publications (mornings in winter offer the best chance to see this elusive beauty). Boats are in operation year-round (though they run less frequently in winter and not at all in stormy weather); the last boat departs around 5pm from the end of March to the end of November. Buses connect Togendai with Moto-Hakone, Odawara, and Shinjuku.

After the boat ride, if you're heading back to Tokyo, buses depart for Odawara near the boat piers in both Hakone-machi and Moto-Hakone. Otherwise, for more sight-seeing, get off the boat in Hakone-machi, turn left, and walk about 5 minutes on the town's main road, following the signs and turning left to **Hakone Check Point (Hakone Seki-sho)** ★ (http://hakonesekisyo.jp; ☏ **0460/83-6635**), on a road lined with souvenir shops. This is a reconstructed guardhouse originally built in 1619 to serve as a checkpoint along the famous Tokaido Highway, which connected Edo (present-day Tokyo) with Kyoto. In feudal days, local lords, called *daimyo,* were required to spend alternate years in Edo; their wives were kept in Edo as virtual hostages to discourage the lords from planning rebellions while in their homelands. This was one of several points along the highway that guarded against the transport of guns, spies, and female travelers trying to flee Edo. Passes were necessary for travel, and although it was possible to sneak around it, male violators who were caught were promptly executed, while women suffered the indignity of having their heads shaven and then being given away to anyone who wanted them. Inside the reconstructed guardhouse, which was rebuilt on the site of the original checkpoint using traditional carpenter tools and architectural techniques of the Edo Period, you'll see life-size models reenacting scenes inside a checkpoint. A small museum displays relating to the Edo Period, including items used for travel, samurai armor, and gruesome articles of torture. Open daily from 9am to 5pm (until 4:30pm Dec–Feb); admission is ¥500 for adults and ¥250 for children. Your Hakone Free Pass gives you a ¥100 discount. It shouldn't take more than 20 minutes to see everything.

Just beyond the Hakone Check Point, at the big parking lot with the traditional gate, is the **Hakone Detached Palace Garden (Onshi-Hakone-Koen),** which lies on a small promontory on Lake Ashi and has spectacular views of the lake and, in clear weather, Mount Fuji. Originally part of an Imperial summer villa built in 1886, the garden is free and open to the public 9am to 5pm and is a great place for wandering. Be sure to stop by the **Lakeside Observation Building** (closed Tuesday), with free displays relating to Hakone Palace, destroyed by earthquakes.

If you take the northernmost exit from the garden, crossing a bridge, you'll see the neighboring resort town, **Moto-Hakone,** down the road. Across the highway and lined with ancient and mighty cedars is part of the old **Tokaido Highway** itself. During the Edo Period, more than 400 cedars were planted along this important road, which today stretches 2.5km (1½ miles) along the curve of Lake Ashi and makes for a pleasant stroll (unfortunately, a modern road has been built right beside the original one). Moto-Hakone is a 5-minute walk from the Detached Palace Garden.

In Moto-Hakone, **Narukawa Art Museum** ★★ (www.narukawamuseum.co.jp; ☏ **0460/83-6828**) is worthwhile and located just after you enter town, up the hill to the right when you reach the orange *torii* gate. It specializes in modern works of the *Nihonga* style of painting, developed during the Heian Period (794–1185) and sparser than Western paintings (which tend to fill in backgrounds and every inch of canvas). Large paintings and screens by contemporary Nihonga artists are on display, including works by Yamamoto Kyujin, Maki Susumu, Kayama Matazo, Hirayama Ikuo, and Hori Fumiko. Changing exhibitions feature younger up-and-coming artists, as well as glassware. I wouldn't miss it; views of Lake Ashi and Mount Fuji are a bonus. Open daily 9am to 5pm; admission is ¥1,200 for adults, ¥900 for high-school and university students, and ¥600 for children.

WHEN YOU'RE DONE SIGHTSEEING FOR THE DAY Buses depart for Hakone Yumoto and Odawara from both Hakone-machi and Moto-Hakone two to four times an hour. Be sure to check the time of the last departure; generally it's around 8pm, but this can change with the season and the day of the week. (The bus also passes two of the accommodations recommended below, the Fujiya Hotel and Ichinoyu, as well as Yunessun hot-springs baths; another bus will take you to Fuji-Hakone Guest House.) Otherwise, the trip from Moto-Hakone takes approximately 30 minutes to Hakone Yumoto and 50 minutes to Odawara, where you can catch the Odakyu train back to Shinjuku or the Shinkansen bullet train onward toward Kyoto.

Where to Stay & Eat

Japan's *ryokan* sprang into existence to accommodate the stately processions of daimyo and shogun as they traversed the roads between Edo and the rest of Japan. Many of these ryokan were built along the Tokaido Highway, and some of the oldest are found in Hakone. Most accommodations cost more during peak travel times like Golden Week, school holidays, New Year's, weekends and national holidays.

For casual dining, the Hakone Open-Air Museum has a pleasant restaurant, **Bella Foresta,** overlooking the park's fantastic scenery and offering a buffet lunch daily from 11am to 3:30pm for ¥1,980. Also sporting a view is the even less formal restaurant **Owakudani Sky,** on the third floor of the Owakudani Ropeway Station, serving curry rice, noodles, and other fare for less than ¥1,200.

But my favorite place for a meal is at **The Fujiya ★★**, located in Hakone's grandest, oldest hotel (see "The Fujiya Hotel," below), serving French food. This main dining hall, dating from 1930, is very bright and cheerful, with a high and intricately detailed ceiling, large windows with Japanese screens, a wooden floor, and white tablecloths. The views of the Hakone hills are impressive, and the service by the bow-tied wait staff is attentive. For lunch you can have such dishes as crab curry, beef stew, fried prawn, rainbow trout, and sirloin steak, or opt for one of the set lunches starting at ¥4,600. The excellent dinners, with seatings at 6 and 8pm (reservations required), feature elaborate set courses (ranging from ¥11,550 to ¥18,000) or a la carte dishes ranging from scallops and grilled lamb to chicken, rainbow trout, and steak. Afterward, be sure to tour the landscaped garden. It's open daily 11:30am to 2pm (to 2:30pm weekends and holidays) and 5:45 to 8:30pm.

Ashinoko Camp Mura ☺ Because you're in a national park, you might be inclined to enjoy nature by roughing it in a cabin beside Lake Ashi, just a 10-minute walk from the ropeway to Sounzan and the boat to Hakone-machi. Operated by Kanagawa Prefecture and also with tent camping, it offers row and detached (more expensive and closer to the lake) cabins that sleep up to six persons, each with two bedrooms, a bathroom, a living room with cooking facilities and tableware, and a deck with picnic table. However, there is no supermarket in nearby Togendai, so you'll either want to bring your own food or dine at the camp's restaurant, which offers both Japanese and Western selections (reservations required for lunch and dinner). There's a hiking trail around the lake. A great place for kids. Open year-round.

164 Hakone-machi, Moto-Hakone, Kanagawa 250-0522. ⓒ **0460/84-8279.** Fax 0460/84-6489. 36 units. Peak season ¥26,250 row cabin, ¥31,500 detached cabin; off season ¥15,750 row cabin, ¥21,000 detached cabin. No credit cards. Bus: Togendai, from Odawara (1 hr.) or Shinjuku (2 hr.), and then a 10-min. walk. **Amenities:** Restaurant; rental bikes; barbecue grills. *In room:* Kitchenette.

Fuji-Hakone Guest House It's a bit isolated, but this Japanese Inn Group member offers inexpensive, spotlessly clean lodging in tatami rooms, all nonsmoking. A 25-year-old house, situated in tranquil surroundings set back from a tree-shaded road, is run by a man who speaks very good English and is happy to provide sightseeing information, including a map of the area with local restaurants. Some of the rooms face the Hakone mountain range. Pluses are the communal lounge area with fridge, microwave, computer (¥100 for 30 min.), TV and even a piano, and the outdoor hot-spring bath (for which there's an extra ¥500 charge).

912 Sengokuhara, Hakone, Kanagawa 250-0631. http://hakone.syuriken.jp/hakone. ⓒ **0460/84-6577.** Fax 0460/84-6578. 14 units (none with bathroom). ¥5,250–¥6,300 single; ¥10,500–¥12,600 double; ¥15,750–¥16,800 triple. Plus ¥150 hot-spring tax per person. Peak season and Sat–Sun ¥1,000–¥2,000 extra. Minimum 2-night stay preferred. Western breakfast ¥840 extra. AE, DC, MC, V. Bus: Hakone Tozan (included in the Hakone Free Pass) from Togendai (10 min.) or from Odawara Station (50 min.) to the Senkyoro-mae stop (announced in English), and then a 1-min. walk. **Amenities:** Hot-spring bath; Wi-Fi (free, in lobby). *In room:* A/C, TV.

The Fujiya Hotel ★★★ 🏨 The Fujiya, established in 1878, is quite simply the grandest, most majestic old hotel in Hakone; indeed, it might be the loveliest historic hotel in Japan. I love this hotel for its comfortably old-fashioned atmosphere, including such Asian touches as a Japanese-style roof and long wooden corridors with photographs of famous guests, from Einstein to Eisenhower. A landscaped garden out back, with a waterfall, pond, greenhouse, outdoor pool, and stunning views over the valley is great for strolls and meditation. There's also an indoor thermal pool and public hot-spring baths (hot-spring water is also piped in to each guest's bathroom). Even if you don't stay here, come for a meal or tea.

There are five separate buildings, all different and added on at various times in the hotel's long history, but management has been meticulous in retaining its historic traditions. Rooms are old-fashioned and spacious with high ceilings and antique furnishings. The most expensive rooms are the largest, but my favorites are those in the Flower Palace, which has an architectural style reminiscent of a Japanese temple and seems unchanged since its 1936 construction. Be sure to ask the front desk for the hotel's map of the surrounding village and leaflets describing how to reach sightseeing spots in Hakone from the hotel.

Note: A limited number of the least expensive rooms in the main building (dating from 1891) are available for foreigners at a special discounted rate, in dollars, based on the hotel's age. However, the special rate is not available on Saturday, the night before national holidays, during Golden Week, the month of August, or New Year's. And if these discounted rooms are sold out, you'll pay the regular rate.

359 Miyanoshita, Hakone-machi, Kanagawa-ken 250-0404. www.fujiyahotel.jp. ⓒ **0460/82-2211.** Fax 0460/82-2210. 146 units. Special rates for foreigners (excluding tax and service charge): $134. Regular rates: ¥20,040–¥44,190 single or double; ¥5,670–¥13,860 extra Sat, night before holiday, and peak season. AE, DC, MC, V. Station: Miyanoshita (Hakone Tozan Railway; 5 min.). Bus: From Odawara or Moto-Hakone to Miyanoshita Onsen stop (1 min.). **Amenities:** 3 restaurants (including The Fujiya, above); lounge; bar; hot-spring baths; Jacuzzi; indoor/outdoor pools; room service; sauna; Wi-Fi (free, in lobby); hotel museum. *In room:* A/C, TV, hair dryer, minibar.

IZU PENINSULA, TOKYO'S PLAYGROUND

Atami: 107km (66 miles) SW of Tokyo; Shuzenji: 140km (87 miles) SW of Tokyo

Whenever Tokyoites want to spend a night or two at a hot-spring spa on the seashore, they head for Izu Peninsula. Jutting into the Pacific Ocean southwest of Tokyo, Izu boasts some fine beaches and a dramatic coastline marked in spots by high cliffs and tumbling surf. It also has a verdant, mountainous interior with quaint hot-spring resorts. However, even though the scenery is at times breathtaking and Izu offers a relaxing respite from bustling Tokyo, there's little of historical interest to lure a short-term visitor to Japan; make sure you've seen both Kamakura and Nikko before you consider coming here.

Keep in mind also that Izu's resorts are terribly crowded during the summer vacation period from mid-July to the end of August, so make accommodations reservations at least several months in advance if you travel during this time. Otherwise, there are hotel, ryokan, and *minshuku* reservation offices in all of Izu's resort towns that will arrange accommodations for you. Be aware, however, that if a place has a room still open at the last minute in August, there's probably a reason for it—poor location, poor service, or unimaginative decor.

Atami

Atami means "hot sea." According to legend, once upon a time, local fishermen, concerned about a geyser spewing forth into the sea and killing lots of fish and marine life, asked a Buddhist monk to intervene on their behalf and to pray for a solution to the problem. The prayers paid off when the geyser moved itself to the beach; not only was marine life spared, but Atami was also blessed with hot-spring water the townspeople could henceforth bathe in. It's rumored that Tokugawa Ieyasu (1543-1616), Japan's most famous shogun, was so enamored by the quality of Atami's hot-spring waters that he ordered barrels of it delivered to his castle in Edo (present-day Tokyo).

Today, Atami—with a population of 40,000—is a conglomeration of hotels, ryokan, restaurants, pachinko parlors, souvenir shops, and a sizable red-light district, spread along narrow, winding streets that hug steep mountain slopes around Atami Bay. Although I find the setting picturesque, the city itself isn't very interesting—in fact, its economy is severely depressed, and because it has none of the fancy shops and nightlife to attract a younger generation, mostly older Japanese vacation here, giving the town an old-fashioned, unpretentious atmosphere. In any case, this is the most easily accessible hot-spring seaside resort from Tokyo, and it has a wide beach flanked by a half-mile boardwalk, a wonderful art museum, and several other attractions that make it popular even on just a day trip.

ESSENTIALS

GETTING THERE From Tokyo Station, it's 40 to 50 minutes by **Shinkansen bullet train;** be sure to check the schedule beforehand, as the Hikari bullet train stops at Atami only three times a day (though the slower Kodama bullet trains run more frequently). The fare is ¥3,570 for an unreserved seat. You can also take the **JR Odoriko** or **Super View Odoriko,** which travels from Tokyo Station to Atami in 1 hour and 15 or 20 minutes, with the fare ranging from ¥3,190 to ¥4,270, depending on the train. Slower is the local **JR Tokaido Line** for ¥1,890, which takes about 1 hour and 45 minutes.

VISITOR INFORMATION The **Atami Tourist Information Office** (adjacent to a coffee shop) is to the left as you exit the train station (☏ **0557/81-5297;** daily 9am–5:30pm; to 5pm Oct–Mar). No English is spoken, but English-language literature and a map are available, including the very useful "Atami Walking Guide." You'll also find information on Atami online at www.atamispa.com.

GETTING AROUND Buses serve major sightseeing attractions in Atami. If you're spending the day here, you might wish to purchase a 1-day ticket for the **YuYu Bus,** which has two routes, both making circuitous trips through town and departing Atami Station every 35 minutes. You can leave and reboard as often as you wish, or you can stay on for a tour of the city. The cost is ¥800 for adults and ¥400 for children.

EXPLORING ATAMI

Atami's must-see is the **MOA Art Museum ★**, 26–2 Momoyama-cho (www.moaart. or.jp; (☏ **0557/84-2511**), housed in a modern building atop a hill with sweeping views of Atami and the bay. It's a 5-minute bus ride from Atami Station on the YuYu Bus; or take a bus from platform 4 to the last stop (fare: ¥160). The museum's entrance is dramatic—a long escalator ride through a tunnel—but the museum itself concentrates on traditional Asian art, including woodblock prints by Hokusai, Hiroshige, and their contemporaries; Chinese ceramics; Japanese bronze religious art; and lacquerware. Although some 200 items from the 3,500-piece private collection are changed monthly, keep an eye out for a few things always on display: the Golden Tea Room (a remake of Toyotomi Hideyoshi's tea room), a Noh theater, and a tea-storage jar with a wisteria design by Edo artist Nonomura Ninsei, a National Treasure. Another National Treasure, displayed only one month a year (Feb), is a gold-leaf screen of red and white plum blossoms by Ogata Korin, whose recreated residence next door is also part of the museum. It takes about an hour to tour the museum, open Friday through Wednesday from 9:30am to 4:30pm; admission is ¥1,600 for adults, ¥1,200 for seniors, ¥800 for university and high-school students, free for children.

I also love **Kiunkaku (起雲閣),** 4–2 Showa-cho (☏ **0557/86-3101;** YuYu bus: Kiunkaku stop), built in 1919 as the private villa of a shipping magnate, converted to a ryokan in 1947, and now open to the public. It's an eclectic mix of Japanese and Western architectural styles, with stained-glass windows, fireplaces, parquet floors, gaily painted European furniture, and tatami rooms, wrapped around a lovely inner garden. It was once a favorite haunt of famous Japanese writers (including Mishima Yukio); who wouldn't feel inspired here? Allow 30 minutes to tour the facilities, open Thursday to Tuesday from 9am to 5pm. Admission is ¥500 for adults, ¥300 for junior-high and high-school students, and free for children.

Finally, if you're here on a Saturday or Sunday, try to catch the 11am dancing performance of the **Atami Geisha,** at Geigi Kenban (across from City Hall), 17–13 Chuo-cho (☏ **0557/81-3575;** YuYu bus: Shiyakusho-mae). Although reservations are not required for the 30-minute show, I advise making one anyway to assure getting a seat, as these performances are very popular with the older generation. Stick around after the show; most of the geisha come out to greet the audience, and you can ask to have your picture taken standing next to a performer. Admission, including tea and a Japanese sweet, is ¥1,300.

WHERE TO STAY & EAT

Home Run Sushi (ほーむらん寿司) 🐟 SUSHI   For excellent sushi, head to this simple, 30-year-old one-room restaurant near the waterfront, with both counter and table seating. There's no English-language menu, but there are plastic-food displays of various sushi sets. I have no idea why this place is called Home Run—one of Japan's many mysteries.

5–1 Nagisacho, Atami City. ℂ **0557/82-7300.** Sushi set meals ¥1,050–¥2,100. AE, DC, MC, V. Daily 11:45am–3pm and 5–9pm. A 10-min. walk from Atami Station, at the end of Ginza Dori St., on a corner to the left.

Taikanso (大観荘) ★★   Located on a pine-shaded mountain slope above the city, this beautiful ryokan was built in 1938 as a private villa. Ten years later it was converted to a Japanese inn; since then, it's been expanded into several buildings connected by covered pathways and meandering streams, adhering to a Kyoto style of architecture popular in the 16th century. Various styles of rooms are available, with the most expensive offering the best views, the most space, and the best meals (Western-style breakfasts available on request). Rooms are tatami, but beds can be installed upon request. The ultimate in luxury is the oldest unit, a three-room suite with a sitting alcove and cypress tub, where Queen Beatrix of the Netherlands stayed with her husband and three sons. Although all the rooms boast hot-spring water for the tubs, there are three public baths with open-air bathing, saunas, and Jacuzzis, as well as three private baths with outdoor baths and views over Atami (extra fee for these: ¥2,100). Be sure to wander the corridors and garden with its 300-year-old pines, stopping off at the footbaths on the third floor of the annex, where you can soak your feet, order drinks, and look out over the town.

7–1 Hayashigaoka-cho, Atami City, Shizuoka 413-0031. www.atami-taikanso.com. ℂ **0557/81-8137.** Fax 0557/83-5308. 44 units. ¥29,550–¥70,000 per person. Rates include 2 meals. ¥3,150–¥5,000 extra per person Sat–Sun, holidays, and peak season. AE, DC, MC, V. Take a taxi from Atami Station, a 4-min. ride. **Amenities:** 2 restaurants; coffee shop; nightclub; indoor/outdoor hot-spring baths; sauna. *In room:* A/C, TV, hair dryer, Internet, minibar.

Shuzenji

Whereas Atami, above, is popular for its seaside setting, Shuzenji Onsen is Izu Peninsula's most famous mountain spa. Nestled in a valley and straddling both sides of a river, it has a history stretching more than 1,200 years, when one of Japan's most revered figures in Japanese Buddhism, Kobo Daishi, discovered a hot spring here and founded Shuzenji Temple. Today, Shuzenji, home to some 16,000 residents, is a small mountain village easily navigated on foot. Most people come for a night or two, staying in a ryokan, soaking in restorative hot-spring baths, strolling along the town's narrow streets to a few historic sights, and feasting on meals featuring local cuisine. Along with Shuzenji Temple, there are several historic sites tied to the Minamoto clan, who established a shogunate government in Kamakura in the 12th century (see "Kamakura," earlier in this chapter).

ESSENTIALS

GETTING THERE   The rail gateway to Shuzenji is Mishima, a minor stop on the Shinkansen bullet train. The Hikari bullet train stops at Mishima about six times a day, though the slower Kodama bullet train stops more frequently; be sure to check the schedule beforehand. In any case, it takes 45 to 60 minutes by bullet train from Tokyo Station to Mishima, where you can then transfer to the **Izu-Hakone Railway**'s Sunzu Line for the 30-minute ride onward to Shuzenji. The fare for the entire journey is ¥4,390 for an unreserved seat. Alternatively, you can save money by taking the slower **JR Tokaido Line** from Tokyo to Mishima, and then board the

Izu-Hakone Railway bound for Shuzenji; the fare for this is ¥2,710 and takes about 3 hours. If you're coming from Atami, take the JR Tokaido Line 12 minutes to Mishima for ¥320, and then transfer to the Izu-Hakone Railway for another ¥500.

You can also reach Shuzenji directly from Tokyo's Shinjuku Station by Odakyu's **Tokai Bus** (𝄐 **0570/01-1255**). Travel time is 2 hours and 35 minutes, and the fare is ¥2,500 one-way or ¥4,500 round-trip. There are two departures daily (at the time of going to press, at 9:15am and 6:35pm), and reservations are required.

VISITOR INFORMATION The **Shuzenji Tourist Information Office** (𝄐 **0558/ 72-2501**) is located inside Shuzenji Station, to the right after exiting the ticket gate. There's no English-speaking staff, but you can pick up a pamphlet with a map. It's open daily 9am to 5pm.

GETTING AROUND Shuzenji Spa (Shuzenji Onsen), with its ryokan, hot-spring baths, Shuzenji Temple, and other sights, is a 30-minute walk from Shuzenji Station, so you'll probably want to take the local bus. Buses depart Shuzenji Station approximately every 10 or 15 minutes from stop no. 1 bound for "Shuzenji Onsen," the last stop. The fare is ¥210. Once you're ensconced in your ryokan, you can walk everywhere. English-language signs direct you to major attractions.

SEEING THE SIGHTS

Shuzenji Onsen spreads along the Katsura River. In the center of the spa town, in the river bed, is **Tokko-no-yu,** the oldest hot spring in Izu. According to legend, in 807 Kobo Daishi saw a young boy washing his ill father in the cold water of Katsura River. Taking pity, Kobo Daishi struck a rock in the riverbed with an iron club (*tokko*), causing the rock to split open and release a hot spring that cured the sick father. Today, a pavilion along the river marks the historic spot.

After discovering Tokko-no-yu, Kobo Daishi founded **Shuzenji Temple,** just steps away from Katsura River on a small hill. Because of its associations with the great Buddhist leader, the temple flourished and a village sprang up around it. During the Kamakura Period (1185–1333), Shuzenji Temple became a stage for two tragic events resulting from the Minamoto clan's bitter family feud. First, Minamoto Yoritomo, who established the Kamakura shogunate but feared that his younger brother Noriyori had ambitions to take over, had Noriyori imprisoned here in 1193. Noriyori, who had proved his bravery by acting as commander in chief in the defeat of the rival Heike clan, subsequently killed himself. Later, Yoritomo's son, Yoriie, the second Kamakura shogun, was assassinated in Shuzenji while enjoying his bath at nearby Hakoyu spa, reportedly through poison added to his bathwater. The present temple building dates from 1883, when it was rebuilt following a mysterious fire. The Shuzenji Treasure House contains items relating to the temple, including the tokko said to have belonged to Kobo Daishi and Yoriie's death mask. You'll also find a statue of Dainichi Nyorai, given to the temple by Hojo Masako, wife of Yoritomo, in honor of her son Yoriie. Admission to the treasure house, open daily 8:30am to 4pm, is ¥300; temple grounds are open daily 6am to 5pm.

Across the river from Shuzenji Temple is **Hakoyu,** now a modern hot-spring public bath housed in an eye-catching tower. You can bathe in its tub made of *hinoki* cypress for ¥350. It's open daily from noon to 9pm. Nearby is the **Bamboo Forest Path,** a pedestrian walkway through a bamboo grove, as well as **Shigetsuden,** the oldest wooden structure in Izu. Yoriie's mother, Masako, ordered construction of Shigetsuden to house several thousand rolls of Buddhist scriptures, donated to console the soul of her son Yoriie. It is thought that most of the scriptures were sent later to Edo (present-day Tokyo) by order of the Tokugawa shogunate, though one roll is displayed at Shuzenji Temple's Treasure House. Beside Shigetsuden is **Minamoto Yoriie's Grave,** marked by a stone pillar erected in 1703 by Shuzenji Temple's head priest to mark the 500th anniversary of Yoriie's death. The eldest son of Yoritomo, Yoriie was only 18 when he became the second shogun and was placed under house arrest in Shuzenji after only 5 years of reign. He was 23 when murdered in his bath by assassins from Kamakura. Three stones behind the pillar mark the graves of Yoriie, his concubine, and their son.

A walking trail leads across the river to **Minamoto Noriyori's Grave.** Other hiking trails lead through the surrounding mountain scenery, including the 5-km (3-mile) Okunoin Walking Trail leading to Okunoin, where Kobo Daishi is said to have practiced meditation as a youth.

WHERE TO STAY & EAT

Walking directions are from Shuzenji Onsen bus terminal.

Nanaban (なヽ番) 🍜 NOODLES   Nanaban is famous in Shuzenji for its buckwheat noodles, but you may have to work a bit to release your meal's special aroma and flavors. Most popular is the Zendera Soba, which you prepare by grinding your own sesame seeds and then grating fresh wasabi root, all of which is added to your soba along with soy sauce (you can take any extra wasabi root home with you). Other soba and *udon* dishes are also available, including those with mountain vegetables and tempura. There's no English-language menu, but there's a plastic food display outside and the menu has pictures. After taking your shoes off at the entrance, you'll be seated at a low table with leg wells, surrounded by antiques and gleaming wood.

761–1–3 Shuzenji Onsen, Izu-shi. 🕭 **0558/72-0007.** Set meals ¥1,260–¥1,890. No credit cards. Fri–Wed 10am–4pm. Across the street from the bus terminal, to the left (1 min.); look for the statue of the raccoon dog and the bamboo fountain.

Arai Ryokan (新井旅館) ★★   Open since 1872, this is one of Shuzenji's most acclaimed inns. It has welcomed many Japanese celebrities over the decades, from writers and artists to Kabuki actors. It's located right in the center of the village, beside the river and just a stone's throw from Shuzenji Temple and the Bamboo Forest Path. Its 15 structures, all registered as national cultural assets and situated around a river-fed pond, include a delightful main building where you're served a welcome tea on an old-fashioned wooden veranda, a wooden covered bridge leading to rooms, and a 90-year-old public bath built in the style of Horyuji Temple in Nara—without the use of nails. Rooms are spread through several buildings constructed during different times in the inn's long history, including standard rooms with and without private bathroom and more elaborate rooms that face the pond and Katsura River. Seasonal meals are served in your room. This inn is highly recommended for its nostalgic atmosphere.

970 Shuzenji Onsen, Izu-shi, Shizuoka 410-2416. www.arairyokan.net. 🕭 **0558/72-2007.** Fax 0558/72-5119. 30 units (15 with bathroom; 12 with toilet only; 3 without bathroom). ¥23,000–¥33,000 per person. Rates exclude tax and service charge. Rates include 2 meals. AE, MC, V. From the bus terminal, turn right and follow the main road; it will be on your left, past Shuzenji Temple (3 min.). **Amenities:** Indoor/outdoor hot-spring baths; indoor hot-spring pool (summer only). *In room:* A/C, TV, hair dryer, minibar.

Goyokan (五葉館)   This family-run inn, in a warehouse-style building of black tiles topped with white mortar, opened about 20 years ago but recently underwent renovation, giving it a contemporary twist on traditional décor and adding a serene hot-spring bath on the top floor. Sandwiched between Shuzenji's main road and the Katsura River, near the bus terminal, it offers nicely decorated and clean tatami rooms, some with views of the river. Note that no single accommodations are available.

765–2 Shuzenji Onsen, Izu-shi, Shizuoka 410-2416. www.goyokan.co.jp. ℂ **0558/72-2066.** Fax 0558/72-8212. 8 units (with toilet only). ¥10,650 per person without breakfast; ¥13,510 per person with breakfast; ¥15,690 with breakfast and dinner. MC, V. Across the street from the bus terminal, to the left (1 min.). **Amenities:** Indoor hot-spring baths. *In room:* A/C, TV, fridge, no phone.

Yagyu-no-Sho (柳生の庄) ★★★   This elegant sanctuary, surrounded by a wall and beautiful garden complete with streams, pond, mossy ground, and bamboo groves, sits on the edge of Shuzenji and feels like it's deep in the countryside. It was built some 40 years ago, a replica of the original Yagyu-no Sato in Nara, and offers 16 rooms, each one with a different atmosphere and unique architectural details, from ceiling designs to door pulls. They range from standard rooms, located in the main building accessible by elevator and decorated with antiques, to villas with their own private garden and open-air bath. The inn's most popular room is Tsukikage, with its own balcony over a pond and open-air bath. Kyoto-style kaiseki meals, with local specialties and mountain vegetables, are served in your room, and the owner's wife speaks English. If you're looking for a pampered mountain retreat, this place fits the bill.

1116–6 Shuzenji Onsen, Izu-shi, Shizuoka 410-2416. www.yagyu-no-sho.com. ℂ **0558/72-4126.** Fax 0558/72-5212. 16 units. ¥42,150–¥68,400 per person. Rates include 2 meals. AE, MC, V. From the bus terminal, turn right and follow the main road; it will be on your right (7 min.). **Amenities:** Indoor/outdoor hot-spring baths. *In room:* A/C, TV, hair dryer, minibar.

6

THE JAPAN ALPS

The several volcanic mountain ranges that lie in central Honshu together comprise Japan Alps National Park (Chubu Sangaku Kokuritsu Koen) ★★★. With the exception of Japan's tallest mountain, Mount Fuji (p. 205), all of Japan's loftiest mountains are in these ranges, making the Japan Alps a popular destination for hikers in summer and skiers in winter (Nagano, near Matsumoto, hosted the XVIII Winter Olympics in 1998). In addition, because some of the villages nestled in these mountains retain much of their traditional architecture, the Japan Alps provide a unique look at mountain life both past and present.

A GOOD STRATEGY FOR SEEING THE JAPAN ALPS Because towns and villages in this region are spread out—with lots of mountains in between—traveling isn't as fast in this part of the country as on Honshu's broad plains. Your best strategy for visiting all the destinations covered in this chapter is to start from Nagoya Station by taking the JR Shinano train in the morning to Nakatsugawa, where you can then board a bus for Magome and spend the day hiking to Tsumago. From Tsumago, it's only a short bus ride to Nagiso, where you can then reboard the Shinano train bound for Matsumoto. From Matsumoto, you'll travel by bus onward to Takayama and then on to Ogimachi (in Shirakawa-go). From there you can return to Takayama to catch the train to Nagoya, or take a bus onward to Kanazawa (see chapter 8 for information on Nagoya and Kanazawa).

THE BEST JAPAN ALP EXPERIENCES

- **Traipsing Around Matsumoto Castle.** Popularly known as the Crow Castle due to its black color, **Matsumoto Castle** boasts the oldest *donjon* (keep) in Japan (more than 400 years old) and contains a superb collection of Japanese matchlocks and samurai armor from the mid 16th century through the Edo Period. See p. 224.
- **Enjoying the Mountain Scenery in Kiso Valley.** There's no finer way to enjoy nature than to be out in it, and the **Nakasendo Highway** linking two old villages provides a close-up view of steep wooded slopes and a rushing stream, not to mention a lesson in history as you traverse this Edo-era footpath. See p. 231.
- **Greeting the Morning at Takayama's Market.** The **Miyagawa Morning Market** along a picturesque riverbank offers everything from flowers and vegetables to locally made crafts. See p. 235.

o **Takayama's Higashiyama Walking Course.** Sure, you should see Takayama's many museums and sights, but you can get away from the crowds on this hiking path that leads past temples and shrines and provides a different perspective on the city. See p. 235.

o **Seeing How Mountain Folk Lived in Ogimachi.** Shirakawago is famous for its thatched-roof farmhouses, but equally fascinating is the history behind them. Learn how they're constructed and about the extended families who once lived in them at Ogimachi's open-air museum and other houses open to the public. See p. 243.

MATSUMOTO, GATEWAY TO THE JAPAN ALPS ★

235km (146 miles) NW of Tokyo

Located in Nagano Prefecture, in the middle of a wide plateau about 590m (1,936 ft.) above sea level and surrounded on all sides by mountain ranges, **Matsumoto ★** boasts a fine feudal castle with the oldest existing *donjon* (keep) in Japan, as well as an outstanding woodblock-print museum. Although the city itself (pop. 240,000) is modern with little remaining from its castle days, it does boast approximately 100 *kura* (storehouses) scattered throughout town, built more than a century ago after a devastating fire destroyed much of the town. Some of the kura, made of earth and straw and then painted many times to protect valuables against future flames, have been renovated into shops, restaurants, and other establishments, especially on Nakamachi Street.

In any event, I find Matsumoto pleasant, the air fresh, and its people among the nicest I've encountered in Japan. Encircled by towering peaks, sparkling mountain lakes, and colorful wildflowers, Matsumoto also serves as the gateway to the hiking trails of Japan Alps National Park; most travelers heading to the more remote regions of the Japan Alps pass through here on their way.

Essentials

GETTING THERE   By Train   The **JR Chuo Honsen Line** runs directly to Matsumoto from Tokyo's Shinjuku Station. Its *Limited Express Azusa*, departing every hour or so, reaches Matsumoto in about 2½ to 3 hours and costs ¥6,200 one-way for an unreserved seat. There's also a direct JR train from Nagoya, the *Limited Express Shinano*, which departs about every hour, takes about 2 hours, and costs ¥5,360 for an unreserved seat.

BY BUS   From Tokyo's Shinjuku Station's west exit, Keio Highway buses (© 03/ **5376-2222**) depart for Matsumoto Bus Terminal (across from Matsumoto Station) approximately every hour, taking about 3¼ hours and costing ¥3,400. From Nagoya, the ride is 2½ hours and ¥3,460; from Osaka, the ride is 5½ hours and ¥5,700; from Takayama, the ride is 2¼ hours and ¥3,100.

VISITOR INFORMATION   You'll find the **Matsumoto City Tourist Informa-tion Center** (© **0263/32-2814;** www.city.matsumoto.nagano.jp or http://welcome. city.matsumoto.nagano.jp; daily 9am–5:45pm) just across from the main ticket gate of Matsumoto Station. It has a good English-language map of the city, and its excel-lent English-speaking staff can provide information on nearby destinations.

GETTING AROUND You can **walk** to Matsumoto Castle, about 1.5km (1 mile) northeast of the station, in about 20 minutes, with signs in English pointing the way. Alternatively, **Town Sneaker Bus** is a dedicated tourist bus, with four routes departing from Matsumoto Station every 30 minutes and making circular routes to all city sights (most useful for the sights below is the Kita, or Northern, Course). It costs ¥190 each time you get off or ¥500 for an all-day pass (half-price for children). To visit the Japan Ukiyo-e Museum, however, you'll have to go by local **train** or **taxi.** Alternatively, free **bicycles** are available daily 9am to 5pm at various locations throughout town, including the Matsumoto City Museum next to Matsumoto Castle and the Former Kaichi School. They're convenient for visiting sights not accessible by Sneaker Bus; ask the Matsumoto Tourist Information staff for details.

Exploring Matsumoto

In addition to the sights below, good places for strolling and shopping include the **Nakamachi** district in the heart of the city with its *kura,* restaurants, and shops selling Matsumoto furniture, crafts, and antiques; and **Nawate Dori,** a narrow pedestrian lane flanking the Metoba River where vendors sell fruit, vegetables, flowers, and souvenirs.

If you want to do some hiking, stop by the Matsumoto Tourist Information for the **"Kamikochi Guide Map,"** which contains a map and recommended hiking trails. It takes a little more than 2 hours via train and bus (not available mid-Nov to mid-Apr) to reach Kamikochi; the fare is ¥2,400 one-way or ¥4,400 round-trip.

Unless otherwise noted, all directions below are from Matsumoto Station.

MATSUMOTO CASTLE & ENVIRONS

Matsumoto Castle ★★ CASTLE   Originally built around 1504 when Japan was in the throes of long and bloody civil wars, Matsumoto Castle is a fine specimen of a feudal castle with a 400-year-old *donjon* that's the oldest existing keep in the country. Surrounded by a moat with ducks and white swans and lined with willow and cherry trees, the outside walls of the donjon are black, earning the place the nickname of Karasu-jo, or Crow Castle. Although it appears to have five stories from the outside, it's actually a six-story structure, with a secret floor that may have hidden warriors. It's rather small as castles go, but English-speaking Goodwill Guides are sometimes on hand to provide free, 1-hour tours outlining the castle's history and **architectural** features. Take your shoes off at the entrance and walk in stocking feet over worn wooden floors and up steep and narrow steps until you finally reach the sixth floor, from which you have a nice view of the city. This would have served as the *daimyo's* (feudal lord's) headquarters in case of enemy attack, while the fifth floor, with views in all directions, was where the generals would have conferred during war. Although the Ishikawa clan rebuilt the castle in the 1590s in anticipation of gun warfare (guns were introduced to Japan in 1543) with many arrow and gun slots and walls thick enough to withstand bullets, the castle was never attacked because civil wars ended with the coming of the Edo Period (1603–1867). Nevertheless, guns were manufactured in Japan throughout the Edo Period, and on display here are approximately 370 matchlocks, armor, and other arms manufactured in Japan from 1543 to the late Edo Era, providing interesting insight into how the import was adapted for domestic use. With war no longer a threat, a moon-viewing room was added to the castle in 1635.

Included in your castle ticket is admission to the **Matsumoto City Museum ★** (© 0263/32-0133) next to the castle. This rather eclectic museum has displays

SEA OF JAPAN

Takojima

Suzu

Wajima

Noto

Anamizu

Toyama-wan

JAPAN

Tokyo

Map area

0   25 mi

0   25 km

Itoigawa

KOGEN NATIONAL PARK

Chikuma-gawa

Nakano

Hime-kawa

Nagano

Suzaka

Kurobe-gawa

19

Koshoku

Sai-gawa

18

Ueda

8

Hakiu

Himi

Takaoka

Toyama

Hida Mts. (Northern Alps)

Matsumoto

Tsubata

Nanto

41

CHUBU SANGAKU NATIONAL PARK

Kamikochi

Matto

Kanazawa

Kamioka

Okaya

Komatsu

8

Ogimachi

Sho-gawa

Furukawa

19

Ina

Shirakawago

HAKUSAN NATIONAL PARK

Takayama

Kiso Mts. (Central Alps)

Kaga

Yamanaka

Kisofukushima

Kiso-gawa

Katsuyama

Hokuno

Gero

Temryu-gawa

Fukui

Ono

Kuzuryu-gawa

Tsumago

Tsukechi

Magome

Nagara-gawa

Nakatsugawa

Imago

41

Yaotsu

Namiai

Seki

Akechi

Tsuruga

Ibigawa

Gifu

19

Seto

Shitara

Mihama

27

NAGOYA

Yahagi-gawa

Toyota

Imazu

Biwa-ko

Tsushima

Chiryu

1

Toyokawa

23

Tokai

Kuwana

23

Moriyama

Nishio

Ohara

Komono

Ise-wan

Mikawa-wan

Enshu-nada

225

A Note on Japanese Characters

Many establishments and attractions in Japan do not have outdoor signs in Roman (English-language) letters. Those that don't are provided with the Japanese equivalent here to help you locate them.

relating to archaeology, history, Matsumoto's many festivals (including the summer Tanabata Festival and a fertility festival held in Sept featuring, well, phalluses), and folklore of the surrounding region, including samurai armor, an ornate palanquin, matchlocks, and farming equipment. You can tour both castle and museum in about 90 minutes.

4–1 Marunouchi. ℂ **0263/32-2902.** Admission ¥600 adults, ¥300 children. Daily 8:30am–5pm. Town Sneaker Bus, Northern Course: Matsumotojo/Shiyakushomae (stop no. 8). To walk, take Agatanomori (also called Ekimae Dori), the main road leading away from Matsumoto Station, and turn left onto Honmachi Dori.

Former Kaichi School (Kyu Kaichi Gakko) HISTORIC SITE   Japan's public school system was founded in 1872 (before that, Buddhist temples were the only source of education). In 1876, this handsome white mortar building of black tile topped by an octagonal turret opened its doors, making it one of the oldest Western-style schools still standing and a fine example of Meiji Era architecture. Serving as an elementary school for 90 years, it remains much as it was, with displays of books, games, desks, abacuses, and other educational items. Most fascinating are the photographs of former pupils (showing how many young girls came to school with young siblings strapped to their backs, as parents were hard at work) and the children's books dating from World War II, with offending passages blackened out by demand of Allied occupational forces after the war. Next to the school is an 1889 parsonage you can see for free. In any case, you can tour everything in about 30 minutes.

2–4–12 Kaichi. ℂ **0263/32-5725.** Admission ¥300 adults, ¥150 children. Daily 8:30am–5pm. Closed Mon Dec–Feb. Town Sneaker Bus, Northern Course: Kyukaichigakko (stop no. 10). Behind the castle, about a 7-min. walk north.

Matsumoto Timepiece Museum (Tokei Hakubutsukan) ★ MUSEUM   I dropped by on a whim but was mesmerized by the pocket watches, sundials, mechanized clocks, early alarm clocks, grandfather clocks, cuckoo clocks (both 18th-c. German and Japanese imitations), Edo-Era Japanese clocks, and hundreds of other timepieces, mostly of Japanese and European origin from the 18th to 20th centuries. Most amazing of all: Most of the 300 or so timepieces on display are actually wound and working. Expect to spend about 40 minutes here.

1–21–15 Chuo. ℂ **0263/36-0969.** Admission ¥300 adults, ¥150 children. Tues–Sun 9am–5pm. Town Sneaker Bus, Eastern Course: Tokei Hakubutsukan (stop no. 15). Btw. Matsumoto Station and Matsumoto Castle, a 10-min. walk from both.

MORE TO SEE & DO
Japan Ukiyo-e Museum (Nihon Ukiyo-e Hakubutsukan) ★★★ 🏛 ART
MUSEUM   Don't miss this ultramodern building housing the private collection of the Sakai family, quite simply one of the best museums of woodblock prints in Japan. With more than 100,000 prints, it's believed to be the largest collection of its kind in the world and includes representative masterpieces of all known Ukiyo-e artists. Exhibitions change every 3 months, with about 100 prints on display at any one time. A 15-minute slide show with English-language explanations introduces the current exhibition, and an English-language pamphlet describes the history of the collection

and how woodblock prints are made. You'll want to spend at least 45 minutes here, longer if you browse the museum shop of reproduction and original prints.

2206–1 Koshiba, Shimadachi. www.ukiyo-e.co.jp/jum-e. ℂ **0263/47-4440.** Admission ¥1,200 adults, ¥600 children. Tues–Sun 10am–5pm. From platform 7 at Matsumoto Train Station, take the local Kamikochi Line 10 min. to Oniwa Station (¥170; JR Rail Pass not accepted) and then walk 15 min. (turn left out of the station, and then left at the T-intersection with the post office; after passing under the bridge, take the 3rd right at the small cemetery and continue straight on, past the underpass); or take a ¥1,500 10-min. taxi ride; or, better yet, come by bike (about 20 min. from Matsumoto Station).

Matsumoto City Museum of Art (Matsumoto-shi Bijutsukan) ART MUSEUM

This inviting museum showcases the talents of artists with connections to Matsumoto, including Kamijyo Shinzan, who elevated calligraphy to an art, landscape artist Tamura Kazuo, and Kusama Yayoi, a female artist known for her exuberant colors and polka-dot modern art. Expect to spend about 30 minutes here.

4-2-22 Chuo. ℂ**0263/39-7400.** Admission ¥400 adults, ¥200 university and high-school students, free for children and seniors. Tues–Sun 9am–5pm. Town Sneaker Bus, Eastern Course: Matsumoto-shi Bijutsukan (stop no. 30); or a 15-min. walk east of Matsumoto Station on Ekimae Dori.

Matsumoto Folkcraft Museum (Matsumoto Mingei-kan 松本民芸館) ★ MUSEUM

Here's a museum worth visiting if you have an extra hour (including the bus ride). Housed in a *kura* built to store fish, it contains folk art made primarily of wood, glass, bamboo, and porcelain from Japan and other countries, with exhibits changed four to five times a year. On display may be items as diverse as combs from around the world to Japanese store signs designed during the Edo Period for people who couldn't read. Particularly beautiful are the wooden chests.

1313–1 Satoyamabe. ℂ**0263/33-1569.** Admission ¥300 adults, free for children 15 and younger. Tues–Sun 9am–5pm. About 15 min. by bus (¥290); from the bus terminal, take the platform 3 bus heading to Utsukushigahara to the Mingeikan stop.

Where to Eat

Matsumoto is famous for its buckwheat noodles, which are fairly thick with a hearty flavor and can be served hot or cold, with several kinds of dips and sauces. It is also known for its *basashi* (raw horse meat), apples, grapes, mountain vegetables, and *oyaki*, rolls filled with mountain vegetables, mushrooms, red bean paste, and other ingredients.

Kura (蔵) ★ 🍴TEMPURA This restaurant occupies the ground floor of one of the largest *kura* in Matsumoto, built in the late Meiji Period and rare for its three stories (most kura are two-storied). Enter the dining room through the thick vault-like door and sit at the dark-wood counter or at one of the tables. The restaurant is known for its delicious tempura, though it also offers sushi, *basashi*, and *kaiseki* on its English-language menu. Best values are set meals, and try to avoid peak mealtimes, when the overworked staff can be brusque.

1–10–22 Chuo. ℂ **0263/33-6444.** Tempura and sushi set meals ¥945–¥2,100; kaiseki ¥3,675–¥5,250. AE, DC, MC, V. Thurs–Tues 11:45am–2pm and 5:30–10pm. Station: Matsumoto (5 min.). Walk down Koen Dori (the small side street to the left of McDonald's) and take the 1st left past the Parco department store; it's on the left.

Nomugi (野麦) ★ NOODLES There are only three tables in this well-known eatery popular with the locals, which means you may have to wait for a seat and can't dawdle over a meal. Its handmade buckwheat noodles are served until they run out, which is why the restaurant has a flexible closing time. You'll be given a sauce to pour into a cup; add green onion, wasabi, and *daikon* radish, and then dip your *soba* into the mix. At the end of your meal, make a soup from the soba water stock (served in a teapot) and the soba sauce. In winter, the soba is served with boiled toppings.

2–9–11 Chuo. ☎ **0263/36-3753.** Soba ¥1,100; half portion ¥700. No credit cards. Thurs–Mon 11:30am to around 2pm. Town Sneaker Bus, Eastern Course: Kuranomachi Nakamachi (stop no. 16, 1 min.). Or a 13-min. walk from Matsumoto Station; walk down Koen Dori (the small side street to the left of McDonald's), turn left at Honmachi, then right at Nakamachi, and then take the 1st right; it's on the left.

Shikimi (しき美) ★ 🍴 EEL/SUSHI   For inexpensive Japanese fare close to Matsumoto Station, try this place specializing in eel and sushi. An atmosphere of old Japan is evoked by its traditional tiled roof, cast-iron lanterns, and interior with wooden sliding doors, small *tatami* rooms, wooden counter, and paper lanterns. I recommend the *unagi donburi* (strips of eel on rice), which comes with soup and pickled vegetables. If sushi is more to your liking, try one of Shikimi's platters of assorted sushi, called *moriawase* (¥1,680–¥3,150), or sushi rolls starting at ¥630.

1–5–5 Chuo. ☎ **0263/36-7716.** Unagi donburi ¥1,890; set lunch (Mon–Fri only) ¥980. No credit cards. Mon–Fri 11:45am–2pm and 4:30–10:30pm; Sat 11:45am–3pm and 4–10pm; Sun 11:45am–9pm. Station: Matsumoto (3 min.). Take Koen Dori (left side of McDonald's) 1 block and turn left; it's on the corner on your left.

Taiman ★★★ FRENCH   If you feel like treating yourself, this ivy-covered, rustic yet elegant restaurant with a view of a garden is an excellent choice. In business for 60 years and located just south of Matsumoto Castle, it offers wonderful French cuisine from a changing menu that might include grilled duck, whitefish in a shrimp cream sauce, scallops, lamb cutlet with pistachio, or grilled steak in a red-wine sauce. My ¥5,250 lunch—which included bread or rice, dessert, and coffee—started with a corn potage, followed by stuffed *ayu* (river fish) and then the main dish, lamb with cèpe mushrooms.

4–2–4 Ote. ☎ **0263/32-0882.** Reservations recommended. Main dishes ¥4,200–¥6,300; set dinners ¥12,600–¥18,900; set lunches ¥5,250–¥9,450. AE, DC, MC, V. Thurs–Tues 11:30am–2pm and 5–9pm (last order 8pm). Town Sneaker Bus, Northern Course: Daimyocho (stop no. 5, 2 min.). Or a 12-min. walk from Matsumoto Station; walk east on Agatanomori (also called Ekimae Dori) and turn left on Honmachi Dori; after the bridge, turn right at the 2nd stoplight where the NTT Building is.

Where to Stay

Because Matsumoto is popular primarily with hikers used to roughing it along nature trails, accommodations are geared mainly toward convenience. Directions are from Matsumoto Station.

EXPENSIVE

Buena Vista ★   Matsumoto's biggest and fanciest hotel is a white gleaming structure popular for its conference and wedding facilities and with those attending the Saito Kinen Festival. Rooms range from very small singles and semi-doubles (cramped for two persons at ¥13,860–¥16,170, depending on the season) to top-floor premier rooms with updated furnishings and the best views of the mountains in the distance. Rates below reflect the seasons, with the highest prices in peak season (July 20–Sept 15) and the lowest in off season (Apr–June and Nov–Mar).

1–2–1 Honjo, Matsumoto, Nagano Prefecture 390-0184. www.buena-vista.co.jp. ☎ **0263/37-0111.** Fax 0263/37-0666. 200 units. ¥9,240–¥11,550 single; ¥19,635–¥27,720 double. AE, DC, MC,

V. Station: Matsumoto (7 min.). Turn right out of the station onto Shirakaba Dori; the hotel will be on a side street to the left. **Amenities:** 4 restaurants; 2 bars; access to nearby fitness club (fee: ¥525); lobby computers w/free Internet; room service. *In room:* A/C, TV, fridge, hair dryer, Internet.

MODERATE

**Matsumoto Hotel Kagetsu ★ ** This hotel, in a newer building reminiscent of the *kura* (storehouse) for which Matsumoto is famous but with a history going back more than 100 years, imparts a pleasant, old-fashioned atmosphere with its antique wooden furnishings and folk crafts in public spaces. Both Western- and Japanese-style rooms are available, comfortably large for the price. For the best views, ask for one of the upper-floor rooms facing the castle and mountains. For a splurge, deluxe corner rooms boast more windows, larger sitting areas, and toilets separate from the bathrooms.

4–8–9 Ote, Matsumoto, Nagano Prefecture 390-0874. http://hotel-kagetsu.jp. ℂ **0263/32-0114.** Fax 0263/33-4775. 80 units. ¥7,350–¥10,500 per person. AE, DC, MC, V. Town Sneaker Bus, Northern Course: Agetsuchimachi (stop no. 7, 1 min.). **Amenities:** 2 restaurants; room service. *In room:* A/C, TV, Internet.

Matsumoto Tokyu Inn Visible from the station, this practical and clean business hotel's main selling point is its convenient location, which probably accounts for rates that are a bit higher than you would expect in Matsumoto. The majority of rooms are singles and twins, all with semi-double-size beds with feather quilts and Swedish pillows (easier to sleep on, perhaps, than the Japanese bean variety). There are also six doubles and five deluxe twins, the latter with sofa, chairs, and a separate vanity area with its own sink. On clear days, higher-priced rooms facing west have views of the Japan Alps.

1–3–21 Fukashi, Matsumoto, Nagano Prefecture 390-0185. www.tokyuhotelsjapan.com. ℂ **0263/36-0109.** Fax 0263/36-0883. 160 units. ¥8,500–¥11,500 single; ¥13,800–¥28,000 double. AE, DC, MC, V. Station: Matsumoto (3 min.). Across the street to the right. **Amenities:** Restaurant; bar; lobby computers w/free Internet. *In room:* A/C, TV, Internet, minibar.

INEXPENSIVE

In addition to the more atmospheric choice below, there's **Toyoko Inn Matsumoto Ekimae Honmachi,** at 2–1–23 Chuo (www.toyoko-inn.com; ℂ **0263/36-1045**), a 6-minute walk west of Matsumoto Station. Charging from ¥5,480 for a single and ¥7,980 for a double, it offers the budget chain's usual freebies, including computers with free Internet access in the lobby, complimentary Japanese breakfast, and free Internet access in the rooms.

A Double or a Twin?

For the sake of convenience, the price for two people in a room is listed as a "double" in this book. Japanese hotels, however, differentiate between rooms with a double bed or two twin beds, usually with different prices. Although most hotels charge more for a twin room, sometimes the opposite is true; if you're looking for a bargain, be sure to inquire about prices for both. Note, too, that hotels usually have more twin rooms than doubles, for the simple reason that Japanese couples, used to their own futon, traditionally prefer twin beds.

Marumo (まるも) ★★ 🎁   This is my top pick for accommodations that epitomize the old-fashioned atmosphere of Matsumoto during the Meiji Era. Located in the traditional district of Nakamachi and occupying a *kura* and traditional Japanese inn constructed after the great 1888 fire that destroyed much of Matsumoto, it boasts a diminutive but eye-catching entryway of polished woods and antiques, very narrow stairs and corridors leading to Japanese-style rooms, and a wonderful coffee shop that has changed little over the decades. Rooms are simple and without the usual creature comforts, but the location is great and the atmosphere is truly one of a kind. If you're searching for "traditional Japan," this is where you'll want to stay.

3–3–10 Chuo, Matsumoto, Nagano Prefecture 390-0811. www.avis.ne.jp/~marumo/index.html. ✆**0263/32-0115.** 8 units, none with bathroom. ¥5,250 per person without breakfast. ¥6,300 with Japanese breakfast. No credit cards. Town Sneaker Bus, Eastern Course: Kurashikkukan (stop no. 17, 2 min.). Or a 15-min. walk from Matsumoto Station. **Amenities:** Coffee shop. *In room:* A/C, TV.

THE NAKASENDO HIGHWAY

About 100km (60 miles) E of Nagoya; 88km (55 miles) SW of Matsumoto

If you're traveling between Nagoya and Matsumoto, you'll most likely pass through Kiso Valley in mountainous Nagano Prefecture. Formed by the Kiso River, the valley has always served as a natural passageway through the Japan Alps and was, in fact, one of two official roads linking Kyoto with Edo (Tokyo) back in the days of the Tokugawa shogunate (the other route was the Tokaido Hwy., which passes through Hakone). Known as the **Nakasendo Highway** ★★, it was the route of traveling *daimyo* and their entourages of samurai retainers journeying between Japan's two most important towns. To serve their needs, 11 post towns sprang up along the Nakasendo Highway in Kiso Valley. Back then, it took 3 days to travel through the valley.

Of the old post towns, **Tsumago** (妻籠) ★★ and **Magome** (馬籠) ★ are two that still survive, with many of the old buildings left intact. An 8km (5-mile) pathway skirting the Kiso River links the two villages, providing hikers with the experience of what it must have been like to travel the 400-year-old Nakasendo Highway back in the days of the shogun. You can visit the two picturesque villages and take the hike in a 1-day excursion from Nagoya or Matsumoto, but I've included an overnight recommendation in case you want to linger. When I took my son, then 14 years old, on this hike he declared it the highlight of our 2-week trip in Japan.

Essentials

GETTING THERE   Because neither Magome nor Tsumago is directly on a train line, you'll have to make the final journey by bus.

To reach **Magome,** take the **JR Shinano express train** (which connects Nagoya and Matsumoto and departs hourly) to Nakatsugawa Station. Trains from Nagoya take about 50 minutes and cost ¥2,430 for an unreserved seat. From Matsumoto, trains take about 75 minutes and cost ¥3,670. The 20-minute bus ride onward to Magome costs ¥540, with buses departing about once an hour.

Because of less frequent train and bus connections, it's harder to reach **Tsumago,** so be sure to check schedules beforehand. Take the **JR Shinano train** to Nagiso Station and then a 10-minute bus ride (¥300). A taxi ride between Tsumago and Nagiso costs about ¥1,400.

Note: Train and bus schedules do not always coincide and not all trains stop in Nagiso or Nakatsugawa, so be sure to plan ahead. Although it's the same JR Shinano train that travels to both Nagiso and Nakatsugawa, express trains stop at Nagiso much less frequently than in Nakatsugawa. Note also that buses between Nagiso and Tsumago are also less frequent than those running between Nakatsugawa and Magome, so inquire about bus schedules beforehand. The Matsumoto Station tourist office has information on bus schedules (see "Visitor Information," on p. 223).

VISITOR INFORMATION   The best way to obtain information about Kiso Valley is to stop by the **Tourist Information Center** in Tokyo or Narita, or Kansai international airports, to pick up the leaflet "Kiso Valley" (or download it as a PDF from JNTO's website at www.jnto.go.jp by looking under "Browse by Destinations"), which provides a rough sketch of the 8km (5-mile) hiking path between Magome and Tsumago and gives basic information about the villages; you can also stop by the tourist office in Matsumoto. Online, more information is available at www.go-nagano. net and www.town.nagiso.nagano.jp.

Otherwise, there's a tourist office in Tsumago (© **0264/57-3123;** open daily 8:30am–5pm) and one in Magome (© **0573-69-2336;** open daily 9am–5pm except Mar–Nov when it opens at 8:30am). No English is spoken, but they do have English-language pamphlets, bus and train schedules, and maps of the hiking trail.

TRAVELING BETWEEN TSUMAGO & MAGOME   If you want to see the post towns of Tsumago and Magome but don't want to hike between the two (or wish to hike the trail, say, from Magome to Tsumago and then return to Magome), a **bus** travels between the two villages for ¥600, but service is infrequent so be sure to get the schedule beforehand. Especially useful for hikers is a **luggage-transfer service** available between Magome and Tsumago daily from mid-March through November. Luggage is accepted at either town's tourist office no later than 11:30am, at a charge of ¥500 per bag, and can be picked up at your destination's tourist office after your hike as early as 1pm, but must be picked up by 5pm. During other times of the year, your bags can be sent by taxi to either tourist office or your *ryokan* for ¥3,000 for one or more bags.

Walking the Nakasendo Highway Between Tsumago & Magome

Allow about 3 hours for the 8km (5-mile) hike between Tsumago and Magome. It doesn't matter which town you start from, though starting from Tsumago is easier if you have heavy luggage being sent via transfer service, as starting in Magome requires an 8-minute walk from the bus stop up a steep slope to the tourist office. I, however, like starting in Magome and ending up in Tsumago, which I consider the crown jewel of the hike.

In any case, the trail is mainly a footpath tracing the contours of the Kiso Valley and crisscrossing a rushing stream over a series of bridges. At times the trail follows a paved road and leads past interesting farming villages, as well as old signposts, watch-house ruins, and other historic remnants, with a short detour leading to two waterfalls, Odaki and Medaki. There are public toilets along the way. Because the trail goes up some steep inclines, wear your walking shoes. And have fun—this is a great walk!

TSUMAGO ★★ Tsumago, the second post town from the south, is the more beautiful and authentic of the two towns. Threatened with gradual decline and desertion after the train line was constructed in 1911, bypassing Tsumago, the town experienced decades of neglect—and that's probably what ultimately saved it. Having suffered almost no modernization in the rebuilding zeal of the 20th century, Tsumago was a perfect target for renovation and restoration in the early 1970s, and in a rare show of insight, electrical wires, TV antennas, and telephone poles were hidden from sight along the main road and strict building codes forbid changes to existing buildings. Thus, Tsumago looks much as it did back in the days of Edo. There are, of course, the ubiquitous souvenir shops, but many sell locally made crafts made of wood and bamboo, including sun hats made from shaved cypress, which started here as a cottage industry in the Edo Era.

On the main street of Tsumago are three separate buildings, called collectively the **Nagiso-machi Museum** (✆ **0264/57-3322**) and open daily from 9am to 5pm for a ¥700 admission. The **Tsumagojuku Honjin** was an officially appointed inn that once served as a way station for the 30 or so *daimyo* who used the Nakasendo Highway to travel to and from Edo. Like all *honjin* (an inn designated as the resting place for daimyo), it's divided into two parts: a large, grand area for the feudal lord and his attendants, and a few smaller, simpler rooms for the Shimazaki family, which managed the inn.

Apparently, the Shimazaki family had plans drawn up to rebuild its inn in 1830. Renovation, however, didn't take place until 160 years later when an heir discovered the plans and gave them to the township, which rebuilt the inn according to the original plans using techniques dating from the period. You'd swear it's the original.

Across the lane is the **Waki-honjin Okuya** ★, the town's secondary inn, used by court nobles or by *daimyo* when the *honjin* was already occupied. The present house, a lovely traditional structure with a garden, dates from 1877 and was rebuilt with *hinoki* cypress trees, a fact that has a special significance for this region. For centuries, all the way through the Edo Period, wood in the Kiso Valley was as good as gold and was used instead of rice to pay taxes. Commoners, therefore, were prohibited from cutting down trees, and those who did so literally lost their heads. When the Meiji Period dawned and the ban was finally lifted, wealthy landowners were quick to rebuild in a statelier manner. Emperor Meiji himself visited the inn in 1880, and though a special tub and toilet were built just for the occasion, he stayed only 30 minutes. Upstairs is a secret room, used for important discussions.

Next door is the **Rekishi Shiryokan,** which serves as a local history museum with displays of lacquerware, porcelain, a model of how the Waki-honjin looked during the Edo Period, diagrams showing how trees were felled and transported from the steep mountainsides, and photographs of buildings in Tsumago before and after they were renovated.

MAGOME The southernmost post town, Magome has old inns, restaurants, and many shops selling beautiful basket work and wooden articles that line both sides of a steeply sloping, cobblestone road. It takes about 20 minutes to stroll through the town.

Where to Stay & Dine

Both Tsumago and Magome have simple *minshuku* and *ryokan* (tourist offices in both towns can make reservations). I love staying at **Ryokan Fujioto** (旅館 藤乙) ★★,

Tsumago, Nagiso-machi 399-5302 (www.takenet.or.jp/~fujioto; ℂ **0264/57-3009;** fax 0264/57-2239), set back from the main road of Tsumago and buffered from foot traffic by a nice Japanese garden. The 100-year-old inn offers nine *tatami* rooms (none with bathroom) for ¥11,550 per person, including two delicious meals (no credit cards accepted). What makes this place a standout is innkeeper Fujihara-san and his daughter Sayaka-san, both of whom speak excellent English, can provide information on the area, and visit with guests in the dining room, explaining all the unique dishes they serve. Even if you don't spend the night, you can sample the inn's local specialties for lunch, served from 10am to 2:30pm daily. An English-language menu with pictures offers broiled trout, carp sashimi, Shinshu beef cooked on magnolia leaf, noodles, and other fare, as well as set meals for ¥1,050 to ¥1,650. Both the inn and restaurant are closed mid-December through February.

In Magome, on the main street through town, **Magome-Chaya** (馬籠茶屋), Magome, Nakatsugawa-shi 4296 (http://magomechaya.com; ℂ **0573/69-2038**), offers 13 simple Japanese-style rooms (none with bathroom) for ¥5,250 for a single and ¥8,190 for a double, without meals (MasterCard and Visa accepted but with a 5% surcharge). The inn's restaurant across the street offers noodles (¥800–¥1,000) and set meals (¥1,600–¥1,800) daily 11am to 3pm.

HIDA TAKAYAMA, LITTLE KYOTO OF THE MOUNTAINS ★★★

533km (331 miles) NW of Tokyo; 165km (103 miles) NE of Nagoya

Located in the Hida Mountains (part of the Japan Alps National Park) in Gifu Prefecture, **Hida Takayama** is surrounded by 3,000m (10,000-ft.) peaks, making the train or bus ride here breathtaking. The town, situated along a river on a wide plateau with a population of 93,000, was founded in the 16th century by Lord Kanamori, who selected the site because of the impregnable position afforded by the surrounding mountains. Modeled after Kyoto but also with strong ties to Edo (Tokyo), Takayama borrowed from both cultural centers in developing its own architecture, food, and crafts, all well preserved today thanks to centuries of isolation. With a rich supply of timber provided by surrounding forests, its carpenters were legendary, creating not only beautifully crafted traditional merchants' homes in Takayama but also the Imperial Palace and temples in Kyoto.

Today, Takayama boasts a delightful and elegant historic district, called **Sanmachi Suji,** with homes of classical design typical of 18th-century Hida. The streets are narrow and clean and are flanked on both sides by tiny canals of running water, which in centuries past were useful for fire prevention, washing clothes, and dumping winter snow, but which now give the town its distinct character. Rising from the canals are one- and two-story homes and shops of gleaming dark wood with overhanging roofs; latticed windows and slats of wood play games of light and shadow in the white of the sunshine. In the doorways of many shops, blue curtains flutter in the breeze.

With its quaint old character, great shopping (including a lively city market), and museums, Takayama is a town that invites exploration. As you walk down the streets, you'll also notice huge cedar balls hanging from the eaves in front of several shops, indicating one of Takayama's sake breweries. Altogether there are seven of them in Takayama, most small affairs. Go inside, sample the sake, and watch the men stirring rice in large vats. There are also a surprising number of museums, most housed in traditional homes and filled with historical relics and antiques of Takayama's past.

Essentials

GETTING THERE By Train The easiest way to reach Takayama is by direct train from Nagoya, with about 10 departures daily for the 2½-hour trip that costs ¥5,360 for an unreserved seat.

BY BUS Nohi buses (www.nouhibus.co.jp; © 03/5376-2222) depart Tokyo's Shinjuku Station five to six times daily spring through autumn, arriving in Takayama 5½ hours later and costing ¥6,500. There are fewer departures in winter, when snow-fall sometimes makes roads impassable. Nohi buses also depart from Kanazawa (© 076/234-0123) twice a day for Takayama, passing through Shirakawa-go on the way and costing ¥3,300 for the 2¼-hour trip. From Nagoya (© 052/563-0489), there are nine departures daily costing ¥2,900 for the 2½-hour ride. Note that reservations are required for these buses. From Matsumoto, both Nohi buses (© 0577/32-1688) and the **Highland Express Bus** (© 0263/35-7400) pass through mountain scenery on the 2-hour and 20-minute trip and cost ¥3,100.

VISITOR INFORMATION The **Takayama Tourist Office** (© 0577/32-5328; daily 8:30am–6:30pm, to 5pm Nov–Mar) is housed in a wooden booth just outside the main (east) exit of Takayama Station. You can pick up an English-language brochure with a map of the town showing the location of all museums and attractions. You can also use the tourist office's laptop for free Internet access, but you have to stand. A small **tourist counter** on Sanno-machi street is open daily 10am to 4pm. More information, including maps, is available at www.hida.jp/english.

GETTING AROUND Takayama is one of Japan's easiest towns to navigate. Most of its attractions lie east of the train station in an area called San-machi Suji and are easily reached from the station in about 10 to 15 minutes **on foot.** Throughout the town are English-language signs pointing directions to the many attractions; they're even embedded in sidewalks and streets.

To reach Hida Folk Village, Hida Takayama Museum of Art, or Teddy Bear Eco Village (see below), you'll have to go by **Takayama City Loop Bus (Sarubobo Bus),** which departs from in front of the train station twice an hour daily from 9am to 4pm. The fare is ¥600 for an all-day pass; a pass that includes admission to the Hida Folk Village costs ¥700. Better yet, ask at the tourist Information Center for the free **London Bus** (operated by the Hida Takayama Museum of Art only for museum customers Apr–Oct), which departs from Takayama Station four times a day. From the museum it's about a 10-minute walk to the folk village.

Alternatively, lots of shops ringing the station rent **bicycles,** with most charging ¥1,200 or ¥1,300 for the day, including **Daily** convenience store right beside the station (© 0577/35-5377) and **Hara Cycling** (© 0577/32-1657) a few minutes' walk from the station on Kokubunji Dori. Note, however, that it's straight up a very long hill to Hida Folk Village, Hida Takayama Museum of Art, and Teddy Bear Eco Village. Personally, I'd rather walk.

Exploring Takayama

Takayama's main attraction is its Old Private Houses (Furui-Machi-nami), which are clustered together in San-machi Suji on three narrow streets called **Ichino-machi, Nino-machi,** and **Sanno-machi.** Be sure to allow time to wander around. In addition to the district's many museums, there are also shops selling Takayama's specialties, including sake, yew woodcarvings, beautiful cypress furniture, and a unique lacquerware called *shunkei-nuri.*

Be sure, too, to visit the **Miyagawa Morning Market,** which stretches on the east bank of the Miyagawa River between Kajibashi and Yayoibashi bridges. Held every morning from 7am (6am in summer) to noon, it's very picturesque, with cloth-covered stalls selling fresh vegetables, flowers, pickled vegetables, locally made crafts, and toys. A smaller morning market is held in front of the Historical Government House (Takayama Jinya; see below).

And if you have more free time still, consider the **Higashiyama Walking Course,** which leads past a string of 13 temples and five shrines nestled on a wooded hill on the east edge of town in an area called Higashiyama Teramachi. It also leads to Shiroyama Park, site of the Kanamori clan castle until it was torn down in 1695 by order of the Tokugawa shogunate. Parts of its stone foundations still remain. The hiking course stretches 3.5km (2¼ miles) end to end, but English-language signs are few and far between and the map provided by the tourist office is hopeless; you could consider getting lost part of the fun.

Fujii Folk Museum (Fujii Bijutsu Mingei-Kan) ★ MUSEUM   This gallery in the heart of San-Machi Suji occupies a traditional merchant's storehouse; its entrance is a replica of an outer gate that once led to Takayama Castle. The eclectic collection from the Edo Period includes beautiful *tansu* (chests) inlaid with mother-of-pearl, sake cups, lacquerware, Imari and Kutani porcelain, tortoiseshell combs, ceremonial Hina dolls, kimono, teakettles, paper lanterns, rice barrels, smoking utensils, matchlocks, swords, farming tools, spinning wheels, and more. Many items are identified in English, making this a very worthwhile museum; you can see it all in about 20 minutes.

Sanno-machi St., 69 Kamisanno-machi. ℂ **0577/35-3778.** Admission ¥700 adults, ¥350 children. Daily 9am–5pm. Station: Takayama (12 min.).

Hida Folk Village (Hida no Sato) ★★ MUSEUM   This is an open-air museum of more than 30 old thatched and shingled farmhouses, sheds, and buildings, many of which were brought here from other parts of the region to illustrate how farmers and artisans used to live in the Hida Mountain range. The entire village is picturesque, with swans swimming in the central pond, green moss growing on the thatched roofs, and flowers blooming in season. Some of the houses have *gassho-zukuri*-style roofs, built steeply to withstand the region's heavy snowfalls; the tops of the roofs are said to resemble hands joined in prayer. All the structures, which range from 100 to 500 years old, are open to the public and are filled with furniture, old spindles and looms, utensils for cooking and dining, instruments used in the silk industry, farm tools, sleds, and straw boots and snow capes for winter. Be sure to ask for the free 20-minute English-language audio guide at the entrance, which describes the social life and architecture of the region.

Workshops set up in one corner of the village grounds demonstrate Takayama's well-known woodcarving, tie-dying, weaving, and lacquer-work industries; some of the artisans even live here. On weekends you can try your hand at sandal-making, weaving, and other crafts; class fees range from ¥500 to¥1,300. You'll want to spend about 1½ hours at the village, but if you're heading to Shirakawa-go, skip it; there's a similar, more accessible open-air museum there.

© **0577/34-4711.** Admission ¥700 adults, ¥200 children 15 and under. Daily 8:30am–5pm. Bus: City Loop Bus to Hida-no-Sato, or the free London Bus to the Hida Takayama Museum of Art (then a 10-min. walk). Or a 30-min. walk southwest of the train station.

Hida Takayama Museum of Art (Hida Takayama Bijutsukan; 飛騨高山美術館) ★★ MUSEUM

Serious glass lovers will not want to miss this museum with its collection of mostly European antique and contemporary glassware from the 16th to the 20th centuries, including works by Tiffany, Lalique, and Gallé, as well as contemporary works by Japanese glassmakers like Fujita Kyohei. Several rooms are furnished in decorative and applied arts by masters such as Louis Majorelle, Mackintosh, and Vienna's Secessionist artists. Don't miss the museum shop with its Japanese and imported glassware and crafts; I also like the Mackintosh-inspired tearoom with outdoor terrace seating. Plan on spending about 45 minutes here.

1–124–1 Kamiokamoto-cho. www.htm-museum.co.jp. © **0577/35-3535.** Admission ¥1,300 adults, ¥1,000 university and high-school students, ¥800 junior-high age and younger. Apr–Nov daily 9am–5pm; Dec–Mar varies (call for open hours). Bus: City Loop Bus to Hida-no-Sato Shita, or take the free London Bus. Station: Takayama (20-min. southwest).

Hirata Folk Art Museum (Hirata Kinen-kan) ★★ MUSEUM

Takayama's most varied and extensive collection of folk art vividly conveys what life was like during the Edo Period by displaying household utensils, crafts, and fine arts found in a typical middle-class home; the house itself, built in 1897 in traditional style with a sunken hearth and both living and working quarters, belonged to a candle-maker. Items are identified in English. On display are folk toys, coin boxes, mirrors, toiletry sets, *geta* sandals, spectacles, hair adornments, *shunkei* lacquerware, and paper and kerosene lamps; my favorite is the room outfitted with items used for travel, including guide maps, portable abacuses, compasses, a traveling pillow, a folding lantern, and even a folding hat. You'll probably spend 20 minutes here.

Ichino-machi St., 39 Kaminino-machi. © **0577/33-1354.** Admission ¥300 adults, ¥150 junior-high age and younger. Daily 9am–5pm. Station: Takayama (10 min.).

Historical Government House (Takayama Jinya) ★★★ GOVERNMENT BUILDING

I highly recommend a visit here to anyone interested in Japanese history. The building served as the Tokugawa government's administrative building for 177 years (1692–1868). Of some 60 local government offices that were once spread throughout Japan, this is the only one still in existence. Resembling a miniature palace with its outer wall and an imposing entrance gate, the sprawling complex consists of both original buildings and reconstructions. In addition to administrative offices, chambers, and courts, the complex contained living quarters, a huge kitchen, an interrogation room with torture devices, and a 400-year-old rice granary, the oldest and biggest in Japan, where rice collected from farmers as a form of taxation was stored. Making visits here especially educational are free guided tours in English, which last about 30 minutes and provide fascinating insight into administrative life of yore.

1–5 Hachi-ken-machi. © **0577/32-0643.** Admission ¥420 for adults, free for high-school age and younger. Mar–Oct daily 8:45am–5pm; Nov–Feb daily 8:45am–4:30pm. Station: Takayama (10 min.).

Shunkei Lacquerware Museum (Hida Takayama Shunkei Kaikan)
MUSEUM This museum, which can be toured in 15 minutes, displays Takayama lacquerware, known for the transparency of its finish, which enhances the grain of the wood. Takayama lacquerware is admired all over Japan for its honey-colored sheen, which becomes lighter and more beautiful over time. The museum displays some 1,000 items dating from the 17th century to the present, including beautifully crafted trays, furniture, vases, rice containers, and lunch boxes; one exhibit explains the multistage production technique and tools of the craft. There's also a shop—and after seeing the time-consuming process to produce *shunkei* ware, you'll know why prices are high.

1–88 Kanda-cho. ✆ **0577/32-3373.** Admission ¥300 adults, ¥200 high-school and junior-high students, free for children. Summer daily 8:30am–5:30pm; winter daily 9am–5pm. Station: Takayama (15 min.).

Lion Dance Ceremony Shishi Hall (Shishi-Kaikan; 獅子會館) MUSEUM More than 300 lion masks from all over Japan, used to perform the lion dance in Japanese festivals, are on display here, as well as Edo-Period screens, ceramics, scrolls, coins, samurai armor, and swords. Best, however, are the 15-minute performances given every half-hour by *karakuri* (automated dolls), which decorate many of Takayama's floats in its two festivals; they're capable of wonderful acrobatics.

53–1 Sakura-machi. ✆ **0577/32-0881.** Admission ¥600 adults, ¥400 junior-high age and younger. Summer daily 8:30am–5:30pm; winter daily 9:05am–4:25pm. A 1-min. walk from Takayama Festival Floats Exhibition Hall (see below).

Merchants' Houses ★★★ HISTORIC HOME In contrast to other castle towns during the Edo Period, Takayama was under the direct control of the Tokugawa government rather than a feudal lord, which meant its homes were built and owned by merchants and commoners rather than the samurai class that dominated other Japanese cities. Located side by side in San-machi Suji and both toured easily in less than 30 minutes, **Yoshijima-ke** or Yoshijima Heritage House (✆ **0577/32-0038**) and **Kusakabe Mingei-kan** (✆ **0577/32-0072**) are merchants' mansions that once belonged to two of the richest families in Takayama. With its exposed attic, heavy crossbeams, sunken open-hearth fireplace, and sliding doors, Yoshijima House is a masterpiece of geometric design. It was built in 1907 as both the home and factory of the Yoshijima family, well-to-do brewers of sake. Notice how the beams and details of the home gleam, a state attained through decades of polishing as each generation of women did their share in bringing the wood to a luster. Yoshijima-ke is also famous for its lattices, typical of Takayama yet showing an elegance influenced by Kyoto. Its walls serve as an art gallery for the lithographs of female artist Shinoda Toko, one of my favorite Japanese artists (and a distant relative of present owner Yoshijima Tadao, who also uses the house for his other passion, jazz, heard softly in the back gallery).

Kusakabe Mingei-kan, built in 1879 for a merchant dealing in silk, lamp oil, and finance, is more refined and imposing. Its architectural style is considered unique to Hida but has many characteristics common during the Edo Period, including a two-story warehouse at the back of the house with open beams and an earthen floor, now filled with folk art and other items. On display, too, are personal items such as lacquerware and chests from Japan and imports from other countries, handed down through the generations and arranged just as they would have been in the 18th and 19th centuries. If you have time for only one house, this one has more to see; free green tea and rice crackers are served in the courtyard.

North end of Nino-machi St., Oshinmachi. Admission to either house ¥500 for adults, ¥300 for junior high and younger. Mar–Nov daily 9am–5pm, Dec–Feb daily 9am–4:30pm (Kusakabe Mingei-kan closes 30 min. earlier). Station: Takayama (20 min.).

Showa Kan (昭和館) ★ MUSEUM   If you're a history or a kitsch buff, check out this eclectic museum packed with items used in daily life during the Showa era (Showa refers to the reign of Emperor Hirohito, 1926–89), including posters, shop signs, bikes, washing machines, rice cookers, clocks, and more, most of it arranged in themed rooms. You can step inside a toyshop, photo studio, doctor's office, dry goods store (it's fun to see what was considered high-tech back then), schoolroom, beauty salon, movie theater, and other establishments, providing a unique perspective on how much Japan has changed in just a few short decades (you'll probably find yourself wishing more from the Showa era remained). After spending about 30 minutes here, be sure to take a look at the small museum shop selling replica tin toys and candies of yesteryear. You'll recognize the museum by the old vehicles and gas pump in the entranceway.

6 Shimoichino-machi. ✆ **0577/33-7836.** Admission ¥500 adults, ¥300 children. Daily 9am–6pm. Station: Takayama (10 min.); just off Kokubunji Dori.

Takayama Festival Floats Exhibition Hall (Takayama Matsuri Yatai Kaikan) ★ MUSEUM   This exhibition hall displays 4 of the 11 huge, elaborate floats used for Takayama's famous Takayama Matsuri (Autumn Festival). Dating mostly from the 17th century and colorfully decorated with carvings, hanging lanterns, and sometimes marionettes, floats are as high as 7m (23 ft.) and are mounted on wheels (it takes 20 people to pull them through the streets). Free 20-minute guided tours in English make the festival hall an interesting stop if you're unable to see the festival itself. The admission price also allows entrance to **Sakurayama Nikko Kan** next door, which houses a replica of the Toshogu Shrine in Nikko (p. 95), built 100 years ago over a period of 15 years at ¹⁄₁₀th the scale. I was initially skeptical, but the 28 buildings—complete with computerized sunsets and sunrises—are works of art.

178 Sakura-machi. ✆ **0577/32-5100.** Admission ¥820 adults, ¥510 high-school students, ¥410 junior-high age and younger. Summer daily 8:30am–5pm; winter daily 9am–4:30pm. In the precincts of Sakurayama Hachimangu Shrine, about a 10-min. walk north of San-machi Suji or a 25-min. walk from the train station.

Hida Takayama Teddy Bear Eco Village ☺ MUSEUM   Kids of all ages might enjoy a 30-minute stopover in this 140-year-old thatched house, where 1,000 bears from around the world are on display, including rare finds like a 1911 Steiff polar bear, a 1903 Steiff named Franz that once belonged to the Habsburg family, a Smokey the Bear, and a bear donated by Patagonia made entirely from excess fleece. Its cafe, with indoor and outdoor seating, offers organic coffee and teas, soy hot dogs, and a very good salad wrap with organic veggies.

3–829–4 Nishino-ishiki. ✆ **0577/37-2525.** Admission ¥600 adults, ¥500 high-school students, ¥400 children. Daily 10am–6pm. Closed irregularly in winter. Bus: City Loop Bus to Hida-no-Sato Shita. Station: Takayama (20 min.); btw. Hida Folk Village and Hida Takayama Museum of Art.

Where to Eat

Takayama has some local specialties you should try while you're here (they may well be served at your *ryokan* or *minshuku*). The best known is *hoba miso,* which is soybean paste mixed with dried scallions, ginger, and mushrooms and cooked on a dry magnolia leaf at your table above a small clay burner. *Sansai* are mountain vegetables, including edible ferns and other wild plants; and *ayu* is river fish, grilled with soy sauce or salt. Other favorite dishes include Takayama's own style of *soba* (buckwheat noodles), *mitarashi-dango* (grilled rice balls with soy sauce), and Hida beef.

In addition to the listings below, stop by **Fujiya Hanaikada (富士屋 花筏),** 46 Hanakawa-cho (ⓒ **0577/36-0339**), a 4-minute walk straight ahead from the station, on a corner to the left. Open Friday to Wednesday from 10am to 6pm, it serves traditional Japanese homemade sweets along with tea and coffee, but what makes this place memorable is its award-winning locally made cypress furniture.

VERY EXPENSIVE

Kakusho (角正) ★★★ 🏠 VEGETARIAN   For a big splurge, dine at Kakusho, established 200 years ago and offering local vegetarian fare called *shojin-ryori,* typically served at Buddhist temples. Situated on the slope of a hill in the eastern part of the city, a 5-minute walk from San-machi Suji, this delightful restaurant serves meals either in small, private *tatami* rooms dating from the Edo Period or in a larger room from the Meiji Period that can be opened to the elements on three sides, all of which overlook a dreamy, mossy garden enclosed by a clay wall. The least expensive meals consist of various mountain vegetables, mushrooms, nuts, tofu, and other dishes, with more dishes added for more expensive meals. The owner speaks some English.

2–98 Babacho. ⓒ **0577/32-0174.** Reservations required. Kaiseki shojin-ryori ¥10,000–¥20,000; set lunches ¥5,500. Prices exclude tax and service charge. No credit cards. Daily seatings at 11:30am and 2pm and 5–7pm (last order). Irregular closing days. Station: Takayama (15 min.). Just north off of San-machi and 1 block east of Kami-ichino-machi.

MODERATE

Le Midi ★★ FRENCH   This tiny, two-level restaurant with red-and-white checkered tablecloths and wood trim, imparts a European flair and delivers delicious food. Its specialty is Hida beef, available as sirloin steak, beef stew, or beef cheek simmered 6 hours in red wine. Even the humble hamburger steak, served on potatoes and with green beans, is quite a presentation. Other dishes include Hida pork, fish of the day, and duck breast.

2–2 Honmachi. ⓒ **0577/36-6386.** Main courses ¥2,000–¥10,000; set dinners ¥4,800–¥12,000; set lunches ¥1,800–¥4,800. AE, DC, MC, V. Mon–Wed and Fri 11:30am–3pm and 6–9:30pm; Sat–Sun and holidays 11:30am–3:30pm and 5–9:30pm. Station: Takayama (9 min.). On Honmachi near Ikadabashi Bridge.

Matsuki Sushi (松喜すし) ★ SUSHI   Takayama is a 90-minute drive from the ocean, but that's where this sushi purveyor shops daily. Seating is at the counter or at low tables with leg wells. An English-language brochure lists various set meals, including a Ninja Course that gives you eight *nigiri-zushi,* one hand-rolled sushi, assorted tempura, and crab miso soup. Or, leave it to chef Kazu and order the *omakase,* which comes with 12 sushi selections along with miso soup; two diners can even split this feast. Oddly, another specialty here is Hida beef—but thank goodness, it's grilled.

1–40 Sowa-cho. ⓒ **0557/34-4766.** Set meals ¥2,980–¥4,980. AE, V. Tues–Sun 11am–2pm; daily 5:30–11pm. Station: Takayama (5 min.). Walk east on Kokubunji St. and turn left after passing Kokubunji Temple; it will be on the right.

Suzuya (寿々や) ★★ LOCAL SPECIALTIES   Darkly lit with traditional Takayama country decor, this restaurant specializing in Takayama cuisine is very popular. There's an English-language menu complete with photographs and explanations of each dish, including such local specialties as mountain vegetables, *hoba miso,* and Hida beef, as well as *shabu-shabu* and sukiyaki.

24 Hanakawa-cho. ✆ **0577/32-2484.** Set meals ¥950–¥4,200. AE, DC, MC, V. Wed–Mon 11am–3pm and 5–8pm (last order). Station: Takayama (6 min.). Just off Kokubunji St. to the right, halfway btw. the station and the Miyagawa River.

INEXPENSIVE

Agura ★★ 🏠 LOCAL SPECIALTIES/PIZZA A converted rice *kura,* with a high-beamed ceiling, wooden floors, slabs of wood for tables, and locally crafted bentwood chairs makes for a lovely, airy setting, heightened by eclectic cuisine, hip waiters, and jazz. The English-language menu lists several salads (I especially like the "Agura Original Salad" with lettuce, shrimp, boiled egg, tomato, ham, tuna, and sprouts), three kinds of pizzas fired in a wood-burning stove, and food that goes down well with beer, including *edamame,* chicken marinated in miso, spring rolls with sweet chili sauce, and Hida beef and miso cooked on a "dead" (I think they mean "dried") Hoba leaf. Note that there's a ¥200-per-person snack charge.

4–7 Shinmeicho. ✆ **0577/37-2666.** Main dishes ¥680–¥1,500. AE, MC, V. Tues–Sun 6–11:30pm (last order). Station: Takayama (12 min.). Just south of Takayama City Memorial Hall; look for the green sign with the yellow seated Buddha.

Myogaya (茗荷舍) VEGETARIAN Just a minute's walk east of the train station, this tiny shop packed with books and some health foods offers a limited selection of homemade organic set meals from an English-language menu, including chicken or veggie curry and stir-fried rice, which come with miso soup and vegetables (takeout available). The friendly proprietress makes this a pleasant place to come even for just a drink, from organic coffee and tea to plum juice and wine made from organic grapes.

5–15 Hanasato-cho. ✆ **0577/32-0426.** Set meals ¥1,000–¥1,100. No credit cards. Wed–Sun 8–10:30am and 11:30am–3pm. Walk straight out of the station 1 block and turn right.

Where to Stay

There are as many *minshuku* and *ryokan* in Takayama as hotels, making it the perfect place to stay in a traditional inn. In fact, staying in a *tatami* room and sleeping on a futon is the best way to immerse yourself in the life of this small community.

You should be aware that in peak season—Golden Week (Apr 29–May 5), August, festival times in April and October, and New Year's—prices will be higher, generally between 10% and 20%, than prices given below.

EXPENSIVE

Best Western Hotel Takayama ★ Purists might decry the size of this chain hotel in such a historic town, but it does have a convenient location just a minute's walk from the train station and could be a lifesaver for those who do not like sleeping on the floor. Besides, at seven stories, it's not even the tallest building around, and its facade, with a replica Meiji-Era design, could be worse. Otherwise, its mostly twin rooms are fairly small and ordinary, though cheerful and bright; ask for a room on a higher floor facing east, where you have a view of mountains in the distance.

6–6 Hanasato-cho, Takayama, Gifu Prefecture 506-0026. www.bestwestern.com. ✆ **0577/37-2000.** Fax 0577/37-2005. 78 units. ¥11,000 single; ¥18,000–¥21,000 double. Rates include breakfast. AE, MC, V. Station: Takayama (1 min.). Walk straight out of the station 1 block and turn left. **Amenities:** 2 restaurants; lounge; lobby computer w/free Internet. *In room:* A/C, TV, fridge, hair dryer, Wi-Fi.

MODERATE

Antique Inn Sumiyoshi (寿美よし) ★★★ 📶   This calls itself a *ryokan,* but its price and homey atmosphere make it seem more like a *minshuku.* Built about 100 years ago by a well-known local carpenter to house a silkworm industry, it opened in 1950 as a ryokan and hasn't changed much since then. An open-hearth fireplace, samurai armor, and antiques fill the reception area, where you are invited to have tea or coffee, and on the second floor there's an outdoor deck facing the river. *Tatami* rooms are comfortable and old-fashioned, many with painted screens and antiques; request one facing the river, across which you have a view of the morning market. Rates are based on room type. Minami-san, the man running the ryokan, is a fourth-generation innkeeper and speaks English. In addition to Japanese and vegetarian dinners (order when making reservations), both Japanese and Western breakfasts are available.

21–4 Honmachi, Takayama, Gifu Prefecture 506-0011. www.sumiyoshi-ryokan.com. © **0577/32-0228.** Fax 0577/33-8916. 8 units (1 with bathroom; 2 with sink/toilet). ¥6,300–¥9,450 per person. Dinner ¥3,150 extra; breakfast ¥1,050 extra. No credit cards. Station: Takayama (10 min. northeast). Across from historic San-machi Suji on the Miyagawa River. *In room:* A/C, TV, minibar, no phone.

Four Seasons 🍴   Although this modern-looking building with an arched roof looks out of place in Takayama, the hotel is a good choice in terms of price. Catering to business travelers during the week and tourists on weekends, it has free coffee in the lobby. Avoid the cheaper rooms on the second and third floors, as these have glazed windows. Rooms on the fourth through sixth floors have views over the city (request a corner room), with those on the sixth floor decorated with wooden furniture and wooden floors (important for the allergy conscious; rooms on the second floor are also with wood floors). A large Japanese bath with Jacuzzi and sauna overlooking a small garden is a plus. (By the way, as you may have guessed by its rates, this place is not part of the famous Four Seasons hotel chain.)

1–1 Kanda-machi, Takayama, Gifu Prefecture 506-0006. www.f-seasons.co.jp. © **0577/36-0088.** Fax 0577/36-0080. 46 units. ¥6,900–¥7,500 single; ¥13,500–¥14,500 twin. AE, MC, V. Station: Takayama (10 min. northeast). **Amenities:** Restaurant; rental bikes (free); hot-spring indoor bath; lobby computer w/free Internet; sauna. *In room:* A/C, TV, fridge, hair dryer, Wi-Fi.

Yamakyu ★   This spotless *minshuku* has a reputation of offering the best meals in town in its price range, served in a communal dining room. Although it's a bit far from the station—about a 20-minute walk or a 5-minute taxi ride—it's located in a quiet residential area near Takayama's many temples and shrines (and Higashiyama Walking Course; see p. 235) and is only a 10-minute walk or short bike ride to the historic district. Its hallways boast a good collection of folk art, antique clocks, glassware, and lamps; eaves above all guest-room doors give it a "village" atmosphere. In the mornings, free coffee is available from the small lobby lounge, where you have a view of a small courtyard garden. As with most *minshuku,* the Japanese-style rooms—nicely done with natural woods and artwork—are without private bathrooms, but the communal baths are large and include tiny outdoor tubs, one ceramic and one wood.

58 Tenshoji-machi, Takayama, Gifu Prefecture 506-0832. © **0577/32-3756.** Fax 0577/35-2350. www.takayama-yamakyu.com. 20 units (all with toilet and sink only). ¥7,980 per person. Rates include 2 meals. No credit cards. Station: Takayama (20 min.). Walk straight up San-machi Suji. **Amenities:** Rental bikes (¥500 per day or ¥300 per half-day); lobby computer w/free Internet. *In room:* A/C, TV.

INEXPENSIVE

Minshuku Sosuke ★   The entryway of this friendly *minshuku* is filled with country knickknacks and has an *irori* (open hearth) in the communal room, where you can warm yourself on chilly days and where guests (85% foreigners) gather to chat in the evening. Although the building housing the minshuku is 180 years old (moved here from a village) and some of the original atmosphere has been preserved, the inside has been remodeled, and all the *tatami* rooms, though simple, are clean and are nonsmoking. Note, however, that some have skylights, and morning arrives awfully early in summer. Also, though it's not far from the station, it's in the opposite direction from the town center, making it less convenient for sightseeing. On the plus side, the owner, who speaks English, will pick you up from the station if he's not busy, and the Green Hotel across the street rents bicycles. Generous meals feature local specialties, with vegetarian choices available if requested in advance.

1–64 Okamoto-cho, Takayama, Gifu Prefecture 506-0054. www.irori-sosuke.com. ☎ **0577/32-0818.** Fax 0577/33-5570. 13 units, none with bathroom. ¥5,040 per person. Japanese dinner ¥2,100–¥4,725 extra; Western or Japanese breakfast ¥735 extra. No credit cards. Station: Takayama (8 min. west). Turn right out of the station onto the main street and then take the 1st right (at the T intersection); it's past the bridge over the tracks, on the right side of the street across from the Green Hotel. **Amenities:** Lobby computer w/free Internet. *In room:* A/C, TV, no phone.

Rickshaw Inn ★★ ☺   In a modern house in a central location, Rickshaw Inn (entirely nonsmoking) is welcoming, due in no small part to the friendly owner, Setoyama Eiko, a Takayama native who lived in the United States and speaks flawless English. A communal living room—with sofas, TV, and newspapers—is a good place to relax with fellow guests. No dinner is served, but Eiko-san can recommend restaurants (ask for her map) and is knowledgeable about museums, crafts, and Takayama's history. Japanese- and Western-style rooms, with sinks or bathrooms, feature Asian artwork and batik shades to block out light. Some Japanese rooms are big enough for three or four people, but best for families or longer stays are the two suites with *tatami* sleeping areas and bathrooms: the Bamboo suite with a kitchenette, table, and chairs; and Sakura with a large living area complete with two sofas, large-screen TV, table, and chairs.

54 Suehiro-cho, Takayama, Gifu Prefecture 506-0016. www.rickshawinn.com. ☎ **0577/32-2890.** Fax 0577/32-2469. 11 units, 8 with bathroom. ¥4,200 single without bathroom; ¥8,900–¥10,200 double without bathroom, ¥11,900 double with bathroom. Suites from ¥19,500 triple; ¥22,000 quad. Western breakfast ¥800 extra. MC, V. Station: Takayama (6 min. east), just off Kokubunji St. **Amenities:** Communal kitchen. *In room:* A/C, TV, Internet, no phone.

Super Hotel Hida Takayama ⚑   Super Hotel is a burgeoning chain offering super-cheap small rooms with few amenities. This one, near the train station and popular with business travelers, is in a modern—if rather stark—building. After checking in via automated machine, you'll pick up a *yukata* and your preferred pillow type from a shelf by the elevator. Other than its rates and location, the only bonus to staying here is its one hot-spring bath, which alternates open hours between the sexes, and coin laundry. Note that rooms must be vacated from 10am to 3pm for cleaning.

4–76 Temmacho, Takayama, Gifu Prefecture 506-0025. www.superhotel.co.jp. ☎ **0577/32-9000.** Fax 0577/32-9090. 77 units. ¥5,480 single; ¥7,980 double. Rates include Japanese breakfast. No credit cards. Station: Takayama (2 min.). Turn right out of the station onto the main street and take the 1st left. **Amenities:** Lobby computer w/free Internet; hot-spring baths. *In room:* A/C, TV, fridge, Internet, no phone.

RURAL SHIRAKAWA-GO & OGIMACHI ★

555km (347 miles) NW of Tokyo

With its thatched-roof farmhouses, paddies trimmed with flower beds, roaring river, and pine-covered mountains rising on all sides, **Shirakawa-go** is one of the most picturesque regions in Japan. Unfortunately, it also has more than its fair share of tour buses (especially in May, Aug, and Oct), with about 1.8 million visitors annually. Still, because of its rather remote location, accessible only by car or bus, Shirakawa-go remains off the beaten path for many foreign tourists. A visit to this rural region in Gifu Prefecture could well be the highlight of your trip.

Although Shirakawa-go stretches about 39km (24 miles) beside the Shokawa River and covers 229 sq. km (88 sq. miles), mountains and forest account for 95% of the region, and Shirakawa-go's 1,800 residents and cultivated land are squeezed into a valley averaging less than 3km (2 miles) in width. Thus, land in Shirakawa-go for growing rice and other crops has always been scarce and valuable. As a result, farmhouses were built large enough to hold extended families, with as many as several dozen family members living under one roof. Because there wasn't enough land available for young couples to marry and build houses of their own, only the eldest son was allowed to marry; the other children were required to spend their lives living with their parents and helping with the farming. But even though younger children weren't allowed to marry, a man was allowed to choose a young woman, visit her in her parents' home, and father her children. The children then remained with the mother's family, becoming valuable members of the labor force.

Before the roads came to Shirakawa-go, winter always meant complete isolation as snow 2m (6 ft.) deep blanketed the entire region. *Irori* (open-hearth fireplaces) in the middle of a communal room were used for cooking, warmth, and light during the long winter months. The family lived, therefore, on the ground floor, while upper floors were used for silk cultivation and storage of utensils. Because of the heavy snowfall, thatched roofs were constructed at steep angles, known as *gassho-zukuri* in reference to the fact that the tops of the roofs look like hands joined in prayer. The steep angle also allowed rain to run off quickly, and the thatch (Japanese pampas grass) dried quickly in the sun, preventing decay. Remarkably, the massive homes were constructed without nails; rather, sturdy ropes held the framework together and helped withstand earthquakes. Because there were no chimneys, smoke from the irori simply rose into the levels above, helping to ward off insects in the thatch and to keep the ropes taut.

Today, there are about 114 thatched farmhouses, barns, and sheds in Shirakawa-go, most of them built about 200 to 300 years ago. The thatched roofs are about .6m (2 ft.) thick and last some 40 years. The old roofs are replaced in Shirakawa-go every April, when one to four roofs are changed on successive weekends. The entire process involves about 200 people, who can replace one roof in a couple of days.

Shirakawa-go's inhabitants live in several small villages. Of these, **Ogimachi ★★★**, declared a UNESCO World Cultural and Natural Heritage site in 1995, boasts the greatest concentration of thatched-roof buildings. With just 600 residents, it's a delightful hamlet of narrow lanes winding past thatched-roof farmhouses, which stand like island sentinels surrounded by paddies. Many of the farmhouses have been turned into *minshuku*, souvenir shops, restaurants, and museums, including an **open-air museum** that depicts life in the region before roads opened it to the rest of the world.

Essentials

GETTING THERE The most common way to reach Ojimachi is by **bus** from Takayama, which takes about 1 hour and costs ¥2,400. There are usually seven departures from Takayama (⌾ **0577/32-1688**) daily (less frequently in winter; heavy winter snowfall sometimes renders the road impassable). From Kanazawa, a bus operates thrice daily; the fare is ¥1,800 for the 1¼-hour trip. In any case, buses arrive at a parking lot next to the Gassho Zukuri Minka-en open-air museum (see below); *minshuku* are located in the village on the other side of the river, reached via pedestrian suspension bridge.

VISITOR INFORMATION There's a **tourist office** (⌾ **05769/6-1013**; daily 8:30am–5pm) located next to the bus parking lot. You can pick up an English-language map, reserve a room in a *minshuku* if you have not already done so, and store luggage here for ¥300 if it won't fit in any of the adjacent lockers. There's a second tourist office across the river on the main road in the center of town, open daily 9am to 5pm. For information online, go to www.shirakawa-go.org/english/index.html.

GETTING AROUND Your own two feet can do it best. You can **walk** from one end of the village to the other in about 15 minutes; English-language signs direct you to the various attractions.

Seeing the Sights in & Around Ogimachi

In addition to an open-air museum, several old farmhouses in Ogimachi are open to the public. *Note:* Because Ogimachi is so small, no addresses are given in this section. This is a very small village, basically just one main street and some side streets.

Doburoku Matsuri no Yakata (**Festival Hall** どぶろく祭の館) MUSEUM This Festival Hall was erected in honor of the Doburoku Matsuri Festival held in Shirakawa-go every year from October 14 to October 19. Centering on locally produced, potent sake, the festival is held just outside the museum's grounds at Hachimanjinja Shrine. If you've never seen a Japanese festival, you might want to come here to see some of the costumes worn during the festival, sample the festive sake, and watch a 20-minute video of the yearly festivities and folk dancing.

⌾ **05769/6-1655.** Admission ¥300 adults, ¥100 junior-high and elementary students. Daily 9am–5pm. Closed Oct 13–16 and Dec–Mar.

 A View of Ogimachi

For an overview (and the best vantage point for photographs) of the entire village, walk along the gently sloping road that leads from the north side of Ogimachi to the **Shiroyama Viewing Point ★★**. There's a souvenir shop/restaurant here, but the best thing to do is to turn left at the crest of the hill and walk to the hill's westernmost point (toward the river), where there are some secluded benches. From here, you'll have a marvelous view of the entire valley. If you're thirsty or hungry, go to the restaurant (also with an outdoor viewing point) to buy a drink or a snack and then take it with you to the lookout.

Gassho Zukuri Minka-en ★★★ MUSEUM To see how rural people lived in centuries past, visit Shirakawa-go's top attraction, this open-air museum with 25 *gassho-zukuri* houses and sheds that were relocated mostly from Kazura village and restored here. Filled with the tools of everyday life and displays ranging from silk production to straw clothing, the buildings are picturesquely situated around ponds, paddies, flower beds, and streams, a photographer's dream. You can occasionally see artisans engage in traditional handicrafts here, and a DVD depicts rural life almost 50 years ago in Kazura, abandoned in 1967. You'll easily spend an hour here.

☏ **05769/6-1231.** Admission ¥500 adults, ¥300 children 7–15. Mar–Nov daily 8:40am–5pm; Dec–Feb 9am–4pm (closed Thurs Dec–Mar; if Thurs is a holiday, it remains open but closes Wed instead). Beside the bus parking lot and tourist office.

Nagase Ke (長瀬家) ★★ Of several homes open to the public, this is my favorite. Built in 1890 using 150- to 200-year-old cypress and 300- to 400-year-old chestnut, the Nagase house is the largest home here, once housing 44 people (a few members of the Nagase family still live here). The enormous cross beam is 18m (59 ft.) long and the height of the house is more than 17m (55 ft.) high. A 15-minute video shows the 2001 rethatching in which 500 people took part, including 40 women involved just in cooking meals for the workers. Because the Nagase ancestors were the personal doctors of the powerful Maeda lords, the house contains gifts from the Maedas as well as medical tools. Like other homes, it also contains a family altar, this one 500 years old and adjoined to the house so it could be quickly removed in case of fire. Upstairs is a mezzanine where 17 laborers lived, while the next level displays various tools used for everything from making rope to making cloth; in this remote area, almost everything people used was handmade. The fourth floor, where silk production once took place, contains tools related to the business, including flat trays where the silk worms were bred.

☏ **05769/6-1047.** Admission ¥300 adults, ¥150 children. Daily 9am–5pm. Occasionally closed. Just north of the main street.

Wada Ke (和田家) ★ This thatched-roof home is Ogimachi's finest—not surprising, as it belonged to the wealthy Wada family, which served as the region's top officials. Still occupied by the Wada family, the 300-year-old house boasts carved transoms, painted sliding doors, lacquerware passed down through generations, a family altar, and *tatami* rooms overlooking a private garden. Upstairs you can see how the heavy roof beams are held together using only rope (no nails were used), as well as containers once used in silkworm cultivation.

☏ **05769/6-1058.** Admission ¥300 adults, ¥150 children. Daily 9am–5pm. Occasionally closed. Just north of the main street.

Where to Stay & Eat

Because huge extended families living under one roof are a thing of the past, many residents of Ogimachi have turned their *gassho-zukuri* homes into *minshuku*. Staying in one gives you the unique chance to lodge in a thatched farmhouse with a family that might consist of grandparents, parents, and children. English is often limited to the basics of "bath," "breakfast," and "dinner," but smiles go a long way. Most likely, the family will drag out their family album with its pictures of winter snowfall and the momentous occasion when their thatched roof was repaired. What I like best about staying overnight is that most tourists (about 4,900 on average daily) are day-trippers, which means you have the village pretty much to yourself by late afternoon. Be sure to take both an evening and early morning stroll.

Most *minshuku* are fairly small, with about four to nine *tatami* rooms open to guests. Rooms are basic without bathroom or toilet, and you may be expected to roll out your own futon. Privacy may be limited, as only a flimsy sliding partition may separate you from the guest next door. All recommended minshuku below are in thatch-roofed homes; rates include breakfast and dinner (add ¥400 in winter—about Nov–Mar—for heating charges), and none accept credit cards or have private bathrooms. Check-in is at 3pm; checkout is 9am. The tourist office can make a reservation for you at these or any of the others around town.

Although all minshuku have public baths, I like soaking in the indoor and outdoor hot-spring baths at **Shirakawa-go no Onsen** (白川郷の温泉; ✆ **05769/6-0026**). Open daily from 7am to 9:30pm, it charges ¥700 for adults and ¥300 for children, but ask your minshuku for a ¥200 discount coupon. If you didn't bring your own towel, you can buy or rent one here.

Juemon (十右エ門) ★　Juemon is a favorite among foreigners traveling in Japan. This attractive *minshuku,* in a 270-year-old farmhouse, features a stone-ringed pond with flowering shrubs and a couple of benches where you can relax and enjoy the view. In addition, there's an *irori* in the dining room; don't be surprised if the outgoing 70-something Mrs. Sakai who runs this place serenades you during dinner with a *shamisen* and folk songs.

Shirakawa Mura, 1653 Ogimachi, Ono-gun, Gifu Prefecture 501-5627. ✆ **05769/6-1053.** 6 units, none with bathroom. ¥8,700 per person. No credit cards. A 15-min. walk from the bus stop, on the south edge of Ogimachi past Doburoku Festival Hall.

Koemon (幸エ門) ★★　This is my top choice for accommodations. English-speaking Otani Shoji is the fifth-generation innkeeper of this 200-year-old farmhouse, which became a *minshuku* 30 years ago and has been modernized with a heated floor, automatic sensor lights, communal Washlet toilets, and even dim switches to enhance the mood around his *irori* fireplace, where you'll have your meals and watch a video during dinner showing the rethatching of the farmhouse. Rooms are spotless, with the best one facing a pond. If you have heavy luggage, you'll be happy to know that this one is closest to the bus terminal.

Shirakawa Mura, 456 Ogimachi, Ono-gun, Gifu Prefecture 501-5627. ✆ **05769/6-1446.** Fax 05769/6-1748. 4 units, none with bathroom. ¥8,400 per person. No credit cards. A 3-min. walk from the bus stop, just over the footbridge.

Ochiudo (落人)　Because minshuku provide dinner and breakfast, all you'll probably need is lunch. With its small front porch overlooking a paddy and welcoming old-fashioned interior in a thatched house, this tea and coffee shop makes for a relaxing place for a snack or light meal. It's owned by charming Miyako-san (whose husband is from the Nagase family; see above), who lets you choose your own cup for tea or coffee and offers a yummy daily curry for ¥1,000 that strays from the usual (with, for example, asparagus), along with a few other healthy choices.

✆ **090/5458-0418.** Main dishes ¥800–¥1,000. No credit cards. Daily 10am–5pm (to 6pm in summer if there are customers). In the middle of Shirakawa Mura, near the Kanda House.

Shimizu (志みづ)   On the edge of town, mercifully far from the tourist crowds and souvenir shops, this small *minshuku* is a good choice for travelers who desire more privacy than that afforded living with a family, as the owner, who speaks some English, lives in the house next door. There's a communal room with an *irori,* where you can serve yourself coffee and tea. Although you can stay here without opting for meals, note that dinner options in the village are minimal. Another plus: If your luggage is heavy or walking is difficult because of heavy rain or snow, the owner can come to the bus terminal to pick you up.

Shirakawa Mura, 2613 Ogimachi, Ono-gun, Gifu Prefecture 501-5627. www.shimizuinn.com. ℂ **05769/6-1914.** Fax 05769/6-1924. 3 units, none with bathroom. ¥8,400 per person with meals; ¥5,900 per person without meals. No credit cards. A 15-min. walk from the bus stop, on the south edge of Ogimachi past Doburoku Festival Hall.

KYOTO & NARA

I f you go to only one place in all of Japan, Kyoto ★★★ should be it. Not only is it the most historically significant town in the nation, this former capital was also the only major Japanese city spared from the bombs of World War II. It's filled with temples, shrines, imperial palaces, gardens, and *machiya* (traditional wooden houses), but what makes it exceptional are scenes from daily life. Spend a few days exploring Kyoto's back streets and neighborhoods, and you'll probably agree that Kyoto is Japan's most romantic city.

Things to Do No fewer than 17 UNESCO World Heritage Sites are located in Kyoto Prefecture, including Kiyomizu Temple, Kinkakuji, Ginkakuji, Ryoanji Temple, Nijo Castle, and Byodoin Temple. Throw in offbeat attractions like the Kyoto International Manga Museum and shops selling some of the nation's finest crafts, and it's easy to see why Kyoto tops the list on any visit to Japan. For more history, head to nearby Nara, an ancient capital even older than Kyoto and famous for its Great Buddha.

Shopping Traditional arts and crafts thrive in Kyoto, where skills are passed down from generation to generation. Home to the nation's greatest concentration of craft artisans, Kyoto boasts specialty shops dealing in textiles, dyed fabrics, pottery, bambooware, cutlery, fans, metalwork, umbrellas, and more. Other favorite haunts are the souvenir shops lining the slope leading to Koyomizu Temple and Kyoto's many markets, including the nation's oldest market at Toji Temple.

Restaurants & Dining Home to the imperial court for 1,000 years, Kyoto is famous for its own style of kaiseki, which blends ceremonial court cuisine with Zen vegetarian food. Some restaurants are more than 300 years old and serve elaborate meals fit for an emperor, but you'll also find plenty of less expensive eateries catering to younger diners, no surprise since the city is home also to Kyoto University.

Nightlife & Entertainment Kyoto is famous for its geisha, and you might catch a glimpse of them as they hurry to their evening appointments in Gion decked out in all their finery. Afterward, head to nearby Pontocho, a narrow pedestrian lane lined with a dazzling collection of restaurants and bars. If it's a warm night, end the evening by sitting along the banks of the Kamo River, popular with Kyoto's young couples. Best of all, these places are all within easy walking distance of each other.

THE BEST KYOTO EXPERIENCES

o **Spending a Night in a Ryokan** Kyoto is one of the best places in Japan to experience a traditional Japanese inn, where you'll sleep on a futon in a *tatami* room and be treated to a beautifully presented multicourse *kaiseki* feast, perhaps with a view of your own private garden. Though expensive, it's the utmost in simple elegance and well worth the splurge.

o **Dining on a Tofu Vegetarian Meal in a Garden Setting** *Shojin ryori*, vegetarian meals served at Buddhist temples, are one of Kyoto's specialties. There are a number of rustic restaurants with outdoor garden seating throughout Kyoto.

o **Visiting a Japanese Garden** Kyoto has a wide range of traditional gardens, from austerely beautiful Zen rock gardens used by Buddhist priests for meditation to the miniature bonsai-like landscape gardens of the ruling classes.

o **Strolling Through Eastern Kyoto** Temples, shrines, gardens, craft shops, traditional neighborhoods—these are highlights of a day spent walking through this historic part of Kyoto. You won't find a slice of old Japan like this in other Japanese cities. See p. 259.

o **Seeing How the Upper Class Lived** Kyoto has more imperial palaces and villas than any other Japanese city. Walk through the shogun's digs at Nijo Castle and if you have time, visit the Kyoto Imperial Palace, Katsura Imperial Villa, or Shugakuin Imperial Villa with their splendid gardens. See p. 257, 264, and 265.

ESSENTIALS

Getting There

FROM KANSAI AIRPORT If you arrive in Japan at Kansai International Airport (KIX) outside Osaka, the **JR Haruka Super Express train** has direct service every 30 minutes to Kyoto Station. The trip takes approximately 75 minutes and costs ¥3,290 for a reserved seat (recommended during busy departure times or peak season) and ¥2,980 for a nonreserved seat, or you can ride free with your JR Rail Pass. A cheaper, though slower and less convenient, alternative is the JR Kanku Kaisoku, which departs every 30 minutes or so from Kansai Airport and arrives in Kyoto 1 hour and 40 minutes later, with a change at Osaka Station. It costs ¥1,830.

If you have lots of luggage, consider taking the **Kansai Airport Limousine Bus** (www.kate.co.jp; ℓ **075/682-4400**) from Kansai Airport; buses depart every hour or less for the 1¾-hour trip to Kyoto Station and cost ¥2,500. More convenient but costlier are **shared-ride vans,** operated by local taxi companies **MK** (www.mk-group.co.jp; ℓ **075/778-5489**) and **Yasaka** (www.yasaka.jp; ℓ **075/803-4800**), which deliver passengers to any hotel or home in Kyoto for ¥3,500, including one suitcase (a second suitcase costs ¥1,000); make reservations 2 days in advance.

FROM ITAMI AIRPORT If you're arriving on a domestic flight at Itami Airport, the Airport Bus takes 1 hour to Kyoto Station and costs ¥1,280.

BY TRAIN FROM ELSEWHERE IN JAPAN Kyoto is a major stop on the Shinkansen bullet train; trip time from **Tokyo** is 2½ hours, with the fare for a nonreserved seat ¥12,710 one-way. Kyoto is only 15 minutes from Shin-Osaka, but you may find it more convenient to take one of the local commuter lines that connect Kyoto directly with Osaka Station in 30 minutes. From **Kobe,** you can reach Kyoto from Sannomiya and Motomachi stations on local JR trains. The strikingly modern **Kyoto Station,** which is like a city in itself with tourist offices, restaurants, a hotel, a department store, a shopping arcade, a theater, and stage events, is connected to the rest of the city by subway and bus.

BY BUS FROM TOKYO   Lots of buses travel between Tokyo and Kyoto; reservations are necessary. **JR Highway buses** (www.jrbuskanto.co.jp; ✆ 03/3844-1950) depart both day and night from Tokyo Station's Yaesu South Exit, arriving at Kyoto Station approximately 8 hours later and costing ¥6,000 to ¥8,300 depending on the bus and time of day. Tickets can be purchased at any major JR station or a travel agency like JTB. In addition, **Willer Express** (willerexpress.com; ✆ 050/5805-0383) buses depart Tokyo, Shinjuku, and Shinagawa stations nightly, arriving at Kyoto Station the next morning. Regular fares start at ¥4,900 for most trips but can vary depending on the date and type of seat selected (tickets purchased online 14 days in advance cost less; reclining seats cost more).

Visitor Information

The **Kyoto Tourist Information Center** (✆ 075/343-0548; daily 8:30am–7pm), on the second floor of Kyoto Station near the ticket gate and Isetan department store, has city and bus maps. There's also a **Tourist Information Counter** at the Kyoto Handicraft Center (p. 280), and you can find free English-language maps of Kyoto at hotels, 7-Eleven or Starbucks.

ON THE WEB   Kyoto city's website is www.kyoto.travel. Kyoto Prefecture's website is www.pref.kyoto.jp/visitkyoto/en.

PUBLICATIONS   A monthly tabloid distributed free at hotels and restaurants is the *Kyoto Visitor's Guide* (www.kyotoguide.com), with maps, a calendar of events, and information on sightseeing and shopping. *Kansai Scene* (www.kansaiscene.com) is a monthly giveaway with information on nightlife, festivals, and other events in Osaka, Kobe, Kyoto and Nara.

City Layout

Most of Kyoto's attractions and hotels are north of Kyoto Station (take the Central exit), spreading like a fan toward the northeast and northwest. The **northern and eastern edges** of the city contain the most famous temples. The heart of the city is in **central Kyoto (Nakagyo-ku ward),** which boasts the largest concentration of restaurants, shops, and bars and which radiates outward from the intersection of Kawaramachi Dori and Shijo Dori. It includes a narrow street called Pontocho, a nightlife mecca that runs along the western bank of the Kamo River. Across the Kamo River to the east is the ancient geisha district of Gion.

FINDING AN ADDRESS   Kyoto's streets are laid out in a grid pattern with named streets (a rarity in Japan) and an address system that's actually quite easy to understand once you get to know the directional terms. The major streets north of Kyoto Station that run east-west are numbered; for example, *shi* means four and *dori* means avenue, so Shijo Dori means "Fourth Avenue." *Agaru* equates to "to the north," *sagaru* to "to the south," *nishi-iru* means "to the west," and *higashi-iru* means "to the east." Thus, an address that reads Shijo-agaru, Teramachi Higashi-iru means "north of Fourth Avenue, east of Teramachi."

On non-numbered streets, addresses generally indicate cross streets. Take the Hotel Monterey, for example: Its address is Karasuma Dori, Sanjo-sagaru, which tells you that the hotel is just south of the intersection of Karasuma Dori and Sanjo Dori. Complete addresses include the ward, or *ku*, such as Higashiyama-ku.

Kyoto's Neighborhoods in Brief

The following are Kyoto's main tourist areas; to locate them, see the "Kyoto" map on p. 286.

Around Kyoto Station The southern ward of **Shimogyo-ku,** which stretches from Kyoto Station north to Shijo Dori Avenue, caters to tourists with its cluster of hotels and to commuters with its shops and restaurants. Kyoto Station, which caused quite a controversy when built because of its size, height, and futuristic appearance, is now this area's top attraction with Isetan department store, a shopping arcade, restaurants, and dramatic public spaces, including a rooftop plaza.

Central Kyoto Nakagyo-ku, the central part of Kyoto west of the Kamo River and north of Shimogyo-ku, embraces Kyoto's main shopping and nightlife districts, with most of the action on **Kawaramachi Dori** and **Shijo Dori** and **Teramachi** and **Shin-kyogoku** covered shopping arcades. Most of Kyoto's legendary craft stores are located here, along with numerous restaurants and bars. Home also to **Nijo Castle,** Nakagyo-ku has a number of exclusive *ryokan* tucked away in delightful neighborhoods typical of old Kyoto. But downtown is changing fast, as Kyoto's younger generation lays claim to new shopping and entertainment complexes, such as **Shin-Puh-Kan,** a renovated telephone company building on Karasuma Dori with shops and an open stage for concerts, and **Kyoto International Manga Museum,** housed in a former elementary school. Nakagyo-ku is one of the most desirable places to stay in terms of convenience and atmosphere.

Pontocho, a narrow lane that parallels the Kamo River's western bank just a stone's throw from the Kawaramachi-Shijo Dori intersection, is Kyoto's most famous street for nightlife. It's lined with bars and restaurants that boast outdoor verandas extending over the Kamo River in summer. Paralleling Pontocho to the east is Kiyamachi, a narrow lane beside a canal lined with bars and restaurants popular with the young.

Eastern Kyoto Eastern Kyoto is a great area for walking, shopping, and sightseeing. East of the Kamo River, the wards of **Higashiyama-ku** and **Sakyo-ku** boast a number of the city's most famous temples and shrines, as well as restaurants specializing in Kyoto cuisine and Buddhist vegetarian dishes, and shops selling local pottery and other crafts. **Gion,** Kyoto's most famous geisha entertainment district, is part of Higashiyama-ku. Customers are entertained in traditional wooden geisha houses that are not open to the public (you can only gain entry through introductions provided by someone who is already a customer)—but the area makes for a fascinating stroll.

Northern Kyoto Embracing the **Kita-ku, Kamigyo-ku,** and **Ukyo-ku** wards, northern Kyoto is primarily residential but contains a number of Kyoto's top sights, including the Kyoto Imperial Palace, Kinkakuji (Temple of the Golden Pavilion), and Ryoanji Temple, site of Kyoto's most famous Zen rock garden.

GETTING AROUND

Kyoto is Japan's most visitor-friendly city, with lots of English-language signs and an easy-to-navigate transportation system.

BY PUBLIC TRANSPORTATION Kyoto's subway and bus networks are efficient and quite easy to use. For more information, stop by the **Bus and Subway Information counter** in front of Kyoto Station to the right of the bus platforms

(**© 075/371-4474;** daily 7:30am–8pm) or check online at www.city.kyoto.lg.jp/kotsu. One of the best ways to explore Kyoto, however, is by foot.

BY SUBWAY   Kyoto has two subway lines, with stops announced in English. The older **Karasuma Line** runs north and south, from Takeda in the south to Kokusai Kaikan in the north, with stops at Kyoto Station and Imadegawa Station (convenient for visiting the Imperial Palace). The newer **Tozai Line** runs in a curve from east to west and is convenient for visiting Nijo Castle and Higashiyama-ku. The two lines intersect in central Kyoto at Karasuma Oike Station (if you find station names cumbersome, go by their numbers; Karasuma Oike, for example, is both K08 on the Karasuma Line and T13 on the Tozai Line). Fares start at ¥210 (children pay half fare) and service runs from about 5:30am to 11:30pm. In addition to subways, the private Keihan Railway runs north-south along the Kamo River on the east side of town and is convenient to Gion and some hotels. Although buses usually get you closer to where you want to go, I sometimes opt for the subway even if I have to walk a bit, simply to avoid hassling with buses and their unknown stops.

BY BUS   The most direct way to get to most of Kyoto's attractions is by bus. Buses depart from Kyoto Station's Central (north/Karasuma) exit, with platforms clearly marked in English listing destinations. Both the Kyoto Tourist Information Center (see "Visitor Information," above) and the Bus and Subway Information counter give out excellent maps showing major bus routes. Some of the buses loop around the city, while others go back and forth between two destinations. Most convenient for sightseeing is Raku bus no. 100 (some of which look like old-fashioned trolleys), which makes a run every 10 minutes from Kyoto Station to major attractions in east Kyoto, including the Kyoto National Museum, Gojo-zaka (the approach to Kiyomizu Temple), Gion, Heian Shrine, Nanzenji, and Ginkakuji. Raku bus no. 101 departs Kyoto Station for Nijo Castle and Kinkakuji, while Raku bus no. 102 cuts across north Kyoto and connects Ginkakuji and Kinkakuji.

The fare for traveling in central Kyoto is ¥220 for a single ride. Board the bus at the rear entrance and pay when you get off (the fare box can make change). If the bus is traveling a **long distance** out to the suburbs, there will be a ticket machine right beside the back door—take the ticket and hold onto it. It has a number on it and will tell the bus driver when you got on and how much you owe. You can see for yourself how much you owe by looking for your number on a lighted panel at the front of the bus; the longer you stay on the bus, the higher the fare.

TRANSIT PASSES   If you think you'll be doing a lot of sightseeing in 1 or 2 days, it may pay to buy a pass. A **city bus all-day pass** costs ¥500. **Passes for both buses and subways** cost ¥1,200 for 1 day or ¥2,000 for 2 days and are available at subway stations or the Bus and Subway Information counter at Kyoto Station. Alternatively, the prepaid Traffica Kyoto Card gives a 10% discount off fares, can be used for city buses and subways, and is available in values of ¥1,000 and ¥3,000; because there's no time limit, it's convenient if you're staying in Kyoto for several days and don't want to fumble for change each ride.

For journeys farther afield, the **Kansai Thru Pass** (**Surutto Kansai;** www.surutto.com) allows foreigners (you must show your passport) to ride subways, private railways (no JR trains), and buses throughout Kansai, including Osaka, Kyoto, Kobe, Nara, Himeji, and Mount Koya, with a 2-day pass costing ¥3,800 and a 3-day pass costing ¥5,000. Children pay half-price. You would have to do quite a bit of traveling to make this worthwhile. It's available at the Kansai International Airport's Travel

Desk (first floor international arrivals) or at the **Bus and Subway Information counter** in front of Kyoto Station.

BY TAXI Taxis in Kyoto come in two different sizes with only slightly different fares. Small ones are ¥660 for the first 2km (1¼ miles), and large ones are ¥710. Taxis can be waved down or, in the city center, boarded at marked taxi stands or at hotels. **MK Taxi** (www.mk-group.co.jp; ✆ **075/757-6212**) also offers individualized English-language guided tours.

BY BICYCLE A popular way to get around Kyoto is by bike, made easy because there are few hills and because most streets are named. During peak season, you might even be faster on a bike than a bus. However, you do have to be on guard for vehicular traffic. **Kyoto Cycling Tour Project,** a 3-minute walk from the Central (north) Exit of Kyoto Station (turn left upon exiting the station and walk past the post office and APA Hotel; www.kctp.net; ✆ **075/354-3636**), open daily 9am to 7pm, rents bikes beginning at ¥1,000 a day, including a cycling map of the city. It also offers guided cycling tours.

[FastFACTS] KYOTO

In addition to the information here, see "Fast Facts: Japan" in chapter 14. You can also make inquiries at one of the tourist offices (see "Visitor Information," above) or the **Kyoto City International Foundation** (www.kcif.or.jp; ✆ **075/752-3010**), which provides information in English for people living in Japan and some tourist information. It's open Tuesday to Sunday from 9am to 9pm.

Area Code If you're calling a Kyoto number from outside Kyoto but within Japan, the area code for Kyoto is 075. For calls within Kyoto, don't dial the area code.

ATMS/Banks In addition to banks, places to exchange money after banks close are large department stores like Isetan, Takashimaya, and Daimaru, and the Kyoto Handicraft Center (p. 280). You can also exchange money at the World Currency Shop on the eighth floor of Isetan at Kyoto Station (✆ **075/365-7750**), open Monday to Friday 11am to 5pm. When changing money, be sure to bring your passport. The most convenient ATMs accepting foreign credit cards are at Kyoto Central Post Office next to Kyoto Station (see "Mail," below) or at one of many 7-Eleven convenience stores in Kyoto.

Climate Kyoto is generally hotter and more humid than Tokyo in summer and colder than Tokyo in winter. For more information, see "When to Go," in chapter 2.

Electricity In both Kyoto and Nara it's 100 volts, 60 cycles, almost the same as in the United States (110 volts, 60 cycles); your two-pronged appliances should work, but they'll run a little slowly (there are no three-pronged plugs in Japan).

Hospitals Most hospitals are not equipped to handle emergencies 24 hours a day, but a system has been set up in which hospitals handle emergencies on a rotating basis. Hospitals in Kyoto include **Japan Baptist Hospital (Nihon Baputesuto Byoin),** north of Kikage, east of Shirakawa, Sakyo-ku (✆ 075/781-5191), **Kyoto University Hospital (Kyoto Daigaku Byoin),** Shogoin Kawahara-cho, Sakyo-ku (www.kuhp.kyoto-u.ac.jp/english; ✆ 075/751-3111), and **Kyoto Municipal Hospital (Kyoto Shiritsu Byoin),** Gojo Dori Onmae, Nakagyo-ku (✆ 075/311-5311). There's also a **holiday emergency clinic** on Shichihonmatsu Street, north of Marutamachi (✆ 075/811-5072). For less urgent care, **Sakabe International Clinic,** Gokomachi, Nijo-sagaru, Nakagyo-ku (✆ 075/231-1624), has an

English-speaking staff. In addition, the **Kyoto City International Foundation** (✆ 075/752-3010) has information on English-speaking doctors and dentists.

Internet Access **Media Café Popeye** has two locations in central Kyoto: next to the Kyoto Royal Hotel & Spa at Sanjo Kawaramachi (✆ **075/253-5300**) and just north of Shijo Dori and east of Teramachi, above a United Colors of Benetton shop (✆ **075/257-5512;** entrance around the back). Both are open 24 hours and charge ¥420 for 1 hour, with discounts for additional hours.

Luggage Storage & Lockers Kyoto Station has lockers for storing luggage beginning at ¥300 for 24 hours, including lockers large enough for big suitcases (¥600) on its south (Shinkansen) side.

Mail The **Kyoto Central Post Office,** located just west of Kyoto Station's Central (north) Exit (✆ **075/365-2471**), is open Monday to Friday 9am to 9pm, Saturday 9am to 7pm, Sunday and holidays 9am to 7pm. You can mail packages bound for international destinations here. To the south

of the Central Post Office's main entrance is a counter offering 24-hour postal service; stamps for letters are also sold from vending machines. There are also ATMs here, where you can obtain currency Monday to Saturday from 5 minutes past midnight to 11:55pm, Sundays and holidays 5 minutes past midnight to 8pm, and consecutive holidays (for example, 3-day weekends) 7am to 8pm.

Police The national emergency telephone number is ✆ **110.**

EXPLORING KYOTO

As Japan's seventh-largest city with a population of about 1.5 million people, Kyoto hasn't escaped the afflictions of the modern age. In fact, if you arrive in Kyoto by train, your first reaction is likely to be great disappointment. There's Kyoto Tower looming in the foreground like some misplaced spaceship. Kyoto Station itself is strikingly modern and unabashedly high tech, looking as though it was airlifted straight from Tokyo. Modern buildings and hotels surround the station on all sides, making Kyoto look like any other Japanese town.

Once you escape to Kyoto's old neighborhoods, however, you'll find yourself in an entirely different place. Kyoto boasts an astonishing 2,000 temples and shrines and 20% of Japan's National Treasures. Because there are so many worthwhile sights, you must plan your itinerary carefully. Even the most avid sightseer can become jaded after days of visiting yet another temple or shrine, no matter how beautiful or peaceful, so be sure to temper your visits to cultural and historical sites with time spent simply walking around. Kyoto is a city best seen on foot; take time to explore small alleyways and curio shops, pausing from time to time to soak in the beauty and atmosphere. If you spend your days in Kyoto racing around in a taxi or a bus from one temple to another, the essence of this ancient capital and its charm may literally pass you by.

Before setting out, be sure to stop by **Kyoto City Tourist Information** at Kyoto Station (✆ **075/344-3300**) to get a detailed map of the city, a bus map, and the *Kyoto's Visitor's Guide* (which also contains maps).

Keep in mind, too, that you must enter Kyoto's museums, shrines, and temples at least a half-hour before closing time. Listings in this section and those that follow give numbers not only for buses departing from Kyoto Station but from elsewhere as well.

For a map of Kyoto's attractions, see p. 286.

Kyoto Illuminated

When the cherry blossoms spring forth or leaves change color, several Kyoto temples are open at night, their buildings and gardens dramatically lit. It's a great way to see these wondrous spaces, literally in a different light. Ask the tourist office or concierge at your hotel for a list of temples offering "light up."

Around Kyoto Station

As strange as it sounds, the biggest tourist draw around Kyoto Station is **Kyoto Station** itself. Japan's second-largest station building (after Nagoya) is a futuristic-looking building with soaring glass atriums, space-age chimes, escalators rising to a rooftop observatory, and open stages for free concerts and other events. In a bold move to attract young Japanese (who nowadays prefer to take their vacations in more exotic or trendier climes), it also has a shopping center selling everything from clothing to Kyoto souvenirs, the fashionable Isetan department store, and restaurants galore. I see more tourists photographing Kyoto Station than any other modern building in town.

Just a 10- and 5-minute walk (respectively) north of Kyoto Station are two massive temple compounds, **Nishi-Honganji** and **Higashi-Honganji** (http://higashi honganji.or.jp). They were once joined as one huge religious center called Honganji, but they split after a disagreement several centuries ago. Higashi-Honganji is Kyoto's largest wooden structure, while Nishi-Honganji, headquarters for 12 million Shin Buddhists, is an outstanding example of Buddhist architecture. A 2-minute walk east of Higashi-Honganji is its garden, **Shosei-en** (© 075/371-2961). Once the private villa of Higashi-Honganji's abbot and designed in part by famous landscape architect Kobori Enshu in the 17th century, it features a pond and several buildings in a park-like setting. Although there are far more beautiful and grander gardens in Kyoto, it provides a nice respite if you're in the area. It's open daily 9am to 4pm, with a ¥500 "donation" expected.

For a personalized English-language tour that takes in Higashi-Honganji, a couple of shrines, a former Geisha area, and back streets of Kyoto before ending near Kiyomizu Temple, join **Johnnie Hillwalker's Kyoto Walking** (© **81/75-622-6803;** http://web.kyoto-inet.or.jp/people/h-s-love) tour, held every Monday, Wednesday, and Friday from 10am to 3:15pm March through November (no walks on national holidays). Led by Hajime Hirooka, with 50 years of guiding experience, and others, tours start from in front of Kyoto Station and cost ¥2,000 for adults, ¥1,000 for 13- to 15-year-olds, and free for children. No reservations are required; pick up his brochure at the tourist office.

Costume Museum MUSEUM   This one-room museum (above a clothing store for monks) is filled with an elaborate, quarter-size replica of the Spring Palace as immortalized by Murasaki Shikibu in *The Tale of Genji,* complete with scenes of ceremonies, rituals, and everyday court life depicted by dolls wearing gorgeous kimono and by miniature furniture and other objects of the Heian Period. The exhibit, including costumes, changes twice a year. In an adjoining room, life-size kimono and costumes can be donned for free, so be sure to bring your camera. You can see everything in about 15 minutes.

Izutsu Building, 5th floor, Shinhanayacho Dori, Horikawa Higashiiru (on the corner of Horikawa and Shinhanayacho sts. just northeast of Nishi-Honganji Temple). www.iz2.or.jp/english/index.htm. ✆ **075/342-5345.** Admission ¥400 adults, ¥300 university and high-school students, ¥200 children 7–12, children 6 and under free. Mon–Sat 9am–5pm. Closed for exhibition change June and Dec. Bus: 9 or 28 to Nishi-Honganji-mae (2 min.), or a 15-min. walk north from Kyoto Station.

Central Kyoto

Much of Central Kyoto has been taken over by the 21st century, but there are a few interesting sites worth investigating.

If you've never been to a street market in Japan, take a stroll down **Nishiki-Koji Dori,** a fish-and-produce market right in the heart of town. A covered pedestrian lane parallel to Shijo Dori to the north and stretching west from Teramachi Dori, Nishiki-Koji has been Kyoto's principal food market for more than 4 centuries. This is where the city's finest restaurants and inns buy their food; you'll find approximately 135 open-fronted shops and stalls selling seasonal vegetables, fish, beans, seaweed, and pickled vegetables, as well as crafts and cooking supplies. Shops are open from the early morning hours until about 6pm; many close on either Wednesday or Sunday.

A Look at the Past

Kyoto served as Japan's capital for more than 1,000 years, from 794 to the Meiji Restoration in 1868. Originally known as Heian-kyo, it was laid out in a grid pattern borrowed from the Chinese with streets running north, south, east, and west. Its first few hundred years—from about A.D. 800 to the 12th century—were perhaps its grandest, a time when culture blossomed and court nobility led luxurious and splendid lives dotted with poetry-composing parties and moon-gazing events. Buddhism flourished and temples were built. A number of learning institutions were set up for the sons and daughters of aristocratic families, and scholars were versed in both Japanese and Chinese.

Toward the end of the Heian Period, military clans began clashing for power as the samurai class grew more powerful, resulting in a series of civil wars that eventually pushed Japan into the Feudal Era of military government that lasted nearly 680 years—until 1868. The first shogun to rise to power was Minamoto Yoritomo, who set up his shogunate government in Kamakura. With the downfall of the Kamakura government in 1336, however, Kyoto once again

became the seat of power, home to both the imperial family and the shogun. The beginning of this era, known as the Muromachi and Azuchi-Momoyama periods, was marked by extravagant prosperity and luxury, expressed in such splendid shogun villas as Kyoto's Gold Pavilion and Silver Pavilion. Lacquerware, landscape paintings, and the art of metal engraving came into their own. Zen Buddhism was the rage, giving rise to such temples as Sai-hoji Temple and the Ryoanji rock garden. And, despite civil wars that rocked the nation in the 15th and 16th centuries and destroyed much of Kyoto, culture flourished. During these turbulent times, *noh* drama, the tea ceremony, flower arranging, and landscape gardening gradually took form.

Emerging as the victor in the civil wars, Tokugawa Ieyasu established himself as shogun and set up his military rule in Edo (presently Tokyo) far to the east. For the next 250 years, Kyoto remained the capital in name only, and in 1868 (which marked the downfall of the shogunate and the restoration of the emperor to power), the capital was officially moved from Kyoto to Tokyo.

Kyoto Imperial Palace (Kyoto Gosho) ★★ PALACE   This is where the imperial family lived from 1331 until 1868 when they moved to Tokyo. The palace was destroyed several times by fire but was always rebuilt in its original style; the present buildings date from 1855. Modestly furnished with delicate decorations, the palace shows the restful designs of the peaceful Heian Period, and the emperor's private garden is graceful. You can visit the palace only on a free, 1-hour guided tour in English, but fair warning: Tours are conducted quickly, leaving little time for dawdling or taking pictures. In addition, tours view buildings only from the outside, though they do impart interesting information on court life and palace architecture.

Kyotogyoen-nai, Karasuma-Imadegawa. http://sankan.kunaicho.go.jp/english. ✆ **075/211-1215.** Free admission. Tours in English Mon–Fri at 10am and 2pm. Closed national holidays. Permission must be obtained from the Imperial Household Agency Office, either online at least 4 days in advance or in person at palace grounds near the northeast corner, Mon–Fri 8:45am–noon and 1–5pm. Foreign visitors can apply in person in advance or on the day of the tour 20 min. before the tour starts (1-day advance application required for Sat tours), but tours can fill up (especially in spring and fall). You must be 18 or older (or accompanied by an adult) and you must present your passport. Subway: Imadegawa (exit 3); turn left and walk south on Karasuma Dori (5 min.).

Kyoto International Manga Museum ☺ MUSEUM   The lofty goal of this museum (with more 300,000 items the largest *manga* museum in the world) is to conduct research on the history and culture of manga and to preserve manga that has appeared through the ages, including historic materials produced since the Edo Period, popular contemporary Japanese works, foreign manga, animation, and other related topics. For most visitors, however, it provides an hour or so of fun, with changing exhibits and approximately 50,000 items on display at any one time. Housed in a former primary school built in 1869, it contains a very popular children's library with manga and picture books kids can enjoy, a memorial hall dedicated to the former elementary school, picture-story shows (popular before the days of TV) three times a day, a Wall of Manga with shelves upon shelves of thousands of manga you can peruse, and—my favorite—an archive that illustrates the long history of Japanese manga. On weekends, manga artists demonstrate their craft. Unfortunately, unless you can read Japanese or are a manga fanatic, you won't be able to take full advantage of this facility. But if you have children, they're likely to feel right at home.

Karasuma Oike, Nakagyo-ku. www.kyotomm.jp. ✆ **075/254-7414.** Admission ¥800 adults, ¥300 junior-high and high-school students, ¥100 children. Thurs–Tues 10am–6pm. Subway: Karasuma-Oike (1 min.).

Museum of Kyoto (Kyoto Bunka Hakubutsukan) ★ MUSEUM   Through video displays, slides, and even holograms, this museum presents Kyoto's 1,200-year history from prehistoric relics to contemporary arts and crafts. I particularly like the various architectural models depicting a local market, merchants' homes, and a wholesale store, but best of all is the vermilion-colored Heian Shrine model with its holographic display of construction workers. An annex, occupying a 1906 bank with its original main hall (complete with teller cages), houses special exhibits and events.

Unfortunately, explanations are in Japanese only, but the museum does offer free English-language guides every day from 10am to 5pm; personal tours last between 30 and 60 minutes depending on your interest (because guides are volunteers, it's a good idea to make a reservation for one). A special feature of the museum is its film library, which houses hundreds of Japanese classics from silent movies to films made up to 20 years ago (the Japanese movie industry was based in Kyoto for decades). Movies, in Japanese only and included in admission price of the museum, are shown twice a

Cultural Immersion

If you're interested in learning firsthand about the tea ceremony, flower arranging, origami, Japanese calligraphy, Japanese cooking, and other cultural pursuits, you can do so with the help of the members of the **Women's Association of Kyoto** (**WAK Japan;** www.wak japan.com; ℭ **075/212-9993**). Courses, conducted in their downtown facility and in members' homes, run 55 minutes to 1½ hours and cost ¥16,000 for one person and up, depending on the class (it's cheaper if there are 2 or more people), including pickup from your hotel. Reservations should be made up to 2 weeks in advance, if possible.

day Thursday through Sunday (at 1:30 and 5pm at last check, but confirm the time). Be sure to browse the Roji Temple Mercantile Street, a re-created merchant's quarters with shops selling crafts and souvenirs and restaurants serving typical Kyoto dishes.

At Sanjo and Takakura sts www.bunpaku.or.jp. ℭ **075/222-0888.** Admission ¥500 adults, ¥400 students, free for children. Special exhibits cost more. Tues–Sun 10am–7:30pm. Subway: Karasuma-Oike (exit 5, 3 min.).

Nijo Castle (Nijojo) ★★★ CASTLE   The Tokugawa shogun's Kyoto home stands in stark contrast to most of Japan's other remaining castles, which were constructed purely for defense. Built by the first Tokugawa shogun, Ieyasu, in 1603, Nijo Castle, a UNESCO World Heritage Site, is considered the quintessence of Momoyama architecture, built almost entirely of Japanese cypress and boasting delicate transom woodcarvings and paintings by the Kano School on sliding doors. Unfortunately, no photos are allowed.

I prefer Nijo Castle to the Imperial Palace because you can explore its interior on your own. The main building, **Ninomaru Palace,** has 33 rooms, some 800 tatami mats, and an understated elegance, especially compared with castles being built in Europe at the same time. All the sliding doors on the outside walls of the castle can be removed in summer, permitting breezes to sweep through the building. Typical for Japan at the time, rooms were unfurnished, and the mattresses were stored in closets.

One of the castle's most intriguing features is its so-called **nightingale floors.** To protect the shogun from real or imagined enemies, the castle was protected by a moat, stone walls and these special floorboards in the castle corridors, which creaked when trod upon. The nightingale floors were supplemented by hidden alcoves for bodyguards. Furthermore, only female attendants were allowed in the shogun's private living quarters. Ironically, it was from Nijo Castle that Emperor Meiji issued his 1868 decree abolishing the shogunate form of government.

Outside the castle is an extensive **garden,** designed by the renowned gardener Kobori Enshu, which is famous in its own right. The original grounds of the castle, however, were without trees—supposedly because the falling of leaves in autumn reminded the shogun and his tough samurai of life's transitory nature, making them terribly sad. Plan on spending 1½ hours here, especially if you decide to rent an audio guide for ¥500 extra, recommended because it describes the significance of what you're seeing.

Corner of Horikawa Dori and Nijo Dori. ⓒ**075/841-0096.** Admission ¥600 adults, ¥350 junior-high and high-school students, ¥200 children. Daily 8:45am–5pm (last entry 4pm). Closed Tues Dec–Jan and July–Aug. Subway: Nijojo-mae Station (1 min.). Bus: 9, 12, 50, or 101 to Nijojo-mae (1 min.).

Nishijin Textile Center (Nishijin-Ori Kaikan) ★ MUSEUM About a 10-minute walk west of the Imperial Palace is this museum dedicated to the weavers who for centuries produced elegant textiles for the imperial family and nobility. The history of Nishijin silk weaving began with the history of Kyoto itself back in 794; by the Edo Period, there were an estimated 5,000 weaving factories in the Nishijin District. Today, the district remains home to one of Japan's largest handmade weaving industries. The museum regularly holds weaving demonstrations at its ground-floor hand looms, which use the Jacquard system of perforated cards for weaving. One of the most interesting things to do here is attend the free **Kimono Fashion Show,** held six or seven times daily from 10am to 4pm, showcasing kimono that change with the seasons. Other activities—for which you need reservations—include dressing up in a kimono for ¥3,600, or as a *maiko* (geisha apprentice) or *geiko* (professional entertainer) for ¥10,000, as well as trying your own hand at producing a textile on a small loom (¥1,800), which you can then take home with you. There's also, naturally, a shop selling kimono, sashes, fabric, and other products and souvenirs.

On Horikawa Dori just south of Imadegawa Dori. www.nishijin.or.jp. ⓒ**075/451-9231.** Free admission. Daily 9am–5pm. Subway: Imadegawa (8 min.). Bus: 9, 12, 59, 101, 102, 201, or 203 to Horikawa Imadegawa (2 min.).

Eastern Kyoto

The eastern part of Kyoto, embracing the area of Higashiyama-ku with its Kiyomizu Temple and stretching up all the way to the Temple of the Silver Pavilion (Ginkakuji Temple), is probably the richest in terms of culture and charm. Although temples and gardens are the primary attractions, Higashiyama-ku also boasts several fine museums, forested hills and running streams, great shopping opportunities, and some of Kyoto's oldest and finest restaurants. I've included two **recommended strolls** through eastern Kyoto later in this chapter that will lead you to the region's best attractions as well as to some lesser-known sights that are worth a visit if you have the time.

Ginkakuji (The Temple of the Silver Pavilion) ★★ TEMPLE Ginkakuji, considered one of the more beautiful structures in Kyoto, was built in 1482 as a retirement villa for Shogun Ashikaga Yoshimasa, who intended to coat the structure with silver in imitation of the Golden Pavilion built by his grandfather. He died before this could be accomplished, however, so the Silver Pavilion is not silver at all but remains a simple, two-story wood structure enshrining the goddess of mercy and Jizo, the guardian god of children. Note the sand mound in the garden, shaped to resemble Mount Fuji, and the sand raked in the shape of waves, created to enhance the views during a full moon.

Ginkakuji-cho. ⓒ **075/771-5725.** Admission ¥500 adults, ¥300 junior-high and elementary students, younger children free. Mid-Mar to Nov daily 8:30am–5pm; Dec to mid-Mar daily 9am–4:30pm. Bus: 5, 17, 102, 203, or 204 to Ginkakuji-michi (10 min.); or 32 or 100 to Ginkakuji-mae (5 min.).

Heian Shrine ★★ SHRINE Although it dates only from 1895, Kyoto's most famous Shinto shrine was built in commemoration of the 1,100th anniversary of the founding of Kyoto and is a replica of the first Imperial Palace, though on a less grand scale. It also deifies two of Japan's emperors: Emperor Kanmu, 50th emperor of Japan, who founded Heian-kyo in 794; and Emperor Komei, the 121st ruler of Japan, who ruled from 1831 to 1866. Although the orange, green, and white structure is interesting for its Heian-Era architectural style, the most important thing to see here is the 3.3hectare (8-acre) **Shinen Garden ★★★**, the entrance to which is on your left as you face the main hall. Typical of gardens constructed during the Meiji Era, it's famous for its weeping cherry trees in spring, its irises and waterlilies in summer, and its changing maple leaves in the fall. Don't miss it.

Nishi Tennocho, Okazaki. www.heianjingu.or.jp. (C) **075/761-0221.** Free admission to grounds; Shinen Garden ¥600 adults, ¥300 children. Daily 8:30am–6pm (to 5pm Nov–Feb). Subway: Higashi-yama (10 min.). Bus: 5, 32, 46, or 100 to Kyoto Kaikan Bijutsukan-mae (2 min.).

Hosomi Art Museum ★ MUSEUM This highly acclaimed private museum houses changing exhibits of Buddhist and Shinto art, primarily from temples and shrines in Kyoto and Nara, including Heian bronze mirrors, Buddhist paintings, lacquerware, tea-ceremony objects, scrolls, folding screens, and pottery. In contrast to the objects it contains, the building itself is starkly modern, complete with automatic doors that open and clang shut with the finality of a prison. The 30 minutes it takes to walk through are worthwhile; be sure to visit the gift shop of finely crafted goods.

6–3 Saishoji-cho Okazaki. www.emuseum.or.jp. (C) **075/752-5555.** Admission ¥1,000 adults, ¥800 students and children. Tues–Sun 10am–6pm. Subway: Higashiyama (exit 2, 7 min.). Bus: 31, 201, 202, 203, or 206 to Higashiyama-Nijo (3 min.). Catty-corner from the Kyoto Museum of Traditional Crafts (Fureaikan).

Kiyomizu Temple (Kiyomizudera) ★★★ TEMPLE This is Higashiyama-ku's most famous temple, known throughout Japan for the grand views afforded from its main hall. Founded in 778 and rebuilt in 1633 by the third Tokugawa shogun, Iemitsu, the temple occupies an exalted spot on Mount Otowa, with its main hall constructed over a cliff and featuring a large wooden veranda supported by 139 pillars, each 15m (49 ft.) high. The main hall is dedicated to the goddess of mercy and compassion, but most visitors come for the magnificence of its height and view, which are so well known to Japanese that the idiom "jumping from the veranda of Kiyomizu Temple" means that they're about to undertake some particularly bold or daring adventure. Kiyomizu's grounds are particularly spectacular (and crowded) in spring during cherry-blossom season and in fall during the turning of the maple leaves.

Also worth checking out are the three-story pagoda and Otowa Falls (known for the purity of its water; *kiyomizu* translates as "pure water"), but be sure not to spite the gods by neglecting to visit **Jishu Shrine ★★** ((C) **075/541-2097**), a vermilion-colored Shinto shrine behind Kiyomizu's main hall that has long been considered the dwelling place of the god of love and matchmaking. Ask for the English-language pamphlet and be sure to take the ultimate test: On the shrine's grounds are two "love–fortune telling" stones placed 9m (30 ft.) apart; if you're able to walk from one to the other with your eyes closed, your desires for love will be granted.

1–294 Kiyomizu. www.kiyomizudera.or.jp. (C) **075/551-1234.** Admission ¥300 adults, ¥200 children 7–15, children 6 and under free. Daily 6am–6pm (until 6:30pm in summer; special evening hours several times a year; Jishu Shrine closes at 5pm. Bus: 100, 202, 206, or 207 to Gojo-zaka (10 min.).

Kodai-ji Temple ★ TEMPLE   Located between Kiyomizu Temple and Yasaka Shrine, this temple was founded in 1605 by Toyotomi Hideyoshi's widow, popularly referred to as Nene, to commemorate her husband and to pacify his spirit. Shogun Tokugawa Ieyasu, who served under Toyotomi before becoming shogun, financed its construction. It contains lovely gardens laid out by Kobori Enshu, as well as teahouses designed by Sen no Rikyu, a famous 16th-century tea master, and the Kodaiji Sho Museum with artifacts from the early Edo Period. A memorial hall enshrines wooden images of Hideyoshi (to the left) and Nene. Nene, by the way, became a Buddhist nun after her husband's death, as was the custom of noblewomen at the time.

526 Shimogawara-cho, Kodai-ji. www.kodaiji.com. © **075/561-9966.** Admission ¥600 adults, ¥250 children 17 and under. Daily 9am–5:30pm (enter by 5pm). Bus: 100, 202, 206, or 207 to Higashiyama Yasui (5 min.).

Kyoto Museum of Traditional Crafts (Fureaikan) ★★ 🏛 MUSEUM   Near Heian Shrine is this excellent museum dedicated to the many crafts that flourished during Kyoto's long reign as the imperial capital. Various displays and videos demonstrate the step-by-step production of crafts ranging from stone lanterns and fishing rods to textiles, paper fans, umbrellas, boxwood combs, lacquerware, Buddhist altars, and *noh* masks. The displays are fascinating, the crafts beautiful, and explanations are in English, making even a 30-minute stop here well worth the effort. Crafts are sold in the museum shop.

In the basement of the Miyako Messe (International Exhibition Hall; look for the bright orange installation outside), 9–1 Seishoji-cho, Okazaki. www.miyakomesse.jp/fureaika. © **075/762-2670.** Free admission. Daily 9am–5pm. Subway: Higashiyama (7 min.). Bus: 5, 32, 46, or 100 to Kyoto Kaikan Bijutsukan-mae (2 min.), or 31, 201, 202, 203, or 206 to Higashiyama-Nijo.

Kyoto National Museum (Kokuritsu Hakubutsukan) ★★ MUSEUM   This museum, housed in a French baroque–style building constructed in 1897, is under renovation until spring of 2014 and is therefore open only for special exhibitions held three or four times a year (check the website for a schedule or ask at the tourist office). Once renovations are complete, it will again feature exhibits highlighting magnificent art objects and treasures, many of which once belonged to Kyoto's many temples and the imperial court, including Japanese and Chinese ceramics, sculpture, Japanese paintings, clothing and kimono, lacquerware, and metalworks.

527 Chaya-machi (across the street from Sanjusangendo Hall). www.kyohaku.go.jp. © **075/541-1151.** Special exhibition fees vary. Contact museum for exhibition dates and times. Bus: 100, 206, or 208 to Hakubutsukan Sanjusangendo-mae (1 min.).

Sanjusangendo Hall ★★★ TEMPLE   Originally founded as Rengeoin Temple in 1164 and rebuilt in 1266, Sanjusangendo Hall has one of the most visually stunning sights I've seen in a Japanese temple: 1,001 wooden statues of the thousand-handed Kannon. Row upon row, these life-size figures, carved from Japanese cypress in the 12th and 13th centuries, make an impressive sight; in the middle is a large seated Kannon carved in 1254 by Tankei, a famous sculptor from the Kamakura Period. Don't expect to actually see a thousand arms on each statue; there are only 40, the idea being that each hand has the power to save 25 worlds. In front of the 1,001 Kannon are a row of 28 guardian deities; not only are they all National Treasures, but it's rare to find a whole set like this one still intact. In any case, to accommodate all these statues, the hall stretches almost 120m (400 ft.), making it the longest wooden building in Japan (no photography or videos are allowed in the building). Its length was too hard to ignore—in the corridor behind the statues, archery competitions have been held for centuries; standing here, you can easily imagine how hard it must be to hit a piece of sacred cloth attached to the wall at the opposite end.

Shichijo Dori. ✆ **075/525-0033.** Admission ¥600 adults, ¥400 junior-high and high-school students, ¥300 children. Apr to mid-Nov daily 8am–5pm; mid-Nov to Mar daily 9am–4pm. Bus: 100, 206, or 208 to Hakubutsukan Sanjusangendo-mae (1 min.).

Northern Kyoto

Two of Kyoto's most famous sights are in the northwestern corner of the city.

Kinkakuji (Temple of the Golden Pavilion) ★★★ TEMPLE   One of Kyoto's best-known attractions—and the inspiration for the Temple of the Silver Pavilion (see above)—Kinkakuji was constructed in the 1390s as a retirement villa for Shogun Ashikaga Yoshimitsu and features a three-story pavilion covered in gold leaf with a roof topped by a bronze phoenix. Apparently, the retired shogun lived in shameless luxury while the rest of the nation suffered from famine, earthquakes, and plague. If you come here on a clear day (best is late afternoon), the Golden Pavilion shimmers against a blue sky, its reflection captured in the waters of a calm pond. However, this pavilion is not the original; in 1950, a disturbed student monk burned Kinkakuji to the ground (the story is told by author Mishima Yukio in his famous novel *The Temple of the Golden Pavilion*). The temple was rebuilt in 1955 and in 1987 was recovered in gold leaf, five times thicker than the original coating: You almost need sunglasses. Be sure to explore the surrounding **park** with its moss-covered grounds and teahouses.

1 Kinkakuji-cho. ✆ **075/461-0013.** Admission ¥400 adults, ¥300 children. Daily 9am–5pm. Bus: 12, 59, 101, 102, 204, or 205 to Kinkakuji-michi (3 min.).

Ryoanji Temple ★★★ TEMPLE   About a 20-minute walk southwest of the Golden Pavilion is Ryoanji—home to what is probably the most famous **Zen rock garden** ★★★ in all of Japan—laid out at the end of the 15th century during the Muromachi Period. Fifteen rocks set in waves of raked white pebbles are surrounded on three sides by a clay wall and on the fourth by a wooden veranda, in an area that measures about 25m (80 ft.) long and 10m (30 ft.) wide. Sit down and contemplate what the artist was trying to communicate. The interpretation of the rocks is up to the individual. (Mountains above the clouds? Islands in the ocean?) My only objection to this peaceful place is that, unfortunately, it's not always peaceful—a loudspeaker on occasion extols the virtue of the garden, destroying any chance for peaceful meditation. If you get here early enough, you may be able to escape both the crowds and the noise.

After visiting the rock garden, be sure to take a walk around the temple grounds. There's a 1,000-year-old **pond,** on the rim of which sits a beautiful little restaurant, **Ryoanji Yudofuya** ★★ (p. 278), with tatami rooms and screens, where you can eat *yudofu* and enjoy the view. There's also a nice landscape garden, with moss so inviting you'll wish you could lie down and take a nap.

Goryoshita-cho. www.ryoanji.jp. ✆ **075/463-2216.** Admission ¥500 adults, ¥300 children 14 and under. Mar–Nov daily 8am–5pm; Dec–Feb daily 8:30am–4:30pm. Bus: 59 to Ryoanji-mae (2 min.); or 12 or 50 to Ritsumeikan Daigaku-mae (4 min.).

Miho Museum on the Mountain

At some museums all the art is inside. At the **Miho Museum,** however, (300 Tashiro Momodani, Shigaraki, Shiga; www.miho.or.jp; ✆ **0748/82-3411;** Tues–Sun 10am–5pm; closed between exhibitions), the gorgeous setting with its harmonic convergence of nature, art, and architecture is part of the experience. After buying your ticket, it's a lovely 10-minute stroll (or ride in an electric-powered tram) through a forest and futuristic tunnel and over a gorge to the museum, designed by I.M. Pei and housing antiquities from East Asia through the Middle East, plus changing exhibitions. To preserve the natural surroundings of mountainous Shiga Prefecture, earth removed during museum construction was replaced, right up to the Japanese red pine on top of the building. Allow up to 2½ hours for your visit, more if you're eating lunch in one the Miho's organic restaurants. Admission is ¥1,000 for adults, ¥800 for college and high-school students, and ¥300 for children (cash only). To reach Miho, take one of many JR trains from Kyoto Station to Ishiyama in 13 minutes (fare: ¥230), where you'll board one of 5 daily Teisan buses (more frequently weekends and holidays; check the website) for the 50-minute ride to the Museum (fare: ¥800).

Toei Kyoto Studio Park (Toei Uzumasa Eigamura) ★ ☺ AMUSEMENT PARK   If your kids are ready to mutiny because of yet another temple, get on their good side by coming to this studio park, owned by one of Japan's three major film companies and where many samurai flicks and TV shows are made. Don't expect the high-tech, polished glitz of American theme parks—rather, this is a working studio where more than 200 TV and movie productions are filmed each year. Indoor and outdoor movie sets re-create the mood, setting, and atmosphere of feudal and turn-of-the-20th-century Japan, complete with photogenic period "villages" lined with samurai houses and old-time shops. Stagehands carry around props, hammers, and saws, and rework sets. You may even see a famous star walking around dressed in samurai garb, or come upon a scene being filmed.

Other popular attractions include the 20-minute ninja show four times a day Monday through Friday (it's in Japanese, but the action is easy to grasp), an exhibition hall of *ukiyo-e* (woodblock prints) with useful explanations in English, and a games arcade (try throwing *shuriken* – round darts used by ninja). You may want to have a Japanese-speaker along for the maze-like "ninja mystery house" full of trap doors and a room tilted on its side, as well as for exhibits on animation, the history of the film industry, a special-effects show and a haunted house. There are also indoor rides and play areas for children. Note that there's an extra charge for some activities, such as having a photo taken of yourself decked out in a kimono or samurai gear for ¥1,800 extra (or, pay ¥8,500 and you'll get the full treatment of wigs, makeup and more, after which you can even stroll walk around the studio park). Come here only if you have a lot of time (you'll probably spend a minimum of 2 hr. here), are a cinema buff, or have youngsters in tow.

10 Higashi-Hachigaokacho, Uzumasa, Ukyo-ku. www.toei-eigamura.com. ✆ **075/864-7718.** Admission ¥2,200 adults, ¥1,300 junior-high and high-school students, ¥1,100 children. Daily 9am–5pm (9:30am–4pm Dec–Feb). Closed Dec 26–Jan 1. Train: JR line to Uzumasa (5 min.) or Hanazono (13 min.) or Keifuku Line to Uzumasa (5 min.). Bus: 75, 91, or 93 to Uzumasa Eigamuramichi (4 min.).

IMPERIAL VILLAS & TEMPLES WITHIN EASY REACH OF KYOTO

If this is your first visit to Kyoto and you're here for only a couple days, you should concentrate on seeing sights in Kyoto itself. If, however, this is your second trip to Kyoto, you're here for an extended period of time, or you have a passion for traditional Japanese architecture or gardens, there are a number of worthwhile attractions in the region surrounding Kyoto. Foremost on my list is **Katsura Imperial Villa.**

Note: The Katsura Imperial Villa, **Shugakuin Imperial Villa,** and **Saihoji** (popularly called Kokedera, the Moss Temple) all require advance permission to visit. To see the Katsura Imperial Villa or Shugakuin Imperial Villa, which are free, you must apply for permission either online in English at http://sankan.kunaicho.go.jp at least 4 days before your intended visit; or go in person to the **Imperial Household Agency Office** (© **075/211-1215;** no English is spoken and no reservations are accepted by phone, but you can have a Japanese speaker call to see whether space is available), located on the northwest grounds of the **Kyoto Imperial Palace** near Inui Gomon Gate, a 5-minute walk from Imadegawa subway station. It's open Monday through Friday from 8:45am to noon and 1 to 5pm. In the off season, you may be able to make a reservation for a tour on the same day, though keep in mind that it takes an hour to reach Katsura Imperial Villa and 30 minutes to reach Shugakuin by taxi from the Imperial Household Agency Office. It's always better, therefore, to make a reservation a day or two in advance if applying in person; in spring and fall, try to make a reservation a week in advance. The time of your tour will be designated when you apply. Parties are limited to four persons, everyone must present their passports, and **participants must be at least 18 years old.** Tours are conducted in Japanese only, but there are videos and a free handheld audio guide in English.

Tours, which take place weekdays (except holidays) and the third Saturday of every month year-round, as well as on Saturdays in April, May, October, and November (even if they are national holidays), are given at Katsura Imperial Villa at 9am, 10am, 11am, 1:30pm, 2:30pm, and 3:30pm and at Shugakuin Imperial Villa at 9am, 10am, 11am, 1:30pm, and 3pm.

For tours of Saihoji, see below.

KATSURA IMPERIAL VILLA ★★★ About a 20-minute walk from Katsura Station on the Hankyu railway line, or a 30-minute bus ride from Kyoto Station (take bus no. 33 to the Katsura Rikyu-mae stop) and then an 8-minute walk, this villa is considered the jewel of traditional Japanese architecture and landscape gardening. It was built between 1620 and 1624 by Prince Toshihito, brother of the emperor, with construction continued by Toshihito's son. The garden, markedly influenced by Kobori Enshu, Japan's most famous garden designer, is a "stroll garden" in which each turn of the path brings an entirely new view.

The first thing you notice upon entering Katsura is its simplicity—the buildings were all made of natural materials, and careful attention was paid to the slopes of the roofs and to the grain, texture, and color of the various woods used. A pavilion for moon viewing, a hall for imperial visits, a teahouse, and other buildings are situated around a pond; as you walk along the pathway, you're treated to views that literally change with each step you take. Islets; stone lanterns; various scenes representing seashores, mountains, and hamlets; manicured trees; and bridges of stone, earth, or wood that arch gracefully over the water—everything is perfectly balanced. No matter where you stand, the view is complete and in harmony. Every detail was carefully planned down to the stones used in the path, the way the trees twist, and how scenes are reflected in the water. Little wonder the Katsura Imperial Villa has influenced architecture not only in Japan but around the world. Sadly, tours are much too hurried (they last only 1 hr.).

SHUGAKUIN IMPERIAL VILLA ★★ Northeast of Kyoto, about a 40-minute bus ride from Kyoto Station (take bus no. 5 from Kyoto Station to the Shugakuin Rikyu-michi bus stop) and then a 15-minute walk, this villa was built in the mid-1600s as a retirement retreat for Emperor Go-Mizunoo, who came to the throne at age 15 and suddenly abdicated 18 years later to become a monk, passing the throne to his daughter in 1629. Amazingly, though the villa was only 2 hours from the Imperial Palace, the emperor came here only on day trips; he never once spent the night. The 53-hectare (133-acre) grounds, among Kyoto's largest, are situated at the foot of Mount Hiei and are famous for the principle known as "borrowed landscape" in which the surrounding landscape is incorporated in the overall garden design. Grounds are divided into three levels (only two of which have compelling features): The **upper garden,** with its lake, islands, and waterfalls, is the most extensive of the three and offers grand views of the surrounding countryside from its hillside pavilion. The **middle garden,** built as a residence for the emperor's daughter, contains a villa with the famous "Shelves of Mist"; in keeping with the Japanese penchant for ranking the best three of everything, this is considered one of the three most beautiful shelves in Japan. The gardens are more spacious and natural than most Japanese-style gardens, which are often small and contrived. Tours, which take 1 hour and 15 minutes and cover about 3km (2 miles), allow ample time for photography.

SAIHOJI ★★ Popularly known as the **Moss Temple (Kokedera),** Saihoji was converted into a Zen temple in 1339 and is famous for its velvety-green moss garden spread underneath the trees. Altogether, there are more than 100 different varieties of moss throughout the grounds, with such popular names as "velvet moss," "water moss," and "snake-stomach moss." They give off an iridescent and mysterious glow that's best just after a rain; indeed, Kyoto's rainy season and high summer humidity create the perfect breeding ground for moss. Before being allowed to visit the grounds, you'll be ushered with other tour participants into a tatami room, where monks light incense, sound the bells, chant for our happiness and ancestry, and instruct participants to write their wishes on a tablet with a calligraphy brush. You can then walk on your own through the moss garden, which looks like it's straight out of a fairy tale and which circles a pond shaped in the Japanese word for heart, and linger as long as you wish; plan on a minimum of 1 hour here.

  Note: Because of fears that huge numbers of visitors would trample the grounds of this UNESCO World Heritage Site to death, permission is needed to visit Saihoji, and you can obtain it only by writing to the temple at least 7 days in advance (applications up to 2 months in advance are accepted). You can write in English to Saihoji Temple, 56 Matsuo, Nishikyo-ku, Kyoto 615-8286 (© **075/391-3631**), and give your name, your (hotel) address in Japan, your age, the number of people in your group, and the date you'd like to visit (plus second and third choices). Include a self-addressed return envelope for the postcard that will certify the approval of your application–and be sure to have it with you when you arrive at the temple! If you want it sent to a hotel in Japan,

Imperial Villas & Temples Within Easy Reach of Kyoto

the monks will send it to you free, but if you want it sent outside Japan to your home, include International Reply Coupons for return postage. The cost of the visit is a "donation" of at least ¥3,000 (no change given), payable when you arrive at the temple on the day of your tour. To reach Saihoji, take the Hankyu Line from Kawaramachi or Karasuma stations 10 minutes to Katsura and then the Arashiyama Line one stop to Kami-Katsura Station, from which it's a 15-minute walk. Or, take bus no. 73 from Kyoto Station or 63 from downtown Kyoto to the Kokedera-michi stop, but it takes longer.

BYODOIN TEMPLE ★★   Located in the town of Uji, about 18km (11 miles) southeast of Kyoto and a 15-minute ride by express JR train from Kyoto Station, Byodoin Temple (www.byodoin.or.jp; ✆ **0774/21-2861**) is a good example of temple architecture of the Heian Period. Originally a villa, it was converted into a temple in 1053. Most famous is the main hall, known as **Phoenix Hall,** the only original building remaining. It has three wings, creating an image of the mythical bird of China, the phoenix; on the gable ends are two bronze phoenixes. On the temple grounds is a National Treasure: one of the most famous bells in Japan (there are no inscriptions on the bell, but it has reliefs of maidens and lions and is thought to contain Korean influences) as well as a monument to Minamoto Yorimasa, who took his own life here after being defeated by the rival Taira clan. Byodoin is best known to Japanese, however, for gracing the back of ¥10 coins. Byodoin is about a 10-minute walk from the Uji JR Station (there's a map of the town in front of the station). Admission to the grounds is ¥600 for adults, ¥400 for junior-high students, and ¥300 for children; ¥300 more to enter Phoenix Hall. Grounds open daily 8:30am to 5:30pm (9am–5pm Dec–Feb); Phoenix Hall open daily 9:10am–4:10pm.

FUSHIMI–INARI SHRINE ★   Just a 2-minute walk from the JR Inari Station (which is just two stops by local commuter train from Kyoto Station), Fushimi-Inari Shrine (✆ **075/641-7331**) is one of Japan's most celebrated Shinto shrines. Founded in 711, it's dedicated to the goddess of rice (rice was collected as taxes during the shogun era) and has therefore long been popular with merchants, who come here to pray for success and prosperity. The 4km (2½-mile) pathway behind the shrine is lined with more than 10,000 red *torii,* (an entrance gate to Shinto shrine) presented by worshipers throughout the ages and by Japanese businesses. There are also stone foxes, which are considered messengers of the gods, usually with a key to the rice granary hanging from their mouths. It's a glorious, almost surreal, walk as you wind through the woods and the tunnel of vermilion-colored torii gates and then gradually climb a hill, where you'll have a good view of Kyoto. At several places along the path are small shops where you can sit down for a bowl of noodles or other refreshments. Admission is free, and the expansive grounds never close. The most popular times to visit are the first day of each month and New Year's, but I prefer weekdays when almost no one is there.

Note: Both Byodoin Temple and Fushimi-Inari Shrine are on the same JR line that continues to Nara. If you plan on spending the night in Nara, you could easily take in these two attractions on the way. Note, however, that the express train to Nara does not stop at JR Inari Station; for that you'll have to take a local train.

WHERE TO EAT

Kyoto cuisine, known as *Kyo-ryori,* is linked to Kyoto's long history and to seasonal foods produced in the surrounding region. Among the various types of Kyo-ryori available, most famous are the vegetarian dishes, which were created to serve the needs of Zen Buddhist priests and pilgrims making the rounds of Kyoto's many temples. Called *shojin ryori,* these vegetarian set meals may include *yudofu* (blocks of tofu simmered in a pot at your table and served with dipping sauce), filmy sheets of *yuba* (soy milk curd), and an array of local vegetables. Kyoto is also renowned for its own style of kaiseki called *Kyo-kaiseki,* originally conceived as a meal to be taken before the tea ceremony but eventually becoming an elaborate feast enjoyed by the capital's nobility with a blend of ceremonial court cuisine, Zen vegetarian food, and simple tea-ceremony dishes. You'll typically need a reservation for kaiseki (though Kyoto's better *ryokan* also serve kaiseki as the evening meal). Simpler restaurants specialize in *obanzai,* home-style Kyoto cooking using traditional seasonal ingredients. For more on kaiseki and other Japanese-style meals, see "Tips on Dining in Japan," beginning on p. 42 in chapter 2.

Remember: Last orders are taken 30 to 60 minutes before the restaurant's actual closing time, even earlier for kaiseki restaurants. Bus information to each restaurant is from Kyoto Station.

Around Kyoto Station

In addition to the restaurants listed here, a good place to browse for dining is **Kyoto Station,** which houses approximately 70 restaurants in underground arcades, at major exits, at Isetan department store (there are more than 20 outlets here alone, mostly on the 10th and 11th floors), in a range of prices. A cheap stand-out is **Ramen Koji** (拉麺小路), where eight of the best ramen shops from around the country are assembled on the 10th floor of Isetan (© **075/361-4401**). Dishes, most priced less than ¥1,000, run from miso ramen (ramen in miso broth) from Sapporo to so-thick-it's-almost-creamy *tonkotsu* (pork broth) from Hakata (Fukuoka). After choosing what you want, buy a ticket from vending machines outside each shop; English-speaking staff is usually on hand to help. Ramen Koji is open daily from 11am to 10pm.

MODERATE

Ichiba Coji (市場小路) VARIED JAPANESE/INTERNATIONAL   This inexpensive beer hall offers a variety of snacks and dishes that go well with its long list of locally brewed beer and sake, as well as *shochu,* wine, and cocktails, listed on an English-language menu and on view in a display case. Sashimi, tofu dishes, grilled whitefish in a balsamic sauce, spareribs served with miso sauce, Vietnamese spring rolls, salads, *nabe* (one-pot meals cooked at your table), and more are offered, along with views north over the city from its ninth-floor perch.

There's another Ichiba Coji in the heart of central Kyoto in the Teramachi covered shopping arcade, in the basement of the Withyou Building (© **075/252-2008**), with a hip, modern decor and set lunches priced from ¥980 to ¥1,980. It's open Monday to Friday 11:30am to 3pm and 5 to 10:15pm; Saturday and Sunday 11:30am to 10:15pm (last order).

9th floor, Isetan department store, Kyoto Station. © **075/365-3388.** Dishes ¥670–¥3,990; set dinners ¥3,150–¥5,250. AE, DC, MC, V. Daily 11am–11pm. Above Kyoto Station.

The Kitchen Salvatore Cuomo ★★ 🍴 ITALIAN   This contemporary eatery with an open kitchen, above Kyoto Station, has a good view toward the north, over rooftops and temples to the hills in the distance. At night, with dimmed lights and an elegant setting, it's a good place for a romantic meal. Its a la carte English-language menu lists pastas, pizzas (like the Diavola with chicken, salami, red pepper, and mozzarella), and main dishes such as the Italian grilled beef with balsamic vinegar sauce.

Where to Dine in Kyoto

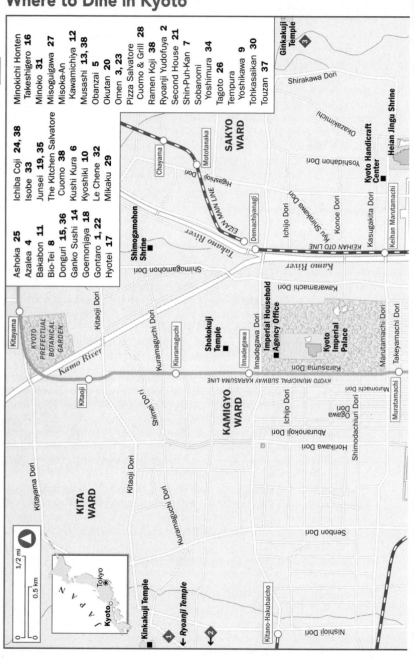

Ashoka **25**
Azalea **4**
Bakabon **11**
Bio-Tei **8**
Donguri **15, 36**
Ganko Sushi **14**
Goemonjaya **18**
Gontaro **1, 22**
Hyotei **17**

Ichiba Coji **24, 38**
Isobe **33**
Junsei **19, 35**
The Kitchen Salvatore
  Cuomo **38**
Kushi Kura **6**
Kyoshiki **10**
Le Chene **32**
Mikaku **29**

Minokichi Honten
  Takeshigero **16**
Minoko **31**
Misoguigawa **27**
Misoka-An
  Kawamichiya **12**
Musashi **13, 38**
Obanzai **5**
Okutan **20**
Omen **3, 23**
Pizza Salvatore
  Cuomo & Grill **28**
Ramen Koji **38**
Ryoanji Yudofuya **2**
Second House **21**
Shin-Puh-Kan **7**
Sobanomi
  Yoshimura **34**
Tagoto **26**
Tempura
  Yoshikawa **9**
Tohkasaikan **30**
Touzan **37**

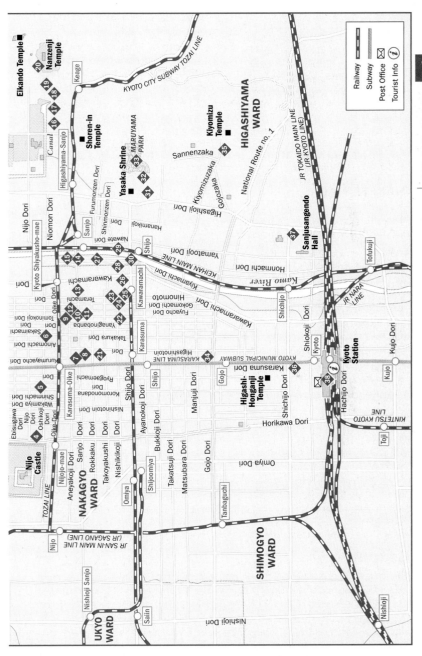

A Note on Japanese Characters

Many hotels, restaurants, attractions, and other establishments in Japan do not have signs giving their names in Roman (English-language) letters. Where they don't, we've given the Japanese script here, next to the restaurant name.

Or, opt for one of the set meals. Set lunches include a trip through an antipasto and a salad bar, along with a choice of main dish.

There's a cheaper, more casual branch, **Pizza Salvatore Cuomo & Grill,** in the heart of the nightlife district alongside the Kiyamachi canal (🕾 **075/212-4965**), offering pizzas, pastas, and outdoor seating.

10th floor, Isetan department store, Kyoto Station. 🕾 **075/365-7765.** Reservations recommended. Main dishes ¥980–¥2,600; set dinners ¥3,800–¥5,800; set lunches ¥1,800–¥3,000. AE, DC, MC, V. Daily 11am–3pm and 5–10pm (last order).

INEXPENSIVE

In addition to these choices, there's a branch of the conveyor-belt sushi shop **Musashi** (p. 274), located in Kyoto Station in the Asty Road concourse on the station's south side across from McDonald's.

Donguri (どんぐり) OKONOMIYAKI   This lively, basement restaurant serves various kinds of okonomiyaki (pancakes filled with your choice of vegetables and meats) from an English-language menu, including the "standard" with ground beef, pork and squid, and the "Italian" with bacon, cheese and corn, served on a *teppan* (steel plate) set into your table. Other dishes include *negiyaki* (with leeks) and *tompei-yaki* (pork ribs with egg, cabbage, leek and ginger), brought to you by staff that looks like ninjas with their black outfits and black kerchiefs on their heads. Wash your meal down with beer, sake or shochu, and cap it with a sundae of black sesame ice cream.

Karasuma Shichijo-sagaru, Nishigawa. 🕾 **075/361-5777.** Dishes ¥630–¥1,050. AE, DC, MC, V. Mon–Sat 5pm–5am; Sun 11am–5am. Just south of Shichijo on Karasuma, 1/2 block north of Yodobashi.

Sobanomi Yoshimura (蕎麦の実よしむら) ★ 🏮 NOODLES   If you thought *soba* was just buckwheat noodles, think again. In addition to regular bowls of soba (choose the thickness), it also makes more unusual dishes made with the sainted grain, from the *amuse bouche* of fried noodles to *soba kawa tsutsumi* (soba crepes filled with julienned vegetables and sauce, like Chinese *mushu*) and even soba ice cream. The house specialty is *yasai-soba*, in which noodles, broth and a plate of vegetables are served separately, allowing you to combine as you wish and dip the remaining ingredients in the broth. Luckily, there's a helpful English-language menu.

Gojo Karasuma Higashi-iru, Kitagawa. 🕾 **075/353-0114.** Set dinners ¥1,800–¥2,300; set lunches ¥880–¥2,800. DC, MC, V. Daily 11am–3pm and 5:30–10:30pm. Subway: Gojo. On Gojo Dori just east of Karasuma Dori and steps from subway Exit 1 (look for the large wooden sign).

Central Kyoto

The heart of Kyoto's shopping, dining, and nightlife district is in Nakagyo-ku, especially on Kawaramachi and Shijo Dori and along the many side streets. In summer, restaurants on the west bank of the Kamo River erect large wooden outdoor platforms that extend over the water and offer open-air dining. Another good bet is Shin-Puh-Kan, a renovated telephone company building on Karasuma Dori between Sanjo Dori and Oike Dori filled with shops and restaurants.

VERY EXPENSIVE

Misoguigawa (禊川) ★★★ 🎁 FRENCH KAISEKI   Dining here could well be the culinary highlight of your trip. For more than 30 years—long before fusion cuisine burst onto the scene—this lovely and exclusive restaurant has been serving nouvelle French cuisine that utilizes the best of Japanese style and ingredients in what could be called French kaiseki. It's located on narrow Pontocho, which parallels the Kamo River and is one of Kyoto's most famous nightlife districts, in a century-old renovated wooden building that once belonged to a geisha. Dishes are the creations of owner/master-chef Teruo Inoue, who trained with a three-star Michelin chef and successfully blends the two cuisines into dishes that are arranged like a work of art and served on Japanese tableware.

   Although four set meals are offered, the chef inquires about allergies and preferences and takes it from there, so no two meals are the same. English-speaking staff explains the ingredients of each dish as it's presented, and the extensive wine list is culled from Inoue's annual visits to France. Seating options include an L-shaped counter with tatami seating and leg wells; an informal counter for customers who prefer to order a la carte dishes (written in French and changing regularly) while watching chefs at work; private tatami rooms; and my favorite, an outdoor summer veranda overlooking the river. Note that the L-shaped counter and veranda add a 10% service charge and private rooms add a 15% service charge, but no service charge is added for the a la carte counter. This is a great place for a splurge.

Sanjo-sagaru, Pontocho. www.misogui.jp. © **075/221-2270.** Reservations required. Set dinners ¥12,600–¥21,000; set lunches ¥4,725–¥10,500. AE, DC, MC, V. Tues–Sun 11:30am–1:30pm and 5:30–8:30pm (last order). Bus: 4, 5, 17, or 205 to Kawaramachi Sanjo (5 min.); on Pontocho, north of the playground.

EXPENSIVE

Kyoshiki ★ KAISEKI/KYO-RYORI   This reasonably priced kaiseki restaurant, with a small garden in the back, was converted from a Meiji-Era private home almost 40 years ago. I recommend the *Hisago obento* for ¥3,150, offered for lunch on the English-language menu. It consists of a variety of seasonal foods served in individual dishes that stack neatly on top of one another to form a gourd; you take the bowls apart to eat. The atmosphere here is relaxed and comfortable, with both tatami and table seating.

Fuyacho Dori, Sanjo-agaru (just north of Sanjo Dori). © **075/221-4840.** Set meals ¥5,250–¥10,500; set lunches ¥3,150–¥5,200. AE, DC, MC, V. Tues–Sun 11:40am–2pm and 5–8pm (last order). Bus: 5 to Shijo-Fuyacho (1 min.). On Fuyacho Dori, just north of Sanjo Dori.

Tempura Yoshikawa ★★ TEMPURA   Located in an old-fashioned part of Kyoto that boasts a number of expensive *ryokan*, this is a tiny, intimate place with a traditional atmosphere that raises tempura to an art. Only 12 lucky diners can sit at the tempura counter, where you can watch the chefs prepare delicate deep-fried morsels. Meals served in tatami rooms, with views of an expansive garden (lit at night), are more expensive.

Tominokoji Dori, Oike-sagaru. www.kyoto-yoshikawa.co.jp. © **075/221-5544.** Reservations required. Set dinners ¥6,000–¥10,000; set lunches ¥3,000–¥4,000. AE, DC, MC, V. Mon–Sat 11am–2pm and 5–8:30pm (last order). Subway: Karasuma Oike Station (6 min.). On Tominokoji St. just south of Oike Dori.

MODERATE

Ashoka ★ INDIAN One of Kyoto's most popular and longest-running Indian restaurants, in business more than 30 years, serves vegetarian and meat curries prepared by Indian chefs, including mutton, chicken, fish, vegetable, and shrimp selections, as well as tandoori. On weekdays, it offers an even cheaper set lunch than given below, only ¥950.

Kikusui Building, 3rd floor, Teramachi Dori. ℂ **075/241-1318.** Main dishes ¥1,500–¥2,400; set dinners ¥2,800–¥6,000; set lunches ¥1,250–¥2,100. AE, DC, MC, V. Daily 11am–3pm and 5–9pm (last order). Bus: 4, 5, 17, or 205 to Shijo Kawaramachi (1 min.). On the north side of Shijo Dori, to the right at the entrance of the Teramachi covered shopping arcade.

Azalea CONTINENTAL Azalea is a pleasant place for a casual Western meal if you're visiting nearby Nijo Castle. Offering an English-language menu and a view of its small, Edo-era landscaped garden, it has inexpensive set lunches that may include a pasta or risotto dish as the main course, along with a la carte selections like sandwiches and beef curry rice. Dinner entrees include salmon and steak. Obviously, at these prices you can't expect perfection, but the setting is nice and it's easy to find. Plus, nightly at 7pm the hotel garden serves as a stage for a free 15-minute dance presentation given by *maiko* (geisha apprentices); if you arrive at 7pm, you can even have someone snap a picture of you standing beside them.

Kyoto Kokusai Hotel, Nijojo-mae, Horikawa Dori. ℂ **075/222-1111.** Set dinners ¥3,000–¥8,000; set lunches ¥1,600–¥3,900. AE, DC, MC, V. Daily 11:30am–2:30pm and 5–9pm. Subway: Nijojo-mae (2 min.). Bus: 9, 50, or 101 to Nijojo-mae. On Horikawa Dori across from Nijo Castle's main entrance.

Ganko Sushi (がんこ寿司) SUSHI/VARIED JAPANESE This popular, lively sushi restaurant offers the usual raw fish selections, as well as an extensive array of Japanese dishes such as grilled *yakitori*, *shabu-shabu*, tempura, tofu, noodles, and shrimp or crab dishes on an English-language menu. Behind the sushi counter is a fish tank with some rather large specimens swimming around happily until their numbers come up.

Kawaramachi-Sanjo, Higashi-iru. ℂ **075/255-1128.** Sushi a la carte ¥180–¥680; set meals ¥1,150–¥2,980. AE, MC, V. Daily 11am–10:30pm (until 11pm Fri and Sat). Subway: Kyoto Shiyakusho-mae (4 min.). Bus: 4, 17, or 205 to Kawaramachi Sanjo (2 min.). On Sanjo Dori, just west of the Kamo River (look for its logo of a face with glasses and a bandanna).

Kushi Kura (串くら) ★ YAKITORI Housed in a 100-year-old warehouse with heavy-beamed, dark-polished wood and whitewashed walls, this refined *kushiyaki* and *yakitori* restaurant serves specially raised chicken grilled over top-grade charcoal. An English-language menu offers set meals and a la carte selections. You can watch the action while comfortably seated at the counter with its leg wells. On weekdays, a lunch costing only ¥840 is also available. A large selection of sake (including the local Fushimi brew) adds to the great atmosphere here.

Takakura Dori, Oike-agaru. ℂ **075/213-2211.** Set dinners ¥1,600–¥4,800; set lunches ¥840–¥2,800; Most skewers a la carte ¥160–¥260. AE, DC, MC, V. Daily 11:30am–2pm and 5–10pm (last order). Subway: Karasuma-Oike (2 min.). Just north of Oike Dori on Takakura Dori.

Tagoto (田ごと) ✦ KYO-RYORI/KAISEKI/OBENTO Nestled in an inner courtyard off busy Shijo Dori and offering a peaceful retreat in the heart of downtown Kyoto, this restaurant has been serving a variety of Japanese dishes at moderate prices since 1868. The English-language menu includes Kyo-ryori set meals (including one with *yuba*, a low-calorie curd made from soy milk, for ¥3,900), seasonal kaiseki meals, mini-kaiseki meals, *obento* box meals, and *soba* noodles (available all day for ¥750–¥1,800).

Shijo-Kawaramachi, Nishi-iru, Kitagawa. http://www.kyoto-tagoto.co.jp. © **075/221-1811.** Set meals ¥3,700–¥12,600; set lunches ¥1,890–¥3,700. AE, DC, MC, V. Daily 11am–8:30pm. Bus: 4, 5, 17, or 205 to Shijo Kawaramachi (1 min.). The entrance is on Shijo Dori just west of Kawaramachi, east of Kyoto Central Inn (look for a narrow passageway to the back courtyard).

INEXPENSIVE

In addition to the choices here, there's a branch of **Ichiba Coji** in the Teramachi covered shopping arcade (on the west side about halfway down), with modern, hip decor and pub food that goes well with beer, sake, and spirits. There's also **Pizza Salvatore Cuomo & Grill,** in the heart of the nightlife district on Kiyamachi canal with outdoor seating. See "Around Kyoto Station," above, for reviews.

Bakabon (ばかぼん) YAKITORI   Dark woods, deeply grained wooden tables and spotlights set the tone for this easygoing izakaya in the heart of downtown, frequented by a 30- and 40-something crowd. The bar food includes grilled dishes (like yakitori) and *kamameshi* (rice and other ingredients served in a kettle), but the real reason you're here is for the selection of Kyoto sakes (try the Kyosansui).

Tominokoji Sanjo-sagaru. © **075/222-0607.** Main dishes ¥450–¥950; set dinners ¥2,850–¥4,850. No credit cards. Daily 6pm–1am. Subway: Kyoto Shiyakushomae (5 min.). On the east side of Tominokoji, south of Sanjo Dori; look for the noren (door curtains) made of rope fringe.

Bio-Tei (びお亭) VEGETARIAN/HEALTH FOOD   For a healthy meal or vegetarian food, head to this very informal second-floor restaurant down the street from the Museum of Kyoto and opposite the post office. Using organic, preservative-free ingredients, it serves only one thing at lunch: a great *teishoku* (fixed-price meal). Last time I was there it came with *genmae* (brown rice), salad, miso soup, pickles, and a curry-based tofu stew with potatoes and carrots. For dinner, a set meal and vegetarian a la carte dishes are offered from a Japanese-language menu. Seating is at sturdy wooden tables hewn from Japanese cypress, and meals are served on tableware from local kilns. As befits a health-food restaurant, smoking is not allowed.

Sanjo Dori Higashinotoin. © **075/255-0086.** Lunch teishoku ¥840; set dinner ¥1,260; dinner main courses ¥700–¥800. No credit cards. Tues–Fri 11:30am–2pm; Tues–Wed and Fri–Sat 5–8:30pm (last order). Closed holidays. Subway: Karasuma-Oike (exit 5, 3 min.). On the southwest corner of Sanjo-Higashinotoin intersection, on the 2nd floor.

Gontaro (権太呂) NOODLES   This shop has been serving its own handmade noodles for a mere 100-some years. A small place with a modern yet traditional interior and an English-language menu, it offers various noodle dishes of either *soba* (buckwheat) or *udon* (a thicker wheat noodle) with such toppings as tempura, as well as *donburi* (a rice casserole with tempura, *yakitori,* or other topping) and *nabe* (udon boiled in broth with seafood, chicken, and vegetables). Those with insatiable appetites can have it all with the Okimari set meal for ¥6,000, which comes with nabe, tempura, barbecue chicken, and noodles.

Fuyacho Dori, Shijo-agaru. © **075/221-5810.** Noodles ¥750–¥1,400; donburi ¥900–¥1,450; nabe ¥4,200 per person. AE. Thurs–Tues 11am–9pm. Bus: 5 to Shijo-Fuyacho (1 min.). On the west side of Fuyacho Dori just north of Shijo Dori; look for lacquered lanterns and a tiny shrine out front, white curtains, and a lone pine tree.

Misoka-An Kawamichiya ★★ NOODLES   Charming and delightful with a central courtyard and cubbyhole rooms, this tiny, 300-year-old noodle shop in a traditional merchant's home makes a great place for an inexpensive meal in the heart of traditional Kyoto. It offers hot or cold buckwheat noodles as well as noodles with such adornments as tempura and chicken and onions. Its specialty is a one-pot noodle dish prepared at your table called *hokoro*, which includes chicken, *yuba*, mushrooms, and vegetables for two. There's an English-language menu.

Fuyacho Dori, Sanjo-agaru. ✆ **075/221-2525.** Noodles ¥650–¥1,580; hokoro ¥8,000 for 2 people. AE, DC, MC, V. Fri–Wed 11am–8pm (last order). Bus: 5 to Shijo-Fuyacho (2 min.). On the west side of Fuyacho Dori just north of Sanjo Dori.

Musashi (むさし) 🍴 SUSHI   For a quick and cheap meal, this conveniently located restaurant can't be beat. Morsels of sushi ranging from tuna to octopus are served via a conveyor belt that moves plates along the counter; reach out and take whatever strikes your fancy. Sushi is priced at ¥137 a plate. Takeout sushi is also available from the sidewalk front counter. You'll find another branch in Kyoto Station (✆075/662-0634), open daily 10am to 10pm.

On the northwest corner of the Kawaramachi-Sanjo intersection. ✆ **075/222-0634.** ¥137 per plate. AE, DC, MC, V. Daily 11am–10pm. Bus: 4, 5, 17, or 205 to Kawaramachi Sanjo (1 min.).

Obanzai (おばんざい) 🍴 HEALTH FOOD/VEGETARIAN   With an all-wood interior, Obanzai offers an all-you-can-eat buffet using primarily organic vegetables. It's very much self-service here; pay by depositing your money into a basket upon entering, and clear your table when you're done. The mostly seasonal, mostly vegetarian dishes may range from pumpkin soup and tofu croquettes to salads, steamed vegetables, and fish catch of the day. A healthy choice near Nijo Castle.

Koromonotana Dori, Oike-agaru. ✆ **075/223-6623.** Lunch buffet ¥840 weekdays, ¥1,050 weekends and holidays; dinner buffet ¥2,100. No credit cards. Daily 11am–2pm; Thurs–Tues 5–8:30pm (last orders). Subway: Karasuma-Oike (exit 2, 5 min.). On the east side of Koromonotana Dori, in the 2nd block north of Oike.

Omen (おめん) ★★ UDON   A casual atmosphere and reasonably priced food make this tiny place popular. *Omen* (vegetable *udon*) is the specialty, and the house's traditional style is to serve the wheat noodles in a flat wooden bowl, the sauce in a pottery bowl, the vegetables delicately arranged (sashimi style) on a handmade platter with a bowl of sesame seeds alongside. You dip and mix yourself, unlike at other udon shops where it all arrives like a stew swimming in one bowl. Tempura, sushi, lightly fried tofu, and *kamonasu dengaku* (fried eggplant topped with a rich miso sauce) are among the other dishes offered. Other branches are located just south of Ginkakuji (✆ 075/771-8994; daily 11am–9pm), and on Pontocho (✆ 075/253-0377; daily 11:30am–3pm and 5–10pm). There's also one in New York.

Gokomachi Dori, Shijo-agaru. ✆ **075/255-2125.** Main dishes ¥650–¥1,050; set meals ¥1,650–¥1,950; set lunches ¥2,300. MC, V. Fri–Wed 11:30am–3pm and 5–9:30pm. Subway: Shijo (5 min.). Bus: 4, 5, 17, or 205 to Shijo Kawaramachi (3 min.). On the east (right) side of Gokomachi Dori, just north of Shijo.

Second House PASTA   Occupying a former *machiya* (merchant's house) with tall ceilings, a large nonsmoking section, and a young staff, this casual restaurant is part of a local chain offering a variety of Western and Asian pasta dishes, such as spaghetti with eggplant, tomato, and bacon; pasta with pork and *kimchi* (Korean-style spicy cabbage); and spaghetti with mushrooms and baby clams. It also has quiche, lunch specials, and homemade cakes and pastries, listed on an English-language menu. There's a pretty cake shop on the ground floor.

Higashinotoin Takoyakushi-agaru. © **075/241-2323.** Dishes ¥830–¥1,200. No credit cards. Daily 11am–10pm (last order). Subway: Shijo. Head north on Karasuma Dori and turn right on Takoyakushi Dori, and left again at the little park. The restaurant is on the left.

Tohkasaikan BEIJING CHINESE This Beijing-style Chinese restaurant popular with families started life as a Western restaurant. The old building features an ancient, manually operated elevator, lots of wood paneling, high ceilings, old-fashioned decor, and a friendly staff. From June to mid-September, you can sit outside on a wooden veranda over the Kamo River, one of the cheapest places along the river to do so. If it's winter or raining, consider sitting in the fourth or fifth-floor dining rooms, which have nice views of the city. The best views, however, are from the rooftop garden (in summer only), where you can order mugs of beer and dine on dishes from the extensive English-language menu, including sweet-and-sour pork, cooked shrimp with arrowroot, and chicken and green pepper. I've had better Chinese food, but the atmosphere is great and is reminiscent of another era.

Nishizume, Shijo Ohashi. © **075/221-1147.** Main dishes ¥1,470–¥2,630; set meals from ¥5,000 (2-person minimum). AE, DC, MC, V. Daily 11:30am–9pm (last order). Bus: 4, 5, 17, or 205 to Shijo Kawaramachi (2 min.). On Shijo Dori just west of the bridge spanning the Kamo River in a large yellow stone building.

Eastern Kyoto
EXPENSIVE

Hyotei (瓢亭) ★★★ 🏮 KAISEKI/OBENTO This 300-year-old restaurant first opened its doors as a teahouse to serve pilgrims and visitors on their way to Nanzenji Temple. Today it consists of two parts: one that offers expensive *Kyo-kaiseki*, which originated with the tea ceremony but is now associated with Kyoto cooking, and an annex offering seasonal obento lunch boxes. The kaiseki meals are served in separate tiny houses situated around a beautiful garden with a pond, maple trees, and bushes; the oldest house, which resembles a small teahouse, is more than 3 centuries old. You'll dine seated on a tatami floor in a private room, the food brought to you by kimono-clad women. The *bekkan* (annex), to the left of the kaiseki restaurant and with its own entrance, serves delicious *shokado bento* (lunch boxes), which change with the season and are served in a communal tatami room with views of a garden.

35 Kusakawa-cho, Nanzenji. © **075/771-4116.** Reservations required for kaiseki, recommended for obento. Kaiseki lunches from ¥23,000, dinners from ¥27,000; obento ¥5,000. AE, DC, MC, V. Kaiseki daily 11am–7:30pm; shokado bento Fri–Wed noon–4pm; closed 2nd and 4th Tues of each month. Subway: Keage (5 min.). Bus: 5 or 100 to Dobutsuen-mae (7 min.). West of Shirakawa Dori Murin-an; look for a plain facade hidden behind a bamboo fence with a sign shaped like a gourd.

Le Chene FRENCH Located on the southwestern edge of Maruyama Park and a good—though pricey—place to stop if you're walking from Kiyomizu Temple to Gion, this restaurant, housed in a building called **Chourakukan** (長楽館), dating from 1909 with elaborate woodwork and marble, is one of the few Western restaurants in eastern Kyoto. Ensconced in an elegant drawing room–style hall with Baccarat chandeliers, Le Chene serves only set menus at mealtimes, but you might consider dropping by the adjoining cafe, a beautiful set of rooms reminiscent of European coffee shops, open daily 10am to 9pm; afternoon tea, served from noon to 6pm, costs ¥3,000.

Chourakukan, Maruyama Park. © **075/561-0001.** Set dinners ¥12,000–¥20,000; set lunches ¥4,000–¥9,000. AE, DC, MC, V. Daily 11:30am–2pm and 5–8pm (last order). Bus: 100 or 206 to Gion (7 min.); after passing Yasaka Shrine, look to the right for a large stone-and-brick, Western-style building behind a wrought-iron gate.

Mikaku (みかく) ★ JAPANESE STEAKHOUSE   Established almost a century ago, this restaurant on the second floor (with counter seating) and third floor (tatami rooms) of a modern building offers sukiyaki, *shabu-shabu*, oil-yaki (sliced beef cooked on an iron griddle and flavored with soy sauce, lemon, and Japanese radish), and *teppanyaki*, all made with high-grade Kobe beef.

Nawate Dori, Shijo-agaru, Gion. © **075/525-1129.** Reservations recommended. Set meals ¥10,000–¥22,000. AE, DC, MC, V. Prices include service charge. Tues–Sun 11:30am–1pm and 5–9pm (last order). Bus: 100 or 206 to Gion (5 min.) or 4, 5, 17, or 205 to Shijo Kawaramachi (5 min.). From Shijo Dori, go 1 block north on Nawate Dori and take the 1st left. The restaurant will be on the right.

Minokichi Honten Takeshigero ★★ KYO-KAISEKI   One of Japan's best-known restaurants for Kyoto cuisine, Minokichi was founded in 1716 as one of eight restaurants licensed to serve freshwater fish and is now in its 10th generation of restaurateurs. With several branches in Japan, this flagship restaurant is an elegantly simple modern building, with tatami rooms reminiscent of those used in tea ceremonies, all with peaceful views of a graceful moss-and-bamboo garden. The specialty is *Kyo-kaiseki* (Kyoto-style kaiseki), emphasizing presentation, selection and preparation of seasonal ingredients. Individual dishes change, but the format is always 10 items: appetizer, raw fish, light soup, food cooked in delicate broth, steamed food, broiled food, deep-fried food, vinegared food, fruit, and green tea with a sweet.

Sanjo-agaru, Dobutsuen-mae Dori. www.minokichi.co.jp/takeshigero. © **075/771-4185.** Reservations required. Kyo-kaiseki dinner ¥15,750–¥31,500; kaiseki lunch ¥7,350–¥15,750. AE, DC, MC, V. Daily 11:30am–2pm and 5–7:30pm (last order). Subway: Keage (10 min.). Bus: 5 or 100 to Dobutsuen-mae (5 min.). Behind beige stucco walls north of Sanjo Dori on the road to the Zoo.

Minoko (美濃幸) ★★★ KAISEKI/OBENTO   This former villa is an enclave of traditional Japan with a simple, austere exterior and an interior of wooden corridors that gently creak underfoot, tatami rooms, and a garden. Opened nearly a century ago by the present owner's father, Minoko retains the spirit of the tea ceremony with *kaiseki* utilizing seasonal ingredients beautifully arranged to please both the palate and the eye and served in a private tatami rooms. Lunch, which is served communally in a large tatami room with a view of a beautiful garden, is more economical and less formal but still draws on the tea ceremony for inspiration. The *chabako-bento* lunch box, for example, is named after the lacquered box it's served in, traditionally used to carry tea utensils. A *hiru-kaiseki*, or mini-kaiseki set meal, is also available at lunch.

480 Kiyoi-cho, Shimogawara-dori, Gion. © **075/561-0328.** Reservations recommended for lunch, required for dinner. Dinner kaiseki from ¥15,697; hiru-kaiseki lunch ¥10,444; obento ¥4,000–¥6,930. AE, DC, MC, V. Daily 11:30am–2:30pm and 5–10pm (last order 8pm). Closed irregularly 3 days a month. Bus: 100 or 206 to Gion (3 min.). A short walk south of Yasaka Shrine.

Touzan ★★★ SUSHI/SUMIBIYAKI/KAISEKI   Next door to Sanjusangendo and across the street from Kyoto National Museum, this eatery is convenient to sightseeing but also worth going out of your way for. Modeled after a traditional Kyoto home but with innovative interior designs (such as pottery shards encased in glass serving as room dividers), it offers views of a traditional rock garden (dramatically lit at night) and specializes in charcoal-grilled foods along with sushi (the latter available in both the restaurant and a sushi counter). A large selection of sake, including 13 local brands, serves as a perfect complement to the meals.

Hyatt Regency Kyoto, 644–2 Sanjusangendo-mawari, Higashiyama-ku. ℂ **075/541-3203.** Set dinners ¥6,000–¥13,000; set lunches ¥2,940–¥4,500. AE, DC, MC, V. Tues–Sun 11:30am–2:30pm and 5:30–10pm. Bus: 100, 206, or 208 to Hakubutsukan Sanjusangendo (1 min.).

MODERATE

Isobe (いそべ) KAISEKI/VARIED JAPANESE A convenient place to stop for lunch if you're walking between Kiyomizu Temple and Gion, this modern, pleasant restaurant offers a nice view of Maruyama Park from its dining room and has an English-language menu with photos listing a variety of set meals featuring sashimi, tempura, and kaiseki.

Maruyama Park, Ikenohata. ℂ **075/561-2216.** Set meals ¥3,150–¥6,090. AE, DC, MC, V. Daily 11am–10pm. Bus: 100 or 206 to Gion (10 min.). On the southeastern edge of the park (if you're walking from Kiyomizu, take a right at the park entrance; if you're coming from Gion, walk past Yasaka Shrine and keep to the right); look for the outdoor red umbrella (up only in dry weather but also depicted on the sign).

Junsei (順正) ★ TOFU/KAISEKI/OBENTO Specializing in tofu, Junsei opened in 1961, but the grounds and garden were originally part of a medical school established in the 1830s during the shogun era. Although tourist-oriented and popular with tour groups, the food is good and an English-language menu makes ordering easy. There are several buildings spread throughout the grounds, and what you want determines where you go; as soon as you arrive, you'll be given a menu and asked what you'll be eating. I chose the house special—a *yudofu* meal—and was directed to an older building with a view of the garden and filled with antiques and tatami mats. My meal came with vegetable tempura and various tofu dishes, including fried tofu on a stick and yudofu boiled in a pot at my table. Other set meals include kaiseki (by reservation only), *yuba, shabu-shabu,* or sukiyaki.

There's a branch, Kiyomizudera Junsei (ℂ **075/541-7111**), located just off Kiyomizu-zaka, the main slope leading to Kiyomizu Temple. Housed in a grand, 1914 former villa with high ceilings, wainscoting, and stained-glass windows, it offers just three set tofu meals priced ¥2,100 to ¥5,250 and is open daily 10:30am to 5pm (last order), closed irregularly.

Nanzenjimon-mae, Sakyo-ku. www.to-fu.co.jp. ℂ **075/761-2311.** Reservations required for kaiseki and shabu-shabu. Yudofu meal ¥3,000-4,000; shabu-shabu or sukiyaki ¥8,000; kaiseki ¥10,000–¥20,000. AE, DC, MC, V. Daily 11am–8pm (last order). Subway: Keage (5 min.). Bus: 5 to Nanzenji-Eikando-michi (7 min.). East of Shirakawa Dori on the road to Nanzenji Temple, north side.

Okutan (奥丹) ★★★ 🏮 TOFU/VEGETARIAN This is one of the oldest, most authentic, and most delightful tofu restaurants in Kyoto. Founded about 350 years ago as a vegetarian restaurant serving Buddhist monks, this thatched-roof wooden retreat in a peaceful setting with pond and garden serves just two things: *yudofu* (a tofu set meal) and a more traditional tofu meal originally from China. Okutan is very simple and rustic with seating either in tatami rooms or outdoors on cushioned platforms, making it especially delightful in fine weather. Women dressed in traditional rural clothing bring your food. The yudofu set meal, which changes slightly with the seasons, includes a pot of tofu boiled at your table, fried tofu on a stick, vegetable tempura, yam soup, and pickled vegetables. It's all highly recommended.

86–30 Fukuchi-cho, Nanzenji. 📞 **075/771-8709.** Reservations recommended (but not accepted in peak season). Yudofu set meal ¥3,150; traditional tofu meal ¥4,200. No credit cards. Fri and Mon–Wed 11am–4pm; Sat–Sun and holidays 11am–4:30pm (last order). Bus: 5 to Nanzenji-Eikando-michi (6 min.). Just north of Nanzenji Temple's main gate (the Sanmon Gate).

INEXPENSIVE

Goemonjaya (五右衛門茶屋) TOFU/TEMPURA/NOODLES Convenient if you're visiting Nanzenji, this four-decade-old, family-run hole-in-the-wall specializes in tofu dishes and tempura. With tatami seating, a miniature garden, and a carp-filled pond, it offers a *yudofu* set meal, a shrimp or vegetarian tempura *teishoku*, and, in summer only, inexpensive noodle dishes ranging from ¥650 for *somen* (thin vermicelli served cold) to ¥800 for *zaru soba* (cold buckwheat noodles). Desserts include *mitarashi dango* (soy-flavored rice dumplings on a stick) and *zensai-mochi* (rice cake with black beans).

67 Kusagawa-cho, Nanzenji. 📞 **075/751-9638.** Set meals ¥1,800–¥3,000. No credit cards. Wed-Mon 11am–6pm. Bus: 5 to Nanzenji-Eikando-michi (2 min.). Across the street from Yachiyo Inn on the road leading to Nanzenji Temple (look for a red lantern beside the road); the restaurant is down a path past a smiling Buddha and a red paper umbrella (open only in dry weather).

Northern Kyoto

In addition to the selection here, there's a branch of **Gontaro,** serving noodles, at Hinomiyashiki-cho 26 (📞 **075/463-1039**), with the same English-language menu as its main shop (p. 273). It's located about halfway down the street that runs between Ryoanji and Ginkakuji, on the west side; look for the red paper lantern. It's open Thursday to Tuesday from 11am to 10pm.

INEXPENSIVE

Ryoanji Yudofuya ★★ 🏠 TOFU/VEGETARIAN If you're visiting Ryoanji Temple in northeastern Kyoto, there's no lovelier setting for a meal than this traditional restaurant, which calls itself the Ryoanji Seven Herb Tofu Restaurant in honor of its signature dish, *yudofu,* boiled tofu and vegetables topped with seven herbs. You can order it by itself, or as a set meal of *shojin ryori* (Buddhist vegetarian) with side dishes. Entrance to the restaurant, situated beside the Kyoyoike Pond on temple grounds, is along a small path that takes you past a stream, a small pond, a grove of

---

 Home-style Cooking Class

So you've eaten your way around town and would now like to cook your own Japanese food. Saeki Taro, who once cooked the meals at a *minshuku* (family-style inn), now teaches homestyle cooking at his **Haru Cooking Class** (www.vegetarian-food-kyoto.com; 📞 **090/4284-7176**). Classes take place in his home in English (he used to live in the United States), and often his wife and adorable young daughter are on hand to help. After instruction in the basics of soy sauce, miso and other common ingredients, you'll have hands-on kitchen time, and within a few hours you'll be eating your creations from the beef, chicken or vegetarian menu. There's a minimum of three persons, so you may be paired with others. Classes cost ¥4,500 to ¥5,900 per person, depending on the ingredients of your meal. Take bus No. 4 or 205 to Shin-Aoibashi bus stop in northeast Kyoto, and Taro will meet you.

maple and pine, and moss-covered grounds, which are also what you see as you dine seated on tatami. You'll know you're getting close to the restaurant when you hear the *thonk* of a bamboo trough fed by a stream, which fills and hits against stone as it empties.

Ryoanji Temple. © **075/462-4742.** Yudofu ¥1,700; yudofu vegetarian set meal ¥3,300. No credit cards. Daily 10am–5pm. Bus: 59 from Shijo Kawaramachi to Ryoanji-mae (2 min.), or 50 to Ritsumei-kan Daigaku-mae (4 min.).

SHOPPING IN KYOTO

As the nation's capital for more than 1,000 years, Kyoto spawned a number of crafts and exquisite art forms that catered to the elaborate tastes of the imperial court and the upper classes. Kyoto today is still renowned for its **crafts,** including Nishijin textiles, Yuzen-dyed fabrics, Kyo pottery (pottery fired in Kyoto), fans, dolls, cutlery, gold-leaf work, umbrellas, paper lanterns, combs, *noh* masks, cloisonné, and lacquerware.

GREAT SHOPPING AREAS   The majority of Kyoto's tiny specialty shops are in central Kyoto. The rectangular grid formed by **Kawaramachi Dori, Shijo Dori, Sanjo Dori,** and **Teramachi Dori** includes two covered shopping arcades and specialized shops selling lacquerware, combs and hairpins, knives and swords, tea and tea-ceremony implements, and more—including, of course, clothing and accessories for customers of all ages.

For antiques, woodblock prints, and art galleries, head toward the high-end **Shinmonzen Dori** and **Furumonzen Dori** in Gion, which parallel Shijo Dori to the north on the eastern side of the Kamo River, as well as **Teramachi Dori** (where prices are generally more reasonable) north of Oike. You'll find pottery and souvenir shops in abundance on the roads leading to Kiyomizu Temple, particulary the hill known as **Chawan-zaka** (Teacup Slope).

For clothing, accessories, and modern goods, **department stores** are good bets. They're conveniently located near Kyoto Station and in central Kyoto near the Shijo-Kawaramachi intersection. Near Kyoto Station are also two large **shopping malls** selling everything from clothing and shoes to stationery and local souvenirs: an underground mall beneath the station and **Aeon** south of the station across Hachijo Dori. **Kyoto-Yodobashi,** on Karasuma Dori a block north of Kyoto Tower, contains the Yodobashi Camera electronics store, fashion boutiques, and restaurants.

Crafts & Specialty Shops

Aritsugu (有次)   The fact that this family-owned business is located at the Nishiki-Koji market is appropriate, as it sells hand-wrought knives and other handmade cooking implements, including sushi knives, bamboo steamers, pots, pans, and cookware used in the preparation of traditional Kyoto cuisine, as well as *ikebana* scissors. In business for 400 years, the shop counts the city's top chefs among its customers. Note that no credit cards are accepted. Open daily 9am to 5:30pm. Nishiki-Koji Dori, Gokomachi Nishi-iru, Nakagyo-ku. © **075/221-1091.** Bus: 4, 5, 10, 11, 12, 17, 32, 46, 201, 203, 205, or 207 to Shijo Kawaramachi (5 min.). 1 block north of Shijo Dori on the north side of Nishiki-Koji Dori, west of Gokomachi.

Ippodo (一保堂)   In business since 1717, this famous shop is a good place not only to buy high-quality Japanese green teas but to learn more about them. Pick up the shop's English-language brochure that explains the different varieties, from *matcha* to *sencha* to *genmaicha*, or sample them at the shop's hands-on tearoom, Kaboku, where you can experience brewing techniques for the different types of tea. Open Monday to Saturday 9am to 7pm; Saturday and holidays 9am to 6pm (Kaboku open daily 11am–5pm). Teramachi Dori, north of Nijo, Nakagyo-ku. www.ippodo-tea.co.jp. ✆ **075/211-3421.** Bus: 4, 10, 17, 32, 59, and 205 to Kyoto Shiyakushomae.

Kasagen Kasagen has been making traditional *bangasa* (umbrellas) since 1861. They're more expensive than elsewhere but are of high quality and made to last a lifetime. Open Thursday to Tuesday 10am to 7pm. 284 Gion-machi, Kitagawa. ✆ **075/561-2832.** Bus: 12, 46, 100, 201, 202, 203, 206, or 207 to Gion. On the north side of Shijo Dori, just west of Yasaka Shrine.

Kikuya Kikuya has a good selection of used kimono, *haori* (short kimono-like jackets, traditionally worn by men), *geta*, and kimono accessories for both adults and children. Although they're not antiques as Kikuya advertises but secondhand, the goods here are beautiful and timeless. Everything is in good condition (Japanese wear kimono only for special occasions), but be sure to look thoroughly for any defects. No credit cards are accepted. Open Monday to Saturday 9am to 7pm. Closed holidays. On Manjuji Dori, east of Sakaimachi. ✆ **075/351-0033.** Take the Keihan Electric Line to Gojo (5 min.).

Kyoto Aburatorishi Senmontenzo (きょうとあぶらとり紙) I realize this is a bit odd, but this shop is dedicated to one of my favorite Japanese cosmetic products: face paper. Kyoto is famous for its face paper, long used by geisha and *maiko*, and this shop sells a bewildering choice of varieties, for everything from dry to troubled skin. I like it for blotting oily skin on hot, humid days. Daily 11am to 8:30pm. Kawaramachi, Shijo-agaru. ✆ **075/213-3322.** Bus: 4, 5, 10, 11, 12, 17, 32, 46, 201, 203, 207, or 205 to Shijo Kawaramachi. On the east side of Kawaramachi Dori, north of Shijo Dori; look for its sign with an elephant.

Kyoto Handicraft Center For one-stop souvenir shopping, your best bet is Kyoto's largest craft, gift, and souvenir center. Four floors of merchandise contain almost everything Japanese imaginable: pearls, lacquerware, dolls, children's toys, kimono (including antique kimono), woodblock prints, pottery, paper products, swords, lanterns, silk and textile goods, painted scrolls, T-shirts, and jewelry boxes—and that's just for starters. You can even buy the socks worn with *geta* wooden shoes and the *obi* sashes worn with the kimono.

You can easily spend an hour or two here just wandering around; artisans also demonstrate their various crafts, including woodblock printing and the production of damascene. You can even try your own hand at 9 different craft activities, including woodblock prints, cloisonné, damascene, and more, with instruction provided. No reservations are necessary, but plan on at least an hour. Lessons run ¥1,890 to ¥3,990 and are a great way for older children to get creative while you shop. And if you spend more yen than you have in your wallet, you can exchange money here at a favorable rate. There's also a tourist office on the ground floor. Open daily from 11am to 6pm. Heian Jingu Kita, Marutamachi Dori, Sakyo-ku. www.kyotohandicraftcenter.com. ✆ **075/761-8001.** Bus: 201, 202, 203, 204 or 206 to Kumano-jinja-mae (1 min.). Just north of Heian Shrine on Marutamachi Dori.

Kyoto Pottery Center (京都陶磁器会館) This modern shop with a glass facade is operated by an association of Kyoto potters who display their wares of Kyo pottery (pottery fired locally), from sake cups and vases to bowls, plates, and chopstick rests. For more shopping, *Chawan-zaka* (Teacup Slope) is just uphill, with 20-some more shops. Daily 9:30am to 5pm. Higashioji Dori, Gojo-agaru. 📞 **075/541-1102.** Bus: 100 or 206 to Gojo-zaka (one of the approaches to Kiyomizu Temple). On Higashioji Dori, north of Gojo Dori.

Miyawaki Baisen-an (宮脇賣扇庵)   This elegant, open-fronted shop has specialized in handmade fans since 1823, particularly fans characteristic of Kyoto. Prices range from ¥2,000 for a small tea-ceremony fan to ¥50,000 for the best that money can buy. Open daily 9am to 7pm (to 6pm in winter). 102 Tominokoji-nishi, Rokkaku-dori, Nakagyo-ku. 📞 **075/221-0181.** Subway: Karasuma Oike (6 min.). On Rokkaku-dori just west of Tominokoji, across from a playground.

Robert Yellin Yakimono Gallery   Robert Yellin may be American-born, but after decades in Japan he's become one of the world's foremost experts on Japanese pottery, published regularly in the *Japan Times* and leading arts journals and selling works by some of Japan's top contemporary ceramic artists. In 2011, he moved his gallery from a remote town in the Kanto region to this gorgeous Taisho-Era house near Ginkakuji Temple, making it easier for visitors to see and learn about the various wares and the artists who created them. Open Monday to Friday from 10:30am to 5pm or by appointment. 39 Ginkakuji-mae-cho, Sakyo-ku. www.japanesepottery.com. 📞 **075/708-5581.** Bus: 5, 17, 102, 203, or 204 to Ginkakuji-michi (5 min.); or 32 or 100 to Ginkakuji-mae (5 min.). Facing Ginkakuji, turn left at the police box to cross the stream, walk right along the stream and make your first left. The gallery is about 100 yds ahead on the left, before the stone stairs.

Zohiko   Zohiko has been in business since 1661, making it a must for those wishing to learn the essence of Japanese lacquerware. The first floor of this flagship store offers exquisitely made pieces for sale, while upstairs is a museum gallery with changing exhibits (admission: ¥300). Although lacquerware for sale at this shop is not cheap, you'll understand why when you understand the labor that goes into each item (ask for the pamphlet in English). Open Thursday to Tuesday from 9:30am to 6pm. 10 Okazaki Saishojicho, Sakyo-ku. www.zohiko.co.jp. 📞 **075/752-7777.** Bus: 201, 202, 203 or 206 to Higashiyama-Nijo (5 min.). Look for the elephant on the side of the building near Heian Shrine and Hosomi Art Museum.

Department Stores

Department stores are good places to shop for Japanese items and souvenirs, including pottery, lacquerware, and kimono as well as clothing, foodstuff, and everyday items.

JR Kyoto Isetan, located in Kyoto Station (http://kyoto.wjr-isetan.co.jp; 📞 **075/352-1111;** daily 10am–8pm), is Kyoto's most fashionable department store, specializing in women's imported and domestic clothing.

In central Kyoto, **Daimaru,** on Shijo Dori west of Takakura (www.daimaru.co.jp/kyoto; 📞 **075/211-8111;** daily 10am–8pm), is Kyoto's largest department store, with everything from clothing to food to electronic goods spread on nine floors. Nearby are **Marui,** on the southeast corner of Shijo-Kawaramachi intersection (📞 **075/257-0101;** Mon–Wed 11am–8pm, Thurs–Sun 11am–9pm), with seven floors of fashion, housewares, and food; and **Takashimaya,** across the street at the southwest corner of the Shijo-Kawaramachi intersection (www.takashimaya.co.jp/kyoto; 📞 **075/221-8811;** daily 10am–8pm), one of Japan's oldest and most respected department stores with a good selection of traditional crafts.

Markets

On the 21st of each month, a flea market is held at **Toji Temple** (✆ **075/691-3325**), about a 15-minute walk southwest of Kyoto Station. Japan's largest flea market, it's also one of the oldest; its history stretches back more than 700 years, when pilgrims began flocking to Toji Temple to pay their respects to Kobo Daishi, who founded the Shingon sect of Buddhism. Today, Toji Temple, a World Heritage Site, is still a center for the Shingon sect, and its market (popularly known as Kobo-san) is a colorful affair with booths selling Japanese antiques, old kimono, ethnic goods, odds and ends, and many other items. Worshipers come to pray before a statue of Kobo Daishi and to have their wishes written on wooden slats by temple calligraphers. Even if you don't buy anything, the festive atmosphere of the market and booths makes a trip memorable. The largest Kobo-san markets take place in December and January. All markets at Toji are held from about 6am to 4pm. A smaller market, devoted entirely to Japanese antiques, is held at Toji Temple on the first Sunday of each month.

Commemorating the scholar and poet Sugawara Michizane, the **Tenjin-san market** held at **Kitano Tenmangu Shrine** (✆ **075/461-0005**) the 25th of every month is a large market offering a little bit of everything—antiques, used clothing, ceramics, food—in a beautiful setting. It's open from about 8am to dusk, but go as early as you can. Kitano Shrine is on Imadegawa Dori between Nishi-oji and Senbon; take bus no. 10, 26, 101, 102, or 203 to the Kitano Tenmangu-mae stop.

Unlike the other temple markets, the **Chion-ji market** (✆ **075/691-3325**), held the 15th of each month from 9am to 4pm, is devoted to handmade goods and crafts, including pottery and clothing. To reach it, take bus no. 17, 102, 201, 203, or 206 to Hyakumanben at the Higashioji and Imadegawa intersection; **Chion-ji Temple** is just to the northeast.

On the first Sunday of every month (though sometimes the date changes), a flea market is held in front of **City Hall** from 10am to 4pm, with local citizens selling unwanted stuff, mostly clothing. Although you may not buy anything to take home with you, a stroll through the **Nishiki-Koji Food Market** is worthwhile just for the atmosphere. With a 400-plus-year history, this covered shopping arcade 1 block north of Shijo Dori in the heart of old Kyoto is lined with vendors selling fish, flowers, eggs, pickled vegetables, fruit, takeout foods, kitchenware and crafts. It's open from 10am to about 6pm; some shops close on either Wednesday or Sunday.

ENTERTAINMENT & NIGHTLIFE

Nothing beats a fine summer evening spent strolling the streets of Kyoto. From the geisha district of Gion to the bars and restaurants lining Pontocho, Kyoto is utterly charming and romantic at night. Begin with a walk along the banks of the Kamo River—it's a favorite place for young couples in love. In summer, restaurants stretching north and south of Shijo Dori along the river erect outdoor wooden platforms on stilts over the water.

There are many annual events and dances, including the very popular geisha dances held in June, the only time of year you can see traditional dances performed by all five of Kyoto's traditional geisha districts; Miyako Odori dances in April and Gion Odori dances in October feature *geiko* and *maiko* (geisha and apprentice geisha) dressed in elaborate costume; and *kabuki* at the Minamiza Theater in December.

To find out what's happening, pick up the **Kyoto Visitor's Guide** (www.kyoto guide.com), a monthly tabloid distributed free at tourist offices, hotels, and restaurants, which contains a calendar of events and performances for the month. **Kansai Scene** (www.kansaiscene.com) is also a monthly giveaway with information on nightlife, festivals, and events.

The Major Nightlife Districts

GION ★★

A small neighborhood of plain wooden buildings in Higashiyama-ku on the eastern side of the Kamo River, Gion doesn't look anything like what you've probably come to expect from an urban Japanese nightlife district; in fact, there's little neon in sight. There's something almost austere and solemn about Kyoto's most famous geisha district, as though its raison d'être were infinitely more important and sacred than mere entertainment. Gion is a shrine to Kyoto's past, an era when geisha numbered in the thousands.

Contrary to popular Western misconceptions, geisha are not prostitutes. Rather, they're trained experts in the traditional arts, conversation, and coquettishness, and their primary role is to make men feel like kings when they're in the soothing enclave of the geisha house. There are now a mere 300 geisha in Gion; after all, in today's high-tech world, few women are willing to undergo the years of rigorous training to learn how to conduct the tea ceremony, to play the *shamisen* (a three-stringed instrument), or to perform ancient court dances.

Gion is about a 5-minute walk from the Shijo-Kawaramachi intersection; to reach it, walk east on Shijo Dori and then take a right on Hanamikoji Dori. Its narrow streets are great for strolling; a good time to take a walk through the neighborhood is around dusk when geisha are on their way to their evening appointments. Perhaps you'll see one—or a *maiko* (a young woman training to be a geisha)—clattering in her high *geta* (wooden shoes). She'll be dressed in a brilliant kimono, her face a chalky white, and her hair adorned with hairpins and ornaments. From geisha houses, music and laughter lilt from behind paper screens, sounding all the more inviting because you can't enter. Don't take it personally; not even Japanese will venture inside without the proper introductions. There are, however, an increasing number of bars and restaurants in Gion that are open to outsiders; it's not hard to imagine that in another 100 years, Gion will look no different from many other nightlife districts.

Gion Corner   After strolling around Gion, visit Gion Corner, which stages special variety programs in the ancient cultural arts. You'll see short demonstrations of the tea ceremony, flower arrangement, *koto* (Japanese harp) music, *gagaku* (ancient court music and dance), *kyogen* (*noh* comic play), *kyomai* (Kyoto-style dance) performed by *maiko,* and *bunraku* (puppetry). The shows cater to tourists, and none of the individual performances beat a full-scale production of the real thing, but this is a convenient and quick introduction to the traditional forms of Japanese entertainment. If you wish, you can also partake in a 30-minute tea ceremony following each performance (available Mar–Nov for an extra fee). Be sure, too, to wander through the Maiko Gallery with its displays relating to maiko hairstyles and accessories. Performances are daily at 6 and 7pm mid-March through November (no performances Aug 16); December through early March performances are only on Friday, Saturday, Sunday, and holidays. Reservations are not necessary, but arrive early (no credit cards accepted), or purchase in advance at most hotels or Gion Corner box office. Yasaka

Hall, 570–2 Minamigawa, Gion. www.kyoto-gioncorner.com. ☏ **075/561-1119.** Tickets ¥3,150 adults, ¥2,200 high-school and university students, ¥1,900 children. Bus: 12, 46, 100, 102, 202, 203, 206, or 207 to Gion (10 min.). Located on Hanamikoji Dori south of Shijo Dori.

PONTOCHO

Pontocho is a narrow alley that parallels the Kamo River's western bank, stretching from Shijo Dori north to Sanjo Dori. Once riddled with geisha houses and other members-only establishments, it is now lined with bars, clubs, restaurants, and hostess bars that fill every nook and cranny. Pontocho makes for a fascinating walk as you watch groups of Japanese enjoying themselves.

Another good place to look for nightlife is **Kiyamachi,** another small street that parallels Pontocho just to the west and runs beside a small canal.

The Club & Live Music Scene

Hello Dolly   With an unlikely location on Pontocho, this dark, tiny club with velvet-upholstered chairs looks like a holdout from the '50s. It has live jazz Friday and Saturday, with classic jazz recordings the rest of the week. To find it, look for an album cover of Doris Day in the window; it's that kind of place. Open daily 6pm to 1am. East side of Pontocho. ☏ **075/241-1728.** Live music cover ¥900–¥1,050 (Fri–Sat only). Bus: 4, 5, 10, 11, 12, 17, 32, 46, 59, 201, 203, 205, or 207 to Shijo Kawaramachi (3 min.).

Le Club Jazz 🎒   For serious jazz fans, this is the real deal, with musicians from Japan and around the world performing on a simple stage six nights a week. It's in a contemporary concrete building on Sanjo Dori, but the entrance—around the back and upstairs—can be hard to find. Its website is in Japanese only, but you can at least get an idea of what you'll pay (or ask a Japanese about performances). Open Tuesday to Sunday 7pm to 1am. Arimoto Building, 2nd floor, Sanjo Dori Gokomachi. http://web. kyoto-inet.or.jp/people/ktsin. ☏ **075/211-5800.** Live music cover ¥1,500–¥3,000. Subway: Kyoto Shiyakusho-mae (3 min.). On the northwest corner of Sanjo Dori and Gokomachi.

Live Spot RAG   Depending on who's playing, the crowd at one of Kyoto's longest-standing live clubs, established in 1981, ranges from an older, more mellow audience to a younger, rowdier bunch. Mostly, however, it's a college-age crowd that comes here to listen to rock, jazz, acoustic, and fusion. Open nightly from 6pm to 2am (to 4:30am on weekends), with live music 7:30 to 10:30pm. Empire Building, 5th floor, Kiyamachi Dori, Sanjo Agaru. www.ragnet.co.jp. ☏ **075/241-0446.** Live music cover ¥1,300–¥4,800 for most performances, plus a 1-drink, 1-dish minimum. Discounts for advance purchases and usually for students. Subway: Kyoto Shiyakusho-mae (3 min.). Bus: 4, 5, 10, 11, 17, 32, 59, or 205 to Kawaramachi Sanjo (2 min.). On the east side of Kiyamachi with its narrow canal, north of Sanjo Dori.

The Bar Scene

Jam Bar ★   Curious about sake but don't know where to start? This friendly, contemporary bar on the edge of Gion is the place. The emphasis is on sake from Kyoto and Niigata, as well as new trends such as infusions of lemon or ginger. A crew of young, knowledgeable sake fans (including some English speakers) offer sake by the glass (or a sampler of three for ¥900), along with snacks, and–should you need it–coffee, tea and beer. It's all served amid cheery, modernist furniture, on the ground floor of Jam Hostel, on the east bank of the Kamogawa River. Open Monday to Friday 5pm to midnight and Saturday to Sunday noon to midnight. 170 Kawabata Tokiwacho. www. sakebar.jp. ☏ **075/201-3374.** Subway: Keihan Shijo. Bus: 100 or 206 to Gion (10 min.) or 4, 5, 17, or 205 to Shijo Kawaramachi (5 min.). From Shijo Dori at the river, head north.

Pig & Whistle   Here's a traditional, noisy, and fun English-style pub where you can play darts, stand at the bar, or sit at a table with your mum. It attracts an older, mixed crowd of both foreigners and Japanese, including foreigners who are networking for employment or business opportunities. Happy hour is from 5 to 7pm nightly. Open daily 5pm to 2am (Fri–Sat to 5am). Shobi Building, 2nd floor, 115 Ohashi-cho, Ohashi, Higashi Iru, Sanjo Dori. www.pigandwhistle.org.uk. ✆ **075/761-6022.** Subway: Sanjo Keihan (2 min.). Bus: 5, 10, 11, 12, or 59 to Sanjo Keihan-mae (2 min.) On the north side of Sanjo Dori, east of the Kamo River.

Rub-A-Dub   This tiny basement bar, decorated like a beach shack with fake palm trees and a corrugated tin roof, has been Kyoto's premier reggae spot for more than 20 years, a laid-back place that plays all genres of Jamaican music. Open Monday to Thursday 7pm to 2am and Friday and Saturday 7pm to 5am. Tsujita Building, 115 Ishi-yamachi, Kiyamachi-sagaru. ✆ **075/256-3122.** Bus: 4, 5, 10, 11, 17, 32, 59, or 205 to Kawaramachi Sanjo. On the east side of Kiyamachi Dori, south of Sanjo Dori.

Tadg's Irish Bar and Restaurant ★ 🍴   Congenial owners Tadg, a professional chef, and Mika, a composer and pianist, lend both their talents and humor to this great bar/restaurant, which offers bar seating, tables with expansive views of Kyoto's temples and mountains, 26 beers on tap (including Guinness and microbrews from around Japan), live music most Friday nights, and a free Wi-Fi connection (and one computer you can use for free). There is also good food, including handmade pizza and vegan and vegetarian choices in addition to the usual Irish stew, bangers and mash, and other pub fare. Open Wednesday to Monday 6pm to 1am. Empire Building, 8th floor, Kiyamachi Dori, Sanjo Agaru. www.kyotoirish.com. ✆ **075/212-6339.** Subway: Kyoto Shiyakusho-mae (3 min.). Bus: 4, 5, 10, 11, 17, 32, 59, or 205 to Kawaramachi Sanjo (2 min.). In the same building as Live Spot RAG, above.

WHERE TO STAY IN KYOTO

Kyoto has a wide variety of accommodations, including some of the best anywhere, but the overall quality of its hotel choices has long lagged behind Tokyo's or Osaka's, surprising for a city where so much of the economy is dependent on tourism. Thankfully, that's changing due to new additions, with more on the way. Western hotels range from luxurious, high-end properties with full facilities to cookie-cutter business hotels and backpacker guesthouses.

On the other hand, if you've never stayed in a *ryokan,* Kyoto is one of the best places to do so. With the exception of hot-spring resorts, Kyoto has more choices of ryokan in all price categories than any other city in Japan. Small, usually made of wood, and often situated in delightfully quaint neighborhoods, these ryokan can enrich your stay in Kyoto by putting you in direct touch with the city's traditional past. Remember that in upper- and midpriced ryokan, the room charge is per person, and though the prices may seem prohibitive at first glance, they do include two meals, tax, and usually the service charge. These meals are feasts, not unlike kaiseki meals you'd receive at a top restaurant where they could easily cost ¥10,000. Ryokan in the budget category, on the other hand, usually don't serve meals unless stated otherwise and often charge per room rather than per person, but they do provide the futon experience.

In any case, be sure to make reservations in advance, particularly in spring when flowers bloom, in autumn for the changing of the leaves, during summer vacation from mid-July through August, and during major festivals (see "Japan Calendar of

Kyoto

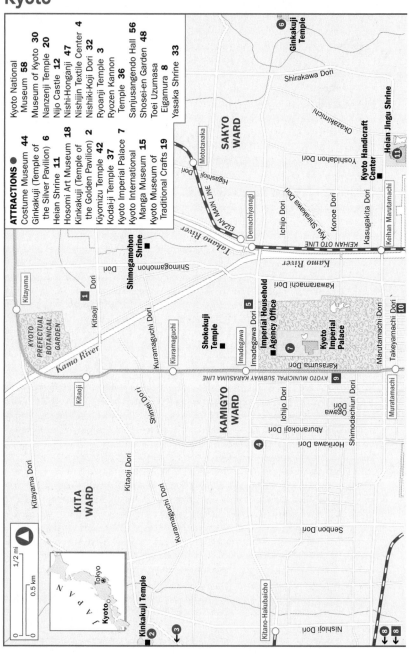

ATTRACTIONS ●

Costume Museum **44**
Ginkakuji (Temple of the Silver Pavilion) **6**
Heian Shrine **11**
Hosomi Art Museum **18**
Kinkakuji (Temple of the Golden Pavilion) **2**
Kiyomizu Temple **42**
Kodaiji Temple **37**
Kyoto Imperial Palace **7**
Kyoto International Manga Museum **15**
Kyoto Museum of Traditional Crafts **19**

Kyoto National Museum **58**
Museum of Kyoto **30**
Nanzenji Temple **20**
Nijo Castle **12**
Nishi-Honganji **47**
Nishijin Textile Center **4**
Nishiki-Koji Dori **32**
Ryoanji Temple **3**
Ryozen Kannon Temple **36**
Sanjusangendo Hall **56**
Shosei-en Garden **48**
Toei Uzumasa Eigamura **8**
Yasaka Shrine **33**

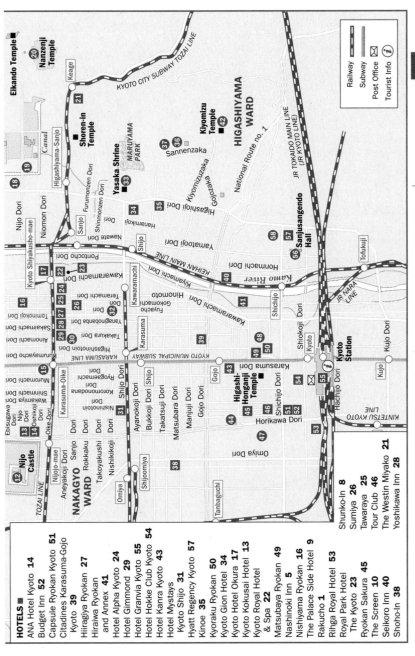

HOTELS ■

ANA Hotel Kyoto **14**
Budget Inn **52**
Capsule Ryokan Kyoto **51**
Citadines Karasuma-Gojo Kyoto **39**
Hiiragiya Ryokan **27**
Hiraiwa Ryokan and Annex **41**
Hotel Alpha Kyoto **24**
Hotel Gimmond **29**
Hotel Granvia Kyoto **55**
Hotel Hokke Club Kyoto **54**
Hotel Kanra Kyoto **43**
Hotel Mystays Kyoto Shijo **31**
Hyatt Regency Kyoto **57**
Kinoe **35**
Kyoraku Ryokan **50**
Kyoto Gion Hotel **34**
Kyoto Hotel Okura **17**
Kyoto Kokusai Hotel **13**
Kyoto Royal Hotel & Spa **22**
Matsubaya Ryokan **49**
Nashinoki Inn **5**
Nishiyama Ryokan **16**
The Palace Side Hotel **9**
Rakucho **1**
Rihga Royal Hotel **53**
Royal Park Hotel The Kyoto **23**
Ryokan Sakura **45**
The Screen **10**
Seikoro Inn **40**
Shoho-In **38**
Shunko-In **8**
Sumiya **26**
Tawaraya **25**
Tour Club **46**
The Westin Miyako **21**
Yoshikawa Inn **28**

A Note on Directions

For all hotel and restaurant listings in this chapter, directions provided are from Kyoto Station unless otherwise indicated. Numbers in parentheses after stations and bus stops refer to the time it takes to reach your destination on foot after alighting from public conveyance.

Events," in chapter 2). Some accommodations raise their rates during these times. In any case, accommodations are expensive in Kyoto, almost on par with Tokyo.

Because Kyoto is relatively small and has such good bus and subway systems, no matter where you stay you won't be too far away from the heart of the city. Most lodgings are concentrated around Kyoto Station (Shimogyo-ku Ward), in central Kyoto not far from the Kawaramachi-Shijo Dori intersection (Nakagyo-ku Ward), and east of the Kamo River (in the Higashiyama-ku and Sakyo-ku wards).

Some properties have shuttle buses to Kyoto Station's south entrance, convenient for train service but not for city buses, which depart from the north side.

TAXES & SERVICE CHARGES   The 5% tax levied by hotels is included in room rates. Mid- and upper-range hotels also add a 10% to 15% service fee. Unless noted otherwise, all rates below include tax and service charge.

Around Kyoto Station
EXPENSIVE

Hotel Granvia Kyoto ★★   Owned by the West Japan Railway Company (Japan Rail pass holders get discounts), this hotel boasts Kyoto's most convenient location for travelers arriving by train: right atop the futuristic-looking Kyoto Station. Only a minute's walk from city buses and trains, it's a good base for exploring Kyoto, Nara, and beyond. The airy lobby is on the second floor, removed from the foot traffic of the station but still buzzing with activity. If you can, avoid the least expensive rooms—they have rather unexciting views of the station's glass roof, and if you're sensitive to noise you'll want to avoid rooms facing the tracks (soundproof windows help but not completely). Otherwise, modern rooms on higher floors facing north have great Kyoto views. Hotel packages are available that include antique shopping, a visit to the inner sanctum of a Shinto shrine, or an evening of entertainment by a geisha.

JR Kyoto Station, Central Exit, Karasuma Dori Shiokoji-sagaru, Shimogyo-ku, Kyoto 600-8216. www.granviakyoto.com. © **075/344-8888.** Fax 075/344-4400. 535 units. ¥28,875–¥43,890 single or double. Granvia Floor ¥43,890–¥49,665 single or double. 20%–36% discount off Superior Twins for holders of Japan Rail Pass (check website for blackout dates). AE, DC, MC, V. **Amenities:** 9 restaurants; bar; 2 lounges; concierge; executive-level rooms; health club w/indoor pool, fitness gym, and sauna (fee: ¥1,050; only guests 21 and older allowed); room service. *In room:* A/C, TV, hair dryer, minibar, Wi-Fi.

Rihga Royal Hotel ★   This has been one of Kyoto's leading hotels since 1969, a particular favorite of Japanese travelers. The building's exterior offers a contemporary rendition of traditional Japanese architecture with its railed ledges, but the lobby is uninteresting and is often busy with tour groups. Still, rooms are comfortable, with adequately sized standard rooms that feature *shoji* screens and window panels that close for darkness. The most expensive rooms, occupying the top two floors, have smart-looking Italian-style furnishings and better city views. Another plus is the frequent shuttle bus to Kyoto Station, though it delivers you to the south side (city buses depart from the north side).

Horikawa Shiokoji, Shimogyo-ku, Kyoto 600-8237. www.rihga.com/kyoto. © **075/341-1121.** Fax 075/341-3073. 484 units. ¥17,325–¥25,410 single; ¥24,255–¥42,735 double. AE, DC, MC, V. Free shuttle bus 4 times an hour 7:30am–9pm from Kyoto Station's Hachijo exit (turn left and walk to the end of the parking lot, past McDonald's), or a 7-min. walk from Kyoto Station. **Amenities:** 6 restaurants; bar; lounge; concierge; executive-level rooms; indoor pool (fee: ¥1,050); room service; sauna (men only; fee: ¥2,625); complimentary shuttle to station. *In room:* A/C, TV, hair dryer, Internet (fee: ¥1,050 for 24 hr.), minibar, Wi-Fi.

MODERATE

Citadines Karasuma-Gojo Kyoto ★ The newly built Kyoto branch of this Singapore-owned "apart-hotel" (apartment hotel) chain is a great choice, evident the moment you enter the stone pathway lined with hanging *washi* paper leading to the mood-lit lobby. Contemporary rooms are actually mini-apartments, complete with small galley kitchens (including rangetop, sink, toaster, microwave, tableware and more) and a fold-out sofa (which can be used as another bed for ¥2,310 extra), separated from the king-size bed by a sliding partition of frosted plexiglass. There's a communal coin-op laundry room. Our only complaint is the underwhelming breakfast buffet for ¥735; with a supermarket 1½ blocks away, you're better off utilizing your kitchen.

432 Matsuya-cho, Gojo Dori, Karasuma Higashi-iru, Shimogyo-ku, Kyoto 600-8105. www.citadines. com. © **075/352-8900.** Fax 075/352-8901. 124 units. ¥23,100–¥29,400 double. AE, DC, MC, V. Subway: Gojo (exit 1, 1 min.). On Gojo Dori, 1½ blocks east of Karasuma Dori. *In room:* A/C, hair dryer, Internet, kitchen.

Hotel Kanra Kyoto ★★★ The Kanra's unassuming façade and discrete entrance around the side give little clue that you are about to enter one of Kyoto's coolest newer properties, artfully designed and with a decidedly hip vibe. Rooms are behind lattice doors in a modern rendition of a *machiya* (merchant house), and even the smallest have plenty of space and oodles of design sense, with black granite floors and wooden soaking tubs and/or showers in the bathrooms. In some, double beds on platforms of white ashwood look like they could sleep four instead of two, and most rooms have tatami spaces with modular furniture. Kitchen Kanra restaurant, on the ground floor, does modern Japanese takes on Italian cuisine and provides the hotel's room service.

185 Kitamachi, Karasuma Rokujo-sagaru, Shimogyo-ku, Kyoto 600-8176. www.hotelkanra.jp. © **075/344-3815.** Fax 075/344-3817. 29 units. ¥17,000–¥25,000 double. AE, DC, MC, V. Subway: Gojo (exit 8, 1 min.); Kyoto Station (Karasuma exit, 8 min). On Karasuma Dori. **Amenities:** Restaurant; room service. *In room:* A/C, hair dryer, fridge, Wi-Fi.

A Double or a Twin?

For the sake of convenience, the price for two people in a room is listed as a "double" in this book. Japanese hotels, however, differentiate between rooms with a double bed or two twin beds, usually with different prices. Most hotels charge more for a twin room, but sometimes the opposite is true; if you're looking for a bargain, therefore, be sure to inquire about prices for both. Note, too, that hotels usually have more twin rooms than doubles, for the simple reason that Japanese couples, used to their own futon, traditionally prefer twin beds.

INEXPENSIVE

Budget Inn ★★ 🛏 Keiji-san and his wife, Hiromi-san, opened this hostelry in 2003 in a former apartment building with six spotless tatami rooms for two to five persons (three of which are gilded in gold and have refrigerators) complete with balconies, plus two dormitory rooms that sleep up to five persons. The level of caring is impressive: a binder full of sightseeing and dining suggestions in each room and little maps to neighborhood restaurants, supermarkets, and more; tips on what's going on and how to spend rainy days; free coffee and tea in the communal kitchen; and the chance to try on a kimono. The location is great, and there's English-speaking staff.

Keiji offers an additional 13 rooms and three dormitory rooms at his nearby **Tour Club,** 362 Momiji-cho, Kitakoji-agaru, Higashi-Nakasuji Dori (www.kyotojp.com; ℂ **075/353-6968**), a 9-minute walk from the station. With similar facilities and amenities, it offers twin rooms from ¥7,770, triples from ¥8,880, quads from ¥11,720, and dormitory beds for ¥2,450. Dorm rooms have shared facilities and an 11pm curfew.

295 Aburanokoji-cho, Aburanokoji, Shichijo-sagaru, Shimogyo-ku, Kyoto 600-8231. www.budgetinn jp.com. ℂ/fax **075/344-1510.** 8 units. ¥8,980–¥9,980 double; ¥10,980 triple; ¥12,980 quad; discounts available for longer stays. MC, V. A 6-min. walk from Kyoto Station's Central (north) exit; turn left on Shiokoji Dori and right at the small parking lot. **Amenities:** Communal kitchen. *In room:* A/C, TV, fridge, no phone, Wi-Fi.

Capsule Ryokan Kyoto In 2010, the owner of Budget Inn opened this combination of two distinct forms of Japanese accommodations—*ryokan* and capsule hotels—and somehow it works. It bills itself as the world's first capsule hotel with tatami and futons, featuring dormitory rooms stacked with human-sized cubbyholes complete with TVs, Internet access, and screens to keep the rest of the world at bay (thoughtfully, earplugs are for sale for ¥100). In any case, this is one of Kyoto's cheapest places to stay, and just think of the stories you'll have to tell the grandkids. Travelers yearning for a little more space can opt for the "ryokan ensuite" rooms, which are minuscule but well designed, with a tall tatami platform (your luggage goes beneath it and futons on top) and a futuristic-looking shower cylinder in the corner of each room (plus sink and toilet). There's no curfew, but the front desk closes from 10pm to 8am.

204 Tsuchihashicho, Shimogyo-ku 600-8226. www.capsule-ryokan-kyoto.com. ℂ **075/344-1510.** 32 units. ¥4,200 capsule beds, ¥4,980 single; ¥7,980 double. Rates higher in peak season. No credit cards. Station: Kyoto (7 min.). On Shichijo Dori just east of Horikawa Dori. **Amenities:** Lobby computer w/free Internet; communal kitchen; Wi-Fi. *In room:* A/C, TV, Internet.

Hiraiwa Ryokan and Annex This *ryokan,* halfway between Kyoto Station and downtown, is one of the best-known and oldest members of the Japanese Inn Group. Although they speak limited English, the Hiraiwa family has been welcoming foreigners from all over the world since opening their doors in 1973. The tatami guest rooms, spread through the century-old traditional main building and a newer annex, are spotless. Note that a Japanese breakfast, which includes *kamameshi* (rice casserole), miso soup, and tofu, must be ordered a day in advance, but you can have coffee and toast until 9am. Shower and bathing facilities are limited (you might opt for the neighborhood public bath and sauna just around the corner) and toilet stalls are unisex, affording little privacy for the shy. And because there's no lounge, there's no chance to meet other guests unless you pass them shuffling down the hall to the bathroom. If you're traveling with a group of friends and would like to hang out in a communal room, stay elsewhere.

314 Hayao-cho, Kaminoguchi-agaru, Ninomiyacho Dori, Shimogyo-ku, Kyoto 600-8114. www2.
odn.ne.jp/hiraiwa. ℂ **075/351-6748.** Fax 075/351-6969. 18 units, none with bathroom. ¥4,200–
¥5,250 single; ¥8,400–¥9,450 double. Japanese breakfast ¥1,050 extra. AE, MC, V. Bus: 17 or 205
(don't take the express 205) to Kawaramachi-Shomen (3rd stop) and then a 4-min. walk (look for
the side street beside Tony Lama), or a 15-min. walk from Kyoto Station. **Amenities:** Lobby computer w/free 30-min. Internet access; communal fridge. *In room:* A/C, TV.

Hotel Hokke Club Kyoto

Hotel Hokke Club Kyoto Popular with tourists thanks to its great location just
opposite Kyoto Station, this chain hotel, friendly and offering reasonable rates, first
opened 90 years ago and provides clean and pleasantly decorated Western-style
rooms with feather quilts and smallish bathrooms. Singles have only tiny glazed windows, but nice semi-double-size beds. The most expensive twins, large for this price
category, face Kyoto Station, but light sleepers may be distracted by train noise.

Kyoto Eki-mae, Shomen Chuoguchi, Karasuma, Shimogyo-ku, Kyoto 600-8216. www.hokke.co.jp.
ℂ **075/361-1251.** Fax 075/361-1255. 187 units. ¥8,400–¥9,450 single; ¥9,870–¥15,750 double. AE,
DC, MC, V. Across from Kyoto Station's Central exit. **Amenities:** 2 restaurants. *In room:* A/C, TV,
fridge, hair dryer, Internet.

Kyoraku Ryokan ★★

Kyoraku Ryokan ★★ Near the Matsubaya (see below), this pleasant and spotlessly clean member of the Japanese Inn Group offers nicely decorated rooms, some
of which look over an inner courtyard garden. Though the English-speaking son is a
fourth-generation innkeeper, the building housing this *ryokan* was erected in 2007
and has the bonus of an elevator and coin-op laundry machines. Guests can help
themselves to free coffee and tea in the dining room. Rooms, all non-smoking and
including one Western style room with private bathroom, are simple, with screened
windows that open. Japanese breakfasts must be ordered the night before, and note
that the ryokan locks its doors at 11pm. The higher rates below are for larger rooms.

231 Kogawa-cho, Shichijo-agaru, Akezu-dori, Shimogyo-ku, Kyoto 600-8149. www.ryokankyoraku.
jp. ℂ **075/371-1260.** Fax 075/371-7161. 16 units, 9 with bathroom. ¥5,200–¥5,600 single without
bathroom, ¥6,000–¥6,600 single with bathroom; ¥9,200–¥10,200 double without bathroom,
¥11,000–¥12,300 double with bathroom. AE, MC, V. A 7-min. walk north of Kyoto Station's Central
exit; walk north on Karasuma Dori, turn right on Shichijo Dori, and then left. **Amenities:** Lobby
computer w/free Internet. *In room:* A/C, TV, no phone, Wi-Fi.

Matsubaya Ryokan ★★★

Matsubaya Ryokan ★★★ 🏠 A member of the Japanese Inn Group, this highly
recommended nonsmoking *ryokan* just east of Higashi Honganji Temple is a great
choice in this category. First opened in the late Edo Period and completely rebuilt in
2008 using architectural details from the old inn, it's owned and managed by the
friendly Hayashi family, now on its fifth generation of innkeepers. Fourteen rooms are
Japanese style, with the best rooms overlooking a garden, while six Western-style
apartments on the fifth floor boast kitchenettes, miniature balconies, free Internet,
and free use of the washing machine. The comfortable lobby lounge is a good place
to meet fellow travelers and chat with the Hayashis, who have made this ryokan the
highlight of many a voyager's trip for many decades.

Higashinotoin Nishi, Kamijuzuyamachi Dori, Shimogyo-ku, Kyoto 600-8150 www.matsubayainn.
com. ℂ **075/351-3727.** Fax 075/351-3505. 20 units (2 without bathroom). ¥4,200–¥4,410 single
without bathroom, ¥6,510–¥9,450 single with bathroom; ¥7,980 double without bathroom,
¥12,180–¥15,960 double with bathroom. AE, MC, V. A 10-min. walk north of Kyoto Station's Central
exit; walk north on Karasuma Dori and take the 3rd right after passing Shichijo Dori. **Amenities:**
Lobby computers w/free Internet. *In room:* A/C, TV, fridge, Internet or Wi-Fi in all rooms, kitchenette (in some).

Ryokan Sakura (さくら) 🎁 Opened in 2009, the smoke-free Sakura has a traditional façade of a *machiya* (merchant's house), but has a comfortably contemporary style inside with gleaming dark woods. Low-key jazz plays in the lobby, and stone corridors lead to tatami rooms, some with an *engawa* (balcony) and others with views of a tiny garden. It's located in an interesting neighborhood of shops selling Buddhist prayer articles; the staff hands out a great bilingual map of local sights and restaurants.

228 Butsuguyacho, Aburanokoji Hanayacho-sagaru, Shimogyo-ku, Kyoto 600-8347. www.kyoto-ryokan-sakura.com. ☏ **075/343-3500.** Fax 075/343-0502. 30 units. ¥7,000–¥10,500 single; ¥12,000–¥15,000 double ¥16,500–¥19,500 triple. AE, DC, MC, V. A 10-min. walk from Kyoto Station's Central (north) exit; turn left on Shiokoji Dori and right at the coffee shop, one block before Horikawa Dori. **Amenities:** Communal kitchen; Wi-Fi (free, in lobby). *In room:* A/C, fridge, Internet.

Central Kyoto
VERY EXPENSIVE

Hiiragiya Ryokan ★★★ This exquisite *ryokan* is as fine an example of a traditional inn as you'll find in Japan. Situated in the heart of old Kyoto, it offers the ultimate in Japanese-style living, with a kind and accommodating staff that's helpful in initiating visitors to the joys of a ryokan. If you're going to splurge just once in Japan, this is one of my top choices. Built in 1818 and an inn since 1861—Ms. Nishimura is the sixth-generation innkeeper—Hiiragiya is a haven of simple design that makes artful use of wood, bamboo, screens, and stones in its spacious, traditionally arranged rooms. Even the remote controls for the lights and curtains are cleverly concealed in specially made lacquered boxes shaped like gourds (invented by the present owner's great-grandfather). Rooms, each one unique, are also outfitted with art and antiques such as gold-painted folding screens or lacquered bathrooms, and most offer garden views and cypress baths. Even the least expensive room—a former tearoom only 4½ tatami-mats big, with a sink but no bathroom and a view of the garden—is good enough for me. A 2006 addition added seven new, elegant rooms connected by gleaming marble corridors. Dinners are exquisite multicourse kaiseki feasts served in your room; Western-style breakfasts are available upon request.

Nakahakusancho, Fuyacho, Anekoji-agaru, Nakagyo-ku, Kyoto 604-8094. www.hiiragiya.co.jp. ☏ **075/221-1136.** Fax 075/221-1139. 28 units, 23 with bathroom; 2 with toilet only. ¥31,500–¥94,500 per person. Rates include 2 meals. AE, DC, MC, V. Located on the corner of Fuyacho and Oike sts. Subway: Kyoto Shiyakusho-mae (4 min.) or Karasuma-Oike (7 min.). Bus: 4, 17, or 205 to Kyoto Shiyakusho-mae (5 min.). Taxi: 10 min. **Amenities:** Lobby computer w/free Internet. *In room:* A/C, TV, hair dryer, Internet (new addition only), minibar.

Sumiya ★★★ Like the other traditional Japanese inns listed here, the 100-year-old Sumiya has a great location in a typical Kyoto neighborhood just a few minutes' walk from bustling downtown. Offering excellent service amid simple yet elegant surroundings, including wooden corridors that wrap around courtyard gardens and several tearooms (a tea ceremony is performed after dinner on the 7th and 17th of each month), it has a variety of rooms, most with wooden tubs and some with wonderful views of tiny private gardens with outdoor benches and platforms for sitting. The oldest rooms employ a striking variety of different woods in their design (be sure to notice the Edo-Era designs on the sliding doors), while rooms in a 1968 addition may have sliding screen doors that open onto a private garden. Meals feature Kyoto kaiseki cuisine (request ahead for special dietary needs); Western breakfasts are also available.

Sanjo-sagaru, Fuyacho, Nakagyo-ku, Kyoto 604-8075. sumiyaryokan@par.odn.ne.jp. ☏ **075/221-2188.** Fax 075/221-2267. 21 units, 16 with bathroom. ¥31,500–¥63,000 per person, including 2 meals. AE, DC, MC, V. On Fuyacho Dori just south of Sanjo St. Subway: Kyoto Shiyakusho-mae (6 min.) or Karasuma-Oike (10 min.). Bus: 4, 5, 17, or 205 to Kawaramachi Sanjo (3 min.). Taxi: 10 min. *In room:* A/C, TV, hair dryer, Internet, minibar.

Tawaraya ★★ Across the street from the Hiiragiya (see above) is another distinguished, venerable old inn, owned and operated by the same family since it opened early in the 1700s (Mrs. Toshi Okazaki Satow is the 11th-generation innkeeper). Unfortunately, fire consumed the original building, so the oldest part of the *ryokan* now dates back a mere 220 years. This inn has had an impressive list of former guests, from Leonard Bernstein to Alfred Hitchcock. Saul Bellow wrote in the ryokan's guest book, "I found here what I had hoped to find in Japan—the human scale, tranquility, and beauty." With refined taste reigning supreme, each room is different and exquisitely appointed. Some have glass sliding doors opening onto a mossy garden of bamboo, stone lanterns, and manicured bushes, with cushions on a wooden veranda where you can sit and soak in the peacefulness. You probably won't ever want to leave, but when you do, the staff will gather to bow and see you off.

Fuyacho, Aneyakoji-Agaru, Nakagyo-ku, Kyoto 604-8094. (©) **075/211-5566.** Fax 075/211-2204. 18 units. ¥42,263–¥84,525 per person, including 2 meals. AE, DC, MC, V. Subway: Kyoto Shiyakusho-mae (4 min.) or Karasuma-Oike (10 min.). Bus: 17 or 205 to Shiyakusho-mae (5 min.). Taxi: 10 min. *In room:* A/C, TV, hair dryer, minibar.

Yoshikawa Inn ★ Known for its tempura (see "Where to Dine in Kyoto," earlier in this chapter), this inn also offers tatami rooms with cypress bathtubs, the best of which look out on the largest garden I've seen in a downtown Kyoto *ryokan.* Built more than 100 years ago and opening as an inn a half-century ago, it offers the extra benefit of leg wells under the tables of its tatami rooms, making dining easier for those not used to sitting on the floor. It offers the usual elegance you'd expect from an inn of this caliber, including a warm, hospitable staff.

Tominokoji Dori Oike-sagaru, Nakagyo-ku, Kyoto 604-8093. www.kyoto-yoshikawa.co.jp. (©) **075/211-5544.** Fax 075/211-6805. 8 units. ¥30,000–¥60,000, including 2 meals. Rates exclude tax & service charge. AE, DC, MC, V. Subway: Karasuma Oike Station (6 min.; on Tominokoji St. just south of Oike Dori). Taxi: 10 min. **Amenities:** Restaurant. *In room:* A/C, TV, hair dryer.

EXPENSIVE

ANA Hotel Kyoto (Zenniku Hotel Kyoto) ★★ Across the street from Nijo Castle and offering rooms with castle views, this hotel has one of the most eye-catching lobby lounges in town, with a glass wall overlooking an impressive waterfall and landscape garden (though we could have done without the deer statue), all to the accompaniment of *koto* (Japanese zither) music. Kimono-clad hostesses greeting guests as they enter the lobby are a welcoming touch. Rooms are attractive if a bit cramped, with roomy bathrooms and unusual extras like shoe dryers, air humidifiers, and ion-free hair dryers and hairbrushes. None of the singles face the castle; double rooms that do start at ¥31,185 during the regular season. Other pluses: great restaurants, a rooftop beer garden in summer, and a complimentary shuttle bus four times an hour to and from Kyoto Station from 8am to 7:45pm (to 9:45pm in summer).

Nijojo-mae, Horikawa Dori, Nakagyo-ku, Kyoto 604-0055. www.ana-hkyoto.com. (©) **800/993-3563** in the U.S. and Canada, or 075/231-1155. Fax 075/231-5333. 298 units. ¥15,015 single; ¥24,255–¥33,495 double. 10%–15% extra per person Apr–May and Oct–Nov; ¥1,155 extra per person Sat and nights before holidays. AE, DC, MC, V. Subway: Nijojo-mae (1 min.). Free shuttle bus from Kyoto Station; or subway or bus: 9, 50, or 101 to Nijojo-mae. **Amenities:** 5 restaurants; bar; lounge; concierge; lobby computer w/free Internet; indoor pool and sauna (fee: ¥1,500); room service. *In room:* A/C, TV, hair dryer, Internet, minibar.

Kyoto Hotel Okura ★★★   First built in 1888, one of Kyoto's oldest hotels underwent a complete metamorphosis in 1994 and is now the city's tallest building, with 17 floors. Its height caused a stir of protest by those who advocate stricter height restrictions; though I usually side with historical preservationists, I must admit that no finer building could have violated the skyline. Its modern facade hints at traditional Japanese latticework, while the spacious lobby, designed after the hotel's original 1920s ballroom, exudes a gracefully elegant old-world ambience. Restaurants on the top floor offer stunning views. Rooms, built around a central atrium, are the utmost in comfort and grandeur. The best views are of the Kamo River, especially from the most expensive rooms on upper floors that also take in the hills of Higashi-yama-ku beyond the city. In short, luxurious accommodations, a great location in the heart of Kyoto, and a hospitable staff come together to make this an excellent choice.

Kawaramachi-Oike, Nakagyo-ku, Kyoto 604-8558. okura.kyotohotel.co.jp. ℂ **075/211-5111,** or 223-2333 for reservations. Fax 075/221-7770. 322 units. ¥21,945–¥24,255 single; ¥31,185–¥56,595 double; from ¥43,890 executive double. AE, DC, MC, V. Subway: Kyoto Shiyakusho-mae (1 min., below the hotel). Bus: 4, 17, or 205 to Shiyakusho-mae (2 min.). **Amenities:** 8 restaurants; 2 bars; lounge; children's day-care center (¥5,250 for 2 hr.); concierge; executive-level rooms; indoor pool w/Jacuzzi and sauna open only 7–10am (fee: ¥2,100; children 17 and younger not allowed); room service. *In room:* A/C, TV, hair dryer, Internet, minibar.

Kyoto Royal Hotel & Spa ★   The main reason to stay here? Location, location, location. In the heart of Kyoto on Kawaramachi Dori, this typical tourist hotel has a friendly staff and has been stylishly renovated to achieve a top-class atmosphere, yet it still can't compete with the facilities and grandeur of Kyoto's other top hotels. However, it's a convenient base for sightseeing and has an information desk to answer guest questions. Chic blonde-and-black furnished rooms feature focused bedside reading lamps, but they are otherwise fairly basic. Note that single rooms and some doubles face an inner courtyard, which cuts down on noise but also on sunshine, while rooms that face the Kamo River have better views but are minuscule; rooms facing busy Kawaramachi are bigger but get more noise. Again, the best reason to stay here is location, though the spa might help you get over jet lag.

Sanjo-agaru Kawaramachi, Nakagyo-ku, Kyoto 604-8005. www.ishinhotels.com. ℂ **075/223-1234.** Fax 075/223-1702. 398 units. ¥20,000 single; ¥30,000–¥40,000 double. AE, DC, MC, V. Subway: Kyoto Shiyakusho-mae (2 min.). Bus: 4, 17, or 205 to Kawaramachi Sanjo (2 min.). **Amenities:** Restaurant; bar; concierge; lobby computers w/free Internet; room service (24 hours); spa; Wi-Fi (free, in lobby). *In room:* A/C, TV, fridge, hair dryer, Internet.

The Screen ★★   If you prefer small hotels and contemporary design, you might enjoy staying at this strikingly modern yet inviting hotel, complete with traditional touches that make it seem like a hybrid between a traditional *ryokan* and a boutique hotel. Each of its 13 rooms, by 13 different international designers, has its own style. Two Japanese-style rooms, for example, have futons on raised tatami platforms along with black lacquered furniture, while another has a playful forest motif and another yet is lined with sheer white curtains. Its location between the Imperial Palace and downtown, on a street lined with craft and antiques stores, is another plus, and I also like the Sky Lounge with its outdoor seating. There aren't many cool hotels like this one in Japan, and after staying in unimaginative rooms, this is a worthy splurge.

640–1 Shimogoryomae-cho, Nakagyoku, Nakagyo-ku, Kyoto 604-0995. www.screen-hotel.jp. ℂ **075/252-1113.** Fax 075/252-1311. 13 units. ¥27,000–¥45,000 single or double. Rates ¥10,000 higher on weekends and peak periods. AE, DC, MC, V. Subway: Karasuma Marutamachi (7 min.). Bus: 4, 17, or 205 to Kawaramachi Marutamachi (7 min.). South of Marutamachi Dori, on Teramachi

Dori. **Amenities:** Restaurant; lounge; lobby computers w/free Internet; spa. *In room:* A/C, TV/DVD, hair dryer, Internet, minibar, MP3 docking station.

MODERATE

Hotel Alpha Kyoto This small, older and unassuming but pleasant brick business hotel has a hidden location near the Kawaramachi-Shijo Dori intersection, and I have always found the staff accommodating. Most rooms, including singles, are outfitted with double-size beds, but because the cheapest singles face an inner courtyard and are fairly dark, it may be worthwhile to dish out extra yen for a brighter room. My favorite rooms overlook a quiet temple and Buddhist cemetery—a fitting view in a town that boasts so many religious structures. There are also three Japanese-style rooms with cedar tubs. In short, this is a good choice if you like to be in the thick of things and are willing to sacrifice space and facilities to be there.

Kawaramachi, Sango-agaru, Nakagyo-ku, Kyoto 604-8006. www.alphakyoto.com. ✆ **075/241-2000.** Fax 075/211-0533. 119 units. ¥8,000–¥9,500 single; ¥12,500–¥19,500 double. AE, DC, MC, V. Subway: Kyoto Shiyakusho-mae (2 min.). Bus: 4, 5, 17, or 205 to Kawaramachi Sanjo (1 min.). Just off Kawaramachi Dori not far from Sanjo Dori; entrance is on a side street called Aneyakoji Dori. **Amenities:** Restaurant; lobby computer w/free Internet; Wi-Fi (free, in lobby). *In room:* A/C, TV, fridge, hair dryer, Internet (in single and twins only).

Hotel Gimmond This small hotel on Oike Dori was built some 30 years ago, but it achieves an even older ambience in its lobby with antique-looking lighting and decor. Though the hotel calls itself a tourist hotel and offers mainly twins, its accommodations and lack of services and facilities place it squarely in the category of business hotel. Simple rooms, all nonsmoking, are soundproof thanks to sliding blackout panels behind the curtains, but I still think those that face away from Oike Dori are quieter; ask for one on a higher floor. Twin rooms are decent sized for the price, while the cheapest rooms are quite small.

Takakura, Oike Dori, Nakagyo-ku, Kyoto 604-8105. www.gimmond.co.jp. ✆ **075/221-4111.** Fax 075/221-8250. 140 units. ¥9,586–¥10,741 single; ¥16,170–¥20,790 double. AE, DC, MC, V. Subway: Karasuma-Oike (2 min.). **Amenities:** 2 restaurants; Wi-Fi (free, in lobby). *In room:* A/C, TV, fridge, hair dryer, Internet.

Hotel Monterey Kyoto ★ In the middle of Karasuma Dori's hubbub is this unexpected choice, located in a former bank. Arched corridors of striated chocolate brown and charcoal gray marble lead to a lobby decorated in the Arts & Crafts style of Edinburgh (Kyoto's sister city). In this country of mostly drab hotel rooms, the Monterey's are remarkably bold, with striped wallpaper done in deep blue or bright red. It's worth paying the extra ¥1,725 to use the top-floor indoor-outdoor hot-spring baths, with surprising views across the city (the hotel drilled more than 1,000m/3,280 ft. below ground to access thermal water).

604 Manjuya-cho, Karasuma Dori, Sanjo-sagaru, Nakagyo-ku, Kyoto 604-8161. www.hotelmonterey. co.jp/kyoto. ✆ **075/251-7111.** Fax 075/251-7112. 327 units. ¥15,000–¥20,000 single; ¥24,000–¥46,000 double. AE, DC, MC, V. Subway: Karasuma Oike (exit 6, 3 min.). Just south of Sanjo Dori on Karasuma Dori. **Amenities:** 2 restaurants; Wi-Fi; lobby computer w/free Internet; spa. *In room:* A/C, TV, fridge, hair dryer. Internet.

Hotel Mystays Kyoto Shijo ★ This tourist/business hotel is a step ahead of older competitors, offering stylish rooms with contemporary furnishings (like red lounge chairs in its single rooms) and black-and-white photos of Kyoto on the walls. Nagomi rooms, with their bamboo floors and low bed, have a traditional Japanese atmosphere, while rooms on the top floors have good city views.

52 Kasaboko-cho, Aburanokoji Higashi-iru, Shijo Dori, Shimogyo-ku, Kyoto 600-8494. ☏ **075/283-3939.** Fax 075/283-3940. 224 units. ¥12,000 single; ¥18,000–¥25,500 double. Rates ¥3,000–¥6,000 higher in peak season. AE, DC, MC, V. Subway: Shijo (4 min.). Bus: 26 to shijo Nishinotoin (2 min.). On the north side of Shijo Dori, east of Aburanokoji. **Amenities:** Restaurant; room service. *In room:* A/C, TV, fridge, hair dryer, Internet.

Kyoto Kokusai Hotel ★   I like this hotel across from Nijo Castle because it offers a few surprises you wouldn't expect in medium-range accommodations. Although its name translates as "International Hotel," and it bills itself as Western-style, the atmosphere is pretty Japanese (more than 90% of its guests are Japanese, and there are many gift shops in the lobby). The large lobby overlooks a pleasant, lush, one-time noble garden, which you can gaze upon from either the tea lounge or restaurant, Azalea (see p. 272; there's also a steak house). Most evenings at 7pm, Azalea hosts dance presentations given by *maiko* (geisha apprentices). Room rates are based on decor and amenities, with higher-priced rooms offering views of Nijo Castle (note, however, that only 50 twins and two doubles face the castle and that none of the singles do). Rooms have comfortable but basic décor, outfitted with *shoji* screens.

Nijojo-mae, Horikawa Dori, Nakagyo-ku, Kyoto 604-8502. www.kyoto-kokusai.com. ☏ **075/222-1111.** Fax 075/231-9381. 274 units. ¥7,000–¥17,000 single; ¥14,000–¥33,000 double. AE, DC, MC, V. Subway: Nijojo-mae (2 min.). Bus: 9, 50, or 101 to Nijojo-mae (2 min.). Across from Nijo Castle. **Amenities:** 3 restaurants, including Azalea (p. 272); lounge; room service. *In room:* A/C, TV, fridge, hair dryer, Internet (in some).

Royal Park Hotel The Kyoto ★   We question the placement of "The" in this hotel's name, but everything else is pretty much on target. Opened in 2011 and close to sightseeing, shopping, nightlife and transportation, it's stylish, comfy and up to date, complete with laundry facilities. Pluses in rooms include custom-designed mattresses, bathrooms with separate showers and soaking tubs, and contemporary décor that includes silver accents, silk bedskirts and curtains, and playful artwork of rabbits jumping over the moon that add a dash of color. *And* the public spaces are non-smoking (including the bar, a rarity in Japan).

Kawaramachi Higashi-iru, Sango Dori, Nakagyo-ku, Kyoto 604-8004. www.rph-the.co.jp/kyoto. ☏ **075/241-1111.** Fax 075/241-1139. 172 units. ¥18,4800–¥31,985 single; ¥28,875–¥39,270 double. AE, DC, MC, V. Subway: Kyoto Shiyakusho-mae (3 min.). On Sanjo Dori just east of Kawaramachi, on the north side. **Amenities:** Restaurant; bar; lobby computer w/free Internet; Wi-Fi (free, in lobby). *In room:* A/C, TV, fridge, hair dryer, Internet.

INEXPENSIVE

Nishiyama Ryokan 🐾   Located just a few minutes' walk north of downtown Kyoto, this 40-year-old property has more soul than a chain hotel, with a traditional atmosphere and a small courtyard garden just beyond the lobby. It even stages cultural events in its lobby for guests free of charge, such as calligraphy lessons or the tea ceremony. It offers mostly Japanese-style tatami rooms and four small Western-style twins, all nonsmoking. A public bath boasts views of a garden waterfall. It's popular with school groups, but if you don't mind the youthful clientele this makes for a good choice for moderately priced Japanese-style accommodations in the heart of the city. Manager Mr. Nishiyama, the third-generation of the family here, speaks English.

Gokomachi, Nijo-sagaru, Nakagyo-ku, Kyoto 604-0933. www.ryokan-kyoto.com. ☏ **075/222-1166.** Fax 075/231-3558. 30 units, 26 with bathroom, 4 with toilet only. ¥6,000 single with toilet, ¥9,000 single with bathroom; ¥12,500–¥16,000 double. Rates ¥1,000–¥3,000 higher in peak season. Japanese dinner ¥7,000 extra; Japanese or Western breakfast ¥1,500 extra. AE, DC, MC, V. Subway: Shiyakusho-mae (3 min.). Bus: 4, 17, or 205 to Shiyakusho-mae (3 min.). 2 blocks northwest of City Hall. **Amenities:** Lobby computers w/free Internet; Wi-Fi (free, in lobby). *In room:* A/C, TV, fridge.

The Palace Side Hotel ★ 🏠 Savvy, budget-conscious travelers have been flocking to this modest hotel with its contemporary lobby and cafe for more than four decades. Although its location just west of the Imperial Palace is not as convenient as our other inexpensive recommendations in central Kyoto, it's near a subway line and offers more facilities than most (including laundry facilities; plus, the palace grounds are great for joggers). Also impressive are the free Japanese-language lessons offered several evenings a month and mini-concerts in the lobby. The rooms (all nonsmoking) are dormitory plain and small (with just the basics of a desk too tiny for any serious work), but half of them have original artwork (by artists who actually stayed there), and all offer windows that open, and tiled bathrooms. The most expensive twins and doubles have kitchenettes.

Karasuma Shimodachiuri-agaru, Kamigyo-ku, Kyoto 602-8011. www.palacesidehotel.co.jp. ☎ **075/415-8887.** Fax 075/415-8889. 120 units. ¥6,000–¥7,000 single; ¥9,000–¥11,800 double. Long-term rates available. AE, DC, MC, V. Subway: Marutamachi (exit 2, 3 min.). **Amenities:** Restaurant; bar; Thai massage room; rental bikes (free 1st hour, then ¥800 for 12 hr.); lobby computers w/free Internet; communal kitchen. *In room:* A/C, TV, fridge, hair dryer.

Eastern Kyoto
EXPENSIVE
Hyatt Regency Kyoto ★★★ Located in Higashiyama-ku near the Kyoto National Museum and Sanjusangendo Hall, this gem combines traditional art and materials with contemporary styles. On the site of the former residence of Emperor Goshirakawa, it also has a beautiful 850-year-old garden, complete with waterfall and pond, visible from some rooms and its top-notch restaurants (Touzan for Japanese and Sette for Italian). Its spa, offering acupuncture, moxibustion, and shiatsu in addition to the usual aromatherapy, boasts more Asian treatments than any other hotel spa in Japan. Classy rooms blend Japanese aesthetics with technical know-how, from kimono-fabric-covered headboards and elegant teaware to large safes with electric hookups for laptops (so you can charge your laptop while it is in storage), control panels for lights, and stone-floored bathrooms. For a splurge, eight deluxe rooms have tatami areas and Japanese-style tubs placed next to balconies, with views of the garden or National Museum. In short, you can't go wrong staying here. Rates below reflect the seasons.

644–2 Sanjusangendo-mawari, Higashiyama-ku, Kyoto 605-0941. http://kyoto.regency.hyatt.com. ☎ **800/233-1234** in the U.S. and Canada, or 075/541-1234. Fax 075/541-2203. 189 units. ¥22,000–¥43,000 single or double; ¥63,000–¥84,000 deluxe rooms. AE, DC, MC, V. Bus: 100, 206, or 208 to Hakubutsukan Sanjusangendo (1 min.). **Amenities:** 3 restaurants, including Touzan (p. 276); 2 bars; babysitting; concierge; gym (free for hotel guests); room service; spa (fee: ¥1,600); Wi-Fi (free, in lobby). *In room:* A/C, TV/DVD (free DVDs), hair dryer, Internet (¥1,575 per day), minibar.

Kinoe (き乃ゑ) ★ This *ryokan* is different from my other high-end Japanese inn recommendations in that it's been in operation only half a century and occupies a modern, 16-year-old building. However, there may be room at this inn when more famous establishments are full, and it has an interesting location on the edge of the Gion geisha district. Under the able management of Ms. Chizuyo Miyata, it offers simple but elegant tatami rooms with all the traditional flourishes such as *shoji* screens, sliding paper doors, calligraphy in the *tokonoma* alcove, and a seating area beside the window. In addition to in-room baths, the shared common baths feature marble walls and a hinoki cypress tub. Meals, including seasonal kaiseki (Western breakfasts on request), are served in your room.

Higashioji, Yasuikado, Higashiyama-ku, Kyoto 605-0812. www.kinoe.co.jp. ☎ **075/561-1230.** Fax 075/561-8719. 13 units. ¥17,850–¥43,050 per person, including 2 meals; ¥11,550–¥23,100 per person with breakfast. AE, DC, MC, V. On Higashioji Dori, south of Yasaka Shrine. Bus: 206 or 207 to Higashiyama Yasui (1 min.). Taxi: 10 min. **Amenities:** Lobby compute w/free Internet; Wi-Fi (free, in lobby). *In room:* A/C, TV, hair dryer, minibar.

Seikoro Inn ★★★ 🏮 This *ryokan* just east of the Kamo River was established in 1831, with the present building dating from a century ago. After passing through a traditional front gate and small courtyard, you'll find yourself in one of the most charming entryways I've seen in Kyoto, which adjoins a cozy parlor replete with an eclectic mix of Japanese and Western antiques. The rooms, also decorated in antiques, are homey and comfortable; some open onto a garden with sliding doors and *shoji* screens. Rooms in an annex built just before the 1964 Olympics are high enough that you can see over the surrounding rooftops, but most of these don't have garden views so I prefer the ones in the oldest buildings. The nice public bath boasts a tub made of 400-year-old hinoki cypress, making it one of the inn's most treasured possessions. The English-speaking, sixth-generation innkeeper doesn't mind if you take your meals elsewhere, especially if you're here for a while. The staff is warm and welcoming and will prepare Western breakfasts on request. If you wish, you can dress up in an elaborate kimono (a 30-min. process) for ¥2,000 so you can take pictures.

Tonyamachi Dori, Gojo-saguru, Higashiyama-ku, Kyoto 605-0907. www.seikoro.com. ☎ **075/561-0771.** Fax 075/541-5481. 22 units. ¥28,875 double room without meals; ¥28,875–¥57,750 per person including 2 meals. AE, DC, MC, V. Bus: 4, 17, or 205 to Kawaramachi Gojo and then a 5-min. walk; cross the bridge over the Kamo River and after Kawabata Dori take the 1st right. Keihan Electric Railway: Gojo Station (2 min.). *In room:* A/C, TV, hair dryer, Wi-Fi.

The Westin Miyako Kyoto ★★★ ☺ One of Japan's best-known hotels, the Miyako opened in 1890 and boasts a guest list that reads like a who's who of visitors to Japan: Douglas Fairbanks, Queen Elizabeth II, Prince Charles and Princess Diana, Ronald & Nancy Reagan, and Ted Kennedy. Even today, half of the guests staying here are foreigners. Still, you'd be hard-pressed to find evidence of that history today (the current building dates from 1992). Rather, this is one of Kyoto's most smartly appointed hotels, on par with the best of Tokyo's hotels. Its setting is as good as it gets: The hotel sprawls over more than 6.4 hectares (16 acres) of hilltop east of the city, close to some of Kyoto's most famous temples (and a subway station). There's a Japanese garden, and families appreciate the indoor and outdoor pools and small playroom equipped with games for toddlers.

Western-style rooms, which come with Westin's trademark Heavenly Beds and one-touch Service Express for everything from room service to messages, come in a variety of styles and prices, with the least expensive occupying the oldest wing and the best on the fifth floor with large terraces overlooking the valley. For those who wish to experience the pleasures of a traditional tatami room but with all the nearby conveniences of a first-rate hotel, the Japanese-style Kasui-en annex is a good bet for *ryokan* first-timers; built in 1959, it offers 20 modern, elegant rooms with views of the Japanese garden and cypress baths.

Keage, Sanjo, Higashiyama-ku, Kyoto 605-0052. www.mikayohotels.ne.jp/westinkyoto. ☎ **800/937-8461** in the U.S. and Canada, or 075/771-7111. Fax 075/751-2490. 499 units. ¥33,500–¥56,000 single or double; from ¥48,500 Executive Club floor; ¥41,500 double in Kasui-en. AE, DC, MC, V. Free shuttle every 30 min. from Kyoto Station's Hachijo exit (8:15am–9:15pm). Subway: Keage (2 min.). **Amenities:** 5 restaurants; bar; concierge; executive-level rooms; gym (fee: ¥500; free for executive level guests); 20m (66-ft.) indoor pool and shallow outdoor pool (fee: ¥500 for either); room service; sauna; sun decks (available also for viewing the full moon); grass tennis court (¥5,250 per hour);

There's another inexpensive lodging option in Kyoto—in one of its temples. Note that payment is in cash only. At **Shunko-In,** 42 Myoshinji-Cho, Hanazono, Ukyo-ku (www.shunkoin.com; ✆ **075/462-5488**), Rev. Kawakami Taka offers Zen meditation classes in English, plus a tour of its gardens, in the sprawling Myoshin-ji monastery. Overnight accommodations include five rooms, two with private shower and toilet, (¥5,000 per person), and three with shared facilities, (¥4,000 per person). No meals are offered, but there are many restaurants nearby. To reach it, take a local train on the JR Sagano Line to Hanazono, and walk two minutes to Myoshin-ji's south gate. It's another two minutes to Shunkoin. It's also served by many bus lines, including bus no. 26 from Kyoto Station to the Myoshin-ji Kitamon stop.

   Shoho-In, Omiya-Matsubara Nishi-iru, Shimogyu-ku (✆ **090/8988-2998**; ask for Kato-san) offers three rooms for two or more persons beginning at ¥5,000 per person, including a large room for up to seven persons and a two-bedroom condo, complete with kitchen and its own entrance, for stays of a week or longer. No meals are served. Be sure to take a peek inside the small 200-year-old temple, famous for its thousand-year-old statue of Amida. Take bus no. 206 to Omiya Matsubara.

wild-bird sanctuary and bird-watching trail; jogging trail; Wi-Fi (free, in lobby). *In room:* A/C, TV, hair dryer, Internet (¥1,575 per 24 hr.), minibar.

MODERATE

Kyoto Gion Hotel   This 40-some-year-old hotel has seen better days, but it's about your only option for mid-range accommodation in Gion, within easy walking distance of the city center, shops, nightlife, and the many sights in Higashiyama-ku. There's no view to speak of, but rooms facing west on the upper floors have floor-to-ceiling windows overlooking the quaint tiled roofs of Gion (corner rooms are best). The single rooms are among the smallest I've seen (I'm not sure there's even room to unpack), and only twins are available for two people (no doubles). A plus is the rooftop beer garden, open in summer.

555 Minamigawa, Gion, Higashiyama-ku, Kyoto 605-0074. www.apahotel.com. ✆ **075/551-2111.** Fax 075/551-2200. 154 units. ¥9,500–¥10,000 single; ¥17,000–¥25,000 double. ¥500 extra on Sat and day before holidays; ¥2,500–¥3,000 extra per person during high season. AE, DC, MC, V. Bus: 100 or 206 to Gion (2 min.). On Shijo Dori, west of Yasaka Shrine. **Amenities:** Restaurant; bar; beer garden; Starbucks; Wi-Fi (free, in lobby). *In room:* A/C, TV, fridge, hair dryer, Internet.

Northern Kyoto

INEXPENSIVE

Nashinoki Inn ★ ☺   In a quiet, peaceful neighborhood north of the Kyoto Imperial Palace, this 100-year-old *ryokan* has been run since 1970 by a warm and friendly elderly lady who speaks some English. Staying here is like living with a Japanese family, as the home looks very lived in and is filled with the personal belongings of a lifetime. Some of the tatami rooms, which feature touches such as vases, Japanese dolls, and pictures, are quite large and adequate for families. Western or Japanese breakfasts are served in your room.

Teramachi Nishi-iru Imadegawa Dori, Futasujime-agaru, Kamigyo-ku, Kyoto 602-0838. www.nande. com/nashinoki. ✆ **075/241-1543.** Fax 075/211-0854. 6 units, none with bathroom. ¥5,700 single;

¥10,100 double. Breakfast ¥950–¥1,050 extra. No credit cards. Subway: Imadegawa Station (10 min. from exit 3); walk past Doshisha University and turn left at Yaomon coffee shop. **Amenities:** Bicycles (free); free guest computer; Wi-Fi (free, in lobby). *In room:* A/C, TV, no phone.

Rakucho ★★ 👔 This member of the Japanese Inn Group isn't as conveniently situated as most of the other inns listed above, but that shouldn't stop anyone from staying in this well-kept 70-year-old *ryokan,* managed by English-speaking Kimiko Urade and her son. All but one of the spotless tatami rooms, decorated with such traditional touches as scrolls, have views of a small peaceful garden. Entrance to the ryokan is through a well-tended tiny courtyard filled with plants. There's a kitchenette with two communal refrigerators, a toaster, microwave, and free instant coffee and tea, as well as laundry facilities.

67 Higashihangi-cho, Shimogamo, Sakyo-ku, Kyoto 606-0824. www.rakucho-ryokan.com. 📞 **075/ 721-2174.** Fax 075/791-7202. 11 units, none with bathroom. ¥5,300 single; ¥8,400–¥9,240 double; ¥12,600 triple. MC, V. Subway: Kitaoji Station (10 min.); walk east on Kitaoji Dori and turn left at the 5th traffic light. Bus: 205 to Furitsudaigaku-mae (2 min. to the north). **Amenities:** Lobby computer w/free Internet; communal kitchenette; Wi-Fi (free, in lobby). *In room:* A/C, no phone.

WALKING TOUR 1: A STROLL THROUGH HIGASHIYAMA-KU

START:	**Sanjusangendo Hall on Shichijo Dori a couple of blocks east of the Kamo River; to get there, walk 20 minutes from Kyoto Station or take bus no. 100, 206, or 208 to Hakubutsukan Sanjusangendo-mae.**
FINISH:	**Gion.**
TIME:	**Allow approximately 5 hours, including stops for shopping and museums.**
BEST TIMES:	**Weekdays, when temples and shops aren't as crowded.**
WORST TIMES:	**There is no worst day for this tour.**

A stroll through Higashiyama-ku will take you to Kiyomizu Temple, one of Kyoto's most famous sights, and other worthwhile attractions like Sanjusangendo Hall. It will also take you through some of Kyoto's most charming neighborhoods, with plenty of shopping opportunities en route.

Note: The second walk, "The Philosopher's Stroll" (see below), includes several attractions that could be combined with this walk if you don't have time for two walks. If you continue walking north from Maruyama Park instead of heading west for Gion, for example, you could take in Heian Shrine and the Kyoto Handicraft Center (covered at the end of the second walk). In any case, because eastern Kyoto has some of the city's most traditional and beautiful restaurants, be sure to read through the dining section to decide beforehand where you want to eat lunch or dinner.

Before setting out, pick up the walking-tour leaflet "Kyoto Walks" at either the Tourist Information Center in Tokyo or Kyoto Tourist Information. It's useful for its maps of four walks, but disregard its claim that you can walk from Kiyomizu Temple to Heian Shrine in 50 minutes. I don't see how it's possible unless you run the entire way. I've walked this route almost a dozen times, and it's always taken me the better part of a day—perhaps I'm slow, but it's a pace that I've found does justice to this wonderful area of Kyoto.

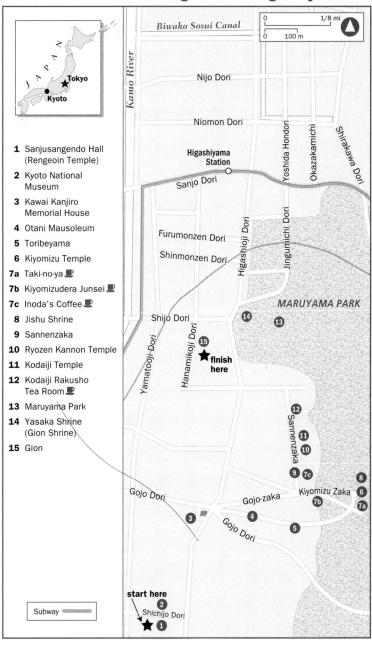

1 Sanjusangendo Hall
(Rengeoin Temple)

2 Kyoto National
Museum

3 Kawai Kanjiro
Memorial House

4 Otani Mausoleum

5 Toribeyama

6 Kiyomizu Temple

7a Taki-no-ya

7b Kiyomizudera Junsei

7c Inoda's Coffee

8 Jishu Shrine

9 Sannenzaka

10 Ryozen Kannon Temple

11 Kodaiji Temple

12 Kodaiji Rakusho
Tea Room

13 Maruyama Park

14 Yasaka Shrine
(Gion Shrine)

15 Gion

Biwako Sosui Canal

0   1/8 mi
0   100 m

Kamo River

JAPAN

Tokyo

Kyoto

Nijo Dori

Niomon Dori

Higashiyama
Station

Yoshida Hondori

Okazakamichi

Shirakawa Dori

Sanjo Dori

Furumonzen Dori

Shinmonzen Dori

Higashioji Dori

Jingumichi Dori

MARUYAMA PARK

Shijo Dori

14

13

15
★ finish
here

Yamatooji Dori

Hanamikoji Dori

Sannenzaka

12

11

10

9 7c

8

6

7b

7a

Kiyomizu Zaka

Gojo Dori

Gojo-zaka

3

4

5

Gojo Dori

start here
2
Shichijo Dori
★ 1

Subway

Start your stroll at:

1 Sanjusangendo Hall

This hall dates from 1266 and is only about 15m (50 ft.) wide, but stretches almost 120m (400 ft.), making it the longest wooden building in Japan. However, it's not the building itself that impresses but what it contains—1,001 life-size images of the thousand-handed Kannon. Seeing so many of them—row upon row of gold figures, glowing in the dark hall—is stunning (unfortunately, no photographs or videos allowed). In the middle is a 3.3m-tall (11-ft.) seated figure of Kannon carved in 1254. At the back of the hall is a 117m (384-ft.) archery range where a competition is held every January 15. (See "Exploring the City," earlier in this chapter, for more information on this and other major sights described in this stroll.)

Across the street is the:

2 Kyoto National Museum (Kokuritsu Hakubutsukan)

In 1889, the Meiji government, fearful that Japan's cultural objects were going the way of the samurai with the increasing import of Western ways and products, established three national museums—one in Tokyo, one in Nara, and this one in Kyoto, which serves as a repository for art objects and treasures that once belonged to Kyoto's temples and royal court. It's presently undergoing renovation, however, with an expected reopening of its permanent collection of ceramics, paintings, lacquerware, textiles, sculptures, and other precious objects after 2013. Until then, special exhibitions are mounted three to four times a year.

East of the Kyoto National Museum (toward the wooded hills) are Higashioji Dori and a stoplight; take a left and walk about 5 minutes until you come to the second stoplight, at a small intersection with a Sunkus convenience store. Turn left here, take the first right down a narrow street, and to your right you'll soon see:

3 Kawai Kanjiro Memorial House

Kawai Kanjiro Memorial House, Gojo-zaka (℃ 075/561-3585), is the former home and studio of one of Japan's most well-known potters, Kawai Kanjiro (1890–1966). Inspired at a young age by Bernard Leach and one of the cofounders of the Japan Folk Crafts Museum in Tokyo, this versatile man handmade much of the furniture in this lovely home, which is a traditional Japanese house with an indoor open-pit fireplace and gleaming woodwork. Pottery, personal effects, and his outdoor clay kiln, built on a slope in the traditional Japanese method, are all on display, but this museum is worth seeing for the house alone, especially if you haven't had much opportunity to see the interiors of traditional Japanese homes. Admission is ¥900 for adults, ¥500 for students, and ¥300 for children. It's open Tuesday to Sunday, 10am to 5pm.

Take a right out of the museum, walk to the busy road with the overpass, and turn right. When you get to the big intersection, look catty-corner across the intersection to the left and you'll see a slope leading uphill between two big stone lanterns. This marks the entrance to the:

4 Otani Mausoleum

It serves as a major mausoleum for members of Shin Buddhism (a Japanese religious sect). In addition to a memorial hall dedicated to victims of World War II, it holds many memorial services for deceased Shin Buddhists from throughout Japan. After passing through a two-story wooden gate, you should turn left and then right for:

5 Toribeyama

Since ancient times it has served as a cremation site and burial ground, with more than 15,000 tombs spread along the slopes.

Follow the pathway uphill through the cemetery for about 10 minutes to the top, where you should then turn left and follow the painted white arrow in the street to the vermilion-colored tower gate, which marks the entrance to:

6 Kiyomizu Temple

This temple is the star attraction of this stroll. First founded in 798 and rebuilt in 1633 by the third Tokugawa shogun, Iemitsu, the temple occupies an exalted spot. The main hall is built over a cliff and features a large wooden veranda supported by 139 pillars, each 15m (49 ft.) high. Take in the view of Kyoto from its deck, but to fully appreciate the grandeur of the main hall with its pillars and dark wood, be sure to walk to the three-story pagoda, which offers the best view of the main hall, built without the use of a single nail. From the pagoda, descend the stone steps to Otowa Falls, where you'll see Japanese lined up to drink from the refreshing spring water. Kiyomizu's name, in fact, translates as "pure water." From here you'll also have the best view of the temple's impressive pillars.

7 Temple Dining 🍴

On the grounds of Kiyomizu Temple, just beside Otowa Falls, is Taki-no-ya (☎ 075/561-5117), an open-air pavilion where you can sit on tatami and enjoy noodles and a beer or flavored shaved ice from the English-language menu. This is a great place to stop (and now you know why this walk takes me all day). If you're lucky to be here in autumn, the fiery reds of the maple trees will set the countryside around you aflame. Open Friday through Wednesday from 10am to 5pm. Or, for something more substantial, wait until after your temple visit to dine on tofu at Kiyomizudera Junsei, located off Kiyomizu-zaka (see p. 277 for a complete review). On Sannenzaka (see below), keep your eyes peeled for Inoda's Coffee (☎ 075/532-5700), where you'll have views of a Japanese-style garden along with pastries, sandwiches, and coffee. It's open daily 9am to 5pm.

Before departing Kiyomizu Temple, be sure to make a stop at the vermilion-colored Shinto shrine located behind the temple's main hall:

8 Jishu Shrine

This shrine is regarded as a dwelling place of the deity of love and matchmaking (ask for the English-language leaflet). Throughout the grounds are English-language signs and descriptions telling about its various parts; for once, you're not left in the dark about the purpose of the various statues and memorials and what Japanese are doing as they make their rounds. It's very enriching. You can buy good-luck charms for everything from a happy marriage to easy delivery of a child to success in passing an examination. On the shrine's grounds are two stones placed about 9m (30 ft.) apart—if you're able to walk from one stone to the other with your eyes closed, you're supposedly guaranteed success in your love life. It sure doesn't hurt to try. There's also a place where you can write down your troubles on a piece of paper and then submerge it in a bucket of water, which supposedly will cause both the paper and your troubles to dissolve. If you failed the rock test, you might make a point of stopping here.

From Kiyomizu Temple, retrace your steps to the vermilion-colored entry tower gate you passed earlier. From here, on a downhill slope called Kiyomizu-zaka, you'll pass shop after shop selling sweets, pottery, fans, ties, hats, souvenirs and curios. If you go crazy shopping here, remember that you're going to have to carry whatever you buy. After a couple of small shrines nestled in among the shops, you'll come to a split in the road and a small shrine on the right shaded by trees, and a taxi rank before you to the left. Just beside this shrine are stone steps leading downhill (north) to a stone-cobbled street called:

9 Sannenzaka

The slope leads past lovely antiques stores, upscale craft shops, and restaurants and winds through neighborhoods of wooden buildings reminiscent of old Kyoto. Keep your eyes peeled for downhill stairs to the right leading to Maruyama Park; after you take these, the street will wind a bit as it goes downhill and eventually end at a T intersection. Take the stairs opposite the road and look to the right for:

10 Ryozen Kannon Temple

This temple (℃ 075/561-2205) has a 24m-high (80-ft.) white statue dedicated to unknown soldiers who died in World War II. Memorial services are conducted four times daily at a shrine that contains memorial tablets of the two million Japanese who perished during the war. There's also a Memorial Hall commemorating the more than 48,000 foreign soldiers who died on Japanese territory. Open daily from 8:45am to 4:20pm; because admission is ¥200, you may only want to take a peek at the statue. Just past Ryozen Kannon Temple, across the parking lot, is:

11 Kodaiji Temple

This temple was founded by the widow Nene in commemoration of her husband, Toyotomi Hideyoshi, who succeeded in unifying Japan at the end of the 16th century. In addition to teahouses and a memorial hall containing wooden images of the couple, there's a beautiful garden designed by master gardener Kobori Enshu. Don't miss it.

Exit Kodai-ji Temple via the main steps leading downhill and turn right, continuing north.

12 Kodajii Rakusho Tea Room

Past Kodai-ji Temple and just before the street ends at a pagoda with a crane on top, keep your eyes peeled for a teahouse on your right with a garden, which you can glimpse from the street through a gate. The Kodaiji Rakusho Tea Room (洛匠) 516 Washiochiyo (℃ 075/ 561-6892), is a lovely place and one of my favorite tearooms in Kyoto. It has a 100-year-old miniature garden with a pond that's home to some of the largest and most colorful carp I've ever seen, some of which are 20 years old and winners of the many medals displayed in the back room. Sit at one of the tables or in the back tatami room and enjoy **matcha** (frothed, powdered green tea), **warabi mochi** (cubes of a jelly-like dessert coated in toasted soy flour), and, in summer, **somen** (finely spun cold noodles). If you're a gardener, you'll probably want to give up the hobby after you've seen what's possible—but rarely achieved. Open from 9:30am to 6pm; closed 1 day a week but, unfortunately, not a fixed day. For coffee or afternoon tea, there's a cafe in Chorakukan, a brick-and-stone Meiji-Era building at the southwest corner of Maruyama Park (described earlier; to the left as you enter the park).

Continuing on your stroll north, turn right at the pagoda with the crane and then take an immediate left, which marks the beginning of:

13 Maruyama Park

An unkempt field of shrubs and weeds until designated a public park in 1886, this is one of Kyoto's most popular outdoor respites, filled with ponds, pigeons, and gardens. In spring, it's one of the most popular spots for viewing cherry blossoms; to the left after you enter the park is one of the oldest, most famous cherry trees in Kyoto. Also farther west is:

14 Yasaka Shrine

Yasaka Shrine is also known as Gion Shrine because of its proximity to the Gion District. Its present buildings date from 1654; the stone *torii* (gates) on the south side are considered among the largest in Japan. But the reason most people come here is one of practicality—the shrine is dedicated to the gods of health and prosperity, two universal concerns. This shrine, free to the public and open 24 hours, is packed during the Gion Festival and on New Year's Eve.

Exit Yasaka Shrine to the west; this brings you to a busy street called Higashioji. Cross it and continue walking west on busy Shijo Dori, until you reach Hanamikoji Dori on your left. This is:

15 Gion

Gion is one of Japan's most famous nightlife districts. It's centered primarily on Hanamikoji Dori, which translates as "Narrow Street for Flower Viewing." This is Kyoto's long-standing geisha district, an enclave of discreet, traditional, and almost solemn-looking wooden homes that reveal nothing of the gaiety that goes on inside—drinking, conversation, and business dealings with dancing, singing, and music provided by geisha and their apprentices, called *maiko*. If it's early evening, you might glimpse one of these women as she small-steps her way in *geta* (a traditional wooden shoe) to an evening appointment, elaborately made up and wearing a beautiful kimono. You might also wish to visit **Gion Corner** on Hanamikoji Dori, which offers performances of dance, puppetry, and other traditional arts nightly; see "Entertainment & Nightlife," later in this chapter, for details.

Winding Down

If all this sightseeing and shopping have made you thirsty, there are many restaurants and bars to the west across the Kamo River, on Pontocho, and near Shijo and Kawaramachi streets. See "Where to Dine in Kyoto" and "Kyoto After Dark" in this chapter for many suggestions in this area.

WALKING TOUR 2: **THE PHILOSOPHER'S STROLL**

START:	**Ginkakuji, the Temple of the Silver Pavilion; from Kyoto Station, take bus no. 32 or 100 to Ginkakuji-mae stop or bus no. 5, 17, 102, 203, or 204 to Ginkakuji-michi stop.**
FINISH:	**Kyoto Handicraft Center, Marutamachi Dori.**
TIME:	**Allow about 5 hours, including stops along the way.**
BEST TIMES:	**Early on weekdays, when crowds aren't as thick.**
WORST TIMES:	**There is no worst time for this walk.**

This stroll takes in the Temple of the Silver Pavilion as well as a couple of other temples, a museum dedicated to Kyoto's traditional crafts, Kyoto's most well-known shrine and its garden, and the best place in town for one-stop souvenir shopping. Linking the Silver Pavilion with the other sights is a canal lined by trees—a path known as the **Philosopher's Pathway.**

From the Ginkakuji-mae or Ginkakuji-michi bus stop, head east (toward the wooded hills) along the canal, and continue east when the canal veers to the (right) south, up the gentle slope to:

1 Ginkakuji, the Temple of the Silver Pavilion

This World Heritage Site is the architectural jewel of this stroll. Contrary to its name, however, Ginkakuji isn't silver at all. It was built in 1482 as a retirement villa for Shogun Ashikaga Yoshimasa, who intended to coat the structure with silver in imitation of the Golden Pavilion built by his grandfather. However, he died before this could be accomplished, which is just as well—the wood of the Silver Pavilion is spectacular just as it is. The entire complex is designed for enjoyment of the tea ceremony, moon viewing, and other aesthetic pursuits, with a beautiful garden of rippled sand, rocks, and moss. One of the small sand-hills is in the image of Mount Fuji. It's easy to imagine the splendor, formality, and grandeur of the life of Japan's upper class as you wander the grounds here. Be sure to take the hillside pathway with its lookout point, dozens of different kinds of moss, and streams; you might be able to escape the crowds that some-times overwhelm this attraction.

Head back to that narrow canal you saw on the way to the temple, heading south lined with cherry, willow, and maple trees and flanked by a small pathway. It's known as the:

2 Philosopher's Pathway

The name Philosopher's Pathway refers to the fact that, throughout the ages, philosophers and priests have strolled this tranquil canal thinking deep thoughts. It's a particularly beautiful sight in spring during the cherry-blossom season. The pathway runs almost 1.6km (1 mile), allowing you to think your own deep thoughts.

3 Café de Sagan 🏃

Approximately 5 minutes down the Philosopher's Pathway, to the right, is Café de Sagan (© 075/751-7968), a coffee shop with an English-language menu listing sandwiches, des-serts, beer, and juices. It's open Friday to Wednesday from 8am to 5pm, with views of the shaded path through its windows.

At the end of the Philosopher's Pathway (a 30-min. walk), near Nyakuoji Shrine, turn right and walk for a few minutes through a residential area until you reach a street with some traffic on it (and a wooden sign pointing toward Eikando and Nanzenji). Here you should turn left. After a couple of minutes, on the left, you'll come to:

4 Eikando Temple (永観堂)

Founded in 863, this temple (also known as **Zenrinji Temple** (禅林寺); www. eikando.or.jp; © **075/761-0007**) derives its popular name from the seventh head priest Eikan (1032–1111), who was loved by the people for attending to the impoverished sick and for planting plum trees as sources of medicine. The temple is famous for a 12th century small statue called the "Mikaeri Amida", a

Walking Tour 2: The Philosopher's Stroll

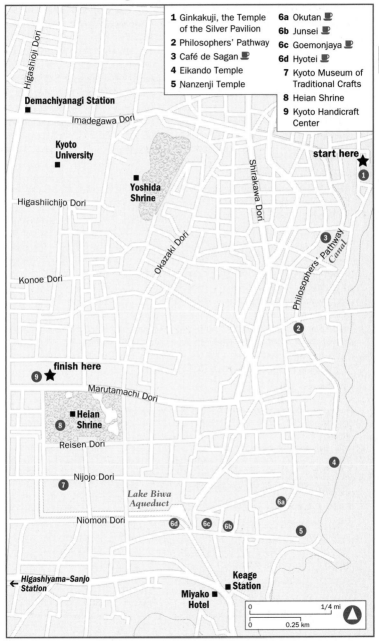

1 Ginkakuji, the Temple of the Silver Pavilion
2 Philosophers' Pathway
3 Café de Sagan 🍴
4 Eikando Temple
5 Nanzenji Temple
6a Okutan 🍴
6b Junsei 🍴
6c Goemonjaya 🍴
6d Hyotei 🍴
7 Kyoto Museum of Traditional Crafts
8 Heian Shrine
9 Kyoto Handicraft Center

Higashioji Dori

Demachiyanagi Station

Imadegawa Dori

Kyoto University

Higashiichijo Dori

Yoshida Shrine

Shirakawa Dori

start here
1

Okazaki Dori

Philosophers' Pathway
Canal
3

Konoe Dori

2

finish here
9

Marutamachi Dori

Heian Shrine
8

Reisen Dori

Nijojo Dori
7

Lake Biwa Aqueduct

Niomon Dori
6d   6c   6b

4

6a

5

Higashiyama-Sanjo Station

Keage Station

Miyako Hotel

0   1/4 mi
0   0.25 km

Buddha with his head turned, looking back over his shoulder. According to popular lore, Eikan, while walking and reciting chants he believed would propel him towards rebirth, was so astonished to see that the Amida Buddha had descended from the altar and was walking ahead of him that he stopped short in his tracks, whereupon the Buddha looked back over his shoulder and admonished, "Eikan, you are dawdling." How typically Zen. The backward-facing Buddha is in the Amidado Hall, reached by a succession of hallways and walkways and past art treasures such as *fusuma* landscape paintings in the temple's various buildings. In autumn, the many maples here are at their most glorious. A detached pagoda, about 125 steps up on a hillside, offers a view over the city. Open daily from 9am to 4pm (last entry); admission is ¥600, except in autumn when it's ¥1,000 and there's also night viewing.

A few minutes' walk farther south brings you to:

5 Nanzenji Temple

Nanzenji Temple (www.nanzenji.com; © **075/771-0365**) is a Rinzai Zen temple set amid a grove of spruce. One of Kyoto's best-known Zen temples, it was founded in 1293, though its present buildings date from the latter part of the 16th century during the Momoyama Period. Attached to the main hall is a Zen rock garden attributed to Kobori Enshu; it's sometimes called "Young Tigers Crossing the Water" because of the shape of one of the rocks, but the association is a bit of a stretch for me. In the building behind the main hall is a sliding door with a famous painting by Kano Tanyu of a tiger drinking water in a bamboo grove. Spread throughout the temple precincts are a dozen other lesser temples and buildings worth exploring if you have the time, including Nanzenin, which was built about the same time as Nanzenji Temple and served as the emperor's vacation house whenever he visited the temple grounds. The temple is open daily from 8:40am to 5pm (to 4:30pm in winter); admission to the main hall is ¥500 and to Nanzen-in ¥300.

6 Nearby Restaurants

Several traditional restaurants near Nanzenji reflect the settings of the temples themselves. Okutan, just north of Nanzenji and with a view of a peaceful pond, has been serving vegetarian tofu meals for 350 years. On the road leading west from Nanzenji are Junsei, serving tofu, obento lunch boxes, and kaiseki in a beautiful garden setting; Goemonjaya, which serves moderately priced set meals and noodles; and Hyotei, which opened more than 300 years ago to serve pilgrims to Nanzenji, offering obento lunches as well as expensive kaiseki. See "Where to Dine in Kyoto" in this chapter for details.

Head straight out (west) from Nanzenji until you see a body of water on your right, the Lake Biwa Aqueduct. Continue west on Niomon Dori (the water will be on your right) to the vermilion-colored bridge to your right, where you'll also see a vermilion-colored *torii*. Turn right here and continue straight ahead to Nijo Dori, where you turn left for one of my favorite museums (look for the bright orange installation outside), the:

7 Kyoto Museum of Traditional Crafts (Fureaikan)

This basement museum in the Miyako Messe building displays all the Kyoto crafts you can think of, from combs, umbrellas, and fans to textiles, sweets, bambooware, and masks. English-language explanations and videos describe how the crafts are made (mostly by hand). The best news: The museum is free. For details, see p. 261.

Across the street to the north, it would be hard to miss:

8 Heian Shrine

If orange and green are your favorite colors, you're going to love Heian Shrine, one of Kyoto's most famous. Although it was built in 1895 in commemoration of the 1,100th anniversary of the founding of Kyoto, Heian Shrine is a replica of the city's first administrative quarters, built in Kyoto in 794, giving you some idea of the architecture back then. The most important thing to see here is the **garden,** the entrance to which is on your left as you face the main hall. Typical of gardens constructed during the Meiji Era, it's famous for its weeping cherry trees in spring, its irises and waterlilies in summer, and its changing maple leaves in the fall. I love sitting on the bench on the wooden bridge topped by a phoenix; you'll probably want to dawdle here, too.

Take a right out of the shrine's main exit onto Reisen Dori and then take the next right, which after 5 minutes will bring you to the:

9 Kyoto Handicraft Center

This center is located behind the shrine on its north side. It's the best place in Kyoto for one-stop shopping for souvenirs of Japan, including pearls, kimono and the less-formal *yukata,* fans, paper products, toys, and more; see p. 280 for complete information. From here, you can take bus no. 206 for Kyoto Station or 203 for downtown Kyoto.

A SIDE TRIP TO NARA ★★

42km (26 miles) S of Kyoto

In early Japanese history, the nation's capital was moved to a new site each time a new emperor came to the throne. In 710, however, the first permanent Japanese capital was set up at **Nara.** Not that it turned out to be so permanent: After only 74 years, the capital was moved first to Nagaoka and shortly thereafter to Kyoto, where it remained for more than 1,000 years. What's important about those 74 years, however, is that they witnessed the birth of Japan's arts, crafts, and literature, as Nara imported everything from religion to art and architecture from China. Even the city itself, laid out in a rectangular grid pattern, was modeled after Chinese concepts. It was during the Nara Period that Japan's first historical account, first mythological chronicle, and first poetry anthology (with 4,173 poems) were written. Buddhism also flourished, and Nara grew as the political and cultural center of the land with numerous temples, shrines, pagodas, and palaces.

Japanese flock to Nara because it gives them the feeling that they're communing with ancestors. Foreigners come here because Nara offers them a glimpse of a Japan that was. Remarkably enough, many of Nara's historic buildings and temples remain intact, and long ago someone had enough foresight to enclose many of these historical structures in the quiet and peaceful confines of a large and spacious park, which has the added attraction of free-roaming deer.

Essentials

GETTING THERE Nara is easily reached from Kyoto Station on two lines: the JR Nara Line and the Kintetsu Limited Express. If you have a Japan Rail Pass, you'll probably want to take the commuter **JR Nara Express,** which departs about four times an hour and takes 43 to 57 minutes depending on the train; if you don't have a pass, the trip costs ¥690 one-way. If speed or luxury is of the utmost importance, the deluxe **Kintetsu Special Limited Express** whisks you to Nara in 35 minutes, guarantees you a seat (all seats are reserved), costs ¥1,110 and departs every 30 minutes (advance purchase suggested in peak season). A slower **Kintetsu ordinary express** takes 45 minutes and costs ¥610. You can also reach Nara from Osaka in about 30 to 50 minutes, depending on the train and the departure station. The **Kintetsu Nara Line,** departing Namba Station, takes 40 minutes and costs ¥540; **JR** trains depart from Osaka Station, take 50 minutes, and cost ¥780.

VISITOR INFORMATION   There are tourist information offices at both **JR Nara Station** (☎ 0742/22-9821; daily 9am–5pm) and **Kintetsu Nara Station** (☎ 0742/24-4858; daily 9am–5pm). Both have good brochures and maps with useful information on how to get around Nara by foot and bus, as well as city magazine *Nara Explorer.* For more detailed information on Nara, visit the **Nara City Tourist Center,** 23–4 Kami-sanjo-cho (☎ 0742/22-3900; daily 9am–9pm), located in the heart of the city on Sanjo Dori between both stations and about a 5-minute walk from each. Finally, there's **Sarusawa Information Center** (☎ 0742/26-1991; daily 9am–5pm), located at Sarusawa-ike Pond, south of Nara Park and not far from Nara's many attractions. Websites with information on Nara include www.pref.nara.jp and www.naraexplorer.jp.

GETTING AROUND   If you take the Kintetsu Line, you'll arrive at **Kintetsu Nara Station;** if you take the JR train, you'll arrive at **JR Nara Station.** Both stations are about a 10-minute walk from each other and are within walking distance of Nara Park and its attractions. Kintetsu Station is slightly closer, about a 5-minute walk to the entrance of the park, while the JR Station is about a 10-minute walk to the park. Keep in mind, however, that Nara Park is quite large and its major attractions are far-flung; it takes about 20 minutes to walk from Kintetsu Nara Station to Todaiji Temple. Around the stations themselves is Nara's small downtown area, with Sanjo Dori serving as the main shopping street and running from JR Nara Station to Nara Park. Alternatively, **Eki Rentacar** (☎ 0742-26-3929; daily 8am–6pm) rents **bikes** outside JR Nara Station's east exit for ¥700 per day.

 Your Own Personal Guide

Nara has many volunteer guides (from students and housewives to retirees), who will happily show you the town's sights in exchange for the chance to practice their English. There's no charge for guiding services, but you pay your own admission and are requested to pay the guide's transportation to meet you, and I suggest you also pay for the guide's lunch (guides do not have to pay admission to attractions). Although a guide is often waiting at Kintetsu Station's tourist office daily from 9am to 5pm, advance reservations are advised at one of the following organizations: **YMCA Goodwill Guides** (http://egg nara.tripod.com; ☎ 0742/45-5920), **Nara Student Guides** (☎ 0742/26-4753) or **Nara SGG Club** (http://nara shikanko.jp/sgg; ☎ 0742/22-5595). If you're visiting Horyuji Temple, cheerful, English-speaking goodwill guides are usually on hand at the iCenter, located near the temple, though reservations are advised via Ikaruga SGG (www4.kcn.ne.jp/~yoppe; ☎ 0745/74-6800).

Nara

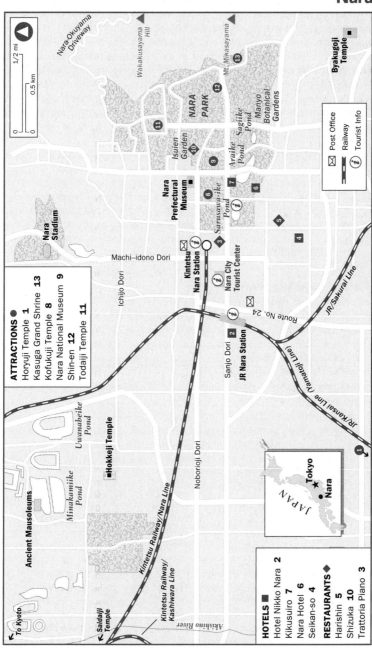

ATTRACTIONS ●
Horyuji Temple **1**
Kasuga Grand Shrine **13**
Kofukuji Temple **8**
Nara National Museum **9**
Shin-en **12**
Todaiji Temple **11**

HOTELS ■
Hotel Nikko Nara **2**
Kikusuiro **7**
Nara Hotel **6**
Seikan-so **4**

RESTAURANTS ◆
Harishin **5**
Shizuka **10**
Trattoria Piano **3**

Post Office
Railway
ⓘ Tourist Info

JAPAN

Tokyo ★
Nara ●

IF YOU'RE HEADING TO HORYUJI   To visit the Horyuji Temple area (see below), the cheapest and fastest way is from JR Nara Station on the JR Yamatoji Line going in the direction of Namba (in Osaka); departures are every 10 to 15 minutes and bring you to Horyuji Station in 13 minutes (fare: ¥210). From there, you can either walk to the temple area in about 20 minutes or take a bus (fare: ¥180), which departs two to three times an hour from 10am. Alternatively, there's bus no. 97, an excursion line that runs between Kasuga Grand Shrine and Horyuji, passing Todaiji Temple and both train stations on the way, but it takes about an hour and costs ¥760 one way (a day pass costs ¥1,000), with 7 departures daily. Because it takes quite a bit of time getting to and from Horyuji, you must limit your sightseeing to only the major attractions if you plan on visiting both Nara Park and Horyuji in 1 day.

Exploring Nara

The best way to enjoy Nara is to arrive early in the morning before the first tour buses start pulling in. If you don't have much time, the most important sites to see are **Todaiji Temple, Kasuga Shrine,** and **Kofukuji Temple's Treasure House,** which you can view in about 3 hours. If you have more time, add **Horyuji Temple.** Or, take a stroll through **Naramachi,** Nara's most historic part of town and boasting many *machiya* (traditional wooden residences). Although a reproduction, **Koshi-no-ie (© 0742/23-4820;** Tues–Sun 9am–5pm) displays common machiya features and is free; ask the tourist office for a Naramachi map.

AROUND NARA PARK

With its ponds, grassy lawns, trees, and temples, Nara Park covers about 520 hectares (1,300 acres) and is home to more than 1,100 deer, which are considered divine messengers and are therefore allowed to roam freely through the park. The deer are generally quite friendly; throughout the park you can buy "deer cookies," which all but the shyest fawns will usually take right out of your hand. All of the below listings are within Nara Park.

Kofukuji Temple ★   Walking east from either the JR or Kintetsu Station, this is the first temple you reach. It was established in 710 as the family temple of the Fujiwaras, the second-most powerful clan after the imperial family from the 8th to 12th centuries. At one time as many as 175 buildings were erected on the Kofukuji Temple grounds, giving it significant religious and political power up until the 16th century; through centuries of civil wars and fires, however, most of the structures were destroyed. Only a handful of buildings remain, but even these were rebuilt after the 13th century.

The **five-story pagoda,** first erected in 730, burned down five times. The present pagoda dates from 1426 and is an exact replica of the original; at 50m (164 ft.) tall, it's the second-tallest pagoda in Japan (the tallest is at Toji Temple in Kyoto). Also of historical importance is the **Eastern Golden Hall (Tokondo),** originally constructed in 726 by Emperor Shomu to speed the recovery of the ailing Empress Gensho. Rebuilt in 1415, it houses several priceless images, including a bronze statue of Yakushi Nyorai, (the healing Buddha) installed by Emperor Shomu on behalf of his sick wife; a 12th-century wooden bodhisattva of wisdom, long worshiped by scholar monks and today by pupils hoping to pass university entrance exams; and the 12 Heavenly Guards, wooden reliefs carved in the 12th century.

But the best thing to see here is the temple's **Treasure House (Kokuhokan) ★★,** which displays many statues and works of art originally contained in the temple's buildings, many of them National Treasures. Most famous are a statue of standing

Ashura carved in the 8th century and a bronze head of Yakushi Nyorai, but my favorites are the six 12th-century carved wooden statues representing priests of the Kamakura Period with fascinating facial features that render them strikingly human.

Nara Park. www.kohfukuji.com. © **0742/22-7755.** Admission to Treasure House ¥600 adults, ¥500 junior-high and high-school students; ¥200 elementary-school students; Eastern Golden Hall ¥300 adults, ¥200 junior-high and high-school students, ¥100 elementary-school student. Combination ticket ¥800, ¥600, and ¥250, respectively. Daily 9am–5pm.

Nara National Museum (Nara Kokuritsu Hakubutsukan) ★ East of Kofukuji, this museum opened in 1895 to house invaluable Buddhist art and archaeological relics and has since expanded into a second building, used for special exhibits. Many masterpieces formerly in Nara's temples are now housed here, including Buddhist sculptures from various periods in Japan's history; paintings, masks, scrolls, calligraphy; and archaeological objects obtained from temple ruins, tombs, and sutra mounds. Unfortunately, although items are identified in English, explanations of their historic significance are not. You'll spend 20 to 30 minutes here.

Nara Park. www.narahaku.go.jp. © **0742/22-7771,** or 050-5542-8600 (request the English-speaking operator). Admission ¥500 adults, ¥250 college students, free for children and seniors. Special exhibits cost more. Tues–Sun 9:30am–5pm.

Todaiji Temple ★★★ Nara's premier attraction is Todaiji Temple and its **Great Buddha (Daibutsu),** Japan's second-largest bronze Buddha. When Emperor Shomu ordered construction of both the temple and Daibutsu in the mid-700s, he intended to make Todaiji the headquarters of all Buddhist temples in the land. As part of his plans for a Buddhist utopia, he commissioned work for this huge bronze statue of Buddha; it took eight castings to complete this remarkable work of art. At a height of more than 15m (50 ft.), the Daibutsu is made of 437 tons of bronze, 286 pounds of pure gold, 165 pounds of mercury, and 7 tons of vegetable wax. However, thanks to Japan's frequent natural calamities, the Buddha of today isn't quite what it used to be. In 855, in what must have been a whopper of an earthquake, the statue lost its head. It was repaired in 861, but alas, the huge wooden building housing the Buddha was burned twice during wars, melting the Buddha's head. The present head dates from 1692.

Be sure to walk in a circle around the Great Buddha to see it from all angles. Behind the statue is a model of how the Daibutsuden used to look, flanked by two massive pagodas. Behind the Great Buddha to the right is a huge wooden column with a small hole in it near the ground. According to popular belief, if you can manage to crawl through this opening, you'll be sure to reach enlightenment (seemingly a snap for children). You can also get your English-language fortune for ¥200 by shaking a bamboo canister until a wooden stick with a number comes out; the number corresponds to a piece of paper. Mine told me that though I will win, it will be of no use, an illness will be serious, and the person for whom I am waiting will not come. And the monk who gave me the fortune said mine was a good one!

The wooden structure housing the Great Buddha, called **Daibutsuden,** was also destroyed several times through the centuries; the present structure dates from 1709. Measuring 48m (160 ft.) tall, 57m (187 ft.) long, and 50m (165 ft.) wide, it's the largest wooden structure in the world—but is only two-thirds its original size. My architect sister, just completing a year's trip around the world with her family, declared the Daibutsuden among the most magnificent buildings she had ever seen.

Nara Park. © **0742/22-5511.** Admission ¥500 adults, ¥300 children. Mar daily 8am–5pm; Apr–Sept daily 7:30am–5:30pm; Oct daily 7:30am–5pm; Nov–Feb daily 8am–4:30pm.

Kasuga Grand (Taisha) Shrine ★　A stroll through the park will bring you to one of my favorite Shinto shrines in the Kyoto area. Originally the tutelary shrine of the powerful Fujiwara family, it was founded in 768 and, according to Shinto concepts of purity, was torn down and rebuilt every 20 years in its original form until 1863. As virtually all empresses hailed from the Fujiwara family, the shrine enjoyed a privileged status with the imperial family. Nestled in the midst of verdant woods, it's a shrine of vermilion-colored pillars and an astounding 3,000 stone and bronze lanterns. The most spectacular time to visit is mid-August or the beginning of February, when all 3,000 lanterns are lit. Here, too, you can pay ¥200 for an *omikuji,* a slip of paper on which your fortune is written in English. If the fortune is unfavorable, you can conveniently negate it by tying the piece of paper to the twig of a tree. Although admission to the grounds is free, admission is charged for the garden of Kasuga Grand Shrine, **Shin-en,** a botanical garden preserving about 300 varieties of native Japanese plants and famous for its wisteria (it's located to the left on the approach to the shrine), and to the **Homotsuden,** a treasure house displaying costumes, swords, and armor. Fork out the extra yen only if you have time and the interest.

Nara Park. www.kasugataisha.or.jp. ℂ **0742/22-7788.** Free admission to grounds; Shin-en ¥500 adults, ¥250 children; Homotsuden ¥500 adults, ¥400 junior- and senior-high students, ¥300 children. Grounds daily 6:30am–6pm summer, 7am–4:30pm winter; Homotsuden and Shin-en Tues–Sun 9am–4pm.

The Horyuji Temple Area ★★★

Founded in 607 by Prince Shotoku as a center for Buddhism in Japan, **Horyuji Temple ★★★** (ℂ **0745/75-2555**) is one of Japan's most significant gems for historic architecture, art, and religion. It was from here that Buddhism blossomed and spread throughout the land. Today about 45 buildings remain in the complex, some of them dating from the end of the 7th century and comprising what are probably the oldest wooden structures in the world. Although they are the main reason people come here, it's the atmosphere of the compound itself that I love—serene, ancient, and a fitting tribute to Prince Shotoku, founder of Buddhism in Japan and much revered still today. Little wonder Horyuji was selected as Japan's first UNESCO World Cultural Heritage Site, in 1993 (for details on reaching Horyuji, see "Essentials," above).

At the western end of the grounds is the two-story, 17m-high (58-ft.) **Kondo,** or main hall, which is considered the oldest building at Horyuji Temple, erected sometime between the 6th and 8th centuries. It contains Buddhas commemorating Prince Shotoku's parents, protected by Japan's oldest set of four heavenly guardians (from the late 7th or early 8th c.). Next to the main hall is Japan's oldest **five-story pagoda,** dating from the foundation of the temple and considered the most important structure of Buddhist temples, as it is here that relics of the Buddha are enshrined; it contains four scenes from the life of Buddha. The **Gallery of Temple Treasures,** or Daihozoden, constructed in 1998, contains statues, tabernacles, and other works of art from the 7th and 8th centuries, many of them National Treasures. On the eastern precincts of Horyuji Temple is an octagonal building called **Yumedono Hall,** or the Hall of Visions, built in 739 as a sanctuary to pray for the repose of Prince Shotoku.

Admission to Kondo, Gallery of Temple Treasures, and Yumedono Hall is ¥1,000 for adults and ¥500 for children. The grounds are open daily from 8am to 5pm (to 4:30pm Nov 4–Feb 21).

Just behind Yumedono is **Chuguji Temple** (中宮寺; ℂ **0745/75-2106**), once part of a large nunnery built for members of the imperial family. It contains two outstanding National Treasures: The wooden statue of **Nyoirin Kannon Bosatsu,** dating from the 7th century, is noted for the serene and compassionate expression on her face. The **Tenjukoku Mandala,** the oldest piece of embroidery in Japan, was originally about 5m (16 ft.) long and was created by Shotoku's consort and her female companions after Shotoku's death at the age of 48. It shows scenes from the Land of Heavenly Longevity, where only those with good karma are invited by the Buddha in the afterlife and where Shotoku surely resides. Only a replica of the fragile embroidery is now on display. Open daily from 9am to 4:30pm (to 4pm Oct–Mar 20); admission is ¥400 for adults, ¥200 for children.

Where to Eat

Harishin (はり新) ★★★ 🏠 OBENTO   Many tourists never see this lovely part of old Nara near Gangoji Temple, called Naramachi and consisting of narrow lanes and traditional wooden homes and shops. The restaurant is a 200-year-old house of ocher-colored walls and a wood-slat facade, and dining is on tatami with a view of a garden. Only an obento that changes with the season, the creation of chef-owner Nakagawa-san, is served (a kaiseki meal is also available only in the evening for ¥6,000 but must be reserved in advance). My obento included an aperitif wine, light tofu flavored with sesame, soup, rice, pickled vegetables, tempura, and various exquisitely prepared bite-size morsels of shrimp, chicken, potatoes wrapped in bacon, and scallops. A meal here is highly recommended.

15 Nakashinya-cho. 🕐 **0742/22-2669.** Reservations required for kaiseki 2 days in advance. Obento ¥2,900. AE, DC, MC, V. Tues–Sun 11:30am–2:30pm and 6–8pm (last order); closed Tues if Mon is a national holiday. A 5-min. walk south of Sarusawa-ike Pond, on the road that leads south from the west edge of the pond (stop at the tourist office for directions).

Shizuka (志津香) KAMAMESHI   This much loved, low-key local shop across from Nara Park is best known for *kamameshi*, rice in a small metal pot and topped with other ingredients. Order from the English menu for dishes like the simple *waka-dori* (chicken with vegetables) or the *Nara nanashu* (seven flavors of Nara), but don't stir it right away until an okoge (crispy rice crust) can form where the rice meets the metal of the pot. An order of *takiawase* (vegetables in seafood broth) costs ¥683 more.

59 Noborioji-cho. www.kamameshi-shizuka.jp. 🕐 **0742/27-8030.** Main dishes ¥892–¥1,207; set meals ¥1,680–¥2,310. No credit cards. Wed–Mon 11am–8pm.

Trattoria Piano ITALIAN   In the center of downtown near the stations and Sanjo Dori, this second-floor restaurant above a bar offers pastas, pizzas (both Napoli style and those with Japanese ingredients), as well as main dishes like veal scaloppini or grilled pork with lemon sauce, along with a fish of the day.

15–1 Hashimoto-cho. 🕐 **0742/26-1837.** Pizza ¥1,480–¥1,680; main dishes ¥1,580–¥1,890. MC, V. Daily 9am–11pm. Station: JR Nara (10 min.) or Kintetsu Nara (3 min.), on the corner of Sanjo Dori and the Higashimuki Shotengai covered shopping arcade.

Where to Stay

Although you can see Nara in a day trip from Kyoto or Osaka, I've included some recommendations for an overnight stay for more leisurely sightseeing. An extra incentive: from mid-July through September, many of Nara's most important historic buildings, like Todaiji Temple, are lit at night, making for a romantic nighttime stroll.

Hotel Nikko Nara ★   This hotel next to the West exit of the JR Nara station is one of Nara's most convenient: Drop off your bags, hop on a rental bicycle to see the sights, and then soak away all cares in the hotel's large public baths. Rooms are comfortable, with fluffy quilted spreads and plenty of desk space. The best rooms are on the 9th and 10th floors with great views toward distant mountains and Nara's temples, especially beautiful when lit at night in summer.

8–1 Sanjo-hommachi, Nara 630-8122. www.jalhotels.com. © **0742/35-8831.** Fax 0742/35-6868. 330 units. ¥12,000 single; ¥21,000–¥30,000 double. AE, DC, MC, V. Station: JR Nara (1 min.). **Amenities:** 4 restaurants; lounge; rental bikes (per day: ¥800 for regular bike, ¥1,500 for electric bike); concierge. *In room:* A/C, TV, fridge, hair dryer, Internet.

Kikusuiro (菊水楼) ★★★   You can hardly find a more beautiful *ryokan* than this inn from 1892, with an ornate Japanese-style roof, surrounded by a white walls, and designated a private cultural asset by the Ministry of Culture. Rooms, some of which face Ara-ike Pond, are outfitted with scrolls and antiques and are connected to one another with rambling wooden corridors. Meals are renowned, there's a beautiful garden, and the manager, Mr. Itoh, speaks English.

1130 Takabatake-cho, Nara 630-8301. www.kikusuiro.com.© **0742/23-2001.** Fax 0742/26-0025. 14 units, 8 with bathroom. ¥36,225–¥48,300 per person, including 2 meals. AE, DC, MC, V. East of Nara Park's Kofukuji 5-story pagoda on Sanjo Dori (corner of Rte. 308 and 369). Station: Kintetsu Nara (10 min.) or JR Nara (20 min.). **Amenities:** 2 restaurants. *In room:* A/C, TV, minibar.

Nara Hotel ★★★   One of the most famous lodgings in Nara (and with staff eager to please), the Nara Hotel sits like a palace atop a hill on the south edge of Nara Park. Built in 1909 in the Momoyama Period style of architecture, it's similar to Japan's other hotels built to accommodate foreigners who poured into the country following the Meiji Restoration, constructed as a Western-style hotel but with many Japanese features. Accommodations in the old part of the hotel feature wide corridors, high ceilings, antique light fixtures, fireplaces (no longer in use), and comfortable old-fashioned decor, while a 1984 addition offers larger, modern rooms and verandas overlooking woods or the old town. I prefer the atmosphere of the older rooms. Those facing the city cost less than those in the new wing, while deluxe twins have more amenities and views of a pond or park (***Note:*** only the newer wing has an elevator).

Nara-Koennai, Nara 630-8301. www.narahotel.co.jp. © **0742/26-3300.** Fax 0742/23-5252. 129 units. ¥18,480 single; ¥28,875–¥57,750 double. 25% discount for holders of Japan Rail Pass. AE, DC, MC, V. An 8-min. taxi ride from the train station. **Amenities:** 2 restaurants; bar; lounge; room service. *In room:* A/C, TV, hair dryer, Internet, minibar.

Seikan-so ★ 🍴   This is a lovely choice in inexpensive Japanese-style accommodations. It boasts a beautiful garden, complete with azalea bushes and manicured trees—the kind of garden usually found only at *ryokan* costing twice as much. Located in quaint Naramachi, a historic neighborhood about a 10-minute walk south of Nara Park, the traditional Japanese building dates from 1916 and wraps around the inner garden. Although the simple rooms are showing their age, all is forgiven if you can get one of the five rooms facing the garden—request one when making your reservation. The friendly owners speak English, and there's a choice of Japanese or Western breakfast.

29 Higashi-Kitsuji-cho, Nara 630-8327. www.nara-ryokanseikanso.com. © **0742/22-2670.** Fax 0742/22-2670. 9 units, none with bathroom. ¥4,200 per person. Breakfast ¥473–¥735 extra. AE, MC, V. Loop bus 1 to Kitakyobate stop (1 min.). 11pm Curfew. Station: Kintetsu Nara (12 min.) or JR Nara (25 min.). **Amenities:** Lobby computer w/free Internet. *In room:* A/C, TV, no phone.

THE REST OF WESTERN HONSHU

8

n addition to Tokyo, Kyoto, and the Japan Alps (covered in previous chapters), the island of Honshu has many other towns and attractions in its western half that are well worth a visit. As the largest of Japan's islands and home to 80% of the country's population, Honshu is where most of the country's important historical events took place; you'll find many castles, gardens, temples, shrines, and other famous sights linked to the past here. Western Honshu's climate ranges from snowy winters in its mountain ranges to subtropical weather in the south. The middle of the island is traversed by Japan's longest river, the Shinano. With all this to offer, it's little wonder that many travelers to Japan never make it off this central island.

THE BEST WESTERN HONSHU EXPERIENCES

o **Seeing Old Architecture at Museum Meiji Mura (Nagoya):** This open-air architectural museum is a treasure with its churches, clapboard homes, bathhouse, kabuki theater, prison, brewery and other original buildings from the Meiji Period, situated on beautifully landscaped grounds. Mail a postcard from a post office from yesteryear and drink tea in the lobby of the original Imperial Hotel, designed by Frank Lloyd Wright. See p. 326.

o **Making a Pilgrimage to Ise Grand Shrines (Ise):** These shrines are the most venerated Shinto shrines in Japan; pilgrims have been flocking here for centuries. Amazingly, the Inner Shrine is razed and reconstructed on a new site every 20 years according to strict rules in the Shinto religion. Follow the age-old route of former pilgrims and stop for a meal in the nearby Okage Yokocho District. See p. 334.

o **Attending a Traditional Tea Ceremony (Kanazawa):** Developed in the 16th century as a way to achieve inner harmony with nature, the ritualized ceremony is performed throughout the country; my favorite locale is Gyokusen-en. See p. 345.

o **Getting Down in Osaka's Nightlife:** Osaka's lively nightlife district centers on a pedestrian lane called Dotombori, but there are plenty of other bars to keep night owls happy. See p. 370.

- **Cycling Through History (Okayama & Matsue):** You can rent bicycles all over Japan, but two of my favorite places for cycling are through the Kibiji District with its ancient burial mounds and paddies and in the village of Omori, home to the Iwami Ginzan Silver Mine World Heritage Site. See p. 400 and 416.

NAGOYA, A HISTORIC & MODERN CROSSROAD

366km (227 miles) W of Tokyo; 147km (92 miles) E of Kyoto; 186km (116 miles) E of Osaka

Nagoya was founded as a castle town almost 400 years ago on orders of Tokugawa Ieyasu, who considered its strategic position on the Tokaido Highway useful for controlling Osaka and other points west. Today, Nagoya is Japan's fourth-largest city with a population of 2.2 million—yet it's a place most foreigners never stop to see. True, it doesn't have the attractions of many of the nation's other cities (it was leveled during World War II), but it does have a castle originally built by the first Tokugawa shogun, as well as one of Japan's most important Shinto shrines. You can also stroll through an aquarium famous for its penguins and sea turtles, visit the world-famous Noritake chinaware display rooms, spend hours at a nearby open-air architectural museum (one of my favorites in Japan), and watch cormorant fishing in summer. Nagoya, capital of Aichi Prefecture, is also home to an international airport and has long served as the gateway to the Japan Alps (see chapter 6) and Ise-Shima National Park (covered later in this chapter).

Essentials

GETTING THERE **By Plane** Known officially as the Central Japan International Airport (NGO) but dubbed **Centrair** (© **0569/38-1195;** www.centrair.jp/en), this airport occupies a man-made island in Ise Bay about 35km (22 miles) outside Nagoya. It boasts two hotels; 130 shops and restaurants (including Japan's largest duty-free store); ATMs in the arrival lobby that accept foreign credit cards; coin-operated computers (¥100 for 10 min.); a health clinic; post office; and even hot-spring baths, Fu-no-Yu (© **0569/38-7070;** daily 8am–9pm), with views of planes landing and taking off. A Tourist Information Center (TIC; © **0569/38-1050;** daily 9am–7pm) is located past the arrivals hall, but little English is spoken.

Meitetsu trains (www.meitetsu.co.jp) connect Centrair with Nagoya Station in 40 minutes by regular train (¥850) or in 28 minutes by express (¥1,200). A taxi from Centrair to downtown Nagoya will run about ¥16,000, including toll charges, and take 50 minutes.

By JR Train The fastest way to get to Nagoya from Tokyo is by Shinkansen bullet train, which takes a little less than 2 hours from Tokyo Station to **JR Nagoya Station** and costs ¥10,070 for an unreserved seat. Nagoya is 40 minutes from Kyoto and about 1 hour from Shin-Osaka Station.

By Bus From Shinjuku Station in Tokyo, the **JR Highway Bus** (© **03/3844-1950;** www.jrbuskanto.co.jp) costs ¥5,100 one-way for the 6-hour trip, with several departures daily. From Kyoto, the Highway Bus costs ¥2,500 and takes 2¾ hours; from Osaka, the trip takes just over 3 hours and costs ¥2,900. **Willer Express** (© **050/5805-0383;** http://willerexpress.com) buses depart Tokyo's Shinjuku Station approximately 12 times daily, arriving at Nagoya Station approximately 5½ hours later. Fares start at ¥3,700, with discounts given to students and seniors.

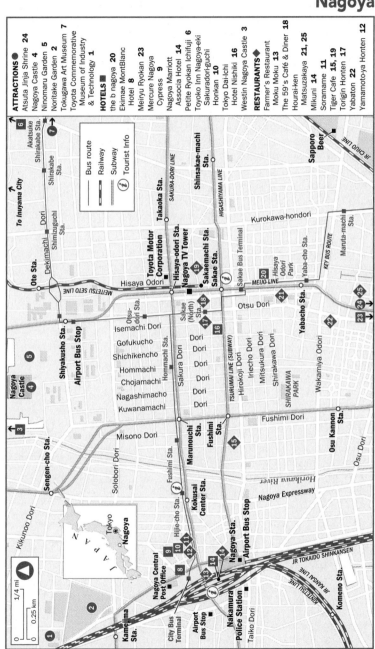

ATTRACTIONS ●
Atsuta Jinja Shrine **24**
Nagoya Castle **4**
Ninomaru Garden **5**
Noritake Garden **2**
Tokugawa Art Museum **7**
Toyota Commemorative
  Museum of Industry
  & Technology **1**

HOTELS ■
the b nagoya **20**
Ekimae MontBlanc
  Hotel **8**
Meiryu Ryokan **23**
Mercure Nagoya
  Cypress **9**
Nagoya Marriott
  Associa Hotel **14**
Petite Ryokan Ichifuji **6**
Toyoko Inn Nagoya-eki
  Sakuradori-guchi
  Honkan **10**
Tokyo Dai-Ichi
  Hotel Nishiki **16**
Westin Nagoya Castle **3**

RESTAURANTS ◆
Farmer's Restaurant
  Moku Moku **13**
The 59's Café & Diner **18**
Houraiken
  Matsuzakaya **21, 25**
Mikuni **14**
Soramame **11**
Tiger Cafe **15, 19**
Torigin Honten **17**
Yabaton **22**
Yamamoto-ya Honten **12**

VISITOR INFORMATION The **Nagoya Station Tourist Information Center** (TIC; ☎ **052/541-4301;** daily 9am–7pm) is located in Nagoya Station's central concourse (look for the "?" signs) and has maps and brochures. There's another Tourist Information Center downtown, in the basement of Oasis 21 (which looks like a spaceship) on Hisaya Dori near Sakae Station (☎ **052/963-5252;** daily 10am–8pm).

Another good source for information is the **Nagoya International Center,** an 8-minute walk from Nagoya Station's Central exit straight down Sakura Dori (or take the subway one stop to Kokusai Center Station), located on the third floor of the Nagoya International Center Building, 1–47–1 Nagono (☎ **052/581-0100;** www.nic-nagoya.or.jp; Tues–Sun 9am–7pm; closed second Sun in Feb and Aug). It's one of Japan's best facilities for foreign visitors and residents, with an English-speaking staff, a lounge area with a TV featuring CNN newscasts, Internet access, and lots of information on the city, including the free monthly publications *Nagoya Calendar* and *Avenues.* The center also offers practical advice on living in Japan, from how to get a visa to which doctors speak English. On the fourth floor, you can apply to visit a Japanese family in their home in the local **Home-Visit System.** You must apply in person, with your passport, no later than 5pm the day before your intended visit. Call ☎ **052/581-5689** for details; the earlier you reserve, the better your chances of finding a family.

For recorded English-language information on events, concerts, festivals, and the arts, call ☎ **052/581-0400;** or go to www.nic-nagoya.or.jp. You can check the city's website at www.ncvb.or.jp.

ORIENTATION Almost completely destroyed during World War II, Nagoya was rebuilt with wide, straight streets, many of which are named.

The ultramodern, twin-towered **JR Nagoya Station,** with its many train lines (including the Shinkansen), soars more than 50 stories above the skyline and contains Takashimaya department store, Tokyu Hands, a Marriott hotel, many restaurants, and an observatory. Built in 1999, it has been recognized by Guinness World Records as being the world's largest building containing a railway station. Clustered nearby are the Meitetsu Bus Terminal, Meitetsu Nagoya (train) Station, Kintetsu Station, and a subway station for the Sakura-dori and Higashiyama lines, as well as many hotels and a huge underground shopping arcade that stretches 6km (3¾ miles) and includes about 600 shops. The city bus terminal here is undergoing renovation; until its completion in 2016, city buses depart from various locations outside Nagoya Station.

Most of the city's attractions spread out east of Nagoya Station (the Central/Sakura-dori exit), including **Sakae,** the city's downtown area, located two subway stops from Nagoya Station and with many shops, restaurants, bars, and department stores. Also in Sakae is **Hisaya Odori,** a wide boulevard that stretches north and south with a park and a TV tower in its green meridian. North of Hisaya Odori is **Nagoya Castle,** while south is **Atsuta Jingu Shrine.**

 A Note on Directions

All directions in the listings below are from Nagoya Station unless otherwise noted; the time in parentheses indicates walking time from the subway or bus stop indicated.

GETTING AROUND The fastest way to get around is via the city's eight-line **subway** system, which is simple to use because station names, written in both English and Japanese, are assigned both a letter (representing the line; H, for example, is for the Higashiyama Line) and a number (so you can count how many stops before

Tourists planning to spend a few days traveling between Nagoya, Osaka, Kyoto, and Ise-Shima can save money by purchasing a **Kintetsu Rail Pass** (www.kintetsu.co.jp; ✆ **052/561-1604**) that covers travel throughout the region on Kintetsu's private lines. Available only for foreign visitors, it must be purchased *before arriving in Japan* at Kintetsu offices or authorized travel agencies (in Japan, it's available only at the Kansai Airport Agency Travel Desk on the first floor of Kansai International Airport). It costs ¥3,700 for adults and ¥1,850 for children and includes 5 days of unlimited travel (but only three trips on limited express trains). For ¥5,700, you can purchase the Kintetsu Rail Pass Wide, which adds a trip from Centrair or Kansai Airport, Mie Kotsu buses, and discount coupons for sightseeing spots.

your destination). There are also English-language announcements and digital signs in trains. Probably the most important line for tourists is the loop **Meijo Line,** which runs through Sakae underneath Hisaya Odori and takes you to both Nagoya Castle (Station: Shiyakusho) and Atsuta Jingu Shrine (Station: Jingu-Nishi), with a branch, the Meiko Line, terminating at Nagoya Port with its aquarium. If you take the Meijo Line in the opposite direction, you'll eventually end up at the—I like this—Ozone stop. Individual tickets for the subway are ¥200 to ¥320, depending on the distance.

The **Nagoya Sightseeing Route Bus** (called **Me-guru** [メーグル] in Japanese) departs from platform 8 in front of Nagoya Station's Sakura Dori/Central exit and is convenient for traveling to the Toyota museum, Noritake Garden, Nagoya Castle, Tokugawa Art Museum, and Sakae. It costs ¥200 per trip or ¥500 for the Me-guru 1-Day (the pass also gives slight discounts to most sights). It operates from 9:30am to about 5pm, every 30 to 60 minutes Tuesday through Friday and every 20 to 30 minutes weekends and holidays.

For **city buses,** you'll pay a flat fare of ¥200. There's also the private **Meitetsu Bus Line** with a terminal located at Nagoya Station; for these buses, take a ticket and pay the exact fare according to the digital panel display at the front when you get off.

There are several **transportation passes** worth considering if you'll be traveling a lot within a single day. For subways, there's the **Ichinichi Jo-sha,** a 1-day pass for ¥740 that allows you to ride as much as you want for a full day; for ¥850 you can ride as much as you want on subways, city buses, and Me-guru sightseeing bus. On the weekends the **Eco Pass** for ¥600 allows unlimited rides on subways and buses. For more information, drop by a Transportation Bureau Service Center (at Nagoya, Sakae, Kanayama, and other major stations), call ✆ **052/522-0111,** or go to the website www.kotsu.city.nagoya.jp/english.

[Fast FACTS] NAGOYA

ATM/Mail   Nagoya's Central Post Office (✆ **052/ 564-2106**), located to the left of the Sakura exit of JR Nagoya Station, is open for mail and money exchange Monday to Friday 9am to 6pm. In addition to a counter open 24 hours for mail, it has ATMs open 12:05am to 11:55pm Monday through Saturday and 12:05am to 9pm on Sunday.

Consulates Several embassies maintain consulates in Osaka, including **Canada** (© 052/972-0450); **New Zealand** (© 052/361-8211); and the **United States** (© 052/581-4501).

Internet Access The Nagoya International Center (see "Visitor Information," above) provides 15-minute Internet access for ¥100. Cheaper is **Media Popeye,** with two locations in downtown Nagoya: across from the TV Tower at 3–6–15 Nishiki (© **052/955-0059**), and on the ninth floor of Become Sakae at 3–32–6 Sakae (© **052/242-8369**). Both are open 24 hours and charge ¥250 for 1 hour.

Exploring Nagoya

Arimatsu Tie-Dyeing Museum (Arimatsu Narumi Shibori Kaikan; 有松・鳴海絞会館) MUSEUM   During the days of the shogun, Arimatsu was a small village on the old Tokaido Highway. Its inhabitants made a living producing *shibori* (tie-dyed cotton cloth), which they then sold as towels to passing travelers. Today, Arimatsu is a suburb of Nagoya on its southeastern edge, yet it still retains its historic core, with several buildings remaining from the Edo Period and more than 2,500 people still involved in this cottage industry. This small museum pays tribute to the painstaking tie-dying process; more than 100 patterns are possible, with a single kimono requiring between 50,000 and 200,000 handmade stitches and taking 4 to 6 months to complete. A short film tells the history of Arimatsu tie-dying and the lengthy process involved in the craft: engraving a pattern, transferring the pattern to the cloth, tying the cloth, dying it, and then taking the stitches out. Several women are usually on hand practicing their trade; a small shop sells their wares. If you want, you can experience tying a handkerchief (¥1,050; allow 1 hr.), a curtain (¥2,625; allow 2 hr.), a table center (¥2,100; allow 2 hr.), or an apron or T-shirt (¥3,150; allow 3 hr.). Your craft will be tie-dyed later and sent to you; reservations are required.

3008 Arimatsu, Midori-ku. www.shibori-kaikan.com. © **052/621-0111.** Admission ¥300 adults, ¥100 children. Daily 9:30am–5pm (closed Wed Dec–Mar). From Meitetsu Nagoya Station, take a local Meitetsu train (not express) 30 min. to Arimatsu Station, walk straight out of the station, turn left at the bottom of the stairs, and then turn left at the sign for HATTORI RESIDENCE; the museum will be on the right (5 min.).

Atsuta Jingu Shrine TEMPLE   Because it contains one of the emperor's Three Sacred Treasures, this is revered as one of the three most important shrines in Japan. Founded in the 2nd century and last rebuilt in 1955, it enshrines the Grass-Mowing Sword (Kusanagi-no-Tsurugi), which is one of the Imperial Regalia of the Emperor. The other two sacred treasures are the Sacred Mirror (in the Ise Grand Shrines; see p. 334) and the Jewels (in the Imperial Palace in Tokyo; see p. 89). According to legend, the Grass-Mowing Sword was presented to a prince named Yamato-Takeru, who used it during a campaign against rebels in eastern Japan; the rebels set a field of grass on fire, and the prince used the sword to mow down the grass, thereby quelling the fire. (*Atsuta* means "hot field" in Japanese.) Actually, there isn't much to see of the shrine—the sword is never on public display—yet this remains one of Nagoya's top attractions (especially on New Year's), and Japanese make pilgrimages here to pay their respects, first purifying their hands or mouths with water, then throwing coins into the money box, clapping to gain the attention of the gods, and bowing as they pray. A Treasure Hall displays exhibits that change monthly of items donated through the ages by members of the Imperial family, shoguns, feudal lords, and common people, including furniture, household goods, and, thanks to the legend of the

Kusanagi-no-Tsurugi, an impressive number of swords and daggers. Surrounded by stately, ancient cypress trees, the shrine provides a nice respite from city life.

1–1–1 Jingu, Atsuta-ku. www.atsutajingu.or.jp. ℂ **052/671-4151.** Free admission to the grounds; Treasure Hall ¥300 adults, ¥150 children. Grounds daily dawn–dusk; treasure house daily 9am–4:30pm (closed last Wed and the following day of every month and Dec 25–31). Station: Jingu-mae (3 min.) via the Meitetsu train line from Meitetsu Nagoya Station or Jingu-Nishi via subway (7 min.).

Nagoya Castle ★ CASTLE   Built for his ninth son by Tokugawa Ieyasu, the first Tokugawa shogun, Nagoya Castle was completed in 1612 and served as both a strategic stronghold on the Tokaido Highway and a residence for members of the Owari branch of the Tokugawa family for almost 250 years, until the Meiji Restoration ended their rule in 1868. A shrewd and calculating shogun, Tokugawa forced feudal lords throughout Japan to contribute to the castle's construction, thereby depleting their resources and making it harder for them to rebel. Although Nagoya Castle was largely destroyed in World War II (only three turrets and three gates escaped destruction), the main *donjon* and other structures, rebuilt in 1959, are almost carbon copies of the original. Like most reconstructed castles in Japan, this replica is made of ferroconcrete, yet it's still impressive from afar. Inside, the 20m-high (66-ft.) donjon is thoroughly modern and even has an elevator up to the fifth floor, where you have fine views of Nagoya and beyond. The castle houses treasures that escaped the bombing during World War II, including beautiful paintings on sliding doors and screens that once adorned the castle's Honmaru Palace (destroyed during World War II but presently being rebuilt the traditional way without the use of nails, a painstaking process that will take 10 years, with an expected reopening in 2018). Also on display are flintlocks, swords, helmets, and exhibits relating to the castle's construction and what life was like during the Edo Period.

Atop the *donjon* roof are two **golden dolphins,** replicas of those that perished during World War II and long thought to protect the castle from dreaded fires. The dolphins each weigh about 1,190 kilograms (2,650 lb.) and are made of cast bronze covered with 18-karat-gold scales. Incidentally, the dolphin on the south end—the favored, warmer side—is considered female, while the one relegated to the colder northern side is male. Through the centuries, the dolphins' gold scales have been stolen three times.

East of the castle is **Ninomaru Garden,** laid out at the time of the castle's construction, converted to a dry Japanese landscape garden in 1716 and today one of the few remaining castle gardens in Japan. Besides providing a beautiful setting, it served as an emergency shelter for the lord in case of enemy attack. Stop by the **Ninomaru Tea House**—it's said that if you drink tea here when it's made with a golden kettle (available only on Fri), 5 years will be added to your life. That should allow you ample time to linger, but otherwise you can tour the castle and grounds in less than 1½ hours.

1–1 Honmaru, Naka-ku. www.nagoyajo.city.nagoya.jp/13_english/index.html. ℂ **052/231-1700.** Admission ¥500 adults, free for junior high and younger. Daily 9am–4:30pm. Station: Shiyakusho (5 min.). Me-guru sightseeing bus: Nagoya Castle (1 min.).

Noritake Garden ★★★ MUSEUM   Nagoya has been a pottery and porcelain production center for centuries; today, the city and its vicinity manufacture 90% of Japan's total export chinaware. The largest chinaware company in Japan is Noritake, founded in 1904 and known the world over for its fine tableware. You can learn more about Noritake by spending about an hour at the site of its former factory, beginning with the Welcome Center's short film depicting the history of Noritake. At the Craft

Center, you'll see displays explaining the manufacturing and decorating processes involved in making porcelain, as well as watch artisans, who, unlike at most modern-day factories where work is largely automated, do almost all their work by hand. The Noritake Museum is probably my favorite part of the complex, with its examples of all the Noritake chinaware ever produced (including a great Art Deco collection). At the Canvas hall, all you ever wanted to know about the role ceramics plays in everyday life—from Washlet toilets to computers—is presented in hands-on displays activated by your own ceramic microchip card. And of course, there are also shops, including those selling Noritake fine chinaware, tableware for everyday use, and an outlet store.

3–1–36 Noritake Shinmachi, Nishi-ku. www.noritake.co.jp/mori. © **052/561-7290.** Admission to Craft Center and museum ¥500 adults, ¥300 high-school students, free for children and seniors; free admission to the Welcome Center, Canvas, and shops. Tues–Sun 10am–5pm (you must enter the Craft Center by 4pm); shops open until 6pm. Subway: Kamejima (5 min.). Me-guru sightseeing bus: Noritake Garden (1 min.). A 15-min. walk north of Nagoya Station.

Port of Nagoya Public Aquarium ★★★ ☺ AQUARIUM

Young Japanese flock to Nagoya's port area on weekends, drawn by a small amusement park, a maritime museum, a shopping complex, and sightseeing boats. But the Public Aquarium, one of Japan's largest, is the major draw for kids of all ages. For the kids there's a touch tank with sea urchins, starfish, and other animals, and an IMAX theater with shows on the hour (included in the entry price). In addition to displays of marine life from the seas around Japan, the aquarium is best known for its penguin tank, which copies the environment of the Antarctic with artificial falling snow and cold temperatures to maintain the penguins' reproductive cycle; the loggerhead and green turtles with a sand beach to encourage them to lay eggs; and its Beluga whales, including the only baby Beluga born in a Japanese aquarium. Not to be missed are the Beluga training sessions, held apparently to keep the Belugas from getting bored. There are also dolphin performances, which you can watch either above or below the water's surface of the second-largest show pool in the world. Count on 3 hours here, including the IMAX.

1–3 Minato-machi, Minato-ku. © **052/654-7080.** Admission ¥2,000 adults, ¥1,000 children. Tues–Sun 9:30am–5:30pm (to 5pm Dec to mid-Mar, to 8pm Golden Week and July 21–Aug). Closed 5 days end of Jan for maintenance. Station: Nagoyako (exit 3, 7 min.).

Tokugawa Art Museum ★★★ 🎁 ART MUSEUM

Located on the grounds of a former mansion owned by the Owari branch of the Tokugawa family—with the original entry gate and a guardhouse still intact—this worthwhile museum houses a changing display of documents, samurai armor, swords, matchlocks, helmets, pottery, lacquerware, *noh* costumes and masks, and paintings that once belonged to the Tokugawa family, including objects inherited from the first Tokugawa shogun, Ieyasu. There are also replicas of structures and items that once adorned Nagoya Castle, including decorative alcoves, a teahouse, and a noh stage. Of the museum's nine National Treasures, most famous is the 12th-century picture scrolls of *The Tale of Genji*, but they're displayed only 1 week a year at the end of November (check with the tourist office); otherwise, replicas are on display. Excellent English-language explanations throughout the museum put the displays in historical context. You can easily spend 90 minutes here and in the museum's garden, the Tokugawaen, with a pond, waterfalls, and strolling paths.

For an even more memorable experience, make reservations to dine at the classy **Garden Restaurant Tokugawaen ★** (© 052/932-7887), overlooking the garden's pond and serving fusion Japanese-French cuisine. Although its wooden veranda and stone foundation give it a traditional atmosphere, candles and jazz music playing in the background lend it a contemporary edge. Only set meals are available, with lunches ranging from ¥2,500 to ¥5,000 and dinners starting at ¥7,000. It's open daily (closed irregularly) from 11am to 2pm and 5 to 10pm (last order).

1017 Tokugawa-cho, Higashi-ku. www.tokugawa-art-museum.jp. © **052/935-6262.** Admission to art museum ¥1,200 adults, ¥1,000 seniors, ¥700 university and high-school students, ¥500 children; combination ticket to museum and garden ¥1,350, ¥1,150, ¥850, and ¥570 respectively. Tues–Sun 10am–5pm. Me-guru sightseeing bus: Tokugawaen (1 min.). Station: Ozone (exit 3, 10 min.).

Toyota Commemorative Museum of Industry and Technology ★★ ☺

MUSEUM   This museum seems an odd marriage: It's devoted to both textile machinery and automobile production and technology. That's because the Toyota Group, founded by Toyoda Sakichi, the inventor of automatic looms, has a long history of producing both. Housed at the site where the Toyota Group had its beginnings, in an attractive brick building dating from the Taisho Period (1912–25), the museum displays approximately 90 looms and textile machinery, from wooden hand looms to air-jet looms that utilize computer graphics. The automobile pavilion provides a historical chronology of automobile production, beginning with a replica of the first Toyota car (1935), early assembly lines using manpower, and automated assembly lines using industrial robots for everything from engine mounting to painting. There's also a display of both old and new Toyota cars and four films of how Toyota makes its cars, including design. Frequent demonstrations of looms (they're loud!), auto-making equipment (including robotics), a Swiss 1898 steam engine, and a trumpet-playing robot make this a fun destination for adults and kids alike. There's also a children's hands-on discovery room. Expect to spend 90 minutes here, longer if you opt for the ¥200 audio guide.

4–1–35 Noritake Shinmachi, Nishi-ku. www.tcmit.org. © **052/551-6115.** Admission ¥500 adults, ¥300 junior-high and high-school students, ¥200 children, free for seniors. Tues–Sun 9:30am–5pm. Me-guru sightseeing bus: Toyota Commemorative Museum of Industry and Technology (Sangyo Gijutsu Kinenkan; 1 min.). Train: Meitetsu Line to Sako (3 min.). Subway: Kamejima (exit 2, 10 min.). Just north of the Noritake Craft Center, about a 25-min. walk from Nagoya Station.

A SIDE TRIP TO INUYAMA CITY

Inuyama City has several worthwhile attractions, so you might want to come for a day of sightseeing and, in summer, top it off with cormorant fishing (see below). The **Inuyama Tourist Information Center,** in Inuyama Station (© **0568/61-6000;** www.inuyama.gr.jp), is open daily 9am to 5pm. To reach Inuyama, take the Meitetsu rapid limited express from Meitetsu Nagoya Station (beside Nagoya Station) 25 minutes to either Inuyama Station (fare: ¥540) or one stop farther to Inuyama Yuen Station (fare: ¥590).

Note: There are no specific addresses in this section, because addresses in smaller Japanese cities do not give exact street addresses. However, everyone will know where these attractions are.

Inuyama Castle ★   CASTLE   Constructed in 1537 atop a bluff overlooking the Kiso River, this four-story *donjon*—much smaller than most of Japan's castles—is Japan's oldest and is a designated National Treasure. It miraculously survived centuries of earthquakes (part of it was damaged by an 1891 earthquake but then repaired) and wars, including in 1584 when Toyotomi Hideyoshi and his 120,000 retainers used it to stage war against Tokugawa Ieyasu, whose forces were spread over Komaki Mountain. Owned by the same family from 1618 to 2004 (it's now under management of a foundation), it displays a few samurai outfits and offers a nice, expansive view over the river that's especially worth a look if you intend to join the nearby cormorant fishing. The castle is so diminutive you can see everything in 15 minutes.

⌀ **0568/61-1711.** Admission ¥500 adults, ¥100 children. Daily 9am–5pm. Station: Inuyama (15 min.).

Museum Meiji Mura ★★★ MUSEUM   Inuyama City's most important attraction is one of my favorite museums in Japan. In fact, it may well be the best reason for a Nagoya stopover. A 100-hectare (250-acre) open-air architectural museum, it features more than 65 buildings and structures dating from the Meiji Period (1868–1912), all beautifully situated on landscaped grounds on the shores of a lake. Before Japan opened its doors in the mid-1800s, unpainted wooden structures dominated Japanese architecture; after Western influences began infiltrating Japan, however, stone, brick, painted wood, towers, turrets, and Victorian features came into play. Unfortunately, earthquakes, war, fire, and developer greed have destroyed most of Japan's Meiji-Era buildings, making this a priceless collection.

On the grounds are Western homes that once belonged to foreigners living in Nagasaki and Kobe, official government buildings and schools, two churches and a cathedral, a post office, a bathhouse, a *kabuki* theater, a brewery, bridges, Japanese-style homes (including one that belonged to Japanese novelists Mori Ogai and Natsume Soseki), a martial-arts hall, an assembly hall used by Japanese immigrants in Hilo, Hawaii, and even a prison. Don't miss the front facade and lobby of the original Imperial Hotel in Tokyo, designed by Frank Lloyd Wright and containing some of the hotel's original Wright-designed furniture. In fact, most of the buildings display furniture and other items related to the building in which they're housed. You can mail a postcard from the post office, buy candy at the old candy shop, have coffee or tea in the Imperial Hotel sitting on original Wright-designed chairs, or stop for a drink at the brewery. Plan on spending at least 3 hours here.

www.meijimura.com. ⌀ **0568/67-0314.** Admission ¥1,600 adults, ¥1,200 seniors, ¥1,000 high-school students, ¥600 junior-high and elementary students. Daily 9:30am–5pm (to 4pm Nov–Feb; closed Mon Dec–Feb). Station: Inuyama, then bus from platform no. 2; 20 min. to Meiji Mura (¥410 one-way).

Watching Cormorant Fishing ★★★

There are two places near Nagoya where you can watch **cormorant fishing** every night in summer (except during a full moon or the 2 or 3 days following a heavy rain). In this ancient, 1,300-year-old Japanese fishing method, trained *ukai* (seabirds) dive into the water in search of *ayu*, a small Japanese trout. At nightfall, wooden fires are lit in suspended cages at the fronts of long wooden boats to attract the ayu, whereupon leashed cormorants are released into the water. To ensure that the cormorants don't swallow the fish, the birds are fitted with neck rings.

In **Inuyama,** cormorant fishing takes place on the Kiso River from June to mid-October. Spectators can board wooden boats departing from 6 to 8:15pm June to August (not available Aug 10), or 5:30 to 7:45pm September and October to observe the spectacle firsthand. While waiting for the full darkness that must descend before the fishing takes place, you can dine on *obento* box meals, which you must order at least 2 days in advance (beer and soft drinks are also sold before boarding). If you don't want to eat on the boat, you can board from 7pm June to August and from 6:30pm September to October. In any case, the actual fishing itself occupies only 20 minutes, so board one of the earlier boats to make it worthwhile. Call **Kiso Gawa Kanko** (⌀ **0568/61-0057**) to make reservations and then pick up your tickets at its ticket office near the bridge (located about a 5-min. walk from Inuyama Yuen Station).

Tickets for boarding the boats, a boxed dinner and watching the fishing cost ¥5,000 for adults and ¥2,750 for children, ¥2,200 and ¥1,100, respectively, without the meal. Alternatively, though it's not traditional, you can also watch cormorant fishing during the day, on Tuesday, Thursday, and Saturday, with boats departing from 11:30am to 1:40pm and costing ¥3,800 for adults and ¥2,900 for children, including lunch.

The city of **Gifu** features cormorant fishing from mid-May to mid-October on the Nagaragawa River, where you can view the entire spectacle aboard a small wooden boat. To reach Gifu, take either the Meitetsu train (fare: ¥540) or the JR train (¥450) from Nagoya 20 minutes to Gifu Station. From there, take a bus (¥200) 16 minutes to Nagara-bashi, where you'll see the ticket office for the **Gifu City Cormorant Fishing Viewing Boat Office** (**Gifu-shi Ukai Kanransen Jimusho;** *✆* **058/262-0104**). To be assured a place, reservations should be made in advance. Tickets cost ¥3,300 for adults and ¥2,900 for children for the 6:15pm boarding daily, as well as for weekend boardings at 6:45pm and 7:15pm. On weekdays, the 6:45 and 7:15pm are discounted to ¥3,000 for adults and ¥2,600 for children. Note that you should bring your own snacks or meal and drinks, as there is no place to purchase them at the boat office. Cormorant fishing begins around 7:45pm. For more information, go to **www.gifucvb.or.jp**.

Where to Eat

One of Nagoya's specialties is *kishimen,* fettuccine-like broad and flat white noodles usually served in a soup stock with soy sauce, tofu, dried bonito shavings, and chopped green onions. Nagoya is also famous for *miso nikomi udon*—udon noodles served in a bean-paste soup and flavored with such ingredients as chicken and green onions. *Cochin* (free-range) chicken and *tonkatsu* (breaded pork cutlets) with a red miso sauce are also Nagoya favorites.

AROUND NAGOYA STATION

The best place for one-stop dining is Nagoya Station itself, on the 12th and 13th floors of one of the twin towers atop the station. Called **Towers Plaza,** it offers about 40 food-and-beverage outlets (in addition to Farmer's Restaurant Moku Moku; see below) serving noodles, sushi, tempura, tofu dishes, grilled eel, *shabu-shabu,* steaks, Chinese food, Indian curries, Italian fare, and more, most with plastic-food displays.

If you reserve early enough (at least 2 months in advance), you might also get one of the coveted tables at French restaurant **Mikuni** on the 52nd floor of the Nagoya Marriott Associa Hotel (*✆* **052/584-1111**). Decorated in Art Nouveau style and considered by some to be the city's finest restaurant due to its celebrated chef Kiyomi Mikuni (who has restaurants also in Tokyo and Sapporo) and healthy *cuisine naturelle,* it offers set lunches for ¥6,800 to ¥14,000 from 11:30am to 1:30pm and set dinners for ¥14,000 to ¥21,000 from 5:30 to 9pm (last order), with a menu that changes monthly.

Farmer's Restaurant Moku Moku ★ VARIED JAPANESE   Boasting its own farm in Mie Prefecture, where it grows organic produce and raises cows, pigs, and chickens, as well as its butcher shop, this buffet restaurant offers lots of choices, including soups, vegetables, fish, breads (from its own bakery), sausages, desserts, and vegetable juices. Note that there are time restrictions for grazing: 90 minutes for lunch and 120 minutes for dinner, which should be enough time to sample just about everything. To find Moku Moku in the "city" that Nagoya Station has become, take an escalator to the second floor and then transfer to an elevator for the 13th floor.

There's a branch downtown, on the seventh floor of La Chic shopping complex, 3–6–1 Sakae (✆ **052/241-0909**).

13th floor, Towers Plaza, Nagoya Station, 1–1–4 Meieki, Nakamura-ku. ✆ **052/587-0909.** Lunch buffet ¥1,850; dinner buffet ¥2,800. AE, DC, MC, V. Daily Mon–Fri 10:30am–3pm; Sat–Sun and holidays 10:30am–4pm; daily 5–9:30pm (last order). Station: Nagoya (inside the station).

Soramame (そら豆) ★ 🍴 VARIED JAPANESE   This former bathhouse, built about 90 years ago, has found a second life as an airy restaurant with split-level dining. Primarily a drinking establishment popular with a young crowd, it offers a wide variety of choices, including avocado gratin, grilled chicken, and lots of vegetable dishes, from radishes to leeks to potatoes. Unfortunately, there's no English-language menu, but the Japanese menu does have hand-drawn pictures of some of its vegetables.

3–17–28 Meieki, Nakamura-ku. ✆ **052/566-5550.** Dishes ¥550–¥1,780. AE, DC, MC, V. Mon–Sat 5pm–midnight (last order). Station: Nagoya: (4 min.). From the Central Exit, walk straight down Sakura-dori and turn left at Junkudo bookstore; it's across the street from Toyoko Inn annex, to the right.

Yamamoto-ya Honten (山本屋本店) UDON NOODLES   This chain noodle shop, a 2-minute walk from Nagoya Station, specializes in *miso nikomi udon*. Its noodles, all handmade, are thick, hard, and chewy and are served in a type of bean paste that's special to Nagoya. You can order it plain or with additions like tofu, cochin chicken, or pork (an English-language menu with explanations makes ordering easy), and if you like your noodles spicy, add spices to your food from the large bamboo container on your table. A small dish of vegetables (cabbage, shaved onion, cucumber) is brought to your table as soon as you're seated and is replenished free of charge.

3–25–9 Meieki, basement of the Horiuchi Building, Sakura Dori, Nakamura-ku. ✆ **052/565-0278.** Udon dishes ¥1,050–¥1,942. AE, DC, MC, V. Daily 11am–9:30pm. Station: Nagoya (Unimall exit, 2 min.); on Sakura Dori's north side, below Junkudo bookstore, in an area called "Gourmet Avenue."

IN SAKAE

In addition to these, **Farmer's Restaurant Moku Moku** (see above) has a branch in Sakae.

The 59's Café & Diner INTERNATIONAL   This place is a hoot. It's worth coming to this small basement bar just to see the waitresses wearing cowboy hats or to gaze at the lava lamps and Spam containers on the counter along with the whiskey. But it serves decent food as well, including a pretty good burger, fish and chips, and other bar fare, and the music is mostly '50s and '60s rock 'n' roll. Wednesday and Friday are Ladies' Nights, when females can drink as much as they want for 100 minutes for ¥1,500, after which those cowboy hats might start looking quite fashionable.

3–15–10 Nishiki, Naka-ku. ✆ **052/971-0566.** Main dishes ¥600–¥1,300. AE, DC, MC, V. Mon–Sat 5pm–4am; Sun 5pm–midnight. Station: Sakae or Hisaya-odori (3 min.); on Hisaya Odori, west of the TV tower.

Hourai-ken Matsuzakaya EEL   A branch of two famous restaurants near Atsuta Shrine, this restaurant offers various *unagi donburi* (rice casserole with eel on top). Most famous is the Hitsumabushi, a set meal for ¥3,100 that includes *unagi donburi*, various condiments, miso soup, and Japanese pickles. Eating it is a ritual: First, dish out some of the eel casserole into the smaller wooden bowl and eat it plain. For the next course, try it with some of the seaweed and green onions that come with it. Finally, add some of the soup and wasabi to the last mixture you tried. The other, more elegant branches are both south of Atsuta Shrine at 2–10–26 Jingu, Atsuta-ku (☎ 052/682-5598; Wed–Mon 11:30am–2:30pm and 4:30–8:30pm); and at 503 Goudo-cho, Atsuta-ku (☎ 052/671-8686; Thurs–Tues 11:30am–2pm and 4:30–8:30pm).

Matsuzakaya, 3–30–8 Sakae, Naka-ku. ☎ **052/264-3825.** Unagi teishoku (set meal) ¥1,575–¥3,780. AE, MC, V. Daily 11am–9pm (last order). Station: Yabacho (1 min.). In the south building of Matsuzakaya department store, in the back on the 10th floor (look for the sign that says UNAGI HORAIKEN).

Tiger Cafe FRENCH   With its antique-looking advertisements for Pernod, tiled walls and floor, small tables, and rattan chairs facing the open facade, this coffee shop is the closest thing in Nagoya to a Parisian cafe. Stop for a drink, a snack of quiche, or dine on more substantial fare such as the fish or meat dish of the day and be glad you're not part of the traffic whizzing by.

A branch, with a slightly different menu, is at 1–8–26 Nishiki (☎ 052/220-0031; station: Fushimi), across from the Hilton Hotel and down a side street with a Starbucks on the corner. It's open Monday to Saturday from 11am to 2:30am and Sunday 11am to 10:30pm.

1–9–22 Higashi-sakura, Higashi-ku. www.tiger-cafe.com. ☎ **052/971-1031.** Main dishes ¥1,300–¥2,000. No credit cards. Mon–Sat 11am–2:30am; Sun 11am–midnight (last order). Station: Sakae (6 min.); north of Oasis 21 on a side street, across from the NHK Building (both of which you can't miss).

Torigin Honten (鳥銀本店) ★ COCHIN CHICKEN   In the heart of Nagoya, this 37-year-old casual restaurant with counter, tatami, or table seating is known for its *Nagoya cochin* (free-range chicken). Although it serves *yakitori,* this is not your usual yakitori restaurant; rather, dining here should be considered a culinary adventure of the chicken, with parts of the bird served in ways you've never imagined. All set meals include raw cochin with real gold flakes, though you're allowed to substitute a cooked dish if you like. The popular Gourmet yakitori (¥1,950) comes with eight different skewers, which may include *tsukune* (meatballs), chicken skin, and breast meat with miso paste. An amiable staff makes it diner-friendly; a black-and-white *kura*-style facade makes it easy to identify. If this main shop (Honten) is full, you may be led to one of three nearby branches, one of which offers tatami rooms with a view of the garden, but I prefer the liveliness of the main restaurant.

3–14–22 Nishiki, Naka-ku. ☎ **052/973-3000.** Cochin main dishes ¥750–¥1,950; set meals ¥2,900–¥5,200. Snack charge ¥300 per person in main shop, ¥500 in its branches. AE, DC, MC, V. Daily 5pm–midnight (last order). Station: Sakae (exit 1, 2 min.).

Yabaton (矢場とん) ★★ TONKATSU   You'll recognize this Everyman's eatery in Nagoya's downtown district immediately by its curtains displaying comical pigs dressed like sumo wrestlers. In operation since 1947, its interior is all about pigs and sumo (I'll let you draw your own conclusions about the connection). It's famous for its *tonkatsu* (pork cutlet), and you'll be asked whether you want yours with its homemade sauce (*sa-u-zu*) or red *miso;* the former is thicker and sweeter, but the latter is the specialty here (if you don't specify, you'll be served the miso, but if you can't decide, ask for a little of both). *Donburi,* a breaded and fried pork cutlet on rice, is the cheapest, but recommended is *hire,* a tender cut with less fat. Main dishes all come with cabbage; rice or miso soup costs extra. Deep-fried vegetables and seafood (scallops, oysters) are also available. And in case you're interested, Yabaton souvenirs—T-shirts, key chains, towels—are for sale, all adorned with comical pigs dressed like sumo wrestlers and baseball players. There's a branch in nearby La Chic shopping complex, on the seventh floor (✆ 052/269-7070; daily 11am–11pm).

3–6–18 Osu. www.english.yabaton.com. ✆ **052/252-8810.** Main dishes ¥735–¥1,785; set meals ¥1,155–¥1,680. No credit cards. Tues–Sun 11am–9pm. Station: Yabacho (exit 4, 3 min.). Turn right at the overpass; it's on the southwest corner of Wakamiya-Otsu Dori intersection.

Where to Stay

EXPENSIVE

In addition to the hotels listed below, the **Nagoya Hilton,** 1–3–3 Sakae, Naka-ku, Nagoya 460-0008 (www.hilton.com; ✆ **800/445-8667** in the U.S. and Canada, or 052/212-1111;), offers 438 units to mostly foreign business travelers.

Mercure Nagoya Cypress (formerly Sofitel The Cypress Nagoya) ★★

With a contemporary, boutiquelike atmosphere, this hotel has a great location near Nagoya Station. Standard rooms are fairly small but comfortable, and because some face other buildings, ask for a room on a higher floor, where you might have an urban view (ones facing the station are my favorite). More deluxe rooms add space, larger windows, and sink and vanity areas separate from the bathrooms. In short, you won't go wrong staying here, especially if you're looking for a small, personable hotel near the station.

2–43–6 Meieki, Nakamura-ku, Nagoya, Aichi Prefecture 450-0002. www.thecypress.co.jp. ✆ **052/ 571-0111.** Fax 052/569-1717. 115 units. ¥25,000–¥32,000 single or double. AE, DC, MC, V. Station: Nagoya (4 min.). Turn left out of the Sakura Dori/Central exit and then the 1st right just before the post office. **Amenities:** 2 restaurants; bar. *In room:* A/C, TV, hair dryer, Internet (fee: ¥1,050 per day), minibar.

Nagoya Marriott Associa Hotel ★★

A location right over Nagoya Station makes this Nagoya's most convenient hotel. Occupying the 15th to 52nd floors of one of Nagoya's tallest buildings, it offers the city's best views (ask for a room facing the castle and downtown; higher floors cost more), not to mention quick access to the many restaurants and shops on the lower floors of this "vertical city." Despite its central location, it doesn't skimp on facilities, offering a health club; good-size, up-to-date guest rooms; and a wide range of in-house dining possibilities (to eat at French restaurant Mikuni, considered Nagoya's top restaurant, make reservations months in advance). Don't miss having a drink at the 52nd-floor Sky Lounge Zenith (daily 11:30am–midnight; ¥1,050 music charge in the evening)—but all this is assuming you can even find the hotel. Guests arriving by train not only have to search for the obscure ground-floor entryway, but have to battle the crowds taking elevators to the many restaurants (reception is on the 15th floor). Luckily, it's worth it.

1–1–4 Meieki, Nakamura-ku, Nagoya, Aichi Prefecture 450-6002. www.associa.com/nma. ✆ **800/228-9290** in the U.S. and Canada, or 052/584-1111. Fax 052/584-1112. 774 units. ¥24,000–¥36,000 single; ¥32,000–¥44,000 double; from ¥40,000 executive-floor double. AE, DC, MC, V. Station: Nagoya (below the hotel). **Amenities:** 6 restaurants, including Mikuni (p. 327), 2 bars; 2 lounges; concierge; executive-level rooms; 20m (66-ft.) 4-lane pool, Jacuzzi, and fitness gym (fee: ¥3,150); room service. *In room:* A/C, TV, hair dryer, Internet (fee: ¥1,575 per day), minibar.

Westin Nagoya Castle ★★

Situated just west of Nagoya Castle, about 2.5km (1½ miles) from Nagoya Station and Sakae, the chief attraction of this 50-some-year-old hotel—a local favorite for special occasions and meetings—is the wonderful views of the moat and castle from its rooms, especially at night when the castle is illuminated. Rooms are spacious enough and feature Heavenly Beds, but it's worth staying here only if you get a room with a view (and for most room types, you won't pay more

A Double or a Twin?

For the sake of convenience, the price for two people in a room is listed as a "double" in this book. Japanese hotels, however, differentiate between rooms with a double bed or two twin beds, usually with different prices. Although most hotels charge more for a twin room, sometimes the opposite is true; if you're looking for a bargain, therefore, be sure to inquire about prices for both. Note, too, that hotels usually have more twin rooms than doubles, for the simple reason that Japanese couples, used to their own futon, traditionally prefer twin beds.

for that view). Otherwise, the location is rather inconvenient, though courtesy shuttle buses to Nagoya Station once an hour are a big plus, and joggers might like the proximity of the castle grounds and an adjacent park; ask the concierge for its map of a 3.6km (2.2-mile) suggested jogging route.

3–19 Hinokuchi-cho, Nishi-ku, Nagoya, Aichi Prefecture 451-8551. www.castle.co.jp/wnc. **800/937-8461** in the U.S. and Canada, or 052/521-2121. Fax 052/531-3313. 195 units. ¥16,000 single; ¥34,000–¥43,000 double; from ¥26,000 executive single; from ¥34,000 executive double. AE, DC, MC, V. Subway: Tsurumai Line to Sengencho (10 min.). Bus: Free shuttle from Nagoya Station every hour on the hour 10am–8pm (15-min. ride). **Amenities:** 5 restaurants; bar; lounge; babysitting; concierge; executive-level rooms; indoor 5-lane 25m (80-ft.) pool and Jacuzzi (fee: ¥1,575) w/exercise room and sauna; room service. *In room:* A/C, TV, hair dryer, minibar, Wi-Fi.

MODERATE

the b nagoya ★   Japanese business hotels used to be dingy, depressing affairs, but this stylish chain illustrates how far they've come. Known for its contemporary, upbeat decor, reasonable rates, and good downtown locations, the b offers smallish, spotless rooms with focused bed lights and deep tubs (two features I especially appreciate), free coffee in the lobby, and a 24-hour convenience store on-site. Sakae, with its shops, restaurants, and nightlife, is a few minutes' walk away.

4–15–23 Sakae, Naka-ku, Nagoya, Aichi Prefecture 460-0008. www.ishinhotels.com/theb-nagoya/en. **052/241-1500.** Fax 052/264-1732. 219 units. ¥8,800–¥10,000 single; ¥12,000–¥16,000 double. AE, DC, MC, V. Station: Sakae (exit 13, 3 min.). On Hisaya Odori, facing the park. **Amenities:** Restaurant; lobby computer w/free Internet. *In room:* A/C, TV, fridge, hair dryer, Internet.

Ekimae MontBlanc Hotel   There isn't a lot to say about this simple hotel except that it's close to the station and offers mostly single functional rooms at reasonable rates. The cheapest singles are minuscule, and though double rooms are adequate in size, there are only 13 of them (there are also 12 semi-double rooms, where two determined people can squeeze in for ¥11,000). The hotel's corner location frees it from proximity to taller buildings, which means you can actually look outside rather than face another building (ask for a room on a higher floor). Otherwise, there's not much to crow about; this is strictly a sleeping machine with a fancy name.

3–14–1 Meieki, Nakamura-ku, Nagoya, Aichi Precture 450-0002. www.montblanc-hotel.jp. **052/541-1121.** Fax 052/541-1140. 277 units. ¥7,800–¥9,000 single; ¥12,600–¥13,600 double. AE, DC, MC, V. Station: Nagoya (2 min.). Turn left out of the Sakura Dori/Central exit and then the 1st right just before the post office. **Amenities:** Restaurant. *In room:* A/C, TV, fridge, hair dryer, Wi-Fi.

Tokyo Dai-Ichi Hotel Nishiki ★★   This smart-looking hotel is my top pick among Nagoya's moderately priced hotels in the city center. Located in the heart of Nagoya's nightlife and business district on Nishiki Dori, it has prices comparable to those of a business hotel but with a much classier atmosphere and decor. Targeting businesspeople as well as female travelers (some may find the flower-patterned bedspreads too feminine), it offers smartly decorated rooms with large desks and larger-than-usual bath towels. There's only one double, but some of the standard twins have two sinks (good for two people trying to get ready at the same time), while deluxe twins are separated into living and sleeping areas and even have two TVs. Rooms facing another building have glazed windows, so if seeing out is important to you, be sure to say so.

3–18–21 Nishiki, Naka-ku, Nagoya Aichi Prefecture 460-0003. www.hankyu-hotel.com/english/index.html. © **052/955-1001.** Fax 052/953-6783. 233 units. ¥9,240–¥11,500 single; ¥15,015–¥25,410 double. AE, DC, MC, V. Station: Sakae (exit 1, 2 min.). **Amenities:** 2 restaurants. *In room:* A/C, TV, fridge, hair dryer, Internet.

INEXPENSIVE

In addition to the choices here, **Toyoko Inn** has six properties in Nagoya, including three near Nagoya Station and one in Sakae. Go to www.toyoko-inn.com for more information and locations.

Meiryu Ryokan   A Japanese Inn Group member and family-owned for more than 60 years, this is a no-nonsense place. Customers are a mix of travelers (including families), students, and during the week, Japanese businessmen. *Tatami* rooms are spotless and cozy, with more space and features than most other hotel rooms in this price category, including a closet, but have glazed windows beyond the *shoji* screens. The men's public bathroom has a sauna, but the female bath doesn't and is smaller (female guests are fewer); and there's also a coin-operated laundry room on site. The owners' son, who often clerks the front desk and is the third-generation innkeeper, speaks English well and is very helpful.

2–4–21 Kamimaezu, Naka-ku, Nagoya 463-0013. www.japan-net.ne.jp/~meiryu.© **052/331-8686.** Fax 052/321-6119. 22 units, none with bathroom. ¥5,250 single; ¥8,400 double. Japanese breakfast ¥630 extra; Japanese dinner ¥2,310 extra (advance dinner reservations required; not available 1st night and Sun). AE, MC, V. Station: Kamimaezu (exit 3, 4 min.). Walk straight out of the station 1 block and turn left; it's on the 2nd block, on the left. **Amenities:** Lobby computer w/free Internet. *In room:* A/C, TV, Internet.

Petit Ryokan Ichifuji ★   This Japanese Inn Group *ryokan* is way out there in Ozone (pronounced *ozon-ay*)—so be sure to get directions before heading out. Ishida Tomiyasu, who speaks a little English, inherited the 50-year-old ryokan from his father and grandfather, and together with his wife, Yoko, has created a restful Japanese interior with wood floors and wainscoting, calligraphy, and coin-operated laundry and a cypress public bath (daily 24 hr.). All except one of the rooms is tatami, with rates that vary depending on the season and room size.

1–7 Saikobashi-dori, Kita-ku, Nagoya Aichi Prefecture 462-0818. http://ichifuji-nagoya.com. © **052/914-2867.** Fax 052/981-6836. 10 units, none with bathroom. ¥6,300–¥8,000 single; ¥10,000–¥14,000 double; ¥16,500–¥20,400 triple. Rates include continental breakfast. AE, DC, MC, V. Station: Heiandori (exit 2, 3 min.); Ozone (10 min.). **Amenities:** Restaurant (w/computer and free Internet until noon). *In room:* A/C, TV, no phone, Wi-Fi (in some).

ISE-SHIMA NATIONAL PARK ★★

465km (289 miles) W of Tokyo; 100km (60 miles) S of Nagoya

Blessed with subtropical vegetation, small islands dotting its shoreline, and the most revered Shinto shrine in Japan, **Ise-Shima National Park** merits a 1- or 2-night stopover if you're anywhere near Nagoya. Located on and around Shima Peninsula and covering 518 sq. km (200 sq. miles), this national park has bays and inlets that make up the home of the Mikimoto pearl and thousands of pearl-cultivating rafts. Although you could conceivably cover the major attractions on a day's outing from Nagoya, I've recommended accommodations in case you'd like to take in the sights at a more leisurely pace.

Ise-Shima's major attractions are concentrated in the small towns of Ise, Futami, Toba, and Kashikojima, all in Mie Prefecture. **Ise** (also called Ise-Shi, which translates as Ise City) is where you'll find the Ise Grand Shrines. **Futami** is famous for a theme park based on Japan's history from 1477 to 1598 and a majestic traditional inn, now a museum. **Toba** contains Mikimoto Pearl Island, which offers a pearl museum and demonstrations by its famous women divers, as well as the Toba Aquarium. In **Kashikojima,** there's an amusement park with a Spanish theme and boat trips around Ago Bay that, with its islets and pearl-cultivating oyster rafts, is one of the most scenic spots in the park.

Essentials

GETTING THERE   By Train   The easiest way to get to Ise-Shima is from Nagoya on the private Kintetsu Railway's **Ise Shima Liner** (✆ 052/561-1604; www. kintetsu.co.jp), which departs every 30 minutes or so from Kintetsu Station, next to the JR Nagoya Station. It takes about 1 hour and 30 minutes via limited express to reach Ise-Shi (with stops at both Ise-Shi and nearby Ujiyamada stations), about 1 hour and 45 minutes to reach Toba, and 2 hours and 10 minutes to reach Kashiko-jima (*Note:* Only JR trains go to Futami; see below). A ticket from Nagoya to the end of the line in Kashikojima costs ¥3,480 one-way. There are also Kintetsu trains to Shima Peninsula from Kyoto (2¼ hr. to Toba; fare: ¥3,780) and from Osaka's Uehon-machi Station (2 hr. to Toba; fare: ¥3,550 and ¥3,450). Most economical, however, is to purchase a Kintetsu Rail Pass *before* arriving in Japan (or, in Japan, it's available only at the Agency Travel Desk at Kansai International Airport). It costs ¥3,700, is valid for 5 days (but only three journeys can be aboard a limited express train), and includes travel to and from Nagoya, Osaka/Kyoto, and Ise (see "Getting Around Japan," in chapter 14, for more information).

If you're traveling on a **Japan Rail Pass,** you can also reach Ise-Shima by **JR Mie Kaisoku** (rapid express) trains, which depart hourly from Nagoya Station, but you'll be charged an extra ¥490. JR trains stop at Ise-Shi and Futami-no-ura before terminating at Toba, where, if you're heading to Kashikojima, you'll have to transfer to the Kintetsu Line (fare from Toba to Kashikojima: ¥460).

By Bus   Buses depart nightly from Tokyo's Ikebukuro Station's east exit at 9:20 and 10:40pm, arriving at Ise-Shi Station at 7:10 and 7:35am respectively and Toba 30 minutes later. The fare to Ise-Shi Station is ¥7,850 one-way. From Kyoto Station, buses depart two times a day for the Ise Grand Shrines and Ise-Shi Station for ¥2,500.

VISITOR INFORMATION   Ise City Tourist Information Offices are located in front of the Outer Shrine Gate (✆ 0596/28-3705) and at Kintetsu Ujiyamada Station in Ise City (✆ 0596/23-9655) both open daily 9am to 5:30pm; or check the website www.ise-kanko.jp. The **Toba Tourist Information Center** at Toba Station (✆ 0599/25-2844; www.toba.gr.jp) is open daily 9am to 5:30pm. More information on the peninsula is available at www.iseshima-kanko.jp.

GETTING AROUND   Transportation within Ise-Shima National Park is either by train or by bus. **Trains** are convenient if your destinations are Ise City, Toba, Futami, and Kashikojima (see "Getting There," above). Some major sites, however, including the Ise Grand Shrines and Ise Azuchi Momoyama Bunkamura, are best reached by bus. For sightseers, there's the **CAN-Bus,** which you can board in front of the JR stations in Ise City and Toba. Buses, departing about once an hour, travel from Uji-yamada and Ise-Shi stations to both Outer and Inner Shrines of the Ise Grand Shrines and Ise Azuchi Momoyama Bunkamura before continuing onward to Toba. One-day passes for ¥1,000 and 2-day passes for ¥1,600 can be bought aboard the buses (unfortunately, the bus timetable is in Japanese only). There are also local buses that run between the Outer and Inner Shrine of the Ise Grand Shrines; you must also take a bus for Parque España.

In Ise-Shi, it makes sense to rent a **bicycle,** available at Ujiyamada Station (¥500 for 4 hr.). Ise-Shi and Ujiyamada stations are a 7-minute walk apart. There are luggage storage facilities at Ujiyamada, Toba, and Ise-Shi stations, as well as at the entrance to the Inner Shrine in Ise.

Exploring Ise-Shima National Park

The easiest way to see the park's sights is to start in Ise-Shi, the northern gateway to Ise-Shima National Park, and work your way down the peninsula to Kashikojima.

ISE CITY (ISE-SHI)

The Ise Grand Shrines (Ise Jingu) ★★ TEMPLE   Tied historically to the imperial family and considered the spiritual home of the Japanese people, Japan's most venerable Shinto shrines, the Ise Grand Shrines (www.isejingu.or.jp/english/index.htm; ✆ **0596/24-111**), consist of an Outer Shrine and an Inner Shrine, plus more than 100 minor shrines spread through a dense forest of Japanese cypress. As the Outer and Inner shrines are about 6.5km (4 miles) apart, your best bet is to first visit the Outer Shrine, which is a 5-minute walk from Ise-Shi Station, and then either cycle or take a bus to the Inner Shrine. In addition to the CAN-Bus (described above in "Getting Around"), a local bus runs between the two shrines every 10 to 15 minutes (fare: ¥410). Because of the distance between the shrines and their large grounds (which take up a whopping 20% of Ise City's land), plan on spending at least 2 hours exploring this area.

The **Outer Shrine (Geku)** was founded in 478 and is dedicated to the Shinto goddess of industry, agriculture, clothing, and housing. The **Inner Shrine (Naiku)** was founded a few centuries earlier and is dedicated to Amaterasu, the sun goddess. Both are among the few Shinto shrines in Japan without any Chinese Buddhist influences and are therefore thought to be the purest style of Shinto architecture. Constructed of plain cypress wood with thick thatched roofs in the oldest style of architecture in Japan, they're starkly simple and have no ornamentation except for gold and copper facing on beams and doors. In fact, if you've come all the way to Shima Peninsula just to see the shrines, you may be disappointed—there's nothing much to see (and no photos are allowed). The shrines are so sacred that no one is allowed near them except members of the imperial family and high-ranking Shinto priests. Both shrines are surrounded by four wooden fences, and lesser mortals are allowed only as far as the third gate.

The fences don't allow you to see much, but that doesn't stop the estimated seven million Japanese who come here annually. They come because of what the shrines represent, which is an embodiment of Japanese Shinto itself. The Inner Shrine is by far the more important because it's dedicated to the sun goddess, considered to be the legendary ancestress of the imperial family. It contains the *Yata-no-Kagami* (Sacred Mirror), one of the Three Sacred Treasures of the emperor.

According to legend, the sun goddess sent her grandson to Japan so that he and his descendants could rule over the country. Before he left, she gave him three insignia—a mirror, a sword, and a set of jewels. As she handed him the mirror, she is said to have remarked, "When you look upon this mirror, let it be as if you look upon me." The mirror, therefore, is said to embody the sun goddess herself and is regarded as the most sacred object in the Shinto religion. It's kept in the deep recesses of the Inner Shrine in a special casket and is never shown to the public. (The sword is in the Atsuta Shrine in Nagoya, and the jewels are in the Imperial Palace in Tokyo.)

Perhaps the most amazing thing about the Outer and Inner shrines is that, even though they were founded centuries ago, the buildings themselves have never been more than 20 years old; for more than 1,300 years, they have been completely torn down and rebuilt exactly as they were on neighboring sites every 20 years. Not only does the practice ensure that the shrines don't deteriorate but also that ancient building techniques are passed down through the generations. The 62nd rebuilding will take place in the fall of 2013.

Even though you can't see much of the shrines, they're still the most important stops in Ise-Shima. The Inner Shrine, considered the more sacred of the two, is approached by crossing the Isuzu River via the elegant Uji Bridge (also rebuilt every 20 years), passing through a manicured garden, and then entering a dark forest of 800-year-old cypress trees. Watch how Japanese stop after crossing the second small bridge on the approach to the shrine to wash and purify their hands and mouths with water from the Isuzu River. Its source lies on the Inner Shrine, and it's considered sacred.

Ise's Historic Districts ★★★ After visiting the Inner Shrine (a 45-min. walk round-trip), turn right after recrossing Uji Bridge for the nearby historic district of **Oharai-machi,** whose 800m-long (½-mile) main street is lined with beautiful wooden buildings and *kura* (storehouses), some dating from the Edo and Meiji periods and others newly constructed but faithful to traditional architecture. This once served as the main pilgrimage road leading to Ise Jingu. During the Edo Period, when travel was strictly controlled, joining a mass pilgrimage to Ise was for many Japanese a once-in-a-lifetime opportunity to venture beyond their homes; it's estimated a fifth of the population joined pilgrimages to Ise during that time. Today it's an interesting area for a stroll, shopping, or a meal.

About halfway down is **Okage Yokocho** (℃ 0596/23-8838) a re-created Meiji Era village with teahouses, restaurants, and shops selling Japanese candies, traditional toys, and folk crafts. If you have time, stop by **Okageza (おかげ座)** ★ (℃ **0596/23-8844;** daily 10am–5:30pm, to 4:30pm in winter), a museum housed in an authentic Edo-Era building that captures the spirit of Oharai-machi during the Edo Period; dioramas of half-scale models and lively street scenes vividly convey what life was like for both the residents and the pilgrims passing through. On a bridge overlooking a model of the city and its shrines, take note of the small man: He's not half-scale; the average Edo man measured 4 feet, 11 inches. Admission is ¥300 for adults and ¥100 for children. You'll spend about 20 minutes here.

Off the beaten tourist track is **Kawasaki,** which served as Ise City's business district during the Edo Period, when boats traversing the Setagawa River delivered goods to storehouses along the river. A grass-roots movement has restored four of these storehouses along with an Edo-Era house, grouped together in the **Merchant's**

House Museum (Ise-Kawasaki Shonin-Kan; 伊勢河崎商人館), 2–25–32 Kawasaki (✆ 0596/22-4810; Wed–Mon 9:30am–5pm), which you can tour for ¥300. In addition to a high-class teahouse, displays include Ise's own paper money, the first paper money in Japan and developed to lessen the load of pilgrims who might otherwise be forced to carry heavy pieces of gold or silver. Surrounding buildings now house restaurants and shops selling crafts, food, and antiques (ask for a map of the area at the museum). In a country where old neighborhoods are disappearing by the minute, the local people who fought to preserve this historic district deserve medals. It's a 15-minute walk north from Ujiyamada Station or northeast from Ise-shi Station.

FUTAMI

Edo Wonderland Ise (Ise Azuchi Momoyama Bunkamura) ★★ ☺

AMUSEMENT PARK   The castle you see on the hill from Futami-no-ura Station is not the former residence of a famous shogun but a replica of Azuchi Castle in Edo Wonderland Ise, one of Japan's many theme parks. If you have youngsters in tow or if you haven't seen one of these period theme parks elsewhere in Japan, go to one—they're fun! This one is among my favorites because, rather than try to re-create a village in Holland or Spain, it's centered on a specific time in Japan's history, the Age of the Warring States—the Sengoku Era (1477–1573), when local warlords struggled for supremacy, and the Azuchi-Momoyama Era (1573–98), when Oda Nobunaga gained control of the land and finally put an end to civil war. In keeping with the theme of this Japanese equivalent of Dodge City, all the staff are dressed in 16th-century costumes, and attractions reflect the pre–Edo Era; visually, it looks just like a movie set. You can watch period dramas such as the action-charged antics of a ninja troupe, be spooked at haunted houses, try to negotiate 11 challenging obstacles in the Ninja Labyrinth, or try your hand at throwing ninja weapons at a target. There are no thrill rides here, but there are old-fashioned game centers, including shooting ranges using bows and arrows and other weaponry of the era. That gold-roofed castle is dedicated to Nobunaga, who built Azuchi Castle; its top-floor, lined with real gold, has a great views. You'll spend 2 to 3 hours here.

1201–1 Mitsu-cho. www.ise-bunkamura.co.jp. ✆ **0596/43-2300.** Admission ¥3,900 adults, ¥2,500 junior-high and high-school students, ¥2,000 children. Daily 9am–5pm (9:30am–4pm mid-Nov to mid-Mar). Station: Futami-no-ura (15 min.). CAN-Bus: to the front entrance.

Hinjitsukan HISTORIC SITE

I used to recommend overnighting at this majestic inn until it sadly closed in 1999, so I'm thrilled it has now reopened as a museum rather than being demolished. Built in 1887 as an inn for important visitors to Ise Grand Shrines, including the imperial family, it faces Futami-ga-ura Beach (popular during the Edo Period as a place for pilgrims to wash and purify themselves before visiting the shrines) and is surrounded by a serene garden. After entering a side entrance (the grand main entryway is reserved for the imperial family), you'll find yourself in a traditional inn consisting of winding corridors leading to tatami rooms. Most impressive are the Grand Hall with its 120 tatami mats and the elaborate Goten, where VIPs of yore stayed. Beyond Hinjitsukan along the beach is Okitama Shrine and one of the region's most famous sites: A large rock and small rock jutting offshore, joined by a huge sacred rope. Called Meotoiwa, or Wedded Rocks, they're considered a symbol of a good and harmonious marriage. The most auspicious time to view them is in summer at sunrise, when the sun rises between them. But you have to get up as early as 4am, so that's one spectacle I haven't seen.

566–2 Chaya Futami-cho. ✆ **0596/43-2003.** Admission ¥300 adults, ¥150 children. Wed–Mon 9am–4:30pm. Station: Futami-no-ura (12 min.). CAN-Bus: Futami-ga-ura Omotesando (10 min.).

TOBA

Mikimoto Pearl Island ★★ MUSEUM   Toba's best-known attraction, located on a small island connected to the mainland by a pedestrian bridge and consisting of several buildings, is touristy but still quite enjoyable, especially if you have a weakness for pearls or have ever wondered how they're cultivated.

To learn about the man who toiled through years of adversity to produce the world's first cultured pearl, visit **Kokichi Mikimoto Memorial Hall,** built in 1993 to commemorate the 100th anniversary of Mikimoto's success. Born in Toba in 1858 as the eldest son of a noodle-shop owner, Kokichi Mikimoto went to Yokohama as a young man and was surprised to see stalls selling pearls with great success. He reasoned that if oysters produced pearls as the result of an irritant inside the shell, why couldn't humans introduce the irritant themselves and induce oysters to make pearls? It turned out to be harder than it sounded. It wasn't until 5 years after he started his research that Mikimoto finally succeeded in cultivating his first pearl, here on what is today called Mikimoto Pearl Island. In 1905, Mikimoto cultivated his first perfectly round pearl, after which he built what is probably the most successful pearl empire in the world.

The **Pearl Museum** tells all you'd probably ever want to know about the creation of pearls, with English-language videos showing the insertion of the round nucleus into the shell and the harvesting of the pearls 2 years later, as well as explanations of the process of making a pearl necklace by hand, from the selection and sorting of pearls to the drilling and stringing. You can learn about the criteria used for pricing pearls (luster is the most important) and color selection. The museum also contains some of Mikimoto's earliest jewelry and models made with pearls, many of which were only recently reacquired by Mikimoto & Co. Ltd. through auctions. My favorite is the brooch made for the 1937 Paris International Exhibition, which can be worn a dozen different ways by employing various clasps. The five-story Pearl Pagoda has 12,760 Mikimoto pearls and took 750 artisans 6 months to complete, after which it was exhibited at the Philadelphia World Exhibition in 1926. The Liberty Bell, a third the size of the original, has 12,250 pearls and was displayed at the New York World's Fair in 1939.

In addition, ***ama* (women divers)** in traditional white outfits demonstrate how women of the Shima Peninsula have dived through the ages in search of abalone, seaweed, and other edibles. They were also essential to the pearl industry, diving to collect the oysters and then returning them to the seabed following insertion of the nuclei. At one time, there were thousands of ama, known for their skill in diving to great depths for extended periods. It is said that there are still about 1,000 of these women divers left in Mie Prefecture, but I've seen them only at demonstrations given for tourists. If you happen to see ama working in earnest (diving for abalone and other food, not pearls), consider yourself lucky. Here you can watch them from the air-conditioned comfort of a viewing room built especially for overseas guests.

Of course, there's also a shop selling Mikimoto pearl jewelry and a restaurant. You can easily spend 1½ hours on Pearl Island.

1–7–1 Toba. www.mikimoto-pearl-museum.co.jp. 🕐 **0599/25-2028.** Admission ¥1,500 adults, ¥750 children 7–15. Jan–Nov daily 8:30am–5pm; Dec daily 9am–4:30pm. Closed 2nd Tues–Thurs of Dec. Station: Toba (3 min.).

Toba Aquarium ★ ☺ AQUARIUM   Next to Pearl Island is one of Japan's largest aquariums, containing more than 850 species of animals and some 20,000 creatures. Various zones and themes make it easy to navigate. The display of marine animals around Ise-Shima and Japan includes giant spider crabs and the finless porpoise, the world's smallest whale. The exhibit of "living fossils"—creatures that have remained relatively unchanged since ancient times—includes sharks, horseshoe crabs, and the nautilus (which are bred here; babies are often on display), while the marine mammal kingdom includes Commerson's dolphins, Russian walruses, Baikal seals, and sea lions, with sea-lion shows several times a day. The aquarium also boasts exotic and rare creatures such as dugongs, African manatees, and Amazonian turtles and frogs. My only complaint is that some tanks look rather bare and outdated in today's world of ever-more-sophisticated aquariums; maybe the animals don't mind, but spectators sure do. Though it's not as sophisticated or complete as the Osaka Aquarium, you can spend 90 minutes here, longer if you have kids.

3-3-6 Toba. www.aquarium.co.jp/english. ☏ **0599/25-2555.** Admission ¥2,400 adults, ¥1,200 junior-high and elementary students, ¥600 children. Nov to mid-Mar daily 9am–4:30pm; mid-Mar to mid-July and Sept–Oct daily 9am–5pm; mid-July to Aug daily 8:30am–5:30pm. Station: Toba (10 min.).

KASHIKOJIMA

At the southern end of the Shima Peninsula, the last stop on the Kintetsu Line is Kashikojima, where one of the main attractions for Japanese is a 50-minute **boat cruise of Ago Bay.** Vessels, built to resemble Spanish galleons or with other Spanish-based themes, depart from the town's boat dock, about a 2-minute walk from the tiny train station, every half-hour or so between 9:30am and 4:30pm (until 3:30pm in winter), weather permitting, and cost ¥1,500 for adults, half-price for children. You'll pass pearl-cultivating rafts, fishing boats, and many small islands along the way. For more information call the **Shima Marine Leisure Co.** (☏ **0599/43-1023**).

Parque España (Shima Spain Mura) ★★ ☺ THEME PARK   You may wonder what this Spanish village is doing in southern Ise Shima. Mie Prefecture has a sister relationship with Valencia in Spain, a relationship that is exploited to the hilt in this ambitious theme park. A huge facility that employs about 40 Spanish-speaking natives, the amusement park includes a shopping area specializing in products from Spain; a plaza that stages dances, festivals, and other outdoor entertainment; a coliseum that features folk dancing and singing; a 360-degree cinema; a clown circus; and amusement rides that range from an adventure lagoon ride through a world of fantasy to the fastest roller coaster I'll ever care to ride (and one of the longest, lasting more than 3 hair-raising min.). Although the park opened to much fanfare in 1994, it has suffered declining attendance ever since, which is bad for business but means there's virtually no waiting time for rides, except during school holidays.

Most educational is the Museo Castillo de Xavier, a reproduction of the castle where Francis Xavier was born (Xavier later brought Christianity to Japan); it presents a brief overlook of highlights in Spanish history, though in Japanese. Still, there's no mistaking the replica of prehistoric drawings from the Altamira caves, the model of the *Santa Maria* that Columbus sailed to America, and a replica of the entrance to the Prado Museum. A film introduces Spain's greatest artists, including Goya, Velázquez, and El Greco. There are amusements geared to all ages, as well as numerous restaurants. Plan to spend about 3 hours here.

www.parque-net.com. ☏ **0599/57-3333.** Passport admission to most attractions ¥4,800 adults, ¥3,800 seniors and children 12–17, ¥3,200 children 4–11; extra charges for gaming houses and flamenco show. Admission only, which includes the museum and most shows but no rides (which you can purchase separately for ¥200–¥600 per ride), ¥2,800, ¥1,800, and ¥1,200 respectively. Hours vary, but generally Mon–Fri 9:30am–5pm, Sat–Sun and holidays 9:30am–6pm (check with the tourist office). Closed last 2 weeks of Feb. Station: Ugata (Kintetsu Line), then a bus that runs 2 or 3 times per hour; or Kashikojima Station, then a bus that runs once an hour. Both buses cost ¥360 for the 15-min. ride.

Where to Eat

ISE

Bon Vivant ★★ 🎁 FRENCH   Occupying a former post office built in the early 1900s near the Outer Shrine, this delightful choice is divided into two parts: an informal brasserie with tall ceilings and antiques (my preference), and a more elegant restaurant. Both feature the creations of owner-chef Kawase-san, made from locally grown products. For lunch, the brasserie is slightly cheaper, with my ¥2,100 set meal including an appetizer of ham, sliced abalone, Matsuzaka beef, and corn mousse; a main course of baked chicken with potato gratin and vegetables; and a dessert. The dinner menu is the same for both the restaurant and brasserie. Or, for a light snack, there's Café de Bon Vivant across the street, open Tuesday to Saturday 9am to 6pm and Sunday 9am to 5pm.

20–24 Honmachi, Ise. ✆ **0596/26-3131.** Reservations required. Set dinners ¥5,000–¥10,000; set lunches ¥2,100–¥6,000 in the restaurant, ¥890–¥2,830 in the brasserie. MC, V. Restaurant Tues–Sun noon–1:30pm; Tues–Sat 5:30–7:30pm (last order). Brasserie Tues–Sun 11:30am–2pm; Wed–Sun 5:30–8pm (last order). Station: Ise-Shi (5 min.). From the JR Ise-Shi Station, take the main exit and walk straight on Geku Sando; it's on a side street to the left (look for a white building with a red roof), just before the Outer Shrine.

Sushi Kyu (すし久) ★★ ☺ SUSHI/LOCAL SPECIALTIES   Located on the main street of Oharai-machi, this traditional restaurant offers tatami seating at low tables with a view out over the river. Waitresses in traditional Japanese worker clothes serve sushi and local cuisine from a Japanese-language menu. Try the *tekone sushi* (raw bonito marinated with soy sauce and mixed with vinegared rice) served in a wooden tub, or the obento of various delicacies.

20 Uji Nakanokiri-machi, Ise. ✆ **0596/27-0229.** Set meals ¥1,050–¥2,500. No credit cards. Wed–Mon 11am–8pm; Tues and on the 1st and last day of every month 11am–5:30pm. Station: Ise-Shi, then local bus or CAN-Bus to the Inner Shrine stop, from which it's a 5-min. walk to Oharai-machi historic district.

TOBA

Oosakaya (大阪屋) SUSHI   Located 2 blocks inland from Mikimoto Pearl Island on the other side of the train tracks, this simple eatery with tatami, table, and counter seating was opened in 1950 by the present owner's grandmother. It offers assorted *nigiri-zushi* (sushi platters) and *maki-sushi* (sushi rolls), but the specialty is *ebi* fry— humungous shrimp deep-fried in batter. The ebi-fry *teishoku*, which includes miso soup, rice, and pickled vegetables, costs ¥1,600 with two ebi fries and ¥2,000 for three ebi fries. Those with voracious appetites can order one of the ¥3,600 set courses, which come with sushi or sashimi in addition to ebi fries and other dishes.

1–4–64 Toba. ✆ **0599/25-2336.** Set meals ¥1,600–¥3,600. AE, DC, MC, V. Fri–Wed 11am–2pm and 4–8:30pm (last order). Station: Toba. Walking in the direction of Mikimoto Pearl Island, turn right under the tracks and take the 2nd street left; Oosakaya will be on the right.

Where to Stay

Kashikojima is the best place to go if you want to escape the crowds and relax in a rural setting, while Toba and Ise have the greatest number of attractions.

ISE

Asakichi (麻吉) ★   Because a pilgrimage to Ise Jingu during the Edo Period was often the only trip a commoner might make in his lifetime, he often lived it up to the hilt in Furuichi, Ise's former red-light district. Located between the Inner and Outer shrines, it was filled with many *ryokan*, brothels, and restaurants. Now only Asakichi remains, founded more than 200 years ago by the present owner's family, on an impossibly narrow street. In any case, the ramshackle ryokan seems little changed since then, built on a slope (and containing steep stairs) and even containing a museum of sorts filled with dusty, Edo-Era family memorabilia which you can request to see. The tatami rooms are simple. Meals are served on request in the privacy of your room or in a dining hall with a view over the rooftops. Western breakfasts are available. The proprietor doesn't speak much English but understands the basics.

109 Nakanocho, Ise-Shi, Mie Prefecture 516-0034. (*) **0596/22-4101.** Fax 0596/22-4102. 10 units (3 with bathroom). ¥12,600 per person. Rates include 2 meals. No credit cards. Station: Ise-Shi, then bus no. 01 or 02 from platform 7 another 9 min. to the Nakanocho stop (1 min.). **Amenities:** Communal fridge; museum. *In room:* A/C, TV, no phone.

Hoshidekan (星出館) ★★ 🏠 Catering to the health conscious, this inexpensive 90-year-old wooden Japanese Inn Group *ryokan* has several tatami rooms with windows framed with gnarled roots and bamboo (they simply don't make windows like this anymore) encircling an inner courtyard. It's nothing fancy, but it's run by a friendly, spry 80-something woman (assisted by her son and his wife) who is a strong advocate of macrobiotic vegetarian meals, which are served in your simple tatami room and the adjoining restaurant. Both Japanese and Western meals are available, but we prefer the ¥1,300 *Genmai teishoku* vegetarian course for dinner. The food, however, is only one of the reasons to stay here. We also like the rental bicycles, perfect for visiting Ise Jingu and nearby Kawasaki historic district.

2–15–2 Kawasaki, Ise-Shi, Mie Prefecture 516-0009. www.hoshidekan.jp. (*) **0596/28-2377.** Fax 0596/27-2830. 10 units (none with bathroom). ¥6,000 single; ¥10,400 double; ¥15,600 triple. Breakfast ¥900 extra; dinner from ¥1,300 extra. AE, MC, V. Station: Ise-Shi, then a 7-min. walk in the opposite direction from the shrine; look for the sign HOSHIDE on the right. **Amenities:** Macrobiotic restaurant (reservations required); rental bikes (¥300 per day). *In room:* A/C, TV, no phone.

TOBA

Thalassa Shima Hotel & Resort ★★ Although the approach to this luxury hotel doesn't seem to promise much, inside it's another story. Everything about this sophisticated seaside hotel is focused on its stunningly beautiful setting on the sea, with nary another building in sight (a public beach, open July–Aug, is a short walk away). It exudes a soothing, subdued atmosphere, fitting for a resort dedicated to healing. Thalassa Shima offers thalassotherapy, which uses seawater, seaweed, and sea-mud treatments to combat stress, fatigue, and excess weight, as well as aromatherapy, reflexology, and other treatments. If your travels have been stressful, a 1-night stay here indulging in a seaweed bath, an underwater-jet treatment, a massage bath, and pressure therapy might just be the mini-vacation you need. Rooms, bathed in cool, crisp whites, have small balconies. Due to the hotel's isolation, you'll want to take your meals here, either at the French restaurant or the classic Japanese restaurant, both with views of the sea.

1826–1 Shirahama, Uramura-cho, Toba-shi, Mie 517-0025. www.thalasso.co.jp. (*) **0599/32-1111.** Fax 0599/32-1109. reservation@thalasso.co.jp. 112 units. ¥20,000–¥48,000 single or double; ¥19,000–¥35,000 per person including 2 meals. Rates higher in peak season. Thalassotherapy treatment from ¥19,000. AE, DC, MC, V. Free 25-min. shuttle bus every hour from JR or Kintetsu Toba Station. **Amenities:** 2 restaurants; bar; exercise room; spa w/glass-enclosed seawater pool and outdoor Jacuzzi overlooking the bay, French thalassotherapy, and other therapies; room service. *In room:* A/C, TV w/free videos/DVDs and players on request, hair dryer, minibar.

KASHIKOJIMA

Ishiyama-So (石山荘) ★ 🏨   If you're looking for an inexpensive, unusual place to stay, a good choice is this family-run *minshuku* located on a small island just a stone's throw from the Kashikojima pier. It can be reached only via the hotel's private boat—call to let them know you've arrived at Kashikojima; the boat will arrive shortly, and you'll be delivered right to the front door. Its location on the water, with a lobby done up in Southeast Asian decor and floor-to-ceiling windows overlooking the water, gives it a slightly exotic atmosphere, right up to the small crabs scurrying through the front door. There's a sun deck overlooking the bay, you can swim off the dock (because of boat traffic, though, you shouldn't go farther than the dock), and footpaths crisscross the small island. Two rooms are Western style and all face the bay. Note that only Japanese meals are served and must be paid for in cash.

Yokoyama-jima, Kashikojima, Ago-cho, Mie 517-0502. Ⓒ **0599/52-1527.** Fax 0599/52-1240. 6 units (3 with bathroom, 3 with sink and toilet only). ¥4,500–¥6,000 per person including breakfast; ¥9,000–¥10,000 per person with 2 meals. MC, V. A 2-min. walk from the station to Kashikojima pier, then a 2-min. boat trip. *In room:* A/C, TV, no phone.

Shima Kanko Hotel Bay Suites ★★★   On a promontory above Ago Bay, this deluxe property offers more luxury and pampering than sister hotel the Classic (see below). In fact, you'd be hard-pressed to find more exclusive (and more expensive) digs anywhere else in Japan. An all-suite hotel, it offers individual pickup from the station, a hushed environment that makes it seem more like a high-class inn rather than a hotel (no children 11 and younger allowed), and a rooftop garden with 360-degree views. Rooms, most with balconies, provide the ultimate in comfort and decor, including to-die-for bathrooms with heated stone floors and tubs overlooking the bay. Because of its isolation, hotel guests generally dine in either the Japanese restaurant (where *kaiseki* meals start at ¥12,000) or the French seafood restaurant (set dinners begin at ¥18,000) or in the nearby Classic. Rates below reflect the seasons.

Kashikojima, Ago-cho, Shima, Mie 517-0593. www.miyakohotels.ne.jp/baysuites/english/index. html. Ⓒ **0599/43-2111.** www.miyakohotels.ne.jp/shima. 50 units. ¥69,000–¥99,000 double; ¥35,000–¥67,500 per person including 2 meals. AE, DC, MC, V. Station: Kashikojima (free pickup from the station). **Amenities:** 2 restaurants; lounge; spa. *In room:* A/C, TV and DVD library, hair dryer, Internet, minibar, MP3 docking station.

Shima Kanko Hotel The Classic ★★★   Sitting on a hill above Ago Bay, this is a resort hotel in the old tradition, established in 1951 and boasting impeccable service and great views (though Bay Suites, above, has robbed some of its views). The hotel boasts its own garden (cared for by three gardeners), at the edge of which is the lovely outdoor pool, free for hotel guests. I especially like the pathway leading down to a private dock where you can sit and watch pearl cultivators at work on their rafts. On the hotel's roof is an observatory, great for watching the beautiful sunsets. In addition, most rooms have views of the bay and are spacious, and despite periodic updating, they retain a pleasant old-fashioned, '50s atmosphere. French restaurant La Mer is famous for its abalone and Mie beef; it's pricey, but there's no other choice in the area.

Kashikojima, Ago-cho, Shima, Mie Prefecture 517-0593. www.miyakohotels.ne.jp/shima-classic/english/index.html. Ⓒ **0599/43-1211.** Fax 0599/43-3538. 117 units. ¥19,058–¥32,918 single; ¥20,790–¥34,650 double. Peak season (Aug and New Year's) ¥5,775 extra; Sat and evenings before holidays ¥3,465 extra. AE, DC, MC, V. Station: Kashikojima (then free shuttle to hotel or a 5-min. walk). **Amenities:** Restaurant; lounge; concierge; outdoor pool w/children's slides; room service; free Wi-Fi in lobby. *In room:* A/C, TV, hair dryer, Internet (in some), minibar.

MORE OF OLD JAPAN: KANAZAWA ★★

622km (386 miles) W of Tokyo; 224km (140 miles) NE of Kyoto

Near the northwest coast of Honshu on the Sea of Japan, Kanazawa is the gateway to the rugged, sea-swept Noto Peninsula. It was the second-largest city (after Kyoto) to escape bombing during World War II, and some of the old city has been left intact, including a district of former samurai mansions, old geisha quarters, Edo-Era canals, and tiny narrow streets that run crookedly without rhyme or reason (apparently to confuse any enemies foolish enough to attack). Kanazawa is most famous for its **Kenrokuen Garden,** one of the most celebrated gardens in all of Japan (and one of my favorites). It's the main reason people come here, though several fine museums are worth a visit, too. Kanazawa is also renowned for its crafts.

Kanazawa first gained notoriety about 500 years ago, when a militant Buddhist sect joined with peasant rebels to overthrow the feudal lord and establish its own autonomous government, an event unprecedented in Japanese history. The independent republic survived almost 100 years before it was attacked by an army commanded by Oda Nobunaga, who was trying to unite Japan at a time when civil wars wracked the nation. Kanazawa was subsequently granted to one of Nobunaga's retainers, Maeda Toshiie, who constructed a castle and transformed the small community into a thriving castle town. The Maeda clan continued to rule over Kanazawa for the next 300 years, amassing wealth in the form of land and rice and encouraging development of the arts. Throughout the Tokugawa shogunate, the Maedas remained the second-most powerful family in Japan and controlled the largest domain in the country. The arts of Kutani ware, Yuzen silk dyeing, lacquerware, and *noh* theater flourished—and enjoy popularity in Kanazawa even today. Japan's fourth-largest city at the end of the Feudal Era, Kanazawa now has a population of 460,000 and is capital of Ishikawa Prefecture. With about 160 rainy days a year, it has a local proverb you'd be wise to heed: "Even if you forget your packed lunch, don't forget your umbrella."

Essentials

GETTING THERE   By Train   Direct **JR trains** from Osaka (via Kyoto) depart hourly; the ride takes about 2 hours and 40 minutes and costs ¥6,930 for an unreserved seat. From Nagoya, direct trains depart for Kanazawa every hour and take about 3 hours; the cost is ¥6,620. From Tokyo, take the Joetsu Shinkansen to Echigo-Yuzawa and switch there for a limited express train to Kanazawa; the trip takes about 4 hours and costs ¥11,840. In 2015, the Shinkansen will extend from Tokyo all the way to Kanazawa, cutting travel time to 2½ hours.

By Bus   JR Highway buses (www.jrbuskanto.co.jp; ✆ **03/3844-1950**) depart five times daily from Shinjuku Station's New South Exit in Tokyo (with a stop also at Ikebukuro Station's east exit), arrive at Kanazawa Station about 8 hours later, and cost ¥7,840. There are also night buses, departing from Tokyo Station's Yaesu South Exit and arriving the next morning for the same price. Buses also depart 10 times daily from Nagoya (¥4,410 for the 4-hr. trip) and six times a day from Osaka's Umeda Station (¥4,300, with trips taking 4 hr. and 40 min.). There are also three buses a day from Takayama (with a stop in Shirakawa-go), which take 2¼ hours and cost ¥3,300.

VISITOR INFORMATION   Near Kanazawa Station, the **Tourist Information Center** (✆ **076/232-3993**) can book hotel rooms and distributes maps, brochures, and the very useful *Eye on Kanazawa* with tips on sightseeing. To find the center, open daily 9am to 7pm (with English-speaking volunteers on duty 10am–6pm), turn right after passing through the wicket (you'll be heading toward the East Gate exit); it will soon be on your left beside a shopping arcade. The **Kanazawa Downtown Tourist Exchange Salon,** on the 3rd floor of the LABBRO shopping mall at 2–2–5 Katamachi (☎ **076/225-8460;** daily 10am–5pm; closed irregularly Wed: Loop Bus: Katamachi), has sightseeing brochures and a lounge. For more information, see **www. kanazawa-tourism.com** and **www4.city.kanazawa.lg.jp**.

GETTING AROUND   Kanazawa's attractions spread south and southeast from the station (take the East Gate exit). Katamachi, 3km (2 miles) southeast of the station, is Kanazawa's downtown. Sights are too far-flung to see everything on foot, so the easiest way to get around Kanazawa is by **bus.** All major lines depart from Kanazawa Station, and as many as 15 lines pass Kenrokuen Garden, including the Kenrokuen Shuttle, which departs from platform 6 at Kanazawa Station. Take a ticket when boarding the bus and pay when you get off; the fare is ¥200.

Easiest for tourists, however, is the **Kanazawa Loop Bus (Shu-yu Bus),** which departs from platform 3 at Kanazawa Station's east exit every 12 minutes and travels to all the tourist sights, making 19 stops in a circular route (stops are announced in English). A single ride costs ¥200 and a 1-day pass, which also allows rides on city buses, costs ¥500. The bus runs daily from 8:36am to 6pm.

Kanazawa is fairly flat, making **cycling** a reasonable alternative. **JR Rental Cycle** (☎ **076/261-1721;** daily 8am–8pm), at the west exit of Kanazawa Station, rents bicycles for ¥1,200 per day.

[Fast FACTS] KANAZAWA

ATM/Mail   The **Kanazawa Central Post Office,** 1–1 Sanja (☎ **076/224-3822**), is Monday to Friday 9am to 9pm, Saturday 9am to 5pm, and Sunday 9am to 3pm. In addition to a counter open 24 hours for mail, it has ATMs open 12:05am to 11:55pm Monday through Saturday and 12:05am to 9pm on Sunday.

Internet Access   The **Ishikawa Foundation for International Exchange,** a 5-minute walk from the east exit of Kanazawa Station (on the road running btw. the Miyako and Nikko hotels), on the third floor of the Rifare building at 1–5–3 Honmachi (☎ **076/262-5931**), has four computers you can use free of charge for 30 minutes daily from 9am to 6pm (to 5pm Sat–Sun). Downtown, **Tourist Exchange Salon** (see above) is a free Wi-Fi hotspot and also has computers you can use for ¥100 for every 10 minutes of surfing.

Exploring Kanazawa

Much of Kanazawa's charm lies in the atmosphere of its old neighborhoods. Be sure to wear your good walking shoes, as the best way to explore various parts of the city is via your own two feet. One suggested itinerary for tackling the city's sights is to take the Loop Bus to the Higashi Chaya district, then another Loop bus onward to Kenrokuen and the sights in its vicinity, and then walk the 15 minutes to the Naga-machi Samurai district. Directional English-language signs to major sights are posted throughout the city. Or, if you wish, call the Tourist Information Center (see above) at least 2 weeks in advance of your visit to request a Goodwill Guide to show you the city; the service is free, but you're expected to pay for the guide's entrance fees, transportation, and lunch.

In addition to the sights below, you should also check out cultural events and classes offered at the **Ishikawa International Lounge,** 1–8–10 Hirosaka (www. ifie.or.jp/english/facilities/lounge; ✆ **076/221-9901;** Loop Bus: Hirosaka), including those that cover origami, calligraphy, Japanese musical instruments, the tea ceremony, Japanese flower arranging, Japanese folk dancing, Japanese cooking, and even Japanese language classes. Classes are free, but you are required to make a reservation and pay for material costs (flower arranging, for example, costs ¥800). The Ishikawa International Lounge, open Monday to Friday 9am to 5pm and Saturday 9am to 4pm, can also answer questions or concerns (such as legal matters) regarding staying or living in Japan.

AROUND KENROKUEN GARDEN

The sights here are listed in the order you'll reach them on foot from Kenrokuen. Kanazawa Castle Park and Gyokusen-en should be seen *before* entering Kenrokuen.

Kanazawa Castle Park PARK/GARDEN   At one time, Kanazawa possessed an impressive castle belonging to the powerful Maeda clan, but it was destroyed by fire several times, the last time in 1881. Ishikawa Gate (Ishikawamon), visible from the northwest corner of Kenrokuen and reached via bridge over a busy thoroughfare, served as the south entrance to the castle and is the castle's only remaining original structure. Observing how big and grand the gate is, you can appreciate the magnitude of the original Maeda castle. Remarkably, its roof tiles are actually lead, in case emergency dictated they be melted down for musket balls. The area just beyond the gate is the newly created Kanazawa Castle Park, which contains a botanical garden with a contemporary layout and reconstructed fortifications (the Hishi Yagura and Hashizume-mon Tsuzuki Yagura watchtowers, and, linking them, the Gojikken Nagaya storehouse) built in 2001 using traditional Japanese construction techniques; an English-language pamphlet and audio buttons make this a fascinating must for architecture buffs, but you can skip these empty buildings if time is of the essence.

Kenroku-machi. ✆ **076/234-3800.** Free admission to Castle Park; watchtowers/storehouse ¥300 adults, ¥100 children. Park Mar to mid-Oct daily 7am–6pm, mid-Oct to Feb daily 8am–5pm; watchtowers/storehouse daily 9am–4:30pm. Loop Bus: Kenrokuen-shita (5 min.).

Kenrokuen Garden ★★★ PARK/GARDEN   Kanazawa's main attraction, the 10-hectare (25-acre) **Kenrokuen Garden,** once served as Kanazawa Castle's outer garden. The largest of what are considered to be the three best landscape gardens in Japan—the other two are Kairakuen Garden in Mito and Korakuen Garden in Okayama—it's considered by some to be the grandest. Its name can be translated as "a refined garden incorporating six attributes"—spaciousness, careful arrangement, seclusion, antiquity, elaborate use of water, and scenic charm. Ponds, trees, winding streams, rocks, mounds, and footpaths have all been combined so aesthetically that the effect is spellbinding. Best of all, unlike most other gardens in Japan, there are no surrounding skyscrapers to detract from splendid views, making this one of my personal favorites.

Altogether, it took about 150 years to complete the garden. The fifth Maeda lord started construction in the 1670s, and successive lords added to it according to their individual tastes. The garden as you now see it was finished by the 13th Maeda lord in 1837; only after the Meiji Restoration was it opened to the public. In addition to pines, cherry trees, irises, ponds, and other elements of natural beauty, there are several historic structures, including a tea-ceremony house dating from 1774 and, most important, Seisonkaku Villa (see below). Plan on 1½ hours of blissful

tea FOR THE SOUL

Just a few minutes' walk from Kenrokuen is a much smaller garden, the **Gyokusen-en,** 8–3 Kosho-Machi (𝒞 **076/221-0181;** Thurs–Tues 9am–4pm). Built during the Edo Period and utilizing water from Kenrokuen, it contains waterfalls, a pond shaped in the *kanji* symbol for water, a stone lantern with a hidden statue of the Virgin Mary (Christianity was banned during the Edo Period), and Kanazawa's oldest teahouse, but what makes this place special in my book is the 1-hour formal tea ceremony (make reservations 2 days in advance), led by women in kimono who explain the history and the process of the ceremony in English. As Nishida Junko, whose husband is the garden's fifth generation of owners, explained: "The tea ceremony is not a show but rather the chance to share our one moment together"; the poignancy of her words brought tears to my eyes and made this my best tea-ceremony experience ever. Admission to the garden is ¥500, with the tea ceremony costing ¥1,000 more.

wanderings. *Tip:* You may want to arrive early in the morning or near the end of the day, as Kenrokuen Garden is a favorite destination of Japanese tour groups, led by flag-carrying guides who explain everything in detail—through loudspeakers.

1–4 Kenroku-machi. 𝒞 **076/234-3800.** Admission ¥300 adults, free for seniors, ¥100 children. Mar to mid-Oct daily 7am–6pm; mid-Oct to Feb daily 8am–5pm. Loop Bus: Kenrokuen-shita (3 min.).

Ishikawa Prefectural Museum for Traditional Products and Crafts (Ishikawa Kenritsu Dento Sangyo Kogeikan) ★★★ MUSEUM   If I had time to visit only one museum in Kanazawa, this would be my choice. It's by far the best place in town to view and learn about all the beautiful handcrafted items for which Kanazawa has long been famous (the Maeda lords promoted crafts over warfare). With the help of a detailed English-language pamphlet, you'll see and learn about the famous Kutani pottery, first produced under the patronage of the Maeda clan in the 1600s and known for its hues of green, red, purple, navy blue, and yellow, as well as Kaga Yuzen dyeing and hand-painting on silk, Kanazawa lacquerware (which uses raised lacquer painting), paulownia woodcrafts, metalwork, family Buddhist altars, Kanazawa gold leaf, *taiko* drums, *koto* and *shamisen* stringed instruments, lion masks, bambooware, fishing lures (using feathers of wild birds), folk toys, *washi* (Japanese paper), umbrellas, and even fireworks. Plan on 1 hour to appreciate everything.

1–1 Kenroku-machi. www.ishikawa-densankan.jp. 𝒞 **076/262-2020.** Admission ¥250 adults, ¥200 seniors, ¥100 children. Daily 9am–5pm (closed 3rd Thurs of every month Apr–Nov and every Thurs Dec–Mar). Loop Bus: Hirosaka (6 min.). Next to Seisonkaku Villa; you can also enter the museum directly from Kenrokuen.

Seisonkaku Villa (成巽閣) ★★ 🏛 HISTORIC HOME   Just outside the Kodatsuno (southeast) exit of Kenrokuen Garden is this must-see villa, built in 1863 by the 13th Maeda lord as a retirement home for his widowed mother. Elegant and graceful, it has a distinctly feminine atmosphere with delicately carved, brightly painted wood transoms and painted shoji screens decorated with seashells, butterflies, flowers, and other motifs. The bedroom is decorated with tortoises painted on the shoji wainscoting; tortoises were associated with long life, and it must have worked—the mother lived to be 84. Expect to linger about 20 minutes here.

1–2 Kenroku-machi. www.seisonkaku.com. ☎ **076/221-0580.** Admission ¥700 adults, ¥300 junior-high and high-school students, ¥250 children. Thurs–Tues 9am–5pm. Loop Bus: Hirosaka (5 min.). Next to the Ishikawa Prefectural Museum for Traditional Products and Crafts.

Ishikawa Prefectural Art Museum (Ishikawa Kenritsu Bijutsukan) ★
ART MUSEUM   One of the Maeda clan's lasting contributions was its encourage-ment of the arts, in full evidence here. After seeing how crafts are made at the Ishikawa Prefectural Museum for Traditional Products and Crafts (see above), stop here to see changing exhibits of the prefecture's most important cultural assets, including Kutani ware, Kaga Yuzen silk, lacquerware, and items such as samurai gear that belonged to the Maeda family, as well as contemporary oil paintings and decora-tive art by artists who were born in Ishikawa, lived here, or had some connection to the prefecture (artists to look for include Nakagawa Kazumasa, Takamitsu Kazuya, and Miyamoto Saburo). One room is reserved solely for the museum's most valuable treasures, a pair of pheasant-shaped incense burners (by a 17th-c. Kyoto potter). Be sure to take advantage of the free English-language audio guides, which provide com-mentary on individual works of art. You'll need 45 minutes here.

2–1 Dewa-machi. www.ishibi.pref.ishikawa.jp/english/index.html. ☎ **076/231-7580.** Admission ¥350 adults, ¥280 seniors and university students, free for children. Daily 9:30am–5pm. Closed 3–4 days monthly during exhibit changes. Loop Bus: Hirosaka (4 min.). Just south of Kenrokuen Garden, not far from Ishikawa Prefectural Museum for Traditional Products and Crafts (discussed above).

21st Century Museum of Contemporary Art, Kanazawa ★★ ART
MUSEUM   In a word, this museum is fun! Centrally located between Kenrokuen Garden and the Katamachi shopping district, Kanazawa's newest museum, with the aim of revitalizing the arts in Kanazawa and attracting young visitors, is ensconced in a striking circular building that has no front or back, allowing visitors to explore it from all directions (and, from time to time, lose themselves in it). Galleries, which range from bright spaces with sunlight pouring through glass ceilings to darkened rooms with no natural light, display a collection that concentrates on works of the past 30 years, particularly of Japanese artists born after 1965, along with contempo-rary works from around the world shown in changing exhibitions. My favorite: Lean-dro Erlich's outdoor "swimming pool" topped with a roof of glass and shallow water; look in, and you might see people who, having entered through a subterranean tun-nel, look like they're walking underwater.

1–2–1 Hirosaka. ☎ **076/220-2800.** www.kanazawa21.jp. Admission ¥350 adults, ¥280 seniors and university students, free for children 17 and under. Special exhibits ¥1,000, ¥800, and ¥400 respec-tively. Sun and Tues–Thurs 10am–6pm; Fri–Sat 10am–8pm. Loop Bus: Hirosaka (2 min.).

THE NAGA-MACHI SAMURAI (BUKE YASHIKI) DISTRICT

About a 15-minute walk west of Kenrokuen Garden and just a couple minutes' walk west of Katamachi (Kanazawa's main shopping district), the Naga-machi Samurai District is basically a few streets lined with beautiful wooden homes hidden behind gold-colored mud walls (higher-ranked samurai had higher walls; the lowest rank had only hedges) and bordered by canals left over from the Edo Period. An unhurried stroll in the neighborhood will give you an idea of what a feudal castle town might have looked like, though on a much reduced scale. Lord Maeda had as many as 8,000 samurai retainers, who in turn had their own retainers, making the samurai popula-tion here very large indeed. To see how those in the lowest military class lived, stop by the **Kanazawa Ashigaru Kinenkan** (金沢市足軽資料館), consisting of two homes open free to the public daily 9:30am to 5pm. In addition, the **Kanazawa**

Shinise Kinenkan (📞 **076/220-2524;** daily 9:30am–5pm), a former Chinese pharmacy established in 1579, displays the old store and family residence and, upstairs, Kanazawa crafts and products from some 60 local stores for ¥100.

To reach the Naga-machi Samurai District from Katamachi, take the side street to the right of the Excel Hotel Tokyu.

Nomura Samurai House (Buke Yashiki Ato Nomura Ke; 武家屋敷跡野村家**)** ★ HISTORIC HOME   Stop 20 minutes here to see how higher-ranking samurai lived back in the Edo Period. Occupied by 11 generations of the Nomura family for 400 years, this traditional Japanese home boasts a drawing room made of Japanese cypress, with elaborate designs in rosewood and shoji screens painted with landscapes, and a tea-ceremony room upstairs (tea costs ¥300). Rooms overlook a small, charming garden with a miniature waterfall, a winding stream, huge carp, and stone lanterns (many people come just for the garden). Personal effects of the Nomura family and objects from the Edo Period are on display, including a samurai outfit, swords, lacquerware, the family altar, and a box for bush warblers (deliberately dark so the birds would sing).

1–3–32 Naga-machi. 📞 **076/221-3553.** Admission ¥500 adults, ¥400 high-school students, ¥250 children. Apr–Sept daily 8:30am–5:30pm; Oct–Mar daily 8:30am–4:30pm. Loop Bus: Korinbo (5 min.). Take the side street to the right of the Excel Hotel Tokyu, turn right at the T, and then turn left.

OTHER SIGHTS

Higashi Chaya District   There are approximately 50 geisha practicing their trade in three old entertainment quarters in Kanazawa, including this one. A walk here reveals rather solemn-looking, wood-slatted facades of geisha houses dating from the 1820s, where men of means have long come to be entertained with music, dancing, songs, the tea ceremony, poem recitals, and other pleasurable pursuits. Geisha still perform at seven houses in the Higashi Chaya District, but most of the other former geisha homes have been turned into shops, inns, and restaurants. For an inside peek at the geisha world, visit the 190-year-old **Shima Geisha House (**志摩**),** 1–13–21 Higashiyama (📞 **076/252-5675;** daily 9am–6pm), a former tearoom where merchants as well as men of letters came to watch geisha perform. Inside, you'll find rooms that were allotted to personal use, as well as to performing, along with displays of ordinary artifacts from hair ornaments, pipes, and game boards to cooking utensils. Architectural details worth noting include several stairways (so that customers could come and go without being seen); a small Shinto shrine at the entrance to the home; a more elaborate family Buddhist altar in a place of honor in a front room; the gleaming wood-lacquered surfaces of furniture; and cloisonné door pulls on sliding doors. Admission is ¥400 for adults, ¥300 for children; but you may also want to enjoy tea in the new addition facing a garden, which, depending on the accompanying sweet, costs ¥500 to ¥700. Plan on 10 minutes or so to tour the house.

Myoryuji Temple (妙立寺**)** ★★ TEMPLE   Myoryuji Temple (1–2–12 Nomachi; 📞 **076/241-0888**) is popularly known as Ninja-dera (Temple of the Secret Agents) because of its secret chambers, hidden stairways, and trick doors. Built by the Maeda clan for family prayer in 1643, it looks small from the outside, just two stories high to comply with height restrictions during the Edo Period. Inside, four stories are evident, but even this is false: Three more levels are concealed. The fortresslike structure contains an amazing 29 stairways and a labyrinth of corridors, along with such trick devices as pitfalls to trap unsuspecting intruders, slatted stairs where lances could stab at passing legs, escape hatches, secret stairways, and rooms that could be opened only from the outside—just one more example of how deep paranoia ran during the Edo Period. Although rumor has it that a tunnel once connected the temple to the castle to serve as an escape route for the feudal lord in case of attack, a river running between them makes it unlikely. Unfortunately, photography is not allowed.

You must phone ahead for a reservation; chances are good that you'll be able to see it the same day you call. To ensure that you don't get lost (which would be quite easy because of all the trick doors), you must join a guided tour. Unfortunately, tours are in Japanese only, but there's an English-language booklet with photos that lets you follow along, and demonstrations of the various trick devices are fairly self-explanatory. Tours, given daily from 9am to 4:30pm (to 4pm in winter), last 30 to 40 minutes and cost ¥800 for adults, ¥600 for children (however, the temple does not recommend tours for children of any age, due to their tendency to talk and make noise, and children 5 and younger are not admitted). To reach it, take the Loop Bus to Jusangenmachi, cross the bridge you see straight ahead of you over the river, take the second left (Teramachi), and then the first right. It will be on your right.

Where to Eat

Kanazawa's local specialties, known collectively as **Kaga Ryori,** consist of seafood, such as tiny shrimp and winter crabs, as well as freshwater fish, duck, and mountain vegetables. Popular in winter is *jibuni,* a duck-and-vegetable stew.

All directions are from Kanazawa Station.

AROUND KANAZAWA STATION

Forus, a shopping center located next to Kanazawa Station (look for *Aeon* on its facade), has a slew of restaurants on its sixth floor, including Mori Mori Zushi and Budoonoki (see below), as well as those serving noodles, *tonkatsu,* and Indian and Korean fare. Most are open daily from 11am to 11pm.

Le Grand Chariot ★★ FRENCH   The highest spot in Kanazawa, this combination lounge and restaurant offers a gorgeous setting and great views, particularly at sunset, making this a good romantic splurge. The sophisticated lounge occupies the center of the room, while dining tables line windows at either side with the best ringside views; from the west windows you can even see the Japan Sea on the horizon. Only changing set meals are available, but they offer a choice of a main dish, artfully presented, along with a buffet of appetizers and desserts. Live music serenades you from 8:30 to 11pm, but the cover charge (¥840 on weekdays and ¥1,365 weekends) is waived for diners.

Hotel Nikko Kanazawa, 30th floor, 2–15–1 Hon-machi. ℂ **076/234-1111.** Reservations recommended. Set lunches ¥2,000–¥2,500; set dinners ¥6,000. AE, DC, MC, V. Daily 11:30am–2pm and 5:30–11pm. Station: Kanazawa (east exit, 1 min.).

Mori Mori Zushi (もりもり寿し) 🔸 SUSHI   This conveyor-belt sushi restaurant has colored plates, each signifying a specific price, but there's also a menu with photos so you can order what you want if it doesn't float past. There are spigots for hot water at the counter; serve yourself and add powdered tea. There's a more colorful branch at Omi-cho Market (ℂ **076/262-7477**), open Monday to Saturday from 10am to 4pm and Sunday from 10am to 8:30pm.

Forus, 6th floor. ℂ **076/265-3510.** Sushi platters ¥120–¥360. No credit cards. Daily 11am–10pm (last order). Station: Kanazawa (east exit, 1 min.). Turn left out of the station.

AROUND KENROKUEN GARDEN

Miyoshian (三芳庵) ★★ 🏠 KAGA KAISEKI   A great place to try the local Kaga cuisine right in Kenrokuen Garden, this 100-year-old restaurant consists of three separate wooden buildings, the best of which is a traditional room extending over a large pond. This is where you'll probably dine, seated on tatami with a view of an ancient pond (giant carp swim in the murky waters). Only set meals of Kaga cuisine are served, all featuring *jibuni*. The more expensive the meal, the more dishes it adds. The ¥1,575 *yugao* meal includes soup, jibuni, sashimi, a seasonal dish such as eel on rice, and pickles. The ¥3,150 *chakaisekifu* meal adds such dishes as salmon, crab, tofu, and various small delicacies. Lunch is served from 11am to 2:30pm, but you can also come just for green tea and sweets for ¥550.

Kenrokuen Garden, 1–11 Kenrokumachi. ⓒ **076/221-0127.** Kaga teishoku ¥1,575–¥3,150. DC, MC, V. Thurs–Tues 9am–4pm. Loop Bus: Kenrokuen-shita (5 min.). Turn right after entering the park's Renchimon Gate.

KATAMACHI

Radiating from Katamachi Shopping Street and Saigawa Odori (called Chuo Dori by the locals) is an area full of restaurants and drinking establishments.

Budoonoki ITALIAN   An informal eatery with a high ceiling and an open facade facing a courtyard, this pleasant restaurant offers salads, pizzas, and pastas, including versions you've probably never thought of, like lotus root salad, pizza with laver seaweed and leek, or spaghetti with duck and horseradish in a thick sauce. Other choices include the fish of the day, fried Iberico pork cutlet, or rice omelet with a sauce of beef and red wine. After 6pm you can nibble on tapas (¥714 for three tapas). Finish it all off with Japanese green-tea parfait. There's a branch on the sixth floor of Forum next to Kanazawa Station (ⓒ **076/265-3521**), open daily 11am to 11pm.

1–3–21 Katamachi. ⓒ **076/232-7878.** Main dishes ¥880–¥1,650; set lunches ¥880–¥1,800. DC, MC, V. Thurs–Tues 11am–9:30pm (last order). Loop Bus: Katamachi (2 min.). In a small alley off Katamachi St. called Prego.

Kincharyo VARIED JAPANESE   This, without a doubt, is Katamachi's easiest restaurant to find: It's located on the third floor of the very visible Excel Hotel Tokyu. Sister restaurant to a famous 80-year-old restaurant in the Teramachi Temple district (near Myoryuji Temple), it offers tempura, *Kaga kaiseki*, sushi, and steak, but most popular are the obento with a variety of dishes for ¥1,732 to ¥2,800.

Excel Hotel Tokyu, 2–1–1 Korinbo. ⓒ **076/263-5511.** Set dinners ¥4,800–¥10,000; set lunches ¥1,800–¥3,800. AE, DC, MC, V. Daily 11:30am–2pm and 5–9pm (last order). Loop Bus: Korinbo (1 min.).

Kitama (きたま) ★ VARIED JAPANESE/KAGA   Sitting on tatami mats, you'll have a pleasant view of moss-covered greenery at this modern restaurant with a 150-year-old history. The *Kojitsu obento* (¥2,100), served in an upright lunch box, features sashimi, small pieces of pork and fish, fried shrimp, a soybean patty, and various seasonal vegetables. The *jibuni teishoku* (¥1,890), with duck stew, clear soup, pickled vegetables, rice, and hors d'oeuvres, is also quite satisfying. The restaurant is also known for its tempura and kaiseki (artfully prepared multicourse meals) starting at ¥4,200.

2–3–3 Katamachi. ⓒ **076/261-7176.** Set meals ¥1,050–¥4,200. AE, DC, MC, V. Daily 11:30am–8:30pm (last order). Closed irregularly. Loop Bus: Katamachi (2 min.). From the intersection of Katamachi and Chuo, walk 1 block west on Chuo Dori and turn right; the restaurant will be on your left with a display case and bamboo fence at its entrance.

HIGASHI CHAYA DISTRICT

Bistro Kanazawa Todoroki-Tei ★ FRENCH   This former bank dating from the Taisho Period (1912–26) has been turned into an attractive restaurant boasting tall ceilings, gleaming dark wood, and period light fixtures. Big-band jazz and swing music playing in the background add to its nostalgic atmosphere. For dinner you might opt for the Caesar salad, prepared tableside and large enough for two to share, followed by confit of duck, grilled beef with a lemon soy sauce, or fish of the day.

1–2–1 Higashiyama. ✆ **076/252-5755.** Main courses ¥2,000–¥6,000; set lunches ¥1,200–¥3,500. AE, DC, MC, V. Daily 11:30am–2:30pm (to 3:30pm Sat–Sun and holidays) and 6–10:30pm. Loop Bus: Hashibacho (1 min.) Beside the bus stop and *Koban* (police box).

Jugatsuya (十月亭) ★ 🍴 KAISEKI/KAGA   Dining in this former teahouse means sitting at a huge wooden slab of a counter, with leg wells for those errant appendages and a view of a small garden. At lunch four meals are offered, which change with the seasons. Summer may feature cold *udon* noodles with sesame sauce, while winter might bring steaming bowls of *jibuni.* Dinners feature kaiseki with local *Kaga* dishes.

1–26–16 Higashiyama. ✆ **076/253-3321.** Reservations recommended. Set lunches ¥1,050–¥2,750; set dinners ¥6,300–¥8,400. AE, DC, MC, V. Tues–Sun 11:30am–3pm and 6–9pm. Loop Bus: Hashi-bacho (4 min.). On the main street of Higashi Chaya District.

ELSEWHERE

Kotobuki-Ya (壽屋) ★★★ 🍴 VEGETARIAN   Specializing in *shojin ryori* (Bud-dhist vegetarian cooking), Kotobuki-ya is in a beautiful 165-year-old merchant's house with a two-story airy entryway. Dining here, on beautiful lacquer and pottery table-ware while seated at tables or on tatami, is a wonderful experience—not surprisingly, they have had many fine reviews. For lunch, you can dine for ¥2,800 on the *shojin ryori obento* or splurge on kaiseki for ¥5,500. Kaiseki dinners are vegetarian or with fish. If you order kaiseki you'll be seated in your own private room (or, if you order the obento lunch, you can have your own room for ¥350 extra per person). Two of the rooms have views of the garden.

2–4–13 Owari-cho. ✆ **076/231-6245.** Reservations required by 4:30pm for dinner. Set lunches ¥2,800–¥5,500; kaiseki dinners ¥7,000–¥15,000. AE, DC, V. Daily 11:30am–2pm and 6–7:30pm (last order). Loop Bus: Musashigatsuji (3 min.). North of Hyakumangoku Dori, on a side street btw. 2 small parking lots.

Shopping

Kanazawa's most famous products are its **Kutani pottery,** with its bright five-color overglaze patterns, and its hand-painted **Yuzen silk.** Kanazawa also produces *maki-e* lacquerware, sweets, toys, wooden products, and almost all of Japan's gold leaf. For convenient shopping for these and other souvenirs, try the **Omiyage Kan shopping arcade** right in Kanazawa Station, open daily 8:30am to 7pm.

For department stores, boutiques, and contemporary shops, visit the **Katamachi and Tatemachi shopping streets,** within walking distance of Kenrokuen Garden and the Naga-machi Samurai district. **Omi-cho Market,** just off Hyakumangoku Dori between the station and Kenrokuen Garden, was established 280 years ago as the "kitchen of Kanazawa" and today is a vibrant city market with more than 170 stalls selling seafood, vegetables, fruit, and more. It's open Monday to Saturday from 10am to 6pm (some shops open also on Sunday).

Ishikawa Prefectural Products Center (Kanko Bussankan)   Located just north of Kenrokuen Garden, this is the place to come for one-stop shopping of all the products Ishikawa Prefecture is famous for. The ground floor sells crafts ranging from lacquerware and pottery to glassware, foodstuff, and toys, while the second floor houses more crafts and a sushi restaurant. Open daily 10am to 6pm (upstairs closes at 4pm; closed some Tues Nov–Mar). 2–20 Kenroku-machi. ℗ **076/222-7788.** Loop Bus: Kenrokuen-shita (2 min.). Backtrack to Hyakumangoku Dori and turn right.

Kaga Yuzen Traditional Industry Center (Kaga Yuzen Dento Sangyo Kaikan; 加賀友禅伝統産業会館) Yuzen dying was brought from Kyoto to Kanazawa in 1712, where a new technique emerged that uses just five colors—indigo, crimson, ocher, green, and purple. A 13-minute English-language video describes the painstaking process of hand-drawing the pattern and its colors and the role Yuzen cloth dying played in Kanazawa history (admission: ¥300 adults, ¥200 children). Otherwise, take the stairs to the left of the entryway to the basement shop, where you can purchase scarves, purses, fans, clothing, *furoshiki* (traditionally used for wrapping presents), and other items made from hand-dyed Yuzen cloth, which borrows heavily from nature for its designs—mainly flowers and landscapes. Open Thursday to Tuesday 9am to 5pm. 8–8 Kosho-machi. www.kagayuzen.or.jp. ℗ **076/224-5511.** Loop Bus: Kenrokuen-shita (2 min.). Cross Hyakumangoku Dori, turn right, and then left after the parking lot.

Kanazawa Crafts Hirosaka Finely crafted glassware, embroidery, fans, jewelry, pottery, umbrellas, and other items by local artisans are sold here. Open Tuesday to Sunday 10am to 6pm. 1–2–25 Hirosaka. ℗ **076/265-3320.** Loop Bus: Hirosaka (1 min.). Beside Kanazawa Noh Museum, near the 21st Century Museum of Contemporary Art.

Kutani Kosen Pottery Studio (Kutani Kosengama; 九谷光仙窯) ★ If your interest lies in pottery, it's worth a visit to this Kutani-ware kiln and shop, open since 1870 and about a 10-minute walk from Myoryuji Temple. In addition to browsing its showroom, you can also take a 15-minute free tour (reservations recommended), led by a guide who speaks some English, to see the entire process of producing handmade Kutani ware, including the potters' wheels, the hand painting of designs, and the kilns. It takes 3 months to produce each piece, sold only here. Open daily 9am to 5pm. 5–3–3 Nomachi. ℗ **076/241-0902.** City Bus No. 1 or 2: 20 min. from Kanazawa Station from platform 8 to the Nomachi Eki stop (3 min.). Walk back toward the city center and take the 1st left (beside a small canal); it's almost immediately on the left.

Sakuda (さくだ) Thinking about wallpapering a room in gold leaf? Then you'll want to pay a visit to Sakuda, located in a modern building in the Higashi Chaya District. (As much as 98% of Japan's entire national output of gold leaf is produced in Kanazawa.) You can watch artisans at work, pounding the gold leaf and spreading it until it's paper-thin and translucent; it's the equivalent of pounding a ¥10 coin into the size of a tatami mat. But most people come here to shop for gold-leafed vases, boxes, chopsticks, bowls, trays, screens, furniture, and—this being Japan—golf balls and clubs. You can even buy gold flakes to add to your coffee or sake. Don't miss the second-floor bathrooms; the women's is done entirely in gold leaf, the men's in platinum. The staff was serving complimentary tea spiked with gold leaf to everyone who dropped by during my last visit. Open daily 9am to 6pm. 1–3–27 Higashiyama. www.goldleaf-sakuda.jp. ℗ **076/251-6777.** Loop Bus: Hashibacho (4 min.).

Shamisen no Fukushima (三味線の福嶋) 👜 There used to be other makers of the three-stringed *shamisen* instrument in Kanazawa to keep the geisha supplied with one of the tools of their trade, but this fourth-generation-owned shop, in the Higashi Chaya District, is the only one remaining. While you may not be in the market for a *shamisen,* from 10am to 4pm you can have a short lesson in English (¥300) and then play as long as you wish, followed by a cup of tea. An upstairs showroom shows how these instruments are made, including the cat and dog skin used to cover the sound box (cat skin is more expensive). Open Monday to Saturday 10am to 4pm; closed holidays, the second and fourth Saturdays of the month, and mid-August. 1–1–8 Higashiyama. ✆ **076/252-3703.** Loop Bus: Hashibacho (2 min.). On Kannon-machi St.

Tawaraya Ame (俵屋あめ) ☺ They've been selling Japanese confectionery from this traditional wood-slatted building since 1830. Tawaraya makes candy from rice and barley, using malt instead of sugar, and now touts the candy as health food. One of the candies, *Jiro Ame,* is soft like honey, purportedly developed for babies who, for one reason or another, could not be breast-fed. *Okoshi Ame* is hard and comes in a wooden bucket; the staff recommends breaking the hard candy with a hammer (kids love this) and putting it in a refrigerator. Soft lollipops and hard candy (true jawbreakers!) and candy flavored with Japanese apricot, ginger, mulberry, and other flavors are also available. Open Monday to Saturday 9am to 6pm; Sunday 9am to 5pm. 2–4 Kobashi-machi. ✆ **076/252-2079.** Loop Bus: Kobashi (2 min.). Cross the bridge and turn left.

Where to Stay

Keep in mind that some accommodations may add a surcharge to the prices below during peak season—New Year's, Golden Week (Apr 29–May 5), and mid-July through mid-November.

Directions are from Kanazawa Station; minutes in parentheses indicate the walking time required from the bus stop.

EXPENSIVE

Hotel Nikko Kanazawa ★★★ Kanazawa's tallest building was designed by a Japanese-French team, who succeeded in giving it a boutique-hotel ambience despite its size. Its lobby exudes a French-colonial drawing room atmosphere, adorned with a bubbling fountain, rattan chairs stuffed with pillows, fake trees, antiques, and Asian decorative art ranging from ginger jars to Japanese lacquered boxes. The English-speaking concierge staff receives high marks, and its location in front of the station can't be beat for convenience. Spacious rooms have decent-size bathrooms, and are decorated with items made with Yuzen cloth, gold leaf, and other Kanazawa handicrafts. Rooms on higher floors offer great views of either mountains or the Japan Sea in the distance.

2–15–1 Hon-machi, Kanazawa, Ishikawa Prefecture 920-0853. www.hnkanazawa.jp. ✆ **800/645-5687** in the U.S. and Canada, or 076/234-1111. Fax 076/234-8802. 254 units. ¥27,000–¥40,000 single or double. AE, DC, MC, V. Station: Kanazawa (east exit, 1 min.). **Amenities:** 5 restaurants, including Le Grand Chariot (p. 348); bar; lounge; concierge; access to next-door health club and spa w/indoor pool (fee: ¥2,100); lobby computer w/free Internet; room service. *In room:* A/C, TV, hair dryer, Internet, minibar.

Kanazawa Miyako Hotel Although the hotel's cheerless exterior could use an update and the lobby is purely functional, all of the rooms are nicely done and its twin rooms (there are only five doubles) are among the largest for their price in Kanazawa. Add to that the Miyako name (synonymous with service), smoke-free restaurants, and a convenient location (across the street from and linked to the station via an underground passage), and you'll see why I like this lodging. There are even rooms for ladies with a vanity, a bigger bed than the standard singles (don't ask me why), and a toiletry bag that includes bath gel and other female-oriented amenities. I also like rooms facing the station's bus terminal; when a Loop Bus pulls out, I know I have 12 minutes to make the next one.

LIVE LIKE A local

For a unique experience, consider spending the night in your own *machiya*, a traditional wooden town house common during the Edo Period. You'll have the entire home, complete with kitchen, futon, and bathroom, plus extras like Japanese umbrellas and *yukata* (not to mention TVs and Internet connection). Homes rent for ¥54,000 for two to three people and ¥72,000 for four to five. Contact **Kikunoya Machiya Kanazawa,** 3–22 Kazue-machi (✆ **076/287-0834;** www.machiya-kanazawa.jp).

6–10 Konohanacho, Kanazawa, Ishikawa Prefecture 920-0852. www.miyakohotels.ne.jp/kanazawa. ✆ **076/261-2111.** Fax 076/261-2113. 193 units. ¥11,550–¥13,860 single; ¥20,790–¥32,340 double. AE, DC, MC, V. Station: Kanazawa (east exit, 1 min.). **Amenities:** 2 restaurants; bar/lounge; room service. *In room:* A/C, TV, fridge, hair dryer, Internet (in some).

MODERATE

APA Hotel Kanazawa-Ekimae　Although just a business hotel, this place does have a special feature that sets it apart: large public baths complete with sauna and open-air bath, all free to hotel guests. Other pluses include a convenient location just steps away from Kanazawa Station (but on the opposite side from where buses depart); bold use of bright colors that are a welcome relief from the usual bland white of most business hotels; and a Seattle's Best Coffee (with free Wi-Fi). If you're not a fan of public baths, however, you might choose to stay elsewhere; the hotel is not geared toward tourists, little English is spoken, and rooms are so minuscule that if you open your luggage you may have to leap to reach your bed. Even the deluxe corner rooms would be considered small in a regular hotel.

If you'd rather be in the heart of the city, the **APA Hotel Kanazawa-Chuo,** 1–5–24 Katamachi (✆ **076/235-2111**), offers similar-size rooms at similar rates and a Seattle's Best Coffee with Wi-Fi, but the water tapped for its indoor and outdoor baths is from hot springs.

1–9–28 Hirooka, Kanazawa, Ishikawa Prefecture 920-0031. www.apahotel.com. ✆ **076/231-8111.** Fax 076/231-8112. 456 units. ¥8,000–¥9,000 single; ¥11,000–¥18,000 double. AE, MC, V. Station: Kanazawa (west exit, 2 min.). **Amenities:** 3 restaurants; bar; sauna. *In room:* A/C, TV, fridge, hair dryer, Internet.

Kanazawa Manten ★ 🍴　A fountain at the entrance, a front desk backed by trees, jazz playing in the hotel restaurant, indoor/outdoor baths, and attentive service all conspire to make this business hotel (located on the opposite side of the station from where the buses depart) seem like it's more expensive than it is. Alas, the mostly single rooms (there are 141 twin rooms and 42 doubles) are no different or larger than those of any other business hotel, with semi-double-size beds that take up most of the floor space. On the bright side, rooms have been stylishly updated (and include ladies' rooms with humidifiers and women's toiletries, as well as queen rooms with massage chairs), the windows can be opened or covered by panels for complete darkness, and on each floor there's a convenience corner with a microwave, trouser press, and vending machines. In short, the cramped quarters and self-serve philosophy of the upper floors reinforce the business-hotel status, but at least in the lobby and the baths you can feel grand.

1–6–1 Kita-yasue, Kanazawa, Ishikawa Prefecture 920-0022. ✆ **076/265-0100.** Fax 076/265-0120. 509 units. ¥6,800–¥7,000 single; ¥13,000–¥15,000 double. AE, DC, MC, V. Station: Kanazawa (west exit, 3 min.). Turn right out of the station and continue along the tracks, past the car park. **Amenities:** Restaurant; lounge; public baths w/Jacuzzi, sauna (men only), and steam room (women only); lounge computer w/free Internet. *In room:* A/C, TV, fridge, hair dryer, Internet.

INEXPENSIVE

In addition to the recommendations here, there are two **Toyoko Inns** in Kanazawa, the **Toyoko Inn Kanazawa-eki Higashi-guchi** (✆ **076/224-1045**) just a 4-minute walk from the east exit of Kanazawa Station and the **Toyoko Inn Kanazawa Kenrokuen Korinbo** (✆ **076/232-1045**) in the heart of the city. Go to www. toyoko-inn.com for more information on this chain.

Murataya Ryokan   This smoke-free Japanese Inn Group *ryokan* is in the heart of Kanazawa, not far from Katamachi and Tatemachi shopping streets and within walking distance of Kenrokuen. It's modern and rather uninteresting from the outside but comfortable and pleasant inside. Note the old-fashioned 50-some-year-old telephone in the reception used to connect Murataya with the outside world; but LAN cables at the Hibachi allow you to hook up your computer. All rooms are clean and are Japanese style with tatami, with extralong futons for tall foreigners. In addition to laundry facilities, a plus is the inn's own map of the Katamachi area, showing the locations of banks, post offices, stores, and restaurants.

1–5–2 Katamachi, Kanazawa, Ishikawa Prefecture 920-0981. www.murataya-ryokan.com/e. ✆ **076/263-0455.** Fax 076/263-0456. 11 units, none with bathroom. ¥4,700 single; ¥9,000 double; ¥12,600 triple. Continental breakfast ¥500 extra; Japanese breakfast ¥800 extra. AE, DC, MC, V. Loop Bus: Katamachi (3 min.). Take the small pedestrian lane on the right side of the APA Hotel and then turn left. **Amenities:** Lobby computer w/free Internet. *In room:* A/C, TV.

Via Inn Kanazawa ★   This business hotel, located inside Kanazawa Station with reception on the third floor, offers all of life's basic necessities, including decent-size rooms and a microwave on each floor (there's a grocery store below the hotel). There are only four twin rooms and no doubles, but two people can stay in a single room for the lowest price below if they don't mind forced togetherness.

Kanazawa Station, Kanazawa, Ishikawa Prefecture 920-0858. ✆ **076/222-5489.** Fax 076/222-5485. 206 units. ¥6,800 single; ¥8,000–¥13,000 double. AE, DC, MC, V. Station: Kanazawa (inside the station). **Amenities:** Lobby computer w/free Internet. *In room:* A/C, TV, fridge, hair dryer, Internet.

Yogetsu ★★ 🏠   Geisha used to live in this 190-year-old *machiya* (traditional wooden home) located on the main street of the Higashi Chaya District, but now it's a charming inn with just a handful of tatami rooms. Remarkably, most of the house retains its original character. Note the entryway door, with a small door built into the larger one; other unique characteristics include an old-style metal tub and a breakfast room overlooking a courtyard garden. Unlike most inns, you have to pay extra for use of a *yukata* (¥200) or a towel (¥100).

1–13–22 Higashiyama, Kanazawa, Ishikawa Prefecture 920-0831. ✆ **076/252-0497.** 3 units, none with bathroom. ¥4,500 per person. Breakfast ¥500 extra. No credit cards. Loop Bus: Hashibacho (4 min.). On the main street of Higashi Chaya District. *In room:* A/C, no phone.

OSAKA, CITY OF MERCHANTS

553km (343 miles) W of Tokyo; 42km (26 miles) SW of Kyoto; 339km (212 miles) E of Hiroshima

Although its history stretches back almost 1,500 years, Osaka first gained prominence when Hideyoshi Toyotomi, the most powerful lord in the land, built Japan's most magnificent castle here in the 16th century. To develop resources for his castle town, he persuaded merchants from other parts of the nation to resettle in Osaka. During the Edo Period, the city became an important distribution center as feudal lords from the surrounding region sent their rice to merchants in Osaka, who in turn sent the rice onward to Edo (present-day Tokyo) and other cities. As the merchants prospered, the town grew and such arts as *kabuki* and *bunraku* flourished. With money and leisure to spare, the merchants also developed a refined taste for food.

Today, with the legacy of the city's commercial beginnings still present, Osaka is the mover and shaker of the Kansai region, known for its international and progressive business and high-tech industries. Capital of Osaka Prefecture and with a population of about 2.6 million, it's the third-most populated city in Japan (after Tokyo and Yoko-hama). Osakans are usually characterized as being outgoing and clever at money affairs. (One Osakan greeting is "Are you making any money?") It's also known for its food, castle, port, underground shopping arcades, and *bunraku* puppet theater, and boasts the oldest state temple in Japan, one of the nation's best aquariums, and the only Universal Studios outside the United States. Because of its international airport, it also serves as a major gateway to the rest of Japan. Indeed, some travelers base themselves in Osaka, taking day trips to Kyoto, Nara, Kobe, Himeji, and Mount Koya.

Essentials

GETTING THERE

BY PLANE Osaka's **Kansai International Airport** (**KIX;** www.kansai-airport. or.jp; ✆ **072/455-2500**) receives both international and domestic flights, with flights from Tokyo's Haneda and Narita airports taking about 1¼ hours.

Constructed on a huge man-made island 5km (3 miles) off the mainland in Osaka Bay and almost 50km (30 miles) from the center of Osaka, this 24-hour airport boasts the latest in technology and, like the city itself, is traveler-friendly. Signs are clear and abundant, and facilities and services—which range from restaurants and shops to a **tourist information center** (see below), **post office, ATMs** that accept foreign credit cards, a children's **playroom** in the international departure area (free of charge), **cellphone** rental counters, computer stations providing Internet access (¥100 for 10 min.), free **Wi-Fi,** and **dental and medical clinics**—are seemingly endless.

GETTING FROM KIX TO OSAKA Taxis are prohibitively expensive: Expect to spend at least ¥17,000 for an hour's cab ride to the city center. Easiest, especially if you have luggage, is the **Kansai Airport Transportation Enterprise** (www.kate. co.jp; ✆ **072/461-1374**), which provides bus service to major stations and a few hotels in Osaka, as well as to Kyoto, Kobe, Nara, Himeji, and Okayama. Most fares to Osaka cost ¥1,500 and tickets can be purchased at counters in the arrival lobby. Another bus service, the **OCAT Shuttle** (www.ocat.co.jp; ✆ **06/6635-3000**), travels from KIX to the Osaka City Air Terminal, located in the heart of Osaka next to JR Namba Station and serving as a major bus terminal for express buses to cities through-out Japan; buses depart KIX every 30 minutes for the 48-minute ride and cost ¥1,000.

If you want to take the **train** into Osaka or even farther to Kyoto, simply walk through KIX's second-floor connecting concourse (baggage carts are designed to go on escalators and as far as train ticket gates). The **JR Airport Express Haruka** (www.westjr.co.jp; ✆ **0570/00-2486**), which travels to Tennoji and Shin-Osaka sta-tions (but not Osaka Station) before continuing to Kyoto, departs about twice an hour; the fare to Shin-Osaka is ¥2,470 for the 50-minute trip. Slower is the **JR Rapid Service (JR Kanku Kaisoku),** which travels from the airport to Tennoji and Osaka stations, with the 68-minute trip to Osaka Station costing ¥1,320. *Note:* When

Osaka

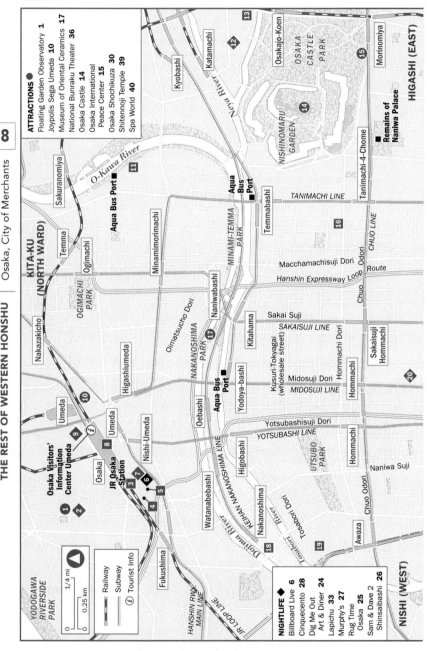

ATTRACTIONS ●
Floating Garden Observatory **1**
Joypolis Sega Umeda **10**
Museum of Oriental Ceramics **17**
National Bunraku Theater **36**
Osaka Castle **14**
Osaka International
  Peace Center **15**
Osaka Shochikuza **30**
Shitennoji Temple **39**
Spa World **40**

NIGHTLIFE ◆
Billboard Live **6**
Cinquecento **28**
Dig Me Out
  Art & Diner **24**
Lapichu **33**
Murphy's **27**
Rug Time
  Osaka **25**
Sam & Dave 2
  Shinsaibashi **26**

YODOGAWA
RIVERSIDE
PARK

Railway
Subway
i Tourist Info

0   1/4 mi
0 0.25 km

Osaka Visitors'
Information
Center Umeda

JR Osaka
Station

KITA-KU
(NORTH WARD)

HIGASHI (EAST)

NISHI (WEST)

Remains of
Naniwa Palace

Osakajo-Koen

OSAKA
CASTLE
PARK

NISHINOMARU
GARDEN

O-Kawa River

Neya River

Dojima River

Tosabori Dori

Aqua Bus Port

TANIMACHI LINE
CHUO LINE
SAKAISUJI LINE
MIDOSUJI LINE
YOTSUBASHI LINE
KEIHAN NAKANOSHIMA LINE
HANSHIN RWY MAIN LINE
JR LOOP LINE

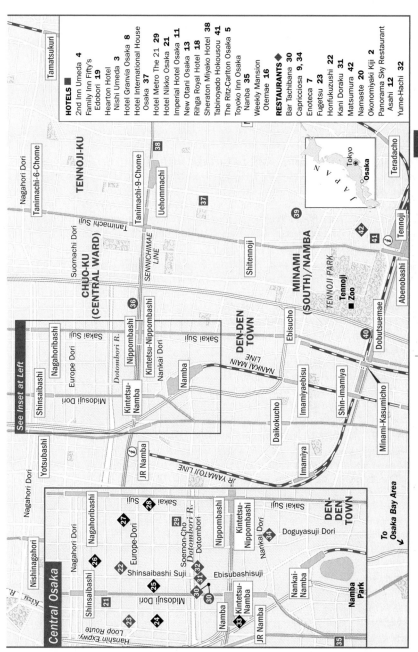

HOTELS ■
2nd Inn Umeda **4**
Family Inn Fifty's Edobori **19**
Hearton Hotel Nishi Umeda **3**
Hotel Granvia Osaka **8**
Hotel International House Osaka **37**
Hotel Metro The 21 **29**
Hotel Nikko Osaka **21**
Imperial Hotel Osaka **11**
New Otani Osaka **13**
Ringa Royal Hotel **18**
Sheraton Miyako Hotel **38**
Tabinoyado Hokousou **41**
The Ritz-Carlton Osaka **5**
Toyoko Inn Osaka Namba **35**
Weekly Mansion Otemae **16**

RESTAURANTS ◆
Bar Tachibana **30**
Capricciosa **9, 34**
Enoteca **7**
Fugetsu **23**
Honfukuzushi **22**
Kani Doraku **31**
Matsumura **42**
Namaste **20**
Okonomiyaki Kiji **2**
Panorama Sky Restaurant Asahi **12**
Yume-Hachi **32**

8

THE REST OF WESTERN HONSHU | Osaka, City of Merchants

returning to the airport from Osaka, make sure you're in a compartment that goes all the way to KIX; not all of them do. If you a have a **Japan Rail Pass,** you can ride these trains for free. Exchange your voucher at the Kansai Airport (rail) Station on the third floor (daily 5:30am–11pm).

Across from the JR trains in the same station at the airport is the private **Nankai Line** (www.nankai.co.jp; ✆ **072/456-6203**), whose sleek **rapi:t a** (pronounced "rapito") train reaches Namba Nankai Station in 35 minutes. There are usually two trains an hour, and ordinary reserved seats cost ¥1,390; if you think you'll be doing some sightseeing that same day, a good deal is the **Osaka Business Ticket,** which combines the trip in to town plus unlimited travel for the day on Osaka's subways, trams and buses for ¥1,500. If you're on a budget, you can also take an ordinary **Nankai Express Line** for ¥890 and reach Namba in 43 minutes.

OSAKA INTERNATIONAL AIRPORT (ITAMI AIRPORT)   If you're arriving on a domestic flight, chances are you'll arrive at Itami Airport (ITM; www.osaka-airport. co.jp; ✆ **06/6856-6781**), north of the city. In addition to a monorail which travels from the airport to Senri-chuo station in 12 minutes for ¥320 (where you can then take the Kita-Osaka Kyuko/Midosuji Line to Umeda Station), buses connect to various parts of Osaka; to Osaka Station, the ride takes 25 minutes and costs ¥620.

BY TRAIN   Osaka is 3 hours from Tokyo by Shinkansen bullet train; tickets are ¥13,240 for an unreserved seat (the Nozomi Shinkansen, which is not valid with a Japan Rail Pass, is faster and more expensive). All Shinkansen bullet trains arrive at **Shin-Osaka Station** at the city's northern edge. To get from Shin-Osaka Station to Osaka Station, Namba, Tennoji, and other points south, use the most convenient public transportation, the **Midosuji Line** subway; the subway stop at Osaka Station is called **Umeda Station. JR trains** also make runs between Shin-Osaka and Osaka stations.

If you haven't turned in your voucher for your **Japan Rail Pass** yet, you can do so at either Osaka Stations or Shin-Osaka Station (daily 5:30am–11pm).

If you're arriving in Osaka from Kobe or Kyoto, the commuter lines, which will deliver you directly to Osaka Station in the heart of the city, are more convenient than the Shinkansen, which will deposit you at out-of-the-way Shin-Osaka Station.

BY BUS   JR "Dream" night buses depart from both Tokyo Station's Yaesu exit and Shinjuku Station's New South exit several times nightly (including buses just for women), arriving at Osaka Station about 8 or 9 hours later and costing ¥9,300. Cheaper still is the nightly **JR Seisyun Eco Dream bus** from both Tokyo and Shinjuku stations, with several departures nightly and costing ¥4,300 to ¥5,000 for the 9-hour trip. There are also **JR day buses** from Tokyo and Shinjuku stations to Osaka Station costing around ¥7,300. Tickets for most buses can be bought at any major JR station, JR bus terminal, or at a travel agency; for inquiries, call ✆ **03/3844-1950** (✆ **03/3844-0489** for reservations) or check www.jrbuskanto.co.jp. In addition, **Willer Express** (http://willerexpress.com; ✆ **050/5805-0383**) operates buses departing Tokyo and Shinjuku stations several times nightly, arriving at Osaka Station the next morning. The cost of these range from ¥4,800 to ¥10,800, depending on the date and type of seat (reclining seats cost more); student and senior discounts are available.

VISITOR INFORMATION

AT KIX AIRPORT   The **Kansai Tourist Information Center** (✆ **072/456-6025;** daily 9am–9pm Nov–Mar, 8:30am–8:30pm Apr–Oct) counters are near both the south and north end of the International Arrivals Lobby. The multilingual staff can help with general travel information about Japan and provides brochures and maps of the larger Kansai area, including Kyoto and Kobe.

IN TOWN At **Osaka Station,** the **Visitors Information Center Umeda** (*C* **06/6345-2189;** daily 8am–8pm) is located in the Central Concourse's north end near the Mitsukoshi Isetan department store. Another center is located in **Shin-Osaka Station** on the third floor (*C* **06/6305-3311;** daily 9am–6pm). At **JR Namba Station,** you'll find the **Visitors Information Center Namba** (*C* **06/6631-9100;** daily 9am–8pm) in the Nankai Namba Station across from Takashimaya Department Store. Another Tourist Information Center is in **JR Tennoji Station** (*C* **06/6774-3077;** daily 9am–6pm).

To find out what's going on in Osaka, *Kansai Scene* (www.kansaiscene.com) is a free bilingual monthly magazine with articles, reviews, listings, and information on the Kansai area; it's available at tourist offices, restaurants, bars, and other places around town. Informtion on Osaka city is also available on the Web at **www.osaka-info.jp,** while **www.kansai.gr.jp** gives information on the Kansai region.

CITY LAYOUT

Osaka is divided into various wards, or *ku,* the most important of which for visitors are Kita-ku (North Ward), which encompasses the area around Osaka Station; and Chuo-ku (Central Ward), where you'll find Osaka Castle and Namba, the heart of the city. Some city maps divide Osaka by location: Kita (North), around Osaka Station; Minami (South), around Namba and Shinsaibashi; Higashi (East), around Osaka Castle; and Nishi (West) which is Osaska's bay area. Shin-Osaka Station, three subway stations north of Osaka (Umeda) Station, is a tourist wasteland with a few hotels.

AROUND OSAKA STATION **Kita-ku** embraces the area around Osaka and Umeda stations and includes many of the city's top hotels, the city's tallest buildings, lots of restaurants, and several shopping complexes, mostly underground. Its maze of buildings and streets, however, make it frustrating to navigate, even for Japanese.

AROUND OSAKA CASTLE Osaka Castle, which lies to the east, is the historic center of the city and is surrounded by a huge park. It's in **Chuo-ku,** which stretches through the city center.

MINAMI/NAMBA Four subway stops south of Umeda Station is Namba (also referred to as **Minami,** or South Osaka), with a cluster of stations serving subways, JR trains, and Kintetsu and Nankai lines, all of which are connected to one another via underground passageways. This is the heart of the city, bustling with the spirit of old Osaka, where you'll find more hotels, Osaka's liveliest eating and entertainment district centered on a narrow street called **Dotombori** (also written Dotonbori), the **National Bunraku Theatre,** and major shopping areas such as the enclosed pedestrian streets **Shinsaibashi-Suji** and **America-Mura** (check out the unique street lamps!) with imported goods from America. Farther south is **Dogayasuji,** famous for

 A NOTE ON directions

For all the attractions, accommodations, and restaurants listed below, I've included the nearest subway or JR station followed by the walking time to the establishment once you reach the indicated station (in parentheses).

cooking supplies; and **Den Den Town,** Osaka's electronics and anime district. Connecting Kita-ku with Namba is Osaka's main street, **Midosuji Dori,** a wide boulevard lined with gingko trees and international name-brand shops.

AROUND TENNOJI   At the south end of the JR Loop Line is **Tennoji-ku,** which was once a thriving temple town with **Shitennoji Temple** at its center. In addition to a park with a zoo, it boasts **Spa World,** one of Japan's biggest and most luxurious public bathhouses, and **Q's Mall.**

OSAKA BAY & PORT   West of the city, Osaka's well-developed waterfront offers a quick getaway for Osakans wishing to escape urban life. In addition to its domestic and international ferry terminals, Osaka Bay is where you will find **Universal Studios Japan,** one of Japan's major draws; and **Tempozan Harbour Village** with its shopping mall and first-class aquarium.

GETTING AROUND

Despite its size, I find Osaka easier to get around than other large Japanese cities because there are lots of English-language signs and information. The exception is Osaka Station, used for JR trains, and its adjoining Umeda Station, used by subway lines and private railway lines Hankyu and Hanshin. Underground passages and shopping arcades complicate navigation; there's no escaping—you will get lost.

When exploring by foot, it helps to know that most roads running east and west end in *"dori"* (street), while roads running north and south end in *"suji,"* which means "avenue."

BY SUBWAY   The **Osaka Municipal Transportation Bureau** (www.kotsu.city. osaka.jp; © **06/6211-9503**) operates Osaka's user-friendly subway network, which is easy to use because all lines are color-coded and the station names are in English (even English-language announcements are on many lines). Lines run from about 5am to midnight. Of the 8 lines, the red **Midosuji Line** is the most important one for visitors; it passes through Shin-Osaka Station and on to Umeda (the subway station next to Osaka Station), Shinsaibashi, Namba, and Tennoji. Fares begin at ¥200 and increase according to the distance traveled; or, purchase a prepaid **Rainbow Card** for ¥500 to ¥3,000 to prevent having to buy an individual ticket each time. For more information on tickets and passes, stop by the **Osaka Municipal Transportation Access** office at Namba Station (© **06/6211-9503**), open Monday to Friday 9am to 7pm and weekends and holidays 10am to 7pm.

Transportation Passes: If you think you'll be traveling a lot by subway on a given day, consider purchasing a **1-Day Enjoy Eco Card** for ¥800 (¥600 weekends and holidays), which allows unlimited rides on subways and buses all day and offers slight discounts to several attractions. Or, there's the **Osaka Unlimited 1-Day Pass,** which costs ¥2,000 and allows unlimited rides on subways, city buses, and private railways in Osaka plus free entrance to 20-some attractions, including Osaka Castle, Floating Garden Observatory, Shitennoji Temple, Museum of Oriental Ceramics, and Osaka International Peace Center. If you're a visitor to Japan, you're also entitled to the **Osaka Unlimited 2-Day Pass** for ¥2,700, valid for travel on subways and buses and providing the same free admission as the 1-Day pass but for 2 days; for this you must show your passport. Passes are available at the Osaka Visitors' Information Centers and at the Osaka Municipal Transportation Access office in Namba (see above). Note that JR trains are not included in any of these passes.

For trips outside Osaka, the **Kansai Thru Pass** (**Surutto Kansai;** www.surutto. com) allows foreigners (you must show your passport) to ride subways, private railways (no JR trains), and buses throughout Kansai, including Osaka, Kyoto, Kobe, Nara, and Mount Koya, with a 2-day pass costing ¥3,800 and a 3-day pass costing ¥5,000. The pass also gives slight discounts to various tourist sights and is available at the KIX Travel Desk (next to the tourist office) or at the Visitor Information Centers in Osaka, but you'd have to do quite a bit of traveling to make this worthwhile.

BY JR TRAIN   A Japan Railways train called the Osaka Kanjo Line, or **JR Loop Line,** passes through Osaka Station and makes a loop around the central part of the city (similar to the Yamanote Line in Tokyo); take it to visit Osaka Castle. Fares begin at ¥120, but you can ride for free with a valid Japan Rail Pass.

[FastFACTS] OSAKA

Consulates   Several embassies maintain consulates in Osaka, including **Australia** (☏ **06/6941-9448**); **Great Britain** (☏ **06/6120-5600**); **New Zealand** (☏ **06/6373-4583**); and the **United States** (☏ **06/6315-5900**).

Internet Access   Near the Midosuji south exit of Osaka Station is an area called Float Court, where on the second floor is **X-Time** (☏ **06/6341-8222**), open daily 10am to 11pm and charging ¥100 for 15 minutes or ¥600 for 2 hours of computer use. In Namba, there's a **Gran Cyber Cafe** on Osaka's nightlife street on the second floor of the Nakaza Cuidaore Building, 1–7–19 Dotombori (☏ **06/6484-2660**), open 24 hours and charging ¥150 for 30 minutes.

Mail & ATM   The Central Post Office, or Osaka Chuo Yubinkyoku, is in the Osaka Ekimae No. 1 Building, 1–3–1 Umeda, Kita-ku (☏ **06/6347-8112**), a 5-minute walk south of Osaka Station. It's open for mail daily 9am to 6pm; its ATM service for international credit cards is available 12:05am to 11:55pm Monday to Saturday and from 12:05am to 9pm Sunday and holidays.

Exploring Osaka
NEAR OSAKA STATION
Floating Garden Observatory (Kuchu Teien Tenbodai) OBSERVATION DECK   This futuristic observatory 167m (557 ft.) high looks like a space ship floating between the two towers of the Umeda Sky Building. Take the superfast glass elevator from the East Tower building's third floor; you'll then take a free-standing, glass-enclosed escalator that bridges the two towers before depositing you on the 39th floor. I'm not afraid of heights, but taking an escalator over thin air in an earthquake-plagued nation always catches my attention; it makes the "floating" observatory feel safe in comparison. From here, you have an unparalleled view of Osaka, making it a popular nightspot for couples on dates. The open-air rooftop deck, famous for its sunset views, features a promenade with phosphorescent stones that glow in the dark and a bench that "measures" the degree of love for couples who sit on it. My own interest in the place, however, has waned since the female attendants stopped wearing cone-shaped hats.

Shin Umeda City, Umeda Sky Building, Oyodo-naka, Kita-ku. www.kuchu-teien.com. ☏ **06/6440-3855.** Admission ¥700 adults, ¥500 junior-high and high-school students and seniors, ¥300 children. Daily 10am–10:30pm. Station: JR Osaka or Umeda (Central North exit of JR Osaka Station, 8 min.). Walk past Yodobashi Camera and the car park to the first intersection, turn left, and take the underpass.

Joypolis Sega Umeda ★ ☺ GAMES ARCADE   I suppose it could be argued that you haven't experienced today's Japan unless you've visited at least one Joypolis, the reigning king of amusement arcades. This one, on the eighth and ninth floors of a youth-oriented shopping arcade complete with a Ferris wheel on top, overloads the senses with lots of flashing lights, bells and whistles, and throngs of squealing kids and teenagers. In addition to arcade games and slot machines, virtual rides simulate gliding through the air or shooting the rapids of a wild river. ***Note:*** Children 15 and under aren't allowed here after 7pm, those 17 and under aren't allowed after 10pm and some "rides" carry height restrictions, with rules enforced by what—the joy police?

HEP FIVE, 5–15 Kakuda-cho, Kita-ku. Ⓒ **06/6366-3647.** Free admission; attractions ¥600. Daily 11am–11pm (you must enter by 10:15pm). Station: JR Osaka or Umeda (4 min.).

Museum of Oriental Ceramics (Toyotoji Bijutsukan) ★★★ 🏛 MUSEUM
This modern facility, about a 15-minute walk south of Osaka Station on Nakanoshima Island in the Dojima River, is my favorite museum in Osaka. Indeed, its 4,000-piece collection of Chinese, Korean, and Japanese ceramics—of which 400 are on display at any one time on a rotating basis—ranks as one of the finest in the world. Built specifically for the collection, the museum does a superb job showcasing the exquisite pieces as the masterpieces they truly are, in darkened rooms that utilize natural light and computerized natural-light simulation. Korean celadon, Chinese ceramics from the Song and Ming dynasties, Chinese snuff bottles, Arita ware from the Edo Period, works by Hamada Shoji, are just some of the items that might be on display. Even if you've never given ceramics more than a passing glance, you're likely to come away with a heightened sense of appreciation. You'll want to spend 30 minutes or more here.

1–1–26 Nakanoshima, Kita-ku. www.moco.or.jp. Ⓒ **06/6223-0055.** Admission ¥500 adults, ¥300 students, free for children. Tues–Sun 9:30am–5pm. Closed during exhibition changes. Station: Naniwabashi on the Keihan Nakanoshima Line (exit 1, 1 min.) or Yodoyabashi (exit 1, 1 min.).

AROUND OSAKA CASTLE

Osaka Castle (Osaka-jo) ★★ CASTLE   First built in the 1580s on the order of Toyotomi Hideyoshi, Osaka Castle was the largest castle in Japan, a magnificent structure used by Toyotomi as a military stronghold from which to wage war against rebellious feudal lords in far-flung provinces. By the time he died in 1598, Toyotomi had accomplished what no man had done before: crushed his enemies and unified all of Japan under his command.

After Toyotomi's death, Tokugawa Ieyasu seized power and established his shogunate government in Edo. But Toyotomi's heirs had ideas of their own: Considering Osaka Castle impregnable, they plotted to overthrow the Tokugawa government. In 1615, Tokugawa sent troops to Osaka where they not only annihilated the Toyotomi insurrectionists but destroyed Osaka Castle. The Tokugawas rebuilt the castle in 1629, but the main tower was destroyed by lightning 36 years later, and the rest burned in 1868 as the shogunate made their last stand against imperial forces in what later became known as the Meiji Restoration.

The present Osaka Castle, surrounded by a massive park famous for its cherry trees and stone-walled moats, dates from 1931 and was extensively renovated in 1997. Built of ferroconcrete, it's not as massive as the original but is still one of Japan's most famous castles and is impressive with its massive stone walls, black and gold-leaf trim, and copper roof. Its eight-story *donjon* (keep) rises 39m (130 ft.), with a top-floor observatory offering bird's-eye views of the city. The rest of the donjon houses a high-tech museum that uses videos, holograms, models, replicas, and artifacts to describe the life and times of Toyotomi Hideyoshi and history of the castle. Be sure to pick up the free audio guide, as some explanations are in Japanese only, but there's plenty to see as well, including a folding screen with meticulously painted scenes of the intense fighting that took place between Toyotomi and Tokugawa forces, samurai armor and gear, a full-scale reproduction of Toyotomi's Gold Tea Room, and a model of Osaka Castle during the Toyotomi Era. If you want, you can have your photo taken in period clothing for ¥300. Plan on about 45 minutes here.

1–1 Osakajo, Chuo-ku. www.osakacastle.net. ℂ **06/6941-3044.** Admission ¥600 adults, free for children 15 and under. Daily 9am–5pm. Station: Osakajo-Koen on the JR Loop Line or Morinomiya (15 min.); or Temmabashi or Osaka Business Park (10 min.).

Osaka International Peace Center (Peace Osaka) ★ MUSEUM Located on the southern edge of Osaka Castle Park, this museum strives for global peace by educating present and future generations about the horrors of war, related by those who survived it. Unlike other museums in Japan dedicated to peace—including those in Hiroshima and Nagasaki—this one does not shy away from Japan's role in the Asian conflict, including its war campaign in China, the abduction of Koreans to work in dangerous areas, and massacres committed by Japanese in Singapore, Malaysia, and elsewhere. But its main focus is on wartime death and destruction, with personal testimonies of air raid survivors (15,000 people died during World War II air raids on Osaka), displays centering on suicide attacks by *kamikaze* pilots at the end of the war, graphic photographs of Hiroshima and Nagasaki after the atomic bombs were dropped, and a section devoted to the horrors of the Auschwitz concentration camp. You'll probably spend 30 sobering minutes here.

2–1 Osakajo, Chuo-ku. www.peace-osaka.or.jp. ℂ **06/6947-7208.** Admission ¥250 adults, ¥150 high-school students, free for children and seniors. Tues–Sun 9:30am–5pm. Closed on days following national holidays and last day of each month. Station: Morinomiya (3 min.) or Osakajo-Koen (8 min.).

AROUND TENNOJI

Shitennoji Temple TEMPLE Founded over 1,400 years ago as the first—and therefore oldest—officially established temple in Japan, Shitennoji Temple is the spiritual heart of Osaka. It was constructed in 593 by Prince Shotoku, who is credited with introducing Buddhism to Japan and remains a revered, popular figure even today. However, like most wooden structures in Japan, the temple's buildings have been destroyed repeatedly through the centuries by fire and war, including the 1615 Tokugawa raid on Osaka Castle and World War II. And through the centuries, the buildings have been faithfully reconstructed exactly as they were in the 6th century, with the Central Precinct (*Garan*) consisting of the Inner Gate, the five-story Buddhist Pagoda, the Main Hall with its statue of Prince Shotoku as the Buddha of Infinite Mercy, and the Lecture Hall all on a north-south axis. Be sure, too, to wander the temple's Gokuraku-Jodo Teien, a restored Japanese landscape garden first laid out during the Tokugawa regime. Buddhists believe that if you follow the path between the two streams representing greed and anger, you will symbolically reach Paradise, a place of sublime beauty, tranquility, and peace.

1–11–18 Shitennoji, Tennoji-ku. ℂ **06/6771-0066.** Admission to either Garan or garden, ¥300 adults, ¥200 students and children. Daily 8:30am–4:30pm (garden daily 10am–4pm). Station: Shitennoji-mae Yuhigaoka (exit 4, 5 min.); or JR Tennoji (north exit, 10 min.).

Spa World ★ ☺ SPA This is one of the most luxurious and ambitious bathhouses I've seen. Accommodating up to 5,000 people, it draws upon hot springs 890m (2,970 ft.) below the earth's surface. On its roof, in a large hangarlike room, is a covered swimming complex that includes a pool, various water slides (¥300 extra for some rides), a kids' pool with aquatic activities, and a sunning terrace with Jacuzzi. You wear your swimming suits here (rental suits available). For a more grown-up experience, the rest of the large complex is divided into themed, geographical bathing zones, which are rotated between the sexes (no suits allowed) and include luxurious locker rooms. At the Asian Zone, for example, Middle Eastern music and tiled mosaics set the tone for the Turkish bath, while Japan is represented by outdoor baths. Massage, sauna, mud packs, and hot stone and moxibustion treatments are available. If you're timid about going to a public bath, this one will convert you. If you're already a fan, you'll want to move in. But sorry, people with tattoos—associated with the Japanese mafia—aren't allowed.

3–2–24 Ebisu-higashi, Naniwa-ku. www.spaworld.co.jp/english. © **06/6631-0001.** Admission weekdays: ¥2,400 adults, ¥1,300 children for 3 hr.; ¥2,700 adults, ¥1,500 children for all day. Weekends: ¥2,700 adults, ¥1,500 children for 3 hr.; ¥3,000 adults, ¥1,700 children for all day. Daily 10am–8:45am the next morning. Station: Shin-Imamiya or Dobutsuenmae (2 min.).

OSAKA BAY AREA

Osaka Aquarium (Kaiyukan) ★★★ ☺ AQUARIUM   Of the many aquariums in Japan, this one is among the best. It's constructed around the theme "Ring of Fire," which refers to the volcanic perimeter encircling the Pacific Ocean. Visits begin through a tunnel filled with reef fish and small sharks, followed by an escalator ride to the eighth floor. From there you'll pass through 15 different habitats ranging from arctic to tropical as you follow a spiraling corridor back to the ground floor, starting with the daylight world—a Japanese forest—above the ocean's surface and proceeding past the Aleutian Islands, Monterey Bay, South American rainforests, Antarctica, the Great Barrier Reef, and other ecosystems as you travel to the depths of the ocean floor. The walls of the aquarium tank are constructed of huge acrylic glass sheets, making you feel as if you're immersed in the ocean; piped-in classical music transforms swimming fish into performances of aquatic choreography. You'll see 30,000 specimens representing 580 species; stars of the show include whale sharks (the largest fish in captivity), Antarctic penguins, the odd-looking ocean sunfish (which has the circumference of a truck tire but is as flat as a pancake), and the Japan giant spider crab with its incredible 3m (9¾-ft.) span. English-spoken audio guides are available for ¥300. Allow about 1½ hours to tour the aquarium, avoiding weekends.

1–1–10 Kaigan-dori, Minato-ku. www.kaiyukan.com. © **06/6576-5501.** Admission ¥2,000 adults, ¥900 children 7–15, ¥400 children 4–6, free for children 3 and under. Daily 10am–8pm. Closed 7 days a year (in June and in winter). Station: Osakako (5 min.).

Mutineers Need Not Apply

The quickest and most scenic way to travel between Osaka Aquarium and Universal Studios is via the *Captain Line* shuttle boat (© **06/6573-8222**) with its all-female crew, which departs every 30 to 60 minutes and charges ¥600 for the 10-minute ride (children ride for half price). Tip: A combination ticket for the boat and aquarium shaves ¥300 off the adult price.

Universal Studios Japan ★★★ ☺

THEME PARK   Following the tradition of Universal's Hollywood and Orlando theme parks, this park takes guests on a fantasy trip through the world of American blockbuster movies, with thrill rides, live entertainment, back-lot streets, restaurants, shops, and other attractions based on actual movies. Board a boat for a harrowing encounter with a great white straight out of *Jaws,* escape a T-Rex as you roller-coaster your way through a setting of *Jurassic Park,* dream your way through the mega-coaster *Hollywood Dream,* fly and leap at high speed among skyscrapers in the 3-D *Amazing Adventures of Spider Man—The Ride,* and see, feel, and smell *Sesame Street 4-D Movie Magic* or *Shrek's 4-D Adventure* (4-D in movie lingo means there are smells and other sensations). Universal Wonderland features rides and attractions (think Snoopy, Hello Kitty, and Elmo) for the wee ones. Unfortunately, most of the attractions have been dubbed into Japanese (I wonder why the original English isn't available on audio guide), so it helps to know the movies beforehand. Plan for an entire day here, but note that it is immensely popular: Avoid weekends, arrive early, and buy a Universal Express Pass Booklet, which allows priority entry into designated rides (the price of these varies by type, age, and advance purchase, so check the website). Alternatively, choose the "single" line for lone riders, which you will get you inside attractions up to three times quicker than regular lines.

2–1–33 Sakurajima, Konohana. www.usj.co.jp. ℗ **06/6465-3000.** Studio Pass to all attractions ¥6,200 adults, ¥5,500 seniors, ¥4,100 children 4–11. Hours vary according to the season; generally daily 10am–5pm in winter, 9am–8:30 or 9pm in summer, and 9 or 10am–7pm the rest of the year. Station: Universal City (5 min.).

IN NEARBY TAKARAZUKA

Northwest of Osaka, the town of Takarazuka (in Hyogo Prefecture) is synonymous with the all-female **Takarazuka Troupe.** Founded in 1914 to attract vacationers to Takarazuka, the troupe proved instantly popular with the general public, whose taste turned from traditional Japanese drama to lively Western musicals and entertainment. Performances are held at the **Takarazuka Grand Theatre;** 1–1–57 Sakaemachi (www.kageki.hankyu.co.jp/english; ℗ **0570/00-5100;** station: Takarazuka) most days throughout the year (closed Wed), usually at 1pm or at 11am and 3pm, depending on the season and days of the week. Tickets range from ¥3,500 to ¥11,000. For more information on the troupe, see "Takarazuka Kagekidan" on p. 160.

Where to Eat

There's a saying among Japanese that whereas a Kyotoite will spend his last yen on a fine kimono, an Osakan will spend it on food, not surprising given Osaka's historic role as a distribution center for rice and produce, earning it the nickname of the "nation's kitchen." You don't have to spend a lot of money, however, to enjoy good food. Local specialties include **Oshi-zushi** (pressed square-shaped sushi), *udon* noodles with white soy sauce, and *takoyaki* (wheat-flour dumplings with octopus).

Osaka is probably best known, however, for *okonomiyaki,* which literally means "as you like it." Its origins date from about 1700, when a type of thin flour pancake cooked on a hot plate and filled with miso paste was served during Buddhist ceremonies. It wasn't until the 20th century that it became popular, primarily during food shortages, and gradually, other ingredients such as pork, egg, and cabbage were added. Today, Osaka is riddled with inexpensive okonomiyaki restaurants—more than 4,000 of them.

AROUND OSAKA STATION
Moderate

Enoteca ★ CONTINENTAL   Shelves filled with wine bottles line the walls of this upscale shop, in the back of which is a casual restaurant specializing in meals that complement our favorite form of the grape. The relaxed ambience and reasonably priced food drew us in (okay, so the wine had something to do with it), but what better way to imbibe a celebratory glass or two than with selections of cheese, salad, quiche, a classic beef stew, lasagne, or the day's lunch? The menu is limited, but the fun part is selecting a bottle from the shop to accompany your meal. A ¥1,000 corkage fee is applied only after 5pm and is waived on Mondays; they also offer wine by the glass.

Herbis Plaza, 2nd floor, 2–5–25 Umeda. ℂ **06/6343-7175.** Main dishes ¥1,000–¥1,800; set lunches ¥840–¥1,155. AE, DC, MC, V. Daily 11am–9:30pm (last order). Station: Nishi-Umeda (3 min.). Southeast of Osaka Station in the Herbis Plaza complex adjacent to the Ritz-Carlton.

Inexpensive

In addition to the choices here, there's a **Fugetsu** okonomiyaki branch on the 8th floor of Yodobashi Camera; see p. 368.

Capricciosa (カプリチオーザ) ☺ PIZZA/PASTA This chain restaurant is very popular with students and families for its pizza and pasta, with pastas available in regular size (good for one person) or large size for hearty appetites or two diners. The English-language menu lists everything from pizza *capricciosa* (with bacon, salami, onion, and more) to spaghetti with eggplant and spinach in meat sauce. The salads are big enough for two to share. While the cheesy decor and fake plants just don't do it for me, a walk through Yodobashi Camera shop with its endless stock is a trip.

There's a branch in the Namba Oriental Hotel Building, 2–8–17 Sennichimae (ℂ **06/6644-8330;** station: Midosuji), open daily 11am to 10:30pm (last order).

Yodobashi Camera, 8th floor, 1–1 Obukacho. ℂ **06/6486-2271.** Pizza ¥1,090–¥1,530; pasta ¥950–¥1,010 for small sizes, ¥1,280–¥1,920 for large sizes. AE, DC, MC, V. Daily 11am–10:30pm (last order). Station: JR Osaka or Umeda (1 min.). Just north of the station.

Okonomiyaki Kiji (お好み焼きじ) OKONOMIYAKI Takimikoji Village, located in the basement of the same building as the Floating Garden Observatory (p. 361), is a fun place for a meal. It's a re-created Showa-Era 1920s and 1930s Japanese village, boasting everything from an old-fashioned sweets shop and a barbershop to a post office and a miniature shrine. There are also about a dozen small restaurants here, including those serving ramen, soba, udon, shabu-shabu and this one offering what some Osakans swear is the best *okonomiyaki* in town. Queues of people waiting to get in are common, but your order is taken while you wait so when you finally sit down at one of the four tables or counter, your order arrives quickly. Until then you can gaze upon customer photos and *meishi* (business cards) that paper the walls and ceiling.

Umeda Sky Building basement, 1–1–90 Oyodo-naka. ℂ **06/6440-5970.** Okonomiyaki ¥600–¥900. No credit cards. Fri–Wed 11:30am–9:30pm. Station: JR Osaka or Umeda (Central North exit of JR Osaka Station, 8 min.). Walk past Yodobashi Camera and the car park to the first intersection, turn left, and take the underpass.

AROUND OSAKA CASTLE
Inexpensive

Panorama Sky Restaurant Asahi 🍴 VARIED WESTERN Views and the beer are the best reasons to pay a visit to this Asahi beer hall. The nonsmoking section has the best views of the castle (unless the space is claimed by a private party), while the more atmospheric smoking section has city views. Popular with area office workers, it offers salads, pizza, spaghetti, grilled spareribs, pan-fried Norwegian salmon, fish-and-chips, fried chicken and a few other choices. Portions aren't large—think tapas—but a couple dishes should do the job. The limited lunch sets come with salad, rice, vegetables, and all-you-can-drink tea, coffee, or juice. Or, come for a snack and wash it down with a mug or two of Asahi beer.

IMP Building, 26th floor, 1–3–7 Shiromi Chuo-ku. © **06/6946-2595.** Main dishes ¥800–¥1,500; set lunches ¥900–¥1,800. AE, DC, MC, V. Mon–Fri 11:30am–2pm and 4:30–10pm; Sat–Sun and holidays 11:30am–10pm. Subway: Osaka Business Park (exit 1, 1 min.). JR train: Osakajo-Koen (4 min.). In Osaka Business Park, across from the New Otani Hotel.

NAMBA

Dotombori (or Dotonbori), a narrow pedestrian lane just off Midosuji Dori that flanks the south bank of the Dotombori River Walk, is the center of Osaka's most famous nightlife district, which radiates from Dotombori on both sides of the canal; you'll find lots of restaurants and bars in this area.

Expensive

Kani Doraku (かに道楽) CRAB   Specializing in *kani* (crab), this restaurant is difficult to miss: It has a huge model crab on its facade, moving its legs and claws. Part of a chain originating in Osaka 50 years ago, this is the main shop of dozens of locations throughout Japan, including another one just down the street at 1–6–2 Dotonbori (© **06/6211-1633**). Dishes range from *kani-suki, ckani-chiri* (a kind of crab sukiyaki), and fried crab dishes to crab croquette, roasted crab with salt, crab salad, crab sushi, and boiled king crab. The easiest thing to do, however, is to order a set meal from the display case outside or from the menu with its photos. This main location occupies several floors, with some tables offering a view of the canal.

1–6–18 Dotonbori. © **06/6211-8975.** Set dinners ¥3,990–¥8,000; set lunches ¥2,000–¥4,000. AE, DC, MC, V. Daily 11am–10pm (last order). Station: Namba (exit 14, 2 min.). On Dotombori beside the Ebisu-bashi Bridge.

Moderate

Yume-Hachi VARIED JAPANESE   I was sad to see the old Cuidaore restaurant, a Dotonbori landmark for more than 50 years, close its doors, but the restaurant's famous clown model, beating a drum and wiggling its eyebrows, still stands at the entrance to the renovated building, making it easy to find this hip restaurant/bar. What I like most is the venue's open-air patio, but it also offers all-you-can-eat-in-2-hours dining options for hearty appetites: From 5 to 9:30pm, it offers a 2-hour buffet for ¥2,980, including drinks like wine and beer (¥3,480 if you prefer whiskey and other drinks); from 9:30pm to 6am, set meals allow you to order as much as you want from a food and drink menu within 2 hours. Or, simply order a drink or snack (like edamame, pasta, salad, pizza, curry rice, desserts), all priced at ¥330, plus a ¥346 table charge for people ordering a la carte. In any case, this is a good place to sober up after a round of drinking in Dotonbori.

Cuidaore Building, 5th floor, 1–7–21 Dotonbori. © **06/6211-0033.** Main dishes ¥330; dinner buffets ¥2,980–¥3,400; all-you-can-eat set courses ¥2,625–¥3,675. AE, DC, MC, V. Open daily 24 hrs. Station: Namba (exit 14, 3 min.). On Dotombori.

Inexpensive

Bar Tachibana (たちばな) TOFU/VARIED JAPANESE   Whether you're sightseeing in Dotombori or here for *kabuki*, this restaurant, in a lovely, typical Japanese setting in the basement of the Shochikuza Theater, is a good pick. A microbrewery that makes its own beer on site (¥450 for a glass of light or dark beer), Tachibana also specializes in tofu (only in Japan!), with tofu included in most of the set meals. In winter it also offers *fugu* (blowfish). There's no English-language menu, but a changing daily lunch and the *tofu teishoku* (¥2,600) are affordable and delicious, and the menu has photos of its set meals. You can see famous kabuki actors dining here, but how could you recognize them without their makeup?

Osaka Shochikuza Theater, 2nd basement, 1–9–19 Dotonbori. ☎ **06/6212-6074.** Main dishes ¥680–¥1,700; set dinners ¥2,600–¥5,800; set lunches ¥850–¥3,800. AE, DC, MC, V. Daily 11:30am–10pm (last order). Station: Namba (exit 14, 2 min.). On Dotombori near the bridge; look for its improbable side entrance to the right and then take the escalator to the second basement.

Fugetsu (風月) OKONOMIYAKI   Big Step is the biggest shopping complex in America-Mura, young Osakans' favorite place to shop for American clothing. As such, this branch of a famous *okonomiyaki* restaurant appeals to young diners with its hip, modern interior, pop music, and individual booths for dining. The English-language menu gives various options, from *yakisoba* to okonomiyaki with pork and egg. There are more than 20 Fugetsu restaurants in Osaka, including outlets in Yodobashi Camera near Osaka Station, 1–1 Obukacho (☎ **06/6377-2319**); at Spa World, 3–2–24 Ebisu-higashi (☎ **06/6631-0373**); and in Universal CityWalk next to Universal Studios, 6–2–61 Shimaya (☎ **06/6463-0030**).

Big Step, 3rd floor, 1–6–14 Nishi-Shinsaibashi. ☎ **06/6258-5189.** Okonomiyaki and yakisoba ¥600–¥1,230. AE, MC, V. Daily 11am–9:30pm (last order). Station: Shinsaibashi (2 min.).

Honfukuzushi (本福寿司) ★★ 🍴 SUSHI   More than just a place to dine, this sushi shop, in operation for more than 180 years, is part of the Osaka experience. Back in the old days, sushi shops were strictly takeout operations, with customers bringing in their own dishes, placing their orders, and then returning home to wait for *geta*-clad deliverers. Nowadays you eat your sushi here; best are the counter seats, where you can watch sushi being pressed in wooden molds, Osaka style. A Japanese-language menu with photos, a display case at the entryway, and a friendly staff can help with ordering. Or, if you just want to try *oshi-zushi* (Osakan sushi), order the *hakozushi*, which comes with six pieces for ¥950. Tokyo-style *nigiri* and *maki*-sushi are also available.

1–4–19 Nishi-Shinsaibashi-suji. ☎ **06/6271-3344.** Sushi sets ¥950–¥3,300; set lunches ¥800–¥1,050. AE, MC, V. Daily 11am–8pm (last order). Station: Shinsaibashi (2 min.). Inside the Shinsaibashi covered shopping arcade, behind the main (oldest) Daimaru department store; look for the old delivery bike parked out front.

Namaste ★★ INDIAN   This is a good place for hot and spicy Indian food, including tandoori and chicken, mutton, prawn, fish, and vegetable curries. The owner, who will wait on you, is so friendly and happy you might think he's reached nirvana. You can reach yours by telling him how hot to make your food. The set lunches are a particularly great deal.

Rose Building, 3–7–28 Minami Semba. ☎ **06/6241-6515.** Main dishes ¥1,080–¥1,500; set dinners ¥2,800–¥4,300; set lunches ¥785–¥1,980. AE, DC, MC, V. Daily 11:30am–3pm and 5:30–11pm. Station: Shinsaibashi (exit 1, 3 min.). 3 blocks north of the Midosuji/Nagahori Dori intersection; walk north on Midosuji Dori, turn east (right) at the Rolex shop and walk past the Shinsaibashi-Suji covered pedestrian shopping street; it will be on the right.

IN TENNOJI
Expensive
Matsumura (まつむら) ★★ 🍴 VARIED JAPANESE/NABE/KAISEKI   Built about 100 years ago for a member of the famous Sumitomo family, this Japanese-style house is a memorable place for a splurge. A kimono-clad hostess will lead you to your low table with tatami seating, where you might have a good view of the courtyard garden. Set meals (available all day) vary with the season, with nabe, fugu, and crab, for example, popular in winter. Although expensive for dinner or for kaiseki, its set lunches are reasonable and delicious.

1–24 Hidennincho. © **06/6771-0421.** Reservations required for kaiseki. Kaiseki meals ¥4,200–¥13,560; set meals ¥3,800–¥9,000; set lunches ¥1,600–¥3,000. AE, DC, MC, V. Daily 11am–10pm. Station: Tennoji (2 min.). Walk north from Tennoji JR Station on Tanimachi-suji St. and turn right at 7-Eleven; it will be on the left, just past the small parking lot.

Shopping

Osaka is famous in Japan for shopping, in no small part because of the discerning nature of the Osakans themselves. Osaka, after all, developed as a commercial town of merchants—and who knows merchandise better than the merchants themselves?

Osaka must rank as one of the world's leading cities in underground shopping arcades. Enter the vast underground arcades in Umeda (where the JR, Hanshin, subway, and Hankyu train lines intersect) with such names as **Whity Umeda, Hankyu Sanbangai, Diamor Osaka,** and **Dojima Underground Shopping Center,** and you may never emerge in this lifetime. **Crysta Nagahori,** connecting Nagahoribashi Station to Yotsubashi-suji, has a glass atrium ceiling, flowing streams of water, and 100 shops, making it one of the largest—if not the largest—shopping malls in Japan. Nearby are **Namba Walk, Nan-nan Town,** and **Namba City,** all interconnected by underground passageways.

There are plenty of aboveground shopping options as well. **Midosuji Dori,** a wide boulevard lined with gingko trees running north and south in the heart of the city, is the city's calling card for name-brand international boutiques, but here, too, is the lovely old **Daimaru** department store, with newer annexes on both sides. Just to the east is **Shinsaibashi-suji,** a covered promenade with many long-established shops, some dating back to the Edo Period. On the other side of Midosuji Dori is **America-Mura,** a popular spot for young Japanese shopping for T-shirts, Hawaiian shirts, ripped jeans, and other American fashions at inflated prices; its biggest marketplace is **Big Step.** Teens also flock to **Marui 0101,** a seven-story department store on the corner of Shinsaibashi-suji and Nankai Dori, and to **HEP FIVE,** a huge shopping complex near Umeda Station with a Joypolis amusement arcade and a Ferris wheel on top. At JR Osaka Station is the 10-story **Isetan Mitsukoshi** department store and **Yodobashi Camera** with computers, watches, bikes, luggage, and more in addition to cameras.

One of the most fun places to shop—or simply browse—is at one of Osaka's famous shopping areas specializing in specific goods. In the heart of the city, just east of Sakaisuji Avenue near Nipponbashi Station, is **Kuromon Ichiba,** a covered street where professional chefs shop for seafood, fruit, vegetables, pickles, and other edibles. It's worth a stroll for local color. To the south, a few blocks east of Nankai Namba Station, is **Sennichimae Doguya-suji,** a covered shopping lane with about 45 open-fronted shops selling all the pots, pans, dishes, and implements you'd ever need to prepare and serve Japanese food. Chopsticks, chopstick rests, pottery, lacquerware, frying pans, aprons, trays, kitchen knives, rice bowls, plastic food, and lots of gift ideas are here at very inexpensive prices.

Just south of that is **Den Den Town,** stretching along Sakaisuji Avenue and its side streets (Station: Ebisucho). This is Osaka's electronics shopping region (*Den* is short for "electric"), similar to Tokyo's Akihabara but not as big. Some 200 open-fronted shops here deal in electrical and electronic equipment, from rice cookers and refrigerators to DVD players, MP3 players, calculators, cameras, and computers. As in Tokyo, shops specializing in *manga, anime,* and costumes have also moved in, especially on Sakaisuji. **Animate,** 4–10–6 Nipponbashi (© **06/6636-0628**), offers two floors of the latest manga and anime books and goods. Like most shops here, Animate is open daily 10am to 8pm. Stop by the **Nipponbashi Information Center,** just north of Ebisucho Station on Sakaisuji (© **06/6655-1717;** daily 11am–7pm) for a free English map of the area. Another fun neighborhood to explore is **Matsuyama-chi-suji** (station: Matsuyamachi), a shop-lined street specializing in dolls, toys, anime figures, and seasonal party decorations.

Of Osaka's many shopping complexes, worth noting is **Rinkan Premium Outlets** near KIX airport (station: Rinku Town), one of the largest outlet malls in Japan and offering some 150 shops and even shuttle bus service from the airport (fare: ¥100). Osaka's largest mall is **Q's Mall** (station: Tennoji), with 250 stores and restaurants, including Tokyu Hands for the home hobbyist and Uniqlo clothing store.

Entertainment & Nightlife

PERFORMING ARTS

BUNRAKU   The **National Bunraku Theater,** 1–12–10 Nipponbashi, Chuo-ku (www.ntj.jac.go.jp; © **06/6212-2531** for information, or 0570/07-9900 for reservations), was completed in 1984 as the only theater in Japan dedicated to Japanese traditional puppet theater. Productions are staged five times a year, with most productions running for about 3 weeks and held daily at 11am for Part 1 and at 4pm for Part 2; each part requires a separate ticket, with prices ranging from ¥2,300 to ¥5,800. English-language programs are available. When *bunraku* is not being performed, other traditional performing arts are often shown, including classical Japanese music. The National Bunraku Theater is located east of Namba and the Dotombori entertainment district, a 1-minute walk from exit 7 of Nipponbashi Station.

KABUKI   The **Osaka Shochikuza,** 1–9–19 Dotombori, Chuo-ku (www.kabuki-bito.jp/eng/contents/theatre/shochiku-za.html; © **06/6214-2211;** station: Namba), was first built in 1923 but was remodeled in 1997 as part of a revival of interest in *kabuki.* Traditional kabuki is performed in January, July, and some other months of the year (the schedule changes yearly), and performances start usually at 11am and 4:30pm, with tickets ranging from ¥5,000 to ¥16,000 for major performances. The theater is located on Dotombori, just west of the Ebisu-bashi Bridge.

LIVE MUSIC   **Billboard Live Osaka,** Basement 2 of the Herbis Plaza ENT Building, 2–2–22 Umeda (© **06/6342-7722;** station: Nishi-Umeda), offers live music ranging from jazz and R&B to J-pop, funk, and soul, with a great sound system and several levels surrounding the stage providing good views. There are usually two shows nightly, with the cheapest tickets (for standing room only) ranging from about ¥5,000 to ¥8,500 for most shows and ¥6,500 to ¥12,500 for reserved seating. Smaller, less high-tech and more affordable is **Rug Time Osaka,** on the fourth floor of the Across Building, 2–6–14 Shinsaibashi Suji (© **06/6214-5306;** station: Namba or Shinsaibashi), which offers a wide range of live jazz bands in three nightly sets, with cover charge ranging from ¥2,000 to ¥3,000. It's open Monday to Saturday 5pm to 2am, Sunday and holidays from 5pm to midnight.

THE BAR SCENE

Osaka's liveliest—and most economical—nightlife district radiates from a narrow pedestrian lane called **Dotombori** (or Dotonbori), which flanks the south bank of the Dotombori Canal. About a 2-minute walk from exit 14 of Namba Station or less than a 10-minute walk from Shinsaibashi Station, it's lined with restaurants and drinking establishments and is good for a lively evening stroll even if you don't wish to stop anywhere.

Cinquecento   This bar is a cut above the rest with its welcoming atmosphere and decent Western fare (including burgers, pasta, pizza, and fish and chips), not to mention that all food and drink are priced at only ¥500. Of note is the red Wall of Shame, where gold plaques identify those crazy enough to have consumed 100 shots in one sitting. Monday to Saturday 8am to 5am, Sunday and holidays 8pm to 3am. Matsumiya Building, 2–1–10 Higashi-Shinsaibashi. © **06/6213-6788.** Station: Nigahoribashi or Nipponbashi (5 min.). Just off Sakaisuji Ave., 1 block south of Suomachi/Europa Dori.

Dig Me Out Art & Diner   In the heart of America-Mura, this casual, friendly bar offers occasional live music, changing art exhibitions, free Wi-Fi, and inexpensive snacks, making it a good place to relax and hang out. It opens at 11am daily, closing at midnight Sunday to Thursday, 12:30am Friday, and 5am Saturday. 2–9–32 Nishi-shinsaibashi. www.digmeout.net/index_3.php. © **06/6213-1007.** Station: Yotsubashi (5 min.) or Shinsaibashi (7 min.). On the same street as Dormy Inn.

Lapichu   This cute bar on a narrow street lined with drinking establishments has something very rare in this neck of the woods—a rooftop beer garden open in summer. But it's worth recommending any time of the year for its good drinks selection, snack menu (from nachos to nabe), and international atmosphere. Monday to Saturday 7:30pm to 3am. 4–8–3 Namba. © **06/6631-8890.** Station: Namba (2 min.) 1 block south of Sennichimae-dori street and 2 blocks west of Midosuji Dori, on a small street paralleling the overhead Hanshin Expressway; look for the white sign with a chili pepper.

Murphy's   Of Osaka's several Irish pubs, this is probably the most popular (and my favorite), drawing a mixed crowd of both Japanese and foreigners and offering a room for nonsmokers, live Irish music the second and fourth Wednesday of each month, a free pool table, and TVs broadcasting major sporting events. Fish and chips or shepherd's pie are reasonable and surprisingly good, but you can also make a meal of the Guinness or Kilkenny Ale. Happy hour is until 7pm daily. Monday through Thursday 5pm to 1am; Friday to Saturday 5pm to about 4am. Lead Plaza Building, 6th floor, 1–6–31 Higashi Shinsaibashi. © **06/6282-0677.** Station: Nagahoribashi (1 min.) or Shinsaibashi (4 min.). 1 block north of Suomachi/Europa Dori and several blocks east of the Shinsaibashi-suji covered arcade, on Shimizumachi Dori (the road south of Daimaru department store) just before the Minami Police Station. Keep your eye out for the sign, as it's easy to miss.

Sam & Dave 2 Shinsaibashi   This dance club is the spot for hip-hop, soul, reggae, and electro. It's open 10pm to 5am (from 9pm Sat). Kawahiro Building, 4th floor, 1–3–29 Shinsaibashi-suji. © **06/6243-6848.** Cover ¥1,500–¥2,000 men, ¥500–¥1,000 women, which includes 1 drink. Station: Shinsaibashi (3 min.). On the street running north of the Daimaru North Annex (Unagidani Minami Dori), just past the Shinsaibashi-suji covered arcade.

Where to Stay

Many hotels are clustered around Osaka Station, but Namba in the center of the city offers more interesting surroundings. In the listings below, the nearest subway or JR station is indicated followed by the number of minutes it takes to walk from the station to the hotel (in parentheses).

AROUND OSAKA & SHIN-OSAKA STATIONS
Very Expensive
The Ritz-Carlton, Osaka ★★★   Opened in 1997, the Ritz-Carlton's first Japanese venture rejected the grandiose marble lobbies popular in Japan at the time, choosing instead a small and intimate one, done in old-world style with overstuffed

sofas, 100-year-old Persian carpets, Italian marble fireplaces, stunning flower arrangements, crystal chandeliers, antiques, and museum-grade landscape paintings and portraits from the 18th and 19th centuries. Unique standouts include the Bar with its 110 kinds of martinis, 150 kinds of single malt whiskey, 50 kinds of cigars, and live music nightly; La Baie, rated by many as Osaka's best French restaurant; a very popular afternoon tea served in the lobby lounge with live classical music; a health club free to hotel guests; and a "check-in" desk just for kids. Stylish rooms—located from the 24th through 37th floors and among the largest in the city—offer panoramic views, especially from deluxe corner rooms.

2–5–25 Umeda, Kita-ku, Osaka 530-0001. www.ritzcarlton.com. **800/241-3333** in the U.S. and Canada, or 06/6343-7000. Fax 06/6343-7001. 292 units. ¥46,273–¥61,698 single; ¥58,138–¥73,936 double. Club floors ¥61,698–¥68,817 single, ¥73,563–¥80,682 double. ¥5,933 extra per room on Sat and nights before holidays. AE, DC, MC, V. Station: Osaka, Umeda, or Nishi-Umeda (7 min.). **Amenities:** 4 restaurants; 2 bars; lounge; concierge; executive-level rooms; health club w/gym, 20m (66-ft.) indoor heated lap pool, and indoor/outdoor whirlpools; room service; spa w/dry and wet saunas and baths (fee: ¥1,050). *In room:* A/C, TV/DVD player, minibar, MP3 docking station, WiFi (¥1,995 for 24 hr.).

Expensive

Rihga Royal Hotel ★   Osaka's oldest and largest hotel, opened in 1935, is located on Nakanoshima, an island in the middle of the Dojima River in the heart of Osaka (a 10-min. ride from Osaka Station). It enjoys a good reputation among Japanese and a high occupancy rate on weekends, due in no small part to the convention center next door. Its facilities include a shopping arcade, a deli, and—at the other end of the extreme—a well-stocked hotel gourmet foods shop with hundreds of eye-popping pastries and delicacies. It also has one of my favorite lobby lounges in the city—a restful oasis where you can sip your drink and watch a cascading waterfall against a backdrop of cliffs and foliage. Comfortable guest rooms have a range of rates and interior designs, from modern to classical drawing-room style. In short, you could do much worse than this hotel, despite the crowds, but for a more intimate experience, go elsewhere.

5–3–68 Nakanoshima, Kita-ku, Osaka 530-0005. www.rihga.com. **06/6448-1121.** Fax 06/6448-4414. 974 units. ¥19,635–¥53,130 single; ¥32,340–¥56,595 double. Executive floor double from ¥48,510. AE, DC, MC, V. Station: Nakanoshima (1 min.); or from JR Osaka Station west exit, free shuttle every 6–15 min. **Amenities:** 18 restaurants; 3 bars; 2 lounges; concierge; dental clinic; executive-level rooms; indoor circular "shape-up" pool, 25m (82-ft.) lap pool, Jacuzzi, and sauna (fee: ¥2,100); room service. *In room:* A/C, TV, hair dryer, Internet (¥1,050 for 24 hr.), minibar.

Moderate

Hearton Hotel Nishi Umeda ★★ 🦵   Just west of JR Osaka Station, the Hearton (pronounced "heart on") is a pleasant business hotel convenient to shops, clubs, and restaurants around the station and offers simple, well-lit, spotless rooms. Train buffs will probably opt for a room facing the tracks with double-paned windows that block out most noise, but otherwise I'd probably choose a room away from the tracks. In addition to the rates below, couples on a budget can stay in a single with a semi-double-size bed for ¥11,800. Although not as new, sister **Hearton Hotel Shinsaibashi,** 1–5–24 Nishi-Shinsaibashi (**06/6251-3711**), has more interesting environs and cheaper rates.

3–3–55 Umeda, Kita-ku, Osaka 530-0001. www.hearton.co.jp. **06/6342-1111.** Fax 06/6342-1122. 471 units. ¥10,600–¥10,800 single; ¥17,000–¥18,500 double; ¥21,600 triple. AE, DC, MC, V. Station: JR Osaka (Sakuradori exit, 3 min.). Walk through the Umesankoji covered arcade; the hotel's straight ahead, on your left. **Amenities:** Restaurant; coffee shop; rental bikes (¥1,000 per day); Wi-Fi (free, in lobby). *In room:* A/C, TV, fridge, hair dryer, Internet.

Hotel Granvia Osaka   You can't get any closer to Osaka Station than this hotel, with discounts for holders of Japan Rail Passes making it even more attractive for train travelers. But there are prices to pay: a ground-floor lobby that's hard to find in the maze that is Osaka Station, and elevators that are crowded with hungry masses on their way to the hotel's many 19th-floor restaurants. Rooms, on floors 21 to 26, are cramped except those on deluxe floors, and many of the cheapest singles face an inner courtyard and are dark. Families may want to opt for one of the huge "Corner Family" rooms (though they're a steep ¥56,595 or more), while those in search of R & R might find relaxation in the 24th-floor Freja rooms, designed with unique Scandinavian furnishings and aromatherapy amenities.

3–1–1 Umeda, Kita-ku, Osaka 530-0001. www.granvia-osaka.jp. ✆ **06/6344-1235.** Fax 06/6344-1130. 648 units. ¥16,170–¥27,720 single; ¥24,255–¥48,510 double. Discounts available for holders of Japan Rail Pass. AE, DC, MC, V. Station: Osaka or Umeda (1 min.; above the station). **Amenities:** 7 restaurants; bar; 2 lounges; room service. *In room:* A/C, TV, hair dryer, minibar, Wi-Fi.

Hotel Laforet Shin-Osaka   I can't think of any reason to stay near Shin-Osaka Station except for the sheer convenience of nearby bullet trains, as there are no attractions here and the rest of Osaka is just a short subway ride away. If you're unconvinced, this modern hotel is your best bet, just a minute's walk from the station and offering comfortable rooms with contemporary decor. Rooms face either a noisy highway or other buildings—take your pick.

1–2–70 Miyahara, Yodogawa-ku, Osaka 532-0003. ✆ **06/6350-4444.** Fax 06/6350-4460. 332 units. ¥15,000–¥17,000 single; ¥18,000–¥22,000 double. AE, DC, MC, V. Station: Shin-Osaka (1 min.). Take the west exit and turn right. **Amenities:** 2 restaurants; bar; room service. *In room:* A/C, TV, hair dryer, Internet (fee: ¥500 per stay), minibar.

Inexpensive
Family Inn Fifty's Osaka ★ 🏮   This motel-like facility, south of Nakanoshima island, offers low prices and no-nonsense small but clean rooms, identically outfitted with double bed, sofa bed, wall-mounted TV, and tiled bathroom (but no closet). Check-in is automated, but humans behind the front desk can help with the process (you'll need a credit card). You pay extra for a smoking room or rooms reserved by phone (rates below are those made online). The catch is that the place is a bit of a chore to reach from Osaka Station (because it's across a footbridge south of the Rihga Royal Hotel's back parking lot, some travelers have been known to use the luxury hotel's shuttle bus). Once you're settled in, you'll find its location fine.

2–6–18 Edobori, Nishi-ku, Osaka 550-0002. www.fiftys.com. ✆ **06/6225-2636.** 86 units. ¥5,250 single; ¥8,400 double; ¥9,450 triple. Smoking rooms ¥1,050 extra. Rates include continental breakfast. AE, MC, V. Station: Nakanoshima (exit 2, 5 min.); walk past the conference center Grand Cube and cross Tosabori-bashi bridge, continue 1 short block, turn left and then right. **Amenities:** Coffee shop; lobby computer w/free Internet; Wi-Fi (free, in coffee shop). *In room:* A/C, TV, hair dryer.

2nd Inn Umeda 🏮   This bare-bones business hotel, next to the Ritz-Carlton, is convenient to the station and offers a coin-operated laundry room and sparse rooms that meet all basic needs, with showers instead of tubs. Determined couples can save money by sharing a semi-double-size bed for ¥7,200.

2–5–16 Umeda, Kita-ku, Osaka 530-0001. ✆ **06/6346-1177.** Fax 06/6346-3006. 128 units. ¥5,800–¥6,200 single; ¥8,400–¥9,000 double. MC, V. Station: Osaka (7 min.) or Nishi-Umeda (exit 10, 4 min.). *In room:* A/C, TV, fridge, Internet, no phone.

AROUND OSAKA CASTLE

Expensive

Imperial Hotel Osaka (Teikoku Hotel) ★★★ One of Osaka's top luxury hotels, the Imperial is situated north of Osaka Castle on the cherry tree–lined Okawa River in a relaxing, resortlike setting, next to a large office complex containing shops and restaurants. Like its Tokyo namesake, its bold interior designs show the same Frank Lloyd Wright inspirations, including an Old Imperial Bar that pays homage to the American architect. The hotel's fitness center is the largest and best equipped in the city, while restaurants take advantage of the river and city views. The high-ceilinged, spacious rooms offer large windows with remote-control drapes and great views (request rooms facing the river), good working desks, down pillows and comforters, fluffy bathrobes, aromatherapy amenities, and marble bathrooms with magnifying mirrors and vanity stools at sinks.

1–8–50 Temmabashi, Kita-ku, Osaka 530-0042. www.imperialhotel.co.jp. © **800/223-6800** in the U.S. and Canada, or 06/6881-1111. Fax 06/6881-1200. 390 units. ¥29,400–¥49,350 single; ¥34,650–¥54,600 double; from ¥48,300 Imperial executive floor double. ¥3,465 more Sat and nights before holidays. Rates exclude service charge. AE, DC, MC, V. Station: JR Sakuranomiya west exit (5 min. to the hotel's riverside entrance); or Osaka Station west exit, free shuttle every 15 min. (every 10 min. on weekends). **Amenities:** 6 restaurants; bar; 2 lounges; children's day-care center (from ¥1,323 per 30 min.); concierge; executive-level rooms; golf driving range (fee: ¥5,250); Osaka's largest state-of-the-art health club w/25m (82-ft.) indoor pool, spa, Jacuzzi, and sauna (fee: ¥2,100); medical clinic; room service; squash courts. *In room:* A/C, TV, fax, hair dryer, Internet, minibar.

New Otani Osaka ★ In a business park that's home to corporate headquarters for telecasting and insurance giants, this Leading Hotel of the World member attracts both business and tourist clientele. Its proximity to Osaka Castle Park, popular with joggers, families, and young Japanese, and its varied public facilities, ranging from a multitude of restaurants to a fitness club, give the property something of an "urban resort" atmosphere. Everything about the hotel's public spaces is visually pleasing, from the airy, four-story atrium lobby with skylights and mirrors that lend it an expansive atmosphere to the indoor pool with its glass-vaulted ceiling. Rooms, however, are rather standard, with rates based on size, height, and view. The best rooms provide the city's most dramatic views of Osaka Castle, which is lit at night, but at fairly hefty prices.

1–4–1 Shiromi, Chuo-ku, Osaka 540-8578. www.hotelnewotaniosaka.jp. © **800/421-8795** in the U.S. and Canada, or 06/6941-1111. Fax 06/6941-9769. 525 units. ¥22,050–¥27,300 single; ¥35,700–¥50,400 double. ¥3,150 extra Sat and nights before holidays. Rates exclude service charge. AE, DC, MC, V. Station: JR Loop Line to Osakajo-Koen (3 min.) or Osaka Business Park Station (3 min.). Across the moat from Osaka Castle. **Amenities:** 10 restaurants; 2 bars; lounge; children's day-care center (¥7,875 for 3 hr.); concierge; executive-level rooms; fitness club w/indoor and outdoor pools and sauna (fee: ¥2,625); room service; 2 outdoor tennis courts. *In room:* A/C, TV, hair dryer, Internet (fee: ¥840 for 24 hr.); minibar.

Inexpensive

Weekly Mansion Osaka at Otemae ☺ West of Osaka Castle on Honmachi Dori, this property is a good choice for groups, families, and long-staying guests. Accommodations, which range from compact studio apartments to three-bedroom units, come with small balconies and kitchenettes, allowing guests to save money and to experience shopping at Osaka's famous food markets. There are even family rooms that combine single beds and futons sleeping up to seven people. The helpful English-speaking staff is happy to provide directions to local shops, restaurants, and tourist attractions. Housekeeping service is available for an extra fee, and there's a coin-operated laundry.

1–3–2 Tokuicho, Chuo-ku, Osaka 540-0025. www.wmt-osaka.jp. © **06/6949-4471.** Fax 06/6942-9373. 111 units. ¥7,000–¥14,100 single; ¥9,000–¥13,000 double; ¥15,000–¥18,000 triple. Weekly and monthly rates available. AE, MC, V. Station: Tanimachi 4 chome (exit 4, 5 min.). Head west on Honmachi Dori and turn right at the 2nd stoplight; it's on your right. **Amenities:** Rental bikes (fee: ¥1,050 per week). In room: A/C, TV, hair dryer, Internet, kitchenette.

NAMBA & SHINSAIBASHI
Expensive
Hotel Nikko Osaka ★   A white monolith soaring 32 stories above ground, the Nikko has a great location atop a subway station right on Osaka's most fashionable boulevard, Midosuji Dori, making its lobby lounge a popular spot for locals meeting friends. In fact, location is mainly what you're paying for here: There is no health club, and guests are overwhelmingly business travelers. Rooms have a pleasing, clean modern design, especially so-called L Floor rooms with their contemporary flair and air purification machines, while Premium rooms add DVD players and Wi-Fi. Because there are no high buildings to obstruct views, city panoramas are a plus from most floors. In short, this is a good choice if you want to be in the midst of Osaka's shopping and nightlife.

1–3–3 Nishi-Shinsaibashi, Chuo-ku, Osaka 542-0086. www.jalhotels.com. © **06/6244-1111.** Fax 06/6245-2432. 642 units. ¥24,000–¥32,000 single; ¥31,000–¥50,000 double; Nikko Deluxe executive floors from ¥53,000 double. AE, DC, MC, V. Station: Shinsaibashi (exit 8 underneath the hotel, 1 min.). **Amenities:** 6 restaurants; 2 bars; 2 lounges; executive-level rooms; access to 2 nearby health clubs (fee: ¥1,050); room service. In room: A/C, TV, hair dryer, Internet, minibar.

Inexpensive
There are more than a dozen **Toyoko Inn** hotels in Osaka, including those near Osaka and Shin-Osaka stations, as well as Toyoko Inn Osaka Nanba, 2–8–7 Motomachi (www.toyoko-inn.com; © **06/4397-1045;** station: Namba), offering singles for ¥6,480 and doubles starting at ¥8,480, including Japanese breakfast.

Hotel Metro The 21 ◢   This hotel has a great location for night owls, just a few minutes' walk from Dotombori, Osaka's main nightlife district, but it's a bit worn around the edges and could do with a sprucing up. Its mostly single rooms, along with 100 twins and doubles, are very small but clean. There's a ladies' floor for extra security, decorated with a more feminine touch and adding women's toiletries. Otherwise, for the best night views, ask for a room on a higher floor facing Dotombori. Stock your empty fridge with purchases from the ground-floor 7-Eleven.

2–13 Soemon-cho, Chuo-ku, Osaka 542-0084. www.metro21.co.jp/e. © **06/6211-3555.** Fax 06/6211-3586. 339 units. ¥9,975 single; ¥14,700–¥21,000 double. AE, DC, MC, V. Station: Nipponbashi (exit 2, 5 min.); cross Dotombori canal and turn left. Or Namba (exit 14, 10 min.); cross Dotombori Canal and turn right. **Amenities:** Bar. In room: A/C, TV, fridge, hair dryer, Internet.

AROUND TENNOJI
Moderate
Sheraton Miyako Hotel Osaka ★★   A multilingual staff providing excellent service, easy access to Kansai International Airport and Shin-Osaka Station, and good dining choices make this hotel popular, especially for business travelers. It's also well located for sightseeing, with Osaka Castle, Shitennoji Temple, the National Bunraku Theater and Namba with its many bars and restaurants all 1.5km (1 mile) away; Nara is just 35 minutes away. Spacious and comfortable rooms offer city views (there are no other high buildings near the hotel), bedside controls for lighting and other functions, and a choice of pillows. The atrium swimming pool, with a sliding roof and free

swimsuit rentals, is a great place to relax, but families will be disappointed to learn that it is not open to children 11 and younger.

6–1–55 Uehonmachi, Tennoji-ku, Osaka 553-0001. www.sheraton.com/miyakoosaka. © **800/325-3535** in the U.S. and Canada, or 06/6773-1111. Fax 06/6773-3322. 575 units. ¥17,325–¥21,945 single; ¥27,720–¥39,270 double. Premium Sheraton rooms from ¥39,270 double. AE, DC, MC, V. Station: Uehonmachi (2 min.). **Amenities:** 6 restaurants; 2 bars; child-care center (¥5,250 for 2 hr.); executive-level rooms; health club w/Jacuzzi, steam and dry sauna (fee: ¥3,450); 25m (82-ft.) atrium pool (fee: ¥1,050); Wi-Fi (free, in lobby). *In room:* A/C, TV, hair dryer, Internet, minibar.

Inexpensive

Hotel International House Osaka 🍴 The International House, providing information and counseling services for foreigners living in Kansai, is a modern facility used also for international seminars, conventions, and meetings. It also includes this hotel, managed by the nearby Sheraton Miyako Hotel Osaka and used mainly by those attending seminars but open to the public; try to book well in advance. Rooms are spartan with about as much personality as those in a business hotel, but they have everything you need, including tiny tiled bathrooms, *yukata,* and a small desk. Some 40 of the 50 rooms are singles, making this a great choice for the single traveler, but note that they don't have closets and are fairly small. The twins, however, are of adequate size; there are also two triples.

8–2–6 Uehommachi, Tennoji-ku, Osaka 543-0001. © **06/6773-8181.** Fax 06/6773-0777. 50 units. ¥6,800 single; ¥13,000 double; ¥16,000 triple. Rates include breakfast. AE, DC, MC, V. Station: Uehommachi (5 min.), Tanimachi 9-chome (8 min.), or Shitennoji-mae (5 min.). **Amenities:** 2 restaurants. *In room:* A/C, TV, fridge, hair dryer, Internet.

Tabinoyado Hokousou (旅の宿葆晃荘) ★★ 🛏 This family-owned ryokan (now in its fourth generation of innkeepers) is a gem. The 120-some-year-old traditional Japanese home has many charming features, including a breakfast room with a soaring ceiling and heavy wooden beams. Rooms, with both Japanese tatami rooms and Western-style rooms with beds available, vary in style and size, with the best, 10-tatami-mat room sleeping up to five people and overlooking a small garden. It has a great location, within walking distance of Shitennoji Temple and Spa World and with direct access to Kansai airport, Osaka and Shin-Osaka Stations, Osaka Castle, and Nara. Finally, the family that's been running the inn for 60 years is warm and welcoming. You can't go wrong staying here.

14–16 Horikoshi-cho, Tennoji-ku, Osaka 543-0056. © **06/6771-7242.** Fax 06/6771-3773. 14 units (none with private bathroom). ¥5,250 single; ¥8,900 double. Japanese breakfast ¥525 extra. No credit cards. Station: Tennoji (1 min.). Walk north from Tennoji JR Station on Tanimachi-suji Street and turn right on the tiny side street between a bank and convenience store (there's an English sign for the ryokan here pointing the way); it will be on the right. In room: A/C, TV.

KOBE, A COSMOPOLITAN PORT

589km (366 miles) W of Tokyo; 75km (47 miles) W of Kyoto; 31km (19 miles) W of Osaka

In January 1995, the world was riveted by news of one of the worst natural disasters of that decade: the Great Hanshin Earthquake that struck Kobe, killing more than 6,400 people and destroying much of the city. In the years since, Kobe has risen from the ashes with more attractions, hotels, and urban redevelopment than ever before and with only a few telltale signs of the city's grimmest hours. Indeed, if it weren't for several earthquake memorials and a museum dedicated to the event, visitors would never guess at the devastation of just 15 years ago.

Blessed with the calm waters of the Seto Inland Sea, Kobe (the capital of Hyogo Prefecture) has served Japan as an important port town for centuries. Even today its port is the heart of the city, its raison d'être. I find Kobe's port fascinating; unlike many harbor cities where the port is located far from the center of town, Kobe's is right there, demanding attention and getting it. One of the first ports to begin accepting foreign traders in 1868 following Japan's 2 centuries of isolation, this vibrant city of 1.5 million inhabitants is quite multicultural, with foreigners from more than 120 different nations residing here. Each group of immigrants has brought with it a rich heritage, and there are a number of fine restaurants serving every kind of cuisine— including Western, Chinese, Korean, and Indian—as well as many steakhouses offering that famous local delicacy, Kobe beef.

Equally famous is Kobe's wonderful nightlife, crammed into a small, navigable, and rather intimate quarter of neon lights, cozy bars, lively pubs, and sophisticated nightclubs. As one resident of Kobe told me, "We don't have a lot of tourist sights in Kobe, so we make up for it in nightlife." Yet the attractions Kobe does offer are unique to Japan, including a neighborhood of Western-style residences built around the turn of the 20th century and museums devoted to fashion and to the city's 1995 earthquake. Kobe is also one of Japan's major sake-producing regions.

Essentials

GETTING THERE   By Plane   If you're arriving at Kansai International Airport (KIX; see "Getting There," under Osaka, on p. 355), there are several options for travel onward to Kobe. Easiest are the **Airport Limousine Buses** operated by Kansai Airport Transportation Enterprise (www.kate.co.jp; ✆ **072/461-1374**), departing KIX every 20 minutes for Sannomiya Station, costing ¥1,900 one-way, and taking about 70 minutes. A more fun option is to take the **Bay Shuttle** (www.kobe-access. co.jp; ✆ **078/304-0033**), a high-speed boat that travels once an hour from Kansai International Airport 31 minutes to Kobe Airport, from which you then take the Portliner Monorail (see below). Cost of the trip is ¥1,800, including the Portliner. Finally, if you want to use your **Japan Rail Pass,** take a *kaisoku* (rapid train making only major stops) to Osaka Station and change there for the JR Kobe Line's 20-minute ride to Sannomiya Station (considered the heart of the city). If you're staying in a hotel closer to Shin-Kobe Station, take the JR Airport Express Haruka train from the airport to Shin-Osaka Station and transfer there for a speedy Shinkansen connection to Shin-Kobe Station (see p. 358 in the Osaka section for information).

If you're arriving at Kobe Airport (UKB; www.kairport.co.jp; ✆ **078/304-7777**), which opened in 2006 on Port Island to serve domestic flights, you can take the **Portliner Monorail** to Sannomiya Station in 17 minutes for ¥320.

By Train   The **Shinkansen** bullet train takes about 3 hours from Tokyo, 30 minutes from Kyoto, and about 14 minutes from Osaka; the fare from Tokyo for an unreserved seat is ¥13,760. All Shinkansen trains arrive at **Shin-Kobe Station,** which is linked to **Sannomiya Station** (the heart of the city) via a 3-minute subway ride (or a 20-min. walk). If you're arriving from nearby Osaka, Kyoto, Himeji, or Okayama, it may be easiest to take a JR express train stopping at Sannomiya Station if you're staying in one of the area's hotels.

By Bus   JR Highway Buses (www.jrbuskanto.co.jp; ✆ **03/3844-1950**) depart from Tokyo Station's Yaesu south exit for Kobe three times nightly (two of the buses make stops also at Shinjuku Station's new South Exit), with the 9:50pm bus arriving at Sannomiya Bus Terminal (near Sannomiya Station) at 7:55am. Fares range from ¥5,000 to ¥8,690, depending on the bus and the season.

VISITOR INFORMATION There are tourist information offices at **Shin-Kobe Station** (© 078/241-9550; daily 9am–6pm) and south of **JR Sannomiya Station**'s east gate, downstairs from the Port Liner station (© 078/322-0220; daily 9am–7pm). English-speaking staff can provide maps and sightseeing information and make hotel reservations. Ask here for your **Kobe Welcome Coupon,** available only to foreigners and containing coupons offering slight discounts to 70 sights and facilities, including the City Loop Line and most museums. You can also download it and obtain more tourist information at www.feel-kobe.jp.

ORIENTATION & GETTING AROUND Squeezed between Mount Rokko rising in the north and the shores of the Seto Inland Sea to the south, Kobe stretches some 29km (18 miles) along the coastline but in many places is less than 3km (2 miles) wide. It's made up of many *ku* (wards) such as Nada-ku, Chuo-ku, and Hyogo-ku. The heart of the city lies around Sannomiya, Motomachi, and Kobe stations in the **Chuo-ku (Central Ward).** It's here you'll find the city's nightlife, its port, many restaurants and shopping centers, and most of its hotels. Unlike most other Japanese cities, many of the major streets in Kobe have names with English-language signs posted, so it's easier to get around here than elsewhere. Additionally, the various maps provided by the tourist office are good.

Because the city isn't very wide, you can walk to most points north and south of Sannomiya Station. South of Sannomiya Station is the **Sannomiya Center Gai** covered-arcade shopping street, beyond which lies Kobe's business and administrative district. North of Sannomiya Station are bars and restaurants clustered around narrow streets such as **Higashimon Street.** Kitano-zaka leads uphill to **Kitano-cho** (usually shortened to Kitano) with its Western-style houses, about a 15-minute walk north of Sannomiya Station. **Shin-Kobe Station** is a 20-minute walk north of Sannomiya. Running from Shin-Kobe Station south through Sannomiya all the way to the port is a flower-lined road—called, appropriately enough, **Flower Road.**

About a 10-minute walk west of Sannomiya Station is **Motomachi Station,** south of which lies the fashionable Motomachi covered-arcade shopping street, **Chinatown,** and **Meriken Park,** established to commemorate the birthplace of Kobe's port. The next stop on the JR line from Motomachi Station is **Kobe Station,** just south of which is **Harborland,** a waterfront development with hotels, restaurants, and the colorful Mosaic outdoor restaurant and shopping complex.

Two train stops east of Sannomiya Station is one of the city's most ambitious urban renewal projects, **HAT Kobe** (an abbreviation of Happy Active Town), a mixed-use neighborhood of apartment complexes, research facilities, schools, and museums, including the Disaster Reduction Museum, which chronicles the Great Hanshin Earthquake. Nearby **Nada Ward** is home of several renowned breweries.

Because of restricted space, Kobe has also constructed two artificial islands in its harbor, Port Island (home of Kobe Airport) and Rokko Island. Farther afield, on Mount Rokko, is the Arima Onsen Spa.

A 13km (8-mile) **City Loop** bus, distinguished by its old-fashioned appearance, passes all major attractions, including Kitano, Chinatown, Meriken Park, and Harborland. Buses run three to four times an hour from about 9:30am to 5:30pm, with the route marked on the map distributed by the tourist office. It costs ¥250 for adults and ¥130 for children per ride. Or, a 1-day pass, allowing you to get off and reboard as often as you like and offering slight discounts to attractions mainly in Kitano, costs ¥650 for adults and ¥330 for children.

You can also use the **JR Local Commuter train,** which stops at Sannomiya, Motomachi, and Kobe stations, if you don't mind walking to destinations north and south of these stations (the City Loop Line buses will get you closer to major attractions). The subway is useful only for transportation between Shin-Kobe and Sannomiya stations. The **Portliner Monorail** connects Sannomiya with Port Island, while the Rokko Liner travels between JR Sumiyoshi Station and Rokko Island.

[Fast FACTS] KOBE

Internet Access   The **Litz Comic Café,** on the sixth floor of the Tatsumi Building at 5–3–2 Asahi Dori (✆ **078/231-2217**), is open 24 hours and charges ¥480 for the first hour and then ¥50 for each subsequent 10 minutes. It's a 2-minute walk southeast of Sannomiya Station, down a small street parallel to the tracks (there's a Starbucks on the corner), on the sixth floor above a pachinko parlor.

Exploring the City

In addition to the sights below, you might wish to drop by **City Hall,** a 6-minute walk south of Sannomiya Station on Flower Road, where on the 24th floor there's an **observatory** (✆ **078/331-8181**) open free to the public Monday to Friday 8:15am to 9pm, Saturday 10am to 10pm, and Sunday and holidays 10am to 9pm.

Evidence of the damage wrought by Kobe's horrific earthquake can be found at **Meriken Park,** a 10-minute walk south of Motomachi Station or a minute's walk from the Meriken Park stop on the City Loop bus. On its eastern edge is the **Port of Kobe Earthquake Memorial,** dedicated to the thousands of people who lost their lives in the tragic 1995 earthquake. Established with the intent of preserving some of the quake's horrific force (240,000 buildings and homes were destroyed), it shows unrepaired damage, including tilted lampposts and a submerged and broken pier.

KITANO

When Kobe was chosen as one of five international ports following the Meiji Restoration, foreign traders and diplomats who settled here built homes in much the same style as those they left behind in their native lands. Approximately 30 of these Western-style homes, called *ijinkan,* remain on a hill north of Sannomiya Station called Kitano-cho, along with a surprising number of churches, synagogues, and other religious centers to serve Kobe's international community. Because the area seems so exotic to young Japanese, this is the number-one draw for domestic visitors, who come also to shop the area's many boutiques, including its many bridal stores (there are also many wedding venues in Kitano).

Approximately 20 Victorian- and Gothic-style homes are open to the public, many with lovely views of the sea from verandas and bay windows. Although you may not be interested in visiting most of them, Kitano is very pleasant for an hour's stroll. It's located about a 15-minute walk north of Sannomiya Station (via Kitano-zaka) or a 10-minute walk west of Shin-Kobe Station. Or take the City Loop bus to Kitano Ijinkan. For orientation purposes, there's the **Kitano Tourist Information Center,** across from the Weathercock House (✆ **078/251-8360;** daily 9am–6pm; Nov–Feb to 5pm), with maps of the area.

Two of the more interesting homes open to the public are the **Moegi House (Moegi no Yakata),** 3–10–11 Kitano-cho (⚹ **078/222-3310**), a pale-green, 110-year-old home built for a former American consul general, Hunter Sharp, and filled with antiques; and **Kazamidori-no-Yakata ★**, 3–13–3 Kitano-cho (⚹ **078/ 242-3223**), popularly referred to as the Weathercock House because of its rooster weather vane. This 1909 brick residence was built by a German merchant and is probably Kobe's most famous home if not its most elaborate. Admission to both homes, located across from one another, is ¥600. Children enter free. They're open daily April to November from 9am to 6pm and December to March from 9am to 5pm (Weathercock House closed the first Tues in June and Feb).

Another home of note (because it contains porcelain, glass, and art, not because of its historical value) is **Uroko no Ie,** 2–20–4 Kitano-cho (⚹**078/242-6530;** daily 9am–6pm Apr–Sept, 9am–5pm Oct–Mar), which has a castlelike exterior and is nicknamed the Fish-Scale House because of its slate walls. It contains lovely antiques, including Meissen porcelain and Tiffany glass, as well as a small private museum of Western 18th- to 20th-century art, with a few works by Andrew Wyeth, Utrillo, and others. Admission is ¥1,000 for adults, ¥300 for children.

JAPAN'S LARGEST HERB GARDEN If you're a gardener, want a respite from city life, or simply want to spend an hour in a cooler climate, take the ropeway located next to Shin-Kobe Station for a 10-minute ride to the **Kobe Nunobiki Herb Garden & Ropeway ★** (www.kobeherb.com; ⚹ **078/271-1160**), with its lovely, meandering, fragrant gardens planted with various flowering shrubs and herbs and offering great views over Kobe. Be sure to take the ropeway to the end (don't get off at the first stop) and then walk downhill past gardens planted with sage, mint, lavender, roses, seasonal herbs, Japanese plants, and a greenhouse. The garden opens daily at 10am, closing at 5pm on weekdays and 8:30pm on weekends, holidays, and peak season (mid-July to Aug). From December to March it closes daily at 5pm. It's closed for 2 weeks in January or February. Admission, including round-trip by ropeway, is ¥1,400 for adults, half-price for children.

CHINATOWN ★

Like the Kitano-cho area, **Chinatown** (called Nankin-machi), a 3-minute walk south of Motomachi Station (or to the Sakaemachi 1-chome stop on the City Loop bus), is worth a walk-through for its lively street scene, with sidewalk vendors selling snacks and with open-fronted souvenir shops and produce stands. If the sidewalk vendors tempt you, eat your snack in the central square called **Nankin Park,** adorned with statues representing the animals of the 12-year Chinese astrological calendar. Chinatown's public restroom, called **Garyoden,** which means "palace of a secluded wise man," is certainly one of Japan's most colorful—its outer wall is decorated with five-clawed dragons and is based on a famous Chinese epic about a dragonlike hero; it's located a block off the main street. You may also want to come to Chinatown for a meal in one of its many restaurants.

KOBE HARBORLAND

Kobe Harborland is a leisure center that's fun to stroll and browse. It's a few minutes' walk from either Kobe Station or Meriken Park, or you can take the City Loop bus to Harborland. For shopping, head to **Mosaic** (http://kobe-mosaic.co.jp; ⚹ **078/360-1722**), a restaurant and shopping complex designed to resemble a Mediterranean village. Through the use of varying architectural and color schemes, it avoids the

Ships Ahoy

What better way to see this port town than by sea? A variety of sightseeing boats depart from Naka Pier Central Terminal, between Meriken Park and Kobe Harborland (take the City Loop bus to Nakatottei Pier). They range from **Luminous Kobe 2** (www.luminouskobe.co.jp; (C) 078/333-8414), known for its French cuisine and departing three times daily for 2-hour cruises costing ¥2,100 to ¥3,150 (meals cost extra), to **Villaggio Italia** ((C) 078/367-2651), mock pirate boats that depart hourly and cost ¥1,000. Children pay half fare.

generic mall atmosphere, and with a diversity of ethnic goods and foods, it mirrors Kobe's international roots. Shops here are open daily from 11am to 8pm.

Beside it is **Mosaic Garden,** a small amusement park for younger children complete with kiddie rides, carousel, roller coaster, enclosed Ferris wheel, and games arcade. It's open daily from 11am to 10pm, with rides costing ¥300 to ¥700. For older kids, there's the Amuseum games arcade inside Mosaic.

MUSEUMS WORTH CHECKING OUT

If you're on your way to the Disaster Reduction Museum, below, it might be worthwhile to check out what's being shown at the **Hyogo Prefectural Museum of Art** practically next door (www.artm.pref.hyogo.jp; (C) 078/262-0901; Tues–Sun 10am–6pm). Designed by renowned Japanese architect Tadao Ando, it displays contemporary art, prints, sculpture, and other works produced by artists with connections to Hyogo Prefecture, as well as temporary exhibits from around the world. It charges ¥500 for adults, ¥400 for university students, and ¥250 for senior-high students and seniors (younger children are free); special exhibits cost more.

Disaster Reduction Museum ★★★ MUSEUM Despite its rather official-sounding name, this facility gives a human dimension to the Great Hanshin Earthquake, which measured 7.3 on the Richter scale. Sheathed in glass and built to withstand both vertical and horizontal earthquakes, it vividly conveys what happened during the first moments of the earthquake and the weeks, months, and years that followed. English-speaking volunteers are on hand to help explain some of the museum's more technical displays; audio guides are also available.

A visit to the museum begins with a powerful 7-minute film that re-creates the exact moment the earthquake struck, with computer-generated scenes that show buildings imploding or bursting into flames and highways collapsing (the graphics might be too much for young children). From the movie theater, visitors emerge into a life-size diorama depicting a typical Kobe neighborhood destroyed by the quake. They then enter another movie theater where a 15-minute documentary shows actual footage shot shortly after the quake and during the weeks that followed, presented through the eyes of a teenage survivor. Other displays in the museum concentrate on the individual experiences of survivors, emergency relief, and reconstruction. A hands-on section helps visitors learn how construction techniques can minimize and even prevent earthquake damage and dispenses information on disaster management. Since 2011 there has also been a special exhibit on the Great East Japan Earthquake. There is no other facility in Japan quite like this one; you can easily spend an hour here.

Silver & Gold

On the opposite side of Mount Rokko is **Arima Onsen,** one of Japan's oldest hot-spring spas. Two public baths here are the **Kin-no-Yu** (金の湯; ✆ **078/904-0680**), or Gold Spring, with copper-colored waters that have twice the salinity and iron of seawater; and the **Gin-no-Yu** (銀の湯; ✆ **078/904-0256**), or Silver Spring, with transparent water rich in carbonic acid. It's said that if you bathe in both these waters and drink carbonated water, you'll be cured of all ailments. The Kin-no-Yu, open daily 8am to 10pm (closed the second and fourth Tues of every month), charges ¥650, while the Gin-no-Yu, open daily 9am to 9pm (closed the first and third Tues of every month), charges ¥550. A combination ticket to both is ¥850. Buses from Sannomiya Station reach Arima Onsen in 40 minutes and cost ¥680 one-way. You can also travel by train to Rokko Station, followed by a trip via cable car, bus, and ropeway. For more information, contact the Kobe Tourist Information office or the Arima Onsen Tourist Information Office (✆ **078/904-0708; www.arima-onsen.com**).

1–5–2 Wakinohama Kaigan-Dori, Chuo-ku. www.dri.ne.jp/english. ✆ **078/262-5050.** Admission ¥600 adults, ¥450 university students, ¥300 high-school students, free for children. Tues–Sun 9:30am–5:30pm (to 7pm Fri–Sat; to 6pm July–Sept). You must enter 1 hr. before closing. Station: JR Nada (12 min. south, toward the harbor).

Hakutsuru Sake Brewery Museum ★ Everything you ever wanted to know about sake production is available at this former brewery, with English-language videos and pamphlets describing the various painstaking steps and comparing the old techniques to those used today. Hakutsuru, established in 1743, is one of many sake breweries in this part of Kobe; its actual brewery is now across the street (closed to the public). Plan on spending 30 minutes on your self-guided tour, which ends with hints on how to enjoy sake and—what would a brewery tour be without this?—free tastings.

4–5–5 Sumiyoshi-minami-machi, Higashinada-ku. ✆ **078/822-8907.** www.hakutsuru-sake.com. Free admission. Tues–Sun 9:30am–4:30pm. Station: Hanshin Sumiyoshi (5 min.); JR Sumiyoshi (15 min.).

Kobe Fashion Museum ★ Located on artificial Rokko Island, this is Japan's first museum devoted to fashion, housed in a contemporary, sophisticated setting that does justice to the highbrow costumes it contains. Temporary displays devoted to individual designers allow closer inspection than you could ever get at a fashion show. Other displays, which are imaginative tableaux complete with visual images, music, and lighting, may feature anything from 20th-century gowns by Christian Dior to extravagant *kabuki* costumes or ethnic clothing worn by indigenous peoples from around the world. Displays change four or five times a year, rotating the many costumes owned by the museum. In all, a very entertaining, unique museum, and a must-see for fashionistas with an hour to spare.

2–9 Koyocho-naka, Rokko Island. www.fashionmuseum.or.jp. ✆ **078/858-0050.** Admission ¥500 adults, ¥250 children and seniors. Thurs–Tues 10am–6pm. Closed 1 week during exhibit changes. Take the local JR train to Sumiyoshi Station, transferring there for the Rokkoliner monorail to Island Center.

Where to Eat

With its sizable foreign population, Kobe is a good place to dine on international cuisine, including French, Indian, and Chinese food. The greatest concentration of Chinese restaurants is along a pedestrian lane in Chinatown, called **Nankin-machi** by the locals, a 2-minute walk south of Motomachi Station. If you're on a budget, you may just want to wander through and buy sticky buns or other cheap fare from the many street stalls. In the center of Nankin-machi is a plaza, good for people-watching.

EXPENSIVE

Kitano Club ★ FRENCH   Located in Kitano on a hill overlooking the city, this well-known, upscale restaurant has been offering meals with a view for more than 55 years. Join the well-heeled who come to soak in the fabulous vistas, listen to live jazz or popular music, and dine on selections that change monthly, with choices that may range from Kobe beef and fresh catch of the day to roast lamb with walnut. Afterward, retire to the bar or adjacent lounge (until midnight). Be sure to call to make sure it's open, as this is a popular wedding venue.

1–5–7 Kitano-cho. ℂ **078/222-5123.** Reservations recommended. Main dishes ¥2,940–¥6,300; set dinners ¥6,300–¥15,750. AE, DC, MC, V. Daily 5:30–10:30pm (last order). Station: Shin-Kobe (7 min.). Go west on Kitano Rd. from ANA Crowne Plaza hotel, taking the 1st street on the right (look for the Kitano Chapel on your left); it will be on your left in the 2nd building.

Wakkoqu ★ TEPPANYAKI STEAKS   This tiny, second-floor restaurant has room for only 30 diners at two counters, where expert chefs cook sirloin, tenderloin, or other cuts of tender Kobe beef on the grill in front of them, which can be paired simply with salt, pepper, mustard, or the restaurant's own sauce. Fixed-course meals come with such side dishes as soup and fried vegetables. This is a good place to try Kobe's most famous product.

Hillside Terrace, 1–22–13 Nakayamate Dori. www.wakkoqu.com/english/index.html. ℂ **078/222-0678.** Reservations recommended. Set dinners ¥7,500–¥13,700; set lunches ¥2,940–¥5,040. AE, DC, MC, V. Daily noon–9:30pm (last order). Station: Sannomiya (7 min.). On Pearl St. just east of Kitano-zaka, in a brick building

MODERATE

Bistro Café de Paris ★ FRENCH   A little bit of Paris in the heart of Kobe is offered by this popular and lively bistro, complete with sidewalk seating and *chansons* in the background. Lunch features set meals that come with soup, salad, a choice of main dish, bread, and coffee or tea, as well as sandwich and pizza sets. Dinner is more substantial, with main dishes ranging from roast lamb with mustard to beef bourguignon. Or, come for the afternoon cake set for ¥1,050, which gives you a choice of 10 different desserts (think tarts, tiramisu, or the mousse of the day) plus coffee, and sit and watch the world parade by.

1–7–21 Yamamoto Dori. ℂ **078/241-9448.** Main dishes ¥1,680–¥1,995; set dinners ¥2,940–¥5,250; set lunches ¥1,050–¥2,415. AE, MC, V. Daily 10am–9pm (last order). Station: Sannomiya (10 min.). On the east side of Kitano-zaka, north of Pearl St.

Ganesha Ghar ◢ NORTHERN INDIAN   This fourth-floor, one-room walk-up is owned by a kind owner/chef, who has made this his cozy home-away-from-home, right down to live Indian broadcasts or movies on the television and a clock set to Indian time. Worth seeking out for its authentic, delicious tandoori and curry at unbeatable prices, it offers a weekday lunch for ¥980, for example, consisting of salad, tandoori, vegetable curry, chicken curry, nan, and saffron rice. By the way, Ganesha Ghar means home of Ganesh (the elephant god of prosperity), and once you've eaten here, you might want to move in, too.

Louvre Bldg. 4F, 1–6–21 Nakayamate Dori. ℂ **078/391-9060.** Curries ¥1,000–¥1,500; set dinners ¥1,980–¥3,300; set lunches ¥980–¥2,000. No credit cards. Daily 11am–2:30m and 5–9:30pm (last order). Station: Sannomiya (4 min.). From the intersection of Kitano-zaka and Ikuta Shinmichi St., walk west past 2 small alleys and turn right at the first real street; it will be on the left.

Steakland Kobe (ステーキランド) STEAKS If you want to eat *teppanyaki* steak but can't afford the high prices of Kobe beef, one of the cheapest places to go is Steakland Kobe, which is used to tourists and offers an English-language menu. Lunch specials, served from 11am to 2pm, feature steak, fried vegetables, miso soup, rice, Japanese pickles, a salad, and coffee. More expensive Kobe beef is also available, with the least expensive fixed-price dinner offering Kobe sirloin costing ¥4,480. You'll sit at a counter, behind which young chefs cook your meal.

1–8–2 Kitanagasa Dori. ✆ 078/332-1653. Steaks ¥1,980–¥5,280; set steak dinners ¥2,680–¥7,480; set lunches ¥980–¥2,980. AE, DC, MC, V. Daily 11am–10pm (last order). Station: Sannomiya (2 min.). On the north side of Sankita, the street that runs along the north side of Hankyu Sannomiya Station, 4 blocks west of Flower Rd. (look for the big, oval hanging sign picturing a steak).

INEXPENSIVE

In addition to the choices here, Mosaic (p. 380) has a variety of restaurants, including **Fisherman's Market** (✆ 078/360-3695) offering buffets of grilled and steamed seafood, rotisserie chicken, pastas, curry, paella, pizza, and other fare. All-you-can-eat buffets cost ¥1,783 for lunch and ¥2,499 for dinner; on weekends it's ¥2,097 and ¥2,709 respectively. It's open daily 11am to 10pm (last order).

Hyotan (瓢たん) ⬆ GYOZA Roll up your sleeves and join the working class at this greasy hole-in-the-wall eatery underneath the tracks of Hankyu Sannomiya Station. It must be doing something right, as it's been selling nothing but *gyoza*—favored for the light texture of its dumpling skin and stuffed with minced pork, leek, and cabbage—for more than 40 years. Gyoza come seven to a serving. At your table will be soy sauce, vinegar, and chili sauce, which you should mix in the little bowl provided; some regulars also mix chili sauce and miso paste. Avoid the noontime rush, when this tiny place is like an assembly line for speed eating.

1–31–37 Kitanagasa Dori. ✆ 078/331-1354. 7-gyoza serving ¥370. No credit cards. Mon–Fri 11:30am–2:30pm and 5–10:30pm; Sat–Sun 11:30am–10:30pm (last order). Closed 2nd Sun and 4th Mon of each month. Station: Sannomiya (2 min.). Underneath the tracks of Hanshin Sannomiya Station in a small passageway called Sun West, at the west end near Ikutasuji; look for its red curtains and phone number.

Nishimura COFFEE SHOP In business some 60 years, Nishimura is a Kobe landmark, but if you can't find it just follow your nose; the smell of roasting coffee broadcasts its location. Some 20 types of coffee are available, as well as snacks, sandwich sets, and desserts. The second floor is nonsmoking.

1–26–13 Nakayamate Dori. ✆ 078/221-1872. Coffee from ¥500. No credit cards. Daily 8:30am–11pm. Station: Sannomiya (9 min.). On the north side of Yamate Kansen Dori (also called Nakayamate Dori), across from Higashimon St. in a mock German half-timbered building.

Pinocchio PIZZA/PASTA This small and cozy corner establishment opened in 1962 and proudly claims to have never fallen victim to the many fads that have come and gone since then. Instead, it still produces handmade pizza, which you can order from the menu or create yourself by ordering the basic pizza for ¥945 and adding ingredients such as garlic, asparagus, mushroom, chicken, or bacon, all priced at ¥105 each. Salads, pasta, pilaf, and gratin are also available from an English-language menu with photos. If the place is full, add your name to the list and wait outside.

2–3–13 Nakayamate Dori. ✆ 078/331-3330. Pizza and pasta ¥1,260–¥1,680; set lunches ¥1,310. AE, DC, MC, V. Daily 11:30am–midnight. Station: Sannomiya (12 min.). On the south side of Yamate Kansen Dori (also called Nakayamate Dori), west of Ikuta Shrine and 1 block east of Tor Rd.

Kobe After Dark

Kobe has a wide selection of English-style pubs, bars, expatriate hangouts, and night-clubs. All the establishments below are easily accessible to foreigners, and most are within walking distance of Sannomiya Station.

THE CLUB & MUSIC SCENE

Garage Paradise Candlelight, gauzy curtains draped from the high ceiling, Roman statues, a copper-and-stone bar, and stone walls set the scene at this base-ment venue with five sets of good, live music nightly. The interesting setting, plus music ranging from R&B to soul and funk, attracts locals and foreigners alike. Open daily 7pm to 3am (Sun to 1am). Kobe Yamashita Building, basement, 1–13–7 Nakayamate Dori. www.garage-paradise.com. ✆ **078/391-6640.** Cover Sun–Thurs ¥520; Fri–Sat ¥520 for women, ¥730 for men. Station: Sannomiya (9 min.). On Yamate Kansen Dori east of Higashimon, catty-corner from Nishimura coffee shop.

Satin Doll This traditional jazz club first opened in 1974 and remains one of the city's top venues. Its sophisticated interior offers table and bar seating with some city views. There are three live music sets nightly (7, 8:30, and 10pm) of mostly Japanese talents; an English-language menu offers mainly snacks. Open Tuesday to Sunday 6pm to midnight. Bacchus Building, 1–26–1 Nakayamate Dori. ✆ **078/242-0100.** Cover from ¥500, more for international acts, plus ¥500 table charge. Station: Sannomiya (9 min.). On Yamate Kansen Dori opposite Higashimon Dori.

Sone Kobe's oldest and best-known jazz club has changed little since its 1969 opening, offering the same traditional jazz, including Dixieland ensembles and piano-vocalist duos, in a clubby, dated atmosphere. There are four stages nightly, and most of its older crowd come to eat; the Japanese-language menu lists pasta, pizza, fish, and Kobe steaks, with set meals starting at ¥2,100. Open daily 5pm to midnight. 1–24–10 Nakayamate Dori. ✆ **078/221-2055.** Cover usually ¥1,200. Station: Sannomiya (5 min.). North of the station on the left side of Kitano-zaka.

THE BAR SCENE

Hobgoblin Kobe This popular British import (there are three branches in Tokyo alone) prides itself on its ales (including its own Hobgoblin brand) and lagers, as well as its British pub decor. It offers a pretty decent menu as well, from sandwiches to tortilla wraps to a homemade pie of the day, bangers and mash, and beer-battered fish and chips. Big screens show major sporting events, from soccer to rugby. Open Mon-day to Saturday from 5pm and Sunday from 3pm to the wee hours. Kondo Building, 7th floor, 4–3–2 Kano-cho. www.hobgoblin.jp. ✆ **078/325-0830.** Station: Sannomiya (1 min.). Across from the station to the north, at the juncture of Ikuta Shinmichi and Flower Rd., above a McDonald's.

Second Chance This all-nighter, in business an astonishing 35 years (which makes it older than virtually all of its customers), is a small, one-room bar favored by night owls who don't mind the rather sparse furnishings. This is where people con-gregate when the other bars have had the good sense to close down for the night. The last Saturday of every month features live music (usually hip-hop or reggae), with a cover charge of ¥3,500 for guys and ¥2,500 for gals, including all you care to drink for both men and women. Open daily 6pm to 5am. Takashima, 2nd floor, 2–1–12 Nakaya-mate Dori. ✆ **078/391-3544.** Station: Sannomiya (10 min.). On Yamate Kansen Dori west of Higashimon and catty-corner from Nishimura coffee shop.

Where to Stay

Some hotels charge more for Saturday nights and nights before holidays, as well as during peak season (Golden Week, summer holidays, and New Year's).

EXPENSIVE

ANA Crowne Plaza Kobe This hotel is directly connected by covered walkway to Shin-Kobe Station—very convenient if you're arriving by Shinkansen train. Rising 37 stories, with rooms on the 14th to 33rd floors, it offers impressive views of Kobe and the bay or the mountains from some of its restaurants and most of its fully equipped rooms. Rates are based on room size and height, with top floors commanding the grandest views at the highest prices (all singles face the wooded mountains). A plus is the large mall occupying the first four floors, with many additional choices in dining.

1 Kitano-cho, Chuo-ku, Kobe, Hyogo Prefecture 650-0002. www.anacrowneplaza-kobe.jp. ℂ **887/227-6963** in the U.S., or 078/291-1121. Fax 078/291-1151. 592 units. ¥15,015 single; ¥21,945–¥38,115 double; from ¥34,650 Crowne Plaza Club double. AE, DC, MC, V. Station: Shin-Kobe (1 min.). **Amenities:** 6 restaurants; 2 bars; lounge; concierge; executive-level rooms; health club w/gym and indoor pool (fee: ¥1,050); room service; spa. *In room:* A/C, TV, fridge, hair dryer, Internet.

Hotel Monterey Amalie ★ Taking its name from a long-ago Danish sailing vessel and decorated in a nautical theme, this property is part of a smart chain of boutique hotels that targets mostly female Japanese travelers with old-world European decor and atmosphere. From its ivy-covered facade to whitewashed walls (some of which could use a fresh coat) and heavy-beamed ceilings, it looks much older than its 1992 construction date. Wood-floored guest rooms feature natural wooden furniture, sheer curtains and heavy wooden shutters, tiled bathrooms, and free-standing wardrobes. Ask for a room overlooking Ikuta Shrine, but because occupancy is enviably high, book early. Otherwise, try nearby sister hotel Monterey Kobe (ℂ **078/392-7111**), with comparable prices and a medieval cloister–like atmosphere.

2–2–28 Nakayamate Dori, Chuo-ku, Kobe, Hyogo Prefecture 650-0004. www.hotelmonterey.co.jp/kobe. ℂ **078/334-1711.** Fax 078/334-1788. 69 units. ¥17,000 single; ¥30,000–¥40,000 double. AE, DC, MC, V. Station: Sannomiya (10 min.). Just west of Ikuta Shrine. **Amenities:** Restaurant. *In room:* A/C, TV, hair dryer, Internet, minibar.

Hotel Okura Kobe ★★ ☺ This majestic 35-story hotel has the prestige of the Okura name, as well as a grand location beside Meriken Park, within easy walking distance of the Motomachi covered shopping arcade and Chinatown. Its inviting lobby has views of a small Japanese garden (the only hotel garden in downtown Kobe) against a backdrop formed by the port. Each elegantly appointed room has all the comforts you'd expect, plus the bonus of great views from its more expensive rooms, which are on higher floors facing either the harbor or the city with Mount Rokko rising behind it (standard rooms provide only city views). In short, this hotel appeals to everyone from businessmen on weekdays to tourists on weekends. Even the imperial family makes this their home base when in Kobe. *Tip:* Upon check-in, ask for immediate free membership in the Okura Club International, which allows late checkout, discounts to its health club, and other privileges.

2–1 Hatoba-cho, Chuo-ku, Kobe, Hyogo Prefecture 650-8560. www.kobe.hotelokura.co.jp. ℂ **078/333-0111.** Fax 078/333-6673. 475 units. ¥21,000–¥42,000 single; ¥26,250–¥47,250 double. Rates exclude service charge. AE, DC, MC, V. Station: Motomachi (10 min. south). City Loop bus: Meriken Park (1 min.). Free shuttle service from Sannomiya Station daily and Shin-Kobe Station (weekends and holidays only) 2–3 times an hour. **Amenities:** 5 restaurants; bar; babysitting; children's day-care center (fee: ¥5,250 for 2 hr.; reservations required 2 days in advance); concierge; health club w/gym, sauna, and heated indoor lap pool (fee: ¥4,200); outdoor pool (fee: ¥1,260); room service; free shuttle service; 2 lit outdoor tennis courts. *In room:* A/C, TV, hair dryer, Internet, minibar.

MODERATE

the b kobe ★★ 🛅   Located just minutes from Sannomiya Station, this hotel wins hands-down as Kobe's most chic moderately priced hotel, offering mostly twin rooms smartly but sparingly done up in brown and red color tones. Reception is on the second floor, where you'll also find a machine dispensing free coffee and a computer you can use for free. In short, a stylish retreat with a convenient location make this a popular business hotel.

2–1–5 Shimoyamatedori, Chuo-ku, Kobe, Hyogo Prefecture 650-0011. www.theb-hotels.com/the-b-kobe/en. ✆ **078/333-4880.** Fax 078/333-4876. 168 units. ¥8,400–¥9,450 single; ¥13,650–¥23,100 double. AE, DC, MC, V. Station: Sannomiya (3 min. south). On Ikuta Shinmichi St. **Amenities:** Lobby computer w/free Internet. *In room:* A/C, TV fridge, hair dryer, Internet.

Kobe Meriken Park Oriental Hotel ★★   An outstanding location on a spit of land jutting seaward from the edge of Meriken Park (it's practically on the water and surrounded by a park) makes this Kobe's best hotel with a view—which it capitalizes on by providing each room with a balcony with views of Kobe's harbor and of the city as it rises up the hills (night views are also good). Popular with couples (weddings are big here), the hotel looks like one of the many cruise ships that dock nearby, rising 14 stories in a lopsided half circle. Its center is hollow, an airy atrium filled with palm trees and bubbling fountains. In addition to standard rooms, there are more expensive Com'fill rooms (designed to "fill you with comfort") and Sea'fill rooms (where earth tones are fused with red and blue, meant to relay sea sunsets) on higher floors, with corner rooms providing views even from bathrooms.

5–6 Hatoba-cho, Chuo-ku, Kobe, Hyogo Prefecture 650-0042. www.kobe-orientalhotel.co.jp. ✆ **078/325-8111.** Fax 078/325-8106. 319 units. ¥16,800–¥21,000 single; ¥19,950–¥36,750 double. Rates exclude service charge. AE, DC, MC, V. Free shuttle service daily from Sannomiya Station and on weekends & holidays from Shin-Kobe Station. Loop Line bus: Nakatottei Pier (5 min.). **Amenities:** 5 restaurants; bar; children's day-care center (¥5,250 for 2 hr.); indoor pool w/sun deck and sauna (fee: ¥2,100); room service; free shuttle service. *In room:* A/C, TV, hair dryer, minibar, Wi-Fi.

Hotel Tor Road ★   Knickknacks, antiques, and dark-wood wainscoting lend an English country atmosphere to this tourist hotel's lobby. The decent-size rooms are clean and tastefully decorated with larger-than-usual bathroom (doubles even provide a separate sink area). Each of the so-called "Concept Rooms" on the ninth floor is designed around a different theme. The "My Room" room, for example, has the logo of a cat repeated on the drapes, pillows, sheets, and elsewhere, but I fail to see why anyone would pay more for it (except that it does have a king-size bed, a rarity in moderately priced hotels, making it a good choice for couples). At the other extreme are the single rooms with semi-double-size beds, where budget-conscious couples can cuddle for ¥10,000.

3–1–19 Nakayamate Dori, Chuo-ku, Kobe, Hyogo 650-0004. www.hoteltorroad.co.jp. ✆ **078/391-6691.** Fax 078/391-6570. 76 units. ¥8,000 single; ¥13,000–¥18,000 double. Rates ¥3,000 more Sat and day before holidays. AE, DC, MC, V. Station: Sannomiya or Motomachi (10 min.). On Tor Rd. just north of Ikuta Shinmichi Dori. **Amenities:** Restaurant. *In room:* A/C, TV, hair dryer, Internet, minibar.

INEXPENSIVE

Green Hill Hotel Urban   Between Sannomiya and Shin-Kobe stations, this simple business hotel with mostly single rooms in a dormitory-like setting is primarily a place to park your head at night (I'd try the other recommendations first). Rather shabby rooms are about as small as they come, most without closets and with glazed windows and minuscule plastic-unit bathrooms. Best are the Japanese rooms. Free tea is dispensed from machines on each floor. Don't confuse this with the older Green Hill Hotel around the corner.

2–5–16 Kano-cho, Chuo-ku, Kobe, Hyogo Prefecture 650-0001. ☏ **078/222-1221.** Fax 078/242-1194. 102 units. ¥4,900 single; ¥9,500–¥10,500 double; ¥12,000 Japanese room double. Rates ¥1,000 more per person in high season. AE, DC, MC, V. Station: Shin-Kobe or Sannomiya (10 min.); btw. the stations, on Flower Rd. **Amenities:** Coffee shop; lobby computer w/free Internet. *In room:* A/C, TV, fridge (singles and twins only), hair dryer, Wi-Fi.

Super Hotel Kobe   This chain comes close to Toyoko Inn's cheap price and ever-expanding network of hotels, but it falls short of its competitor when it comes to atmosphere and amenities. You have to ring the doorbell to gain admission, and rooms—all singles—are minuscule with just the basics.

2–1–11 Kano-cho, Chuo-ku, Kobe, Hyogo Prefecture 650-0001. www.superhotel.co.jp. ☏ **078/261-9000.** Fax 078/231-9090. 87 units. ¥5,460 single. Rates include breakfast. AE, MC, V. Station: Shin-Kobe or Sannomiya (8 min.); btw. the stations, on the west side of Flower Rd. (its entry is on a side street). *In room:* A/C, TV, fridge, hair dryer, Internet, no phone.

Toyoko Inn Kobe-Sannomiya II 🏃   One of Japan's fastest-growing business hotel chains surpasses others for such perks as computers in the lobby guests can use for free, semi-double-size beds in singles, free domestic phone calls (for calls up to 3 min.), and free Japanese breakfasts. Rooms are small but clean, and female travelers even get a cosmetic set geared just for them. If this one's full, Toyoko Inn Kobe-Sannomiya I, 2–2–2 Gokodori (☏ **078/271-1045**), is only 5 minutes away.

5–2–2 Kumoi Dori, Chuo-ku, Kobe, Hyogo Pref. 651-0096. www.toyoko-inn.com. ☏ **078/232-1045.** Fax 078/232-1046. 334 units. ¥5,985–¥6,480 single; ¥7,480–¥9,480 double. Rates include Japanese breakfast. DC, MC, V. Station: Sannomiya (east exit, 2 min.). Behind Daiei department store; turn left onto the busy thoroughfare in front of JR Sannomiya Station and then another left. **Amenities:** Lobby computer w/free Internet; smoke-free rooms. *In room:* A/C, TV, fridge, hair dryer, Wi-Fi.

THE TEMPLES OF MOUNT KOYA ★★★

748km (465 miles) W of Tokyo; 199km (124 miles) S of Osaka

If you've harbored visions of wooden temples nestled in among trees whenever you've thought of Japan, the sacred mountain of **Mount Koya** is the place to go. It's all here—head-shaven monks, religious chanting at the crack of dawn, the wafting of incense, temples, towering cypress trees, tombs, and early morning mist rising above the treetops. Mount Koya—called Koyasan by Japanese—is one of Japan's most sacred places and the mecca of the Shingon Esoteric sect of Buddhism. Standing almost 900m (3,000 ft.) above the world, the top of Mount Koya is home to more than 115 Shingon Buddhist temples scattered through the mountain forests. Some 50 of these temples offer accommodations, making this one of the best places in Japan to observe temple life firsthand.

A World Heritage Site, Koyasan first became a place of meditation and religious learning almost 1,200 years ago when Kukai, known posthumously as Kobo Daishi, was granted the mountaintop by the imperial court in 816 as a place to establish his Shingon sect of Buddhism. Kobo Daishi was a charismatic priest who had spent 2 years in China studying esoteric Buddhism before returning to his native land to spread his teachings among Japanese. Revered for his excellent calligraphy, his humanitarianism, and his teachings, Kobo Daishi remains one of the most beloved figures in Japanese Buddhist history. When he died in the 9th century, he was laid to rest in a mausoleum on Mount Koya. His followers believe Kobo Daishi is not dead but simply in a deep state of meditation, awaiting the arrival of the last bodhisattva (Buddha messiah). According to popular belief, priests opening his mausoleum decades after his death found his body still warm.

Through the centuries, many of Kobo Daishi's followers, wishing to be close at hand when the great priest awakens, have had huge tombs or tablets constructed close to Kobo Daishi's mausoleum, and many have had their ashes interred here. Pilgrims over the last thousand years have included emperors, feudal lords, samurai, and common people, all climbing to the top of the mountain to pay their respects. Women, however, were barred from entering the sacred grounds of Koyasan until 1872.

Essentials

GETTING THERE The easiest way to get to Koyasan is from Osaka. **Nankai Railway's** ordinary express (*kyuko*) **Koya Line** trains depart from Osaka's Namba Station every half-hour or hour bound for Gokurakubashi, and the trip south takes about 1 hour and 40 minutes. If you want to ride in luxury, Nankai limited-express trains with reserved seating depart about five times daily and arrive in Gokurakubashi about 1 hour and 15 minutes later. After arriving at the last stop, Gokurakubashi, you continue your trip to the top of Mount Koya via a 5-minute ride in a cable car. The entire journey from Namba Station to Mount Koya costs ¥1,230 one-way, including the cable car; if you take the faster limited express, it'll cost ¥760 extra. You'll save money, however, with Nankai's **discount ticket** called **Koyasan World Heritage Ticket** (available at Namba Station), which includes round-trip travel from Namba Station and the cable car, plus unlimited rides on Koya's buses for 2 days and a 20% discount to the attractions listed below. The cost is ¥2,780 if you travel by ordinary express and ¥3,310 by limited-express. Children pay half fare. For more information on travel to and around Koyasan, go to **www.nankaikoya.jp**.

VISITOR INFORMATION At the top of Mount Koya is Koyasan Station, where you'll find a booth of the local tourist office, the main office of which is located approximately in the center of Koyasan village near Kongobuji Temple. You can pick up a map of Koyasan and book a room in a temple at either office, but it is recommended that you email or fax for a reservation at least 7 business days before your visit (see "Where to Stay & Eat," below). Both offices are open daily from 8:30am to 4:30pm in winter (Nov–Feb), to 5pm the rest of the year. The main office has a computer with Internet access you can use for free, as well as a 90-minute rental audio guide for ¥500 that's highly useful for learning more about what you're seeing throughout Koyasan, including the location of famous mausoleums and tombstones in Okunoin. For more information, contact the **Koyasan Tourist Association** (*©* **0736/56-2616**) or check the websites **www.koya.org/eng** and **http://eng. shukubo.net**.

GETTING AROUND   Outside the cable car station, you must board a **bus** that travels 2km (1¼ miles) along a narrow, winding road to the village of Koyasan and then continues along the main street all the way through town to the Okunoin-guchi and Okunoin-mae bus stops, the location of Kobo Daishi's mausoleum. The bus passes almost all the sights along the way, as well as most temples accommodating visitors and the Koyasan Tourist Association's main office. Buses depart every 30 or 40 minutes between 6:29am and 7pm; the trip to Okunoin-mae takes 20 minutes and costs ¥400. Otherwise, once you're settled in at your temple accommodations, you can probably walk to Okunoin and other locations mentioned below. Otherwise, rental bicycles are available at the main tourist office costing ¥400 for one hour and an additional ¥100 for every 30 minutes after that (because the number of bikes are limited, you might want to reserve one in advance by calling the tourist office).

Exploring Mount Koya

THE TOP ATTRACTION   The most awe-inspiring and magnificent of Koyasan's many structures and temples, **Okunoin ★★★** contains the mausoleum of Kobo Daishi. The most dramatic way to approach Okunoin is from the Okunoin-guchi bus stop, where a pathway leads 1.5km (1 mile) to the mausoleum. Swathed in a respectful darkness of huge cypress trees forming a canopy overhead are monument after monument, tomb after tomb—approximately 200,000 of them, all belonging to faithful followers from past centuries. The audio guide from the tourist office (see "Visitor Information," above) will guide you to the most famous tombstones, including those of the Toyotomi, Shimadzu, Maeda, Asano, and Matsudaira clans.

I don't know whether being here will affect you the same way, but I am always awe-struck by the sheer density of tombstones, the iridescent green moss, the shafts of light streaking through the treetops, the stone lanterns, and the gnarled bark of the old cypress trees. Together, they present a dramatic picture representing more than a thousand years of Japanese Buddhist history. If you're lucky, you won't meet many people along this pathway. Tour buses fortunately park at a newer entrance to the mausoleum at the bus stop called Okunoin-mae. I absolutely forbid you to take this newer and shorter route; its crowds lessen the impact of this place considerably. Rather, make sure you take the path farthest to the left, which begins near the Okunoin-guchi/Ichinohashi stops. Much less traveled, it's also much more impressive and is one of the main reasons for coming to Koyasan in the first place. And be sure to return to the mausoleum at night; the stone lanterns (now lit electrically) create a mysterious and powerful effect.

At the end of the pathway, about a 30-minute walk away, is the **Lantern Hall,** or Torodo, which houses about 21,000 lanterns, donated by prime ministers, emperors, and others. Two sacred fires, which reportedly have been burning since the 11th century, are kept safely inside. The mausoleum itself is behind the Lantern Hall. Buy a white candle, light it, and wish for anything you want. Then sit back and watch respectfully as Buddhists come to chant and pay respects to one of Japan's greatest Buddhist leaders. Many who have successfully completed the pilgrimage to Shikoku Island's 88 Buddhist temples, often dressed in white and carrying a staff, conclude their journey here.

MORE TO SEE & DO   **Kongobuji Temple** (金剛峯寺) **★★**, located near the main Koyasan Tourist Association office in the center of town (© **0736/56-2011**), is the central monastery headquarters of the Shingon sect in Japan. Although Kongobuji was originally built in the 16th century by Toyotomi Hideyoshi to commemorate his mother's death, the present building is 150 years old, reconstructed following a fire. Pictures by famous artists from long ago decorate the rooms, including those depicting Kobo Daishi's trip to China, and the huge kitchen, big enough to feed multitudes of monks, is also on view. The most important thing to see, however, is the temple's magnificent rock garden, reputedly the largest in Japan and said to represent a pair of dragons in a sea of clouds. If it's raining, consider yourself lucky—the wetness adds sheen and color to the rocks. Admission is ¥500 for adults, ¥200 for children.

Another important site is the **Garan ★** (*(℗* **0736/56-3215**), the first buildings constructed on Koyasan and still considered the center of religious life in the community. It's an impressive sight with a huge *kondo* (main hall), first built in 819 by Kobo Daishi; a large vermilion-colored *daito* (pagoda), which many consider to be Koyasan's most magnificent structure and which is very much worth entering (¥200 each for the kondo and daito); and the oldest building on Mount Koya, the Fudodo, which was built in 1197. Next to the complex is the **Reihokan Museum** (霊宝館; www.reihokan.or.jp; *℗* **0736/56-2254**), displaying wooden Buddha sculptures, scrolls, art, and other Koyasan treasures spread through two buildings, with exhibitions changed four times a year. Admission here is ¥600 for adults, ¥350 for students, and ¥250 for children.

All of the sites above are open daily: 8:30am to 4:30pm November to April, and 8:30am to 5 or 5:30pm May to October.

Where to Stay & Eat

Although this community of 4,000 residents has the usual stores, schools, and offices of any small town, there are no hotels here. The only place you can stay is at a temple, and I strongly urge you to do so.

Japanese who come here have almost always made reservations beforehand, and you should do the same. You can make reservations by calling the temple directly or through travel agencies such as the **Japan Travel Bureau** (www.jtbgmt.com). You can also make reservations upon arrival in Koyasan at either Tourist Association office before 4pm (see "Essentials," above), but I suggest emailing or faxing a minimum of 7 days in advance to be sure you can get a space (fax **0736/56-2889**), especially during peak travel seasons; include your name, address, phone and fax numbers, e-mail address, dates of stay, and number of people.

WHAT IT'S LIKE TO STAY AT A KOYASAN TEMPLE   Prices for an overnight stay in one of the temples, including two vegetarian meals, range from ¥9,500 to ¥15,000 per person, depending on the temple, the room, and the meal. You may need to supply your own towel and toiletries. Check-in is around 3pm (5pm at the latest) and checkout is at 9am (you can leave your luggage at the temple while sightseeing).

Your room will be tatami and may include a nice view of a garden. Both baths and toilets are communal. High-school and college students attending Koyasan's Buddhist university live at the temple; they'll bring your meals to your room, make up your futon, and clean your room. The *shojin ryori* (Buddhist vegetarian meals) are generally quite good, and because Buddhist monks are vegetarians but not teetotalers (beer and sake are made of rice and grain), alcoholic drinks are readily available at the temples for an extra charge. Meals are at set times. Dinner is at 5:30pm, and because the students must leave for school, breakfast is usually served by 7:30am. The morning religious service is at 6 or 6:30am; you don't have to attend, but I strongly recommend that you do. There's something uplifting about early morning meditative chanting, even for nonbelievers; some temples include sacred fire ceremonies as well.

Below are just a few of the dozens of area temples open to overnight guests (rates are based on two people to a room). They're all located very near the indicated bus stop. All of them have public baths, as it's rare for temples to offer rooms with bathrooms.

Ekoin (恵光院) ★   This 100-year-old temple, with origins stretching back almost 1,100 years when Kukai was said to have erected a stupa on this site, has nice grounds and is nestled in a wooded slope an easy walk from Okunoin. For centuries it enjoyed support of the Shimadzu clan of southern Kyushu. It's known for its excellent Buddhist cuisine, and the master priest will give *zazen* meditation lessons if his schedule permits (make advance reservations). Every morning there's both a chanting service and a fire ceremony. Most rooms have nice sitting alcoves. Reservations should be made in advance, especially for peak season; there's always someone here who speaks a little English.

497 Koyasan, Koya-cho, Ito-gun, Wakayama Prefecture 648-0211. www.ekoin.jp. ☎ **0736/56-2514.** Fax 0736/56-2891. 37 units, none with bathroom. ¥10,000–¥15,000 per person. Rates include 2 meals. AE, MC, V. Bus: Karukayado-mae. **Amenities:** Computer w/free Internet access; hot-spring bath. *In room:* TV (most rooms), no phone (in some).

Rengejoin Temple (蓮華定院) ★★   This temple's head priest speaks English, so a lot of foreigners are directed here; it's a good place to meet people and to find out about Buddhism. It's also one of the few temples that may take you in without a reservation. Established 900 years ago, it was rebuilt 150 years ago after a fire. Rooms have views of a nice garden with a pond; pluses are the English-language videos placed in some rooms that explore the history and significance of Mount Koya and Kongobuji Temple, as well as both evening and morning services conducted in both Japanese and English. The disadvantage is that it's on the opposite end of town from Okunoin, about a 40-minute walk away.

700 Koyasan, Koya-cho, Ito-gun, Wakayama Prefecture 648-0211. ☎ **0736/56-2233.** Fax 0736/56-4743. 48 units, none with bathroom. ¥9,500–¥15,750. Rates include 2 meals. No credit cards. Bus: Ishinguchi stop. *In room:* TV, no phone.

Shojoshinin (清浄心院) ★★★   Of all Koyasan's temples, this one has the most curb appeal. Originating as a thatched hut built by Kukai almost 1,200 years ago and once the second-largest temple in Koyasan after Kongobuji, today it boasts attractive 152-year-old buildings against a wooded backdrop, including a large wooden structure with rooms overlooking a small garden and pond. It's usually full in August and peak seasons, so make reservations early (rare among temple lodgings, it has one room with a private bathroom, for the highest price listed below). It has a great location at the beginning of the tomb-lined pathway to Okunoin, making it convenient for your late-night stroll to the mausoleum.

566 Koyasan, Koya-cho, Ito-gun, Wakayama Prefecture 648-0211. ☎ **0736/56-2006.** Fax 0736/56-4770. 30 units, 29 without bathroom. ¥9,500–¥15,100 per person. Rates include 2 meals. No credit cards. Bus: Okunoin-guchi. *In room:* TV (most rooms), no phone (in most rooms).

Tentokuin (天徳院)   The rooms of this temple, which dates from 1622, are located in a new annex. Most look out onto the garden, which in the 1930s was described as one of the most beautiful places in Japan. With a natural mountain background, the garden is of the "borrowed landscaping" style and retains its layout design dating from the Momoyama Period. Rates depend on room size and garden view.

370 Koyasan, Koya-cho, Ito-gun, Wakayama Prefecture 648-0211. ☎ **0736/56-2714.** Fax 0736/56-3618. 55 units, none with bathroom. ¥9,500–¥15,000 per person. Rates include 2 meals. AE, V. Bus: Senjuin-bashi. *In room:* TV, no phone.

HIMEJI, A CASTLE TOWN ★

640km (400 miles) W of Tokyo; 130km (81 miles) W of Kyoto; 87km (54 miles) E of Okayama

The main reason tourists come to Himeji, in Hyogo Prefecture, is to see its 400-year-old beautiful **castle,** which embodies better than any other castle the best in Japan's military architecture. If you were to see only one castle in Japan, this is my pick (note, however, that the castle's main keep is under wraps until 2014, though parts remain open inside and a special exhibit of the restoration project is equally fascinating).

Because of the castle's proximity to Himeji Station on the Shinkansen line, many tourists stop only long enough to see the castle and maybe a few other sites before continuing onward. I've included a few recommendations, however, for those wishing to make an overnight stop.

Essentials

GETTING THERE A stop on the **Tokaido/Sanyo Shinkansen** bullet train, which runs between Tokyo and Kyushu, Himeji is about 3½ hours from Tokyo, 1 hour from Kyoto, and less than a half-hour from Okayama. The fare from Tokyo is ¥14,700 for a nonreserved seat. If you're arriving at Kansai International Airport outside Osaka, there are 10 Airport Limousine Buses daily to Himeji Station; the trip takes a little over 2 hours and costs ¥3,200 one-way (half fare for children).

VISITOR INFORMATION The **Himeji Kanko Navi Port** tourist information center (✆ 079/287-0003) is located at the central exit of the station's north (castle) side, to the right after you exit from the ticket gate. Open daily from 9am to 7pm, the staff answers questions, hands out maps, and even rents bikes free of charge (see below). For online information see **www.himeji-kanko.jp/en**; some information is also provided at **www.city.himeji.lg.jp/en**.

There are coin lockers at the station for those stopping in Himeji only for a few hours to see the castle.

GETTING AROUND You can **walk** to Himeji's attractions. The main road in town is Otemae Dori, a wide boulevard stretching from Himeji Station north to Himeji Castle (you can walk the distance in about 15 min.). To the east (right) of Otemae Dori are two parallel streets, Miyukidori and Omizosuji, both covered shopping arcades. If you want, you can use a **bicycle** free of charge from 9am to 5:30pm by filling out an application form before 4pm at Himeji Kanko Navi Port, where you'll be given a ticket and told where to pick up the bike. Finally, the retro-looking **Himeji Castle Loop Bus** makes runs daily from 9am to 5pm (only on weekends and holidays Dec–Feb) every half-hour (every 15 min. weekends and holidays) from the station to the castle, Koko-en, and beyond. It costs ¥100 per ride; an all-day ticket for ¥300 includes discounts to Himeji Castle and Koko-en.

[FastFACTS] HIMEJI

Internet Access **Jyukukan Himeji,** beside the APA Hotel Himejieki-Kita (see p. 396 for directions), 98 Higashi Ekimai-cho (✆ 079/286-6006), is open 24 hours and charges ¥290 for the first 30 minutes and then ¥100 for each subsequent 15 minutes. The **Library Corner** of the Himeji International Exchange Center, 4th floor of the Egret Himeji building, 68–290 Honmachi (✆ 079/287-0820), offers an hour of free Internet use daily from 10am to 6pm.

Exploring Himeji

Himeji Castle ★★★ CASTLE As soon as you exit from Himeji Station north exit, you'll see Himeji Castle straight ahead at the end of a wide boulevard called Otemae Dori. Perhaps the most beautiful castle in all of Japan, Himeji Castle is nicknamed "White Heron Castle" in reference to its white walls, which stretch out on either side of the main *donjon* (castle keep) and resemble a white heron poised in flight over the plain. Whether it looks to you like a heron or a castle, the view of the white five-story donjon under a blue sky is striking, especially when the area's 1,700 cherry trees are in bloom. This is also one of the few castles in Japan that has remained virtually as it was since its completion in 1618, surviving even World War II bombings that laid Himeji in ruins. In 1993, the castle, along with Horyuji Temple in Nara, became Japan's first UNESCO's World Heritage Sites. **Note:** Himeji Castle's donjon is under renovation until March 2014, necessitating the erection of a protective shroud over the keep and occasional partial shutdowns of the castle's interior. However, inside the scaffolding is Egret's Eye View, reached via elevator and affording close-up views of the painstaking renovation of plaster walls and roof tiles, done using traditional methods. The opportunity to see such work is so rare, it has been drawing crowds. Once renovation is complete, it will take a year to dismantle the scaffolding.

Originating as a fort in the 14th century, Himeji Castle took a more majestic form in 1581 when a three-story donjon was built by Toyotomi Hideyoshi during one of his military campaigns in the district. In the early 1600s, the castle became the residence of Ikeda Terumasa, one of Hideyoshi's generals and a son-in-law of Tokugawa Ieyasu. He remodeled the castle into its present five-story structure. With its extensive gates, three moats, turrets, and a secret entrance, it had one of the most sophisticated defense systems in Japan. The maze of passageways leading to the donjon was so complicated that intruders would find themselves trapped in dead ends. The castle walls were constructed with square or circular holes through which gun muzzles could poke; the rectangular holes were for archers. There were also drop chutes where stones or boiling water could be dumped on enemies trying to scale the walls.

On weekends (and sometimes weekdays), volunteers hanging around the castle ticket office offer guided tours of the castle for free. It gives them an opportunity to practice their English while you learn about the history of the castle and even old castle gossip. But even if you go on your own, you won't have any problems learning about the history of the castle, as there are good English-language explanations throughout the castle grounds. With or without a guide, you'll spend at least 2 hours here. But beware, there are lots of stairs. **Tip:** A combination ticket, allowing discounted admission to both the castle and Koko-en (see below), is available at either entrance.

68 Honmachi. www.himeji-castle.gr.jp. ℂ **079/285-1146.** Admission ¥400 adults, ¥100 children; Egret's Eye View ¥200 and ¥100 extra, respectively. Combination ticket to both Himeji Castle and Koko-en ¥560 adults, ¥200 children. May 27–Aug daily 9am–6pm; Sept–May 26 daily 9am–5pm. You must enter 1 hr. before closing time. A 15-min. walk straight north of Himeji Station via Otemae Dori.

Koko-en (好古園) ★★★ 🛗 PARK/GARDEN Although laid out only in 1992, this is a wonderful garden, occupying land where samurai mansions once stood at the base of Himeji Castle, about a 5-minute walk away. Actually it's composed of nine separate small gardens, each one different and enclosed by traditional walls, with lots of rest areas to soak in the wonderful views. The gardens, typical of those in the Edo

Dining in Style

Shojin ryori vegetarian feasts are served in Juryoin Temple (✆ **079/266-3553**) for ¥5,250 or more (cash only), on special lacquerware that can be 200 years old. Although it's for groups of four or more (reservations required), you might be able to join an existing group. The full-course lunch is served Friday to Wednesday between noon and 1pm, but plan on 90 minutes for your meal. After paying an admission of ¥500 for admission to temple grounds (children get in free), you'll walk 20 minutes to reach the Maniden, the main temple building. An impressive, cliff-side wooden structure dedicated to the Goddess of Mercy, it was first constructed in 970, burned to the ground almost 1,000 years later, and was reconstructed in the 1930s. Other highlights among the many other structures spread along the mountaintop are the Jikido, a former dormitory for priests-in-training (this, together with Jogyodo and Daikodo, make up the Three Temples, where *The Last Samurai* was filmed) and the five mausoleums of the Honda clan, rulers of Himeji Castle in the 17th century.

Period, include a garden of deciduous trees, a garden of pine trees, a garden of flowers popular during the Edo Period, tea-ceremony gardens, and traditional Japanese gardens with ponds, waterfalls, and running streams. If you wish, relax at the Souju-an teahouse in the Cha-no-niwa (tea-ceremony garden) with tea and a sweet (¥500; daily 10am–4pm) or dine at a restaurant overlooking a carp pond (see "Where to Eat," below). In any case, I wouldn't miss this special place. If you don't stop (but how could you resist?), you can stroll through all the gardens in about 45 minutes.

68 Honmachi. ✆ **079/289-4120.** Admission ¥300 adults, ¥150 children. Combination ticket to both Himeji Castle and Koko-en ¥560 adults, ¥200 children. Daily 9am–5pm (to 6pm May–Aug). A 15-min. walk north of Himeji Station; turn left in front of Himeji Castle (the entrance will be on your right).

A Pilgrimage to Mount Shosha & Engyoji Temple

If you're staying overnight, you might consider a half-day trip to **Mount Shosha** (called Shoshazan in Japanese; ✆ **079/266-3327**), the 370m-high (1,214-ft.) mountain retreat of Engyoji Temple, founded more than 1,000 years ago by a holy man who received enlightenment from the God of Wisdom and Intellect. Since then, Japanese have flocked to the mountain to seek purification of both body and spirit. Many make it a fun day's outing as well, bringing obento lunch boxes with them to enjoy under the wooded trees (you'd be wise to do the same, as the only dining facilities on temple grounds is at Juryoin Temple; see below). No doubt, the fact that scenes from *The Last Samurai* starring Tom Cruise were shot here boosted its popularity. But I like this 3- to 4-hour excursion mainly for the lovely hike. The various temple buildings spread along the mountaintop are a bonus.

To reach Shoshazan, take bus no. 8 from Himeji Station, Himeji Castle, or Koko-en 25 minutes to the last stop (fare: ¥260). From there, board the Mt. Shosha Ropeway cable car (✆ **079/266-2006**) that departs every 15 minutes and costs ¥900 round-trip (half-price for children). Be sure to check when the last ropeway departs the mountain (5pm in winter; 6 or 7pm in summer).

Where to Eat

In addition to the choices below, consider stopping by **Kassui-ken** (活水軒; **079/289-4131**). To be honest, this charmless restaurant would not have much to recommend it except for one overwhelming feature: It overlooks a koi pond in lovely Koko-en Garden.

It's certainly the most picturesque place in town to try Himeji's specialty, conger eel. If that's too exotic, it also serves a few noodle dishes and beef curry. Or you can stop just for dessert or a refreshing drink of beer, soda, or coffee; but avoid the busy lunchtime crowd. In any case, set meals range from ¥1,575 to ¥2,625 (no credit cards accepted), and it's open daily 9:30am to 4:30pm (to 5:30pm from Apr 27 through Aug).

In the listings below, directions are from Himeji Station.

Menme (めんめ) ★ ♦ NOODLES   The friendly husband-and-wife team here has been dishing out udon noodles at this same spot for more than 30 years, with tempura udon, curry udon, and other various udon listed on the English menu. Tanimoto-san makes all of his udon on the spot, so though you might have to wait, it's interesting to watch the process. And though the restaurant's location draws in many passing tourists, it's also popular with locals.

68 Honmachi. © **079/225-0118.** Udon ¥550–¥950; set meal (Mon–Fri only) ¥730. No credit cards. Thurs–Tues 11:30am–6pm. On Otemae Dori, on the left just before Himeji Castle; look for the sign board showing plates of noodles.

Mille ★★ 🍴 VARIED JAPANESE/WESTERN   Great views of Himeji Castle are the trademark of this fancy but reasonably priced restaurant offering set meals. Although the menu is in Japanese, there are photos of various options that may include sashimi, tempura, and other fare, as well as set meals of Western food.

Egret Himeji Building, 4th floor, 68 Honmachi. © **079/225-0030.** Set dinners ¥3,150–¥6,300; set lunches ¥1,575–¥4,200.AE, DC, MC, V. Mon–Fri 11:30am–2:30pm; Sat–Sun and holidays 11am–2:30pm; daily 5–9pm (last order). Walking north on Otemae Dori, turn right at the next-to-last streetlight before Himeji Castle; it's the soaring glass building on the right.

Sainte Vierge ★★ FRENCH   This is Himeji's swankiest place for French cuisine, with an elegant drawing-room ambience, white table-clothed tables spaced far apart for privacy, and classical music. Only set meals are served, giving choices of fish, meat, or both as main courses, along with side dishes. My ¥2,300 set lunch consisted of bread, an appetizer of homemade ham with organic vegetables, sweet potato soup, and seabass. Because this is a popular wedding venue, especially on weekends, be sure to call first to see whether it's open to the public.

Konyamachi 23. © **079/223-1122.** Set dinners ¥3,999–¥10,500; set lunches ¥2,300–¥5,000. AE, DC, MC, V. Wed–Mon noon–2pm and 6–8pm (last order). Walk north on Otemae Dori toward the castle and after the Shirogane intersection take the 2nd right (Mizuho and Tokyo-Mitsubishi UFJ banks are on the corner here); it's past the 2 covered shopping arcades, on the right.

Where to Stay

APA Hotel Himejieki-Kita   This business hotel offers rooms that aren't much bigger than their beds, windows that open (though the cheapest singles face another building), panels that close for complete darkness, and inserts for slippers (an APA chain hotel original). The lobby is on the second floor, above an Internet cafe.

98 Higashi Ekimae-cho, Himeji, Hyogo Prefecture 670-0926. www.apahotel.com. © **079/284-4111.** Fax 079/284-4112. 152 units. ¥7,500–¥8,000 single; ¥13,000–¥14,000 double. AE, DC, MC, V. Station: Himeji (north exit, 5 min.). Walk north on Otemae Dori toward the castle; turn right at the 1st large intersection, Shirogane, on a street called Junishomae (a one-way street with a traffic

light) and walk past 2 covered shopping arcades and Starbucks; it will be on the left. **Amenities:** Restaurant; Internet cafe. *In room:* A/C, TV, fridge, hair dryer, Internet.

Claire Higasa This family-owned hotel is a good bet. Although distinctly a business hotel with its 50 single rooms, laundry room (use of the washing machine is free), and soda and noodle vending machines, several pluses—such as soothing music and flower arrangements in the lobby and an accommodating, English-speaking staff—take it out of the ordinary. Rooms are tiny; even tinier bathrooms have a shower/sink combination faucet that's a bit mind-boggling for the technically challenged, but who cares when the large seventh-floor public baths with Jacuzzi jets have castle views? There's only one double room; alternatively, couples can squeeze into a semidouble bed for ¥9,450 or, better yet, opt for a Japanese-style room.

22 Junishomae-cho, Himeji, Hyogo Prefecture 670-0911. www.hotel-higasa.com. ℂ **079/224-3421.** Fax 079/289-3729. 60 units. ¥7,035 single; ¥13,650–¥14,700 double; ¥12,600 Japanese-style double. MC, V. Station: Himeji (north exit, 5 min.). Walk north on Otemae-Dori toward the castle and after the first big intersection (Shirogane intersection, the one with a large, one-way street named Junishomae Dori and a traffic light) take the next left; it's 4 short blocks farther, on the left across from a small park. *In room:* A/C, TV, fridge, hair dryer, Wi-Fi.

Hotel Nikko Himeji ★★ The Nikko is Himeji's most luxurious hotel. Its location only a 1-minute walk from Himeji Station's Shinkansen side is a definite plus, as are its dining options, its top-floor lounge with a view of the castle, and its health club. For castle views in the distance, splurge on a twin (type B) or double on the 10th floor or higher facing north (single rooms do not offer castle views). Rooms are small but comfortable, with large windows.

100 Minami-ekimai-cho, Himeji, Hyogo Prefecture 670-0962. www.hotelnikkohimeji.co.jp. ℂ **079/222-2231.** Fax 079/224-3731. 257 units. ¥10,925–¥11,200 single; ¥20,700–¥26,850 double. AE, DC, MC, V. A 1-min. walk from the south (Shinkansen) central exit of Himeji Station. **Amenities:** 4 restaurants; bar; lounge; health club w/20m (66-ft.) indoor lane pool, sauna, whirlpool, and exercise room (fee: ¥1,500). *In room:* A/C, TV, hair dryer, Internet, minibar.

Toyoko Inn Himeji-eki Shinkansen Minami-guchi ★ ✦ This budget chain beats all the rest with its tiny immaculate rooms, free services, and coin-operated laundry room. Next to Himeji Station's south (Shinkansen) exit, it offers tiny rooms, with singles from the ninth floor boasting views of the castle in the distance.

97 Minami-ekimae-cho, Himeji, Hyogo Prefecture 670-0962. www.toyoko-inn.com. ℂ **079/284-1045.** Fax 079/284-1046. 210 units. ¥5,480–¥8,880 single; ¥7,980–8,890 double. Rates include free Japanese breakfast. AE, DC, MC, V. A 1-min. walk from the south (Shinkansen) exit of Himeji Station, to the left. **Amenities:** Lobby computer w/free Internet, Wi-Fi (free, in lobby). *In room:* A/C, TV, fridge, hair dryer, Internet.

OKAYAMA: GATEWAY TO SHIKOKU

733km (455 miles) W of Tokyo; 218km (136 miles) W of Kyoto; 160km (100 miles) E of Hiroshima

With a strategically important location as the major gateway to the island of Shikoku (see chapter 9), Okayama Prefecture is a center of trade, industry and crafts. In 1988, it got a further boost thanks to the Seto Ohashi Bridge, which measures almost 9.5km (6 miles) in length and connects Okayama Prefecture on Honshu Island with Sakaide on Shikoku. Before the bridge was built in 1988, it took an hour by ferry to reach Shikoku, whereas traveling by train or car along the double-decker bridge cuts travel time down to just 15 minutes, and it remains the only rail bridge to the island.

For those of you less interested in bridges, Okayama city, with a population of 701,000 and the capital of Okayama Prefecture, boasts one of the most noted gardens in Japan. It's an easy jaunt to Bizen, one of Japan's most famous pottery towns, and in nearby Kurashiki (see "Kurashiki, Market Town of Many Charms," beginning on p. 405), its historic quarter ranks as one of the most picturesque neighborhoods in Japan. And scattered through Okayama Prefecture are a couple so-called **International Villas,** accommodations located primarily in rural areas with amazingly low rates.

Essentials

GETTING THERE Okayama is a major stop on the **Shinkansen** Tokaido/Sanyo Line, about 3½ hours from Tokyo (fare: ¥15,850 for an unreserved seat), 1 hour and 20 minutes from Kyoto (fare: ¥6,820), and 45 minutes from Hiroshima (fare: ¥5,350).

Buses depart nightly from Shinjuku Station's west exit in Tokyo: at 9:30pm (Shimoden Bus Co.; ✆ **03/5438-8511**) and at 9:45pm (Ryobi Bus Co.; ✆ **03/3928-6011**), both arriving at Okayama Station the next day at 7:50am and costing ¥9,800 one-way. From Tokyo Station, JR buses (✆ **03/3844-0489**) depart from the Yaesu south exit at 8:40pm and arrive in Okayama at 7:18am for ¥10,000.

Flights from Tokyo to Okayama Airport (OKJ; www.okayama-airport.org; ✆ **086/294-5201**) take about 1 hour and 15 minutes. An Airport Limousine Bus shuttles passengers to Okayama Station in about 30 minutes for ¥740.

VISITOR INFORMATION The **Okayama City Tourist Information Office** (✆ **086/222-2912;** daily 9am–6pm) is inside Okayama Station near the central exit of the east side (look for the sign displaying a question mark). The office is well prepared for foreign visitors, supplying English-language maps and brochures.

Just a 5-minute walk from Okayama Station is the **Okayama International Center,** 2–2–1 Hokancho, Kita-ku, where at the first-floor Information Counter (www.opief.or.jp; ✆ **086/256-2914;** Mon–Sat 9am–5pm) you can also obtain tourist information, get maps, and access the Internet. To find the center, take the west exit of the station's central gate and turn right (north) onto the main street running in front of the station until you come to a 7-Eleven, where you should turn left; the center is the big building on your right. More information on Okayama is available on the Internet at **www.pref.okayama.jp** and **www.city.okayama.jp**.

GETTING AROUND Okayama's sights are all clustered within walking distance of each other, due east of Okayama Station. You can walk from Okayama Station to Okayama Castle in about 30 minutes via Momotaro Odori. Otherwise, board a **streetcar** from Okayama Station's east side bound for Higashiyama (platform 1) and disembark about 6 minutes later at the Shiroshita streetcar stop (the third stop; to your right will be the very noticeable, cylindrical Okayama Symphony Hall building). Pay the ¥100 fare when you get off. From here you can continue walking straight ahead (east) 15 minutes to Okayama Castle and then visit nearby Korakuen Garden and Yumeji Art Museum.

[Fast FACTS] OKAYAMA

Internet Access You can access the Internet for free at the Okayama International Center, but you're limited to 30 minutes of usage and because there are only two computers, you may have to wait. Otherwise, head to Club Mont Blanc on the sixth floor of the OPA building across from Okayama Station's east exit, 6–3 Honmachi (✆ **086/224-7050**), open 24 hours and charging ¥290 for 30 minutes.

Exploring Okayama

Korakuen Garden ★★★ PARK/GARDEN   Okayama's claim to fame is this garden, considered one of Japan's three most beautiful landscaped gardens (the other two are in Kanazawa and Mito). Completed in 1700 by the Ikeda ruling clan after 14 years of work, its 11 hectares (28 acres) are graced with a pond, running streams, pine trees, plum and cherry trees, flowering bushes such as azaleas and hydrangeas, bamboo groves, teahouses, and tea plantations. The surrounding hills, as well as Okayama's famous black castle, are incorporated into the garden's design (luckily, laws limiting the size of surrounding buildings protect the views). Its name, Korakuen, means "the garden for taking pleasure later," which has its origins in an old saying: "Bear sorrow before the people; take pleasure after them." This garden differs from most Japanese gardens in that it has large expanses of grassy open areas—the first Japanese garden to do so and still a rarity in crowded Japan. Other unusual features worth seeking out are the Ryuten, a wooden pavilion that straddles a stream where you can soak your feet, and an enclosure of red-crested cranes. You can easily spend an hour here.

1–5 Korakuen. www.okayama-korakuen.jp. ℂ **086/272-1148.** Admission ¥400 adults, ¥140 children, free for seniors. Combination ticket to Okayama Castle and Korakuen Garden ¥560 adults, ¥260 children. Apr–Sept daily 7:30am–6pm; Oct–Mar daily 8am–5pm. Streetcar stop: Shiroshita (20 min.). Continue walking straight east and then turn left for the footbridge.

Okayama Castle   Originally built in the 16th century, Okayamajo was destroyed in World War II and rebuilt in 1966. Thanks to its black exterior, it has earned the nickname "Crow Castle"; it was painted black to contrast with neighboring Himeji's famous White Heron castle. Unlike castles of yore, an elevator whisks you up to the fourth floor of the *donjon*. Take the stairs to the top floor for views of the park and the city beyond; other floors contain a few swords, samurai outfits, lacquerware, and other Edo-Period items, most identified in Japanese only and quickly seen in 15 minutes or so. There's also a children's play area with old-fashioned toys, but probably the most rewarding thing to do here is to try on a kimono and have someone snap a picture of you with your own camera. Donning costumes is free, but only five participants are accepted at 10 and 11am, and 1, 2, and 3pm. Frankly, if you've seen other Japanese castles, you might just want to photograph this one from the outside and move on. For a fairytale fantasy indulgence, you can rent swan-shaped paddle boats on the river below the castle (just be glad your neighbors aren't here to see you).

2–3–1 Marunouchi. ℂ **086/225-2096.** Admission ¥300 adults, ¥120 children. Combination ticket to Okayama Castle and Korakuen Garden ¥560 adults, ¥260 children. Daily 9am–5:30pm. Streetcar stop (15 min.). Continue walking east; it will be on your right.

> ## When You're Done Sightseeing
>
> The fastest way to return to Okayama Station is by bus no. 1 from the Korakuen-mae bus stop, located outside Korakuen Garden just before the bridge to Yumeji Art Museum.

Yumeji Art Museum (Yumeji-Kyodo Bijutsukan; 夢二郷土美術館**)** ART MUSEUM   This museum, in a brick building topped by a cock weather vane just a few minutes' walk north of Korakuen, is dedicated to the works of Yumeji Takehisa. Born in Okayama Prefecture in 1884, Yumeji is sometimes referred to as Japan's Toulouse-Lautrec and is credited with developing the *fin de siècle* Art

Nouveau movement in Japan. This collection includes some of his most famous works (beautiful women were his favorite subjects, often painted with larger-than-life eyes), mostly in the sparse, Nihonga style of painting. The small three-room exhibition displays a selection of about 100 of his works, changed every 3 months; allow about 15 minutes.

2–1–32 Hama. www.yumeji-art-museum.com. ℂ **086/271-1000.** Admission ¥700 adults; ¥400 junior-high to college students; ¥300 children. Tues–Sun 9am–5pm. Streetcar: Shiroshita stop (23 min.). Just north of Korakuen Garden, a short walk across Horai-bashi Bridge.

A Cycling Excursion

For some rural R & R, head west from Okayama city to the historic Kibiji District, once home to the ancient Kibi kingdom and known today for its huge *kofun* (burial mounds), temples, shrines, and five-story pagoda, all connected via a marked biking path that traverses this pastoral landscape. It's fun to cycle from one historic destination to the next, but what I like most about this ride is its rural setting, through villages, past peach groves, and along paddies (much of the bike path is actually on the same raised walkways farmers use to separate and dam their paddies and to get to their fields).

Rental bikes (ℂ **0866/92-0233**) are available daily 9am to 6pm to the right outside Soja Station, which you can reach in 34 minutes by JR train from Okayama Station (fare: ¥400), with trains running two to three times an hour. Bikes rent for ¥400 for 2 hours, plus ¥200 each additional hour. Although you can return bikes to Soja Station, I suggest forking out an additional ¥600 drop-off fee and cycling the bike path's entire 15km (10 miles) to Ichinomiya Station, where you can ditch the bike and hop on a train for an 11-minute ride back to Okayama Station (fare: ¥200). It takes 3 to 4 hours to bike the entire path and stop at sights along the way. **Caveat:** Although the bike path is well marked most of the way, with signs in English saying KIBIJI DISTRICT with a picture of a bike, I got lost trying to find Ichinomiya Station. Villagers are apparently used to lost cyclers and soon had me merrily on my way. Be sure to pick up a cycling map when you rent your bike; the Okayama International Center also has information on the Kibiji District (see "Visitor Information," above).

Where to Eat

Okayama's most famous dish is Okayama *barazushi,* which features Seto Inland Sea delicacies and fresh mountain vegetables. Traditionally served during festive occasions and therefore sometimes called *matsuri* (festival) *sushi,* it consists of a rice casserole laced with shredded ginger and cooked egg yolk and is topped with a variety of goodies, including conger eel, shrimp, fish, lotus root, and bamboo.

EXPENSIVE

Kuriya Sen ★★ KAISEKI/TEPPANYAKI   For a memorable meal with a view, head to this 20th-floor restaurant with sweeping views over the city, located in the ANA Hotel across from Okayama's west exit. With a modern, minimalist design, it offers changing kaiseki meals for lunch and dinner, along with grilled steaks and seafood prepared at a 12-seat *teppanyaki* counter. A stylish bar on the same floor offers cocktails with the same mesmerizing views.

ANA Hotel Okayama, 20th floor, 15–1 Ekimoto-machi. ℂ **086/898-2284.** Reservations recommended. Set lunches ¥2,100–¥8,000; set dinners ¥4,100–¥17,325. AE, DC, MC, V. Daily 11:30am–2pm (to 3pm Sat–Sun) and 5:30–10pm. Okayama Station (west exit, 1 min.).

MODERATE

Fukuzushi (福寿司) ★★ SUSHI   It's worth reserving a day or more in advance for *barazushi* at this spotless sushi shop beloved by locals and just a short walk from Okayama Station. The precise ingredients change daily (they've been at it for more than half a century), but on our visit barazushi included marble-sized potatoes, *koya-dofu* (freeze-dried tofu), mushrooms, *anago* (sea eel), clams, carrots and more, artfully served in rustic Bizen-yaki bowls with a side of miso soup. There's an English menu with more standard sushi choices.

2-16-17 Hokancho. fukuzushi-okayama.jp. © **086/252-2402.** Reservations required for *barazushi* at least 1 day in advance. *Barazushi* ¥3,000; other sushi sets ¥950–¥2,500. MC, V. Tues–Sun 11am–2:30pm and 5–10pm. Station: Okayama (west exit, 5 min.). Walk north along the main street and look for the green awning just past "Big American Shop."

Matsunoki-Tei (まつのき亭) ★★ 🍴 KAISEKI/SHABU-SHABU   This refined, family-run restaurant occupies a traditional-style house. Dining here is a luxurious experience, as you sit in a private tatami room (some with leg wells under the table, though you can also request a Western-style table when making reservations) and enjoy well-prepared dishes brought by an efficient and courteous staff. Although kaiseki is one of the most expensive meals you can have in Japan, it's quite reasonable here, and the all-you-can-eat *shabu-shabu* has a 2-hour time limit (indicate whether you want kaiseki or shabu-shabu when making your reservation). Even more economical are the obento lunch boxes for ¥1,700 and more elaborate mini-kaiseki lunches.

20–1 Ekimotomachi. © **086/253-5410.** Reservations required by noon for evening meals. Kaiseki ¥3,700–¥10,000; all-you-can-eat shabu-shabu ¥3,400; set lunches ¥1,700–¥4,000. No credit cards. Daily 11am–2pm and 5–10pm; closed 1st and 3rd Monday of each month. Station: Okayama (west exit, 2 min.). Walk west on the street to the north of NHK; it's just past the New Station Hotel, on the right.

Petite Mariée ★ FRENCH   Brick walls, a beamed ceiling, French music, a large bouquet of flowers, and numerous European knickknacks set the mood at the tiny (nonsmoking) Petite Mariée, which serves inexpensive yet good French bistro cooking. The set meals change every 3 days, but my ¥1,250 set lunch consisted of creamy mushroom potage, bread, seafood soufflé, vegetables, and coffee or tea. A glass of wine with lunch costs only ¥150 extra. Unfortunately, set meals are written in Japanese only (though the main dishes of set meals are displayed outside), while the a la carte menu (think roast lamb or scallops), is in French.

1–3–8 Yanagimachi. © **086/222-9066.** Main dishes ¥1,950–¥5,550; set lunches ¥1,250–¥2,300; set dinners ¥2,950–¥9,850. MC, V. Thurs–Tues 11:30am–2pm and 5–9pm (last order 8:30pm). Closed 3rd Tues of every month. Station: Okayama (8-min. walk southeast). Take the central (east) exit, turning right (south) onto Shiyakusho-suji; go 1 block past the gas station (it will be on your right) and turn left onto Akura Dori. It's 2 blocks farther on your right.

INEXPENSIVE

In addition to the choices below, there are some inexpensive, rustic snack houses along the moat that separates Okayama Castle and Korakuen Garden, at Tsukimi Bridge, where you can order a drink, noodles, or ice cream and relax with a view of the castle. Most are open daily 8:30am to 5pm (to 4:30pm in winter). If you're looking for a quick take-out meal, including *barazushi*, try the box-lunch stands in Okayama Station near the Shinkansen gate and across the corridor at Sun Station Terrace shopping pavilion and its adjacent supermarket.

Okabe (おかべ) 🍴 TOFU   This informal eatery in the heart of Okayama is a local institution for its specialty, homemade tofu. There's no problem ordering, as it serves only two *teishoku* (set meals), both with soup, rice, and pickled vegetables: the Okabe teishoku with two kinds of tofu, the other a *donburi* (rice bowl) topped with *nama-yuba*, the delicate skin that forms atop tofu, like a light noodle. Seating is along one long counter with only a dozen seats, behind which an army of women scurry to get out orders. It's simple but atmospheric.

1–10–1 Omotecho. ℂ **086/222-1404.** Okabe teishoku ¥800; donburi ¥850. No credit cards. Mon–Wed & Fri–Sat 11:30am–2pm. Closed national holidays. Streetcar: Shiroshita (2 min.). Walk south through the Omotecho covered shopping arcade 2 min. to the stoplight and turn right (west); it's on the left, on a corner. You'll see Okabe's open-fronted tofu shop; the restaurant is around the corner, next to a mural of a porter carrying baskets.

Shikisai (四季彩) VARIED JAPANESE   Located just outside the entrance to Korakuen Garden (its name translates as "Four Seasons of Color"), this up-to-date two-story building is decorated with Bizen pottery and Japanese *ikebana* and is a good place to try Okayama specialties for lunch, including *barazushi* (¥1,575), tempura, and seasonal dishes such as *nabe* (a one-pot stew eaten in winter), *anago* (sea eel), and mini-kaiseki meals, as well as *soba* and *udon* noodles, all listed on an English-language menu. Top it off with Doppo, a locally brewed beer. *Note:* Given its location, it can be busy with bus tours.

1–5 Korakuen-gaien. ℂ **086/273-3221.** Set lunches ¥1,260–¥2,100. No credit cards. Daily 11am–3pm. Streetcar: Shiroshita (11 min.). Located just north of the main entrance gate, next to a souvenir shop.

Yamadome (山留) ★ KUSHIAGE   This restaurant has been around since the late 1960s, but its renovated interior is classy and contemporary, with classical background music and local artists' work on the walls. It serves fried foods on sticks, from beef to fish to vegetables, with a variety of dipping sauces. The menu is in Japanese only, but a 10-stick (*juppon*) *kushikatsu* course costs ¥1,350. It's also worth trying *zosui*, a fragrant rice porridge with chicken and egg.

1–22 Tenjincho. ℂ **086/224-6886.** Kushikatsu sticks ¥120–¥170; set lunches ¥630–¥1,270; kushikatsu sets ¥1,350–¥2,290. No credit cards. Mon–Sat 11am–2:15pm and 5–9:30pm. Closed 1 week in mid-Aug. Streetcar: Shiroshita (1 min.). Just north of the streetcar stop, on a side street across from an Eneos gas station (which you can see from the stop).

Shopping

You can choose from a sampling of products and crafts made in Okayama Prefecture at the **Okayama Prefectural Local Products Center (Harenokuni Okayamakan;** 岡山県観光物産センター**),** 1–1–22 Omotecho (ℂ **086/234-2270;** Wed–Mon 10am–7pm), conveniently located beside (south of) the Shiroshita streetcar stop. Bizen pottery (see below), *igusa* (rush-grass mats), wooden trays, bambooware, papier-mâché toys, sake, and more are all for sale here.

For general shopping, there's a large underground shopping arcade called **Ichiban-gai** beneath Okayama Station, with boutiques selling clothing, shoes, and accessories. Across from the station and connected to Ichibangai is **Takashimaya** department store. In the heart of the city, just south of Shiroshita streetcar stop, is the 1km (half-mile) **Omotecho** covered shopping arcade, where you'll find **Tenmaya,** Okayama's largest department store.

THE pottery TOWN OF BIZEN

Japan's pottery tradition dates back millennia, and one of the most historic centers, with a 1,000-year history, is an easy train ride from Okayama. *Bizen-yaki* (Bizen pottery) is distinctive in that no glaze is applied to the clay. Rather, it's fired in a kiln for 10 to 15 painstaking days at nearly 2,300°F, with each piece achieving an unpredictable and distinctive look due to accumulations of ash, charcoal, and leaves wrapped around the pottery and even direct contact with flame. Bizen ware's rustic quality makes it well suited for the tea ceremony: Food looks great on it, too.

The center of the Bizen region is the village of **Imbe**, home to about 400 regional artisans and 35 minutes from Okayama by local train via the JR Ako Line (fare: ¥570). You don't even need to leave the train station to see their work; upstairs, the large gallery **Bizen-yaki Dento Sangyo Kaikan** (備前焼伝統産業会館; www.touyuukai.jp; ℂ **0869-64-1001;** Wed–Mon 9:30am–5:30pm) has row after row of it you can peruse for free. Next door, the four-story

Bizen Pottery Traditional and Contemporary Art Museum (岡山県備前陶芸美術館; ℂ **0869-64-1400;** Tues–Sun 9:30am–5:30pm) is full of new and old masterpieces. While an excellent English-language leaflet explains Bizen pottery, lack of English signage may limit your appreciation of individual pieces. Admission is ¥700 for adults, ¥400 high-school and university students, and free for children.

Across the street, dozens of working studios and galleries welcome visitors (pick up a map at the tourist office in the station). **Toukeidou** (℃ **0869/64-2147;** tokeido@mx3.tiki.ne.jp) is the shop of Hideaki Kimura, who can trace his pottery lineage back at least 17 generations, speaks English, and can guide you around his studio and kiln. Contact him a few days ahead of your visit to confirm that he'll be in.

For more information, contact the Okayama Tourist Information office or the **Bizen Potters Association** (www.touyuukai.jp; ℂ **0869/64-1001**).

Where to Stay
EXPENSIVE

Hotel Granvia Okayama ★★ Owned by the West Japan Railway Group and offering a discount for Japan Rail Pass holders, this hotel boasts a great location just east of Okayama Station (take the east central exit and look for it on your right). Rooms, on the 8th to 18th floors, with the best city views offered by more expensive twins and doubles on higher floors (most singles face another building), have snappy carpeting, duvet-covered beds, blackout curtains, and good bedside reading lamps. Of the hotel's several food-and-beverage outlets, best are those on the 19th floor with great views; among these, Applause, a classy cocktail lounge with a glass rotunda, serves a buffet lunch (¥1,890) and is a favorite for drinks (but note that there's a ¥1,050 music charge after 8pm).

1–5 Ekimoto-cho, Okayama 700-8515. www.granvia-oka.co.jp. ℂ **086/234-7000.** Fax 086/234-7099. 328 units. ¥14,437–¥15,939 single; ¥25,410–¥36,960 double. 20% discount for JR Pass holders. AE, DC, MC, V. Okayama Station (east central exit, 1 min.). **Amenities:** 5 restaurants; bar; 2 lounges; computer w/free Internet (in business center); concierge; 20m (66-ft.) indoor pool, sauna, and Jacuzzi (fee: ¥1,000); room service. *In room:* A/C, TV, hair dryer, Internet, minibar.

MODERATE

ANA Hotel Okayama ★★   The ANA could get away with charging significantly more for its up-to-date rooms in a contemporary tower just steps from Okayama Station. Its splashy décor would be at home in Tokyo or Osaka and its staff goes out of its way to be accommodating. Rooms are classy yet subdued, while 20th-floor restaurants have some of the region's best views, including Kuriya-sen (p. 400), where a diverse Japanese/western breakfast buffet is served for ¥1,500. There's no fitness center, but the hotel hands out a jogging map.

15–1 Ekimoto-machi, Okayama 700-0024. www.anahotel-okayama.com. ℂ **086/898-1111.** Fax 086/898-1200. 217 rooms. ¥7,875–¥8,925 single; ¥12,600–¥16,800 double. AE, DC, MC, V. Station: Okayama (west exit, 1 min.), via covered overpass. **Amenities:** 2 restaurants; bar; lobby computers w/free Internet; room service. In room: A/C, TV, hair dryer, Internet, minibar.

Kooraku Hotel ★   This business hotel is used to foreign guests and has much more design sense than most, with museum-style display cases of Bizen ware ceramics throughout the building. Rooms range from tiny singles (from 14 sq. m./150 sq. ft.), to deluxe 36-sq.-m. (387-sq.-ft.) corner twins with lots of light and big bathrooms. Couples who want to stay very close can sleep in a single room for ¥8,000. Ask for a room facing the front. Pluses include a post office and pharmacy next door and a bar in the basement. It's conveniently located about halfway between Okayama Station and the Shiroshita streetcar stop (the heart of the city), on a street lined with cherry and willow trees beside the small Nishigawa River.

5–1 Heiwa-cho, Kita-ku, Okayama 700-0827. www.hotel.kooraku.co.jp. ℂ **086/221-7111.** Fax 086/221-0007. 211 units. ¥6,750–¥7,700 single; ¥11,000–¥20,000 double. AE, DC, MC, V. A 7-min. walk east of Okayama Station. Take the central (east) exit, walk straight ahead on Momotaro Odori, and turn right on Nishigawa Ryokudo Koen Suji. **Amenities:** Restaurant; bar; lobby computer w/ free Internet. In room: A/C, TV, fridge, hair dryer, Internet.

Mitsui Garden Hotel Okayama ★   This smart-looking business hotel near Okayama Station distinguishes itself from most in this category with handsome public baths on the 10th floor and small rooms with a muted color scheme and crisp, modern decor. There are mostly singles and a few twins and doubles; because most face another building and are dark, you might want to request one that doesn't. You'll have the most space in superior doubles, with sofas and air purifiers.

1–7 Ekimoto-cho, Kita-ku, Okayama 700-0024. www.gardenhotels.co.jp. ℂ **086/235-1131.** Fax 086/225-8831. 352 units. ¥8,000–¥9,000 single; ¥15,200–¥16,800 double. AE, DC, MC, V. A 2-min. walk southeast of Okayama Station. Take the central (east) exit and turn right; it's behind Hotel Granvia. **Amenities:** Buffet restaurant open only for breakfast; lobby computer w/free Internet; Wi-Fi (free, in lobby). In room: A/C, TV, fridge, hair dryer, Internet.

INEXPENSIVE

Comfort Hotel 🗹   This simple business hotel has a great location for sightseeing, across from the Shiroshita streetcar stop and halfway between Okayama Station and the castle, a 15-minute walk from each. It offers small but modern mostly double rooms (a rarity in Japan, as most Japanese couples prefer twin beds), along with such perks as free rental bikes, free breakfast, and free coffee in the lobby from 3pm to midnight.

1–1–13 Marunouchi, Okayama 700-0823. www.comfortinn.com. ℂ **877/424-6423** in the U.S. and Canada, or 086/801-9411. Fax 086/801-9495. 208 units. ¥5,800 single; ¥8,500–¥12,000 double. Rates include breakfast buffet. AE, DC, MC, V. Streetcar: Shiroshita (1 min.; across the intersection to the right). **Amenities:** Free rental bikes; lobby computers w/free Internet. In room: A/C, TV, fridge, hair dryer, Wi-Fi.

countryside DELIGHTS: OKAYAMA INTERNATIONAL VILLA GROUP

If you're not on a tight schedule and you don't mind roughing it a bit, you might consider treating yourself to a few days in the countryside of Okayama Prefecture in one of two **International Villas.** Established in 1988 by the Okayama Prefectural Government to provide international guests the opportunity to experience rural Japan, the two villas are now managed by the local municipalities. Meals are not provided, so guests are expected to either dine out or cook and clean up after themselves.

In Hattoji, a village reached in about an hour via train and then bus or taxi, there's the **Hattoji Villa,** a 19th-century renovated thatched farmhouse with four Japanese-style rooms. Shiraishi Island in the Seto Inland Sea, which features beaches, shrines, and hiking trails, is home to the **Shiraishi Villa,** an airy, early 1990s, glass-and-wooden building with four twin rooms and one Japanese-style room and with great views of the Seto Inland Sea. To reach Shiraishi from Okayama requires a 45-minute train ride, a 7-minute walk to the port, and a 22- to 35-minute ride on a ferry.

If these villas were privately owned, you'd easily pay more than twice what you'll be charged: ¥3,500 per person (¥4,000 for single travelers). Rooms, all without private bathroom, are rented individually, or you can rent the entire villa. Note, however, that only non-Japanese visitors and their Japanese guests are allowed to stay at Shiraishi Villa, while Hattoji Villa is open to both non-Japanese and Japanese guests. The maximum stay is 7 nights. For more information, including locations, rates, and reservations, contact the **Okayama International Villa Reservation Desk** (www.international-villa.or.jp; © **086/256-2535;** fax 086/256-2576).

KURASHIKI, MARKET TOWN OF MANY CHARMS ★★★

26km (16 miles) W of Okayama

If I were to select the most picturesque town in Japan, **Kurashiki** would certainly be a top contender. Here, in the heart of the city, clustered around a willow-fringed canal, is a delightful historic district of old buildings and *ryokan* perfect for camera buffs.

As an administrative center of the shogunate in the 17th century, Kurashiki blossomed into a prosperous market town where rice, sake, and cotton were collected from the surrounding region and shipped off to Osaka and beyond. Back in those days, wealth was measured in rice; large granaries were built to store the mountains of granules passing through the town, and canals were dug so that barges laden with grain could work their way to ships anchored in the Seto Inland Sea. Kurashiki, in fact, means "Warehouse Village."

It's these warehouses, still standing, that give Kurashiki its distinctive charm. Kurashiki is also known throughout Japan for its art museums, including the prestigious Ohara Museum of Art with its collection of European and Japanese art. For these reasons, Kurashiki is hardly undiscovered, and Japanese flock here in droves, especially in summer months. Yet despite its overcrowdedness, Kurashiki still rates high on my list of places to see in Japan.

Essentials

GETTING THERE **By Train** Although Kurashiki has a Shinkansen station (**Shin-Kurashiki**), most Shinkansen trains do not stop there, and the station is inconveniently located about 9.5km (6 miles) west of the city center. From most destinations, you're better off getting off the Shinkansen in Okayama and transferring to the **JR Sanyo Line** to **Kurashiki Station,** in the heart of the city; trains depart frequently and take about 13 minutes (fare: ¥320). Otherwise, a local train runs between Shin-Kurashiki and Kurashiki stations about every 15 minutes and takes 9 minutes.

By Bus The same buses that depart from Tokyo's Shinjuku station for Okayama (see "Okayama: Gateway to Shikoku," earlier in this chapter) continue onward to Kurashiki, arriving in Kurashiki about 40 minutes after their Okayama stop and costing ¥10,000 one-way.

VISITOR INFORMATION There's a **tourist information office** in Kurashiki Station (✆ 086/424-1220), open daily 9am to 7pm. Another information office, called the **Kurashiki-Kan** (✆ 086/422-0542), is right on the canal in the historic district and has a rest area with tables and vending machines; open daily 9am to 6pm (to 5:15pm in winter), it was built in 1916 and is ironically the only Western-looking wooden building in the area. Both offices distribute maps and brochures, including the useful "Walking Map of Kurashiki." Although it's mostly for residents, www.city. kurashiki.okayama.jp has some information that might prove useful.

ORIENTATION The willow-lined canal, called the **Bikan Historical Quarter,** is only a 10-minute walk from Kurashiki Station; take the south exit and walk south on Chuo Dori, turning left just before the Kurashiki Kokusai Hotel. In fact, you can walk virtually everywhere of interest in Kurashiki; the Bikan Historical Quarter is zoned mostly for pedestrians.

Exploring Kurashiki's Bikan Historical Quarter & Environs

Kurashiki's **historic old town** is centered on a canal lined with graceful willows and 200-year-old granaries made of black-tile walls topped with white mortar. Many of the granaries have been turned into museums, *ryokan*, restaurants, and boutiques selling handblown glass, Bizen pottery, papier-mâché toys, women's ethnic clothing imported from Bali and India, and mats and handbags made of *igusa* (rush grass), a local specialty. Street vendors sell jewelry, their wares laid out beside the canal, and healthy young men stand ready to give visitors rides in rickshaws.

A resident advised me that because of the crowds that descend upon Kurashiki during the day (about four million tourists come here a year), I should get up early in the morning before the shops and museums open and explore this tiny area while it's still under the magic spell of the early morning glow. "Real lovers of Kurashiki come on Monday," he added. "Because that's when most everything is closed, and there are fewer people." I've found that early evening is also a magical time to walk the streets, especially after sunset when many buildings along the canal are illuminated.

Do try to avoid weekends, but no matter when you come, you're likely to fall under the city's spell. One of the most rewarding things to do in Kurashiki is simply explore (don't neglect the side streets btw. the canal and Achi Shrine on Tsurugatayama Park; even rain only enhances the contrasting black and white of the buildings).

Japan Rural Toy Museum (Nihon Kyodogangu-Kan) ★★ ☺ MUSEUM
Almost next to the Folkcraft Museum (below) is this museum with its delightful and colorful display of traditional and antique Japanese toys from every prefecture. Opened in 1967, it has thousands upon thousands of items crammed into four rooms, including kites (200 of them!), miniature floats, antique Japanese dolls, masks, and spinning tops. Incidentally, the huge top in the corner helped the owner of the museum, Ohga Hiroyuki, gain entry into the *Guinness World Book of Records* in 1983—by spinning 1 hour, 8 minutes, and 57 seconds. You can tour the museum in much less time than that—30 or 40 minutes. A large store at the entrance sells great traditional Japanese toys.

1–4–16 Chuo. ✆ **086/422-8058.** Admission ¥400 adults, ¥300 junior-high and high-school students, ¥200 children. Daily 9am–5pm. On the canal.

Kurashiki Folkcraft Museum (Kurashiki Mingei-Kan) MUSEUM Under the slogan USABILITY EQUALS BEAUTY, this museum contains folk crafts not only from Japan but from various other countries as well, giving unique insight into their cultural similarities and differences as reflected in the items people make and use in daily life. Spread through three old rice granaries, displays change three times a year and may include baskets, ceramics, glass, textiles, and woodwork. Unfortunately not all items are identified in English, but you'll appreciate their beauty. Plan on 30 minutes here.

1–4–11 Chuo. ✆ **086/422-1637.** Admission ¥700 adults, ¥400 university and high-school students, ¥300 children. Tues–Sun 9am–5pm (to 4:15pm Dec–Feb). On the canal, beside the Kurashiki-Kan tourist office.

Ohara Museum of Art (Ohara Bijutsukan) ★★★ ART MUSEUM This is by far Kurashiki's most impressive museum, a must-see even on a short list of sightseeing. Ohara Magosaburo, who believed that even people in remote Kurashiki should have the opportunity to view great works of art (that's his beautiful mansion across the canal from the museum), founded it in 1930 as Japan's first museum of Western art. The main building, a two-story stone structure resembling a Greek temple, is small but manages to contain the works of such greats as Picasso, Matisse, Vlaminck, Chagall, Manet, Monet, Degas, Pissarro, Sisley, Toulouse-Lautrec, Gauguin, Cézanne, El Greco, Renoir, Miró, Kandinsky, Klee, Pollack, Jasper Johns, Oldenburg, Frank Stella, Rothko, De Kooning, Warhol, and Hundertwasser. The museum has expanded so much since its founding that several annexes have been added over the years. A *Mingei* (Japan's 20th-century folk crafts) gallery housed in a renovated granary contains works by some of my favorites, including ceramics by Hamada Shoji, Bernard Leach, and Kawai Kanjiro; and woodblock prints by Munakata Shiko, who lived in Kurashiki 3 years. An annex is devoted to Japanese artists painting in the Western style and to contemporary Japanese artists, which makes for a fascinating comparison. Yet another building displays ancient Chinese art, primarily from prehistoric times to the Tang Dynasty (A.D. 618–907), and your ticket also includes entry to the Kojima Torajiro Memorial Hall (see below). Allow up to 2 hours to see everything, but your ticket is good all day so you don't have to see it all at once. An audio guide (¥500) covers important works in the main gallery.

1–1–15 Chuo. www.ohara.or.jp. ✆ **086/422-0005.** Admission ¥1,300 adults, ¥800 university and senior-high students, and ¥500 children. Tues–Sun 9am–5pm. On the canal.

Ohashi House (Ohashi-ke; 大橋家住宅) Built in 1796 by a wealthy salt and rice merchant, this traditional mansion is typical of the era, with front rooms used for entertaining guests and for business (the doorsill leading to the warehouse can be removed for easy transport), and the rear used as family living quarters. An imposing front gate, usually allowed only in homes belonging to the samurai class, is proof how important the Ohashi family was; another unique feature is a guesthouse, rare in merchant's homes. Once much larger (a hotel occupies the former garden), the home's 20 remaining rooms contain family heirlooms but are otherwise fairly empty. It's the only merchant's house open to the public, so come for a 15-minute spin through if you've never seen the inside of a traditional Japanese home.

3–21–31 Achi. www.ohashi-ke.com. © **086/422-0007.** Admission ¥500 adults, ¥300 seniors and children. Daily 9am–5pm (Sat to 6pm June–Aug). Closed on Fri Dec–Feb. Across Chuo Dori from the Bikan Historical Quarter, behind the Nikko Hotel.

IVY SQUARE

A 1-minute walk from the canal and museums is a complex called **Kurashiki Ivy Square.** Built as a cotton mill by a local spinning company in 1889, this handsome redbrick complex shrouded in ivy has been renovated into a hotel, restaurants, museums, and a few boutiques and galleries selling crafts. It's especially romantic in the evening when, from mid-July to the end of August, there's a beer garden in the inner courtyard (daily 6–9:30pm) and classical music wafts from loudspeakers built into the courtyard's brick floors.

Museums at Ivy Square include **Kojima Torajiro Memorial Hall** (© **086/422-0010**), named for and displaying paintings by the local artist who went to Europe to purchase most of the pieces in the Ohara museum (he died, however, before completion of the museum). It is open Tuesday to Sunday from 9am to 5pm and is included in the admission ticket for the Ohara Museum of Art. Most unique, however, in my opinion, is the one-room music-box museum, **Orgel Musée** (オルゴールミュセ; © **086/427-3904**), where 30-minute concerts on 30 antique organs, player pianos, and music boxes from Europe, the United States, and Japan take place. You must enter on the hour, at 10am, 11am, 1pm, 2pm, 3pm, 4pm, and 5pm (closed Tues). Admission here is ¥500 for adults and ¥300 for children.

Where to Eat

In addition to the following options, **Ryokan Kurashiki** (see "Where to Stay") serves elegant, seasonal set lunches (¥1,850–¥2,500) with views of its garden. In summer, consider dining at an evening beer garden, located in the courtyard of Ivy Square and on the lawn of the Kokusai Hotel.

MODERATE

Hachikengura ★★ FRENCH Occupying a converted rice granary that once belonged to the Ohashi family (described above in the Ohashi House review), this is my top pick for an atmospheric meal, boasting a soaring wood-beamed ceiling, tiled walls, and a worn wooden floor. Traditional French cuisine, such as seafood fricasee or steak of beef or veal, is served in a nouvelle style and listed on the English-language menu. You can eat here more economically if you come for lunch.

Hotel Nikko Kurashiki, 3–21–19 Achi. www.nikko-kurashiki.com. © **086/423-2400.** Reservations recommended. Main dishes ¥2,800–¥6,300; set lunches ¥1,500–¥3,800; set dinners ¥5,000–¥15,000. AE, DC, MC, V. Daily 11:30am–3pm and 5:30–10pm. Across from the Bikan Historical Quarter.

INEXPENSIVE

El Greco Coffeehouse COFFEE SHOP El Greco is Kurashiki's most famous coffee shop, open since 1959 and simply decorated with a wooden floor, wooden tables and benches, vases of fresh flowers, and El Greco photos. It serves coffee, fruit juice, milkshakes, ice cream, and cake from an English-language menu.

1–1–11 Chuo. ✆ **086/422-0297.** Coffee ¥500. No credit cards. Tues–Sun 10am–5pm. Next door to the Ohara Museum in an ivy-covered stone building.

Kamoi (カモ井) ★ VARIED JAPANESE   This restaurant, occupying a 200-year-old rice granary on Kurashiki's willow-fringed canal, is simply decorated with stark-white walls, dark wooden beams, and a collection of cast-iron teapots. An English-language menu has photos of sushi set meals, noodle dishes, a *tempura teishoku*, the *Kamoi teishoku* (featuring sashimi and *chirashi-zushi*—seafood rice bowl), and—my favorite—the *Kurashiki bento* with tempura, vegetables, rice, and soup.

1–3–17 Chuo. ✆ **086/422-0606.** Set meals ¥1,365–¥2,625. No credit cards. Thurs–Tues 10am–6pm (closed 2nd Mon of each month). Catty-corner across the canal from the Ohara Museum of Art.

Kanaizumi (かな泉) UDON   Kanaizumi, housed in a warehouse-style building with tall ceilings, is easy to spot: Just look for its chef rolling out *udon* behind a large window open to the street (though he's on duty only from 11am–1pm daily). In addition to the thick, handmade wheat udon noodles, tempura, sashimi, and local cuisine is served, but all fixed-price meals come with udon. As the menu is in Japanese only, make your selection from the display case or from pictures in the menu.

8–33 Honmachi. ✆ **086/421-7254.** Udon ¥480–¥1,150; set meals ¥750–¥1,800. AE, MC, V. Tues–Sun 11am–8pm. Behind (east of) Ryokan Kurashiki.

Kiyutei (亀遊亭) STEAK   Enter through the front gate just off the canal, pass through the small courtyard, and go into a small room dominated by a counter with cooks grilling steaks, the specialty of the house. There's an English-language menu; you're probably best off ordering one of the set meals, which offer also grilled salmon, Japanese curries, the day's fish, and other choices in addition to steak.

1–2–20 Chuo. ✆ **086/422-5140.** Set dinners ¥1,300–¥5,000; set lunches ¥1,000–¥4,200. AE, DC, MC, V. Mar–Nov Tues–Sun 11am–9pm; Dec–Feb Tues–Sun 11:30am–8:30pm. On the canal, across from the main entrance of the Ohara Museum of Art.

Kuku CURRY   This cute, 30-year-old mom & pop shop with just a counter and three tables and jazz background music is an inexpensive alternative if you're searching for something different. Its curries on the English-language menu are mostly Indian style (served on stainless steel *thali* trays), plus a few from Thailand and there's an assortment of Asian beers. Set lunches include curry, salad, chai and dessert (no smoking allowed during lunch time). It's down a picturesque lane (if it weren't for those darn overhead electric/telephone lines) a few minutes' walk from the Bikan Historical District; ask the tourist office for directions.

11–19 Honmachi. ✆ **086/424-3075.** Curries ¥750–¥900; set lunches ¥980–¥1,200. No credit cards. Thurs–Tues 11:30am–8pm. A 4-min. walk northeast of the historic district.

Ristorante Rentenchi PIZZA/PASTA   This cozy, tiny restaurant (with an English-language menu), run by a kind husband-and-wife team, is a good choice for inexpensive dining between Kurashiki Station and the Bikan Historical Quarter. Neapolitan-style, thick-crusted pizza from a wood-burning oven is the specialty, and the sommelier can make suggestions from a list of some 200 Italian wines.

2–19–18 Achi. ✆ **086/421-7858.** Reservations recommended. Pizza and pasta ¥950–¥2,500; set lunches ¥1,050–¥2,800. AE, DC, MC, V. Wed–Mon 11:30am–2pm and 6–10pm. An 8-min. walk south of Kurashiki Station on Chuo Dori, on the left side (look for the Italian flag).

Where to Stay

EXPENSIVE

Ryokan Kurashiki (旅館くらしき) ★★★ 🎁   The best place to stay to get a feeling for old Kurashiki is right in the heart of it—in one of the old warehouses on Kurashiki's picturesque willow-lined canal. This venerable *ryokan* consists of an old mansion and three converted rice-and-sugar warehouses more than 250 years old, all in its own little compound connected by a corridor of black marble polished to a sheen. Filled with antiques and curios, it has long, narrow corridors, nooks and crannies, and the peaceful sanctuary of an inner garden. There's no other ryokan in Japan quite like this one. Its five rooms, which are actually two- and three-room suites consisting of a tatami living room and sleeping quarters with Western-style beds, are simply elegant, with antiques placed here and there, two TVs, and Jacuzzi tubs. Two are big enough for up to six people (though no children younger than 13 are allowed). Guests can elect to eat in their room, in a tatami room overlooking the canal, or in a delightful terrace tea lounge overlooking a small garden (Western-style breakfasts are available).

4–1 Honmachi, Kurashiki, Okayama Prefecture 710-0054. www.ryokan-kurashiki.jp. © **086/422-0730.** Fax 086/422-0990. 5 units. ¥28,000–¥48,000 per person. Rates include 2 meals but exclude service charge. Rates ¥1,000 higher in peak season. AE, DC, MC, V. In the Bikan Historical Quarter. **Amenities:** Restaurant; tea lounge; lobby computer w/free Internet. *In room:* A/C, TV, fridge.

Tsurugata (鶴形) ★★   Rustic furniture, aged wood and memorable meals of seasonal specialties are trademarks of this *ryokan,* on the canal in the Bikan Historical Quarter's oldest building, constructed in 1744. It was once a merchant's house and shop selling rice, cotton, seafood, and cooking oil. The most expensive rooms have a view of the garden with its 400-year-old pine trees and stone lanterns, while the least expensive, rather ordinary six tatami mat rooms are on the second floor without a view. All rooms have private toilets, but for most of them you'll be using the common baths.

1–3–15 Chuo, Kurashiki, Okayama Prefecture 710-0046. © **086/424-1635.** Fax 086/424-1650. 11 units, all with toilet, 3 with bathroom. ¥14,800–¥33,600 per person. Rates include 2 meals. AE, DC, MC, V. In the Bikan Historical Quarter, on the canal. **Amenities:** Restaurant. *In room:* A/C, TV.

MODERATE

Kurashiki Ivy Square Hotel ★   When this 1882 brick cotton mill was converted to a hotel in 1974, much of the old architectural style was left intact, making for an interesting setting. Rooms are simple but clean (and could do with some updating), with some facing a tiny expanse of green grass and an ivy-covered wall or a koi-filled canal. Rooms range from inexpensive rooms without private bath (though guests can don the hotel's cotton *yukata* robes and use the common baths) to deluxe two-room suites. The Bikan Historical Quarter is just a minute's walk away, but the train station is a 20-minute hike away.

7–2 Honmachi, Kurashiki, Okayama Prefecture 710-0054. www.ivysquare.co.jp. © **086/422-0011.** Fax 086/424-0515. 161 units, all with toilet, 67 with bathroom. ¥7,875 single with toilet, ¥10,500 single with bathroom; ¥13,125 twin with toilet; ¥16,800–¥28,350 twin/double with bathroom. AE, DC, MC, V. A minute's walk south of the Bikan Historical Quarter. **Amenities:** Restaurant; bar; summer beer garden; lobby computer w/free Internet; access to nearby sports club w/gym and pool (fee: ¥800). *In room:* A/C, TV, fridge, hair dryer, Internet.

Kurashiki Kokusai Hotel ★★   This has long been Kurashiki's most popular Western-style hotel—and it's easy to see why. Built in 1963, it blends into its surroundings with black-tile walls set in white mortar, while the interior pays tribute to the mid-19th-century Japanese modernist style with an old-fashioned charm and huge woodblock murals in the lobby by Mingei artist Munakata Shiko (you can see more of his work at the Ohara Museum). Rooms are a bit dated and are slated for renovation by 2014, but have nice touches of locally made crafts that lift them out of the ordinary, including woven place mats, Kurashiki glass lampshades, and woodblock prints by a local artist. A newer annex offers slightly larger (mostly) twin rooms with larger bathrooms, but I prefer the smaller (and cheaper) rooms in the old building facing the back with a pleasant view of the Ohara Museum, garden greenery, and the black-tile roofs of the old granaries.

1–1–44 Chuo, Kurashiki 710-0046, Okayama Prefecture. www.kurashiki-kokusai-hotel.co.jp. ✆ **086/422-5141.** Fax 086/422-5192. 106 units. ¥10,395 single; ¥16,170–¥26,565 double. Add ¥1,155 per person in peak season. AE, DC, MC, V. A 10-min. walk south of Kurashiki Station, on Chuo Dori past the entrance to the Bikan Historical Quarter. **Amenities:** Restaurant; bar; lounge; summer barbecue garden; business center computer w/free Internet. *In room:* A/C, TV, fridge, hair dryer, Internet.

INEXPENSIVE

Toyoko Inn Kurashikieki Minamiguchi 🐟 This inexpensive business hotel has a good location between Kurashiki Station and the Bikan Historical Quarter, above a convenience store. It also tries harder than most business hotels to draw in customers, offering free Internet access from computers in the lobby, free domestic calls from lobby phones, free Wi-Fi in the lobby, free breakfast and coin-op laundry machines. Rooms are tiny, with most of the room taken up by double- or queen-size beds, but the price is right. Ask for a room on a top floor for unobstructed city views.

2–10–20 Achi, Kurashiki, Okayama Prefecture 710-0055. www.toyoko-inn.com. ✆ **086/430-1045.** Fax 086/430-1046. 154 units. ¥4,980–¥6,300 single; ¥6,300–¥8,350 double. Rates include breakfast. AE, DC, MC, V. A 3-min. walk south of Kurashiki Station, on Chuo Dori on the left side. **Amenities:** Lobby computer w/free Internet. *In room:* A/C, TV, fridge, hair dryer, Wi-Fi.

OFF THE BEATEN PATH: MATSUE ★

724km (450 miles) SW of Tokyo; 186km (116 miles) NW of Okayama; 402km (251 miles) NE of Hakata (Fukuoka)

Capital of Shimane Prefecture and with a population of just over 200,000, **Matsue** lies near the northern coast of western Honshu. It's off the beaten track for most foreign tourists, who tend to keep to a southerly route in their travels toward Hiroshima and Kyushu. Japanese, however, are quite fond of Matsue, and a fair number of them choose to spend their summer vacation in and around this pleasant town, visiting its castle and other sights, including a nearby museum highlighting contemporary Japanese art in a fantastic garden setting. Hugging the shores of Lake Shinji and Nakaumi Lagoon, cut in half by the Ohashi River, and crisscrossed by a network of canals, Matsue is a pretty castle town blessed with Edo-Era architecture, particularly along the castle moat where many samurai settled. All these things conspire to make a trip to Matsue—despite its out-of-the-way location—very worthwhile.

Essentials

GETTING THERE   By Train   The easiest way to reach Matsue is from Okayama via the 2½-hour **JR limited express Yakumo train** ride that costs ¥5,360 for an unreserved seat.

BY BUS   A bus departs from Tokyo's Shibuya Station nightly at 8pm, arriving at Matsue Station at 6:26am and costing ¥11,550 one-way. There are also buses from Hiroshima (taking about 3½ hours and costing ¥4,000 one-way), Okayama (about 3 hr. for ¥3,400) and Osaka (4½ hr. for ¥5,050).

BY PLANE   Flights from Tokyo to **Izumo Airport** (IZO; ☎ **0853/72-7500**) take about 80 minutes. From there, buses deliver passengers to Matsue Station in about 25 minutes for ¥1,000.

VISITOR INFORMATION   Upon arrival at **Matsue Station,** stop at the **Matsue International Tourist Information Office** (☎ **0852/21-4034;** daily 9am–6pm), located in a contemporary-looking kiosk in front of the station's north exit, where you can pick up English-language brochures on Matsue and Shimane Prefecture and a good map of the city. Be sure also to ask for the pamphlet listing discounts (up to 50%) available to international visitors for 18 tourists sights in and around Matsue, including the Adachi Museum of Art (see "Exploring Matsue," below). In town, there's a Tourist Office counter at the Matsue History Museum (p. 413), open daily 8:30am to 6:30pm (to 5pm Oct–Mar). Go to **www.city.matsue.shimane.jp** and **www.kankou-shimane.com/en** for online information on Matsue.

GETTING AROUND   Matsue's attractions lie northwest of the station and across the Ohashi River, and although buses run virtually everywhere, you can easily cover most distances **on foot.** Matsue Castle is about a 30-minute walk from Matsue Station, with most attractions located just north of the castle along a picturesque moat on a street called Shiomi Nawate. West of Matsue Station, about a 10-minute walk away, is Lake Shinji, famous for its sunsets.

If you prefer to ride, ¥500 buys you an all-day pass for the **Lakeline Sightseeing Bus** (☎ **0852/60-1111**), which features red, old-fashioned buses running every 20 minutes in a 50-minute loop through the city beginning at Matsue Station and stopping at most tourist sights daily between 8:40am and 5:48pm, with longer hours September through March so visitors can enjoy sunsets on Lake Shinji. Single trips cost ¥200. Pick up a map of the bus route at the Tourist Information Office; a signboard at the front of the bus shows the next stop (I've provided both the Japanese and English names for all stops listed below). Note that buses travel in only one direction (counterclockwise), so plan your sightseeing accordingly (I've listed the attractions below also in a counterclockwise order to match the bus route).

[FastFACTS] MATSUE

ATM/Mail   The main post office is a 3-minute walk from the north exit of Matsue Station, reached by turning right (east) on the street that runs in front of the station. It's open Monday to Friday 9am to 7pm, Saturday 9am to 5pm, and Sunday and holidays 9am to 12:30pm (its ATM facilities are open Mon–Fri

7am–11pm, Sat 9am–9pm, Sun and holidays 9am–7pm.

Goodwill Guides
Although Matsue's sights are concentrated in one area of town and are easy to find on your own, you may want a "goodwill guide" to show you around, especially if you're going to Izumo Taisha Shrine or the Adachi Museum. The

goodwill guide network is composed of volunteers with foreign-language abilities who act as guides in their city. All you have to do is pay their transportation costs and entrance fees into museums and sights—and it's nice if you buy them lunch, too. Apply for a Matsue Goodwill Guide 4 days in advance at ✆ **090/8998-5746** or **090/1013-4319.**

Internet Access On the third floor of **Town Plaza Shimane** is the International Center, 8–3 Tonomachi (www.sic-info.org/en/service/internet; ✆ **0852-31-5056;** Lakeline stop: Karakoro Kobo Mae), offering computers with free Internet connection Monday to Friday from 9am to 7pm and Sunday from 9am to 5pm for a maximum of 1 hour.

Exploring Matsue

International visitors are entitled to 50% discounts at Matsue Castle, Matsue History Museum, Teahouse Meime-an, Buke Yashiki, Lafcadio Hearn Memorial Museum and Old Residence, Gesshoji Temple, Adachi Museum of Art, and other attractions by showing their passport at attraction entrances. The prices below are the regular fare, without the discount.

ATTRACTIONS AROUND MATSUE CASTLE

Most of these attractions are located on Shiomi Nawate, a small, picturesque street beside the castle's north moat.

Matsue Castle ★★ CASTLE   First built in 1611 and partly reconstructed in 1642 and again in the 1950s, Matsue Castle is the only castle along this northern stretch of coast built for warfare as opposed to serving merely as a residence. It's also one of Japan's few remaining original castles—that is, it's not a ferroconcrete reconstruction. Rising up from a hill about 1.5km (1 mile) northwest of Matsue Station with a good view of the city, the five-story *donjon* (which actually conceals six floors to give its warriors a fighting advantage) houses the usual *daimyo* and samurai gear, including armor, swords and other weaponry, helmets, and lacquerware that belonged to the Matsudaira clan, who ruled for 10 generations. Plan on 30 minutes here.

Lafcadio Hearn (a European who lived in Matsue in the 1890s, adopted Japanese citizenship, and wrote extensively about Japan) said of Matsue Castle: "Crested at its summit, like a feudal helmet . . . the creation is a veritable architectural dragon, made up of magnificent monstrosities." As you walk through the castle up to the top floor, notice the staircase. Although it looks sturdy, it's light enough to be pulled up to halt enemy intrusions. Concealed holes on the second floor could serve as drop chutes for raining stones down on invaders. The top floor, with windows on all four sides from which the feudal lord could command his army (and today provides city views), is one of the few original watchtowers remaining in Japan. And to think the castle almost met its demise during the Meiji Restoration when the ministry of armed forces auctioned it off, hoping to rid the city of its feudal-era landmark. Luckily, former vassals of the clan pooled their resources and bought the castle. In 1927, the grounds were donated to the city.

1–5 Tonomachi. ✆ **0852/21-4030.** Admission ¥550 adults, ¥280 children. Daily 8:30am–5pm (to 6:30pm Apr–Sept). Lakeline bus: Matsue-jo Otemae/Matsue Castle (1 min.). Or a 30-min. walk northwest of Matsue Station.

Matsue History Museum (Matsue Rekishikan) MUSEUM   Housed in a replica Edo-era building, this museum showcases Matsue's 400 years as a castle town with a film describing the construction of Matsue Castle (in Japanese only, but interesting nevertheless), city maps from the past 4 centuries (the town's moats remain remarkably little changed) and other displays. Be sure to pick up the free audio guide, which gives insight into how commoners lived during the Edo era and other interesting information, and to relax on the circle of sofas where you can see old photographs projected on the ceiling. In truth, there's not a lot to see here; if you don't want to pay admission, stop by the tourist office here or to see the cafe's fantastic confectionary creations. Famous for its tea ceremony, Matsue is also famous for its long history of confectionaries.

279 Tonomachi. ✆ **0852/32-1607.** Admission ¥500 adults, ¥250 children. Daily 8:30am–6:30pm (to 5pm Oct–Mar). Lakeline bus: Otemae Horikawa Yuransen Noriba/Horikawa boat boarding point (1 min.). Southeast of the castle.

Teahouse Meimei-an (明々庵) TEAHOUSE   This is one of Japan's most renowned and well-preserved thatch-roofed teahouses, built in 1779 upon orders of a 29-year-old lord of the Matsudaira clan. It's located at the top of a flight of stairs, from which you have a good view of Matsue Castle (read: photo op). Note the waiting room (and its ancient toilet), for guests awaiting a summons to the teahouse. A separate building offers bitter Japanese green tea and sweets for an additional ¥400, which you might find refreshing before you move on to your next destination.

278 Kitahori-cho. ✆ **0852/21-9863.** Admission ¥400 adults, ¥200 students, free for children. Daily 8:30am–6:30pm (to 5pm Oct–Mar; tea served until 4:30 and 4pm, respectively). Lakeline bus: Koizumi Yakumo Kinenkan-mae/Lafcadio Hearn Museum (4 min.). Or a 5-min. walk northeast of Matsue Castle, back from Shiomi Nawate on a small side street and up a flight of stairs to the left.

Buke Yashiki (武家屋敷) ★ HISTORIC HOME   This ancient samurai house, facing the castle moat, was built in 1730 and belonged to the Shiomi family, one of the chief retainers of the Matsudaira feudal clan residing in the castle. High-ranking samurai, the Shiomi family lived pretty much like kings themselves, having separate servants' quarters, a tearoom, a room for bathing, and even a shed for their palanquin. Compared with samurai residences in wealthier regions of Japan, however, this samurai house is considered rather austere. As you walk around it, peering into rooms with their wooden walls slid open to the outside breeze, you'll see furniture and objects used in daily life by samurai during the Edo Period. You can see it all in 15 minutes.

305 Kitahori-cho. ✆ **0852/22-2243.** Admission ¥300 adults, ¥150 children. Daily 8:30am–6:30pm (to 5pm Oct–Mar). Lakeline bus: Koizumi Yakumo Kinenkan-mae/Lafcadio Hearn Museum (3 min.). Northeast of Matsue Castle across the moat, on Shiomi Nawate.

Lafcadio Hearn Memorial Museum (Koizumi Yakumo Kinenkan) MUSEUM/HISTORIC HOME   Here you'll see a 10-minute video about the life of writer Lafcadio Hearn (1850–1904) and his possessions, including his desk, manuscripts, clothing, photographs of his family, and smoking pipes. Japanese are fascinated with this man who married the daughter of a Matsue high-ranking samurai, became a Japanese citizen, and adopted the name Koizumi Yakumo. He was one of the first writers to give Japanese the chance to see themselves through the eyes of a foreigner and to describe Japan to the outside world. His books still provide insight into Japanese life at the turn of the 20th century and are available at all bookstores in Japan with an English-language section.

Because most Japanese will assume it's out of respect for Hearn that you've come to Matsue, you may want to read one of his books before coming here. His volume *Glimpses of Unfamiliar Japan* contains an essay called "In a Japanese Garden," in which he gives his impressions of Matsue, where he lived for 15 months before moving to Kumamoto to teach English. You can see the small garden immortalized in Hearn's essay at the **Lafcadio Hearn's Old Residence** (✆ **0852/23-0714**) next door, a Japanese-style house (and former samurai mansion) where Hearn lived in

1891. Admission here is ¥300 for adults, ¥150 for children. It's open the same hours as the museum. You can tour both the museum and the residence in 30 minutes.

322 Okudani-cho. ☏ **0852/21-2147.** Admission ¥300 adults, ¥150 children. Daily 8:30am–6:30pm (to 5pm Oct–Mar). Lakeline bus: Koizumi Yakumo Kinenkan-mae/Lafcadio Hearn Museum (1 min.). On Shiome Nawate north of Matsue Castle.

ELSEWHERE IN MATSUE

Gesshoji Temple (月照寺) ★★ 🎒 TEMPLE   This is the family temple and burial ground of the Matsudaira clan, feudal lords of Matsue and the surrounding region. It was established in 1664 by Matsudaira Naomasa, whose grandfather was the powerful Tokugawa Ieyasu. Nine generations of the Matsudaira clan are buried here, each in his own small compound spread throughout the solemn grounds; Naomasa's grave, the grandest and largest, is the one at the far left (allow 20 min. to see all of them). What I like most about this cemetery is that it seems ancient and forgotten; you might find yourself the only living soul here. At the grave of the sixth lord is a stone turtle (described by Hearn as "the monster tortoise") famous for midnight strolls that terrorized residents; if you rub its head, you'll have good luck. Stop for ceremonial green tea (¥400) in a room of a modern building facing a great little garden, and be sure to see the one-room treasure house with items belonging to the Matsudairas. In June, the grounds are famous for stunning hydrangeas—don't miss it.

Sotonakabara-cho. ☏ **0852/21-6056.** Admission ¥500 adults, ¥300 high-school students, ¥150 junior-high school and children. Daily 8:30am–5:30pm (to 5pm Nov–Mar). Lakeline bus: stop Gesshoji-mae/Gesshoji Temple (4 min.). A 15-min. walk west of Matsue Castle.

Boat Trips

The **Horikawa Sightseeing Boat** (**Horikawa Meguri;** www.matsue-horikawa meguri.jp; ☏ **0852/27-0417**) is a tour of the castle moat aboard flat-bottom boats (take off your shoes and sit on tatami) with a rooftop canopy that lowers for tight squeezes under bridges. It's a picturesque, relaxing way to travel, with trips around the castle lasting about 50 minutes. In winter, you can keep warm huddled under a *kotatsu* (a kind of heated blanket). Note, however, that commentary is in Japanese only. There are three boarding spots along the moat: between the main entrance to Matsue Castle and the Matsue Museum of History; Matsue Horikawa Fureai Hiroba northeast of the castle (near Ji Beer Kan, p. 418), and Karakoro Hiroba near the Kyobashi Bridge. Boats run every 15 minutes daily from 9am to 6pm in summer (to 4 or 5pm the rest of the year). An all-day ticket allowing you to disembark and embark as much as you like costs ¥1,200 for adults and ¥600 for children, but foreigners can ride for ¥800 and ¥400, respectively, by showing their passport.

Easy Side Trips

ADACHI MUSEUM ★★★ 🎒 MUSEUM   I was blown away the first time I laid eyes on the Adachi Museum, 320 Furukawa-cho, Yasugi (www.adachi-museum. or.jp/e; (☏ **0854/28-7111;** daily 9am–5:30pm, to 5pm Oct–Mar), which houses one of Japan's premier collections of Japanese modern art (from the Meiji, Taisho, and Showa periods) amid the meticulously sculpted garden that I consider one of Japan's finest. Exhibitions in the main building, which are changed four times a year to reflect the seasons, are comprised of some 300 early modern and contemporary Japanese works and include the largest collection of distinguished painter Yokoyama Taikan, with at least 20 of his 120 works here always on display. Also on display are

Japanese *douga,* or illustrations from children's books and magazines, as well as pottery by Kawai Kanjiro and Kitaoji Rosanjin. An annex displays works by promising emerging artists, purchased by the museum to support contemporary Japanese-style painting (*nihonga*).

But what makes this museum truly unique is its perfectly landscaped **Adachi Museum Garden ★★★**, crafted to complement Taikan's masterpieces and continually visible through cleverly designed windows to incorporate it into the museum's artwork. The effect is surreal, as though the garden is a still picture, a scroll, a Taikan painting. There are several outdoor viewing spots, as well as a coffee shop overlooking a koi pond and two teahouses serving traditional cakes and powdered green tea (one with a nice view of a moss garden). You'll want to spend at least 2 hours here, more if you opt for the ¥300 audio guide that provides commentary of garden and exhibit highlights.

Admission to the museum is ¥2,200 for adults, ¥1,700 for university students, ¥900 for high-school students, and ¥400 for children, but foreigners get a 50% discount by showing their passport. To get there, take the JR train from Matsue Station 20 minutes to Yasugi, and then board one of the free shuttle buses that depart 10 times a day for the 20-minute ride to the museum. (At last check, buses departed for Adachi at 9:05, 10, 11, and 11:55am; and at 12:30, 1, 2, 2:25, 3:05, and 4:15pm, but you'd be wise to verify this.) Alternatively, the Yakumo limited express train traveling between Okayama and Matsue also stops at Yasugi Station, so you could disembark here, deposit your luggage in one of the station's coin lockers (or leave it with the Yasugi City Tourist Information Office in the station if lockers are full), and then travel onward after visiting the museum.

IWAMI GINZAN SILVER MINE ★ RUINS Iwami Ginzan was mined for its high-quality silver from 1526 to 1923. By the late 16th century, Japan was producing one-third of the world's silver, most of it from Iwami Ginzan, which was traded throughout East Asia. While silver mining certainly added to the coffers of the Tokugawa shogunate, it was backbreaking work for the miners, who over the centuries dug 600 mine shafts throughout the area by hand. In 2007, Iwami Ginzan Silver Mine was declared a World Heritage Site, not only because of its well-preserved overview of silver production—from digging and refining to transportation to local ports—but also because of its well-preserved natural environment, thanks to feudal-era reforestation programs to ensure the necessary timber for fuel needed for refining.

Disappointingly, the Iwami Ginzan World Heritage Center, tasked with introducing the area's history and mining techniques, has no displays in English and is isolated from the rest of Iwami Ginzan. I suggest skipping it and heading straight to Omori village (population 400), nestled along a river valley and established during the shogun era for the mining magistrate's office and settled by samurai and merchants. After renting an audio guide and bicycle, you can explore picturesque Omori with its old homes, a few shops, the former magistrate's office (not much in English, so not worth going inside), the Kawashima samurai residence (admission: ¥200), and the House of the Kumagai merchant family (¥500). But the best thing to do is head south out of town (there are signs pointing the way) to the Ryugenji Mabu Mine Shaft (¥400), part of which you can walk through on your own and marvel at the chisel marks (miners could advance only 30cm/11 inches a day) as you listen to your audio guide describe hardships faced by miners, who considered themselves lucky if they reached 30 years of age. In fact, the audio guide describes 50 spots along the 2.9km (1.8 mile) stretch from the north end of Omori to the Ryugenji mine shaft in the south, making you feel like you're with your own personal guide. This is a fun outing, but because it's a bit far from Matsue, it will take the better part of a day. Note that most attractions close around 4 or 5pm and some are closed on Monday.

To reach Omori, take the train from Matsue to Oda in about an hour (¥820 via the JR San-in Line, with a transfer in Izumoshi), and then board the bus outside Oda Station for 25 minutes to the Omori stop (¥650; there are usually 2 buses an hour). Audio guides (¥500) are available at nearby Iwami Ginzan Park; staff can point you to the bike kiosk, where ordinary bikes cost ¥500 for 3 hours and electric bikes cost ¥700 for 2 hours (the road to the mine is an incline; I went with the latter).

IZUMO TAISHA GRAND SHRINE (IZUMO TAISHA) SHRINE The most important religious structure in the vicinity of Matsue is easy to see on a half-day side trip, but come only if you have time to spare. **Izumo Taisha,** 195 Kizuki Higashi, Taisha-cho, Izumo-shi (© **0853/53-3100;** daily sunrise–sunset), is considered one of Japan's holiest shrines because, according to popular lore, all the gods in the Shinto pantheon gather here for 1 month every autumn to determine the world's fate for the upcoming year. In Izumo this month is called the "Month with the Gods." Everywhere else in Japan, it's referred to as the "Month without Gods," because they're all away performing their duty here, housed in those long buildings flanking both sides of the main shrine. Otherwise, like the Ise Grand Shrines, the main shrine here, reconstructed in 1744, is considered too sacred for mere mortals and is hidden away from close inspection. You'll have to content yourself with a picture showing how it looked 1,000 years ago, when it was reputedly 24m (79 ft.) higher to heaven on top of huge pilings. This makes it the oldest site of a Shinto Grand Shrine displaying the Taisha style of architecture. It's dedicated to Okuninushi-no-mikoto, the Shinto deity responsible for medicine, farming, and happiness. To the left of the main shrine is the marriage shrine, where you'll see people throwing coins up into the bristled ends of thick, twisted rice ropes adorning the entrance; legend has it that if a coin gets stuck in the bushy end, the thrower will have good luck in marriage. Admission to the shrines is free.

It's a 30- to 40-minute JR train ride from Matsue Station to Izumoshi Station (¥570), followed by a 30-minute bus ride (¥510) bound for Izumo Taisha ("Taisha-yuki"; get off at the last stop). Or, for a more atmospheric journey, you can reach Izumo Taisha Grand Shrine via the private Ichibata Railway from Matsue Shinjiko Onsen Station (departures are once or twice an hour) 55 minutes to Izumo Taisha-mae Station (¥790). Note, however, that you'll have to change trains at Kawato Station, but there's an immediate transfer to a waiting train. It's an interesting ride, with the train stopping at stations no larger than American closets. From Izumo Taisha-mae Station it's a 3-minute walk to the shrine entrance.

Where to Eat

Much of Matsue's regional cuisine comes from Lake Shinji, including sea bass, smelt, carp, freshwater eel, and a small black clam (*shijimi,* popular in soups). *Warigo soba,* which comes with stacked layers of noodles to which you add grated *daikon* radish, yam, fish flakes, seaweed, and other condiments, is also popular.

MODERATE

Kyoragi (京らぎ) ★★ LOCAL SPECIALTIES Located across from Ji Beer Kan (see below), this modern restaurant with a wood interior, lots of windows, and both tatami and table seating specializes in dishes based on original Izumo recipes, using organic meats and vegetables whenever possible. There are pictures of some of the set meals and sushi and sashimi dishes offered on the Japanese-language menu, including the very tasty *Hanahibiki* set lunch for ¥1,680 with lots of local delicacies. The *kokoro* set meal, served only for dinner (¥2,625), allows you to choose from almost a dozen different kinds of fresh fish for your main course, along with side dishes that change weekly.

512–5 Kuroda-cho. ⌂ **0852/25-2233.** Reservations required for kaiseki. Set dinners ¥2,625; set lunches ¥1,260–¥2,100; kaiseki from ¥4,200. DC, MC, V. Tues–Sun 11am–2pm and 5–9:30pm (open on holiday Mon, closing Tues instead). Lakeline bus: Horikawa Yuransen Noribo/Horikawa Boat Boarding Point (1 min.).

INEXPENSIVE

Bankichi (番吉) ★ 🏮YAKITORI   Bankichi is a lively, friendly place, presided over by the grinning, English-speaking owner/cook for 25 years. Customers seem to be content, too, as they crowd into this small restaurant with counter and booth seating. A branch of an Osaka *yakitori-ya*, Bankichi offers an English-language menu of various yakitori, including chicken, minced chicken meatballs, chicken thigh with plum sauce, or shiitake mushrooms. There's a ¥200 snack charge.

491–1 Asahimachi. ⌂ **0852/31-8308.** Yakitori ¥200–¥300. MC, V. Daily 5pm–midnight. From Matsue Station's north exit, turn left out of the station's north exit on the main street; it will be on your right (look for the red lantern and sign), before Toyoko Inn (2 min.).

Ji Beer Kan VARIED JAPANESE   In a large, airy setting beside the castle moat west of the Hearn Memorial Museum, this microbrewery/restaurant is on the second floor above a souvenir shop. Four different kinds of beer are brewed, with a sampler of three costing ¥950. The English-language menu has photos of various soba and udon dishes (¥700–¥1,000) and set meals that may include yakiniku, fried shrimp, ginger-flavored fried pork, or other main dishes. Be forewarned that this place is popular with tour groups; avoid the lunch-time rush. Or, if all you want is a beer, buy one from a counter in the souvenir shop and take it outside to enjoy at a table beside the moat. By the way, nearby is a boarding dock for the Horikawa Sightseeing Boat.

509–1 Kuroda-cho. ⌂ **0852/55-8877.** Set meals ¥900–¥2,800. AE, MC, V. Daily 11am–5pm (last order). Lakeline bus: Horikawa Yuransen Noribo/Horikawa Boat Boarding Point (1 min.).

Kaneyasu (かねやす) ★ 🐟 FISH/VARIED JAPANESE   This modest one-counter place with tatami rooms upstairs has good food and is run by grandmotherly, bustling women. It has been around for more than 50 years, and most of its customers are local working people, so avoid the noontime rush. It has a great lunch *teishoku*, which includes a piece of *yakizakana* (grilled fish), vegetable, soup, tofu, rice, and tea. In the evening, such dishes as grilled fish, yam, bamboo, seasonal dishes, and various vegetables are available, but it's probably easier to order one of the two set meals, both of which feature locally caught seafood, the restaurant's specialty.

569–3 Otesemba-cho. ⌂ **0852/21-0550.** Set dinners ¥1,500–¥2,000; lunch teishoku ¥650–¥860. No credit cards. Mon–Fri 11am–2pm; Mon–Sat 5–9pm. Closed holidays. Take the underground passage to cross the main street that runs in front of Matsue Station's north exit; it's 1 block farther north.

Pasta Factory Ortaggio ITALIAN   Located in the hip Kiyomise neighborhood with its restaurants and shop, this small and casual restaurant with an open kitchen offers a few choices of pizza and meat dishes (like grilled lemon chicken), but pasta is mostly what this place is about, with lots of choices on the English-language menu. In addition to usual choices like spaghetti carbonara and spaghetti Bolognese, there's also Japanese-style pasta, including spaghetti with bacon, Japanese pickles, and garlic soy sauce.

82 Suetsugu Honmachi. ☏ **0852/28-0101.** Pizza, pasta, and main dishes ¥650–¥1,000. Set lunches ¥850–¥1,280. MC, V. Mon–Fri 11:30am–2:30pm; Sat–Sun and holidays 11:30am–3pm; Mon–Sat 5:30–10pm; Sun and holidays 5:30–9pm (last order). Lakeline bus: Karakoro Kobo-mae/Karakoro Art Studio (2 min.). 1 block south of the moat, near Kyobashi bridge and the Horikawa Sightseeing Boat dock.

Yakumoan (八雲庵) ★★ 🍴 SOBA NOODLES A wonderful place to stop off for lunch if you're sightseeing along Shiomi Nawate north of Matsue Castle, this lovely *soba* shop with a teahouselike atmosphere is surrounded by a stone wall with a large wooden entryway, a small Japanese garden, and a pond full of prize carp. Part of the restaurant, a former samurai residence, dates from 200 years ago. Its specialty is noodles, all handmade, including the local specialty Warigo *soba* and *udon*.

308 Kitabori-cho. ☏ **0852/22-2400.** Noodles ¥600–¥900. No credit cards. Daily 11am–3:30pm. Lakeline bus: Koizumi Yakumo Kinenkan-mae/Lafcadio Hearn Museum (1 min.). On Shiomi Nawate St., beside the Buke Yashiki samurai house.

Where to Stay

Directions for listings below start from Matsue Station.

EXPENSIVE

Minamikan (皆美館) ★★ 🍴 You'll be treated like royalty at this *ryokan,* located right beside Lake Shinji and boasting an original structure dating from 1888. On the second floor are the so-called "Classic" (and cheapest) tatami rooms, most with nice wood detailing; one floor up are the "Retro rooms," combination rooms with both beds and tatami areas; most expensive are the fourth-floor "Modern" rooms, with sofas, beds, and Jacuzzi onsen baths overlooking the lake. In fact, most rooms face the lake, but if you really want to feel special, opt for the two-room cottage right beside the lake with views of the lake and a garden. Minamikan is also renowned for its restaurant, open to the public daily from 11:30am to 2:30pm and 5:30 to 9:30pm (last order), with set lunches starting at ¥1,575.

14 Suetsugu Honmachi, Matsue, Shimane Prefecture 690-0843. ☏ **0852/21-5131.** Fax 0852/26-0351. 10 units; 1 cottage. ¥23,250–¥30,180 per person, including 2 meals. Rates exclude service charge. ¥4,620 extra on Fri–Sat and nights before holidays. AE, DC, MC, V. Taxi: 8 min. Lakeline bus: Karakoro Kobo-mae/Karakoro Art Studio (2 min.). Off the Kyomise shopping/dining street in the heart of Matsue. **Amenities:** Restaurant; hot-spring baths. *In room:* A/C, TV, minibar.

MODERATE

Hotel Ichibata ★ Matsue's best-known tourist hotel is the Hotel Ichibata, which first opened its doors almost 45 years ago in a part of town called Matsue Shinjiko Onsen, a hot-spring spa. Pluses include the hotel's indoor and outdoor hot-spring public baths with views over Lake Shinji, top-floor bar, and a nearby jogging path that hugs the shores of the lake. Just behind the hotel is the private Ichibata Line train to Izumo Taisha. None of the singles or doubles have a view of the lake, but the more expensive twins and all the 43 Japanese-style rooms do, including some combination-style rooms with both beds and tatami area. After checking in, you can choose which color *yukata* you wish to wear during your stay.

30 Chidori-cho, Matsue, Shimane Prefecture 690-0852. www.ichibata.co.jp/hotel. ☏ **0852/22-0188.** Fax 0852/22-0230. 142 units. ¥9,390 single; ¥17,100–¥27,600 double; from ¥23,400 Japanese style for 2. ¥1,050 extra per person Sat and nights before holidays. AE, DC, MC, V. Lakeline bus: Chidori Minami Koen/Park (1 min., in front of the hotel). **Amenities:** Restaurant; bar; lounge; outdoor beer

garden (summer only); indoor/outdoor hot-spring baths; room service; Wi-Fi (free, in lobby). *In room:* A/C, TV, fridge, hair dryer, Internet.

Matsue Tokyu Inn   Part of a national business hotel chain, the Tokyu Inn is a good choice for travelers who want to spend the night close to Matsue Station. Rooms are small and generic but have everything you need, including Tempur-Pedic Comfort Pillows that mold to your head, phone chargers (including for iPhone), air purifiers, and bigger bathrooms than in most business hotels. Paying slightly higher rates in each category will get you a larger bed in single rooms and a larger room in double and twin rooms. There's also a ladies' floor, with rooms equipped with irons and female-oriented toiletries.

590 Asahimachi, Matsue, Shimane Prefecture 690-0003. www.tokyuhotels.com/locations/Shimane. ✆ **0852/27-0109.** Fax 0852/25-1327. 181 units. ¥8,800–¥10,500 single; ¥15,300–¥31,500 double. AE, DC, MC, V. Across the street (you have to take the underground passageway) from Matsue Station's north exit, to the right. **Amenities:** Restaurant; lounge; Wi-Fi (free, in lobby). *In room:* A/C, TV, fridge, hair dryer, Internet.

INEXPENSIVE

Toyoko Inn Matsue Ekimae, 498–10 Asahimachi (www.toyoko-inn.com; ✆ **0852/60-1045**), offers tiny rooms with all the basics, with singles starting at ¥4,980 and doubles at ¥6,480, including breakfast. It's a 3-minute walk from Matsue Station's north exit (walk past the buses to the main road and turn left).

Matsue New Urban Hotel   This business hotel near Lake Shinji and within walking distance of Matsue Castle and other tourist sights offers large hot-spring baths, free bikes for guests (electric bikes cost ¥500 for 4 hr.), and a convenience store. There are two buildings, with the main building being cheaper but providing only city views, and an annex with both city and (more expensive) lake views. It has a shuttle bus to Matsue Station in the mornings (but not from the station).

40–1 Nishi-chamachi, Matsue, Shimane Pref. 690-0845. ✆ **0852/23-0003.** Fax 0852/23-0018. 169 units. ¥4,725–¥7,140 single; ¥8,400–¥13,650 double. AE, DC, MC, V. Lakeline bus: Karakoro Kobomae/Karakoro Art Studio (5 min.). **Amenities:** 3 restaurants; rooftop beer garden (summer only); free rental bikes; hot-spring baths; lobby computer w/free Internet. *In room:* A/C, TV, fridge, hair dryer.

Ryokan Terazuya (旅館寺津屋) ★★★ 🍴   Terazuya offers good value for your money, but it also offers something money can't buy: true hospitality. This Japanese inn has been in business since 1893, owned by the Terazu family, who has shown so much kindness to foreigners that many consider their stay here a highlight of their trip. The Terazus treat guests like family, teaching them the tea ceremony, giving calligraphy lessons, and singing traditional *noh* songs in the tatami party room. They've even been known to escort guests to the *onsen.* The postwar building, while nothing special on the outside, is spotless and colorfully decorated inside. Located across from a small shrine and train tracks (yes, you'll hear trains), it's also near Lake Shinji, making it convenient for watching those famous sunsets. And although it's only a 7-minute walk from Matsue Station (head west along the north side of the railroad tracks and keep to the left when you reach the plaza), the Terazus will pick you up if you call ahead (or ask staff at the Matsue tourist office to call for you).

60–3 Tenjin-machi, Matsue, Shimane Prefecture 690-0064. www.mable.ne.jp/~terazuya/english. ✆ **0852/21-3480.** Fax 0852/21-3422. 9 units, none with bathroom. ¥4,500 per person with coffee and bread, ¥5,000 with Japanese breakfast, ¥7,350 with breakfast and dinner. No credit cards. Lakeline bus: Kenritsu Bijutsukan-mae/Prefectural Museum (3 min.). *In room:* A/C, TV, Wi-Fi.

HIROSHIMA, THEN & NOW ★★

894km (554 miles) W of Tokyo; 376km (235 miles) W of Kyoto; 279km (174 miles) E of Hakata/Fukuoka

With a population of 1.18 million, Hiroshima, capital of Hiroshima Prefecture, looks just like any other city in Japan. With modern buildings and an industry that includes the manufacture of cars and ships, it's a city full of vitality and purpose with a steady flow of both Japanese and foreign business executives in and out. But unlike other cities, Hiroshima's past is clouded: It has the unfortunate distinction of being the first city ever destroyed by an atomic bomb. (The second city—and it is hoped the last—was Nagasaki, on Kyushu island.)

It happened one clear summer morning, August 6, 1945, at 8:15am, when a B-29 approached Hiroshima from the northeast, passed over the central part of the city, dropped the bomb, and then took off at full speed. The bomb exploded 43 seconds later at an altitude of 600m (1,980 ft.) in a huge fireball, followed by a mushroom cloud of smoke that rose 8,910m (29,700 ft.) in the air.

There were approximately 350,000 people living in Hiroshima at the time of the bombing, and almost a third lost their lives on that day. The heat from the blast was so intense that it seared people's skin, while the pressure caused by the explosion tore clothes off bodies and caused the rupture and explosion of internal organs. Flying glass tore through flesh like bullets, and fires broke out all over the city. But that wasn't the end of it: Victims who survived the blast were subsequently exposed to huge doses of radioactive particles. Even people who showed no outward signs of sickness suddenly died, creating panic and helplessness among the survivors. In the years that followed, blast survivors continued to suffer from the effects of the bomb, with a high incidence of cancer, disfigurement, scars, and keloid skin tissue.

Ironically, Hiroshima's tragedy is now the city's largest tourist draw and visitors from around the world come to see Peace Memorial Park with its haunting museum and memorials. But Hiroshima, laced with rivers and wide, tree-lined boulevards, boasts a few other worthwhile attractions as well and is the most popular gateway for trips to nearby Miyajima, a jewel of an island considered to be one of Japan's most scenic spots, covered later in this chapter.

Essentials

GETTING THERE **By Plane** Flights to Hiroshima take about 1½ hours from Tokyo and 2¼ hours from Sapporo. Limousine buses connect **Hiroshima Airport** (HIJ; www.hij.airport.jp/english; ✆ **0848/86-8151**) with Hiroshima Station's Shinkansen (north) exit in 48 minutes, costing ¥1,300 one-way.

By Train Hiroshima is about 5 hours from Tokyo by **Shinkansen** bullet train (you have to change trains in Okayama or Shin-Osaka if you have a Japan Rail Pass, because only the Nozomi, which is not covered by the pass, covers the entire distance in 4 hr.), 2 hours from Kyoto, and 1 hour and 10 minutes from Hakata Station on Kyushu. The fare from Tokyo is ¥17,540 for an unreserved seat; ¥10,280 from Kyoto.

By Bus Buses depart from Tokyo Station every night at 8 and 9pm, both reaching Hiroshima Station at 7:30am the next morning for ¥11,600. Willer Express has a bus nightly from Shinjuku at 8:20pm, arriving at Hiroshima Station at 7:40pm for ¥7,400 and up, depending on the seat. From Osaka, buses depart six times a day, taking 5 hours to reach Hiroshima and costing ¥4,000 and up.

By Boat You can reach Hiroshima by **high-speed boat** from Matsuyama on Shikoku in 1 hour and 10 minutes for ¥6,900, but slower ferries, which cover the distance in 2 hours and 30 minutes, are cheaper (¥3,500) and provide better views of the Seto Inland Sea. Hiroshima Port, in Ujina, is connected to Hiroshima Station by streetcar in 43 minutes.

VISITOR INFORMATION There are two Hiroshima City Tourist Information centers at **Hiroshima Station,** one at the north exit where Shinkansen bullet trains arrive and the main one at the station's south exit, where the streetcars are (📞 082/261-1877). Both are open from 9am to 5:30pm daily. A third tourist office is located in **Peace Memorial Park** in the Rest House (📞 082/247-6738). It's open daily from 9:30am to 6pm April to September (to 7pm Aug 1–15) and from 8:30am–5pm the rest of the year. All three facilities have English-language brochures of Hiroshima and Miyajima with maps. Online information on Hiroshima is available at **www. hcvb.city.hiroshima.jp.**

GETTING AROUND One legacy of Hiroshima's total destruction was its rebirth into one of Japan's most navigable cities, with wide, open boulevards instead of the usual cramped streets. Hiroshima's main attractions, including Peace Memorial Park, Hiroshima Castle, Shukkei-en Garden, and Hiroshima Museum of Art, lie to the west and southwest of Hiroshima Station. The most convenient mode of transportation in the city is **streetcar,** which costs only ¥150 one-way; children pay half fare. If you need to transfer to another line, ask the driver for a *norikae* (transfer) card, which you then pass through the card machine upon alighting from the first streetcar and again when boarding the second streetcar. When you arrive at your destination, return the card to the streetcar driver. A 1-day pass, which you can buy from the conductor, costs ¥600. Be sure to pick up a streetcar map from the tourist office.

It's probably easiest to make the circuit to Hiroshima's centrally located attractions **on foot.** From Hiroshima Station, you can walk to Shukkei-en Garden in about 15 minutes, from which it's another 10-minute walk to Hiroshima Castle. You can walk onward to Peace Memorial Park in about 15 minutes, passing the Hiroshima Museum of Art and the A-Bomb Dome on the way. Just east of Peace Park is the **Hondori** covered shopping arcade and its neighboring streets, considered the heart of the city with its many department stores, shops, and restaurants. Alternatively, due to its flat terrain and wide streets, Hiroshima is also easy to navigate by bike. **Bicycles,** available at a handful of hotels (including Hotel Granvia and Hotel Sunroute; see p. 432), cost ¥1,000 for the day (9am–5pm) and are available to everyone.

[Fast FACTS] HIROSHIMA

ATM/Mail Hiroshima's main post office, 2–62 Matsubara-cho (📞 082/261-6401), is located to the right after exiting from Hiroshima Station's south side and is open 24 hours for mail. Its ATM services are available Monday to Saturday 12:05am to 11:55pm and Sunday and holidays 12:05am to 9pm.

Consulates There's a Canadian consulate in central Hiroshima (📞 082/246-0057).

Internet Access **Media Café Popeye,** located in the Hondori covered shopping arcade (📞 082/545-0369) above a shop called Beams, is open 24 hours and charges ¥100 for the first 30 minutes, and then ¥60 for each subsequent 10 minutes.

Hiroshima

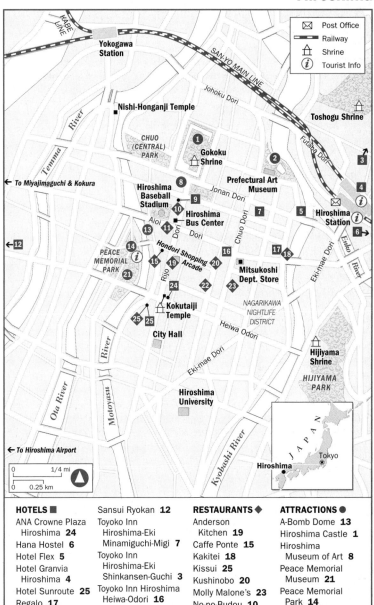

Legend:
- ⊠ Post Office
- ▬ Railway
- ⛩ Shrine
- ⓘ Tourist Info

Map labels:

Yokogawa Station

KABE LINE

SAN-YO MAIN LINE

Johoku Dori

Nishi-Honganji Temple

CHUO (CENTRAL) PARK

Gokoku Shrine

Toshogu Shrine

Futaba Dori

← To Miyajimaguchi & Kokura

Temma River

Prefectural Art Museum

Hiroshima Baseball Stadium

Jonan Dori

Hiroshima Bus Center

Aioi Dori

Hiroshima Station

Chuo Dori

Rijo Dori

PEACE MEMORIAL PARK

Hondori Shopping Arcade

Mitsukoshi Dept. Store

Ekienko River

Eki-mae Dori

NAGARIKAWA NIGHTLIFE DISTRICT

Kokutaiji Temple

City Hall

Heiwa Odori

Hijiyama Shrine

HIJIYAMA PARK

River

Motoyasu

Ota River

Eki-mae Dori

Hiroshima University

← To Hiroshima Airport

Kyobashi River

JAPAN

Tokyo ✷

Hiroshima

0   1/4 mi
0   0.25 km

HOTELS ■
ANA Crowne Plaza Hiroshima **24**
Hana Hostel **6**
Hotel Flex **5**
Hotel Granvia Hiroshima **4**
Hotel Sunroute **25**
Regalo **17**
Rihga Royal Hiroshima **9**
Sansui Ryokan **12**
Toyoko Inn Hiroshima-Eki Minamiguchi-Migi **7**
Toyoko Inn Hiroshima-Eki Shinkansen-Guchi **3**
Toyoko Inn Hiroshima Heiwa-Odori **16**

RESTAURANTS ◆
Anderson Kitchen **19**
Caffe Ponte **15**
Kakitei **18**
Kissui **25**
Kushinobo **20**
Molly Malone's **23**
No-no-Budou **10**
Okonomi-Mura **22**
Sushi Tei **11**

ATTRACTIONS ●
A-Bomb Dome **13**
Hiroshima Castle **1**
Hiroshima Museum of Art **8**
Peace Memorial Museum **21**
Peace Memorial Park **14**
Shukkei-en Garden **2**

Exploring Hiroshima

As you walk around Hiroshima today, you'll find it hard to imagine that the city was the scene of such widespread horror and destruction just 60-some years ago. On the other hand, Hiroshima doesn't have the old buildings, temples, and historic structures that other cities have, yet it draws a steady flow of travelers, including Japanese school groups, who come to see Peace Memorial Park, the city's best-known landmark. Dedicated to peace, the city also seems committed to art: In addition to art museums, you'll find statues, stone lanterns, memorials, and sculptures lining the streets.

PEACE MEMORIAL PARK

Peace Memorial Park (Heiwa Koen) ★★★ lies in the center of the city. English-language signs all over the city indicate how to reach it. From Hiroshima Station's south side, take streetcar No. 1 or 2 to the Genbaku-Domu-mae stop, which is just north of the park. The first structure you'll see as you alight from the streetcar is the **A-Bomb Dome (Genbaku Domu),** the skeletal ruins of the former Industrial Promotion Hall, left as a visual reminder of the death and destruction caused by the atomic bomb and now on the World Heritage List. Across the river is the park; it takes about 10 minutes to walk from its northern end to the museum.

Along the way you'll see the park's many statues and memorials. Most touching is the **Children's Peace Monument,** dedicated to the war's most innocent victims, not only those who died instantly in the blast but also those who died afterward from the effects of radiation. It's a statue of a girl with outstretched arms, and rising above her is a crane, a symbol of happiness and longevity in Japan. The statue is based on the true story of a young girl, Sadako, who suffered from the effects of radiation. She believed that if she could fold 1,000 paper cranes she would become well again. However, even though she folded more than 1,000 cranes, she still died of leukemia. Today, all Japanese children are familiar with her story, and around the memorial are streamers of paper cranes donated by schoolchildren from all over Japan. To the east of the statue is the **Rest House,** where you'll find a branch of the Hiroshima Tourist Office.

Also in Peace Memorial Park is a **Cenotaph for Korean Victims.** It's a little-publicized fact that 20,000 Koreans were killed that fateful summer day, most of them brought to Japan as forced laborers. It's significant to note that for 29 years, the cenotaph remained outside the park. In 1999, Hiroshima's mayor, calling for an end to prejudice against Korean residents in Japan, gave the memorial a new home here.

Between the Children's Peace Monument and the museum is the **Cenotaph for the A-bomb Victims,** designed by Japan's famous architect Kenzo Tange (who also designed the Tokyo Metropolitan Government offices in Shinjuku; see p. 98). Shaped like a figurine clay saddle found in ancient tombs, it shelters a stone chest, which in turn holds the names of all of those killed by the bomb and its afteraffects (more than 280,000 names have been registered so far). An epitaph, written in Japanese, carries the hopeful phrase, "Let all the souls here rest in peace, for we shall not repeat the evil." If you stand in front of the cenotaph, you'll have a view through the hollow arch of the Flame of Peace and the A-Bomb Dome. It is said that the **Flame of Peace** will continue to burn until all atomic weapons vanish from the face of the earth and nuclear war is no longer a threat to humanity.

East of the Peace Flame is the **Hiroshima National Peace Memorial Hall for the Atomic Bomb Victims** (www.hiro-tsuitokinenkan.go.jp; ✆ 082/543-6271).

Its Hall of Remembrance, a 360-degree panorama re-creating the bombed city as seen from the hypocenter, is made of 140,000 tiles, the number of people estimated to have died by the end of 1945. The rest of the memorial is a vast, computerized audiovisual library with information on victims, their histories, and photos. Admission is free and it's open the same hours as the Peace Memorial Museum.

Just beyond is the main focus of the park, the **Peace Memorial Museum (Heiwa Kinen Shiryokan)** ★★★, 1–2 Nakajima-cho, Naku-ku (www.pcf.city. hiroshima.jp; ✆ **082/241-4004;** daily 8:30am–6pm Mar–Nov [until 7pm in Aug], daily 8:30am–5pm Dec–Feb). It comprises two buildings: the East Building, which tells of Hiroshima before the bomb fell and what happened to the city in the following months and years, and the Main (west) Building, which concentrates on that fateful August day. Entrance to the museum is in the East Building; admission is ¥50. Although an audio guide is available for ¥300, you can learn just as much by reading the excellent English-language descriptions throughout the museum. You must enter 30 minutes before closing time, but you'll need at least 1 hour to do the museum justice.

The East Building addresses Hiroshima's militaristic past, challenging the city's former self-characterization as a blameless victim. In great detail, it explains why Hiroshima was selected as the blast site: As Imperial Headquarters, Hiroshima was home to Japan's military command center as well as a military supply base (Mitsubishi, which produced warships, was based here). It also gives food for thought as to why the bomb was dropped, suggesting that the high cost to develop the bomb (called the Manhattan Project), coupled with the desire to establish U.S. supremacy over the Soviet Union and facilitate defeat in Japan, all played a role. There are photographs of Hiroshima prior to the bomb; a model shows what Peace Park (near the hypocenter) looked like before the bomb, with tightly packed houses and temples. TV screens show actual footage of the bomb being dropped and its aftermath, while photographs show Hiroshima's utter destruction. The museum also documents Hiroshima's current dedication to the abolition of nuclear weapons; a globe of the world provides a chilling map of nuclear proliferation.

The Main Building concentrates on the suffering caused by the atomic bomb, beginning with panoramas of scorched earth and seared victims and photographs of the atomic bomb that destroyed the city and the intensity of the blast's epicenter (90% of Hiroshima's buildings were destroyed or burned). It then shows in graphic detail the effects of the blast on bodies, buildings, and materials. Most of the photographs in the exhibit are of burned and seared skin, charred remains of bodies, and people with open wounds, while displays explain the effects of radiation, including hair loss, keloid scars, leukemia, and cancer. There's a bronze Buddha that was half-melted in the blast; on the stone steps of a bank is a shadow, all that remains of the person who had been sitting there. Tattered clothing and other personal effects are accompanied by short biographies of their owners, many of them children and teenagers and many of whom died in the blast.

Needless to say, visiting Peace Memorial Park is a sobering and depressing experience but perhaps a necessary one. And to think that what was dropped on Hiroshima is small compared to the bombs of today; as early as 1961, the Soviet Union had tested a hydrogen bomb 3,300 times more powerful than the atomic bomb dropped on Hiroshima. From the museum, the closest streetcar stop is Fukuro-machi, where you can catch streetcar no. 1 for Hiroshima Station.

More Sights & Attractions

Hiroshima Castle ★★ CASTLE   Completed in 1591 but destroyed in the atomic blast, Hiroshima Castle was reconstructed in 1958. Its five-story wooden *donjon* is a faithful reproduction of the original, but the main reason to come here is the museum housed in the castle's modern interior, which can be toured in about 30 minutes and is devoted to Hiroshima's history as a flourishing castle town, with good English-language presentations. It also gives a good explanation on castles in Japan, including differences in architecture between those built on hills (for defense) and those built on plains (mainly administrative; Hiroshima's is an example of a flatland castle). Videos, with English translations via earphones, describe Hiroshima's founding and the construction of Hiroshima Castle, while displays explain the differences in lifestyle between samurai and townspeople, the hierarchy of the feudal administration system, and other aspects of Edo life. There's also samurai gear, swords, models of old Hiroshima and the castle, as well as a kimono and helmet and breast plate you can try on for free. The top of the donjon provides a panoramic view of the city.

21–1 Moto-machi, Naka-ku. www.rijo-castle.jp/rijo/main.html. ℂ **082/221-7512.** Admission ¥360 adults, ¥180 children, free for seniors and children under 6. Daily 9am–6pm (to 5pm on weekdays Dec–Feb, 6pm weekends). A 15-min. walk north of Peace Memorial Park, or a 25-min. walk west of Hiroshima Station. Streetcar: Kamiya-cho-higashi (10 min.).

Hiroshima Museum of Art (Hiroshima Bijutsukan) ★★ 🎨 ART MUSEUM
This gem of a private museum is located in a park in the heart of the city and housed in a modern round building. Its permanent collection of some 200 paintings, half by French painters from Romanticism to Ecole de Paris, is presented in chronological order in four rooms. Though small, virtually every piece is by a well-known artist, including Delacroix, Courbet, Corot, Manet, Monet, Renoir, Sisley, Degas, Toulouse-Lautrec, Rousseau, Cézanne, Gauguin, van Gogh, Matisse, Picasso, Braque, Utrillo, Chagall, and Modigliani. Changing exhibits may feature the museum's collection of Japanese art in the Western style from the Meiji Era to the present, including works by Kuroda Seiki and Kishida Ryusei. You'll spend an hour here.

3–2 Motomachi, Naka-ku. www.hiroshima-museum.jp. ℂ **082/223-2530.** Admission ¥1,000 adults, ¥500 university and high-school students, ¥200 junior-high and elementary students. Prices may change due to special exhibits. Daily 9am–5pm. Streetcar: Kamiya-cho-higashi (3 min.). In Chuo Park, across from the Rihga Royal Hotel (Hiroshima's tallest building).

Shukkei-en Garden PARK/GARDEN   Shukkei-en Garden, which means "landscape garden in miniature," was first laid out in 1620 by a master of the tea ceremony, with a pond constructed in imitation of famous Lake Xi Hu in Hangzhou, China. Using streams, ponds, islets, and bridges, the feudal lord's garden was designed to appear much larger than it actually is and is best viewed on a 30-minute circular stroll. Like everything else in Hiroshima, it was destroyed in 1945, but amazingly, it looks like it's been here forever. Unfortunately, like most gardens in Japan, tall neighboring buildings detract from the garden's beauty (there ought to be a law), but it's still a pleasant respite from city traffic. A fun thing to do, especially if you're with children, is to buy food for the carp (¥100) and watch them swarm.

2–11 Kaminobori-cho, Naka-ku. ℂ **082/221-3620.** Admission ¥250 adults, ¥150 university and high-school students, ¥100 children. Daily 9am–6pm (to 5pm Oct–Mar). Streetcar: Shukkeien-mae. A 15-min. walk from Hiroshima Station.

Exploring Sights of the Seto Inland Sea

Stretching between Honshu and the islands of Shikoku and Kyushu, the Inland Sea is dotted with more than 3,000 pine-covered islands and islets, part of which is protected as Seto-Naikai (Seto Inland Sea) National Park. Hiroshima Prefecture serves as a departure point for ferries traveling to islands throughout the Seto Inland Sea and to Shikoku. A more active way to see the Seto Inland Sea is to cycle part or all of the **Shimanami Kaido,** a 70km (43-mile) dedicated cycling path between Onomichi in Hiroshima Prefecture and Imabari on Shikoku Island.

CYCLING THE SHIMANAMI KAIDO   The Shimanami Kaido route travels over six islands connected by seven bridges, with numerous temples, sightseeing spots, and restaurants along the way; be sure to pick up the English brochure at the Hiroshima tourist office with maps, the location of bike rental shops along the path, and other information about the route. Bikes cost ¥500 for a day, plus a ¥1,000 deposit. If you wish to cycle one-way and leave your bike in Imabari or at one of the 13 cycle-rental stops along the way, you forfeit your deposit. Electric bikes are also available at some bike shops for ¥800, but they are only for 4 hours and must be returned to the original rental location. Bridges along the route charge a toll, which you deposit into a box on the honor system, for a total of ¥500 if you go all the way to Shikoku, which takes about 8 hours (you can buy prepaid toll tickets at cycling shops so you don't have to fish for change). For more information on the Shimanami Kaido, see p. 458 in chapter 9.

Rental bikes (including electric bikes) are available in Onomichi City at **Onomichi Ekimae Kowan Chushajo** (尾道駅前港湾駐車場; ✆ **0848/22-5332;** daily 7am–6pm), a 3-minute walk from Onomichi Station, located to the right in a parking garage (see below for information on getting to Onomichi from Hiroshima). Here, too, is the port, where you'll board the 4-minute ferry (fare: ¥110, plus ¥150 for the bike) to the first island, Mukaishima, to begin your ride. Or, you can rent a bike at the **Onomichi Citizens Center Mukaishima** (✆ **0848/44-0110;** daily 8:30am–5pm), to the left after exiting the dock, but no electric bikes are available here.

If you wish to cycle but have no interest in going all the way to Shikoku, another interesting option is to take the Shinkansen 30 minutes from Hiroshima to Mihara (fare: ¥2,220), from which you can take a **high-speed boat** operated by Mihara-Setoda Kyodo Line (✆ **0848/64-0564)** 30 minutes to Setoda on Ikuchijima island. Ferries depart approximately once an hour, with one-way fares costing ¥800. You can then rent a bike at **Setoda-cho Tourist Information (Kanko Annaisho)** in front of the Hirayama Ikuo Museum (✆ **0845/27-0051;** daily 9am–5pm), visit Choseizan Kosanji Temple (see below), and cycle around Ikuchijima in a couple of hours. Or, you can bike from Kosanji Temple over the Tatara Ohashi bridge to Omomishima island's Oyamazumi Shrine with its fantastic collection of samurai weaponry (see p. 458) in about 2 hours. You can then cycle back to the Tatarai Ohashi bridge, deposit your bike at **Michi no Ike Tatara Shimanami Koen** bike station (✆ **0897/87-3855;** daily 9am–5pm), and catch a bus at the nearby Omishima bus station for the almost 2-hour ride back to Hiroshima (fare: ¥2,900); there are only 3 buses a day weekdays and 6 buses weekends and holidays, so be sure to check the schedule (at press time, the last bus departs at 7:16pm). More frequent are hourly buses reaching Fukuyama Station in 1 hour (fare: ¥1,700), where you can then catch the train back to Hiroshima.

HIGHLIGHTS ALONG THE SHIMANAMI KAIDO From Hiroshima, take the JR Sanyo Line 1½ hours to Onomichi Station (fare: ¥1,450). Direct trains are only once an hour, so you might have to change in Itozaki, but transfer is just across the tracks. If you have a Japan Rail Pass, it's quicker to take the Shinkansen 30 minutes to Mihara, followed by the 13-minute Sanyo local line (ask for the train schedule in advance). At Onomichi Station, the **Onomichi Tourist Office** (www.city.onomichi. hiroshima.jp/english/en_index.html; ☎ **0848/20-0005;** daily 9am–6pm) has information on the Shimanami Kaido and an English map of the city.

Onomichi is an old-fashioned port town, a bit rough (neglected) around the edges but infinitely more photogenic than most towns here. That's due to its steep hills rising directly from the port, packed with old houses, winding lanes, and some 20 temples along the 2km **Old Temple Course,** which you can reach in a few minutes' walk from Onomichi Station. Highlights include **Senkoji Temple,** founded in 806 and commanding views over the harbor, and, beside the nearby wood pagoda, whimsical **Cat Alley (Nekono Hosomichi),** with its painted cat stones and alternative-looking cafes hidden among the overgrowth like fairy enclaves.

Ikuchijima Island boasts what I consider a definite must on the Shimanami Kaido, **Choseizan Kosanji Temple ★★**, located in the town of Setoda (www. kousanji.or.jp; ☎ **0845/27-0800**). Even if you're not renting a bike, this is a great excursion. You can reach it by ferry from Mihara (see above) or from Onomichi port (¥800 for the 40-min. ride), from which it's a 10-minute walk from Setoda's pier. This place is like no other, a re-creation of famous historic buildings from throughout Japan, erected by a former businessman-turned-Buddhist-priest over a 30-year period beginning in 1936 in honor of his mother. Occupying a picturesque hillside setting with many flowering trees, the grounds contain remakes of Byodoin Temple outside Kyoto, Nikko's Yomeimon Gate, Horyuji's Hall of Visions in Nara, and other important buildings, all expertly crafted. Be sure to tour **Choseikaku Villa,** built in 1927 as the home of the priest's beloved mother and employing an amazing variety of woods for its intricately carved transoms, paneling, and other traditional features. Another highlight is the **grotto cave** (beside Byodoin Temple). Stretching 350m (1,155 ft.), it depicts unfortunate souls in hell being burned, chopped to pieces, eaten by animals, and suffering other gruesome forms of torture, for crimes ranging from murder and thievery to drinking too much or having sex with a nun. After passing through caves and Buddhist statues, you then emerge to see a 15m (50-ft.) statue of the Goddess of Mercy, hoping by now that she is, indeed, merciful. On the crest of the hill is the Heights of Eternal Hope for the Future, a huge white-marble installation by a Hiroshima sculptor; its jagged edges resemble a glacier and there's a coffee shop here—Café Cuore—in what looks like an igloo. Other things to see include museums showcasing art relating to Buddhism, the tea ceremony, and modern Japanese art. You can spend an easy 2 hours here. Admission to Kosanji Temple, open daily 9am to 5pm, is ¥1,200 for adults, ¥700 for high-school students, and free for children.

Near the front gate to Kosanji is a branch of a famous ice-cream shop, **Dolce (ドルチェ),** Kosanji-mae Ten (☎ **0845/26-4036**), renowned for its *Hakata-no-shio,* an ice cream that contains salt obtained from seawater (and tastes much better than it sounds). Ikuchijima is also known for its many outdoor sculptures placed around the island and for its 800m (2,640-ft.) Sunset Beach, a popular swimming destination.

For information on Oyamazumi Shrine on Omishima Island, see p. 458.

Where to Eat

Although the people of Osaka claim to have made *okonomiyaki* popular among the masses, the people of Hiroshima claim to have made it an art. Okonomiyaki is a kind of Japanese pancake filled with cabbage, meat, and other fillings. Whereas in Osaka the ingredients are mixed together, in Hiroshima each layer is prepared separately, which means the chefs have to be quite skilled at keeping the entire thing together. Hiroshima is also famous for oysters (among the largest I've ever seen), with thousands of rafts cultivating oysters in Hiroshima Bay and producing 20,000 tons of shelled oysters yearly.

MODERATE

Kissui ★★ KAISEKI   Convenient to Peace Memorial Park, great 15th-floor views, an English-language menu, and beautifully prepared kaiseki meals make this an optimal choice for tourists. For lunch, the Kissui Set for ¥2,500 is a great choice, but no matter what you choose, you can't go wrong here. Alternatively, Viale, also on the 15th floor, offers Italian fare with the same great views.

Hotel Sunroute, 15th floor, 3–3–1 Otemachi. © **082/249-5657.** Kaiseki set dinners ¥5,800–¥9,899; set lunches ¥2,500–¥7,800. AE, DC, MC, V. Daily 11:30am–2pm and 5–8pm (last order). Streetcar: Chuden-mae (see directions to hotel in review of Hotel Sunroute, below).

INEXPENSIVE

Anderson Kitchen INTERNATIONAL   Occupying an old, renovated bank building in the Hondori covered shopping arcade, this popular place not far from Peace Memorial Park has a gourmet food department on its ground floor offering baked goods, wine, and imported delicacies, while the second floor has a cafeteria with various counters specializing in different types of food—salads, sandwiches, pizza, pasta, steaks, Chinese dishes, desserts, or drinks. Just pick up a tray and select the items you want. You pay at the end of each counter.

7–1 Hondori. © **082/247-4800.** Dishes ¥850–¥1,700. No credit cards. Daily 11am–9pm (last order). Streetcar: Hondori (1 min.); in the Hondori covered shopping arcade 1 block to the east.

Caffé Ponte ITALIAN   What I like most about this smoke-free restaurant is that it's easy to find (just across the river from the tourist office in Peace Park) and offers outdoor seating under white umbrellas, making a meal here seem like a mini-vacation. Its English-language menu with photos offers lots of choices, including oysters, pasta, fish, and meat dishes.

1–9–21 Otemachi. www.caffeponte.com. © **082/247-7471.** Main dishes ¥1,200–¥2,800; set dinners ¥3,800–¥6,500; set lunches ¥1,280–¥1,980. AE, DC, MC, V. Mon–Fri 10am–10pm, Sat–Sun and holidays 8am–10pm (7:30am–10pm daily in Aug). Streetcar: Hondori (3 min., through the covered shopping arcade) or Genbaku Dome-mae (2 min.). East of Peace Park, on the bank of Motoyasu-gawa river at the Motoyasu-bashi bridge.

Kakitei (牡蠣亭) ★ 🍴 OYSTERS   Calling itself the "Oyster Conclave," this hip pavilion restaurant, perched beside the tree-lined Kyobashi-gawa river with views of passing streetcars, has a distinct retro atmosphere, with outdoor seating in summer. It's famous for its oysters prepared in a Western style. You might, for example, try grilled oysters on the half shell served with tomato and cheese, champagne cream, or vegetables in a mustard-butter blend, though the oyster quiche is probably my favorite.

11 Hashimoto-cho. © **082/221-8990.** Grilled oysters ¥700–¥850 for 2, ¥900–¥1,280 for 3; set lunch ¥1,200. AE, DC, MC, V. Wed–Mon 11am–2:30pm and 5–10:30pm. Streetcar: Kanayama-cho (1 min.). Or a 13-min. walk from Hiroshima Station.

Kushinobo (串の坊) ★★ KUSHIYAKI   This is a friendly, rub-elbows-with-the-locals kind of place, lively and crowded and decorated with Japanese knickknacks. Although kushiyaki connoisseurs like ordering skewers a la carte, you'll probably be better off ordering from the English-language menu listing only set meals. I always enjoy the Kushinobo-gozen with 10 skewers of vegetables, meat, and seafood plus fresh vegetables, rice, soup, and dessert, but what I like most is watching skewers being prepared behind the counter and the friendly interactions between customers. The chef is a serious fellow, but he speaks English and somehow manages to keep all the orders straight. It's located off the east end of the Hondori covered arcade.

Parco-mae, 7–4 Horikawa-cho. ⊘ **082/245-9300.** Reservations recommended. Set dinners ¥2,350–¥3,200; set lunches ¥1,200–¥1,500. AE, DC, MC, V. Daily 11:30am–1:30pm and 5–9:30pm (last order). Streetcar: Hatchobori (2 min.). Walk south on Chuo Dori 2 blocks to Parco department store and turn right into a covered shopping arcade; take the 1st left and then the 1st right. Look for its Chinese-style red facade.

Molly Malone's VARIED WESTERN   An Irish pub with good food—what more do you need? In addition to 10 beers on tap (a sampler of three costs ¥1,000), it offers soups, salads (like a poached salmon salad), pastas (including vegetarian choices like the yummy pasta with brocolli, peppers, oven-dried tomato, olives, roasted eggplant, artichoke, basil, garlic, pine nuts and parmesan), burgers, and classic pub fare ranging from fish and chips and bangers and mash to cottage pie and Irish stew. Add happy hour Monday to Saturday from 5 to 7pm and screens showing international soccer and rugby games, and this could be your new favorite hot spot.

Teigeki Building, 4th floor, 1–20 Shintenchi. ⊘ **082/244-2554.** Main dishes ¥800–¥1,200. MC, V (¥3,000 minimum order). Mon–Thurs 5pm–1am, Fri 5pm–2am, Sat 11:30am–2:30am, Sun and holidays 11:30am–midnight (last order). Streetcar: Hatchobori (1 min.). Walk south on Chuo Dori Ave.; it's on the left (across from Parco) and is easy to miss.

No-no-Budou (野の葡萄) ★ 🔥 JAPANESE BUFFET   This popular buffet restaurant in the Pacela shopping complex (next to Righa Royal Hotel) specializes in healthy, organic foods, with some 50 choices that change daily but always include choices of Chinese and Japanese dishes, from noodles and tempura to soups and salads. Some seats beside windows provide city views, but avoid the lunchtime rush.

Motomachi CRED complex, 7th floor of Pacela, 78–6 Motomachi. ⊘ **082/502-3340.** Buffet lunch ¥1,575; buffet dinner ¥1,890. AE, DC, MC, V. Daily 11am–3pm and 5–9pm (last order). Streetcar: Kamiya-cho-nishi (1 min.); follow the underground signs for the Astram Line and take the exit on your left.

Okonomi-Mura (お好み村) ★★ 🎎 OKONOMIYAKI   This is the best place in town to witness okonomiyaki short-order cooks at their trade, although the building doesn't look as though it contains restaurants. Its name means "okonomiyaki village," and that's what it is—floors of individual stalls, dishing out okonomiyaki. All offer basically the same menu—sit down at one of the counters and watch how the chef first spreads pancake mix on a hot griddle; follows it with a layer of cabbage, bean sprouts, and bacon; and then adds an egg on top. If you want, you can have yours with Chinese noodles. The portions are enormous; this is one of Hiroshima's most beloved establishments. I suggest wandering through and stopping at one that catches your fancy. Or, for a specific recommendation, try **Chii-chan** (ちいちゃん; ⊘ **082/249-8102**) on the second floor, offering food from an English-language menu until 1am (closed on Tues); Chii-chan and his female staff sell 200 to 500 okonomiyaki a day.

5–13 Shintenchi. ☏ **082/241-2210.** Set meals ¥735–¥1,365. No credit cards. Daily 11am–9pm, but some stalls stay open later. Streetcar: Hatchobori (2 min.). Walk south on Chuo Dori 4 blocks (you'll see Yamada on the corner) and turn right.

Sushi Tei (すし亭) ★ 🍴 SUSHI Excellent sushi at reasonable prices is the reason this establishment is so popular. You'll be seated at the counters, as cooks shout greetings and orders back and forth. Ordering is made easy by an English-language menu, offering rolled sushi (like the crab salad roll), sashimi, and soup. There are many Sushi Tei restaurants in town, but this is one is easy to find, near the A-Bomb Dome.

1–4–31 Otemachi. ☏ **082/545-1333.** Sushi sets ¥840–¥2,100. AE, DC, MC, V. Mon–Sat 5pm–midnight; Sun and holidays 11:30am–10pm. Streetcar: Kamiya-cho-nishi (1 min.). Take the small street beside the Deo Deo building (with the overhead "Deo Deo" sign) and turn right; it's on the left.

Where to Stay

Directions are from Hiroshima Station.

EXPENSIVE

ANA Crowne Plaza Hiroshima ★★ I like this hotel's location, near Peace Park and the Hondori covered shopping arcade. Rooms, too, are a good reason to stay here, comfortably outfitted with blackout drapes, a choice of pillows, and aroma-therapy products ranging from bath powder and mint tea to eye warmers (available on request if not already in your room). Standard rooms occupy lower floors, while some twins on top-floor Premier floors even provide views as far away as Miyajima. Add a helpful staff and a wide range of facilities, and you have one of Hiroshima's top choices.

6–20 Nakamachi, Naka-ku, Hiroshima 730-0037. www.anacrowneplaza-hiroshima.jp/en. ☏ **082/241-1111.** Fax 082/241-9123. 409 units. ¥16,170–¥17,325 single; ¥25,410–¥33,495 double. AE, DC, MC, V. Streetcar: 1 to Fukuro-machi (1 min.). Walk south (the same direction as your streetcar) on Rijo Dori to Heiwa Odori (there's a small shrine on the corner) and turn left. **Amenities:** 5 restaurants; bar; lounge; concierge; dental clinic; health club w/gym, heated lap pool and sauna (fee: gym is free; ¥2,000 for pool and sauna); room service. *In room:* A/C, TV, hair dryer, Internet, minibar.

Rihga Royal Hotel Hiroshima ★★★ The 33-story Rihga Royal stands out as Hiroshima's tallest hotel, has a convenient location in the heart of the city between Hiroshima Castle and Peace Park, and is connected to a large complex that includes the Pacela shopping mall and Sogo department store. A sophisticated, European atmosphere and polished service make it a favorite among foreign travelers; even the lobby lounge—with its tall ceiling and circular glass facade—makes for a cheerful meeting place. Large rooms with luxurious furnishings come with plenty of features, including magnifying mirrors and lots of counter space in the bathrooms. Rates are based on floor height and room size, but even some of the cheapest twins have views of the castle or Peace Park. The best views, however, are from top floors with panoramas of the Seto Inland Sea (you can even see Miyajima). A nice touch are the pictorial maps in each room describing the view, but the best view of all is afforded from the 33rd-floor Rihga Top lounge (no cover charge if you sit at the bar).

6–78 Motomachi, Naka-ku, Hiroshima 730-0011. www.rihga-hiroshima.co.jp. ☏ **082/502-1121.** Fax 082/228-5415. 486 units. ¥16,170–¥18,480 single; ¥23,100–¥40,425 double; from ¥40,425 executive double. AE, DC, MC, V. Streetcar: 1, 2, or 6 to Kamiya-cho-nishi (1 min.). **Amenities:** 7 restaurants; 2 bars; lounge; babysitting; concierge; executive-level rooms; health club w/gym, atrium-style 25m (82-ft.) 5-lane pool, Jacuzzi, and sauna (fee: ¥3,150 for pool and sauna; ¥6,300 for everything); health and dental clinic; room service. *In room:* A/C, TV, fridge, hair dryer, Internet (fee: ¥1,050 per 24 hr.).

MODERATE

Hotel Flex ★★ 🏦 This is Hiroshima's most unconventional hotel, apparent the first moment you walk in and find yourself in a cafe that opens out onto the tree-lined Kyobashi-gawa river and doubles as the check-in lobby. A concrete structure that bills itself as "SBC" (small but comfortable), it offers laundry facilities and tiny but fashionable single, twin, and double rooms (some of which offer relaxing river views), as well as three top-floor rooms that are almost like mini-apartments without the kitchen (one even has an outdoor terrace).

7–1 Kaminobori-cho, Naka-ku, Hiroshima 730-0014. www.hotel-flex.co.jp. Ⓒ **082/223-1000.** Fax 082/223-5678. 65 units. ¥6,825–¥15,750 single; ¥11,550–¥22,000 double. AE, DC, MC, V. Hiroshima Station (7 min.). From the station's south exit, turn right and then left after the post office; after crossing the pedestrian Ekinishi-koka-bashi bridge and turning right to cross another bridge, it will be immediately on your right. **Amenities:** Cafe/restaurant; lobby computer w/free Internet; Wi-Fi (free, in cafe). *In room:* A/C, TV, fridge, Internet.

Hotel Granvia Hiroshima ★ Owned by JR West (and offering discounts to holders of the Japan Rail Pass), this hotel is convenient for short stays because it's connected to the Shinkansen (north) side of the station. Inconvenient, however, is that to get to Hiroshima's sights and streetcars, which are on the other side of the station, you have to navigate a confusing underground passage (if you have a rail pass, you can pass through the station, which is much quicker). Rooms are comfortable but have no view, unless you count views of the Shinkansen pulling into the station. A plus are the hotel's many dining options, including one serving Hiroshima-style *okonomiyaki.*

1–5 Matsubara-cho, Minami-ku, Hiroshima 732-0822. www.hgh.co.jp. Ⓒ **082/262-1111.** Fax 082/262-4050. 403 units. ¥11,319–¥16,747 single; ¥17,902–¥31,185 double. 20% discount for holders of Japan Rail Pass. AE, DC, MC, V. Attached to Hiroshima Station. **Amenities:** 9 restaurants; 2 bars; lounge; outdoor beer terrace (summer only); rental bikes (¥1,000 per day); access to health club in Hiroshima Station w/gym, indoor pool, and sauna (discount ticket at concierge desk ¥2,650); room service. *In room:* A/C, TV, Internet, minibar.

Hotel Sunroute ★★ Although most hotels in this chain are strictly business hotels, this hotel's excellent location, next to the river and catty-corner from the museum in Peace Memorial Park, plus two very good restaurants with great views, makes it a popular choice for tourists as well. The highest-priced rooms have the additional advantage of views of the park and river; the cheapest rooms, however, are on low floors and have no views whatsoever.

3–3–1 Otemachi, Naka-ku, Hiroshima 730-0051. www.sunroutehotel.jp/hiroshima. Ⓒ **082/249-3600.** Fax 082/249-3677. 284 units. ¥9,450–¥11,550 single; ¥12,600–¥26,250 double. AE, DC, MC, V. Streetcar: 1 to Chuden-mae (3 min.). Backtrack north to Heiwa Odori and turn left; it's on your left before the river. **Amenities:** 2 restaurants, including Kissui (p. 429); bar; rental bikes (¥1,000 per day). *In room:* A/C, TV, fridge, hair dryer, Internet.

INEXPENSIVE

There are four Toyoko Inns in Hiroshima. Check www.toyoko-inn for locations.

Hana Hostel This former business hotel turned backpacker's hostel offers 10 small private rooms (in addition to multi-bed dormitories), all with either wash basin and toilet or bathroom and consisting of both Western-style and Japanese tatami rooms. Pluses include its location near Hiroshima Station, laundry facilities, communal kitchen with free tea and coffee, a fifth-floor lounge with TV and DVDs, and a rooftop terrace where you can hang out and hang laundry. If I were you, I'd ask for a room facing the front of the building, away from the train tracks.

1–15 Kojin-machi, Minami-ku, Hiroshima 730-0015. http://hiroshimahostel.jp. ℂ **082/263-2980.** Fax 082/298-2988. 13 units, 4 with toilet only, 6 with bathroom, 3 dormitory rooms without bathroom. ¥3,700 single with toilet only, ¥3,900 with bathroom; ¥6,400 double with toilet only, ¥6,800 double with bathroom; ¥10,200 triple with bathroom; ¥11,600 quad with toilet ony; ¥2,500 dormitory bed. MC, V. Hiroshima Station (3 min). Turn left out of the station's south exit and follow the tracks; after passing by the road that crosses the tracks (don't cross the tracks), take the 1st right and then 1st left at the small parking lot. **Amenities:** Rental bikes (¥500 per day); lobby computer w/free Internet. *In room* (private rooms only): A/C, TV, hair dryer, no phone.

Regalo ★ ☙ Located on one of Hiroshima's many rivers, about halfway between Hiroshima Station and downtown, this small hotel capitalizes on its river views with an atmospheric Italian restaurant and, across the street beside the river, an open-air pavilion cafe. While the cheapest rooms have glazed windows facing the back and are dark, rooms only slightly more expensive have refreshing views of the river. In the lobby are telephones with free domestic calls to land lines (in-room phones are only for receiving calls, not for making calls). In short, this establishment is a pleasant alternative to most inexpensive lodgings, with more personality than the cookie-cutter Toyoko Inn chain.

9–2 Hashimoto-cho, Naka-ku, Hiroshima 730-0015. ℂ **082/224-6300.** Fax 082/224-6301. info@ regalo-h.com. 63 units. ¥6,500–¥7,000 single; ¥9,500–¥10,000 double; ¥12,000 triple. Rates include breakfast. AE, DC, MC, V. Streetcar: 1, 2, or 6 to Kanayama-cho (2 min.). Walk back toward the bridge but don't cross it; turn left at the river. Or a 13-min. walk from Hiroshima Station. **Amenities:** Restaurant; cafe; lounge; lobby computer w/free Internet. *In room:* A/C, TV, fridge, hair dryer, no phone.

Sansui Ryokan ★ This is a good choice for travelers who like meeting locals rather than staying in impersonal hotels. It's run by the motherly and very hospitable Kato-san, who cheerfully oversees operations, has kimono you can try on for free, and can even arrange 1-hour lessons in calligraphy or the tea ceremony (¥1,500 each) if you make reservations 3 weeks in advance. It has a cozy communal room offering free coffee and tea, but note that tatami rooms on the second floor are reached by steep stairs. Best of all, it's only a few minutes' walk west of Peace Memorial Park.

4–16 Koami-cho, Naka-ku, Hiroshima 730-0855. www.sansui-ryokan.com. ℂ **082/293-9051.** Fax 082/233-2377. 6 units, none with bathroom. ¥4,200 single; ¥7,500 double; ¥10,500 triple. Breakfast ¥600 extra. MC, V. Streetcar: 2 to Koami-cho (1 min.). Walk toward and turn left at the river and then the 1st left. **Amenities:** Rental bikes (¥300 per day). *In room:* A/C, TV, no phone.

MIYAJIMA, SCENIC ISLAND IN THE SETO SEA ★★★

13km (8 miles) SW of Hiroshima

Easily reached in about 40 minutes from Hiroshima, **Miyajima** is a treasure of an island only 2km (1¼ miles) off the mainland in the Seto Inland Sea. No doubt you've seen pictures of its most famous landmark: a huge red *torii*, or shrine gate, rising out of the water. Erected in 1875 and made of camphor wood, it's one of the largest *torii* in Japan, measuring more than 16m (53 ft.) tall. It guards Miyajima's main attraction, Itsukushima Shrine, designated a World Heritage Site in 1996.

With the Japanese penchant for categorizing the "three best" of virtually everything in their country—the three best gardens, the three best waterfalls, and so on—it's no surprise that Miyajima is ranked as one of the three most scenic spots in Japan (the other two are Matsushima in Tohoku; and Amanohashidate, a remote sand spit, on the Japan Sea coast). Only 31 sq. km (12 sq. miles) in area and consisting mostly of steep, wooded hills, it's an exceptionally beautiful island, part of the Seto-Naikai (Inland Sea) National Park that is mostly water, islands, and islets. Of course, this distinction means it can be quite crowded with visitors, particularly in summer and autumn.

Miyajima has been held sacred since ancient times. In the olden days, no one was allowed to do anything so human as to give birth or die on the island, so both the pregnant and the ill were quickly ferried across to the mainland. Even today there's no cemetery on Miyajima. Covered with cherry trees that illuminate the island with snowy petals in spring, and with maple trees that emblazon it in reds and golds in autumn, Miyajima is home to tame deer that roam freely through the village. It's a delightful island for strolls and hikes—but avoid coming on a weekend.

Essentials

GETTING THERE   The easiest way to reach Miyajima is from Hiroshima. You can travel from Hiroshima by JR train, streetcar, bus, or boat, but the fastest and most reliable method is the **train,** which departs from Hiroshima Station approximately every 15 minutes and costs ¥400 (free for JR Rail Pass holders) for the 26-minute ride to Miyajimaguchi (if you're downtown or in Peace Memorial Park, you might find it easier to catch the train at Nishi-Hiroshima Station). Otherwise, **streetcar no. 2** takes about an hour from Hiroshima Station to Hiroden Miyajimaguchi, the last stop, and costs ¥270. Both the train and streetcar deposit you at Miyajimaguchi, from which it's just a 2-minute walk to the **ferry** bound for Miyajima. There are two ferry companies (JR and Matsudai) offering the 10-minute ride to Miyajima for ¥170, but if you have a **Japan Rail Pass,** you can ride on the JR ferry for free.

Alternatively, boats travel from downtown Hiroshima directly to Miyajima in about 45 minutes. Operated by **Aqua Net Hiroshima** (www.aqua-net-h.co.jp; ✆ **082/240-5955**), boats depart from Motoyasu-bashi bridge, near the A-Bomb Dome, 10 to 12 times daily. Fare is ¥1,900 one-way; children pay half fare. Note that service is suspended during inclement weather and when the tide is low.

VISITOR INFORMATION   On Miyajima island, stop off at the **Tourist Information Office** (www.miyajima.or.jp; ✆ **0829/44-2011**), located in the Miyajima ferry terminal and open daily 9am to 6pm. It has an English-language brochure and a map, and the helpful staff can show where restaurants and accommodations are located.

GETTING AROUND   You can **walk** to all the sights, accommodations, and restaurants listed below. If you wish to visit one of the island's beaches or explore more of the island, rental **bicycles** are available daily 8am to 5pm (last checkout is 3pm) from both ferry companies at the island's ferry terminal. JR rents bikes for ¥320 for 2 hours or ¥1,050 for the entire day (no Rail Pass discounts), while Matsudai charges only ¥300 for 3 hours plus ¥100 for each additional hour. Inquire at each ferry company ticket window. It takes about 20 minutes to cycle to the nearest beach. Otherwise, shuttle **buses** travel to the beaches year-round and twice an hour from mid-July through August for ¥300. Ask the Tourist Information Office for a schedule.

Exploring Miyajima Island

There are no addresses in this and the dining sections because the village is small, and the address would only be meaningful to the postman.

SEEING THE SIGHTS

Miyajima's major attraction, **Itsukushima Shrine** ★★ (© 0829/44-2020), is about a 10-minute walk from the ferry pier (turn right from the terminal), at the end of a long narrow pedestrian street called Omotesando Dori that is lined with souvenir shops and restaurants. Founded in 593 to honor three female deities, the wooden shrine is built over the water so that, when the tide is in, it appears as though the shrine is floating. A brilliant vermilion, it contrasts starkly with the wooded hills in the background and the blue of the sky above, casting its reflection in the waters below. If you do happen to see Itsukushima Shrine when the tide is in and it's seemingly floating on water, you should consider yourself very lucky indeed—most of the time the lovely shrine floats above a surface that's only a little more glamorous than mud. That's when imagination comes in handy (the Hiroshima tourist offices may have a tide calendar).

The majority of the shrine buildings are thought to date from the 16th century, preserving the original style of 12th-century architecture, but they have been repaired repeatedly through the centuries. Most of the shrine buildings are closed, but from 6:30am to sunset daily (usually 6pm in summer, to 5 or 5:30pm in winter), you can walk along the 230m (770-ft.) covered **dock,** which threads its way past the outer part of the main shrine and one of the oldest *noh* stages in Japan. From the shrine, you'll have a good view of the red *torii* standing in the water. **Bugaku** (festival dances) are staged here 10 times a year (expect those days to be crowded with tour groups). An ancient dance performed to the accompaniment of court music, Bugaku was introduced to Japan centuries ago from India through China and Korea. The performer's costume is orange, matching the shrine around him. Admission to the shrine is ¥300 for adults, ¥200 for high-school students, ¥100 for children.

Turn right upon exiting the shrine. After a few minutes, you'll come to the **History and Folklore Museum** (Rekishi Minzoku Shiryokan; © 0829/44-2019; Tues–Sun 8:30am–5pm). It has a colorful, English-language brochure to guide you through the 170-year-old house (which once belonged to a wealthy soy-sauce merchant and is built around a small Japanese garden), as well as through several other buildings. Packed with items donated by the people of Miyajima, the museum is a window into commoners' daily lives in ages past, with farm tools, cooking objects, furniture, lacquerware, combs, and much more. Another exhibit focuses on a popular TV series that takes place on Miyajima. Be sure to see the narrow, three-room dwelling in the back of the museum complex, typical of the island. Admission is ¥300 for adults, ¥170 for high-school students, and ¥150 for junior-high and elementary students. It will take about 30 minutes to see everything.

Another sight worth exploring is **Daisho-in Temple,** on the slope of Mount Misen (© 0829/44-0111; daily 8am–5pm). One of the most famous Shingon temples in western Japan, it has numerous worthwhile sights spread on its leafy grounds, including a mandala made of colored sand that was created by Tibetan priests, a main hall where worshipers pray for health and contentment, and a hall dedicated to Kobo Daishi, founder of the Shingon sect (his remains are interred on Mount Koya). In Henshokutsu Cave are Buddhist icons and sand gathered from all

88 pilgrimage temples on Shikoku; making a round here is considered as auspicious as visiting the temples themselves. Other halls contain deities thought to bring good health and to save humans from earthly sexual desires. Every April 15 and November 15 there are fire-walking festivals here, in which worshipers walk over hot coals; in March there's a ceremony to give thanks to retired old kitchen knives. An excellent brochure at the entrance describes the various sights, free to the public. From Daisho-in, there's a pathway leading to the summit of Mt. Misen, which you can hike in about 90 minutes.

ENJOYING MIYAJIMA'S NATURAL WORLD

The other popular thing to do on Miyajima is to visit its highest peak, 535m (1,755-ft.) **Mount Misen,** which seems lightyears away from the crowds down below. Signs direct you to Momijidani Park, a pleasant hillside park covered with maple trees (spectacular in autumn) and cherry trees (heavenly in spring) and marked by a picturesque stream. From here, you can take the **Miyajima Ropeway** (www.miyajima-ropeway.info; ✆ **0829/44-0316**) to Mount Misen; round-trip tickets cost ¥1,800 for adults and ¥900 for children. However, you might wish to enjoy more scenery by walking back down (it takes about 60–90 min., down one of three different pathways); one-way tickets cost ¥1,000 and ¥500, respectively. In any case, the actual summit of Mount Misen, a 30-minute walk from the cable car terminus over a strenuous up-and-down pathway, offers splendid 360-degree views of the Seto-Naikai (Inland Sea) National Park. Mt. Misen is best known for Kobo Daishi's visit in 806, when he spent a 100-day retreat here and is said to have lit the Eternal Fire (located in the Kiezu-no Reikado Hall), which has reputedly been burning for more than 1,200 years and was used to light the Peace Flame in Hiroshima's Peace Memorial Park. Plan on at least 2 hours roundtrip for the ropeway and hike to the summit, noting the last ropeway departure from Mt. Misen (5 or 5:30pm most of the year). If you're hiking back down, plan on a total of 3 to 4 hours.

Miyajima is also known for its beaches. If you're looking to swim, there are two beaches west of the town and shrine: **Suginoura** and **Tsutsumigaura Natural Park** (you can also camp here). Ask at the tourist office for a schedule of shuttle buses that will bring you to the beaches.

Where to Eat

Grilled conger eel and oysters are two of Miyajima's specialties (it even celebrates an oyster festival in early Feb).

Kakiya OYSTERS   Located on Miyajima's main shopping street, this open-fronted shop is easy to spot with cooks working over a grill laden with humongous oysters. An English-language menu offers oysters prepared a half-dozen ways, including raw (¥400 for one), barbecued in the shell (¥1,000 for four), and breaded and fried (¥1,500 for three). It even offers wine, beer, shochu, sake, and other drinks to wash it all down. How civilized!

✆ **0829/44-2747.** Oyster set meals ¥1,000–¥1,500. No credit cards. Daily 10am–6pm. On Omotesando Dori, about a 6-min. walk from the ferry pier.

Koumitei (好味亭) OKONOMIYAKI   Convenient to the ferry pier, this simple restaurant with counter, table, and tatami dining stays open later than most restaurants on the island. Hiroshima-style okonomiyaki (which is prepared for you) is available from the English-language menu.

☏ **0829/44-0177.** Okonomiyaki ¥780–¥1,300; set meals ¥1,100–¥1,300. No credit cards. Thurs–Tues 11am–2:30pm and 5–9pm. A 1-min. walk from the ferry pier, catty-corner to the right.

Mizuha (水羽) VARIED JAPANESE   Occupying an old rice granary, this bustling restaurant offers local specialties like conger eel and oysters, as well as more ordinary choices like tempura and *kamameshi* (rice casserole with toppings) from an English-language menu, with a choice of table and tatami seating.

☏ **0829/44-1570.** Set meals ¥1,470–¥1,300. No credit cards. Daily 9am–5pm. A 10-min. walk from the ferry pier, behind Itsukushima Shrine and near the 5-story pagoda.

Tonookajaya (塔之岡茶屋) NOODLES   Dine inside or out at this tiny teahouse-like shop next to the five-story pagoda. The shop serves mostly *udon* (thick wheat noodles), including udon with tempura, but it also offers a few other choices on its English-language menu, including *amazake* (a sweet rice porridge; served Nov–Apr). What makes this place especially interesting is the 210-year-old pine tree out front that has been guided through the centuries to attain its unique, horizontal shape. You can also come here just for drinks.

☏ **0829/44-2455.** Main dishes ¥600–¥750. No credit cards. Daily 10am–5pm. A 10-min. walk from the ferry pier, on the hill with the 5-story pagoda, down some steps leading toward the bay.

Where to Stay

You can see Miyajima easily on a day's trip from Hiroshima, but because it's such a beautiful respite from city life and because most tourists are day-trippers, you'll enjoy the island much more if you stay behind after the last ferry leaves. An added benefit of a longer stay: Itsukushima Shrine is illuminated at night, a gorgeous sight over-nighters should not miss. I've therefore included a few recommendations on where to stay, but avoid Golden Week and weekends in July, August, October, and November (when maple leaves are in full color), because accommodations are usually full.

EXPENSIVE

Iwaso Ryokan (岩惣旅館) ★★★ 🎁   This is the most famous *ryokan* on the island, and with a history stretching back to 1854, it was also the first ryokan to open on Miyajima, which explains its idyllic location in Momijidani Park. It's highly recommended for a splurge, with the price dependent on the room, its view, and the meals you select (be sure to specify any dietary needs such as vegetarian food only, whether you want a Western breakfast, or whether there are Japanese foods you cannot eat). The newest part of the ryokan was built in 1981, and though some of its rooms have very peaceful and relaxing views of a stream and woods and even Itsukushima Shrine, I prefer the rooms dating from the 1920s and '30s; although equipped with only toilets (no tub) they have more individuality (some even face a small waterfall). If you really want to go all out and live like a feudal lord, there are also three separate *hanare* (cottages) that are 60 to 90 years old, all exquisitely decorated. Open your shoji screens to see maples, a gurgling brook, and woods, all in utter privacy. You'll be treated like royalty here, but of course you have to pay for it. Dinner is served in your room, while breakfast is served in its restaurant (open also for lunch to the public).

Momijidani, 345 Miyajima-cho, Hatsukaichi-shi, Hiroshima-ken 739-0522. www.iwaso.com. ☏ **0829/44-2233.** Fax 0829/44-2230. 38 units, 7 with toilet only. ¥19,950–¥32,500 per person. Cottages ¥36,900–¥42,150 per person. Rates are higher during peak season and nights before holidays. Rates include 2 meals. AE, DC, MC, V. A 15-min. walk from the ferry pier in Momijidani Park. Pickup service available. **Amenities:** Restaurant; lounge; indoor/outdoor hot-spring baths. *In room:* A/C, TV, fridge, hair dryer (in rooms with tub).

Kurayado Iroha ★★★   Opened in 2009 on the main Omotesando Dori pedestrian shopping street, this is modern Japanese elegance at its finest, with service so flawless you feel like staff has been waiting just for you. Before arrival you'll be asked your food preferences and allergies, and with good reason since dinners (served in a dining room) are a feast of organic vegetables, seafood from the Seto Inland, and other dishes; the meal typically lasts 2 hours and is a highlight of staying here. Several types of rooms are available, with the cheapest on the second floor offering only inner courtyard views and the best offering both beds and tatami with sweeping views of the sea or mountains. In any case, don't miss the top-floor baths.

589–4 Miyajima-cho, Hatsukaichi-shi, Hiroshima 739-0559. www.iroha.to. ℂ **0829/44-0168.** Fax 0829/44-0169. 18 units. ¥31,500–¥36,750 per person. Rates are higher in peak season. Rates include 2 meals. AE, DC, MC, V. A 5-min. walk from the ferry pier. **Amenities:** Restaurant. *In room:* A/C, TV, hair dryer, Internet, minibar.

MODERATE

Momiji-so ★★   This small, Japanese-style house has a great location in Momiji-dani Park, not far from the ropeway to Mount Misen, and has been in business for 100 years. Tatami rooms vary in size, though all have artwork, flowers, and views of the surrounding park; the best looks out over a koi pond. A plus is the nice outdoor Japanese restaurant serving noodles, barbecued conger eel on rice, and other dishes—weather permitting, you'll dine outside. Not much English is spoken, but they're used to foreigners and are very kind.

Momijidani-koennai, Miyajima-cho, Hatsukaichi-shi, Hiroshima 739-0500. www.gambo-ad.com. ℂ **0829/44-0077.** Fax 0829/44-0076. 7 units. ¥8,400 per person without meals; ¥12,400 per person with breakfast; ¥16,800 per person with 2 meals. No credit cards. A 25-min. walk from the ferry pier in Momijidani Park. Pickup service available. *In room:* A/C, TV, minibar, no phone.

Ryoso Kawaguchi (旅荘かわぐち) ★★ 🎒   This 300-year-old home, with white-washed walls, wood floors, and exposed beams, has a traditional atmosphere, and modern updates like Wi-Fi and two private-use baths make it comfortable. Tatami accommodations include two airy rooms with lofts for sleeping and a two-room suite good for families. The dining room and bar overlook a garden courtyard, while the third-floor lounge has a view of the five-story pagoda. The ninth-generation innkeepers speak English and are gracious and welcoming.

469 Miyajima-cho, Hatsukaichi-shi, Hiroshima 739-0554. http://ryoso-kawaguchi.jp. ℂ **0829/44-0018.** Fax 0829/44-2361. 7 units, all with toilet, none with bathroom. ¥7,000 single; ¥13,650–¥14,700 double; ¥20,475–¥22,050 triple. Breakfast ¥1,050 extra; dinner ¥4,200 extra. No credit cards. A 10-min. walk from the ferry pier, on Machiya Dori. **Amenities:** Bar. *In room:* A/C, TV, Wi-Fi.

INEXPENSIVE

Miyajima Morinoyado (みやじま杜の宿) ★★ 🍃   You're forgiven if you pass this place by, thinking it must be an exclusive *ryokan*. Indeed, if it weren't a municipally owned People's Lodge (Kokumin Shukusha), rates here could easily be three times as much as they are. Though modern, it has a lovely Japanese design with a lobby overlooking a carp pond. On the other hand, the many school groups and families staying here leave no doubt that it's a public lodge, and it's quite a hike from the ferry pier. Both tatami rooms and Western-style twins—simple but spacious and spotless—are available, some with views of the bay. The public baths look onto rock gardens. Reservations should be made 11 months in advance, especially for August, but sometimes there are cancellations; when I dropped by on a weekday in June, rooms were available. Both Western and Japanese breakfasts, served in a restaurant, are available; dinners are Japanese and are served in your room.

Miyajima-cho, Hatsukaichi-shi, Hiroshima-ken 739-0588. www.morinoyado.jp. © **0829/44-0430.** Fax 0829/44-2248. 30 units, 26 with bathroom, 4 with toilet only. ¥5,040–¥5,775 per person room only; ¥9,555–¥11,865 per person with 2 meals. ¥735 more per person on Sat, nights before holidays, and during peak season (New Year's and mid-July to Aug). Discounts given for children. No credit cards. A 25-min. walk from the ferry pier, across from the aquarium and just before the tunnel. **Amenities:** Restaurant. *In room:* A/C, TV, fridge, hair dryer.

SHIKOKU

The smallest of Japan's four main islands, Shikoku is also the one least visited by foreigners. That's surprising considering the natural beauty of its rugged mountains, its mild climate, and its most famous monuments—88 sacred Buddhist temples.

Many Japanese wish to make a pilgrimage to all 88 temples at least once in their lifetime as a tribute to the great Buddhist priest Kobo Daishi, who was born on Shikoku in 774 and who founded the Shingon sect of Buddhism.

This pilgrimage has been popular since the Edo Period, as many believe that a successful completion of the tour exonerates Buddhist followers from rebirth. It used to take almost 2 months to visit all 88 temples on foot. Even today, you can see pilgrims making their rounds dressed in white—only now they're more likely to go by organized tour buses, which cut travel time down to 2 weeks.

THE BEST SHIKOKU EXPERIENCES

- **Trekking to Kotohiragu Shrine (Kotohira):** One of Japan's oldest and most popular shrines beckons at the top of 785 granite steps on the Yashima Plateau with great views of the Seto Inland Sea, but for most Japanese, it's the "I made it!" that counts. See p. 445.
- **Feeling Like a Giant Among the Bonsai (Takamatsu):** Most of us are used to seeing bonsai in pots, but at Japan's largest bonsai-growing area, in business since the Edo Period, you'll see them planted in rows, too. See p. 445.
- **Viewing Art at Benesse Art Site Naoshima:** This is not a museum, but rather an island in the Seto Inland Sea that's devoted to cutting-edge art, with two museums (both designed by Tadao Ando) and interactive art installations in traditional Japanese buildings. There's no other place in Japan quite like this. See p. 446.
- **Bathing in Dogo Onsen Honkan (Matsuyama):** This wooden 1894 bathhouse has baths, yes, but it's the upstairs tatami relaxation rooms where people lounge in yukata and drink tea that make a visit here special. See p. 455.
- **Walking the Streets of Uchiko:** Uchiko is a traditional village with an historic district that remains remarkably intact. Visit the residence of a former wax merchant, have lunch at the local farmers' market, and even spend the night. See page 456.

GETTING TO SHIKOKU For most of history, the only way to reach Shikoku was by boat. However, the 1988 completion of the Seto Ohashi Bridge, which links Shikoku with Okayama Prefecture by road and rail, changed Shikoku forever. In 1999, the completion of a series of bridges spanning six scenic islands in the Seto Inland Sea connected Shikoku with Hiroshima Prefecture (complete with cycling paths offering scenic views and now one of Shikoku's hottest attractions), followed by a third bridge, for cars only, linking Shikoku with Kobe.

It has all made Shikoku much more accessible. Shinkansen travelers can simply transfer in Okayama to trains bound for either Takamatsu or Matsuyama. The energetic can cycle from Honshu to Shikoku on the Shimanami Kaido, the bike path stretching from Hiroshima Prefecture to Ehime Prefecture.

GETTING AROUND SHIKOKU For travelers without a Japan Rail Pass, the All Shikoku Rail Pass is a good alternative. Whereas a regular one-way fare between Takamatsu and Matsuyama costs ¥5,500, the Shikoku rail pass costs ¥6,700 for two days and ¥9,700 for five days. Furthermore, unlike Japan Rail Passes, the Shikoku pass is also valid on local streetcars in Takamatsu and Matsuyama. Passes can be purchased overseas through Japanese travel agencies such as JTB or in Japan at JR Shikoku Travel Agencies in major stations on the island. For more information, visit www.tourismshikoku.org/all-shikoku-rail-pass.

TAKAMATSU ★

805km (500 miles) W of Tokyo; 71km (44 miles) S of Okayama

The second-largest town on Shikoku, with a population of 427,000, Takamatsu is the capital of Kagawa Prefecture and is located on the northeastern coast of the island, overlooking the Seto Inland Sea. Takamatsu means "high pine," and the city served as the feudal capital of the powerful Matsudaira clan from 1642 until the Meiji Restoration in 1868 (back in those days it was called Sanuki province, and the Sanuki name is still widely used). The Matsudairas are responsible for Takamatsu's most famous site, Ritsurin Garden, one of Japan's most outstanding gardens. Takamatsu also boasts more bonsai nurseries than anywhere else in Japan, while nearby is Kotohiragu Shrine, a popular mountaintop destination that requires a real workout just to see.

Essentials

GETTING THERE **By Plane** JAL and ANA fly from Tokyo's Haneda Airport to Takamatsu Airport (TAK; www.takamatsu-airport.com; ✆ 087/835-8110) in 1 hour and 20 minutes. There is also air service from Okinawa. An airport bus delivers passengers downtown in about 45 minutes for ¥740.

By Train **JR's Marine Liner** trains depart from Okayama Station approximately twice an hour, reaching Takamatsu in an hour; the fare is ¥1,470. From Matsuyama, trains take about 2½ hours and cost ¥5,500.

By Bus JR buses (www.jrbuskanto.co.jp. ✆ 03/3844-1950) depart Tokyo Station's Yaesu south exit nightly at 8:20 and 8:50pm (the latter bus also picks up passengers at Shinjuku Station at 9:30pm), reaching Takamatsu Station at 5:51am and 7:14am respectively the next day. The one-way fare is ¥10,000.

VISITOR INFORMATION The **Takamatsu Information Plaza** (✆ 087/851-2009; daily 9am–6pm), located outside the main exit of the train station in a small building on the left side of the circular plaza, offers an English-language map of the city. You can also pick up the Shikoku Passport; although in Japanese only, it gives slight discounts to some of the listings below, including Ritsurin Garden, Shikoku Mura and JR Hotel Clement. In addition, the Kagawa Welcome Card gives discounts to foreigners; you must download it at **www.21kagawa.com/visitor**.

Information is available online at **www.city.takamatsu.kagawa.jp/kankou** and **www.pref.kagawa.lg.jp**.

If you crave a bit of news from home or plan to remain in the area, head for **I-Pal Kagawa,** 1–11–63 Bancho (www.i-pal.or.jp/en; © **087/837-5908;** Tues–Sun 9am–6pm), located about a 15-minute walk south of Takamatsu Station on Chuo Dori in the northwest corner of Central (Chuo) Park. Here you'll find magazines and newspapers in many languages, CNN on the tube, and three computers you can use free of charge for 30 minutes. This is also a good place to find out what's going on in the area.

ORIENTATION & GETTING AROUND Takamatsu Station, Takamatsu Port, and the local streetcar terminus are clustered at the north edge of the city on the coast of the Seto Inland Sea, in a modern urban development called Sunport Takamatsu, which also includes the 30-story Takamatsu Symbol Tower, exhibition and concert facilities, restaurants, shops, and offices. Office workers take respite along the Waterfront Harbor Walk and Tamamo Park, site of Takamatsu Castle's remains.

Most hotels and restaurants listed below, as well as Ritsurin Garden, are located south and southeast of Sunport Takamatsu. **Chuo Dori** is the town's main avenue, running south from Sunport to Ritsurin Garden and beyond. Bisecting Chuo Dori and paralleling it to the east are shopping arcades. In fact, a total of 2.7km (1⅔ miles) of covered shopping arcades make Takamatsu's among the longest in Japan.

Although the main attractions of Takamatsu are spread out, they're easily reached from Takamatsu Station by **JR train** or by a commuter streetcar called the **Kotoden Line.** The Kotoden streetcar terminus, called **Takamatsu Chikko Station,** is a 2-minute walk from JR Takamatsu Station's main exit, past the JR Hotel Clement and to the right. Fares start at ¥180. Two stops south on the Kotoden streetcar (or a 25-min. walk from Takamatsu Station) is **Kawaramachi Station,** the heart of the city where you'll find many department stores, restaurants, and nightspots.

[FastFACTS]TAKAMATSU

Internet Access   In addition to I-Pal Kagawa (above), E-Topia Kagawa (© **087/822-0111;** Tues–Sun 10am–8pm), on the fourth and fifth floors of Symbol Tower next to Takamatsu Station, has some 20 computers you can use for 1 hour for free (be sure to bring your passport with you for identification).

Exploring Takamatsu

Ritsurin Garden ★★★ PARK/GARDEN   Work on Ritsurin Garden, once the summer retreat of the Matsudaira family, began in the 1600s and took about 100 years to complete. Using the backdrop of adjacent Mount Shiun in a principle known as "borrowed landscaping," the 75-hectare (185-acre) park, Japan's largest Cultural Heritage Garden, incorporates the pine-clad mountain into its overall visual design. Basically, the garden, arranged around six spring-fed ponds (home to some 3,000 koi) and 13 scenic mounds, can be divided into two parts: a traditional, classical, southern garden; and a modern, northern garden, once a lord's private hunting grounds and

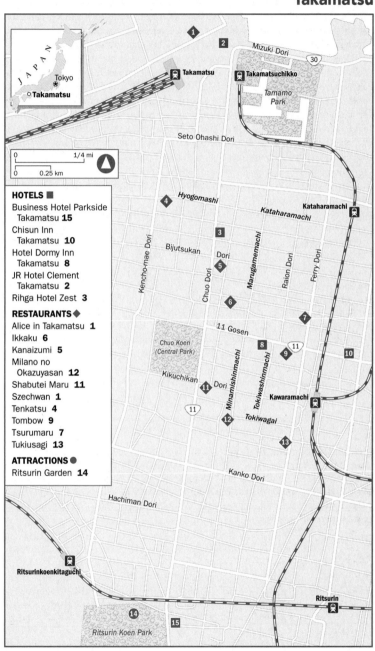

HOTELS ■

Business Hotel Parkside
  Takamatsu **15**
Chisun Inn
  Takamatsu **10**
Hotel Dormy Inn
  Takamatsu **8**
JR Hotel Clement
  Takamatsu **2**
Rihga Hotel Zest **3**

RESTAURANTS ◆

Alice in Takamatsu **1**
Ikkaku **6**
Kanaizumi **5**
Milano no
  Okazuyasan **12**
Shabutei Maru **11**
Szechwan **1**
Tenkatsu **4**
Tombow **9**
Tsurumaru **7**
Tukiusagi **13**

ATTRACTIONS ●

Ritsurin Garden **14**

with wide grassy lawns and huge lotus ponds. No matter the season, something is always in bloom, from plum and cherry trees in spring to camellias in winter (a bulletin board at the entrance identifies what's in bloom). English-speaking volunteers are on hand most days to provide free tours if you wish, but there's also an English-language audio guide for ¥200 that explains 30 key sights around the garden.

The **southern garden** is the more interesting one, a strolling garden in which each bend of the footpath brings another perspective into view, another combination of rock, tree, and mountain. The garden is absolutely exquisite, and what sets it apart are its twisted, contorted pines. On one of my visits, a mist was rolling off Mount Shiun, lending mystery to the landscape; what better fits the image of traditional Japan than mist and pine trees? Altogether, there are some 1,400 pine trees and 350 cherry trees in Ritsurin Garden, which you should tour in a counterclockwise fashion to fully appreciate the changing views. Although I consider this garden just as beautiful as those in Okayama and Kanazawa, tall buildings on its eastern periphery detract from its overall effect; without them I would give this garden top rating.

There are a couple of things you can stop and see during your tour of the park. In the Meiji Era northern garden are the **Sanuki Folk Art Museum (Sanuki Mingei Kan),** which is included in the park's admission fee and displays local folk art and handicrafts such as ceramics, lacquerware, furniture, and items used in daily Edo life (regrettably, there are no English-language descriptions); and the **Commerce and Industry Hall (Shokoshoreikan),** which sells local products, including kites, masks, woodcarvings, umbrellas, fans, and food items and sponsors craft-making demonstrations on weekends and holidays. But my favorite thing to do is drop by **Scooping the Moon House (Kikugetsu-tei)** in the southern garden, with its teahouse dating from the 17th century overlooking a pond. Powdered tea, used in tea ceremonies, costs ¥710 for adults and ¥550 for children. It takes about an hour to see the southern garden; add another half-hour if you also take in the northern garden.

1–20–16 Ritsurin-cho. http://ritsuringarden.jp. (C) **087/833-7411.** Admission ¥400 adults, ¥170 children. Daily sunrise–sunset (schedule changes monthly, but approx. 7am–5pm in winter, 5:30am–7pm June–Aug). Kotoden streetcar: Ritsurin-koen Station (10 min.). JR train: If you have a Japan Rail Pass, go by JR train toward Tokushima; get off at Ritsurin-koen Kita Guchi, turn right out of the station, follow the tracks to the 1st street, and turn right (4 min.).

Shikoku Mura Village ★★   On the northeastern edge of town, this open-air museum boasts more than 30 traditional houses, sheds, and storehouses dating from the Edo Period and collected from all over Shikoku. The structures, picturesquely situated amid bamboo groves, stone walls and flower beds on the wooded slope of Yashima Hill, include thatch-roofed homes of farmers and fishermen, an 1893 lighthouse and the keepers' cottages, a rustic pavilion for tea-ceremony, a 250-year-old rural *kabuki* stage, rice and soy-sauce storehouses, and sheds for pressing sugar and for producing paper out of mulberry bark. There's also a rickety suspension bridge made of vines, once a familiar sight in Shikoku as a means for crossing the island's many gorges and ravines (if you look closely, however, you'll see that this one is reinforced by cables). It takes at least 1½ hours to stroll through the village (and there are lots of stairs). I heartily recommend a visit if you haven't had the opportunity to see similar villages in Takayama or Shirakawago, as they convey, better than anything else, rural life in Japan in centuries past.

Bonsai Is Big in Kinashi

If you've admired the art of **bonsai**—miniature pines and other trees crafted through skillful manipulation—you might wish to stroll through **Kinashi**, a western suburb of Takamatsu. Kinashi has been a hub of bonsai since the Edo Period and remains the largest bonsai-growing location in Japan; of the 70 nurseries here, more than two-thirds are in the bonsai business. To reach it, take a local JR train from Takamatsu Station two stations to Kinashi (fare: ¥210 for the 7-min. trip), and cross the tracks and street. This is the only place I've ever seen bonsai groves, with hundreds of tiny pine trees planted in rows awaiting trimming. One of the largest nurseries, **Nakanishi Chinshouen** (中西珍松園; http://chinshoen.jp; ℂ **087/882-0526**) across from the station (look for the sign near the footbridge), is owned by a fifth-generation bonsai cultivator. You're welcome to walk through this and other nearby nurseries. Between September 15 and June 25, on the 5th, 15th, and 25th of each month, there's a bonsai auction at the Bonsai Center, about a 12-minute walk uphill from the station via Bonsai Dori, from 9am until stocks run out.

91 Yashima-naka-machi. ℂ **087/843-3111.** Admission ¥800 adults, ¥500 high-school students, ¥300 children. Daily 8:30am–6pm (Nov–Mar to 5:30pm). Kotoden streetcar: Kotoden Yashima Station (about a 20-min. ride) and then a 5-min. walk. JR train: Take a JR train bound for Tokushima and get off at Yashima Station (15 min.).

Easy Side Trips from Takamatsu

KOTOHIRA ★★   If you have 4 hours to spare, one of the best historical side trips you can take is to Kotohira, home of Japan's oldest kabuki theater and of **Kotohiragu Shrine** ★★, 892 Kotohira-cho (ℂ **0877/75-2121**), one of Japan's oldest and most popular shrines with a history stretching back to the 11th century. It takes about an hour and costs ¥830 to reach Kotohira by ordinary JR train from Takamatsu (35 min. and ¥1340 by limited express), but that isn't the end of it—the shrine itself is at the top of 785 granite steps, which on average take 40 minutes to ascend. If that's too much for you, you can hire one of the porters who wait at the bottom of the steps, but they'll take you only to the *omon* (main gate), which is reached after climbing 365 steps. It costs ¥5,300 one-way and ¥6,800 round-trip to ride in palanquins. What decadence.

Otherwise, begin the long trek up to Kotohiragu Shrine by taking JR Kotohira Station's only exit, walk straight past a small park (with a wooden pagoda-shaped lighthouse, built in 1860, which served as a beacon for traveling pilgrims), and pass the Kotoden Station. (You can also travel from Takamatsu in 1 hr. by Kotoden streetcar.) Turn left at the T-junction with a post office. You'll soon see, to the right, a sloping, narrow street lined with souvenir shops. Eventually, you'll reach the first flight of stairs. If you're making a detour to the kabuki theater (described below), turn left after the 22nd step and follow the directions below.

At about the 475th step (in case you're counting), just past the stables, to the right you'll find **Shoin,** built in 1659 to receive important visitors. Its doors and alcoves contain paintings by Maruyama Okyo, a famous 18th-century landscape artist. Especially famous is the painting of two tigers drinking from a stream. It's open daily from 8:30am to 5pm; admission is ¥800 for adults, ¥400 for students, and free for children.

After another 15-minute workout, you'll reach **Hongu,** the main shrine, where you'll be rewarded with a sweeping view of the surrounding countryside as well as of the shrine itself. Kompira-San was originally founded in the 11th century but has been rebuilt many times, with the main shrine buildings re-erected about 100 years ago. It's dedicated to the Shinto god of seafarers and voyagers (look for the **Emado,** Votive Picture Pavilion, with photos of ships and other vessels that have asked for blessings and returned safely). In recent years, it has even become revered as the protector of foreign travelers. For my part, I was just thankful for having successfully traveled the stairs to the shrine. And to be honest, the shrine itself is not the main draw; most of the three million annual hikers, it seems, come for the hike itself and the comradeship it inspires. If you're still game (and want to say you went the entire distance), you can continue another 583 steps to **Okunoyashiro.** You can say your prayers here, but the inner shrine is closed to the public. Kotohiragu Shrine is open daily from sunrise to sunset (7pm in summer; 5pm in winter).

Because you're in the vicinity, make every effort to see the highly recommended **Kompira Grand Playhouse ★** (金毘羅大芝居 金丸座); **Kompira O-Shibai** or Kanamaruza, (© 0877/73-3846), which was built to entertain the masses flocking to Kotohiragu Shrine. Located about 300m (985 ft.) to the left of the 22nd step as you ascend, and then up the hill on the right, it's the oldest existing kabuki stage in Japan, stunning in its simplicity and delightful in its construction. As there was no electricity when it was built in 1835, the sides of the hall are rows of *shoji* screens and wooden coverings, which can be opened and closed to control the amount of light reaching the stage. Notice the check-in counter at the entrance for *geta* (wooden sandals), *tatami* seating, paper lanterns, and revolving stage, which was turned by four men in the basement (be sure to check out the basement). You can also tour the various makeup and dressing rooms behind the stage and watch a video in Japanese. It's open daily from 9am to 5pm (except for 16 days in Apr when kabuki is performed to sellout crowds) and charges an admission of ¥500 for adults, ¥300 for junior-high and high-school students, and ¥200 for children (the Shikoku Passport offers a discount). Ask for the English-language handout.

BENESSE ART SITE NAOSHIMA ★★★　Naoshima, a small island in the Seto Inland Sea, is devoted to contemporary art in a big way, with three striking museums, interactive installations housed in traditional buildings, and outdoor sculptures spread throughout the island, making it a major destination for cutting-edge art in Japan. More than that, Naoshima is a place of discovery, with a unique symbiotic relationship between natural scenic beauty and art. Plan on at least 7 hours for the experience, including the 50-minute ferry from Takamatsu. Note that for art venues

Making Candy for 27 Generations

The first 365 steps to Kotohiragu Shrine are lined with souvenir shops, but inside shrine precincts it's blissfully free of commercialism. The exception: five simple wooden stands operated by local families selling homemade, fan-shaped hard candies. No one knows how long they've been there, but the best guess is 27 generations. If that longevity doesn't merit special consideration, we don't know what does.

DOGGEDLY faithful

In the olden days, the faithful who could not manage a trip to Kotohiragu Shrine in person would set a barrel adrift at sea, along with an offering and a plea for passing fishermen to take the offering to the shrine on their next pilgrimage. The more resourceful would even send dogs on the pilgrimage, with a tag that read "Kotohira Pilgrimage" and a pouch of money around their necks. Travelers who encountered the dogs used the money to buy the animals food and passage on boats until the dogs reached their destination.

closed on Monday, if Monday is a national holiday, they stay open but will close the next day, on Tuesday, instead.

Shikoku Kisen ferries (© 087/821-6798) depart Takamatsu Port at least five times daily for Miyanoura Port on Naoshima. The trip takes 50 minutes by regular ferry (fare: ¥510) or 25 minutes by high-speed ferry (¥1,200). You can also reach Naoshima from Uno in Okayama Prefecture in 20 minutes for ¥220. At Miyanoura there's a **Tourist Information Center** (Umi-no-eki Naoshima), open daily 8:30am to 6pm and offering an English-language map of the island, rental bikes (¥500 for the day), and schedules for buses that travel to all art sites (bus fare: ¥100 per ride).

From Miyanoura Port, you can take the bus 5 minutes (stop: Nokyo-mae, in front of JA Bank) or walk 30 minutes to Honmura, where you'll find a handful of **Art House Projects ★★★**, old buildings that have been remodeled by artists into interactive art installations. At Kadoya (by Miyajima Tatsuo), you'll see a 200-year-old farmhouse that contains a darkened room with a shallow pool of water and submerged colored numbers that blink on and off at varying frequencies, with the speed of each number controlled by an islander and each number representing a human life. Go'o Jinja is an Edo-Era shrine that has been transformed by Sugimoto Hiroshi, with glass stairs, white rocks, and a narrow underground passageway that leads to a tomblike space. Ishibashi is a restored family home of a salt-producing family now housing paintings of waterfalls by Senju Hiroshi, while Gokaisho, where residents once gathered to play the Japanese game *go*, contains Suda Yoshihiro's sculpture *Camelia*. Haisha is a former dental clinic transformed by Ohtake Shinro into an eclectic "sculptural scrapbook" of found objects and graphic art. But my favorite is Minamidera, a stark wooden building designed by famed architect Tadao Ando, with an installation by James Turrell called *Backside of the Moon*. After being led into a pitch-black room by staff, you wait about 10 minutes until your eyes adjust, when you finally see a faint glow ahead. You're told you can walk to the light to touch it, only to find . . . well, you'll have to "see" for yourself. Art House Projects are open Tuesday to Sunday 10am to 4:30pm and cost ¥1,000 for a combination ticket for all six (children 14 and younger get in free to all of Naoshima's art museums). Buy tickets at the tourist office above, at Ueda's Tobacconist (across from Nokyo-mae bus stop), or the Honmura Lounge & Archive beside the bus stop.

From Honmura, it's a 10-minute bus ride and a walk uphill to **Benesse House ★★★**, a museum designed by Tadao Ando and containing an expensive hotel (© 087/892-3223; rates begin at ¥35,000 for a twin, but less expensive is Benesse House Park Hotel nearby), cafe, restaurant, and art by Jasper Johns, Robert Rauschenberg, Frank Stella, Jackson Pollock, Andy Warhol and others, many of

A Note on Japanese Characters

Many establishments and attractions in Japan do not have outdoor signs in Roman (English-language) letters. Those that don't are provided with the Japanese equivalent to help you locate them.

whom created site-specific art that works in marvelous harmony with Ando's architecture and Naoshima's natural beauty. It's open daily 8am to 9pm, with admission costing ¥1,000 (free for overnight guests).

The **Chichu Art Museum ★★★** (✆ **087/892-3755**), 3 minutes away by bus (free shuttle bus btw. the two museums weekends and holidays) or a 30-minute walk, was also designed by Ando. Built underground so as not to interfere with Naoshima's natural beauty, it's a maze-like structure of concrete with sharp angles and contemplative spaces, accented by a few pieces of large installation art: a light installation by James Turrell, a room containing a huge granite ball and gold-leaf covered bars by Walter De Maria, and a room of giant water lily paintings by Claude Monet. This museum is open Tuesday to Sunday 10am to 6pm (to 5pm Oct–Feb) and costs ¥2,000. From here, the bus back to Miyanoura Port takes 20 minutes.

Halfway between Benesse House and Chichu Art Museum is Naoshima's newest attraction, the **Lee Ufan Museum ★★** (✆ **087/840-8285**), which displays paintings and sculpture by this seminal artist of minimalism, born in Korea but working as an artist and professor in Japan. Another Ando building, it's open Tuesday to Sunday 10am to 6pm (to 5pm Oct–Feb). Admission is ¥1,000.

Information on Benesse Art Site Naoshima is available at **www.benesse-artsite. jp**; ✆ **087/892-2887**. General information on Naoshima is available from the Naoshima Tourism Association at **www.naoshima.net**; ✆ **087/892-2299**.

Where to Eat

EXPENSIVE

Alice in Takamatsu ★★ FRENCH   You could come here just for the views, soaring over the city through floor-to-ceiling windows or close at hand in a smart restaurant with contemporary chandeliers, tables covered in crisp white tablecloths, and polished concrete floors. But that would negate the contemporary French cooking (think tomato and herb-steamed dorade, or roast veal with whole grain wheat salad) by the French-trained Japanese chef from TV's Iron Chef program. Menus are in French and Japanese.

30th floor, Takamatsu Symbol Tower, 2–1 Sunport. ✆ **087/823-6088.** Set lunches ¥1,500–¥5,000; set dinners ¥6,300–¥8,400. AE, DC, MC, V. Daily 11am–3pm and 5:30–10:30pm. Station: Takamatsu (1 min.).

Szechwan ★★★ CHINESE   Classic standards, such as bird's-nest soup, sweet-and-sour pork, and chicken with cashew nuts, receive innovative makeovers at this elegant 29th-floor restaurant with white tablecloths and background jazz music. Add panoramic views of the Seto Inland Sea, excellent service, reasonably priced set lunches, and you're in for a memorable dining experience.

29th floor, Takamatsu Symbol Tower, 2–1 Sunport. ✆ **087/811-0477.** Main dishes ¥1,600–¥3,500; set lunches ¥1,500–¥3,500; set dinners ¥5,250–¥10,500. AE, DC, MC, V. Daily 11am–3pm and 5–10pm. Station: Takamatsu (1 min.).

MODERATE

Tenkatsu (天勝) TEMPURA/SUSHI   This restaurant has been in business since 1866, though you'd hardly guess that by its modern-looking building with a plastic-food display case and a window where passersby can watch a chef prepare sushi. Inside the restaurant are tatami mats and tables, but I suggest sitting at the counter, which encircles a large pool filled with fish. As customers order, fish are swept out of the tanks with nets—they certainly couldn't be fresher. A photo menu (along with prices for fish in the tanks) and a display case help you choose. For a splurge, order a *kaiseki* course, beginning at ¥5,250.

7–8 Hyogomachi. ☎ **087/821-5380.** Reservations required for kaiseki. Set lunches ¥840–¥2,100; set dinners ¥1,575–¥3,675. AE, DC, MC, V. Mon–Fri 11am–2pm and 4–10pm; Sat–Sun 11am–9pm. Station: Takamatsu (a 5-min. walk south from the station). Walk south on Chuo Dori until it intersects with a large covered pedestrian shopping arcade called Hyogomachi. Turn right and walk all the way through the arcade; upon emerging, you'll find the restaurant on your left.

Tukiusagi (月うさぎ) ★ CONTEMPORARY IZAKAYA Exchange your shoes for slippers as you enter this cozy, friendly drinking establishment that also serves small plates ideal for sharing. Standouts on the expansive, English-language menu lists local chicken in garlic, *chijimi* (savory, Korean-style pancakes with seafood and vegetables), dumplings and more. An evening of eating, drinking, and merriment here should set you back about ¥3,000 per person, including the obligatory ¥300 snack charge. Seating is at tables, on the floor with a well beneath for your feet, or at the counter to watch the action in the open kitchen.

1–4–13 Tokiwa-cho. ☎ **087/861-7623.** Main dishes ¥550–¥900. Cash only. Mon–Sat 5:30–11:30pm. Kotoden streetcar: Kawaramachi Station (1 min.). Take the west exit (with the BUS STOP signs), use the upper promenade deck to cross the street, take the elevator to street level; and turn right for the small alleyway; look for the round windows on the left with rabbits etched into the glass.

INEXPENSIVE

Ikkaku (一鶴) HONE-TSUKI TORI One of Takamatsu's top chains for *hone-tsuki tori* has a location right in the city center, with a lively atmosphere reminiscent of an *izakaya* (tip: if tobacco smoke bothers you, sit under an A-frame roof at one of the U-shaped counters). There's no English menu, but all you really need to know is *hinadori* (leg and thigh of tender young hen,) redolent with salt, pepper and garlic, *torimeshi* (chicken fried rice), which comes with a side of flavorful chicken broth, and pointing skills for anything else that looks good.

Udon All Day, Udon All Night

The people of Takamatsu are so proud of their local Sanuki udon that Kagawa Prefecture has nicknamed itself *Udon-ken* (Udon Prefecture) in tourist literature. In addition to being thick and chewy like elsewhere in Japan, these handmade, wheat-based noodles can be over 2 feet long, making slurping a talent. **Tsurumaru** (鶴丸), in the Kawaramachi neighborhood at 9–34 Furubabamachi (☎ **087/821-3780;** daily 8pm–3am), is a classic noodle shop with an English-language menu offering basic niku udon with sliced beef and *curry udon* in thick curry broth. At the cafeteria-style **Kanaizumi** (かな泉), a 15-minute walk south of Takamatsu Station at 9–3 Konyamachi (☎ **087/822-0123;** Mon–Sat 9am–5pm), order noodles, choose side dishes from tempura to sushi, and help yourself to condiments like dried bonito flakes, ground ginger, chopped green onion and sesame seeds. No credit cards are accepted, but these places are cheap.

5th floor, Festa 2 Building, Kajiya-cho. © **087/823-3711.** Main dishes ¥300–¥980. AE, DC, MC, V. Mon–Fri 4–11pm, Sat–Sun 11am–11pm. Station: Kawaramachi (6 min.). Walk north on Ferry Dori, turn left on Route 11, right into the Marugamemachi covered arcade and left at Starbucks; look for the five-story Festa 2 bulding on the left.

Milano No Okazuyasan ★ ITALIAN   In this cozy second-floor restaurant, hospitable chef-owner Mr. Takeda serves mainly homemade pastas, from the usual spaghetti Bolognese with meat sauce to spinach fettuccine with cream sauce or veal ragout with white fettuccine, as well as a handful of pizzas and main dishes that might include seafood saffron risotto. Set lunches include all the salad and great, fresh-baked bread you can eat, plus a choice of soup, dessert, or coffee. There's no English-language menu, but the photo menu suffices for most visitors.

Egou Building, 11–14 Kamei-cho. © **087/837-1782.** Main dishes and pasta ¥800–¥1,000; set lunches ¥840–¥945; set dinners ¥2,030–¥5,880. AE, DC, MC, V. Daily 11am–3pm and 5–10pm. Kotoden streetcar: Kawaramachi (4 min.). Take the west exit (with the BUS STOP sign) and walk through the covered walking arcade (Tokiwa-cho) until the awning ends; continue straight and then start looking carefully for Milano on your left.

Shabutei Maru (しゃぶ亭まる) 🍴 SHABU-SHABU   This casual, small, second-floor eatery has inexpensive lunches of chicken, pork, and beef, with second helpings of rice included in the price. From 5pm, it offers all-you-can-eat *shabu-shabu* (and in winter, sukiyaki) with a 90-minute time limit—kind of like an "on-your-mark, get-set, go" spree of uninhibited gorging. Ditto with all the beer, sake, or soft drinks you can drink if you pay ¥1,200 more. Various grades of meat are available, from beef and pork (the cheapest) to top-grade *wagyu* beef. Seating is at counters or tables and the place is often very crowded; many of the servers are English-speaking students.

8–8 Kamei-cho. © **087/835-9842.** Set lunches ¥499–¥3,200; all-you-can-eat shabu-shabu dinners ¥1,800–¥3,500 for men, ¥1,700–¥3,300 for women. AE, DC, MC, V. Daily 11:30am–2pm and 5–10pm (last order). Kotoden streetcar: Kawaramachi (5 min.). Take the west exit and walk through the Tokiwa-cho covered arcade; it's on the 2nd floor, catty-corner from the southeast corner of Chuo (Central) Park, just off Chuo Dori on Kikuchikan Dori. Look for the large red circle logo next to the House 809 building.

Tombow (とんぼ) KUSHIAGE   The red umbrella outside is your landmark to this dark wooded, homey spot offering deep-fried skewers and four dipping sauces to choose from. Ordering is easy from the English-language menu, or just go with the *omakase* (chef's choice) course for ¥150 per skewer that continues until you say "stop." There's a non-smoking section in the upstairs tatami rooms, but we prefer to be around the action at the counter.

1-12-6 Kawaramachi. © **087/835-1315.** Skewers ¥150 each; set lunches ¥2,100; set dinners from ¥3,150. AE, DC, MC, V. Mon–Fri 11:30am–1:30pm, Mon–Sat 4–10:30pm. Station: Kawaramachi (3 min.). Walk north from the station, turning left off Ferry Dori one block before Route 11; the restaurant is on the left in the middle of the block.

Shopping

Arts, crafts and specialty products of Kagawa Prefecture are available at **Sun Quelaque** (サン・クラッケ), 4-9 Minami-Shinmachi (© **087/887-0306;** Wed–Mon 10am–7pm), located where the Minami-Shinmachi shopping arcade meets Kikuchikan Dori (look for the olive tree). Nearby is the network of covered arcades that make up Takamatsu's central shopping district. It's all just west of Kataharamachi and Kawaramachi stations on the Kotoden line, or about a 10-minute walk south of Takamatsu Station.

A DOUBLE OR A twin?

For the sake of convenience, the price for two people in a room is listed as a "double" in this book. Japanese hotels, however, differentiate between rooms with a double bed or two twin beds, usually with different prices. Although most hotels charge more for a twin room, sometimes the opposite is true; if you're looking for a bargain, therefore, be sure to inquire about prices for both. Note, too, that hotels usually have more twin rooms than doubles, for the simple reason that Japanese couples, used to their own futon, traditionally prefer twin beds.

Where to Stay

EXPENSIVE

JR Hotel Clement Takamatsu ★★   Across from Takamatsu Station (and offering a discount to holders of a Japan Rail Pass), the city's most expensive hotel is also its most conspicuous: sleek, 21 stories high, cutting across the landscape like a white sail, and by far the best place in town. It's designed with an aquatic theme, with a cascading fountain in the sunlit lobby lounge, carpets and chandeliers with wavy patterns, bubbled or crackled glass in public places, and curving, seductive lines. Room rates are based on size, floor, view, and amenities, with the best twin and double rooms offering views of the sea or nearby Tamamo Park, even from the bathroom. But the least expensive rooms are also recommendable—spacious and chic with contemporary furnishings and good bedside reading lamps (note, however, that the cheapest double has only a semi-double bed). Ask for a room on the highest available floor.

1–1 Hamano-cho, Takamatsu, Kagawa Prefecture 760-0011. www.jrhotelgroup.com. ✆ **087/811-1111.** Fax 087/811-1100. 300 units. ¥12,470–¥18,480 single; ¥20,790–¥40,425 double. 10% discount with Japan Rail Pass, Kagawa Welcome Card, or Shikoku Passport. AE, DC, MC, V. Station: Takamatsu (1 min.). **Amenities:** 4 restaurants; bar; lounge; beer garden (summer only); concierge; room service. In room: A/C, TV, hair dryer, Internet, minibar.

MODERATE

Chisun Inn Takamatsu   This business hotel, with imitation Art Deco decor in its lobby and hallways, offers mostly single rooms in a convenient location near Kawaramachi Station in the heart of the city's shopping and nightlife district. Rooms, though small, are pleasantly decorated, but it's been awhile since I've seen pink-tiled bathrooms like those here. The hotel's seven twins are all corner rooms, bright and large for the price with vanity/sink separate from the—you guessed it—pink bathrooms (which also have a sink).

11–1 Fukudamachi, Takamatsu, Kagawa Prefecture 760-0048. www.solarehotels.com. ✆ **087/823-1111.** Fax 087/823-1123. 117 units. ¥5,500–¥7,850 single; ¥13,860–¥16,200 double. AE, DC, MC, V. Kotoden streetcar: Kawaramachi (5 min.). Take the west exit (toward the bus stop), walk north on Ferry Dori, and turn right at the 1st traffic signal to cross the tracks; it's on the left. **Amenities:** 2 free rental bikes; lobby computers w/free Internet. In room: A/C, TV, fridge, hair dryer, Internet.

Rihga Hotel Zest   This beige-brick hotel appeals to both business and leisure travelers with its convenient location on Chuo Dori next to Hyogomachi shopping arcade. It has an accommodating staff and offers a variety of rooms at different price ranges, but you'll probably want to hand out more yen for more space, as the cheapest rooms, including all singles, are rather narrow with tiny bathrooms.

9–1 Furujinmachi, Takamatsu, Kagawa Prefecture 760-0025. www.rihga-takamatsu.co.jp. ℭ **087/822-3555.** Fax 087/822-7516. 122 units. ¥7,854–¥9,471 single; ¥15,015–¥28,875 double. 10% discounts with the Kagawa Welcome Card; be sure to mention the card when making your reservation and show it when you check in. AE, DC, MC, V. Station: Takamatsu (a 10-min. walk south of the station, on Chuo Dori just past Hyogomachi arcade). **Amenities:** 3 restaurants; lounge; rooftop beer garden (summer only); lobby computer w/free Internet. *In room:* A/C, TV, fridge, hair dryer.

INEXPENSIVE

Business Hotel Parkside Takamatsu ★ ⚑   This small business hotel has a great location across from Ritsurin Garden. Rooms are small, but who cares when you can open the window and look out over the fabled garden? Some rooms have only a partial view or none at all, so be sure to request a ringside seat on an upper floor (smoke-free rooms, unfortunately, are on the third floor). Staff doesn't speak much English but aims to please. Bonus: The hotel has discount tickets to Ritsurin Garden.

1–3–1 Ritsurin-cho, Takamatsu, Kagawa Prefecture 760-0073. ℭ **087/837-5555.** Fax 087/837-3000. 116 units. ¥4,950–¥5,400 single; ¥7,950–¥8,400 double; ¥11,900 triple. AE, DC, MC, V. Kotoden streetcar: Ritsurin Koen (10 min.). Walk straight from the west exit and turn right on Chuo Dori; the hotel will be on the right. **Amenities:** Restaurant; free rental bikes; lobby computers w/free Internet. *In room:* A/C, TV, fridge, hair dryer, Internet.

Hotel Dormy Inn Takamatsu ⚑   Rooms at this business hotel are a teeny tiny 14 to 15 sq. m. (150–160 sq. ft.), and most have just one bed, but if you're OK with that there are lots of perks: central location to Kawaramachi's restaurants, nightlife and shopping, an up-to-date design, cheerful staff, late-night ramen and breakfast (*sanuki udon,* tempura and more) included in rates, and contemporary common baths on the top floor that even include a tiny outdoor bath. Most rooms have shower stalls, but you'll pay less for one of the rooms with toilet and sink only.

1–10-10 Karwaramachi, Takamatsu, Kagawa Prefecture 760-0052. ℭ **087/832-5489.** Fax 087/835-5657. 151 units, 25 with toilet only. ¥7,000–¥8,000 single; ¥11,000–¥16,000 double; ¥21,000 triple, including breakfast and late-night snacks. AE, DC, MC, V. Kotoden streetcar: Kawaramachi (5 min.). Take the west exit, walk north (right) two blocks to the next main street (Route 11), and turn left; the hotel is in the second block on the left. **Amenities:** Lobby computers w/free Internet. *In room:* A/C, TV, fridge, hair dryer, Internet.

MATSUYAMA CASTLE & DOGO SPA ★★

947km (588 miles) W of Tokyo; 192km (120 miles) E of Takamatsu; 211km (132 miles) SW of Okayama

Although Matsuyama is Shikoku's largest town and the capital of Ehime Prefecture with a population of more than 515,000, it has the relaxed atmosphere of a small town. Located on the island's northwest coast, Matsuyama features one of Japan's best-preserved feudal castles and what I consider to be the most delightful, historic public bathhouse in the country, located in Dogo Onsen. Nearby Shimanami Kaido, a series of bridges connecting Ehime and Hiroshima prefectures, has a dedicated cycling lane with fantastic views of the Seto Inland Sea, while a side trip to the village of Uchiko with its Edo-era buildings and traditional setting makes for a relaxing excursion.

Essentials

GETTING THERE **By Plane** Flights connect Matsuyama Airport (MYJ; ✆ 089/971-5439) with Tokyo, Sapporo, Osaka, Nagoya, Fukuoka, Kagoshima and Okinawa. Buses connect the airport to downtown in 30 minutes for ¥400.

By Train The easiest way to reach Matsuyama is by **JR train** from Okayama (on Honshu island); the trip takes 2 hours and 40 minutes and costs ¥6,120. There are hourly departures from Takamatsu, taking 2½ hours and costing ¥5,500.

By Bus A **JR bus** (www.jrbuskanto.co.jp; ✆ 03/3844-1950) departs nightly from Tokyo Station at 8:20pm and a **Nishi Tokyo Bus** (✆ 03/5376-2222) departs nightly from Shinjuku Station at 7:10pm; they arrive respectively at Matsuyama Station the next day at 8:35am and at Matsuyama Shieki (City Station) at 7:10am. One-way fare for either is ¥12,000.

By Boat Matsuyama is also linked by ferry to several ports on Honshu and Kyushu islands, including Osaka (overnight: 8⅔ hr.), Oita (near Beppu; 3¾ hr.), and Hiroshima (70 min. by high-speed boat). The fare to Matsuyama is ¥6,300 from Osaka, ¥6,900 from Hiroshima and ¥3,200 from Beppu. Boats dock at **Matsuyama Port (Matsuyama Kanko Ko),** where buses transport passengers to Matsuyama Station in about 20 minutes for ¥450.

VISITOR INFORMATION The **Matsuyama City Tourist Information Office** (✆ 089/931-3914; daily 8:30am–8:30pm) is inside JR Matsuyama Station to the left as you exit the wicket. Be sure to pick up the booklet "Shikoku Passport"; although in Japanese only, it provides many discounts on attractions, hotels, and restaurants. The **Dogo Tourist Information Center** (✆ 089/943-8342; daily 8am–8pm) is across the street from the Dogo Onsen streetcar stop. The **Ehime Prefectural International Center (EPIC),** located between Matsuyama Castle and Dogo Onsen (www.epic.or.jp; ✆ 089/917-5678; Mon–Sat 8:30am–5pm), provides information on Ehime Prefecture, including Uchiko and the Shimanami Kaido cycling path. You'll also find English-language newspapers and three computers you can use for free. To reach EPIC, take streetcar no. 3, 5, or 6 heading toward Dogo Onsen to the Minami-machi stop. Backtrack and look to the right for the INFORMATION sign with a question mark; the office is in a barrack partially hidden behind another building. More information is available online at **www.pref.ehime. jp/izanai/english/index.htm**; **www.city.matsuyama.ehime.jp** and at **www.mcvb. jp/convention**, the latter also with good city maps.

ORIENTATION & GETTING AROUND **JR Matsuyama Station,** which serves long-distance trains, is on the west edge of town, with most attractions, hotels, shopping, and restaurants spreading to the east. **Matsuyama Castle** lies less than 2.5km (1½ miles) due east of the station. Just southwest of the castle is the **Okaido** shopping arcade, a covered pedestrian passageway lined with restaurants and shops and considered to be the heart of the city. **Dogo Onsen,** Japan's oldest hot-spring spa, is on the eastern edge of the city.

The easiest and most convenient form of transportation in Matsuyama is **streetcar** operated by Iyo Tetsudo. The no. 5 line runs from Matsuyama Station to the Okaido arcade, Matsuyama Castle, and Dogo Onsen. The fare is ¥150 per trip or ¥400 for a **1-day pass (Ichinichi Joshaken).** An old-fashioned locomotive-style streetcar nicknamed Botchan (after a novel by Natsume Soseki set in Matsuyama; see below) runs between Matsuyama Station and Dogo Onsen and costs ¥300 per ride (discounted to ¥100 if you have the 1-day pass).

[FastFACTS] MATSUYAMA

Internet Access   In addition to EPIC, above, you can also check e-mail at **COMS,** on the second floor at 6–4–20 Sanbancho (📞 **089/943-5776;** Tues–Sat 9am–8:30pm and Sun/holidays 9am–5pm) for ¥100 an hour. It's a 7-minute walk from either Matsuyama Station or Matsuyama Shieki; or take the streetcar to the Minami-horibata-cho stop. By the way, in the same building is the Matsuyama International Center (📞 **089/943-2025**), which also offers information about the area.

Exploring Matsuyama

The Shikoku Passport gives discounts for both Matsuyama Castle and Dogo Onsen.

Matsuyama Castle ★★ CASTLE   Right in the heart of the city, Matsuyama Castle crowns the top of a 131m (435-ft.) hill, commanding an impressive view. It was built by feudal lord Kato Yoshiaki beginning in 1603, falling in 1635 into the hands of the powerful Matsudaira family, which ruled the surrounding region from here through the Edo Period. Like most structures in Japan, Matsuyama Castle has suffered fire and destruction through the ages, but this one was renovated with original materials in the 1850s, unlike many other castles (such as those in Osaka and Nagoya) that were renovated after World War II. There's only one entrance, a pathway leading through a series of gates that could be swung shut to trap attacking enemies. A secret gate allowed a surprise rear attack, while drop chutes could be used to rain stones onto the enemy. Drums were used to communicate, whether it was to warn of invaders or simply give the time. The granary could store enough rice to feed 2,000 people for a year. The three-story *donjon* houses some samurai gear, swords, screens, and scrolls from the Matsudaira family, as well as photographs of Japan's other castles. Allow yourself 30 minutes to tour the inside.

Surrounding the castle is a park; if you're feeling energetic, walk uphill through the park to the castle in about 15 minutes. Otherwise, the easiest way to the castle is to take the streetcar to the Okaido stop, walk 5 minutes north on the street next to Starbucks, and then, from the east side of Katsuyama Hill, take a cable car or chairlift (more fun!) from the cable station on the left side of the street (there's also a walking path to the castle from here). A round-trip ticket for either the cable car or the chairlift, including castle admission, costs ¥1,000 for adults and ¥400 for children.

📞 **089/921-4873.** Admission ¥500 adults, ¥150 children. Daily 9am–5pm (to 4:30pm Dec–Jan and 5:30pm in Aug.). Streetcar: Okaido stop, then chairlift.

DOGO ONSEN ★★★

Dogo Onsen boasts a 3,000-year history and claims to be the oldest hot-spring spa in Japan. According to legend, the hot springs were discovered after a white heron healed an injured leg by soaking it in the thermal mineral waters. Located in the city's northeast, about a 20-minute streetcar ride from Matsuyama Station (take streetcar no. 5 to Dogo Onsen, the last stop), Dogo Spa can accommodate about 7,000 people in 34 hotels and *ryokan,* which means the narrow streets resound at night with the slap of thonged slippers and the occasional clatter of *geta* (wooden platform sandals) as vacationers go to the various bathhouses dressed in *yukata* (cotton robes). Friendly conversations start as tourists gather on the hour to see the Botchan clock (located across from the historic 1895 Dogo Onsen streetcar station), an animated clock featuring characters from Natsume Soseki's novel, and soak their feet in the nearby foot bath, one of 10 foot baths scattered through the area. Be sure to stop at the Dogo Onsen Tourist Information Center, located at the entrance to the shopping arcade.

Most of the hotels and ryokan in Dogo have their own onsen, but I suggest that no matter where you stay, you make at least one trip to **Dogo Onsen Honkan ★★★**, 5–6 Yunomachi, Dogo (**© 089/921-5141**), a wonderful three-story public bathhouse built in 1894. A wooden structure with shoji screens, tatami rooms, creaking wooden stairways, and the legendary white heron topping the crest of its castlelike roof, this Momoyama-style building is as much a social institution as it is a place to soak and scrub. On busy days, as many as 7,000 people pass through its front doors. The water here is transparent, colorless, tasteless, and alkaline, helpful for rheumatism and neuralgia. At the very least, it makes your skin feel soft and smooth. The hottest spring water coming into the spa is 131°F (55°C); the coolest, 68°F (20°C). But don't worry—the waters are mixed to achieve a comfortable 110°F (43°C).

Bathing in the ground-floor granite bath, however, is just a small part of the experience here. Most people come to relax, socialize, and while away an hour or more, and I suggest you do the same. Although you can bathe for as little as ¥400 for adults and ¥150 for children 2 to 11, it's worth it to pay extra for the privilege of relaxing on tatami mats in a communal room on the second floor, dressed in a rented *yukata*, drinking tea from a lacquered tea set, and eating Japanese rice crackers. If the weather is fine, all the shoji screens are pushed open to let in a breeze, and as you sprawl on the tatami, drinking your tea and listening to the voices of people coming and going, you can imagine that you've landed in ancient Japan. To my mind, the entire scene resembles an old woodblock print suddenly come to life. Be sure to take a peek inside the Botchan Room, said to be the favorite room of novelist Natsume Soseki and decorated with photos from his sojourn here in 1895.

The cost of the bath, yukata, crackers, and tea for 1 hour is ¥800. Use of a smaller, more private bath and lounging area for an hour where tea and crackers are also served costs ¥1,200 and includes a visit to Yushinden (see below). And if you really want to splurge for 1 hour and 20 minutes, you can rent a private tatami room on the third floor, which also comes with tea, sweets, and yukata, for ¥1,500. Children 2 to 11 years old pay half-price for all these fares. This differentiation in luxury probably

 botchan IN MATSUYAMA

Botchan, by Natsume Soseki (1867-1916), is by many estimations Japan's most widely read novel, with a cultural importance akin to the works of Mark Twain in America. The title character is a young teacher from Tokyo who finds himself in the sticks of Matsuyama in the 1890s, largely paralleling Natsume's own life. The novel's colorful characters, including fellow teachers Redshirt and Porcupine and the beautiful but unattainable Madonna, now populate Matsuyama as wooden cutouts and costumed locals at tourist attractions. Never mind that Botchan generally looked down on Matsuyama; the city has adopted the novel as its own.

dates from the early days when there were separate baths for the upper class, priests, commoners, and even animals.

While at the spa, be sure to see **Yushinden,** special bathing, changing and relaxation quarters built for the imperial family in 1899 and last used in 1952. You can tour Yushinden for an extra ¥250 for adults and ¥120 for children.

The spa is open daily 6am until 11pm, but you must enter by 10:30pm. You must enter the second and third floors (both of which close at 10pm), by 9 and 8:40pm respectively; you must enter the Yushinden by 9pm.

A NEARBY TEMPLE After your bath, you may want to visit **Ishiteji Temple** ★, 2–9–21 Ishite (✆ **089/977-0870**), about a 15-minute walk east of Dogo Onsen Station; from the station, walk under the neon archway and keep going straight east. Established in 728, it's the 51st of Shikoku's 88 sacred temples. Its main Nio-mon Gate, built in 1318 with a blend of Chinese and Japanese styles, is a good example of architecture of the Kamakura Period. You'll see statues of Kobo Daishi, as well as an old-fashioned arcade of stalls that seems little changed over the decades. Notice the huge straw sandals at the main gate; those with feet or leg ailments are thought to regain their health by touching them. You'll also see regular-size sandals at the temple, donated by older Japanese in hopes of regaining new strength in their legs (who knows, maybe they've been walking the pilgrimage). Behind the main temple is a tunnel containing stone statues representing the 88 temples of Shikoku; pausing in front of each statue is considered a short circuit to the actual pilgrimage, convenient for those who don't have time for the real thing but still hope for the pilgrimage's blessings. And by the way, all those paper cranes you see in front of the main hall were folded in prayer for world peace, a practice that started with the American invasion of Iraq in 2003. The temple is open 24 hours.

An Easy Side Trip to Uchiko ★★★

If you have time for a side trip, I strongly recommend an excursion to the village of Uchiko, which has some fine old homes and buildings dating back to the Edo Period and the turn of the 20th century. Whereas about 70% of Matsuyama was destroyed during World War II, Uchiko was left intact, and a tiny part of the old historic district, now designated a preservation zone by the Japanese government, is a living memorial to days of yore. During the Edo and Meiji periods, Uchiko gained fame as a center of candle-making and wax production, producing about 30% of the country's wax, used for lighting, umbrellas, and for the styling of elaborate feudal-era hairdos. Even the 25-minute express train ride from JR Matsuyama Station (departing hourly costing ¥1,250) is enjoyable as you weave through valleys of wooded hills past grape, *mikan* orange, persimmon, rice, and tobacco farms.

At Uchiko Station, ask for the Visitors' Guide at the ticket window; it contains a map showing the 15-minute walk to Yokaichi, the historic district. There are also signs in English pointing the way. Otherwise, a retro-style shuttle bus circles through town for ¥300 per ride, while rental cycles available at the station from 9:30am to 5pm cost ¥300 for two hours, plus ¥200 for each additional hour. Because addresses in this village of 18,000 souls are only for postmen, I've omitted them. All sights listed below are open daily 9am to 4:30pm.

Your first stop from the station (a 5-minute walk away) is **Uchiko-za** (内子座; ✆ **0893/44-2840**), a kabuki theater built in 1916 (look for the signpost on the left after you pass the creek). Though not as grand as the one at Kotohira near Takamatsu

(p. 445), it's a good example of how townspeople used to enjoy themselves years ago. It features a revolving stage, windows that can be opened and closed to control the amount of light reaching the stage, and a small display of memorabilia (note the ultimate platform shoes, *geta,* used by *bunraku* puppeteers). Admission is ¥400 for adults, half-price for children. You're better off, however, with a combination ticket for ¥900 and ¥450 respectively that allows admission to the theater, Museum of Commercial and Domestic Life, and the Kami-Haga Residence listed below. The Shikoku Passport also offers discounted admissions.

A 5-minute walk farther along the main street, on the right, is the **Museum of Commercial and Domestic Life (Akinai to Kurashi Hakubutsukan; ℂ 0893/44-5220).** This museum—once housing a pharmacy and built in typical Uchiko style—uses life-size figures, recordings (alas, in Japanese only), and authentic artifacts in its dioramas depicting the daily lives of a merchant and a druggist's family. One of the dioramas, for example, is of a Taisho-Era pharmacy, with two figures kneeling on a tatami floor as they discuss the business at hand, while another shows a family eating, the servant seated on a step below to show a lower status. But my favorite is of the woman in the kitchen, complaining about all the work she has to do. Admission here is ¥200 for adults, half-price for children.

As you continue your walk along Yokaichi's quaint main street, you'll pass galleries and shops, some offering bamboo ware, fresh produce, and other products from shelves on the sidewalk (payment is on the honor system; deposit your money in the proffered bamboo shaft). You might want to stop by the **Machi-ya Shiryokan** (ℂ 0893/44-5212), a restored merchant's home open free to the public, but the highlight of a trip to Uchiko is the **Kami-Haga Residence ★ (ℂ 0893/44-2771).** Built in 1894 without the use of nails by a wealthy merchant who made his fortune exporting wax, the grand house boasts massive posts and beams and contains four toilets (two for the family, one for children, and one for guests) and even a room used only for giving birth. You can see the traditional methods for wax production out back. Admission is ¥500 if purchased separately.

Today only one shop carries on the wax-making tradition, run by the **Omori** (大森) family. Following techniques developed by their ancestors 200-some years ago, the sixth and seventh generations of this family collect and process *haze* berries (a kind of sumac) and make candles by hand. You can observe the process and buy their wares at their workshop, located on the right as you head back to the train station (ℂ 0893/43-0385; 9am–5pm, closed Tues & Fri).

WHERE TO EAT & SLEEP A 10-minute walk east of Yokaichi (or a 15-min. walk from the train station), across the Oda River, **Karari** (ℂ 0893/43-1122; daily 11am–8pm) is a farmers' market plus bakery and a restaurant offering both Western and Japanese dishes featuring local ingredients. Nestled among trees beside the river and with large windows that almost make you feel like you're dining in a treehouse, the restaurant offers a weekend buffet for ¥1,575 with 50 choices of dishes, while weekdays set meals start at ¥1,200. If you want to have Uchiko to yourself after the day-trippers leave, **Kokoro** (ℂ 0893/44-5735) is a beautifully restored 1889 warehouse with two contemporary guest rooms featuring walls covered in swatches of *washi* paper and fabulous barrel-style baths. Rates range from ¥9,500 to ¥12,000 per person, depending on the season, and include breakfast in the charming café across the street. No credit cards accepted at either establishment.

Cycling the Shimanami Kaido ★★★

If you're a bicyclist—and even if you're not—you owe it to yourself to ride one of Japan's most rewarding cycling routes: a dedicated biking and pedestrian lane that connects Ehime Prefecture on Shikoku with Onomichi in Hiroshima Prefecture on Honshu (Japan's main island). Part of the Shimanami Kaido route (also called the Setouchi Shimanami Sea Route), which is actually a series of six bridges that hopscotch across the Seto Inland Sea via six islands, the cycling path runs beside vehicular traffic on the bridges but often diverges from the highway on the islands. Needless to say, views of the sea and surrounding countryside are great, even from the bridges, and the pathway, clearly marked in green, is easy to follow (though steep in some areas). If you want, you can cycle the entire 70km (43-mile) distance between Shikoku and Honshu in less than 7 hours, whereupon you could either return to Shikoku by bus or continue your travels onward (send your luggage beforehand to your next hotel by *takkyu-bin;* see p. 630). Or, you may wish to simply cycle for a few hours and then head back; or, you can go as far as you wish, leave your rental bike at one of 14 bike drop-off sites along the cycling path, and then catch a bus back (check bus schedules beforehand, as buses don't go to all drop-off sites). In my opinion, of the entire cycling path, the stretch from Shikoku is more scenic and easier to follow than the stretch closer to Hiroshima (for information on cycling the Shimanami Kaido from Hiroshima Prefecture, see p. 427). Note that the Shikoku Passport gives discounts for Shiyoden Treasure Museum, bike rentals, and accommodations at Sunrise Itoyama.

If you're not going the distance, for a fun day's outing I suggest bicycling to Omishima, an island you'll reach in about 2 hours, where another 30 minutes of cycling will bring you to **Oyamazumi Shrine,** guarded by a 2,600-year-old tree. Worshiped through the years by samurai, the shrine is home to the **Shiyoden Treasure Museum ★★** (© 0897/82-0032), with an astounding collection of helmets, armor, and swords, all donated to the shrine by warriors who wished to express thanks for victories in battle. The museum contains about 80% of Japan's samurai gear designated National Treasures (eight items; look for the red mark) or National Important Cultural Assets, including items once worn by Minamoto Yoshitsune and Minamoto Yoritomo (who donated his sword and outfit just before establishing his Kamakura shogunate in 1192). The museum is open daily 8:30am to 5pm; admission is ¥1,000 for adults, ¥800 for university and high-school students, and ¥400 for children. By the way, there's a bike drop-off center, called Shimanami-no-eki Mishima, just before the shrine, where you can leave your bike and catch a bus to Imabari (check bus schedules beforehand).

Rental bikes are available at the foot of the first bridge (the Kurushima Kaikyo Bridge) at **Sunrise Itoyama** (www.sunrise-itoyama.jp; © 0898/41-3196), which also offers a restaurant, showers, and rooms without private bathrooms beginning at ¥4,200 for a single and ¥6,300 for a twin (no credit cards accepted). Bikes rent for ¥500 a day, plus a ¥1,000 deposit which you forfeit if you decide to ditch your bike at one of the drop-off sites; be sure to ask the folks at Sunrise Itoyama for a bus schedule back. You'll also have the annoyance of bridge toll fees at varying distances, which you deposit into boxes on the honor system (or, you can purchase a coupon for ¥500 covering all the tolls at Sunrise Itoyama). There are also power-assisted bikes for ¥800; I've rented one (in the interest of research, of course—twice) and found it

Matsuyama Castle & Dogo Spa

SHIKOKU

helpful on the circular ramp that climbs 65m (213 ft.) just to meet the first bridge. However, power-assisted bikes must be returned to Sunrise Itoyama, and they have only enough juice to run about 4 hours or so. Sunrise Itoyama is open for bike rentals daily 8am to 8pm (to 5pm Oct–Mar).

To reach Sunrise Itoyama, take an express train from Matsuyama Station 30 minutes to Imabari, from where there are only three to five buses a day to Sunrise Itoyama. You'll probably find it easier, therefore, to take a local train 5 minutes onward from Imabari to Hashihama Station, from which the cycling center is a 20-minute walk; or, if you notify Sunrise Itoyama in advance, they offer pickup and drop-off service at Hashihama Station (not available during peak periods).

Where to Dine
EXPENSIVE
Kadota ★ FRENCH   Chef Kadota, a gold medalist in the Culinary Olympics, worked at both the Okura Hotel and ANA Hotel Matsuyama before opening his own restaurant here in 1993. Small and cozy, with classical music playing in the background, flowers on every table, and French cuisine served on elegant tableware, it offers homemade appetizers, organic vegetables whenever possible, and—the house specialty—steaks and seafood in season. Your dinner may start with yellowtail sashimi in mandarin orange sauce or fish bouillabaisse, followed by local sea bream in white-wine sauce or steak in red-wine sauce with sweet-potato gratin.

3-4-25 Sanban-cho. ✆ **089/931-3511.** Reservations recommended. Main dishes ¥1,365–¥2,625; set dinners ¥5,250–¥15,750; set lunches ¥2,100–¥3,675. AE, DC, MC, V. Daily 11am–2pm and 5–9pm (last order). Closed 2 days in Aug. Streetcar: Kencho-mae (5 min.). Take the side road to the east of the ANA hotel, continue straight 7 blocks, and then turn right where you'll see the restaurant with a tree lit in tiny white lights.

MODERATE
Kushihide (くし秀) 🍴YAKITORI/CHICKEN   Behind the counter of this 50-year-old eatery are some 400 individual sake cups inscribed with the names of regular customers; the cook joked that this way, the cups didn't have to be washed. Washed or unwashed, they're testimony to the popularity of this simple eating and drinking venue. The restaurant elevates chicken cuisine to an obsession, raising its own chickens and serving them in endless variety. It's best known for *hone-tsuki ashi* (fried chicken leg and thigh) for ¥850), but there's also chicken sukiyaki, chicken burgers, *senzanki* (fried chicken), even chicken sashimi (the restaurant claims it's safe as the chickens are served on the day of their demise). In fact, chicken or chicken broth is a part of virtually every dish offered here—even ice cream. There's a photo menu, or just sit at the counter to point at what you like.

3-2-8 Nibancho. ✆ **089/921-1587.** Yakitori ¥210–¥265; set meals ¥1,890–¥4,725. AE, MC, V. Tues–Sun 4:30–11pm. Streetcar: Okaido (2 min.). Walk down Okaido Arcade and take the 1st right after the stoplights; it's 1 block farther on your left (look for the wooden sign over the door).

Sushimaru (すし丸) SUSHI   Located just east of the Okaido shopping arcade, Sushimaru has Japanese *noren* (shop curtains), a display case outside, and old-fashioned architecture. A *higawari* (today's lunch) consisting of sushi, *nigiri* sushi (sushi rolls), salad, and soup for ¥800, is available most days, but even more popular is the changing *tsukigawari* (monthly lunch), served daily until 2pm and including various dishes in addition to sushi. A Japanese-language menu with photos shows other set meals. In the evening, kaiseki featuring sashimi are also available. Another Sushimaru is located in the Hotel Patio Dogo (see below).

2–3–2 Nibancho. ☎ **089/941-0447.** Set meals ¥1,050–¥3,700; kaiseki ¥3,700–¥10,000. AE, DC, MC, V. Mon–Fri 11am–2pm and 4:30–10:30pm; Sat–Sun and holidays 11am–10:30pm. Streetcar: Okaido (4 min.). Walk south along the Okaido shopping arcade. After you cross Nichiban-cho (the 1st light), take the 1st small street on your left; it will be on your right a few shops down.

INEXPENSIVE

Dogo Beer Bakushukan 🍴 If you agree that "One gulp of beer taken just after a bath is the time when you feel most refreshed," as proclaimed on this microbrewery's banner, then after bathing at Dogo Onsen Honkan head straight across the street for some sake or beer. (The parent company has been a sake producer for more than a century.) Upbeat, eclectic decor mixes the traditional (bamboo ceilings) and the modern (artwork), while the menu mixes German-style beers (Cologne-style Kolsch, alt, and stout), with Japanese pub grub. About half the picture menu is regional specialties like *taimeshi* (Seto Inland Sea sea bream over rice) and *jakoten* (deep-fried cakes of fish paste), along with items like *kushiyaki* (grilled skewers) and fried chicken.

20–13 Yuno-machi, Dogo. ☎ **089/945-6866.** Main dishes ¥370–¥2,100. AE, DC, MC, V. Daily 11am–10pm. Streetcar: Dogo Onsen. Across from Dogo Onsen Honkan; look for "Brewery Restaurant" sign.

Where to Stay

The Shikoku Passport provides discounts for ANA Hotel and Hotel Patio Dogo; mention the discount when making reservations and show the passport upon check-in.

VERY EXPENSIVE

Yamatoya Besso (大和屋別荘) ★★★ The ultimate *ryokan* experience awaits you at this famous inn in Dogo Onsen. It's the little things that make it special: the rustle of kimono as you're met by bowing, smiling women in the front courtyard; pillars of salt at the front door in good Shinto fashion; lit shoji lanterns guiding the way through hushed hallways; scrolls of haiku poems, in beautiful calligraphy, decorating all the rooms and changed seven times a year to fit the season. With a history dating back 140 years—it was rebuilt in 1988 as a refined, luxurious inn—it offers rooms that preserve the integrity of the past with TVs hidden behind shoji screens and old-fashioned cypress tubs that use water from hot springs. For a real splurge, four rooms have their own open-air tubs. Lavish *kaiseki* meals feature Seto Inland Sea seafood, served on Arita-style porcelain dishes.

2–27 Dogo Sagidani-cho, Matsuyama, Ehime Prefecture 790-0836. ☎ **089/931-7771.** Fax 089/931-7775. 19 units. ¥46,350–¥81,000 per person. Rates include 2 meals. Weekday and off-season discount available. AE, DC, MC, V. Streetcar: Dogo Onsen (5 min.). **Amenities:** Indoor/outdoor hot-spring baths, Internet terminal. *In room:* A/C, TV, hair dryer.

EXPENSIVE

ANA Hotel ★ Matsuyama's premier hotel (called Zenniku Hotel in Japanese) has a great location in the heart of the city, just a few minutes' walk to the Matsuyama Castle ropeway and the Okaido covered shopping arcade; streetcars heading for Dogo Onsen pass right in front of the hotel. It offers business hotel-like inexpensive singles (the cheapest listed here), as well as larger and well-appointed singles, twins, and doubles; ask for a double or twin with a castle view.

3–2–1 Ichiban-cho, Matsuyama, Ehime Prefecture 790-8520. www.anahotelmatsuyama.com. ☎ **800/993-3563** in the U.S. and Canada, or 089/933-5511. Fax 089/921-6053. 327 units. ¥6,930–¥17,094 single; ¥19,635–¥40,425 double; ¥21,368–¥32,340 twin. AE, DC, MC, V. Streetcar: Okaido (1 min.). **Amenities:** 3 restaurants; bar; tea lounge; rooftop beer garden (summer only); room service. *In room:* A/C, TV, hair dryer, Internet, minibar.

MODERATE

Hotel Patio Dogo ★ With a great location across from Dogo Onsen Honkan, this comfortable and contemporary hotel offers semi-double beds in singles, and queens in the more expensive double rooms. Ah, space at last! Best are rooms on the second through fourth floors whose windows overlook the historic spa. The most expensive corner deluxe twin rooms have the most space and the best views. In the evening, join the other tourists staying in Dogo and wear your *yukata* across the street for a soak in the historic spa.

20–12 Yuno-machi, Dogo, Matsuyama, Ehime Prefecture 790-0842. www.patio-dogo.co.jp. ☎ **089/941-4128.** Fax 089/941-4129. 101 units. ¥7,665–¥9,450 single; ¥11,550–¥26,250 double. AE, DC, MC, V. Streetcar: Dogo Onsen (5 min.). Walk though the covered shopping arcade and turn left. **Amenities:** Restaurant (a branch of Sushimaru; see "Where to Dine," above); lobby computer w/free Internet. *In room:* A/C, TV, fridge, hair dryer, Wi-Fi.

Old England Dogo Yamanote Hotel ★★ An outdoor terrace cafe; a lobby decorated in old-world style with wainscoting and antique-filled cabinets; and classical music playing in the background transport a touch of England to the heart of Dogo Onsen. A sign outside declaring SINCE 1886 refers to a *ryokan* that once stood here, but alas, the owner tore it down and opened this hotel. Still, this is a classy choice if you prefer a bed to a futon, with rooms sporting brocade bedspreads and curtains, wood floors, and roomy bathrooms (note that the cheapest doubles are with semi-double-size beds). Although most people staying here pay rates that include meals in the hotel's good French restaurant (meals cost ¥12,800–¥15,800 per person), rates below are for rooms only.

1–13 Dogosagidani-cho, Dogo, Matsuyama, Ehime Pref. 790-0836. ☎ **089/998-2111.** Fax 089/998-2112. 70 units. ¥10,700–¥19,050 single; ¥15,100–¥38,100 double. Rates ¥2,100 higher per person on nights before holidays. AE, DC, MC, V. Streetcar: Dogo Onsen (10 min.). Walk though the covered arcade; it's uphill and around the bend behind Dogo Onsen Honkan. **Amenities:** Restaurant; coffee shop, Wi-Fi (free, in lobby). *In room:* A/C, TV, fridge, hair dryer, Internet.

INEXPENSIVE

Hotel No. 1 Matsuyama ⚡ Close to restaurants and bars and about a 10-minute walk from the castle, this hotel offers facilities that more expensive hotels lack, including roof-top hot-spring baths with views across the city, laundry machines on most floors, and spotless rooms with blackout panels and a surprising amount of space. We could do without those statues in the lobby, but at these prices…

2-7-3 Chifune-machi, Matsuyama, Ehime Prefecture 790-0011. ☎ **089/921-6666.** Fax 089/921-7788. 315 units. ¥5,140 single; ¥7,350–¥7,870 double. AE, DC, MC, V. Streetcar: Okaido (6 min.). Walk though the covered shopping arcade and turn left when it ends. **Amenities:** Restaurant; indoor/outdoor hot-spring baths. *In room:* A/C, TV, fridge, hair dryer, Internet.

Minshuku Miyoshi (民宿みよし) Run by a sweet *obaasan* (granny), this aging '70s-era inn is in Dogo Onsen near Ishiteji Temple. It's hard to spot, but if you call ahead, someone may be able to pick you up at the Dogo Onsen streetcar stop or meet you in front of Ishiteji Temple. Not much English is spoken, but they're used to foreigners and offer clean, basic tatami rooms, all with sink and toilet. Staff will even wash and dry your clothes for free if you have a lot of laundry.

3–7–23 Ishite, Matsuyama, Ehime Prefecture 790-0852. ©/fax **089/977-2581.** 6 units, none with bathroom, all with toilet. ¥4,000 without meals; ¥5,000 with breakfast; ¥7,350 with 2 meals. All rates are per person. No credit cards. Streetcar: Dogo Onsen (10 min.). Bus: 52 to Ishiteji. Across from Ishiteji Temple, painted olive green and set back across the parking lot to the left of the store selling tombstones. *In room:* A/C, TV, no phone.

KYUSHU

The southernmost of Japan's four main islands, Kyushu offers a mild climate, hot-spring spas, beautiful countryside, national parks, unique museums, and warm, friendly people. With the 2011 opening of a new Shinkansen bullet train connecting Fukuoka and Kagoshima, travel in Kyushu is easier and faster than ever before (see p. 609 for information on Kyushu rail passes).

Historians believe that Japan's earliest inhabitants lived on Kyushu before gradually pushing northward. According to local legend, it was from Kyushu that the first emperor, Jimmu, began his campaign to unify Japan. Kyushu is therefore considered to be the cradle of Japanese civilization. And because Kyushu is the island closest to Korea and China, it has served through the centuries as a point of influx for both people and ideas from abroad, including those from the West. Many of the island's museums and attractions are tied to Kyushu's international heritage.

10

THE BEST KYUSHU EXPERIENCES

- **Acting Scholarly in Dazaifu (Dazaifu, near Fukuoka):** Established in 905 to deify the god of scholarship, **Dazaifu Tenmangu Shrine** has a festive atmosphere and is popular with students wishing to pass school exams. Learn about Japan's early cultural exchange with Asia at the **Kyushu National Museum**. See p. 468.
- **Cheering the Local Baseball Team (Fukuoka):** Baseball in Japan is a completely different spectator experience; join avid fans cheering on the Fukuoka Softbank Hawks at Fukuoka Yahoo! Japan Dome. If they win, there's fireworks. See p. 469.
- **Being Brave on an Active Volcano: Mt. Aso** was larger than Mt. Fuji before blowing its stack; its massive caldera is home to Naka-dake, an active cone drawing thousands of sightseers. **Mount Sakurajima,** Kagoshima's most famous landmark, is just a short ferry ride away for up-close looks at its lava fields. See p. 495 and 505.
- **Exploring Chiran (Chiran, near Kagoshima):** This former castle town is famous for seven diminutive gardens laid out by samurai during the Edo Period, as well as for the **Peace Museum for Kamikaze Pilots** dedicated to young pilots who died in suicide missions in World War II. See p. 506.

- **Being Buried in Sand:** Being buried up to your neck in hot, steaming sand is considered relaxing and curative. In Ibusuki it's available beachside, while in Beppu it's done in an old wooden bathhouse. See p. 513 and 518.

FUKUOKA, GATEWAY TO KYUSHU & BEYOND

1,174km (730 miles) W of Tokyo; 450km (281 miles) W of Hiroshima

With a population of 1.8 million and capital of Fukuoka Prefecture, Fukuoka is Kyushu's largest city and serves as a major international and domestic gateway to the island. On the northern coast of Kyushu, it lies closer to Seoul, Korea, than to Tokyo. Although it's not a must-see tourist destination, there are some interesting museums, shrines, and a temple worth seeing if you've arrived in Fukuoka on the Shinkansen.

During Japan's feudal days, Fukuoka was divided into two distinct towns separated by the Naka-gawa river. Fukuoka was where the samurai lived since it was the castle town of the local feudal lord. Merchants lived across the river in Hakata, the commercial center of the area. Both cities were joined in 1889 under the common name of Fukuoka. Fukuoka's main train station, which serves both Shinkansen bullet trains and commuter trains, is in Hakata and is therefore called Hakata Station.

In the 13th century, Fukuoka was selected by Mongol forces under Kublai Khan as the best place to invade Japan. The first attack came in 1274, but Japanese were able to repel the invasion. Convinced the Mongols would attack again, Japanese built a 3m-high (10-ft.) stone wall along the coast. The second invasion came in 1281. Not only did the Mongols find the wall an impediment, but a typhoon blew in and destroyed the entire Mongol fleet. Japanese called this gift from heaven "divine wind," or *kamikaze,* a word that took on a different meaning during World War II when young Japanese pilots crashed their planes into American ships in a last-ditch attempt to win the war.

Today, Fukuoka is a modern, internationally oriented commercial and business center with a highly developed port and coastal area. It is also recognized for its many environmental efforts, including a project to cover buildings with flowers and greenery (its downtown ACROS building with its terraced façade is a much-photographed example), Japan's first ordinance for water conservation, and its own method for waste landfill that cuts greenhouse gases by 50%.

Essentials

GETTING THERE   By Plane   Direct flights connect **Fukuoka Airport** (**FUK;** www.fuk-ab.co.jp; © **092/621-6059**) to a variety of international cities, including Beijing, Shanghai, Hong Kong, Seoul, and Bangkok, as well as numerous domestic cities; flying time from Tokyo's Haneda Airport is about 1 hour and 40 minutes. In addition to JAL and ANA, **Skymark** (www.skymark.co.jp; © **050/3116-73703**), a small airline serving Fukuoka, offers 10 flights daily from Haneda to Fukuoka. To transfer to town, there's a subway station called Fukuoka-kuko Station directly under the domestic terminal of **Fukuoka Airport** (if you've arrived at the international terminal, take the free shuttle bus departing every 10 minutes to the domestic terminal). The trip takes only 5 minutes to Hakata Station and 11 minutes to Tenjin and costs ¥250; or, you can purchase a 1-day subway pass for ¥600 if you plan to

Kyushu

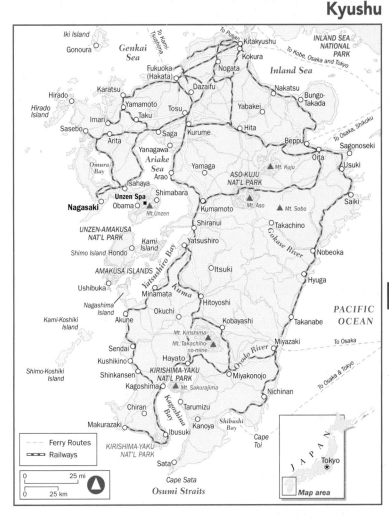

sightsee the same day. Alternatively, there's bus service directly from the domestic terminal every 20 to 30 minutes to Hakata Station's bus terminal; the cost is ¥250.

By Train Fukuoka's **Hakata Station** is connected to the JR Hakata City, a shopping and dining complex that includes Amu Plaza and Hankyu department store. It's the last stop on the Nozomi Shinkansen bullet train from Tokyo, with the trip taking a little over 5 hours. If you have a Japan Rail Pass, which doesn't cover Nozomi trains, you'll have to take the slower Hikari Shinkansen and change trains in Osaka, Himeji, or Okayama, which takes almost 6 hours not including transfers. Regardless of which bullet train you take, the fare from Tokyo is ¥21,210 for an unreserved seat. Hiroshima is 1 hour and 10 minutes away; Kagoshima is 1½ hours away.

KYUSHU | Fukuoka, Gateway to Kyushu & Beyond

465

By Bus A Nishitetsu "Hakata" bus (www.nishitetsu.co.jp/bus/highway/gb; ✆ 0120/489-939;) departs from Tokyo's Shinjuku Station nightly at 9pm, arriving at Hakata Bus Terminal (next to Hakata Station) at 11:10am the next morning. The fare is ¥15,000 one-way. Buses from Kagoshima Chuo Station take about 4 hours and cost ¥5,300),

VISITOR INFORMATION The **Fukuoka City Tourist Information Office** in Hakata Station is located in a free-standing kiosk in the central passageway near the East Gate (✆ 092/431-3003; daily 8am–9pm), as well as in the center of town in Lion-Hiroba, 2–1–1 Tenjin (✆ 092/751-6904; daily 10am–6:30pm; station: Tenjin). Both have maps and sightseeing pamphlets. Ask for **Rainbow,** a free monthly with concert, exhibition, events, and festival information; and **Fukuoka Now,** good for restaurant and nightlife listings. More information by phone is available at the Tourist Information Call Center for Foreign Travelers daily from 10am to 6:30pm at ✆ **092/751-6904.** On the Internet, sightseeing information is available at **www. yokanavi.com** and, to a lesser degree, at **www.city.fukuoka.jp.** Another useful site is **www.fukuoka-now.com,** good for restaurants, exhibitions, events, and nightlife.

ORIENTATION Although Hakata Station is the terminus for Shinkansen bullet trains and trains departing for the rest of Kyushu, with many hotels clustered nearby, the heart and business center of Fukuoka is an area to the west called **Tenjin.** It's home to several department stores, its own train station and bus center, a large underground shopping arcade, and restaurants. Just a few minutes' walk from Tenjin is **Nakasu,** one of Japan's most famous nightlife districts, with more than 2,000 bars, restaurants, and small clubs clustered on what's actually an islet bounded by the Naka-gawa river.

Across the river from Nakasu (and a 10-min. walk west of Hakata Station) is **Canal City Hakata,** an intriguingly designed (by award-winning American architect Jon Jerde) entertainment, hotel, and shopping complex with 125 shops and restaurants. Also nearby and within walking distance are Tochoji Temple, Hakata Machiya Folk Museum, Kushida Shrine, and the Fukuoka Asian Art Museum.

GETTING AROUND You can **walk** from Hakata Station to most of the attractions recommended below.

By Subway Fukuoka City Subway (http://subway.city.fukuoka.lg.jp; ✆ **092/734-7800**) is the fastest and easiest method of transportation because there are only three major lines and stops are announced in English. The red-colored Kuko Line is the most useful for tourists. It travels from Fukuoka Airport to Hakata Station, Gion, Nakasu-Kawabata, Tenjin, and Tojin-Machi stations, stops for all the attractions listed below. Fares start at ¥200, but if you think you'll be riding a lot, a 1-day subway pass for ¥600 allows unlimited rides.

By Train Whereas Hakata Station serves as the terminus for the Shinkansen and JR trains departing for the rest of Kyushu, Tenjin has its own station, called **Nishitetsu Fukuoka Station,** located inside the Mitsukoshi department store building and useful for trips to Dazaifu.

By Bus The city's two bus terminals are located beside Hakata Station at the Hakata Bus Terminal and in Tenjin near Nishitetsu Fukuoka Station and Mitsukoshi department store. Buses running inside the central Hakata-Tenjin District charge a flat fare of ¥100. Most useful for tourists is the "¥100 Bus," which sports a big ¥100 coin on its side and travels a circular route going both directions from Haktaka

Station to 18 stops in the downtown area, including Gion-machi, Tenjin, and Canal City. Pick up a bus map at the tourist office.

[FastFACTS] FUKUOKA

Consulates You'll find both an Australian consulate (*☎* **092/734-5055**) and a US consulate (*☎* **092/751-9331**) in Fukuoka.

Internet Access You can check e-mail 24 hours a day at **Media Café Popeye,** located on the eighth floor

of the Hakata Bus Terminal, next to Hakata Station (*☎* **092/432-8788**). It charges ¥410 for 1 hour.

Mail & ATM An international post office is located next to the Hakata (west) exit of Hakata Station, open Monday to Friday 9am to

7pm, Saturday 9am to 5pm, and Sunday 9am to 12:30pm. ATMs that accept international credit cards are in service Monday to Saturday 12:05am to 11:55pm and Sunday and holidays 12:05am to 9pm.

Exploring Fukuoka

About an 8-minute walk northwest of Hakata Station and located on the right side of Taihaku-Dori is **Tochoji Temple** (東長寺), 2–4 Gokushomachi (*☎* **092/291-4459;** daily 9am–5pm; subway: one stop from Hakata Station to Gion, exit 1, 1 min.; ¥100 Bus: Gion-machi, stop no. 16; look for a picture of a Buddha near the front gate). This modern reconstruction of a long-established temple, established by Kobo Daishi, may not look like much, but up on the second floor is Japan's largest seated wooden Buddha, measuring 10m (33 ft.) tall and carved in 1988. Admission is free, but you are asked to refrain from taking photographs. Particularly interesting is the trip through the Hells of Buddhism, upon which you can embark by entering the small room to the left of the Buddha. After viewing colored reliefs of unfortunate souls burning in hell, being boiled alive, and suffering other tortures, enter the totally dark, twisting passageway and walk through it guided by a rail, whereupon you'll reach the end—enlightenment! It's fun for older kids.

On the other side of Taihaku-Dori, farther down the side street with a 7-Eleven and marked by a large cement *torii,* is the **Hakata Machiya Folk Museum (Hakata Machiya Furusato-Kan;** 博多町屋ふるさと館) ★, 6–10 Reisen-machi (www.hakatamachiya.com; (*☎* **092/281-7761;** daily 10am–6pm; subway: Gion, exit 2, 4 min.; ¥100 Bus: Okunodo, stop no. 15). This museum celebrates the history and cultural heritage of Hakata, the old merchants' town, concentrating primarily on the Meiji and Taisho eras. It occupies three buildings, two of which are Meiji-Era replicas; the third is an authentic, 150-year-old house of a weaver. On display are items used in everyday life like baskets and clothing, as well as dioramas depicting festivals, everyday street scenes, and a home typical of a Hakata merchant family. On a replica 1899 telephone, you can listen to *Hakata-ben,* the local dialect, which is quite difficult even for native Japanese speakers to understand. In the old house you can watch artisans at work on Hakata's most famous wares, including *Hakata-ori* cloth, used for *obi* sashes and famous for

A Note on Japanese Characters

Many establishments and attractions in Japan do not have outdoor signs in Roman (English-language) letters. Those that don't are provided with the Japanese equivalent to help you locate them.

loincloths worn by sumo wrestlers. Be sure to see the 22-minute film of the Yamakasa Festival, Fukuoka's most famous festival, featuring races of men carrying enormous floats. Add another 30 minutes to see the museum itself and its small crafts shop. Admission is ¥200 for adults and free for children.

Beyond the Hakata Machiya Folk Museum, to the right, you can see more local products at the **Hakata Traditional Craft Center (Hakata Dentou-Kougeikan)**, 6–1 Kamikawabata-machi (http://hakata-kentou-kougeikan.jp; ✆ **092/409-5450;** Thurs–Tues 10am–6pm; subway: Gion or Nakasu-Kawabata, 5min.; ¥100 Bus: Canal City Hakata-mae or Gion-machi, 4 min.). In addition to galleries showing Hakata-ori, Hakata *Ningyo* (dolls), and other crafts, there's a café with free Wi-Fi. Admission is free. Next door is **Kushida Shrine,** 1 Kamikawabata-machi (✆ **092/291-2951;** shrine grounds daily 24 hr.), Fukuoka's oldest shrine. Site of the Yamakasa Festival, it has long been the shrine for merchants praying for good health and prosperity. Most interesting is a tall, towering float on view (except in June when it is being rebuilt) that is used in the Yamakasa Festival held in mid-July and decorated with dolls made by Hakata doll makers. Incredibly, the elaborate floats are made anew every year.

Walk through Kushida Shrine and turn right into the **Kawabata-dori covered shopping arcade.** Linking Canal City Hakata and Hakata Riverain, it was once the city's main shopping street but has been overtaken by the two complexes it connects. At the end of the arcade, across the street, is Riverain, where up on the seventh and eighth floors is the **Fukuoka Asian Art Museum ★★★**, 3–1 Shimokawabata-machi (http://faam.city.fukuoka.lg.jp; ✆ **092/263-1100;** Thurs–Tues 10am–8pm; subway: Nakasu-Kawabata, exit 6; ¥100 Bus: Kawabata-machi Hakataza-mae), the only museum I've seen in Japan devoted to contemporary and modern art from around Asia. From folk pop art to political art, the permanent exhibition presents the cutting edge of art from the Philippines, Indonesia, Malaysia, Singapore, Thailand, China, Mongolia, Korea, India, and other Asian countries, with changing displays culled from the museum's own collection. It's very much worth the hour you'll spend here and the ¥200 admission for adults, ¥150 for college and high-school students, and ¥100 for junior-high students and younger (special exhibits cost more).

If you're ready for dining or shopping, retrace your steps through Kawabata-dori arcade and take the escalator leading to **Canal City Hakata** (see below), a virtual city-within-a-city complete with hotels, shops, restaurants, and a 177m-long (590-ft.) canal that runs through its center.

An Easy Side Trip from Fukuoka
DAZAIFU

If you have 4 or more hours to spare, I heartily recommend taking a side trip to **Dazaifu,** a pleasant village that is home to a shrine that is immensely popular with Japanese, and the Kyushu National Museum. Dazaifu has a festive atmosphere, and one of the main reasons to visit, in my opinion, is to see everyone else.

The best way to reach Dazaifu is from Nishitetsu Fukuoka Station in Tenjin (in the Mitsukoshi department store). Take a *tokkyu* (limited express) of the Nishitetsu Tenjin Omuta Line (there are departures every 30 min.) 12 minutes to Futsukaichi (the second stop); transfer there for the 8-minute train ride on the Nishitetsu Dazaifu Line (two stops) to Dazaifu Station, the last stop (a few trains go directly from Fukuoka Station to Dazaifu). If you don't catch a limited express, the trip to Dazaifu can take about 50 minutes. In any case, the fare is ¥390 one-way. The **Dazaifu City Tourist Information Desk** (✆ **092/925-1880;** daily 9am–5pm), located inside Dazaifu Station, has an English-language pamphlet with a map.

TAKE ME OUT TO THE ballgame

If you're in town April through mid-October, consider seeing the **Fukuoka Softbank Hawks** baseball team play one of its 60-some home games in Fukuoka Yahoo! Japan Dome (www.softbank hawks.co.jp; ☏ **092/847-1006**), the first retractable-roof stadium in Japan. Tickets start at ¥1,000 for an unreserved seat in the outfield and are available at major convenience stores or at the box office. Personally, I find watching the spectators as much fun as watching the game, with their coordinated cheering, flag waving, trumpet blowing, and more. Oddly enough, the roof is kept closed (in case it rains and so that players aren't distracted by their shadows), but when the Hawks win, they open the roof and celebrate with fireworks. And this being Japan, the dome is near **Hawks Town Mall** with many restaurants, shops, and other amusements. To reach Hawks Town, take the subway to the Tojin-machi stop, from which it's about a 13-minute walk. Or take bus no. 306 from gate 6 of the Hakata Bus Terminal beside Hakata Station, or bus no. 300, 301, 303, or 305 from in front of Hakata Station or the Tenjin Bus Center.

Dazaifu Tenmangu Shrine ★★★, 4–7–1 Saifu Dazaifu (www.dazaifu tenmangu.or.jp; ☏ **092/922-8225**), is a 5-minute walk from the station, reached by taking a right onto a pedestrian lane lined with shops selling souvenirs, sweets, and crafts, followed by three bridges (representing the past, present, and future) spanning a turtle-filled pond shaped in the kanji for "heart." The shrine itself was established in 903, soon after the death of Michizane Sugawara, who was demoted from his position as Minister of the Right in Kyoto and exiled to Dazaifu, where he continued his scholarly studies despite extreme hardship. Today, Michizane is deified as the god of literature and calligraphy, which explains why this shrine is so popular. As the head office of 12,000 Tenmangu shrines spread throughout Japan and presided over by the 39th-generation Michizane descendant, it draws six million visitors a year, many of them high-school students praying to pass tough entrance exams into universities. Behind the main hall, which dates from 1591, hang wooden tablets, written with the wishes of visitors—mostly for successful examination scores. Also behind the main hall is an extensive plum grove with 6,000 trees; the plum blossom, in bloom from late January to March, is considered the symbol of scholarship.

Whatever you do, a must-see is **Komyozenji Temple** ★ (☏ 092/922-4053), just a 2-minute walk from the shrine. This Zen temple, built in 1275, boasts Kyushu's sole rock garden, arranged to form the Chinese character for "light." In the back is also a combination moss-rock garden, representing the sea and land and shaded by maple trees. It's a glorious sight and is almost never crowded, except in autumn when changing maple leaves make it even more spectacular. To see it, take your shoes off at the entrance to the right, throw ¥200 into the donation box, and walk to the wooden veranda in back where you can sit and meditate. It's open daily 8am to 5pm.

Behind Dazaifu Tenmangu Shrine, to the right, is an escalator that will take you to the **Kyushu National Museum** ★★, 4–7–2 Ishizaka (www.kyuhaku.jp; ☏ 092/918-2807), which in 2005 opened as Japan's first new national museum in 100 years (the other three national museums are in Tokyo, Kyoto, and Nara). Perched on a hillside, it's a strikingly modern structure that undulates down the slope like a gentle wave, with surrounding woods reflected on its glass facade. Through permanent and special exhibits, it focuses on Japan's cultural heritage, how that heritage has been influenced by other Asian cultures through the ages, and the role Kyushu has played in cultural exchange (be sure to ask for the free 30-minute audio guide, but you'll probably spend at least an hour here). Religious objects, musical instruments, ceramics, lacquerware, art, and other items from ancient to modern times from a number of nations are on display, including goods that reached Japan via the Silk Road and European trading ships. Don't miss the ground-floor interactive corner Ajippa, where volunteers are on hand to introduce you to toys, musical instruments, clothing, and other items from Korea, Indonesia, China, and other Asian countries. If possible, sign up for the free 1-hour Backyard Tour, offered twice a week, which takes visitors behind the scenes to the museum's huge conservation complex that keeps 50 curators and 100 volunteers busy and to the seismic isolation structure built to keep its collections safe. The museum is open Tuesday to Sunday from 9:30am to 5pm and costs ¥420 for adults, ¥130 for university students (free for children). Special exhibits cost more.

Where to Eat

For one-stop dining, head to **Canal City Hakata** (www.canalcity.co.jp/eg/; (**© 092/ 282-2525**), a 10-minute walk west of Hakata Station or a 1-minute walk from the ¥100 Bus stop Canal City Hakata-mae stop. You'll find 50-some restaurants in this shopping complex, situated around a canal and water fountains and offering everything from Chinese, Italian, and Japanese cuisine to fast food and bar snacks. On the fifth floor is **Ramen Stadium,** with eight ramen shops offering noodles, *gyoza* (dumplings), and other fare from different regions of Japan. Pick your meal from the ticket vending machine outside each shop; there are photos of most selections, priced from ¥650 to ¥1,050. Like most restaurants in Canal City, they're open daily from 11am to 11pm. At Hakata Station, there's **JR Hakata City** (© 092/431-8484), with dozens of outlets on the 9th and 10th floors of Amu Plaza offering everything from Mexican and Thai to tempura and shabu-shabu, most open daily 11am to 11pm.

For a bit more local flavor, head to one of Fukuoka's famous 200 *yatai* **stalls** ★ (street-side food stalls). Most are located in Tenjin, Nakasu Island along the bank of the Naka-gawa river, and just to the east near Reizen Park. Most stalls sell only ramen, while others serve *oden,* gyoza, tempura, and other simple fare. They're open daily from about 6pm to 2am. Many nighttime revelers stop here before or after a spin through the Nakasu entertainment district. Choose a stall and sit down, and you'll be served a steaming bowl of ramen, most of which average about ¥700.

Aroma's ★ EUROPEAN   Located in the Grand Hyatt, with its great location in Canal City, this upbeat, modern restaurant has a great lunch buffet serving mostly Mediterranean-inspired cuisine using local ingredients, including salads, soup and vegetables, and many fish and meat choices. Dinner buffets add more choices, and by paying ¥400 extra, you can drink all the wine you want (thank goodness there's a 90-min. time limit). Or, there's an all-day a-la-cart menu offering everything from sandwiches, *udon* noodles, and curry rice to heavier fare like rack of lamb.

Grand Hyatt Fukuoka, 1–2–82 Sumiyoshi. www.fukuoka.grand.hyatt.com. © **092/282-2803.** Main dishes ¥1,800–¥3,900; buffet dinner ¥3,500; buffet lunch Mon–Fri ¥2,100, weekends and holidays ¥2,300. AE, DC, MC, V. Daily 11:30am–2:30pm and 5:30–9pm. Station: Hakata (12 min.). ¥100 Bus: Canal City Hakata-mae (stop no. 4; 2 min.).

Kazaguruma (かざぐるま) 🏮 LOCAL SPECIALTIES   In a relocated 200-year-old farmhouse accented with heavy wooden beams, this lively *izakaya* specializes in locally brewed *shochu* (an *izakaya* is a Japanese bar with beer, sake, and Japanese food, generally open only from 5 or 6pm). It offers a fish of the day, *yakitori*, sashimi, grilled chicken, tomato salad, *niku-jaga* (a beef and potato stew) and other local favorites, including my favorite, *fu-wa fu-wa Satsuma-age* (a delicious deep-fried tofu pocket filled with delicate vegetables, originally from Kagoshima). Because menu descriptions are in Japanese, ask a waiter or neighboring diner for help with translations; this is a friendly place. Dishes are generally meant to be shared, so I'd order two dishes per person and go from there. There's a ¥320 snack charge.

Dangam Building, 1–13–1 Hakata-eki Higashi. ☏ **092/481-3456.** Main dishes ¥420–¥680. AE, DC, MC, V. Mon–Sat 5pm–3am. Station: Hakata (1 min). From the station's east Chikushi exit, walk straight ahead, cross the main street, and take the 1st alley left; it's immediately on the right.

Murata (むらた) NOODLES   Across from Hakata Machiya, this traditional eatery specializes in homemade buckwheat noodles, served by a friendly staff to customers sitting at counters made of wood slabs or on *tatami*. Although traditional soba is usually made with 80% buckwheat and 20% wheat, the tasty and delicate *kikouchi* offered here is 100% buckwheat and is served cold with vegetables. The English-lanuage menu also offers the usual soba and udon, which you can order hot or cold and topped with such items as tempura or duck and leek.

2–9–1 Reisen-machi. ☏ **092/291-0894.** Soba ¥600–¥1,750. MC, V (cash only during lunch). Daily 11:30am–8:30pm (closed 2nd Sun of each month). Subway: Gion (exit 2, 4 min.); ¥100 Bus: Okunodo (stop no. 15, 3 min.). Across from Hakata Machiya Folk Museum.

Ume no Hana (梅の花) VEGETARIAN/TOFU   Although located on a busy street, this restful and low-key chain is a world apart, simply decorated in that sparse yet elegant Japanese way and known for its appetizing low-calorie, light vegetarian cuisine. Its English-language menu centers around tofu and vegetables, though some set meals may include fish; for dinner there's also a shabu-shabu set.

Ayasugi Building, 1–15–6 Tenjin. ☏ **092/737-4080.** Set dinners ¥3,100–¥8,000; set lunches ¥1,400–¥2,600. AE, MC, V. Daily 11am–3pm and 5–9pm (last order). Subway: Tenjin (5 min.). ¥100 Bus: Shiyakusho-kita-guchi ACROS Fukuoka-mae (stop no. 10; 1 min.). On Meiji Dori Ave., across from the ACROS building.

Where to Stay

EXPENSIVE

Grand Hyatt Fukuoka ★★★   Fukuoka's top hotel commands a grand setting in the innovative Canal City Hakata, with easy pedestrian access to the city's main sights. Its black-marbled lobby has a curved facade that overlooks the shopping complex, but for guests who desire solitude, the hotel also has its own private roof garden. Service throughout the hotel is superb—along the order of "Your wish is our command." Small but stylish rooms provide views of the private garden or the river and its night scenes. Besides all the luxury, a stay at the Grand Hyatt is fun, with Canal City's many shops and restaurants right outside the door.

1–2–82 Sumiyoshi, Hakata-ku, Fukuoka 812-0018. www.fukuoka.grand.hyatt.com. ☏ **888/591-1234** in the U.S., or 092/282-1234. Fax 092/282-2817. 370 units. ¥28,000–¥31,000 single; ¥34,000–¥43,000 double; from ¥45,000 Grand Club double. AE, DC, MC, V. Station: Hakata (12 min.). ¥100 Bus: Canal City Hakata-mae (stop no. 4; 2 min.). **Amenities:** 3 restaurants, including Aroma's (p. 470); 2 bars; lounge; concierge; executive-level rooms; fitness center and spa w/25m (82-ft.) indoor pool (fee: ¥2,100); room service; Wi-Fi (free, in lobby). *In room:* A/C, TV, hair dryer, Internet, minibar.

A Double or a Twin?

For the sake of convenience, the price for two people in a room is listed as a "double" in this book. Japanese hotels, however, differentiate between rooms with a double bed or two twin beds, usually with different prices. Although most hotels charge more for a twin room, sometimes the opposite is true; if you're looking for a bargain, therefore, be sure to inquire about prices for both. Note, too, that hotels usually have more twin rooms than doubles, for the simple reason that Japanese couples, used to their own futon, traditionally prefer twin beds.

Hakata Miyako Hotel ★　Near Hakata station's east Chikushi Shinkansen exit, this property with the famous Miyako name offers a convenient connection to Fukuoka Airport (just 5 min. via subway) and is close to shops and restaurant complexes. Single rooms are tiny, with no place to unpack a suitcase, but doubles and twins add more space and most rooms have floor-to-ceiling windows that let in plenty of light (though city views are not spectacular). The one disadvantage: Tourist sights are on the west side of the station, so you have to go through the station concourse to reach them.

2–1–1 Hakataeki-higashi, Hakata-ku, Fukuoka 812-0013. www.miyakohotels.ne.jp/hakata. ✆ **092/441-3111.** Fax 092/481-1306. 266 units. ¥12,474 single; ¥21,945–¥25,410 double. AE, DC, MC, V. Station: Hakata (Chikushi exit, 1 min.). **Amenities:** 2 restaurants; bar/lounge; Wi-Fi (free, in lobby). *In room:* A/C, TV, hair dryer, Internet, minibar.

MODERATE

Canal City Fukuoka Washington Hotel 🗲　Though part of a nationwide business-hotel chain, this property has more style: it's located in Canal City Hakata, Fukuoka's number-one shopping-and-entertainment complex, offering convenience right outside the front door. The cheapest singles face the Grand Hyatt above the Canal City complex, while higher-priced and larger singles and all twins and doubles have views outward toward the city. The downside: Its good location makes it popular; you'll find the lobby crowded at check-in and checkout times. At press time, I was told there was a "foreigner discount" to the rates below, so call the hotel directly and ask.

1–2–20 Sumiyoshi, Hakata-ku, Fukuoka 812-0018. www.wh-rsv.com/english. ✆ **092/282-8800.** Fax 092/282-0757. 423 units. ¥7,800–¥10,400 single; ¥15,000–¥19,000 double. Rates ¥1,000 higher per person Fri–Sat and nights before holidays. AE, DC, MC, V. Station: Hakata (10 min.). ¥100 Bus: Canal City Hakata-mae (stop no. 4; 1 min.). **Amenities:** Coffee shop. *In room:* A/C, TV, hair dryer, Internet, minibar.

Dukes Hotel Hakata ★　Flower boxes, plants, and evergreens outside the entrance hint that this is no ordinary hotel. Indeed, it's a reasonably priced hotel with class, with a small but very civilized lobby that exudes charm and invites you to linger among its Chinese vases, palm trees, antiques, and classical music. Most of the rooms, tiny but comfy with a simple decor that suggests an English-style countryside manor, are singles, with only nine twins and nine doubles (though two people can squeeze into a single room for ¥10,185). In the world of cloned business hotels, this establishment is a welcome relief. Farther from Hakata Station but in the heart of the city (4 min. from the Nakasu-kawabata subway stop or Higashi-Nakasu/stop no. 11 of the ¥100 Bus), **Dukes Hotel Nakasu,** 1–1 Nakasunakashima-machi, Hakata-ku (✆ **092/283-2800**), offers the same amenities and style at a cheaper price.

2–3–9 Hakataeki-mae, Hakata-ku, Fukuoka 812-0011. www.dukes-hotel.com. ✆ **092/472-1800.** Fax 092/472-1900. info@dukes-hotel.com. 153 units. ¥8,190–¥9,450 single; ¥12,600–¥13,650 double. AE, DC, MC, V. Station: Hakata (2 min.). From the west (Hakata) exit, take the wide road straight ahead (Hakata Ekimae-dori); it's down this street on your right in the 2nd block. **Amenities:** Restaurant. *In room:* A/C, TV, fridge, hair dryer, Internet.

JR Kyushu Hotel Blossom Fukuoka ★★ ✍

You're forgiven for thinking you've stumbled into the wrong hotel, since recent renovations have elevated this once-boring property into an entirely different place. Two sit-down desks (usually found only in fancy hotels) have replaced the front check-in counter, while the high-ceilinged entryway and lobby impart an Old-World-meets-chic elegance. Rooms, too, are impressively designed, with framed Hakata-ori cloth adorning walls and even stylish phones, but they don't sacrifice comfort either, with focused lights trained on comfortable beds. There's a ladies' floor offering specialized amenities and a laundry room. Holders of JR Rail Passes receive substantial discounts (at last check, singles starting at ¥7,100 and doubles from ¥11,000).

2–2–4 Hakataeki-Higashi, Hakata-ku, Fukuoka 812-0013. www.jrhotelgroup.com. ✆ **092/413-8787.** Fax 092/413-9746. 90 units. ¥10,000–¥12,000 single; ¥17,000–¥30,000. Discount with Japan Rail Pass. AE, DC, MC, V. Station: Hakata (a 2-min. walk from the east Chikushi Shinkansen exit, behind the Miyako Hotel). **Amenities:** Restaurant, lobby computer w/free Internet; Wi-Fi (free, in lobby). *In room:* A/C, TV, fridge, hair dryer, Internet.

INEXPENSIVE

In addition to the choices here, **Toyoko Inn** (www.toyoko-inn.com) has four locations within walking distance of Hakata Station and two near Tenjin Station. As with most Toyoko Inns, they all offer computers in the lobby providing free Internet access, complimentary breakfast, and free Internet or Wi-Fi in small rooms.

Hakata JBB Hotel

In the heart of the city, beside the Hakata Machiya Folk Museum and within easy walking distance of Canal City Hakata, the Asian Art Museum, and other attractions, this is a simple but well-managed establishment, offering free coffee every morning in the lobby (and a microwave and table in case you've brought your own food). Open-air passageways lead to tiny but well-kept rooms complete with toothbrush, shampoo, and pajamas. Beds are semi-double-size and are for single use, but married couples or two women can room together for ¥5,500. You won't find anything in the city center cheaper than this.

6–5–1 Reisen-machi, Hakata-ku, Fukuoka 812-0039. www.jbbhotel.com. ✆ **092/263-8300.** Fax 092/263-8301. 59 units. ¥3,980 single; ¥5,500 double. ¥4,500 and ¥6,000, respectively, on Sat. Sun discount available. No credit cards. Station: Hakata (10 min.). Subway: Gion (exit 2, 4 min.). ¥100 Bus: Okunodo (stop no. 15; 3 min.). **Amenities:** Wi-Fi (free, in lobby). *In room:* A/C, TV, fridge, hair dryer, no phone.

Wafu Ryokan Kashima Honkan ★ 🏠

It comes as something of a surprise to find a traditional inn in the heart of Kyushu's largest city, and an inexpensive one to boot. Housed in a 90-year-old building with a homey atmosphere, an enclosed garden, and rambling hallways leading to simple *tatami* rooms, each one different, it's a good choice for budget-seeking traditionalists. Its convenient location, down the street from the Hakata Machiya Folk Museum, and laundry room, are a bonus.

3–11 Reisen-machi, Hakata-ku, Fukuoka 812-0039. ℂ **092/291-0746.** Fax 092/271-7995. kashima-co@mx7.tiki.ne.jp. 27 units, none with bathroom. ¥4,725 single; ¥8,400 double; ¥1,050 more per person Sat and nights before holidays. Japanese breakfast ¥1,050 or Western breakfast ¥735 extra; dinner ¥3,675 extra. MC, V. Station: Hakata (10 min.). Subway: Gion (exit 2; 4 min.). ¥100 Bus: Okunodo (stop no. 15; 3 min.). **Amenities:** Lobby computers w/free Internet; Wi-Fi (free, in lobby). *In room:* A/C, TV, fridge.

NAGASAKI, WINDOW TO THE WORLD ★★

1,329km (826 miles) SW of Tokyo; 152km (95 miles) SW of Fukuoka

Unlike Kumamoto, Kagoshima, Beppu, and other well-known Kyushu destinations, Nagasaki doesn't have a castle, a famous landscaped garden, or hot-spring spas. Rather, its charm is much more subtle. Many people in Japan—including foreign residents—consider this city one of the country's most beautiful. It's a place of hills rising from the deep, U-shaped harbor with boats and ferries chugging back and forth, of houses perched on terraced slopes, of small streets and distinctive neighborhoods, and of people extremely proud of their hometown. Without a doubt, Nagasaki is one of Japan's most livable cities, despite its population of 443,000 residents. It's also perhaps Japan's most cosmopolitan city, with a unique blend of outside cultures interwoven into its history, architecture, food, and festivals.

Nagasaki, capital of Nagasaki Prefecture and located on the northwest coast of Kyushu, opened its harbor to European vessels in 1571 and became a port of call for Portuguese and Dutch ships; Chinese merchants soon followed and set up their own community. Along with traders came St. Francis Xavier and other Christian missionaries, primarily from Portugal and Spain, who found many converts among the local Japanese. During Japan's more than 200 years of isolation, only Nagasaki was allowed to conduct trade with outsiders and thus served as the nation's window on the rest of the world. Even today, Japanese come to Nagasaki for a dose of the city's intermingled cultures. Its harbor remains one of Japan's most active, with shipbuilding one of its major industries.

All the city's major attractions are connected to its diversified, and sometimes tragic, past. Nagasaki is best known as the second city to be destroyed by an atomic bomb.

Essentials

GETTING THERE   By Plane   JAL and **ANA** serve Nagasaki Airport (NGS; www.nabic.co.jp; ℂ **0957/52-5555**) from Tokyo's Haneda Airport, with a flight time of about 1 hour and 50 minutes. Airport **buses** travel to Nagasaki Station in about 45 minutes for ¥800.

By Train   Trains depart Hakata Station in **Fukuoka** approximately once or twice an hour, arriving at Nagasaki Station about 2 hours later at a cost of ¥4,080 for an unreserved seat. From **Tokyo,** take the Shinkansen bullet train to Hakata Station and transfer there for a train to Nagasaki; travel time is about 7½ to 8½ hours, depending on connections, and the fare is ¥23,930 for an unreserved seat.

By Bus   Buses depart frequently from Fukuoka's Hakata Bus Terminal, arriving at the Nagasaki Station Bus Terminal (across from Nagasaki Station) 2½ hours later and costing ¥2,500. From Osaka, buses depart nightly at 9pm, arriving in Nagasaki at 8:05am.

Nagasaki

Map Legend

- ✝ Church
- ⛩ Shrine
- ✉ Post Office
- ⓘ Tourist Info
- ▬ Railway

NAGASAKI PARK

Suwa Shrine

Honrenji Temple

Ken-ei Bus Station **5**

6

Nagasaki Station

7 **8** Central Post Office

Nishi Nakamachi

City Hall

Umamachi Dori

Nagasaki River

Chamber of Commerce

Imauomachi Dori

GOTO MACHI **9** **10**

Kofukuji Temple **11**

Fukuromachi Dori

KOZEN MACHI

City Hall Street

Manzaimachi Dori

Nakajima Gawa

Megane-bashi **12**

Teramachi Dori

Nagaski Port Terminal

Ohato Dori

Prefecture

Kanko Dori **13**

17

DEJIMA MACHI **14**

Dejima Wharf **15**

Hamanomachi Arcade

16 **16**

Sofukuji Temple **18**

19

20

CHINA TOWN

■ Nagasaki Bus Station

21

■ Nagasaki Prefectural Art Museum

Nagasaki Harbor

MOTOKAGO MACHI

23

22

Oura Gawa

24

26 **25**

27

28

10

KYUSHU | Nagasaki, Window to the World

HOTELS ■

Best Western Premier Hotel Nagasaki **1**
Hotel Majestic **27**
Hotel New Nagasaki **7**
Hotel Wingport Nagasaki **5**
JR Kyushu Hotel Nagasaki **6**
Nagasaki International Hostel Akari **11**
Nagasaki Hotel Monterey **24**
Nishikiso Bekkan **22**
Sakamoto-ya **10**
Toyoko Inn Nagasaki Ekimae **9**
Victoria Inn Nagasaki **16**

RESTAURANTS ◆

Gohan **20**
Harbin **13**
Kagetsu **21**
Red Lantern **15**
Nihonkai Shoya **8**
Shikairo **26**
Shippoku Hamakatsu **19**
Tia **16**
Yossou **17**

ATTRACTIONS ●

Confucius Shrine **25**
Dejima **14**
Glover Garden **28**
Hollanders Slope **23**
Nagasaki Atomic Bomb Museum **2**
Nagasaki Ropeway to Mt. Inasa **4**
Nishizaka Hill **3**
Peace Park (Hirano-machi) **2**
Sofukuji Temple **18**
Spectacles Bridge **12**
Twenty-Six Martyrs Museum **3**

VISITOR INFORMATION The **Nagasaki City Tourist Information Office** (℡ **095/823-3631;** daily 8am–8pm) is located just outside the main ticket gates of Nagasaki Station, to the right in the Seattle's Best coffee shop. It offers a luggage delivery service for ¥200 per bag to many hotels (excluding those within walking distance) daily from 8am to 2pm, allowing you to begin sightseeing right away. Information on Nagasaki is available online at **www.at-nagasaki.jp.** See **www.ngs-kankanren.com/eng** for information on Nagasaki Prefecture, including Unzen.

ORIENTATION Nagasaki is one of Japan's most navigable cities, with lots of English-language signs pointing the way to attractions. City layout follows natural boundaries set by the Urakami River, the long and narrow Nagasaki Bay, and the many steep-sloped hills. **Nagasaki Station,** along with AMU Plaza next door offering shopping and dining options, isn't located in the downtown part of the city. Rather, most nightspots, shops, and restaurants are located southeast of the station, clustered around an area that contains **Shianbashi Dori** and **Kanko Dori streets,** the **Hamano-machi** and **Kanko** covered shopping arcades, a waterfront area called **Dejima Wharf,** and **Chinatown** with Chinese restaurants and souvenir shops. Near the Hamano-machi arcade is the iconic **Spectacles Bridge,** a stone-arched bridge built in 1634 by a Chinese Zen priest and named for the reflection its two arches cast in the water. South of downtown is **Glover Garden,** where many foreigners settled in the 19th century. Nearby is **Hollander Slope** (**Oranda-zaka,** also referred to as Dutch Slope), undoubtedly Nagasaki's prettiest street, a cobbled lane lined with wooden houses built by former European residents (back then, the people of Nagasaki referred to all Europeans as Hollanders). **Peace Park** and its atomic-bomb museum are located north of Nagasaki Station on the other end of town.

GETTING AROUND **By Streetcar** Streetcars have been hauling passengers in Nagasaki since 1915 and have changed little in the ensuing years; they're still the easiest—and most charming—way to get around. Four lines run through the heart of the city, with stops written in English. Because streetcars have their own lanes of traffic here, during rush hour they're usually the fastest on the road. It costs a mere ¥120 (half-price for children) to ride one no matter how far you go; pay at the front when you get off. You are allowed to transfer to another line only at **Tsuki-machi Station** (ask the driver for a transfer ticket, a *norisugi,* when you disembark from the first streetcar); otherwise, you must pay each time you disembark. If you think you'll be riding more than five times in 1 day, you can save a few yen with a ¥500 **pass,** which you must buy in advance at the tourist office or at many hotels, which allows unlimited rides for 1 day. Streetcars run from about 6:15am to 11:30pm.

On Foot With the exception of Peace Park, you can also get around Nagasaki easily on foot, which is certainly the most intimate way to experience the city and its atmosphere. You can walk from the Hamano-machi downtown shopping district to Glover Garden, for example, in 20 minutes, passing Chinatown, Dejima, and Hollander Slope on the way.

By Bike I've been told that many Nagasaki residents never learned how to ride a bike because of the city's hilly terrain. Most tourist destinations, however, lie around the port and are easy to reach by bike. The JR Midori-no-madoguchi office at Nagasaki Station (across from the tourist office) rents six electric bikes. An all-day rental (9am–5pm) costs ¥900 if you have a JR train ticket or rail pass, ¥1,500 if you don't.

[FastFACTS] NAGASAKI

ATM Between Nagasaki Station and AMU Plaza, on the second floor behind Royal Host restaurant, is a CD Corner that accepts international credit cards. It's open Monday to Friday 8am to 9pm, and Saturday, Sunday and holidays from 9am to 7pm.

Internet Access Located in the Hamano-machi covered shopping arcade in the heart of downtown Nagasaki, **Internet** **Café Cybac,** 2–46 Aburaya-machi (℃ **095/818-8050**), open 24 hours, charges a one-time ¥300 fee and then ¥300 for the first 30 minutes, plus ¥100 for each additional 15 minutes.

Exploring the City

NEAR NAGASAKI STATION

Twenty-Six Martyrs Museum ★ MUSEUM   After Nagasaki opened its port to European vessels, missionaries arrived to convert Japanese to Christianity. Gradually, however, the Japanese rulers began to fear that these Christian missionaries would try to exert political and financial influence through their converts. Who was to say that conversion to Christianity wasn't the first step toward colonization? So in 1587, Toyotomi Hideyoshi, ruler of Japan, officially banned Christianity. In 1597, 26 male Christians (20 Japanese and 6 foreigners) were arrested in Kyoto and Osaka, marched 30 days through the snow to Nagasaki, and crucified on **Nishizaka Hill** as examples of what would happen to offenders. Through the ensuing decades, there were more than 600 documented cases of Japanese, Portuguese, and Spanish Christians being put to death in the Nishizaka area. In 1862, the 26 martyrs were canonized by the pope.

Today, Nishizaka Hill is home to the Monument to the 26 Saints, with statues of the martyrs carved in stone relief. Immediately striking is that three of them look very young; indeed, the youngest was only 12. Behind the relief is the Twenty-Six Martyrs Museum housing artifacts relating to the history of Christianity in Japan, including Edo-era decrees prohibiting Christianity, reward notices for those turning in Christians to authorities, religious objects, and information about each of the 26 martyrs, as well as remains of Japanese martyrs returned to Nagasaki in 1995 after more than 380 years of interment in Macau. Perhaps most amazing about the history of Christianity in Japan is that the religion was practiced secretly by the faithful throughout Japan's isolation policy, surviving more than 200 years underground without the benefits of a church or clergy. You'll spend at least 30 minutes here.

7–8 Nishizaka-machi. www.26martyrs.com. ℃ **095/822-6000.** Admission ¥500 adults, ¥300 junior- and high-school students, ¥140 children. Daily 9am–5pm. From Nagasaki Station, cross the main street via the pedestrian bridge and head north; it will be on the right, up a steep hill.

PEACE PARK (HIRANO-MACHI) ★★

On August 9, 1945, at 11:02am, American forces dropped an atomic bomb over Nagasaki, 3 days after they had dropped one on Hiroshima. The bomb, which exploded 480m (1,600 ft.) aboveground, destroyed about a third of the city, killed an estimated 74,000 people, and injured 75,000 more. Today, Peace Park, located north of Nagasaki Station, serves as a reminder of that day of destruction with a museum, memorials, and statues. Nagasaki's citizens are among the most vigorous peace activists in the world; a peace demonstration is held in Peace Park every year on the anniversary of the bombing, along with a declaration for peace by the city mayor.

Near the Nagasaki Atomic Bomb Museum (see below), a black pillar marks the exact epicenter of the atomic blast; a black casket contains names of the bomb's victims. Ironically, the bomb exploded almost directly over the Urakami Catholic Church, built after centuries of persecution in Japan and of which only a fragmented wall remains. A few minutes' walk farther north, separated by several streets, is the largest part of Peace Park (the nearest streetcar station to this section is Matsuyama). It occupies the site of a former prison; all 134 inmates died in the blast. A fountain is dedicated to the wounded who begged for water; many of them died thirsty. Statues donated by countries from around the world line a pathway leading to Peace Statue, a 9m-high (30-ft.) statue of a male deity. One hand points to the sky from where the bomb came (meant as a warning?), and the other hand points to the horizon (representing peace? hope? the future?).

Nagasaki Atomic Bomb Museum ★★★ MUSEUM Visiting this museum, with English-language displays, is by far the most important thing to do in Peace Park. Upon entering, guests circle an empty, glass-dome foyer via a spiraling ramp—bringing to mind, perhaps, the atomic mushroom cloud? This is followed by photographs of the city as it looked before the bomb, accompanied by the ominous, loud ticking of a clock. Displays illustrate events leading up to the bombing, the devastation afterward, the effects of radiation, Nagasaki's postwar restoration, the history of nuclear weapons, and the subsequent peace movement. Objects, photos, and artifacts graphically depict the bomb's devastation, including a clock stopped precisely at 11:02am, personal belongings ranging from mangled spectacles to a student's singed trousers, hand bones encased in a clump of melted glass, and photographs of victims, including a dead mother and her baby and a 14-year-old whose face has been hideously burned. Survivors describe personal experiences on that fateful day. The adjoining Peace Memorial Hall for Atomic Bomb Victims contains a Remembrance Hall, with portraits of those who lost their lives. The museum is by no means pleasant, but something every concerned individual should see. Plan on an hour here, more if you opt for the ¥150 audio guide. (If you've already seen the far more comprehensive Peace Memorial Museum in Hiroshima, this one will be largely repetitive.)

7–8 Hirano-machi. www1.city.nagasaki.nagasaki.jp/peace. © **095/844-1231.** Admission ¥200 adults, ¥100 children. Daily 8:30am–5:30pm (until 6:30pm May–Aug). Streetcar: Hamaguchi-machi (5 min.). Across the street and up the hill.

DOWNTOWN NAGASAKI

Dejima—Site of the Former Factory ★★ MUSEUM When the Tokugawa shogunate adopted a national policy of isolation in the 1630s, only Nagasaki was allowed to remain open as a port of trade with foreigners. Because the Portuguese and Spaniards were associated with the outlawed Christian religion, they were expelled in 1639; only the Dutch and the Chinese were allowed to remain and continue trading. In 1641, all the Dutch (employees of the Dutch East India Company) were confined to a tiny fan-shaped artificial island called Dejima, where they remained for 218 years (at any given time, about 15 Dutchmen were in residence; no wives were allowed). This was Japan's only official contact with the outside world; the director of Dejima was required to travel to Edo every 1 to 4 years to report to the shogun. Otherwise, the only people allowed to cross the bridge into the Dutch community were Japanese prostitutes and traders.

Today, after having become part of the mainland through land reclamation and decades of languishing as little more than a streetcar stop, Dejima is being reborn

Ghostly Battleship Island

Looking like a scene in a novel by Murakami Haruki, Hashima is a deserted island 19km (12 miles) from Nagasaki Port. After coal was discovered around its seabed in 1810, the island expanded as a community, with highrise apartments housing up to 5,300 people, a hospital, school, and even a shrine. In 1974 the coalmine closed and the island was abandoned. In 2010, Yamasa Kaiun Co. harbor cruiseboats (✆ **095/822-5002**) that had long sailed around the island were granted permission to make short landings. The 170-minute trips (in Japanese only, but there's an English pamphlet) depart Nagasaki Port (streetcar: Ohato) twice daily, weather permitting, and cost ¥4,000 plus a ¥300 landing fee. Hashima looms like a warship abandoned at sea, earning it the nickname **Gunkanjima (Battleship Island).**

through an ambitious project to re-create the island as it was in the early 19th century, with more than 15 structures resurrected (a total of 25 are planned). After picking up an English-language brochure and map, you'll be greeted by staff dressed in period clothing as you explore the First Ship Captain's Quarters with furnishings of the period, Head Clerk's Quarters with examples of equipment and knowledge brought to Japan from Europe, a re-created kitchen, and stone warehouses. One warehouse describes Dejima's role in the introduction of Western science and culture to Japan and the export of Japanese gold, silver, and copper, while another displays artifacts excavated on Dejima, including earthenware, pipes, and bones of cows, dogs and other animals kept on the island. Be sure to see the 12-minute video about Dejima's history and daily life (English-language audio phones provided). Plan on about an hour here.

6–3 Dejima-machi. www1.city.nagasaki.nagasaki.jp/dejima. ✆ **095/821-7200.** Admission ¥500 adults, ¥200 high-school students, ¥100 children. Daily 8am–6pm. Streetcar: Dejima (1 min.) or Tsuki-machi (2 min.).

Sofukuji Temple ★ TEMPLE   About a 7-minute walk from the Hamano-machi downtown shopping street, Sofukuji is Nagasaki's most famous temple. Distinctly Chinese with its Ming architecture, it dates back to 1629, when it was founded by Chinese residents. Its Buddha Hall, painted a brilliant red and decorated with Chinese lanterns, was designed and cut in China before transportation to Nagasaki. Erected in 1646, it's the oldest building in Nagasaki and is a National Treasure. Another National Treasure is the temple's beautiful gate, which employs a complex jointing system and features brightly painted detailing. But most fascinating, in my opinion, is the temple's gigantic cauldron, built by a priest during a terrible famine in the 1680s to cook enough porridge to feed more than 3,000 people a day.

7–8 Kayjiya-machi. ✆ **095/823-2645.** Admission ¥300 adults, ¥200 junior-high and high-school students, ¥100 children. Daily 8am–5pm. Streetcar: Shokakuji-shita (4 min.); head back toward the bay, turning right at Sofukuji St.

AROUND GLOVER GARDEN

Confucius Shrine (Koshi-byo) ★ SHRINE   Chinese residents living in Nagasaki built this colorful, red-and-yellow shrine in 1893, aided by the Ch'ing Dynasty in China. This is the only Confucian mausoleum outside China built by the Chinese. In fact, the land upon which it stands belongs to China and is administered by the

Chinese embassy in Tokyo. The main hall contains a statue of Confucius, attended by courtyard statues representing his 72 disciples. Behind the main hall is the small Museum of Chinese History with a changing exhibit of bronze jars, ceramics, jade and ivory carvings, and other treasures on loan from Beijing's National Museum of Chinese History and Beijing Palace's Museum of Historical Treasures. You can see everything in a half-hour.

10–36 Oura-machi. ⓒ **095/824-4022.** Admission ¥600 adults, ¥400 high-school students, ¥300 children. Daily 8:30am–5:30pm. Streetcar: Oura Tenshodo-shita (3 min.). Walk inland (continuing in the same direction as your streetcar if coming from downtown), and turn left when you reach a small playground on your right near Hollander Slope.

Glover Garden ★★ ICON   After Japan opened its doors to the rest of the world and established Nagasaki as one of a handful of international ports, Nagasaki emerged as one of the most progressive cities in the country, with many foreign residents. A number of Western-style houses were built during the Meiji Period (1868–1912), many of them on a hill overlooking Nagasaki and the harbor. Today, that hill has been developed into Glover Garden, which showcases nine Meiji-Era buildings and homes on lushly landscaped grounds. Some of the structures stand on their original site; others have been moved here. The stone-and-clapboard houses have sweeping verandas, Western parlors, the most modern conveniences of the time, and Japanese-style roofs. Most famous is **Glover Mansion,** Japan's oldest Western-style house, built in this location in 1863 and romanticized as the home of Madame Butterfly, the fictitious, tragic heroine of Puccini's opera. Married to a Japanese woman (and much more faithful than his Puccini counterpart), Thomas Glover was a remarkable Scotsman who, among other things, financially backed and managed ship-repair yards in Nagasaki, brought the first steam locomotive to Japan, sold guns and ships, and exported tea. The **Ringer House,** dating from the early Meiji Period, contains a display of photos, clothes, and artifacts of Kiba Teiko, a Japanese opera singer who played Madame Butterfly.

Among other buildings, a former boys' academy houses photographs of Glover and his family, while the Mitsubishi Dock House, built in 1896 to serve as a rest house for ship crews, offers great views of the harbor. One of Nagasaki's first Western

 A View from the Top

The best panoramic view of Nagasaki is from atop 330m (1,090-ft.) Mount Inasa, which you can reach in 7 minutes from Nagasaki Station by taking bus no. 3 or 4 to the Ropeway-mae stop (fare: ¥150) or one of the free evening shuttle buses (get the schedule at the tourist office). A 2-minute walk from the bus stop is Fuchi Shrine, where believers come to pray for a good marriage, safe childbirth, and academic success. Beside the shrine is the Nagasaki Ropeway (www.nagasaki-ropeway.jp; ⓒ **095/861-3640;** daily 9am–10pm), which delivers you to the top of Mount Inasa in 5 minutes (round-trip fare: ¥1,200 adults, ¥900 junior-high and high-school students, ¥600 children). A hilltop observation deck provides 360-degree panoramic views; we recommend you arrive before sunset and stay for the zillion twinkling lights. To make the most out of your trip, consider dining at **Hikari** (ⓒ **095/862-1050;** daily 11am–9pm), a restaurant with great views offering a champon set (¥1,400), curry rice, and other inexpensive fare (see "Where to Eat," below, for information on champon).

restaurants, the Jiyu-Tei, is now a quaint cafe. Don't miss the **Nagasaki Traditional Performing Arts Museum,** which displays floats and dragons used in Nagasaki's most famous festival, the Okunchi Festival, held in October. The museum's highlight is an excellent film of the colorful parade, featuring massive ships deftly maneuvered on wheels and Chinese dragon dances. At any rate, views from Glover Garden of the harbor are among the best in the city. Plan on spending about 1 hour here.

8–1 Minami Yamate-machi. www.glover-garden.jp. © **095/822-8223.** Admission ¥600 adults, ¥300 high-school students, ¥180 children. Daily 8am–6pm (to 9:30pm Golden Week and mid-July to mid-Oct). Streetcar: Oura Tenshudo-shita (7 min.); cross the bridge, turn left after the ANA Hotel Nagasaki Glover Hill, and walk uphill, following the signs.

A Side Trip to Huis Ten Bosch ★★★

If you're ready for some R & R from your travels in Japan but have only 1 day to spare, perhaps **Huis Ten Bosch,** in Sasebo (www.huistenbosch.co.jp; © **0956/27-0546**), will do the trick. This replica of a 17th-century Dutch village boasts tree-lined canals, brick houses, city squares, brick-paved roads, churches, museums, shops, restaurants, hotels, gardens, and even stately private homes—proof at how adept Japanese are at imitation. Most of the buildings are faithful reproductions of originals back in the Netherlands; even the bricks were imported from Holland. Although I was a bit skeptical about visiting an imitation Dutch village in Japan, I must admit that the grounds and craftsmanship are beautifully done (Huis Ten Bosch is also environmentally conscious, with its own desalination and sewage treatment plants; it also generates much of its own energy). Even Holland itself isn't this pristine. In fact, I consider this the country's premier theme park designed for adults. Although there are some rides and attractions, this is not an amusement park in disguise.

Highlights include **Palace Huis Ten Bosch,** a replica of the formal residence of Queen Beatrix of the Netherlands, which boasts an art gallery, period rooms showing how upper-class Dutch lived, and a baroque garden; **museums** with collections of porcelain, ornamental glass, teddy bears, and trick art; the **Thriller Fantasy Museum** horror house; and **theaters** that re-create the flooding of a Dutch town, introduce M. C. Escher's works with a 3-D film, and show a movie in which the audience is the cast (each visitor's face is scanned and instantly digitalized using computer processing). There are also cruises of the village's canals; parades, dances, concerts, and other events; more than 50 shops; and more than 40 restaurants (including beer and wine gardens). The park is so vast there are shuttle buses and other forms of transportation, but to really feel like you're in Holland, rent a bicycle (¥1,000 for 3 hr.).

A 1-day Toku-Toku passport ticket to Huis Ten Bosch and its attractions costs ¥5,400 for adults, ¥4,400 for children 12 to 17, and ¥3,400 for children 4 to 11 (3 and under are free). The best time to visit is spring, during—what else?—tulip season. Open daily 9 or 10am to 9 or 10pm, depending on the season and day of the week. To reach Huis Ten Bosch, take the **JR Sea Side Liner Express** from Nagasaki Station to Huis Ten Bosch Station (about 1 hr. and 20 min.); trains depart approximately every hour and cost ¥1,430 one-way.

Where to Eat

Nagasaki's most famous food, called *shippoku,* is actually an entire meal of various courses with Chinese, European, and Japanese influences. It's a feast generally shared by a group of four or more and includes such dishes as fish soup, sashimi, and fried, boiled, and seasonal delicacies from land and sea. Other local specialties are **champon,** a Chinese noodle usually served in soup with meat, seafood, and vegetables, and **sara udon,** a plate of thick or thin noodles with cabbage, bean sprouts, pork, and more.

Nagasaki's nightlife district centers on a small area south of Hamano-machi known as **Shianbashi,** which begins just off the streetcar stop of the same name and is easily recognizable by the neon arch that stretches over the entrance of a street called Shianbashi Dori. Shianbashi shimmers with the lights of various drinking establishments and *yakitori-ya,* which are often the cheapest places to go for a light dinner. Another good hunting ground for restaurants is **Chinatown;** although smaller than those in Yokohama and Kobe, it's just the tip of the iceberg of Nagasaki's highly visible Chinese heritage.

EXPENSIVE

Kagetsu (花月) ★★★ 🍴 SHIPPOKU/KAISEKI   This traditional restaurant is the ultimate Japanese dining experience, an oasis of dignified old Japan, where kimono-clad waitresses shuffle down wooden corridors and serve guests seasonal exquisite dishes in *tatami* rooms. First established in 1642 and formerly a geisha house, Kagetsu is one of Japan's longest-running restaurants; the oldest part of the present wooden building is about 200 years old. Display cases exhibit treasures related to Kagetsu's history. Behind the restaurant, which is set back from the road, is a beautiful 250-year-old garden. I'll never forget my evening stroll here as a half-moon rose above gnarled, stunted pines. The back of the restaurant, consisting mainly of glass, was lit up, so I could see into a multitude of private tatami rooms all on different levels. It was like a woodblock print suddenly sprung to life. There must be at least two of you if you want to feast on *shippoku* or *kaiseki.*

2–1 Maruyama-machi. ☏ **095/822-0191.** Reservations required at least a day (a week is better) in advance. Lunch obento (available only weekdays) ¥5,200; shippoku set lunch ¥10,080; shippoku or kaiseki set meals ¥13,860–¥18,900. AE, DC, MC, V. Daily noon–3pm and 6–10pm (last order). Closed irregularly. Streetcar: Shianbashi (3 min.). Head under the neon arch of a bridge onto Shianbashi Dori, continue straight, and then take the road btw. the cute *koban* police box and small Maruyama park; it's straight ahead where the street ends, with the traditional gate.

MODERATE

Gohan (御飯) ★★ ORIGINAL JAPANESE   The English-speaking owner-chef here is a musician, so you'll hear interesting music as you dine on creative, original meals. The interior of this restaurant is authentically old; salvaged beams and pieces from five different houses were given new lives here. Only set meals are served, which change daily and may include such items as sashimi, new potato with sesame seed, grilled fish with soy sauce and ginger, tofu, soup, and rice. The dishes themselves are by a talented local potter of some renown. This place is so tiny, you'll feel like a local insider dining here.

2–32 Aburayamachi. ☏ **095/825-3600.** Set dinners ¥4,200–¥6,300. No credit cards. Mon–Sat 6pm–midnight (last order 9pm). Streetcar: Shokakujishita (1 min.). Walk 1 block down Sofukuji-dori toward the temple and take the 1st left; it's the 2nd building on your right with the name on the *noren* (short curtains hung outside a shop or restaurant to signify it is open)—look carefully, it's easy to miss.

Harbin ★★ FRENCH/RUSSIAN   Established in 1959, Harbin is a Nagasaki tradition. Its owner was born in Manchuria and named his restaurant after Harbin, a town close to his birthplace that was once an international city of Russian, Chinese, and Japanese residents. His family-run restaurant serves a unique blend of French and Russian cuisine, due to his French-trained chef son, who brought his own interpretations to the menu. A small, unpretentious-looking establishment, it offers a menu written in Japanese, English, and Russian offering dishes like fried chicken Kiev style, Georgian spicy lamb pot, and roasted French duck in a red currant sauce, along with homemade sausages and bread. The *coulibiac* (traditional Russian salmon pie), when available, is perhaps the best thing on the menu, but Russian customers never pass up the pork jelly.

4–13 Yorosujamachi, 2nd floor. ℂ **095/824-6650.** Main dishes ¥1,575–¥3,625; set meals ¥3,675–¥6,300; set lunches ¥1,050–¥3,150. No credit cards. Daily 11:30am–2pm and 5:30–10pm (last order). Closed some Wed. Streetcar: Kanko Dori. Walk straight through Kanko Dori covered shopping arcade (which bisects Hamano-machi arcade) to the 3rd block; it's on the left, above a Doutour coffee shop.

Nihonkai Shoya (日本海正や) SUSHI/LOCAL SPECIALTIES   This down-home restaurant specializes in dishes from Kyushu and Okinawa, with an evening a-la-carte menu showing pictures of dishes commonly served in a local *izakaya* (Japanese-style pub). There's ramen and *gyoza* (dumplings) from Fukuoka, *Satsuma-age* (fried fishcakes) from Kagoshima, *basashi* (raw horsemeat) and *karashi renkon* (deep-fried lotus root) from Kumamoto, *sara udon* from Nagasaki, and *goya* champon (champon with bittermelon) from Okinawa, along with regular fare like sashimi, *niku-jaga* (beef and potato stew), and *kushiyaki* (skewered meats). My ¥1,000 lunch consisted of sashimi, tempura, soup, rice, and *chawan-mushi* (egg custard).

10–10 Daikoku-machi. ℂ **095/818-6731.** Main dishes ¥470–¥800; set lunches ¥720–¥1,500. AE, DC, MC, V. Daily 11:30am–2pm and 5–11:30pm (last order). Station: Nagasaki (1 min.). Over the pedestrian bridge and across from New Nagasaki Hotel; look for its blue sign with a fish.

Shikairo (四海楼) ★★ CHAMPON   If you're interested in eating *champo*, this is the Chinese restaurant that claims to have invented it. First opened in 1899, it occupies a five-story modern building, with two red pillars and other hints of Chinese-influenced architecture, not far from Glover Garden. Unless you've made a reservation for a private room, take the elevator to the fifth floor, where you'll be treated to great harbor views and delicious food (be sure to dine at off-peak hours to snag a table with the best views). The English-language menu, complete with pictures, offers several champon set meals (including one for ¥1,470 that also includes *gyoza*, rice, and pickled vegetables, available all day), along with dishes like shredded and braised meats wrapped in lettuce and *sara udon*. After eating, stop by the restaurant's free museum on the second floor, where displays depict the restaurant's history.

4–5 Matsugae-machi. ℂ **095/822-1296.** Main dishes ¥997–¥1,985; set meals ¥1,470–¥3,150. AE, DC, MC, V. Daily 11:30am–3pm and 5–8pm (last order). Streetcar: Oura Tenshudo-shita (1 min.).

Shippoku Hamakatsu (卓袱浜勝) SHIPPOKU   This modern, elegant restaurant, just a minute's walk from the Hamano-machi covered shopping arcade, is one of Nagasaki's best-known *shippoku* restaurants. The ground floor, with Western-style table seating, is made private with alcoves and bamboo screens; upstairs is a large *tatami* room with individual low tables and seat cushions. It offers shippoku set meals for lone diners for both lunch and dinner (¥2,940), making it a good place to try this unique cuisine if you're alone. The English-language menu, with photos, also shows more extensive set meals for parties of two or more.

6–50 Kajiya-machi. www.shippoku.co.jp. $\mathcal{C}$ **095/826-8321.** Dinner shippoku set meals ¥2,940–¥10,500; set lunches ¥1,000–¥2,940. AE, DC, MC, V. Daily 11:30am–8:30pm (last order). Streetcar: Shianbashi (4 min.). Walk under the arch with the clock and take the 2nd right; it's in the middle of the block on the left (look for a black facade and a lattice door).

Yossou (吉宗) ★★ VARIED JAPANESE   The scene at this 145-year-old restaurant is timeless. After taking off your shoes at the entrance, you'll be led upstairs to a large, old tatami room (more picturesque than the ground-floor dining room), where you then dine on set meals of tempura, unagi (grilled eel), *kakuni* (braised pork), or mini-shippoku (the Japanese menu has photographs). But the real reason everyone comes is for its specialty, *chawan-mushi*, a piping hot egg custard topped with pork, eel, shrimp, fish cake and mushroom, served with most of the restaurant's set meals.

8–9 Hamano-machi. $\mathcal{C}$ **095/821-0001.** Set meals ¥1,260–¥3,150; set lunch ¥1,050. AE, MC, V. Daily 11am–8pm (last order). Streetcar: Kanko Dori. Walk down the Kanko Dori covered shopping arcade, taking the next right after passing the bisecting Hamano-machi covered arcade; it's on the right, in a traditional building with red lanterns.

INEXPENSIVE

Red Lantern 🍴 LOCAL SPECIALTIES/CHINESE   On a fine summer's evening, one of the most picturesque places for a meal is at an outside table at Dejima Wharf, a complex of restaurants and bars strung along a boardwalk near the Dejima historic district, where you have a view of the harbor and city lights. Its Japanese menu, with pictures of some of its dishes, includes dim sum (like spring rolls and shrimp dumplings), *mapa tofu* (tofu and minced pork in a spicy chili sauce), champon, sara udon, and a delicious *pari-pari wafu-wafu* salad, which comes with crispy-thin noodles, deepfried lotus, pork, shrimp, and other goodies (and is big enough for two to share). With its delicious local fare, generous servings, great atmosphere, and reasonable prices, it's a popular choice for locals and tourists alike.

Dejima Wharf, 1–1 Dejima. $\mathcal{C}$ **095/829-0475.** Main dishes ¥700–¥1,800; set dinner ¥2,900; set lunches ¥700–¥850. AE, MC, V. Tues–Sun 11:30am–2:30pm and 5:30–10pm (last order). Streetcar: Dejima (2 min.).

Tia (ティア) ★ ORGANIC JAPANESE BUFFET   This restaurant's name ("aunt" in Spanish) reflects the homey atmosphere and home-cooked food your aunt might serve. With about 30 organic dishes, from fish and pork to brown rice, tofu and vegetables, there's enough variety to please everyone. In a rustic room with wooden tables, this restaurant has a diverse clientele and is very popular for lunch; if you're into speed eating, you can opt for a 30-minute buffet time limit for ¥800. Or, if you like beer, wine, or *nihonshu* (sake), go for the all-you-can-drink dinner buffet.

Victoria Inn, 6–24 Doza-machi. $\mathcal{C}$ **095/828-1234.** Buffet dinner ¥1,600; ¥3,500 all-you-can-drink dinner buffet; obento lunch box ¥650; lunch buffet ¥1,300. AE, DC, MC, V. Daily 11:30am–3pm and 6–9pm. Streetcar: Kanko Dori (1 min.). Take the side street with the dragon over it (entrance to China Town); it's almost immediately on your left, on the second floor.

Where to Stay

Nagasaki has reasonably priced hotels, but keep in mind that some accommodations may raise their rates during peak times, which are Golden Week (Apr 29–May 5), Obon (mid-Aug), the Okunchi Festival (Oct 7–9), and the Lantern Festival (Chinese New Year, which changes annually).

EXPENSIVE

Best Western Premier Hotel Nagasaki ★★★ One of Nagasaki's finest hotels, the Best Western's marbled lobby, decorated with large Oriental vases, has a distinct Asian flair. Good-size rooms offer the usual comforts, though business travelers should take note that two upholstered chairs and a small table take the place of a desk. One floor is reserved for women, with higher-grade sheets and towels, bathrobes, and toiletries geared toward female travelers. There are only three single rooms in the hotel, though discounts are given for single use of twins and doubles. Rooms on the 14th Sky Floor, with so-called Hollywood twins (two singles pushed together) or double beds, have the best views (ask for a room facing the port). Or, visit the 15th-floor buffet restaurant or bar for panoramic vistas.

2–26 Takara-machi, Nagasaki 850-0045. www.bestwestern.co.jp/nagasaki. ⓒ **800/528-1234** in the U.S. and Canada, or 095/821-1111. Fax 095/823-4309. 181 units. ¥15,000–¥18,000 single; ¥23,000–¥35,000 double. AE, DC, MC, V. Streetcar: Takara-machi (1 min.); or, from Nagasaki Station, turn left and walk north 8 min. **Amenities:** 4 restaurants; bar; lounge; beer hall (summer only); babysitting; Japanese roof garden; room service; Wi-Fi (free, in lobby). *In room:* A/C, TV, fridge, hair dryer, Internet.

Hotel Majestic ★★ 🎁 The Majestic is a small, charming, quiet hotel. The beautifully appointed rooms are decorated in different themes; the country-living room, for example, sports wooden floors, light-oak furnishings, and claw-foot bathtubs. However, there are no singles, the cheapest twins offer no views, and even more expensive rooms overlook a parking lot toward views of the harbor, glimpsed between buildings (best are the ten superior twins with small balconies and larger-than-average bathrooms.). No matter. The best things about this getaway are its small size—which means no tour-bus groups in the lobby—and its great location near Glover Garden. Its cozy, European-style restaurant/bar will make you feel at home.

2–28 Minami Yamate-machi, Nagasaki 850-0931. ⓒ **095/827-7777.** Fax 095/827-6112. 23 units. ¥21,945–¥31,185 double. AE, DC, MC, V. Streetcar: 1 to Tsuki-machi, then 5 to Oura Tenshudo-shita (2 min.); cross the bridge and walk straight past the ANA Hotel Nagasaki Glover Hill. **Amenities:** Restaurant; bar. *In room:* A/C, TV, minibar.

Hotel New Nagasaki ★★ The deluxe New Nagasaki beats Best Western in location, right next to the train station. Its rooms are among the city's largest, with some offering great views of Nagasaki's busy port and Mount Inasa. Add the hotel's helpful staff, souvenir shop offering local specialties, and restaurants serving Japanese, Chinese, and Western food, and you have what amounts to one of Nagasaki's best choices. The huge, marbled lobby, however, can be crowded and noisy.

14–5 Daikoku-machi, Nagasaki 850-0057. www.newnaga.com. ⓒ **095/826-8000.** Fax 095/823-2000. 130 units. ¥27,300 double; ¥34,650 executive double. Rates exclude service charge. AE, DC, MC, V. Station: Nagasaki (1 min., to the right). **Amenities:** 3 restaurants; bar; executive-level rooms; room service; business center computer w/free Internet. *In room:* A/C, TV, hair dryer, minibar, Wi-Fi.

Sakamoto-ya (坂本屋) ★★★ 🎁 This beautiful 118-year-old *ryokan* (Nagasaki's oldest) right in the heart of the city is a wonderful place, especially when you consider how rare traditional ryokan are nowadays in major Japanese cities. Most of the rooms, which are named after plants, flowers, and trees, have a Japanese-style bathtub made of wood, as well as traditional artwork on the walls. The best room is *Matsu No Ma* (Pine Room), which even has its own miniature garden with a tiny shrine. Rates vary according to the room and the meals served; you may opt for the *shippoku* dinner, a Nagasaki specialty consisting of a variety of dishes showing European and Chinese influences. Western breakfasts are also served on request.

2–13 Kanaya-machi, Nagasaki 850-0037. © **095/826-8211.** Fax 095/825-5944. 10 units. ¥15,750–¥31,100 per person. Rates include breakfast and dinner. AE, DC, MC, V. Station: Nagasaki (9 min.). Take the streetcar or turn right out of the station and follow the streetcar tracks south to the 1st streetcar stop (Goto-machi); take the road between Shinwa Bank and a Toyota dealer and follow it as it curves uphill to the right; it's ahead at the end of the 2nd block, on a corner. **Amenities:** Restaurant. *In room:* A/C, TV, minibar.

MODERATE

JR Kyushu Hotel Nagasaki 🍴   You can't get closer to Nagasaki Station than this business hotel on the station's second floor; those traveling with a Japan Rail Pass will also profit from a discount. Otherwise, rooms are your basic boxes, with alcoves serving as closets and small bathrooms. Try to get a room on a high floor facing the train tracks and the port. Those wishing to avoid any quality time in their rooms might take advantage of adjoining Amu Plaza's many shops and restaurants (the hotel's Royal Host coffee shop is also a good bet for breakfast).

1–1 Onoue-machi, Nagasaki 850-0058. www.jrhotelgroup.com. © **095/832-8000.** Fax 095/832-8001. 144 units. ¥6,900 single; ¥12,600 double. 10% discount with Japan Rail Pass. AE, DC, MC, V. **Amenities:** Coffee shop; lobby computer w/ free Internet. *In room:* A/C, TV, fridge, hair dryer, Internet.

Nagasaki Hotel Monterey ★   Step into old Portugal in this whimsical place complete with whitewashed walls, imported tiles, a small chapel with decorations imported from Portugal, and a restaurant with courtyard seating. There's even a kerosene lamp museum on hotel premises, free to hotel guests. Popular with young women, the hotel fits the historic past of Nagasaki and is conveniently located at the bottom of Hollander Slope. Rooms, too, give hints of Portugal with terra-cotta-colored floor tiles, dark-wood or painted furniture, and, in fancier rooms, shuttered windows.

1–22 Oura-machi, Nagasaki 850-0918. www.hotelmonterey.co.jp. © **095/827-7111.** Fax 095/820-7017. 123 units. ¥12,000–¥12,500 single; ¥16,500–¥37,500 double. AE, DC, MC, V. Streetcar: 1 to Tsuki-machi, then 5 to Oura Kaigan Dori (1 min.); walk inland. **Amenities:** Restaurant; café. *In room:* A/C, TV, fridge, hair dryer, Internet.

Victoria Inn Nagasaki ★★ 📷   Right in the heart of the city, this small hotel has an intimate lobby that resembles a rich merchant's home in old Nagasaki rather than a place to check in. Beds are at least double-size (some are even queen-size or king-size), but note that some of the cheapest singles and doubles face a wall 3m (10 ft.) away; if you're claustrophobic, specify a room with an outdoor view. One of the best things about this hotel is its convenient location, near Chinatown and just a stone's throw from the Hamano-machi shopping arcade and nightlife. You can walk to many sites, including Glover Mansion, Dejima, and Sofukuji Temple. We also like its buffet restaurant specializing in seasonal organic dishes.

6–24 Doza-machi, Nagasaki 850-0841. www.victoria-inn.jp. © **095/828-1234.** Fax 095/828-0178. 87 units. ¥11,000–¥12,500 single; ¥13,500–¥20,000 double. AE, DC, MC, V. Streetcar: Kanko Dori (1 min.). The hotel is across from the streetcar stop, behind a building; look for its sign. **Amenities:** Restaurant (Tia, p. 484); bar; room service; Wi-Fi (free, in lobby). *In room:* A/C, TV, hair dryer, Internet, minibar.

INEXPENSIVE

In addition to the choices below, the **Toyoko Inn Nagasaki Ekimae,** 5–45 Goto-machi (www.toyoko-inn.com; (© **095/825-1045**), is a 6-minute walk south of Nagasaki station. It offers small singles starting at ¥5,480 and doubles at ¥7,980, plus lobby computers with free Internet access and free Japanese breakfast.

Hotel Cuore Nagasaki Ekimae (ホテルクオレ長崎駅前)   This business hotel is popular with female tourists as well, who even have their own top floor with key-card access, different amenities, and, from front rooms, views of Mount Inasa. Rooms are tiny but spotless, with white walls and window panels that can be closed for complete darkness.

7–3 Daikoku-machi, Nagasaki 850-0057. © **095/818-9000.** Fax 095/818-9006. 161 units. ¥6,300–¥6,800 single; ¥8,000–¥12,000 double. AE, DC, MC, V. Station: Nagasaki (1 min.). Across from the station, via pedestrian overpass. **Amenities:** Lobby computer w/free Internet; Wi-Fi (free, in lobby). *In room:* A/C, TV, fridge, hair dryer, Internet.

Nagasaki International Hostel Akari ★★ 🎒   With the best prices in central Nagasaki, this family-owned, nonsmoking establishment near temples and the land-mark Spectacles Bridge is run by a friendly, English-speaking young couple, who provide more than just a bed, including a warm welcome. Bonuses include the hos-tel's own guide map, a bulletin board posting information, free tea and coffee in the communal kitchen, and free daily "Short Walks with Nagasaki Locals," led by volun-teers wishing to meet foreigners. Rooms (doubles, twins, and triples) have *tatami* floors but are outfitted with beds. There are also two dormitory rooms on the 4th floor (no elevator), one with bunk beds sleeping four people and the other sleeping eight.

2–2 Kojiyamachi, Nagasaki 850-0871. www.nagasaki-hostel.com. © **095/801-7900.** 11 units (9 with bathroom). ¥5,900–¥6,500 double; ¥8,700–¥9,000 triple; ¥2,500–¥2,900 per person in dormitory. MC, V. Streetcar: Kokaido-mae (2 min.). Walk straight ahead on the road without tram tracks, cross the river and turn left; it will be on the right. **Amenities:** Communal room w/free Wi-Fi and com-puters w/free Internet; kitchen; library. *In room:* A/C, no phone.

Nishikiso Bekkan   This Japanese inn, managed by the same friendly family for 50 years, has a comfortable, lived-in atmosphere. Its simple *tatami* rooms have chairs for relaxing and vary in price depending on size and view, with the best views over rooftops from the *ryokan*'s hilltop location. It's located near the Hamano-machi shop-ping arcade in the heart of the city.

1–2–7 Nishikoshima, Nagasaki 850-0837. © **095/826-6371.** Fax 095/828-0782. 11 units, 6 with bathroom. ¥4,200–¥5,250 per person. Breakfast ¥750 extra; dinner ¥3,675 extra. AE, DC, MC, V. Streetcar: Shianbashi (4 min.). Head under the neon arch on the right onto Shianbashi Dori, turn right at the cute *koban* police box, walk 1 block past Maruyama Park and turn left; it will be on your right up a flight of stone steps. *In room:* A/C, TV, minibar.

UNZEN SPA & ITS HELLS ★★

66km (41 miles) SE of Nagasaki

Unzen Spa is a small hot-spring resort town located about 700m (2,300 ft.) above sea level in the pine-covered hills of the Shimabara Peninsula. Thanks to its high altitude, cool mountain air, great scenery, and hot sulfur springs, Unzen became popular in the 1890s as a summer resort for American and European visitors, who came from as far away as Shanghai, Hong Kong, Harbin, and Singapore to escape the oppressively humid summers. They arrived in Unzen by bamboo palanquin from

Obama, 11km (6¾ miles) away. In 1911, Unzen became the first prefectural park in Japan. In 1934, the area became **Unzen-Amakusa National Park ★★**, one of the nation's first national parks, covering 282 sq. km (113 sq. miles). In 2009, it became part of the new **Unzen Volcanic Area Geopark,** which covers the entire Shimabara Peninsula.

I like Unzen Spa because it's small and navigable. It consists basically of just a few streets with hotels and *ryokan* spread along them, a welcome relief if you've been spending hectic weeks rushing through big cities and catching buses and trains. Hiking paths wind into the tree-covered hills, and dense clouds of steam arise from solfataras (vents) and fumaroles, evidence of volcanic activity. For visitors, the best result of all that thermal activity is the abundance of hot springs: Unzen's name derives from *"Onsen,"* meaning "hot spring."

Essentials

GETTING THERE The only way to get to Unzen via public transportation is by bus. From Nagasaki, buses depart three times a day (at 9am, 1pm, and 4pm) from the Ken-ei Bus Terminal (📞 **095/826-6221**) across the street from Nagasaki Station (sit on the right side of the bus for the most panoramic views). The ride takes about 1 hour and 40 minutes and costs ¥1,900. If you have a rail pass, save money by taking the train from Nagasaki to Isahaya Station, where at the nearby Shimatetsu Bus Center (📞 **0957/22-4091**) you can catch one of 10 buses a day to Unzen at a cost of ¥1,300 for the 80-minute trip. Ask for bus and train schedules at the tourist information counter at Nagasaki Station. By the way, both these buses pass through Obama, which flew flags commemorating US President Obama after his 2008 election win.

You can also reach Unzen from Kumamoto. From Kumamoto Port (which you can reach in 25 min. by bus from Kumamoto Station for ¥420), take the Kyushu Ferry (📞 **096/326-6111;** 1 hr.) for ¥680 or the faster 30-minute Ocean Arrow Kumamoto Ferry (📞 **0957/63-8008**) for ¥800 to Shimabara Port, where you can catch a bus to Unzen, which takes an another 40 minutes and costs ¥730.

VISITOR INFORMATION The **Unzen Tourist Association** (www.unzen.org; 📞 **0957/73-3434;** daily 9am–5pm), is located in the heart of Unzen next to the Unzen Spa House and across from the police station (bus stop: Nishi-Iriguchi). Not much English is spoken, but it has a good English-language map of Unzen and rents English-language low-tech audio guides for ¥200 per day that cover different areas of Unzen and the national park. Most useful is The Talking Guide to Unzen A, which covers 41 sights in and around town, including the Hells where you can hear about murder and intrigue, how to extend your life, and the optimal spot for getting rid of jealousy. Guide B provides commentary on the Hells and the trip to Nita Pass, while C and D are farther afield for people with cars. You should also stop by the octagonal-shaped **Unzen Visitor Center (Unzen Oyama-no-Johokan;** 📞 **0957/73-3636;** Fri–Wed 9am–5pm), with displays and brochures on the national park for those interested in bird watching, flora, and hiking.

GETTING AROUND Buses from Nagasaki make several stops in Unzen before terminating at Unzen's Shimatetsu Bus Center (📞 **0957/73-3366**), so let the bus driver know where you're staying. I've provided the bus-stop name for accommodations, but otherwise, Unzen is so small you can walk from one end to the other in about 20 minutes. Buses from Kumamoto go only to the Bus Center.

[FastFACTS]UNZEN

Internet Access   **Kaseya Café,** near Shimatetsu Bus Center (*©* **0957/73-3321**; Thurs–Tues 7am–6pm), has a computer you can use for ¥100 for 10 minutes; or purchase a drink or sandwich, and you can use it or Wi-Fi for free.

What to See & Do

When the area around Unzen Spa was designated a national park in 1934, it was named after what was thought to be an extinct volcanic chain, collectively called Mount Unzen. In 1990, however, a peak in Mount Unzen—Mount Fugen—erupted for the first time in almost 200 years, killing several dozen people on its eastern slope and leaving behind a huge lava dome. Unzen Spa, on the opposite side, was untouched and remains the area's most popular resort town.

THE HELLS (JIGOKU)   Unzen Spa literally bubbles with activity, as sulfurous hot springs erupt into surface cauldrons of scalding water in an area known as the Hells (Jigoku). Indeed, in the 1600s, these cauldrons were used for hellish punishment, as some 30 Christians were boiled alive here after Christianity was outlawed in Japan. Today, Unzen Spa has more than 30 solfataras and fumaroles, with the Hells providing the greatest show of geothermal activity, making this spot Unzen's number-one attraction. It's a favorite hangout of huge black ravens, and the barren land has been baked a chalky white through the centuries. Pathways lead through the hot-spring Hells, where sulfur vapors rise thickly to veil pine trees on surrounding hills. A simple cross erected on stones serves as a memorial to the Christians killed here. A kiosk sells eggs boiled in the hot springs (¥200 for 2); it's said that if you eat one, you'll live three years longer.

TAKING THE WATERS   On the main street of Unzen are a finger spa and two foot spas, where you can soak the appropriate appendages in outdoor baths for free. If you'd like to get more than your feet wet (though all accommodations below offer hot-spring baths), the **Unzen Spa House,** across from the Unzen Kanko Hotel (*©* **0957/73-3131**), is open Monday to Saturday 10am to 6pm; on Sundays and holidays (including summer school vacation from mid-July through Aug), it's open to 7pm. Indoor cypress baths and *rotenburo* (outdoor hot-spring baths) cost ¥800. In the Spa House is also the impressive **Vidro Museum ★** (daily 9am–6pm), with Edo-Era Nagasaki glass and Bohemian, Italian, French, and other glassware. Admission here is ¥700; or, buy a ticket for the spa and museum for ¥1,100.

FARTHER AFIELD ★   If you feel like taking an excursion, head for Mount Fugen, Unzen's most popular destination outside Unzen Spa. To reach it, make reservations for a shared taxi with Heisei Kanko Taxi (*©* **0975/73-2010**), which departs Unzen three times a day for **Nita Pass,** about a 23-minute ride (round-trip fare: ¥860). From Nita Pass, board the 3-minute ropeway for ¥1,220 round-trip to go up higher to **Mount Myoken,** which at 1,333m (4,399 ft.) offers spectacular panoramic views. If you're ready for some real climbing, however, continue for another hour or so along a marked path leading starkly uphill to the summit of **Mount Fugen,** once Unzen's highest peak at 1,359m (4,485 ft.) above sea level—this is the peak that erupted in 1990. On a clear day, you'll be rewarded with splendid views of other volcanic peaks as far away as Mount Aso in the middle of Kyushu, as well as Mount Heisei Shinzan,

I was looking for an easy hike, somewhere quiet to write in my journal, and settled for Konohanasakuya-Hime Jinja, a hillside shrine established 300 years ago above the Gensei-Numa Marsh on the edge of Unzen Spa. Unknowingly, I had picked a shrine dedicated to the deity of flowers, where people come to pray for fertility, safe childbirth, and family harmony. So imagine my delight when I reached the shrine's small clearing to discover two unmistakable statues of—well, you'll just have to see for yourself. Benches provide views over Unzen to Mount Myoken and the ropeway.

a lava dome born during Mount Fugen's last eruption and now Unzen's loftiest peak at 1,483m (4,894 ft.). Allow at least 2½ hours for the hike to Mount Fugen and back.

If you're a golfer, the **Unzen Golf Course** (© 0957/73-3368) was established in 1913 as Japan's first public golf course. Green fees are ¥6,500 Monday to Friday, ¥8,500 weekends and holidays.

Where to Eat & Stay

Most overnight visitors eat dinner and breakfast in their *ryokan*. For lunch, there are several places mentioned elsewhere in this chapter that offer meals. Even if you don't stay at the **Unzen Kanko Hotel,** its old-fashioned dining hall with a high ceiling, wainscoting, wooden floors, white tablecloths, and flowers on each table make it memorable for a meal. It serves both Japanese and Western selections, including set lunches from ¥2,500 to ¥4,900 and a la carte items such as club sandwich and beef curry, served daily from noon to 2pm. In the historic **Kyushu Hotel** is Centenary Dining (Hyaku-nen Dining), a period dining room with a tall ceiling, deco-style lamps and views of the Hells. Its Japanese fusion cuisine may include dishes like sashimi with pine nuts, crushed chips, and sesame sauce, with lunch sets priced from ¥1,600 to ¥3,000 and available daily 11:30am to 2:30pm. In the Spa House, the most popular dish in the **Spa House Restaurant** is *guzoni* (a stew of pounded rice cake, mushrooms, fish cake, and vegetables), but set meals featuring udon noodles, fried oysters, or tonkatsu are also available, most priced ¥750 to ¥1,000 and served daily from 11am to 4pm. You go up to the counter to order (cash only accepted here), serve yourself tea or water, and take a seat at a table or on tatami where you can look upon greenery through the window façade.

As for accommodations, keep in mind that, as with most resort areas in Japan, Unzen tends to be crowded and sometimes even fully booked during Golden Week and New Year's and from mid-July to August. The best times of year are late April to June, when Unzen's famous azalea bushes are in glorious bloom, and late October and early November, when the maple leaves turn brilliant reds.

With the exception of Seiunso at the end of this section, all the *ryokan* and hotels listed here are within an easy walk of bus stops along the route traversed by the bus from Nagasaki, so I've included the bus stops for each establishment below. You can also tell the bus driver where you're staying, and he'll drop you off at the nearest stop (if you're arriving from Kumamoto, buses go only to the bus terminal).

Kyushu Hotel ★★★ Built in 1917, the Kyushu Hotel is a lovely, old-style property with a view of a lovely traditional garden from its luxurious lobby. Pluses include a gracious and accommodating staff (the fourth-generation owners speak English) and fusion cuisine served in Hyaku-nen Dining (see above) that successfully blends Western and Japanese styles, but you can also opt for Japanese meals served in your room or the Japanese restaurant. Best of all, the Kyushu Hotel offers some of the most scenic views in town; many of its rooms boast great views of the hills as well as the Hells. Almost half the rooms are *tatami*, featuring alcoves with Western-style chairs next to large windows to take in the view. There are also Western-style rooms with beds, as well as combination rooms with tatami areas and beds. The communal baths are spacious and inviting with both indoor and outdoor bathing, but if you don't care to bathe with everyone, reserve the private family bath, also with outdoor bath, for ¥2,100 (there's a 40-min. time limit), or—for real luxury—stay in one of two rooms with their own indoor/outdoor baths.

Obamacho, Unzen City 320, Nagasaki Prefecture 854-0697. www.kyushuhtl.co.jp. *©* **0957/73-3234.** Fax 0957/73-3733. 97 units. ¥13,000–¥28,000 per person, excluding tax and service. Rates include breakfast and dinner. AE, DC, MC, V. Bus: Oyama-no-Johokan (2 min.). **Amenities:** 2 restaurants; bar; lounge; indoor/outdoor hot-spring baths. *In room:* A/C, TV, hair dryer, minibar.

Miyazaki Ryokan (宮崎旅館) ★★   One of the largest Japanese inns in Unzen, this modern *ryokan* first opened 80 years ago and overlooks a beautiful, gracefully manicured garden with hills and sulfur vapors rising in the background—absolutely exquisite when the azaleas are in bloom. Upon arrival, you'll be served green tea and sweets by graceful women in kimono. Afterward, you'll want to ease into the large, marble hot-spring bath overlooking a rock-lined outdoor bath, separated for men and women. Or, if you're shy about bathing with others or want to make it a family affair, make a reservation, at no extra charge, for the private family bath. Although breakfast (Western style, if desired) is served in a communal dining area, an excellent *kaiseki* dinner is served in your own room in true ryokan fashion. About half the rooms are *tatami* rooms, while the others are combination rooms with twin beds and a separate tatami area. Ask for a room on the 6th floor overlooking the garden or, barring that, the Hells (views are not as good, however, as from the Kyushu Hotel, above).

Obamacho, Unzen City 320, Nagasaki Prefecture 854-0692. www.miyazaki-ryokan.co.jp. *©* **0957/73-3331.** Fax 0957/73-2313. 96 units. ¥18,000–¥40,000 per person. ¥2,000 extra per person Sat, nights before holidays, and ¥3,000 extra per person peak season. Rates exclude tax. Rates include breakfast and dinner. AE, MC, V. Bus: Oyama-no-Johokan (3 min.). **Amenities:** Lounge; indoor/outdoor hot-spring baths; sauna. *In room:* A/C, TV, fridge, hair dryer.

Seiunso Kokumin Shukusha (青雲荘国民宿舎) ☺ 🍴   This public lodging offers as much comfort and as many facilities as a moderately priced resort hotel. Large rooms are pleasant, Japanese style (you lay out your own futon here); half have a small balcony offering views of the surrounding woods, and all have sinks and toilets. There are also three combination rooms with both beds and *tatami* areas that are quite spacious, are accessible to travelers with disabilities, and have the best views; you can stay in these rooms for the same charge if they're not booked. In addition to public baths, there are two private family baths (¥1,050 for 50 min.). Reserve early to stay here. The main disadvantage is that the location is outside Unzen, about a 25-minute walk from the Hells, and check-in isn't until 4pm.

Obamacho, Unzen City 500–1, Nagasaki Prefecture 854-0621. *©* **0957/73-3273.** Fax 0957/73-2698. 63 units (without bathroom but with toilets). ¥7,920 per person with 2 meals. MC, V. Bus: Nishi-Iriguchi (20 min.). Pickup service available from Shimatetsu Bus Center. **Amenities:** Restaurant; indoor/outdoor hot-spring baths w/relaxation room; playground. *In room:* A/C, TV.

Unzen Kanko Hotel ★★★ 🏠 If you're the least bit romantic, you won't be able to resist staying at this old-fashioned mountain lodge, built in 1935 of stone and wood, covered in ivy, and resembling a Swiss chalet. No wonder it's been designated an Important Tangible Cultural Heritage Site. The lobby, main dining hall, and public spaces have changed little over the decades, with whitewashed walls, dark-beamed ceilings, and inviting sofas and chairs. The rooms are rustic and old-fashioned, too, most with reproduction William Morris wallpaper, clawfoot tubs, and, in twins facing the front, heavy ceiling-to-floor curtains tied back to reveal a balcony.

Obamacho, Unzen City 320, Nagasaki Prefecture 854-0621. www.unzenkankohotel.com. ☎ **0957/73-3263.** Fax 0957/73-3419. 44 units. ¥13,860 single; ¥23,100–¥43,890 double. Rates ¥3,465–¥5,775 higher Sat and nights before holidays. AE, DC, MC, V. Bus: Nishi-Iriguchi (1 min.). **Amenities:** Restaurant; bar; lounge; billiard room; concierge; hot-spring indoor/outdoor baths (including a family bath for ¥2,100 for 1 hr.); library w/books and DVDs. *In room:* A/C, TV, fridge, hair dryer.

Unzen Sky Hotel ★★★ 🏠 Despite its name, this nondescript medium-priced property just off the main road offers only tatami rooms (though some also have beds in a corner), nicely yet simply furnished, with the best views facing the Hells. Japanese meals are served in its restaurant, but to save money you can also stay here without meals (keep in mind, though, that dinner options in Unzen are limited).

Obamacho, Unzen City 323-1, Nagasaki Prefecture 854-0621. www.unzen-skyhotel.com. ☎ **0957/73-3345.** 53 units. Per person, ¥8,550 with 2 meals, ¥6,500 with breakfast, ¥5,400 without meals. MC, V. Bus: Shimatetsu Bus Center (1 min.). **Amenities:** Restaurant; lounge; hot-spring indoor/outdoor baths; Wi-Fi (free, in lobby). *In room:* A/C, TV, fridge, hair dryer.

KUMAMOTO, CASTLE TOWN ★

1,293km (804 miles) SW of Tokyo; 189km (118 miles) S of Fukuoka

Located roughly halfway down Kyushu's western side, Kumamoto boasts a fine castle and a landscaped garden, both with origins stretching from the first half of the 17th century. Once one of Japan's most important castle towns, Kumamoto today is the progressive capital of Kumamoto Prefecture, with a population of 700,000. Yet it retains a small-town atmosphere, which is precisely why I like it.

Essentials

GETTING THERE **By Plane** **JAL, ANA, Skymark,** and **Solaseed Air** fly to Kumamoto Airport (KMJ; ☎ **096/232-2810;** www.kmj-ab.co.jp) from Tokyo in about 2 hours. Airport shuttle buses travel to Kumamoto Station and the Kumamoto Kotsu (bus) Center downtown in about 54 minutes and cost ¥670.

By Train Depending on the trains, it takes a little over 6 or 7 hours to reach Kumamoto from **Tokyo,** not including transfers, at a cost of ¥24,750 for an unreserved seat. From **Fukuoka's Hakata Station,** Shinkansen bullet trains travel to Kumamoto in 40 minutes and cost ¥4,480. There are also four express trains daily both ways between **Beppu** and Kumamoto; stopping at Aso Station along the way, they take about 3 hours and cost ¥4,800.

VISITOR INFORMATION Stop by the **Kumamoto Tourist Office** inside Kumamoto Station near the Shirakawa (east) ticket gate (☎ **096/352-3743;** daily 8:30am–7pm) for an English-language map, brochures and streetcar map. In the city center, there's another **Kumamoto Tourist Information** center at Sakura-no-Baba Josaien, a souvenir complex at the base of Kumamoto Castle (☎ **096/322-5060;** daily

Bus & Ferry from Unzen Spa

From Unzen Spa, the fastest way to reach Kumamoto is to take a bus 40 minutes to Shimabara Port (fare: ¥730), where you can then board a 1-hour ferry (fare: ¥680) or a 30-minute Ocean Arrow (fare: ¥800) to Kumamoto Port. Buses connect Kumamoto Port with Kumamoto Station in 25 minutes for ¥420 and then travel onward to the Kotsu bus center in downtown Kumamoto for ¥480.

8:30am–6:30pm, to 5:30pm Nov–Mar). If you're coming by plane, stop by the **Kumamoto Airport Information Office** (ⓒ 096/232-2810; daily 6:55am–9:30pm).

More information is available on the city's website at **www.city.kumamoto. kumamoto.jp** and Kumamoto Prefecture's website at **www.visitkumamoto.com**.

ORIENTATION & GETTING AROUND Kumamoto Station lies far south of the city's downtown area, but transportation between the two is easy via streetcar, which departs from in front of the station and reaches the downtown area in about 15 minutes. **Downtown** centers on three covered shopping streets called Shimotori, Kamitori, and Sunroad Shinshigai, with many department stores, shops, hotels, bars, pachinko parlors, and restaurants in the area. Here, too, is the city's bus station, the **Kumamoto Kotsu Center,** from which all buses in the city depart. Just north of downtown, within walking distance, rises **Kumamoto Castle,** which is surrounded by moats, turrets, and expansive greenery, on the edge of which are several museums and historic sites. **Suizenji Garden** lies far to the east.

Getting around Kumamoto via old-fashioned **streetcar** is easy because there are only two lines, each stop has a number, and stops are announced in English. The A-Line is most convenient for tourists; the only one departing from Kumamoto Station, it passes through downtown and near Kumamoto Castle before going onward to Suizenji Garden. Streetcar fare is a flat rate of ¥150; pay when you get off.

Because the grounds surrounding Kumamoto Castle encompass 97 hectares (242 acres), with a circumference of 9km (5½ miles), many visitors opt to see sights via the **Kumamoto Castle Loop Bus** (Shiro-megurin), which departs every 20 minutes from Kumamoto Station, operates daily from 8:30am to about 5pm, and stops at Sakura-no-Baba Josaien, Kumamoto Castle, Hosokawa Mansion, and other places of interest. This bus costs ¥130 for a single journey, or ¥300 for the entire day along with discounts to attractions on its route. However, if you plan on taking public transportation at least four times in 1 day, you can save money by purchasing a **1-day pass** for unlimited travel on streetcars and buses for ¥500. It includes a 20% discount to six sights, including Kumamoto Castle.

[FastFACTS] KUMAMOTO

Internet Access The **Kumamoto City International Center,** 4–8 Hanabatacho (ⓒ **096/359–2121;** streetcar: Hanabata-cho), offers three computers with free Internet access on the second floor daily from 9am to 9pm (closed the second and fourth Mon of every month). Otherwise, **Media Café Popeye,** located near the north end of the Kamitori covered shopping street (ⓒ **096/326-6767;** streetcar: Toricho-suji), is open 24 hours and charges ¥420 for one hour.

Mail & ATMs There's a convenient post office at Kumamoto Station's north end, open Monday to Friday 9am to 5pm for mail; its ATMs are open Monday to Friday 8am to 7pm and weekends 9am to 7pm.

Exploring Kumamoto

Contemporary Art Museum, Kumamoto ★ 📖 ART MUSEUM   Because it's free (except for special exhibitions) and centrally located in downtown Kumamoto, consider taking a 30-minute jaunt through this forerunner in contemporary art, where art is treated as an experience rather than something to be viewed passively. Showcasing works by local talent Ide Nobumichi, as well as commissioned installations by Kusama Yayoi (look for her *Infinity Mirrored Room*) and Miyajima Tatsuo (with a pillar of flashing diodes) and special exhibits, it seems more like a community center than a museum, with a children's play corner and a Ping-Pong table designed by Ishii Hiroshi that responds digitally to the ball. My favorite area is the library, with art, books, and comfortable sofas (a favorite place, apparently, for dozing off), where there's nightly piano music from 7 to 7:30pm, followed by 10 minutes of darkness in which a ceiling light installation, by James Turrell, slowly transforms from blue to red.

2–3 Kamitori-cho. www.camk.or.jp. ✆ **096/278-7500.** Free admission, except for some special exhibits. Wed–Mon 10am–8pm (you must enter by 7:30pm). Streetcar: Toricho-suji (1 min.). Between Hotel Nikko and Kamitori covered shopping arcade.

Hosokawa Mansion (Kyu-Hosokawa Gyobutei) ★ HISTORIC HOME   A 10-minute walk north of Kumamoto Castle, this imposing 300-year-old samurai mansion was built by a subsidiary member of the Hosokawa clan, Lord Gyobu, and was enlarged in the 1800s. After picking up the English-language pamphlet, you can wander past some 20 rooms, including the lord's study and reception room, kitchen, and servants' quarters. You'll see Edo-Era furnishings and personal items including an Edo clock, a suitcase, clothing, games, a woman's cosmetic case, lacquerware, a kimono chest, and more, giving you a good idea of how feudal lords lived during the Edo Period. Afterwards, have tea and a sweet in the 1889 teahouse located outside the main gate, served 10am to 3:30pm by elderly volunteers dressed in kimono and a bargain at only ¥200.

3–1 Furukyo-machi. ✆ **096/352-6522.** Admission ¥300 adults, ¥100 children. Combination ticket for Hosokawa Mansion and Kumamoto Castle ¥640 adults, ¥240 children. Daily 8:30am–5:30pm (to 4:30pm Nov–Mar). Castle Loop Bus: Kyu-Hosokawa Gyobutei, stop 8 (1 min.).

Kumamoto Castle ★★ CASTLE   Completed in 1607, Kumamoto Castle is massive. It took 7 years to build, under the direction of Kato Kiyomasa, a great warrior who fought alongside Tokugawa Ieyasu in battle and was rewarded for his loyalty with land. The castle was built atop a hill and had two main towers, 49 turrets, 29 gates, and 18 two-story gatehouses; to make the walls impossible for enemies to scale, they were built with curves at the bottom and nearly vertical at the top and were crowned with an overhang. More than 100 wells ensured water even during a siege, while camphor and gingko trees were planted for firewood and edible nuts. The castle passed into the possession of the Hosokawa family in 1632 and remained an important stronghold for the Tokugawa shogunate throughout its 250 years of rule, particularly in campaigns against the powerful and independent-minded lords of southern Kyushu. During that time, 11 generations of the Hosokawa clan ruled over Kumamoto.

Much of the castle was destroyed in 1877 during the Seinan Rebellion led by Saigo Takamori, a samurai who was unhappy with the new policies of the Meiji government in which ancient samurai rights were rescinded. Saigo led a troop of samurai in an attack on the castle and its imperial troops, who remained under siege for 53 days before government reinforcements finally arrived and quelled the rebellion. When the smoke cleared, most of the castle lay in smoldering ruins.

While the Uto Turret, which is three-tiered and five stories, is the original, the main keep was reconstructed in 1960 of ferroconcrete, and although it's not nearly as massive as before, it's still quite impressive and remains Kumamoto's star attraction (famous Japanese director Kurosawa Akira used it for his epic dramas *Ran* and *Kagemusha*). The interior houses a museum with elaborately decorated palanquins, models of Kumamoto and the castle during the Edo Period, armor, swords, former possessions of both Kato Kiyomasa and the Hosokawa family, and rifles and other artifacts from the Seinan Rebellion. Beside the castle, reached via the "Passage of Darkness," a dark and narrow corridor meant to thwart intruders, is a replica of Honmaru Goten Palace, which served as the feudal lord's living quarters after completion in 1610. Painstakingly restored using traditional methods and even local materials and craftsmen, it features rooms with gorgeous paintings and a kitchen. If you intend to visit Hosokawa Mansion (see above), buy a joint ticket for entrance to both sights (¥640 for adults and ¥240 for children).

1–1 Honmaru. ☎ **096/352-5900.** Admission ¥500 adults, ¥200 children. Apr–Oct daily 8:30am–6pm; Nov–Mar daily 8:30am–5pm. Castle Loop Bus: Kumamoto Castle, stop 6 (5 min.). Streetcar: Kumamoto Castle (10 min., or 3 min. to Sakura-no-Baba Josaien and then free shuttle bus to the castle).

Suizenji Garden (Suizenji Jojuen) ★ PARK/GARDEN   Laid out in the 1630s by Hosokawa Tadatoshi as a retreat for the tea ceremony and grounds for a nearby temple, Suizenji Garden took about 80 years to complete. The garden wraps itself around a cold spring-fed lake (considered particularly good for making tea). But what makes the place especially interesting is that its design is said to incorporate famous scenes in miniature from the 53 stages of the ancient **Tokaido Highway,** which connected Kyoto and Tokyo. (The 53 stages were also immortalized in Hiroshige's famous woodblock prints.) Most recognizable are cone-shaped Mount Fuji and Lake Biwa; near the garden's entrance is Nihon Bashi (Bridge of Japan), Edo's starting point on the Tokaido Road. The park is small—almost disappointingly so—and for the life of me, I can't figure out more than a handful of the 53 stages. Maybe you'll have better luck. Pastoral views are also marred by—my pet peeve—surrounding buildings. Take solace by sipping tea in a traditional thatched-roof teahouse with views of the pond (¥600, including a sweet). Also on garden grounds is **Izumi Shrine,** built in 1878 and dedicated to the Hosokawa lords, as well as a *noh* theater, where noh is performed in spring and fall ceremonies. A stroll of the garden takes about 20 minutes.

8–1 Suizenji Koen. ☎ **096/383-0074.** Admission ¥400 adults, ¥200 children. Mar–Oct daily 7:30am–6pm; Nov–Feb daily 8:30am–5pm. Streetcar: about a 12-min. ride from downtown to Suizenji Jojuen (3 min.). Backtrack the way you've come, take the 1st right and then right again onto a narrow shop-lined street with a stone *torii* gate.

A Side Trip to Mt. Aso ★

In the center of Kyushu, between Kumamoto and Beppu, is **Mt. Aso-Kuju National Park,** encompassing two groups of mountains, volcanic Mt. Aso and Mt. Kuju, as well as sweeping grasslands populated by horses, forests, and hot springs. Mt. Aso is the chief attraction of the park: It possesses one of the largest calderas (crater basins) in the world, measuring some 25km (15 miles) north to south and 18km (almost 12 miles) east to west, with a 120km (75-mile) circumference. Mt. Aso must have been one mighty mountain before blowing its stack in four massive eruptions some 90,000 to 300,000 years ago—larger even than Mt. Fuji.

The caldera is so large, in fact, that more than 50,000 people call it home. It also contains a handful of volcanic cones, including the still-active **Naka-dake,** Mt. Aso's main draw. Constantly spewing forth high-temperature gas, sulfurous fumes, and ash, it offers visitors the rare chance to peer into an active volcano from its lunar-like rim. Cement bunkers on its slopes are testimony to the fact that Naka-dake occasionally explodes, including in 2011 when ash plumes billowed 2,400m (8,000 ft.) into the air.

To reach Naka-dake, take one of four daily JR express trains that travel between Kumamoto and Beppu, to Aso Station. From Kumamoto it takes a little over1 hour and costs ¥1,680 for an unreserved seat; from Beppu it takes 2 hours and costs ¥3,270. The **Aso Tourist Office** (© **0967/35-5088;** daily 9am–6pm), reached by turning left out of Aso Station, has a map of the area and bus schedules. If lockers at Aso Station are full, the tourist office will keep your luggage for you (¥500 per bag), useful if you're traveling onward, say, to Beppu. Staff can also make hotel reservations. From Aso Station, buses depart seven times a day for Naka-dake between 9:05am and 3:20pm; the trip takes 40 minutes and costs ¥540 one way. You can then take a ropeway (¥600 one way or ¥1,000 roundtrip), but there's also a pathway you can hike in about 30 minutes.

Alternatively, there are also four buses that travel daily from Kumamoto Station or Kotsu bus center directly to the ropeway (Asosan Nishi Station stop) in slightly less than 2 hours for ¥1,760. If you're traveling onward to Beppu, note that a bus departing Kumamoto Station at 11:20am makes a 90-minute stop at the ropeway, arriving in Beppu at 6:38pm (fare: ¥3,850). Finally, **SUNQ Bus** (© **096/354-4845**) offers two guided tours (in Japanese) of Mt. Aso for ¥5,900, including lunch. Contact the Kumamoto tourist office for more information on Mt. Aso.

Where to Eat

Kumamoto's specialties include *dengaku* (tofu, and sometimes taro and fish, coated with bean paste and grilled on a fire), *karashi renkon* (lotus root that has been boiled, filled with a mixture of bean paste and mustard, and then deep-fried), and *basashi* (raw horse meat sliced thin and then dipped in soy sauce flavored with ginger or garlic).

MODERATE

Aoyagi (青柳) ★★ LOCAL SPECIALTIES/KAISEKI   Everyone in Kumamoto knows this restaurant, located in the downtown area just off the Shimotori covered shopping arcade. The modern, classy building offers seating on *tatami*, at the counter, or at low tables with leg wells. *Kamameshi* (rice casseroles) and local dishes are highly featured on its English-language menu, like the Kamameshi set meal for ¥2,800 that comes with sashimi, shrimp and vegetable tempura, daikon salad, kamameshi, steamed egg custard, soup, and dessert. Horsemeat is served raw, grilled, and in sukiyaki, and the a la carte menu lists everything from tempura and deliciously spicy *karashi renkon* to—my favorite—tofu salad with burdock root, soybeans and fresh mesclun greens with sesame dressing.

1–2–10 Shimotori. © **096/353-0311.** Kaiseki meals ¥5,250–¥6,300; set lunches ¥1,000–¥3,150. AE, DC, MC, V. Daily 11:30am–10pm. Streetcar: Toricho-suji (2 min.). Walk down Shimotori shopping arcade 2 blocks to Sannenzakadori (just past Daiei) and turn right; it's in the 2nd block on the right.

Senri (泉里) ★ LOCAL SPECIALTIES/VARIED JAPANESE You can try Kumamoto's local dishes at this restaurant right in Suizenji Garden, available from a Japanese menu featuring set meals. For lunch, you can choose main dishes such as eel or river fish, served with side dishes of vegetable, soup, rice, and tea. Or order the ¥3,150 *kyodo-ryori* course, which includes local specialties such as *basashi* and *dengaku*. In the evening, only *kaiseki* cuisine is available and it must be ordered at least 1 day in advance. Dining is in small *tatami* rooms; choice rooms face the garden.

Suizenji Garden. ✆ **096/381-1415.** Reservations recommended, a must for kaiseki. Kaiseki set dinners from ¥5,250; set lunches ¥2,100–¥3,150. No credit cards. Tues–Sun 11am–2pm and 5–9pm. Streetcar: Suizenji Jojuen (4 min.). Senri has its own entrance to the right of Suizenji Garden's main gate and also an entrance inside Suizenji Garden.

INEXPENSIVE

Ginnan (ぎんなん) 🍴 LOCAL SPECIALTIES/VARIED JAPANESE Sakura-no-Baba Josaien is a tourist compex at the base of Kumamoto Castle with shops selling souvenirs, sake, sweets, tea, and other local goods. Here, too, is this buffet reaturant, where you can dine on *karashi renkon*, *niku-jaga* stew made with horsemeat instead of the usual beef, chicken from Aso, and other regional dishes, as well as tempura, salads, pizza, and more. Dinner buffets add more substantial fare like *shabu-shabu* and *nabe*.

1–14 Ninomaru. ✆ **096/312-2691.** Dinner buffet ¥2,000; lunch buffet ¥1,500. AE, DC, MC, V. Daily 11am–3pm and 5–10pm. Castle Loop Bus: Sakura-no-Baba Josaien, stop 5 (1 min.). Streetcar: Kumamoto Castle (3 min., across the moat).

Higo Fukunoya (肥後福のや) ★ 🍱 ORGANIC JAPANESE Although its location is not convenient to either Kagoshima Station or downtown (it lies on the streetcar route btw. them), people who like healthy, organic meals go out of their way to dine at this restaurant, simply decorated with rough wooden floors, contemporary Japanese background music, and tables overlooking the Tsuboi river. It's located at the back of a complex of Edo-Era buildings, which also contain the Purely organic health-food store and shops selling natural, environmentally friendly products. For lunch there's a vegetarian set lunch, two *obento* choices, and a *kaiseki* meal, while dinner features a set meal for ¥2,100 and three kaiseki meals starting at ¥3,150.

15 Nakatoji-machi. ✆ **096/323-1552.** Reservations required for kaiseki dinner. Set dinners ¥2,100–¥7,350; set lunches ¥1,260–¥3,150. AE, DC, MC, V. Thurs–Tues 11:30am–2pm and 6–8:30pm (last order). Streetcar: Gofukumachi (1 min.). If coming from Kumamoto Station, walk straight ahead (instead of turning like the tracks); go 1 block to the 1st light and turn right; it will be on your left.

Kokutei (黒亭) 🍴 RAMEN Located in a simple black-and-white building, this famous ramen restaurant has been serving homemade ramen since 1959. Its name means "in the black" house—they must have known they'd be a success. Popular with locals from office workers to grandmothers, it's small and can get quite crowded (avoid the lunch rush). The English menu with pictures lists a few simple choices, with prices dependent on the number of pork slices you choose to eat with your ramen or whether you add an egg or vegetables. If you wish, buy a package of dry ramen to take home as a souvenir.

1–2–29 Nihongi. ✆ **096/352-1648.** Noodles ¥590–¥1,080. No credit cards. Daily 10:30am–8:30pm (closed 1st and 3rd Thurs of every month). Kumamoto Station (6 min.) Turn right out of the station's Shirakawa (east) exit and left at the 1st (Nihongi-guchi) streetcar stop; it's a few blocks ahead, on the right on the corner.

Tateki (楯己) ★ 🍢 KUSHIAGE   Located on a street filled with striptease clubs (be sure to match the *kanji* with the sign outside the door—otherwise you'll get more than skewered food), this 30-year-old restaurant serves *kushiage*, or skewered meats and vegetables. Although kushiage isn't unusual in Japan, Tateki's method of cooking and serving it is: Instead of counter seating, behind which the cook prepares your food, here you sit on *tatami* while a waiter in a beret kneels at your personal hibachi and grills your meal in front of you. The least-expensive set dinner comes with 10 sticks of meat and vegetables plus appetizer, salad, and *soba*, while the set lunch consists of seven sticks, two sauces, rice, soup, appetizer, and salad.

Kaishika Building, 1–11–8 Shimotori. ✆ **096/325-4989.** Set lunch ¥1,050; set dinners ¥2,100–¥4,200. No credit cards. Daily 11:30am–11pm. Streetcar: Hanabatacho (5 min.). Walk east on Ginza Dori 2 blocks, take a right on Sakae Dori and then the 1st left onto an unmarked street called Korinjidori; Tateki will be on the right at the end just before the covered arcade, to the right and toward the back of a dog statue.

Trattoria Rosso ★ 🎒 ITALIAN   You can come for pizza, pasta, or one of the main dishes like grilled scampi or saltimbocca, but better yet are the good-value set meals, which let you choose your main dish from the English-language menu. The ¥1,050 set lunch, for example, gets you a salad, bread or rice, a drink, and a main dish selected from four different kinds of pasta or eight choices of fish and meat selections. It's a cheerful little place in a cute, European-style shopping center.

Suidocho Village, 1–19 Suidocho. ✆ **0120/348-906.** Main dishes ¥1,800–¥2,600; set dinners ¥2,500–¥5,000; set lunches ¥1,050–¥2,100. AE, DC, MC, V. Daily 11am–2:30pm and 5–9:30pm (last order). Streetcar: Suidocho (1 min.). Head north on the busy street (Highway 3); it will be on the left, just past the church, in the back of the small Suidocho Village shopping center.

Shopping

One of Kumamoto's most famous products is Higo Zogan, or **damascene,** in which gold, silver, and copper are inlaid on an iron plate to form patterns of flowers, bamboo, and other designs. Originally used to adorn sword guards and armor, damascene today is used on such accessories as paperweights, jewelry, and tie clasps. Another Kumamoto product is the **Yamaga lantern,** made of gold paper and used during the Yamaga Lantern Festival held in August. Other local products include Amakusa pearls, pottery, knives, toys, sake, and bamboo items.

You can shop for damascene, pottery, toys, ceramics, knives, tea, *shochu*, sake, and confections in the **Kumamoto Prefecture Product Center (Kumamoto-ken Bussankan; 熊本県物産館),** located on the ground floor of the NTT Building at 3–1 Sakura-machi (✆ **096/353-1168;** daily 10am–6:30pm). It's a 1-minute walk west of the Hanabatacho streetcar stop. Otherwise, the **Prefectural Traditional Crafts Center,** east of Kumamoto Castle at 3–35 Chibajo-machi (✆ **096/324-4930;** Tues–Sun 9am–5pm) offers a wider selection of traditional crafts from throughout the prefecture, including Yamaga paper lanterns, Amakusa pearls, bambooware, ceramics, woodworks, toys, pearls, knives, damascene, and more. It's a 5-minute walk from the Kumamoto Castle streetcar stop; or, take the Castle Loop Bus to the KKR Hotel Kumamoto stop no. 8.

Where to Stay

EXPENSIVE

Hotel New Otani Kumamoto ★★ 🍢   The area around Kumamoto Station has nothing to offer sightseers, but if you like the convenience of being near the station, this property belongs to one of Japan's most respected names. Its standard rooms are fairly ordinary but do have large comfortable beds, individual bedside reading lights with dimmer switches, windows with blinds to block light and double-paned glass to block noise. For the best view, ask for a room on a higher floor facing the station.

1–13–1 Kasuga, Kumamoto 860-0047. www.newotani.co.jp. © **800/421-8795** in the U.S. and Canada, or 096/326-1111. Fax 096/326-0800. 130 units. ¥12,705 single; ¥20,790–¥36,960 double. AE, DC, MC, V. Station: Kumamoto (1 min. from the Shirakawa exit, to the left). **Amenities:** 4 restaurants, bar; concierge; lobby computer w/free Internet; men's sauna (fee: ¥1,050). *In room:* A/C, TV, hair dryer, Internet, minibar.

Hotel Nikko Kumamoto ★★★   Right next to the Contemporary Art Museum in the heart of downtown and within walking distance to the castle, this is the city's most luxurious hotel, evident the moment you enter its spacious, artfully designed lobby. Rooms, many with views of Kumamoto Castle or Mount Aso in the distance (ask for a room above the 8th floor), offer sitting areas, closets that light up as soon as you open them, focused bedside reading lights so your partner can sleep, blackout curtains for total darkness, and excellent insulation from traffic noise. The standard twins are especially roomy, with separate tub/shower/toilet areas.

2–1 Kamitori-cho, Kumamoto 860-8536. www.nikko-kumamoto.co.jp. © **800/645-5687** in the U.S. and Canada, or 096/211-1111. Fax 096/211-1175. 191 units. ¥17,325 single; ¥31,185–¥43,890 double. AE, DC, MC, V. Streetcar: Toricho-suji (1 min.). **Amenities:** 4 restaurants; lounge; concierge; room service; Wi-Fi (free, in lobby). *In room:* A/C, TV, hair dryer, Internet, minibar.

MODERATE

JR Kyushu Hotel Kumamoto 🍴   This business hotel right next to Kumamoto Station offers convenience, reasonable prices, and 10% discounts for holders of the Japan Rail Pass. As a whopping 140 of its 150 rooms are singles, make reservations in advance for its one double or eight twin rooms. (It also has one room for those with limited mobility.) Singles are small but have surprisingly roomy bathrooms, while twins are corner rooms with windows on two sides and a sofa.

3–15–15 Kasuga, Kumamoto 860-0047. www.jrhotelgroup.com. © **096/354-8000.** Fax 096/354-8012. 150 units. ¥6,500 single; ¥12,600 double. AE, DC, MC, V. Station: Kumamoto (1 min. from the Shirakawa east exit, to the right). **Amenities:** Restaurant; lobby computer w/free Internet. *In room:* A/C, TV, fridge, hair dryer, Internet.

KKR Hotel Kumamoto ★★ 🏮   Located north of Kumamoto Castle across the street, this trendy hotel buzzes with activity as a popular wedding and banquet venue (weekdays are quieter and also cheaper). The best reason to stay here is its up-close view of the castle, with the absolute best views provided by twin and triple rooms above the hotel's rooftop garden (visible also from the hotel's Japanese restaurant). Unfortunately, none of the hotel's 11 single rooms have castle views (solo travelers can stay in a castle-view twin for ¥11,500), and there are no double rooms.

3–31 Chibajo-machi, Kumamoto 860-0001. www.kkr-hotel-kumamoto.com. © **096/355-0121.** Fax 096/355-7955. 54 units. ¥8,000 single; ¥14,500–¥16,000 double. ¥1,000 extra per person on Sat and nights before holidays. AE, DC, MC, V. Castle Loop Bus: KKR Hotel Kumamoto (1 min.). Streetcar: Kumamoto Castle (8 min.). Follow the streetcar tracks north and then the 1st left over the bridge; the hotel is straight ahead. **Amenities:** 2 restaurants. *In room:* A/C, TV, fridge, hair dryer, Internet.

Waskuki Tsukasa-kan (和数奇) **★★** 🏮   Located in a modern rendition of an Edo-era castle with a whitewashed façade accented with black trim, this is a hip address in downtown Kumamoto. Take the elevator to reception on the third floor, where you'll be greeted by staff wearing traditional Japanese clothing. Rooms, most with Western beds plus a tatami area, feature latticework, shoji screens, dark wooden beams, and other traditional touches. There's a big public bath, and shopping and restaurants are just footsteps away.

7–35 Kamitoricho, Kumamoto 860-0845. ☎ 096/352-5101. Fax 096/354-8105. 59 units. ¥8,400 single; ¥12,600–¥16,800 double. Rates ¥2,100 more per person on nights before holidays. AE, DC, MC, V. Streetcar: Toricho-suji (3 min.). Take the Kamitori covered shopping arcade and then the second right. **Amenities:** Restaurant. *In room:* A/C, TV, fridge, hair dryer, Internet.

INEXPENSIVE

There are four Toyoko Inns in Kumamoto, including **Toyoko Inn Kumamoto Eki-mae** just a 2-minute walk from the station (☎ 096/351-1045) and **Toyoko Inn Kumamoto-jo Toricho Suji** (☎ 096/325-1045; streetcar: Suidocho) downtown. See www.toyoko-inn.com for more information.

Nakashimaya ★★ 🎁   Where else can you sleep on tatami and batik dye a T-shirt (¥3,000), handkerchief or sneakers in a basement art room? This artsy inn offers lots of surprises, including a large common room with a huge TV and DVD library, communal kitchen, laundry room, and a rooftop terrace complete with a hammock, free coffee and distant views of the castle. In addition to simple tatami rooms for one to two people, there's a dormitory room Japanese style, with screens and chests separating futons. Note that children younger than 12 are not allowed.

2–11–6 Shinmachi, Kumamoto 860-0004. http://nakashimaya.ikidane.com. ☎ fax **096/202-2020.** 7 units, none with bathroom. ¥3,000 single; ¥5,500 double; ¥2,500 dormitory bed. ¥200 extra June–Sept for A/C and Dec–Feb for heating. ¥500 discount if you bring a sleeping bag. No credit cards. Streetcar: Gofukumachi (5 min.). If coming from Kumamoto Station, walk straight ahead (instead of turning like the tracks), cross Meihachi-bashi bridge, turn right and then an immediate left (there's a corner fruit market here); it's ahead, on the left. **Amenities:** Rental bikes (¥500 per day); communal kitchen. *In room:* A/C, no phone.

KAGOSHIMA, PLAYGROUND OF THE SOUTH ★★

1,483km (927 miles) SW of Tokyo; 315km (197 miles) S of Fukuoka; 197km (123 miles) S of Kumamoto; 343km (214 miles) SW of Beppu

Capital of Kagoshima Prefecture and with a population of 600,000 residents, Kagoshima is a city of palm trees, flowering trees and bushes, wide avenues, and people who are like the weather—warm, mild-tempered, and easygoing. The city spreads along Kinko Bay and boasts one of the most unusual bay vistas in the world: Sakurajima, an active volcano, rising from the waters. During summer vacation (July 21–Aug), there are nightly fireworks displays over the bay (with a huge one held the end of Aug). Kagoshima is also home to Sengan-en, one of my favorite gardens.

Because of its relative isolation at the southern tip of Japan, far away from the capitals of Kyoto and Tokyo, Kagoshima has developed an independent spirit through the centuries that has fostered a number of great men and accomplishments. Foremost is the Shimadzu clan (also spelled Shimazu), a remarkable family that for 29 generations (almost 700 years) ruled over Satsuma (as the region was known then) and its vicinity before the Meiji Restoration in 1868. Much of Japan's early contact with the outside world was via Satsuma, first with China and then with the Western world. Japan's first contact with Christianity occurred in Kagoshima when St. Francis Xavier landed here in 1549; although he stayed only 10 months, he converted more than 600 Japanese to Christianity. Kagoshima is also where firearms were introduced to Japan.

By the mid–19th century, as the Tokugawa shogunate began losing strength and the confidence of the people, the Shimadzu family was already looking toward the future and the modernization of Japan. In the mid-1850s, the Shimadzu family built the first Western-style factory in the country, employing 200 men to make cannons, glass, ceramics, land mines, ships, and farming tools. In 1865, while Japan's doors were still officially closed to the outside world and all contact with foreigners was forbidden, the Shimadzu family smuggled 19 young men to Britain so they could learn foreign languages and technology. After these men returned to Japan, they became a driving force in the Meiji Restoration and Japan's modernization (a statue of them stands outside Kagoshima Chuo Station).

Another historical figure who played a major role during the Meiji Restoration was Saigo Takamori, who was born in Kagoshima Prefecture. A philosopher, scholar, educator, and poet, he helped restore Emperor Meiji to power, but because he was also a samurai, he subsequently became disillusioned when the ancient rights of the samurai class were rescinded and the wearing of swords was forbidden. He led a force of samurai against the government in what is called the Seinan Rebellion but was defeated. He then withdrew to Shiroyama in Kagoshima, where he committed suicide in 1877. Today, Saigo has many fans among Japanese, who still visit the cave on Shiroyama Hill where he died.

Essentials

GETTING THERE   By Plane   You can reach Kagoshima Airport (KOJ; www.koj-ab. co.jp) from Tokyo (flight time: 1 hr. 45 min.), Osaka (1 hr. 10 min.), and Sapporo (2 hr. 35 min.) in addition to other cities in Japan. The airport is linked to Kagoshima Chuo Station in 1 hour by **limousine bus,** which departs every 10 to 15 minutes and costs ¥1,200.

By JR Train   Thanks to the new Kyushu Shinkansen, completed in 2011, travel time is approximately 7 hours from Tokyo (if you have a Rail Pass, travel time will be slower because you can't take the Nozomi), about 4½ hours from Osaka, 1 hour and 40 minutes from Fukuoka, and about 45 minutes from Kumamoto. Tickets from Tokyo cost ¥28,030 for an unreserved seat, ¥9,660 from Fukuoka, and ¥6,250 from Kumamoto. All trains travel to Kagoshima Chuo (Central) Station.

By Bus   Buses connect Kyushu's cities more cheaply than the train. From Fukuoka's Tenjin Station, 24 buses depart daily and cost ¥5,300 one-way for the 4-hour trip to Kagoshima's bus center, next to Kagoshima Chuo Station. There are also buses from Nagasaki (¥6,500) and Kumamoto (¥3,600), among others.

VISITOR INFORMATION   There's a Tourist Information Center at **Kagoshima Chuo Station** (© 099/253-2500; daily 8am–8pm), as well as at the airport (© 0995/58-2114; daily 7am–9:15pm). They have good English-language maps and a hefty guide that covers everything from public transportation to recommended sightseeing itineraries.

The **Kagoshima Prefectural Visitors Bureau** is located in the Sangyo Kaikan Building, 9–1 Meizan-cho (www.kagoshima-kankou.com/for; © 099/223-5771; Mon–Fri 8:30am–5:15pm), where you can obtain information on the city as well as the prefecture, including Ibusuki and Chiran. Take the streetcar to the Asahi-Dori stop and walk east (toward the bay) on Road 58; it will be on your left in the second block.

GETTING AROUND Downtown Kagoshima lies between Kagoshima Chuo Station with its adjacent Amu Plaza (a shopping, restaurant, and recreation complex—you'll see the Ferris wheel on top) and Kinko Bay, northeast of the station, with **Tenmonkan-Dori** (a covered shopping street) serving as the heart of the city.

You can walk from the station to downtown in about 20 minutes, but the city is also easy to get around by **streetcar** and **bus.** There are two streetcar lines (fare: ¥160), as well as two types of buses—City View buses and Kagoshima City buses. The **Kagoshima City buses** are regular buses used as commuter transportation by the people living here, while the **City View buses** are geared toward tourists, with stops announced in English and two slightly different routes departing from Kagoshima Chuo Station's Shirakawa (east) exit. The retro-looking Shiroyama/Iso line runs every 30 minutes from 9am to about 5:20pm, while the Waterfront Course bus, designed with a motif of water and dolphins, runs every 75 minutes from 8:40am to 5:25pm. Both travel to Sengan-en garden, the Kagoshima aquarium, Sakurajima Ferry Terminal, and Tenmonkan-Dori covered shopping street along different routes, but only the Shiroyama/Iso line goes to Shiroyama, and only the Waterfront Course stops by the Museum of Meiji Restoration. The fare is ¥180, and you pay when you get off. Or, invest in a 1-day pass for ¥600 allowing unlimited travel on City View buses, streetcars and city buses, plus slight discounts to the top attractions, including the ferry to Sakurajima and Sengan-en. Children pay half fare. Passes can be purchased at the tourist office in Kagoshima Chuo Station and aboard buses and streetcars.

[FastFACTS] KAGOSHIMA

Internet Access Comic Buster, 3–1 Chuo-cho (☎ **099/250-6369**), is about a 1-minute walk to the left after exiting from Kagoshima Chuo Station's Shirakawa (east) exit, on the fourth floor next to Sunkus convenience store. Open 24 hours, it charges ¥100 for a member's card (passport required), then ¥280 for 30 minutes and ¥100 for every 15 minutes after that.

Mail & ATMs Kagoshima's main post office is located just north of Kagoshima Chuo Station (turn left from the Shirakawa exit), past Amu Plaza. It's open for mail Monday to Friday 9am to 7pm, Saturday 9am to 5pm, and Sunday and holidays from 9am to 12:30pm. ATMs are open Monday to Friday 7am to 11pm, Saturday 9am to 9pm, and Sunday 9am to 7pm.

Exploring Kagoshima

SuizokuKan (loworld) ☺ AQUARIUM   This aquarium, within walking distance of downtown and located beside the Sakurajima Ferry Terminal, concentrates on sea life from waters surrounding Kagoshima Prefecture. The largest tank is home to stingrays, bluefin tuna, Japanese anchovy, a whale shark, and other creatures from the Kuroshio (Black Current), which flows from the East China Sea past Kagoshima to the Pacific Ocean. Another tank contains squid, octopuses, the Japanese giant crab (the world's largest crab), and fish that inhabit the Kagoshima seas. Other highlights include the world's only display of tube worms (which inhabit the deep sea by hydrothermal vents), the world's largest eel, a children's touch pool, and a tot's play area. Dolphins, which have access to open waters, are used only for educational shows (conducted in Japanese only). Expect to spend at least an hour here, more if you have kids.

3–1 Honko-Shinmachi. ☎ **099/226-2233.** Admission ¥1,500 adults, ¥750 junior-high and high-school students, ¥350 children. Daily 9:30am–6pm (you must enter by 5pm). Closed 1st Mon in Dec and the following 4 days. Streetcar: Suizokukan-guchi (8 min.); walk toward the harbor. City View Bus: Kagoshima Suizokukan-mae (2 min.).

Kagoshima Prefectural Museum of Culture (Reimeikan; 黎明館) ★

MUSEUM Presenting an overview of Japanese history in general and Kagoshima Prefecture in particular, this museum occupies the former site of Tsurumaru Castle, of which only the stone ramparts and moat remain. Upon entering the museum, you'll walk over a glass floor above a map of Kagoshima Prefecture (much of it is islands). The museum then traces regional history over the last 30,000 years, including the rise of the Shimadzu clan in the 11th century, Kagoshima's preeminence as a pottery center after Korean potters were brought here in the late 1500s, and Kagoshima's role in the overthrow of the shogunate government. There are models of an 18th-century samurai settlement, Tsurumaru Castle, and, best of all, Tenmonkan-Dori as it might have looked 90 years ago. The second floor is devoted to folklore and everyday life with bambooware, festival objects, and farming and fishing implements, while the third floor shows Satsuma swords, pottery, scrolls, and paintings. A hands-on learning room for children has old-fashioned toys, musical instruments, and samurai outfits that can be tried on, including one for adults that weights a hefty 15.6kg (32 pounds). You'll spend about an hour here.

7–2 Shiroyama-cho ☎ **099/222-5100.** Tues–Sun 9am–5pm. Closed 25th of each month unless it falls on Sat or Sun. Admission ¥300 adults, ¥190 college and high-school students, ¥120 children. Streetcar: Shiyakusho-mae (4 min.). Walk inland. City View Bus: Satsuma Gishihimi-mae (2 min.).

Museum of the Meiji Restoration (Ishin Furusato-kan) ★★ MUSEUM

The importance of the Meiji Restoration, which marked Japan's turbulent transition from an isolated society ruled by a shogun to the restoration of imperial rule and the dawning of Japan's industrial age, cannot be overstated. This high-tech museum is devoted to those instrumental in the overthrow of the shogunate, including Saigo Takamori, Okubo Toshimichi, and others from Satsuma. Although there are plenty of displays, including sophisticated dioramas with holograms, they're frustratingly only in Japanese. There are two animatronic shows, however, featuring life-size figures and dramatic sound and light effects, with English-language earphones. In the 25-minute

---

 Fishy Business

Tsukiji Fish Market may be famous, but it has also become too popular for its own good, prompting authorities there to limit public access to its tuna auctions. In contrast, the **Kagoshima Fish Market Tour** provides an up-close guided tour of the Kagoshima City Fish Market, including rows of swordfish, mahi mahi, octopus, and other specimens from around the world laid out for auction and the adjoining wholesale market. One-hour tours take place every

Saturday at 7am March through November and cost ¥800. Participants must be junior-high-school age and older and must sign up by 5pm the day before (Friday) at the front desk of any participating hotel, including the Furusato Kanko Hotel (see below), Hotel & Residence Nanshukan, 19–17 Sengoku-cho (☎ **099/226-8188;** streetcar: Izuro-Dori), and a handful of other hotels. Contact tourist information for more details.

Road to the Restoration, you'll hear from Saigo himself as he talks about his childhood, the alliance of clans to overthrow the shogun, and Emperor Meiji's rise to power, while the 20-minute *Satsuma Students, Go West* follows 19 young men who were smuggled out of Japan and recounts their first experiences with Western clothing, food, and the world as they travel 66 days at sea to study Western technology in England. Plan on about an hour here.

23–1 Kajiya-cho. ℂ **099/239-7700.** Daily 9am–5pm. Admission ¥300 adults, ¥150 children. Kagoshima Chuo Station: 8 min. Across from the station, walk down wide Napoli Dori to the Tourism Exchange Center and then left. City View Bus: Ishinfurusatokan-mae (1 min.).

Nagashima Museum ★★★ 🏛ART MUSEUM Although it's not conveniently located (you'll want to take a taxi), this is a very worthwhile private museum on a hill high atop the city with great views of Sakurajima and Kagoshima. While its focus is mostly on works by such Kagoshima artists as Kuroda Seiki, Wada Eisaku, and Togo Seiji, it also contains some works by well-known Western artists like Picasso, Cezanne, Renoir, and Chagall, as well as pottery from South America. But most impressive, in my opinion, is an outstanding collection of mainly 19th-century white Satsuma pottery, including many pieces that were originally imported to London, Paris, and New York, and the more utilitarian 17th- to 20th-century black Satsuma pottery. An hour is enough time to see everything, but try to time your visit so you can eat lunch in the museum's French restaurant, **Camellia** (ℂ 099/259-0883; daily 11am–3pm), with set meals starting at ¥1,800 weekdays and ¥2,000 weekends and with great views over the city.

3–42–18 Take (ℂ **099/250-5400.** Daily 9am–5pm. Admission ¥1,000 adults, ¥800 college and high-school students, ¥500 seniors, ¥400 children. Taxi: 7 min. from Kagoshima Chuo Station.

Sengan-en ★★★ GARDEN/PARK Whereas Sakurajima, rising dramatically out of the bay, is Kagoshima's best-known landmark, Sengan-en is its most widely visited attraction. A countryside villa and garden, it was laid out in 1658 by the Shimadzu clan, incorporating Sakurajima and Kinko Bay into its design scheme in a principle known as borrowed landscape (too bad, however, about those modern overhead electric wires). There's a lovely grove of bamboo, a waterfall located a 30-minute walk up a nature trail with good views over the bay, and the requisite pond, but my favorite is a particularly idyllic spot, site of famous poem-composing garden parties. Guests seated themselves on stones beside a gently meandering rivulet and were requested to have completed a poem by the time a cup filled with sake came drifting by on the tiny brook; if they failed, they had to drink it. Ah, those were the days! Today it remains Japan's only garden with its original *kyokusui* (poem-composing garden) still intact.

The good life is also apparent in the **Iso Residence,** which was built as a villa by the Shimadzu clan more than 350 years ago and became the family's main residence when the Meiji Restoration made feudal lords obsolete. Now only one-third its original size, the stately manor can be viewed by joining a tour conducted every 20 minutes and given in Japanese only (but with an English-language information sheet). You'll see 10 of the villa's 25 rooms, including a bedroom, a bathroom, a dressing room, living quarters, and reception rooms, furnished with possessions once belonging to the Shimadzu clan. Ceremonial green tea and a sweet are included in the 20-minute tour. The 32nd generation of the Shimadzu family, incidentally, now resides in Kagoshima.

The other important thing to see here is the **Shoko Shuseikan,** built in the mid-1850s by the Shimadzus as Japan's first industrial factory. Displays explore the Shuseikan's production of cannons, textiles, glass, iron, printing, and other products that made Kagoshima a forerunner in Japan's modernization. Also housed here are items relating to the almost 700-year history of the Shimadzu clan, including family heirlooms ranging from lacquerware to tea-ceremony objects, palanquins used to carry Shimadzu lords back and forth to Edo (present-day Tokyo; the trip from Kagoshima took 40–60 days), everyday items used by the family, and photographs. In all, you'll probably spend at least 2 hours seeing everything, especially if you stop off at souvenir shops selling Satsuma glassware, pottery, and other Kagoshima products.

9700–1 Yoshino-cho. www.senganen.jp. ℭ **099/247-1551.** Daily 8:30am–5:30pm (to 5:20pm Nov–Mar). Tours of Iso Residence daily 9am–4:40pm (last tour). Admission ¥1,000 adults, ¥500 children. Iso Residence tours cost an extra ¥500 adults, ¥250 for children. City View Bus (30 min. from Kagoshima Chuo Station): Sengan-en-mae (1 min.).

Sakurajima

With ties to Naples, Italy, as its sister city, Kagoshima bills itself the "Naples of the Orient." That's perhaps stretching things a bit, but Kagoshima is balmy most of the year and even has its own Mount Vesuvius: Mount Sakurajima, an active volcano across Kinko Bay that has erupted 30 times through recorded history and continues to puff steam into the sky and occasionally cover the city with fine soot and ash. In 1914, Sakurajima had a whopper of an eruption and belched up 3 billion tons of lava. When the eruption was over, the townspeople were surprised to discover that the flow was so great it now blocked the 500m-wide (1,700-ft.) channel separating the volcano from a neighboring peninsula; Sakurajima, which had once been an island, was now part of the mainland. As a precaution (the volcano does occasionally release some heavy particles), all children living in Sakurajima wear yellow helmets to and from school (as opposed to yellow hats children usually wear), and every home has a shelter.

Magnificent from far away and impressive if you're near the top, Sakurajima can be visited by taking the **Sakurajima Ferry** (www.sakurajima-ferry.jp; ℭ **099/293-2525**) for ¥150 for adults and ¥80 for children. Ferries depart from the Sakurajima Ferry Terminal, about an 8-minute walk from downtown Kagoshima or either the Shiyakusho-mae or Suizokukan-guchi streetcar stop, or just a 2-minute walk from the City View Kagoshima Suizokukan-mae bus stop. Ferries run 24 hours, departing every 10 to 15 minutes during most of the day and once an hour through the night. Trips take 15 minutes, enough time to down a bowl of the ferry's famous udon noodles! Alternatively, there's a daily Yorimichi Cruise that departs Kagoshima's Sakurajima Ferry Terminal daily at 11:05am for a cruise around the bay and terminates at Sakurajima port 50 minutes later and costs ¥500 for adults and ¥250 for children.

 Evening Cruises

A popular way to enjoy summer nights in Kagoshima is on a boat cruise of Kinko Bay, offered mid-July through August nightly from 7 to 9pm (except during Obon in mid-Aug), the highlight of which are fireworks over the water. Boats depart from the Kagoshima side of the Sakurajima Ferry Terminal and charge ¥1,000 for adults, half fare for children. Call ℭ **099/293-2525** for more information.

Mount Sakurajima's Produce

Mount Sakurajima's rich soil grows the world's largest radishes, averaging about 17 kilograms (37 lb.) but sometimes weighing in at as much as 36 kilograms (80 lb.), and the world's smallest oranges, only 3 centimeters (1¼ in.) in diameter.

Upon reaching Sakurajima, stop off at the **Ferry Terminal Tourist Information Center** (✆ **099/293-4333;** daily 8:30am–5pm) for a map of the island and time schedule for buses to Furusato Onsen and beyond.

There are lava fields with walking paths near Sakurajima's ferry pier. A 10-minute walk away are **Yogan Nagisa Park,** with its 100m- (328 ft-) long foot spa where you can soak your feet, relax and gaze upon bay views, and the **Sakurajima Visitor Center** (✆ **099/293-2443;** daily 9am–5pm), with English-language displays and a film relating the history and natural history of Sakurajima, including its 1914 eruption. From here, the 3km (1.5-mile) **Nagisa Lava Trail** hugs the coast as it travels past huge lava boulders and pine trees, terminating at the **Karasumima Observation Point.**

If you wish to go farther or don't wish to hike, the **Sakurajima Island View** tour bus departs Sakurajima's ferry pier approximately once an hour from 9am to 4:35pm. It makes 8 stops on the island's west side, including the Sakurajima Visitor Center and several lookout points, such as the Yunohira Lookout Point halfway up the volcano, where it makes a 15-minute stop. An all-day pass, available at the ferry ticket counter or on the bus, costs ¥500 (children pay half fare); single tickets, which increase the farther you go, are ¥110 to ¥430. Alternatively, the **Sakurajima Nature Sightseeing Tour** (✆ **099/257-2111**) departs from Kagoshima Chuo Station at 9am and 1:40pm daily and takes in the Sakurajima Ferry and visits lava fields, lookout points like Yunohira, a shrine gate half-buried in lava, and other sights. It costs ¥2,200 for adults, half price for children. You can also join this tour on Sakurajima island for ¥1,700 and ¥850, respectively.

Another fun thing to do on Sakurajima is to visit **Furusato Onsen ★★**, at the Furusato Kanko Hotel (see p. 510), with indoor hot-spring baths with windows overlooking the bay and open-air hot-spring baths set amid lava rocks right beside the sea. Note that the outdoor bath is for both sexes, and although you'll completely disrobe, you'll be provided a white cotton *yukata* (an English-language handout provides guidelines). Furusato Onsen is open to visitors daily 8am to 6pm (hotel guests can use the baths also evenings). Note, however, that various parts of the *onsen* are closed for cleaning on different days of the week: The outdoor bath is closed Monday and Thursday until 3pm, while the indoor hot-spring bath is closed Wednesday until 2pm. Admission is ¥1,050 including yukata; bring your own towel or buy one for another ¥210. You can reach Furusato Onsen by taking the free **Furusato Kanko Hotel shuttle bus** departing daily from the Sakurajima Ferry Terminal on the hour between 10am and 5pm. Otherwise, take the **Kagoshima Kotsu Bus** that departs daily once or twice an hour from the ferry terminal, costing ¥300.

A Side Trip to the Gardens of Chiran

If you have an extra day, I suggest taking an excursion to **Chiran ★★**, 31km (19 miles) south of Kagoshima. Surrounded by wooded hills and rows of neatly cultivated tea plantations, it's one of 102 castle towns that once bordered the Shimadzu kingdom during the Edo Period. Although the castle is no longer standing, seven old gardens and samurai houses have been carefully preserved.

Apparently, the village headman of Chiran had the opportunity to travel with his lord Shimadzu in the mid-1700s to Kyoto and Edo, taking with him some of his samurai retainers. The headman and his retainers were so impressed with the sophisticated culture of Kyoto and Edo that they invited gardeners to Chiran to construct a series of modestly sized gardens on samurai estates surrounding the castle.

Some of these gardens remain and are located on a delightful road nicknamed **Samurai Lane,** which is lined with moss-covered stone walls and hedges. As descendants of the samurai are still living in the houses, only the gardens are open to the public. There are two types of gardens represented: One, belonging to the Mori family, is of the miniature artificial-hill style, in which a central pond symbolizes the sea and rocks represent the mountains; the others are "dry" gardens, in which the sea is symbolized not by water but by white sand that is raked to give it the effect of rippling water. The gardens are masterful demonstrations of the borrowed-landscape technique, in which surrounding mountains and scenery are incorporated into the general garden design. Although the tidy gardens are small, they are exquisite and charming. Notice, for example, how the tops of hedges are cut to resemble rolling hills, blending with the shapes of mountains in the background.

The seven gardens open to the public are indicated by a white marker in front of each entry gate. All seven can be visited for ¥500 for adults, ¥300 for children, daily from 9am to 5pm. Plan on about an hour to see them. For more information on the samurai gardens, call ✆ **0993/58-7878.**

I also recommend a visit to Chiran's **Peace Museum for Kamikaze Pilots (Heiwa Kaikan; ✆ 0993/83-2525;** daily 9am–5pm), dedicated to 1,036 pilots who died in World War II suicide missions in Okinawa, steering bomb-laden planes into Allied warships and other targets (439 of them trained in Chiran). In addition to *kamikaze* aircraft and uniforms, it displays photographs of pilots, all between the ages of 17 and 22, along with farewell letters, personal memorabilia, and a film showing actual footage of the kamikaze pilots in action. Although most displays are in Japanese, an English-language audio guide for ¥100 gives interesting background information about the war, kamikaze operation in Okinawa, and individual pilots, while touchscreens give English translations of pilots' letters, poems and other writings. Not all pilots were eager to die for their country; one display relates how one pilot's wife was so distraught, she lost her breast milk and her son died at 8 months old. Plan on an hour here. Admission is ¥500 for adults, ¥300 for children.

Chiran, which was merged with several other towns in 2007 to form the new city of Minamikyushu, can be reached in about 1½ hours by one of 8 buses that depart daily from Kagoshima Chuo Station (the tourist office in the station has a timetable and a map showing location of bus departures). It costs ¥850 to the Samurai Gardens (bus stop: Bukeyashiki-Iriguchi) and ¥920 to the Peace Museum (bus stop: Tokko-heiwa-kannon-Iriguchi). There are also local buses that travel between the two for ¥150. Finally, there are five buses a day between Chiran and Ibusuki (see p. 512 later in this chapter), with the fare costing ¥940.

Where to Eat

While in Kagoshima, be sure to try its local dishes, known as *Satsuma ryori* and named after the original name of the Kagoshima area. This style of cooking supposedly has its origins in food cooked on battlefields centuries ago; if that's the case, it certainly has improved greatly since then. Popular Satsuma specialties include *Satsuma-age* (ground fish mixed with tofu and sake and then deep-fried), *tonkotsu*

KYUSHU | Kagoshima, Playground of the South

(pork that has been boiled for several hours in miso, *shochu*, and brown sugar—absolutely delicious), ***sakezushi*** (a rice dish flavored with sake and mixed with vegetables and seafood), and ***Satsuma-jiru*** (miso soup with chicken and locally grown vegetables including Sakurajima radishes). ***Kibinago*** is a small fish belonging to the herring family that can be caught in the waters around Kagoshima; a silver color with brown stripes, it's often eaten raw and arranged on a dish to resemble a chrysanthemum. ***Kurobuta*** is pork from a black pig.

MODERATE

Ajimori (あぢもり) ★ KUROBUTA This 30-year-old establishment specializes in pork from small black pigs, which the locals claim is more tender and succulent than regular pork. The restaurant is divided into two parts: the upper floors, with both table seating and private *tatami* rooms, serve *Satsuma Kuroshabu*, a Kagoshima specialty of black-pork *shabu-shabu*; the first floor is a casual dining room specializing in *tonkatsu*, breaded black-pork cutlet. If you order the Kuroshabu, you'll eat it just like the more common beef shabu-shabu, cooking it yourself at your table by dipping it into a boiling broth and then in raw egg or sauce. Otherwise, go to the first floor for perhaps the lightest, best-tasting tonkatsu you'll ever have; the tonkatsu set lunch, available every day except Sundays and holidays for ¥750, is a bargain.

13–21 Sennichi-cho. 📞 **099/224-7634.** Shabu-shabu set dinners ¥4,200–¥8,400; set lunches ¥750–¥3,150. AE, DC, MC, V (for shabu-shabu set meals only). Wed–Mon 11:30am–2:15pm (last order; noon–1pm for shabu-shabu) and 5:30–8:30pm (8pm last order for shabu-shabu). Streetcar: Tenmonkan-Dori (3 min.). Walk south all the way through the covered Sennichi Arcade (also called Senmonkan-Dori; it's opposite the Tenmonkan-Dori arcade) and keep going past the *koban* police box onto Ginza St.; it's on the left just before the next arch with the eyeglasses motif.

Kumasotei ★★ SATSUMA RYORI Located in the city center, this restaurant has been specializing in local Satsuma cuisine for 45 years but carries them one step further by featuring them as part of *kaiseki* set meals. It reminds me more of a private home or *ryokan* because dining is in individual *tatami* rooms. If there isn't a crowd, you'll probably have your own private room; otherwise, you'll share. The main menu is in Japanese, but there's a smaller English-language menu with photos of the various set meals, which may include such local dishes as *Satsuma-age, tonkotsu, Satsuma-jiru, kibinago,* or *sakezushi*. For lunch there's also *shabu-shabu*.

6–10 Higashi Sengoku-cho. 📞 **099/222-6356.** Set dinners ¥2,800–¥10,000; set lunches ¥1,500–¥2,800. AE, DC, MC, V. Daily 11am–2:30pm and 5–9:30pm (last order). Streetcar: Tenmonkan-Dori (4 min.). Walk north through the Tenmonkan-Dori covered shopping street 4 blocks and turn left; it will be on your right.

INEXPENSIVE

Noboruya (のぼる屋) 🍜 RAMEN This popular, inexpensive restaurant in the center of town is Kagoshima's best-known *ramen* (noodle) shop, in business since 1947. It's a simple place, occupying one room of a small, wooden home with one counter and an open kitchen. As only one dish is served, there's no problem ordering. A big bowl of ramen comes with noodles (made fresh every day) and slices of pork, all seasoned with garlic (you can add extra garlic if you want). You also get as much pickled radish as you want (supposedly good for the stomach) and tea. As you eat your ramen at the counter, you can watch an army of women peeling garlic and cooking huge pots of noodles over gas flames—it's a great place to soak up local atmosphere.

2–15 Horie-cho. 📞 **099/226-6695.** Ramen ¥1,000. No credit cards. Mon–Sat 11am–7pm. Streetcar: Izuro-Dori (1 min.). Walk down the wide street (Miami Dori) marked by stone lanterns on each side and take the 1st right; Noboruya is at the end of the 2nd block on the left, with its entrance around the corner.

No-no-Budou (野の葡萄) ★ 🖊 JAPANESE BUFFET   Of the dozen or so restaurants located on the fifth and sixth floors of Amu Plaza adjoining Kagoshima Chuo Station, this is one of the more interesting, featuring 70 dishes that change every few months, with various offerings of tempura, soups, salads, fish, noodles, vegetables, and much, much more. Evening buffets also include sashimi and sushi, and if you really want to make an evening of it, pay ¥1,000 extra for all the beer, shochu and chuhai you can drink in two hours (¥1,500 if you want wine and higher-grade alcohol). There's even a large nonsmoking section. Other choices in Amu Plaza run the gamut from pork *shabu-shabu* and *tonkatsu* to Italian and Chinese fare.

Amu Plaza, 5th floor, 1–1 Chuo-cho. 🕿 **099/206-7585.** Dinner buffet ¥2,180; lunch buffet ¥1,480. AE, MC, V. Daily 11am–4pm and 5–10pm. Beside Kagoshima Chuo Station.

Yako-Hai ITALIAN   I confess I have no idea what its name means, but if you have a hankering for Western food, this restaurant is easy to find and is especially good if you come for the Saturday buffet, which lets you choose a pasta, fish or meat main course and augment it with lots of choices of veggies. Otherwise, chow down on pasta, pizza, or a main dish like grilled pork, sautéed salmon, or chicken cutlet.

14–28 Sennichi-cho. 🕿 **099/239-0070.** Pizza and pasta ¥700–¥980; main dishes ¥1,000–¥2,980; Sat. buffet ¥1,400. AE, DC, MC, V. Daily 11am–3pm (to 5pm for Sat buffet) and 5pm–midnight (last order). Streetcar: Tenmonkan-Dori (2 min.). Walk south through the Sennichi Arcade (also called Senmonkan-Dori; it's opposite the Tenmonkan-Dori arcade); it will be on your left, on a corner.

Shopping

Satsuma pottery is probably Kagoshima Prefecture's most famous ware, produced in the Kagoshima area for more than 400 years. It comes in two styles: black, which was used by townspeople in every day life; and white, which is more elegant and was thus used by former lords and made for export. Other Kagoshima products include *oshima tsumugi,* beautiful silk made into such items as clothing, handbags, and wallets; *shochu,* an alcoholic drink made from such ingredients as sweet potatoes and drunk on the rocks or mixed with hot or cold water; furniture, statues, and chests made from **yaku cedar;** and **Satsuma cut glass,** first produced during the Edo Period and available in stunning shades of blue, red, purple and many other colors.

A good place to shop for local items is the **Kagoshima Brands Shop,** downtown in the Sangyo Kaikan Building (the same building housing the Kagoshima Prefectural Visitors Bureau) at 9–1 Meizan-cho (🕿 099/225-6120; daily 9am–6pm). This one-room shop offers tinware, handmade knives, Satsuma pottery, glassware, *oshima tsumugi,* yaku cedar, *shochu,* and other items. To reach it, take the streetcar to the Asahi-Dori stop, from which the shop is a 1-minute walk away toward the bay.

The most famous cake of Kagoshima (the one all Japanese tourists must buy before returning home) is *karukan,* a delicious spongy white cake made from rice, with Chinese and Korean origins. The most famous maker of karukan today is **Akashiya** (明石屋), 4–16 Kinseicho (🕿 099/226-0431; daily 9am–7pm), which began selling the cakes 160 years ago. It has the solemnity of a first-rate jewelry store and is just as refined. It's located on the side street to the right of Yamakataya department store, a 1-minute walk from the Asahi-Dori streetcar stop. Although cakes are now available made with an *anko* (sweet red-bean paste) center, old-timers insist that only the plain white square ones are the real thing (you can sample a small one for ¥126).

Where to Stay

EXPENSIVE

Castle Park Hotel (Shiroyama Kanko Hotel) ★★ Kagoshima's foremost hotel sits 106m (353 ft.) high atop the wood-covered Shiroyama Hill and commands a great view of the city below and Sakurajima across the bay. Opened 50 years ago, it offers updated, comfortable rooms, the most recommended (and more expensive) of which face the volcano and city with the best views in town. Note, however, that all single rooms face inland and have double-size beds that take up much of the space. Pluses include hot-spring (including open-air) baths with views of Kinko Bay and good restaurants that take advantage of the hotel's views and gardenlike setting (I especially like the buffet restaurant with its outdoor terrace and the microbrewery with its summer beer garden). In short, this is a great respite from city life, and to offset the hotel's main drawback—an isolated location away from the city center—it offers free shuttle buses to Tenmonkan-Dori in the heart of the city and Kagoshima Chuo Station every half hour (it's also served by both daytime and the night City View buses).

41–1 Shinshoin-cho, Kagoshima 890-8586. www.shiroyama-g.co.jp. ℂ **099/224-2211.** Fax 099/224-2222. 365 units. ¥12,000 single; ¥22,000–¥49,000 double. ¥1,000 extra per person Fri; ¥2,000 extra per person Sat and night before holidays. AE, DC, MC, V. Taxi or free shuttle bus 12 min. from Kagoshima Chuo Station. City View Bus: Shiroyama (1 min.). **Amenities:** 5 restaurants; lounge; bar; outdoor/indoor hot-spring baths; room service; sauna; Wi-Fi (free, in lobby & some restaurants). *In room:* A/C, TV, hair dryer, Internet, minibar.

Furusato Kanko Hotel (故里観光ホテル) ★★ 🎁 Although this *ryokan* on Sakurajima is inconvenient for sightseeing, it's great for relaxation. It boasts open-air hot-spring baths set amid rocks right beside the sea and indoor hot-spring baths overlooking Kinko Bay (see "Sakurajima" earlier in this chapter). Afterward, retire to the shrinelike Meditation Room for spiritual cleansing as well. Rooms are Japanese style, all with balconies overlooking great bay views. Some even boast views from their bathrooms, while the very best (and most expensive) have private terraces with open-air hot-spring baths. Breakfast features *kamameshi* (rice casseroles) made with the inn's own hot-spring water; dinner consists mainly of seafood from Kinko Bay, *tonkotsu* (slowly stewed pork), and other local specialties.

1076 Furusato-cho, Kagoshima 891-1592. ℂ **099/221-3111.** Fax 099/221-2345. info@furukan. co.jp. 24 units. ¥13,800–¥23,350 per person. ¥2,100 extra per person weekends and holidays. Rates include breakfast and dinner. AE, DC, MC, V. For directions to Furusato Kanko Hotel, see Sakurajima, earlier in this chapter. **Amenities:** Restaurant (serving lunch only); great indoor/outdoor hot-spring baths. *In room:* A/C, TV, hair dryer, minibar.

MODERATE

JR Kyushu Hotel Kagoshima 🦐 Convenient to Kagoshima Chuo Station (you can enter it right from the station), this business hotel gives Japan Rail Pass holders a 10% discount. Recently renovated, it offers clean, mostly single rooms, ranging from standard rooms devoid of character to deluxe rooms in a newly added tower that have classier furnishings, blinds instead of curtains, and duvets instead of bedspreads, including SOHO single rooms equipped with computers, ladies' rooms with amenities geared to females, and executive doubles with separate living/sleeping areas, sofas, and large desks.

1–1–2 Take, Kagoshima 890-0045. www.jrhotelgroup.com. ℂ **099/213-8000.** Fax 099/213-8029. 248 units. ¥6,500–¥8,000 single; ¥12,000–18,000 twin. AE, DC, MC, V. Station: Kagoshima Chuo Station (west exit, 1 min.). **Amenities:** Restaurant; café/bar; lobby computer w/free Internet. *In room:* A/C, TV, fridge, hair dryer, Internet.

remm Kagoshima ★ 🎁   Opened in 2011, this hotel with a third-floor reception and an equal number of singles, doubles, and twins is located in the heart of downtown, with easy access from Kagoshima Chuo Station via streetcar passing right outside the front door. Although small, rooms, with a gray and black color scheme, make good use of space, with (rain) showers instead of tubs, red tables instead of desks (and a massage chair), focused bed lights, and bathrooms that seem larger due to windows or glass facades open to the room.

1–32 Higashisengoku-cho, Kagoshima 892-0842. www.hankyu-hotel.com. *℗* **099/227-4123.** Fax 099/224-0611. 251 units. ¥9,450–¥10,500 single; ¥13,650–¥23,100 twin. AE, DC, MC, V. Streetcar: Tenmonkan-Dori (1 min.). Backtrack toward the station; it's on the right. **Amenities:** Coffee shop. *In room:* A/C, TV, fridge, hair dryer, Internet.

Richmond Hotel Kagoshima Kinseicho   This business hotel is located on downtown's main street. Check-in and checkout are accomplished via automatic machines, though humans are on hand to help guide you through the process or you can opt to check in at the front desk. Rooms are small, though there are special single rooms for ladies (reservations required) featuring Tempur-Pedic pillows, terry-cloth robes, and female-oriented toiletries. Note that the cheapest singles and doubles are actually the same room, fine for one person but cramped for two. *Tip:* Join the Richmond Club, which requires a ¥500 one-time membership fee, to qualify for cheaper rates on reservations made online or by phone. Applications are available online or at check-in.

5–3 Kinseicho, Kagoshima 890-0828. www.richmondhotel.jp. *℗* **099/219-6655.** Fax 099/219-6668. 220 units. ¥7,800–¥9,300 single; ¥9,400–¥20,000 double. AE, DC, MC, V. Streetcar: Asahi-Dori (1 min.). **Amenities:** Restaurant; lobby computer w/free Internet. *In room:* A/C, TV, fridge, hair dryer, Internet.

INEXPENSIVE

In addition to the choices here, there are two **Toyoko Inns** near the Tenmonkan Dori covered shopping street and two near Kagoshima Chuo Station, all offering the usual lobby computers with free Internet access, free Wi-Fi in the lobby, free in-room Internet, and free Japanese breakfast. Check www.toyoko-inn.com for more information.

Gasthof Hotel ★   After traveling to Europe about 40 years ago, the proprietor of his hotel decided to re-create the coziness of a German bed-and-breakfast with a cafe in the lobby, antiques in the hallway, and rooms that vary in decor, furniture, and bedspreads, including four-poster beds in some. Although it falls short, the Gasthof has a lot more character than a regular business hotel and has a convenient location near Kagoshima Chuo Station. In fact, so little has changed here over the decades, it seems like it's caught in a time warp of '80s Europe. Now managed by the original owner's son, it boasts a private Asian art museum overflowing with priceless treasures from pottery to Buddha statues, and the buffet breakfasts are a bargain. Another plus is the Japanese restaurant and two *izakaya* (Japanese pub) in the same building.

7–1 Chuo-cho, Kagoshima 890-0053. www.gasthof.jp. *℗* **099/252-1401.** Fax 099/252-1405. info@ gasthof.jp. 48 units. ¥5,250–¥5,565 single; ¥8,900 double; ¥12,600 triple. Breakfast ¥525 extra. MC, V. Station: Kagoshima Chuo (3 min.). Take the underground passageway and Exit E to wide, tree-lined Napoli Dori (beside Daiei department store), walk 3 blocks, and turn left at the Mobil gas station; it's at the end of the street on the left. **Amenities:** 4 restaurants/bars; lobby computer w/free Internet, Wi-Fi (free, in lobby). *In room:* A/C, TV, fridge, Internet.

Nakazono Ryokan A member of the Japanese Inn Group, this simple, laid-back, non-smoking *ryokan* with Japanese-style rooms is located near Kagoshima Station (not to be confused with Kagoshima Chuo Station), about a 10-minute walk from the Tenmonkan-Dori covered shopping street and a 3-minute walk from the ferry to Sakurajima. Its English-speaking owner is knowledgeable about area sightseeing and has even prepared handouts on how to get to Ibusuki and Chiran. No meals are served, but there's free coffee and tea and a communal refrigerator, as well as a laundry room, and the owner will direct you to nearby restaurants or, if you wish, help you order delivery pizza or sushi.

1–18 Yasui-cho, Kagoshima 892-0815. ✆ **099/226-5125.** Fax 099/226-5126. www.satsuma.ne.jp/myhome/shindon. 10 units, none with bathroom. ¥4,200 single; ¥8,400 double; ¥11,970 triple. AE, MC, V. Streetcar: Shiyakusho-mae (3 min.). Take the small alley that runs between a parking lot and a temple with a big bell and then the 1st left. **Amenities:** Lobby computer w/free Internet; Wi-Fi (free, in kitchen). *In room:* A/C, TV (some rooms).

SOUTHERN KYUSHU'S TOP SPA: IBUSUKI ★

50km (31 miles) S of Kagoshima

At the southern tip of Satsuma Peninsula, Ibusuki is southern Kyushu's most famous hot-spring resort and is home to 45,000 residents. With a pleasant average temperature of 66°F (19°C) throughout the year due to warm ocean currents, it's a region of lush vegetation, flowers, and palm trees. It also boasts Japan's best natural hot-sand bath and beaches, making it a fine choice for a low-key vacation.

Essentials

GETTING THERE Ibusuki is approximately an hour from Kagoshima Chuo Station by **JR train,** with the fare costing ¥970 one-way. Alternatively, and traveling the same tracks as the regular train, there's the **Ibusuki no Tamatebako** (Ibusuki Treasure Box), a sightseeing train outfitted with upholstered chairs positioned to take advantage of views of Sakurajima and Kinko Bay. There are three departures daily (you should make reservations) and the fare is ¥2,070, free with a JR Rail Pass. **Buses** depart from Kagoshima's Yamagataya Bus Center in the heart of the city (near the Asahi-Dori streetcar stop) seven times a day (some make stops at Kagoshima Chuo Station before traveling onward), reaching Ibusuki's train station 1½ hours later and costing ¥930 one-way. You can also reach Ibusuki by bus via Chiran with its samurai garden and kamikaze museum (see p. 506 for more information).

VISITOR INFORMATION Ibusuki Tourist Information (✆ 0993/22-4114; daily 7:30am–7pm) is located in Ibusuki Station. In addition to a map of Ibusuki, it offers a luggage transfer service to local hotels (¥400 per bag) until 3:30pm daily, luggage storage (¥300 per bag), and rental bikes (see below). For online information, go to **www.city.ibusuki.lg.jp** and **www.kagoshima-kankou.com/for**.

GETTING AROUND The small town of Ibusuki is spread along the coast, north and south of the train station. Public **buses** run along the coast to the south, where most hotels are located, but not to the north, though t**axis** are also readily available. Probably the easiest way to get around is by **rental bike,** available at the tourist office daily 8am to 6pm for ¥1,000 for 4 hours (¥600 if you have a Rail Pass or train ticket) and at the JR car-rental office at Ibusuki Station daily 8am to 5pm for ¥1,500 for the day (¥900 with a Rail Pass or train ticket). By bike it takes about 7 minutes south to the Natural Sand Bath and about 25 minutes north to Chiringashima.

Exploring Ibusuki

TAKING A HOT-SAND BATH   The most popular thing to do in Ibusuki is to have yourself buried up to your neck in black sand at Yunohama Beach, heated naturally by hot springs that surface close to the ground before running into the sea. To take part, head to the **Natural Sand Bath (Suna Mushi Kaikan) ★★★** (© 0993/23-3900; daily 8:30am–noon and 1–9pm), a modern facility nicknamed **Saraku** by the locals (*saraku* has two meanings: to walk around, and to enjoy the sand). Head to the second-floor reception, pay ¥900 for the baths and rental *yukata* (add another ¥200 if you didn't bring a towel), change into the yukata in the dressing room, and then head down to the beach. One of the women there will dig you a shallow pit. Lie down, arrange your yukata so no vulnerable areas are exposed, and then lie still while she piles sand on top of you. It's quite a funny sight, actually, to see nothing but heads sticking out of the ground. The water, a hot 185°F (85°C), contains sodium chloride and is considered beneficial in alleviating rheumatism, arthritis, gastrointestinal troubles, neuralgia, and female disorders. It is also valued as a beauty treatment for the skin. After your 15-minute sand bath, go indoors for a relaxing hot-spring bath and the sauna. The Natural Sand Bath is a 20-minute walk or 7-minute bike ride from Ibusuki Station; from the main exit, head straight down Chuo Dori to the beach and turn right. You can also take a bus to the Suna Mushi Kaikan-mae stop.

SATSUMA DENSHOKAN (薩摩伝承館) **★★★**   You'd expect to find this world-class private gallery in a big city like Tokyo, but Satsuma Denshokan (© 0993/23-0211; daily 9am–5pm), is at home instead in this small resort town's Hakusuikan ryokan (see below), thanks to the *ryokan's* owners who spent the past 65 years amassing this amazing 3,000-piece collection. Housed in a restful, Kyoto-style building set within a reflective pond (and stunningly illuminated at night), it shows some 380 pieces on a rotating basis, including Satsuma ceramics created especially for export and made popular by the 1867 Paris Exposition, Chinese ceramics and porcelain spanning 5,000 years, woodblock prints, and artifacts dating from the Meiji Restoration (including Saigo Takamori's *haori* jacket). You can easily spend an hour or more here, twice that if you take full advantage of the free audio guide and a spin through the museum shop. Admission is ¥1,000 for adults, ¥800 for university students, ¥600 for high-school students, and ¥300 for children (staying guests pay half price). There's no public transportation here, so you'll have to take a taxi 5 minutes from Ibusuki Station or ride about 20 minutes by bike.

SWIMMING & HIKING   Several resorts listed below have their own beach. Otherwise, ask the tourist office for an update on Sun-Beach Ibusuki, a public beach that's unfortunately been closed due to a typhoon that deposited large rocks. Another popular destination is Chiringashima, a small, uninhabited island and national park. During low tide from March to November, you can walk to the island via an 800m (2,625-ft.) sand-bridge in about 15 minutes. Be sure to inquire beforehand what time the tide comes in, however, so you don't get stranded.

Where to Eat

Aoba LOCAL SPECIALTIES/VARIED JAPANESE   This simple restaurant near Ibusuki Station offers a variety of *teishoku* set meals and dishes from its Japanese menu with photos, virtually all of which come with *onsen tamago*, eggs soft-boiled in hot-spring water, an Ibusuki specialty. Onsen tamago is even served on the Caesar salad. Other dishes include yakitori, black pork *tonkatsu*, and *chige nabe*, a very spicy (and yummy) soup with vegetables, *tonkotsu* (see the dining section in the Kagoshima section earlier for a description of local cuisine) and—what else?—tamago onsen. Set meals feature tonkatsu, shabu-shabu, *unagi* (grilled eel), and kaiseki.

1–2–11 Minato. ✆ **0993/22-3356.** Set meals ¥1,080–¥3,000. No credit cards. Thurs–Tues 11am–3pm and 5:30–10:30pm. Station: Ibusuki (1 min.). Turn left out of the station; it's on the main road to the left.

Chozjuan (長寿庵) LOCAL SPECIALTIES/VARIED JAPANESE   Tempura, *somen* (cold noodles), udon, soba, and other typical Japanese dishes are available at this modern restaurant, as well as regional specialties. There's a set meal for ¥1,000 that features *onsen tamago* (see above) served with minced meat, plus two side dishes and noodles. The expanded dinner menu includes yakitori, sashimi, tonkotsu, tonkatsu, noodles, shabu-shabu, and more, along with set meals.

2167–1 Omase Jyuni-cho. ✆ **0993/22-5272.** Main dishes ¥500–¥2,000; set meals ¥1,000–¥2,500. AE, DC, MC, V. Daily 11am–2:30pm and 5–10pm. Ibusuki Station (1 min.). Behind (west of) the station to the right, behind bamboo.

Ristorante Fenice di Acqua Pazza ★ 🍴 ITALIAN   This restaurant is not as easy to get to as those above, but if you're visiting Satsuma Denshokan (see above), this restaurant is in the same cool building and is a great choice for lunch. With its white tablecloths, brick and glass walls, artwork, and attentive service, it looks much more expensive than it is. The ¥1,980 set lunch, for example, includes an appetizer featuring Kagoshima ingredients, soup, pasta of the day, dessert, and coffee. Or, dine on salad, pasta, or the day's fish or meat from the a-la-carte-menu, available also for dinner.

Chirin-no-Sato. ✆ **0993/23-0214.** Main dishes ¥1,210–¥2,860; set dinners ¥3,300–¥9,350; set lunches ¥1,980–¥3,080. AE, DC, MC, V. Daily 11:30am–2:30pm and 6–9pm (last order). Ibusuki Station: 5 min. by taxi or 20 min. by bike (no public transportation).

Where to Stay
EXPENSIVE

Ibusuki Hakusuikan (指宿白水館) ★★★ 🎒   A driveway lined with pine trees sets the mood for this modern, elegant, and resortlike *ryokan* right on the beach with landscaped lawns and one of the most impressive hot-spring baths I've ever seen. Established in 1960 and expanded over the years, the ryokan seems like a village, with several buildings connected by corridors. The public bath—a reproduction of an Edo-Era hot-spring spa—is classy and refined, also designed like a small village with a large bathing area made of cypress wood and stone with pools of varying temperatures, a huge *rotenburo* (outdoor hot-spring pool), a sand bath, a steam room, and a replica Edo-Era sauna with a round dome. Even the dressing rooms are faithfully styled after the Edo Period, though naturally with all the latest conveniences. Other pluses: the ryokan's own museum, Satsuma Denshokan (see above), and its own beach.

Several room types are available. Least expensive are the 30 Western-style twins, all of which face inland and are rather ordinary looking. Better are the Japanese-style *tatami* rooms facing the sea, as well as the ryokan's 115 combination rooms, spacious with both beds and separate tatami areas and available in various price categories (or, stay in nearby sister property **Augerbe Gatayama Club,** ✆ **0993/23-0122,** a former summer retreat for bank employees offering seclusion, just 8 twin and tatami rooms, and a French restaurant for ¥15,000 per person, including two meals). Meals are served in a wide choice of Japanese and Western restaurants. This place is the perfect getaway; you'll want to change into your *yukata* as soon as you arrive. No wonder former Prime Minister Koizumi chose this ryokan for a summit meeting with Korea.

Chirin-no-Sato, Ibusuki, Kagoshima Prefecture 891-0404. www.hakusuikan.co.jp/en. ✆ **0993/22-3131.** Fax 0993/23-3860. 205 units. ¥15,900–¥36,900 per person. ¥1,050–¥2,100 extra on weekends. Rates include breakfast and dinner. AE, DC, MC, V. Taxi: 5 min. from Ibusuki Station. (No public transportation.) **Amenities:** 6 restaurants; coffee shop; 2 bars (including a shochu tasting bar); 2 lounges; nightclub; lobby computer w/free Internet; fantastic indoor/outdoor hot-spring and sand bath; museum; outdoor swimming pool. *In room:* A/C, TV w/pay movies, hair dryer, Internet, minibar.

Ibusuki Iwasaki Hotel ★ ☺ This is Ibusuki's best-known spa hotel, a self-contained resort on 50 hectares (125 acres) of lush tropical grounds with pleasant walking trails throughout. Open for 40 years, it's very popular with Japanese tour groups for its facilities, including huge public baths, outdoor swimming pools kids love (they like the amusement hall with table tennis, 10-pin bowling, and video games, too), a beach, and the Ibusuki Golf Club (hotel guests get discounts; or ask about golf packages). During the off season, however, you have the hotel seemingly to yourself. Another plus is the resort's private, eclectic museum featuring Japanese artists painting in the Western style, some Western artists (Gauguin), crafts from Papua New Guinea, and Satsuma pottery. All rooms have either a full or partial view of the sea and a balcony; the best rooms also have views of the wonderful grounds, one of the resort's best features and well worth a stroll. Nights here are nice, with the sound of waves and frogs croaking in the lotus pond.

3755 Juni-cho, Ibusuki, Kagoshima Prefecture 891-0493. http://ibusuki.iwasakihotels.com/en. ✆ **0993/22-2131.** Fax 0993/24-3215. 285 units. ¥15,015–¥25,410 double. AE, DC, MC, V. Taxi: 5 min. from Ibusuki Station. Bus (does not have a number) 1 to 3 times hourly to Ibusuki Iwasaki Hotel stop. **Amenities:** 4 restaurants; coffee shop; rental bikes (¥525 for 2 hr.); bowling arcade; fitness room (fee: ¥500); indoor/outdoor hot-spring baths overlooking the sea; hot-sand baths (fee: ¥1,050); Ibusuki Golf Club; Jacuzzi; minigolf (fee: ¥1,050 for 2 hr.); museum and craft gallery (admission: ¥600); elaborate outdoor pool w/waterslide and children's pool; room service; soccer field; outdoor lighted tennis courts; Wi-Fi (free, in lobby). *In room:* A/C, TV, hair dryer, minibar.

MODERATE

Ibusuki Kyuka-Mura (指宿国民休暇村) ⟋ This government-owned lodge is located right at the water's edge near Chiringashima and the public beach (but a bit far from town) and offers reasonably priced, basic accommodations, making it a popular choice with Japanese families. During summer vacation months, on New Year's, in March during spring vacation, and in May during school trips, you should reserve 6 months in advance. At other times, it's relatively easy to get a room here. The cheapest rooms are the eight Western-style rooms, which face inland and have toilets but no bathrooms, but I prefer the Japanese-style rooms for the same price (also with toilet only) that are the size of 7½ *tatami* mats and have glass sliding doors opening seaside. Most expensive are roomy, 10-mat Japanese-style rooms facing the sea with bathroom (you can even see the water from the tub); some even have a balcony with chairs.

10445 Higashikata, Ibusuki, Kagoshima Prefecture 891-0404. www.qkamura.or.jp. 🕿 **0993/22-3211.** Fax 0993/22-3213. 65 units (7 with bathroom, 58 with toilet only). ¥4,800–¥6,400 per person. Buffet breakfast ¥1,300 extra. Japanese dinner ¥2,500–¥6,000 extra. AE, DC, MC, V. Free shuttle buses depart from in front of Ibusuki Station 3 times a day. **Amenities:** Restaurant; lounge; rental bikes (¥500 for 2 hr.); indoor/outdoor hot-spring baths; Ping-Pong; sand baths (fee: ¥945; Wi-Fi (free, in lobby). *In room:* A/C, TV, fridge.

INEXPENSIVE

Weekly Mansion Kaisui (ウィークリーマンション海水)   The two brick buildings here are a former apartment complex, so their rooms, which can hold up to four persons, feature kitchenettes (they're unequipped, so ask management for pots, pans, plates, and utensils if you plan to cook), beds and tatami areas, laundry machines, and separate rooms for the tub and toilet. There's also a cafeteria, but best of all is the location, right on the sea near the Natural Sand Bath, where you can see the sunrise from your room. A good choice if you're the independent type; not much English is spoken.

5–24–15 Yunohama, Ibusuki, Kagoshima Prefecture 891-0405. 🕿 **0993/22-6001** or 080/3950-9262. 43 units. ¥3,500–¥4,500 per person. Breakfast ¥500 extra. Dinner ¥1,500 extra. No credit cards. Station: Ibusuki (20 min.); from the main exit, walk straight on Chuo Dori to the beach and turn right. Bus: Shieonsen-mae (1 min). Going in the direction of the Ibusuki Iwasaki Hotel (ask for the Ibusuki Iwasaki Hotel *yuki* bus; the bus does not have a number), get off at the Shieonsen-mae stop and turn left for the beach. Pickup service available. **Amenities:** Cafeteria w/free Wi-Fi. *In room:* A/C, TV, no phone.

BEPPU, KING OF THE HOT-SPRING SPAS ★★

1,228km (763 miles) SW of Tokyo; 186km (116 miles) SE of Fukuoka

Beppu gushes forth more hot-spring water than anywhere else in Japan. With approximately 2,832 hot springs spewing forth 130,000 kiloliters (34 million gal.) of water daily, it has long been one of the country's best-known spa resorts. Some 11.5 million people come to Beppu every year to relax and rejuvenate themselves in one of the city's 100-some public bathhouses, and they do so in a number of unique ways: They sit in mud baths up to their necks, they bury themselves in hot black sand, they soak in hot springs, and on New Year's they bathe in water filled with floating orange peels. They even drink hot-spring water and eat food cooked by its steam.

Bathing reigns supreme here—and I suggest you join in the fun. After all, visiting Beppu without enjoying the baths would be like going to a world-class restaurant with your own TV dinner.

Not a very large town, with a population of 120,000, Beppu is situated on Kyushu's eastern coast in a curve of Beppu Bay, bounded on one side by the sea and on the other by steep hills and mountains. On cold days, steam rises everywhere throughout the city, escaping from springs and pipes and giving the town an otherworldly appearance. Indeed, eight of the hot springs look so much like hell that that's what they're called—Jigoku, the Hells. But, rather than a place most people try to avoid, the Hells are a major tourist attraction. In fact, everything in Beppu is geared toward tourism, and if you're interested in rubbing elbows with Japanese on vacation—particularly older Japanese and multi-generational families—this is one of the best places to do so.

Essentials

GETTING THERE **By Plane** The nearest airport is Oita Airport (OIT; www. oita-airport.jp), a 45-minute bus ride away (bus fare: ¥1,450).

By Train From Tokyo, take the Shinkansen to Kokura and transfer there to a limited express bound for Beppu; the trip takes 6 hours by Nozomi and more than 7 hours by Hikari (not including transfers) and costs ¥22,940 for unreserved seats. There are also direct trains daily from Hakata Station in Fukuoka (trip time: 2 hr.) and Kumamoto (3 hr.), with the latter making stops also at Aso Station, gateway to Mount Aso (p. 495). From Kagoshima, as counterintuitive as it sounds, it's faster to take the Shinkansen up to Kokura and change there for the limited express to Beppu.

By Bus There are two buses departing Kumamoto Station daily (at 11:20am and 3:20pm) for ¥3,850, arriving at Beppu Station at 6:38 and 8:35pm, respectively, with the first bus making a 90-minute stop at the Mount Aso ropeway.

By Ferry Ferries make nightly runs from Osaka at 7:09pm Monday to Thursday and at 7:55pm Friday to Sunday, arriving at Beppu at 6:55am and 7:45am, respectively. Fares begin at ¥9,600. Contact tourist offices in Osaka (see chapter 8) or the **Ferry Sunflower** in Osaka (© 06/6572-5181) for more information.

From Shikoku, the most practical ferry is from Yahatahama, running six times daily and costing ¥3,020 one-way for the almost 3-hour trip; contact the **Uwajima Unyu Co.** for information (© 0894/23-2536).

VISITOR INFORMATION The **Beppu Foreign Tourist Information Office** (© 0977/21-6220; daily 9am–5pm) is located in Beppu Station at the east (main) exit. A second tourist office, 1–3–17 Kitahama (© 0977/23-1119; daily 10am–5pm) is a 5-minute walk due east of the main exit on Beppu's main street, in the Sol Paseo Ginza shopping arcade. Finally, a third office is near the Hells at 5 Furomoto (© 0977/66-3855; daily 9am–5pm; closed 3rd Wed of every month) and has free hot-spring water to drink (it has a salty taste), a footbath, and a kitchen where you can steam-cook your own food (p. 520). The latter two offices also have computers with free Internet access. Online, go to **www.beppu-navi.jp** and **www.visit-oita.jp**.

ORIENTATION & GETTING AROUND **Beppu Station** is located near the center of the city. Its main exit is to the east and the sea, while to the west lie the Hells and the majority of hot-spring baths. Because most destinations are not within walking distance, the easiest ways to get around Beppu are by bus and by taxi. Of the two bus companies serving Beppu, the **Kamenoi Bus Company** (© 0977/23-0141) is the largest and serves most of the city. Fares begin at ¥140 and increase according to the distance, with stops announced in English, but if you plan on doing a lot of sightseeing there's a 1-day pass called **My Beppu Free**—which nonetheless costs ¥900 for adults, half-price for children 11 and under, and allows unlimited travel on Kamenoi Company buses (which are blue) in the city. You can purchase the passes at the Tourist Information Office in the station.

Taking the Waters

Beppu is divided into eight hot-spring areas, each with its own mineral content and natural characteristics. Although any hot-spring bath can help stimulate metabolism and blood circulation and create a general feeling of well-being, there are specific springs with various mineral contents that Japanese believe help relieve ailments ranging from rheumatism and diabetes to skin disease. The tourist office has a pamphlet so you can select the baths that will benefit you the most. And whatever you do, don't rinse off with plain water after taking your bath because this will wash away all those helpful minerals. You should bring your own towel and, for some places, a *yukata* (cotton kimono), though the latter is also available for sale or for rent.

HOT-SPRING BATHS

SUGINOI PALACE A 15-minute bus ride from Beppu Station, **Suginoi Palace** ★★ (www.suginoi-hotel.com; ℂ **0977/24-1141**) is an amusement center with one of the best-known baths in all of Japan. Called **Tanayu** and built of natural woods and glass, it's refined and spacious, with different kinds of baths both inside and out that take advantage of its hillside perch with great views out over the town toward the sea. In addition to an indoor bath, Jacuzzi, and sauna with panoramic views, there are outdoor cypress tubs, waterfall massages (great for shoulders and backs), and even shallow pools with headrests so you can recline to gaze upon the view. It's open daily 9am to 11pm (longer hours for guests staying at Suginoi Hotel).

If you're shy about disrobing in front of strangers or have kids in tow, the adjoining **Aqua Garden** has a huge, open-air hot-spring pool, also with views over the city, as well as a kids's pool, saunas, and a Float Healing Bath (an indoor, Zen-like experience with mood lighting and underwater music). Hours here are daily 10am to 10pm. One admission covers both facilities for ¥1,500 for adults and ¥900 for children on weekdays, ¥2,000 and ¥1,200 respectively on weekends and holidays. If, however, you're staying at the Suginoi Hotel (p. 521), you can use all baths for free (note that people with tattoos are now allowed).

From mid-July through August, there's also Suginoi's **Aqua-Beat,** a water park with water slides (great fun!), children's pools, a simulated wave pool, and a Jacuzzi. Admission here is ¥2,800 for adults, ¥1,600 for junior-high and high-school students, and ¥1,000 for children 4 to 12 (free for hotel guests). It's open daily 9am to 6pm.

To reach Suginoi Palace, take the hotel's free shuttle from Beppu Station's west exit (to the right, in a parking lot), running hourly from 9am to 9pm. By the way, much of the energy to run the vast complex, including the hotel, is steam generated.

TERMAS SPA (KITAHAMA ONSEN) A hot-spring public spa beside the sea, Termas Spa, 11–1 Kyomachi (ℂ **0977/24-4126;** Fri–Wed 10am–10pm), offers indoor baths and a sauna, as well as a large outdoor hot-spring pool and Jacuzzi for both sexes overlooking the sea (you wear your swimsuit here; rental suits cost ¥150). Admission is ¥500 for adults, half-price for children. It's a 20-minute walk from Beppu Station (take the east exit and turn left when you reach the sea; it will be on the right); or take bus no. 20 or 26 to Matogahama Koen stop.

HOT-SAND BATHS

One of the unique things you can do in Beppu is to take a "bath" in hot sand, considered useful for treating muscle pain, arthritis, and indigestion. Although several public baths offer the experience, one of the most atmospheric places is the **Takegawara Bathhouse** ★★★, 16–23 Motomachi, Beppu 874 (ℂ **0977/23-1585;** daily 8am–10:30pm, closed 3rd Wed of each month). Established in 1879 and reconstructed in 1938 in traditional, Meiji-Era architecture, this beautiful wooden structure is one of the oldest public baths in the city and has an interior that resembles an ancient gymnasium, dominated by a pit filled with black sand. The attendants are used to foreigners here; they'll instruct you to change into the provided *yukata* and lie down in a hollow they've dug in the sand. An attendant will then shovel sand on top of you and pack you in until only your head and feet are sticking out. I personally didn't find the sand all that hot, but it is relaxing as the heat soaks into your body. You stay buried for 10 minutes, contemplating the wooden ceiling high above and hoping you don't get an itch somewhere. When the time is up, the attendant will tell you to stand up, shower off the sand, and then jump into a bath of hot water. The cost is ¥1,000. To reach the bathhouse, a 10-minute walk from Beppu Station, take the station's main (east) exit and walk toward the sea, turning right at the street just before the big intersection (across from Tokiwa department store). The bathhouse is a couple of blocks down this street on the right, with its entrance around the corner.

More to See & Do

THE HELLS (JIGOKU)   You might as well join everyone else and go to the Hells, boiling ponds created by volcanic activity. Their Japanese name, Jigoku, refers to the burning hell of Buddhist sutras. Six of the eight Hells are clustered close together in the Kannawa hot-spring area, within walking distance of each other, and they can be toured in about 90 minutes or so. Each hell has its own attraction, but because a few are kind of hokey, you might just want to visit a couple (the first three below are my favorites).

Umi Jigoku, or Sea Hell, has a nice garden setting (spectacular in spring when azaleas are in bloom), a cobalt-blue pond, a greenhouse with giant lotus plants, and a footbath where you can soak your feet in hot springs. **Oniishibozu Jigoku** features bubbling mud (said to resemble a shaved monk's head), a footbath, and its own hot-spring baths (extra admission charged for the baths). **Kamado Jigoku,** the Oven Hell, was used for cooking and has a statue of a red devil (read: photo op). Skip **Yama Jigoku,** featuring animals living in deplorable conditions; **Oniyama Jigoku,** featuring much of the same for crocodiles; and **Shiraike Jigoku,** the White Pond Hell, with fish tanks that look like they haven't been cleaned in ages. To reach this cluster of hells, located in Kannawa, take bus no. 2 from Beppu Station's west exit 20 minutes to Umijigoku-mae bus stop (fare: ¥320). If you wish to see more, you can then take bus no. 16 from the Kannawa bus stop 6 minutes onward to the Chinoike-Jigoku-mae bus stop (fare: ¥180), where you'll find **Chinoike Jigoku,** the Blood-Pond Hell, which is blood red in color because of the red clay dissolved in the hot water; and **Tatsumaki Jigoku,** or Waterspout Hell, which has one of the largest geysers in Japan but is unimpressive due to a stone roof erected over the geyser.

The Hells are open daily 8am to 5pm. Admission fee to each is ¥400 for adults, ¥350 for high-school students, ¥160 for junior-high students, and ¥160 for children, but if you think you'll visit all of them, buy the combination ticket for ¥2,000, ¥1,300, ¥1,000, and ¥900, respectively. For more information, contact the **Beppu Jigoku Association** at © **0977/66-1577** or visit its website at www.beppu-jigoku.com.

BEPPU CITY TRADITIONAL BAMBOO CRAFTS CENTER (BEPPU-SHI TAKEZAIKU DENSTO SAINGYO KAIKAN)   Beppu is famous for its bamboo crafts, and the best place to shop for bambooware and to learn more about this amazingly durable material is this museum at 8–3 Higashisoen (© **0977/23-1072;** Tues–Sun 8:30am–5pm). Exhibits explain how bamboo grows, the different varieties of bamboo (620 kinds are found in Japan; 1,250 grow worldwide), and the role bamboo has played in daily Japanese life, with displays that include palanquins, fish traps, lunch boxes, toys, fans, hats, bows, arrows, and a beautiful 1920s stationery box by

National Living Treasure Sato Chiyota. Even Edison's electric light bulb used a bamboo filament. You can see it in 15 minutes, but with your new appreciation for bamboo, you'll easily spend an additional 15 minutes in its shop. Admission is ¥300 for adults and high-school students, ¥100 for children. To reach it, take bus no. 1 from Beppu Station's west exit to the Minabaru stop (fare: ¥230), backtrack to the traffic light, and walk 3 minutes on the downhill street on the right.

MONKEYS & AN AQUARIUM   On Beppu's southern border rises **Mount Takasaki,** home to some 1,200 wild monkeys and one of Japan's largest monkey habitats (℃ **097/532-5010;** daily 8:30am–5pm). At the base of the mountain where they're fed, however (to keep them from raiding farmers' fields), it's nothing but concrete and they don't seem particularly wild or concerned about the humans walking among them. Admission is ¥500 for adults (half-price for children). Come here only if you have children, combining it with a trip to **Umitamago,** Kaigan, Takasakiyama-shita (℃ **097/534-1010;** daily 9am–6pm, to 9pm some weekends and holidays), across the highway via pedestrian bridge. This aquarium features an 8m-high (26-ft.) circular tank with 3,000 fish and sea creatures from the seas around Kyushu, as well as seals, sea lions, dolphins, sea otters, sea turtles, penguins, a Japanese giant salamander (the world's largest amphibian), a touch pool with harmless sharks and rays, a discovery room for small children, and shows. Admission is ¥1,890 for adults, ¥950 for junior-high and elementary students, and ¥630 for children (free for children 3 and younger). To reach Mount Takasaki and the aquarium, take an Oita Kotsu bus that departs from Beppu Station for Oita Station about once an hour (more frequently from Kitahama, about a 10-minute walk south of Beppu Station) for 10 minutes to Takasakiyama stop; unfortunately, your My Beppu Free pass isn't accepted on this bus, so you'll have to pay ¥230.

Where to Eat

In addition to the choices here, a fun place for a meal is **Jigoku-Mushi Kobo Kannawa,** 5 Furomoto (℃ **0977/66-3775**), which allows you to cook your own food in traditional steam ovens and is located in the same building as the tourist office near the Hells, on Ideyuzaka slope (bus stop: Kannawa). You can bring your own food, or buy tickets from the vending machine for crab, shrimp, chicken, potatoes and vegetables (¥500–¥1,000 per dish; tourist office staff can help). You then go to a counter for bamboo baskets laden with your food, pay ¥500 for 30 minutes of cooking time, and lower your baskets into ovens powered by geothermal steam. This self-service facility, open daily from 9am to 8pm (closed 3rd Wed of every month), is so do-it-yourself, you're even responsible for clearing your table and washing your dishes in the communal sink.

Biliken (ビリケン) VARIED JAPANESE   It is easy to spot this casual restaurant, on the main street halfway between the station and the sea and popular with shoppers, businessmen, and families, because of the gold statue to the left of the doorway of Biliken—a curious-looking, bald-headed, round-tummied god who is said to bring good luck. A display case and English-language menu make ordering easy for Japanese set meals that include tempura, broiled eel, sashimi, *tonkatsu*, and more, with seating on *tatami* or at dark lacquered tables.

2–1–18 Kitahama. ℃ **0977/21-2088.** Set meals ¥650–¥2,100; set lunch ¥600. No credit cards. Fri–Wed 11:30am–9pm. Station: Beppu (4 min.). From the east exit, on the left side of the main road leading to the sea, across from the Foreign Tourist Information Office.

Mitsu Boshi (三ツ星) ★★ FRENCH This small, cozy restaurant on the main road leading south of the six clusters of Hells has an English-language menu offering grilled lobster, grilled prawn, the local Bungo beef, and other dishes expertly executed by the owner-chef, Otsuka-san. For a special treat, order the ¥2,100 set lunch or ¥3,990 set dinner featuring the chef's original creations of French cuisine with a Japanese twist, presented in a *kaiseki* style and using regional ingredients. Vegetarian meals are also available on request.

284 Kannawa. ⓒ **0977/67-3536.** Main dishes ¥1,260–¥3,100; set dinners ¥2,520–¥6,300; set lunches ¥1,050–¥5,250. AE, MC, V. No credit cards. Wed–Mon 11am–3pm and 5–9pm. Bus: Kannawa stop (1 min.). In front of the bus stop, on Miyuki Zaka.

Where to Stay

As with most hot-spring spas, Beppu levies a hot-springs tax: ¥150 per person, per night. In addition, some places raise their rates for New Year's, Golden Week (Apr 29–May 5), Obon (mid-Aug), Saturdays, and evenings before holidays.

EXPENSIVE

Sennari Inn (千成) ★★★ 🎴 This 70-year-old inn was originally built as a vacation villa and still serves as a serene haven from the outside world with its traditional architecture and beautiful garden views from every room, three of which have their own private outdoor bath. It's also known for its elaborate meals that may include specialties like *fugu* (blowfish), though the second-generation owner will accommodate personal tastes and allergies if given advance notice. Dinner is served true *ryokan* style in the comfort of your room if you wish, while breakfast is offered in a communal *tatami* room. One room is a combination room with tatami and a bed, while the rest are all tatami. Note that there's an 11pm curfew.

2–18 Noguchimoto-machi, Beppu, Oita Prefecture. 874-0933. ⓒ **0977/21-1550.** Fax 0977/21-1542. 8 units. ¥15,750–¥25,000 per person including 2 meals; ¥8,400 per person without meals off season, ¥10,500 per person without meals in high season. AE, DC, MC, V. Station: Beppu (2 min.). From the west exit, walk cattycorner to the right and take the small street between the slanted stone wall and Fujiyoshi Hotel; it's on the right, on a corner. **Amenities:** Indoor/outdoor hot-spring baths. *In room:* A/C, TV, fridge.

Suginoi Hotel ★★ ☺ One of the best-known hotels in Kyushu, Suginoi is famous for its adjoining Suginoi Palace with its hot-spring indoor and outdoor baths and summer water park, all free to hotel guests (p. 518). Situated on a wooded hill with a sweeping view of the city and sea below, it's a lively and noisy hotel, filled with good-natured vacationers; if you like being in the middle of the action, this is the place for you. The complex is actually two hotels in one, each with its own check-in counter and both offering Japanese-style, Western-style (with beds), and combination (with both beds and *tatami* area) rooms. Rates are based on season, room type, and view; those facing inland are slightly cheaper. The older main building (Hon-Kan) is larger, catering primarily to families and groups (its Western-style rooms face only inland), while the Hana-kan is smaller and has mostly Western-style rooms, including those facing the sea. Linking the two is the upscale middle wing, Naka-Kan, offering Ceada Floor rooms with a modern twist on traditional Japanese design complete with open-air baths; stylish Grace Floor rooms with semi-open balcony baths; and the so-called Good Time Floor geared toward multi-generational families with its disabled-access facilities. With all the kiddie diversions—water park, game room, and cheap eats in Suginoi Palace—this is a perfect choice for families. The downside is that the place is so vast you have to hike to its various facilities or take the free shuttle bus, and it's inconvenient to the rest of Beppu.

Kankaiji, Beppu, Oita Prefecture. 874-0822. www.suginoi-hotel.com. ☎ **0977/24-1141.** Fax 0977/21-0010. 592 units. ¥12,150–¥40,050 per person, including 2 meals. Rates higher in peak season. AE, DC, MC, V. From Beppu Station, free hotel shuttle bus every hour (daily 9am–9pm). Taxi: 8 min. **Amenities:** 5 restaurants; bar; lounge; Suginoi Palace with hot-spring baths (see "Taking the Waters," above); 2 24-hr. hot-spring baths for hotel guests only; spa w/hot sand baths (extra fee charged); water park (mid-July to Aug only). *In room:* A/C, TV, hair dryer, Internet (some rooms), minibar.

MODERATE

Hotel Arthur   I like the location of this hotel, just a 3-minute walk from Beppu Station but tucked away on a side street near restaurants and bars. A warmly decorated lobby sporting a medieval suit of armor leads to the usual small rooms, which have shades in addition to curtains for extra darkness. The cheapest singles have narrow beds and no closets, but some higher-priced singles from the seventh floor have views of the sea between buildings. Extras include a 10th-floor restaurant with good views from three sides and decent Western food, plus two small hot-spring baths, one with a sauna (and the first I've ever seen with a TV in it), with alternating hours for men and women. The hotel does a good job explaining all its services in English.

1–2–5 Kitahama, Beppu, Oita Prefecture. 874-920. www.hotel-arthur.co.jp. ☎ **0977/25-2611.** Fax 0977/24-0073. 120 units. ¥5,500–¥7,500 single; ¥9,500–¥14,000 double. Rates higher on Sat and holidays for double occupancy. AE, DC, MC, V. Station: Beppu (3 min.). From the station's main east exit, walk straight ahead for 2 blocks to a stoplight just past Ekimae Onsen and turn right. **Amenities:** Restaurant; indoor hot-spring bath; lobby computer w/free Internet; sauna; smoke-free rooms. *In room:* A/C, TV, fridge, hair dryer, Internet.

Sakaeya (サカエ屋) ★★ 🏠   The oldest *minshuku* (family-run inn) in the city, this place near the Hells is full of local character. Like many older homes in Beppu, it utilizes hot springs for a number of in-house uses, including old radiators heated naturally from hot springs and a *jigokugama* (stone oven) in the courtyard that uses steam from hot springs for cooking. Rooms are all Japanese style, with two choices for accommodations. The cheapest option is a room without a bathroom in the oldest part of the inn, dating from the Meiji Period (1868–1912), where you lay out your own futon and cook your own meals in the jigokugama or in a modern communal kitchen. If you can afford it, however, opt for rates that include meals. Not only will your accommodations be nicer, with a traditional atmosphere with sitting alcoves and bathrooms, but also your dinner will be steamed using the hot springs and then served in a Japanese dining room with whitewashed walls and a heavy timbered ceiling. In winter, the *kotatsu* (a table with a heating element and covered with a blanket to keep legs warm) in the dining room is steam heated. But no matter your choice, a stay here is sure to be memorable.

Ida, Kannawa, Beppu, Oita Prefecture. 874-0043. ☎ **0977/66-6234.** Fax 0977/66-6235. 12 units, 6 with bathroom, 1 with toilet only. ¥13,650–¥21,000 per person with 2 meals; ¥3,675 per person without meals. Rates exclude service charge. Rates higher on weekends and holidays. No credit cards. Bus: Jigokubaru (2 min.); take the 1st left. **Amenities:** Indoor hot-spring baths. *In room:* A/C, coin-op TV, fridge.

Yamada Bessou (山田別荘) ★★ 🍴   Built in 1930 as a wealthy person's second home and becoming a ryokan some 65-years ago, this stately house offers traditional tatami rooms, the best of which have views of the private garden, as well as an outdoor hot-spring bath. It's located in a quiet neighborhood, not far from Beppu's main shopping street and within walking distance of the station.

3–2–18 Kitahama, Beppu, Oita Prefecture. 874-0920. ℂ**0977/24-2122.** Fax 0977/24-2122. 9 units, 2 with bathroom. ¥10,000–¥12,000 per person with 2 meals. AE, DC, MC, V. Beppu Station: 7 min. From the east exit, take the main street until you reach Sol Paseo and the Foreign Tourist Information Office (which will be on your right), turn left and then right at the tire and bike shop. **Amenities:** Indoor/outdoor hot-spring baths. *In room:* A/C, TV, fridge, Wi-Fi (most rooms).

INEXPENSIVE

Khaosan Beppu   This backpacker's hostel within walking distance of Beppu Station has both dormitory and private rooms on four floors (no elevator). These include two single rooms without bathrooms and 12 rooms with and without bathrooms that sleep two or more people and come with a bunkbed, sofa, and a small table, plus room to throw out a couple more futons. It has information on how to reach regional attractions, and pluses include free coffee and tea, a footbath at the front door, its nearby Hot Pepper bar, a communal kitchen, and a lounging area with a big TV, DVDs, and video and Wii games.

3–3–10 Kitahama, Beppu, Oita Prefecture. 874-0920. www.khaosan-beppu.com. ℂ **0977/23-3939.** 16 units, 8 with bathroom. ¥3,000 single without bathroom; ¥5,000 double without bathroom; ¥6,000 double with bathroom; ¥2,000 dormitory. No credit cards. Station: 7 min. From the east exit, walk down the main street, turn left at Kaimonji Park, and right when you reach Hot Pepper bar; it will be on the right. **Amenities:** Free bike rental; hot-spring baths; lobby computer w/free Internet. *In room:* A/C, no phone.

Yokoso (陽光荘) ★ 🥢   Housed in a beige-colored, two-story building on Ideyuzaka, the main road between the two group of Hells, Yokoso offers simple, clean Japanese-style rooms and is run by kind, English-speaking, third-generation innkeepers. Air-conditioning in summer is coin-operated, but steam heating is free. No meals are served, but a communal open-air kitchen is available, complete with a hot-springs-powered oven and suggestions for how long to cook food in bamboo steamers (there's a grocery store across the street). It boasts four hot-spring baths and one of the most interesting saunas I've ever seen, so tiny you have to crawl inside; heated naturally with hot springs, it even has a grass floor, as in the days of yore. You're also welcome to head over to the nearby annex (where there are eight more rooms) to use another hot-spring bath, and, best of all, a *rotenburo* (outdoor bath) tucked in a corner of the garden that you can use privately. Note that there's an 11pm curfew here.

Ida 3 Kumi, Kannawa, Beppu 874-0043. ℂ **0977/66-0440.** Fax 0977/66-0440. www.coara.or.jp/~hideharu. 35 units. ¥3,800 per person 1st night, ¥3,300 2nd night. No credit cards. Bus: Jigokubaru (3 min.). Take the 1st immediate left and go up the slope; it will be on the right. **Amenities:** Indoor/outdoor hot-spring baths. *In room:* Coin-op A/C, coin-op TV, no phone.

OKINAWA

O kinawa Prefecture, an archipelago of 160 islands between Kyushu and Taiwan, seems like its own country. Maybe that's because once upon a time, it was its own kingdom—the Ryukyu Kingdom—with dynasties and castles (constructed mostly btw. the 14th–18th c.), as well as its own languages, culture, and cuisine. Although it was invaded by Satsuma (in what is now Kagoshima in southern Kyushu) in the early 1600s, the Ryukyu Kingdom retained domestic autonomy, trading freely with China and elsewhere, until it was annexed to Japan after the 1868 Meiji Restoration; in 1879 it was renamed Okinawa Prefecture.

You might know Okinawa as a site of brutal combat during World War II (several sites and memorials recount the horrific battle and massive casualties). If you're a diver, you might know Okinawa as one of the best diving spots in the world. But what I've always liked about Okinawa—apart from its unique museums, historic sites, tropical weather, and the finest beaches I've seen in Japan—is its laid-back, rural atmosphere. In fact, parts of Okinawa are so off the beaten path, they seem like they're caught in a time warp of a few decades past.

Of Okinawa's 160 islands (part of the Ryukyu Island chain), only 49 are inhabited. The largest, **Okinawa Island** (Okinawa-honto), is home to Naha, capital of Okinawa Prefecture and gateway to the rest of the islands by sea and by air. After visiting Okinawa Island's many attractions, you might wish to fly or take a ferry onward to one or more of my other favorites, like **Kume Island,** renowned for its beaches, sugar cane fields, and historic sites relating to the Ryukyu Kingdom. **Iriomote** is famous for its vast pristine wilderness and for scuba diving.

Information on Okinawa is available at **www.pref.okinawa.jp** and **www.ocvb.or.jp**.

THE BEST OKINAWA EXPERIENCES

o **Learning About Okinawa's Ancient Ryuku Kingdom:** Part of a World Heritage Site, **Shuri Castle** served as the center of the Ryukyu Kingdom, which thrived for about 500 years before Okinawa became part of Japan. Learn more about Ryukyu at the **Okinawa Prefectural Museum.** See p. 528 and 528.

o **Visiting WWII Memorial Sites:** Learn about the horrific Battle of Okinawa and how it impacted Okinawans at the **Okinawa Prefectural Peace Memorial Museum,** then visit the **Himeyuri Peace**

Museum for a moving account of women and girls assigned to cave hospitals to care for the wounded. See p. 529 and 529.

○ **Spending a Day at the Beach:** Okinawa is famous for its white sandy beaches, including those on Okinawa Island, Kume, Ishigaki and Iriomote. Many offer snorkeling around coral reefs as well. See individual islands for more information.

○ **Dining on Local Specialties:** Okinawa has its own cuisine, with many dishes made from pork (like pigs' feet simmered in soy sauce and sake) and goya (bittermelon), as well as dishes influenced by stationed U.S. military like taco rice and spam sandwiches. See p. 531.

○ **Kayaking in Iriomote:** You can kayak in Japan's largest mangrove swamp followed by a trek and lunch at a waterfall in one of several guided tours in Iriomote. See p. 537.

OKINAWA ISLAND ★

1,539km (956 miles) SW of Tokyo

On April 1, 1945, Allied forces landed on Okinawa Island in an attempt to seize control of the island and use it as a base for an invasion of mainland Japan. The Battle of Okinawa, the only land battle on Japanese territory, raged for the next 82 days, with many Japanese troops and drafted Okinawans, including high-school students, ensconced in the island's many caves. By the time the horrific fighting was over, more than 200,000 people had lost their lives. Just a few weeks later, after atomic bombs were dropped on Hiroshima and Nagasaki, the Japanese surrendered.

Okinawa was then placed under control of the U.S. government until 1972, when sovereignty reverted back to Japan. Remaining, however, are American military bases, which were greatly expanded during the Korean War and that occupy land that had belonged to Okinawans for generations (75% of American bases in Japan are in Okinawa). Many protests have been lodged against the U.S. presence, especially following rapes of local women and girls by U.S. servicemen; as part of ongoing negotiations, about 9,000 troops will transfer from Okinawa to Guam, Hawaii, and other locations in coming years, leaving about 10,000 Marines in Okinawa.

Okinawa Island has a number of sites and attractions that make a 2- or 3-day stay particularly worthwhile, including nine castle sites dating from the Ryukyu Kingdom era that are on the UNESCO World Heritage list, a world-class aquarium, a theme park containing Japan's second-longest limestone cave and exhibits related to Okinawa history and culture, and several memorials for victims of the Battle of Okinawa. There are also more lighthearted pursuits, including shopping and dining in downtown Naha, sunning and swimming on the island's many white sandy beaches, and snorkeling and scuba diving among the island's surrounding coral reefs.

Essentials

GETTING THERE   By Plane   Flights to Naha Airport (OKA; ☏ **098/840-1151**) take 2 hours and 50 minutes from Tokyo's Haneda Airport, 2 hours from Osaka's Kansai Airport, and 1½ hours from Fukuoka. After stopping by the **Visitor Information Center** in either the international terminal (☏ **098/859-0742;** daily 10:30am–7:30pm) or the domestic terminal (☏ **098/857-6884;** daily 9am–9pm), head to Naha Kuko Station in the domestic terminal, where the Yui Rail monorail delivers you to Kencho-mae Station in downtown Naha in 12 minutes for ¥260. There are also Airport Limousine Buses going to major resorts on the island; it costs ¥1,860 and takes 2 hours to travel to Busena on the northwest coast.

If you plan to visit at least two Okinawan islands in addition to Okinawa Island, you can save money by purchasing an Okinawa Island Pass, valid on five specific routes within the Okinawan island chain, including flights from Naha to Kume or Ishigaki, on Japan Transocean Air (a subsidiary of JAL). A minimum of two flights, at ¥9,000 each, is required. **Note:** Tickets must be purchased from JAL before arriving in Japan.

By Ferry   Ferries travel to Naha from various ports on Honshu and Kyushu, including Tokyo, Osaka, and Kagoshima. Most frequent are those from Kagoshima, which depart every day or two and take about 25 hours, with prices starting at ¥13,200 for the cheapest class.

VISITOR INFORMATION   In addition to Visitor Information Centers at the airport, you'll find the **Naha Tourism Information Center** on Okiei Street, just off Kokusai Dori, at 2–1–4 Makishi (www.naha-navi.or.jp; (℃ **098/868-4887;** Mon–Fri 8:30am–8pm; Sat–Sun 10am–8pm), where you can pick up city maps and brochures. Be sure, too, to get the free **Okinawa Island Guide,** with information on sightseeing, marine sports, dining, accommodations, events, and more, along with maps.

ORIENTATION & GETTING AROUND   Naha, in the south part of Okinawa Island, is home to Naha Airport and the island's major attraction, Shurijo Castle. Its most famous boulevard is **Kokusai Dori** (Yui Rail stop: Kencho-mae or Makishi), lined with souvenir shops, department stores, hotels, restaurants, and bars.

For the Okinawa Prefectural Museum and Shurijo Castle, you'll have to take the **Yui Rail** monorail. It runs from Naha Airport through downtown Naha to Shuri Station, the last stop, in 27 minutes for ¥320. In operation daily 6am to 11:30pm, trains depart every 6 to 15 minutes and start at ¥220. One-day passes with unlimited rides cost ¥600; children pay half fare.

Also in the southern part of Okinawa are sites relating to World War II, as well as Okinawa World, a theme park with a cave and restored Okinawan homes housing galleries and exhibitions. U.S. military bases are located mostly in central Okinawa Island, where you'll also find Okinawa City, the island's second-largest town, and Chatan, both with many establishments, shops, and services geared toward military personnel and their families. Chatan is especially trendy, with its American Village shopping mall, dive and surf shops, international restaurants, beaches, and other amusements. North Okinawa Island, the least populated, is a hilly region with resorts, golf courses, beaches, snorkeling and diving spots, and Okinawa Churaumi Aquarium.

For destinations outside Naha, you'll have to take a **bus** from the Naha Bus Terminal (℃ **098/867-7386;** Yui Rail stop: Asahibashi). The Tourist Information Centers have pamphlets with bus information (those with numbers 20 and higher service outlying areas). Take a ticket upon boarding (fares, which increase with the distance covered, are posted up front) and pay when you get off.

If you have an international driver's license, you might wish to **rent a car.** There are many rental agencies, with locations at the airport, in Naha, at hotels and other locations. Prices start at ¥2,800 for 24 hours in a subcompact, plus ¥1,575 per day for insurance and an extra ¥1,050 in high season. For more information contact

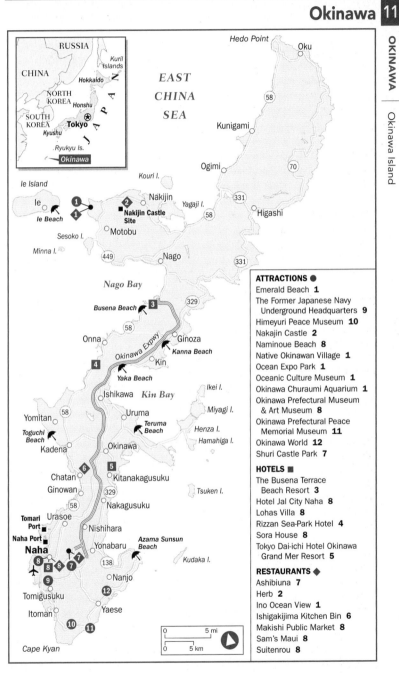

ATTRACTIONS ●

Emerald Beach **1**
The Former Japanese Navy
 Underground Headquarters **9**
Himeyuri Peace Museum **10**
Nakajin Castle **2**
Naminoue Beach **8**
Native Okinawan Village **1**
Ocean Expo Park **1**
Oceanic Culture Museum **1**
Okinawa Churaumi Aquarium **1**
Okinawa Prefectural Museum
 & Art Museum **8**
Okinawa Prefectural Peace
 Memorial Museum **11**
Okinawa World **12**
Shuri Castle Park **7**

HOTELS ■

The Busena Terrace
 Beach Resort **3**
Hotel Jal City Naha **8**
Lohas Villa **8**
Rizzan Sea-Park Hotel **4**
Sora House **8**
Tokyo Dai-ichi Hotel Okinawa
 Grand Mer Resort **5**

RESTAURANTS ◆

Ashibiuna **7**
Herb **2**
Ino Ocean View **1**
Ishigakijima Kitchen Bin **6**
Makishi Public Market **8**
Sam's Maui **8**
Suitenrou **8**

ABC-Rent-A-Car (www.abc-car.net/en; ℘ **098/859-5555**), **Budget Rent A Car** (℘ **0120/130 543**); or **Okinawa Tourist Rent-A-Car** (℘ **0120/34-3732**).

Otherwise, you can hire a **taxi** (℘ **098/831-9007**) for ¥3,150 per hour or ¥21,300 for the whole day. Mr. Takara is an English-speaking driver who knows the island well; make a reservation and negotiate the fare at ℘ **098/868-7508.**

Exploring Okinawa Island
IN NAHA
Okinawa Prefectural Museum & Art Museum (Okinawa Kenritsu Hakubutsukan & Bijutsukan) ★ ☺

Make these two museums under one roof your first stop. While the art museum is interesting for its changing exhibitions of contemporary art, including works by artists with a connection to Okinawa, the Prefectural Museum is a must if you wish to learn more about Okinawa's history, culture, and natural history and therefore gain a better understanding for what you'll see elsewhere. You'll learn about the formation of the Ryukyu archipelago; the rise and fall of the mighty Ryukyu Kingdom with its extensive trade routes to China, Japan, and Southeast Asia; the Battle of Okinawa and subsequent U.S. occupation; and Okinawan folklore, crafts, and culture. A discovery room for children is equipped with traditional toys, clothing, musical instruments, and more. Be sure to ask for the free audio guides to both museums, where you'll spend at least 1½ hours to see both.

Omoromachi 3–1–1, Naha. www.museums.pref.okinawa.jp. ℘ **098/941-8200.** Admission to Prefectural Museum ¥400 adults, ¥250 university and high-school students, ¥150 children; art museum ¥300, ¥200, and ¥100 respectively (special exhibits cost more). Daily 9am–6pm (Fri–Sat to 8pm). Yui Rail: Omoromachi Station (10 min.). West of the station toward the port.

Shuri Castle Park (Shurijo Koen) ★★★

Naha's top attraction was first constructed between the 13th and 14th centuries and served as the epicenter of the Ryukyu Kingdom for about 500 years, until the establishment of Okinawa Prefecture in 1897. Serving as both a residence for the king and an administrative and religious center, it shows architectural influences from both China and Japan but is uniquely Ryukyuan in style. Unfortunately, the original structures were destroyed in the Battle of Okinawa, but as a reflection of the site's importance, this partial re-creation, along with eight other historic properties in Okinawa Prefecture, has been designated as a World Heritage "Gusuku Sites and Related Properties of the Ryukyu Kingdom." Lots of information and pamphlets in English explain the significance of what you're seeing; you'll probably spend about an hour here, longer if you catch one of the 40-minute traditional court dances (performed, at last check, on Wed, Fri–Sun, and holidays at 11am, 2pm, and 4pm).

1–2 Kinjocho, Shuri, Naha. www.oki-park.jp/shurijo-park. ℘ **098/886-2020.** Admission ¥800 adults, ¥600 high-school students, ¥300 children. July–Sept daily 8:30am–8pm; Apr–June and Oct–Nov daily 8:30am–7pm; Dec–Mar daily 8:30am–6pm. Closed 1st Wed & Thurs in July. Yui Rail: Shurijo Station, then a 15-min. walk or bus 8 to Shurijo-mae stop.

IN SOUTH OKINAWA ISLAND
Buses for the following destinations depart from Naha Bus Terminal.

The Former Japanese Navy Underground Headquarters (Kyukaigun Shireigo) ★

This is where the Japanese Navy, under Rear Admiral Ota, took its last stand in the Battle of Okinawa. A system of underground tunnels stretching 450m (1,475 ft.) and built by civilians using shovels and pickaxes, it remains almost exactly as it was, including the operations room and where Ota killed himself with a grenade. Rather than surrender, many staff also committed suicide; 2,400 bodies were recovered after the war. Before touring the tunnels, which are rather bare but convey what it must have been like to live here (audio explanations throughout the tunnels are available in English, but you have to request them to be turned on), first tour the one-room museum. Most poignant are farewell letters written to family members.

236 Aza Tomishiro. ✆ **098/850-4055.** Admission ¥420 adults, ¥210 children. Daily 8:30am–5pm. Bus: 33, 46, or 101 to Tomigusuku Park-mae, then a 10-min. walk.

Himeyuri Peace Museum (Himeyuri Heiwa Kinen Shiryokan; ひめゆり平和祈念資料館) ★★★ Of all the war memorials, this one affects me the most, perhaps because it gives a personal dimension to the tragedy of war. It tells the story of 240 girls and teachers who in March 1945 were assigned to serve as nurse assistants in an army hospital buried inside a series of caves, where they were faced with indescribably filthy conditions and duties, including disposal of amputated limbs and burying the dead. As U.S. forces approached, the girls were thrown out of the caves to fend for themselves, where they were killed in battle or, fearing rape, took their lives. In all, 226 perished; this museum, filled with portraits and personal accounts, was founded by the survivors. You'll spend about 40 minutes here, but note that it also takes time to get here.

671–1 Aza-Ihara, Itoman. ✆ **098/997-2100.** Admission ¥300 adults, ¥200 high-school students, ¥100 children. Daily 9am–5pm. Bus: 34 or 89 to Itoman Bus Terminal (40 min.), then bus 82, 107, or 108 15 min. to Himeyuri Memorial Tower in front of the museum.

Okinawa Prefectural Peace Memorial Museum (Heiwa Kinen Shiryokan) ★★★ Through dioramas, video screens, photographs, testimonials, and a free audio guide in English, this museum vividly conveys the impact of the Battle of Okinawa on the Okinawan people, from their forced mobilization to the last days of battle, when many died in caves from artillery fire, flamethrowers, or starvation; at the hands of Japanese soldiers; or from forced suicide. But it doesn't stop there: the museum also describes Okinawan life before and after the war, from forced assimilation under the Japanese to postwar protests over the vast seizure of land for U.S. occupation. An hour and 30 minutes at this must-see will make you reflect not only on the human cost of war, but also on what Okinawans have endured for more than a century.

614–1 Aza-Mabuni, Itoman. www.peace-museum.pref.okinawa.jp. ✆ **098/997-3844.** Admission ¥300 adults, ¥150 children. Daily 9am–5pm. Bus: 89 to Itoman Bus Terminal (40 min.), then 82 to Heiwa-kinendo-iriguchi.

Okinawa World ★★ ☺ Okinawa's largest theme park promotes the region's history, culture, and natural sciences with a variety of attractions, including Gyokusendo Cave, which you can walk through in about 30 minutes along an 890m (2,900-ft.) walkway suspended above water and filled with impressive stalagmite and stalactite formations; a museum devoted to the *habu*, Okinawa's indigenous poisonous snake; an orchard of 450 tropical fruit trees; an outdoor plaza for performances of the local Eisa dance; and workshops for potters, glass blowers, weavers, and other artisans housed in restored century-old Okinawan homes. Plan on 3 hours to see everything.

1336 Maekawa, Tamagusuku, Nanjo. www.gyokusendo.co.jp/okinawaworld/en/. ✆ **098/949-7421.** Open Pass to everything ¥1,600 adults, ¥800 children. Apr–Oct daily 9am–6:30pm; Nov–Mar daily 9am–6pm. Bus: 54 or 83 to Gyokusendo-mae.

IN NORTH OKINAWA ISLAND

Ocean Expo Park (Kaiyohaku Kinen Koen) ★★ ☺   This expansive park on the northwestern coast, site of the 1975 International Ocean Expo, contains several attractions, most important of which is the **Okinawa Churaumi Aquarium ★★** (http://oki-churaumi.jp; ✆ 098/48-3740; daily Mar–Sept 8:30am–8pm, Oct–Feb 8:30–6:30pm), which concentrates on the oceans and currents surrounding the Ryukyu Islands, from coral reef habitats to the deep sea. Highlights include huge whale sharks and manta rays, dolphin shows, a touch pond for kids, a movie theater, and a close look at the colorful tropical fish that call the surrounding waters home. Admission is ¥1,800 for adults, ¥1,200 for high-school students, and ¥600 for children. Plan on 1½ hours here.

I also recommend strolling through the park's free **Native Okinawan Village (Okinawa Kyoudo Mura),** featuring more than a dozen sites modeled after a village from the Ryukyu Kingdom period, including thatch-roofed houses and storehouses, grand homes where the manor lord and priestess lived, and an *utaki* (sacred forest). Nearby, the **Oceanic Culture Museum (Kaiyo Bunka-kan;** ✆ 098/48-2741; daily May–Aug 8:30am–7pm, Sept–Apr 8:30am–5:30pm), displays items relating to oceanic people from Asia through the South Pacific, including replica boats and canoes, fishing gear, money (like the Yap's stone currency), clothing, and more. Admission is ¥170 for adults, ¥50 for children. There's also **Emerald Beach,** where you can swim free (open only Mar–Oct).

To reach Ocean Expo Park, take express bus no. 111 from Naha Bus Terminal 105 minutes to Nago Bus Terminal, followed by a 55-minute ride on bus no. 65, 66, or 70.

MARINE SPORTS

BEACHES   Okinawa, with a swimming season that runs from about March through October, has a huge variety of white sandy beaches, most with gentle slopes. Most accessible is **Naminoue Beach,** located right in Naha (bus no. 5 or 15 to Seibumon stop), but there are prettier beaches outside the city, especially to the north. Some are public beaches and some are resort beaches open to the public; many also have coral reefs popular with snorkelers. Some charge small fees. Favorites include **Okuma Beach, Emerald Beach** (in Ocean Expo Park, above), **Manza Beach, White Beach, Ikei Beach** (on Ikei Island), **Busena Beach** (popular for its watersports like windsurfing) and beaches on outlying islands like **Ie Island, Minna Island, Izena Island,** and **Iheya Island.** Ask the tourist office for bus and ferry information.

DIVING & SNORKELING   Due to its crystal-clear waters and coral reefs teeming with marine life, Okinawa is a diving mecca year-round, with Maeda Point the most popular dive spot on Okinawa Island. There are numerous dive shops offering instruction in English for everything from certification courses to *taiken* diving (experience dives for uncertified divers) to guided dives for those already certified. **Piranha Divers Okinawa,** 2277-75 Aza-Nakama, Onna Village (http://piranha-divers.jp; ✆098/967-8487), offers a variety of options, including an all-day trip to the Kerama Islands, considered one of the premier dive spots in the world, for ¥17,000 and the chance to dive with whale sharks for ¥12,000. **Reef Encounters International,** 1–273 Miyagi, in Chatan (✆ 098/936-8539; www.reefencounters.org) offers diving around Okinawa Island, to the Kerama Islands, and to islands farther afield, as well as night diving. A half-day of beach diving or snorkeling costs ¥9,800. *Note:* Dangerous sea creatures include the box jellyfish, lionfish, the crown-of-thorns starfish, and the Erabu black-banded sea krait.

Where to Eat

Okinawan cuisine is big on pork, including *tebichi* (pigs' feet), simmered for hours in soy sauce and sake to make it soft and glutinous, and *rafute,* pork belly simmered in fish broth and *awamori* liquor. Other favorites include Okinawa *soba,* made with white flour instead of the mainland's usual buckwheat; and dishes made with *goya* (bittermelon), like stir-fried *goya champuru* containing tofu, pork, egg, and other ingredients. Champuru means to "mix together" in Okinawan dialect, with the ultimate example being taco rice, an adaptation of Mexican tacos (introduced by Americans stationed here) served with rice instead of tortillas. *Kyutei* cuisine, blending Chinese and Okinawan flavors and ingredients, originated with the Ryukyuan royal court.

Pair it with the local Orion Beer or awamori, Japan's oldest distilled liquor, introduced to the Ryukyu Kingdom from Siam (present-day Thailand) in the early 15th century and made with Thai rice. By the way, Okinawan food and drink must be healthy—Okinawans live longer than anywhere else in the world.

In addition to choices below, other good bets are **Makishi Public Market,** where food vendors sell local specialties on the second floor; and **Ino Ocean View Restaurant** in the Okinawa Churaumi Aquarium (𝓒 **098/48-2745**), offering a buffet of Okinawan specialties daily 11:30am to 3pm for ¥1,260 and panoramic views.

Ashibiuna (あしびな) ★ OKINAWAN DISHES   Located south of the Shurijo Castle exit, this quaint restaurant occupies a wooden house with a red-tiled roof, a reconstructed home of a high-ranking official of the Ryukyu Kingdom. Its English-language lunch menu offers set meals of all the local favorites, including tebichi, Okinawa noodles, and goya champuru, all served with white rice or *jyushi* (rice with pork and vegetables). The dinner menu, in Japanese only, offers set courses that include sashimi, grilled fish, and other fare, along with local specialties.

2–13 Tounokura Shuri, Naha. 𝓒098/884-0035. Set dinners ¥3,150–¥5,250; set lunches ¥800–¥900. AE, MC, V. Daily 11:30am–3pm and 5:30pm–midnight. Yui Rail: Shurijo (15 min.). Turn right out of the south exit, cross the intersection, and continue straight on Ryutan Dori until you see Family Mart on the right, where you should turn left; it will be almost immediately on the right, behind a stone wall and entryway covered with bougainvillea.

Herb ★ 🍴VEGETARIAN   This cute restaurant, perched on a hill with great views over treetops toward the sea, is a destination in itself, which is good because it takes some effort to get here. Located in north Okinawa Island across from Nakajinjo Castle (on the World Heritage list and worth a visit for its rock-strewn ruins and visitor center), it offers two set meals of mostly raw seasonal fruit and vegetables (like dragon fruit, aloe, or *goya*), herbs from its own garden, and whole-grain bread and brown rice, as well as a daily pasta with salad (the menu is in Japanese only, but there are photos). Drinks include soybean milk and juice made from apples, oranges, carrots, or aloe and lemon. You must make reservations by 9am the day of your visit.

1471 Imadomari Nakajin-son. 𝓒 **098/56-5681.** Set meals ¥1,200–¥2,000. No credit cards. Sun–Thurs 11am–5pm. From Hwy. 515, across from Nakajin Castle, 1.5km (almost 1 mile) on a winding road.

Ishigakijima Kitchen Bin 🍴 HAMBURGERS   This burger joint in Chatan offers large and regular-size burgers made with local Ishigaki beef and topped with choices like avocado, cream cheese, or bacon and cheese. Or, you might opt for taco rice or pork bowl with *kimchi* and mayonnaise. Instead of fries, try the *goya* chips.

1–11–1 Chatan. 𝓒098/936-7587. Dishes ¥640–¥1,480. AE, MC, V. Daily 11am–10pm. Bus: 20, 28, 29, or 120 to Chatan (5 min.). On one of Chatan's main streets, in a bright yellow building.

Sam's Maui TEPPANYAKI   With Polynesian decor complete with Tiki torches and Hawaiian music, this restaurant is popular with tourists and locals alike. Set meals from the English-language menu offer steak, prawns, scallops, and other entrees, cooked on a *teppanyaki* grill in front of you, along with seasonal vegetables (like green papaya *kimchi*), soup (including an East Indian curry soup), salad, and potatoes or rice.

1–3–53 Makishi, Naha. www.sams-okinawa.jp/maui.© **098/861-9595.** Set dinners ¥2,850–¥5,500. AE, DC, MC, V. Daily 5pm–midnight. Yui Rail: Makishi (8 min.). On Kokusai Dori, across from OPA.

Suitenrou (首里天楼) ★ KYUTEI   A dramatic stone entryway and an interior reminiscent of the days of the Ryukyu Kingdom set the tone for the elaborate meals served here. Set meals containing famous Okinawan dishes and photographs make ordering easy. The ¥5,250 dinner is a 12-course meal that may include pork ear salad, fermented tofu, sesame-flavored pork, duck, and fish wrapped in kelp, but the highlight is a nightly performance (at 7 and 8pm) on the second floor, of folk dancing and court dances once performed for Chinese envoys visiting Shurijo Castle.

1–3–60 Makishi, Naha.© **098/863-4091.** Reservations required. Set dinners ¥3,150–¥10,500; set lunches ¥2,100–¥3,150. AE, DC, MC, V. Daily 11am–11pm (last order). Yui Rail: Makishi (8 min.). On Kokusai Dori, near Hotel Jal City.

Shopping

Okinawa is famous for a variety of crafts, including *bingata* (stencil-dyed fabric with bright tropical motifs made into clothing and accessories), pottery, Ryukuan lacquerware, Ryukyuan glassware, *kariyushi* shirts (the Okinawan version of the Hawaiian Aloha shirts), *Shisha* (lion dogs, used to ward off evil spirits), *shuri-ori* weaving, and *awamori* (a potent spirit made from Thai rice and black-*koji* mold). There are many souvenir shops along the 1.5km (1 mile) **Kokusai Dori,** but for one-stop shopping, be sure to visit **Tenbusu Naha,** in the Naha-shi Dento Kogei-kan building on Kokusai Dori at 3–2–10 Makishi (© **098/868-7866**), which contains the Naha Municipal Arts and Crafts Museum with English-language descriptions of Okinawa's various crafts (open daily 9am–6pm; admission ¥300 adults, ¥200 students, ¥100 children); the Traditional Arts & Crafts Center where you can try your hand at Bingata stencil dying and other crafts; a shop selling local crafts; and a theater with performance art three times daily Monday to Friday.

Just a few minutes' walk south of Kokusai Dori via the covered Heiwa Dori shopping arcade is **Makishi Public Market (Makishi Kousetsu Ichiba)** with food items unique to Okinawa (including pig's face, feet, and stomach), while another 7-minutes' walk farther south on Heiwa Dori brings you to **Tsuboya Yachimun Dori** with its 20-some ceramic-art workshops and galleries, definitely worth the stroll.

Where to Stay

Most hotels charge extra during peak season (New Year's, Golden Week, and summer school vacation), with discounts in the off season. Directions are from Naha Airport.

EXPENSIVE

The Busena Terrace Beach Resort ★★ ☺   Located on the northern tip of Okinawa Island and surrounded on three sides by water, this resort with an elegant yet tropical atmosphere is the ultimate getaway. In addition to many on-site facilities, including a spa and indoor and outdoor pools, Busena Beach and Busena Marine Park with an underwater observatory and glass-bottom boats are just a short walk or free shuttle ride away. The resort also offers a wide range of activities, from a kids' club to sunset cruising and fishing, along with rentals for beach umbrellas, sea kayaks, and windsurfing. Rooms range from standard ones facing inland toward a distant cape to more expensive rooms facing the ocean with balconies, but for true luxury there are "cottage" suites (from ¥103,950) with huge balconies and views from both bedroom and living room. Restaurants also take advantage of the beautiful views, making this a good choice for a romantic retreat.

1808 Kise, Nago City, Okinawa 905-0026. www.terrace.co.jp/en/busena. ⓒ **098/51-1333.** Fax 098/51-1331410 units. ¥42,735–¥56,595 double; club floor from ¥72,765 double. Rates ¥11,550 higher in peak season. AE, DC, MC, V. 120 min. via Airport Limousine from the airport. **Amenities:** 6 restaurants; lounge; 2 bars; rental bikes (¥2,625 for 3 hr.); children's center (¥7,350 per day); executive-level rooms; gym; indoor/outdoor pools; spa. *In room:* A/C, TV, hair dryer, Internet, minibar.

Rizzan Sea-Park Hotel ☺   This behemoth (it claims to have more rooms than any other hotel in Okinawa) has a great location on an 800m (½-mile) white sandy beach about halfway up the western coast. It offers lots of activities for the entire family, including marine sports, but it's too big for my tastes (just the distance from your room to the elevator can be quite a trek). Rooms (twins, suites, and family rooms) have balconies but are rather standard; it's worth splurging for a view of the ocean.

1496 Aza Tancha, Onna Village, Kunigami-gun, Okinawa 904-1496. www.rizzan.co.jp/english. ⓒ **098/964-6611.** Fax 098/964-6660. 558 units. ¥17,000–¥19,000 per person, including 2 meals. Rates higher in peak season; off-season discounts available. AE, DC, MC, V. 70 min. via Airport Limousine from the airport. **Amenities:** 9 restaurants; lounge; 2 bars; children's center for ages 5 and younger (¥1,050 per hr; parents must remain on hotel property; concierge; computer corner w/free Internet; minigolf; indoor/outdoor pools; spa; tennis courts. *In room:* A/C, TV, fridge, hair dryer.

MODERATE

Hotel Jal City Naha   It seems a shame to come all this way just to spend the night in Naha, but this is a good choice if you're in transit to another island or prefer this hotel's location right on Kokusai Dori. Rooms are small but stylish, with good views out over the city from its higher floors.

1–3–70 Makishi, Naha, Okinawa 900-0013. www.jalhotels.com/naha/. ⓒ **098/866-2580.** Fax 098/867-8491. 304 units. ¥15,015–¥16,745 single; ¥18,480–¥30,030 double. Rates higher in peak season; off-season discounts available. AE, DC, MC, V. Yui Rail: Makishi Station (8 min.). **Amenities:** Restaurant. *In room:* A/C, TV, fridge, hair dryer, Internet.

Tokyo Dai-ichi Hotel Okinawa Grand Mer Resort ★★ 🛍   It isn't on the coast, but this family hotel on top of a hill outside Okinawa City has lots of pluses, including free shuttle service from the airport (you can also take it to the airport and then board the monorail for Naha), a multilingual staff, laundry facilities on every floor, a summer beer garden on a grassy lawn, and shuttle services to Araha and Sunset beaches July through September (and even free use of beach gear). All rooms have balconies; best are studio rooms for two people, complete with kitchenette.

1205–2 Yogi, Okinawa City, Okinawa 904-2174. www.daiichihotel-okinawa.com. ⓒ **098/931-1500.** Fax 098/931-1509. 297 units. ¥16,000–¥19,000 double. Rates higher in peak season; off-season discounts available. AE, DC, MC, V. 50 min. via free shuttle from Naha Airport (reservations required). **Amenities:** 2 restaurants; lounge; children's day-care center (¥1,050–¥2,100 per hour); computer corner w/free Internet; concierge; 24-hr. fitness center; indoor pool w/children's pool; sauna; spa. *In room:* A/C, TV, fridge, hair dryer, Internet.

INEXPENSIVE

Of four Toyoko Inns (www.toyoko-inn.com) in Naha, most centrally located are **Toyoko Inn Naha Asahibashi Ekimae,** 2–1–20 Kume (𝄢 **098/951-1045;** Yui Rail: Asahibashi Station), with doubles starting at ¥7,980, and **Toyoko Inn Naha Miebashi-eki,** 1–20–1 Makishi (𝄢 **098/867-1045;** Yui Rail: Miebashi), with doubles for ¥6,280. Both rates include Japanese breakfast.

Lohas Villa ★   With an easy-to-find convenient location on Okiei Dori, near the tourist office and a stone's throw from Kokusai Dori, this nonsmoking guesthouse attracts a backpacking crowd and exudes a laid-back Southeast Asian atmosphere with a third-floor reception filled with fake plants and wooden furniture. There's a communal fridge and microwave. Each room is slightly different, with a double bed, futon, or bunk beds; seven dormitory rooms stack 'em in three deep.

2–1–6 Makishi, Naha, Okinawa 900-0013. www.lohas-cg.com. 𝄢 **098/867-7757.** 35 units (none with bathroom). ¥4,500 single; ¥6,000 double; ¥1,500 dormitory bed. Off-season and 1-week discounts available. No credit cards. Yui Rail: Miebashi (5 min.). **Amenities:** Lobby computer w/free Internet. *In room:* Coin-op A/C, TV, no phone.

Sora House ★★ 📖   The building is old, but this fifth-floor walk-up is grand, with a friendly proprietor and a large, comfy communal room with a kitchen, dining area, sofas, and free use of computers, as well as a rooftop courtyard. It's the kind of place where you don't mind hanging out. There are four dormitory rooms sleeping six to eight people each, along with four simple but bright and cheerful rooms with bunk beds (which you can also book as a single).

2–24–15 Kumoji, Naha, Okinawa 900-0015. www.mco.ne.jp/~sora39. 𝄢 **098/861-9939.** 8 units (none with bathroom). ¥3,500 single; ¥5,000 double; ¥1,700 dormitory bed. No credit cards. Yui Rail: Miebashi (1 min. from the north exit). **Amenities:** Rental bikes (¥500 per day); lobby computer w/free Internet; communal kitchen. *In room:* A/C, no phone.

KUME ISLAND ★

94km (58 miles) W of Okinawa Island

I first visited **Kume Island (Kumejima)** in the mid-1980s, when it was still considered rather remote, but I have to say that with the exception of more attractions, it hasn't changed much since then. What always comes to mind whenever I picture the island is its natural beauty, its rows of sugar cane accented against red-colored earth, majestic Ryukyu pines, white sandy beaches, and azure seas. A port of call for trade between China and the Ryukyu Kingdom in Naha, Kume Island still displays traces of Chinese influence, from graves and buildings that follow the principles of *feng shui* (geomancy) to guardian dogs placed virtually everywhere. It's the perfect destination if you want to get away from the hustle and bustle of everyday life, though sights and activities like castle ruins, the historic Uezu Residence, an outlying island popular for snorkeling, a public bath boasting deep-sea mineral water, and a facility dedicated to local weaving would make it hard to remain idle for long. I think the most telling testimony to the down-to-earth, unpretentious nature of the island's 9,300 residents is the products they're known for: deep-sea salt, handmade textiles, their own miso paste and *awamori,* and—unsurprising for an island that's been inhabited for more than 1,000 years—mineral water. If you want, there's a "school" where you can learn more about the island from islanders themselves.

Essentials

GETTING THERE & GETTING AROUND Flights from Naha take 30 minutes; or, from Naha's Tomari Port, **Kume Line Ferries** (📞 098/868-2686) arrive at Kanegusuku Terminal about 4 hours later and cost ¥3,000 one-way or ¥5,700 round-trip.

Kume Airport is located on the north end of the island, the ferry terminal is on the west side, and Kume Town and Eef Beach on the southeast end. An infrequent **bus,** with a schedule that coincides with flights to and from the airport, travels from the airport and Kanegusuku Terminal to various locations on the island, including Eef Beach Hotel, the Bade Haus, and Kume Town, with a ride all the way to the last stop costing ¥390. Another bus circles part of the island four or five times a day, but only on certain days. Otherwise, **taxis** start at ¥450; a taxi from the airport to Eef Beach will cost about ¥2,200. Most convenient is to rent a car. **Japaren Rent-A-Car** (📞 0120/41-3900 toll-free) offers its cheapest subcompact for ¥4,725 for 24 hours, plus ¥1,050 for insurance, with free pickup at the airport.

VISITOR INFORMATION The Kumejima Town Tourist Association (📞 098/985-7115; bus stop: Eef Beach Hotel-mae; Mon–Fri 8:30am–5:30pm) is located on the main road of Kume Town.

Exploring Kume Island

It's probably safe to say most tourists come to Kume Island for its **beaches.** Most famous is **Eef Beach** (bus stop: Eef Beach Hotel-mae) on its southeast end, the island's largest beach at 2km (1¼ miles) long and certainly one of Japan's best. Most people make a point, too, of taking a boat to **Hate-no-Hama,** a treeless sandy island surrounded by crystal-clear, aquamarine water just 7km (4 miles) east of Kume Town (bus stop: Tomari Fisherina). You can rent snorkeling equipment here for ¥1,500 from May through October, but there isn't much else to do (pack a picnic lunch). Hate-no-Hama Kanko Service (📞 090/8292-8854) is one of several boat companies that will take you round-trip for ¥3,500 on a flexible schedule.

Just off the eastern coast is another island, **Oujima,** connected to Kume Island by bridge and home to several sites (bus stop: Nishi-oujima). **Bade Haus Kume-Island ★** (📞 098/985-8600; daily 10am–10pm) has the distinction of being the only bathing facility in the world that uses 100% deep-ocean water (from depths of 612m/2,020 ft.). Its main pool opens toward a white sandy beach with outdoor deck chairs and open-air Jacuzzi; there's also a steam room, dry sauna, a spa with indoor and outdoor baths, and a treatment room for oil body massages, hot-stone therapy, and other treatments. Admission is ¥2,000; add ¥500 for the spa. Free shuttles run from several resorts, including Cypress Hotel and Eef Beach Hotel. Next to the Bade Haus is the **Sea Turtle Museum (Kumejima Umigame Kan)** (📞 098/985-7513; Wed–Mon 9am–5pm), with tanks of baby and adult loggerhead, green, and hawksbill sea turtles. Explanations are in Japanese only, but a 10-minute film shows Kume Island as a major breeding ground. Admission is ¥300 for adults, ¥200 for children. Nearby on the beach is a natural phenomenon, the **"Tatami Ishi,"** a field of hardened lava divided into distinct pentagonal and hexangular shapes.

My favorite attraction is the **Yuima-ru Pavilion (Yuima-ru-kan) ★★** north of Kume Town (📞 098/985-8333; bus stop: Maja; daily 9am–5pm), where you can observe women engaged in making *tsumugi,* a type of silk textile. Of about 250

You can mingle with the islanders at **Shimanogakko** (© 098/985-3551), which offers excursions and classes for everything from trekking and sea kayaking to trying your hand at *tsumugi* weaving or playing the *sanshin* (a three-string instrument). Three-hour kayaking costs ¥6,300, while the 2-hour sanshin lesson costs ¥3,150. Your teacher may not speak English, but you could find the experience priceless.

Okinawan artisans engaged in the craft, 150 of them live on Kume Island. A 30-minute film shows the painstaking steps of collecting the silk and forming the thread, making the dyes from vegetation found on the island, dying each string according to the selected pattern, and then weaving them together on a loom. Remarkably, the women here are engaged in every step, right down to the cultivation of silk worms. You can watch them at work; a shop sells their products.

If you have a car, be sure to stop by the **Uezu Residence (Uezuke)** on Hwy. 242 (daily 8am–6pm; to 5pm in winter), built in the 1720s as the home of an important lord during the Ryukyu Kingdom and noted for its tiled roof and—to protect it from typhoons—limestone wall and *fukugi* trees. Admission is ¥300 for adults, ¥200 for junior-high students, and ¥100 for children. The Gushikawa and Uegusuku castle ruins are also worth a stop.

Where to Eat

Kameyoshi (亀吉) VARIED JAPANESE   There's table and *tatami* seating at this local restaurant that seems to offer a bit of everything, including sushi, *katsudon* (fried pork), *unagi-shu* (eel on rice), *gyoza*, pizza, and Okinawan specialties like *rafute*, all from a Japanese-language menu with photos. Ordering is easiest with one of the set meals, like the ramen and gyoza set, the Okinawa set with sashimi, or the sushi set.

160–39 Aza, Higa, Kumejima Town. © 098/985-8703. Set meals ¥800–¥2,300; set lunches ¥700. No credit cards. Wed–Mon 11:30am–9:30pm (last order). Bus stop: Eef Beach Hotel-mae. Beside the tourist office.

Where to Stay

You'll pay more in peak season, generally from about June through October, Golden Week, and New Year's.

Cypress Resort   Near the airport, this is as upscale as it gets on Kumejima. In addition to lazing by the pool or walking to the beach, you can sign up for activities, including snorkeling trips to Hate-no-Hama, scuba diving, and free shuttle service and discount tickets to Bade Haus. All rooms are with balcony facing the sea.

803–1 Ohara, Kumejima, Okinawa 901-3132. © 098/985-3700. Fax 098/985-3701. info.kume jima@urhm-inc.jp. 84 units. Peak season ¥27,500–¥35,500 single, ¥34,000–¥47,000 double; low season ¥10,500–¥18,500 single, ¥17,000–¥30,000 double. Rates include breakfast. AE, DC, MC, V. Bus stop: Cypress Resort, or a 3-min. taxi ride or 15-min. walk from the airport. **Amenities:** Restaurant; rental bikes (¥3,000 per day in peak season, ¥2,000 in low season); fitness room; outdoor pool; spa. *In room:* A/C, TV, hair dryer, Internet.

Eef Beach Hotel ☺   This is Kume Island's oldest hotel, with a great location right on Eef Beach. It offers trips to Hama-no-Hata and shuttles to Bade Haus, while a sports club rents beach chairs, snorkeling gear, and other equipment. Most rooms are ocean views with balconies, but the so-called "garden-view" rooms are cheaper. A good, solid choice for families.

548 Janado, Aza, Kumejima Town, Okinawa 901-3107. ✆ **098/985-7111.** Fax 098/985-7111. 80 units. Peak season ¥29,850 single, ¥37,400–¥40,800 double; low season ¥18,480 single, ¥25,410–¥28,875 double. Rates include breakfast. AE, DC, MC, V. Bus stop: Eef Beach Hotel-mae. **Amenities:** Restaurant; rental bikes (¥1,000 for 2 hr.); computer and Wi-Fi free in lobby; 2 outdoor pools; outdoor tennis courts. *In room:* A/C, TV, hair dryer, fridge.

Nankurunaisa (なんくるないさあ)   Its name translates as "everything's going to be all right," which pretty much sums up this laid-back *minshuku* just a block from the tourist office and Eef Beach (though the water is pretty shallow here). A modern building, it has a pleasant covered terrace where breakfast is served and both Japanese and Western-style rooms.

160–68 Aza, Higa, Kumejima Town, Okinawa 901-310. ✆/fax **098/985-7973.** 9 units. ¥5,500 per person peak season, ¥5,000 low season. No credit cards. Bus stop: Eef Beach Hotel-mae. *In room:* A/C, TV, hair dryer.

THE YAEYAMA ISLANDS— ISHIGAKI & IRIOMOTE ★★

450km (279 miles) SW of Okinawa Island; 2,000km (1,240 miles) SW of Tokyo

The **Yaeyama archipelago,** closer to Taiwan than to Okinawa Island, is a chain of 27 islands, most of them small and uninhabited. **Ishigaki Island,** with 80% of the Yaeyama Islands' population, serves as the area's gateway and administrative center. Most famous of the Yaeyama Islands is **Iriomote ★★★**, a rather mysterious island covered mostly with subtropical primeval forests preserved in a national park that you can explore by kayak and on foot. At about the same latitude as the Bahamas, the Yaeyama Islands are also blessed with beautiful beaches and coral reefs. Come here to commune with nature.

Essentials

GETTING THERE & GETTING AROUND   Two **flights** daily from Tokyo's Haneda airport land at Ishigaki Airport 3½ hours later. Otherwise, planes depart Naha every hour or less for the 65-minute trip. A bus travels from the airport to the bus terminal (in downtown Ishigaki near the port) in 15 minutes for ¥200.

VISITOR INFORMATION   The **Ishigaki Tourist Office,** located across from Shinei Park about a 5-minute walk from the bus terminal and Outer Islands Ferry Terminal (www.city.ishigaki.okinawa.jp; ✆ **0980/82-2809;** Mon–Fri 8:30am–5:30pm), has maps and information in English and can help with bus schedules around Ishigaki and ferry schedules to Iriomote.

Exploring Ishigaki and Iriomote

ISHIGAKI   **Ishigaki City,** on the south end of the island and where most of the island's 48,000 residents live, has an interesting **public market** just a few blocks inland from the bus terminal and ferry terminal. Of the island's many beaches, **Maezato Beach,** in front of the ANA Hotel (bus stop: ANA Hotel & Resort), is closest to the city center, but other popular destinations include **Sukuji Beach** with its long, sandy shoreline (bus stop: Seamen's Club); **Kabira Bay,** famous for its black pearl cultivation (bus stop: Kabira), and the **Yonehara Coast,** with its beach, campground, and grove of Yaeyama Palm Trees, found only on these islands (bus stop: Yonehara Palm Grove). Buses are infrequent, so check schedules beforehand; 5-day bus passes range from ¥1,000 to ¥2,000 depending on the route.

Ishigaki is also famous for its corals, many manta rays, and drop-offs. The **Umicoza Diving School,** 827–15 Kabira (*©* **0980/88-2434;** www.umicoza.com) offers diving excursions for the novice and expert alike. Its two-tank dive trip to "manta ray point" costs ¥12,600, including lunch.

IRIOMOTE   Your main reason for coming this far is **Iriomote Island (Iriomotejima),** which at 289 sq. km (115 sq. miles) is the second-largest Okinawan island but is almost entirely covered by a dense subtropical forest laced by rivers that drain into Japan's largest mangrove swamp. Its most famous resident is the Iriomote cat, a shy, nocturnal wildcat found only here, but your only chance of seeing one of the 100 or so remaining animals is only a picture of it on many road signs. There are, however, many crabs, birds, butterflies, and other things to see in what is sometimes called "Asia's Amazon."

You can reach Iriomote by ferry ride from the Outer Islands Ferry Terminal in Ishigaki City, with boats departing two to four times an hour for the 40-minute trip. Operated by three different ferry companies, boats travel to Ohara Port on the east coast for ¥1,770 one-way and, less frequently, to Uehara Port on the west coast for ¥2,300. The Iriomotejima Kotsu Bus travels approximately six times a day between the two ports for ¥680; or, purchase a 3-day pass for ¥1,000. Otherwise, each of the ferry companies operates its own buses on Iriomote, which you can ride free only if you purchased their ferry ticket (some drivers, however, don't seem to care).

In any case, because Iriomote is not easy to navigate on your own, this is one of the few times I recommend an organized tour. **Hirata Tourism Company,** 2 Misakicho in Ishigaki City (www.hirata-group.co.jp/english; *©* **0980/82-6711**), offers several guided tours in English into Iriomote's remote wilderness that involve hiking and boat trips. The Urauchi River/Maryudo Canoe Experience, for example, available April to September, includes a 30-minute kayak ride along a river beside a mangrove forest followed by a hike over rough terrain to a waterfall, where you have the chance to swim and eat a sack lunch before heading back. Departing Ishigaki at 8:30am and returning at 5:40pm, it costs ¥14,500 for adults and ¥12,500 for children, including the ferry and lunch.

Although tours provide an up-close view of Iriomote's wilderness, you might want to stay another day or two to enjoy the island's beaches. **Hoshizuma no Hama,** located north of Uehara Port, is known for its coral and star-shaped sand. **Pension Hoshinosuna,** a pension/restaurant on the beach (see below) rents snorkeling equipment for ¥1,050 for 3 hours, plus a ¥1,000 deposit, and offers diving trips, like a two-tank boat dive for ¥11,000.

Where to Eat

Hitoshi VARIED JAPANESE   This *izakaya* (Japanese drinking establishment) is well known among the locals; anyone can point you in the right direction. It specializes in *maguro* (tuna) served as sushi and sashimi but also offers Okinawan specialties like *gurukan* (deep-fried local fish), *shima rakkyo* (pickled Okinawan scallion), *jimami* (peanuts) tofu, *ikka sumi yakisoba* (squid black-ink fried noodles), and *fu* (wheat gluten) *champuru* from a Japanese menu. Seating is at the counter or at tables with leg wells.

197–1 Okawa, Ishigaki City. ✆ **0980/88-5807.** Main dishes ¥450–¥800. No credit cards. Mon–Sat 5–10pm (last order). Bus stop: Bus Terminal (5 min.). On the road west of the post office, past Yui Road on the left.

Where to Stay

Guest House Rakutenya 🐟 Located inland about a 6-minute walk from the Outer Islands Ferry Terminal, this comfortable inn occupies two buildings, one of which is a rare, two-story wooden dwelling that belonged to the English-speaking owner's grandparents and the other a typical Okinawan home with a red-tiled roof. Both are filled with quirky collectibles and antiques. Two of the rooms are twins, while the rest are *tatami*.

291 Okawa, Ishigaki City, Okinawa 907-0022. www3.big.or.jp/~erm8p3gi/english/english.html. ✆/fax **0980/83-8713.** 10 units (none with bathroom). ¥3,000 per person. ¥500 extra per person in peak season. No credit cards. Bus stop: Ishigaki Bus Terminal (6 min.); walk inland a few short blocks; it's past busy Yui Road, on the other side of a parking lot behind a rock wall. **Amenities:** Free computer and Wi-Fi in lobby. *In room:* Coin-op A/C, TV, no phone.

Hotel East China Sea   Near the bus terminal, Outer Islands Ferry Terminal, and downtown Ishigaki City, this convenient choice offers rooms with rattan furniture that impart a slight South Seas look, as well as Japanese-style rooms. But the best feature, in my opinion, is the balconies from all rooms facing the busy port with its fleet of ferries, fishing boats, and pleasure boats.

2–8 Misakicho, Ishigaki City, Okinawa 907-0012. www.eastchinasea.jp. ✆ **0980/88-1155.** Fax 098/88-1156. 79 units. ¥17,000 single; ¥24,000–¥52,000 double. Rates ¥1,000–¥2,000 higher per person in peak season; off-season discounts available. Rates include breakfast buffet. AE, DC, MC, V. Bus stop: Ishigaki Bus Terminal, then a 2-min. walk east. **Amenities:** Restaurant. *In room:* A/C, TV, hair dryer.

Pension Hoshinosuna ★ 🎏 On a hill, above the famous Hoshizuma no Hama beach with its pretty islet-studded bay and sand shaped like stars, this pension is popular for its dive shop, rental snorkeling equipment, and restaurant with an outdoor terrace facing the sea offering Okinawan specialties. It even offers outdoor yoga sessions. It has Western- and Japanese-style rooms with dreamy views of the ocean. A great, inexpensive getaway.

289–1 Uehara, Iriomote, Okinawa 907-1541. ✆ **0980/85-6448.** hoshizuna@lime.ocn.ne.jp. 10 units. ¥7,500–¥10,000 per person, including 2 meals. Higher rates in peak season. AE, MC, V. Pickup available from Uehara Port. **Amenities:** Restaurant; yoga sessions ¥1,500. *In room:* TV, fridge.

NORTHEASTERN HONSHU: TOHOKU

12

Because so many of Japan's historic events took place in Kyoto, Nara, Kamakura, Tokyo, and other cities in south-western Honshu, most visitors to Japan never venture farther north than Tokyo. True, northeastern Honshu (called the Tohoku District) does not have the famous temples, shrines, gardens, and castles of southern Japan, but it does have spectacular mountain scenery, national parks, hot springs in abundance, excellent ski resorts, many hiking trails, and its own list of impressive historic sites. Its rugged, mountainous terrain, coupled with cold, snowy winters, has also helped preserve the region's traditions. You won't find any of Tokyo's edgy flashiness here, but rather a down-to-earth practicality, warm hospitality, and a way of life that harks back generations. And although Tohoku was the site of the 2011 Great East Japan Earthquake, it's business as usual at the destinations listed below, most of which are far from the coast damaged by the tsunami. And although Fukushima Prefecture is still undergoing radiation removal and cleanup around the damaged power plant—a process that could take decades—the destinations covered in this chapter are free of elevated radiation levels.

Matsushima, about 3 hours north of Tokyo, is considered one of Japan's most scenic spots, with pine-covered islets dotting its bay; in fact, although it suffered some damage from the tsunami, these islets shielded it from widespread destruction. Farther north and inland is **Hiraizumi,** once capital of a 12th-century domain that stretched across much of Tohoku and now home to several treasures together listed as a World Heritage Site. The pleasant village of **Kakunodate** was once a thriving castle town and is famous for its remaining samurai houses and cherry trees. Occupying 862 sq. km (333 sq. miles) of northern Tohoku is the resplendent **Towada-Hachimantai National Park,** best visited for its scenic lakes; rustic hot-spring spas that seem little changed over the decades; skiing; and hiking, including a trail that flanks the picture-perfect Oirase Stream. And after a day of trekking or skiing, what could be better than a soothing hot-spring soak?

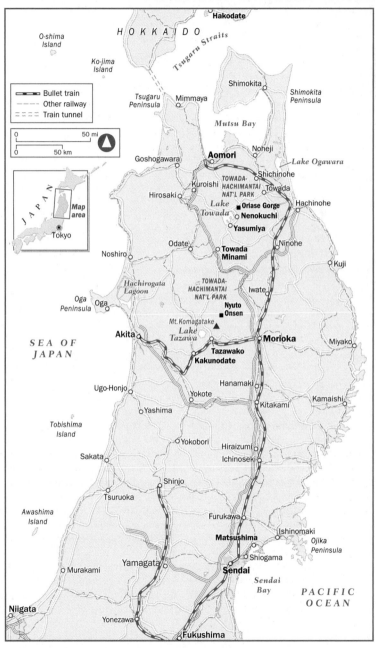

THE BEST TOHOKU EXPERIENCES

○ **Strolling the Pure Land Garden (Hiraizumi):** This garden was created in the 12th century as a representation of a Buddhist utopia. As you walk around the serene pond with its simple layout, it's easy to imagine monks achieving nirvana here. See p. 552.

○ **Exploring Samurai Houses (Kakunodate):** Several thatched-roof samurai houses filled with items from Japan's feudal past remain in this former castle town, famous also for its cherry trees and crafts made of cherry-tree bark. See p. 554.

○ **Swimming and Cycling (Lake Tazawa):** This small lake offers a small beach, rental bikes, and a microbrewery, making for a pleasant summer's day. See p. 558.

○ **Spending the Night at Nyuto Onsen:** There is no other hot-spring spa quite like this one, nestled in a valley and consisting of a string of new and ancient inns; many people come just for a dip in the many rustic outdoor baths. See p. 557.

○ **Hiking Along the Oirase Stream (Lake Towada):** This is one of my favorite hiking paths in Japan, beside a rushing stream and under a dense canopy of trees; go early in the morning or avoid summer vacation, however, to beat the crowds. See p. 562.

Tohoku Essentials

GETTING THERE & GETTING AROUND   Tohoku's major airports are in Sendai (SDJ), Aomori (AOJ), and Akita (AXT). You can also travel to Tohoku via **Shinkansen** bullet train from Tokyo's Ueno or Tokyo Station to Shin-Aomori or Akita, with stops at Sendai, Kakunodate, Ichinoseki (for Hiraizumi), Hachinohe, and Tazawako (the latter two are convenient springboards for travel onward to Towada-Hachimantai National Park).

Although there is bus service in the national park, buses to some of the more remote areas are infrequent or nonexistent. For that reason, Tohoku is one of the few regions in Japan where **rental cars** are a great convenience, if not a necessity. In addition to car-rental agencies at both Aomori and Akita airports, there are JR Eki Rent-A-Car offices at train stations throughout Japan, including Aomori, Morioka, Kakunodate, and Tazawako stations, which offer 20% discounts for train fares booked in conjunction with car rentals. You'll also find Toyota Rent-A-Car (www.toyotarentacar.net) offices virtually everywhere. If you want to keep your driving to a minimum, I suggest taking a Shinkansen as far as Tazawako or Kakunodate and then, after seeing the sights there, drive to Nyuto Onsen for the night before continuing northward to Lake Towada. A 2-day rental of a subcompact car costs about ¥14,700, including mileage and insurance. Drop-off fees can add ¥4,000 to ¥9,000, depending on the distance. Keep in mind that Tohoku's winter season, from November to March, can bring below-freezing temperatures and up to a foot of snowfall virtually overnight. Some mountain passes are occasionally closed due to snowfall, though access to major ski resorts is generally open. See "Getting Around" in chapter 14, for information on renting a car. Contact information for rental agencies in Tohoku is provided under destination listings below.

THE PINE-CLAD ISLANDS OF MATSUSHIMA ★

375km (234 miles) NE of Tokyo

Because the trip to northern Tohoku or onward to Hokkaido is such a long one, a pleasant place to break up the journey with an overnight stay is **Matsushima ★**. Matsushima means "Pine Islands"—and that's exactly what this region is. More than 260 pine-covered islets and islands dot Matsushima Bay, giving it the appearance of a giant pond in a Japanese landscape garden where twisted and gnarled pines sweep upward from volcanic tuff and white sandstone, creating bizarre and beautiful shapes.

Matsushima is so dear to Japanese hearts that it's considered one of the three most scenic spots in Japan (the other two are Miyajima in Hiroshima Bay and Amanohashi-date on the north coast of Honshu)—and was so designated about 370 years ago in a book written by a Confucian philosopher of the Edo government. Basho (1644–94), the famous Japanese haiku poet, was so struck by Matsushima's beauty that it's almost as though he were at a loss for words when he wrote: "Matsushima, Ah! Matsushima! Matsushima!"

Unfortunately, motorboats have been invented since Basho's time, detracting from the beauty that evoked such ecstasy in him long ago.

Essentials

GETTING THERE   From Tokyo, take the **Tohoku Shinkansen** train from Ueno or Tokyo Station to Sendai, which costs ¥10,080 for an unreserved seat and will take from 1½ to 2¼ hours, depending on the number of stops. In Sendai (there's a tourist office in Sendai Station, open daily 8:30am–8pm, where you can pick up a map of Matsushima and boat and train schedules), change to the **JR Senseki Line**—it's on the other side of the station but well marked in English; trains depart approximately every half-hour. From Sendai, the trip to **Matsushima Kaigan Station** takes about 25 minutes by express train and costs ¥400.

After the Quake

Matsushima is on the Tohoku Pacific coast where the tsunami struck on March 11, 2011, but it was relatively lucky. Those 260 islands in the bay provided a natural breakwater, so while the tsunami towered nearly 17 meters (55 feet) elsewhere, it reached only about 2.9 meters (9½ feet) here. Two towns-people perished, which, while tragic, was mild compared to the approximately 16,000 confirmed dead and 3,300 missing from that fateful day. Although Matsushima's downtown flooded, and energy, transport, food, and fresh water supplies were cut off for more than a month, Matsushima's wealth of hillside inns sheltered evacuees and, later, repair workers. Matsushima is about 100km (60 miles) from the stricken Fukushima nuclear power plant; to allay fears of radiation, the city installed a radiation meter outside city hall that shows radiation readings comparable to places far from the disaster zone. The best way visitors can support the rebuilding efforts, locals say, is to keep visiting. In acknowledgement of its relative good fortune, Matsushima sends a portion of its rebuilding funds to neighboring towns.

A Note on Japanese Characters

Many establishments and attractions in Japan do not have outdoor signs in Roman (English-language) letters. Those that don't are provided with the Japanese equivalent to help you locate them.

A more picturesque way to get to Matsushima, however, is to take the Senseki Line from Sendai only as far as **Hon-Shiogama** (about 18 min. by express), where you can catch a **sightseeing boat** operated by the Marubun Matsushima Kisen Co. (www.marubun-kisen.com/english; ✆ **022/365-3611**) for a 50-minute trip to **Matsushima Kaigan Pier;** tickets cost ¥1,400 for adults, ¥700 for children. You'll pass an unsightly thermal power station, which, for many years, touted that it was built in such a way so "as not to distract from Matsushima Bay's beauty, but rather harmonize with it." I don't even have to tell you my thoughts on this. Otherwise, it's a pleasant trip, despite the nonstop commentary in Japanese. Boats depart from both Hon-Shiogama and Matsushima Kaigan piers in both directions daily every half-hour from 9am to 3:30pm but only once an hour from 9am to 3pm December through March. From Hon-Shiogama Station, it's a 10-minute walk to the boat pier; take a right out of the station, cross the street, turn right at the first red light (crossing under the tracks), and continue straight on.

VISITOR INFORMATION   Upon arrival in Matsushima, stop off at one of the two **Matsushima Tourist Association offices,** to pick up an English-language map with information on major sites and get directions to your hotel. One is a booth to the right after you exit **Matsushima Kaigan Station** (www.matsushima-kanko.com/en; ✆ **022/354-2263;** weekdays 9:30am–4:30pm, weekends and holidays 9am–5pm). Adjoining this tourist office is a hotel-reservation counter where you can book rooms for free; you can also leave your luggage here (¥200–¥300 per bag), useful if you're making a quick stopover (there are also lockers in Sendai Station).

If you're arriving in Matsushima by boat, you'll find another information office in the modern building to the left of **Matsushima Kaigan Pier** (✆ **022/354-2618;** daily 8:30am–5pm, to 4:30pm in winter).

ORIENTATION & GETTING AROUND   All of Matsushima's major attractions are within walking distance of both the station and the pier (the two are about six minutes apart on foot, though the pier is more centrally located). You can cover the entire area on foot in a half-day of sightseeing. Some farther-flung hotels have shuttle services to the town center.

Exploring Matsushima

CRUISING THE BAY   Arriving in Matsushima by **sightseeing boat** is a good introduction to the bay because you'll pass pine-covered islands and oyster rafts along the way. Board the boat in Hon-Shiogama for the 50-minute trip to Matsushima Kaigan Pier (see "Getting There," above). Other sightseeing boats make 50-minute round trips around the bay from Matsushima's pier once an hour between 9am and 4pm; they charge ¥1,400 for adults, half-price for children.

Entsuin (円通院) ★★ 🏛 TEMPLE   Perhaps not as well known as Zuiganji (see below), this temple was also built in the early Edo Period, more than 360 years ago by the powerful Date clan that ruled over a large swath of the Tohoku region. It features a small rock garden (with seven rocks representing the Seven Deities of Good

Fortune), a moss garden with six different types of moss, a lovely rose garden, an Edo-Period garden with a pond and "borrowed landscaping," and a small temple housing an elaborate statue of Lord Date Mitsumune, grandson of Lord Date Masamune (who founded the Sendai fief). Depicted here on a white steed, Mitsumune was reportedly poisoned by the Tokugawa shogunate and died at the tender age of 19 in Edo Castle. The seven statues surrounding him represent retainers who committed ritual suicide to follow their master into death. The interior walls are all covered with an overlay of gold. The painting of an occidental rose on the right-hand door is thought to be the first in Japan (hence the rose garden); other Western flowers include narcissus and corona. Be on the lookout for "hidden" joined crosses above the door that are slanted; because Christianity was banned in Edo Japan, the Date clan used crosses as a symbol for silent revolt. Expect to spend about 45 minutes here, enjoying the serenity and views of the wonderful gardens. You can also enjoy vegetarian cuisine (see Ungai, below).

67 Aza-chonai. ✆ **022/354-3206.** Admission ¥300 adults, ¥150 high-school students, ¥100 children. Daily 8:30am–5pm (to 4pm in winter). Next to Zuiganji Temple (to the left as you face it).

Kanrantei HISTORIC SITE   This famous landmark is just a 1-minute walk from the pier. A simple wooden teahouse, Kanrantei, the "Water-Viewing Pavilion," was used by generations of the Date family for such aesthetic pursuits as viewing the moon and watching the ripples on the tide. Originally it belonged to warlord Toyotomi Hideyoshi as part of his estate at Fushimi Castle near Kyoto, but he presented it to the Date family at the end of the 16th century; it was moved here in 1645, where it remains one of the largest teahouses in Japan. For an additional ¥300 or more (depending on the accompanying sweet), you can drink ceremonial green tea while sitting on *tatami* and contemplating the bay, its islands, and the boats carving ribbons through the water. After tea, wander through the small museum containing samurai armor, ceramics, lacquerware, and tea-ceremony utensils belonging to the Date family.

56–1 Aza-chonai. ✆ **022/353-3355.** Admission ¥200 adults, ¥150 university and high-school students, ¥100 children. Daily 8:30am–5pm (to 4:30pm Nov–Mar).

Michinoku Date Masamune Historical Museum (Michinoku Date Masamune Rekishikan; みちのく伊達政宗歴史館) ★ MUSEUM   This wax museum details the life and times of Date Masamune (1567–1636) through 25 life-size, audiovisual diorama displays, with good explanations in English. Showing everything from how he lost sight in one of his eyes at age 5 to his marriage at age 13 to his victories in battle (he fought his first battle at age 15), the dioramas bring to life what might otherwise be dull history. At the very least, you get to see how people dressed back then and learn why Date Masamune was nicknamed the One-Eyed Dragon. Of less interest are wax figures of early-19th- and 20th-century personalities of northern Japan. Plan on spending 30 minutes here.

Matsushima Kaigan. www.date-masamune.jp. ✆ **022/354-4131.** Admission ¥1,000 adults, ¥600 junior-high and high-school students, ¥500 children; foreigners with passports pay ¥500 adults, ¥300 junior-high and high-school students, children free. Daily 8:30am–5pm (9am–4:30pm in winter). Across from Godaido Temple (see below), set back from the main street.

Zuiganji Temple (瑞巌寺) ★★★ TEMPLE   Matsushima's best-known attraction is the most famous Zen temple in northern Japan. Located just a couple minutes' walk from Matsushima Kaigan Pier and 10 minutes from the train station, its entrance is shaded by tall cedar trees. On the right side of the pathway leading to the temple are caves and grottoes dug out by priests long ago; adorned with Buddhist statues and memorial tablets, they were used for practicing *zazen* (sitting meditation) and are an impressive sight. Here, too, you'll find what is probably Japan's only monument to . . . eels!

Now a National Treasure and the highlight of a stay in Matsushima, Zuiganji Temple was originally founded in the Heian Period (828) as a Tendai temple but became a Zen temple in the 13th century. After a period of decline, it was remodeled in 1604 by order of Date Masamune, the most powerful and important lord of northern Honshu (see above). Unifying the region known as Tohoku, Date built his castle in nearby Sendai, and today almost all sites in and around Sendai and Matsushima are tied to the Date family. It took hundreds of workers 5 years to build the impressive main hall, a large wooden structure that was constructed in the *shoin-zukuri* style typical of the Momoyama Period and served as the Date family temple. But it's the temple's interior that impresses, especially the wood-carved transoms and brilliantly painted, gold-plated *fusuma* (sliding doors). A room at the back is dedicated to the samurai who were laid to rest here, having followed their Date lord into death by committing ritualistic suicide. (**Note**: The main hall is closed for renovation until 2016; however, other parts of the temple normally closed to the public will be open during that time). On temple grounds is also the **Zuiganji Art Museum (Seiryuden),** which houses temple and Date family treasures displayed on a rotating basis, including painted sliding doors, portraits and statues of the Date clan, teacups, scrolls, calligraphy, and woodblock prints, many of Matsushima as it looked in former times. In all, you'll probably spend an hour at Zuiganji Temple.

Under the supervision of Zuiganji Temple is **Godaido,** a small wooden worship hall on a tiny island not far from the pier. Connected to the mainland by a short bridge, its grounds are open night and day and are free, but there's not much to see other than the bay. Nevertheless, Godaido is often featured in brochures of Matsushima, making this delicate wooden temple one of the town's best-known landmarks.

91 Aza-chonai. © **022/354-2023.** Admission for both Seiryuden and Zuiganji Temple ¥700 adults, ¥400 children. Daily 8am–3:30pm Dec–Jan, to 4pm Nov and Feb, to 4:30pm Oct and Mar, to 5pm Apr–Sept.

ISLANDS

On the southern edge of Matsushima, about an 8-minute walk from Matsushima Kaigan Station, is **Oshima,** a small island once used as a retreat by priests. Long ago there were more than 100 hand-dug caves carved with scriptures, Buddhist images, and sutras, but today the island and its remaining 50 caves and stone images are rather neglected. It's a nice quiet spot in which to sit and view the harbor; you can walk around the entire island in about 20 minutes. There's no fee, there's no gate, and the island never closes (although the bridge was washed away by the tsunami, plans are in the works for its resurrection; check with the tourist office). Because it was a Buddhist retreat, women were forbidden on the island until after the Meiji Restoration in 1868.

At the other end of Matsushima, about a 10-minute walk from the boat pier, is **Fukuurajima,** another island connected to the mainland, this time by a long red concrete bridge with orange-colored railings. It's a botanical garden of sorts, with several hundred labeled plants and trees, but mostly it's unkempt and overgrown—which comes as a surprise in cultivated Japan. It will take you less than an hour to circle the island, and there are many resting spots along the way, including a snack shop selling ice cream and drinks. The island gate is open daily 8am to 5pm (4:30pm in winter) and admission is ¥200 or adults, half-price for children.

Where to Eat

In summer, stalls on the main street of Matsushima sell grilled octopus, corn on the cob, and crab. In addition, look for *donburi* (rice bowls) topped with *anago* (sea eel) in summer or *kaki* (oysters, in various preparations) in winter.

Donjiki Chaya (どんじき茶屋) NOODLES/ODANGO   This rustic noodle with an English-language menu is a convenient place for an inexpensive lunch if you're visiting Zuiganji and Entsuin temples. Built about 400 years ago, it's easy to spot because of its thatched roof, with sliding doors pushed wide-open in summer and *tatami* seating. In addition to buckwheat noodles, it also serves *odango,* pounded rice balls covered with sesame, red-bean, or soy sauce (¥480 for five pieces). Or, stop by for a refreshing plum vinegar drink—it's better than it sounds.

89 Chonai, Matsushima. ☏ 022/354-5855. Noodles ¥380–¥580. No credit cards. Apr–Nov daily 9am–5pm; Dec–Mar Sat–Sun and holidays 9am–4pm. A 5-min. walk from Matsushima Kaigan Station or the pier; across from Entsuin Temple.

Santori Chaya (さんとり茶屋) ★ SEAFOOD/SUSHI   October through March is oyster season in Matsushima, and you can scarcely throw a shell without hitting a place selling *kaki-don* (oysters on a bowl of rice). This family-run shop serves a great *kaki-ten-don* with tempura-fried oysters and vegetables in a special sauce made from Sendai miso for ¥1,260. The rest of the year, local *anago* (sea eel) is similarly featured. Sit at the ground floor counter, or as you head upstairs for seating on cushions on wood floors, note the sticker at eye level indicating the height of the 2011 tsunami (the downstairs was gutted and rebuilt). There's a picture menu for easy ordering.

24-4-1 Aza Senzui. ☏ 022/353-2622. Main dishes ¥980–¥1,980. AE, DC, MC, V. Thurs–Tues 11:30am–3pm and 5–10pm. A 4-min. walk east of the pier.

Shiosai ★★ 🍷 FRENCH   Located atop a hill, this hotel restaurant has the best view in town. Book a table at sunset close to the floor-to-ceiling windows overlooking Matsushima, where you can watch the day fade and lights in the town below begin to glimmer. Only set meals are available, but they're very good and surprisingly inexpensive. My ¥2,940 dinner consisted of pumpkin soup, seafood cocktail and steak, salad, bread, dessert, and coffee or tea. It's a good place for a romantic meal. Or, from 3 to 5pm, come for teatime and enjoy the view.

Taikanso Hotel, 7th floor, 10–76 Aza Inuta. ☏ 022/354-2161. Set lunches ¥1,785–¥3,990; set dinners ¥2,500–¥5,355. AE, DC, MC, V. Daily 11:30am–3pm and 5:30–8:30pm (last order). For directions, see "Where to Stay," below.

Ungai ★ 🎁 BUDDHIST VEGETARIAN   Located on the grounds of Entsuin Temple (dining here gets you free admission to the temple), this is a great place for a peaceful meal, as you dine in a modern *tatami* room and look out over a garden. It serves three set meals typical of Buddhist vegetarian cuisine (which features many small dishes with vegetables and tofu that change with the seasons); let your budget be your guide. Although reservations should be made 1 day in advance, your hotel may be able to reserve on the same day.

Entsuin Temple, 67 Aza-chonai. ☏ 022/353-2626. Reservations required. Set meals ¥4,000, ¥5,500, and ¥8,000. AE, DC, MC, V. Thurs–Tues 11:30am–2pm (last order). To the right just past Entsuin's entrance.

Where to Stay

Because this is a popular tourist destination, accommodations in Matsushima are not cheap, especially during the peak months of May through November. For the Tanabata Festival (Aug 6–8 in Sendai) and the Toronagashi Festival (Aug 15–16 in Matsushima), rooms may be fully booked 6 months in advance and rates are at their highest. Rates are generally lower during the off-season months (Dec–Apr).

Directions are given from the boat pier or train station, whichever is closer. The pier and station are about a 6-minute walk apart.

EXPENSIVE

Hotel Ichinobo (ホテル一の坊) ★★ Despite its large size, modern facilities, and the word "hotel" in its name, this property has the atmosphere of a traditional *ryokan* (albeit a rather large, modern one) and offers mostly Japanese-style rooms. It's surrounded by pine trees and boasts lovely landscaped grounds and ponds, with views of the sea and islands from all its rooms and the wonderful public baths, including outdoor baths. It also offers 26 aesthetically furnished Matsushima Club twin rooms that include DVD players (and free DVD rentals); some of these boast glassed-in, private hot-spring baths off private balconies. Dinners are served in one of two restaurants, one featuring a pond where hapless fish await their fate and the other offering *teppanyaki* cuisine. Glass buffs should not miss the hotel's Kyohei Fujita Museum of Glass, dedicated to the only glass artist designated a National Living Treasure until his death. Although Ichinobo's location on the northern edge of Matsushima—about a 20-minute walk from the pier—is inconvenient, staff will fetch you upon arrival.

1–4 Takagi Azahama, Matsushima-cho, Miyagi Prefecture 981-0215. www.ichinobo.com/matsushima. ✆ **022/353-3333.** Fax 022/353-3339. 126 units. ¥16,850–¥25,850 per person (higher during Golden Week and Obon holidays, late Apr to early May, and mid-Aug). Rates include 2 meals. AE, DC, MC, V. Free shuttle bus from pier or train station with reservation. **Amenities:** 2 restaurants; bar; tea lounge; glass museum; outdoor pool; sauna; Wi-Fi (free, in lobby). *In room:* A/C, TV, DVD players (in some), fridge, hair dryer.

MODERATE

Matsushima Century Hotel ★ This gleaming hotel, near Fukuurajima island, is popular with families. I recommend taking a combination room with both *tatami* area and beds or a Japanese-style room facing the bay, as these all have a balcony and chairs. The cheapest Western-style rooms, though sunny and cheerful, face inland, are small with unit baths, and have no balconies. Public baths have views of the bay. Meals are served in a restaurant; breakfast is an all-you-can-eat Japanese/Western buffet.

8 Aza Senzui, Matsushima-cho, Miyagi Prefecture 981-0213. www.centuryhotel.co.jp. ✆ **022/354-4111.** Fax 022/354-4191. 135 units. ¥13,600–¥24,150 per person, including 2 meals. ¥3,000 extra Sat and nights before a holiday. AE, DC, MC, V. A 5-min. walk east of the pier. Call for a pickup from the station. **Amenities:** Restaurant; bar; coffee shop; children's pool; sauna overlooking the bay. *In room:* A/C, TV, hair dryer, minibar.

Taikanso (大観荘) ★★ 🏊 Able to accommodate 1,100 guests, Matsushima's largest hotel sprawls atop a plateau surrounded by pine-covered hills and offers the best views in town, including views of the island-studded bay from its recently renovated indoor and outdoor public baths. Although it's a bit of a hike from attractions, it is served by a shuttle bus. Both Western- and Japanese-style rooms are available, though the cheapest rooms (singles and twins) face inland. All the Japanese-style rooms face the sea (though views are marred for some by a bus parking lot), including wonderful combination rooms (the most expensive) that offer the best of both worlds with *tatami* areas and beds. A plus here is that you can choose from several restaurants to dine in (including one that offers a crab dinner); room rates vary with the meal and restaurant. One of the least expensive is one of my favorites: Shiosai (see above), which has the best view in town of both Matsushima Bay and the surrounding hills. The front desk is very helpful with English-language sightseeing information.

10–76 Aza Inuta, Matsushima-cho, Miyagi Prefecture 981-0213. www.taikanso.co.jp. © **022/354-2161.** Fax 022/353-3431. 256 units. ¥10,500–¥21,000 per person. ¥2,000–¥4,000 extra weekends and peak season. Rates include 2 meals. AE, DC, MC, V. Station: Matsushima Kaigan (15 min.) or via shuttle bus. **Amenities:** 4 restaurants, including Shiosai; bar; 2 lounges; outdoor pool (summer only); room service; Wi-Fi (free in lobby). *In room:* A/C, TV, fridge, hair dryer.

INEXPENSIVE

Hotel Daimatsuso   This somewhat worn, '80s-era hotel, with a lobby crowded by a souvenir shop and vending machines (and with free coffee in the morning), is homey nonetheless and close to the train station. The cheapest rooms (both Japanese and Western style) have no bathrooms and look unceremoniously onto another building; this is where you'll probably end up if you opt for a room without meals. Otherwise, best are Japanese-style rooms with balconies on the fifth floor facing the sea, some of which are combination rooms with beds and *tatami* areas. Hot-spring-fed common baths have murals of the pine-clad islands. Rooms come with the basics, though some of the bathrooms are so small you have to wonder how some people fit into them. Dinner is served in your room, while breakfast is in the dining room.

25 Azachonai Matsushima, Matsushima-cho, Miyagi Prefecture 981-0213. © **022/354-3601.** Fax 022/354-6154. 41 units, 3 with toilet only, 29 with bathroom. ¥6,300–¥7,350 per person without meals; ¥10,500–¥12,600 per person with 2 meals. AE, DC, MC, V. Station: Matsushima Kaigan (1 min.). Walk straight out of the station; the hotel will be on your left. **Amenities:** Hot-spring baths; Wi-Fi (free in lobby). *In room:* A/C, TV, fridge.

Resort Inn Matsushima 🦶   This modern, airy budget hotel with spacious Western-style rooms is located on a steep hill above the train station and has a nice outdoor terrace where you can have breakfast. Catering mostly to couples and families, it offers only twins (though solo travelers can stay in a twin room) and larger family rooms with two twin beds and two sofa beds, all with views of the sea. Higher rates below are for peak season and weekends. Dinner is not served on site, but for ¥2,000 the hotel can arrange dinner at local restaurants and a shuttle to get you there and back.

17 Sanjukari, Matsushima Aza, Matsushima-cho, Miyagi Prefecture 981-0213. © **022/355-0888.** Fax 022/355-0889. 29 units. ¥8,000–¥10,000 single; ¥14,000–¥18,000 twin; ¥18,000–¥24,000 triple; ¥20,000–¥28,000 quad. Rates include breakfast. AE, DC, MC, V. Station: Matsushima Kaigan (10 min.). Take a right out of the station, then another right under the tracks, and continue straight up the hill; the hotel will be on your left. Free shuttle from the station daily 3–6pm. **Amenities:** Wi-Fi (free in lobby). *In room:* A/C, TV, fridge, hair dryer, no phone, Wi-Fi.

HIRAIZUMI, 12TH-CENTURY BUDDHIST UTOPIA ★

Imagine a Buddhist heaven on earth, created long ago, where the souls of both friend and foe, human and animal, could gather to find peace and consolation. That is what Fujiwara Kiyohira, who had lost his father, wife, and at least one son in battle and treachery, set out to do in the early 12th century when he became supreme ruler of a vast area in Tohoku called Oshu. Rather than continue to build military power, Fujiwara decided to embrace the Buddhist principles of peace. Using wealth he had gained from area gold mines, he created a domain of temples and gardens in **Hiraizumi** that were to symbolize the Buddhist Pure Land, the epitome of which was Chuson-ji Temple with its Golden Hall. His son and grandson continued work on this utopian paradise, constructing a massive temple complex called Motsu-ji, as well as countless other temples, pagodas, and gardens, earning Hiraizumi respect and admiration from Kyoto and beyond. Sadly, that's where the grand achievements end. After only 100 years and three generations of Fujiwara rulers, Hiraizumi was attacked in 1189 by Minamoto Yoritomo, who would subsequently succeed in seizing power and establishing his shogunate government in Kamakura in 1192. Although Hiraizumi lost most of its treasures through fires in the ensuing centuries, shoguns and feudal lords made concerted efforts to preserve the Golden Hall and other buildings, testimony to Hiraizumi's significance all those years ago.

In 2011, just a few months after the Great East Japan Earthquake, Hiraizumi's treasures were declared a World Heritage Site, heartwarming news in what was otherwise a devastating time for one of Tohoku's hardest-hit prefectures, Iwate (Hiraizumi was untouched). Although the Golden Hall is undeniably impressive and an incredible work of art, Fujiwara's vision of Hiraizumi as a land of peace and purity is what impresses me the most; the impact of this short-lived but amazing northern stronghold cannot be overstated. Hiraizumi, an unpretentious town of 8,400 residents with surprisingly few accommodations, restaurants, and souvenir shops (which seem to plague Japan's other tourist spots), could well be the most important Japanese village you've never heard of. But while Hiraizumi may have escaped the international radar until now, it's well known among Japanese, attracting 1.8 million visitors a year.

Essentials

GETTING THERE   From Tokyo, take the **Shinkansen** bullet train from Ueno or Tokyo Station about 2½ hours to Ichinoseki, then transfer to a local train (trains depart about every hour) for the 8-minute ride to Hiraizumi. The fare from Tokyo is ¥11,960. If you're coming from Hokkaido or northern Honshu, catch the local train from Morioka, which takes about 80 minutes and costs ¥1,450.

VISITOR INFORMATION   Surprising for a town this size, there's a **tourist office** inside Hiraizumi Station (✆ 0191/46-2100; daily 9am–4pm) and another one just outside the station to the right (✆ 0191/46-5086; daily 8:30am–5pm), where you can pick up good English maps and brochures. Online, go to **www.japan-iwate.info/index.html**.

ORIENTATION & GETTING AROUND   Hiraizumi is not large and you can **walk,** but its sights are spread out. Due east of Hiraizumi Station is Motsu-ji, 700m (less than half a mile) away along a tidy residential street. From Motsuji, it's a 1.6km- (1 mile-) walk north to Chusonji, passing the Hiraizumi Cultural Heritage Center along the way. You can get around faster on **bicycle,** which you can rent at the tourist office outside the station from 9am to 4pm, costing ¥500 for 2 hours or ¥1,000 all day. Additionally, Gold Rental (✆ 0191/46-4031; daily 9am–5pm) straight out from the station offers bikes for the same price, as well as electric bikes that cost ¥600 and ¥1,300, respectively (it's a slight incline to Chuson-ji). Finally, the **Loop Bus Run Run** departs Hiraizumi Station every 30 minutes from 9:45am to 4:15pm and travels a one-way circular loop to Motsu-ji, Hiraizumi Cultural Heritage Center, Chuson-ji, and other sites. It costs ¥140 for one ride, ¥400 for an all-day pass.

Exploring Hiraizumi

Chuson-ji Temple ★★★ After killing his half-brother for taking the lives of his family, Lord Kiyohira decided to create a peaceful Buddhist paradise on earth to console the souls of the dead. Chuson-ji, constructed from 1105 to 1126, was a massive complex of more than 40 halls, pagodas, monks' quarters, and other structures. Sadly, most of Chuson-ji was destroyed by fire in 1337. Today, the only surviving structure remaining from the Fujiwara era is the Golden Hall.

The approach to the temple is up steep Tsukimizaka (Moon Viewing Slope), lined with 400-year-old cedars planted by orders of the Date clan, whose later fiefdom included this area and who vowed to protect Hiraizumi's legacy. After a 10-minute walk you'll reach the **Hondo (Main Hall),** dedicated to Amida Nyorai (Buddha of Infinite Light) and used for religious ceremonies and prayer. Farther along is **Sankozo,** a museum containing treasures of Chuson-ji, including statues of Buddha, sutras, and the Thousand-Armed Kannon goddess, which used to be housed in the Golden Hall.

Completed in 1124, the **Golden Hall (Konjikido)** has come to symbolize the golden years of the Fujiwara era and was declared Japan's first architectural National Treasure in 1929. Measuring just 5.5m by 5.5m (18x18ft.), it is almost entirely covered in gold leaf (chosen not only because Fujiwara possessed so much gold but also because gold is considered the symbolic color of the Pure Land) and decorated with lacquer, mother-of-pearl, metalwork, and ivory. Inside are statues of Amida and her attendants, as well as peacocks and floral displays meant to represent paradise. Entombed beneath the statues are the mummified bodies of Kiyohira, his son, and grandson, as well as the head of his great-grandson, which had been sent to Kamakura as proof that he had been assassinated, thus bringing the Fujiwara rule to an end. Alas—and this is a big alas—the Golden Hall sits protected inside a concrete building. Yet even in 1288, the Kamakura shogunate, recognizing the magnificence of the Golden Hall, ordered that it be shielded from the elements with a protective building, which was later replaced in the 15th century with the **Oido,** which today stands nearby. Other important sites include the **Kyozo** (Sutra Hall) and a rare, open-air, thatch-roofed Noh stage, rebuilt in 1853 in traditional style by the Date clan.

202 Koromonoseki. www.chusonji.or.jp. ⓒ **0191/46-2211.** Admission ¥800 adults, ¥500 high-school students, ¥300 junior-high students, ¥200 children. Daily 8:30am–5pm (to 4:30pm in winter). Run-Run bus: Chuson-ji.

Hiraizumi Cultural Heritage Center (Hiraizumi Bunka Isan Center) ★★
Make this one of your first stops, since it's your best bet for assimilating Hiraizumi's vast cultural and historic significance. Good explanations in English and a free audio guide tell you how Kiyohira's personal loss compelled him to create the Pure Land, how his son and grandson carried on his vision, how his great-grandson, pursued by Minamoto Yoritomo, fled to the north of Hiraizumi to spare the village from becoming a battlefield, and how Yoritomo was so impressed by Hiraizumi, it influenced his development of Kamakura. Archeological finds round out the exhibits.

44 Hanadate. www.chusonji.or.jp. ⓒ **0191/46-4012.** Admission free. Daily 9am–5pm. Run-Run bus: Bunka Isan Center.

Zazen Meditation

One-hour sessions of sitting Zen meditation are available at both Chuson-ji (Apr–Oct only) and Motsu-ji by applying at least 1 week in advance and paying ¥1,000. Motsu-ji accepts a minimum of four people, but Chuson-ji accepts lone practitioners. Bonus: Zazen participants get to enter the Hondo at both places.

Motsu-ji Temple ★   Kiyohira's son, Motohira, began construction of this temple complex in the mid-12th century, work that was completed by Motohira's son. It's said that Motsu-ji was unparalleled, even larger and grander than Chuson-ji, with dozens of halls, stupas, and quarters for 500 monks. Tragically, numerous fires reduced all of Motsu-ji's buildings to ashes. You'll have to content yourself with how it must have looked 850-some years ago with the huge illustrated map near the entrance and the **Hondo (Main Hall),** a reconstruction of a 12th-century Heian Buddhist temple and home of Yakushi, the Buddha of healing. But the most important thing to see here is the **Pure Land Garden,** which has survived relatively intact and is thus an outstanding display of garden techniques from the Heian Period (794-1192). It's centered on a large pond meant to evoke the ocean, with a rocky cliff, artificial mountain, beaches, boulders, and islands. Compared to Japanese landscape gardens of today, it seems simple and uncontrived, kind of what you'd expect a Buddhist paradise to look like. Still, I wish I could have seen Motsu-ji in its heyday. The great haiku poet Basho probably expressed it most succinctly when he visited Motsuji more than 500 years after its downfall and wrote: "The summer grass—'Tis all that's left—of ancient warrior's dreams."

58 Osawa. www.motsuji.or.jp. ✆ **0191/46-2331.** Admission ¥500 adults, ¥300 high-school students, ¥100 children Daily 3:30am–5pm (to 4:30pm in winter). A 10-min. walk east of Hiraizumi Station. Run-Run bus: Motsu-ji.

Where to Eat

Chuson-ji Temple has a simple self-serve restaurant, **Kanzan-tei,** located next to the outdoor Noh stage and offering good views of the countryside from its hillside perch. It offers curry udon and a few other noodle dishes, but the specialty is soba topped with Japanese yam, which you can order with a set lunch for ¥1,200 (no credit cards accepted). It's open daily from 10am to 3:30pm (last order).

Minka (民家) VARIED JAPANESE   This tiny place near the station, in a 90-year-old building filled with antiques, offers ramen, curry rice, soba, and udon, served at low tables on tatami. It also serves the local specialty, *hatto-jiru,* a soup made here by boiling mushrooms, carrots, onions, and other vegetables in a chicken broth flavored with soy and miso, along with thick and chewy handmade noodles. If you want, you can even order yours with gold flakes *(ogon-batto).*

31–1 Suzusawa. ✆ **0191/46-3186.** Main dishes ¥300–¥650. No credit cards. Daily 10am–7pm. A 5-min. walk from Hiraizumi Station. Take the first right onto Chuson-ji street; it's on the left, just before the street crosses the tracks (look for the miniature water wheel outside).

Oku no Yorimichi (奥のより道) ✦ VARIED JAPANESE   The ¥650 set lunch here (not available Sundays) is a steal, coming with soup, rice, a main dish (fish or meat), coffee, and dessert. There are plenty of other options, too, including *tonkatsu,* ramen, tofu salad, and the local (and famous) Maesawa beef, along with *yoshoku* (Japanese versions of Western food) choices like hamburger, omelet rice, pasta, and a spicy Pakistani chicken curry. In the evening, it also serves as a neighborhood bar. It's name, by the way, is a play on Basho's *Oku no Hosomichi* (*Narrow Road to the Interior*), meaning, instead, to take a detour.

82–3 Suzusawa. ✆ **0191/46-34996.** Main dishes ¥530–¥2,000; steak set meals ¥2,200–¥6,000. No credit cards. Wed–Mon 11:30am–2pm and 5:30–10pm. Run-Run bus: Yukyu no Yu Hot Spring. On the road opposite Hotel Musashibo, towards town.

Where to Stay

Hiraizumi may receive 1.8 million tourists a year, but hardly any of them stay the night, due, most likely, to the town's surprisingly limited supply of accommodations. Here are a couple of my favorites.

Hotel Musashibo (ホテル武蔵坊) ★　This place would be just ordinary elsewhere, but here it's Hirazumi's best accommodation (and tallest building), nothing fancy but with a prime spot overlooking wooded hills not far from Motsu-ji. Despite its name, most of its rooms are tatami, though it does offer six single rooms with beds (and toilets but no tubs) and one spacious combination corner room with beds, a tatami area, and tub right beside a window.

15 Osawa, Hiraizumi, Iwate Prefecture 029-4102. www.musasibou.co.jp. ✆ **0191/46-2241.** Fax 0191/46-2250. 48 units, 6 with toilet only. ¥8,550–¥9,600 single; ¥12,750–¥14,850 per person in tatami room. Rates include 2 meals. AE, MC, V. Run-Run bus: Yukyu No Yu Hot Spring. Up the hill on the left. **Amenities:** Restaurant; lounge; bar; hot-spring baths. *In-room*: AC, TV, fridge, hair dryer.

Maizuruso (舞鶴荘)　This place started taking in boarders almost 40 years ago, when hired laborers working the local farms needed a place to stay. Though the boxy structure lacks character and is worn in places, it has a good location near Motsu-ji Temple, with some of its tatami rooms facing an ancient garden across the street (ask for a room facing the front).

23–1 Shirayama, Hiraizumi, Iwate Prefecture 029-4102. www6.ocne.ne.jp/~maiduru. ✆ **0191/46-3375.** 9 units, none with bathroom. ¥3,500 per person without meals, ¥5,500–¥7,500 per person with 2 meals. No credit cards. A 10-min. walk from Hiraizumi Station. Walk straight from the station toward Motsu-ji, turning right when you reach the park (Kanjizaio-in Ato); it will be on the right. **Amenities:** Lobby computer w/free Internet. *In room*: A/C, TV, no phone.

KAKUNODATE, TOWN OF SAMURAI HOMES ★

Kakunodate was founded in 1620 by feudal lord Ashina Yoshikatsu, who chose the site for its river and easily defended mountain. His samurai retainers settled just south of his hilltop castle, in modest thatched-roof homes behind wooden fences along wide, fine streets, which they lined with weeping cherry trees imported from Kyoto. To help support themselves, the samurai engaged in cottage industry, crafting beautiful products made from cherry bark. Meanwhile, merchants settled in their own district, in narrow, cramped quarters. Many of the town's 13,000 residents are direct descendants of the town's original samurai and merchants.

Although the castle is long gone, Kakunodate's castle-town architectural layout remains remarkably intact, with one of the country's best-preserved (though regrettably small) samurai districts. It's also famous for its cherry trees, not only in the samurai district but also along the banks of the Hinokinai River, and for cherry-bark crafts. Yet Kakunodate is an unpretentious village, with only a few of the souvenir and tourist shops that plague other picturesque towns.

Essentials

GETTING THERE   From Tokyo, take the **Akita Shinkansen** from Tokyo or Ueno stations directly to Kakunodate. The trip takes about 3½ hours and costs ¥15,850 for a reserved seat (some trains require reservations). Kakunodate is just one stop after Tazawako. (See "Towada-Hachimantai National Park," below.) If coming from elsewhere in Tohoku, you can also take the **Tohoku Shinkansen** train to Morioka and transfer.

VISITOR INFORMATION   After you exit Kakunodate Station, look for the **Kakunodate Tourist Information Center** to the right, housed in a replica of a traditional warehouse (© **0187/54-2700;** daily 9am–6pm), where you can pick up an English-language map from the helpful, English-speaking staff and reserve a hotel room (in person only). More information is available at **www.kakunodate-kanko.jp**.

ORIENTATION & GETTING AROUND   You can walk to all the sights and lodging and dining recommendations below (though you might opt for a short taxi ride to your accommodations if you're weighed down by luggage). To reach the samurai district, a 15- to 20-minute walk from the station, walk straight out of the station and continue until it ends at a T-intersection (you'll see a post office across the street; this is the former merchant district and the heart of the city). Here, you turn right. Or, you might wish to tour by **rental bike,** available in a shop on the plaza in front of the train station next to the police *koban* for ¥300 per hour.

Seeing the Sights

Kakunodate is at its most glorious (and crowded) in late April, when its hundreds of cherry trees are in full bloom. The most popular viewing spot is along the Hinokinai River, where two rows of some 400 cherry trees form a shimmering tunnel of blossoms for 2km (1¼ miles). They were planted in 1933 to commemorate the birth of the present emperor, Akihito.

THE SAMURAI DISTRICT (BUKEYASHIKI) ★★   Of Kakunodate's 80-some samurai mansions built during the Edo Period, only six remain. Still, the district retains its feudal atmosphere to an amazing degree, thanks to its wide streets flanked by weeping cherry trees and dark wooden fences. These fences and traditional entry gates are employed even today to conceal more-modern homes, giving a clean, crisp line of vision throughout the district. It's a strong contrast to the jumble of most Japanese cities, and even to the merchant district that's just a short walk away.

If you're walking from the station, you'll pass several samurai houses on Bukeyashiki Dori that are open free to the public (though admittance inside is restricted), including the **Odano Samurai House** to the right, the **Kawarada Samurai House** next door, the **Matsumoto Samurai House** across the street (where you can usually see craftsmen at work), and the city-owned **Iwahashi Samurai House** on the right, which has appeared in movies.

But the first major place of interest will be the **Aoyagi Samurai Manor (Kakunodate Rekishi-mura Aoyagi;** 角館歴史村青柳家) ★★★, 26 Higashi Katuraku-cho (© **0187/54-3257**), to the right through an impressive entry gate that serves as testimony to the Aoyagi family's high samurai status. This is more than a mere manor, however, as it's actually a compound of several traditional buildings spread throughout an unkempt garden, each filled with a wealth of eclectic treasures from the 17th to 20th centuries, collected through the ages by the Aoyagi family and well documented in English. As you wander through the buildings, you'll see samurai armor, rifles, swords, dolls, kimono, sake cups, *ukiyo-e* (woodblock prints), scrolls and screens, Meiji-Era uniforms and medals, farm tools, antique phonographs, and cameras. Other buildings hold shops, a teahouse, and a restaurant. You'll want to spend at least an hour exploring here. Open daily 9am to 5pm (to 4pm in winter). Admission is ¥500 for adults, ¥300 for junior-high and high-school students, and ¥200 for children.

Next door is the **Ishiguro Samurai House** ★★, Omotemachi (© 0187/55-1496). In contrast to the Aoyagi Samurai Manor, this thatched-roof home remains almost exactly as it might have looked when it was constructed 200 years ago by the Ishiguro samurai family. After the Meiji Restoration, the family became landlords and collected rice as rent. Today, English-speaking, 12th-generation Ishiguro Naotsugi continues to live here; he has opened five simple but elegant rooms to the public in the main house. Family heirlooms, including samurai gear, winter *geta* (fur-lined and with spikes), scales for weighing rice, and old maps of Kakunodate are on display in a former warehouse. The medical illustrations (copies), by the way, are from Japan's first book on anatomy, copied from a Dutch book in 1774 by Kakunodate samurai Odano Naotake. You can see everything in less than 30 minutes, though if Ishiguro-san is on hand to answer questions, you might linger longer. Open daily 9am to 5pm. Admission is ¥300 for adults and ¥150 for children.

Where to Eat

Kakunodate's local specialties include *inaniwa udon,* hand-pulled wheat noodles far more delicate than the more typical, hearty Osaka-style udon, and *oyakodon* (rice topped with local chicken and egg). In addition to the restaurants below, a simple dining room at the Aoyagi Samurai Manor, called **Mori no Shokushin-kan** (森の食心館; © **0187/52-8015**), offers noodle dishes, including tempura *soba* (¥1,260) and *inaniwa udon* (with mountain vegetables, ¥900). Open daily 10am to 4pm (but only on weekends in winter), it has an English-language menu. **Folkloro Kakunodate** next to the train station (see below) has a simple restaurant open daily from 11am to 9pm offering set meals for ¥500 to ¥1,500 from its English-language menu, including *inaniwa udon, oyakodon,* and curry rice.

Nishinomiyake (西宮家) ★ VARIED JAPANESE   This pleasant and inexpensive restaurant is located in the family compound of the Nishinomiya clan, a samurai family that later became merchants and built the main house and five warehouses that are on display today. The restaurant is in a warehouse dating from 1919 and offers a limited menu of *inaniwa udon,* beef hash with rice, hamburger steak, *ebi* (shrimp) fry, and other dishes. Best, perhaps, is to order one of the *obento* lunch boxes. After your meal, be sure to wander through the other warehouses, including a small museum housing family treasures and a crafts shop.

11–1 Tamachi Kami-cho. © **0187/52-2438.** Obento ¥1,050–¥1,575. No credit cards. Daily 10am–5:30pm (last order; 4:30pm in winter). Station: Kakunodate (8 min.). Walk straight out of the train station and turn left at the 3rd street; the restaurant will be almost immediately on your right.

Shichibe (しちべえ) ★ LOCAL SPECIALTIES Take your shoes off at the entrance and then head for one of the tables with chairs or *tatami* seating with leg wells towards the back, where you'll have a view of a small garden. Traditionally decorated with white walls, wood crossbeams, and *shoji*, it serves most of Kakunodate's local specialties, including *inaniwa udon, oyakodon,* and *kiritampo nabe* (a one-pot stew consisting of rice pounded into a paste and then charcoal grilled before simmering in chicken broth with vegetables), along with Akita Prefecture beef and pork (like in *tonkatsu*), and a tofu set meal. The menu is in Japanese only, but there are pictures.

15 Yokomachi. ✆ **0187/54-3295.** Main dishes ¥1,200–¥2,000; set lunch ¥900; set meals ¥1,600–¥5,250. No credit cards. Mon–Sat 11am–7pm; Sun 11am–5pm. Station: Kakunodate (15 min.). Just before the Samurai District to the right, catty-corner from the City Office marked on the map; look for the bamboo gate.

Shopping

Kakunodate has been famous for *kabazaiku* (cherry-bark crafts) since the Edo Period. You can observe artisans at work on this painstaking craft at the **Kakunodate-machi Denshokan** (角館町伝承館) (10–1 Omotemachi Shimocho; ✆ **0187/54-1700;** daily 9am–5pm, to 4:30pm in winter), in a red-brick building a couple minutes' walk from the samurai houses on Bukeyashiki Street. In addition to seeing how strips of cherry bark are applied to tea canisters, boxes, vases, and other goods in live demonstrations, you can tour a museum devoted to the craft along with displays of samurai outfits and items that once belonged to the Kakunodate feudal lord, as well as everyday items used by common people such as straw raingear and *geta* ice skates, and wonderful photos of days long past. And of course, you can also browse for cherry-bark products in its large shop. Admission to the *denshokan* is ¥300 for adults and ¥150 for children; there's no admission for the shop.

Where to Stay

Although you can tour Kakunodate's sights in a day, I've included accommodations in case you're arriving from Tokyo or seeking respite in a small town. Book well ahead if you hope to stay here during peak seasons: cherry-blossom season (roughly late Apr through early May) and summer holidays (mid-July through Aug).

Folkloro Kakunodate No English is spoken at this JR-affiliated hotel, but its location next to Kakunodate Station and its clean, modern, and inexpensive Western-style rooms make it a logical choice for a 1-night stopover, especially if you have a Japan Rail Pass, which gives a 10% discount. Two types of rooms are available: 11 twins and 15 deluxe twin family rooms that sleep up to four. Note, however, that the family rooms, with twin beds and two sleeper sofas, seem cramped for four but are roomy for two. Higher rates below are for peak season.

14 Naka-sugasawa, Kakunodate, Senboku-shi, Akita Prefecture 014-0368. www.jre-hotels.jp. ✆ **0187/53-2070.** Fax 0187/53-2118. 26 units. ¥7,350–¥10,500 single; ¥12,600–¥18,900 twin; ¥18,270–¥27,720 triple; ¥21,000–¥32,760 quad. Rates include breakfast buffet. AE, DC, MC, V. To the left after you exit the train station. **Amenities:** Restaurant. *In room:* A/C, TV, fridge, hair dryer, Wi-Fi.

Ishikawa Ryokan (石川旅館) One of Kakunodate's oldest *ryokan,* open since the Edo Period and now in its fifth generation of innkeepers, it now occupies a dated building constructed in 1920. Although corridors suggest the ordinary, the Japanese-style rooms are fine, simple but with nice wood details. And the elderly owners are every bit as self-effacing and hospitable to guests as their ancestors must have been to traveling samurai and other high officials. Though they don't speak English, they make your stay here a real treat. Meals, should you opt for them, are served in your room. Prices remain the same here all year.

32 Iwasemachi, Kakunodate, Senboku-shi, Akita Prefecture. © **0187/54-2030.** Fax 0187/54-2031. 11 units (2 with bathroom, 1 with toilet only). ¥6,500 per person without meals; ¥13,500 per person with 2 meals. No credit cards. Station: Kakunodate (12 min.). Walk straight out of the train station and turn left when you reach the covered benches (1 block before the T intersection); the ryokan will be on your right. *In room:* A/C, TV.

Tamachi Bukeyashiki Hotel (田町武家屋敷ホテル) ★★ 🎒 This delightful hotel is deceiving—it looks as though it has been here since the Edo Period, with its whitewashed walls, open wooden beams, and rustic ambience, but it was built in 1999. It combines tradition with modern comfort, with gleaming wood floors, contemporary Japanese art, and Japanese- and Western-style rooms that exude class, from sensuously curving paper lampshades to ceramic tissue holders. Breakfast (Western breakfast is available) is served in a restaurant with dark-wood tables overlooking a garden. This small, intimate establishment is a perfect choice for experiencing Kakunodate's relaxed, small-town charm.

23 Tamachi Shimocho, Kakunodate, Senboku-shi, Akita Prefecture. © **0187/52-1700.** Fax 0187/52-1701. 12 units. ¥17,850–¥21,999 per person with 2 meals; ¥12,600–¥15,750 per person with breakfast only. AE, DC, MC, V. Station: Kakunodate (12 min.). Walk straight out of the train station and turn left at the 3rd street; the hotel will be 2 blocks down, on your right. **Amenities:** Restaurant. *In room:* A/C, fridge, hair dryer, Internet.

TOWADA-HACHIMANTAI NATIONAL PARK

Towada-Hachimantai National Park, spreading 862 sq. km (333 sq. miles) through north-central Tohoku and shared by three prefectures, is blessed with mountain ranges, lakes, streams, and hot-spring spas. It's perfect for the outdoor enthusiast, offering hiking in summer and skiing in winter. Most easily accessible from Tokyo is **Lake Tazawa** at the southern end of the park, with its nearby ski lifts, hot-springs, and biking and hiking opportunities. Far to the north, and a good choice if you're heading onward to Hokkaido, are the pristine **Lake Towada** and delightful **Oirase Stream** with its riverbank hiking trail.

Unfortunately, bus service in the national park is either infrequent or nonexistent. Train and bus connections are reasonably fast, or you might consider renting a car.

Lake Tazawa, Nyuto Onsen & Mount Komagatake

Lake Tazawa (Tazawako) has the distinction of being the deepest lake in Japan, 423m (1,387 ft.) deep. Crystal clear, the caldera offers swimming as well as cycling along its rim. Nearby are several ski resorts, as well as the Nyuto Onsen ★★ rustic hot-spring spa area at the base of Mount Nyuto, which make good bases for exploring the area. Mount Komagatake is a popular destination for trekkers.

ESSENTIALS
GETTING THERE From Tokyo, take the **Akita Shinkansen** from Tokyo or Ueno stations directly to Tazawako. The trip takes about 3 hours and costs ¥15,240 for a

reserved seat (some trains require reservations). Tazawako is one stop before Kakunodate (see the "Kakunodate, Town of Samurai Homes" section earlier). If coming from elsewhere in Tohoku, you can also take the **Tohoku Shinkansen** train to Morioka and transfer. You can also reach Tazawako Station by Towada Taxi **sightseeing van or bus** (© **0186/35-2111**) from Yasumiya on Lake Towada (information on Lake Towada below) from late April to October for ¥6,000 per person (two or more passengers, weather permitting). Vehicles depart Yasumiya at 9am and reach Tazawako Station at 4pm, with stops at scenic spots along the way; reservations are required. From Tazawako Station you must then board a bus to all the recommendations below, including Nyuto Onsen.

VISITOR INFORMATION   For information on Lake Tazawa and vicinity, including skiing and bus schedules throughout the region, or for hotel reservations, stop by the **Tazawako Tourist Information Center** inside Tazawako Station (www.tazawako.org; © **0187/43-2111;** daily 8:30am–5:30pm). They also offer one computer with free Internet access and a topographical model of the area. For information on Nyuto Onsen, see its website at **www.nyuto-onsenkyo.com**.

ORIENTATION & GETTING AROUND   The town of Tazawako, in Akita Prefecture, is the transportation launching pad for visiting the southern region of Towada-Hachimantai National Park. **Buses** depart from the Tazawako Bus Terminal, outside Tazawako Station, for Lake Tazawa, area ski resorts, Mount Komagatake, and Nyuto Onsen hot-spring spas. Ask for bus schedules in English at the Tazawako Tourist Information Center.

Lake Tazawa is just a 15-minute bus ride from Tazawako Station; some buses stopping here go onward to Tazawako Skijo ski resort and Nyuto Onsen (Nyuto Spa), both northeast of the lake. Otherwise, a bus departs Tazawako Station approximately every hour for Tazawako Skijo (a 30-min. ride), Kogen Onsen (for Mount Komagatake, 37 min.), and Nyuto Onsen (45 min.).

CAR RENTALS   Tazawako is a good starting point for driving excursions through Towado-Hachimantai National Park. **JR Eki Rent-A-Car** (© **0187/43-1081**) is located beside Tazawako Station. For **Toyota Rent-A-Car** in Tazawako, call © **0187/43-2100;** staff will pick you up from the station.

WHAT TO SEE & DO

SWIMMING & CYCLING AT LAKE TAZAWA   Just 20km (13 miles) in circumference, Lake Tazawa is popular for its small swimming beach a couple minutes' walk from the bus stop. Outside the swimming season—mid-July through August—you'll find nary a soul there. You can rent bicycles here for ¥400 for the first hour and ¥300 for every additional hour; mountain bikes run ¥600 per hour. It takes about 2 hours to ride around the lake; unfortunately, you have to share the road with vehicular traffic, but because this is a popular cycling route, motorists know to keep a lookout. (Still, it may be prudent to avoid weekends and the mid-July and Aug vacation crunch.) Except for one small stretch, the road is mostly flat and is pleasantly wooded and relatively unspoiled; circle the lake counterclockwise in the left lane, which puts you on the inside track closer to the lake. Along the way you'll pass a nice restaurant (see "Where to Eat," below) and a golden statue of the legendary Princess Tatsuko, a nymphlike beauty just off the shoreline. According to myth, the princess drank from Lake Tazawa hoping for eternal beauty; instead, she was turned into a dragonlike serpent as punishment for her vanity.

Rustic Spas in the Wild

One of the main reasons for coming to this neck of the woods is Nyuto Onsen ★★, one of the most rustic hot-spring areas in Japan. Located deep in the woods, it boasts a string of seven inns with hot-spring spas, including some very atmospheric outdoor baths. All are open to the public, with admission starting at ¥500, but the Yumeguri-cho ticket book for ¥1,500 allows entry to all 7 baths and free use of a shuttle bus (Yumeguri-go) connecting them. This is a truly unique experience, but to truly enjoy it you should plan to spend the night (see "Where to Stay," below).

Sightseeing boats, some of which make stops to explore the surrounding woods, operate on Lake Tazawa from late April to early November; a 40-minute trip costs ¥1,170.

Laka Tazawa is a 15-minute bus ride from Tazawako Station. All buses going to Nyuto Onsen stop here—the bus stop at the lake is Tazawakohan—and the fare is ¥350.

SKIING   Of several area ski resorts, largest is **Tazawako Skijo** (© 0187/46-2011), with nine lifts. A 1-day lift ticket costs ¥3,800 and ski-equipment rental costs ¥6,000 for everything; snowboarding is also available. Buses from Tazawako Station (traveling in the direction of Nyuto Onsen) reach Tazawako Skijo in about 30 minutes and cost ¥510.

CLIMBING MOUNT KOMAGATAKE   Visible from Lake Tazawa, Akita Prefecture's tallest mountain is actually a 1,637m-high (5,402-ft.) dormant volcano. It's a popular destination for hikers, though a bus that deposits hikers at the 8th Station makes it a fairly quick hike—you can reach the top in about 1½ hours. At the peak, you're rewarded with grand vistas of the surrounding mountains, as well as more hiking trails. It's also said to be the best in northern Japan for alpine plants. Because the path is steep at times, wear nonslip soles. (All Japanese you see will be outfitted head to toe in hiking regalia.) From Tazawako Station, six buses a day make the 1-hour trip directly to Mount Komagatake's 8th Station for ¥1,000. Or, take a more frequent 37-minute ride to Kogen Onsen (¥600) and transfer there for a 25-minute ride to the 8th station (¥410). Buses run daily July and August but only on weekends June, September, and October.

WHERE TO EAT

Orae ★ WESTERN/VARIED JAPANESE   Located beside Lake Tazawa, a 15-minute walk counterclockwise from the bus stop or a short bike ride, this casual restaurant is my top pick for lunch, due in no small part to its on-site Kohan no Mori microbrewery (it makes an award-winning Akita Komachi Lager, and the *dunkel* is very good), free Wi-Fi, and views of the lake from both its airy, glass-enclosed dining room and outdoor terrace. The menu, in Japanese only, offers seasonal selections of Western dishes, including pizza, pasta, salads, hamburger steak, and baked chicken, along with Japanese dishes. *Korokke* (croquettes) are a specialty, changing with the season, from those filled with *edamame* (soybean) in summer to taro in autumn.

37–5 Haruyama, Tazawako. © **0187/58-0608.** Main dishes ¥500–¥1,800; set meals ¥1,210–¥2,060. AE, DC, MC, V. Daily 11:30am–8:30pm (last order). Bus: Tawazakohan (15 min.). Walk around the lake to the right.

WHERE TO STAY

Qkamura National Park Resort Village **(Kyukamura Tazawako-Kogen;**
休暇村田沢湖高原)** ◢   Conveniently located on Nyuto Onsen's main road (buses
from Tazawako Station stop right outside), this sprawling government-owned public
lodging makes up in heart what it lacks in ambience compared to the rustic inns
nearby. Its public spaces mix the cheerful with the institutional   think pink and rose
industrial carpeting and blond woods—and rooms are very well maintained. It's the
only place to stay if you prefer Western-style rooms (they're also the only ones here
with bathrooms), though Japanese tatami rooms are also available (Japanese guests
lay out their own futon, but staff will do it on request). Rooms in the east wing
have forest views, while west wing *tatami* rooms get great afternoon light through
the mountains. In addition to serving buffet-style meals in the dining room, it
offers easy access to hiking paths and welcoming, wood-built indoor and outdoor
hot-spring baths.

2–1 Komagatake, Tazawako, Senboku-shi, Akita Prefecture 014-1201. www.qkamura.or.jp.
℃ **0187/46-2244.** Fax 0187/46-2700. 38 units (all with toilet, 3 with bathroom). ¥11,800 per person
single or double. Rates include 2 meals. AE, MC, V. Bus: From Tazawako Station, 50 min. to Qka-
mura-mae stop (look for the sign that reads NATIONAL PARK RESORT VILLAGE). **Amenities:** Indoor/out-
door hot-spring baths; lobby computer w/free Internet; Wi-Fi (free, in lobby). *In room:* A/C, TV,
fridge, hair dryer.

Taenoyu **(妙乃湯)** ★★   This inn merges old-fashioned comfort with classy elegance (updated *tatami* rooms, polished wood floors, antiques), making it a good
choice for those who find Qkamura too pedestrian and Tsuru-no-yu too rustic. Next
to a river and a man-made waterfall, it offers 7 indoor and outdoor baths, including a
private family outdoor bath available for 1 hour and a mixed-sex bath (shy females can
wrap a towel around them, but men are supposed to bathe in the buff). Meals, which
include Akita Prefecture specialties and edible wild plants gathered from around the
hotel, are served communally in a tatami room with tables, chairs and river views or
in a cozy lounge with antiques and a fireplace. Best rooms have a view of the river.

2–1 Komagatake, Tazawako, Senboku-shi, Akita Prefecture 014-1201. http://taenoyu.com/web-
english.html. ℃ **0187/46-2740.** Fax 0187/46-2207. 17 units, 10 with toilet, none with bathroom.
¥11,000–¥18,000 per person including 2 meals. Rates exclude tax and service charge and are
¥1,000 higher on weekends and in peak season. AE, DC, MC, V. Bus: From Tazawako Station, 53
min. to Taeno-onsen stop. **Amenities:** Indoor/outdoor hot-spring baths; Wi-Fi. *In room:* A/C, TV.

Tsuru-no-yu Onsen **(鶴の湯温泉)** ★★★ ▮   By far, this is the best place to stay
in Nyuto Onsen, if not in all of Tohoku. Contrary to what you might think, however,
it's neither refined nor elegant; it's not even expensive. Rather, nestled in a wooded
valley more than 2.5km (1½ miles) off the already isolated main Nyuto Onsen road,
this is about as remote as you can get in Japan. With its thatched-roof row house of
tatami rooms lit by oil lamps, complemented by the sound of rushing water and steam
rising from the outdoor baths, it seems positively ancient. I've never seen anything
like it.

Tsuru-no-yu opened as an *onsen* (hot-spring spa) 350 years ago; its oldest building—a thatch-roofed row house of 5 tatami rooms with blackened walls and *irori*
(open-hearth fireplaces)—is 100 years old. Additions that ramble along the hillside
were constructed over the years, along a rushing stream that serenades you to sleep.
Dinners are cooked over the irori, either in your room or in a tatami dining hall, with
all the guests dressed in *yukata* (cotton kimono). If you're on a budget, you can stay

in the self-cooking wing, which offers simple tatami rooms and lets you cook meals in a communal kitchen. Eleven outdoor sulfurous baths are separated for men and women, but there is one mixed bath where you can wrap a towel around you. Unfortunately, day-trippers spoil some of the fun of staying here (baths are open to the public daily 10am–3pm for ¥500). Evenings, however, are magical.

If you're more about creature comforts, about 10 minutes down the road there's the modern annex Yama no Yado, the only inn in Nyuto Onsen with private bathrooms in each room. Its baths, however, don't compare to those above; if you've come this far, you'll at least want to amble over to Tsuru-no-yu's baths.

50 Kokuyurin, Tazawako, Senboku-shi, Akita Prefecture 014-1204. www.tsurunoyu.com. ℂ**0187/46-2139.** Fax 0187/46-2761. 35 units (14 with toilet, none with bathroom). ¥8,550–¥15,900 per person including 2 meals. ¥2,780 per person in the self-cooking wing, plus ¥200 for kitchen use and ¥735 futon charge. Winter heating charge ¥1,050 extra. MC, V. Pickup available from Arupa Komakusa bus stop. **Amenities:** Indoor/outdoor hot-spring baths. *In room:* No phone (in most).

Lake Towada & Oirase Stream ★★

Located at the northern end of Towada-Hachimantai National Park, on the border between Aomori and Akita prefectures, **Lake Towada** (Towadako in Japanese) is one of the park's top scenic gems. It's one of Japan's least spoiled lakes, with only two small villages on its perimeter and encircled by wooded cliffs and mountains. Best, however, is **Oirase Stream,** the only river flowing out of Lake Towada. A shaded mountain stream that courses over boulders and is fed by numerous waterfalls, it is flanked by a hiking trail offering one of the prettiest walks in Tohoku. In autumn, leaves of gold and red render the scenery truly spectacular. **Note:** Avoid winter, when inns and restaurants close for the season due to deep snow.

ESSENTIALS

GETTING THERE As Lake Towada does not lie close to a train station, your final journey to the lake must be by **bus** to the JR Towadako bus terminal in Yasumiya, a small village on Lake Towada with a tourist office and a few accommodations. The bus rides are through scenic, mountainous terrain (you might want to pack some Dramamine).

From Tokyo, take the 3-hour **Shinkansen train** to Hachinohe (fare: ¥15,350), and then board a **JR Tohoku bus** from the station's west exit. It takes about 2¼ hours and costs ¥2,600 to Yasumiya. If you're arriving from Hokkaido, take the train to Aomori. Outside Aomori Station, to the left, you can board a **JR bus** from platform no. 8 bound for Lake Towada, with the last stop at Yasumiya 4 hours later and costing ¥3,000. If you have a Japan Rail Pass, you can ride both these buses for free (but not with a JR East Pass). Both these buses travel on the road beside the hiking trail along Oirase Stream (see below) and make several stops there (stops and a simple narration of the sights are announced in English), with about five or six runs daily. For more information, contact the **JR bus** company in Aomori at ℂ **017/723-1621** (in Japanese) or visit **www.jrbustohoku.co.jp**.

CAR RENTALS Travel by car is quicker than by bus and may be less expensive depending on the number in your group. **JR Eki Rent-A-Car** has offices at Aomori Station (ℂ **017/722-3930**) and Hachinohe Station (ℂ **0178/28-2882**). **Toyota Rent-A-Car** also has offices in Aomori Station (ℂ **017/739-0115**) and in Hachinohe (ℂ **0178/27-0100**), with free pickup from the station.

VISITOR INFORMATION   In Yasumiya, the **Lake Towada Information Center** (© 0176/75-2425; daily 8am–5pm) is located next to the JR Bus Center, has great brochures in English, and can tell you which inns have space available.

ORIENTATION & GETTING AROUND   The village of Yasumiya, on the south-eastern shore of Lake Towada, has a bus terminal, a tourist office, and a handful of accommodations and restaurants. On the eastern side of the lake is Nenokuchi, trail head for hikes along Oirase Stream. The **JR buses** that run between Yasumiya and Aomori or Hachinohe also stop at Nenokuchi and several locations along the Oirase hiking trail, making approximately a dozen runs a day from April to early November. Otherwise, your best bet for travel between Yasumiya and Nenokuchi is via **sightsee-ing boat** (see below).

SEEING THE SIGHTS

In Yasumiya, the major point of interest is **Towada Jinja Shrine,** surrounded by giant cedars and boasting marvelous woodcarvings of animals. A curious custom here is to buy a keyhole-shaped paper amulet called a *hitogata*, write your name and birth date on it, twist it into the shape of a tadpole and then throw it into the lake. If it sinks, legend says, your wish will come true. Near the shrine is a well-known sculp-ture of two young women by Takamura Kotaro. Unlike the golden nymph at Lake Tazawa, these broad-shouldered, wide-hipped figures were sculpted to honor the sturdy women who can withstand northern Tohoku's harsh winters. My Japanese friends, however, think they're very unflattering.

SIGHTSEEING BOATS ON LAKE TOWADA   The best way to enjoy the pristine beauty of crystal-clear **Lake Towada,** a double caldera formed some 20,000 years ago by a volcanic eruption, is aboard excursion boats that cruise the waters. About 46km (28½ miles) of undulating coastline marked by capes, inlets, cliffs, and trees that put on a spectacular autumn show make this one of Towada-Hachimantai National Park's major draws. Two cruises are available: a 50-minute cruise between Yasumiya and Nenokuchi (available only Apr to early Nov), and a 60-minute cruise that begins and ends at Yasumiya (available when the lake is not frozen). The cost of either cruise is ¥1,400. A surcharge of ¥500 is levied if you wish to sit in the top lounge. Children pay half fare.

HIKING OIRASE STREAM ★★   To my mind, hiking along the Oirase Stream (Oirase Keiryu in Japanese) is the major draw for a trip to Lake Towada. A clear-running, gurgling stream that runs 65km (40 miles) on its way from the lake to the Pacific Ocean, it's at its picture-perfect best in **Oirase Gorge,** where hikers are treated to 13 waterfalls, rapids coursing over moss-covered boulders, and a dense wood of ferns, Japanese beech, oaks, and other broad-leaved trees, particularly stun-ning in autumn. A trail runs beside the stream from Nenokuchi on the lakeshore 14km (8¾ miles) northeast to Yakeyama; there are kilometer markers along the path in English. Since the waterfalls are between Nenokuchi and Ishigedo, most hikers cover just these 9km (5½ miles), in about 2 hours. Disappointingly, a road runs through the gorge beside the stream, but the pathway often diverges from the road, and the roar of the swift-running river and falls masks the sound of vehicles. The hike upstream (toward Nenokuchi) is considered the most picturesque, as it affords a full view of the cascading rapids.

There are eight bus stops on the road beside Oirase Stream, including Nenokuchi, Ishigedo, and Yakeyama. Because buses run only once an hour or so, you might con-sider taking a bus first and then hiking back. Between Nenokuchi and Yakeyama, for example, the bus ride costs ¥590 (free with your Japan Rail Pass) and takes about 15 minutes.

WHERE TO EAT

Most accommodations serve breakfast and dinner, with *himemasu* (Lake Towada trout) a favored dish. For an inexpensive meal on the Oirase Gorge trail, a small snack bar at Ishigedo sells ramen noodles, tempura *soba*, ice cream, and drinks.

Shinshuya LOCAL SPECIALTIES   This restaurant above a large souvenir shop is pretty darn basic and could do with some sprucing up, but it has dead-on lakeside views, an English-language menu, and a convenient location near the path to Towada Jinja Shrine. *Inaniwa udon* (noodles with mountain vegetables), *kiritampo nabe* (a one-pot stew consisting of rice pounded into a paste and then charcoal grilled before simmering in chicken broth with vegetables), Aomori beefsteaks, and fish are just some of the local specialties. To order, purchase your meal ticket at the counter.

16–11 Yasumiya. **℃ 0176/75-3131.** Main dishes ¥945–¥3,150. MC, V. Daily 8am–6pm (10am–4pm in winter). Bus: Towadako (3 min.). On the 2nd floor above a souvenir shop beside the lake.

WHERE TO STAY

Peak season is August and October; book far in advance for these months. Most lodgings in the area close during winter.

Himemasu Sanso (ひめます山荘) 🔔   This neat and spacious *minshuku* at the entrance to Yasumiya offers *tatami* rooms, most with views of the surrounding wooded hills (once you open the frosted glass windows). Meals are served communally and usually feature local trout and wild mountain vegetables; Western-style breakfasts are available on request. The owners will pick you up when you arrive by bus, but because they don't speak much English, you should go to the Lake Towada Information Center (see above) and have someone from there place the call.

16–15 Towada Kohan Yasumiya, Oaza Okuse, Towada-shi, Kamikita-gun, Aomori Prefecture 018-5501. **℃ 0176/75-2717.** Fax 0176/75-2717. 8 units, none with bathroom. ¥6,500 per person, including 2 meals. No credit cards. Bus: Towadako in Yasumiya (15 min., inland from the JR bus station). **Amenities:** Hot-spring bath. *In room:* TV, no phone.

Oirase Keiryu Hotel   The main reason for staying in this large, rather ordinary hotel is its lovely location beside Oirase Stream, making it an easy base for hiking the trail. There's a bus stop right outside with connections to Aomori and Hachinohe stations, along the gorge and to the lake, but the hotel also offers its own free shuttle bus from Shin-Aomori and Hachinohe stations (reservations must be made at least 3 days in advance). The hotel is divided into two sections: an older, rustic Daiichi (first) Wing with 105 rooms, and the newer Daini (second) Wing with 85 (more expensive) rooms. I prefer the Daini with its lobby overlooking the stream and maple trees and its hard-to-overlook giant fireplace sculpture by eccentric Okamoto Taro. It offers both Japanese *tatami* and twin rooms, about half with views of Oirase Stream. Public hot-spring baths also take advantage of river views. Meals are served communally in a dining room. Rates vary according to the season, room type (twins are less expensive than *tatami* rooms), and whether it's a weekday, Friday, or night before a holiday. The rates below reflect the full price range.

231 Aza Tochikubo, Oaza Okuse, Towada-shi, Aomori Prefecture 034-0398. www.oirase-keiryuu.jp. **℃ 0176/74-2121.** Fax 0176/74-2128. 189 units. ¥12,000–¥27,000 per person, including 2 meals. AE, DC, MC, V. Bus: Yakeyama (1 min.). **Amenities:** 2 restaurants; lounge; indoor and outdoor hot-spring baths. *In room:* A/C, TV, fridge, hair dryer.

Towada Hotel ★★★   This imposing, elegant hotel is my top choice for a splurge on Lake Towada. Secluded on a wooded hill overlooking the lake (and practical only if you have your own car), it was built in 1938 using huge cedar logs in a mix of Western-lodge-meets-Japanese-temple style, with a modern addition built years later. Former U.S. ambassador Edwin Reischauer and Emperor Showa have stayed here; nowadays most American guests are high-ranking officers from a nearby U.S. military base. Although all rooms face the lake, best are the Japanese rooms, all in the older part of the hotel and elegant with great views. Western-style rooms, though spacious and beautifully designed, do not have as good a view; be sure to ask for a room on the top floor and be sure, too, to wander over to the older wing for a look at its beautiful wood details in the old lobby (crafted by shrine and temple carpenters). Unfortunately, the public baths do not have hot-spring waters (instead, it's heated water from a mountain stream), but they do have lakeside views and outdoor tubs. Meals, served in a communal dining room with a mix of Japanese and Western dishes, are substantial. Western-style breakfasts are available.

Kosaka-machi, Towadako Nishi-kohan, Akita Prefecture 018-5511. ℂ **0176/75-1122.** Fax 0176/75-1313. 50 units, 8 with toilet, 42 with bathroom. Peak season ¥18,900–¥24,150 per person; regular season ¥15,750–¥18,900. Off-season discounts available. Rates include 2 meals. AE, DC, MC, V. Pickup service available from JR bus terminal in Yasumiya. **Amenities:** Restaurant and lounge; sauna; Wi-Fi (free, in lobby). In room: A/C, TV, fridge, hair dryer.

Tsuta Onsen ★   This classic, north-country inn dates from 1909 and is one of Tohoku's most famous traditional *ryokan*. *Tsuta* means "ivy" in Japanese, a theme carried out not only in pillars, transoms, and other architectural details but also in the dense, surrounding beech forest. Rooms in the oldest wooden structure (built in 1918) and an annex (1960), both up a long flight of stairs, have beautiful wood-carved details and good views but are without bathrooms (they're also cheaper), while the west wing 1988 addition, with gleaming wood floors salvaged from an old ryokan, has an elevator and toilets (a few have bathrooms), but its rooms lack the character of the older rooms. For the best views, be sure to request a room facing away from the street. For those who don't like sleeping on futons, three combination units offer *tatami* areas, beds, and bathrooms. The hot-spring baths are new but preserve traditional bathhouse architecture, with high ceilings and cypress walls; they're considered beneficial for healing scars and other skin problems. Breakfast is served in a dining room, while dinner is served in your room. Although not on the Oirase Stream and not as conveniently located as, say, the Oirase Keiryu Hotel (see above), the Tsuta is one of a kind and is served by the same JR bus that travels between Aomori and Lake Towada (it's about a 15-min. bus ride to Yakeyama). It also has its own 1-hour hiking trail to a nearby lake.

Aza Tsutanoyu, Okuse, Towada-shi, Aomori Prefecture 034-0301. ℂ **0176/74-2311.** Fax 0176/74-2244. info@thuta.co.jp. 50 units (3 with bathroom, 20 with toilet only). ¥10,650–¥26,400 per person, including 2 meals. AE, DC, MC, V. Bus: From Aomori Station, a 2-hr. JR bus ride to Tsuta Onsen stop (1 min.). **Amenities:** Hot-spring indoor bath; Wi-Fi (free, in lobby). In room: TV, fridge (in some).

HOKKAIDO

Hokkaido, the northernmost of Japan's four main islands, has a landscape strikingly different from that of any other place in Japan. With more than 83,000 sq. km (32,000 sq. miles) and accounting for 22% of Japan's total landmass, it has only 4.3% of its population. In other words, Hokkaido has what the rest of Japan doesn't: space. The least developed of Japan's four islands, it's your best bet for avoiding the crowds (and the summer heat) that plague Japan's more well-known playgrounds during peak travel season.

Hokkaido didn't open up to development until after the Meiji Restoration in 1868, when the government began encouraging Japanese to migrate to the island (at the expense of Hokkaido's indigenous people, the Ainu). Even today, Hokkaido has a frontier feel to it, and many young Japanese come here to backpack, ski, camp, and tour the countryside on motorcycles or bicycles. There are dairy farms, silos, and broad, flat fields of wheat, corn, and potatoes. Where the fields end the land puckers up, becoming craggy with bare volcanoes, deep gorges, and hills densely covered with virgin forests and dotted with clear spring lakes, mountains, rugged wilderness, wild animals, bubbling hot springs, and rare plants. The people of Hokkaido are as open and hearty as the wide expanses of land around them.

Much of Hokkaido's wilderness has been set aside as national and prefectural parkland. Of these areas, Shikotsu-Toya, Daisetsuzan, and Akan national parks are among the best known, offering a wide range of activities from hiking and skiing to bathing at *onsen,* or hot-spring spas.

Hokkaido's main tourist season is in July, when days are cool and pleasant with an average temperature of 70°F (21°C). While the rest of the nation is afflicted by the rainy season, Hokkaido's summers are usually bright and clear. Winters are long and severe; still, ski enthusiasts flock to slopes near Sapporo and to resorts such as Niseko and Daisetsuzan National Park. February marks the annual Sapporo Snow Festival, featuring huge ice and snow sculptures.

With its New Chitose Airport, the city of Sapporo—Japan's largest city north of Tokyo—serves as a springboard to Hokkaido's national parks and lakes. Yet despite all the island has to offer, Hokkaido remains virtually undiscovered.

THE BEST HOKKAIDO EXPERIENCES

○ **Dining on Hokkaido Specialties:** Hairy crab, corn on the cob, potatoes, salmon, and *Jingisukan* (mutton and vegetables that you grill at your table) are just some of the foods for which this northern island is famous. In Sapporo, you'll also want to try its ramen. See p. 579.

○ **Learning About the Ainu:** Hokkaido's indigenous Ainu have lost much of their culture due to assimilation, but an excellent museum near **Noboribetsu** and a great performance theater featuring songs and dance in **Akanko Onsen** bring Ainu traditions to life. See p. 588 and 596.

○ **Hitting the Slopes:** There are lots of skiing opportunities right outside Sapporo, but Hokkaido's most famous ski town is **Niseko,** renowned for its powdery snow. See p. 578 and 579.

○ **Exploring Daisetsuzan National Park:** The largest of Japan's 28 national parks—and some say Hokkaido's most beautiful—**Daisetsuzan** boasts three volcanic chains, fir- and birch-covered hillsides, impressive Sounkyo Gorge, and plenty of skiing and hiking opportunities. See p. 591.

○ **Fishing in Hokkaido:** Most foreigners laugh when they see Japanese fishing spots—a stocked pool in the middle of Tokyo or a cement-banked river, lined elbow to elbow with fishermen. For more sporting conditions, head to Lake Akan in Hokkaido's **Akan National Park,** where you can fish for rainbow trout or white spotted char; in winter there's even ice fishing. See p. 597.

ESSENTIALS

GETTING THERE & GETTING AROUND The fastest way to reach Hokkaido is to fly. Flights from Tokyo's Haneda Airport to Sapporo's **New Chitose Airport** take about 1½ hours. Overland, for centuries, the only way to travel between Honshu and Hokkaido was via a 4-hour ferry ride, but the opening of the Seikan Tunnel in 1988 allowed the entire trip between the islands to be made by train in little more than 2 hours—more than a fourth of which is in the 55km (34-mile) tunnel. Today, travel to Hokkaido by land is generally via the **Shinkansen** bullet train from Ueno or Tokyo Station in Tokyo to Shin-Aomori in Tohoku, followed by the **limited express Hakucho train** to Hakodate on Hokkaido, with the entire trip taking about 6 hours. In Hakodate, you must change trains for travel onward to Sapporo (see individual cities for train fares). Future plans call for a new Hokkaido Shinkansen to reach Hakodate by 2015, with eventual extension to Sapporo.

There are also **overnight sleeper trains** connecting Osaka, Kyoto, Tokyo and other Honshu cities with Hakodate and Sapporo on Hokkaido, with individual compartments for one or more people. Daily *Hokutosei* trains, for example, depart Tokyo's Ueno Station at 7:03pm, arriving in Hakodate the next morning at 6:35am and in Sapporo at 11:15am, with fares for a basic single or twin compartment starting at ¥23,600 and ¥27,170, respectively (there are also more luxurious compartments). If you have a Japan Rail Pass, you pay only the sleeping car surcharge (¥14,570 to Sapporo). Every two or three days, luxury *Cassiopeia* trains depart Ueno at 4:20pm and arrive in Hakodate at 5:02am and Sapporo at 9:25am (surcharge to Sapporo with Japan Rail Pass starts at ¥21,620; add ¥17,930 if you don't have a Japan Rail Pass). The *Twilight Express,* Japan's longest train route (nearly 1,500km/930 miles along the

coast of the Sea of Japan) connects Osaka and Kyoto with Sapporo and Hakodate every two or three days, departing Osaka at 11:50am and arriving in Sapporo at 9:52am. For more information on overnight sleeper trains, go to www2.jrhokkaido.co.jp/global/english/travel/index.html.

Public transportation around Hokkaido is by train and bus. In addition to regular bus lines, sightseeing buses link some national parks and major attractions. Although they're more expensive than regular buses, and although commentaries are in Japanese only, they offer unparalleled views of the countryside and usually stop at scenic wonders, albeit sometimes only long enough for the obligatory photo. Keep in mind that bus schedules fluctuate with the seasons and can be infrequent; some lines don't run during snowy winter months. Get bus and train schedules before setting out on each leg of your journey. In small towns, everyone knows the local bus schedules, even clerks at front desks. Otherwise, you might find yourself waiting to make a transfer.

JR HOKKAIDO PASSES If you plan to travel a lot within Hokkaido and don't have a Japan Rail Pass (see chapter 14 for information on rail passes), consider purchasing one of several special passes issued by JR Hokkaido that allow unlimited travel on JR trains and buses in Hokkaido. The **Hokkaido Rail Pass**, for example, works just like the Japan Rail Pass (you must be a foreign tourist visiting Japan) but can be purchased either abroad (at JTB and other authorized travel agencies) or at train stations in Hakodate, Sapporo, New Chitose Airport and a few other cities in Hokkaido. It costs ¥15,000 for 3 days, ¥19,500 for either 5 consecutive days or any 4 days within a 10-day period, or ¥22,000 for 7 consecutive days. Alternatively, the **JR Hokkaido Round Tour Pass (Hokkaido Furii Pasu)** can be used by anyone (including Japanese and foreigners living in Japan) and can be purchased in Hokkaido and at major JR stations nationwide. Allowing unlimited travel in Hokkaido, the 7-day pass costs ¥25,500, but note that it's not valid during peak holiday periods at the beginning of May, in mid-August, and over New Year's. For more information visit **www2.jrhokkaido.co.jp/global**.

RENTING A CAR   Because distances are long and traffic is rather light, Hokkaido is one of the few places in Japan where renting a car is actually recommended. Because it's expensive, however, it's economical only if there are several of you. Rates for a 1-day rental of a compact car in July or August with unlimited mileage and insurance begin at ¥9,975 per day, with each additional day costing ¥7,350; rates run about ¥3,000 cheaper the rest of the year. Car-rental agencies are found throughout Hokkaido, often near train stations as well as at Chitose Airport outside Sapporo and at Kushiro Airport in Kushiro. In Sapporo, **Toyota Rent-A-Car** (www2.toyotorentacar.net/english; ✆ **011/281-0100**) has multiple locations. **JR Hokkaido Rent A Lease** (✆ **011/241-0931**), near the east exit of Sapporo Station, offers "Rail & Rentacar" discount packages for train and car rentals booked in conjunction with each other. For routes and road conditions, go to **www.northern-road.jp/navi/eng**.

A GOOD STRATEGY FOR SEEING HOKKAIDO   To take in all the sights in this chapter, your first destination should be **Hakodate,** where history, views and seafood make for a great introduction to the island. From there, board a train bound for **Sapporo,** stopping off at **Shikotsu-Toya National Park** along the way. From Sapporo, two worthwhile destinations are **Sounkyo Onsen** in **Daisetsuzan National Park** and **Akan National Park.** To follow this plan, you'll need at least a week. You can also do this tour in reverse by flying into eastern Hokkaido (such as Kushiro) and taking the train toward Sapporo and Hakodate; see chapter 3 for a sample itinerary.

INFORMATION   Additional information on Hokkaido is available online at **www.visit-hokkaido.jp**.

HAKODATE, SOUTHERN GATEWAY TO HOKKAIDO ★

888km (549 miles) NE of Tokyo; 283km (177 miles) SW of Sapporo

Hakodate, the southern gateway to Hokkaido (and Hokkaido's third-largest city with a population of 285,000), is about as far as you may care to get in a day if you arrive in Hokkaido from Tokyo by train. This busy fishing port makes a good 1-night stopover because it has a famous nighttime attraction and one early morning attraction, which means you can easily see a little of the city before setting out for your next destination. For those who want to linger longer, it also boasts quaint historic districts of renovated warehouses (now housing restaurants and shops) and century-old Western-style homes, churches, and administrative buildings. Founded during the

Feudal Era, Hakodate was one of Japan's first ports opened to international trade following the Meiji Restoration. With its clanking streetcars, sloping streets lined with historic buildings, and port, it retains the atmosphere of a provincial outpost even today.

Essentials

GETTING THERE By Plane JAL and **ANA** fly from Tokyo's Haneda Airport to Hakodate Airport (HKD) in 1¼ hours. Limousine buses travel to JR Hakodate Station, stopping near some hotels en route, in 20 minutes for ¥400.

By JR Train From Tokyo, take the **Shinkansen** bullet train to Shin-Aomori (3½ hrs.), and then transfer to a direct train for Hakodate (about 2½ hr.). The total fare for a reserved seat is ¥18,990. There are also overnight sleeper trains from Honshu (see p. 566 for information). Hakodate is about 3¼ hours from Sapporo and costs ¥8,080 for an unreserved seat.

GETTING AROUND With the exception of Mount Hakodate, the most pleasant way to see Hakodate is on foot. The city is easy to navigate, and there are many English-language signs. Otherwise, streetcars are the major form of transportation (stops are announced in English), with fares starting at ¥200; take a ticket upon entering the back door and pay when you get off. There's also a 1-day streetcar pass for ¥600.

VISITOR INFORMATION The **Hakodate Tourist Office** (www.hakodate-kankou.com; ✆ **0138/23-5440;** daily 9am–7pm, to 5pm Nov–Mar) is inside the station to your left as you exit the wicket. It has excellent English-language maps and brochures of Hakodate and can help with same-day accommodations.

What to See & Do

In addition to the sights here, you might wish to soak away the aches of travel in one of Hakodate's hot-spring spas. Yunokawa Spa is Hokkaido's oldest, but it's 25 minutes away by streetcar (ask the tourist office for a map and list of baths). More accessible is **Yachigashira Public Hot-Springs Bath,** located at the foot of Mount Hakodate (✆ **0138/22-8371;** daily 6am–9:30pm; closed second and fourth Tues of every month; streetcar: Yachigashira). It's famous for its rust-colored waters, but what strikes me most is its size, capable of accommodating—I shudder at the thought—more than 500 bathers.

EXPLORING HISTORIC HAKODATE You can take the streetcar to the Jujigai or Suehiro-cho stops to explore Hakodate's historic districts, but more fun is to walk 12 minutes from the station (past the morning market and continuing along the seaside promenade) to the renovated **waterfront warehouse district** with its shops and restaurants and the nearby **Meijikan** (✆ **0138/27-7070**), a former 1911 brick post office now housing craft and glassware boutiques. A few minutes' walk further is historic **Motomachi,** a picturesque neighborhood of steep slopes, cobblestone and slate-lined streets, and turn-of-the-20th-century Western-style clapboard homes, consulates, churches, and other buildings, many open to the public with artifacts of the time (admission varies from free to ¥300). Most impressive is the gray-and-yellow gingerbread building of the **Old Public Hall of Hakodate Ward**, just uphill from Motomachi Park. In the park itself is **Old Branch Office of the Hokkaido Government**, which contains a Tourist Information Center (✆ **0138/27-3333;** daily 9am–7pm, to 5pm in winter).

MOUNT HAKODATE AFTER DARK Hakodate is probably most famous for its night view from atop Mount Hakodate, which rises 334m (1,100 ft.) about 3km (1¾ miles) southwest of Hakodate Station, so you should time your visit just at sunset (though note that it can be chilly up there, even in Aug). Few vacationing Japanese spend the night in Hakodate without taking the cable car to the top of this lava cone, which was formed by the eruption of an undersea volcano. From the peak, the lights of Hakodate shimmer and glitter like jewels on black velvet. I wouldn't miss it, not only for the view, but for the camaraderie shared by everyone making the pilgrimage. There's an informal restaurant here (where you can indulge in a drink or a snack while admiring the spectacular view) as well as the usual souvenir shops.

You can reach the foot of Mount Hakodate via a 5-minute streetcar ride from Hakodate Station to the Jujigai stop. From there, walk about 6 minutes to the rope-way that will take you to the top. The round-trip costs ¥1,160 for adults and ¥590 for children. Ropeway hours are daily 10am to 10pm late April through mid-October (from 9am during Golden Week and July 25–Aug 20), and 10am to 9pm mid-October through late April. From mid-April to mid-November you can also reach the top of Mount Hakodate directly by bus from Hakodate Station; the 30-minute trip costs ¥360 for adults and half-price for children.

THE MORNING MARKET ★ The other must-see is Hakodate's morning market, which is spread out just southwest of the train station daily from about 5am to noon. Walk around and look at the variety of foods for sale from about 300 vendors, especially the hairy crabs for which Hokkaido is famous. Dozens of small restaurants sell *donburi* (rice bowls) topped with local seafood (salmon roe, sea urchin, crab, squid and more), making for an only-in-Hakodate breakfast.

Where to Eat

Several of Hakodate's harborfront warehouses have been renovated into smart-looking shopping and dining complexes. They're about a 12-minute walk from Hakodate Station, past the morning market and continuing along the seaside promenade.

Bluemoon Diner VARIED JAPANESE/SEAFOOD Located in the waterfront warehouse district, this buffet restaurant offers sweeping views of the bay and dishes ranging from sushi to grilled steaks. Its all-you-can-eat grazing comes with a time limit (60 minutes for lunch and 80 minutes for dinner); pay ¥1,200 more for all the drinks you can consume, including alcoholic beverages. A little more sedate is the adjoining **Hakodate Kaisen Club,** a seafood restaurant managed by local fishmongers offering a wide range of fresh seafood, including king crab, fried fish, and *kaisen-don,* a bowl of rice topped with seafood, from a Japanese menu with picture.

14-17 Suehirocho. ⓒ **0138/24-8104.** Buffet lunch ¥1,500; buffet dinner ¥1,980. AE, DC, MC, V. Daily 11:30am–2:30pm and 5–8pm. Streetcar: Jujigai (5 min.). Walk toward the harbor and turn left at the waterfront.

Hakodate Beer ★ BAR FOOD/SEAFOOD In a brick building about halfway between the waterfront warehouse district and the station, this beer hall has four kinds of beer brewed in the large copper vats before you, as you dine on Hokkaido specialties, fish and chips, sirloin steak, sausages, or a "steamboat"—seafood, sliced meat, vegetables, and dumplings cooked in boiling broth at your table and dipped in chili sauce (¥3,500 for up to three people). There's also more standard pub fare on the English menu like *karaage* (fried chicken pieces) and pasta. There's live piano music in the evenings and outdoor seating in summer. A local institution.

For the sake of convenience, the price for two people in a room is listed as a "double" in this book. Japanese hotels, however, differentiate between rooms with a double bed or two twin beds, usually with different prices. Although most hotels charge more for a twin room, sometimes the opposite is true; if you're looking for a bargain, therefore, be sure to inquire about prices for both. Note, too, that hotels usually have more twin rooms than doubles, for the simple reason that Japanese couples, used to their own futon, traditionally prefer twin beds.

5–22 Ohtemachi. ✆ **0138/23-8000.** Main dishes ¥650–¥890. AE, DC, MC, V. Daily 11am–10pm. Station: Hakodate (6 min.).

Seiryuken (星龍軒) RAMEN   Hokkaido is famous for ramen, and different cities have their own style. In Hakodate it's *shio-ramen* (ramen in lightly salted pork broth), topped with slices of roast pork and bamboo shoots. This local favorite has only 20 seats at simple tables or a red Formica counter, which means you'll have to wait in line at peak times, but the light-as-air broth is worth it. There's no English menu, so ask for *shio-ramen* (¥530), *gyoza* (¥450), or *shio-ramen-chahan setto* (ramen with a side of fried rice, ¥780). Note: the shop may close early if the soup runs out.

7–3 Wakamatsu-cho. ✆ **0138/22-0022.** Main dishes ¥530–¥750. No credit cards. Mon–Sat 11am–6pm. Station: Hakodate Station (3 min.). Walk to the main street where the streetcar runs, and turn right; turn right again just before the Aqua Garden Hotel (it's the white building across from the hotel).

Shinmura (新村) SUSHI   Two things make this conveyor-belt sushi bar in the morning market unusual: The sushi chefs are mostly women (women's hands are said to be too hot to make sushi), and you can choose your fish or seafood from tanks out front and have it diced into sashimi right before your eyes. Otherwise, prices are determined by the color of the plate on the belt.

22–2 Otemachi. ✆ **0138/27-7885.** 2 pieces of sushi ¥126–¥630. No credit cards. Daily 9am–10pm (9am–9:30pm in winter). Hakodate Station (2 min.). From the west exit, walk past the morning market; Shinmura is past the 1st small intersection on the right-hand side (look for the tanks out front).

Where to Stay

Some hotels raise their rates during Hakodate's peak tourist season, July and August.

EXPENSIVE

Hakodate Danshaku Club Hotel & Resorts (函館男爵倶楽部) ★★ ☺
Though "Resorts" is an overstatement, this locally owned boutique hotel offers a convenient location near Hakodate Station and the morning market. It's named after a Hokkaido potato; a 1902 horseless carriage that once belonged to the farmer/shipbuilder who developed the *danshaku* graces the modern lobby. Its tile- and wood-floored standard rooms would qualify as suites elsewhere, with one or two bedrooms (sleeping up to four persons) that can be closed off from the living area by opaque, shoji-like doors, well-equipped kitchens, balconies facing Mount Hakodate, and spacious bathrooms complete with generous tubs and windows providing views.

22–10 Otemachi, Hakodate, Hokkaido, 040-0064. www.danshaku-club.com. ✆ **0138/21-1111.** Fax 0138/21-1212. 52 units. ¥22,000–¥38,000 double. Winter discounts available. AE, DC, MC, V. Station: Hakodate (3 min., past the morning market). **Amenities:** Cafe; lobby computer w/free Internet access; spa. *In room:* A/C, TV, hair dryer, Internet, kitchen.

MODERATE

B&B Pension Hakodate-Mura   This immaculate, mostly Western-style Japanese Inn Group member, decorated with whitewashed walls, wood furniture, and fresh and dried flowers, is built around a courtyard. In addition to Western-style rooms with wood floors (including a triple and a quad with a loft bed), there are two *tatami* rooms; only one double has a bathroom. Rules are similar to a youth hostel's (check-in at 3pm, checkout at 10am, and the door locks at 11pm), but what I like is its location near the waterfront warehouse district and Motomachi, only a 15-minute walk from Hakodate Station.

16–12 Suehiro-cho, Hakodate, Hokkaido, 040-0053. www.bb-hakodatemura.com. ✆ **0138/22-8105.** Fax 0138/22-8925. 16 units (1 with bathroom). ¥5,580 single; ¥8,960–¥11,560 double. Breakfast ¥800 extra per person. AE, MC, V. Streetcar: Jujigai (2 min.); follow the streetcar tracks for 1 block, turn right, and then turn left. **Amenities:** Lobby computer w/free Internet; Wi-Fi (free in lobby).

Hotel Route Inn Grantia Hakodate Ekimae (ホテルルートイングランティア 函館駅前) ★   Despite a no-flair atmosphere and small rooms, this hotel rises above the ordinary with a convenient location near the station, reasonable prices, good views (reserve a room above the fourth floor for the best harbor views), and large hot-spring baths on the 13th floor, which look out over the station to the bay and mountains. Family rooms have one king-size bed (and not much else) that you are welcome to put the entire family in. In-room pluses include good bedside reading lamps and cards sold in vending machines for ¥1,000 that allow you to watch movies (including Hollywood releases in English) all night long.

21–3 Wakamatsu-cho, Hakodate, Hokkaido, 040-0063. www.route-inn.co.jp. ✆ **0138/21-4100.** Fax 0138/21-4101. 286 units. ¥6,900 single; ¥12,500 double; ¥14,500 family room. Off-season discounts available. AE, DC, MC, V. Station: Hakodate (1 min. from main exit, to the left). **Amenities:** 2 restaurants; lobby computers w/free Internet. *In room:* A/C, TV, fridge, hair dryer, Internet.

> ### 📎 A Note on Japanese Characters
>
> Many establishments and attractions in Japan do not have signs in English. Where they don't, we've given the Japanese script here, next to the name in English.

La Vista Hakodate Bay ★★
Opened in 2008 on the site of former warehouses, this 13-story hotel gives a nod to history with its brick and wood motifs, art deco accents, and in-room nostalgic touches like hand-cranked coffee grinders for your morning joe. Single rooms are compact though stylish, while double rooms have plenty of space, including some with windowside low tables complete with leg wells from which to enjoy the views. Most bathrooms have showers instead of tubs, since most guests opt for the rooftop hot-spring baths (where they even receive popsicles for cooling down afterwards). The hotel's breakfast buffet (¥1,900) is well known for its dazzling array of fresh Hakodate seafood. After checkout, there's free shuttle service to the station.

12–6 Toyokawa-cho, Hakodate, Hokkaido, 040-0065. www.hotespa.net. ✆ **0138/23-6111.** Fax 0138/23-6222. 350 units. ¥10,000-20,000 single; ¥16,000–¥26,000 double. AE, DC, MC, V. Streetcar: Uoichiba (4 min.). Walk toward the bay and look for the tower to the left. **Amenities:** Restaurants; indoor/outdoor hot-spring baths; lobby computer w/free Internet; spa. *In room:* A/C, TV, fridge, hair dryer, Internet.

INEXPENSIVE

In addition to the choices here, two locations of **Toyoko Inn** (www.toyoko-inn.com) are within a few minutes' walk of the station, both with the usual freebies like breakfast, lobby computers, and in-room Internet access, plus winter discounts.

Comfort Hotel Hakodate ⚑ This business hotel sits across from the station and a few minutes from the Morning Market. Rooms don't break any records for style or size (though higher-priced twin rooms are large enough to fit a third bed), and only upper floor rooms have any view to speak of. However, the property is modern and spotless, there's free coffee in the lobby, and rates include a simple breakfast of bread, eggs, onigiri (rice balls), homemade soup and more.

16.3 Wakamatsu-cho, Hakodate 040-0063. www.choicehotels.com. ✆ **0138/24-0511.** Fax 0138/24-0512. 139 units. ¥6,600 single; ¥6,800–¥12,000 double. AE, DC, MC, V. Station: Hakodate (1 min.). From the main exit, walk straight along the right side of the buses; it's on the corner in front of the streetcar stop. **Amenities:** Lobby computer w/free Internet. *In room:* A/C, TV, fridge, hair dryer, Wi-Fi.

Niceday Inn ⚑ Kind Mrs. Saito gives a warm welcome, and staying here is like living in a Japanese home. Although Mrs. Saito's English is limited, she offers tourist information and a map and tries to help with whatever you need. The inn is very plain but offers clean Japanese- and Western-style rooms. No meals are served, but free instant coffee, a fridge, and public phone are in the small communal entry room.

9–11 Otemachi, Hakodate 040-0064. ✆ **0138/22-5919.** 3 units, none with bathroom. ¥3,000 per person. No credit cards. Station: Hakodate (8 min.). Take the west exit out of the station and walk straight past the morning market; after crossing the wide, tree-lined avenue, take the 3rd left (across from the Kokusai Hotel entrance). The inn is a white, 2-story building on your right. *In room:* A/C or fan, no phone.

SAPPORO

1,200km (746 miles) NE of Tokyo; 283km (177 miles) NE of Hakodate

Sapporo is one of Japan's newest cities. About 142 years ago, it was nothing more than a scattering of huts belonging to Ainu and Japanese families. With the dawning of the Meiji Period, however, the government decided to colonize the island, and in 1869 it established the Colonization Commission. The area of Sapporo (the name comes from the Ainu word meaning "big, dry river") was chosen as the new capital site, and in 1871, construction of the city began.

During the Meiji Period, Japan looked eagerly toward the West for technology, ideas, and education, and Hokkaido was no exception. Between 1871 and 1884, 76 foreign technicians and experts (including 46 Americans) who had colonization experience were brought to this Japanese wilderness to aid in the island's development. Sapporo was laid out in a grid pattern of uniform blocks similar to that of an American city. In 1876, the Sapporo Agricultural College was founded to train youth in skills useful to Hokkaido's colonization and development.

The Sapporo of today, capital of Hokkaido Prefecture, has grown to 1.9 million residents, making it the largest city north of Tokyo (and the fifth largest in Japan). In 1972, it was introduced to the world when the Winter Olympics were held here, and its many fine ski slopes continue to attract winter vacationers, as does the Snow Festival, held every February (see the "Japan Calendar of Events," in chapter 2). In August, when the rest of Japan is sweltering under uncomfortably high temperatures and humidity, Sapporo stays pleasantly cool.

Essentials

GETTING THERE By Plane Flights take 1½ hours from Tokyo's Haneda Airport, 2 hours from Hiroshima, and 2¼ hours from Fukuoka. Sapporo's **New Chitose Airport** (www.new-chitose-airport.jp; ☎ **0123/23-0111**), located about 43km (27 miles) southeast of the capital, is connected to downtown by either **Airport Limousine Bus,** which delivers passengers to a few major hotels in about 70 minutes for ¥1,000; or **JR trains** that operate every 15 minutes between Chitose Airport Station and Sapporo Station, with the 36-minute trip costing ¥1,040.

By JR Train Most trains from Honshu arrive in Hakodate, where you'll transfer to a train departing every hour or so for Sapporo. From Tokyo, the trip to Sapporo costs ¥22,670 and averages 10 hours, including transfers. Trains from Hakodate take about 3½ hours and cost ¥8,080 for an unreserved seat. See p. 566 earlier in this chapter for information about overnight train services with sleeper cars.

VISITOR INFORMATION In JR Sapporo Station, the excellent **Hokkaido-Sapporo Tourist Information Center** (☎ **011/213-5088;** daily 8:30am–8pm), located opposite the west ticket gate, offers a wealth of information not only on Sapporo but all of Hokkaido, making it a must stop for travelers to anywhere on the island. Here, too, is a JR information counter (daily 8:30am–7pm), where you can pick up JR train and bus schedules or get rail passes validated. Additionally, the **Sapporo International Communications Plaza,** on the third floor of the MN Building across from the Clock Tower at N1 W3, Chuo-ku (☎ **011/211-3678;** Mon–Sat 9am–5:30pm; closed holidays), provides maps and information on tourist attractions, daily life, and transportation. Online, you can check **www.welcome.city.sapporo.jp** or **www.sta.or.jp.**

ORIENTATION & GETTING AROUND After the jumble of most Japanese cities with their incomprehensible address systems, Sapporo will come as a welcome surprise. Its streets are laid out in a grid pattern, making the city easy to navigate. Addresses in Sapporo refer to blocks that follow one another in logical, numerical order.

Sapporo Station lies on the north side of the city center, with downtown and many of its attractions, hotels, and restaurants spreading to the south. The center of Sapporo is **Odori,** a park-lined avenue south of Sapporo Station that runs east and west and bisects the city into north and south sections. **North 1st Street,** therefore, refers to the street 1 block north of Odori. The other determinant landmark is the **Soseigawa River,** which marks addresses east and west. **West 1st Street** runs along the west bank of the Soseigawa River, while **East 1st Street** runs along the east bank.

Addresses in Sapporo are generally given by block. **N1 W4,** for example, is the address for the Sapporo Grand Hotel, means it's located in the first block north of Odori and 4 blocks west of West 1st Street. To be more technical about it, the entire, formal address of the hotel would read N1-jo W4-chome. "Jo" refers to blocks north and south of Odori, while "chome" refers to blocks east and west of the river. Better yet, street signs in Sapporo are in English.

Central Sapporo is easy to cover on foot. You can walk south from Sapporo Station to **Odori Park** in less than 10 minutes (even quicker via an underground passage) and on to **Susukino,** Sapporo's nightlife district, in another 7 or 8 minutes. For longer distances, transportation in Sapporo is via **bus,** three **subway** lines (which interchange at **Odori Station**), and one **streetcar** line. Fares begin at ¥200 for buses and

Sapporo

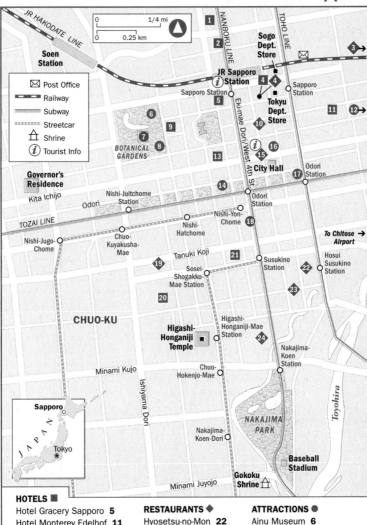

Map legend:
- ✉ Post Office
- Railway
- Subway
- Streetcar
- ⛩ Shrine
- ⓘ Tourist Info

Map labels:
JR HAKODATE LINE, NANBOKU LINE, TOHO LINE, Soen Station, Sogo Dept. Store, JR Sapporo Station, Sapporo Station, Sapporo Station, Tokyu Dept. Store, Eki-mae Dori/West 4th St., City Hall, Odori Station, Governor's Residence, Kita Ichijo, Odori, Nishi-Juitchome Station, BOTANICAL GARDENS, TOZAI LINE, Chuo-Kuyakusha-Mae, Nishi-Jugo-Chome, Nishi-Hatchome, Nishi-Yon-Chome, Odori Station, To Chitose Airport, Tanuki Koji, Susukino Station, Hosui Susukino Station, CHUO-KU, Sosei-Shogakko-Mae Station, Higashi-Honganji-Mae Station, Higashi-Honganji Temple, Minami Kujo, Chuo-Hokenjo-Mae, Ishiyama Dori, Nakajima-Koen Station, Toyohira, Sapporo, JAPAN, Tokyo, Minami Juyojo, Nakajima-Koen-Dori, NAKAJIMA PARK, Baseball Stadium, Gokoku Shrine

HOKKAIDO | Sapporo

13

HOTELS ■
- Hotel Gracery Sapporo **5**
- Hotel Monterey Edelhof **11**
- JR Tower Hotel Nikko Sapporo **4**
- Nada **20**
- Nakamuraya Ryokan **9**
- Sapporo Aspen Hotel **2**
- Sapporo Grand Hotel **13**
- Toyoko Inn Sapporo Nishi-Guchi-Hokudai-mae **1**
- Watermark **21**

RESTAURANTS ◆
- Hyosetsu-no-Mon **22**
- Kita-no-Fuji **24**
- Komugi-no-Ie La Pausa **15**
- Mikuni Sapporo **4**
- Ramen Yokocho **23**
- Sapporo Bier Garten **3**
- Sky J **4**
- Taj Mahal **10**
- Tokumaru **19**

ATTRACTIONS ●
- Ainu Museum **6**
- Aurora Town **17**
- Botanic Garden **8**
- Clock Tower (Tokeidai) **16**
- Natural Science Museum **7**
- Odori Koen (Park) Promenade **14**
- Pole Town **18**
- Sapporo Factory **12**

subways and ¥170 for streetcars, but easier are prepaid cards available in denominations beginning at ¥1,000 and valid for all conveyances. **One-day cards,** allowing unlimited rides on all modes of transport, are also available for ¥1,000. A 1-day card for subways only costs ¥800, discounted to ¥500 on weekends and holidays. Children pay half fare. Cards can be purchased at subway stations and on buses and streetcars.

Finally, the white-colored **Sapporo Stroll Bus** (Burari Sapporo Kanko Bus), operating early May to early November, and the blue- or orange-colored **Sapporo Walk Bus** (operating year-round) are **tourist buses** that travel in a loop to tourist sites around the city (unfortunately, neither goes to Nopporo Forest Park). Single fares are ¥200 for adults, half-price for children. A 1-day pass (available only when the Sapporo Stroll Bus is in operation), ¥750 for adults and ¥380 for children, allows you to get on and off as many times as you want between 9am and 7pm. Stops are announced in English and bus stops are clearly marked. Pick up a map showing stops and routes at the Tourist Information Center.

[Fast FACTS] SAPPORO

Consulates   You'll find consulates for Australia (☏ **011/242-4381**), Canada (☏ **011/643-2520**), New Zealand (☏ **011/802-9272**), and the United States (☏ **011/641-1115**) in Sapporo.

Internet Access   Inside the Hokkaido-Sapporo Tourist Information Center (see above) is Café Norte, open daily 8:30am to 8pm with five coin-operated computers (¥100 per 10 min.). Also, on the first floor of the Century Royal Hotel (1 min. west of Sapporo station's south exit), **i-café** (☏ **011/221-3440**) charges ¥180 for 30 minutes and is open 24 hours a day.

Mail & ATMs   Sapporo Central Post Office, N6 E1 (☏ **011/748-2380**), 2 blocks east of Sapporo Station, has a 24-hour window for stamps and mail and ATMs for international credit cards (weekdays 7am–11pm; Sat 9am–9pm; Sun and holidays 9am–7pm). Otherwise, there's a smaller post office in the east end of Sapporo Station's Paseo shopping mall, also with ATMs.

Exploring Sapporo

One of the first things you should do in Sapporo is walk around. Starting from **Sapporo Station** (which contains a chic shopping and restaurant complex) take the road leading directly south called **Eki-mae Dori** (which is also West 4th). This is one of Sapporo's main thoroughfares, taking you south through the heart of the city.

Four blocks south of the station, turn left on N1, where after a block you'll find Sapporo's most famous landmark, the **Clock Tower (Tokeidai),** N1 W2, Chuo-ku (☏ **011/231-0838**). This Western-style wooden building was built in 1878 as a drill hall for the Sapporo Agricultural College (now Hokkaido University). The large clock at the top was made in Boston and was installed in 1881. In summer, it attracts tourists even at night; they hang around the outside gates just to listen to the clock strike the hour. Inside the tower is a local-history museum, not worth the price of admission. By the way, across the street is **Sapporo International Communications Plaza** (see "Visitor Information," above).

If you continue walking 1 block south of the Clock Tower, you'll reach **Odori Koen Promenade,** a 103m-wide (344-ft.) boulevard stretching almost 1.6km (1 mile) from east to west. In the middle of the boulevard is a wide median strip that has been turned into a park with trees, flower beds, and fountains. This is where much of the **Sapporo Snow Festival** is held in early February, when ice and packed snow are carved to form statues, palaces, and fantasies. Begun in 1950 to add a bit of spice and life to the cold winter days, the Snow Festival now features some 240 snow and ice sculptures and draws about 2.1 million visitors a year. One snow structure may require as much as 300 6-ton truckloads of snow, brought in from the surrounding mountains. The snow and ice carvings are done with so much attention to detail that it seems a crime they're doomed to melt (see "Japan Calendar of Events," in chapter 2).

Odori Park is also the scene of the **Sapporo Summer Festival,** celebrated with beer gardens set up the length of the park from late July to mid-August and open every day from noon. Various Japanese beer companies set up their own booths and tables under the trees, while vendors put up stalls selling fried noodles, corn on the cob, and other goodies. Live bands serenade the beer drinkers under the stars. It all resembles the cheerful confusion of a German beer garden, which isn't surprising considering Munich is one of Sapporo's sister cities (Portland, Oregon, is another one). Some of the other festivals held in Odori Park are the **Lilac Festival** in late May heralding the arrival of summer, and **Bon-Odori** in mid-August with traditional dances to appease the souls of the dead.

Botanic Garden (Shobutsu-en) GARDEN   This 13-hectare (32-acre) garden contains some virgin forest and more than 4,000 varieties of plants gathered from all over Hokkaido, arranged in marshland, herb, alpine, and other gardens. Of greater interest, perhaps, is the section devoted to plants used by the Ainu, whose extensive knowledge of plants covered not only edible ones but also those with medicinal use and other properties, including organic poison used for arrows to kill bears and other game. Unfortunately, there's no English-language explanation of plant usage. Still, with lots of trees and grassy lawns, it's a good place for a summer picnic.

Worth visiting on garden grounds is Japan's oldest **natural science museum,** founded in 1882 to document the wildlife of Hokkaido and housed in a turn-of-the-20th-century, Western-style building. Be sure, too, to visit the small, one-room **Ainu Museum,** which displays some fine examples of Ainu artifacts, including traditional clothing, jewelry, farming tools, hunting traps, harpoons, a canoe, and bamboo mouth harps (played by women and children). A 13-minute video, filmed in 1935, shows the ritualistic killing of a brown bear, a ceremony to give thanks and send the bear's soul to the afterlife, and the skinning. In any case, you'll probably want to spend an hour touring the garden and its museums. Note that from November 4 to April 28, only the greenhouse is open (Mon–Fri 10am–3pm; Sat 10am–noon); admission then is ¥110 for everyone.

N3 W8 Chuo-ku. ✆ **011/221-0066.** Admission ¥400 adults, ¥280 children. Apr 29–Sept 30, Tues–Sun 9am–4pm; Oct–Nov 3, 9am-3:30pm. Station: Sapporo (10 min.).

Nopporo Forest Park (Nopporo Shinrin Koen)

If you have an extra half-day or more, I heartily recommend this park on the outskirts for its two very worthwhile attractions. To reach the park, fastest is to take one of the frequent **JR trains** 10 minutes to Shin-Sapporo Station (¥260), and then transfer to **JR bus** no. 22 (from stop no. 10) for a 15-minute ride to the last stop, Kaitaku-no-Mura (¥200; free with the Japan Rail Pass). You can also take the **Tozai subway line** 20 minutes to Shin-Sapporo Station and board the same bus. A few of these buses per day originate at JR Sapporo Station and reach the park in about one hour for

¥260. Get bus and train schedules at the tourist office in Sapporo Station. All buses stop at Kinenkan Iriguchi (near the Historical Museum of Hokkaido), before Kaitaku-no-Mura. It's about a 10-minute walk between the two attractions.

Historical Museum of Hokkaido (Kaitaku Kinenkan) ★ MUSEUM   This museum does a great job detailing Hokkaido's development from prehistory to the 1960s, with lots of information in English, including a great audio guide (¥130 extra). The section on the indigenous Ainu is especially good, with displays of clothing, a house, items used for trade with the Japanese and other artifacts, along with descriptions of their forced assimilation into Japanese culture (see p. 586 for more information on the Ainu). You'll also learn about Hokkaido's early contacts with Russia, the lives of 19th-century Japanese pioneers (including former samurai who had lost their land and stipends with the Meiji Restoration), the opening of Hakodate Port, the establishment of Sapporo Agricultural College, and more. The Living Experience Room provides hands-on experience with tools, including a hand loom, and interactive displays. If history's your thing, you'll easily spend 2 hours here. *Note:* as we went to press, the museum was slated to close in 2013 for a 2-year renovation (the exact dates were undetermined). Check the website or tourist offices for updated information.

Konopporo 53-2, Atsubetsu-cho. www.hmh.pref.hokkaido.jp. *C* **011/898-0456.** Admission ¥500 adults, ¥170 university and high-school students, free for seniors and children. Tues–Sun 9.30am–4:30pm. Closed some national holidays.

Historical Village of Hokkaido (Kaitaku-no Mura) ★★ ☺ MUSEUM   This open-air museum of more than 50 historical Japanese- and Western-style buildings, dating mostly from the Meiji and Taisho eras and brought here from around Hokkaido, includes homes, farmhouses, a shrine, a church, a newspaper office, a post office, a police box (manned by a sword-wielding police officer), and many small businesses, including a blacksmith, brewery, barbershop, grocery, inn, and sleigh factory—all outfitted as they would have looked in the past. Highlights include the Matsuhashi Family Residence, Hokkai Middle School, the Aoyama fisherman's family complex, and the Hokuseikan Silkworm house. In summer, staff members dressed in Meiji-Era clothing are on hand to answer questions. Kids like being able to run and explore; there's an old-fashioned playground with a seesaw and other traditional play equipment; nearby is the Traditional Activities Room, where children can make crafts and play games at no extra charge. There are horse-drawn carriage rides on weekends in summer and horse-drawn sleighs during the Snow Festival (extra fee charged). You can easily spend 2 hours here, wandering "villages" themed by fishing, farm, mountain and town. *Tip:* Wear slip-on shoes, as they must be removed to enter many of the structures.

Konopporo 50–1, Atsubetsu-cho. www.kaitaku.or.jp. *C* **011/898-2692.** Admission Apr–Nov ¥830 adults, ¥610 university and high-school students; Dec–Mar ¥680 and ¥550, respectively. Free for children and seniors; free also for high-school students on Sat. May–Sept daily 9am–5pm; Oct–Apr Tues–Sun 9am–4:30pm. Bus: Kaitaku-no-Mura (1 min.).

Hitting the Slopes

Skiing is big around Sapporo, site of the 1972 Winter Olympics and easily accessible by plane from many cities in Japan—there are slopes within city limits and more than a dozen skiing areas less than 2 hours away, most open from early December to late April. On the west edge of town are Okurayama Jump Hill and Miyanomori Jump Hill, both sites of the 1972 Winter Olympics. Here, too, is the **Sapporo Bankei Ski**

Area (www.bankei.co.jp/ski/english.html; ℂ 011/641-0071), just 20 minutes from downtown Sapporo and popular for after-work and night skiing (it stays open to 10pm). You can reach them by subway to Maruyama Koen Station, followed by a 15-minute bus ride. Just 2.5km (1½ miles) south of Sapporo Station is **Nakajima Park** (Station: Nakajima Koen), with free use of cross-country skis in winter.

Farther afield to the west, the **Sapporo Teine** ski areas (www.sapporo-teine.com; ℂ 011/682-6000) were the sites of the alpine, bobsled, and toboggan events for the Olympics. A lift joins the two areas, creating Hokkaido's longest run (6km/3¾ miles). A 4-hour, 6-hour, or 1-day lift pass costs ¥3,500, ¥3,900, or ¥4,800 respectively; ski-rental equipment is available from ¥4,950 in the day and ¥3,000 at night. Snowboarding gear costs ¥4,950 per day. Keep in mind that gear sizes are generally smaller than in the West (ski boots up to 30cm, size 12 in the U.S., and snowboard boots up to 28.5cm, size 10½ in the U.S.). Take the JR Ishikari Liner train from Sapporo Station 20 minutes to Teine Station and then take JR bus no. 70 another 19 minutes to Teine Olympia-mae.

Niseko (www.niseko.ne.jp), 90km (56 miles) and a 3½-hour bus ride west of Sapporo, is considered by our skiing and snowboarding friends as the best ski resort in Hokkaido for its fine powder, extensive night skiing, and hot-spring spas (it's also very popular with Aussies wishing to ski in their off season). Three skiing regions (An'nupuri, Niseko Village, and Grand Hirafu/Hanazono), joined by a network of some 60 runs, 38 gondolas and lifts, and shuttle buses that provide easy exploration of the different areas, offer a variety for skiers of all levels. An 8-hour lift ticket costs ¥4,900, with rental prices comparable to those at Teine. To get there, reserve a seat with Chuo (ℂ 011/231-0500) or Donan (ℂ 011/865-5511 or 0123/46-5701) bus company; both go to Niseko from either Chitose Airport or Sapporo Station and cost ¥3,850. Alternatively, you can also go by JR Niseko Express train (operating daily from mid-Dec through mid-Feb) from Sapporo Station to Niseko in about 2 hours, followed by a shuttle bus. JR offers a great "Tebura Skip" Niseko package, costing ¥5,500 for the Niseko Express train or ¥4,500 for a local train (available mid-Feb to mid-Mar) that includes the round-trip train and shuttle bus from Sapporo, an 8-hour lift ticket, and ski or snowboard rental with boots. For more information on skiing and snowboarding around Sapporo, stop by the Hokkaido-Sapporo Tourist Information Center in Sapporo Station or go to **www.snowjapan.com**.

Where to Eat

In addition to Hokkaido specialties like crab, corn on the cob, potatoes and salmon, Sapporo is known for *Jingisukan* (Genghis Khan—Mongolian-style mutton and vegetables that you grill yourself at the table). It's also famous for its ramen, and the most popular place to try them is at one of the 18 tiny shops crammed into the narrow alley known as **Ramen Yokocho,** located just 1 short block east of the Susukino Station. It doesn't matter which shop you choose—just look for an empty seat. Shops have photos of various dishes outside the front door (many labeled in English). Ramen in miso broth (*miso ramen*) or topped with seafood are the most typical styles, with a steaming bowlful starting at ¥750. Most are open daily from 11:30am to 3am.

VERY EXPENSIVE

Mikuni Sapporo ★★ FRENCH   Mikuni Kiyomi has a reputation as *the* Japanese authority on French food. Hokkaido-born and the proprietor/chef of several Mikuni restaurants in Tokyo and elsewhere, Mikuni has brought his expertise home to triumphant reviews. Though access is less than stellar (via a hard-to-find elevator to the ninth floor of Stellar Place in Sapporo Station), the restaurant compensates with city views and great cuisine, available only as set meals. A seasonal, autumn lunch, for example, may include cappuccino-style mushrooms and chestnuts, either pan-fried codfish with potatoes and lentils or braised pork garnished with French beans and sweet-potato purée, plus dessert and coffee. There are an extensive wine list and knowledgeable sommeliers to advise you.

Stellar Place 9F, W2 N5. ☎ **011/251-0392.** Reservations strongly suggested. Set dinners ¥8,000–¥17,000; set lunches ¥3,200–¥10,000. AE, DC, MC, V. Daily 11:30am–2:30pm and 5:30–9pm (last order). Above Sapporo Station.

EXPENSIVE

Hyosetsu-no-Mon KING CRAB   This well-known restaurant, in business more than 40 years in Sapporo's Susukino nightlife district, specializes in giant king crab caught in the Japan Sea north of Hokkaido. Its English-language menu consists almost entirely of king crab dishes, with set meals including cooked crab, sashimi, crab soup, crab tempura, and vegetables. Although set dinners are expensive, they are a good deal compared to ordering a la carte, and there are also usually seasonal specials for ¥3,520. There's a Hokkaido sakes to accompany your meal.

S5 W2 (next to Sluggers Batting Stadium). www.hyousetsu.co.jp. ☎ **011/521-3046.** Set dinners ¥3,520–¥13,860; set lunches ¥1,980–¥4,000. AE, DC, MC, V. Daily 11am–10pm (last order). Subway: Susukino (2 min.).

Sky J ★★★ INTERNATIONAL   Breathtaking views, reasonable prices, and a wide array of tempting dishes make this sleek restaurant a popular place to dine. The lunch buffet gets top ratings, with a range of Western and Asian dishes, all identified in English and utilizing lots of organic veggies, along with nine kinds of bread and two dessert tables. For dinner (last order 9pm), both set meals and an a la carte menu are available, with an example of the former including Hokkaido specialties such as salmon and seasonal ravioli with caviar as a starter, followed by steak with a cumin flavor and eggplant fondue. From 8pm, the Sky J morphs into a classy cocktail lounge, with live music (and a ¥750 cover charge unless you dine before 8pm). But it's the views that set this place apart.

35th floor, JR Tower Hotel Nikko Sapporo, N5 W2. ☎ **011/251-6377.** Lunch buffet ¥2,200; set dinners ¥4,500–¥8,000; main dishes ¥1,600–¥3,600. AE, DC, MC, V. Daily 11:30am–2:30pm and 5:30pm–midnight. Station: Sapporo.

MODERATE

Kita-no-fuji (北の富士) 🍴 CHANKO NABE   Located in the heart of the Susukino nightlife district and named after a famous sumo wrestler born in Hokkaido, this restaurant decorated with sumo memorabilia specializes in the famous hearty stews favored by sumo wrestlers, *chanko nabe*, which you cook at your table. There's a picture menu in Japanese only, with more expensive nabe featuring crab, but you can also tell them how much you want to spend per person. The set dinner might include chanko nabe, salad, mini croquettes, onigiri (rice balls) and dessert. Although other dishes include sashimi, yakitori, and shabu-shabu, it's the nabe you'll want to order.

Susukino Plaza, S7 W4. ☎ **011/512-5484,** or 512-1339 for reservations. Reservations recommended. Chanko nabe ¥2,300–¥3,200; set dinner ¥1,980. AE, DC, MC, V. Daily 4–11pm. Subway: Susukino (7 min.). To the left of a building with a Maya-like facade; look for the black slate, boulder and wooden lattice front.

Tokumaru (徳丸) ★★ 🍢 YAKITORI/VARIED   As you exit the Tanuki-koji Arcade, you may wonder whether you're on the right track, but stick with it for another 1½ blocks to the rustic wooden building on the left. Inside you'll find some of the city's best *yakitori*, served in a rustic setting of wooden beamed ceilings and bamboo accents. The English-language menu offers yakitori by the skewer and as a set, along with other grilled dishes, salads, *oden* (fish cake stew), and king crab legs. The downside: it can be smoky indoors, but in summer there's an outdoor beer garden.

Tanuki-koji, S3 W9. ℂ **011/281-1900.** Yakitori ¥110–¥290; main dishes ¥300–¥1,627. AE, DC, MC, V. Daily 5–11:30pm. Subway: Susukino (7 min.).

INEXPENSIVE

Komugi-no-ie La Pausa 🍴 ITALIAN   Right across the street from the Clock Tower, this light and airy restaurant serves Neapolitan pizza baked in a stone kiln and homemade pasta, and though there's no English menu, photos make it easy to point and order. Pizzas come with a variety of toppings; my sausage pizza came with lots of cheese, eggplant, tomatoes, and capers. Or, go with the all-you-can-eat pizzas and pastas in 120 minutes for ¥1,580, available all day. There are other branches around town, including in Susukino (S3 W3, ℂ **011/290-3012**).

N1 W3. ℂ **011/252-2231.** Pasta and pizza ¥730–¥1,090; set dinners ¥1,480–¥1,680; set lunches ¥580–¥1,280. AE, DC, MC, V. Daily 11am–11:30pm. Subway: Odori (1 min.). In the same building as International Communications Plaza, on the 2nd floor via outdoor staircase.

Sapporo Bier Garten ★ JINGISUKAN   If you think of beer when you hear the word "Sapporo," then a trip here is a must. World-famous Sapporo beer was brewed in the handsome, ivy-covered brick buildings here from 1890 to 2003. Today they hold restaurants, shops, and the free Sapporo Beer Museum (ℂ **011/731-4368;** daily 9am–6pm), with displays unfortunately in Japanese only (samples cost ¥200 each, or ¥500 for a set of three). Still, this is a good destination for beer and a meal, especially in the historic, cavernous Kessel Hall, where you dine underneath a huge 1912 mash tub. The specialty here is *Jingisukan*, which you cook yourself on a hot skillet at your table. The best deal is the King Viking course, which for ¥3,770 gives you as much Jingisukan and draft beer as you can consume in 100 minutes. Otherwise, for all you timid drinkers, draft beer starts at ¥400 for a small and ¥530 for a half liter, with the all-you-can-eat Jingisukan sans drinks priced at ¥2,720. You and your clothes will smell like Jingisukan afterwards, but you can mitigate that in summer by dining outdoors. By the way, a 12-minute walk away (or a short ride on the Sapporo Walk Bus) is **Sapporo Factory,** N2 E4 (ℂ **011/207-5000**), a complex centered on another old Sapporo Beer brick building housing more restaurants and 160 shops (daily 11am–8pm).

N7 E9, Higashi-ku. www.sapporo-bier-garten.jp. ℂ **011/742-1531.** All-you-can-eat *Jingisukan* ¥2,620–¥3,770. AE, DC, MC, V. Kessel Hall daily 11:30am–10pm. Bus: Chuo Bus no. 88 or 188 from platform 2 (north of Sapporo Station) or Sapporo Walk.

Taj Mahal 🍴 INDIAN   This second-floor Indian restaurant tries too hard with its Indian mirrored fabrics, brass lamps, and Indian music, as the food alone is reason enough to come here. The service is friendly and the choices are varied—in addition to tandoori and kabobs, they serve chicken, lamb, seafood and vegetable curries (but no pork or beef), as well as "soup curry," a Sapporo-style take on Indian curries. Choose how spicy you want it, from very mild to very, very hot. Tasty lunch specials are served until 3pm, but not on Sundays or holidays. There's a branch in Sapporo Factory (see above; ☎ **011/207-0765**), open daily 11am to 9:30pm.

N2 W3. www.tajmahalgroup.com. ☎ **011/231-8850.** Curries ¥1,270–¥1,750; set dinners ¥1,600–¥2,580; set lunches ¥680–¥1,650. AE, DC, MC, V. Daily 11am–10pm. Station: Sapporo (6 min.). Walk south on the left side of Eki-mae Dori and when you come to JTB, turn left; it will be on the right after the next narrow street.

Shopping

Sapporo is famous for underground shopping malls, appreciated especially during inclement weather and Hokkaido's long, cold winters. Near Odori Park are three underground shopping arcades, known collectively as Sapporo Chikagai, with about 140 shops open daily 10am to 8pm. The one underneath Odori Park, from the Odori Station all the way to the TV tower in the east, is **Aurora Town,** with boutiques and restaurants. Even longer is the 390m (1,300-ft.) **Pole Town,** which extends from the Odori Station south all the way to **Susukino,** Sapporo's nightlife amusement center, where you'll find many restaurants and pubs. Before reaching Susukino, however, you may want to emerge to street level at **Sanchome** (you'll see escalators going up), where you'll find more shopping at the 1km-long (½-mile) **Tanuki-koji** covered shopping arcade's 200 boutiques, traditional specialty shops, and restaurants.

Where to Stay

The busiest tourist seasons are summer and early February during the annual Snow Festival. If you plan to attend the festival, book your room at least 6 months in advance. Most other times you should have no problem finding a room, but it's always wise to reserve in advance. Outside of peak seasons, some upper- and medium-priced hotels lower their room rates, sometimes by 50% or more; be sure to ask for a discount.

EXPENSIVE

Hotel Monterey Edelhof ★★ Although opened in 2000, this elegant hotel embraces the architectural exuberance of early 1900s Vienna, with lots of marble, stained-glass windows, Art Deco embellishments, and Otto Wagner–inspired designs. Elevators have old-fashioned floor dials, classical music plays in public spaces, and even the function rooms carry such names as Belvedere. Forgive me a sudden craving for Sacher torte. Located in downtown Sapporo, on the upper floors of an office building, the hotel offers small but smartly decorated rooms with a slight Art Deco motif. Corner twins have sweeping views of Odori Park and the city lights. The hotel spa, which uses hot springs tapped deep below ground, is a huge (though pricey) plus.

N2 W1, Chuo-ku, Sapporo 060-0002. www.hotelmonterey.co.jp/eng. ☎ **011/242-7111.** Fax 011/232-1212. 181 units. ¥17,325 single; ¥32,340–¥43,890 double. AE, DC, MC, V. Station: Sapporo (8 min.). **Amenities:** 2 restaurants; hot-spring spa w/sauna and Jacuzzi (fee: ¥1,500); lobby computer w/free Internet. *In room:* A/C, TV, hair dryer, Internet, minibar.

JR Tower Hotel Nikko Sapporo ★★★ Contemporary elegance and convenience—not to mention top-class restaurants, a deluxe spa (offering everything from reflexology to indoor hot-spring baths), and spectacular views from all rooms—make this the best place to stay in Sapporo. Located above Sapporo Station and presided over by a walkie-talkie-toting staff who makes sure everything runs smoothly, it offers rooms (23rd–34th floors) with all the latest in hotel design, including desks with flip tops that double as mirrored vanities, separate tub/shower areas, and towels embroidered with different-colored insignia to take out the guessing game of which towel belongs to whom. The best rooms are south-facing twins, where in-room maps identify Susukino's buildings, nearby mountains and even stars in the sky, while singles are tiny for the price, face the train tracks, and are noisy even at 30 stories high. *A caveat:* Train passengers must undergo a roundabout hike to reach hotel elevators, though strategically placed signs assure them they're on the right track.

JR Tower, N5 W2, Chuo-ku, Sapporo 060-0005. www.jrhotels.co.jp/tower/english. ✆ **011/251-2222.** Fax 011/251-6370. 350 units. ¥20,000 single; ¥29,000–¥52,000 double. 20% discount for holders of Japan Rail Pass. AE, DC, MC, V. Above Sapporo Station. **Amenities:** 4 restaurants, including Sky J (p. 580); hot-spring spa w/sauna and Jacuzzi (¥1,500); room service. *In room:* A/C, TV, hair dryer, Internet, minibar.

Sapporo Grand Hotel ★   Open since 1934, this dignified hotel is Sapporo's oldest and largest, with a central downtown location near the Botanic Garden and Odori Park. An appealing choice of dining and drinking outlets (including those serving Hokkaido specialties) and a helpful English-speaking staff help make your stay enjoyable. The hotel's three buildings were constructed at various times: Many Japanese travelers prefer the traditional (we'd say dated) digs in the main building; for the same price you can stay in the smoke-free annex with its renovated twin rooms. In the east building are family rooms (with four beds) and so-called "Comfort Rooms" on top floors that provide added luxuries like humidifiers and big-screen TVs. Most rooms are fairly large but—a sign of the hotel's age—have small windows and small bathrooms. Note, too, that many rooms face other buildings.

N1 W4, Chuo-ku, Sapporo 060-0001. www.grand1934.com. ✆ **011/261-3311.** Fax 011/231-0388. 562 units. ¥18,480 single; ¥27,145–¥63,525 double. AE, DC, MC, V. Station: Sapporo (8 min.). **Amenities:** 5 restaurants; 2 bars; lounge; room service; spa; Wi-Fi (free, in lobby). *In room:* A/C, TV, hair dryer, Internet, minibar.

MODERATE

Hotel Gracery Sapporo ★   With a great location across from Sapporo Station's south side, this property starts with a seventh-floor lobby where free coffee is served, with guest rooms rising to the 16th floor. A no-contact key card allows you to enter your room with a simple wave, check out on departure day at lobby kiosks, and even buy beer. Rooms are small but stylish, and there are also Ladies Rooms with feminine décor and extra amenities like humidifiers. Add the some 150 movies-on-demand, and this hotel succeeds as an affordable urban getaway. The range of rates reflects the seasons.

N4 W4-1, Chuo-ku, Sapporo 060-0004. www.wh-rsv.com. ✆ **011/251-3211.** Fax 011/241-8238. 440 units. ¥12,000–¥14,000 single; ¥18,500–¥24,000 double; rates higher during Snow Festival. AE, DC, MC, V. Station: Sapporo (1-min. south of the station, across the street to the right). **Amenities:** Restaurant; lobby computers w/free Internet. *In room:* A/C, TV, fridge, hair dryer, Internet.

Nakamuraya Ryokan (中村屋旅館) ★   This modern and comfortable Japanese inn, just a stone's throw from the Botanic Garden, first opened more than 110 years ago but now occupies a nondescript 50-some-year-old building. Inside, it exudes a mid-20th-century throwback charm, with pleasant Japanese-style *tatami* rooms, some with a sitting area near the window. The hallways with eaves and slatted wooden doors to each room are a nice touch. Although rooms have their own tub, you might want to take advantage of the marble public baths here. If you order dinner, it will be served *ryokan* style in your room by kimono-clad women.

N3 W7, Chuo-ku, Sapporo 060-0003. www.nakamura-ya.com. ✆ **011/241-2111.** Fax 011/241-2118. 26 units. Rates for foreign guests ¥7,350 single; ¥13,650 double; rates higher during Snow Festival. Breakfast ¥1,500 extra; dinner ¥2,100–¥5,000 extra. AE, MC, V. Station: Sapporo (10 min.).

Located btw. the Botanic Garden and Old Government Building. **Amenities:** Restaurant; lounge; Wi-Fi (free, in lobby). *In room:* A/C, TV, fridge.

Sapporo Aspen Hotel ☺   This hotel has a convenient location just two minutes north of Sapporo Station. Rooms are rather small for the price but are comfortable enough, with windows that open, heavy curtains to block light, sitting areas and desks, and plenty of counter space in bathrooms. Families take note: 14 so-called "quartet" rooms have four twin beds and roomy bathrooms with two sinks and separate rooms for the toilet and tub. The best views are from the west side overlooking Hokkaido University and distant mountains.

N8 W4-5, Kita-ku, Sapporo 060-0808. www.aspen-hotel.co.jp. ✆ **011/700-2111.** Fax 011/700-2002. 302 units. ¥9,500–¥14,500 single, ¥17,500–¥21,000 twin, ¥39,000 quad; June–Sept and Snow Festival ¥11,500–¥17,500 single, ¥21,500–¥28,000 twin, ¥53,000 quad. AE, DC, MC, V. Station: Sapporo (a 2-min. walk straight north of the station, on the left). **Amenities:** Restaurant; coffee shop; rental bicycles (fee: ¥1,500 per day); Wi-Fi (free, in lobby). *In room:* A/C, TV, fridge, hair dryer, Internet.

INEXPENSIVE

In addition to the choices below, there are five branches of **Toyoko Inn** (www.toyoko-inn.com) in Sapporo. Our favorite location is **Toyoko Inn Sapporo-eki Nishi-Guchi Hokudai-Mae** across from the park-like campus of Hokkaido University. All have freebies like breakfast, lobby computers, and Wi-Fi in the tiny rooms (rooms are so small, a sign suggests stowing luggage under the bed). The Business Twins are great for friends traveling together (or couples who wish they weren't)—the bathroom splits the room in halves, each containing its own bed, TV, mirror, hair dryer, and more. Rates start at ¥5,480 for a single and ¥7,480 for a double, but they're even cheaper in winter (except during the Snow Festival).

Nada ⚑   A bit of a hike from the station (a 30-min. walk southwest), this little family inn has friendly hosts who offer Japanese-style rooms (some up a steep flight of stairs), all non-smoking and including dormitory-style rooms with bunk beds at cheaper prices if you're willing to share with strangers. The communal kitchen has a cozy, wooden dining area. There is no curfew. Backpackers from all over the world have found their way here.

S5 W9 Chuo-ku, Sapporo 064-0805. www.sapporonada.com. ✆ **011/551-5882.** Fax 011/551-0303. 10 units, none with bathroom. ¥3,500 per person; ¥2,700 per person in dormitory. Winter heating charge ¥200 extra. Breakfast ¥500 extra. MC, V (5% extra if you pay by credit card). Subway: Susukino (10 min.). Walk west on South 4 (Rte. 36) 5 blocks to West 9 (there's a gas station on the corner), turn left, and then right on the 4th street. **Amenities:** Rental bikes (fee: ¥500 per day); communal kitchen. *In room:* TV, no phone.

Watermark ⚑ 🏨   In downtown Sapporo near the Tanuku Koji shopping arcade, this boutique-like hotel offers rooms that are the same size as those in business hotels, but with much more panache. Black-and-white photographs of trees are set in black-colored alcoves above each duvet-covered bed, and bathrooms have separate areas for the sink, toilet, shower, and tub. If you want to sleep next to your sweetie but need more space than that afforded by a double room, "Hollywood" twins with the two beds next to each other are a good choice.

S3 W5-16 Chuo-ku, Sapporo 060-0063. http://watermarkhotel-sapporo.com. ✆ **011/233-3151.** Fax 011/233-2181. 153 units. May–Sep ¥7,500 single, ¥10,000–¥14,000 double; Oct–Apr ¥5,500 single, ¥7,000–¥9,000 double; ¥1,000 extra on Sat and day before holiday all-year. AE, DC, MC, V. Subway: Susukino (4 min.). Walk north on West 5 (Eki-mae Dori) and turn left at Mos Burger; it's 1½ blocks ahead on the right. **Amenities:** Restaurant. *In room:* A/C, TV, fridge, hair dryer, Internet.

NOBORIBETSU SPA & SHIKOTSU-TOYA NATIONAL PARK

If you have only a couple days to visit one of Hokkaido's national parks, head to **Shikotsu-Toya National Park ★★**, which lies between Hakodate and Sapporo. This 987-sq.-km (381-sq.-mile) national park encompasses lakes, volcanoes, and the famous hot-spring resort of **Noboribetsu Onsen ★★**, home to 800 people. Famous for the variety of its hot-water springs ever since the first public bathhouse opened here in 1858, Noboribetsu Spa is one of Japan's best-known spa resorts and is the most popular of Hokkaido's many spa towns. It boasts 11 different types of hot water, each with a different mineral content, and gushes 10,000 tons a day. With temperatures ranging between 113°F (45°C) and 197°F (90°C), the waters contain all kinds of minerals, including sulfur, salt, iron, and gypsum, and are thought to help relieve such disorders as high blood pressure, poor blood circulation, rheumatism, arthritis, eczema, and even constipation.

Also known for its seasonal beauty, Noboribetsu is an impressive sight in spring, when 2,000 cherry trees lining the road into the *onsen* are in full bloom. In autumn, thousands of Japanese maples burst into flame. In the nearby village of **Shiraoi** on Lake Poroto, a museum and village commemorate the native Ainu and their culture.

Essentials

GETTING THERE Noboribetsu Onsen is accessible only by **bus.** The nearest train station is **Noboribetsu Station**, which lies on the main **JR train** line that runs between Hakodate and Sapporo, a little more than 2 hours from Hakodate and 70 minutes from Sapporo. Fares for a reserved seat are ¥4,360 from Sapporo, ¥6,700 from Hakodate. From Noboribetsu Station it's a 10- to 15-minute bus ride to the last stop of Noboribetsu Onsen (¥330; departures once or twice an hour).

There is also one direct bus, the **Kosoku Onsen-go,** from Sapporo Station to Noboribetsu Onsen costing ¥1,900 for the 1¾-hour trip. Contact **Donan Bus** (📞 011/865-5511) for more information.

VISITOR INFORMATION & GETTING AROUND The **Noboribetsu Tourist Association** (www.noboribetsu-spa.jp; (📞 0143/84-3311; daily 9am–6pm) is on

---

  Un-Bearable Park

As you wander around Noboribetsu Onsen, you'll see advertisements for a bear park. The best thing about this place is the trip via ropeway—the bear park occupies one of the tallest hills around. Of the 135 bears who live here, a few dozen are crowded together in concrete pens in one of the saddest sights I've ever seen. Although the bears, many of them rescued from extermination or brought here as orphaned cubs, are luckier than some of their peers (government policy advocated the extermination of Hokkaido brown bears in the 1950s and still allows some of the remaining wild bears to be hunted and culled annually), the admission (including ropeway) of ¥2,520 is too high a price for this joyless place. Skip it—you're better off spending your money elsewhere.

ANOTHER ISLAND, ANOTHER PEOPLE: THE ainu OF HOKKAIDO

Hokkaido is the ancestral home of the Ainu, the native inhabitants of Japan's northernmost island. Not much is known about their origins; it's not even clear whether they're Asian or Caucasian, but they are of different racial stock than the Japanese. They're round-eyed and light-skinned, and Ainu males can grow thick beards and mustaches.

Early Ainu inhabited an area from Sakhalin in Russia through present-day Tohoku, and Japan "discovered" them when trade with Hokkaido began some 800 years ago. Living in a harsh environment with few resources, Ainu grew skilled at using the plants and animals around them for everything from medicine to utensils. Traditionally, they lived as hunters and fishermen, using dogs to help in the hunt and setting up trip traps with arrows to catch wild animals. Arrows were carved with wooden "knives" and then dipped in poison to increase their efficiency. Clothes were fashioned from bark, nettles, or even salmon skin. Animistic, they had gods for every object and phenomenon, whether sun, thunder, fire, or animals. Most important to Ainu

culture were bear cubs, kept in captivity before being killed, with elaborate ceremonies held to send the cub's spirit to the next life.

After Japan opened Hokkaido for development in the late 1800s, Ainu were forcibly assimilated into Japanese society, and many died of smallpox, measles, cholera, and other newly introduced diseases. Like Native Americans, they faced discrimination and their culture was largely destroyed. Hunting and fishing on lands they had used for generations was prohibited, tattoos and earrings were banned, and male Ainu were taken from their families for forced labor. Eventually, Ainu adopted Japanese names, language and clothing. Today, some 23,000 people in Hokkaido claim Ainu roots (it's estimated that many more deny their ancestry for fear of lingering discrimination). While a small proportion earn their living from tourism, selling woodcarvings and other crafts or performing traditional dances and songs, today most Ainu live lives no different from those of other Japanese.

Noboribetsu Onsen's main street, just a minute's walk north of the bus depot (continue up the hill; it will be on your left side with a clock above the door). In addition to a map, ask for the useful pamphlet "A Guide to Walking Trails in Noboribetsu Onsen." You may not encounter anyone who speaks English, but luckily the town is so small you shouldn't have any problem getting around.

Exploring Noboribetsu
ENJOYING NOBORIBETSU'S NATURAL WONDERS

TAKING THE LOCAL WATERS   Although all the spa hotels and *ryokan* have their own taps into the spring water, almost everyone who comes to Noboribetsu Onsen makes a point of going to the most famous hotel bath in town, **Dai-ichi Takimoto-kan ★★** (www.takimotokan.co.jp; ℂ **0143/84-2111**), one of the first bathhouses to open at the hot springs. Now a huge, modern bathing hall with some 35 tubs and pools containing different mineral contents at various temperatures, it's an elaborate affair with hot-spring baths and Jacuzzis both indoors and out, saunas, steam rooms, and waterfall massage (this is one of my favorites—you sit under the shooting water and let it pummel your neck and shoulders). Although the baths are separate for men and women, there's an indoor swimming pool for families with a slide and play area for children, so be sure to bring your swimsuit. If you're staying at the Dai-ichi Takimotokan or Takimoto Inn (see "Where to Stay," below), you can use the baths for free at any time—in the evenings, don't miss bathing in the outdoor baths, where you can order beer, soft drinks, or sake and enjoy the nice mountain scenery. Otherwise, Daiichi Takimotokan is open to the public daily from 9am to 6pm (you must enter by 5pm); the charge is ¥2,000 for adults, half-price for children 3 to 12.

HELL VALLEY (JIGOKUDANI) ★ To get an idea of what all this hot water looks like in its natural state, visit Hell Valley at the north edge of town past Dai-ichi Takimotokan. This volcanic crater 446m (1,485 ft.) in diameter has a huge depression full of bubbling, boiling water and rock formations of orange and brown. As you walk the concrete path called Hell Valley Promenade which winds along the left side of the crater keep an eye down below to the right for a tiny shrine dedicated to the deity that protects eyes (those most in need are apt to miss it); local lore says that if you rub some of the protective water over ailing eyes, they'll be cured. Farther along, you'll soon reach a sign for OYUNUMA and a path leading uphill to the left through lush woods; if you follow it for about 10 minutes, you'll come to a lookout point over a large pond of hot bubbling water called Oyunuma (the lookout is across the road; it's another 5-min. walk to the pond). Return to the road and turn right (west) and then right again on the road leading downhill, where you will soon see a hiking path on the left that runs alongside the steaming Oyunuma River; halfway down is a natural foot bath. If you want to take a different route back, return to the road and the Oyunuma path but look for the Funamiyama (Mount Funami) Promenade to the right. It traces the backbone of several ridges, passing a number of small stone guardians before ending up back at Hell Valley.

ESPECIALLY FOR KIDS

Noboribetsu Date Jidai Mura ★★ ☺ THEME PARK A visit to this reproduction of a Feudal-Era village is the closest you can get to taking a time machine back to the late Edo Period. Facades of shops and restaurants, theaters, the downtown, and a samurai district are a meticulous reproduction from the days of yore, and the cheerful staff is dressed in period clothing. See ninja warriors fighting in a trick mansion or outdoor theater, local merchants hawking their wares, Edo-Era tenements with life-size models (I especially like the one of the boy in the outhouse), a small ninja museum showing tricks of the trade, and courtesans performing in a Disneyesque re-creation of how Japan might have looked when the shogun reigned. Shows are in Japanese (the ninja shows are probably the only ones that would interest children), but the various attractions are fun for the entire family, and if you haven't seen another historical theme village elsewhere in Japan, this rather small one is worth a 2-hour visit (an English-language timetable gives show times). To commemorate the day forever, don a kimono, samurai, or ninja outfit and have your photo taken in front of a traditional backdrop for ¥3,500.

53–1 Naka-Noboribetsu-cho, Noboribetsu-shi. www.edo-trip.jp. ℭ **0143/83-3311.** Admission ¥2,900 adults, ¥2,100 seniors, ¥1,500 children. Apr–Oct daily 9am–5pm; Nov–Mar Thurs–Tues 9am–4pm. You must enter 1 hr. before closing. Bus: A few buses daily from Noboribetsu Onsen or JR Noboribetsu Station to Jidai Mura (fare: ¥180); or, take a more frequent bus to San-ai Byoin, from which it's a 10-min. walk partially up hill. Located halfway btw. Noboribetsu Onsen and Noboribetsu city.

Noboribetsu Marine Park Nixe ★ ☺ AQUARIUM/THEME PARK   Small children love this combination Danish theme park and aquarium, located near Noboribetsu Station. The aquarium, one of the largest in northern Japan, is inside Castle Nixe, modeled after a Danish castle, where you'll see sharks (from an underwater tunnel), morays, salmon, sturgeon, king crab, giant octopus, and other sea creatures. More attractions include touch pools with small sharks, rays, and horseshoe crabs; a reptile house with snakes, turtles and lizards; dolphin and sea lion shows; a king penguin parade; a game arcade; the ubiquitous souvenir shops (selling Danish and aquarium-related gifts); and a handful of kiddie rides (¥200–¥300 extra). You can see everything in about 2 hours.

1–22 Noboribetsu Higashi-machi, Noboribetsu-shi. www.nixe.co.jp. (C) **0143/83-3800.** Admission ¥2,400 adults, ¥1,200 children. Daily 9am–5pm. Closed 5 days in early Dec. Station: Noboribetsu (7 min.). Walk straight out the exit and turn right after 1 block.

LEARNING ABOUT THE AINU IN NEARBY SHIRAOI

Poroto Kotan and the Ainu Museum (ポロトコタン) **★★** CULTURAL INSTITUTION   Shiraoi (an Ainu word meaning "Place of Many Horseflies") was settled by the Ainu long before Japanese arrived; today, it's a small town of some 22,000 inhabitants, including Ainu. Poroto Kotan ("Big Lake Village" in Ainu), on the shores of Lake Poroto, is a mock village of native houses made entirely from wood and reeds, a native plant garden, a dance area, probably the most important Ainu museum anywhere, and a research center dedicated to preserving Ainu culture. If you're lucky, your visit will coincide with two annual festivals: one, in the spring, to pray for life's necessities; the other in the fall to give thanks for the harvests (call for festival dates).

Highlights of a visit here include demonstrations of Ainu weaving techniques, woodworking, and other crafts, and native dances and performances of the *mukkari* (Ainu mouth harp) performed by Ainu in traditional costume. Unfortunately, bears (and dogs) are kept in captivity here in filthy metal cages, but even this is an Ainu tradition—in spring, when the mother bear left her cave in search of food, Ainu fetched the cubs to keep in a wooden cage in the village until they were old enough for slaughter. Bears were revered as gifts from the gods. The most important thing to see, however, is the excellent museum, with English-language descriptions of Ainu history, culture, society, and traditions, videos (Japanese-language only) and displays of utensils, clothing (from salmon-skin boots to intricately embroidered kimono), fish hooks (the Ainu excelled at fishing), jewelry, and other everyday artifacts.

If you wish, you can lunch on dried salmon, *peneimo* (pancakes of local potato), *ohau* (broth containing mountain vegetables, meat, and fish), and herb tea bought from one of the stalls. Although the village is small and can be toured in about an hour, it's an important stop for those wishing to learn about Ainu culture and the indigenous people who have little left of what was once a rich heritage.

2–3–4 Wakakusa-cho, Shiraoi-cho, Hokkaido 059-0902. www.ainu-museum.or.jp. (C) **0144/82-3914.** Admission ¥750 adults, ¥550 high-school students, ¥450 junior-high students, ¥300 children. Daily 8:45am–5pm. Closed 1 week for New Year's. Train: 13 min. by JR express train or 25 min. by local train from JR Noboribetsu Station to JR Shiraoi Station, and then a 10-min. walk. Exit straight out of the station, turn left at the first traffic signal and left again at the next signal. Cross the tracks and then turn right at the next intersection. **Note:** Only 5 express trains running btw. Hakodate and Sapporo daily stop at Shiraoi (if coming from Sapporo, you can also transfer to a local train at Tomakomai Station).

Where to Eat

Fukuan (福庵) SOBA   This small, traditional *soba* shop (take your shoes off at the entrance) serves its own buckwheat noodles. From the English-language menu, recommended is the *tenseiro*, tempura soba with shrimp and vegetables; or the *Ebi-ten-oroshi soba*, a summertime meal of cold soba, shrimp tempura, seaweed, dried fish flakes, and Japanese daikon radish.

30 Noboribetsu Onsen-machi. ✆ **0143/84/2758.** Soba ¥680–¥1,400. No credit cards. Daily 11:30am–2pm and 6–10:30pm (closed irregularly 1 day a month). A 1-min. walk from the bus terminal, on the main street across from the tourist information office.

Poplar WESTERN   For an inexpensive Western-style lunch, draft beer, or coffee, this simple restaurant has a limited English-language menu with pictures. While they may not win any culinary awards, items include beefsteak, hamburger steak, pastas, fried shrimp, grilled salmon, and pork cutlet. There's a monthly special set for ¥1,000.

Takimoto Inn. ✆ **0143/84-2205.** Main dishes ¥700–¥1,200. AE, DC, MC, V. Daily 11am–2pm (last order). Inside Takimoto Inn (see below).

Where to Stay

During the busiest tourist seasons (Golden Week, July through September, and New Year's), hotel rates are at their highest, particularly on weekends. October, when the leaves are changing, is also popular. All places below charge a daily ¥150 hot-springs tax in addition to the rates given.

EXPENSIVE

Oyado Kiyomizu-ya (御やど清水屋) ★★   You'll be royally welcome at this elegantly modern *ryokan* with traditional touches, one of our favorites in Hokkaido. You'll be ushered down a long corridor decorated with plants, stones, and paper lanterns to the elevator that will whisk you up to your room. Least expensive are average-looking Western-style rooms, making the simple but pleasant Japanese *tatami* rooms a better choice. For a splurge, combination rooms are actually two-room suites with a tatami room where you'll dine and a separate bedroom. Some accommodations on the 6th and 7th floors even boast snuggly fur-lined futons and down covers.

The ryokan is beside a roaring river, the sounds of which will sing you to sleep. But it's the delicious seasonal *kaiseki* meals that assure the ryokan many repeat guests; the parade of beautifully prepared dishes includes local specialties. Service is impeccable, and the second-generation owner, Mr. Iwai, speaks excellent English; he can answer your questions regarding Noboribetsu and the surrounding area. (A sake connoisseur, he can also recommend which of the 14 different kinds of sake he keeps on hand might go best with your meal.) If you're looking for a place far from tour groups, souvenir shops, and impersonal service, you'll be happy here.

173 Noboribetsu Onsen-machi, Noboribetsu-shi, Hokkaido 059-0551. www.kiyomizuya.co.jp. ✆ **0143/84-2145.** Fax 0143/84-2146. 43 units. ¥10,000 single; ¥16,000 double. Rates exclude tax. Breakfast ¥2,000 extra; dinner ¥5,000–¥10,000 extra. Rates including 2 meals and tax ¥13,800–¥21,150 (rates ¥2,100 higher on nights before holidays). AE, DC, MC, V. Pick-up service available from Noboribetsu Onsen bus terminal, or it's a 10-min. walk. **Amenities:** Coffee shop; indoor/outdoor hot-spring baths (the outdoor bath alternates days for men and women); Wi-Fi (free in lobby). *In room:* TV.

MODERATE

Dai-ichi Takimotokan ★   This is Noboribetsu Onsen's best-known *ryokan*, thanks to its long history (opened in 1858) and its gigantic public baths. Today, however, it's a large, modern facility with little personality and lots of noisy tour groups. The most compelling reasons to stay here are its location near Hell Valley and its famous hot-spring baths, which hotel guests are entitled to use free anytime, night or day. Another plus: shuttle bus service from downtown Sapporo for only ¥500 (call the hotel for reservations). Most rooms are simple *tatami*, spread throughout four buildings. Oldest and cheapest are those in the East Building, without bathrooms (but with toilets; some also have views of an enclosed garden), while rooms in the West Building are a step up with private bathroom. The South Building has Japanese-style rooms and eight Western-style rooms, but it's a hike to the hot-spring baths. Most luxurious are rooms in the Main Building, with top floors offering the best views. Guests staying in the East and West buildings or Western-style rooms dine in a buffet restaurant offering Japanese, Chinese, and Western food (or can pay more for a traditional Japanese meal served in your room), while those staying in tatami rooms in the South and Main building can opt for seasonal dinners of Hokkaido specialties served in their rooms.

55 Noboribetsu Onsen-machi, Noboribetsu-shi, Hokkaido 059-0595. www.takimotokan.co.jp. ℰ **0143/84-3322.** Fax 0143/84-2202. 399 units, 342 with bathroom, 57 with toilet only. ¥9,150–¥16,150 per person off season; ¥13,275–¥23,715 per person peak season. Sat and holidays ¥2,100 extra per person. Rates include 2 meals. AE, DC, MC, V. A 5-min. walk uphill from the bus station, beside Hell Valley. **Amenities:** 3 restaurants; lounge; 2 bars; 24-hr. indoor/outdoor hot-spring baths; indoor pool; Wi-Fi (free, in lobby). *In room:* A/C, TV, minibar or fridge.

Kashoutei Hanaya (花鐘亭はなや) ★　This modern *ryokan* has traditional touches like a small Japanese garden off the lobby, flower arrangements, bamboo, carpets patterned like leaves flowing on a stream, and Japanese music playing softly in public areas. Most rooms are Japanese style, with or without bathroom, while the two combination Japanese/Western-style rooms are without bathroom (all rooms, however, have toilet and sink). Meals are served in your room. The owner speaks English. The ryokan is on the edge of town, about a 5-minute walk from the bus terminal.

134 Noboribetsu Onsen-machi, Noboribetsu-shi, Hokkaido 059-0551. www.kashoutei-hanaya. co.jp. ℰ **0143/84-2521.** Fax 0143/84-2240. 21 units (5 with bathroom, 16 with toilet only). ¥12,750–¥26,400 per person. Rates include 2 meals. AE, DC, MC, V. Bus: From Noboribetsu Station to Byoin-mae (one stop before the terminal—the ryokan will be close behind you, across the road). Pickup service also available from Noboribetsu Onsen bus terminal. **Amenities:** Coffee shop; indoor/outdoor hot-spring baths; Wi-Fi (free, in lobby). *In room:* A/C, TV, minibar.

INEXPENSIVE

Takimoto Inn　If you prefer a hotel with beds to a *ryokan* with futons, this quiet hotel shows its age (1977) but has a friendly staff and allows guests to use Dai-chi Takimotokan's famous baths across the street for free any time, as well as its shuttle bus from Sapporo. All rooms are twins with narrow beds (but can be used as singles or triples) and spartan, with metal doors that clang shut with the finality of a prison and minuscule bathrooms. There's no view, but windows do open. Buffet meals offer a mix of Japanese and Western food.

76 Noboribetsu Onsen-machi, Noboribetsu-shi 059-0551. www.takimotoinn.co.jp. ℰ **0143/84-2205.** Fax 0143/84-2645. 47 units. ¥7,500 per person, including 2 meals. Sat ¥1,050 extra (rates higher New Year's, Golden Week, Obon). AE, DC, MC, V. A 5-min. walk uphill from the bus station, across the street from Dai-ichi Takimotokan. **Amenities:** Restaurant; hot-spring bath (guests can also use Dai-ichi Takimotokan's baths free). *In room:* TV, fridge.

SOUNKYO SPA & DAISETSUZAN NATIONAL PARK

Although I find it difficult to rank nature in terms of beauty, there are some who maintain that **Daisetsuzan National Park ★★★** is the most spectacular of Hokkaido's parks. With its tall mountains covered with fir and birch trees and sprinkled with wildflowers, its river gorge laced with waterfalls, and hiking trails, Daisetsuzan National Park is the perfect place to come if you've been itching to get some exercise in relatively unspoiled countryside. Lying in the center of Hokkaido (east of Sapporo), this national park—Japan's largest—contains three volcanic mountain groups, including the highest mountain in Hokkaido, Mount Asahi, 2,254m (7,513 ft.) high. Hiking in summer and skiing in winter are the primary pursuits of the park's visitors.

Nestled at the very edge of Sounkyo Gorge, Daisetsuzan's most famous natural attraction, is **Sounkyo Onsen ★**, the perfect base for exploring the national park. Once rather unattractive with a hodgepodge of ugly cement buildings, Sounkyo has reinvented itself with attractive and compatible alpine-style buildings and stone and wood paths that do justice to the magnificent scenic backdrop and its soothing hot springs. Yet it remains a mountain village, home to 600 residents and only a dozen or so accommodations, most of them small affairs. More important, Sounkyo Spa serves as the starting point for the cable-car trip to the top of a neighboring peak with its hiking trails and easy ski slope. From late January to mid-March, the spa is the scene of the Ice Falls Festival, a winter fantasyland with giant ice sculptures, frozen waterfalls lit with colored lights, and weekend fireworks.

Essentials

GETTING THERE   The only way to reach Sounkyo Onsen by public transportation is by **bus.** If you're coming from Sapporo, take the **JR train** 2½ hours to Kamikawa (four departures daily; ¥6,180 one-way), transferring there for the 30-minute bus ride (¥800) directly to Sounkyo Onsen. Buses depart about 11 times a day and generally connect with train arrivals, but it's always wise to check ahead with the JR counter in Sapporo Station's Hokkaido-Sapporo Tourist Information Center (or, have a Japanese call the Kamikawa bus terminal at ℂ **01658/2-1316**).

There are two buses a day—called the Sunrise Asahikawa-Kushiro-go—connecting Sounkyo Onsen with Akanko Onsen in Akan National Park (p. 595), with the one-way fare costing ¥3,260 for the 3½-hour trip. Reservations are required; call ℂ **01658/5-3321** in Sounkyo, or 0154/67-2205 in Akan; or drop by the bus terminal in either town. All bus fares are half-price for children.

VISITOR INFORMATION & ORIENTATION   The **tourist information office** (ℂ **01658/5-3350**; daily 10:30am–5pm) is located in the bus terminal, called the Kanko Center (there's a post office next door). The staff's English is limited, but they have maps and can point you in the direction of your lodging or even make reservations for you. In any case, the village is so tiny that you won't have any difficulty getting around; it's basically two streets leading up to the ropeway, and a pedestrian lane, called Canyon Mall Street, that wanders through the center of town.

Exploring Sounkyo Onsen

Before exploring the environs, you might want to pop into Sounkyo's free **Daisetsuzan National Park Visitor Center,** located across from the ropeway (ℂ **01658/9-4400;**

June–Oct daily 8am–5:30pm, Nov–May Tues–Sun 9am–5pm), with displays on the park's animals, plants, and geological wonders, most with explanations in English. A topographical map shows the layout of Daisetsuzan National Park, and videos show the park's geological history and changes through the seasons. If you plan on hiking, you might ask the staff for recommended trails, as well as a rundown on places where brown bears are often spotted (you'll want to avoid those!).

SOUNKYO GORGE The Sounkyo Gorge is a river valley hemmed in on both sides by rock walls rising almost 150m (500 ft.) and extending some 19km (12 miles). Unfortunately, a major rock slide has closed most of the gorge to sightseers (you used to be able to cycle much of the gorge), but you can still see a small portion by walking 3km (2 miles) from Sounkyo Spa (walk down to the highway and turn right) and keeping to the right when the highway disappears into a tunnel. This will bring you to a parking lot beside the roaring river and a view of two famous waterfalls side by side: the Ginga no Taki (Silver River Falls) and the Ryuusei no Taki (Shooting Star Falls). At the far end of the parking lot is a fence, beyond which you can see the gorge. Bring some drinks or a picnic lunch. There's one daily bus here from Sounkyo Spa (ask the tourist office for details). And though there are bicycles for rent in town, the short trip to the gorge doesn't warrant the rental price.

GOING TO THE TOP OF MOUNT KURODAKE ★ Take the **cable car** directly from Sounkyo Onsen to Mount Kurodake, where you'll be rewarded with sweeping views. The tops of the mountains are really beautiful here, covered with wildflowers and alpine plant life. It would be a shame to come to Sounkyo and not spend a few hours amid its lofty peaks. The trip by cable car takes 7 minutes, with round-trip tickets costing ¥1,850 for adults and ¥950 for children. From the cable-car station, walk a few minutes farther up the mountain, where you'll come to a chairlift. The chairlift ride (my favorite part) takes 15 minutes, swinging you past lush forests of fir and birch. Round-trip fare here is ¥600 for adults and ¥400 for children. Ropeway and lift operating hours vary; in the summer the ropeway runs daily 6am to 7pm, in winter it's 9am to 4pm (call ✆ **01658/5-3031** for more information).

DAY HIKES You can forgo the cable car and chairlift up **Mount Kurodake** and hike instead; plan on the entire day up and back. Or, for a short hike, forgo the chairlift on Mount Kurodake and hike about 1 hour from the fifth stage (where the chairlift begins) to the seventh stage (where the chairlift ends). If you're prepared to exert yourself climbing over boulders, however, the most rewarding journey is the 1½-hour hike from the seventh stage onward to the peak of Kurodake, 1,950m (6,500 ft.) high. There, if the weather is clear, you'll greeted with views of the surrounding mountain ranges. If you feel like taking a day hike, there's the circular Ohachi-daira path along the top of mountain ridges that you can hike in about 8 hours. Be sure to note lift operating hours before setting out. *Note:* If you plan on hiking past the seventh stage, you must first check in at the hut to the left of where the chairlift ends, where you sign your name and give your route so that tabs can be kept on you while on the mountain (hiking from here is recommended only in July–Aug, as snow can cover the ground other months of the year). Hiking boots are essential, but you can also rent rubber boots here for ¥500, a must if you don't have hiking boots because trails are slippery and wet (small streams from winter snows cascade down the trail even in July). Note, however, that rental sizes only go up to 28 centimeters (12 in.).

As for other hiking possibilities, across the highway and river from Sounkyo Spa is the **Panoramadai** hiking course, where you can hike to a panoramic lookout in about an hour. Past the Taisetsu Hotel above Sounkyo Spa is the Momidijani Course, which takes about 1-hour round-trip and follows a mountain stream to a waterfall.

For more information on these and other hiking trips, stop by the **Daisetsuzan National Park Visitor Center.**

SKIING **Mount Kurodake** becomes a skier's haven from November through April (and sometimes into May), with beginner-to-intermediate slopes. Although you can rent skis up on the mountain at the cable-car station, keep in mind that your feet may be too big (at last check, boots went up to 28cm/12 in.). Skis and boots rent for ¥3,000, while a 1-day cable-car and chairlift ticket goes for ¥3,700.

TAKING THE WATERS In the village Community Center, you'll find **Kurodake-no-yu** (✆ 01658/5-3333), a public hot-spring bath with large, spotless, and attractive indoor and outdoor baths plus a sauna. The spa charges ¥600 for adults (half-price for children) and is open daily 10am to 9:30pm (last entry 9pm; closed Wed Nov–Apr, except during Ice Falls Festival). Buy your tickets at the vending machine on the ground floor before going up to the baths.

Where to Dine

Beergrill Canyon ITALIAN-JAPANESE Located in the same building as Spa Kurodake, this casual restaurant serves various pizzas, pastas, and Hokkaido fare from its English-language menu. Choices include pizza with mushrooms and prosciutto, spaghetti with rainbow trout and mushrooms, spicy curry with chicken or Hokkaido vegetables, venison stroganoff, and Hokkaido sirloin steak. For a complete meal, add a mini-salad, bread, or rice to your entree by paying ¥250 extra. Wash it all down with beer. There's a computer you can use for free if you order something.

Sounkyo. ✆ **01658/5-3361.** No credit cards. Daily 11:30am–3:30pm and 5:30–9pm (last order); 9:30am–9pm on weekends in summer. Closed Wed Nov–Apr except during Ice Falls Festival.

Ramen House Tozanken (登山軒) RAMEN For an inexpensive, quick meal, stop by this ramen shop located at the bottom of the pedestrian slope (look for its red *noren*). Its English-language menu with pictures lists nine different kinds of ramen, such as the deep-fried chicken ramen or Asahikawa ramen (with handmade miso soup, vegetables, and roast pork), as well as rice bowls and *gyoza*. In nice weather you can sit at the outdoor tables.

Sounkyo. ✆ **01658/5-3005.** Main dishes ¥700–¥1,100. No credit cards. Daily 10am–10pm. Closed Nov–May except during Ice Falls Festival.

Where to Stay

There are plenty of inexpensive pensions and hotels in Sounkyo. The army of college-age Japanese you see working in the area comes from other parts of Japan to work for the summer. They may not know a lot about the area, but most of them speak some English. If you want to stay here in July, August, or September, be sure to make advance reservations. Rates below include the ¥150 *onsen* tax.

MODERATE

Hotel Taisetsu ★★ ✦ This hotel's ridge-top location above town gives it good views of the surrounding gorge and mountains from some rooms. What makes this a top pick, however, are its three gorgeous baths, two of which are open 24 hours; best are the seventh-floor indoor and outdoor baths with great views and the newer outdoor baths overlooking expansive greenery (you can use the baths even if you don't stay here for ¥800). Most rooms are Japanese style, spread in a west wing (ask for a room on a top floor facing the front toward the gorge) and an east wing (request a room facing the back toward the hills, as those facing the front overlook a characterless *ryokan*). Best of all are the *Yukihana* two-room suites on the sixth floor, complete with a huge bathroom with a hot-spring bath affording panoramic views; guests staying here dine in private rooms in an exclusive Japanese restaurant. Otherwise, rates are based on meals, with the cheapest served buffet style in a characterless dining hall and the more expensive in Top of the Canyon, which serves a mix of Japanese and Western dishes. You can also choose to dine in your room for ¥2,000 more.

Sounkyo Onsen, Kamikawacho, Kamikawa-gun 078-1701. www.taisetsu-g.com. ℂ **01658/5-3211.** Fax 01658/5-3420. 216 units. ¥10,000–¥35,000 per person. Rates include 2 meals. AE, DC, MC, V. Shuttle bus pickup from bus terminal (call on arrival), or an 8-min. walk. **Amenities:** 4 restaurants; Japanese-style pub; indoor/outdoor hot-spring baths; sauna; whirlpool baths; Wi-Fi (free, in lobby). *In room:* TV, fridge, hair dryer.

INEXPENSIVE

Onsen Pension Ginga ★ 🍴 This cute lodge is bright and airy, with a glass-enclosed communal dining room decorated in European drawing-room style and both Japanese- and Western-style rooms, most with large windows providing great panoramic views (best are the corner rooms, and room no. 208). Rooms without bathrooms do have sinks. Japanese meals, served in the dining room, feature local fish and seasonal homegrown vegetables. Unfortunately, the hot-spring bath here is small.

Sounkyo Onsen, Kamikawacho, Kamikawa-gun 078-1701. ℂ **01658/5-3775.** 18 units (5 with bathroom). ¥7,500 per person without bathroom, ¥8,865 per person with bathroom. Rates include 2 meals. No credit cards. A 2-min. walk from the bus terminal. **Amenities:** Small indoor hot-spring bath. *In room:* TV, no phone.

Resort Pension Yama-no-ue (リゾートペンション山の上) This pension offers simple *tatami* rooms with just the basics. There are communal toilets, sinks, and showers; but for a real hot-spring bath, guests staying here are entitled to use the Spa Kurodake next door for free. In summer, the small dining room serves ample meals of Hokkaido cuisine. If you stay more than 1 night (or in winter), you'll dine also at Beergrill Canyon (see above). Breakfast is Western style. Because the owner is an avid photographer and butterfly collector, you'll see gorgeous shots of the area and captured butterflies on the walls. Call for special rates, which might include 2 nights with no meals plus a pass for the ropeway for ¥9,400 single, ¥16,800 double.

Sounkyo Onsen, Kamikawacho, Kamikawa-gun 078-1701. www.p-yamanoue.com. ℂ **01658/5-3206.** Fax 01658/5-3207. 14 units, none with bathroom, 1 with toilet. ¥8,800–¥12,600 per person. Rates include 2 meals. No credit cards. A 3-min. walk from the bus terminal. **Amenities:** Coin laundry; Wi-Fi (free in lobby). *In room:* TV, no phone.

AKANKO SPA & AKAN NATIONAL PARK

Spreading through the eastern end of Hokkaido, **Akan National Park** ★★ features volcanic mountains, dense forests of subarctic primeval trees, and three caldera lakes, including Lake Akan. The best place to stay in the park is **Akanko Onsen,** a small hot-spring resort on the edge of Lake Akan and home to some 1,400 residents. It makes a good base for active vacations ranging from fishing to hiking and from which to explore both Akan National Park and nearby Kushiro Marshland National Park, famous for its red-crested cranes. It also has a re-created Ainu village, with one of the best music and dance performances I've seen.

Essentials

GETTING THERE **By JR Train & Bus** Because there's no train station at Akanko Onsen itself, transportation to the resort town is by train to Kushiro or Kitami and then by bus to Akanko. Kushiro is about 4 hours from Sapporo by JR train (¥8,610 for an unreserved seat); Kitami is 4½ hours away (¥8,290 for an unreserved seat). From **JR Kushiro Station,** buses depart four or five times a day for Akanko; the 2-hour trip costs ¥2,650 one-way. From **Kitami,** buses depart twice a day (at last check at 9:30am and 3pm), and the 70-minute trip costs ¥1,800. You must make a reservation for this bus by calling 🕿 **0157/23-2181** in Kitami or 🕿 **0154/67-2205** in Akanko.

Two Sunrise buses a day depart Sounkyo Onsen for Akanko Onsen (at last check at 9:27am and 4:57pm), with the one-way fare costing ¥3,260 for the 3½-hour trip. Reservations are required; call 🕿 **01658/5-3321** in Sounkyo, or 0154/67-2205 in Akan, or drop by the bus terminal in either town. All bus fares are half-price for children.

By Plane Because Akan National Park lies at the eastern extremity of Hokkaido, you may wish to fly at least one-way between here and Tokyo. The closest airport to Akanko Onsen is **Kushiro Airport** (KUH), with the flight from Tokyo taking about 1½ hours. From Kushiro Airport, 5 buses a day travel to Akanko in about 1 hour and 20 minutes for ¥2,090.

VISITOR INFORMATION **Akanko Onsen's Tourist Association** (www.lake-akan.com; 🕿 **0154/67-2254;** daily 9am–6pm) is located a few minutes' walk from the Akanko Onsen bus terminal (turn left out of the bus terminal and take the first right, then left on the main street; the building, on your left, looks like a massive yellow barn, across from the post office and the New Akan Hotel Shangri-La). Occasionally there's an English-speaker here, and in any case you can pick up an English-language pamphlet about Akan National Park with a map of the town and foldouts on hiking. The staff will also make reservations for hotels and *ryokan*; Wi-Fi is available here.

For information on the park and its natural wonders, drop by the **Akankohan Eco Museum Center** (🕿 **0154/67-2785;** Wed–Mon 9am–5pm), located beside the lake about a 7-minute walk from the bus terminal. Displays, in Japanese only, show off native flora and fauna, including the Hokkaido brown bear and sika deer (both stuffed), *marimo* (duckweed), and live freshwater fish such as white-spotted char and kokanee salmon. Admission is free.

GETTING AROUND Akanko Onsen is small, and walking is the best way to get around. It consists primarily of one main street that snakes along the lake, with *ryokan* and souvenir shops lining both sides.

Exploring Akan
SEEING THE SIGHTS

RED-CRESTED CRANES Red-crested cranes, the official birds of Hokkaido, are regarded as both a good omen and a national symbol of Japan. Because they mate for life, they're also considered a symbol for love. Once threatened with extinction, these graceful and beautiful creatures now lead protected lives in and around **Kushiro**

Marshland National Park (Kushiro Shitsugen), Japan's largest marshland, as well as a few other places in the area. The best place to learn about cranes is at the excellent **Akan Kokusai Tsuru Center (Akan International Crane Center)** ★, 23–40 Akan (✆ **0154/66-4011; daily 9am–5pm).** In addition to a film showing their beautiful courtship dance and nesting habits, it has fun, interactive displays, most with English-language explanations. You'll learn just about everything you'd ever want to know about red-crested cranes here, from why they fly to how much an egg weighs. Best of all, if you're visiting between about November and March, there's an **observatory** on the often snow-covered expanse behind the building, where 200 red-crested cranes live, court, and mate. This is a great opportunity to photograph the birds in action, and you'll be surprised at how large they actually are; try to arrive for the daily 2pm feeding. Admission to the International Crane Center is ¥460 for adults, half-price for children. Plan on staying at least an hour in winter, less in summer when the birds have returned to their native marshlands. The International Crane Center is some 40 minutes from Akanko Onsen by bus; get off at the Tancho-no-Sato stop (fare: ¥1,570). The same bus runs between Akanko Onsen, Kushiro Airport and Kushiro Station, so it's possible to stop here, visit, and then catch the next bus (buses are infrequent, however, so get the schedule beforehand).

In summer, your best bet for observing cranes outside the marshland is the **Japanese Crane Reserve (Tancho-Tsuru Koen),** Kushiro-cho (✆ **0154/56-2219; daily 9am–6pm, to 4pm in winter),** a marshy area set aside in 1958 for breeding and raising cranes. It now has about a dozen cranes—some of them second and third generation—living in natural habitats behind high meshed fences. They are fed at least twice a day. Admission is ¥460 for adults and ¥110 for children. Also on the way to Kushiro airport and station, it's located 1 hour by bus from the Akanko Onsen bus terminal; get off at the Tsuru-koen stop. For just a quick look, one bus a day makes a 15-minute stop at this park, which is all you really need.

AINU SITES IN AKANKO ONSEN   Although the Ainu originally lived near Kushiro, not Akan, they have built the **Ainu Kotan Village** in Akanko Onsen (✆ **0154/67-2727)** and now number about 130 individuals, making this one of Hokkaido's largest Ainu communities. Although Ainu Kotan Village itself is just one street lined with souvenir shops (selling mostly woodcarvings), just beyond is the **Akanko Ainu Theater Ikor** ★★, where you can see Ainu performing traditional songs, dances and instruments like the *mukkuri* (bamboo mouth harp). This is the most professional Ainu production I've seen, and because the dances aren't the same as those performed at Poroto Kotan in Shiraoi (p. 588), this theater is highly recommended even if you've already been to Poroto Kotan. Thirty-minute shows are performed six times a day in summer (including evenings), less frequently in winter (at 8:30pm Dec to late Apr). Admission is ¥1,000 for adults, half-price for children. Near the theater is the **Seikatsu Kinenkan** (May–Oct, daily 10am–10pm), an Ainu home and outbuildings that display various Ainu utensils and crafts. Admission here is ¥300 for adults, ¥100 for children (skip it if you've been to Poroto Kotan).

ENJOYING THE OUTDOORS

BOATING   For Japanese visitors, one of the most popular activities in Akanko Onsen is a **boat cruise of Lake Akan,** which provides close-up views of the mountains, islands, and shoreline, all stunningly beautiful. Lake Akan is famous for its very rare spherical green algae, spongelike balls of duckweed called *marimo* that have been designated a Special Natural Monument. Found in only a few places in the world, marimo are formed when many separate and stringy pieces of algae at the bottom of the 43m-deep (144-ft.) lake roll around and eventually come together to form a ball, gradually growing larger and larger. It takes 150 to 200 years for marimo to grow to the size of a baseball; some in Lake Akan are as much as 29 centimeters (12 in.) in diameter—meaning they are very old indeed. Supposedly, when the sun shines, the marimo rise to the surface of the water, giving Lake Akan a wonderful green shimmer. The **Marimo Discovery Cruise** makes a 15-minute stop at Churui Islet to see the **Marimo Exhibition Center** with a few tanks of marimo. One-hour cruises operate from May to mid-November and cost ¥1,850 for adults and ¥960 for children, including the exhibition center. Boats depart every hour or so, with the last boat departing at 5pm in summer. If you want to see both the Marimo Exhibition Center and travel through more scenic narrow passages between islands and islets, there's a 35-minute **High Speed Cruise** by motorboat which costs ¥3,500. That being said, I hope you'll think twice about taking this cruise, as motorboats disturb the peace and quiet of this nature's wonderland (maybe the price alone will deter you).

CANOEING   To get a real feel for Akan Lake at duck and goose level, take a tour in a two-person Canadian canoe, available May to October. For beginners, a 45-minute trip costs ¥2,100 for adults and ¥1,600 for children. There's also a 90-minute Adventure Course for ¥5,300 for adults and ¥3,700 for children that goes farther afield, while the 2½-hour Yaitai island course includes a trip to uninhabited Yaitai island in the lake. You may see carp spawning, deer, or—if you are really lucky—bear. Make canoe reservations at the **Akan Nature Center** (© **0154/67-2801**), shown on the English-language map.

FISHING ★★   Lake Akan is one of Japan's most famous fishing lakes. In addition to kokanee salmon, said to have originated in the lake, sport fish include rainbow trout, steelhead trout, and white spotted char, a native fish. If you want to fish, contact **Fishing Land** (© **0154/67-2057**), located beside the New Akan Hotel Shangri-La. A fishing permit costs ¥1,500 per day and includes fishing in Akan River and Hiotan Pond, as well as the lake. A rental rod and lures cost ¥1,000. Add ¥3,000 if you want to be dropped off at a fishing spot by boat. Fly-fishing season is from May to the end of November, except from mid-July to mid-August when it's too hot. From January to March, you can ice fish.

HIKING TRAILS   Akanko Onsen's easiest walk begins and ends right in town. Start at the **Akankohan Eco Museum Center** at the east end of town, where to the left you'll find an easy, 30-minute footpath leading through a primeval forest of pines and ferns, past *bokke* (volcanic, bubbling mud), and along the lakeshore. It ends at the boat dock with cruises of Lake Akan (see above). If you want to make this an hour's hike, take the steps to the right of the Eco Museum Center leading uphill at the orange *torii* gate to the Inari Shinto Shrine and follow the path through woodlands along a ridge before descending to the lake and joining the path described above. Both paths are shown on the English-language pamphlet describing the Akankohan Eco Museum Center.

For more serious hiking, while out on your boat trip you'll see two cone-shaped volcanoes: **Mount Oakan (Oakandake)** to the east and **Mount Meakan (Meakandake)** to the south. Both are surrounded by virgin forests and are popular daylong destinations for hikers. **Mount Oakan** (called "male mountain" by the Ainu for its supposed manly features) is dormant, with a summit about a 4½-hour hike from Akanko Onsen. You can reach the trail entrance, Takiguchi, in 5 minutes via one of the buses going in the direction of Kushiro (get off at the Takiguchi stop). Plan about 6 hours for the ascent and descent. **Mount Meakan** (which the Ainu called "female mountain") is an active volcano, so check before you go. It's the highest mountain in the Akan area at 1,500m (4,900 ft.) above sea level and is covered with primeval forests of spruce and fir. There are three hiking trails up Mount Meakan. If you're hiking the entire distance, the trail access closest to Akanko is located at the west end of town, where you can follow the Furebetsu Woodland Road, a former transport road, to an old sulfur mine for 3 hours to get to the trail entrance, from which it's another 3 hours to the peak where you'll be rewarded with panoramic views of the surrounding area. Pick up English-language alpine guides with maps to Mount Oakan and Mount Meakan at the tourist association.

A shorter hike follows a trail to **Mount Hakuto-zan,** from which you also have a good view of the town and lake. It takes about 20 minutes to reach Akan's skiing area and another 50 minutes to reach Mount Hakuto-zan observatory, a grassy and moss-covered knobby hill that remains slightly warm throughout the year because of thermal activity just below the surface. The woods of birch and pine here are beautiful, and what's more, you'll probably find yourself all alone. Stop at the local tourist office for directions to the trail head and a map in Japanese.

WINTER ACTIVITIES   In winter, Lake Akan freezes over and becomes a playland for winter sports. **Cross-country skiing** (rental equipment ¥1,000 for 2 hr.), **ice-skating** (¥1,000 for 1 hr.), and **ice fishing** (¥1,500 a day) are popular. For downhill skiers, the **Lake Akan National Ski Area** (www.akan-ski.com; ℂ **0154/67-2881**) is blessed with a magnificent view of Mount Oakan rising behind Lake Akan. The F.I.S.-certified slalom course attracts ski teams and individuals in training, while the intermediate and beginner slopes are popular with less demanding skiers. A one-day lift pass costs ¥2,500; ski equipment rents for ¥4,000 per day.

During the **Lake Akan Ice Festival** (late January through early March), illuminated ice sculptures, traditional dance, fireworks over the frozen lake, and stalls selling food make for a fun midwinter festival. Contact the tourist office for more details.

Where to Eat

One local specialty to look for is *"yakitori-don,"* a rice bowl with local venison replacing the usual chicken.

Poronno (ポロンノ) AINU   For a different kind of lunch, head to the Ainu Kotan Village and look for a souvenir shop with a sign reading HANDMADE FOLKCRAFT & TRADITIONAL AINU FOODS. In the back you'll find five tables, a counter, and funky decor and music. The English-language menu lists *rataskepp,* (warm pumpkin with beans and corn); *pochie imo,* dense little pancakes of local potato; curry with venison and local vegetables; pumpkin cakes; and drinks such as *shikerebe* (cork bark tea). The Ainu *teishoku* set meal is rice with red beans and deer soup. I did not love the food, but I found it interesting to eat items gleaned from the natural surroundings.

Ainu Kotan Village, Akanko Onsen. ℂ **0154/67-2159.** Dishes ¥400–¥1,200; Ainu teishoku ¥850. No credit cards. Daily noon–11pm (noon–9:30pm winter).

Where to Stay

EXPENSIVE

Tsuruga Wings (formerly Yuku-no-Sato Tsuruga; 鶴賀ウィングス) ★★★ 🎁
Ainu patterns are the main motif throughout Akanko Onsen's largest property. But what makes it a standout are its beautiful and fantasy-provoking hot-spring baths in

the West Wing. One is designed as a village, spread on several levels and including a cavelike room and an outdoor bath beautifully landscaped with stones and pines overlooking the lake. Another includes a rooftop hot-spring bath with 360-degree panoramic views (the baths alternate for the sexes, so guests staying here can try both). Even if you don't stay here, you can visit the baths from noon to 5pm for ¥1,470. Additional baths in the East Wing are more traditional but have a spa zone.

The rest of the hotel, including well-appointed guest rooms, does not disappoint. Most rooms are Japanese style, the best (and most expensive) of which have lakeside views, large bathrooms (some with open-air tubs), bar areas for entertaining, and seating around an indoor hearth. There are also more than 50 combination rooms with *tatami* area and beds, as well as a floor called Rera ("wind" in Ainu) decorated with Ainu carvings. Meals can be served in your room, which you should specify the time of making your reservation, but most people opt for the buffet restaurant serving Japanese, Chinese, and Western fare that includes live music at dinnertime and would be right at home on a cruise ship.

4–6–10 Akanko Onsen, Akancho, Kushiro-shi 085-0467. www.tsuruga-g.com. ✆ **0154/67-2531.** Fax 0154/67-2754. 370 units. ¥16,950–¥39,375 per person, including 2 meals. Off-season discounts available. AE, DC, MC, V. Free pick-up or a 10-min. walk from the bus terminal; turn left out of the terminal, take the 1st right to the main street, and turn left. There are also free shuttle buses operating from Kushiro and Kitami stations and a ¥2,500 shuttle from Sapporo station (reservations required). **Amenities:** 4 restaurants; bars; lounge; indoor/outdoor hot-spring baths; Wi-Fi (free, in lobby). *In room:* A/C, TV, hair dryer, Internet (in some rooms), minibar or fridge.

INEXPENSIVE

Onsen Minshuku Kiri (温泉民宿桐)   Located above a souvenir shop on the main street (look for a wooden, roofed sign with black lettering on white), these simple accommodations include clean Japanese-style rooms in a variety of sizes and a small cypress hot-spring bath crafted by the owner. They're all connected by shiny wooden floors and walls with faux-wood wallpaper.

4–3–26 Akanko Onsen, Akancho, Kushiro-shi 085-0467. ✆ **0154/67-2755.** Fax 0154/67-2755. 7 units (none with bathroom). ¥3,500 per person. Breakfast from ¥500 extra. AE, DC, MC, V. A 9-min. walk from the bus terminal; turn left out of the terminal, take the 1st right to the main street, and turn left on the main street. **Amenities:** Indoor hot-spring bath. *In room:* TV, no phone.

Onsen Minshuku Yamaguchi (温泉民宿山口) 🔌   Taro-chan the mynah bird may be the first to greet you at this homey family-owned inn near Ainu Kotan Village. Its Japanese rooms are spacious for the price, and there's free coffee in the lounge. Neither the owners nor Taro-chan speak English, but there's a detailed folder in English of sights and activity suggestions. If you'd like the more expensive special dinner featuring local seafood, order it in advance, as the owners prepare only a limited number each night.

5-3-2 Akanko Onsen, Kushiro-shi 085-0467. www.goodinns.com/yamaguchi. ✆ **0154/67-2555.** Fax 0154/67-2506. 10 units (none with bathroom). ¥5,925 per person including two meals, ¥9,600 per person with the seafood dinner. No credit cards. A 10-min. walk from the bus terminal; turn left out of the terminal, take the 1st right down to the main street, and turn left. It's the two-story gray building past Tsuruga Wings and over the bridge. **Amenities:** Indoor hot-spring bath. *In room:* TV, no phone, Wi-Fi.

PLANNING YOUR TRIP TO JAPAN

14

Since the March 2011 earthquake and tsunami—and subsequent nuclear power-plant meltdown in Tohoku—the overriding concern for many visitors to Japan is how the disaster will impact their visit and whether radiation continues to be a threat. After all, coastal towns and villages were obliterated on that fateful day, and the 20km (12 mile) evacuation zone surrounding the Fukushima power plant remains a virtual ghost town. Otherwise, it's back to business as usual in all other areas of Japan, including areas of Tohoku, and some regions like southern Kyushu have even seen a surge in tourism. I, for one, had no qualms about spending a month in Tokyo two months after the Great East Japan Earthquake and traveling to the Tohoku region four months later. Radiation levels monitored on the ground and in the food system have been deemed safe in Tokyo and elsewhere; many foreign travelers who visited Japan after the 2011 disaster did so as a show of support and were warmly welcomed by innkeepers, shop owners, restaurant staff, and others who want the world to know that Japan is open for business. Of course, travel is a personal decision (chances of an earthquake measuring 7.3 in Tokyo Bay occurring in the next 3 decades stands at 70%, according to the Japanese government), and all travelers are responsible for keeping abreast of the latest developments that could affect their plans. If you're reading this, you've probably already decided that a trip to Japan lies in your future. This chapter provides the nuts and bolts of what you need to know (for information on radiation, see "Health," on page 624.

Probably two of the most common worries first-time visitors have about a trip to Japan are the language barrier and the high cost of living. To help alleviate fears about the first, I've provided a glossary of useful words and phrases (p. 639), given the Japanese characters for establishments that do not have English-language signs so you can recognize their names, outlined tips for dealing with the language barrier (see "Dealing with the Language Barrier", p. 30), given brief instructions on how to reach most of the places I recommend, made suggestions for ordering in restaurants without English-language menus, and provided prices for everything from subway rides to museums.

As for costs, probably everyone has heard horror stories about Japan's high prices. Ever since the dramatic fall of the dollar against the yen in the 1980s and 1990s, Tokyo and Osaka have been two of the world's most expensive cities, with food and lodging costing as much as in New York or London, maybe more. But after Japan's economic bubble burst in the early 1990s, something happened that would have been unthinkable during the heady spending days of the 1980s: Japanese became bargain conscious, ushering a new era of inexpensive French bistros, secondhand clothing stores, 100-yen shops, and budget hotels. Since the Great East Japan Earthquake, prices have fallen even further in an attempt to lure back foreign tourists.

Still, it's difficult not to suffer an initial shock from Japan's high prices, which will seem especially exorbitant if you insist on living and eating exactly as you do back home. The secret is to live and eat as Japanese do. This book will help you do exactly that, with descriptions of eateries and Japanese-style inns that cater to the native population. While you may never find Japan cheap, you will find it richly rewarding for all the reasons you chose Japan as a destination in the first place.

Furthermore, Japan remains one of the safest countries in the world; in general, you don't have to worry about muggers, pickpockets, or crooks. In fact, I sometimes feel downright coddled in Japan. Everything runs like clockwork: Trains are on time, and the service—whether in hotels, restaurants, or department stores—ranks among the best in the world. I know if I get truly lost, someone will help me and will probably even go out of his or her way to do so. Japanese are honest and extremely helpful toward foreign visitors. Indeed, it's the people themselves who make traveling in Japan such a delight.

GETTING THERE
By Plane

Japan has four international airports. Outside Tokyo is **Narita International Airport** (NRT; www.narita-airport.jp; ✆ **0476/34-8000**), where you'll want to land if your main business is in the capital, the surrounding region, or points north or east such as Hokkaido. Much closer to central Tokyo is Haneda Airport (HND; www. tokyo-airport-bldg.co.jp; ✆ **03/5757-8111**), which has long served as Tokyo's domestic airport but began accepting international flights in 2010. Most international flights, however, land at Narita.

Outside Osaka, **Kansai International Airport** (KIX; www.kansai-airport.or.jp; ✆ **072/455-2500**) is convenient if your destination is Osaka, Kobe, Nara, Kyoto, or western or southern Japan; it is also convenient for connecting to domestic air travel within Japan, since most domestic flights out of Tokyo depart from Haneda Airport, necessitating an airport transfer if you arrive at Narita International Airport. In between Narita and Kansai airports, outside Nagoya, is the **Central Japan International Airport** (NGO; www.centrair.jp/en; ✆ **0569/38-1195**), nicknamed Centrair, which offers the advantage of slick airport facilities (including hot-spring baths!) and easy access to Nagoya, the Shinkansen bullet train, Japan Alps, and beyond.

Because the flight to Tokyo is such a long one (about 11 hr. from Los Angeles, 12 hr. from Chicago or London, and 13 hr. from New York), you may wish to splurge for a roomier seat and upgraded service, including special counters for check-in, private

COPING WITH jet lag

A major consideration for visitors flying to Japan, especially on long flights from North America, is jet lag. Flying west has slightly less effect than flying east, which means you'll have a harder time recovering from your flight from Japan back to North America. Here are some tips for combating jet lag:

○ **Reset your watch** to your destination time before you board the plane.

○ **Drink lots of water** before, during, and after your flight. Avoid alcohol and caffeine.

○ **Exercise and sleep well** for a few days before your trip.

○ If you have trouble sleeping on planes, **fly eastward on morning flights.**

○ This is strictly personal, but I find that taking an over-the-counter **nighttime pain reliever** also helps me sleep onboard.

lounges at the airport, and better meals, though these come with a price. You should also consider a mileage program, because you'll earn lots of miles going to Japan.

Japan's major carriers are **Japan Airlines (JAL**; www.jal.com) and **All Nippon Airways (ANA**; www.ana.co.jp**).** Together they offer more international flights to Japan than any other airline. One advantage to flying with JAL or ANA to Japan is that you can purchase your Japan Rail Pass through them. More importantly, flying to Japan with JAL (or another Oneworld fare partner such as American Airlines) or ANA (or a Star Alliance member such as United Airlines) means you are then eligible for deep discounts on domestic flights within Japan. See "Getting Around," below, for more on rail passes and domestic flights.

By Ferry

Several cities in Japan are connected by ferry to China, Korea, and Russia, a viable option if you're on a budget and have time to spare. The **Shanghai Ferry Company** (www.shanghai-ferry.co.jp/english), for example, departs Shanghai every Tuesday at 11am and arrives in Osaka on Thursday at 9am. One-way fares range from ¥22,000 to ¥42,000, depending on the class of service. Other companies ply the waters between China and Kobe or Shimonoseki. From Korea, several companies offer service from Busan to Kyushu, with most boats docking in Fukuoka. Fastest is the daily **JR Kyushu Beetle** hydrofoil (www.jrbeetle.co.jp/english), which makes the journey in less than 3 hours and costs ¥14,500 one way. From June to about mid-September, **Heart Land Ferry** (www.heartlandferry.coj/english) makes runs from Sakhalin in Russia to Wakkanai on the northern tip of Hokkaido, with the 5½-hour trip starting at ¥25,000 one way in economy class.

GETTING AROUND

Japan has an extensive transport system, the most convenient segment of which is the nation's excellent rail service. You can also travel by plane (good for long-distance hauls but expensive unless you plan ahead), bus (the cheapest mode of travel), ferry, and car.

By Train

The most efficient way to travel around most of Japan is by train. Whether you're being whisked through the countryside aboard the famous Shinkansen bullet train or are winding your way up a wooded mountainside in an electric tram, trains in Japan are punctual, comfortable, safe, and clean. All trains except local commuters have washrooms and toilets. Bullet trains even have telephones and carts selling food and drinks. And because train stations are usually located in the heart of the city next to the city bus terminal or a subway station, arriving in a city by train is usually the most convenient method. Furthermore, most train stations in Japan's major cities and resort areas have tourist offices. The staff may not speak English, but they usually have maps or brochures in English and can point you in the direction of your hotel. Train stations also may have a counter where hotel reservations can be made free of charge. Most of Japan's passenger trains are run by six companies (such as JR East) that make up the **Japan Railways (JR) Group**, which together cover 20,000km (12,400 miles) and operate about 20,000 departures daily. There are also private regional companies, like **Kintetsu (Kinki Nippon Railway)** operating around Osaka, Kyoto, Nagoya, and Ise and **Odakyu Electric Railway** operating from Tokyo to Hakone.

SHINKANSEN (BULLET TRAIN) The Shinkansen is probably Japan's best-known train. With a front car that resembles a space rocket, the Shinkansen hurtles along at a maximum speed of 300kmph (187 mph) through the countryside on its own special tracks.

There are five basic Shinkansen routes in Japan, plus some offshoots. The most widely used line for tourists is the **Tokaido Shinkansen,** which runs from Tokyo and Shinagawa stations west to such cities as Nagoya, Kyoto, and Osaka. The **Sanyo Shinkansen** extends westward from Osaka through Kobe, Himeji, Okayama, and Hiroshima before reaching its final destination in Hakata/Fukuoka on the island of Kyushu. There are several types of trains that travel along this route. The *Nozomi Super Express* Shinkansen is the fastest and most frequent train and is the only one that covers the entire 1,179km (730 miles) between Tokyo and Hakata. Frustratingly, the *Nozomi* is not covered by the Japan Rail Pass (see "Japan Rail Pass," below). Instead, holders of the Japan Rail Pass must take the *Hikari*, which makes more stops than the Nozomi, or the *Kodama,* which stops at every station. Rail-pass travelers wishing to go the entire distance between Tokyo and Hakata must therefore take the Hikari or Kodama and transfer in Osaka or Okayama. Trains run so frequently—as often as four times an hour during peak times not including the *Nozomi*—that it's almost like catching the local subway. From Hakata, the newest train line, the **Kyushu Shinkansen,** runs from Hakata to Kagoshima in about 1½ hours; although the *Mizuho* is faster and runs between Osaka and Kagoshima, it's also not covered by

---

📎 TRAVEL TIP

To help you reach the hotels, restaurants, and sights recommended in this book, I've included the nearest train or subway station or bus or streetcar stop, followed in parentheses by the approximate number of minutes it takes to walk from the station or bus stop to your destination.

the Japan Rail Pass. The **Sakura Shinkansen**, however, covers the same distance in a little more than 4 hours.

The **Tohoku Shinkansen Line** runs north from Tokyo and Ueno stations to Sendai, Morioka, Kakunodate, Hachinohe, and Aomori (some trains require reservations), with branches extending to Shinjo and Akita. Future plans call for a new Hokkaido Shinkansen to extend from Aomori all the way to Sapporo; the stretch between Aomori and Hakodate is expected to open by 2015. The **Joetsu Shinkansen** connects Tokyo and Ueno stations with Niigata on the Japan Sea coast, while the **Nagano Shinkansen,** completed in time for the 1998 Winter Olympics, connects Tokyo and Ueno stations with Nagano in the Japan Alps.

Shinkansen running along these lines usually offer two or more kinds of service—trains that stop only at major cities (like the *Nozomi* on the Tokaido-Sanyo Line) and trains that make more stops and are therefore slightly slower. ***Note:*** If your destination is a smaller city on the Shinkansen line, make sure the train you take stops there. As a plus, each stop is announced in English through a loudspeaker and on a digital signboard in each car.

REGULAR SERVICE   In addition to bullet trains, there are also two types of long-distance trains that operate on regular tracks. The **limited-express trains,** or LEX *(Tokkyu),* branch off the Shinkansen system and are the fastest after the bullet trains, often traveling scenic routes, while the **express trains** *(Kyuko)* are slightly slower and make more stops. Slower still are **rapid express trains** *(Shin-Kaisoku)* and the even slower **rapid trains** *(Kaisoku).* To serve the everyday needs of Japan's commuting population, **local trains** *(Futsu)* stop at all stations.

For long distances, say, between Tokyo and Sapporo, JR operates overnight **sleeper trains** *(Shindai-sha),* which offer compartments and berths.

INFORMATION   For the most comprehensive site covering rail travel in Japan, go to **www.japanrailpass.net**, which provides links to the websites of all six JR Group companies and contains information on rail passes. For information on routes (including transfers), fares, and timetables for trains and planes in Japan, I use **www.hyperdia.com** and sometimes **www.jorudan.co.jp/english**.

In Japan, stop by the **Tourist Information Center** in downtown Tokyo or at the international airports in Narita or Osaka (see chapters 4 and 8 for locations and open hours) for the invaluable *Railway Timetable,* published in English and providing train schedules for the Shinkansen and limited express JR lines throughout Japan. To be on the safe side, I also stop by the train information desk or the tourist information desk as soon as I arrive in a city to check on train schedules onward to my next destination. Another good resource is the **JR East InfoLine** (www.jreast.co.jp/e; (📞 **050/2016-1603**), available daily 10am to 6pm to answer questions about train schedules, fares, how to buy tickets, and more.

TRAIN DISTANCES & TRAVELING TIME   Japan is much longer than most people imagine. Its four main islands, measured from the northeast to the southwest, cover roughly the distance from Boston to Atlanta. Thank goodness for the Shinkansen bullet train! In addition, transportation can be slow in mountainous regions, especially if you're on a local train.

The chart below measures rail distances and traveling times from Tokyo to principal Japanese cities. Traveling times do not include the time needed for transferring and are calculated for the fastest trains available, excluding the *Nozomi* and *Mizuho* Shinkansen trains because most tourists to Japan use the JR Rail Pass, which is not valid on either the *Nozomi* or the *Mizuho.*

Train Travel from Tokyo to Principal Cities

CITY	DISTANCE (MILES)	TRAVEL TIME
Beppu*	763	7 hr.
Fukuoka (Hakata Station)*	730	6 hr.
Hakodate*	549	6 hr. 10 min.
Hiroshima*	554	4 hr. 50 min.
Kagoshima*	912	7 hr. 40 min.
Kanazawa*	386	4 hr. 30 min.
Kobe (Shin-Kobe Station)	366	3 hr. 20 min.
Kumamoto*	804	9 hr.
Kyoto	319	2 hr. 36 min.
Matsue*	578	5 hr. 45 min.
Matsumoto	146	2 hr. 30 min.
Matsuyama*	589	7 hr.
Nagoya	227	1 hr. 55 min.
Narita Airport	49	1 hr.
Nikko	93	1 hr. 59 min.
Okayama	455	3 hr. 52 min.
Osaka (Shin-Osaka Station)	343	2 hr. 54 min.
Sapporo*	746	10 hr.
Takamatsu*	500	5 hr. 10 min.
Takayama*	331	4 hr.
Toba*	303	3 hr. 40 min.
Yokohama	18	30 min.

* Destination requires a change of trains.

TRAIN FARES & RESERVATIONS   Ticket prices are based on the type of train (Shinkansen bullet trains are the most expensive), the distance traveled, whether your seat is reserved, and the season, with slightly higher prices (usually a ¥200 surcharge) during peak seasons (Golden Week, July 21–Aug 31, Dec 25–Jan 10, and Mar 21–Apr 5) and a ¥200 discount during low season. Children (ages 6–11) pay half fare, while up to two children 5 and younger travel free if they do not require a separate seat. I've included train prices from Tokyo for many destinations covered in this book (see individual cities for more information). Unless stated otherwise, prices in this guide are for adults for **nonreserved seats** on the fastest train available during regular season (for unreserved seats, fares are the same for the Nozomi and slower Shinkansen like the Hikari). You can buy JR tickets and obtain information about JR trains traveling throughout Japan at any Japan Railways station (in Tokyo this includes major stations along the Yamanote Line, which loops around Tokyo). If you wish to purchase a ticket using a credit card, go to a Ticket Reservation Office (*Midori-no-madoguchi*) at any major JR station.

No matter which train you ride, be sure to hang onto your ticket—you'll be required to give it up at the end of your trip as you exit through the gate.

SEAT RESERVATIONS   You can reserve seats for the Shinkansen, as well as for limited-express and express trains (but not for slower rapid or local trains, which are on a first-come, first-served basis) at any major Japan Railways station in Japan. Reserved seats cost slightly more than unreserved seats (¥300–¥510 for the

Shinkansen and express trains). The larger stations have a special reservation counter called **Midori-no-madoguchi (Ticket Reservation Office)** or View Plaza (Travel Service Center), easily recognizable by their green signs with RESERVATION TICKETS written on them. If you're at a JR station with no special reservation office, you can reserve your seats at one of the regular ticket windows. You can also purchase and reserve seats at several travel agents, including the giant **Japan Travel Bureau (JTB),** which has offices all over Japan. Finally, **JR East** (serving the area around Tokyo and north through Tohoku) offers Internet reservation for its trains at http://jreast-shinkansen-reservation.eki-net.com; unfortunately, the reservation system does not apply to lines run by other JR companies, including the popular Tokaido/Sanyo Shinkansen to Kyoto and beyond.

It's a good idea to reserve your seats for your entire trip through Japan as soon as you know your itinerary if you'll be traveling during peak times; however, you can only reserve 1 month in advance. If it's not peak season, you'll probably be okay using a more flexible approach to traveling—all trains also have nonreserved cars that fill up on a first-come, first-seated basis. You can also reserve seats on the day of travel up to departure time. I rarely reserve a seat when it's not peak season, preferring instead the flexibility of being able to hop on the next available train (or, sometimes I reserve a seat just before boarding). In any case, nonreserved seats (*jiyuuseki*) are located in cars at the front or back of Shinkansen trains. To determine where you should stand to board the train, look for the platform display showing a diagram of the train cars and which ones are reserved and nonreserved. Then look for signs—either on digital boards overhead or written on the platform itself—that shows the location for each car. If you want to sit in the nonsmoking car of the Shinkansen bullet train, ask for the *kinensha,* though nowadays most trains are completely smoke free.

TIPS FOR SAVING MONEY If your ticket is for travel covering more than 100km (62 miles), you can make as many stopovers en route as you wish as long as you complete your trip within the period of the ticket's validity. Tickets for 100 to 200km (62–124 miles) are valid for 2 days, with 1 day added for each additional 200km (124 miles). Note, however, that stopovers are granted only for trips that are not between major urban areas, such as Tokyo, Yokohama, Osaka, Nagoya, Kyoto, Kobe, Hiroshima, Kitakyushyu, Fukuoka, Sendai, or Sapporo. Moreover, stopovers are not permitted when traveling by express and limited express. Ask about stopovers when purchasing your ticket.

You can also save money by purchasing a round-trip ticket for long distances. A round-trip ticket by train on distances exceeding 600km (373 miles) one-way costs 20% less than two one-way tickets.

If you don't qualify for a Japan Rail Pass (see below), the **Seishun 18 (Seishun ju-hachi kippu)** is a 5-day rail pass for ¥11,500 for travel anywhere in Japan as long as you use JR local and rapid trains (that is, no Shinkansen, limited express, or express trains), making it a good bet for day excursions in the countryside, albeit very slow ones (the trip from Tokyo to Kyoto would take 9 hr. and requires three or more changes of trains, compared to 2 hr. 20 min. on the Shinkansen). The biggest drawback, however, is that it's available only during Japan's three major school holidays: spring break (Mar 1–Apr 10); summer break (July 20–Sept 10); and winter break (Dec 10–Jan 10). You can use it on 5 consecutive days or on any 5 days within the school break period; people traveling together can share the five rides (for example, two people can travel for 2 days and one person can travel for 1 day). Tickets can be purchased at JR Ticket Reservation Offices (Midori-no-Madoguchi) and Travel View Centers.

You can save quite a bit by purchasing a rail pass, even if you only plan to travel a little. How economical is a Japan Rail Pass? If you were to buy a round-trip reserved-seat ticket on the Shinkansen from Tokyo to Kyoto, it would cost ¥26,440, which is almost as much as a week's ordinary rail pass. Thus, if you plan to see more than just Tokyo and Kyoto, it pays to use a rail pass, **which you must buy outside Japan** (some regional rail passes, however, described below, can be purchased in Japan if you're a tourist).

With a Rail Pass, you can make seat reservations for free, which otherwise costs up to ¥510 per ride on the Shinkansen. Another advantage to a rail pass is that it offers a 10% discount or more off room rates at more than 50 JR Hotel Group hotels, including the Hotel Granvia in Kyoto, Okayama, and Hiroshima; the JR Tower Hotel Nikko Sapporo; Nara Hotel; JR Kyushu Hotel Fukuoka; JR Kyushu Hotel Kumamoto; JR Kyushu Hotel Nagasaki; JR Kyushu Hotel Kagoshima; and ANA Hotel Clement Takamatsu. A Japan Rail Pass booklet, which comes with your purchase of a rail pass, lists member hotels (or go to www.jrhotelgroup.com). Note that regional rail passes, however, do not qualify for the hotel discount.

There are also regional tickets good for sightseeing. The **Hakone Free Pass,** for example, offered by Odakyu railways (www.odakyu.jp/english), includes round-trip transportation from Tokyo and unlimited travel in Hakone for a specific number of days. The **Hokkaido Round Tour Pass (Hokkaido Furii Pasu**; www.jrhokkaido.co.jp) valid for 7 days of JR train and bus travel in Hokkaido, costs ¥25,500, though some restrictions and blackout dates apply. If you qualify, the Japan Rail Pass, however, is a much better deal than these alternatives.

JAPAN RAIL PASS The Japan Rail Pass is without a doubt the most convenient and most economical way to travel around Japan. With the rail pass, you don't have to worry about buying individual tickets, and you can reserve your seats on all JR trains for free. The rail pass entitles you to unlimited travel on all JR train lines including the Shinkansen (except, regrettably, the *Mizuho* and *Nozomi Super Express*), as well as on most JR buses and the JR ferry to Miyajima.

There are several types of rail passes available; make your decision based on your length of stay in Japan and the cities you intend to visit. You might even find it best to combine several passes to cover your travels in Japan, such as a 1-week standard pass to journey around Honshu, plus a regional pass just for Kyushu. Online pass information is available at **www.japanrailpass.net**.

THE STANDARD PASS If you wish to travel throughout Japan, your best bet is to purchase the standard Japan Rail Pass. It's available for ordinary coach class and for the first-class Green Car and is available for travel lasting 7, 14, or 21 days. Rates for the ordinary pass (as of March 2012) are ¥28,300 for 7 days, ¥45,100 for 14 days, and ¥57,700 for 21 days. Rates for the Green Car are ¥37,800, ¥61,200, and ¥79,600 respectively. Children (ages 6–11) pay half fare. Personally, I have never traveled in the first-class Green Car in Japan and don't consider it necessary. However, during peak travel times (New Year's, Golden Week, and Obon in mid-Aug), you may find it easier to reserve a seat in the first-class Green Car, which you can get by paying a surcharge in addition to showing your ordinary pass.

BEFORE YOU LEAVE HOME   The standard Japan Rail Pass is available only to foreigners visiting Japan as tourists and *can be purchased only outside Japan*. It's available from most travel agents, including **Kintetsu International** (www.kintetsu.com; ✆800/422-3481) and **JTB USA** (www.jtbusa.com; ✆ 800/235-3523). If you're flying **Japan Airlines** (**JAL;** www.jal.com; ✆ 800/525-3663) or **All Nippon Airways** (**ANA;** www.ana.co.jp; ✆ 800/235-9262), you can also purchase a rail pass from them. A full list of authorized travel agents is available at **www.japanrailpass. net**.

Upon purchasing your pass, you'll be issued a voucher (called an **Exchange Order**), which you'll then exchange for the real pass after your arrival in Japan. Note that once you purchase your Exchange Order, you have 3 months until you must exchange it in Japan for the pass itself. When obtaining your actual pass, you must then specify the date you wish to start using the pass within a 1-month period.

ONCE YOU'VE ARRIVED   In Japan, you can exchange your voucher for a Japan Rail Pass at more than 40 JR stations that have Japan Rail Pass exchange offices, at which time you must present your passport and specify the date you wish to begin using the pass; most offices are open daily from 10am to 6 or 7pm, some even longer.

At both Narita Airport (daily 6:30am–9:45pm) and Kansai International Airport (daily 5:30am–11pm), you can pick up Japan Rail Passes at either the Travel Service Center or the Ticket Office. Other Travel Service Centers or Ticket Offices, all located in JR train stations, include those at Tokyo (daily 7:30am–8:30pm), Ueno, Shinjuku, Ikebukuro, Shibuya, and Shinagawa stations in Tokyo; Kyoto Station; Shin-Osaka and Osaka stations; and Sapporo, Hakodate, Nagoya, Kanazawa, Okayama, Matsue, Hiroshima, Takamatsu, Matsuyama, Hakata, Nagasaki, Kumamoto, and Kagoshima Chuo stations. Stations and their open hours are listed in a pamphlet you'll receive with your voucher.

REGIONAL PASSES FOR FOREIGN VISITORS   In addition to the standard Japan Rail Pass above, there are regional JR rail passes available for ordinary coach class that are convenient for travel in eastern or western Honshu, Kyushu, or Hokkaido. They can be purchased before arriving in Japan from the same vendors that sell the standard pass. All but the Kintetsu Rail Pass can also be purchased inside Japan, usually only within the area covered by the pass but also at Narita airport for some passes. These regional passes are available only to foreign visitors and require that you present your passport to verify your status as a "temporary visitor"; you may also be asked to show your plane ticket. Only one pass per region per visit to Japan is allowed.

In the Tokyo area, the **JR Kanto Area Pass** (www.jreast.co.jp) is a 3-day pass for ¥8,000 that allows you travel on JR trains, including Shinkansen bullet trains traveling north from Tokyo, as far away as Utsunomiya (useful for trips to Nikko), Karuizawa, Mt. Fuji, Izu Peninsula, Narita (including the airport), and other areas.

If you're arriving by plane at the Kansai Airport outside Osaka and intend to remain in western Honshu, you may opt for one of two different **JR-West Passes** (www. westjr.co.jp/english), available at Kansai Airport, Osaka JR station, Kyoto Station, and other locations, as well as online. The **Kansai Area Pass,** which can be used for travel between Osaka, Kyoto, Kobe, Nara, Himeji, and other destinations in the Kansai area, is available as a 1-day pass for ¥2,000, 2-day pass for ¥4,000, 3-day pass for ¥5,000, or 4-day pass for ¥6,000. Travel is restricted to JR rapid and local trains, as well as unreserved seating in the Kansai Airport Express Haruka operating between Kansai Airport, Shin-Osaka, and Kyoto (that is, Shinkansen are not included in the pass). The other JR-West Pass available is the **Sanyo Area Pass,** which covers a larger area, allows travel via Shinkansen (including the superfast *Nozomi* and *Mizuho*) and JR local trains from Osaka as far as Hakata (in the city of Fukuoka on Kyushu), and includes Hiroshima, Okayama, Kurashiki, Himeji, and Kobe. It's available for 4 days for ¥20,000 and for 8 days for ¥30,000. Children 6 to 11 years of age pay half-price for all passes; up to two children 5 years old and younger can travel free with a paying adult.

There are also a couple other non-JR passes available for Kansai. The **Kansai Thru Pass** (www.surutto.com) is valid on city subways, private railways (*not* JR trains), and buses throughout the Kansai area, including Kansai Airport, Osaka, Kyoto, Nara, Himeji, and Mount Koya, and provides slight discounts to hundreds of tourist facilities (usually ¥100 or 10%). Available only to tourists, it costs ¥3,800 for a 2-day pass and ¥5,000 for 3 days and is sold at Kansai International Airport, Tourist Information Centers in Osaka and Nara, and the Kyoto Station Bus Information Center. Or, if you plan to spend a few days traveling farther afield between Nagoya, Osaka, Kyoto, Nara, and Ise-Shima, you can save money by purchasing a **Kintetsu Rail Pass** (www.kintetsu.co.jp), which covers travel throughout the region on Kintetsu's private lines. Available only for foreigners, it must be purchased before arriving in Japan at Kintetsu offices or authorized travel agencies. It costs ¥3,700 and includes 5 days of unlimited travel (but only 3 trips on limited express trains). For ¥5,700, you can purchase the Kintetsu Rail Pass Wide, which adds roundtrip travel from Centrair or Kansai Airport, Mie Kotsu buses, and discount coupons for sightseeing spots.

Though not as popular as western Honshu, eastern Honshu also offers its own **JR-East Pass** (www.jreast.co.jp), which includes travel from Tokyo to Nagano in the Japan Alps and throughout the Tohoku District, including Sendai, Kakunodate, and Aomori via Shinkansen and local JR lines. Passes for travel in ordinary coach cars are available for 5 days for ¥20,000 and 10 days for ¥32,000; a 4-day flexible pass (valid for any 4 consecutive or nonconsecutive days within a month) costs ¥20,000. Discounts are provided for children and youths up to 25 years of age. Passes are available online and at Narita airport, JR stations in Tokyo (including Tokyo, Shinagawa, and Shinjuku), and several JR stations in Tohoku, including Sendai, Shin-Aomori, and Nagano.

If your travels are limited to the island of Kyushu, consider the **JR-Kyushu Rail Pass** (www.jrkyushu.co.jp), valid for 3 days for ¥14,000 and 5 days for ¥17,000 (¥7,000 and ¥9,000, respectively, for passes for northern Kyushu only). Passes include rides on the Kyushu Shinkansen and are available for purchase at Hakata, Nagasaki, Kumamoto, and Beppu JR stations, among others. Likewise, there's a **Hokkaido Rail Pass** (www.jrhokkaido.co.jp), valid for 3 days of travel (including some JR buses) for ¥15,000, 5 days (or 4 flexible days within a 10-day period) for ¥19,500, and 7 days for ¥22,000. It's sold at Narita Airport and Hakodate, Sapporo, and Kushiro JR stations.

By Plane

Because it takes the better part of a day and night to travel by train from Tokyo down to southern Kyushu or up to northern Hokkaido, you may find it faster—not to mention cheaper if you buy your ticket in advance (see below)—to fly at least one stretch of your journey in Japan. You could, for example, fly internationally into Osaka and then onward to Fukuoka on Kyushu, from where you can take a leisurely 2 weeks to travel by train through Kyushu and Honshu before returning to Osaka. I don't, however, advise flying short distances—say, from Tokyo to Osaka—because the time spent getting to and from airports can be longer than the time spent traveling by Shinkansen.

Almost all domestic flights from Tokyo leave from the much more conveniently located **Haneda Airport.** If you're already in Tokyo, you can easily reach Haneda Airport via Airport Limousine Bus, monorail from Hamamatsucho Station on the Yamanote Line, or the Keikyu Line from Shinagawa. If you're arriving on an international flight at Narita Airport, therefore, make sure you know whether a connection to a domestic flight is at Narita or requires a transfer to Haneda Airport via the Airport Limousine Bus (see chapter 4 for details).

Two major domestic airlines are **Japan Airlines** (**JAL;** www.jal.co.jp; ✆ **0570/025-071** in Japan) and **All Nippon Airways** (**ANA;** www.ana.co.jp; ✆ **0570/029-709** in Japan). Regular fares with these two companies are generally the same no matter which airline you fly domestically and are more expensive for peak season including New Year's, Golden Week, and summer vacation. However, bargains do exist. Some flights early in the day or late at night may be cheaper than flights during peak time; there are also discounts for seniors 65 and over. Your best bet on snagging a discount, however, is to purchase your ticket in advance. ANA's *Tabiwari* and JAL's *Sakitoku* are discount fares on reservations made 28 days in advance, while the Super Tabiwari and Super Saitoku give deep discounts on tickets purchased 45 days in advance. Regular one-way fares from Tokyo to Naha, Okinawa, for example, are ¥40,800 but go as low as ¥13,800 for a Super Tabiwari or Super Saitoku on selected flights. There are also slight discounts on tickets booked 3 days before departure and on round-trip fares.

Otherwise, there are small regional airlines that generally offer fares that are cheaper than the standard full fare charged by JAL or ANA. These include **Skymark** (www.skymark.co.jp; ✆ **050/3116-7370**), operating out of Fukuoka; **Solaseed Air** (www.skynetasia.co.jp; ✆ **0570/037-283**), connecting Nagasaki, Kumamoto, and Kagoshima with Tokyo and Okinawa; **Air Do** (✆ **0120/057-333**), out of Sapporo; and **Jetstar Japan,** owned by JAL, the Qantas Group, and Mitsubishi and offering domestic flights out of Narita and Kansai airports beginning in 2012.

Tickets can be purchased directly through the airline or at a travel agent such as **Japan Travel Bureau (JTB),** which has offices virtually everywhere in Japan.

SPECIAL DOMESTIC FARES FOR FOREIGNERS Purchasing domestic tickets in advance in connection with your international flight is by far the most economical way to go. JAL's "oneworld Yokoso/Visit Japan Fare" ticket, purchased in conjunction with a flight to Japan with JAL or one of its Oneworld fare partners (such as American Airlines) and sold only outside Japan, provides discount fares of ¥10,000 per flight for domestic travel to more than 30 cities in Japan served by JAL and its subsidiary Japan Transocean Air (JTA, based in Okinawa).

Visitors flying other airlines into Japan can take advantage of JAL's "Welcome to Japan Fare," which provides discounts on JAL's domestic flights regardless of which international airline is used to reach Japan. Also sold only outside Japan, this costs ¥13,000 per flight, with a minimum of two flights required.

ANA offers a similar program, with its Star Alliance Japan Airpass ticket costing ¥10,000 per flight if you fly ANA or one of its Star Alliance partners such as United Airlines; if you fly another airline, its Visit Japan Fare is ¥13,000 per ticket, with a minimum of two flights required.

Note that fares exclude airport taxes and booking fees and that there are blackout dates for all these fares, mostly in mid-March, during summer vacation (mid-July through Aug), and New Year's, though oneworld Yokoso/Visit Japan Fare and Japan Airpass tickets are less stringent. You should first purchase your international ticket and then contact JAL or ANA to purchase and book your Japan domestic tickets (oneworld Yokoso/Visit Japan Fare can also be booked online).

If you plan to visit at least two Okinawan islands in addition to Okinawa Island, you can save money by purchasing an Okinawa Island Pass, valid on five specific routes within the Okinawan island chain, including flights from Naha to Kume or Ishigaki, on Japan Transocean Air (a subsidiary of JAL). A minimum of two flights, at ¥9,000 each, is required, and tickets must be purchased from JAL before arriving in Japan. For more information, including blackout dates, contact your nearest JAL office.

Solaseed Air also offers Visit Japan fares for foreign visitors on limited routes: between Tokyo's Haneda Airport and Miyazaki, Kumamoto, Nagasaki, Kagoshima and Oita; and between Naha (Okinawa) and Miyazaki, Kumamoto, Nagasaki and Kagoshima. Fares are just ¥10,000 and can be purchased in Japan at Solaseed Air airport ticketing counters, but note that they are for stand-by seating only.

By Bus

Buses often go where trains don't and thus may be the only way for you to get to the more remote areas of Japan, such as Shirakawa-go in the Japan Alps. In Hokkaido, Tohoku, Kyushu, and other places, buses are used extensively.

Some intercity buses require you to make reservations or purchase your ticket in advance at the ticket counter at the bus terminal. For others (especially local buses), when you board a bus you'll generally find a ticket machine by the entry door. Take a ticket, which is number-coded with a digital board displayed at the front of the bus. The board shows the various fares, which increase with the distance traveled. You pay when you get off.

In addition to serving the remote areas of the country, **long-distance buses** (called *chokyori basu*) also operate between major cities in Japan and offer the cheapest mode of transportation. Although **Japan Railways** (www.jrbuskanto.co.jp) operates almost a dozen bus routes eligible for JR Rail Pass coverage, the majority of buses are run by private companies (some of which do not have English-language websites). The **Nihon Bus Association** (www.bus.or.jp) is comprised of bus companies throughout Japan and is a good place to start when researching fares. Willer Express (http://willerexpress.com) offers service from Sendai, Tokyo, Nagoya, Kanazawa, Kyoto, Osaka, Matsuyama, Hiroshima, and Fukuoka. Some long-distance buses travel during the night and offer reclining seats and toilets, thus saving passengers the price of a night's lodging; double decker buses may even have salons or bars on the first floor. Long-distance buses departing from Tokyo, for example, cost ¥3,000 to ¥9,400 for Kyoto, depending on the company, time of day (weekdays are generally cheaper), and season. Long-distance bus tickets can be purchased at View Plazas at major JR stations (for JR buses), at travel agencies such as JTB, or at bus terminals.

For more information on local and long-distance buses, refer to individual cities covered in this guide, contact the **Tourist Information Center** in Tokyo (see "Visitor Information" on p. 636) or the local tourist office, or check the websites above.

By Car

With the exception, perhaps, of Izu Peninsula, the Tohoku region, Hokkaido, and Okinawa, driving is not recommended for visitors wishing to tour Japan. Driving is British style (on the left side of the road), which may be hard for those not used to it;

traffic can be horrendous; and driving isn't even economical. Not only is gas expensive, but all of Japan's expressways charge high tolls—the one-way toll from Tokyo to Kyoto is almost the same price as a ticket to Kyoto on the Shinkansen. And whereas the Shinkansen takes only 3 hours to get to Kyoto, driving can take about 8 hours. In addition, you may encounter few signs in English in remote areas. Driving in cities is even worse: Streets are often hardly wide enough for a rickshaw, let alone a car, and many roads don't have sidewalks so you have to dodge people, bicycles, and telephone poles. Free parking is hard to find, and garages are expensive. Except in remote areas, it just doesn't make sense to drive.

If you're undeterred, a good roundup of more than 800 car-rental agencies in Japan, including those located at airports and train stations and those with GPS voice guidance in English, is provided at **www2.tocoo.jp**, where you can make reservations, see pictures and descriptions of rental cars, and review your knowledge of international traffic signs. Otherwise, major car-rental companies in Japan include **Toyota Rent-A-Car** (www.rent.toyota.co.jp; ✆ **0800/7000-815** toll-free); **Nippon Rent-A-Car Service** (www.nipponrentacar.co.jp; ✆ **03/3485-7196** for the English Service Desk), **Nissan Rent-A-Car** (✆ **0120/00-4123** toll-free), and **Avis** (www.avis-japan.com; ✆ **0120/31-1911** toll-free). In Hokkaido, Kyushu, and some other areas, there is also **JR Eki Rent-A-Car,** located beside JR train stations and offering 20% discounts on train fares booked in conjunction with car rentals; you can reserve these cars at any JR Travel Service Center (located in train stations) anywhere in Japan.

Rates vary, but the average cost for 24 hours with unlimited mileage is about ¥10,500 for a subcompact including insurance but not gas; in some tourist areas, such as Hokkaido, rates are more expensive in peak season.

If you do intend to drive in Japan, you'll need either an **international** or a **Japanese driving license.** Remember, cars are driven on the left side of the road, and signs on all major highways are written in both Japanese and English, though some rental companies offer GPS with English voice guidance. It is against the law to drink alcohol and drive, all passengers must wear seat belts, and it's prohibited to use a mobile phone while driving. Be sure to purchase a bilingual map, as back roads often have names of towns written in Japanese only. Recommended is the *Shobunsha Road Atlas Japan,* available in bookstores that sell English-language books; it also contains maps of major cities, including Tokyo, Sapporo, Hiroshima, and others.

BREAKDOWNS & ASSISTANCE   The **Japan Automobile Federation (JAF;** www.jaf.or.jp) is one of several road service providers maintaining emergency telephone boxes along Japan's major arteries to assist drivers whose cars have broken down or drivers who need help. Calls from these telephones are free and will connect you to JAF's operation center at your request. English is spoken.

By Ferry

Because Japan is an island nation, an extensive ferry network links the string of islands. Although travel by ferry takes longer, it's also cheaper and can be a pleasant, relaxing experience. For example, you can take a ferry from Osaka to Beppu (on Kyushu), with fares starting at ¥9,600 for the 12-hour trip. Unfortunately, information in English is hard to come by. Contact the **Tourist Information Center** (see "Visitor Information" in chapter 4) for details concerning routes, prices, schedules, and telephone numbers of the various ferry companies.

TIPS ON ACCOMMODATIONS

Accommodations available in Japan range from Japanese-style inns to large Western-style hotels, in all price categories. Although you can travel throughout Japan without making reservations beforehand, it's essential to book in advance if you're traveling during peak travel seasons and is recommended at other times (see "When to Go," p. 46, for peak travel times). If you arrive in a town without reservations, most local tourist offices—generally located in or near the main train station—will find accommodations for you at no extra charge. Note that in popular resort areas, most accommodations raise their rates during peak times. Some also charge more on weekends.

A *note on reservations:* When making reservations at Japanese-style accommodations and small business hotels, it's usually best if the call is conducted in Japanese or by e-mail if available, as written English is always easier for most Japanese to understand. First-class hotels, however, always have English-speaking staff, as do many of the less expensive hotels and Japanese inns recommended in this guide.

A *note about taxes and service charges:* A 5% consumption tax is included in all hotel rates, including those given in this book. Furthermore, upper-end hotels and some moderately priced hotels also add a 10% to 15% service charge to their published rates, while expensive *ryokan* will add a 10% to 20% service charge. No service charge is levied at business hotels, pensions, and *minshuku* (accommodations in a private home) for the simple reason that no services are provided. In resort areas with hot-spring spas, an *onsen* (spa) tax of ¥150 is added per night. Tokyo levies its own local hotel tax (¥100–¥200 per person per night). Unless otherwise stated, the prices given in this guide include all consumption taxes and service charge, but not onsen or local hotel tax.

Japanese-Style Inns

Although an overnight stay in a *ryokan* (traditional Japanese inn) can be astoundingly expensive, it's worth the splurge at least once during your stay. Nothing quite conveys the simplicity and beauty—indeed the very atmosphere—of old Japan more than these inns with their gleaming polished wood, *tatami* floors, rice-paper sliding doors, and meticulously pruned gardens. Personalized service by kimono-clad hostesses and exquisitely prepared *kaiseki* meals are the trademarks of such inns, some of which are of ancient vintage. Indeed, staying in one is like taking a trip back in time.

If you want to experience a Japanese-style inn but can't afford the prices of a full-service ryokan, a number of alternatives are described below. Although they don't offer the same personalized service, beautiful setting, or memorable cuisine, they do offer the chance to sleep on a futon in a simple tatami room and, in some cases, eat Japanese meals.

RYOKAN Ryokan developed during the Edo Period, when *daimyo* (feudal lords) were required to travel to and from Edo (present-day Tokyo) every 2 years. They always traveled with a full entourage including members of their family, retainers, and servants. The best ryokan, of course, were reserved for the daimyo and members of the imperial family. Some of these exist today, passed down from generation to generation.

Traditionally, ryokan are small, only one or two stories high, contain about 10 to 30 rooms, and are made of wood with a tile roof. Most guests arrive at their ryokan around 3 or 4pm. The entrance is often through a gate and small garden; upon

The proper way to wear a yukata is to first fold the right side over your body and then wrap over it with the left side on the outside; the opposite is done only when a person has died.

entering, you're met by a bowing woman in a kimono. Take off your shoes, slide on the proffered plastic slippers, and follow your hostess down the long wooden corridors until you reach the sliding door of your room. After taking off your slippers, step into your tatami room, almost void of furniture except for a low table in the middle of the room, floor cushions, an antique scroll hanging in a *tokonoma* (alcove), and a simple flower arrangement. Best of all is the view past rice-paper sliding screens of a Japanese landscaped garden with bonsai, stone lanterns, and a meandering pond filled with carp. Notice there's no bed in the room.

Almost immediately, your hostess serves you welcoming hot tea and a sweet at your low table so you can sit there for a while, recuperate from your travels, and appreciate the view, the peace, and the solitude. Next comes your hot bath, either in your own room or in the communal bath. Because many ryokan are clustered around onsen, many offer the additional luxury of bathing in thermal baths, including outdoor baths. (For bathing, be sure to follow the procedure outlined in "Minding Your P's & Q's" in chapter 2—soaping and rinsing *before* getting into the tub.) After bathing and soaking away all travel fatigue, aches, and pains, change into your *yukata,* a cotton kimono provided by the ryokan. You can wear your yukata throughout the ryokan, even to its restaurant (in Western-style hotels, however, never wear a yukata outside your room unless you're going to its public bath, or it's in a resort onsen setting like the Suginoi Hotel in Beppu).

When you return to your room, you'll find the maid ready to serve your *kaiseki* dinner, an elaborate spread that is the highlight of a ryokan stay. It generally consists of locally grown vegetables, sashimi (raw fish), grilled or baked fish, tempura, and various regional specialties, all spread out on many tiny plates; the menu is determined by the chef. Admire how each dish is in itself a delicate piece of artwork; it all looks too wonderful to eat, but finally hunger takes over. If you want, you can order sake or beer to accompany your meal (but you'll pay extra for drinks).

After you've finished eating, your maid will return to clear away the dishes and to lay out your bed. The bed is really a futon, a kind of two-layered mattress with quilts, and is laid out on the tatami floor. The next morning, the maid will wake you, put away the futon, and serve a breakfast of fish, pickled vegetables, soup, dried seaweed, rice, and other dishes. Feeling rested, well fed, and pampered, you're then ready to pack your bags and pay your bill. Your hostess sees you off at the front gate, smiling and bowing as you set off for the rest of your travels.

Such is life at a good ryokan. Sadly, the number of upper-class ryokan diminishes each year. Unable to compete with more profitable high-rise hotels, many ryokan in Japan have closed down, especially in large cities; very few remain in such cities as Tokyo and Osaka. If you want to stay in a Japanese inn, it's best to do so in Kyoto, smaller towns like Takayama, or at a hot-spring spa.

In addition, although ideally a ryokan is an old wooden structure that once served traveling daimyo or was perhaps the home of a wealthy merchant, many today—especially those in hot-spring resort areas—are actually modern concrete affairs with as many as 100 or more rooms, with meals served in communal dining rooms. What they lack in intimacy and personal service, however, is made up for with cheaper prices and such amenities as modern bathing facilities and perhaps a bar and outdoor recreational facilities. Most guest rooms are fitted with a TV, a telephone, a safe for locking up valuables, and a cotton yukata, as well as such amenities as soap, shampoo, a razor, a toothbrush, and toothpaste.

Rates in a ryokan are always per person rather than per room and include breakfast, dinner, and often service and tax. Thus, while rates may seem high, they're actually competitively priced compared to what you'd pay for a hotel room and comparable meals in a restaurant. Although rates can vary from ¥9,000 to an astonishing ¥150,000 per person, the average cost is generally ¥12,000 to ¥20,000. Even within a single ryokan the rates can vary greatly, depending on the room you choose, the dinner courses you select, and the number of people in your room. If you're paying the highest rate, you can be certain you're getting the best room, the best view of the garden or perhaps even your own private garden with an outdoor bath, and a much more elaborate meal than lower-paying guests. All the rates for ryokan in this book are based on double occupancy; if there are more than two of you in one room, you can generally count on a slightly lower per-person rate; small children who sleep in the same bed as their parents often receive a discount as well. Although most Japanese would never dream of checking into an exclusive ryokan solo, lone travelers may be able to secure a room if it's not peak season.

Although I heartily recommend you try spending at least 1 night in a ryokan, there are a number of **disadvantages** to this style of accommodations. The most obvious problem is that you may find it uncomfortable sitting on the floor. And because the futon is put away during the day, there's no place to lie down for an afternoon nap or rest, except on the hard, tatami-covered floor. In addition, some of the older ryokan, though quaint, can be cold in the winter and—though increasingly rare—may have only Japanese-style toilets (see "Toilets" on p. 636). As for breakfast, you might find it difficult to swallow raw egg, rice, and seaweed in the morning. (I've even been served grilled grasshopper—quite crunchy.) Sometimes you can get a Western-style breakfast if you order it the night before, but more often than not the fried or scrambled eggs will arrive cold, leading you to suspect they were cooked right after you ordered them.

A ryokan is also quite rigid in its **schedule.** You're expected to arrive sometime between 3 and 5pm, take your bath, and then eat at around 6 or 7pm. Breakfast is served early, usually by 8am, and checkout is by 10am. That means you can't sleep in, and because the maid is continually coming in and out, you have a lot less privacy than you would in a hotel.

You should always make a **reservation** if you want to stay in a first-class ryokan (and even in most medium-priced ones), because the chef has to shop for and prepare your meals. Ryokan staff members often do not look kindly upon unannounced strangers turning up on their doorstep (though I did this on a weekday trip to Nikko without any problems at all). You can make a reservation for a ryokan through any travel agency in Japan or by contacting a ryokan directly. You may be required to pay a deposit. For more information on ryokan in Japan, including destinations not covered in this guide, pick up the *Japan Ryokan Guide* at one of the Tourist Information Centers in Japan, which lists some 1,200 members of the **Japan Ryokan Association** (www.ryokan.or.jp; ✆ **03/3231-5310**). Another useful resource is **Japanese Guest Houses** (www.japaneseguesthouses.com), with more than 600 member high-end and moderately priced Japanese inns.

JAPANESE INN GROUP　If you want the experience of staying in a Japanese-style room but cannot afford the extravagance of a ryokan, you might consider staying in one of the participating members of the Japanese Inn Group—an organization of more than 80 Japanese-style inns and hotels throughout Japan offering inexpensive lodging and catering largely to foreigners. Although you may balk at the idea of staying at a place filled mainly with foreigners, keep in mind that some inexpensive Japanese-style inns are not accustomed to guests from abroad and may be reluctant to take you in. I have covered many Japanese Inn Group members in this book over the years and have found the owners for the most part to be an exceptional group of friendly people eager to offer foreigners the chance to experience life on tatami and futons. In many cases, these are good places in which to exchange information with other world travelers and are popular with both young people and families.

Although many of the group members call themselves ryokan, they are not ryokan in the true sense of the word, because they do not offer the trademark personalized service and only rarely the beautiful setting common to ryokan. However, they do offer simple tatami rooms that generally come with TVs and air conditioners; most have towels and cotton yukata. Some offer Western-style rooms as well, and/or rooms with private bathrooms. Facilities generally include a coin-operated washer and dryer, a public bath, and sometimes a computer for checking e-mail. The average cost of a 1-night stay is about ¥5,000 to ¥6,000 per person, without meals. Breakfast is usually available if you pay extra; dinner is also sometimes available.

You can view member inns at **www.japaneseinngroup.com**. Or, upon your arrival in Tokyo, head to the Tourist Information Center for the free pamphlet called *Japanese Inn Group*. Make reservations directly with the inn in which you wish to stay (most have faxes and e-mail). In some cases, you'll be asked to pay a deposit (most accept American Express, MasterCard, and Visa).

MINSHUKU　Technically, a *minshuku* is inexpensive Japanese-style lodging in a private home—the Japanese version of a bed-and-breakfast. Usually located in tourist areas, rural settings, or small towns, minshuku can range from thatched farmhouses and rickety old wooden buildings to modern concrete structures. Because minshuku are family-run affairs, there's no personal service, which means you may be expected to lay out your own futon at night, stow it away in the morning, and tidy up your room. Most also do not supply a towel or *yukata,* nor do they have rooms with a private bathroom. There is, however, a public bathroom, and meals, included in the rates, are served in a communal dining room. Because minshuku cater primarily to domestic travelers, they're often excellent places to meet Japanese. Keep in mind, however, that many minshuku owners have day jobs, so it's important for guests to be punctual for meals and checkout.

Officially, what differentiates a ryokan from a minshuku is the level of service and corresponding price, but the differences are sometimes very slight. I've stayed in cheap ryokan providing almost no service and in minshuku too large and modern to be considered private homes. The average per-person cost for 1 night in a minshuku, including two meals, is generally ¥7,000 to ¥9,000 with two meals; most do not accept credit cards.

Reservations for minshuku should be made directly with the establishment. Or, contact the **Minshuku**

Roller Bag Etiquette

I love my roller bag, but under no circumstances should you roll a bag on tatami or on old wooden floors of Japanese inns.

Tips on Accommodations

PLANNING YOUR TRIP TO JAPAN

Network Japan (www.minshuku.jp; ☎ **0120/07-6556**) for a reservation in one of its 3,000 members throughout Japan.

KOKUMIN SHUKUSHA & QKAMURA A *kokumin shukusha* can be translated as a people's lodge—public lodging found primarily in or around national parks and resort and vacation areas. Established by the government (though some are privately managed), there are more than 300 of these facilities throughout Japan. Catering largely to Japanese school groups and families, they offer basic, Japanese-style rooms at an average daily rate of about ¥8,000 to ¥9,000 per person, including two meals. Because they're usually full during the summer, peak seasons, holidays, and weekends, reservations are a must and can be made directly at the facility or through a travel agency. There are also 36 National Park Resort Villages (nicknamed Qkamura; www.qkamura.or.jp) located exclusively in national parks and popular with families. The drawback for many of these lodges is that because they're often located in national parks and scenic spots, the best way to reach them is by car.

SHUKUBO These are lodgings in a Buddhist temple, similar to inexpensive ryokan, except they're attached to temples and serve vegetarian food. There's usually an early morning service at 6am, which you're welcome—in some *shukubo*, required—to join. Probably the best place to experience life in a temple is at Mount Koya (see chapter 8). Prices at shukubo generally range from about ¥7,000 to ¥15,000 per person, including two meals.

Western-Style Accommodations

Western-style lodgings range from luxurious first-class hotels to inexpensive ones catering primarily to Japanese business travelers.

When selecting and reserving your hotel room, contact the hotel directly to inquire about rates, even if a North American toll-free 800 number is provided; sometimes there are special deals, such as weekend or honeymoon packages, that central reservation desks are not aware of. It's a must, too, to check the hotel's website, where there's often discounted rates or packages. In any case, always check to see what kinds of rooms are available. Almost all hotels in Japan offer a wide range of rooms at various prices, with room size the overwhelming factor in pricing. Other aspects that often have a bearing on rates include bed size, floor height (higher floors are more expensive), and in-room amenities. Rooms with views—whether of the sea or a castle or even of cityscapes—are also generally more expensive. In Japan, a **twin room** refers to a room with twin beds, and a **double room** refers to one with a double (or larger) bed; most hotels charge more for a twin room, but others charge more for doubles. Because Japanese couples generally prefer twin beds, doubles are often in short supply, especially in business hotels. A **Hollywood twin** means two twin beds pushed together side by side. ***Note:*** For the sake of convenience, the "double" rates for hotels listed in this book refer to two people in one room and include both twin and double beds.

Some of the upper-priced hotels also offer executive floors, which are generally on the highest floors and may offer such perks as a private lounge with separate check-in, more in-room amenities, complimentary breakfast and evening cocktails, extended checkout time, and privileges that can include free use of the health club. At just a few thousand yen more than regular rates, these can be quite economical.

When making your reservation, therefore, check the hotel website or inquire about the differences in room categories and rates and what they entail. Once you decide on the type of room you want, ask for the best in that category. For example, if you want a standard room, and deluxe rooms start on the 14th floor, ask for a standard on the 13th floor, which may give better views than standards on the 10th. In addition, be specific about the kind of room you want, whether it's a nonsmoking room, a room with a view of Mount Fuji, or a room with Internet connections for your laptop.

Be sure to give your approximate time of arrival, especially if it's after 6pm, or they might give your room away. Check-in ranges from about 1 or 2pm in first-class hotels to 3 or 4pm for business hotels. Checkout is generally about 10am for business hotels and 11am or noon for upper-range hotels. In any case, it's perfectly acceptable to leave luggage with the front desk or bell captain if you arrive early or want to sightsee after checking out.

HOTELS Both first-class and mid-priced hotels in Japan are known for excellent service and cleanliness. The first-class hotels in the larger cities can compete with the best hotels in the world and offer a **wide range of services,** from health clubs and aesthetic spas with massage services to business centers and top-class restaurants and shopping arcades. Unfortunately, health clubs and swimming pools usually cost extra—anywhere from ¥1,050 to an outrageous ¥5,000 per single use. In addition, outdoor pools are generally open only from about mid-July through August (the school holiday season). Rooms come with such **standard features** as a minibar, bilingual cable TV with pay movies and English-language channels like CNN or BBC, high-speed Internet or wireless connections (usually at a charge at expensive hotels but often free in less expensive ones), clock, a radio, *yukata,* a hot-water pot and tea (and occasionally coffee, though you usually have to pay extra for it), a hair dryer, and a private bathroom with a tub/shower combination. (Because Japanese are used to soaping down and rinsing off before bathing, it would be rare to find tubs without showers; similarly, showers without tubs are practically nonexistent in this nation of bathers.) Virtually all hotels also have "Washlet" toilets, which are combination toilets and spray bidets with a controllable range of speeds and temperatures. Because they're accustomed to foreigners, hotels in this category employ an English-speaking staff and offer nonsmoking floors or rooms. Services provided include room service, same-day laundry and dry cleaning, and often English-language newspapers such as the *Japan Times* delivered free to your room. Note that in medium-range hotels, same-day laundry service is not available Sundays and holidays and you must turn in your laundry by 10am to receive it by 5pm that day.

The most expensive hotels in Japan are in Tokyo and Osaka, where you'll pay at least ¥32,000 for a double or twin room in a first-class hotel and ¥16,000 to ¥32,000 for the same in a mid-priced hotel. Outside the major cities, rooms for two people range from about ¥20,000 to ¥30,000 for first-class hotels and ¥10,000 to ¥20,000 for mid-priced hotels.

Although some internationally known high-end chains have a presence in Japan, including Four Seasons, Hyatt, and Ritz-Carlton, Japanese chains naturally dominate, including New Otani (www.newotani.co.jp; ✆ **0120/22-7021**), Okura (www.okura. com; ✆ **0120/00-3741**), Nikko/JAL Hotels (associated with Japan Airlines; www. jalhotels.com; ✆ **0120/58-2586**), Prince (www.princehotels.com/en; ✆ **0120/00-8686**), Tokyu (www.tokyuhotels.com; ✆ **03/3462-0109**), and the Japan Railways Hotel Group (www.jrhotelgroup.com/eng; ✆ **0120/58-2586**), which owns hotels adjoining train stations throughout Japan and provides discounts to those with a Japan Rail Pass.

TIPS FOR saving ON YOUR HOTEL ROOM

Although Japanese hotels have traditionally remained pretty loyal to their published **rack rates,** which are always available at the front desk, the Great East Japan Earthquake and on-going recession have introduced floating rates (the lower the demand, the lower the price) and bargains.

○ **Check the Internet.** If the hotel has a website, check to see whether discounts or special promotions are offered. Some hotels offer discounts exclusively through the Internet. In addition, check hotel booking sites such as Expedia and Rakuten Travel (see below).

○ **Contact the hotel directly.** In addition to calling a hotel's toll-free number, call the hotel directly to see where you can get the best deal.

○ **Always ask politely whether there's a room less expensive than the first one offered.** Because there are usually many categories, ask what the difference is, say, between a standard twin and a superior twin. If there are two of you, ask whether a double or a twin room is cheaper. Find out the hotel's policy on

children—do children stay free in the room or is there a special rate?

○ **Ask about promotions and special plans.** Hotels frequently offer special "plans," including "Spring Plans," "Ladies' Plans," and even "Shopping Plans" that provide cheaper rates or throw in extras like breakfast.

○ **Remember the law of supply and demand.** Resort hotels are more crowded and therefore more expensive on weekends and during peak travel periods such as Golden Week. Discounts, therefore, are often available for midweek and off-season stays. Business hotels, on the other hand, are sometimes cheaper on weekends.

○ **Ask about hotel membership plans.** Some chain business hotels offer hotel memberships with discounts on meals and free stays after a certain number of nights. Others, such as the New Otani, Okura, and the Imperial in Tokyo, allow free use of the hotel swimming pool simply if you become a member at no extra charge. Ask the concierge or front desk.

In addition to the recommendations in this guide, you can also check out the 400-some members of the Japan Hotel Association listed in the booklet *The Hotel Index* available from the Tourist Information Centers in Japan or online at **www.j-hotel. or.jp**.

BUSINESS HOTELS   Catering traditionally to Japanese business travelers, a "business hotel" is a no-frills establishment with tiny, sparsely furnished rooms, most of them singles but usually with some twin and maybe double rooms also available. Primarily just places to crash for the night, these rooms usually have everything you need, but in miniature form—minuscule bathroom, tiny bathtub/shower, small bed (or beds), TV, telephone, radio, clock, yukata, Wi-Fi or Internet connections (usually free but sometimes charged), empty fridge, and barely enough space to unpack your bags. If you're a large person, you may have trouble sleeping in a place like this. There are no bellhops, no room service, and sometimes not even a lobby or coffee shop, although usually there are vending machines selling beer, soda, cigarettes, and snacks. Most business hotels have nonsmoking rooms, but a few may not. The advantages of staying in business hotels are price—starting as low as ¥6,000 or ¥7,000 for a single—and location—usually near major train and subway stations. Check-in is usually not until 3 or 4pm, and checkout is usually at 10am; you can leave your bags at the front desk.

As for business-hotel chains, I'm partial to the Toyoko Inn chain (www.toyoko-inn. com), which boasts more than 160 locations around Japan and always employs female managers. They offer minuscule rooms outfitted with about everything you need, including free Internet access, and have raised the bar in business-hotel amenities by adding lobby computers with free Internet access, free domestic calls from lobby phones (but limited to 3 min.), and usually free Japanese breakfast. Other budget and medium-priced chains to look for are Tokyu Inns, all with specially designed Ladies Rooms with female-oriented toiletries and amenities (www.tokyu hotels.com; ☏ 03/3462-0109), the Ishin Group Hotels with its classy business hotels (www.ishinhotels.com), Washington Hotels (www.wh-rsv.com), the Sunroute Hotel Chain (www.sunroute.jp/WelcomeSV), Mitsui Garden Hotels (www.garden hotels.co.jp), APA Hotels & Resorts (www.apahotel.com) and Super Hotel (www. superhotel.co.jp) with the lowest rates around.

PENSIONS   Pensions are like *minshuku,* except that accommodations are Western-style with beds instead of futons, and the two meals served are usually Western. Often managed by a young couple or a young staff, they cater to young Japanese and are most often located in ski resorts and in the countryside, sometimes making access a problem. Averaging 10 guest rooms, many seem especially geared to young Japanese women and are thus done up in rather feminine-looking decor with lots of pinks and flower prints. In recent years, *Wa-fu* Pensions (with Japanese-style rooms) have also made an appearance. The average cost is ¥8,000 per person per night, including two meals.

GUESTHOUSES   Virtually nonexistent just a decade ago, low-cost guesthouses have opened in major cities around the country, catering primarily to backpackers and travelers who don't mind close quarters. Although they often have a few tiny private rooms with tatami or beds for one or two people, the majority are known primarily for their dormitory rooms, with shared bathrooms down the hall. They often have communal kitchens and lounging areas as well. Some are better than others; I've included a few that rise above the rest in some of Japan's more expensive cities.

YOUTH HOSTELS   There are some 320 youth hostels in Japan, most of them privately run and operating in locations ranging from temples to concrete blocks. There's no age limit (though children 3 and younger may not be accepted), and although most of them require a youth hostel membership card, some let foreigners stay without one at no extra charge or for ¥600 extra per night (after 6 nights you automatically become a YH member). Or, buy an International Hostel Card for ¥2,800. Youth hostels are reasonable, averaging about ¥3,360 per day without meals, and can be reserved in advance. However, there are usually quite a few restrictions, such as a 9 or 10pm curfew, a lights-out policy shortly thereafter, an early breakfast time, and closed times through the day, generally from about 10am to 3pm. In addition, rooms generally have many bunk beds or futons, affording little privacy. On the other hand, they're certainly the cheapest accommodations in Japan. For a "splurge," there are seven Youth Guest Houses in Japan, offering rooms with private bath and averaging ¥6,500 per night.

Because youth hostels are often inconveniently located, I have included only one, in Tokyo, but if you plan on staying almost exclusively in hostels, pick up a pamphlet called "Youth Hostel Map of Japan," available at the **Tourist Information Centers** in Japan, or check www.jyh.or.jp. For youth hostel membership in the U.S., contact **Hostelling International USA** (www.hiusa.org; (✆ **301/495-1240**).

CAPSULE HOTELS　Capsule hotels, which became popular in the early 1980s, are used primarily by Japanese businessmen who have spent an evening out drinking and missed the last train home—costing about ¥3,000 to ¥4,000 per person, a capsule hotel is sometimes cheaper than a taxi to the suburbs. Units are small—no larger than a coffin and consisting of a bed, a private TV, an alarm clock, and a radio—and are usually stacked two deep in rows down a corridor; the only thing separating you from your probably inebriated neighbor is a curtain. A cotton kimono and a locker are provided, and bathrooms and toilets are communal. Most capsule hotels do not accept women, but those that do have separate facilities.

LOVE HOTELS　Finally, a word about Japan's so-called "love hotels." Usually found close to entertainment districts and along major highways, such hotels do not provide sexual services themselves; rather, they offer rooms for rent by the hour to couples. You'll know that you've wandered into a love-hotel district when you notice hourly rates posted near the front door, though gaudy structures shaped like ocean liners or castles are also a dead giveaway. Because many of them have reasonable overnight rates as well, I have friends who, finding themselves out too late and too far from home, have checked into love hotels, solo.

Finding a Hotel or Inn

If all my recommendations for a certain city are fully booked, or if you're traveling to destinations not covered in this guide, there are several ways to find alternative accommodations.

SURFING FOR HOTELS　In addition to well-known booking sites like Travelocity, Expedia, Orbitz, and Hotels.com, you should also check Asia-specific sites like Asiatravel.com, Asia-hotels.com, and agoda.com. Of course, you'll also want to check all the websites mentioned earlier, such as www.j-hotel.or.jp for members of the Japan Hotel Association. Japan's largest online hotel reservations company for budget and moderately priced accommodations is **Rakuten Travel** (http://travel.rakuten.co.jp/en/index.html; ✆ **050/2017-8977**).

In any case, it's always a good idea to **get a confirmation number** and **make a printout** of any online booking transaction.

FINDING A ROOM WHEN YOU'RE IN JAPAN　High-end hotels and *ryokan* can be booked through travel agencies in Japan, including the ubiquitous Japan Travel Bureau. Otherwise, if you arrive at your destination without accommodations, most major train stations contain a tourist information office or a hotel and ryokan reservation counter where you can book a room. Although policies may differ from office to office, you generally don't have to pay a fee for their services, but you usually do have to pay a percentage of your overnight charge as a deposit. The disadvantage is that you don't see the locale beforehand, and if there's space left at a ryokan even in peak tourist season, there may be a reason for it. Although these offices can be a real lifesaver in a pinch and in most cases may be able to recommend quite reasonable and pleasant places in which to stay, it pays to plan in advance.

[FastFACTS] JAPAN

Area Codes All telephone area codes for Japanese cities begin with a zero (03 for Tokyo, 06 for Osaka, 075 for Kyoto), but drop the first zero if calling Japan from abroad. The country code for Japan is 81.

Business Hours Banks are open Monday through Friday 9am to 3pm (but usually will not exchange money until 10:30 or so, after that day's currency exchange rates come in). Neighborhood post offices are open Monday through Friday 9am to 5pm. Major post offices, however (usually located near major train stations), have longer hours and may be open weekends as well. (Some central post offices, such as those in Tokyo and Osaka, are open 24 hr. for mail.)

Department stores are open from about 10am to 8 or 9pm (but note that some have been closing earlier to conserve energy, while others close some floors but keep their food halls open later); most are open daily but may close irregularly. Smaller stores are generally open from about 10am to 8pm, closed 1 day a week (Monday and Wednesday are the most common off days). Convenience stores such as 7-Eleven and Family Mart are open 24 hours.

Keep in mind that museums, gardens, and attractions stop selling admission tickets at least 30 minutes before the actual closing time. Similarly, restaurants take their last orders at least 30 minutes before the posted closing time (even earlier for *kaiseki* restaurants). Most national, prefectural, and city museums are closed on Monday; if Monday is a national holiday, however, they'll remain open and close on the following day, Tuesday, instead. Privately owned museums, however, usually close on holidays.

Car Rental See "Getting Around," earlier in this chapter.

Cellphones See "Mobile Phones," later in this section.

Crime See "Safety," later in this section.

Customs Visitors entering Japan must fill out a "Customs Declaration" form (handed out on incoming flights). If you're 20 or older, you can bring duty-free into Japan up to 400 non-Japanese cigarettes or 500 grams of tobacco or 100 cigars; three bottles (760cc each) of alcohol; and 2 ounces of perfume. You can also bring in goods for personal use that were purchased abroad whose total market value is less than ¥200,000. For more information, check the website www.customs.go.jp.

Disabled Travelers For those with disabilities, traveling can be a nightmare in Japan, especially in Tokyo and other large metropolises. City sidewalks can be so jam-packed that getting around in a wheelchair is exceedingly difficult; some busy thoroughfares can be crossed only via pedestrian bridges.

Most major train and subway stations now have elevators, but they can be difficult to locate. Otherwise, smaller stations, especially in rural areas, may be accessible only by stairs or escalators, though in recent years some have been equipped with powered seat lifts. Only half of Japan's train stations have barrier-free toilets. While some buses are now no-step conveyances for easy access, subway and train compartments are difficult for solo wheelchair travelers to navigate on their own due to a gap or slight height difference between the coaches and platforms. In theory you can ask a station attendant to help you board, though you might have to wait if he's busy; you can also request an attendant at your destination to help you disembark. Although trains and buses have seating for passengers with disabilities—called "Priority Seats" and located in the first and last compartments of the train—subways can be so crowded that there's barely room to move. Moreover, Priority Seats are almost always occupied by commuters, so unless you look visibly handicapped, no one is likely to offer you a seat.

As for accommodations, only 10% of the nation's hotels have barrier-free rooms (called a "universal" room in Japan and used primarily by seniors), mostly in the expensive category, and even then there are usually only one or two such rooms. Only a scant 1% of Japanese inns have such rooms. Lower-priced accommodations may also lack elevators.

Restaurants can also be difficult to navigate, with raised doorsills, crowded dining areas, and tiny bathrooms that cannot accommodate wheelchairs. Best bets for ramps and easily accessible bathrooms include restaurants in department stores and upper-end hotels. Even Japanese homes are not very accessible, since the main floor is always raised about a foot above the entrance-hall floor.

For information on traveling with a wheelchair, including limited information on a handful of sights and hotels offering facilities for travelers with disabilities, visit the Accessible Japan website at www.tesco-premium.co.jp/aj/index.htm.

When it comes to facilities for the blind, Japan has a very advanced system. At subway stations and on many major sidewalks in large cities, raised dots and lines on the ground guide blind people at intersections and to subway platforms. In some cities, streetlights chime a theme when the signal turns green east-west, and chime another for north-south. Even Japanese yen notes are identified by a slightly raised circle—the ¥1,000 note has one circle in a corner, while the ¥10,000 note has two. Many elevators have floors indicated in Braille, and some hotels identify rooms in Braille.

Doctors   Many first-class hotels offer medical facilities or an in-house doctor. Otherwise, your embassy or the AMDA International Medical Information Center (www.amda-imic.com; ✆ **03/5285-8088;** daily 9am–8pm) can refer you to medical professionals who speak English.

Drinking Laws   The legal drinking age is 20. Beer, wine, and spirits are readily available in department stores, grocery stores, some convenience stores, and liquor stores. Many bars, especially in nightlife districts such as Shinjuku and Roppongi, are open until dawn. If you intend to drive in Japan, you are not allowed even one drink.

Drugstores   Drugstores, called *yakkyoku,* are found readily in Japan. Note, however, that you cannot have a foreign prescription filled in Japan without first consulting a doctor in Japan, so it's best to bring an adequate supply of important medicines with you. No drugstores in Japan stay open 24 hours. However, ubiquitous convenience stores like 7-Eleven, Lawson, and Family Mart, open day and night throughout Japan, carry such nonprescription items as aspirin.

Earthquakes   See "Safety," later in this section.

Electricity   The electricity throughout Japan is 100 volts AC, but there are two different cycles in use (which ended up playing havoc during electricity shortages after the Great East Japan Earthquake): In Tokyo and in regions northeast of the capital up through Hokkaido, it's 50 cycles, while in Nagoya, Kyoto, Osaka, and all points to the southwest, it's 60 cycles. In any case, it's close enough to the American system that I've never encountered any problems plugging in my American electronics, including laptops and camera rechargers. Leading hotels in Tokyo often have two outlets, one for 110 volts and one for 220 volts (with the appropriate plugs used in the U.S. and Europe), so you can use most American or European appliances (electric razors, travel irons, laptops, and so forth) during your stay. Note, too, that the flat, two-legged prongs used in Japan are the same size and fit as in North America, but three-pronged appliances are not accepted (for my laptop, I bring the small two-prong attachment so I can plug into a Japanese socket).

Embassies & Consulates   Most embassies are located in Tokyo (see "Fast Facts: Tokyo" in chapter 4). There are, however, Australian consulates in Osaka, Fukuoka, and Sapporo; British consulates in Osaka and Nagoya; Canadian consulates in Nagoya, Sapporo, and Hiroshima; consulates for New Zealand in Osaka, Nagoya, Fukuoka and

Sapporo; and U.S. consulates in Osaka, Nagoya, Fukuoka, Naha (Okinawa), and Sapporo. See individual city listings for contact information.

Emergencies The national emergency numbers are (✆) **110** for **police** and (✆) **119** for **ambulance** and **fire** (ambulances are free in Japan unless you request a specific hospital). You do not need to insert any money into public telephones to call these numbers. However, if you use a green public telephone, it's necessary to push a red button before dialing. If you call from a gray public telephone or one that accepts only prepaid cards, you won't see a red button; in that case simply lift the receiver and dial. Be sure to speak slowly and precisely.

Family Travel Japanese are very fond of children, which makes traveling in Japan with kids a delight. All social reserve seems to be waived for children. Taking along some small and easy-to-carry gifts (such as colorful stickers) for your kids to give to other children is a great icebreaker.

Safety also makes Japan a good destination for families. Still, plan your itinerary with care. To avoid crowds, visit tourist sights on weekdays. Never travel on city transportation during rush hour or on trains during popular public holidays. And remember that with all the stairways and crowded sidewalks, strollers are less practical than baby backpacks.

Children 6 to 11 years old are generally charged half-price for everything from temple admission to train tickets, while children 5 and under are often admitted free. Tourist spots in Japan almost always have a table or counter with a stamp and inkpad so that visitors can commemorate their trip; you might wish to give your children a small notebook so they can collect imprints of every attraction they visit. There are many attractions throughout Japan geared just toward kids, including sophisticated theme parks. And what teenager could resist Japan's pop culture, fashion, and fads?

Although it's not advertised, many hotels and *ryokan* (Japanese-style inns) give discounts to young children (up to 5 or 9 years of age) or allow them to stay for free, but only if they sleep with you and do not require an extra bed. Ryokan may also give discounts for meals. At budget chain Toyoko Inn, for example, elementary-age children and younger can stay free, but only if they share a bed with a parent. Only one child per bed is allowed (one child can share a double bed; two children are allowed in rooms with twin beds). An extra pillow or other amenities are not provided, but can be supplied for an extra ¥1,050. In any case, it's advisable to ask in advance. Many upper-range hotels in major cities like Tokyo and Osaka provide babysitting services, although they are prohibitively expensive. Expect to fork over a minimum of ¥5,000 for 2 hours of freedom.

As for food, the transition from kid-favorite spaghetti to *udon* noodles is easy, and udon and *soba* shops are inexpensive and ubiquitous. In addition, most family-style restaurants, especially those in department stores, offer a special children's meal that often includes a small toy or souvenir. For those real emergencies, Western fast-food places such as McDonald's and KFC are seemingly everywhere in Japan.

To locate those accommodations, restaurants, and attractions that are particularly kid-friendly, see the "Kids" icon throughout this guide. For a suggested itinerary in Japan with kids, see chapter 3.

Gasoline Gas prices can fluctuate, but are generally significantly higher than in North America. A price of ¥150 per liter is not unusual.

Health Foremost in most people's minds since the 2011 Great East Japan Earthquake, and the subsequent struggle to contain the damaged Fukushima nuclear power plant, is fear of radiation. After all, reports of contaminated food plagued the country after the disaster, including contaminated tea, beef, spinach, rice, mushrooms, milk, and even infant formula. Although the detected amounts of radiation were so low that they would cause health problems only if consumed in large quantities for more than a year, and the Fukushima power plant achieved a cold shutdown by the end of 2011, contaminated foods raised fears that the government was not doing enough to protect the public. That being said, measures are in place to protect food and water safety (Japan's standards for radioactive contamination are the same as in the US), including a suspension of fishing around the Fukushima reactors, measuring drinking water for radiation levels, and measuring radiation levels at various locations around Tokyo and prefectures around the damaged power plants. My personal take on the radiation situation is that a month's stay will have no long-term effects on my longevity, and frankly, you're likely to get more radiation on the flight to Japan than being in most areas of Japan, which, as an island nation, stretches about 2,900km (1,800 miles) from northeast to southwest. On the other hand, if I were a mother living in eastern Fukushima Prefecture, I probably would have left long ago.

In any case, at the time of going to press, radiation levels in eastern Japan (excluding the area immediately surrounding the defunct Fukushima power plant) had stabilized and were considered normal. Safecast (http://maps.safecast.org) provides daily radiation levels throughout Japan utilizing more than 600,000 radiation detection points around the country. In any case, if a radiation emergency does occur, you're advised to stay inside, shower and change into clean clothes, and tune in to radio and television networks. Your embassy's website (see "Embassies & Consulates," above) is also a good resource. For advice on what to do during an earthquake or tsunami, see "Safety," later.

Otherwise, it's safe to drink tap water and eat to your heart's content everywhere in Japan (pregnant women, however, are advised to avoid eating raw fish and to avoid taking hot baths). Although Japan had nine cases of mad cow disease after its first confirmed case in 2001, all slaughtered cows must now be checked for the disease before the meat is authorized for consumption. To prevent the spread of avian and H1N1 flu, all incoming passengers are monitored upon arrival at Narita Airport for fever; those with a higher than normal temperature may be quarantined. To be on the safe side, therefore, you may opt for an influenza vaccine before departing from home.

You don't need any inoculations to enter Japan. **Prescriptions** can be filled at Japanese pharmacies *only if they're issued by a Japanese doctor.* To avoid hassle, bring more prescription medications than you think you'll need, clearly labeled in their original containers, and be sure to pack them in your carry-on luggage. But to be safe, bring copies of your prescriptions with you, including generic names of medicines in case a local pharmacist is unfamiliar with the brand name. Over-the-counter items are easy to obtain, though name brands are likely to be different from those back home, some ingredients allowed elsewhere may be forbidden in Japan, and prices are likely to be higher.

Insurance   For information on traveler's insurance, trip cancellation insurance, and medical insurance while traveling, please visit www.frommers.com/planning/.

Internet & Wi-Fi   Narita International Airport, Haneda Airport, and Kansai International Airport all offer free **Wi-Fi** (wireless fidelity), as well as computer terminals (¥100 per 10 min.).

With the exception of resort hotels in remote areas, many ryokan, and some budget hotels, most accommodations in Japan, especially in major cities, provide Internet access in their guest rooms. While most provide dataports, more and more are going with **Wi-Fi.** I'm also happy to report that more and more are also offering Internet connections for free (see individual hotel listings for each city; if no fee is given, usage is free). Otherwise, expect to pay anywhere from ¥500 to ¥1,050 for 24 hours. Although you might want to pack a phone cord and spare Ethernet network cable just to be safe if you're staying in cheap accommodations, you probably won't need them otherwise, as most hotels supply them to guests free of charge. Most hotels also have computers for guest use, either for a fee (in the hotel business center, which can be exorbitant, or coin-operated, usually ¥100 for 15 min.) or—mostly in cheaper accommodations—for free (free use of lobby computers is noted in individual hotel listings). Note that accommodations that charge for Internet in their rooms sometimes offer Wi-Fi in their lobby for free, so it always pays to ask.

Outside hotels, more and more restaurants, cafes, and bars also offer free Wi-Fi; you'll probably have to ask for the password. Otherwise, cybercafes can be found in most cities, though they're often nonexistent in small towns. I've listed cybercafes for many destinations when I could find them (see individual chapters), but more may have opened by the time you travel. Ask local tourist offices for updated locations. For information on Japan's electricity requirements, see "Electricity," above.

Language   English is widely understood in major hotels, restaurants, and shops, but it's hit-or-miss elsewhere. Be sure to pick up the free "Tourist's Language Handbook," at the Tourist Information Center. Also, see "Dealing with the Language Barrier," in chapter 2 and the glossary of useful phrases in chapter 15.

Legal Aid   Contact your embassy if you find yourself in legal trouble. The **Legal Counseling Center,** 1–4 Yotsuya, Shinjuku (www.horitsu-sodan.jp; (ℂ **03/5367-5280**; station: Yotsuya), is operated by three bar associations and provides legal counseling with English interpreters Monday to Friday from 1 to 4pm.

LGBT Travelers   While there are many gay and lesbian establishments in Tokyo (concentrated mostly in Shinjuku's Ni-chome district; see chapter 4), the gay community in Japan is not a vocal one, and in any case, local information in English is hard to come by. A useful website for information on the gay scene in Japan, as well as gay and lesbian club listings in cities around the country, is **www.utopia-asia.com/tipsjapn.htm**.

Luggage & Lockers   Storage space on Shinkansen bullet trains is limited, so travel with the smallest bag you can get away with. Coin-operated lockers are located at major train stations as well as at most subway stations, but most lockers are generally not large enough to store huge pieces of luggage (and those that do are often taken). Lockers generally cost ¥300 to ¥800 depending on the size. Some major stations also have check-in rooms for luggage, though these are rare. If your bag becomes too much to handle, you can have it sent ahead via *takkyu-bin,* an efficient forwarding service available at upper- and mid-range hotels and all convenience stores in Japan. At Narita and Kansai international airports, service counters will send luggage to your hotel the next day (or vice versa) for about ¥2,000 per bag.

Mail   If your hotel cannot mail letters for you, ask the concierge for the location of the nearest post office, recognizable by the red logo of a capital T with a horizontal line over it. Mailboxes are bright orange-red. It costs ¥110 to airmail letters weighing up to 25 grams and ¥70 for postcards to Australia, North America, and Europe. Domestic mail costs ¥80 for letters up to 25 grams, and ¥50 for postcards. Post offices throughout Japan are also convenient for their ATMs, which accept international bank cards operating on the PLUS and Cirrus systems, as well as MasterCard and Visa.

Although all **post offices** are open Monday through Friday from 9am to 5pm, international post offices (often located close to the central train station) have longer hours, often until 7pm or later on weekdays and with open hours also on weekends (in Tokyo and Osaka, counters are open 24 hr.). If your hotel does not have a shipping service, it is only at these larger post offices that you can mail packages abroad. Conveniently, they sell cardboard boxes in several sizes with the necessary tape. Packages sent via surface mail cannot weigh more than 20 kilograms (about 44 lb.) and take about a month to reach North America, with a package weighing 10 kilograms (about 22 lb.) costing ¥6,750. Express EMS packages, which take 3 days to North America and can weigh up to 30 kilograms (66 lb.), cost ¥14,000 for 10 kilograms (22 lb.); the same package to Australia also costs ¥14,000 while to Europe it costs ¥16,200. For more information, visit **www.post. japanpost.jp**.

Measurements   Before the metric system came into use in Japan, the country had its own standards for measuring length and weight. Rooms are still measured by the number of *tatami* straw mats that will fit in them. A six-tatami room, for example, is the size of six tatami mats, with a tatami roughly .9m (3 ft.) wide and 1.8m (6 ft.) long.

Medical Requirements   Unless you're arriving from an area known to be suffering from an epidemic (particularly cholera or yellow fever), inoculations or vaccinations are not required for entry into Japan. Note, however, that the temperature of all arriving passengers is taken upon entering the customs area; if you have a fever, you may be quarantined as a protection against H1N1 or avian flu. Also see "Health," above.

Mobile Phones   The three letters that define much of the world's wireless capabilities are GSM (Global System for Mobiles). Unfortunately, Japan uses a system that is incompatible with GSM, and foreigners are not allowed to buy cellphones in Japan. You can, however, use your **own mobile phone number** in Japan by bringing your own SIM card from home and inserting it into a handset rented from **Softbank Global Rental** or **NTT DoCoMo.** Note, however, that this works *only* if you rent a phone at the airport (in-town Softbank and DoCoMo outlets cannot handle this) or you make an online rental reservation and have the phone delivered to your destination in Japan. In addition, for it to work, your home service provider must have a roaming agreement with Softbank or NTT and you must subscribe to your provider's roaming service. You'll pay for the phone rental, but your calls will be billed through your home provider.

Another option is to **bring your own mobile phone** and rent a 3G SIM card from Softbank **at the airport.** This works also with the iPhone 4 (you should ensure that your phone SIM is unlocked and available for international roaming). Alternatively, some phones (they must support W-CDMA) with roaming agreements with NTT can work simply by choosing "DOCOMO" from the mobile phone operator selection screen when you arrive in Japan. Of course, these conveniences can be expensive. For more information, contact your mobile phone company, NTT DoCoMo (http://roaming.nttdocomo.co.jp), or Softbank Global Rental (www.softbank-rental.jp), where you can also find out about rental costs and make online reservations.

You can also rent a phone in Japan. If you're in Japan for only a few days and are staying in an upper-class hotel, most convenient but most expensive is to rent a mobile phone from your hotel. A check of several hotels in Tokyo turned up rental fees ranging from ¥525 to ¥1,575 per day (the more expensive the hotel, the more expensive the rental), plus charges for calls (incoming calls are free).

I suggest, therefore, that you rent a phone at the airport. Lots of companies maintain counters at Narita and Osaka international airports, including NTT DoCoMo and Softbank Global Rental (see above), as well as **G-Call** (www.g-call.com/e), **Telecom Square** (www. telecomsquare.co.jp/en), and **PuPuRu** (www.pupuru.com/en), which have the extra convenience of easy pickup and drop-off and offer online reservations. Most rentals start at ¥525 per day, though bargains are often offered online or on-site. Charges for domestic and international calls vary; incoming calls are usually free.

For travelers staying in Japan a week or longer, **Go Mobile** (www.gomobile.co.jp) offers 1-week, 2-week, and 30-day rentals, including a limited number of free local calls. A 1-week rental costs ¥2,995 and includes 15 minutes of free local calls. Phones are shipped to an address in Japan (such as your hotel) and returned via a prepaid, pre-addressed envelope.

   Over & Out

If you're traveling with a buddy, consider bringing along walkie-talkies. They're cheaper than phones, could be a lifesaver if you get separated, and make it easier to rendezvous, especially in big cities.

THE VALUE OF THE YEN VS. OTHER POPULAR CURRENCIES

Yen	Aus$	Can$	Euro (€)	NZ$	UK£	US$
100	A$1.17	C$1.20	€88	NZ$1.47	£78	$1.20

Money & Costs Frommer's lists exact prices in the local currency. The currency conversions quoted above were correct at press time. However, rates fluctuate, so before departing consult a currency exchange website such as **www.oanda.com/currency/converter** to check up-to-the-minute rates.

There's no getting around it: Japan is expensive; the exchange rate makes it even pricier. In various surveys of the most expensive cities around the world, Tokyo is always among the top 10, while Osaka, Nagoya, Yokohama, and Kobe have also had their spot in the top 10. Luckily, rural areas are generally much cheaper than the big cities, and hopefully this guide will help reduce some potential costs by showing you how to take advantage of deals on public transportation, dine more cheaply, and, when available, see sights with reduced admission.

In any case, you'll probably want to arrive in Japan with cash, credit cards, and maybe even traveler's checks. Luckily, it's much easier to obtain yen than it used to be even just a decade ago.

Currency The currency in Japan is called the *yen*, symbolized by ¥. Coins come in denominations of ¥1, ¥5, ¥10, ¥50, ¥100, and ¥500. Bills come in denominations of ¥1,000, ¥2,000, ¥5,000, and ¥10,000, though ¥2,000 notes are rarely seen. You'll find that all coins get used (though it's hard to get rid of ¥1 coins). Keep plenty of change handy for riding local transportation such as buses or streetcars. Although change machines are virtually everywhere, even on buses where you can change larger coins and ¥1,000 bills, you'll find it faster to have the exact amount on hand.

Some people like to arrive in a foreign country with that country's currency already on hand, but I do not find it necessary for Japan. **Narita, Haneda, Kansai,** and **Nagoya international airports** all have exchange counters for all incoming international flights that offer better exchange rates than what you'd get abroad, as well as ATMs. I usually change enough money to last several days.

Personal checks are not used in Japan. Most Japanese pay with either credit cards or cash—and because the country overall has such a low crime rate, you can feel safe walking around with money (though of course you should always exercise caution). The only time you really need to be alert to possible pickpockets in Japan is when you're riding a crowded subway during rush hour or walking in heavily visited areas of Tokyo and other large cities.

In any case, although the bulk of your expenses—hotels, train tickets, major purchases, meals in tourist-oriented restaurants—can be paid for with credit cards, you'll want to have cash on hand for those times when you might not have easy access to an ATM for cash withdrawals, especially in rural areas.

ATMs The best way to get cash away from home is from an ATM (automated teller machine). Because most bank ATMs in Japan accept only cards issued by Japanese banks, your best bet for obtaining cash is the ubiquitous **7-Eleven** convenience store (www.sevenbank.co.jp/intlcard), most of which are open 24 hours and have ATMs that accept foreign bank cards operating on the **Cirrus** (www.mastercard.com) and **PLUS** (www.visa.com) systems, as well as American Express. Note, however, that not all cards, even those issued through Visa or MasterCard, are accepted. For that reason, I suggest traveling with at least two cards from different issuers.

WHAT THINGS COST IN TOKYO	JAPANESE YEN
Narita Express from airport to Tokyo Station	2,940
Metro subway ride from Ginza to Asakusa	190
Double room at Mitsui Garden Hotel Ginza (moderate)	25,200
Double room at Hotel Asia Center (inexpensive)	12,390
Dinner for one, without drinks, at Waentei-Kikko (moderate)	6,825
Dinner for one, without drinks, at Maisen (inexpensive)	1,420
Glass of beer	500–800
Cup of coffee	250–600
Admission to Tokyo National Museum	600

More user-friendly are the 21,000-some **post offices** in Japan, all of which have ATMs accepting foreign bank cards operating on the Cirrus and PLUS systems and with instructions in English. Although major post offices, usually located near main train stations, have long open hours for ATMs (generally 7am–11pm weekdays and 9am–7 or 9pm on weekends, though some are open almost 24 hours a day), small post offices may have only limited hours for ATMs (depending on the post office, that may be until 6 or 7pm weekdays and until 5pm on weekends).

Other places with ATMs that might accept foreign-issued cards include Citibank and large department stores in major cities. Note that there is no public American Express office in Japan.

Be sure you know your four-digit personal identification number (PIN) and your daily withdrawal limit before leaving home. Also keep in mind that many banks impose a fee every time a card is used at a different bank's ATM, and that fee can be higher for international transactions than for domestic ones. In addition, the bank from which you withdraw cash may charge its own fee. Because Japan is expensive and there's a limit to how much money you can withdraw with each transaction, you'll find these bank fees especially annoying here. For international withdrawal fees, ask your bank.

Credit Cards   Credit cards are a safe way to carry money, provide a convenient record of all your expenses, and generally offer relatively good exchange rates. The most readily accepted cards are **American Express, Diners Club, MasterCard** (also called Eurocard), **Visa,** and the Japanese credit card **JCB** (Japan Credit Bank). Shops and restaurants accepting credit and charge cards will usually post which cards they accept at the door or near the cash register. However, some establishments may be reluctant to accept cards for small purchases and inexpensive meals, so inquire beforehand. Note, too, that the vast majority of Japan's smaller and least-expensive businesses, including many restaurants, noodle shops, fast-food joints, ma-and-pa establishments, and the cheapest accommodations, do not accept credit cards.

In any case, beware of hidden credit-card fees while traveling. Check with your card issuer to see what fees, if any, are charged for overseas transactions. Recent reform legislation in the U.S., for example, curbed some exploitative lending practices, but many banks responded by increasing fees in other areas, including fees for customers using credit and debit cards while out of the country—even if those charges were made in U.S. dollars. Fees can amount to 3% or more of the purchase price. Check with your bank before departing to avoid any surprise charges on your statement.

Traveler's Checks It's hard to imagine, but 20 years ago there were hardly any ATMs in Japan that accepted foreign credit cards, making traveler's checks a must. Today, I find traveler's checks still useful in Japan. Traveler's checks help you avoid annoying credit card fees, generally fetch a better exchange rate than cash, and offer protection in case of theft (be sure to keep a record of the traveler's checks' serial numbers separate from your checks in the event that they are stolen or lost); *you may need your passport to exchange traveler's checks.* Note, however, that in some very remote areas, even banks won't cash them. Before taking off for small towns, be sure you have enough cash.

Exchanging Money All banks in Japan displaying an AUTHORIZED FOREIGN EXCHANGE sign can exchange currency and traveler's checks, with exchange rates usually displayed at the appropriate foreign-exchange counter. **Banks** are generally open Monday through Friday from 9am to 3pm, though business hours for exchanging foreign currency usually don't begin until 10:30 or 11am (be prepared for a long wait; you'll be asked to sit down as your order is processed). More convenient—and quicker—are **Travelex** (www.travelex.com) foreign-exchange kiosks, with locations in several cities in Japan, including Tokyo, Kyoto, Nagoya, Osaka, and Sapporo.

If you need to exchange money outside banking hours, inquire at your **hotel.** Likewise, large **department stores** also offer exchange services and are often open until 7:30 or 8pm. Note, however, that hotels and department stores may charge a handling fee, offer a slightly less favorable exchange rate, and require a passport for all transactions.

For help with currency conversions, tip calculations, and more, download Frommer's Travel Tools app for your mobile device. Go to http://www.frommers.com/go/mobile/ and click on the Travel Tools icon.

Newspapers & Magazines

Three English-language newspapers are published daily in Japan: the **Japan Times** and the **Daily Yomiuri,** as well as the **International Herald Tribune** with a section devoted to Japan. Major bookstores carry the international editions of such newsmagazines as *Time* and *Newsweek*. You can also read the *Japan Times* online at www.japantimes.co.jp and the *Daily Yomiuri* at www.yomiuri.co.jp/dy. I personally also like reading http://newsonjapan.com, which gives a roundup of the daily news—business, politics, travel, society, and more—with excerpts drawn from Japanese news sources.

Packing

The first thing you'll want to do when you're packing is select the smallest bag you can get away with and **pack as lightly as you can.** Storage space is limited on Japan's trains, including the Shinkansen bullet train, business hotels sometimes lack closets, and there are multitudes of stairs and overhead and underground passageways to navigate in virtually every train station in the country.

The most important item is **a good pair of walking shoes,** well broken in. You will probably be walking much more than you do at home. Keep in mind, too, that because you have to remove your shoes to enter Japanese homes, inns, shrines, and temples, you should bring a pair that's easy to slip on and off. And since you may be walking around in stocking feet, save yourself embarrassment by packing socks and hose without holes.

Take a Load off Heavy Bags

If your bag becomes a burden but you don't want to mail items home, an alternative is to send a bag onward to your next or last stop by *takkyu-bin,* available at larger hotels, train stations, and convenience stores. Bags reach most destinations in 1 or 2 nights, with the delivery cost of an average-size bag weighing 10 kilograms (22 lb.) ¥1,400. I love this amazingly efficient service—it's a lifesaver!

Passport Savvy

Safeguard your passport in an inconspicuous, inaccessible place, such as a money belt, and keep a photocopy of your passport's information page in your luggage. If you lose your passport, visit your nearest consulate as soon as possible for a replacement (see "Embassies & Consulates," on p. 623). *Note:* All foreigners must present their passports for photocopying when checking into lodging facilities. In addition, foreigners are required to carry with them at all times either their passports or, for those who have been granted longer stays, their alien registration cards. Police generally do not stop foreigners, but if you're caught without an ID, you'll be taken to local police headquarters. It happened to me once, and believe me, I can think of better ways to spend an hour and a half than explaining in detail who I am, what I am doing in Japan, where I live, and what I plan to do for the rest of my life. I even had to write a statement explaining why I rushed out that day without my passport, apologizing and promising never to do such a thoughtless thing again.

As for **clothes,** you'll need a coat in winter and very light clothing for the hot and humid summer months. Jackets are necessary for spring and autumn; I've seen it snow in March in Tokyo, and even May can be quite crisp. Japan's top French restaurants often require jackets and ties for men. Although the older generation considers it inappropriate for women to wear dresses without hose or tops without sleeves, the younger generation ignores this, especially in resort areas. Jeans and capris are okay for casual dining and sightseeing.

Virtually all hotels and Japanese-style inns—save youth hostels and some budget-priced inns—provide towels, soap, washcloths, toothbrushes, toothpaste, shampoo, a cotton kimono (called a *yukata* and not a giveaway), and usually razors. If you run out of something, you'll have no problem finding it in Japan. Most hotels and inns also provide a thermos of hot water or a water heater as well as some tea bags. Free coffee is rare, so if you're a coffee addict, you can save money by buying instant coffee and drinking your morning cup in your hotel room. Hair dryers are a standard feature in virtually all rooms with private bathrooms, including business hotels. Because the sun rises early in summer (as early as 4am), you might want to include a pair of eyeshades.

It's also good to carry a supply of pocket tissues, change for local buses (faster than trying to change ¥1,000 notes), a folding umbrella, and a compass for getting your bearings and following directions using local maps. Finally, pack small, inexpensive gifts from home that can be given to those who show unexpected kindness, including candy, postcards, and hometown souvenirs.

Passports As of 2007, all foreigners entering Japan are fingerprinted and photographed in a measure to prevent terrorism, despite the fact that terrorism in Japan has been mostly homegrown. Exceptions include children younger than 16, diplomats, and some permanent residents of Japan.

For most tourists, including those from the United States, Canada, Australia, New Zealand, and the United Kingdom, the only document necessary to enter Japan is a passport. Foreign visitors from many countries can enter Japan without a visa for purposes of tourism. **Americans, Australians,** and **New Zealanders** traveling to Japan as tourists for a stay of 90 days or less need only a valid passport to gain entry into the country. **Canadians** don't need a visa for stays of up to 3 months, and **United Kingdom** and **Irish citizens** can stay up to 6 months without a visa.

For information on obtaining passports, contact the following agencies:

Australia: **Australian Passport Information Service** (☎ **131-232,** or visit www.passports.gov.au).

Canada: **Passport Office,** Department of Foreign Affairs and International Trade, Ottawa, ON K1A 0G3 (☎ **800/567-6868;** www.ppt.gc.ca).

Ireland: **Passport Office,** Setanta Centre, Molesworth Street, Dublin 2 (☎ **01/671-1633;** www.foreignaffairs.gov.ie

New Zealand: **Passports** Office, Department of Internal Affairs, 47 Boulcott Street, Wellington, 6011 (☎ **0800/225-050** in New Zealand or 04/474-8100; www.passports.govt.nz).

United Kingdom: Visit your nearest passport office, major post office, or travel agency or contact the **Identity and Passport Service (IPS),** 89 Eccleston Square, London, SW1V 1PN (☎ **0300/222-0000;** www.ips.gov.uk).

United States: To find your regional passport office, check the U.S. State Department website (travel.state.gov/passport) or call the **National Passport Information Center** (☎ **877/487-2778**) for automated information.

Police The national emergency number for police is ☎ **110.**

Safety The tragic 2011 Great East Japan Earthquake brought world-wide attention to the fact that Japan is earthquake-prone, but in reality, most earthquakes are too small to detect (of the more than 100,000 earthquakes annually in Japan, only 1% are big enough to feel). In any case, Japan has the world's best early-warning systems for impending earthquakes and tsunamis (the death toll would have been much higher without it) and has strict building codes (it's worth noting that not one skyscraper was felled by the 3/11 earthquake; the tsunami caused most of the damage). If you're around other people, you'll most likely hear everyone's phones going off at once for an earthquake alert, as most people are signed up for the warning that an earthquake may take place. In any case, in the event of a warning or an earthquake, there are a few precautions you should take. If you're indoors, the three rules of thumb are Drop, Cover, and Hold On. In other words, you should drop to the ground, take cover under a sturdy table, a piece of furniture or under a doorway, and then hold on until the shaking stops. Do not go outdoors, as the greatest danger is from falling debris, collapsing walls, and flying glass. Never use elevators during a quake.

If you're outdoors, stay away from trees, power lines, streetlights, and the sides of buildings; if you're surrounded by tall buildings, seek cover in a doorway. If you're in a coastal area, move away from the beach. The authorities will issue a tsunami warning if dangerous waves seem imminent. And expect aftershocks. Although secondary shockwaves are generally not as severe as the first one, they can damage weakened structures and can occur in the first hours or days—and even months—after the first quake. In the case of major emergencies, there are shelters throughout Japan, mostly schoolyards and other public facilities. Other precautions include noting emergency exits wherever you stay; all hotels supply flashlights, usually found attached to your bedside table. For more information on earthquakes, tsunamis, volcanic information, the weather, and warnings and advisories, see the Japan Meteorological Agency's website at www.jma.go.jp/jma/indexe.html.

As for crime, Japan has long been recognized as one of the safest countries in the world. In all the years I've lived and worked in Japan, I've never had even one fearful encounter, and I never hesitate to walk anywhere at any time of the night or day. After the 2011 tsunami, the possibility of looting occurring along the damaged coast never even crossed my mind; in fact, millions in yen and other valuables found in the rubble was turned over to authorities. When a friend of mine forgot her purse in a public restroom in Osaka, someone turned it in to the police station complete with money, digital camera, and passport. In other words, if you lose something—say on a subway or in a park—chances are good that you'll get it back (to find out how, go to the nearest police station or contact the local tourist office).

That being said, crime—especially pickpocketing—is on the increase, and there are precautions you should always take when traveling: Stay alert and be aware of your immediate surroundings. Be especially careful with cameras, purses, and wallets in congested areas like Narita airport, subways, department stores, or tourist attractions (like the retail district around Tokyo's Tsukiji Market). Some Japanese caution women against walking through parks alone at night.

Senior Travel   More and more attractions are offering **free admission** or **discounts** to seniors 65 or 70 and over (be sure to have your passport handy). However, discounts may not be posted, so be sure to ask. Seniors also receive discounts on domestic plane fares.

Older visitors to Japan should be aware that there are many stairs to navigate in metropolitan areas, particularly in subway and train stations and even on pedestrian overpasses.

Smoking   The legal age for purchasing tobacco products and smoking in Japan is 20. Smoking is banned in most public areas, including train and subway stations and office buildings. In many cities, ordinances also ban smoking on sidewalks but allow it in marked areas, usually near train stations. Many restaurants have nonsmoking sections, though bars do not. Entirely smoke-free restaurants are on the rise; your best chance of finding one is in a hotel. Virtually all medium-priced and upper-range hotels have designated nonsmoking floors, though Japanese-style inns, because of their small size, usually do not; some business hotels also don't. If you want to sit in the nonsmoking car of the Shinkansen bullet train, ask for the *kinensha* (some lines are completely smoke-free); during peak times, be sure to reserve a seat in the nonsmoking car in advance.

Student Travel   Students sometimes receive discounts at museums, though occasionally discounts are available only to students enrolled in Japanese schools. Furthermore, discounted prices may not be displayed in English. Your best bet is to bring along an **International Student Identity Card (ISIC)** with your university student ID and show them both at museum ticket windows. For information on the card and where and how to obtain one, check the website www.isic.org.

Taxes   Although there's long been discussion about whether to raise Japan's consumption tax (a debate that intensified after the 3/11 earthquake), the current tax imposed on goods and services, including hotel rates and restaurant meals, is 5%. Although hotels and restaurants are required to include the tax in their published rates, you might come across one that has yet to comply (especially on English-language menus which may not be updated regularly). In Tokyo, hotels also levy a separate accommodations tax of ¥100 to ¥200 per person per night. In hot-spring resort areas, a ¥150 *onsen* tax is added for every night of your stay.

In addition to these taxes, a 10% to 15% **service charge** will be added to your bill in lieu of tipping at most of the fancier restaurants and at moderately priced and upper-end hotels; in *ryokan*, service charge can be as high as 20%. Business hotels, *minshuku*, youth hostels, and inexpensive restaurants do not impose a service charge.

As for **shopping,** a 5% consumption tax is also included in the price of most goods. (Some of the smaller vendors are not required to levy tax.) Travelers from abroad, however, are eligible for an exemption on goods taken out of the country, although only the larger department stores and specialty shops seem equipped to deal with the procedures. In any case, most department stores grant a refund on the consumption tax only when the total amount of purchases for the day at their store exceeds ¥10,001. You can obtain a refund immediately by having a sales clerk fill out a list of your purchases and then presenting the list to the tax-exemption counter of the department store; *you must present your passport*. Note that no refunds for consumption tax are given for food, drinks, tobacco, cosmetics, toiletries, film, and batteries.

Telephones **To call Japan:** First, dial the international access code: **011** from the U.S.; **00** from the U.K., Ireland, or New Zealand; or **0011** from Australia. Next, dial the country code for Japan, **81.** Finally, dial the city code (3 for Tokyo, 6 for Osaka; for other area codes, check the listings for each city in this guide) and then the number. If you're calling a Japanese cellphone from overseas, which generally starts with **090** (080 has been recently added), you should drop the first zero and just dial **90** after the country code.

Domestic calls: If you're making a long-distance domestic phone call, all telephone area codes for all Japanese cities begin with a zero (03 for Tokyo, 06 for Osaka).

Despite the proliferation of cellphones, you can still find public telephones in telephone booths on the sidewalk, in or near train stations, in hotel lobbies, restaurants and coffee shops, and even on the bullet train (the latter require a prepaid card; see below). A local call costs ¥10 for each minute; a warning chime will alert you to insert more coins or you'll be disconnected. It's best, therefore, to insert two or three coins so that you won't have to worry about being disconnected; ¥10 coins that aren't used are returned at the end of the call. Most public phones accept both ¥10 and ¥100 coins. The latter is convenient for long-distance calls, but no change is given for unused minutes. All gray ISDN telephones are equipped for international calls.

If you think you'll be making a lot of domestic calls from public phones and don't want to deal with coins, purchase a magnetic **prepaid telephone card.** These are available in a value of ¥1,000 and are sold at vending machines (sometimes located right beside telephones), station kiosks, and convenience stores. Green and gray telephones accept telephone cards. In fact, many nowadays accept telephone cards exclusively. Insert the card into the slot. On the gray ISDN telephones, there's a second slot for a second telephone card, which is convenient if the first one is almost used up or if you think you'll be talking a long time. Domestic long-distance calls are cheaper at night, on weekends, and on national holidays for calls of distances more than 60km (37 miles).

Toll-free numbers: Numbers beginning with **0120** or **0088** are toll-free. Calling a 1-800 number in the U.S. from Japan is not toll-free but costs the same as an international call.

To make international calls from Japan: For a collect call or to place an operator-assisted call through KDDI, dial the international telephone operator at ℂ **0051.** From a public telephone, look for a specially marked INTERNATIONAL AND DOMESTIC CARD/COIN TELEPHONE. Although many of the specially marked green or gray telephones, the most common public telephone, accept both coins and magnetic telephone cards for domestic calls, most do not accept magnetic cards for direct overseas calls (due to illegal usage of telephone cards), especially in big cities, except for those in a few key facilities such as the airport and some hotels. You'll therefore either have to use coins, or purchase a special prepaid international telephone card that works like telephone cards issued by U.S. telephone companies. That is, an access number must first be dialed, followed by a secret telephone number, and then the number you wish to dial. Such cards are often sold from vending machines next to telephone booths in hotels or in convenience stores such as Sunkus, Circle K, Family Mart, or Lawson. There are numerous such cards (with instructions in English), including the rechargeable **Brastel Smart Phonecard** (www.brastel.com; ℂ **0120/659-543**), which charges ¥48 per minute from a payphone to a landline in the U.S.; or the **KDDI Super World Card** (www.kddi.com; ℂ **0057**), which charges ¥6 for every six seconds for the first three minutes and ¥4.7 for every six seconds after that. Some hotels have special phones equipped to accept credit cards.

International rates vary according to when you call, which telephone company you use, and what type of service you use. Direct-dial service is cheaper than operator-assisted calls. The cheapest time to call is between 11pm and 8am Japan time, while the most expensive time is weekdays from 8am to 7pm.

If you're not using a prepaid card (which has its own set of instructions and access numbers), to make a direct-dial international call, you must first dial one of the international access codes offered by the various telephone companies—**001** (KDDI), **0033** (NTT Communications), or **0061** (Softbank Telecom)—followed by **010** and then the country code. The country code for the United States and Canada is **1;** for the United Kingdom, it's **44;** for Australia, it's **61;** and for New Zealand, it's **64.** Next you dial the area code and number. For example, if you wanted to call the British Embassy in Washington, D.C., using KDDI you would dial 001-010-1-202-588-6500. If you're dialing from your hotel room, you must first dial for an outside line, usually 0.

Television   If you enjoy watching television, you've come to the wrong country. Almost nothing is broadcast in English; even foreign films are dubbed in Japanese. Most upper-range hotels, however, offer **bilingual televisions,** whereby you can switch from Japanese to English if the program or movie was *originally in English*, though only a few (and fairly dated) English movies and sitcoms are broadcast each week. The plus of bilingual TVs is that you can listen to the nightly national news broadcast by NHK at 7 and 9pm. Otherwise, major hotels in larger cities have cable or satellite TV with English-language programs including CNN broadcasts (sometimes in Japanese only) and BBC World as well as in-house pay movies. But even if you don't understand Japanese, I suggest that you watch TV at least once; maybe you'll catch a samurai series or a sumo match. Commercials are also worth watching.

A word on those **pay video programs** offered by hotels and many resort *ryokan:* Upper-range hotels usually have a few choices in English, and these are charged automatically to your bill. Most business hotels, however, usually offer only one kind of pay movie—generally "adult entertainment." If you're traveling with children, you'll want to be extremely careful about selecting your TV programs. Some adult video pay channels appear with a simple push of the channel-selector button, and they can be difficult to get rid of. Increasingly, however, many business hotels have vending machines offering prepaid cards for their adult movies. Although rare, you may also come across televisions with coin boxes attached to their sides; some must be fed to activate the TV, while others are for adult entertainment videos. Now you know.

Time   Japan is 9 hours ahead of Greenwich Mean Time, 14 hours ahead of New York, 15 hours ahead of Chicago, and 17 hours ahead of Los Angeles. Although there's been discussion of initiating daylight saving time to conserve energy in wake of the 2011 disaster, Japan currently does not use daylight saving time, so subtract 1 hour from the above times in the summer when calling from countries that have daylight saving time such as the United States.

Because Japan is on the other side of the international date line, you lose a day when traveling from the United States to Asia. (If you depart the United States on Tues, you'll arrive on Wed.) Returning to North America, however, you gain a day, which means that you arrive on the same day you left. (In fact, it can happen that you arrive in the States at an earlier hour than you departed from Japan.)

Tipping   One of the delights of being in Japan is that there's no tipping—not even to waitresses, taxi drivers, or bellhops. If you try to tip them, they'll probably be confused or embarrassed. Instead, you'll have a 10% to 15% service charge added to your bill at higher-priced accommodations and restaurants. That being said, you might want to tip, say, your room attendant at a high-class *ryokan* if you're making special requests or meals are served in your room; in that case, place crisp, clean bills (¥3,000–¥5,000) in a white envelope on the table of your room at the beginning of your stay; but it's perfectly fine if you choose not to tip.

Toilets   If you need a restroom, your best bets are at train and subway stations (though these can be dirty), big hotels, department stores, and fast-food restaurants. Use of restrooms is free in Japan, and though most public facilities supply toilet paper, it's a good idea to **carry a packet of tissues.**

In parks and some restaurants in rural areas, don't be surprised if you go into some restrooms and find men's urinals and private stalls in the same room. Women are supposed to walk right past the urinals without noticing them.

Many toilets in Japan, especially those at train stations, are **Japanese-style toilets:** They're holes in the ground over which you squat facing forward toward the end with a raised hood. Men stand and aim for the hole. Although Japanese lavatories may seem uncomfortable at first, they're actually more sanitary because no part of your body touches anything.

Western-style toilets in Japan are usually very high-tech. Called **Washlets,** these combination bidet/toilets have heated toilet seats, buttons and knobs directing sprays of water of various intensities to various body parts, blow dryers, and even lids that raise when you open the stall. But alas, instructions are usually in Japanese only. Listen to the voice of experience: Don't stand up until you've figured out how to turn the darn spray off.

VAT   See "Taxes" above.

Visas   Most foreign tourists, including Americans, Canadians, Australians, New Zealanders, and citizens of the United Kingdom and Ireland, do not need visas to visit Japan. Nationals of countries that do not have reciprocal visa exemption arrangements with Japan must obtain a visa. A Temporary Visitor's Visa allows tourists to stay in Japan for up to 90 days. Applicants must apply in person to a Japanese Embassy or a consulate with a valid passport, two passport photos taken within the past 6 months, two official visa application forms, and documents certifying the purpose of the visit.

Visitor Information   The **Japan National Tourist Organization (JNTO)** is the single best source for travel information on Japan. I also recommend the comprehensive www.japan-guide.com, with links to many other websites.

JNTO Online: You can reach JNTO via the Internet at **www.jnto.go.jp** (and at **www.japantravelinfo.com** for North American travelers; **www.seejapan.co.uk** for British travelers; and **www.jnto.org.au** for Australian travelers), where you can read up on what's new, view maps, get the latest weather report, find links to online hotel reservation companies and tour companies, and browse through information ranging from hints on budget travel to regional events. JNTO also showcases local tourism attractions, Japanese cuisine, and other topics (including yours truly, twice in 2011) on YouTube at www.youtube.com/visitjapan.

JNTO Overseas: If you'd like information on Japan before leaving home, contact one of the following JNTO offices:

In the **United States:** 11 West 42nd Street, 19th Floor, New York, NY 10036 (© **212/757-5640;** visitjapan@jntonyc.org); and Little Tokyo Plaza, 340 E. Second St., Ste. 302, Los Angeles, CA 90012 (© **213/623-1952;** info@jnto-lax.org).

In **Canada:** 481 University Ave., Ste. 306, Toronto, ON M5G 2E9, Canada (© **416/366-7140;** info@jntoyyz.com).

In the **United Kingdom:** Fifth Floor, 12 Nicholas Lane, London EC4N 7BN, England (© **020/7398-5678;** info@jnto.co.uk).

In **Australia:** Level 4, 56 Clarence St., Sydney NSW 2000, Australia (02/9279-2177; travelinfo@jnto.org.au).

JNTO in Japan: Your best bet for general or specific information on Japan is at one of JNTO's three excellent **Tourist Information Centers (TICs).** They're located in downtown Tokyo, at Narita Airport outside Tokyo, and at Kansai International Airport outside Osaka (see chapters 4 and 8 for locations and open hours). All distribute leaflets on destinations throughout Japan and can provide train, bus, and ferry schedules and leaflets on major attractions and sights—for example, Japanese gardens, hot springs, museums, and art galleries. Be sure to ask for "The Tourist's Language Handbook," a phrase booklet to help foreign visitors communicate with the Japanese, as well as the invaluable "Railway Timetable," which contains timetables for Shinkansen trains and major train lines throughout Japan.

Local Information: You'll also find locally run tourist offices in nearly every city and town throughout Japan, most of them conveniently located at or near the main train station. Look for the logo of a red question mark with the word INFORMATION written below. Although the staff at a particular tourist office may not speak English (many do), they can point you in the direction of your hotel, perhaps provide you with an English-language map (usually free), and, in many cases, even make hotel bookings for you. Note, however, that they're not equipped to provide you with information on other regions of Japan (for that, go to a TIC). I've included information on local tourist offices throughout this book (see "Visitor Information," in the regional chapters), including how to reach them after you disembark from the train and their open hours.

Water The water is safe to drink anywhere in Japan, although some people claim it's too highly chlorinated. Bottled water is also readily available.

Wi-Fi See "Internet & Wi-Fi," earlier in this section.

Weather The **Japan Meteorological Agency** (www.jma.go.jp) provides a wealth of information, including daily forecasts, location and magnitude of the latest earthquakes, and tsunami and typhoon warnings, along with estimated dates for the cherry blossom and rainy season and other fun data.

AIRLINE WEBSITES

Aeroméxico
www.aeromexico.com

Air Canada
www.aircanada.com

Air France
www.airfrance.com

Air India
www.airindia.com

Air New Zealand
www.airnewzealand.com

Alitalia
www.alitalia.com

All Nippon Airways
www.ana.co.jp

British Airways
www.british-airways.com

Cathay Pacific
www.cathaypacific.com

China Airlines
www.china-airlines.com

Delta Air Lines
www.delta.com

Japan Airlines
www.jal.com

Jetstar Airways
www.jetstar.com

KLM Royal Dutch Airlines
www.klm.com

Korean Air
www.koreanair.com

Lufthansa
www.lufthansa.com

Philippine Airlines
www.philippineairlines.com

Qantas Airways
www.qantas.com

Singapore Airlines
www.singaporeair.com

Skymark
www.skymark.co.jp

Skynet Asia Airways
www.skynetasia.co.jp

Swiss Air
www.swiss.com

Thai Airways International
www.thaiair.com

Turkish Airlines
www.thy.com

United Airlines
www.united.com

US Airways
www.usairways.com

Virgin Atlantic Airways
www.virgin-atlantic.com

Airline Websites

PLANNING YOUR TRIP TO JAPAN

A GLOSSARY OF USEFUL JAPANESE TERMS

Needless to say, it takes years to become fluent in Japanese, particularly in written Japanese, with its thousands of kanji, or Chinese characters, and its many hiragana and katakana characters. If you know even a few words of Japanese, however, they will not only be useful but will delight Japanese people you meet in the course of your trip.

Pronunciation

In Japanese, there's very little stress on individual syllables. Here's an approximation of some of the sounds of Japanese:

a	*as in* father
aa	*held slightly longer than a*
e	*as in* pen
i	*like e as in* need
ii	*held slightly longer than i*
o	*as in* oh
oo (or ou)	*held slightly longer than o, never oo as in moon*
u	*like oo as in moon, not yu as in cute (unless after a y)*
uu	*held slightly longer than u*
ai	*as in* I
ei	*as in* hey
g	*as in* go, *never j as in* gel

Vowel sounds are almost always short unless they are pronounced doubled, in which case you hold the vowel a bit longer. Similarly, double consonants are given more emphasis than only one consonant by itself. Vowels do not need to be paired with a consonant. Consonants must be paired with a vowel (as in *ka* or *te*), except the final *n*.

Useful Words & Phrases

BASIC TERMS

Yes	**Hai**	はい
No	**Iie**	いいえ
Good morning	**Ohayo gozaimasu**	お早うございます
Hello (Good afternoon)	**Konnichiwa**	今日は
Good evening	**Konbanwa**	今晩は
Good night	**Oyasumi nasai**	おやすみなさい
Hello	**Konnichiwa**	こんいちは
Nice to meet you.	**Hajimemashite.**	はいめめして
Goodbye	**Sayoonara** (or Bye-Bye)	さようなら、バイバイ
Excuse me/Pardon me/ I'm sorry	**Sumimasen**	すみません
Please (when offering something)	**Doozo**	どうぞ
Please (when requesting something)	**...o kudasai**	...を下さい
Thank you	**Arigatoo gozaimasu**	ありがとうございます
You're welcome	**Doo-itashimashite**	どういたしまして

BASIC QUESTIONS & EXPRESSIONS

(I'm) American	**Amerikajin desu**	アメリカ人です
(I'm) Canadian	**Canadajin desu**	カナダ人です
(I'm) English	**Igirisujin desu**	イギリス人です
Sorry, I don't speak Japanese	**Sumimasen, Nihongo wa hanasemasen**	すみません、日本語は話せません
Do you understand English?	**Eigo wa wakarimasu ka?**	英語は分かりますか?
Where is the toilet?	**Toire wa doko desu ka?**	トイレはどこですか?
My name is . . .	[Your name] **...to mooshimasu**	...と申します
What is your name?	**O-namae wa nan desu ka?**	お名前は何ですか?
What time do you open/ close?	**Nanji ni akimasuka? Nanjini shimarimasuka?**	何時に開きますか?何時に閉まりますか?
This one	**Kore** (something near you)	これ
That one	**Sore** (something near the person you're talking to)	それ
That one	**Are** (something away from both of you)	あれ
How much does it cost?	**Ikura desu ka?**	いくらですか?

TRAVEL TERMS

Train station	**Eki**	駅
Airport	**Kuukoo**	空港
Subway	**Chikatetsu**	地下鉄
Bus	**Basu**	バス

Taxi	**Takushii**	タクシー
Airplane	**Hikooki**	飛行機
Train	**Densha**	電車
Ticket	**Kippu**	きっぷ
One-way ticket	**Katamichi-kippu (or katamichiken)**	片道きっぷ(片道券)
Round-trip ticket	**Oofuku-kippu (or oofukuken)**	往復きっぷ (往復券)
I would like to buy a ticket.	**Kippu ichimai o kaitai no desu.**	きっぷ一枚を買いたいのです。
Tourist Information Office	**Kanko annaijo**	観光案内所
Police	**Keisatsu**	警察
Police box	**Koban**	交番
Post office	**Yuubin-kyoku**	郵便局
I'd like to buy a stamp.	**Kitte o kaitai no desu.**	切手を買いたいのです。
Internet	**Intaanetto**	インターネット
Wi-fi	**Waifai (or musenran)**	ワイファイ(無線ラン)
Bank	**Ginkoo**	銀行
Hospital	**Byooin**	病院
Drugstore	**Yakkyoku**	薬局
North	**Kita**	北
South	**Minami**	南
East	**Higashi**	東
West	**Nishi**	西
Left	**Hidari**	左
Right	**Migi**	右
Convenience store	**Konbiniensu stoaa (or konbini)**	コンビニエンスストアー (コンビニ)

LODGING TERMS

Hotel (western-style)	**Hoteru**	ホテル
Japanese-style inn	**Ryokan**	旅館
Japanese home-style lodging	**Minshuku**	民宿
Youth hostel	**Yuusu hosuteru**	ユースホステル
Cotton kimono	**Yukata**	浴衣
Room	**Heya**	部屋
Do you have a room available?	**Heya ga arimasu ka?**	部屋がありますか?
I'd like a private bathroom.	**Basu toire tsuki no heya o onegaishimasu.**	バストイレ付きの部屋をお願いします。

DINING TERMS & PHRASES

Restaurant	**Resutoran** (usually serves Western-style food)	レストラン
Dining hall	**Shokudoo** (usually serves Japanese food)	食堂

Coffee shop	**Kissaten**	喫茶店
Japanese pub	**Izakaya** or **Nomiya**	居酒屋、飲み屋
Breakfast	**Chooshoku**	朝食
Lunch	**Ohiru/ranchi**	お昼、ランチ
Dinner	**Yuushoku**	夕食
Japanese green tea	**Ocha**	お茶
Black (Indian) tea	**Koocha**	紅茶
Coffee	**Koohii**	コーヒー
Cold water	**Mizu**	水
I would like a fork, please.	**Fooku o kudasai.**	ホークを下さい。
I would like a spoon, please.	**Supuun o kudasai.**	スプーンを下さい。
I would like a knife, please.	**Naifu o kudasai.**	ナイフを下さい。

NUMBERS

one	**Ichi**	一
two	**Ni**	二
three	**San**	三
four	**Shi** (or **yon**)	四
five	**Go**	五
six	**Roku**	六
seven	**Shichi** (or **nana**)	七
eight	**Hachi**	八
nine	**Kyuu**	九
ten	**Juu**	十
eleven	**Juuichi**	十一
twelve	**Juuni**	十二
twenty	**Nijuu**	二十
thirty	**Sanjuu**	三十
forty	**Yonjuu**	四十
fifty	**Gojuu**	五十
sixty	**Rokujuu**	六十
seventy	**Nanajuu**	七十
eighty	**Hachijuu**	八十
ninety	**Kyuujuu**	九十
one hundred	**Hyaku**	百
one hundred one	**Hyakuichi**	百一
one hundred eleven	**Hyakujuuichi**	百十一
two hundred	**Nihyaku**	二百
one thousand	**Sen**	千
ten thousand	**Ichiman**	一万
twelve thousand three hundred forty-five	**Ichiman-nisen-sanbyaku-yonjuu-go**	一万二千三百四十五

Index

See also Accommodations and
Restaurant indexes, below.

General Index

A

A Bathing Ape (Tokyo), 154
A-Bomb Dome (Genbaku Domu;
  Hiroshima), 424
Academic trips, 55
Accommodations, 613–621. *See
  also* Accommodations Index
  best traditional, 6–7
  finding, 621
  kokumin shukusha (Okamura),
    617
  minshuku, 616–617
  reservations, 613
  ryokan (traditional Japanese
    inns), 613–615
  taxes and service charges, 613
  Western-style, 617–621
Acupuncture, Tokyo, 105
ACURA Acupuncture Clinic
  (Tokyo), 105
Adachi Museum (Yasugi), 415–416
Adachi Museum Garden (Yasugi),
  416
Adventure and wellness trips, 56
Advocates (Tokyo), 166
Ago Bay, 338
The Ainu, 586, 588, 596–597
Ainu Kotan Village, 596
Ainu Museum (Hokkaido), 588
Ainu Museum (Sapporo), 577
Air travel, 72–74, 601–602,
  609–611
Akamonkai Japanese Language
  School, 55
Akan, Lake, 596–597
Akanko Ainu Theater Ikor, 596
Akankohan Eco Museum Center,
  597
Akan Kokusai Tsuru Center (Akan
  International Crane Center),
  596
Akanko Spa and Akan National
  Park (Hokkaido), 594–599
Aka Renga (Red Brick Warehouse;
  Yokohama), 203
Akasaka (Tokyo), 80
  accommodations, 171–172, 184
  restaurants, 143–144
Akashiya (Kagoshima), 509
Akihabara (Tokyo), 78
  restaurant, 144
  shopping, 145, 146, 151
Akihabara Gamers (Tokyo), 146
Akinai to Kurashi Hakubutsukan
  (Museum of Commercial and
  Domestic Life; Uchiko), 457
AKKY International (Tokyo), 152
Albatross (Tokyo), 165

Ama (women divers), Toba, 337
America-Mura (Osaka), 369
American Pharmacy (Tokyo), 88
Ameya Yokocho (Tokyo), 154–155
Amida (Kamakura), 190
Amusement parks, 5
Amuse Museum (Tokyo), 94, 111
Animate (Osaka), 369
Anime
  films, 36
  shopping for, 146
  Tokyo International Anime
    Fair, 49
Antique Mall Ginza (Tokyo), 146
Antiques and curios, 9
  Tokyo, 146–147
Aoi Matsuri (Hollyhock Festival;
  Kyoto), 50
Aoyagi Samurai Manor (Kaku-
  nodate Rekishi-mura Aoyagi;
  Kakunodate), 554–555
Aoyama (Tokyo), 80
  accommodations, 178
  restaurants, 133–138
  walking tour, 112–116
Apple Store (Tokyo), 87
Aqua-Beat (Beppu), 518
Aqua Garden (Beppu), 518
Aquariums, 5
  Okinawa Churaumi Aquarium,
    530
  Osaka Aquarium (Kaiyukan),
    364
  Port of Nagoya Public
    Aquarium, 324
  SuizokuKan (Ioworld;
    Kagoshima), 502–503
  Toba Aquarium, 337–338
  Umitamago (Beppu), 520
Arc Academy, 55
Area codes, 622
Arima Onsen (near Kobe), 382
Arimatsu Tie-Dyeing Museum
  (Arimatsu Narumi Shibori
  Kaikan; Nagoya), 322
Aritsugu (Kyoto), 279
Art House Projects (near
  Takamatsu), 447
Artisans of Leisure, 56
Arty Farty (Tokyo), 166
Asahi Shoten (Tokyo), 155
Asakusa (Tokyo), 79
  accommodations, 176, 178,
    180–181
  nightlife, 164
  restaurants, 126–128
  walking tour, 108–112
Asakusa Information Center
  (Tokyo), 108
Atami, 216–218
Atami Geisha, 217
A Taste of Culture, 56
ATMs (automated teller
  machines), 628–629
Atomic Bomb Museum, Nagasaki,
  478
Atsuta Jingu Shrine (Nagoya),
  322–323

Aurora Town (Sapporo), 582
Autumn, 46
Autumn Festival (Takayama
  Matsuri), 52

B

Bade Haus Kume-Island, 535
Ball-Catching Festival (Tamaseseri;
  Fukuoka), 48
Bamboo Forest Path (Shuzenji),
  219
Bar Six (Tokyo), 164
Baseball, 5
  Dazaifu, 469
  Tokyo, 102
Bathing, 29–30
Battledore Fair (Hagoita-Ichi;
  Tokyo), 53
Bauhaus (Tokyo), 161
Beaches
  Iriomote, 538
  Ishigaki, 537–538
  Kume Island, 535
  Okinawa, 530
Bean-Throwing Festival
  (Setsubun), 49
Bears, Noboribetsu Onsen, 585
Beer, 42
Benesse House (near Takamatsu),
  447
Benten-kutsu Cave (Kamakura),
  190
Beppu, 516–523
Beppu City Traditional Bamboo
  Crafts Center (Beppu-Shi
  Takezaiku Densto Saingyo
  Kaikan), 519–520
Bic Camera (Tokyo), 152
Big Step (Osaka), 369
Bike Tours Japan, 56
Biking, 4, 8
  Ibusuki, 512–513
  Kakunodate, 554
  Kyoto, 253
  Lake Tazawa, 558
  Miyajima, 434
  Nagasaki, 476
  Nara, 310
  Okayama, 400
  Shimanami Kaido, 427, 458–459
  Takayama, 234
  tours, 56
Billboard Live Osaka, 370
Billboard Live Tokyo, 161
Bizen, 403
Bizen Pottery Traditional and
  Contemporary Art Museum,
  403
Bizen-yaki Dento Sangyo Kaikan
  (Imbe), 403
Blue Note (Tokyo), 161
Boat travel and cruises, 602, 612
  Hiroshima, 422
  Huis Ten Bosch, 481
  Kagoshima, 505
  Laka Tazawa, 559
  Lake Akan, 596–597

Restaurants